XUÉXÍ HÀNYĪNG CÍDIǍN

学习汉英词典

LEARNER'S CHINESE ENGLISH DICTIONARY

修訂本

REVISED EDITION

学习汉英词典 XUÉXÍ HÀNYĪNG CÍDIÁN
LEARNER'S CHINESE–ENGLISH DICTIONARY

11th Edition (revised) 1999 第十一版 （修订本） 1999

Jointly Published by 联合出版者：
NANYANG SIANG PAU 南洋商報

UMUM PUBLISHER PTE. LTD.
普及出版社（私营）有限公司

Sole Distributor 总发行：THE SHANGHAI BOOK CO. (PTE) LTD.
上海书局
Blk.231, Bain Street, #02-73, Bras Basah Complex, Singapore 180231.
Tel: 3360144 Fax: (65) 3360490 Tlx: RS 29297 KHNCO SHOOBOOK
63-C, Jalan Sultan, Kuala Lumpur, Malaysia. Tel: 2384642/2308602

Printed by 承印者: Vinlin Press Sdn. Bhd.
永联印务有限公司
56, 1st Floor Jln. Radin Anum 1,
Bandar Baru Seri Petaling,
57000 Kuala Lumpur.

再　版　说　明

本词典出版之后，深获各界人士的爱护和支持，第一版数月内便告售罄。借此再版机会，我们参考了各界人士提供的意见，重新校订全书。

这次再版，我们除了校正因排版、印刷上的疏忽所造成的一些错误之外，也力求将全书第一版中还未以简体字排印的文字改为简体字。此外，也更正了一些文字释义方面不够贴切、完善的地方。

尽管有了这些努力，我们相信这本词典仍会有些瑕疵，希望各界人士继续给我们提出批评，以使本词典更臻完善。

普及出版社

Preface to the Second Edition

The publication of the First Edition of this dictionary has met with such a favourable response from our readers that copies published were sold out within a period of a few months. To show our appreciation for the love and support given to us, we have embarked on this Second Edition, incorporating many changes as a result of the useful and valuable comments and suggestions offered.

Besides corrections of typesetting and printing errors, we have also made another thorough check on the Chinese characters in order to ensure that all of them are in the simplified form. Furthermore, we have re-examined many of the translations and modified quite a number of them so that they are more apt and precise.

However, we are only too conscious of the fact that the compilation of a good dictionary is no easy task and that there is still plenty of room for improvement. We sincerely hope that our dear readers would continue to give us their criticisms and comments to enable us to meet the needs of our readers in future editions.

The Editorial Board,

Umum Publisher

目　录

CONTENTS

前 言

华文是世界四份之一人口的语文，随着简体字和汉语拼音的推行，华文的学习日趋普遍。在我国，广大受英文教育的学生与社会人士已将华文视为必须学好与掌握的语文。

我们为了配合广大读者的需求，特邀请数位教育与学术界先进，依现代汉语拼音法及最新的汉语拼音词典，共同编辑了这本「学习汉英词典」。本词典共选入五千个单字及一万五千余个词组、成语与谚语。为了进一步协助学习者明了这些字及词的意义与用法，我们除了加以注释之外，并特地给那些常用字加上中英文示范例句及词类说明。

我们希望这本词典的出版除了协助受英文教育的学生及社会人士学习华文之外，对受华文教育者在学习英文写作及翻译方面也会有所裨益。

鉴於学识有限，加上工作匆忙，我们相信这本词典难免会有缺点，希望各界前辈能随时给我们提供意见。

普及出版社

FOREWORD

The Chinese Language is the language of a quarter of the world population, and with the promoting of the simplified form of the Chinese Characters and the Chinese Phonotic Transcription, there is a tremendous increase in the number of people learning it. In our country, English educated students and people from all walks of life have probably realized it is important to master Chinese Language.

In order to meet the need of our readers, our editorial board had invited a few linguisticians and educators to compile this "Learner's Chinese-English Dictionary" which is based on the Modern Chinese Phonetic Transcription System and references are also made on a number of currently noted dictionaries with Phonetic Transcription. This dictionary contains five thousand words and over fifteen thousand phrases and idioms. In order to aid the learners in the understanding of these words and the usage of the phrases, besides providing explanations for these words, sentence illustrations and explanations for phrases are also supplied.

We hope that the publishing of this dictionary would benefit the English stream students who take Chinese as a Second Language and the public in general; and those Chinese educated people,who are interested in English composition writing and translation, would also find this dictionary a great help.

Due to the limit of our time and knowledge, some mistakes are inevitable. We sincerely hope that our readers would generously give us their advice and constructive criticism.

Umum Publisher

编 辑 说 明

（一）编辑目的

「学习汉英词典」主要是为协助汉、英语文的学习者而编，适宜中、小学生及社会上工作的各阶层人士。

（二）文字的排列(查字法)

1 本词典共选入五千个单字及一万五千余个词组、成语及谚语。每个单字都用比较大的字体排列在最前面。其所属的词组则以较小的方体字列出。

2 本词典的全部文字皆按其汉语拼音的字母次序排列。查字时，可依其汉语拼音在汉语拼音音节表中查明其页数。如「巴」「bā」字，从汉语拼音音节表中可查知其页数是第８。

3 凡字形相同而读音不同的字，都依其拼音法分别归类到不同的范畴。如「阿」字可分别在「ā」、「á」、「ǎ」、「à」、「ē」等五个范畴内查阅。

4 凡一个字具有两种或多种不同的拼音，在其中英文注释之后，都有加上另见「xx」，即请查阅另一拼音范畴。如「呆」「ái」字在其中英文注释之后，有写上另见「dāi」，意即在「dāi」的范畴内，可查到「呆」字的另一种解释。

5 本词典附有汉语拼音方案简介，供读者学习汉语拼音。

6 本词典附有笔画查字表。不谙汉语拼音者，可依文字笔画的多寡查用本词典。如「安」字可从笔画查字表中查知是编於词典正文的第３页。

7 本词典所采用的字体系通用的简体字，在简体字旁边有将其繁体字标在括号（　）内，供不谙简体字的读者查阅。

（三）文字的注释

1 每个字都有中英文注释，所属的词组则只有英文注释。

2 凡有两个意义以上的文字，都分别以１、２、３、４…标明其数个不同的意义。

3 每个单字之后，都有其词性说明。如「阿」(part)，意即「阿」这个字是属於质词(particle)。如果一个字有两个或两个以上的词性，也分别在1、2、3……之后逐个说明其词性。

4 词性以略语方式标明，请查阅词性简称表。

5 在常用字的注释之后，附有中英文例句或其用法示例。例子的开端以 * 号表示。

6 在释义时，若有碰到比喻或引申义，则以(fig)标明。

(四)词类简称表

词性以略语方式标明

(n)	noun	名词	[míngcí]
(pron)	pronoun	代词	[dàicí]
(v)	verb	动词	[dòngcí]
(auxv)	auxiliary verb	助动词	[zhùdòngcí]
(adj)	adjective	形容词	[xíngróngcí]
(adv)	adverb	副词	[fùcí]
(prep)	preposition	介词	[jiècí]
(conj)	conjunction	连词	[liáncí]
(interj)	interjection	叹词	[tàncí]
(part)	particle	质词	[zhìcí]
(pref.)	prefix	词头	[cítòu]
(suf.)	suffix	词尾	[cíwěi]

(五)参考书

1 现代华语词典——上海书局出版
2 远东英汉大辞典——远东图书公司印行
3 汉英大辞典——中国图书出版公司发行
4 麦氏汉英大辞典——东南亚书店股份有限公司出版
5 通用汉英辞典——中华书局出版
6 现代汉英词典——Cosmos Books Ltd. 出版
7 通用新字典——商务印书馆出版
8 英译汉语成语词典——商务印书馆出版
9 袖珍汉英词典——中华书局出版

EDITOR'S NOTE

(1) Aim

The Learner's Chinese-English Dictionary is compiled mainly to meet the need of beginners in Chinese and English. It is suitable for Primary, Secondary students and people from all walks of life.

(2) Directions On the use of the Dictionary

a. This dictionary has selected five thousand words and fifteen thousand phrases and idioms. The word is bigger in size and placed at the most front while the phrases and idioms that belong to this word are smaller, and placed in separate rows from the single word.

b. All the words in this dictionary have been arranged in the alphabetical order of the Chinese Phonetic Alphabet. When looking up for a word, the Chinese Phonetic Transcription (or PINYIN) of the word should be used/ and "the Table on the Syllables of Chinese Phonetic Transcription" should be used as a guide to look for the page where the word is, for example the word 巴 [bā], in the Table it indicates that it is in page 8.

c. Words that are the same in form but different in sounds are arranged into different categories, according to PINYIN (Chinese Phonetics) alphabetical order. For example, the word 阿 can be found in five categories of [ā], [á], [ǎ], [à], and [ē]

d. When a word has two or more PINYIN (Chinese Phonetic Transcription) REFERRING TO [ ] is placed after the Chinese and English explanations. This is to indicate to the readers to look up more about the word in another category of PINYIN. For example, the word 呆 [ái], after its Chinese and English explanations, REFERRING TO [dāi] is added. This means that in the category of [dāi], a different explanation of 呆 can be obtained.

e. This dictionary has a table of a "Scheme for the Chinese Phonetic Alphabet" for the readers to acquaint themselves with Chinese Phonetics.

f. A "Character Stroke Index" is also supplied. Readers who are not yet familiar with the scheme for the Chinese Phonetic Alphabet, can still look up words according to the number of strokes of the characters. For example, the word 安 can be found in Pg. 3. of the dictionary by using the table.

g. The common simplified Chinese characters are adopted. At the side of the simplified form, the original complex form of the characters are put in brackets ( ). This is for the convenience of those readers who are not familiar with the simplified Chinese characters.

(3) The Explanation of Words

a. Every word is supplied with Chinese and English explanations. The idioms and phrases belonging to the word are given English explanations.

b. Words that have two or more meanings, the numbering (1,2,3,4, ...) is used to note their various meaning.

c. Every word is followed by its part of speech. For example 阿 (part.) indicates that this word 阿 is a particle. If a word has two or more parts of speech, they are indicated after the numbers 1,2,3 ....

d. Abbreviations are used to indicate parts of speech. A table of Abbreviations of Parts of Speech is for such a purpose.

e. After the explanations of commonly used words, English and Chinese exemplary sentences are listed, preceded by the mark *

f. In our translation, when figurative language occurs the abbreviation (fig.) is marked.

(4) Abbreviations of Parts of Speech

(n)	noun	名词	[míngcí]
(pron)	pronoun	代词	[dàicí]
(v)	verb	动词	[dòngcí]
(aux. v)	auxiliary verb	助动词	[zhùdòngcí]
(adj)	adjective	形容词	[xíngróngcí]
(adv)	adverb	副词	[fùcí]
(prep)	preposition	介词	[jiècí]
(conj)	conjunction	连词	[liáncí]
(part)	particle	质词	[zhìcí]
(interj)	interjection	叹词	[tàncí]
(pref)	prefix	词头	[cí tòu]
(suf.)	suffix	词尾	[cí wěi]

(5) Reference Books

1. XIÀNDÀI HUÁYǓ CÍDIǍN
2. Far East English-Chinese Dictionary
3. A New Complete Chinese-English Dictionary
4. Mathews' Chinese-English Dictionary
5. General Chinese-English Dictionary
6. A Current Chinese-English Dictionary
7. 通用新字典
8. Chinese Idioms and Phrases
9. A Pocket Chinese-English Dictionary

汉语拼音音节索引

The Table on the Syllables of Chinese Phonetic Transcription

Syllable	Character	Page
A		
ā	阿	1
	啊	1
	腌	1
á	啊	1
à	啊	1
a	啊	1
āi	唉	1
	埃	1
	挨	1
	哀	1
	哎	2
ái	皑	2
	捱	2
	呆	2
	挨	2
	癌	2
ǎi	蔼	2
	霭	2
	嗳	2
	矮	2
ài	艾	2
	爱	2
	嗳	3
	嫒	3
	瑗	3
	暖	3
	隘	3
	唉	3
	碍	3
ān	厂	3
	庵	3
	鹌	3
	安	3
	鞍	4
	谙	4
	氨	4
ǎn	俺	4
	铵	4
àn	岸	5
	按	5
	胺	5
	案	5
	暗	5
	黯	6
āng	肮	6
ǎng	昂	6
àng	盎	6
āo	凹	6
	熬	6
áo	嗷	7
	熬	7
	遨	7
	翱	7
ǎo	袄	7
	拗	7
	媪	7
ào	傲	7
	骜	7
	奥	7
	懊	7
	澳	7
	坳	7
B		
bā	巴	8
	芭	8
	笆	8
	疤	8
	八	8
	叭	8
	扒	8
	捌	8
bá	拔	8
	跋	9
bǎ	把	9
	靶	9
bà	把	9
	耙	9
	鲃	9
	爸	9
	罢	9
	霸	10
	坝	10
ba	吧	10
bái	白	11
bǎi	百	11
	佰	11
	柏	11
	摆	11
bài	败	12
	拜	12
	稗	12
bān	般	12
	搬	12
	瘢	12
	颁	12
	班	12
	斑	12
	扳	13
bǎn	阪	13
	坂	13
	板	13
	版	13
	钣	13
bàn	半	13
	伴	14
	拌	14
	绊	14
	办	14
	扮	14
bāng	邦	14
	梆	14
	帮	14
bǎng	榜	15
	膀	15
	绑	15
bàng	傍	15
	谤	15
	磅	15
	镑	15
	棒	15
	蚌	15
bāo	包	15
	孢	16
	胞	16
	炮	16
	苞	16
	龅	16
	煲	16
	褒	16
	剥	16
báo	雹	16
	薄	16

bǎo 保 16 褓 17 堡 17 葆 17 鸨 17 宝 17 饱 18
bào 抱 18 鲍 18 刨 18 暴 18 爆 19 豹 19 报 19
bēi 卑 20 碑 20 杯 20 背 20 悲 20
běi 北 20
bèi 倍 21 焙 21 蓓 21 悖 21 贝 21 狈 21 被 21 背 21 备 21 辈 22
bēn 奔 22
běn 本 22 畚 22
bèn 奔 22 笨 22
bēng 绷 23 崩 23
běng 绷 23
bèng 绷 23 蹦 23 迸 23 泵 23
bī 逼 23
bí 鼻 23
bǐ 匕 23 比 24 秕 24 俾 24 彼 24 鄙 24 笔 24
bì 必 25 庇 25 陛 25 毕 25 哔 25 蓖 25 篦 25 婢 25 睥 25 裨 25 髀 25 畀 25 痹 25 辟 25 避 25 壁 26 嬖 26 璧 26 臂 26 襞 26 甓 26 敝 26 弊 26 蔽 26 币 26 毙 26 愎 26 闭 26 贲 27 碧 27
biān 编 27 蝙 27 鳊 27 鞭 27 邊 27 砭 28
biǎn 扁 28 匾 28 贬 28
biàn 卞 28 遍 28 辨 28 辩 28 辫 28 便 28 变 29
biāo 骠 29 镖 29 膘 29 标 29 镳 30 飙 30 彪 30
biǎo 表 30 表 30 婊 30 裱 30
biào 鳔 30
biē 憋 31 鳖 31
bié 别 31 蹩 31
biě 瘪 31
bīn 宾 31 傧 31 滨 31 缤 31 槟 31 濒 32 彬 32
bìn 摈 32 膑 32 殡 32 髌 32 鬓 32
bīng 兵 32 冰 32
bǐng 丙 32 柄 32 炳 33 饼 33 屏 33 秉 33 禀 33
bìng 并 33 並 33 病 33
bō 拨 33 波 34 玻 34 菠 34 播 34 饽 34 钵 34 剥 34
bó 伯 34 泊 34 舶 34 帛 34 箔 34 博 34 搏 35 膊 35 薄 35 礴 35 脖 35 鹁 35 勃 35 钹 35 驳 35
bǒ 跛 35 簸 35
bò 擘 35 薄 35 柏 35 簸 35
bū 逋 36
bǔ 捕 36 哺 36 卜 36 補 36
bù 部 36 簿 36 不 36 布 39 怖 39 步 39 埠 39

C

cā 擦 40

Pinyin	字	页
cāi	猜	40
cái	才	40
	材	40
	财	40
	裁	40
cǎi	采	41
	睬	41
	踩	41
	采	41
cài	菜	41
	蔡	42
cān	参	42
	餐	42
cán	残	42
	蚕	42
	惭	42
cǎn	惨	42
càn	粲	43
	灿	43
cāng	伧	43
	仓	43
	沧	43
	舱	43
	苍	43
cáng	藏	43
cāo	糙	44
	操	44
cáo	曹	44
	嘈	44
	漕	44
	槽	44
cǎo	草	44
cè	侧	44
	测	45
	厕	45
	策	45
	册	45
cēn	参	45
cén	岑	45
	涔	45
céng	曾	45
	层	45
	蹭	45
chā	叉	45
	插	45
	锸	46
	差	46
chá	查	46
	茶	46
	搽	46
	楂	46
	察	47
chǎ	衩	47
chà	诧	47
	杈	47
	岔	47
	刹	47
	差	47
chāi	钗	47
	拆	47
	差	47
chái	柴	48
	侪	48
	豺	48
chài	虿	48
	瘥	48
chān	掺	48
	搀	48
chán	谗	48
	巉	48
	馋	48
	单	48
	婵	48
	禅	48
	蝉	48
	廛	48
	缠	48
	孱	48
	潺	49
	蟾	49
chǎn	阐	49
	产	49
	铲	49
	谄	49
chàn	忏	49
	颤	49
chāng	昌	49
	猖	49
	娼	49
	鲳	49
	菖	49
cháng	徜	50
	常	50
	嫦	50
	裳	50
	尝	50
	偿	50
	肠	50
	长	50
chǎng	场	51
	敞	51
	厂	51
chàng	唱	51
	怅	51
	畅	51
	倡	52
chāo	抄	52
	钞	52
	超	52
cháo	朝	52
	嘲	52
	潮	53
	巢	53
chǎo	吵	53
	炒	53
chē	车	53
chě	扯	53
chè	撤	53
	澈	54
	彻	54
	坼	54
	掣	54
chēn	嗔	54
	瞋	54
	琛	54
chén	辰	54
	晨	54
	忱	54
	沉	54
	陈	55
	尘	55
	臣	55
	榇	55
	衬	55
	趁	55
	称	55
	谶	55
chēng	撑	55
	瞠	56
	赪	56
	称	56
	蛏	56
	铛	56
	铮	56
chéng	成	56
	盛	57
	诚	57
	城	57
	呈	57
	程	57
	橙	57
	澄	57
	承	57
	惩	58
	乘	58
chěng	逞	58
	骋	58
chèng	秤	59
chī	嗤	59
	吃	59
	痴	59
chí	池	59
	持	59
	迟	59
	踟	59
	弛	59
	驰	59
	匙	59
chǐ	侈	60
	尺	60
	齿	60
	耻	60
	褫	60
chì	敕	60
	翅	60
	叱	60
	啻	60
	趩	60
	斥	60
	赤	60
	饬	61
	炽	61
chōng	冲	61
	忡	61

	憧	61
	充	61
	舂	61
chóng	虫	61
	崇	62
	重	62
chǒng	宠	62
chòng	冲	62
	铳	62
chōu	抽	62
	瘳	63
chóu	俦	63
	畴	63
	踌	63
	筹	63
	惆	63
	绸	63
	稠	63
	仇	63
	雠	63
	愁	63
	酬	63
chǒu	丑	63
	瞅	64
chòu	臭	64
chū	出	64
	初	65
chú	刍	65
	雏	65
	除	66
	蜍	66
	厨	66
	橱	66
	锄	66
chǔ	楚	66
	础	66
	处	66
	储	66
	杵	67
chù	畜	67
	触	67
	处	67
	绌	67
	黜	67
	怵	67
	矗	67
chuài	揣	67
chuǎi	揣	67
chuài	踹	67
chuān	川	67
	穿	68
chuán	船	68
	传	68
	椽	69
chuǎn	舛	69
	喘	69
chuàn	钏	69
	串	69
chuāng	创	69
	疮	69
	窗	69
chuáng	床	69
chuǎng	闯	70
chuàng	怆	70
	创	70
chuī	吹	70
	炊	70
chuí	垂	70
	捶	71
	锤	71
	槌	71
chūn	春	71
chún	淳	71
	鹑	71
	醇	71
	纯	71
	唇	71
chǔn	蠢	71
chuō	戳	72
chuò	啜	72
	辍	72
	绰	72
cī	疵	72
cí	磁	72
	糍	72
	慈	72
	瓷	72
	词	72
	祠	72
	雌	72
	辞	72
cǐ	此	73
cì	刺	73
	次	73
	伺	73
	赐	73
cōng	囱	73
	骢	73
	聪	74
	匆	74
	葱	74
	从	74
cóng	从	74
	丛	74
	淙	74
	琮	74
còu	凑	74
	辏	75
	腠	75
cū	粗	75
cú	簇	75
	醋	75
	猝	75
	蹙	75
	蹴	75
	促	75
cuān	蹿	75
cuán	攒	76
cuàn	窜	76
	篡	76
cuī	崔	76
	催	76
	摧	76
cuǐ	璀	76
cuì	悴	76
	啐	76
	淬	76
	粹	76
	萃	76
	翠	76
	瘁	76
	脆	76
cūn	皴	76
	村	76
cún	存	77
cǔn	忖	77
cùn	寸	77
cuō	搓	77
	蹉	77
	撮	77
cuó	痤	77
cuò	措	77
	错	77
	厝	78
	挫	78
	锉	78

D

dā	搭	79
	答	79
dá	怛	79
	答	79
	达	79
	鞑	79
	打	79
dǎ	打	79
dà	大	80
dāi	呆	81
	待	81
dǎi	歹	81
	逮	81
	傣	81
dài	殆	81
	怠	81
	代	81
	贷	81
	袋	82
	玳	82
	黛	82
	逮	82
	大	82
	带	82
	戴	82
	待	82
dān	单	82
	禅	83
	眈	83
	耽	83
	丹	83
	担	83
dǎn	掸	83
	胆	83

dàn 旦 84
但 84
担 84
惮 84
弹 84
啖 84
淡 84
澹 84
诞 84
石 84
蛋 84
dāng 当 84
裆 85
dǎng 党 85
挡 85
dàng 荡 85
当 85
挡 85
档 85
dāo 刀 85
dǎo 岛 86
捣 86
祷 86
导 86
蹈 86
倒 86
dào 到 86
倒 86
道 86
盗 87
悼 87
稻 87
dé 得 87
锝 87
德 87
de 的 87
地 88
得 88
děi 得 88
dēng 登 88
蹬 88
灯 88
děng 等 88
dèng 澄 89
镫 89
瞪 89
凳 89
邓 89
dī 低 89
堤 89
提 89
滴 89
镝 89
dí 嫡 89
敌 89
籴 89
迪 89
笛 89
的 89
涤 89
dǐ 邸 90
诋 90
抵 90
底 90
dì 帝 90
缔 90
蒂 90
弟 90
睇 90
第 90
递 90
的 90
地 91
diān 颠 91
巅 91
掂 91
diǎn 点 91
踮 92
典 92
diàn 玷 92
店 92
惦 92
钿 92
淀 92
靛 92
殿 92
电 92
垫 93
奠 93
diāo 凋 93
雕 93
刁 93
貂 93
diào 吊 93
钓 93
调 94
掉 94
diē 跌 94
爹 94
dié 谍 94
堞 94
喋 94
牒 94
碟 94
蹀 94
鲽 94
迭 94
dīng 丁 95
叮 95
盯 95
钉 95
dǐng 顶 95
鼎 95
dìng 定 95
锭 96
碇 96
订 96
钉 96
diū 丢 96
dōng 冬 96
东 96
dǒng 董 96
懂 97
dòng 峒 97
恫 97
洞 97
胴 97
冻 97
栋 97
动 97
dōu 兜 97
都 97
dǒu 斗 97
抖 98
陡 98
dòu 豆 98
痘 98
逗 98
窦 98
斗 98
dū 督 98
都 98
dú 读 98
椟 98
牍 98
犊 98
黩 98
独 99
毒 99
dǔ 堵 99
赌 99
睹 99
笃 99
肚 99
dù 杜 99
肚 99
度 100
渡 100
镀 100
妒 100
duān 端 100
duǎn 短 100
duàn 段 100
缎 100
锻 101
断 101
duī 堆 101
duì 对 101
兑 102
队 102
dūn 惇 102
敦 102
墩 102
礅 102
吨 102
蹲 102
盹 102
dùn 炖 102
钝 102
顿 102
囤 102

盾 102
遁 102
duō 掇 102
裰 103
咄 103
多 103
哆 103
duó 度 103
踱 103
夺 103
duǒ 朵 103
躲 103
duò 惰 103
堕 103
跺 103
舵 103
驮 104

E

ē 阿 105
婀 105
é 俄 105
哦 105
峨 105
娥 105
蛾 105
锇 105
鹅 105
讹 105
额 105
ě 恶 106
è 谔 106
愕 106
腭 106
锷 106
鳄 106
鹗 106
萼 106
厄 106
扼 106
呃 106
遏 106
恶 106
噩 107
饿 107
ēi 诶 107
éi 诶 107
èi 诶 107
ēn 恩 107
èn 摁 107
ér 而 107
儿 107
ěr 耳 107
饵 108
尔 108
迩 108
èr 二 108
贰 108

F

fā 发 109
fá 伐 110
垡 110
筏 110
阀 110
乏 110
罚 110
fǎ 法 110
砝 111
fà 发 111
fān 番 111
幡 111
翻 111
蕃 111
藩 111
帆 111
fán 璠 111
燔 111
蹯 111
蕃 111
凡 111
钒 112
繁 112
烦 112
樊 112
fǎn 反 112
返 113
fàn 饭 113
贩 113
范 113
犯 113
梵 113
泛 113
fāng 方 114
坊 114
妨 114
钫 114
芳 114
fáng 防 114
坊 115
肪 115
房 115
fǎng 仿 115
访 115
纺 115
昉 115
舫 115
fàng 放 115
fēi 非 116
绯 116
菲 116
霏 116
扉 116
飞 116
妃 117
féi 肥 117
腓 117
fěi 诽 117
蜚 117
翡 117
菲 117
匪 117
fèi 沸 117
费 117
肺 117
废 118
吠 118
fēn 分 118
吩 119
纷 119
氛 119
雰 119
芬 119
fén 坟 119
濆 119
焚 119
fěn 粉 119
fèn 偾 119
愤 119
分 120
份 120
忿 120
粪 120
奋 120
fēng 峰 120
烽 120
蜂 120
锋 120
风 120
枫 121
疯 121
丰 122
封 122
féng 逢 122
缝 122
冯 122
fěng 讽 122
凤 122
奉 122
俸 123
缝 123
fó 佛 123
fǒu 否 123
缶 123
fū 夫 123
肤 123
敷 123
孵 124
跗 124
fú 弗 124
拂 124
佛 124
绋 124
孚 124
俘 124
浮 124
莩 125
符 125
伏 125
袱 125
幅 125
辐 125

	福	125
	夫	125
	扶	125
	芙	126
	服	126
	芾	126
	凫	126
	枹	126
fǔ	拊	126
	府	126
	俯	126
	腐	126
	甫	126
	辅	126
	脯	126
	釜	126
	抚	126
	斧	127
fù	付	127
	附	127
	驸	127
	复	127
	覆	128
	腹	128
	鳆	128
	馥	128
	讣	128
	赴	128
	阜	128
	富	128
	副	128
	负	129
	父	129
	傅	129
	缚	129
	妇	129
	赋	129

G

gá	噶	131
gāi	该	131
	赅	131
gǎi	改	131
gài	丐	132
	溉	132
	概	132
	盖	132
gān	干	132
	杆	133
	肝	133
	竿	133
	甘	133
	柑	133
	尴	133
gǎn	杆	133
	秆	133
	赶	133
	敢	134
	橄	134
	感	134
gàn	干	134
gāng	冈	135
	刚	135
	纲	135
	钢	135
	扛	135
	肛	135
	缸	135
	岗	136
	港	136
gàng	杠	136
gāo	高	136
	膏	137
	篙	137
	糕	137
	睾	137
gǎo	搞	137
	槁	137
	稿	137
	告	137
	诰	138
	膏	138
	郜	138
gē	咯	138
	胳	138
	搁	138
	哥	138
	歌	138
	戈	138
	鸽	138
	割	138
gé	格	138
	阁	138
	搁	139
	隔	139
	嗝	139
	蛤	139
	葛	139
	革	139
	舸	139
	盖	139
	个	139
	合	139
	葛	139
gè	各	139
	个	140
gěi	给	140
gēn	根	140
	跟	140
gèn	亘	141
gēng	更	141
	庚	141
	赓	141
	耕	141
	羹	141
gěng	哽	141
	绠	141
	梗	141
	鲠	141
	耿	141
gèng	更	142
gōng	工	142
	功	142
	攻	142
	供	143
	龚	143
	弓	143
	躬	143
	公	143
	恭	143
	宫	143
	肱	144
gǒng	拱	144
	巩	144
gòng	贡	144
	共	144
	供	144
gōu	勾	144
	沟	144
	钩	145
gǒu	狗	145
	枸	145
	苟	145
	笱	145
gòu	勾	145
	构	145
	购	145
	够	145
	垢	146
	觏	146
	媾	146
gū	估	146
	咕	146
	沽	146
	姑	146
	酤	146
	辜	146
	菇	146
	骨	146
	呱	146
	孤	146
	箍	147
gǔ	古	147
	诂	147
	牯	147
	骨	147
	股	147
	鼓	147
	臌	148
	瞽	148
	蛊	148
	谷	148
	贾	148
	鹄	148
gù	固	148
	痼	148
	梏	148
	估	148
	故	149

H

jǐng 景 223
憬 223
井 223
阱 223
儆 223
警 223
刭 223
颈 223
jìng 径 224
胫 224
劲 224
靖 224
静 224
竞 224
竟 224
境 224
镜 225
敬 225
净 225
jiǒng 迥 225
窘 225
jiū 啾 225
揪 226
纠 226
赳 226
鸠 226
究 226
jiǔ 久 226
灸 226
九 226
韭 226
酒 226
jiù 臼 227
舅 227
旧 227
就 227
鹫 227
疚 227
柩 227
厩 228
咎 228
救 228
jū 狙 228
疽 228
居 228
拘 228
驹 228
掬 228
鞠 228
车 229
jú 局 229
菊 229
橘 229
jǔ 咀 229
矩 229
沮 229
举 229
龃 230
jù 巨 230
讵 230
炬 230
拒 230
距 230
倨 230
据 230
锯 230
踞 231
剧 231
遽 231
具 231
俱 231
惧 231
飓 231
屦 231
聚 231
句 231
juān 圈 232
捐 232
涓 232
娟 232
juǎn 卷 232
juàn 倦 232
卷 232
眷 232
圈 232
绢 232
juē 撅 232
嗟 232
jué 厥 232
决 233
诀 233
抉 233
倔 233
掘 233
崛 233
攫 233
谲 233
角 233
爵 234
嚼 234
绝 234
觉 234
juè 倔 234
jūn 均 234
钧 235
君 235
菌 235
军 235
jùn 俊 235
峻 235
骏 235
竣 235
郡 235

K

kā 咖 236
kǎ 卡 236
咯 236
kāi 开 236
揩 238
kǎi 凯 238
恺 238
铠 238
楷 238
慨 238
kān 堪 238
勘 238
戡 238
刊 238
看 238
龛 239
kǎn 坎 239
砍 239
槛 239
kàn 瞰 239
看 239
kāng 康 239
慷 239
糠 239
káng 扛 239
kàng 亢 240
伉 240
抗 240
炕 240
kǎo 考 240
拷 240
烤 240
kào 铐 240
靠 240
kē 珂 241
柯 241
苛 241
疴 241
颗 241
窠 241
磕 241
瞌 241
科 241
ké 颏 241
壳 241
咳 241
kě 可 241
渴 242
kè 恪 242
客 242
课 243
克 243
刻 243
kěn 垦 243
恳 243
肯 243
啃 244
kēng 坑 244
吭 244
铿 244
kōng 空 244
kǒng 孔 244
恐 245
kòng 空 245
控 245
kǒu 口 245
kòu 寇 246

叩 246
扣 246
kū 枯 246
骷 246
窟 246
哭 246
kǔ 苦 246
kù 酷 247
库 247
裤 247
kuā 夸 247
kuá 胯 248
跨 248
kuài 会 248
侩 248
狯 248
脍 248
块 248
快 248
筷 248
kuān 宽 248
kuǎn 款 249
kuāng 匡 249
诓 249
筐 249
kuáng 狂 249
诳 249
kuàng 旷 249
矿 249
况 250
框 250
眶 250
kuī 亏 250
窥 250
盔 250
kuí 揆 250
暌 250
睽 250
葵 250
魁 251
逵 251
kuǐ 傀 251
kuì 馈 251
愦 251
溃 251
聩 251
篑 251
喟 251
愧 251
kūn 昆 251
坤 251
kǔn 捆 251
kùn 困 251
kuò 括 251
阔 252
廓 252
扩 252

L

lā 垃 253
拉 253
啦 253
邋 253
lá 拉 253
lǎ 喇 253
là 辣 253
瘌 254
腊 254
蜡 254
落 254
la 啦 254
lái 来 254
lài 徕 254
睐 254
赖 254
濑 255
癞 255
lán 兰 255
拦 255
栏 255
阑 255
谰 255
澜 255
褴 255
蓝 255
篮 255
婪 255
岚 255
lǎn 览 255
揽 255
缆 255
懒 255
làn 烂 256
滥 256
lāng 啷 256
láng 狼 256
琅 256
郎 256
榔 256
鎯 256
廊 256
lǎng 朗 256
làng 浪 256
lāo 捞 256
láo 劳 257
唠 257
痨 257
牢 257
醪 257
lǎo 老 257
佬 258
姥 258
潦 258
lào 络 258
烙 258
酪 258
唠 258
涝 258
lè 勒 258
乐 258
le 了 259
lēi 勒 259
擂 259
léi 累 259
雷 259
擂 259
镭 259
羸 259
lěi 累 259
垒 260
耒 260
蕾 260
磊 260
lèi 类 260
累 260
擂 260
肋 260
泪 260
léng 棱 260
lěng 冷 260
lèng 楞 261
lí 离 261
缡 261
篱 261
梨 261
犁 261
黎 261
黧 261
藜 261
骊 261
狸 261
厘 261
蠡 262
罹 262
lǐ 里 262
俚 262
理 262
鲤 262
醴 262
礼 262
李 263
lì 历 263
呖 263
沥 263
厉 263
励 263
蛎 263
粝 263
疠 263
戾 264
唳 264
利 264
痢 264
立 264
粒 264
笠 265
莅 265
栗 265
砾 265
丽 265
俪 265
郦 265
力 265

M

N

O

殴 322
鸥 322
ǒu 偶 322
耦 322
呕 322

P

pā 趴 323
啪 323
葩 323
pá 耙 323
爬 323
扒 323
pà 怕 323
帕 323
pāi 拍 323
pái 排 324
徘 324
牌 324
pài 派 324
pān 潘 325
攀 325
pán 磐 325
盘 325
蟠 325
蹒 325
pàn 畔 325
判 325
叛 326
盼 326
pāng 滂 326
乓 326
páng 旁 326
膀 326
磅 326
螃 326
彷 326
庞 327
pàng 胖 327
pāo 抛 327
páo 泡 327
咆 327
炮 327
袍 327
刨 327
pǎo 跑 327
pào 泡 327
炮 327
pēi 呸 328
胚 328
péi 陪 328
培 328
赔 328
pèi 沛 328
配 328
佩 329
辔 329
pēn 喷 329
pén 盆 329
pèn 喷 329
pēng 抨 329
怦 329
砰 329
澎 329
烹 329
péng 朋 329
鹏 329
棚 329
膨 330
蓬 330
篷 330
pěng 捧 330
pèng 碰 330
pī 坯 330
披 330
批 331
霹 331
砒 331
劈 331
pí 枇 331
毗 331
琵 331
啤 331
脾 331
皮 331
疲 332
pǐ 痞 332
癖 332
匹 332
pì 辟 332
僻 332
譬 332
屁 332
媲 332
piān 扁 332
偏 332
翩 333
篇 333
片 333
pián 胼 333
便 333
piàn 骗 333
片 333
piāo 漂 333
剽 334
飘 334
piáo 嫖 334
瓢 334
piǎo 漂 334
瞟 334
殍 334
piào 票 334
漂 334
骠 334
piē 撇 334
瞥 334
piě 撇 334
pīn 拼 335
姘 335
pín 频 335
贫 335
pǐn 品 335
pìn 牝 335
聘 335
pīng 乒 336
píng 瓶 336
屏 336
平 336
坪 337
评 337
苹 337
萍 337
凭 337
pō 坡 338
颇 338
泼 338
泊 338
pó 婆 338
pǒ 叵 338
pò 魄 338
迫 338
破 338
pōu 剖 339
pū 仆 339
扑 339
铺 339
pú 璞 339
脯 339
蒲 339
匍 339
葡 340
仆 340
菩 340
pǔ 浦 340
圃 340
普 340
谱 340
朴 340
蹼 340
pù 暴 340
瀑 340
铺 340

Q

qī 欺 341
期 341
戚 341
蹊 341
妻 341
凄 341
萋 341
栖 341
七 342
漆 342
缉 342
qí 其 342
骐 342
棋 342
琪 342
祺 342

麒 343
旗 343
奇 343
崎 343
骑 343
琦 343
祈 343
颀 343
歧 343
齐 343
脐 343
鳍 343
qǐ 杞 343
起 343
企 344
绮 344
岂 344
启 344
乞 344
qì 契 344
讫 344
迄 344
汽 344
泣 344
葺 344
砌 344
器 344
气 345
弃 345
憩 345
qiā 掐 345
qiǎ 卡 345
qià 洽 346
恰 346
qiān 千 346
阡 346
钎 346
芊 346
迁 346
搴 346
签 346
谦 346
悭 347
铅 347
牵 347
愆 347
qián 钳 347
黔 347
钱 347
潜 347
前 347
虔 348
掮 348
qiǎn 遣 348
谴 348
浅 348
qiàn 欠 348
歉 348
慊 348
倩 348
堑 348
纤 348
茜 348
嵌 348
qiāng 呛 349
枪 349
腔 349
锵 349
羌 349
戕 349
镪 349
qiáng 墙 349
樯 349
强 349
qiǎng 强 350
襁 350
抢 350
qiàng 呛 350
qiāo 跷 350
悄 350
敲 350
锹 350
qiáo 憔 350
樵 350
瞧 350
乔 350
侨 350
桥 350
荞 351
翘 351
qiǎo 悄 351
愀 351
巧 351
qiào 诮 351
俏 351
峭 351
鞘 351
壳 351
窍 351
翘 351
撬 351
qiē 切 351
qié 茄 352
qiě 且 352
qiè 切 352
窃 352
挈 352
锲 352
惬 352
箧 352
妾 352
怯 352
qīn 侵 353
钦 353
亲 353
衾 353
qín 勤 353
琴 353
禽 353
噙 353
擒 353
qǐn 寝 354
qìn 沁 354
揿 354
qīng 青 354
清 354
蜻 354
氢 354
轻 354
倾 355
qíng 情 355
晴 355
擎 355
黥 355
qǐng 顷 355
请 355
qìng 罄 356
庆 356
亲 356
qióng 穷 356
琼 356
qiū 秋 356
丘 356
邱 357
蚯 357
qiú 求 357
球 357
裘 357
逑 357
酋 357
遒 357
囚 357
泅 357
qū 祛 357
区 357
驱 357
躯 358
蛆 358
曲 358
屈 358
趋 358
qú 渠 358
qǔ 取 358
娶 358
曲 358
qù 觑 359
去 359
趣 359
quān 圈 359
悛 359
quán 全 359
诠 360
痊 360
蜷 360
鬈 360
拳 360
颧 360
权 360
泉 360
quǎn 犬 360
quàn 劝 360
券 360
quē 缺 361
què 确 361

榷 361
阙 361
阕 361
却 361
雀 361
qún 裙 361
群 361
麇 361

R

rán 髯 362
然 362
燃 362
rǎn 染 362
ráng 瓤 362
rǎng 壤 362
攘 363
嚷 363
ràng 让 363
ráo 娆 363
饶 363
rǎo 扰 363
rào 绕 363
rě 喏 363
惹 363
rè 热 364
rén 人 364
仁 365
rěn 忍 365
稔 366
荏 366
rèn 刃 366
纫 366
韧 366
轫 366
认 366
妊 367
饪 367
衽 367
任 367
rēng 扔 367
réng 仍 367
rì 日 367
róng 容 368
溶 368
熔 368
榕 368
蓉 369
戎 369
绒 369
荣 369
融 369
茸 369
rǒng 冗 369
róu 柔 369
揉 369
糅 369
蹂 370
鞣 370
ròu 肉 370
rú 儒 370
孺 370
濡 370
襦 370
蠕 370
如 370
茹 370
rǔ 汝 371
辱 371
乳 371
rù 缛 371
蓐 371
褥 371
入 371
ruǎn 软 371
ruǐ 蕊 371
ruì 蚋 372
锐 372
睿 372
瑞 372
rùn 闰 372
润 372
ruò 若 372
偌 372
箬 372
弱 372

S

sā 撒 373
sǎ 洒 373
撒 373
sà 萨 373
卅 373
飒 373
sāi 腮 373
鳃 373
塞 373
sài 塞 373
赛 374
sān 三 374
叁 374
sǎn 散 374
伞 374
sàn 散 374
sāng 桑 375
丧 375
sǎng 嗓 375
sàng 丧 375
sāo 搔 375
骚 375
臊 375
缫 375
sǎo 扫 375
嫂 375
sào 臊 375
扫 375
埽 375
sè 啬 376
穑 376
涩 376
色 376
瑟 376
塞 376
sēn 森 376
sēng 僧 376
shā 纱 376
砂 376
沙 376
杉 377
鲨 377
痧 377
杀 377
刹 377
煞 377
shǎ 傻 377
shà 霎 377
啥 377
厦 377
煞 378
shāi 筛 378
shài 晒 378
shān 删 378
姗 378
珊 378
苫 378
杉 378
衫 378
扇 378
搧 379
煽 379
山 379
舢 379
膻 379
芟 379
shǎn 䀹 379
陕 379
闪 379
shàn 善 379
缮 380
膳 380
蟮 380
鳝 380
禅 380
擅 380
讪 380
疝 380
扇 380
赡 380
苫 380
shāng 伤 380
商 381
shǎng 晌 381
上 381
赏 381
shàng 上 381
尚 382
shāo 捎 382

梢 382
稍 382
艄 382
鞘 382
筲 382
烧 382
sháo 勺 383
芍 383
韶 383
shǎo 少 383
shào 绍 383
邵 383
哨 383
少 383
shē 赊 383
奢 383
shé 折 383
蛇 384
舌 384
佘 384
shě 舍 384
shè 摄 384
慑 384
舍 384
设 384
射 384
麝 385
社 385
涉 385
赦 385
shēn 申 385
伸 385
呻 386
绅 386
砷 386
参 386
深 386
莘 386
身 386
娠 386
shén 神 387
什 387
甚 387
shěn 审 387
婶 387
哂 387
shèn 甚 388
蜃 388
贤 388
渗 388
慎 388
shēng 生 388
牲 389
甥 389
笙 389
升 389
昇 389
声 389
shéng 绳 389
shěng 省 389
shèng 乘 390
剩 390
盛 390
胜 390
圣 391
shī 师 391
狮 391
施 391
尸 391
诗 392
虱 392
失 392
湿 392
shí 时 392
鲥 393
石 393
十 393
什 393
食 393
蚀 393
实 394
识 394
拾 394
shǐ 史 394
驶 394
使 394
矢 395
豕 395
屎 395
始 395
shì 式 395
试 395
拭 395
轼 395
弑 395
侍 395
恃 395
噬 396
氏 396
舐 396
市 396
柿 396
释 396
士 396
仕 397
世 397
是 397
嗜 397
适 397
逝 398
势 398
誓 398
示 398
视 399
饰 399
室 399
谥 399
似 399
事 399
shōu 收 400
shǒu 手 400
首 401
守 401
shòu 受 402
授 402
绶 402
狩 402
寿 402
售 402
兽 402
瘦 402
shū 抒 403
舒 403
梳 403
疏 403
蔬 403
叔 403
淑 403
菽 403
输 403
姝 404
殊 404
书 404
枢 404
倏 404
shú 孰 404
塾 404
熟 404
赎 405
shǔ 署 405
曙 405
薯 405
暑 405
蜀 405
鼠 405
属 405
黍 406
数 406
shù 术 406
述 406
束 406
漱 406
树 406
数 407
戍 407
竖 407
庶 407
恕 407
墅 407
shuā 刷 407
shuǎ 耍 407
shuà 刷 407
shuāi 衰 407
摔 408
shuǎi 甩 408
shuài 率 408
帅 408
shuān 拴 408
闩 408
shuàn 涮 408
shuāng 双 408
霜 409
孀 409
shuǎng 爽 409

shuí 谁 409
shuǐ 水 409
shuì 说 410
税 410
睡 410
shǔn 吮 410
shùn 舜 410
瞬 410
顺 410
shuō 说 411
shuò 朔 411
铄 411
数 411
硕 411
sī 斯 411
撕 412
嘶 412
厮 412
思 412
丝 412
司 412
私 412
sǐ 死 413
sì 伺 413
饲 413
嗣 413
四 413
泗 414
驷 414
巳 414
祀 414
似 414
肆 414
俟 414
寺 414
食 414
si 厕 414
sōng 松 415
sǒng 怂 415
悚 415
耸 415
sòng 宋 415
送 415
颂 415
诵 415
讼 416
sōu 搜 416
艘 416
嗖 416
sǒu 叟 416
sòu 嗽 416
sū 稣 416
酥 416
苏 416
sú 俗 416
sù 速 417
簌 417
素 417
宿 417
肃 417
粟 417
溯 418
塑 418
诉 418
suān 酸 418
suàn 蒜 418
算 418
suī 虽 418
suí 隋 419
随 419
绥 419
遂 419
suǐ 髓 419
suì 遂 419
隧 419
碎 419
穗 420
岁 420
祟 420
sūn 孙 420
sǔn 损 420
榫 420
笋 420
suō 唆 420
梭 420
蓑 420
缩 420
suǒ 唢 421
锁 421
琐 421
索 421
所 421

T

tā 它 423
他 423
她 423
塌 423
tǎ 塔 423
獭 423
tà 踏 423
榻 423
蹋 423
拓 423
呔 423
tāi 胎 424
tái 苔 424
台 424
抬 424
苔 424
台 424
台 424
tài 太 424
汰 424
态 424
泰 424
tān 摊 425
滩 425
瘫 425
贪 425
坍 425
tán 谈 425
痰 425
谭 425
潭 425
坛 425
坛 426
昙 426
弹 426
檀 426
tǎn 毯 426
坦 426
袒 426
忐 426
tàn 碳 426
炭 426
探 426
叹 427
tāng 汤 427
táng 唐 427
塘 427
搪 427
糖 427
溏 427
棠 427
堂 427
膛 427
螳 427
tǎng 傥 428
倘 428
淌 428
躺 428
tàng 烫 428
趟 428
tāo 滔 428
掏 428
涛 428
táo 桃 428
逃 428
陶 428
淘 429
tǎo 讨 429
tào 套 429
tè 特 429
téng 誊 430
腾 430
疼 430
藤 430
tī 梯 430
剔 430
踢 430
tí 提 430
题 431
啼 431
蹄 431
tǐ 体 431
tì 惕 432
剃 432
涕 432

屜 432
倜 432
嚏 432
替 432
tiān 天 432
添 433
tián 田 433
填 433
甜 433
恬 433
tiǎn 舔 433
殄 433
tiāo 佻 433
挑 433
tiáo 迢 434
条 434
调 434
tiǎo 挑 434
窕 434
tiào 眺 434
跳 435
tiē 贴 435
帖 435
tiě 帖 435
铁 435
tiè 帖 435
tīng 厅 436
听 436
tíng 廷 436
蜓 436
霆 436
庭 436
亭 436
停 436
婷 436
tǐng 挺 436
铤 437
艇 437
tōng 通 437
tóng 同 438
桐 439
铜 439
童 439
僮 439
瞳 439
彤 439
筒 439
tǒng 桶 439
桶 439
统 439
tòng 痛 439
恸 440
tōu 偷 440
tóu 投 440
骰 441
头 441
tòu 透 441
tū 突 441
凸 442
秃 442
tú 涂 442
荼 442
途 442
图 442
徒 442
屠 443
tǔ 土 443
吐 443
tù 兔 443
吐 443
tuān 湍 444
tuán 团 444
团 444
tuī 推 444
tuí 颓 445
tuǐ 腿 445
tuì 蜕 445
退 445
tūn 吞 445
tún 屯 446
囤 446
豚 446
臀 446
tuō 托 446
脱 446
拖 446
tuó 陀 447
驼 447
鸵 447
驮 447
tuǒ 椭 447
妥 447
tuò 拓 447
唾 447

W

wā 哇 448
洼 448
蛙 448
挖 448
娲 448
wá 娃 448
wǎ 瓦 448
wà 袜 448
瓦 449
wa 哇 449
wāi 歪 449
wài 外 449
wān 剜 449
蜿 449
弯 449
湾 450
wán 玩 450
顽 450
完 450
丸 450
纨 451
wǎn 宛 451
惋 451
婉 451
碗 451
挽 451
晚 451
绾 451
皖 451
wàn 蔓 451
万 451
wāng 汪 452
wáng 亡 452
王 452
wǎng 罔 453
惘 453
魍 453
网 453
往 453
枉 453
wàng 旺 454
望 454
妄 454
忘 454
往 454
wēi 偎 454
煨 454
委 454
萎 455
威 455
微 455
危 455
巍 455
wéi 韦 456
帏 456
违 456
围 456
惟 456
唯 456
帷 456
维 456
为 457
桅 457
wěi 伟 457
纬 457
委 457
诿 457
萎 457
痿 458
猥 458
伪 458
尾 458
娓 458
唯 458
wèi 尉 458
蔚 458
慰 458
胃 458
谓 458
猬 459
畏 459
喂 459
未 459
味 459
卫 459
为 460
位 460

魏 460
wēn 温 460
瘟 460
wén 文 461
纹 461
蚊 461
雯 461
闻 461
wěn 紊 462
刎 462
吻 462
稳 462
wèn 问 462
wēng 翁 462
嗡 462
wèng 瓮 462
wō 涡 463
蜗 463
窝 463
倭 463
喔 463
wǒ 我 463
wò 握 463
幄 463
龌 463
沃 463
卧 463
斡 463
wū 乌 464
呜 464
污 464
屋 464
巫 464
诬 464
wú 吾 464
梧 464
鼯 464
无 464
芜 466
吴 466
蜈 466
毋 466
wǔ 午 466
武 466
妩 466
舞 466
五 466
伍 466
捂 467
侮 467
wù 悟 467
晤 467
骛 467
务 467
雾 467
勿 467
物 467
坞 467
误 467
恶 468
戊 468

X

xī 希 469
稀 469
奚 469
溪 469
嘻 469
嬉 469
熹 469
西 469
牺 469
析 469
晰 470
蜥 470
息 470
熄 470
夕 470
汐 470
吸 470
昔 470
惜 470
悉 470
锡 470
曦 470
兮 470
熙 471
膝 471
蟋 471
犀 471
xí 习 471
熄 471
席 471
袭 471
檄 471
xǐ 徙 471
喜 472
禧 472
洗 472
玺 472
xì 隙 472
细 472
戏 473
系 473
阋 473
xiā 虾 473
瞎 473
xiá 瑕 473
暇 473
霞 473
遐 473
侠 473
狭 473
峡 474
狎 474
匣 474
辖 474
黠 474
xià 下 474
吓 475
夏 475
xiān 先 475
纤 475
仙 475
掀 476
鲜 476
xián 闲 476
娴 476
弦 476
舷 476
咸 476
嫌 476
涎 477
衔 477
贤 477
xiǎn 冼 477
险 477
鲜 477
藓 477
显 477
蚬 477
xiàn 现 478
苋 478
宪 478
羡 478
限 478
陷 478
县 478
线 479
馅 479
腺 479
献 479
xiāng 襄 479
镶 479
相 479
湘 480
箱 480
厢 480
乡 480
香 480
xiáng 详 480
祥 480
翔 480
降 480
xiǎng 响 481
饷 481
享 481
想 481
xiàng 象 481
像 481
橡 482
向 482
相 482
项 482
巷 482
xiāo 削 482
消 482
销 483
硝 483
宵 483
霄 483
逍 483
萧 483

箫 483
潇 483
骁 483
嚣 483
哮 483
枭 483
xiáo 淆 483
xiǎo 晓 483
小 483
xiào 肖 484
校 484
效 484
啸 484
孝 485
笑 485
xiē 歇 485
些 485
蝎 485
xié 协 485
胁 485
偕 486
谐 486
挟 486
携 486
邪 486
斜 486
xiě 写 486
xiè 懈 486
蟹 486
泄 486
屑 486
泻 487
械 487
谢 487
亵 487
卸 487
xīn 欣 487
辛 487
心 487
新 488
薪 489
馨 489
xìn 衅 489
芯 489
信 489
xīng 星 489
猩 489
惺 490
腥 490
兴 490
xíng 刑 490
形 490
型 490
行 490
xǐng 省 491
醒 491
xìng 幸 491
悻 491
性 491
姓 492
杏 492
兴 492
xiōng 凶 492
汹 492
胸 492
兄 493
xióng 雄 493
熊 493
xiū 休 493
羞 493
修 493
xiǔ 朽 494
宿 494
xiù 臭 494
嗅 494
秀 494
绣 494
锈 494
袖 494
宿 494
xū 吁 494
虚 494
墟 495
嘘 495
须 495
需 495
xú 徐 495
xǔ 许 495
栩 496
诩 496
xù 序 496
恤 496
畜 496
蓄 496
叙 496
煦 496
续 496
酗 496
旭 496
绪 496
絮 496
婿 497
xuān 宣 497
喧 497
暄 497
萱 497
轩 497
xuán 旋 497
漩 497
玄 497
悬 498
xuǎn 烜 498
癣 498
选 498
xuàn 炫 498
眩 498
券 498
旋 498
绚 498
渲 498
xuē 削 499
靴 499
xué 学 499
穴 499
噱 499
xuě 雪 499
xuè 血 500
xùn 熏 500
醺 500
勋 500
xún 旬 500
询 500
寻 500
浔 501
驯 501
循 501
巡 501
xùn 殉 501
讯 501
汛 501
迅 501
训 501
逊 502
蕈 502

Y

yā 押 503
鸭 503
呀 503
鸦 503
压 503
yá 牙 504
蚜 504
芽 504
涯 504
崖 504
衙 504
yǎ 雅 504
哑 504
yà 轧 504
讶 505
迓 505
亚 505
揠 505
yān 淹 505
腌 505
焉 505
阉 505
嫣 505
咽 505
烟 505
胭 506
湮 506
殷 506
yán 延 506
筵 506
阎 506
妍 506
研 506
言 506
檐 507

沿 507
严 507
岩 507
炎 507
盐 507
颜 508

yǎn
偃 508
鼹 508
奄 508
掩 508
演 508
俨 508
衍 508
眼 508

yàn
燕 509
咽 509
宴 509
谚 509
厌 509
艳 509
焰 510
堰 510
雁 510
赝 510
砚 510
唁 510
验 510

yāng
央 510
殃 510
秧 510

yáng
羊 510
佯 510
洋 510
扬 511
杨 511
疡 511
阳 511

yǎng
氧 511
痒 511
养 511
仰 512
样 512
恙 512
漾 512
怏 512
鞅 512

yāo
要 512
腰 512
夭 512
妖 512
吆 513
邀 513

yáo
谣 513
徭 513
摇 513
瑶 513
遥 513
窑 513
尧 513
肴 513

yǎo
咬 513
窈 514
舀 514

yào
耀 514
药 514
要 514
钥 515

yē
耶 515
椰 515
掖 515
噎 515

yé
耶 515
爷 515

yě
也 515
冶 515
野 515

yè
夜 516
掖 516
液 516
腋 516
谒 516
业 516
曳 516
叶 516
页 516

yī
医 516
衣 517
依 517
漪 517
伊 517
咿 517
一 517
壹 520
揖 520

yí
夷 520
咦 520
姨 520
胰 520
痍 520
饴 520
怡 520
贻 520
移 521
颐 521
疑 521
仪 521
宜 521
遗 521

yǐ
倚 522
椅 522
旖 522
迤 522
蚁 522
乙 522
以 522
已 523
矣 523

yì
意 523
臆 523
译 523
驿 523
益 523
溢 523
缢 524
亿 524
忆 524
艺 524
呓 524
邑 524
悒 524
亦 524
奕 524
役 524
毅 524
疫 524
翼 524
异 525
屹 525
裔 525
翌 525
易 525
义 525
议 526
诣 526
抑 526
谊 526
逸 526
肄 526

yīn
因 526
姻 527
茵 527
音 527
阴 527
荫 527
殷 527

yín
银 527
龈 527
寅 527
淫 527
霪 528
吟 528

yǐn
隐 528
瘾 528
引 528
饮 528

yìn
印 528
荫 528

yīng
婴 528
缨 528
樱 529
鹦 529
罂 529
英 529
莺 529
膺 529
鹰 529
应 529

yíng
莹 529
萤 530
营 530
赢 530
盈 530
迎 530
蝇 530

yǐng 颖 530
影 531
yìng 应 531
映 531
硬 531
yō 唷 531
哟 532
yōng 雍 532
臃 532
壅 532
庸 532
慵 532
佣 532
拥 532
痈 532
yóng 喁 532
yǒng 甬 532
俑 533
涌 533
蛹 533
踊 533
勇 533
永 533
泳 533
咏 533
yòng 用 533
佣 534
yōu 忧 534
优 534
悠 534
幽 535
yóu 尤 535
犹 535
鱿 535
由 535
邮 535
油 536
柚 536
铀 536
游 536
yǒu 黝 536
有 536
酉 538
友 538
莠 538
yòu 宥 538
右 538
幼 538
佑 538
柚 538
釉 538
鼬 538
诱 538
又 539
yū 迂 539
淤 539
瘀 539
yú 俞 539
愉 539
渝 539
瑜 539
榆 539
逾 539
隅 539
愚 539
于 540
盂 540
舆 540
谀 540
腴 540
余 540
鱼 540
渔 540
虞 541
娱 541
yǔ 语 541
宇 541
伛 541
与 541
屿 541
予 541
羽 541
雨 541
yù 域 542
鹬 542
浴 542
裕 542
欲 542
谕 542
喻 542
愈 542
尉 543
预 543
育 543
寓 543
遇 543
妪 543
芋 543
吁 544
玉 544
御 544
与 544
誉 544
郁 544
驭 544
狱 544
yuān 鸳 544
渊 544
冤 544
yuán 原 545
援 545
猿 545
元 545
源 546
园 546
辕 546
员 546
圆 546
缘 546
yuǎn 远 546
yuàn 苑 547
怨 547
院 547
愿 547
媛 547
yuē 曰 547
约 547
yuè 月 548
钥 548
悦 548
阅 548
越 548
乐 548
跃 548
岳 549
粤 549
yūn 晕 549
yún 云 549
耘 549
芸 549
匀 549
yǔn 陨 549
殒 549
允 549
yùn 愠 549
蕴 549
晕 549
酝 549
运 549
韵 550
孕 550
熨 550

Z

zā 扎 551
咂 551
zá 杂 551
砸 551
zāi 栽 551
灾 552
zǎi 宰 552
仔 552
载 552
zài 载 552
再 552
在 552
zān 簪 553
zán 咱 553
zǎn 攒 553
zàn 赞 553
暂 554
錾 554
zāng 脏 554
赃 554
zàng 藏 554
脏 554
葬 554
zāo 糟 554
遭 554
záo 凿 555
zǎo 澡 555
藻 555
早 555
枣 555

蚤 555
zào 噪 555
燥 555
躁 555
造 555
皂 556
灶 556
zé 责 556
啧 556
泽 556
择 556
则 556
贼 557
zěn 怎 557
zēng 曾 557
增 557
憎 557
赠 557
zhā 喳 558
渣 558
zhá 扎 558
札 558
轧 558
闸 558
炸 558
铡 558
zhǎ 眨 558
zhà 乍 558
诈 558
咋 558
炸 558
蚱 558
榨 559
栅 559
zhāi 斋 559
摘 559
zhái 宅 559
zhǎi 窄 559
zhài 债 559
寨 559
zhān 占 559
沾 559
粘 560
毡 560
瞻 560
zhǎn 展 560
辗 560
斩 560
崭 560
盏 560
zhàn 占 560
站 561
战 561
栈 562
绽 562
颤 562
湛 562
zhāng 章 562
樟 562
蟑 562
彰 562
张 562
zhǎng 掌 563
长 563
涨 563
zhàng 帐 563
账 564
胀 564
涨 564
障 564
瘴 564
丈 564
仗 564
杖 564
zhāo 招 564
昭 565
朝 565
zháo 着 566
zhǎo 爪 566
找 566
沼 566
zhào 兆 566
召 566
诏 566
照 566
罩 567
赵 567
肇 567
zhē 蜇 567
遮 567
zhé 折 567
折 567
蜇 568
哲 568
蛰 568
辙 568
摺 568
zhě 者 568
褶 568
zhè 鹧 568
这 568
zhe 着 568
zhēn 贞 568
侦 569
斟 569
砧 569
珍 569
针 569
真 569
甄 570
zhěn 诊 570
疹 570
缜 570
枕 570
zhèn 振 570
赈 571
震 571
镇 571
阵 571
zhēng 争 571
挣 572
狰 572
峥 572
铮 572
睁 572
筝 572
正 572
怔 572
征 572
征 573
症 573
蒸 573
zhěng 拯 573
整 573
正 574
zhèng 正 574
证 575
政 575
症 576
郑 576
zhī 支 576
枝 576
肢 576
知 576
蜘 577
之 577
芝 577
只 577
织 577
汁 577
脂 677
zhí 直 577
值 578
植 578
殖 578
职 578
执 578
侄 579
zhǐ 止 579
址 579
趾 579
纸 579
只 579
旨 579
指 579
zhì 至 580
桎 581
蛭 581
致 581
窒 581
痔 581
质 581
帜 581
秩 581
挚 581
制 581
制 582
志 582
志 582
痣 582
置 582
智 583

拼音	字	页
	稚	583
	滞	583
	治	583
	掷	583
	炙	583
	栉	583
zhōng	中	583
	钟	584
	钟	584
	忠	585
	盅	585
	衷	585
	终	585
zhǒng	肿	585
	种	585
	踵	585
	冢	585
zhòng	中	585
	仲	586
	种	586
	众	586
	重	586
zhōu	周	587
	舟	587
	州	587
	洲	587
	诌	587
	粥	587
zhóu	妯	587
	轴	588
zhǒu	帚	588
	肘	588
zhòu	宙	588
	绉	588
	皱	588
	咒	588
	昼	588
	骤	588
	胄	588
zhū	朱	588
	侏	588
	诛	588
	珠	588
	株	589
	蛛	589
	诸	589
	猪	589
zhú	烛	589
	竹	589
	逐	589
zhǔ	主	590
	嘱	590
	瞩	591
	煮	591
zhù	住	591
	注	591
	驻	591
	柱	591
	蛀	592
	贮	592
	苎	592
	著	592
	箸	592
	祝	592
	助	592
	筑	592
	铸	592
zhuā	抓	593
zhuān	专	593
	砖	593
zhuǎn	转	594
zhuàn	传	594
	转	594
	篆	595
	撰	595
	赚	595
zhuāng	装	595
	庄	595
	桩	595
	妆	595
zhuàng	撞	595
	壮	596
	状	596
zhuī	椎	596
	锥	596
	追	596
zhuì	缀	597
	坠	597
	惴	597
	赘	597
zhūn	谆	597
zhún	准	597
zhuō	卓	597
	桌	597
	捉	598
	拙	598
zhuó	浊	598
	啄	598
	琢	598
	灼	598
	镯	598
	擢	598
	茁	598
	酌	598
	着	598
zī	咨	599
	姿	599
	资	599
	髭	599
	孜	599
	兹	599
	滋	599
	辎	600
	吱	600
zǐ	子	600
	仔	600
	紫	600
	姊	600
	滓	600
zì	字	600
	自	600
	恣	602
	渍	602
zi	子	603
zóng	宗	603
	综	603
	棕	603
	踪	603
	鬃	603
zǒng	总	603
zòng	纵	604
	粽	604
zǒu	走	604
zòu	奏	605
	揍	605
zū	租	605
zú	卒	605
	族	605
	足	605
zǔ	诅	606
	阻	606
	组	606
	祖	606
zuān	钻	606
zuǎn	纂	607
zuàn	钻	607
zuǐ	嘴	607
zuì	醉	607
	最	607
	罪	607
zūn	尊	608
	樽	608
	遵	608
zúo	昨	608
zǔo	左	608
	佐	608
	撮	608
zùo	作	608
	坐	609
	座	610
	做	610

A

ā

阿 [ā] (part) 加在称呼前面的词 an initial particle ; prefix to names of people. 阿姨，真高兴见到你! Auntie, how glad to see you!

阿飞 [āfēi] a hoodlum

阿片 [āpiàn] opium

阿司匹林 [asīpǐlín] aspirin

啊 [ā] (interj) 叹词，表示赞叹或惊异 to express admiration or surprise *啊，多么惊奇! Oh, what a surprise!

腌 [ā] (腌臜) [āzā] (adj) 肮脏，不干净 filthy; unclean

另见 [yān]

á

啊 [á] (interj) 叹词，表示疑问或反问 to express doubts or to question *啊，这是你的吗？ Is this yours, eh?

à

啊 [à] (interj) 叹词，表示答应或醒悟 to express a promise or to show realization. * 啊，就这么办吧！ Ah, let's do it this way. * 啊，原来是这么回事！ Ah, this is what the matter is about!

·a

啊 [·a] (part) 助词，表示语气或感情，用于句末 used at the end of a sentence, as an accent, or a stress * 大家看啊！ Look, everyone!

āi

唉 [āi] (interj) 表示答应 to express a promise * 唉，去吧 。 Aye, go ahead.

另见 [ái]

埃 [āi] 1 (n) 尘土，灰土 dirt; dust 2 (n) 长度单位，一万万分之一厘米 angstorm, a unit of length, equal to 0.00000001 cm.

挨 [āi] 1 (v) 靠拢 lean to * 大家挨着坐。We sit leaning against one another. 2 (adv) 依次，顺次 in order; in sequence * 挨户通知。Inform one after another.

挨次 [āicì] in order

另见 [ái]

哀 [āi] 1 (n, adj) 悲痛，悲伤 sorrow; grief; pity; sad; woeful; distressing 2 (v) 悼念，怜悯 to grieve for; to sympathize with; to pity

哀辞 [āicí] eulogies written for the death of friends

哀悼 [āidào] to condole; to mourn

哀的美敦书 [āidìměidūnshū] ultimatum

哀歌 [āigē] an elegy

哀号 [āiháo] to wail loudly

哀泣 [āiqì] to weep bitterly
哀求 [āiqíu] to appeal to; to implore
哀诉 [āisù] to appeal; to petition; to complain
哀痛 [āitòng] to feel grief

哎 [āi] (interj) 叹词，表示不满或提醒 to express discontent or to remind ＊哎，你太慢了。Hey, you are too slow.

ái

皑(皚) [ái] (adj) 洁白，常叠用 dazzling white ＊皑皑白雪盖满了街道 The streets are covered with dazzling white snow.

捱 [ái] (v) 遭受 to suffer 困难地度过 to pass with difficulty ＊他终於捱过了年关。He finally passed the New Year festival with difficulty.

呆 [ái] (adj) 不灵活 idiotic
呆板 [áibǎn] clumsy
另见[dāi]

挨 [ái] (v) 遭受 to suffer ＊那个学徒常挨老板的打骂 The apprentice often suffers scoldings and beatings by his master.
另见[āi]

癌 [ái] (n) 上皮细胞所形成的恶性肿瘤（医）cancer

ǎi

蔼(藹) [ǎi] (adj) 和气 friendly ＊他是个和蔼的老人。He is a friendly old man.
藹然可親 [ǎirán kěqīn] friendly ; lovable.

霭(靄) [ǎi] (n) 云气 cloudiness

嗳(噯) [ǎi] (interj) 叹词，表示否定或不同意 to express denial or disagreement ＊嗳，别那么说。Oh, please don't say that.
另見 [ài]

矮 [ǎi] 1 (adj) 高度小 short ＊十七岁的孩子才四尺高是太矮了。Four feet is too short for the height of a seventeen-year-old child. 2 (adj) 等级低 low as of rank or position ＊中士比上士矮一级A Corporal is one rank lower than a sergeant
矮子 [ǎi·zi] a shorty

ài

艾 [ài] (n) 草本植物可供药用，叶可制艾绒 artemisia, a herb which produces punk
艾绒 [àiróng] moxa punk, used with castor-oil
另见 [yì]

爱(愛) [ài] (n, v, adj) 对人或事物具有深厚的，亲密的感情 love; affection;to be fond of; beloved ＊爱你的邻居。Love thy neighbours. ＊母爱是伟大的。Great is mother's love.
爱戴 [àidài] to love with special respect
爱抚 [àifǔ] to caress; to fondle
爱国 [àiguó] patriotic
爱国心 [àiguó xīn] 爱国精神 [àiguó jīngshén] patriotic spirit; patriotism
爱国运动 [àiguó yùndòng] a patriotic movement
爱国者 [àiguó zhě] 爱国志士 [àiguó zhìshì] a patriot
爱国主义 [àiguó zhǔyì] patriotism
爱好 [àihào] take delight in
爱护 [àihù] to take care for; to protect with loving care
爱己主义 [àijǐ zhǔyì] （利己主义）egoism
爱敬 [àijìng] to affect and respect
爱克斯光 [àikèsī guāng] X-rays
爱怜 [àilían] to pity; to be compassionate
爱恋 [àiliàn] in love; have a passion for
爱莫能助 [ài mò néng zhù] willing but have no ability to render assistance
爱慕 [àimù] to long for; have ardent desire for
爱情 [àiqíng] love; affection

爱人 [ài·ren] lover; sweetheart
爱人如己 [ài rén rú jǐ] love others as oneself
爱神 [àishén] the blind deity; Cupid; Eros; Venus
爱斯基摩人 [àisījīmórén] an Eskimo

爱他主义 [àitā zhǔyì] (利他主义) altruism
爱屋及乌 [ài wū jí wū] when one loves another the affection extends to his friend
爱惜 [àixī] to be sparing of; to be economical of
爱悦 [àiyuè] like; be pleased with; take delight in

嗳(噯) [ài] (interj) 叹词，表示懊恼，悔恨 to express regrets ＊嗳，这话我不应该说的。Alas, I should not have said such a thing. 另見 [ǎi]

媛(嬡) [ài] (n) 〔令媛〕旧时对别人女儿的敬称 a respectful term for the daughter of a friend, used in olden days

瑷(璦) [ài] (n) 美玉 jade

暧(曖) [ài] (adj) 昏暗 obscure
暧昧 [àimèi] ambiguous; vague; secretive

隘 [ài] 1 (n) 险要的地方 a pass; a defile 2 (adj) 狭窄 narrow; confined; obstructed; contracted ＊你的视野很狭隘 Your view is too narrow.
隘口 [àikǒu] the entrance to a pass
隘巷 [àixiàng] a narrow lane

唉 [ài] (interj) 叹词，表示失望或惋惜 to express disappointment or to feel sorry ＊唉，这么容易他也办不到。Ah, he can't even do such an easy job. ＊唉，她这么年轻就死了。Alas, she died so young!
另见 [āi]

碍(礙) [ài] (v) 妨害，阻拦 to obstruct; to impede; to block ＊他的病妨碍了学业的进步。His illness impeded his progress of study.
碍口 [ài kǒu] not convenient to speak
碍事 [ài shì] to be in the way; to obstruct; to meddle; inconvenient
碍手碍脚 [ài shǒu ài jiǎo] to impede in the process of work

ān

厂 [ān] 同"庵"（本页） similar to "庵"
另见 [chǎng]

庵 [ān] 1 (n) 小草屋 a thatched cottage 2 (n) 佛庙，多指尼姑居住的地方 a Buddhist temple, especially a Buddhist nunnery
庵堂 [āntáng] a convent; a Buddhist shrine

鹌(鵪) [ān] (n)〔鹌鹑〕[ānchún] 鸟类 a quail

安 [ān] 1 (adj) 平静，稳定 calm; still; quiet ＊请让我在安静的地方写诗 Please let me write poems in a quiet place. 2 (adj) 平安没有危险 safe ＊我们都平安无事，请勿担心 We are all safe; please do not worry. 3 (v) 使平静，使安定 to pacify; to settle ＊去安抚那受惊的小孩吧 Go and pacify the frightened child 4 (v) 装置 to install ＊我家里最近安了一个电话。Recently

my home has been installed a telephone. 5(adv) 怎么，哪里 how; where ∗安得而知之？How could [I] know it? ∗而今安在？Where is [he] now?

安瓿 [ānbù] an ampoule

安步当车 [ān bù dàng chē] to walk slowly and regard it as taking a car

安插 [ānchā] to find a place or position for one; to insert

安抵 [āndǐ] to arrive in safety

安定 [āndìng] at rest; tranquility

安顿 [āndùn] to accommodate; to arrange

安放 [ānfàng] to put in a safe place

安分 [ānfèn] contented with one's lot; take things easily

安分守己 [ān fèn shǒu jǐ] to keep one's duty and self-restraint; to mind one's own business

安好 [ānhǎo] well; in peace; in good health

安家费 [ānjiāfèi] an allotment or advance to support the family

安静 [ānjìng] repose; peaceful; quiet

安居 [ānjū] to settle down

安居乐业 [ān jū lè yè] to live in peace and be content with one's occupation

安乐 [ānlè] joyful; at ease; content

安谧 [ānmì] quiet; in repose

安眠 [ānmián] placid sleep; sound sleep

安眠药 [ānmiányào] a sleeping drug

安宁 [ānníng] peace; tranquillity

安排 [ānpái] to arrange; to appoint

安培 [ānpéi] ampere

安培计 [ānpéijì] amperemeter

安培小时 [ānpéi xiǎoshí] ampere-hour

安贫乐道 [ān pín lè dào] to stand poverty and keep straight

安琪儿 [ānqí'ér] angel

安全 [ānquán] safe; safety; security

安全玻璃 [ānquán bō·li] safety glass

安全灯 [ānquándēng] a safety lamp; a Davy lamp

安全感 [ānquángǎn] a sense of security

安全理事会 [ānquánlǐ shì huì] Security Council

安全系数 [ānquán xìshù] coefficient of safety; safety factor

安如磐石 [ān rú pán shí] firm as a rock

安身立命 [ān shēn lì mìng] to settle down physically and mentally

安神 [ānshén] to calm the spirit

安神药 [ānshényào] a soothing medicine

安适 [ānshì] to feel at home

安慰 [ānwèi] to comfort; to soothe; to afford consolation; to set at ease

安稳 [ānwěn] secure

安息 [ānxī] to rest

安息香 [ānxīxiāng] gum benzion

安闲 [ānxián] repose and leisure

安歇 [ānxiē] to lodge at; to rest

安心 [ānxīn] put the mind at rest; have no anxiety about

安逸 [ānyì] indolent

安营 [ānyíng] to pitch a camp

安葬 [ānzàng] to bury

安置 [ānzhì] to place; to appoint to

安装 [ānzhuāng] to install

鞍 [ān](n) 放在骡马背上的坐垫 a saddle

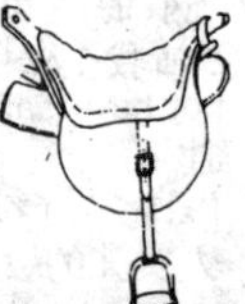

谙（諳） [ān](v) 熟悉 fully acquainted with; commit to memory

谙练 [ānliàn] skilled in; accustomed to; versed in; experienced; proficient

谙晓:谙悉 [ānxiǎo] [anxī] have a good knowledge of

氨 [ān] (n) 氮氢化合气体，也称阿摩尼亚 ammonia 〔化〕

ǎn

俺 [ǎn] (pronoun) 方言，我，我们 I or We in dialect

铵（銨） [ǎn] (n) 一种带阳电荷的基 ammonium; a positively

charged radical

àn

岸 [àn] 1 (n) 江，河，湖，海等水边的地 a bank; a shore; a beach; a coast ＊ 一些孩子在河岸上捉蚯蚓。Some children were catching worms on the bank of the river. 2 (adj) 高大 lofty

岸然 [ànrán] loftily; solemnly

按 [àn] 1 (v) 用手或指头压 to press with one's hand or finger ＊ 你只需按电钮一下，就会有人来开门。You need only to press the button once and someone will come to open the door. 2 (v) 压住，搁下 to put down; to put aside ＊ 因为大家都没空，此事就按下不谈。Discussion of the matter was put aside because all of us were busy. 3 (adv) 依照 according to; as ＊ 就按你所说的去做吧。Do according to what you say. 4 (v) 考查 to examine 5 (v) 抑制 to stop ; to control ＊ 我按不住心头怒火，打了他一顿。Unable to control my anger, I beat him up. 6 (n) 对书或文章所作的说明，评论 notes on a book or an article

按兵不动 [àn bīng bù dòng] to withhold the troops from action

按部就班 [àn bù jiù bān] orderly; well-behaved; careful to follow the prescribed way

按法惩办 [àn fǎ chéng bàn] to punish according to the law

按理 [ànlǐ] theoretically

按脉 [àn mài] to feel the pulse

按名发給 [ànmíng fāgěi] to distribute according to the list of names

按摩 [àn mó] to massage

按捺 [ànnà] to press down firmly; to control; to repress

按说 [ànshuō] generally speaking

按图索骥 [àn tú suǒ jì] to search for something basing on the hints given

按语 [ànyǔ] introductory words to an editorial note

按月分繳 [ànyuè fēnjiǎo] 按月摊还 [ànyuè tānhuán] monthly instalments

按照 [ànzhào] according to; as

按值 [ànzhí] advalorem

胺 [àn] (n) 氨的有机化合物 amine〔化〕

案 [àn] 1 (n) 长桌子或代替桌子用的长木板 a table, usually long ＊ 他伏在书案上睡着了。He fell asleep on the table. 2 (n) 涉及政治或法律的事件 a case in law ＊ 这宗谋杀案终於审完了。The trial of this murder case is finally over. 3 (n) 提出计划，办法等的文件 a plan; a proposal ＊ 他提出了未来五年的教育方案。He suggested the plan for education for the coming five years. 4 (n) 记事的文件 records of cases ＊ 秘书保有整个开会过程的案卷 The secretary kept a record of what was done at the meeting.

案板 [ànbǎn] a long board for making wheaten food

案牍 [àndú] documents

案件 [ànjiàn] a case in law

案卷 [ànjuán] documents kept for reference

案情 [ànqíng] the details of a legal case

案头 [àntóu] on the table

案由 [ànyóu] the outline of a legal case

暗 [àn] 1 (adj) 不明亮 dark; gloomy ＊ 这么暗的房间，怎能看书？ How can one read in such a dark room? 2 (adv) (adj) 秘密的，不公开的 secret ; private ＊ 那些间谍正在传暗号。Those spies were sending secret codes. 3 (adj) 藏在里面或底下的，看不见的 hidden ＊ 船只航近暗礁是危险的。It is dangerous for ships to sail near the hidden reefs. 4 (adj) 愚昧糊涂 stupid; ignorant ＊ 兼听則明，偏信則暗。It is wise to be open to all proposals but it is stupid to believe one- sidedly

暗藏 [àncáng] to conceal

暗潮 [ànchāo] a secret disaffection; an

undercurrent
暗淡 [àndàn] dark; gloomy
暗地里 [àndì·li] 暗中 [ànzhōng] in secret
暗斗 [àndòu] secret enmity
暗访 [ànfǎng] a secret inquiry
暗沟 [àngōu] a culvert; an underdrain
暗害 [ànhài] to injure secretly
暗号 [ànhào] a secret sign; a password; a code word; a cipher
暗合 [ànhé] to agree with accidentally; to coincide with
暗疾 [ànjí] a secret sickness, a sickness of which the patient is shy to tell
暗箭 [ànjiàn] a secret arrow — a covert attack
暗箭伤人 [àn jìan shāng rén] to hit below the belt
暗箭难防 [àn jiàn nán fǎng] it is difficult to watch out for people's cunning tricks
暗礁 [ànjiāo] a hidden reef
暗码 [ànmǎ] a cipher; a code
暗盘 [ànpán] a price fixed secretly
暗器 [ànqì] a small weapon which was used in olden time to shoot covertly
暗杀 [ànshā] assasination; murder
暗射 [ànshè] to insinuate
暗射地图 [ànshè dìtú] a blank map
暗示 [ànshì] a hint
暗室 [ànshì] 暗房 [ànfáng] a darkroom
暗算 [ànsuàn] a machination; to plot privately against others
暗探 [àntàn] a detective
暗无天日 [àn wú tiān rì] skylessly and sunlessly black (to describe a corruptive society)
暗线光谱 [ànxiàn quāngpǔ] 吸收光谱 [xīshōu guang pǔ] absorption spectrum〔物〕
暗箱 [ànxiāng] a part of a camera
暗笑 [ànxiào] to laugh in one's sleeve
暗語 [ànyǔ] a secret language
暗中摸索 [àn zhōng mō suǒ] groping in the dark

黯 [àn] (adj) 深黑 black; dark

黯然 [ànrán] gloomily; sadly; in a melancholic way

āng

骯(骯) [āng] (adj)〔骯脏〕[āng·zang] 不干淨, 不清洁 dirty; filthy

áng

昂 [áng] 1 (v) 仰，抬起 to raise; to lift ＊昂头看那道美丽的彩虹！Lift up your heads to see the rainbow! 2 (adj)（价格）高，贵 expensive, referring to prices ＊ 太昂贵的，我买不起。I can't afford to buy the expensive ones. 3 (adj) 振奋，有时叠用 high in spirits ＊ 战场上的士兵个个斗志昂扬。Every soldier in the battlefield is in high fighting spirit.

昂然 [ángrán] proudly; elatedly; stately
昂貴 [ángguì] costly; high in price

àng

盎 [àng] (n) 一种盛水的陶器 a pot

盎然 [àngrán] abundantly
盎斯 [àngsī] ounce

āo

凹 [āo] 周围高中间低，跟“凸”相对 (n) a depression; an indentation (adj) concave; hollow

凹版 [āobǎn] an engraving; a copper or steel plate
凹地 [āodì] a hollow
凹刻 [āokè] cut in intaglio
凹坑 [āo kēng] a pit
凹透镜 [āotòujìng] concave lens

平
凹

凹凸不平 [āotúbùpíng] concave and convex; unevenness
凹陷 [āoxìan] hollow

敖 [āo] (v) 以多量的汤水久煮 to boil: to simmer
另见 [áo]

áo

嗷 [aó] 〔嗷嗷〕(n) 哀号的声音 a sound of wailing
嗷嗷待哺 [áo'áodàibǔ] to wail for food

熬 [áo] 1 (v) 久煮 to simmer; to decoct ＊熬粥的时候，水份越来越少。In making porridge, the water content becomes less and less. 2 (v) 忍受，勉强支持 to endure; to bear ＊在考试前夕，他熬夜把功课读完。On the day before the examination, he endured a sleepless night to finish studying his lessons.
熬煎 [ānjiān] to boil ; to ill-treat ; to afflict; to gall
熬痛 [áotòng] endure pain
熬炼 [áoliàn] to boil and smelt; to discipline
熬药 [áoyào] to decoct herbs

遨 [áo]〔遨游〕[áoyóu] (v) 漫游，游历 to ramble; to travel

翱 [áo]〔翱翔〕[áoxiáng] (v) 展开翅膀盘旋地飞行 to hover ＊雄鹰在空中翱翔觅食。The eagle hovered in the sky to look for food.

ǎo

袄(襖) [aǒ] (n) 有衬里的上衣 a coat; a jacket ＊这件棉袄很合身。This cotton jacket is very fitting.

拗 [ǎo] (v) 弄弯 to bend; to break into two ＊他把竹竿拗断了。He has broken the bamboo into two.
另见 [ào]
[niù]

媪 [ǎo] (n) 老年妇女 an old woman ＊那老媪慢吞吞地走着。That old woman moves very slowly.

ào

傲 [ào] (adj) 自高自大 proud; overbearing; insolent ＊高傲自大的人常看不起别人。An overbearing person always looks down upon others.
傲慢 [àomàn] scorn; arrogant; insolence; haughtiness
傲气 [àoqì] haughtiness; proud feeling
傲然 [àorán] haughtily; proudly; arrogantly

骜(驁) [ào] 1 (n) 骏马 a noble steed 2 (adj) 不驯良，傲慢，不服从 untamed; indomitable; disobedient

奥 [ào] (adj) 意思很深，不容易懂 with profound meaning; incomprehensible; difficult to understand
奥秘 [àomì] mysterious
奥妙 [àomiào] subtle; hidden

懊 [ào] (v) 懊恨，烦恼 to regret ; to be vexed
懊悔 [àohuǐ] regret ; reproach oneself
懊恼 [àonǎo] angry; vexed
懊丧 [àosàng] disappointed; dissatisfied

澳 [ào] (n) 海边弯曲可以停船的地方 a bay; a harbour

坳 [ào] (n) 山间的平地 a depression; a hollow; a cavity

B

bā

巴 [bā] 1 (v) 巴望，盼望 to hope; to wish ＊我肚子很饿，巴不得早点吃饭。Feeling very hungry, I hope to take a meal soon 2 (prep) 靠近 near ＊这里前不巴村，后不近店。This place is neither near a village nor any shop. 3 (n) 粘接的东西 a paste 4 (v) 紧贴 ＊壁虎巴在墙上。The lizard stuck itself to the wall

巴不得 [bā·bu de] earnestly hope

巴结 [bā·jie] to flatter; toady; to curry favour

巴蛇 [bā shé] a python （动）

巴掌 [bā zhǎng] the open hand; the palm; a slap on the face

芭 [bā] 一种香草 a fragrant herb

芭蕉 [bā jiāo] the banana plant

芭蕾舞 [bā lěi wǔ] ballet.

笆 [bā] 1 (n) 用竹子或柳条编成的器物 an article made of bamboo or willow strips 2 (n) 竹篱 bamboo fence

笆斗 [bā dǒu] a semispherical basket

另见 篱笆 [líbā]

疤 [bā] (n) 伤口或疮长好后留下的痕迹 a scar. ＊伤口是復原了，但是却永远留下一个疤。Although the wound is healed, it will leave a scar forever.

八 [bā] (n) 数目 a numeral; eight

八月 [bāyuè] August

叭 [bā] (n) 表示声音 to denote a sound ＊枪"叭"的一声响了。The gun was fired with a "叭"

另见巴 [bā]

扒 [bā] 1 (v) 抓着可依附的东西，紧握着 to take hold of 2 (v) 挖掘 to dig ＊人人扒沟，让污水流走。Everyone digs drains to let the filthy water flow away.

捌 [bā] "八"的大写 the complicated form of "八"

bá

拔 [bá] 1 (v) 抽出，拉出 to pluck; to pull out ＊农夫在烈日下拔草。The farmer is pulling weeds out under the hot sun. 2 (v) 挑选，提升 to select; to promote ＊由于经理的提拔，他终於得到一份高职。With the promotion given by his manager, he was finally able to get a high post. 3 (v) 吸出 to root up; to extirpate; to eradicate ＊医生替他拔毒之后，他感到好点了。After the doctor has extirpated the poison, he feels better now.

拔除 [bá chú] to uproot; to eradicate

拔河 [bá hé] tug of war

拔尖儿 [bá jiān ēr] outstanding; top-notch ; self-glorification

拔苗助长 [bá miáo zhù zhǎng] to try to make rice shoots grow by pulling or stretching ; to spoil things by being too impatient and subjective

跋 [bá] 1 (v) 翻山越岭 to travel; to walk. 2 (n) 题在书后的文字 post-script (in a book)

跋扈 [bá hù] arrogant ; domineering ; bossy

跋涉 [bá shè] to cross land and water (a difficult journey)

bǎ

把 [bǎ] 1 (v) 抓住，掌握住 to grasp; to hold; to seize * 把住栏杆慢慢下来。Grasp the railings and go down slowly. 2 (v) 用来移置句中宾词于动词之前的字。to have (somebody or something done) * 把这封信寄了去 Have this letter sent out · (Send this letter out.) 3 (v) 守卫 to guard. * 我们去看戏，留下妈妈把守门户。We went to see the show, leaving mother to look after the house. 4 (n) 手推车，自行车的柄 a handle; the grip of a handcart or a bicycle 5 量词 a measure word (for things usually with handles) piece * 拿一把刀来切蛋糕。Take a knife to cut the cake.

把臂之交 [bǎ bì zhī jiāo] a very intimate friendship * 我们同事十年，可说是把臂之交。We have been colleagues for ten years and our friendship can be said to be an intimate one.

把柄 [bǎ bǐng] proof; evidence ; the secret in the possession of one party; something that can be used as a hold over somebody

把持 [bǎ chí] to control; to keep a tight grip

把风 [bǎ fēng] to scout ; to act as an informer

把手 [bǎ·shǒu] a handle; a knob ; a hand grip

把守 [bǎ shǒu] to guard; to defend; to hold on

把舵 [bǎduò] to steer; to pilot

把握 [bǎ wò] to have a thorough grasp of; to be sure of something

把戏 [bǎ xì] magical and acrobatic performances; fuggery trick; game

另见 [bà]

靶 [bǎ] (n) 练习射击用的目标 a target; a mark

靶子场 [bǎ·zi chǎng] the rifle range

bà

把 [bà] (n) 器物上便于手拿的部份，柄 a handle

另见 把 [bǎ]

耙(耚) [bà] (n) 把土块弄碎的农具 a rake; a harrow

龅(齙) [bà] (adj) 牙齿不整齐，向外露出 irregular and protruding teeth

爸 [bà] (n) 爸爸，儿子对父亲的称呼 dad; father

罢(罷) [bà] 1 (v) 休止 to stop; to cease * 欲罢不能 wishing to stop but unable to do so 2 (v) 免去(职位) to dismiss; to suspend; to discharge. (from office) 3 (v) 完了 to finish * 听罢妈妈讲她以前贫苦的生活，我觉得我比她幸福多了。After having listened to mother's story of her past poverty, I feel that I am so much more fortunate than she was.

罢工 [bà gōng] to go on strike; a strike;

罢官 [bàguān] to dismiss officials from their posts

罢课 [bàkè] a student strike ; a walk out staged by students

罢了 [bà liǎo] a modal particle placed at the end of a declarative ; sentence meaning "that's all" "only" etc

罢免 [bà miǎn] to dismiss from office

罢市 [bà shì] stoppage of trade; suspension of business ; to close up shops ;to go on strike

罢休 [bàxiū] to give up ; to stop; let the matter drop

霸(覇) [bà]1 (n) 诸候的首领 a feudal chief 2 (n) 强横无理，依仗恶劣势力欺压人民的人 a tyrant; an oppressor ＊人们再也忍受不住这恶霸的欺侮，于是团结起来把他赶走。The people could not bear the bullying of the tyrant any-more , so they united to dispose of him. 3 (v) 强力独占 to rule by force; to dominate over; to encroach on

霸道 [bà dào]despotisim; tyranny; over bearing; high-handed

霸权 [bà quán] supremacy; hegemony

霸权主义 [bà quán zhǔ yì] hegemon-ism

霸占 [bà zhàn] to encroach upon ; to usurp ; to annex; to occupy by force

坝(壩) [bà] (n) 拦住河流的堤 an embankment; a dike; a dam

ba

吧(罢、罷) [·ba] (particle) 助词 1 表示可以，允许 to express permission granted ＊就让他去吧 All right , let him go 2 表示命令 to denote an order or instruction ＊快去找吧。 Go and find it quickly. 3 表示推测 to denote a guess or speculation ＊我想他会来吧。I think he will come.

bái

白 [bái] 1 (adj) 象雪或乳汁那样的颜色 white ; snowy 2 (adj) 空的，没有加上其他东西的 plain; empty; blank ＊这只是一张白纸，没有写上什么东西。 This is only a blank sheet of paper with nothing written on it. 3 (adj) 亮 bright ＊在大白天，他还敢偷东西？Dare he steal in broad daylight? 4 (adj) 清楚 clear ＊经过一番调查后，事情真相大白了。After some inves-tigation , the truth of the matter becomes clear. 5 (adj) 没有效果的 useless ＊跟你这种不讲理的人说话是白费气力的。 It is use-less to talk to an unreason-able person like you. 6 (v) 陈述，说话 to express; say ＊我向他表白我的心事。 I told him my con-cerns

白菜 [bái cài] Chinese cabbage

白痴 [bái chī] an idiot; mentally sub-normal

白鸽 [bái gē] a domestic pigeon

白宫 [bái gōng] the White House

白喉 [bái hóu] diphtheria

白话 [bái hùa] vernacular, the vernacu-lar language

白痢 [bái lì] diarrhoea

白茫茫 [bai mang mang]in an endless whiteness (snow, cloud, etc.)

白皮书 [bái pí shū] white paper; a white-book

白热化 [bái rè huà] to get into a state of white heat

白刃 [bái rèn] naked blade ; a sharp knife

白色恐怖 [bái sè kǒng bù] white terror

白手成家 [bái shǒu chéng jiā] to start from scratch;to buildup from nothing

白天 [bái tiān] daytime

白血球 [bái xué qíu] white blood cell; white corpuscle

白蚁 [bái yǐ] a white ant; a termite

白字 [bái zì] a wrongly written or pronounced word

白昼 [bái zòu] broad daylight; in open day

bǎi

百 [bǎi] 1 数词 hundred 2(adj)众多的，所有的 many; numerous ＊百花齐放的景色真美。Many flowers in full bloom presents a beautiful scene.

百般 [bǎi bān] all manners of; in a hundred and one ways; by all means.

百发百中 [bǎi fā bǎi zhòng] to hit the bull's eye every time; to shoot with great accuracy

百分比 [bǎi fēn bǐ] percent

百分率 [bǎi fēn lǜ] percentage

百分数 [bǎi fēn shù] the percentage system

百分之百 [bǎi fēn zhī bǎi] a hundred percent; absolutely; out and out

百害 [bǎi hài] harmful in many ways

百花齐放，百家争鸣 [bǎi hūa jí fàng bǎi jīa zhēng míng] let a hundred flowers blossom and a hundred schools of thought contend

百花齐放，推陈出新 [bǎi hūa jí fàng tuī chén chū xīn] let a hundred flowers blossom, weed through the old to bring forth the new

百货公司 [bǎi hùo gōng sī] a depart-mental store; an emporium

百计 [bǎi jì] many different plans

百科全书 [bǎikē quán shū] an encyc-lopedia

百孔千疮 [bǎi kǒng qiān chuāng] riddl-ed with a thousand gaping wounds

百炼成钢 [bǎi liàn chéng gāng] tem-pered in repeated struggles; tough-ened and hardened

百年 [bǎi nián] a century

百年大计 [bǎi nián dà jì] fundamental task, crucial for generations to come; matters of vital and lasting importance

百万 [bǎi wàn] million

百闻不如一见 [bǎi wén bù rú yī jiàn] better to see once than hear a hund-red times

百姓 [bǎi xìng] the common people

百叶窗 [bǎi yè chuāng] venetian shutter

百战百胜 [bǎi zhàn bǎishèng] a hund-red battles, a hundred victory; invincible

百折不挠 [bǎi zhé bèi náo] undaunted by repeated setbacks; long and persistent effort

百足 [bǎi zú] centipede

佰 [bǎi] (n) "百"的大写 the compli-cated form of "百"

柏 [bǎi] (n) 常绿乔木 the cypreso, the cedar

柏树 [bǎi shù] a cypress tree

柏油 [bǎi yóu] pitch; asphalt; tar

摆(擺、襬) [bǎi] 1 (v) 放置，陈列 to place; to display; to spread out ＊把这花瓶摆在桌子上。Place the vase on the table. 2 (v) 摇动 to swing; to move to and fro; to oscillate ＊快摆手让他注意你。Quickly wave your hand so that he wil notice you. 3 (v) 故意表现 tc exhibit; to manifest; tc show＊他升级后，便摆出一副了不起的样子。He showed a proud manner since he had been promoted. 4 (n) 悬挂在细线上来回摇摇摆的锤 a pendulum

摆布 [bǎi bù] to place; to arrange in order

摆动 [bǎi dòng] to oscilate; to swing

摆渡 [bǎi dù] to ferry across; a ferry boat

摆架子 [bǎi jià·zi] to put on air; to assume air

摆列 [bǎi liè] array; exhibit; to display

摆弄 [bǎi nòng] to play or meddle with; to fiddle about with

摆设 [bǎi shè] to furnish and decorate; furnishings; decoration; decor

摆事实，讲道理 [bǎi shì shí jiǎng dào lǐ] to present the facts and reason things out

摆脱 [bǎi tuō] get rid of; break away

bài

败(敗) [bài] 1 (n) 输，失利，跟"胜"相对 a defeat; a loss ＊只要你尽力去做，胜败我是不计较的。 You only need to put in your best efforts to do it , I do not mind if it will be a success or a failure. 2 (v) 损毁 to destroy ; to spoil; to ruin; to rout; to defeat ＊你为人冲动，常常会败事。 As an impulsive person, you often spoil the matters.

败坏 [bài huài] to spoil; to corrupt; to ruin

败家 [bài jīa] to ruin a family

败类 [bài lèi] bad characters; scoundrels; dregs; scum

败露 [bài lù] be exposed; be uncovered

败兵 [bài pīng] defeated troops

败退 [bài tuì] to retreat in defeat

败战 [bài zhàng] a lost battle; a defeat

拜 [bài] 1 (v) 以礼会见 to pay respect; to visit ＊很久没问候你母亲了，有空一定到府上拜访她。 I have not seen your mother for a long time; when I am free , I shall call at your home to pay her a visit. 2 敬礼 to do obeisance; to salute; to worship

拜倒 [bài dǎo] to bow before

拜访 [bài fǎng] to visit someone

拜会 [bài huì] to make an official visit; to pay a courtesy call

拜托 [bài tuō] to entrust; to make a request

稗 [bài] (n) 也叫"稗子"，"稗草"稻田的主要杂草 weeds; tares

bān

般 [bān] (n) 样，种类 sort; kind; class; manner ＊在百般威迫利诱下他毫不动摇He was not in the least moved by all sorts of threats and temptations

搬 [bān] (v) 移动，迁移 to remove; to transport; to move ＊请你把这箱水果搬到我的摊位前面。 Please move this crate of fruits to the front of my stall.

搬迁 [bānqiān] to move

搬家 [bān jiā] to move house

搬弄是非 [bānnòng shìfēi] to tell tales; to make mischief

搬运 [bānyùn] to carry; to convey; to transport

瘢 [bān] (n) 疮和伤口好了后留下的痕迹 a mark ; a scar on the skin

颁(頒) [bān] (v) 发下 to send out; to issue; to grant; confer ＊上级颁布命令要防守小镇。 The superiors issued orders to defend the town.

颁布 [bānbù] to issue; to promulgate

颁发 [bānfā] to confer ; to award ; to promulgate

颁赏 [bānshǎng] to give rewards or bounties

班 [bān] 1 (n) 一群人按次序排成的行列 a team 2 (n) 按工作学习等第需要编成的组织 a class ＊我是三年级甲班学生。 I am a student in grade III, Class A. 3 (n) 军队编制中最小的单位，在排以下 a squad 4 (n) 工作服务的次数 a shift; a duty ＊矿工分两班工作。 The miners work in two shifts. 5 (n) 量词 a measure word (eg. a number bus, etc.) ＊第二路巴士每五分钟一班。 No. 2 buses run every five minutes.

班车 [bānchē] a bus on regular schedule

班机 [bānjī] a schedule flight

班级 [bānjí] class or grade in a school

班门弄斧 [bān ménnòng fǔ] trying to show off in front of those better than ourselves

班师 [bānshī] to withdraw troops

班长 [bānzhǎng] a monitor (class) ; a squad leader

斑 [bān] (n) 一种颜色中杂有别种颜色 variegated

斑点 [bāndiǎn] spots
斑马 [bān mǎ] a zebra

斑纹 [bānwén] stripes

扳 [bān] 1 (v) 拉 to pull; to draw ＊枪手急扳枪掣，子弹正中靶心。The gunman pulled the trigger immodiately and the bullet hit accurately at the bull's eye. 2 (v) 扭转 to turn
扳子 [bān·zi] a wrench; a spanner

bǎn

阪 [bǎn] 同"坂" a slope

坂 [bǎn] (n) 山坡，斜坡 a slope

板 [bǎn] (n) 成片的硬物体 a board; a plank; a slab ＊午饭后建筑工人躺在木板上休息。The construction workers lay down on the wooden planks and rest after lunch.
板壁 [bǎnbì] a wooden partition
板擦 [bǎncā] a (blackboard) duster
板凳 [bǎndèng] a wooden bench
板眼 [bǎnyǎn] a beat or rest in music

版 [bǎn] 1 (n) 名册，户籍 a register 2 (n) 上面有文字或图形的供印刷用的底子 a block for printing 3 (n) 印刷物排印或修订的次数 an edition＊这部小说很受欢迎，目前已出了第三版。This novel is very popular; the third edition is out now 4 (n) 报纸的分页 the page in newspaper ＊太空船降落在火星上的消息，当然是头版新闻啦。 It is certain that the news about the landing of the space-craft on Mars will appear in the first page of the newspapers.
版本 [bǎnběn] an editiion; a printed book
版画 [bǎnhuà] a print; a block print; an engraving
版面 [bǎnmiàn] layout or make-up of a pointed sheet
版权 [bǎnquán] author's rights; copyright
版图 [bǎntú] territory; dominions

钣 [bǎn] (n) 金属板 sheet (of metal)

bàn

半 [bàn] 1 (adj) 二分之一 half; semi-; mid- 2 (adj) 不完全的 half; incomplete; partly ＊我们在热带林中碰见了一些半开化的土族。 We met some half-civilized tribes in the tropical forests.
半成品 [bànchéngpǐn] semi-finished product; semi-manufactured product
半岛 [bàndǎo] a peninsula
半导体 [bàndǎotǐ] transistor; semiconductor
半封建 [bànfēngjiàn] semi-feudalism
半工半读 [bàngōngbàndú] part-work and part-study
半截 [bànjié] a half
半斤八两 [bànjīn-bāliǎng] six of one and half a dozen of the other- there is not much to choose between the two
半径 [bànjìng] radius
半路 [bànlù] half-way; midway
半旗 [bànqí] flag at half-mast
半球 [bànqiú] hemisphere
半身不遂 [bànsēn-bùsuí] hemiplegia; hemiplegy
半生 [bànshēng] half of one's life-time
半数 [bànshù] half the total number
半天 [bàntiān] half a day; (for) a long time
半透明 [bàntòumíng] translucent
半途而废 [bàntú ér fèi] to abandon halfway
半信半疑 [bànxìnbànyí] half-believing and half-doubting; not quite convinced

半学年 [bànxuénián] semester
半夜 [bànyè] mid-night
半意识 [bànyìshí] sub-consciousness
半圆 [bànyuán] semi-circle
半元音 [bànyuányīn] a semi-vowel
半身像 [bànshēnxiàng] bust
半月形 [bànyuèxíng] crescent-shaped; semilunan; semicircular
半殖民地 [bànzhímíndì] a semi-colony

伴 [bàn] 1 (n) 同在一起的人 a partner; a companion; an associate ＊她怕黑，你就给她作伴吧。She is afraid of the dark, so you will keep her company. 2 (v) 陪着，配合 to accompany; to associate ＊她唱歌很好听，如果有音乐伴奏会更美妙 She sings very well but it will be much more wonderful if accompanied by music.
伴唱 [bànchàng] to accompany (a singer)
伴郎 [bànláng] a bestman
伴侣 [bànlǚ] a partner; a companion; a mate
伴娘 [bànniáng] a bridesmaid
伴随 [bànsuí] to follow; to be in the wake of; simultaneously
伴奏 [bànzòu] to accompany (a singer or a player); to play to the accompaniment of

拌 [bàn] (v) 搅和 to mix; to mix in ＊公升水拌三茶匙杀虫剂，用来喷射农作物。Mix 3 teaspoonful of water into the insecticide and spray it on the crop.
拌和 [bànhuó] to mix
拌嘴 [bàn zuǐ] to quarrel

绊（絆）[bàn] (v) 脚被挡住或缠住 to trip over; to stumble; to hinder
绊倒 [bàndǎo] to stumble and fall
绊脚石 [bànjiǎoshí] a stumbling-block; an obstruction

瓣 [bàn] 1 (n) 花的分片和草木的叶子 petal of a flower 2 (n) 种子果实或鳞茎可以分裂的片子 the segments or sections (of a seed, a fruit or a bulb)
瓣膜 [bànmó] the valves of the heart

办（辦）[bàn] 1 (v) 处理 to do; to manage; to handle; to go about ＊这件工作一定要找个有经验的人去办。You must look for an experienced person to do this task. 2 (v) 创设 to set up; to found ＊大家都筹欵来为村民办学校。We raise funds to set up a school for the villagers. 3 (v) 处分，惩治 to punish; to bring to justice.＊他杀人，应该依法惩办。He should be punished by the law for killing.
办不到 [bànbùdào] unfeasible; impossible; impermissible; never
办得到 [bàndédào] can be done; feasible; possible
办法 [bànfǎ] way; means; measures
办公 [bàn gōng] to do office work; to work in an office; to be in office
办公室 [bàngōngshì] an office
办貨 [bànhuò] to buy goods
办理 [bànlǐ] to take in hand; to transact; to manage; to do;
办事 [bànshì] to run affairs
办事处 [bànshìchù] a local office; an office

扮 [bàn] (v)化装 to disguise oneself; to adorn; to dress up as ＊她扮作可怜的老妇人，像极了。She dresses up as a poor old lady and it looks genuine.
扮演 [bànyǎn] to act a part in a play; to have a role (in a play, etc.)

bāng

邦 [bāng] (n) 国 a state; a country; a nation ＊我们的邻邦包括泰国与马来西亚。Our neighbouring countries include Thailand and Malaysia
邦交 [bāngjiāo] diplomatic relations between sovereign states

梆 [bāng] (n) 子，打更用的响器 a watchman's rattle

帮（幫）[bāng] 1 (v) 相助 to help; to assist ＊她是个好学生，常帮同学温课。As a good student she often helps her classmates in their studies. 2 (n) 伙，群，集团 a group; a party; a gang ∗山头盘据着一帮恶名远扬的土匪。The hill-top was occupied by a group of notorious bandits.

帮忙 [bāng máng] to help; to land a (helping) hand

帮腔 [bāngqiāng] choral accompaniment; to back (something up); to chime in with

帮手 [bāng shǒu] an assistant; a helper; an accomplice

帮凶 [bāngxiōng] an accomplice or an accessary (in crime)

帮助 [bānzhù] to help; to assist; help; assistance; aid

bǎng

榜 [bǎng] (n) 公布出来让大家知道的文告或名单 a notice; an announcement of a list of names(e.g. candidate) ∗会考后，同学们焦急地等待当局放榜。After the Government Examination, the students waited anxiously for the ministry to announce the list of successful candidates.

榜样 [bǎngyàng] a model; a pattern; an example

膀 [bǎng] (n) 膀子，胳膊上部靠肩的部份 the upper arms

膀肋 [bǎnglèi] the lower ribs

另见 [páng]

绑 (綁) [bǎng] (v) 捆扎，缚 to tie to bind; to fasten together

绑匪 [bǎng fěi] kidnappers; brigands

绑架 [bǎng jià] to kidnap

绑票 [bǎng piào] to seize for ransom; a person held for ransom by brigands

bàng

傍 [bàng] (prep.) 挨着，靠近 near

傍晚 [bàngwǎn] dusk; evening; night fall

谤 (謗) [bàng] (v) 恶意地说别人的坏话 to slander; to speak ill of; to defame ∗业务上的竞争竟使他诽谤对手。It was business competition that made him slander his rivals.

磅 [bàng] (n) 英美制重量单位 a measure word — pound

磅秤 [bànchèng] a scale (for weighing)

另见 [páng]

镑 (鎊) [bàng] (n) 译音字，英国的货币单位 pound sterling (£) the unit of British currency

棒 [bàng] 1 (n) 棍子 a stick; a club; a cudgel; a staff 2 (adj) 漂亮；好；强壮；能干 smart; bright; excellent; strong; capable∗这小伙子真棒，什么事都办得很好。This young man is very smart; he manages everything well.

棒球 [bàngqiú] baseball

蚌 [bàng] (n) 软体动物，可供食用 oysters; mussels

蚌蛤 [bànggé] a clam or mussel

蚌珠 [bàngzhū] a pearl from the oyster

bāo

包 [bāo] 1 (v) 用纸，布等把东西裹起来 to wrap; to envelope; to pack ∗用布把伤口包起来。Use a cloth to wrap up the wound. 2 (n) 裹成的东西 a parcel; a package ∗把行李包拿到关口接受检查。Bring your luggage to the Customs for checking 3 (n) 装东西的袋 a wrapper; a container; a bag ∗开学了，孩子要买新书包。When school reopens, the children want to buy new school bags. 4 (v) 总括在一起 to hold; to embrace; to include ∗这部百科全书很完整，无所不包。This set of encyclopedia is a complete one; there is nothing unincluded. 5 (v) 负全部责任，保证 to undertake; to insure; to be responsible; to take charge of ∗这件事包在我身上。I shall take full charge of the matter.

包庇 [bāobì] to screen; to harbour; to shield

包藏 [bāocáng] to conceal; to store up
包丰 [bāofēng] a kind of fruit

包袱 [bāo·fu] a cloth wrapper; a bundle; a burden (mental)
包工 [bāogōng] contract work; to contract for a job.
包裹 [bāoguǒ] a parcel; a package
包含 [bāohán] to include; to comprise; to contain
包涵 [bāo hán] to excuse someone out of good manners
包伙食 [bāohuǒshí] to get or supply all meals at a fixed rate; table board
包括 [bāokuò] to include; to involve; to embrace; to cover
包罗万象 [bāo luó wànxiàng] very rich in content; everything conceivable; all-embracing; all-inclusive
包围 [bāowéi] to surround; to besiege; to outflank
包厢 [bāoxiāng] boxes or stalls in a theatre
包扎 [bāozā] to dress (a wound); to wrap up; to pack up
包装 [bāozhuāng] to pack; to wrap up
包子 [bāo·zi] steamed stuffed buns

孢 [bāo] (n) 孢子，植物无性生殖中所产生的生殖细胞 spore

胞 [bāo] 1 (n)胎衣 the placenta 2 (adj) 同父母的 of the same parents ＊这两个同胞兄弟，经过了二十年的隔离又重聚了。The two brothers, both of the same parents, reunited after twenty years of separation.

炮 [bāo] (v) 把东西放在器物上烘烤或焙 to roast; to bake
炮制 [bāozhì] to decoct, (Chinese medicine)
另见 [páo]
[pào]

苞 [bāo] (n) 花没有开时包着花朵的小叶片 the bract

龅 [bāo] (n) 龅牙，长得不整齐向外突出的牙齿 projecting teeth

煲 [bāo] 1 (n) 壁较陡直的锅 a pot; a saucepan 2 (v) 煮或熬 to boil; to cook; to heat

褒 [bāo] (v) 赞美，夸奖 to praise; to commend
褒贬 [bāo biǎn] to praise and censure; to criticise
褒奖 [bāojiǎng] to praise and reward
褒扬 [bāoyáng] to praise; to commend

剥 [bāo] (v) 去掉外面的皮壳 to tear; to peel off; to strip; to pull off; to rind ＊吃苹果不必剥皮。 There is no need to peel off the skin of apples before eating.
另见 [bō]

báo

雹 [báo] (n) 冰雹，空中水蒸气遇冷结成的冰粒或冰块，常在夏季随暴雨下降 hail; hailstones

薄 [báo] 1 (adj) 不厚的 thin ＊她衣着單薄，冷得发抖。Dressed in thin clothes, she shivered in cold. 2 (adj) 冷淡（指感情） indifferent; heartless; cold (emotions) ＊在金钱至上的城市里，人情薄得很。 In the city where money is most important, people are indifferent to one another 3 (adj) 微小 small ＊父亲死后只留下一点薄产给他。After the death of his father, he inherited a small estate from him.
另见 [bó]
[bò]

bǎo

保 [bǎo] 1 (v) 守卫 to defend; to protect ＊军队驻扎在边界保卫国土。 The troops stationed at the boundary to defend their territory. 2 (v) 负责，有把握 to insure; to guarantee ＊他做事认真，我保他这次能完成任务。He is serious in his work; I guarantee he will accomplish his mission this time. 3 (v) 保持 to maintain; to hold ;to keep＊毛线衫穿了能保暖。Wearing a sweater will keep us warm.

保安 [bǎoān] preservation (maintenance) of public peace or security

保镖 [bǎo biāo] an armed escort; a body-guard

保藏 [bǎocáng] to preserve; to keep

保持 [bǎochí] to keep; to remain; to maintain; to hold

保存 [bǎocun] to preserve; to keep

保管 [bǎoguǎn] to conserve; to preserve; safekeeping; care

保护 [bǎohù] to protect ; to safeguard

保护国 [bǎo hù guó] a protectorate

保护贸易主义 [bǎohùmàoyì zhǔyì] protectionism

保护色 [bǎohùsè] protective colouring; disguise; camouflage

保健 [bǎojiàn] health protection ; health case

保留 [bǎolíu] to reserve; to shelve; to maintain; to keep back

保密 [bǎo mì] to keep secret; to maintain secrecy

保姆 [bǎomǔ] a nurse; a baby-sitter

保票 [bǎo piào] a guarantee

保全 [bǎoquán] to preserve; to keep from injury ; to keep something intact

保释 [bǎoshì] to bail a security; to stand bail

保守 [bǎoshǒu] to keep; to maintain; conservative

保送 [bǎosòng] send on recommendation (e.g. to college)

保温 [bǎowēn] to keep warm

保险 [bǎoxiǎn] insurance; sure; security; safe and sound; secure

保险费 [bǎoxiǎnfèi] premium

保险丝 [bǎoxiǎnsī] a fuse; a fuse-wire

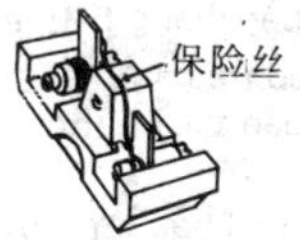

保险箱 [bǎoxiǎnxiāng] a safe; a strong box

保养 [bǎoyǎng] to maintain; to keep fit

保有 [bǎoyǒu] to retain, to occupy; to possess; to keep; to hold

保育员 [bǎoyùyuán] a kindergarten nurse; a childcare cook

保障 [bǎozhàng] to ensure; to guarantee; to safeguard

保证 [bǎozhèng] to guarantee ; to pledge; to assure; assurance

保重 [bǎozhòng] to look after oneself

褓 [bǎo] (n) 小儿的衣被 a swaddling cloth

堡 [bǎo] (n) 土筑的小城，现泛指军事上防守用的建筑物 an earthwork ; a castle; a station for defense

堡垒 [bǎolěi] a fort; a fortification

葆 [bǎo] (n) 草木茂盛 luxuriant foliage

鸨(鴇) [bǎo] (n) 指那些开设妓院对妓女进行残酷剥削和虐待的女老板 a procuress

宝(寶) [bǎo] 1 (n) 玉器的总称 a jewel; a gem 2 (n) 珍贵的东西 a treasure; a highly-prized article 3 (adj) 珍贵的 precious; valuable ＊博物院里陈列着古代将军的宝剑。Valuable swords of ancient generals are being displayed in the museum.

宝贝 [bǎobèi] a treasure; a treasured object;little darling (of child)

宝贵 [bǎoguì] valuable; precious

宝库 [bǎokù] a treasure house

宝石 [bǎoshí] precious stones; a

gem
宝塔 [bǎotǎ] a pagoda
宝藏 [bǎozhàng] treasure - trove; buried treasure
宝座 [bǎo zuò] a throne; a seat of power

饱(飽) [bǎo] 1 (v) 吃夠了 to eat; to the full 2 (adj) 充满，充分 full of; satisfied ＊他饱读诗书仍勤恳不倦地学习。He is very well-educated, yet he does not stop learning.
饱和 [bǎohé] saturated
饱经风霜 [bǎo jīng fēng shuāng] to have experienced a long period of trial and tribulation in life
饱满 [bǎomǎn] full-flush; filled
饱暖思淫欲 [bǎo nuǎn sī yín yù] lewd thoughts arise from fullness of food and the comfort of warm clothing, that is, easy living
饱食 [bǎoshí] be sated with food; be well-fed

bào

抱 [bào] 1 (v) 用臂膀围住 to hug; to hold in the arms; to embrace ＊母亲紧抱着孩子。The mother hugs the child tightly. 2 (v) 环绕 to surround ＊山环水抱。Surrounded by mountains and water. 3 (v) 谨守 to cherish ＊那老妪抱着一个希望：儿子有一天会回来。The old woman cherished the hope that her son would come back one day
抱病 [bào bìng] to be sick
抱不平 [bào bùpíng] to be outraged by an injustice done to another person; to champion the cause of a wronged person
抱负 [bàofù] aspiration; ambition; lofty aim
抱歉 [bàoqiàn] to regret; to feel apologetic; to be sorry
抱恨 [bào hèn] to bear hatred
抱恨终身 [bàohènzhōngshēn] to harbour regret (or sorrow) throughout one's life
抱头鼠窜 [bào tóu shǔ cuàn] to cover the head and sneak away like a rat back to its hole; to skulk away in shame
抱头痛哭 [bào tóu tòngkū] to weep bitterly
抱薪救火 [bào xīn jìu huǒ] to employ erroneous methods to eradicate disaster, and causing it to spread further
抱怨 [bàoyuàn] to bear malice; to complain; to grumble

鲍(鮑) [bào] (n) 鲍鱼，生活在海里的一种软体动物，肉可供食用 the abalone

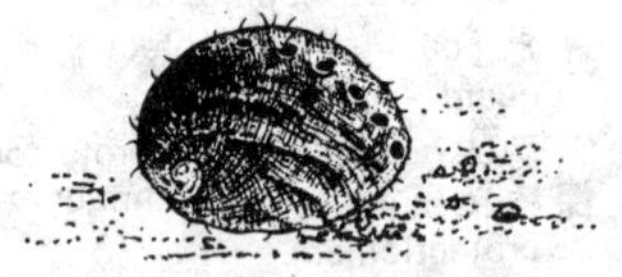

刨 [bào] 1 (n) 刨子或刨床，刮削木料或金属的工具 a plane; a carpenter's plane 2 (v) 用刨子或刨床刮削 to plane; to level; to make smooth ＊先刨平板面才涂清漆。Plane the surface of the plank before varnishing.
刨床 [bàocnuáng] a planning machine
刨花 [bàohuā] shaving; wood chips
刨子 [bào·zi] (carpenter's) plane

暴 [bào] 1 (adj) 又猛又急 violent ＊几间亚答屋在暴风雨中倒坍。Some attap houses collapsed during a violent storm. 2 (adj) 凶残 cruel; tyrannical ＊古代奴隶主的残暴行为数之不尽。The cruel deeds done by the ancient slave masters were innumerable. 3 (v) 显露 to show; to appear; to expose ＊他急得头上的青筋都暴出来了。He was so anxious that his head showed lines of veins. 4 (v) 损害，糟蹋 to injure ＊吸毒是自暴自弃的行为。Drug-taking is an act of injuring and abandoning oneself. 5(adj.) 急躁 hot-tempered; hot-headed; hasty ∗碰到象他这样暴性子的人有理也说不清。 It cannot help the situation to reason with a hot-tempered person like him.

暴动 [bàodòng] riot; an uprising; to resort to insurrection

暴发户 [bàofāhù] an upstart

暴风雨 [bàofēngyǔ] a storm

暴富 [bàofù] an upstart

暴君 [bàojūn] a tyrant; a despot

暴力 [bàolì] violence; force

暴利 [bàolì] extravagant profits; sudden wealth acquired by profiteering

暴戾 [bàolì] atrocious; inhuman; cruel; brutal

暴露 [bào lù] to expose; to reveal; to lay bare

暴乱 [bàoluàn] insurrection; riot

暴跳如雷 [bào tiào rú léi] to stamp with rage

暴徒 [bàotú] ruffians; hoodlums; delinquents

暴行 [bàoxíng] atrocity; savage act; outrage

暴风雪 [bàofēngxuě] a blizzard; a snow-storm

暴雨 [bàoyǔ] a rainstorm; torrential rain

暴躁 [bàozào] short-tempered; irascible

暴政 [bàozhèng] tyranny

暴卒 [bàozú] sudden death

另见 [pù]

爆 [bào] (v) 爆炸，炸裂 to crack; to explode; burst; blow up; scorch ∗要爆掉山坡的石头才可採矿。 The rocks on the hillslope must be blown up before any mining can be carried out.

豹 [bào] (n) 哺乳动物 a leopard; a panther; a species of wild cat

豹死留皮 [bào sǐ líu pí] the leopard dies but leaves its skin - as a man leaves his reputation

报(報) [bào] 1 (v) 告知 to inform; to report ∗当我一听到爸爸平安归来，立刻跑回家报喜。 Once I heard that dad was back safely, I immediately ran home to report the good news. 2 (n) 传达消息的文件或信号 a document or signal messages or news 3 (n) 报纸，刊物 a newspaper; a gazette 4 (v) 回答 to recompense; to revenge; to repay ∗他以怨报德 实在是个薄情寡义的人 Repaying kindness with hatred, he is in actual fact a very heartless man.

报仇 [bào chóu] to revenge; to avenge; to redress a grievance

报酬 [bào chóu] remuneration; a reward; a pay; a fee

报答 [bào dá] to repay

报到 [bào dào] to report one's arrival; to report for duty

报道 [bào dào] information; a report; news; tidings; to report; to cover

报恩 [bào ēn] to repay one's kindness; to requite favours

报贩 [bàofàn] newspapers vendor

报废 [bào fèi] to be declared or classified worthless

报复 [bàofù] to retaliate; to revenge

报告 [bào gào] to inform; to give a report; speech or talk

报关 [bào guān] to declare at the custom

报告文学 [bàogào wénxué] reportage

报话机 [bàohuàjī] a walkie-talkie

报捷 [bào jié] to announce a victory

报警 [bào jǐng] to report to the police

报刊 [bào kān] newspapers and periodicals; the press

报名 [bào míng] to register; to enter one's name

报幕 [bào mù] to annouce (items in a programme)

报社 [bàoshè] a newspaper office

报税 [bàoshuì] to declare goods for the payment of duty

报头 [bàotóu] masthead
报喜 [bào xǐ] to announce good news; to report success
报销 [bàoxiāo] to put in an expense account; to be destroyed;to be finished off
报信 [bào xìn] to deliver a message; to give information
报纸 [bào zhǐ] newspaper; the press

bēi

卑 [bēi](adj) 低下，低劣 low ; base; vulgar; inferior; mean ＊班上的同学都比她富有得多，使她感到自卑。Her classmates are all so much richer than she that she feels herself inferior.
卑鄙 [bēibǐ] mean; vulgar; base; despicable; contemptable
卑躬屈膝 [bēi gōng qū xī] servile; cringing; subservient
卑贱 [bēijiàn] mean; ungentlemanlike, vulgar; lowly
卑劣 [bēiliè]sordid; abject; base; mean-vulgar; despicable and unscrupulous
卑谦 [bēiqiān] humble; yielding
卑怯 [bēiqiè] cowardice
碑 [bēi] (n) 刻上文字作为纪念事业，功勋或作为标志的石头 a monument; a large stone tablet
碑铭 [bēimíng] the inscription on a tablet
碑文 [bēiwén] an epitaph
杯 [bēi] (n) 盛水，茶，酒等的器皿 cup
杯盘狼藉 [bēi pán láng jí] cups and plates all in disorder after a feast
杯水车薪 [bēishuǐ chē xīn] a cup of water to put out a load of burning fire-wood-utterly inadequate
杯中物 [bēizhōngwū] the contents of the wine cup, i.e. wine
背 [bēi] (v) 人用肩背驮东西 to be burdened; to carry on the back (or shoulder) ＊早餐后，小强背起书包，上学去了。After breakfast, small Liang carried his schoolbag on the shoulder and went to school.
背包 [bēibāo] a knapsack; a rucksack
背包袱 [bēibāofù] to take on heavy burdens;to become a burden on one's mind
背负 [bēifù]to carry on the back; to bear ; to be ungrateful
另见 [bèi]
悲 [bēi] (n) 哀痛，伤心 sadness; sorrow; grief ＊我见到了失散多年的妹妹，一时悲喜交集。When I saw my sister who had been lost for many years, I was at once full of joy intermingled with sorrow
悲哀 [bēiāi] sorrowful; sad; grieved; grievous
悲惨 [bēicǎn] miserable; tragic
悲愤 [bēifèn] grievous and indignant; resentment; grief-stricken and enraged
悲歌 [bēigē] a sad tune; a sad piece of music
悲观 [bēiguān] pessimistic
悲剧 [bēijù] a tragedy; a tragic drama
悲伤 [bēishāng] sad; sorrowful
悲痛 [bēitòng]grievous; deeply grieved over; distressing; sorrowful
悲喜剧 [bēixǐjù] a tragic-comedy
悲壮 [bēizhuàng] solemn and stirring ; tragic and moving

běi

北 [běi] (n) 方向 north
北冰洋 [Běi Bīng Yáng] the Artic Ocean
北斗星 [běidǒuxīng] the Dipper; the Plough 〔天〕
北方 [běifāng] the northern part of; the north
北回归线 [běihuíguīxiàn] tropic of cancer
北极 [běijí] north pole
北京 [běijīng] Peking
北极星 [běijíxīng] the Polar Star〔天〕
北京猿人 [Pěijīng yuán rén] Peking Man
北极熊 [běijíxióng] polar bear
北美洲 [Běiměizhōu] North America

bèi

倍 [bèi] 1 (n) 照原数增加的次数 double; time; -fold *工厂加班，产量立刻增加二倍。The factory arranged an additional shift, and production immediately increased two-fold. 2 (v) 更加 to increase; to double; to multiply *战士们受到家信的鼓励，勇气倍增。Inspired by the letters from home, the soldiers felt that their courage was doubled.

倍数 [bèishù] multiple

焙 [bèi] (v) 用小火烘烤 to dry over a fire; to bake

蓓 [bèi] (n)〔蓓蕾〕[bèilěi] 含苞未放的花 flower buds.

悖 [bèi] (adj) 背理的; 逆乱的 perverse; rebellious; contrary to what is right

贝(貝) [bèi] 1 (n) 软体动物中的腹足瓣腮两类统称 cowries; shells 2 (n) 珍物 valuables; precious things

狈(狽) [bèi] (n) 传说中前脚短的野兽 a legendary wolf with short fore legs

被 [bèi] 1 (n) 被子，睡觉时盖身体的东西 a quilt; a blanket 2 (v) 盖，遮 to cover; to wear 3 (prep) 介词，表示被动语态 by (indicating passive voice) *这难题被他解决了。This problem is solved by him.

被乘数 [bèichéngshù] a multiplicant

被除数 [bèichúshù] a dividend

被单 [bèidān] a bedsheet; a bedspread; a counter-pane

被动 [bèidòng] passive

被告 [bèigào] the defendent; the accused

被害 [bèihài] be injured; be misused

被迫 [bèipò] to be forced; to be compelled; to be coerced

被褥 [bèirù] bedding; coverlet; mattress

背 [bèi] 1 (n) 胸部的反面 the back of the body *整天弯着身子的人，到晚上往往会感到背痛。Those who bend the body for one whole day always suffer from backache at night. 2 (n) 东西的反面 the back of things; the reverse side *椅背写着一些东西。There is something written on the rear of the chair. 3 (v) 不当面 to go behind one's back *不要背着人乱说。Don't go behind somebody's back and talk nonsense. 4 (v) 离开 to leave; to abandon *为了生计，许多人不得不背井离乡到外地工作。In order to survive, many people had to abandon their hometowns. 5 (v) 把文字熟记后再凭记忆读出 to learn by heart; to recite *学生们很怕背诵课文。Students are afraid of learning the text by heart.

背道而驰 [bèi dào ér chí] to run in the opposite direction; to run counter to

背后 [bèihòu] behind

背景 [bèijǐng] background; setting; backdrop

背离 [bèilí] to turn one's back on; to deviate from

背弃 [bèiqì] to betray

背信弃义 [bèixìnqìyì] treachery; perfidy; breach of faith

背诵 [bèisòng] to recite; to say by heart

背心 [bèixīn] a waistcoat; a vest; a sleeveless sweater

另见 [bēi]

备(備) [bèi] 1 (v) 预防，预办 to prepare; to get ready *宿舍只供住宿，寄宿者得自备伙食。The hostel is only for lodging, the occupants must prepare their own food. 2 (v) 配置; 装置 to provide; to fit out; to be equipped with *很难找到才德兼备的人。It is hard to find a person equipped with both the talents and the virtues.

备存货物 [bèicúnhuòwù] provision stock

备考 [bèikǎo] remarks; appendix for reference

备课 [bèikè] to prepare lessons

备忘录 [bèiwànglù] memorandum; a

written reminder
备用 [bèiyòng] for use
备战 [bèi zhàn] to prepare for war; to be prepared against war
备注 [bèi zhù] remarks; appendix
辈(輩) [bèi] 1 (n) 世代 a generation ＊能使到后辈受益才是个好的长远计画。A long term plan is only good when it can benefit future generations. 2 (n) 毕生 life; lifetime ＊我爷爷辛苦了一辈子，却不曾过过好日子。Having had toiled for life, my grandfather had never lived a comfortable life.

bēn

奔 [bēn] 1 (v) 急走，跑 to hurry; to run quickly; to rush ＊野猪中枪后，狂奔了一公里，才倒下。 After having been shot, the boar ran madly for a kilometre and fell down. 2 (v) 逃亡 to flee ＊不少少女离家出奔，寻求自由。Quite a number of young girls fled from their homes to look for freedom.
奔波 [bēnbō] to be on the go; to be busy running about
奔驰 [bēnchí] to speed on; to gallop
奔放 [bēnfàng] bold and unrestrained
奔流 [bēnliú] to flow on at a great speed; to pour
奔走 [bēnzǒu] to hasten; to rush about on business; busy running around
另见 [bèn]

běn

本 [běn] 1 (n) 草木的根或茎 roots or stems of plants 2 (n) 事物的根源 origin; source; basis; foundation 3 (adj) 指这方面或自己方面的 native (this; I; my; we; our) ＊有兴趣者请到本公司办事处面洽。 The interested party may call at the offices of this company for personal contact. 4 (n) 量词（用于书籍刊物等）a measure word, copy (for books, pictorials, etc.) 5 (n) 母财：本钱，资本 capital; cost
本地 [běndì] local; native
本分 [běnfèn] one's duty
本行 [běnháng] one's own profession; in one's line
本籍 [běnjí] original domicile
本来 [běnlái] original; originally
本领 [běnlǐng] ability; capacity
本末倒置 [běnmòdàozhì] to confuse cause and effect; to put the cart before the house
本能 [běnnéng] instinct
本人 [běnrén] oneself; in person
本色 [běnshǎi] original colour; true self, intrinsic character
本身 [běnshēn] oneself; itself
本事 [běnshì] ability; skill
本位 [běnwèi] standard; basis; unit
本文 [běnwén] the original text
本性 [běnxìng] nature, the true (original) character
本义 [běnyì] original meaning; literal sense
本意 [běnyì] original meaning; original intention
本旨 [běnzhǐ] aim; object; the main idea
本质 [běnzhì] essence; substance
本质 [běnzhì] nature; innate character; intrinsic quality
畚 [běn] (n) 盛土的器具 a basket or hod used by bricklayers and farmers for earth, manure, grass, etc
畚箕 [běnjī] a basket or hod for earth, manure, grass, etc

bèn

奔 [bèn] (v) 直往，投向 to head for ＊他顺着小道直奔山头。He headed for the hilltop along the small path.
另见 [bēn]
笨 [bèn] 1 (adj) 不聪明，愚蠢 stupid; foolish; silly; slow-witted 2 (adj) 不灵巧 awkward; clumsy
笨蛋 [bèndàn] a fool; a stupid fellow
笨手笨脚 [bènshǒubènjiǎo] clumsy
笨重 [bènzhòng] heavy; clumsy; cumbersome
笨拙 [bènzhuō] clumsy; stupid

bēng

绷(綳) [bēng] (v) 包扎，拉紧 to bind; to tie

绷带 [bēngdài] a bandage

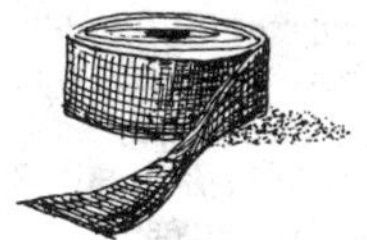

另见 [běng]
[bèng]

崩 [bēng] 1 (v) 倒塌，垮 to collapse; to fall in ruins ＊地震时，山崩土裂，日月无光。When the earth quakes, mountains collapse and lands split and the sun and moon darken. 2 (v) 破裂 to breakdown

崩裂 [bēngliè] to crack; to burst apart

崩溃 [bēngkuì] to collapse; to breakdown

崩塌 [bēngtā] to cave in; to crumble; to collapse

běng

绷(綳) [běng] (v) 板着 to harden one's countenance) ＊你整天绷着脸，究竟是生谁的气？Whom are you angry with that you harden your countenance for the whole day?

另见 [bēng]
[bèng]

bèng

绷(綳) [bèng] (v) 裂开 to crack; to split ＊他一转身，就把衬衣给绷裂了。Once he turned his body, he split his shirt.

另见 [bēng]
[běng]

蹦 [bèng] (v) 跳 to jump; to bounce; to hop

迸 [bèng] (v) 溅出，喷射 to burst forth; to spurt ＊潮水冲激着礁石，迸起乳白色的浪花。When the tide comes, milky sprays burst forth at the side of the reefs.

泵 [bèng] (n) 吸入和排出流体的机器 a pump

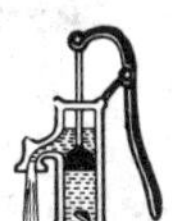

bī

逼 [bī] 1 (v) 强迫，威胁 to press for; to force; to compel ＊他被逼躲进垃圾堆里，避过歹徒的追杀。He was forced to hide himself inside the rubbish dump to avoid being killed by the gangsters. 2 (v) 强迫索取 to extort ＊那人逼债，凶得像只老虎。That person was as fierce as a tiger when he was extorting his debtors.

逼供 [bīgòng] to extort evidence

逼近 [bījìn] to crowd on; to draw near; to approach; to press forward

逼迫 [bīpò] to force; to compel; to coerce; to constrain

逼上梁山 [bī shàng Liáng Shān] to be driven to join the rebels on Liangshan; to be compelled to revolt

逼真 [bīzhēn] life-like; true to life; vivid

bí

鼻 [bí] (n)动物司嗅觉的器官 nose; trunk (elephant); muzzle (dogs, horses)

鼻鼾 [bíhān] snore

鼻孔 [bíkǒng] the nostrils

鼻腔 [bíqiāng] nasal cavity; nasal twang

鼻涕 [bítì] nasal mucus, snivel

鼻烟 [bíyān] snuff

鼻音 [bíyīn] nasal sound; nasal

鼻祖 [bízǔ] the founder of a family; the first ancestor

bǐ

匕 [bǐ] 1 (n) 汤匙 a spoon; used more often in ancient time 2 (n) 短剑 a dagger

匕首 [bǐshǒu] a dagger

比 [bǐ] 1 (v) 较量 to compare; a contrast; a comparison * 你怎能拿今天的一块钱和十年前的相比？How can you compare the one dollar today with that ten years ago? 2 (v) 做手势 to gesture (with hands), to make a gesture (with hands) *他比一比这条衬衣的大小 He made a gesture of the size of the shirt. 3(v) 兩個数目的比较 ratio 4 (prep) 介词，表示两种事物状态的不同程度…… ...... than * 椰树比油棕树高。The coconut tree is taller than the oil palm tree.

比比皆是 [bǐ bǐ jiē shì] such is found everywhere; such ...... can be found everywhere

比不上 [bǐ bù shàng] cannot compare with; no match for

比得上 [bǐ déshàng] comparable

比方 [bǐ fāng] for instance; analogy; example

比较 [bǐjiào] to compare; comparatively

比例 [bǐlì] ratio; proportion; scale

比例尺 [bǐlìchǐ] a scale (e.g. on a map)

比目鱼 [bǐmùyú] soles

比拟 [bǐnǐ] to compare; to draw a parallel; to metaphor

比如 [bǐrú] for example; for instance; such as; if; suppose

比赛 [bǐsài] to compete; a contest; a match; a race; a competition

比喻 [bǐyù] a parable; a metaphor; an illustration; an allegory

比重 [bǐzhòng] specific gravity

秕 [bǐ] (n) 秕子，不饱满的谷粒。blasted or withered grain; unripe grain

俾 [bǐ] (v) 使（达到某种效果） to cause; to enable

彼 [bǐ] 1 (pronoun) 他，对方 he; she 2 (adj) 那，那个 that; those

彼岸 [bǐ àn] yonder shore; nirvana

彼此 [bǐcǐ] this and that; now and then; you and I; each other; one another

彼一时，此一时 [bǐ yī shí, cǐ yī shí] times have changed; that was one time, and this is another

鄙 [bǐ] 1 (adj) 粗俗 rustic 2 (adj) 低劣 low; base; mean

鄙薄 [bǐbó] to despise; to speak ill of

鄙见 [bǐjiàn] my humble opinion

鄙劣 [bǐliè] unpolished; mean; vile; worthless

鄙视 [bǐshì] to despise; to disdain; to look down upon

鄙意 [bǐyì] my humble opinion

笔（筆）[bǐ] 1 (n) 写字的一种用具 a pen; a pencil; a writing brush 2 (v) 写 to write; compose 3 (n) 组成汉字的笔划 the strokes that form the Chinese characters * "天"字有四笔划。There are four strokes in the character "天" 4 (n) 量词 a measure word, a sum (of money) *她捐了一笔钱给医院 She donated a sum of money to the hospital.

笔法 [bǐfǎ] penmanship; pencraft

笔伐;笔诛 [bǐfá; bǐzhū] denouncing one in writing; chastise (punish) one with the pen

笔杆 [bǐgǎn] holder of a writing brush

笔迹 [bǐjī] handwriting

笔记 [bǐjì] notes; memorandum

笔尖 [bǐjiān] a pen nib

笔记本 [bǐjìběn] a notebook

笔名 [bǐmíng] pen-name

笔墨 [bǐmò] pen and ink; writing; words; articles

笔试 [bǐshì] written examination

笔顺 [bǐshún] order of strokes in writing a chinese character

笔误 [bǐwù] slip of the pen

笔译 [bǐyì] written translation

笔者 [bǐzhě] the writer; the author

笔直 [bǐzhí] perfectly straight; upright

bì

必 [bì] (part) 一定，肯定 certainly; must; will; necessarily*专制和侵略必须结束。Overbearing and aggression must come to an end.

必不可免 [bìbùkěmiǎn] unavoidable

必不可少 [bìbùkěshǎo] absolutely necessary; indispensable; essential

必定 [bìdìng] certainly; surely; be bound to; undoubtedly

必将 [bìjiāng] surely will

必可 [bìkě] certainly possible

必然 [bìrán] be bound to; inevitable; necessarily; certainly

必然性 [bìránxìng] necessity, inevitability; certainly

必修课 [bìxiūkè] compulsory subject; required course

必需 [bìxū] essential; indispensable

必须 [bìxū] must; have to; necessary

必需品 [bìxūpǐn] necessaries; necessities; requisites

必要 [bì yào] necessary; indispensable; essential

必要性 [bìyàoxìng] necessity

必由之路 [bìyóuzhīlù] the road one must follow; the only road to; the only way

必争之地 [bìzhēngzhīdì] a hotly contested spot

庇 [bì] (v) 遮蔽，掩护 to protect; to cover; to shelter; to shield; to hide; to harbour

庇护 [bì hù] to shelter; to shield; to put under one's protection

庇祐 [bìyòu] divine protection and assistance

陛 [bì] (n) 帝王朝廷的台阶 the steps to the throne

陛下 [bìxià] a respectful address to the emperor; majesty; your (his, her) Majesty

毕（畢） [bì] 1 (v) 结束，完了 to finish; to close; to complete ; to terminate *毕业后，你打算做什么？What do you intend to do after your graduation? 2 (adj) 全部 entire; all; total *我毕生难忘这个教训。I will not forget this lesson in all my life

毕竟 [bìjìng] after all; at last; finally; in the long run

毕生 [bìshēng] all one's life; life-long; life-time

毕业 [bì yè] to finish school; to complete study; to graduate

毕业证书 [bìyèzhèngshū] (graduation) certificate; diploma

哔（嗶） [bì]〔哔叽〕[bìjī] (n) 斜纹的纺织品 beiges; serge

蓖 [bì]〔蓖麻〕[bìmá] (n) 草本植物 the castor-oil plant

蓖麻油 [bìmáyóu] castor oil

篦 [bì] 1 (n) 篦子，齿很密的梳头用具 a fine-toothed comb 2 (v) 用篦子梳 to comb

婢 [bì] (n) 婢女，社会上受压迫，供人役使，丧失人身自由的女孩子 a slave girl; a maid servant

睥 [bì]〔睥睨〕[bìnì] (v) 斜着眼睛向旁边看，有蔑视的意思 to look askance; to take a scornful look

裨 [bì] (v)(adj) 补益; 补助 to benefit; to aid; advantageous; profitable

裨补 [bìbǔ] to support; to aid; to make up a deficiency

裨益 [bìyì] of great advantages ; be advantageous

髀 [bì] (n) 大腿 the thigh; the buttocks

畀 [bì] (v) 给，与 to give to; to confer to

痹（痺） [bì] (adj) 麻木 numb

辟 [bì] (n) 君主 the king; the emperor 另见 [pì]

避 [bì] (v) 躲开 to avoid; to shun; to flee; escape; leave;to keep away *她辞掉那份工作以避免交上坏朋友。She quitted that job to shun evil company.

避而不谈 [bìérbútàn] to evade the question; to keep silent about the matter
避风所 [bìfēngsuǒ] a typhoon shelter; a refuge from the storm
避讳 [bì huì] to evade the issue
避开 [bì kāi] to evade ; to dodge ; to steer clear of; to keep away from
避雷器 [bìléiqì] a lightning arrester; a lighting conductor
避雷针 [bìléizhēn] a lightning rod
避免 [bì miǎn] to avoid; to avert; to refrain from
避难 [bìnàn] to take refuge; to seek shelter
避匿 [bìní] to abscond
避暑 [bì shǔ] to avoid the summer heat; to take a summer holiday
避嫌 [bìxián] to avoid suspicion
避孕 [bì yùn] birth control; contraception
避重就轻 [bì zhòng jiù qīng] to take up the minor issue; to evade the major one

壁 [bì] (n) 墙 a wall
壁报 [bìbào] a wall newspaper
壁橱 [bìchú] a built-in wardrobe or cupboard
壁灯 [bìdēng] decoration lamp
壁虎 [bìhǔ] a house lizard
壁画 [bìhuà] fresco; wall painting; mural
壁垒 [bìlěi] a strongly fortified barrier; rival camps confronting each other; two sharply opposed sides
壁毯 [bì tǎn] tapestry; wall hanging

嬖 [bì] (v) 宠爱 to treat as a favourite

璧 [bì] (n) 扁平，圆形，中间有孔的玉 a kind of jade

臂 [bì] (n) 胳膊，从肩到腕的部分 the arm
臂章 [bì zhāng] an arm-badge; a brassard
臂助 [bìzhù] to give a helping hand; to help

襞 [bì] (n) 衣服上的褶痕 creases; folds or pleats in a garment

躄 [bì](adj)两腿残废 不能行走 lame; crippled

敝 [bì] 1 (adj) 破的,坏的, 差的 bad; poor; unworthy; defeated; ruined; worn out ＊那小乞丐一身敝衣，根本不能耐寒。That small beggar's clothes were too worn out for him to stand the cold. 2 (Pron) 自称谦词 a modest term for "my", "our"

弊 [bì] 1 (n) 害处，毛病 defeat 2 (n) 恶行，不艮行为，欺骗行为 malpractice
弊病 [bìbìng] corruption; abuse; defects ; viciousness
弊害 [bìhài] evils; vices; abuses

蔽 [bì] (v) 遮盖，掩藏 to cover; to conceal; to shelter

币 (幣) [bì] (n) 钱财 money; coins ; currency ＊这书包值马币五元。This schoolbag costs five Malaysia dollars.
币制 [bìzhì] currency system; monetary system
币值 [bìzhí] currency value

毙 (斃) [bì] (v) (adj)死 to die; dead ＊在一场血战中，警察击毙了三名私会党徒。 The police shot three secret society members dead in a bloody clash.

愎 [bì](adj) 任性，固执 perverse; self-willed; obstinate

闭 (閉) [bì] 1 (v) 关上，合上 to close; to shut 闭嘴！keep your mouth shut! 2 (v) 塞住，不通 to obstruct; to stop up
闭关政策 [bì guān zhéngcè] a policy of seclusion; a closed- door policy
闭门羹 [bìméngēng] refused of entrance; cold shoulder treatment
闭门思过 [bìménsīguō] reflect one's misdeeds in private
闭门造车 [bì mén zào chē] to make a cart behind closed doors; to work behind closed doors; to draw up a plan

without considering the actual condition

闭幕 [bì mù] to drop the curtain; to close a meeting

闭塞 [bìsè] close up; stop up; cut off from the world; out of touch

贲（賁）[bì] (adj) (adv) 光明的样子 bright; brightly

另见 [bēn]

碧 [bì] (n) (adj) 青绿色 green; blue

碧绿 [bìlù] jade green

碧血 [bìxuè] dark blood

biān

编（編）[bian] 1 (v) 织造 to weave; to braid; to knit; to plait ＊这盲人编得一手好竹篮。The blind man can weave excellent bamboo baskets with his own hands. 2 (v) 按次序排列 to arrange ＊我在编排班上同学的名单。I am arranging a list of students' names in the class. 3 (v) 排列整理资料，使成作品 to edit ; to compose ; to compile ＊他所编的书受到读者的欢迎。The book he edited is well-liked by the readers.

编号 [biān hào] to number; to classify

编辑 [biānjí] to edit; to compile; an editor; a compiler

编辑部 [biānjíbù] editorial board

编结 [biānjié] to tie; to bind

编剧 [biānjù] a playwright; a script writer; a scenario-writer

编目 [biān mù] to make a catalogue of; a catalogue; a list

编排 [biān pái] to arrange; to lay out

编入 [biān rù] to enlist; to enroll

编写 [biānxiě] to compile

编译 [biānyì] to edit and translate

编造 [biānzào] to make; to prepare; to fabricate; to create out of imagination

编者 [biānzhě] an editor; a compiler

编者按 [biānzhěàn] an editorial's note; a comment

编制 [biānzhì] to weave; to work out; organisation

编织 [biānzhī] to knit; to weave; to plait

编著 [biānzhù] to compile; to write

编纂 [biānzuǎn] to compile

蝙 [biān]〔蝙蝠〕[biānfú] (n) 哺乳动物，有翼膜，能飞 bat

鳊（鯿）[biān] (n) 鱼类 the bream ; the carp

鞭 [bian] 1 (n) 形状细长，軟勒或可摺曲的用具，兵器或刑具 a whip; a lash ＊毒贩被判监禁三年，兼受五鞭。The drug trafficker served a sentence of three years' imprisonment and five lashes. 2 (v) 用鞭子打 to flog; to slash; to whip

鞭长莫及 [biān cháng mòjí] beyond the reach of the whip or the law

鞭策 [biāncè] to berge on; to spur on

鞭笞 [biānchī] to whip; to lash; to flog

鞭炮 [biānpào] firecrackers; strings of firecrackers

鞭子 [biān·zi] a whip

边（邊）[biān] 1 (n) 物体周围的部份 a side; an edge; a margin ＊谁把花瓶放在桌子边? Who put the vase on the edge of the table? 2 (n) 交界的地方 a border; a boundary ＊在边界，发生了激烈的战事。Fierce battles broke out at the border.

边防 [biānfáng] frontier - garrison frontier defence

边患 [biānhuàn] troubles on the frontier

边疆 [biānjiāng] the frontier; the borderland

边界 [biānjiè] border; boundary; borderline; boundary line

边境 [biānjìng] border; frontier

边区 [biānqū] border area

边塞 [biānsài] a frontier-pass

边外 [biānwài] beyond the frontier

边沿 [biānyán] the edge ; along the bank
边音 [biānyīn] a lateral sound
边缘 [biānyuán] a rim; an edge; brink

砭 [biān] (n) 石针 a stone probe

biǎn

扁 [biǎn] (adj) 平薄 flat ＊鸭子有扁喙。 The duck has a flat beak.
扁桃腺 [biǎntáoxiàn] tonsils
另见 [piān]

匾 [biǎn] (n) 长方形的木牌，上面题字，横挂在门的上头或墙的上部 a tablet; a board with an inscription; a signboard hung above the door

贬(貶) [biǎn] 1 (v) 减少，降低 to demote; to reduce; to devaluate ＊美国货币又一次贬值了。 The American currency had devaluated again 2 (v) 给予低的，不好的评价 to disparage; censure; to depreciate ＊朋友犯了错误，我们可以批评他，但不应该贬低他。We could criticise a friend for his mistakes , but should not degrade him.
贬黜 [biǎnchù] to degrade from office; degradation
贬词 [biǎncí] an expression of censure
贬低 [biǎndī] to disparage; to belittle; to play down
贬评 [biǎnpíng] pass adverse judgement
贬义 [biǎnyì] derogatory sense
贬义词 [biǎnyìcí] derogatory word
贬值 [biǎn zhí] to devalue; to depreciate

biàn

卞 [biàn] (n) 姓 a surname

遍 [biàn] 1 (adj)(v) 到处，全面 all over ＊我们的朋友遍天下。 Our friends are all over the world. 2 (n) 次 a time ＊[根]这本书我已经读过两遍了。 I have already read the book 'Roots' twice .
遍地 [biàndì] everywhere
遍及 [biànjí] to reach as far as; to reach every place
遍体鳞伤 [biàntǐlínshāng] the body is covered wth wounds all over

辨 [biàn] (v) 分别，分析 to distinguish ; to recognise ＊我们待人处事，都必须明辨是非。 In dealings with any persion and any matter , we must distinguish between right and wrong.
辨别 [biànbié] to distinguish
辨明 [biànmíng] to distinguish
辨认 [biànrèn] to make out

辩(辯) [biàn] (v) 说理，争论 to dispute; to debate; to argue; to discuss ＊真理是越辩越明的。 The more we debate , the more we become clear about the truth.
辩白 [biànbái] to try to justify
辩驳 [biànbó] to argue and refute
辩才 [biàncái] the gift of eloquence ; oratorical talent
辩护 [biànhù] to come out in defence of; to defend
辩护士 [biànhùshí] an apologist
辩解 [biàn jiě] to explain; to make an excuse; to clear oneseif from a charge ; to justify
辩论 [biànlùn] to discuss; to debate; to argue; to moot
辩明 [biànmíng] explain clearly
辩证法 [biàn zhèng fǎ] dialectics

辫(辮) [biàn] (n) 分股交叉编成的长条 a queue; a braid

便 [biàn] 1 (adj) 顺利，容易 convenient; handy; easy ＊巴士站就在我家附近，我每天上班回家，都很方便。The bus stop is near my house ; it is convenient for me to go to office and come back home every day. 2 (adv) then; so; thus; readily; forthwith ＊为求办事快捷，他说到便做到，从不拖延。To be quick in action, he said it and then did it without delay. 3 (adj) 简单的，普通的 ordinary;

common; informal 4 (v) 排泄屎，尿 to ease nature
便秘 [biànbì] constipation
便道 [biàndào] a sidewalk; a pavement
便饭 [biàn fàn] an informal meal
便服 [biànfú] informal dress; plain clothes
便利 [biàn lì] convenience; facilities; handiness
便条 [biàntiáo] a short note
便衣 [biànyī] ordinary clothes; plain clothes; informal dress
便于 [biànyú] to be convenient to
便酌 [biànzhuó] an informal dinner
另见 [pián]

变（變）[biàn] (v) 和原来不同 to change; to transform; to vary *这个世界不断在变化中。 This is an ever changing world.
变本加历 [biàn běn jiā lì] to go from bad to worse; with ever-increasing intensity
变成 [biànchéng] to become; to change into; to be converted into
变调 [biàndiào] to change the tune or tone
变动 [biàndòng] change; alteration; variation; fluctuation
变法 [biàn fǎ] reform
变革 [biàngé] transformation; reformation
变更 [biàngēng] to alter; to change
变故 [biàngù] calamity; alteration; variation; fluctuation
变卦 [biàn guà] to change one's mind; to change one's tune
变化 [biànhuà] change; variation; transformation
变换 [biànhuàn] to change; to substitute
变幻莫测 [biànhuànmòcè] unpredictable; erratic
变节 [biàn jié] change of loyalty
变乱 [biànluàn] rebellion; insurrection; disturbance
变卖 [biànmài] to turn into money; to dispose by sale
变迁 [biànqiān] to change in trends or condition
变态 [biàntài] an anomaly; abnormality
变态叶 [biàntàiyè] metamorphosis of the leaf
变通 [biàn tōng] to fall in with; to change method; to do in another way
变相 [biànxiàng] to change appearance; to change form
变形 [biàn xíng] to change form
变形虫 [biàn xíng chóng] amoeba

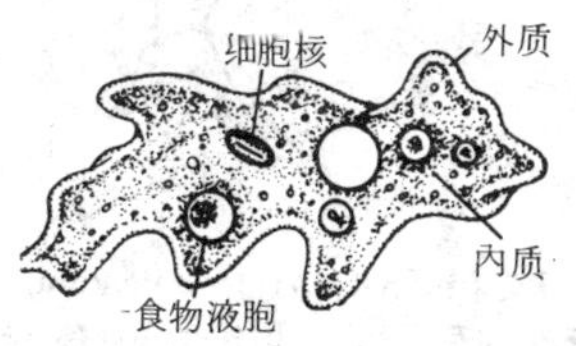

变形虫

变压器 [biànyāqì] a transformer
变质 [biàn zhì] change in quality; deterioration
变质岩 [biànzhìyán] metalmorphic rocks
变种 [biànzhǒng] variation; mutation

biāo

骠（驃）[biāo] (n) 黄白色的马，战马 a cream coloured horse
另见 [piào]

镖（鏢）[biāo] (n) 旧时一种投掷武器 a throwing weapon; a dart

膘 [biāo] (n) 牲畜的肥肉 fat of a stock animal

标（標）[biāo] 1 (n) 树梢 the topmost branches of a tree 2 (n) 事物的表面 thing's surface 3 (v) 揭出，写明 to mark; to label *这玩具的标价是两块钱。 The marked price of this toy is two dollars. 4 (n) 表记，记号 a mark; a label; a sign; a signal
标榜 [biāobǎng] to publish the list of successful candidates; to brag about;

to give favourite publicity to
标本 [biāoběn] a specimen; a sample
标点符号 [biāodiǎn fúhào] punctuation marks
标记 [biāojì] to mark
标价 [biāo jià] to mark a price on
标明 [biāomíng] clearly indicated or stated
标签 [biāoqiān] a label
标枪 [biāoqiāng] javelin

标题 [biāo tí] a title; a heading
标新立异 [biāo xīn lì yì] to create what is new and original
标语 [biāoyǔ] a motto; a slogan; a watchword
标志 [biāozhì] to show; to symbolize; a symbol; a distinguishing mark
标致 [biāo zhì] very beautiful; very pretty
标注 [biāozhù] a top-note
标准 [biāo zhǔn] a standard; a norm
标准化 [biāozhǔnhuà] standardization

镳（鑣）[biāo] 1 (n) 马嚼子，也指马头的方向 bit for a horse 2 (n) same as 镖

彪 [biāo] 1 (n) 小老虎 a tiger-cat 2 (n) 斑纹 stripes; streaks; veins

biǎo

表 [biǎo] 1 (n) 外部 surface; exterior ＊他外表凶恶，可是心地仁慈。He has a harsh exterior but a kind heart. 2 (v) 显示 to make known; to show; to express ＊他听了老妇的不幸遭遇深表同情。After having heard about the misfortune of the old lady, he expressed deep sympathy with her. 3 (n) 榜样 an example 4 (n) 分类，分项记录事物的文件 a table; a list
表白 [biǎobái] to vindicate; to justify oneself; to profess
表层 [biǎocéng] top layer
表达 [biǎodá] to express; to voice
表弟 [biǎodì] a male younger cousin
表哥 [biǎogē] a male elder cousin
表格 [biǎogé] table; form; chart
表记 [biǎojì] a signal; a sign; a mark
表姐 [biǎojiě] a female elder cousin
表决 [biǎojué] to determine by vote; to put to the vote
表里如一 [biǎo lǐ rú yī] the consistency in one's words and deeds; integrity
表妹 [biǎomèi] a female younger cousin
表面 [biǎomiàn] surface; superficial; ostensible
表面化 [biǎomiànhuà] to become overt; to come out into open
表面性 [biǎomiànxìng] superficiality
表明 [biǎomíng] to make clear
表皮 [biǎopí] epidermis; bark
表情 [biǎoqíng] expression of emotion; facial expression
表示 [biǎoshì] to indicate; to express; to mean
表率 [biǎoshuài] good example
表现 [biǎoxiàn] to show; to behave
表演 [biǎoyǎn] to perform; to exhibit; to play; to show
表扬 [biǎoyáng] to praise; to commend
表彰 [biǎo zhāng] to cite; to commend

表（錶）[biǎo] (n) 计时，计量的器具 a meter; a watch; a timepiece.

婊 [biǎo] (n) 婊子：妓女 a prostitute

裱 [biǎo] (v) 裱糊，用纸，布或丝织物把墙壁，书面，画等粘糊衬托起来。to mount map or scrolls to paste

biào

鳔（鰾）[biào] (n) 鱼体内的器官，使鱼能在水中浮沉 the air

bladders of fishes

biē

憋 [biē] 1 (v) 闷，不通风 to choke; to stifle 2 (v) 忍住，不发泄出来 to restrain; to hold; to hold back ＊他憋着一口气，潜游了一百公尺。 He held his breath and swam 100 metres underwater.

憋闷 [biē mèn] bored; depressed

憋气 [biēqì] short of breath; suffocated

鳖（鱉）[biē] (n) 爬行动物，龟属，背甲有软皮，生活在河湖，池沼里 the freshwater turtle

bié

别 [bié] 1 (v)离别 to leave; to depart to ＊我们的祖先得离别家乡，到海外来谋生 Our forefathers had to leave their homeland and went abroad to make a living. 2 (v) 区分，分类 to distinguish; to classify ＊所有的标本都经过专家们鉴别和分门别类 然后陈列在博物院里。 All the specimens were distinguished and classified by the experts and then displayed in the museum. 3(adj)另外 other; another; some other ＊我不要这个手表，有没有别个牌子的？ I don't want this watch; is there any other brand? 4 (v) 不要 do not; must not ＊别光说不做。Don't just talk and do nothing. 5 (v)穿过，扣定 to pin

别处 [biéchǔ] elsewhere; other place

别出心裁 [bié chū xīn cái] to have an unconventional idea

别的 [biédì] other

别管 [biéguǎn] no matter; however; whatever

别具一格 [bié jù yī gé] a unique style of its own

别开生面 [bié kāi shēng miàn] in a novel way

别离 [biélí] to leave; to part; to separate; to depart

别名 [biémíng] another name; an alias

别人 [biérén] others

别墅 [bié shù] a villa; a country seat; a summer house

别有用心 [bié yǒu yòng xīn] with ulterior motives

别针 [biézhēn] a pin

别致 [biézhì] new; unusual; interesting and novel

别字 [biézì] a wrongly written or mispronounced character

蹩 [bié] (v) 脚没踏平而扭伤 to limp

蹩脚 [biéjiǎo] inforior in skill or quality; poor and incompetent

biě

瘪（癟）[biě] (adj) 不饱满，凹下去 empty; shrivelled up

bīn

宾（賓）[bīn] (n) 客人 a visitor; a guest ＊总理在招待外宾。 The prime minister is entertaining guests from abroad.

宾馆 [bīnguǎn] guest house

宾客 [bīnkè] a visitor; a guest

宾至如归 [bīn zhì rú guī] the guests are feeling perfectly at home

宾主 [bīnzhǔ] guest and host; secondary and principal

傧（儐）[bīn] (v) 迎接和招待客人 to entertain

傧接 [bīnjiē] receive guest respectfully

傧相 [bīnxiàng] bridegroom's best man or bride's maid of honour

滨（濱）[bīn] 1 (n) 水边 a shore; a beach; a coast; a bank ＊在星期日，海滨挤满了人。On Sundays, the beach is crowded with people. 2 (v) 临近 to be on the verge of

缤（繽）[bīn] (adj) 华丽，繁多，杂乱的样子 mixed colours; in confusion

缤纷 [bīnfēn] confused

槟（檳）[bīn] (n) 常绿乔木，羽状复叶，生长在热带 the areca nut palm

槟榔 [bīnláng] the betel nut; the areca nut

濒（瀕）[bīn] (v) 临近，接近 to be on the verge (brink) of; to be at the point of

濒死 [bīnsǐ] to be on the brink of death

濒於破产 [bīnyúpòchǎn] to be on the verge of bankruptcy

彬 [bīn]（同斌）(adj) 文雅有礼貌的样子 ornamental ; refined (manner)

彬彬有礼 [bīnbīnyǒulǐ] in a refined manner

bìn

摈（擯）[bìn] (v) 排斥，抛弃 to reject; to expel; to throwaway; to exclude; to renounce

摈斥 [bìnchì] to reject; to expel; to exclude

摈弃 [bìnqì] to cast away; to reject

摈逐 [bìnzhú] to drive out; to expel

膑（臏）[bìn] (n) 膝盖骨 the knee-cap

殡（殯）[bìn] (v) 停放棺材或把棺材运往埋葬的地方去 to make a funeral; to encoffin a corpse; to carry to burial

殡仪馆 [bìnyíguǎn] funeral parlour

髌（髕）[bìn] (n) 髌骨，就是"膝盖骨" the knee-cap

鬓（鬢）[bìn] (n) 面颊的两旁靠近耳朵的头发 the hair on the temples; curls

bīng

兵 [bīng] 1 (n) 战士，军队 soldiers; a force; an army * 谁说好男不当兵？Who say that a good man should not become a soldier? 2 (n) 武器，军械 weapons ; arms 3 (adj) 关于军事的 military; warlike

兵变 [bīng biàn] troops in mutiny

兵不血刃 [bīng bù xuè rèn] the battle went smoothly ; and victory easily won without bloodshed

兵工厂 [bīnggōng chǎng] arsenal; an armoury

兵荒马乱 [bīnghuāng - mǎluàn] chaos in times of war

兵力 [bīnglì] force; military strength

兵连祸结 [bīnglián huò jié] repeated wars and calamities

兵团 [bīngtuán] army corps

兵饷 [bīngxiǎng] soldiers' ration

兵役 [bīngyì] military service

冰 [bīng] (n) 水摄氏零度或零度以下凝结成的固体 ice

冰雹 [bīngbáo] hailstones

冰车 [bīngchē] a sledge; a sleigh

冰川 [bīngchuān] a glacier

冰冻 [bīngdòng] frozen

冰河时代 [bīnghé shídài] the glacial epoch; the ice age

冰冷 [bīnglěng] ice-cold; very cold

冰凉 [bīngliáng] very cool; very cold

冰片 [bīngpiàn] Borneo Camphor

冰淇淋 [bīngqílín] ice-cream

冰清 [bīngqīng] clear as ice; pure and incorrupt

冰山 [bīngshān] an iceberg

冰释 [bīngshì] solved; finished

冰霜 [bīngshuāng] frost; ice

冰糖 [bīngtáng] crystallized sugar

冰天雪地 [bīngtiān-xuědì] icy and snowy field

冰箱 [bīngxiāng] ice box; refrigerator

冰消瓦解 [bīngxiāo - wǎjiě] fully vanished or eliminated

冰柱 [bīngzhù] icicle

bǐng

丙 [bǐng] (n) 天干的第三位，用作次序的第三 the third of the ten stems, used as indicating third in position; number three; third

柄 [bǐng] (n) 器物的把儿 a handle; a hilt * 那悍妇用伞柄敲打她的丈夫。That shrew hammered her husband with the hand of an umbrella.

炳 [bǐng] (adj) 光明，显著 bright; brilliant; luminous

饼(餅) [bǐng] (n) 扁圆形的面制食品 cake; pastry

饼干 [bǐnggān] biscuit

屏 [bǐng] 1 (v) 除去 to get rid of; to put aside; to reject 2 (v) 忍住，抑制住 to keep in control; to hold back

屏斥 [bǐngchì] to blame

屏息 [bǐngxī] to hold one's breath

屏逐 [bǐngzhú] to drive out; to expel

另见 [píng]

秉 [bǐng] (v) 拿着 to hold; to maintain

秉公办理 [bǐnggongbànlǐ] to administer with justice

秉直 [bǐngzhí] to adhere to correct principles

稟 [bǐng] 1 (n) 天性所赋 natural endowment 2 (v) 对署长或上司报告 to report to a superior ＊官吏必须向皇帝稟明国家大事。The officials must report to the emperor (superior) the affairs of the government.

稟赋 [bǐngfù] be endowed by nature

bìng

并(併) [bìng] (v) 合在一起 join together; combine ＊他主张将两间公司合并为一。He suggests to combine the two companies into one.

并吞 [bìngtūn] to annex; to gobble up

并 [bing] 1 (adv) 一齐，平排着 together 2 (conj) 和 and ＊我们做事，应该手脑并用 。As we work, we should use our hands and brain together. 3 用在否定词前，表示不象预料的那样 an intensive particle placed before a negative word to show not as might be expected ＊虽然是七月了，但天气并不太热。Although it is already July, the weather is in no sense hot.

并存 [bìngcún] to coexist

并非 [bìngfēi] by no means; in no sense

并驾齐驱 [bìng jià qí qū] to keep pace with; to keep up with; to match with

并肩 [bìng jiān] shoulder to shoulder; side by side; abreast

并举 [bìngjǔ] to promote or work simultaneously

并立 [bìnglì] to stand side by side

并列 [bìngliè] to put... on a par with...; to parallel

并排 [bìngpái] to keep abreast of; to be side by side; to lie alongside

并且 [bìngqiě] moreover; and also

并未 [bìng wèi] by no means as yet

并行 [bìngxíng] to go side by side

并重 [bìngzhòng] to regard both as equally important

病 [bìng] (n) (v) 生物体发生不健康的现象 an ailment; sickness; illness; a disease; to fall ill

病毒 [bìngdú] virus

病根 [bìnggēn] cause of disease; root of trouble

病故 [bìnggù] to die of illness

病号 [bìnghào] a sick person

病假 [bìngjià] sick leave

病剧 [bìngjù] seriously or dangerously ill

病菌 [bìngjūn] disease germs

病历 [bìnglì] case history

病理学 [bìnglǐxué] pathology

病情 [bìngqíng] sympton

病人 [bìngrén] a patient; a sick person

病入膏肓 [bìng rù gāo huāng] gravely ill; beyond treatment; irretrievable

病室 [bìngshì] a ward; a sick-room

病态 [bìngtài] physiologically or psychologically abnormal; morbid

病痛 [bìngtòng] the pain (torment) of a disease

病愈 [bìngyù] cured; convalescent; recover from sickness; get well

病症 [bìngzhēng] illness

病状 [bìngzhuàng] symptons of disease

bō

拨(撥) [bō] 1 (v) 挑动，推转 to poke; to stir 2 (v) 分给，支付 to distribute; to appropriate ＊学校每年都得拨款举办运动会。The school has to appropriate a fund to hold a sports meet every year.

拨交 [bōjiāo] to hand over to; to appropriate to

拨款 [bō kuǎn] to allot or appropriate funds

拨弄 [bō nòng] to stir up; to fiddle with; to provoke; to manipulate

波 [bō] (n) 水的起伏现象 waves; surges

波长 [bō cháng] wave length

波动 [bōdòng] undulation; a fluctuation; rise and fall

波及 [bōjí] to involve; to implicate; to entangle

波浪 [bōlàng] waves; surges; billows

波澜壮阔 [bōlán zhuàngkuò] on a magnificent scale; to surge forward with tremendous momentum

波涛 [bōtāo] huge waves

波纹 [bōwén] ripples

波折 [bōzhé] obstacles; difficulties; setbacks

玻 [bō] (n)〔玻璃〕用炭酸钠,炭酸钾,或铅丹和石灰白砂等烧鎔制成的物体 glass

玻璃器 [bō líqì] glass-ware

玻璃纤维 [bō lí xiān wéi] glass fibre

玻璃紙 [bō lízhǐ] cellophane

菠 [bō] (n)〔菠菜〕草本植物,供食用 spinach

菠萝 [bōluó] pineapple

菠罗密 [bōluó mì] the jack-fruit

播 [bō] 1 (v) 撒开,撒种 to sow; to scatter ＊农夫们正在稻田里播种。The farmers are sowing seeds in the padi fields. 2 (v) 散布,传扬 to spread; to broadcast＊这人散播谣言,应受处分。This man spreads rumours, therefore he should be punished.

播送 [bōsòng] to broadcast

播音 [bō yīn] to broadcast

播种 [bō zhǒng] to sow

饽(餑) [bō]〔饽饽〕[bōbō] (n) 糕点 cakes

钵(鉢) [bō] (n) 陶盛器,像盆而小 a small earthware basin

剥 [bō] (v) 削下,去皮 to peel; to skin

剥夺 [bōdúo] to deprive; to expropriate

剥削 [bōxuē] to extort; to exploit

剥削者 [bōxuēzhě] exploiter

另见 [bāo]

bó

伯 [bó] 1 (n) 父亲的哥哥,对老年人的尊称 a paternal elder uncle; an address of a senior to show respect 2 (n) 兄弟中排行最大的 the eldest of brothers

伯爵 [bójué] a count; an earl

伯仲之间 [bózhòngzhījiān] be nearly equal; be well-matched

泊 [bó] (v) 停船靠岸 to anchor; to touch at; to moor

泊岸 [bóàn] disembark

泊船税 [bóchuánshuì] keelage

另见 [pō]

舶 [bó] (n) 大船,海船 sea-going vessels

舶来品 [bóláipǐn] imported goods

帛 [bó] (n) 丝织物的总称 silk

箔 [bó] 1 (n) 竹帘;门帘 a bamboo screen; a door screen 2 (n) 金属打成的薄片 metal foil

博 [bó] 1 (adj) 多,丰富 extensive; ample; rich ＊中国地大物博。China has vast territory and rich resources. 2 (v) 取得 to obtain; to aim *他的文章博得老师与同学的好评。 His article won the praises from his teacher and classmates.

博爱 [bó'ài] universal love; charity

博得 [bódé] to win (praise, applause etc)

博览会 [bólǎnhuì] an exhibition; an exposition; a fair

博士 [bóshì] a doctor of philosophy

博闻 [bówén] extensive knowledge

博物馆 [bówùguǎn] a museum

博学 [bóxué] well-learned

搏 [bó] (v) 对打 to fight; to combat *双方博斗多时，不分胜负。 Both parties fought hand-to-hand for a long time, yet neither side could win.

博斗 [bódòu] wrestle; fight

膊 [bó] (n) 上肢，近肩的部分 the upper arm

薄 [bó] 1 (adj) 不厚 thin 2 (v) 迫近 to approach; to go near

薄弱 [bóruò] too weak; vulnerable

薄视 [bóshì] to slight; to look down upon; to despise; to regard with contempt

另见 [bǎo]
[bò]

礴 [bó] (v) 充塞 to fill; to extend.

脖 [bó] (n) 脖子，就是"颈项" the neck

脖子 [bó·zi] neck

鹁（鵓） [bó] (n) 鸟类 a wood-pigeon

鹁鸽 [bógē] a dove; a pigeon

鹁鸪 [bógū] a wood-pigeon

勃 [bó] 1 (adj) 旺盛 flourshing; prosperous 2 (adv) 突然，忽然 suddenly; abruptly; unexpectedly

勃发 [bófā] to rise suddenly

勃然 [bórán] suddenly; abruptly; on or of a sudden

勃谿 [bóxī] quarrel in the family

钹（鈸） [bó] (n) 一种打击乐器 cymbals

驳（駁） [bó] 1 (v) 说明事实理由，否定别人的意见 to dispute; to contradict; to argue; to refute *在辩论会中，辩论者举出许多理由来反驳对方。 In the debate, the debaters brought out many reasons to refute their opponents. 2 (v) 大批货物用小船分载转运 to lighter

驳斥 [bóchì] to repudiate; to refute

驳船 [bóchuán] barge

驳倒 [bódǎo] to run (somebody) down in argument; to refute

驳回 [bóhuí] to reject

驳运 [bóyùn] transport; trans-ship

bǒ

跛 [bǒ] (adj) 瘸脚或脚有毛病，走路身体不平衡 lame; crippled

跛子 [bǒ·zi] a lame (crippled person); a cripple

簸 [bǒ] (v) 扬去谷粒中的杂物 to winnow

另见 [bò]

bò

擘 [bò] 1 (n) 大拇指 the thumb 2 (v) 剖，分开 break; tear; pierce

擘画 [bò huà] to make a plan

薄 [bò] 〔薄荷〕 [boha] (n) 草本植物可入药 the peppermint

另见 [báo]
[bó]

柏 [bò] (n) 木名，叶小如鳞，成片状 the cypress; the cedar

另见 [bǎi]

簸 [bò] (n) 用竹篾，柳条或铁皮等制成的器具，用来扬去糠麸或清除垃圾 a winnowing fan

簸箕 [bò jī] a winnowing fan; a basket for dust, etc
另见 [bǒ]

bū

逋 [bū] 1 (v) 逃亡 to flee; to abscond 2 (v) 拖欠 to owe
逋逃薮 [būtáosǒu] a refugee; a harbour for criminals
逋租 [būzū] unpaid rent

bǔ

捕 [bǔ] (v) 捉 to seize; to catch; to arrest ＊孩子们捕捉萤火虫，装进瓶子里。The children caught fireflies and put them in bottles.
捕风捉影 [bǔ fēng zhuō yǐng] to catch at shadows; to beat the air; to make accusation on hearsay
捕获 [bǔhuò] to succeed in catching; to capture
捕拿 [bǔná] to arrest; to catch
捕捉 [bǔzhuō] to catch

哺 [bǔ] (v) 喂 to feed
哺乳 [bǔrǔ] suckle one's young
哺乳动物 [bǔrǔ-dòngwà] mammals
哺育 [bǔyù] to bring up; to nurture

卜 [bǔ] (v) (n) 從預兆推定吉凶 to divine; to foretell
卜卦 [bǔguà] to divine by the eight diagrams

补(補) [bǔ] 1 (v) 添上材料修整破损的东西 to make up; to repair; to mend; to patch ＊请你给我补好这条裤子的破洞。Please patch up the hole on this pair of trousers for me. 2 (v) 把缺少的充实起来或添上。to make up; to fill up; to fill a vacancy ＊老师今天病了，要在星期天补课。Our teacher is sick today, so we have to make up for the lesson on Sunday. 3 (v) 营养 to nourish
补偿 [bǔcháng] to compensate (indemnify) a person for his loss
补充 [bǔchōng] to supplement; to fill up; to replenish
补给 [bǔjǐ] a supply to meet a deficit; material supply
补救 [bǔjiù] to rectify shortcomings; to reform abuses to save the situation
补考 [bǔkǎo] re - examination
补鞋匠 [bǔxiejiàng] a cobbler
补药 [bǔyào] tonic; restoratives
补注 [bǔzhù] supplementary notes
补助公债 [bǔzhū gōngzhài] subsidy bonds
补足 [bǔ zú] to make up; to make good a deficiency; to supply

bù

部 [bu] 1 (n) 区分，方位 a section; a part ＊加东位於星加坡东部。Katong is situated in the eastern part of Singapore. 2 (n) 常用为机关或组织单位的名称 a ministry; a department; a board 3 量词 a measure word (set of books, etc)
部队 [bùduì] a corps; a detachment
部分 [bù-fen] part; section
部件 [bùjiàn] parts; component parts
部落 [bùluò] a tribe; a clan
部门 [bùmén] a class; a department; a section
部首 [bùshǒu] radicals of Chinese characters
部署 [bùshǔ] to arrange the parts; to assign places to
部位 [bùwèi] locality
部下 [bù xià] those under the command; subordinates
部长 [bùzhǎng] a minister; head of a department

簿 [bù] (n) 本子 a book; a register
簿册 [bùcè] registers; lists
簿记 [bùjì] bookkeeping
簿籍 [bùjí] books and records

不 [bù] (adv) 表示反面的意义 not; no ＊你不大声说话，别人怎会听得见？If you do not speak louder, how

can others hear you?
不安 [bùān] uneasy; uncomposed; very uncomfortable
不比 [bùbǐ] different from
不必 [bùbì] not necessary; need not
不成文法 [bùchéngwénfǎ] unwritten law
不耻下问 [bù chǐ xià wèn] not ashamed of learning from those who are inferior to us in learning and status
不辞劳苦 [bùcíláokǔ] to spare no pains; to take pains
不但 [bùdàn] not only
不导体 [bùdǎotǐ] nonconductor; insu lator
不倒翁 [bùdǎowēng] a tumbler
不打自招 [bùdǎzì zhāo] to confess without duress
不得不 [bù dé bù] to have no choice but
不得了 [bù déliǎo] terrible
不等 [bùděng] not of the same kind; in variety
不得要领 [bù dé yào lǐng] not to the point; irrelevant; fail to grasp the main points
不得已 [bùdéyǐ] forced to; compelled to
不动产 [bùdòngchǎn] immovable property; fixed assets
不法 [bùfǎ] lawless; unlawful; illegal
不妨 [bùfāng] harmless ; there is no objection; it does not matter
不乏其人 [bù fáqírén] not short / lack of that kind of people
不分皂白 [bù fēn zào bái] indiscriminate
不服 [bùfú] to disobey; to resist; not to submit
不甘 [bù gān] to be unwilling to
不敢当 [bù gǎndāng] I am not worthy of such compliments; not equal to the honour
不甘后人 [bù gān hòu rén] unwilling to be back ward
不共戴天 [bù gòng dài tiān] not to live under the same sky (with one's enemy); sworn (enemy)
不顾 [bùgù] to disregard
不管 [bùguǎn] no matter
不关痛痒 [bù guān tòng yǎng] do not care a bit; be not affected
不过 [bùguò] only; merely; but
不寒而慄 [bùhánérlì] very frightened
不好意思 [bù hǎoyì-si] ashamed to; shy; embarrassed; reluctant to
不和 [bùhé] discord
不合时宜 [bùhéshíyí] outdated
不慌不忙 [bùhuāng bùmáng] no hurry
不即不离 [bù jí bù lí] neutrality; a middle of-the-road attitude
不禁 [bùjīn] cannot help; cannot refrain from
不胫而走 [bù jìng ér zǒu] spreading rapidly without promotion work
不景气 [bùjǐngqì] depression; dullness
不济事 [bùjìshì] it does not help the matter; of no use
不咎既往 [bùjiùjì wǎng] to forgive the past faults
不拘 [bùjū] without restraint ; no matter; irrespective of
不堪 [bùkān] unenduarable; unbearable
不堪设想 [bùkān shèxiǎng] inconventionable; unimaginable
不可告人 [bùkě gào rén] ulterior motives that cannot bear the light of day
不可救药 [bù kě jiù yào] incorrigible; incurable
不可开交 [bù kě kāi jiāo] unmanagable; to be terribly (busy)
不客气 [bù kè qì] don't mention it, impolite
不可胜数 [bùkě shēng shù] uncountable; too many
不可思议 [bù kě sīyì] unimaginable; difficult to understand
不可一世 [bù kě yī shì] overbearing
不可终日 [bù kě zhōng rì] in a desperate situation
不愧 [bùkuì] to be worthy of; to live up to
不料 [bùliào] unexpectedly
不劳而获 [bù láo ér huò] to reap with-

out sowing
不力 [bù lì] half-hearted
不利 [bùlì] disadvantage; improfitable
不艮 [bùliáng] bad ; unhealthy; undesirable
不了了之 [bù liǎo liǎo zhī] concluding the affair by not attending to it
不论 [bùlùn] no matter
不伦不类 [bùlún-bùlèi] neither fish nor fowl
不满 [bùmǎn] to pass censure on ; to discontent
不毛之地 [bù máo zhī dì] barren and desolated place
不免 [bùmiǎn] to bound to; to have to
不灭 [bùmiè] immortal; indestructible
不能自拔 [bù néng zì bá] cannot break out of
不偏不倚 [bùpiān-bùyǐ] without bias
不平 [bùpíng] unjust; unfair; uneven
不求甚解 [bù qiú shèn jiě] not bothering to understand
不屈 [bùqū] not to surrender ; undaunted
不屈不挠 [bùqūbùnáo] unswerving; unyielding
不然 [bùrán] otherwise
不仁 [bùrén] inhumanity ; cruelty ; merciless
不忍 [bùrěn] cannot bear
不如 [bùrú] not equal to ; cannot do better than
不入虎穴，焉得虎子 [bù rù hǔ xué, yān dé hǔ zǐ] nothing ventured, nothing gained
不三不四 [bùsan bùsì] neither one thing nor the other; dubious
不慎 [bùshèn] heedless; careless; unscrupulous
不胜枚举 [bù shèng méi jǔ] too numerous to mention
不时 [bùshí] now and then; occasionally; frequently
不时之需 [bù shí zhī xū] a need that could arise anytime
不速之客 [bù sùzhī kè] casual visitor; uninvited guest
不通 [bùtōng] not correct; bad grammar
不透明 [bùtòumíng] opacity; opaque
不外 [bùwài] not beyond; nothing more than
不问 [bùwèn] no matter what
不祥 [bùxiáng] ominous; ill omen
不相干 [bùxīnggān] to have nothing to do with
不像话 [bù xiàng huà] absurd
不肖 [bùxiào] degenerate; fall short of a coventional standard
不肖之徒 [bùxiàozhītú] worthless characters
不行 [bùxíng] cannot be done; out of the question
不幸 [bùxìng] unlucky; unfortunate
不省人事 [bù xǐng rén shì] unconscious
不朽 [bùxiǔ] immortality; eternity
不锈钢 [bùxrùgāng] stainless steel
不宣而战 [bù xuān ér zhàn] undeclared war
不学无术 [bù xué wú shù] lack of learning and capabilities
不扬 [bùyáng] ugly or awkward in appearance
不一 [bùyī] different
不宜 [bùyí] it is not right that ......
不意 [bùyì] suddenly; unexpectedly
不义 [bùyì] injustice; impropriety
不以为然 [bùyǐwèirán] to disagree; to doubt its correctness
不由分说 [bùyóufēnshuō] not permitted to explain
不由自主 [bùyóuzìzhǔ] unable to control oneself
不悦 [bùyuè] displeased
不择手段 [bù zé shǒuduàn] by any means; by fair or foul means
不正 [bùzhèng] wrong
不知所以 [bù zhī suǒ yǐ] do not know why
不治之症 [bǔ zhì zhī zheng] a hopeless case; an incurable disease

不自量力 [bù zìliànglì] not according to one's ability and strength

不足挂齿 [bù zú guà chǐ] not worth mentioning

不足为奇 [bù zú wéiqí] nothing surprising (quite common)

布 [bù] 1 (n) 用棉纱，麻纱等织成的可以做衣服或其他东西的材料 cloth 2 (v) 散着排列 to spread; to arrange ＊花了一天的时间，才把客厅布置好。It takes one day to arrange the living room in order 3 (v) 宣告 to publish; to make known. ＊成绩将在月底公布。The results will be published at the end of the month.

布告 [bùgào] announcement; to make known to the public

布景 [bùjǐng] built-up scenery; setting

布局 [bùjú] overall arrangement

布匹 [bùpǐ] cloth

布鞋 [bùxié] cloth-shoes

布置 [bùzhì] to arrange

怖 [bù] (adj) 害怕 afraid; frightened; alarmed ＊吃活猴子的脑是很可怖的。To eat the brains of a living monkey is frightening.

步 [bù] 1 (n) 脚步，行走时两脚之间的距离 a step; a pace 2 (v) 走路 to walk; to go on foot; to march ＊市场离我家不远，步行就能到达。The market is not far from my house, it is within the walking range. 3 (n) 进行的程度或阶段 steps or stages in a process ＊这算术题可分三步去做。This sum can be solved in three steps.

步步高升 [bù bù gāo shēng] rise step by step

步伐 [bùfá] measured steps; march

步人后尘 [bù rén hòu chén] follow or imitate others

步骤 [bùzhòu] steps, procedure

埠 [bù] 1 (n) 停船的码头 a jetty; a port 2 (n) 指大城市 a city

埠头 [bùtóu] a wharf; a port

C

cā

擦 [cā] 1 (v) 揩，抹 to wipe; to clean ; to erase ＊他拿手帕擦干脸上的汗。 He wiped the sweat on his face with a handkerchief. 2 (v) 磨 to rub ＊他把错字擦净，重写一遍。 He rubs away the wrong words and rewrites.

cāi

猜 [cāi] (v) 推测，料想 to guess ＊我猜那瓶子里有一千零一粒豆。 I guess that there are 1001 grains of bean in the bottle.

猜度 [cāiduó] to guess ; to venture an opinion; to conjecture

猜忌 [cāijì] to envy

猜谜 [cāimí] to guess riddles

猜疑 [cāiyí] to doubt; to suspect

cái

才(纔) [cái] 1 (n) 能力 ability; talent; endowment ＊師长们都称赞他是个才德兼备的好学生。 All the teachers praise him for being a good student having both talents and virtues. 2 (n) 指具有某种才能的人 a person of a certain ability or talent ＊蠢才。 an idiot ; 天才。a genius; 专才。an expert 3 (adv) 只有，刚刚 only; just ＊才走了一个站，巴士就坏了。Having just travelled to another stop the bus broke down.

才干 [cáigàn] practical ability

才华 [cáihua] rich talent; brilliance of mind

才能 [cáinéng] talent; capacity; ability

才是 [cáishì] that is it; very well

才子 [cáizi] a man of talent

材 [cái] (n) 原料 materials＊教材。 teaching materials ; 木材。 timber ; 钢材。 steel materials

材料 [cáiliào] materials; stuff

财(財) [cái] (n) 金钱和物质的总称 property ; valuables ; wealth＊一场大火，造成财物的损失达一百万元。The fire caused a loss of one million dollars worth of property.

财产 [cáichǎn] property; estate

财富 [cáifù] wealth; fortune; riches

财库 [cáikù] treasury

财力 [cáilì] financial capability; financial resources

财迷 [cáimí] money-mad

财势 [cáishì] wealth and influence

财团 [cáituán] financial group; a consortium ; a foundation

财务 [cáiwù] financial affairs

财物 [cáiwù] money and property

财源 [cáiyuán] a source of riches; a resource; financial resource

财政 [cáizhèng] finance

财政年度 [cáizhèngniándū] a fiscal year

裁 [cái] 1 (v) 剪割 to cut ; to trim ＊她小心裁衣，以避免浪费。 She cut the cloth carefully to avoid wastage. 2 (v) 减去，除掉 to reduce; to cut off; to diminish ＊超级强国从来没有裁减核子武器生产。The superpowers have never reduced the production of nuclear weapons. 3 (n) 决定，判断 decision; determination ;judgement ＊公证人的裁决是双方都有错。The judgement of the referee is that both are in the wrong.

裁度 [cái duó] to decide; to plan

裁缝 [cái·feng] a tailor; a dressmaker; to sew

裁减 [cáijiǎn] to cut down

裁剪 [cáijiǎn] to cut (a dress)

裁决 [cáijué] to judge; to decide; to verdict; to make a ruling

裁军 [cáijūn] disarmament

裁判 [cáipàn] to judge; to decide; judgement; referee

裁判权 [cáipànquán] jurisdiction; judicial right

裁员 [caí yuán] to cut down the number of persons employed

cǎi

采(採) [cǎi] 1 (v) 摘取 to pick; to pluck ＊他在花园里采了一束胡姬花。He picked a bundle of orchids in the garden. 2 (v) 搜集，选取 to collect ; to select ; to choose ＊我们在郊外采集了许多植物标本。We collected a lot of botanical specimens in the wilds.

采伐 [cǎifá] to fell timber

采访 [cǎifǎng] to make inquiries; to cover news

采访员 [cǎifǎngyuán] a correspondent ; a reporter

采购 [cǎigòu] to purchase

采矿 [cǎi kuàng] to obtain (coal, etc) from a mine ; mining

采纳 [cǎinà] to accept ; to adopt; to take

采取 [cǎiqǔ] to adopt; to take (action) ; to follow (a policy)

采石 [cǎishí] quarrying

采用 [cǎiyòng] to adopt; to appoint; to put to use; to employ

采摘 [cǎizhāi] to pluck; to pick

睬 [cǎi] (v) 答理，理会 to bother; to take note; to care for ＊假使你还是自私，便不会有人睬你。Nobody will care for you so long as you remain selfish.

踩 [cǎi] (v) 脚踏 to step upon; to tread on; to stamp ＊我一脚踩在烂泥里把袂弄脏了。I dirty my trousers when I step on the mud.

彩(綵) [cǎi] 1 (n) 各种颜色 colours 2 (n) 称赞夸奖的表示 an expression of praises ＊喝彩。to applaud; applause ＊在全区常年运动会上，我们为校队喝彩。In the district annual sport meet, we applauded our school team. 3 (n) 指赌博性的奖品 lottery prize ＊他买了一张彩票，希望得彩后就不用來工作。Having bought a lottery ticket, he hoped that he might win a prize and be free from coming to work. 4(adj) 神色，精神 countenance; spirit or energy of mind

彩旗 [cǎiqí] coloured flags; streamers

彩票 [cǎipiào] lottery ticket

彩排 [cǎipái] to dress rehearsal

彩色 [cǎisè] colour

彩色片 [cǎisèpiàn] colour film

彩饰 [cǎishì] adorn; ornament

彩霞 [cǎixiá] roseate clouds

彩绣 [cǎixiù] coloured embroidery

cài

菜 [cài] 1 (n) 可供烹食的草本植物 vegetables 2 (n) 盛在盘里的熟食 a dish (of cooked food)

菜单 [càidān] a menu; a bill of fare

菜刀 [càidāo] a cook's chopper

菜市场 [càishìchǎng] a market

菜肴 [càiyáo] food eaten along with rice

菜园 [càiyuán] a vegetable garden

菜油 [càiyóu] cabbage oil; rape-seed oil

菜子儿 [càizǐr] vegetable seeds

蔡 [cài] (n) 姓 a Chinese surname

cān

参(參) [cān] (v) 加入 to take part in ; to participate; to join ＊要参加乒乓队的请来这里报名。Those who wish to join the ping pong team may register their names here.

参观 [cānguān] to take a view of;to visit ; to pay a visit to

参考 [cānkǎo] to refer to; reference

参加 [cānjiā] to join; to take part in

参军 [cānjūn] to join the army

参谋 [cānmóu] staff officers

参谋长 [cānmóuzhǎng] chief of staff

参议院 [cānyìyuàn] senate

参与 [cānyù] to participate; to share; to take part in; to join

参阅 [cānyuè] to read for reference

参赞 [cānzàn] a councillor

参战 [cānzhàn] to participate in war

参照 [cānzhào] to confer; to consult

另见 [cēn] [shēn]

餐 [cān] 1 (v) 吃 eat 2 (n) 饭食 a meal

餐具 [cānjù] a dinner-set

餐室 [cānshí] a dining-room; an eating place

餐厅 [cāntīng] a large dining hall ; a restaurant

cán

残(殘) [cán] 1 (v) 毁坏，伤害 to destroy; to spoil; to ruin ; to injure ＊这个村在第二次世界大战时已被侵入者摧残。This village had been ruined by invaders during the Second World War. 2 (adj) 凶恶 cruel; oppressive; savage ＊想不到歹徒那么残忍，把看守人也杀了！ I have never expected the culprit to be so cruel as to kill the watchman. 3 (adj) 不完整的 incomplete; disabled ＊他身残志更坚。He is physically disabled but mentally strong. 4 (adj) 剩下的remnant; remaining＊家里的女佣人常等我們吃完后 才吃残馀的饭菜。The servant in my house usually eats the remains after we have had our meals.

残暴 [cánbào] tyrannical; brutal; merciless

残兵 [cánbīng] disabled (defeated)soldiers; remnant troops

残存 [cáncún] to survive

残废 [cánfèi] physically disabled; deformed; crippled

残酷 [cánkù] cruelty; brutality; atrocity

残疾 [cán·ji]deformed; maimed

残局 [cánjú] the last stages (e.g. of a chess game); a lost situation

残缺不全[cánquēbù quǎn] incomplete; deficient

残忍 [cánrěn] brutal; cruel; merciless

残杀 [cánshā] slaughter; massacre

残余 [cányú] remnants; survivals

残滓 [cánzǐ] leftovers; remnants; leavings

蚕(蠶) [cán] (n) 一种昆虫，它的茧可抽丝 the silkworm

蚕豆 [cándòu] broad beans

蚕茧 [cánjiǎn] silkworm cocoon

蚕食 [cánshí] to nibble up

蚕丝 [cánsī] silk

惭(慚) [cán] (adj) 害羞，羞愧 ashamed; blushful

惭愧 [cánkuì] ashamed; abashed

cǎn

惨(慘) [cǎn] 1 (adj) 悲伤，悲痛 miserable; wretched ＊集中营里的囚犯过着悲惨的生活。The prisoners in the concentration camp lived a miserable life. 2 (adj) 凶狠恶毒 cruel ; inhuman ＊希特勒惨无人道地杀害了许多的善良人民。 Hitler had killed many innocent people in a cruel and inhuman manner. 3 (a; adv) 严重 seriously; badly ＊由于平时不多练习，所以校队在这次比赛中惨败了。Because of the lack of usual practices, the school team lost the match badly this time.

惨案 [cǎnàn] massacre ; tragical incident

惨白 [cǎnbái]ghostly pale; hazy; dim

惨不忍睹 [cǎnbùrěndǔ] so tragic that it is unbearable to look at

惨酷 [cǎnkù] cruel; hard-hearted

惨剧 [cǎnjù] a tragedy; a tragic event

惨死 [cǎnsǐ] to meet with a tragic death ; to die distressingly

惨痛 [cǎntòng] bitter ; grievous

惨无人道 [cǎnwúréndào] cruel and inhuman; brutal and callous

惨刑 [cǎnxíng] cruel punishment; torture

惨重 [cǎnzhòng] grievous and heavy (loss)

càn

粲 [càn] 1 (adj) 鲜明，美好 beautiful; bright; splendid 2 (adv) 笑的样子 smilingly

粲粲 [càncàn] clean and bright; fresh looking

粲然 [cànrán] laughingly; smilingly

灿（燦）[càn] (adj) [灿烂] 色彩鲜明耀眼 glorious; bright; brilliant ; lustrous

cāng

伧（傖）[cāng] (adj) 粗野

伧夫 [cāngfū] a worthless fellow ; reckless fellow

仓（倉）[cāng] (n) 储藏粮食或其他物资的地方 a barn; a granary; a storehouse

仓卒 [cāngcù] hurried; quick; at the spur of the moment

仓促 [cāngcù] hasty; hurried

仓房 [cānfáng] a storehouse ; a granary

仓皇 [cānghuáng] fearful; in a hurry; in haste

仓库 [cāngkù] a warehouse

沧（滄）[cāng] (adj) 暗绿色（指水） blue; green(colour of water)

沧海桑田 [cāng hǎi sāng tián] seas change into mulberry fields — the world is changing all the time

沧海一粟 [cāng hǎi yī sù] a grain (drop) in the ocean; very minute

舱（艙）[cāng] (n) 船或飞机内部分隔开的部位 the hold of a ship or an aeroplane

苍（蒼）[cāng] 1 (n) (adj) 深绿色 deep-green 2 (adj) 深蓝色 blue; the azure of the sky 3 (adj) 灰白色 groy; hoary

苍白 [cāngbái] pale (complexion) grey (hair)

苍翠 [cāngcuì] verdant green

苍老 [cānglǎo] ravaged by age; age-worn

苍茫 [cāngmáng] boundless and indistinct; vast and hazy

苍蝇 [cāng yíng] flies

cáng

藏 [cáng] 1 (v) 躲，隐避 to hide away; to conceal ; to harbour ＊他们把毒品藏在轮胎里。 They hid the drugs in the tyres . 2 (v) 收存 to store; to accumulate; to hoard ＊北方人每年都得贮藏煤块来准备过冬。 Every year the northern people have to store up coal for the winter.

藏匿 [cángní] concealment; to hide; to lie hidden

藏身 [cángshēn] hide oneself

藏头露尾 [cángtóulùwěi] to give a partial account of

藏书 [cángshū] collection of books

藏污纳垢 [cángwūnàgòu] a sewer in which all that is evil finds a home; a vehicle for filth; to shelter evil people or things

另见 [zàng]

cāo

糙 [cāo] (adj) 不细致的，不光滑的 coarse; rough

糙米 [cāomǐ] unhulled rice; coarse rice

操 [cāo] 1 (v) 拿，掌握 to take in hand; to hold; to keep; to manage 2 (v) 限制 to restrain 3 (v) 训练，锻炼 to train; to drill

操场 [cāochǎng] parade ground; playground

操劳 [cāoláo] to labour painstakingly; to do something industriously

操练 [cāoliàn] to drill

操守 [cāoshǒu] unswerving integrity; chastity; virtue

操心 [cāoxīn] to worry about; to be concerned over

操行 [cāoxíng] conduct; behaviour

操业 [cāoyè] do one's duty

操之过急 [cāo zhī guò jí] to act with undue haste; too hasty

操纵 [cāozòng] to control

操舟；操舵 [cāozhoū; cāoduò] to steer

操作 [cāozuò] do manual labour; to work; to operate; to practise

cáo

曹 [cáo] 1 (n) 等，辈 a company; a class; a generation 2 (n) 姓 a Chinese surname

嘈 [cáo] (adj) 声音杂乱，有时叠用 bustling; tumultuous; noisy ＊巴刹里很嘈杂 It is very noisy in the market.

漕 [cáo] (n) 运河 a canal

漕河 [cáohé] a canal

漕运 [cáoyùn] canal transportation

槽 [cáo] 1(n) 一种较大的长方形或方形的容器 a manger; a trough 2 (n) 两边高起，中间凹下的部分 a groove

cǎo

草 [cǎo] 1 (n) 一种根部柔软，结实后即枯死的植物 weeds; grass; straw 2 (adj) 粗略，粗率 careless; rough ＊他办事草率，经常出错。Being careless in what he does, he often makes mistakes. 3 (adj)（字体）不整洁 slipshod (writing) 4(adj) 未定的（文稿） unauthorized or rough (manuscript) 5 (n) 稿子 manuscript

草案 [cǎo'àn] draft copy of a document; a draft

草包 [cǎobāo] straw bag; a sack loaded with straw; an incapable person

草本植物 [cǎoběn zhíwù] herbs

草草了事 [cǎocǎoliǎoshì] rashly done

草地 [cǎodì] a lawn; a grass field

草稿 [cǎogǎo] a rough draft; a manuscript

草菅人命 [cǎo jiān rénmìng] regard human lives to be of little importance

草帽 [cǎomào] a straw hat

草莓 [cǎoméi] strawberry

草木皆兵 [cǎomùjiēbīng] see every grass and tree as an enemy soldier—a state of imaginary fears

草拟 [cǎonǐ] to draft

草坪 [cǎopíng] a lawn

草人 [cǎorén] a scarecrow

草书 [cǎoshū] a rapid cursive style of writing; a running hand

草率 [cǎoshuài] rash; careless

草图 [cǎotú] a sketch

草鞋 [cǎoxié] straw sandals

草原 [cǎoyuán] a grassland; a prairie (in North America); a steppe (in Central Asia)

草约 [cǎoyuē] a draft treaty; a provisional contract

cè

侧（側） [ce] 1 (n) 旁边 the side 2 (v) 倾斜 to incline towards ＊他侧身向那讲话者，以便听得更清楚些。He inclined toward the speaker to hear more clearly.

侧门 [cèmén] a side door

侧面 [cèmiàn] side view; side dimension; profile

侧面图 [cèmiàntú] a lateral view; side elevation

侧视 [cèshì] side look

侧重 [cèzhòng] to lay emphasis on

测(測) [cè] (v) 度量 to survey

测度 [cèduò] to estimate; to measure ; to calculate

测绘 [cèhuì] to survey and make maps

测量 [celiáng] to survey

测量员 [celiángyuán] a surveyor

测望台 [cèwàngtaí] observation platform

测验 [cèyàn] to check; to test

厕(厠) [cè] (n) 厕所，大小便的地方 a toilet; a lavatory 另见 [·si]

策 [cè] 1 (n) 计谋，办法 a method; a plan 2 (n) 行政方针 a policy 3 (v) 推动 to cause somebody to do something

策动 [cèdòng] to incite; to instigate; to engineer

策反 [cèfǎn] to instigate rebellion within the enemy camp

策画 [cèhuà] to hatch plot

策进 [cèjìn] to urge ; to hasten; to push

策略 [cèluè] a strategy ; a plan ; a device ; a scheme

策应 [cèyìng] to afford assistance to; to relieve; to act in concert with (a person)

策源地 [cè yuán dì] a hotbed ; a source; a cradle; a place of origin

册 [cè] 1 (n) 书本 a book 2 (n) 量词 a measure word (for books)

册子 [cè·zi] a pamphlet; a book

cēn

参(參) [cēn] (adj) 长短，高低不齐 unequal; not uniform; varied ; irregular

参差不齐 [cēn cī bù qí] not uniform ; untrimmed ; uneven

参杂 [cēnzá] mixed; blended; confused 另见 [cān]
[shēn]

cén

岑 [cén] 1 (n) 小而高的山 a small but lofty hill 2 (n)姓 a Chinese surname

涔 [cén] (n) 雨水，溢水 overflow; rain water

涔涔 [céncén] continuous (dropping or flowing of water, rain, sweat, tears, etc)

céng

曾 [céng] (adv) 已然 already ; at some time in the past ＊我曾看过那部电影，所以很清楚它的内容。 I have already seen that picture so I am very clear about its contents. 另见 [zēng]

层(層) [céng] 1 (n) 量词 a measure word: layer 2 (adj) 重迭 laminated; repeated

层出不穷 [céngchūbùqióng] appearing time and again

层次 [céngcì] order; degrees; series

蹭 [céng] (v) 磨擦 to rub

chā

叉 [chā] 1 (n) 尖端分歧，便于刺物的用具 a fork; a prong 2 (v) 用叉或矛刺取東西 to pick (with a fork or a spear) 3 (v) 交错 to cross; to intersect

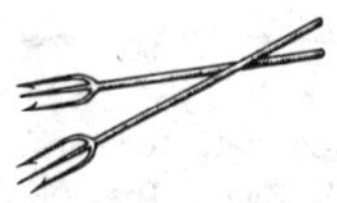

叉路 [chālù] forked road

叉手 [chāshǒu] to interlace the hands

叉腰 [chāyāo] to put the arms akimbo

插 [chā] 1 (v) 扎进去 to insert; to pierce ＊他把锁匙插进锁洞。He inserted the key in the lock. 2 (v) 加入 to take part in; to interfere ＊他不喜欢

别人插手处理他的家事。 He is not happy to have others interfering in his family affairs.

插班 [chābān] to classify a student from another school according to his grade

插翅难飞 [chā chì nán fēi] even with wings (he) couldn't escape

插花 [chā huā] to arrange flowers

插口 [chākǒu] to interrupt in speaking

插曲 [chāqǔ] interlude; a song from a film or a play

插手 [chāshǒu] to meddle; to have a hand in

插图 [chātú] an illustration

插秧 [chāyāng] to transplant rice shoots

插座 [chāzuò] socket

锸 [chā] (n) 掘土的工具 a spade

差 [chā] 1 (v; n) 错误 to err; to mistake; error; discrepancy 2 (v;n) 不同 to differ; difference *汉语发音跟英语有很大的差别。There is a great difference in pronunciation between Chinese and English.

差别 [chābié] difference

差错 [chācuò] a mistake; a mishap; an untoward accident

差额 [chāé] a deficit

差距 [chājù] a gap (lagging behind); leeway

差异 [chāyì] difference; diversity

另见 [chà]

[chāi]

chá

查 [chá] 1 (v) 考察，检点 to examine; to investigate; to search *港务员在检查货物。The port operater was examining the cargoes. 2(v) 翻看 to inquire into; to refer to *不懂字的意思，那就应该去查字典。You should refer to the dictionary if you don't know the meaning of words.

查办 [chabàn] to investigate and prosecute

查察 [cháchá] to inquire officially into

查抄 [cháchāo] to seize and confiscate property

查出 [cháchū] to discover; find out

查点 [chádiǎn] to check item by item

查对 [cháduì] to check up

查封 [cháfēng] to confiscate and seal up

查究 [chájiū] to try and examine

查看 [chákàn] to look into; to inspect

查探 [chátàn] to find out by inquiries

查问 [cháwèn] to investigate; to inquire

查询 [cháxún] to investigate; to make inquiry

查验 [cháyàn] to examine ; to scrutinize

查阅 [cháyuè] to read for information; to consult (books)

查帐 [cházhàng] to audit accounts

茶 [chá] (n) 常绿灌木，叶可制成饮料 a tea plant; tea

茶杯 [chábēi] a tea cup

茶匙 [cháchí] a teaspoon

茶点 [chádiǎn] a light meal ; dainties served with tea; refreshments

茶房 [cháfáng] a servant ; a waiter; a waitress

茶馆 [cháguǎn] a tea-house

茶花：山茶花 [cháhuā shānch© huā] camellia

茶会 [cháhuì] a tea-party

茶具 [chájù] a tea-set

茶礼 [chálǐ] betrothal presents

茶钱 [cháqián] a tip

茶水 [cháshuǐ] drink (tea, water, etc)

茶叶 [cháyè] tea leaf

茶余饭后 [chá yú fàn hòu] leisure hours

搽 [chá] (v) 涂抹 to smear; paint on

搽粉 [cháfěn] to powder the face

搽药 [cháyào] to apply medicine

槎 [chá] (n) 用竹木编成的筏 a raft made of bamboo or wood

察 [chá] (v) 细看，调查，研究to examine; to inquire into ; to observe ; to inspect＊一位卫生官员在上午视察本校。A health officer inspected our school in the morning.

察办 [chábàn] investigate and act

察出 [cháchū] to find out; to detect ; to discover

察访 [cháfǎng] to go about finding out; fact-finding

察觉 [chájué] to realize; to sense

察看 [chákàn] to look over; to examine

察验 [cháyàn] to examine

察言观色 [chá yán guān sè] to examine a man's words and observe his countenance

chǎ

衩 [chǎ] (n) 衣服旁边开叉处 the open seam, slit, slash or crotch of a garment

chà

诧(詫) [chà] (v) 惊讶，奇怪 to wander at; to be astonished

诧异 [chàyì] to be surprised at

杈 [chà] (n) 树干树枝的分叉 branches of a tree

岔 [chà] 1 (adj) 分歧的，由主干分出的 (point) where roads fork ＊我在岔路口徘徊了十分钟还不能肯定那一条是通往医院的路。Having wandered for ten minutes at the point where the roads fork, I still could not be sure of the way to the hospital. 2 (adj) 迷失(话题)astray(as of topic of conversation) ＊打岔(＝插嘴)。to lead astray in conversation; to interrupt

岔道 [chàdào] a fork in the road a branch road

岔子 [chàzi] unexpected and undesirable turn of events

刹 [chà] (n) 佛寺 a buddhist temple

刹那 [chànà] a very short moment 另见 [shā]

差 [chà] 1 (adj) 不相同，不相合 different＊他的第二本书和第一本差不多。His second book is not much different from his first. 2(adj)缺乏 short of 3 (adj) 不好，不够标准 poor; not up to standard ＊这收音机质量很差，用不到一年就坏了。This radio is poor in quality:it breaks down within a year of use.

差不多 [chàbùduō] more or less; not too much difference

差点儿 [chàdiǎnr] almost; narrowly; nearly

差劲儿 [chàjìnr] worthless; poor in quality; hard (condition, etc.)

chāi

钗(釵) [chāi] (n) 妇女的发夹 a hairpin

拆 [chāi] 1 (v) 打开 to tear open 2 (v) 使分散，使瓦解 to tear down

拆除 [chāichú] to dismantle; to demolish

拆穿 [chāichuān] to expose; to reveal

拆股 [chāigǔ] to dissolve partnership

拆毁 [chāihuǐ] to demolish; to destroy ; to pull down

拆开 [chāikāi] to disclose; to break apart; to break open

拆平 [chāipíng] to raze to the ground; to demolish ; to level

拆散 [chāisǎn] to disperse; to scatter; to break away; to break up

拆台 [chāi tái] to undermine; to disrupt

拆卸 [chāixiè] to unload; to dismount; to take into parts

拆字 [chāizì] fortune telling by dissection of characters

差 [chāi] 1 (v) 派遣 to send 2 (n) 被派遣的人 a messenger ＊邮差。a postman. 3 (n) 被派遣的任务 a mission ＊出差。be sent on a mission.

差遣 [chāiqiǎn] to dispatch; to send

差使 [chāishǐ] official employment

差事 [chāishì] an assigned duty

差役 [chāiyì] an official servant; a messenger; a runner
另见 [chā]
[chà]

chái

柴 [chái] (n) 烧火用的木 firewood

柴火 [cháihuo] kindling; firewood
柴米油盐 [cháimǐyóuyán] firewood,oil rice and salt- necessities of life
柴油机 [cháiyóujī] diesel engine
柴油 [cháiyóu] diesel oil

侪(儕) [chái] (n) 同辈，同类的人 a class; a company; people of the same sort

chái

豺 [chái] (n) 哺乳动物，狼属 a ravenous beast, akin to jackal

豺狼当道 [chái láng dāng dào] the wolves stop the road--rascals in power

chài

虿(蠆) [chài] (n) 蝎子一类的毒虫 an insect like a scorpion

瘥 [chài] (v) 病愈 to recover from sickness

chān

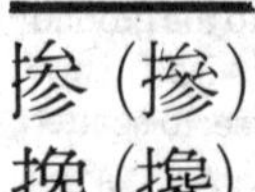

掺(摻) [chān] (v) 混合，拌和 to mix; to mingle; to blend

搀(攙) [chān] (v) 扶 to support; to sustain ＊她痛得站不起来，快搀住她。 Give her some support quickly as she feels too painful to stand.

chán

谗(讒) [chán] (v) 说别人的坏话 to slander; to defame; to misrepresent ; to speak maliciously

谗谤 [chánbàng] slander; talk scandal ; libel
谗害 [chánhài] injure by misrepresentation
谗诬 [chánwū] make a false charge against one
谗言 [chányán] calumny; slander; false charge

崨 [chán] (adj) 山势高险的样子 steep

崨岩 [chányán] a cragged steep cliff; a high precipice

馋(饞) [chán] (v) 贪吃 to love to eat; to be greedy

馋涎 [chánxián] saliva

单(單) [chán] (n)[单于]古代匈奴的君主 a chieftain or a khan of the ancient Hun
另见 [dān]

婵(嬋) [chán] (adj) 姿态美好 beautiful; graceful

禅(禪) [chán] 1 (n) 静思 meditation; abstraction 2 (n) 佛教 Buddhism

禅法 [chánfǎ] Buddhism
禅经 [chánjīng] Buddhist scriptures
禅堂 [chántáng] a hall of contemplation
禅心 [chánxīn] the mind in a state of abstraction
另见 [shàn]

蝉(蟬) [chán] (n) 虫名，翅膜质，可发声 the cicada ; broad locust

蝉联 [chánlián] continuous; connected
蝉纱 [chánshā] a kind of thin gauze
蝉蜕，蝉衣 [chántuì; chányī] the exuviae of the cicada , used for medicinal purposes

廛 [chán] (n) 城市平民的住屋 the houses of urban dwellers

缠(纏) [chán] 1 (v) 围绕 to wrap round ; to coil 2 (v) 搅扰，牵绊 to invlove; to entangle ; to annoy

缠绵 [chánmián] sentimental
缠绕 [chánnǎo] to bind round ; to entangle; to twine
缠扰 [chánrǎo] to annoy; to vex

孱 [chán] (adj) 瘦弱，软弱，弱小 weak ＊小乞丐饿了好几天，身体很孱弱。 Having starved for a few days , the small beggar became very weak.

潺 [chán] (adj) 水流动的样子 water flowing

潺潺 [chán chán] gurgling and babbling; purling

蟾 [chán] 一种蛙 a toad

蟾蜍 [chánchú] a toad

chǎn

阐(闡) [chǎn] (v) 说明白 to express;to disclose;to enlighten

阐明 [chǎnmíng] to clarify

产(產) [chǎn] 1 (v) 生出 to produce; to give birth to * 她在医院产下了一个男婴。 She gave birth to a male baby in the hospital.* 印尼出产石油。Indonesia produces petroleum. 2 (n) 生出來的东西 products; produce;resources* 榴梿是一种著名的土产。 The durian is one of the well known local produces. 3 (n) 财物 an estate; property * 大富翁一死，他的家人就争地产。 Once the rich man died , his family members fought for his estate.

产地 [chǎndì] where things are produced

产额 [chǎné] the amount of production; yield; output

产科 [chǎnkē] obstetrics

产量 [chǎnliàng] volume of production; output

产品 [chǎnpǐn] product

产生 [chǎnshēng] to produce ; to give rise to; to result from; to originate in results

产物 [chǎnwù] products; outcome

产业 [chǎnyè] property; estate

产业工人 [chǎnyègōngrén] industrial worker

产值 [chǎnzhí] value of output

铲(鏟) [chǎn] 1 (n) 用来推前兜削的工具 a spade; a shovel 2 (v) 推前兜削 to spade

铲除 [chǎnchú] to uproot ; to eradicate; to exterminate

谄(諂) [chǎn] (v) 用卑贱的态度奉承，讨好 to flatter ; to curry favour ; to cajole * 那花花公子只晓得向女孩子谄谀献媚。That playboy knew nothing but to flatter girls.

谄上欺下 [chǎnshàngqīxià] to flatter the superiors and bully the subordinates

谄笑 [chǎnxiào] to laugh and joke in order to please

谄言 [chǎnyán] flattering words ; flattery

谄谀 [chǎnyú] adulation ; cajole and flatter

chàn

忏(懺) [chàn] (v) 悔过 to regret; feel sorry for; to repent

忏悔 [chànhuǐ] to repent

颤(顫) [chàn] (v) 振动 to shiver; to tremble; to shake

颤动 [chàndòng] to shake; to tremble; to vibrate

另见 [zhàn]

chāng

昌 [chāng] (adj) 发达，兴旺 prosperous; flourish

昌盛 [chāngshèng] flourishing ; prosperous ; abundant

昌言 [chāng yán] good words

猖 [chāng] (adj) 疯狂 mad

猖獗 [chāngjué] rampant

猖狂 [chāngkuáng] frantic; on the rampage

娼 [chāng] (n) 妓女 a prostitute

娼妓 [chāngjì] prostitute

鲳(鯧) [chāng] (n) 一种食用鱼 a pomfret

菖 [chāng] (n) 草本植物 the sweet flag

菖蒲 [chāngpú] the calamus

cháng

徜 [cháng] (v) 交脚而坐 to sit cross legged

徜徉 [chángyáng] to go to and fro ; undecided

常 [cháng] 1 (adj) 长久 always; ever ∗好花不常开，好景不常在。Beautiful flowers do not always bloom, a good situation will not last forever. 2 (adv) 时时，多次 frequently ∗我常运动，以使身体强壮。I exercise frequently to keep my body strong. 3 (adj) 普通的，一般的 common; general ∗她缺乏常识。She has no common sense.

常备不懈 [chángbèibùxiè] all-time preparedness; be always vigilant

常备军 [chángbèijūn] regular army; standing army

常常 [chángcháng] often ; frequently

常规 [chángguī] convention; regular; conventional

常价 [chángjià] current rates

常客 [chángkè] a regular patron (customer)

常年 [chángnián] all the year round; annual

常事 [chángshì] a common affair

常识 [chángshí] common sense

常态 [chángtài] normal state

常务委员会 [cháng wù wěi yuán huì] a standing committee

嫦 [cháng] 〈嫦娥〉[chángé] (n) 神话中由人间飞到月亮里去的仙女 a legendary beauty who flew to the moon from the earth

裳 [cháng] 下身的衣裙 skirts; petticoats; garments especially the lower ones

尝(嘗) [cháng] 1 (v) 辨别滋味，体会 to taste; to test ∗她毕业后去工作，开始尝到赚钱难的滋味。After having left school, she got a job and began to taste the hardship of earning money. 2 (adj) 曾经 already; formerly; ever

尝试 [chángshì] to try; to attempt; to endeavour

偿(償) [cháng] (v) 归还，补还 to make up; to compensate; to pay back

偿还 [chánghuan] to repay ; to compensate; to make good

偿金 [chángjīn] indemnity

偿期 [chángqī] time of payment

偿命 [chángmìng] to forfeit one's life

偿心愿 [chángxīnyuàn] to fulfill one's wishes

肠(腸) [cháng] (n) 内脏之一 the intestines

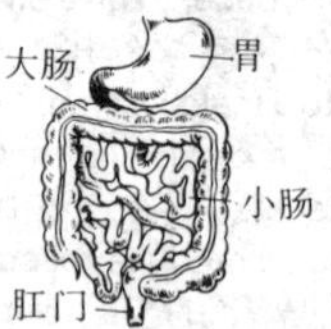

肠炎 [chángyán] enteritis

长(長) [cháng] 1 (adj) 短的相对 long 2 (n) 距离 distance ∗星柔长堤全长1.609公里。The length of the Singapore-Johore causeway is 1.609 Kilometres 3 (n) 优点，专门技能 a strong point ; a skill ∗油彩画是他的特长。 Oil painting is the skill he excels. 4 (adv) 永远 forever∗他已经与世长辞了。He has left the world forever. 5 (adv) 常 always; constantly

长臂猿 [chángbìyuán] a gibbon

长波 [chángbō] long waves

长城 [chángchéng] the great wall

长处 [chángchù] a merit;strong points ; good qualities

长此以往 [chángcǐyǐwǎng] if things go on like this

长度 [chángdû] lengtn

长短 [chángduǎn] length ; long and short; right and wrong

长方形 [chángfāngxing] rectangle

长工 [chánggōng] regular employment ; long-term labourers
长颈鹿 [chángjǐnglù] a giraffe

长龙 [chánglóng] a long queue
长年累月 [chángniánlěiyuè] all the year round
长跑 [cángpǎo] long distance running
长篇大论 [cháng piān dà lùn] long winded tirade ; lengthy (writing, speech, etc)
长篇小说 [chángpiānxiǎoshuō] a novel
长期 [chángqī] long-term
长驱直入 [chángqūzhírù] to drive straight in
长射程 [cháng shè chéng] a long range
长生不老 [chángshēngbùlǎo] immortality
长时间 [chángshíjiān] for many hours ; for a long time (while)
长寿 [chángshòu] longevity; long life
长途 [chángtú] long distance
长远 [chángyuǎn] long-range
长征 [chángzhēng] to go on an expedition
另见 [zhǎng]

chǎng

场(塲) [chǎng] 1(n) 平坦的空地 a courtyard ; a n open space; a field 2 量词 a measure word* 一场雨 a fall of rain; *一场足球赛 a foodball game *一场战 a battle *一场戏 a play
场地 [chǎngdì] an area of a level ground
场合 [chǎnghé] occasion
场面 [chǎngmiàn] scene; occasion; a stage
场所 [chǎngsuǒ] a place; a location
场中 [chǎngzhōng] in the arena
敞 [chǎng] (adj) 地方宽绰，沒有遮拦 spacious
厂(廠) [chǎng] (n) 通常指用机械制造生产资料或生活资料的地方 a factory ; a plant ; a workhouse
厂工 [chǎnggōng] workmen
厂章; 厂规 [chǎngzhāng -chǎngguī] factory regulations
厂主 [chǎngzhú] a manufacturer; an owner of a factory
另见 [ān]

chàng

唱 [chàng] 1 (v) 高呼而延长声音 sing 2 (v) 大声叫 to call loudly
唱段 [chàngduàn] arias;a singing passage
唱对台戏 [chàngduìtáixì] to put on a rival show ; to set oneself up against
唱反调 [chàngfǎndiào] to harp on a discordant tune
唱高调 [chànggāodiào] to chant bombastic words
唱歌 [chànggē] to sing (a song)
唱片 [chàngpiàn] a phonograph record; a disc
唱票 [chàngpiào] to count the votes orally
唱腔 [chàngqiāng] aria
唱诗班 [chàngshībān] a choir;a glee club
唱咏 [chàngyǒng] to chant; to sing
怅(悵) [chàng] (adj) 烦恼，不如意 despaired; dissatisfied
怅惘 [chàngwǎng] in low spirits; depressed
畅(暢) [chàng] 1 (adj) 沒有阻碍 smooth; fluent 2 (adj) 尽情，痛快 joyful; happy; contented *我把一切不满都告诉了你后，心里感到畅快了。Having told you all my dissatisfaction, I feel happy.

畅怀 [chànghuái] light-hearted; gratified

畅快 [chàngkuài] delightful; pleased

畅流 [chàngliú] freely flowing

畅所欲言 [chàngsuǒyùyán] to speak one's mind freely

畅谈 [chàngtán] to talk pleasantly

畅通 [chàngtōng] unimpeded

畅销 [chàngxiāo] a good sale

畅行 [chàngxíng] to advance unimpededly

畅饮 [chàngyǐn] to drink with gusto

畅游 [chàngyóu] to swim to one's heart's content; to tour to one's heart's content

畅志 [chàngzhì] a feeling of pleasantness; amenity of mind

倡 [chàng] (v) 带头，发动 to introduce; to lead; to initiate ＊很多华校都是华人倡办的。Many Chinese schools were initiated by the Chinese.

倡导 [chàngdǎo] to advocate; to propagate

倡议 [chàngyì] to make a motion; to initiate

chāo

抄 [chāo] 1 (v) 誊写 to copy; to transcribe ＊把这几句抄在你的笔记簿上。Copy these sentences in your notebook. 2 (v) 走(近路) to take (a short cut) ＊如果抄近路，我只要步行五分钟便到学校。If I take a short cut, I can walk to school for only five minutes. 3 (v) 搜查，没收 to search and confiscate

抄稿 [chāogǎo] to copy a draft

抄获 [chāohuò] to search and capture

抄录 [chāolù] to copy

抄没 [chāomò] to confiscate

抄袭 [chāoxí] to copy; to plagiarize; to follow(somebody's footsteps)

抄写 [chāoxiě] to copy; to transcribe

钞(鈔) [chāo] (n) 钱 money; paper money

钞票 [chāopiào] paper money; bank notes

超 [chāo] (v) 高出，越过 to exceed; to overtake; to surpass; to transcend ＊有些汽车超过速度限制。Some of the autos exceed the speed-limit.

超出 [chāochū] to exceed

超等 [chāoděng] first-class; super class

超额 [chāoé] to overfulfil

超凡 [chāofán] unusual

超过 [chāoguò] to surpass; to overtake; to surmount

超级 [chāojí] super grade

超级大国 [chāo jídà guó] a superpower

超龄 [chāolíng] over-age

超群 [chāoqún] above the average; distinct

超然 [chāorán] aloof; transcendent

超声波 [chāoshēngbō] ultrasonic waves; supersonic

超支 [chāozhī] over-expenditure

超越 [chāoyuè] to transcend; to excel; to surmount

超重 [chāozhòng] overweight

超自然 [chāozìrán] supernatural

cháo

朝 [cháo] 1 (prep) 对，向 towards; facing; direct ＊他正匆匆忙忙朝我家走来。He is walking quickly towards my house. 2 (n) 封建君主一姓世代 a dynasty 3 (n) 朝廷 the imperial court

朝代 [cháodài] a dynasty

朝贡 [cháogòng] to present tribute

朝见 [cháojiàn] to have an audience with the emperor

朝野 [cháoyě] government and people

另见 [zhāo]

嘲 [cháo] (v) 讽刺，讥笑 ridicule; laugh and joke at; mock at ＊嘲弄残废的人是一件残酷的事。It is a cruel practice to ridicule a handicapped person.

嘲骂 [cháomà] to abuse; to scold

嘲弄 [cháonòng] to mock; to ridicule

嘲笑 [cháoxiào] to jeer at; to mock at; to ridicule

潮 [cháo] 1 (n) 海水定期涨落的现象 the tide * 他在低潮时採集贝类。He collected shellfish at low tide. 2 (adj) 微湿 moist; damp; humid

潮解 [cháojiě] deliquesce; melt away; deliquescence

潮流 [cháoliú] a tidal current; the current trend

潮气 [cháoqì] moisture

潮湿 [cháoshī] damp

潮水 [cháoshuǐ] the tide; the tidal waters

潮信 [cháoxin] fix time of the tides; a tide period; time for high tide

巢 [cháo] (n) 鸟或昆虫等的窝 a nest

巢穴 [cháoxuè] a den; a lair

chǎo

吵 [chǎo] 1 (v) 声音杂乱打扰人 to disturb by making noise * 他给收音机吵醒了。 He was disturbed and awakened by the radio. 2 (v) 口角 to quarrel * 何必为小事而吵架呢? Why quarrel over small matters? 3 (adj) 声音杂乱 noisy

吵架 [chǎojià] to quarrel

吵闹 [chǎonào] to make a great noise; to kick up a fuss; to wrangle

炒 [chǎo] (v) 烹调方法 to fry ; to wast

chē

车 (車) [chē] 1 (n) 陆地交通运输工具 a vehicle; a carriage 2 (n) 某些机械或机器 a machine; a mill * 荷兰以风车出名。Holland is famous for its windmills. 3 (v) 用机器切削 to shape with a lathe

车床 [chēchuáng] a lathe; a machine tool

车次 [chēcì] number (of train journey)

车夫 [chēfū] a coachman; a driver

车工 [chēgōng] a lathe turner

车间 [chējiān] a workshop

车辆 [chēliàng] cars; vehicles

车轮 [chēlún] a wheel

车票 [chēpiào] a (train or bus) ticket

车房 [chēfáng] a garage

车身 [chēshēn] the body of a car

车水马龙 [chēshuǐmǎlòng] a great deal of traffic; heavy traffic

车厢 [chēxiāng] railway carriage; coach (of a train)

车载斗量 [chē zài dǒu liáng] a huge quantity

车站 [chēzhao] a bus stop; a railway otation

车轴 [chēzhóu] the axle

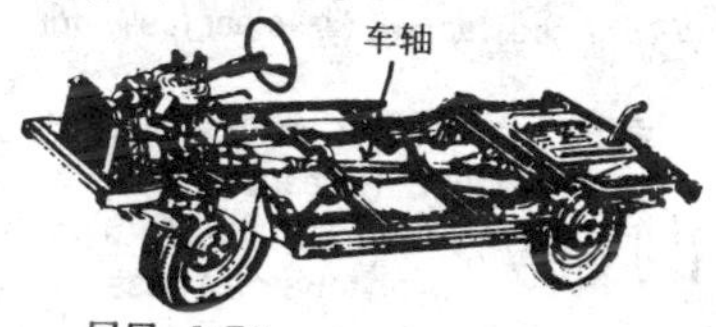

另见 [jū]

chě

扯 [chě] 1 (v) 拉 to pull * 小孩子扯着母亲去买雪糕。The child pulls its mother to buy ice-cream. 2 (v) 撕 to tear * 他在打篮球时扯破了衣服。 He tore his clothes in a basket-ball game. 3 (v) 闲谈 to talk casually * 大家一直在东拉西扯，避谈正题。 We keep talking casually to avoid the main subject.

扯皮 [chěpí] to haggle over trifles

扯平 [chěpíng] to take an average

扯上 [chěshàng] to pull up; to hoist

扯下 [chěxià] to pull down ; to haul down

chè

撤 [chè] 1 (v) 除去，去掉 to remove * 上司对他的工作表现不满，把他撤职了。 His superior is dissatisfied with his performance and therefore remove him from office. 2 (v) 收回，退走 to withdraw * 和平谈判成功后，双方都撤兵。 After the success of the peace negotiations, both sides withdraw their troops.

撤换 [chèhuàn] to dismiss and replace

撤回 [chèhuí] to withdraw; to draw back; to pull back

撤离 [chèlí] to withdraw

撤军 [chèjūn] to withdraw troops

撤退 [chètuì] to evacuate; to withdraw ; to retreat

撤销 [chèxiāo] to cancel ; to annul ; to abolish; to dismiss

撤职 [chèzhí] to remove somebody from office ; to dismiss somebody from his post; dismissal

澈 [chè] (adj) 水清 clear (as water)

澈查 [chèchá] to make a thorough investigation; to search out

彻(徹) [chè] (v) 通，透 to pervade ; to penetrate; to pass through ＊妈妈彻夜不睡，等待妹妹回家。 My mother did not sleep all the night to wait for my sister's returning home.

彻底 [chèdǐ] thorough; thoroughgoing ; complete

彻头彻尾 [chètóu-chèwěi] out and out ; from head to foot

彻夜 [chèyè] all night

坼 [chè] (v) 裂开 to crack; to split; to break

坼裂 [chèliè] crack; split

掣 [chè] (v) 拉、扯 to pull ; to obstruct ; to hinder

掣动带 [chèdòngdài] driving band

掣肘 [chèzhǒu] to pull somebody's arm- to obstruct (somebody from doing something)

chēn

嗔 [chēn] (v) 生气 to be angry at

瞋 [chēn] (v) 发怒时睁大眼睛瞪人 to glare at angrily; be angry at

琛 [chēn] (n) 珍宝 a precious stone

chén

辰 [chén] (n) 时间 time

晨 [chén] (n) 清早 morning ; dawn; daybreak

晨昏颠倒 [chénnūndiāndǎo] turn night into day ; topsy-turvy

晨曦 [chénxī] daybreak

晨星 [chénxīng] morning stars-few ; scarce; rare

晨钟暮鼓 [chénzhōngmùgǔ] morning bell and evening drum-something to keep people awake

忱 [chén] (n) 真诚的情意 sincerity; honesty; heart ＊朋友们的热忱使我十分感动。 The sincerity of my friends touched me.

沉 [chén] 1 (v) 往水里落下去，跟"浮"相对 to sink in water ; to submerge; to immerse ＊木不沉于水。 Wood does not sink in water . 2 (v) 下陷 to sink ＊威尼斯一年又一年地在下沉。Venice is sinking year after year. 3 (adj) 深 deep; profound ＊她在沉思中，听不到我说什么。Being deep in thought, she does not hear what I say .

沉静 [chénjìng] quiet; poised

沉沦 [chénlún] to perish

沉闷 [chénmèn] boring; dull; tedious

沉默 [chénmò] silent

沉没 [chénmò] to submerge

沉默寡言 [chénmòguǎyán] habitually silent; taciturn

沉溺 [chénnì] to drown oneself (in pleasure, etc); to indulge in

沉睡 [chénshuì] to sleep soundly

沉思 [chénsī] to ponder ; to think deeply ; to contemplate

沉痛 [chéntòng] grievous ; extremely painful; deep in sorrow

沉重 [chénzhòng] heavy

沉着 [chénzhuó] cool; composed

沉醉 [chénzuì] heavily drunk; be intoxicated with

沉香 [chénxiāng] aloes wood

陈(陳) [chén] 1 (v) 排列，摆设 to arrange; to exhibit ＊图书馆的书陈列得有条有理 The books in the library are arranged systematically. 2 (v) 叙说 to tell; to narrate; to express carefully ＊他陈述骑劫的始末。He told the story of the hijack. 3 (adj) 时间久的，旧的 old; stale ＊当局要拆掉这座陈旧的屋子。The authority wanted to pull down this old house. 4 (n) 姓 a surname

陈辩 [chénbiàn] explain; plead

陈词滥调 [chéncí-làndiào] platitude; senseless prate; cliche; often-repeated rubbish

陈腐 [chénfǔ] stale; antiquated; outworn (views; opinions)

陈规陋习 [chén guī lòu xí] outdated irrational rules and customs

陈货 [chénhuò] old stock

陈迹 [chénji] old traces; old ruins

陈旧 [chénjiù] out of date; stale (ideas); outmoded

陈酒 [chénjiǔ] old wine

陈列 [chénliè] arrange; show; exhibit; display; demonstrate

陈列馆 [chénlièguǎn] an exhibition hall

陈设 [chénshè] to display; to arrange; arrangement

陈述 [chénshù] to state; to explain; to recount

陈述句 [chénshùjù] declarative sentence

尘(塵) [chén] (n) 飞扬的灰土 dust; dirt; earth

尘埃 [chénāi] dust

尘世 [chénshì] this world; mortality

尘土 [chéntǔ] dust

臣 [chén] (n) 君主制国家的官员的统称 a statesman; a vassal; a courtier

臣民 [chénmín] subjects

臣仆 [chénpū] servants and slaves

臣子 [chénzǐ] a minister of state; courtiers

chèn

榇(櫬) [chèn] (n) 棺材 a coffin

衬(襯) [chèn] 1 (v) 在里面托上一层 to line 2 (n) 附在衣服第一部份里面的专制品 lining 3 (v) 对照，烘托 to contrast; to be the background of ＊这图样蓝黄相衬，很美观。Blue and yellow contrast prettily in this design. 4 (v) 帮助 to assist

衬衫 [chènshān] a shirt

衬托 [chèntuō] to serve for contrast or as background

衬衣 [chènyī] a shirt

趁 [chèn] (v) 利用机会 take advantage of

趁便 [chènbiàn] take advantage of the conveniences

趁火打劫 [chènhuǒdǎjié] to fish in trouble waters; to take advantage of a bad situation; to loot

趁机 [chènjī] make use of the times; take advantage of the chance

趁热打铁 [chènrèdǎtiě] to strike while the iron is hot

趁势 [chènshì] to take advantage of

趁早 [chènzǎo] while there's yet time; before it is too late

称(稱) [chèn] (adj) 适合 suitable; fit ＊他经验丰富，一定很称职。With the rich experience he has, he is very fit for this job.

称心 [chènxīn] to one's liking; just as one wishes

另见 [chēng]

谶(讖) [chèn] (n) 预言，预兆 a prophecy; an omen

chēng

撑 [chēng] 1 (v) 抵住，支持 to support; to prop(up) 2 (v) 用篙使船前进 to pole a boat 3 (v) 张开 to open ＊下雨了，快撑伞。It's raining, open the umbrella quickly. 4 (v) 使过，饱满 to overfill

撑持 [chēngchí] to support; to prop up
撑竿跳 [chēnggāntiào] pole vault
撑腰 [chēngyāo] to support ; to back up

瞠 [chēng] (v) 瞪着眼睛看 to stare at

瞠目结舌 [chēng mù jié shé] to be stunned

赪(赬) [chēng] (adj) 红色 red

称(稱) [chēng] 1 (v) 量轻重 to estimate; to weigh 2 (v) 叫，说 to call; to address; to name; to say *那瘋子自称王中王。That madman called himself the king of kings. 3 (v) 赞扬 to commend; to praise; to express * 人人都称赞他的舍己为人的精神。Every one praised him for his spirit of sacrificing himself for others.

称霸 [chēngbà] to dominate ; to play the tyrant; to seek hegemony
称号 [chēnghào] a name; a title
称呼 [chēnghū] to call ; to name ; to style
称颂 [chēngsòng] to pay tribute to; to praise
称王称霸 [chēng wáng chēng bà] to rule supreme; to lord it over
称赞 [chēngzàn] to praise ; to commend
另见 [chèn]

蛏(蟶) [chēng] (n) 贝类，壳长方形，肉可供食 mussel

铛(鐺) [chēng] 1 (n) 温器 a pot for keeping wine or tea warm 2 (n) 一种平底浅锅 a flat cooking pot
另见 [dāng]

琤 [chēng] (n) 玉石撞击声，形容琴声或流水声 sound of music of the lute; sound of flowing water

chéng

成 [chéng] 1 (v) 做完，实现 to finish; to complete; to accomplish 2 (v) 变为 to become; to turn into * 他完成使命，成为一名英雄。He accomplished his mission and became a hero. 3 (v) (n) 造就 to win; to succeed; success * 成者为王，败者为寇。Those who won the battle are named kings and those who lost, bandits. 4 (n) 十分之一 one tenth; tenths * 这话有九成可信。Nine tenths of this statement is believable

成败 [chéngbài] success or failure
成败不计 [chéng bai bùjì] success or failure not taken into consideration
成本 [chéngběn] cost of production
成分 [chéngfèn] elements; ingredients ; compositions
成风 [chéngfēng] to become a common practice
成功 [chénggōng] to succeed
成规 [chéngguī] a regular rule or custom
成果 [chéngguǒ] result; accomplishment
成绩 [chéngjī] achievement; results
成家立业 [chéngjiālìyè] to live independently by having one's own family and enterprise
成见 [chéngjiàn] prejudice; biasness
成交 [chéngjiāo] to close a bargain; to strike a deal
成吉思汗 [chéng jí sī hàn] Genghis Khan
成就 [chéng jiù] achievements to make progress; to achieve success
成立 [chénglì] to establish; to found; to set up; to come into existence
成名 [chéngmíng] to become famous
成年 [chéng nián] an adult; all year round
成批 [chéngpī] in groups; in large number
成品 [chéngpǐn] production
成千上万 [chéngqiānshàngwàn] hundreds of thousands
成亲 [chéngqīn] to be married; to marry

成全 [chéngquān] to facilitate; to lend a helping hand; to complete
成群结队 [chéngqúnjiéduì] to form into groups; to flock; to herd
成人 [chéngrén] an adult
成日 [chéngrì] the whole day
成熟 [chéngshú] to ripe; mature
成套 [chéngtào] a complete set (of machinery or equipment)
成天 [chéngtiān] all day long
成为 [chéngwéi] to become; to turn into; to grow into
成效 [chéngxiào] effect
成形 [chéngxíng] to take shape
成议 [chéngyì] settle; come to agreement
成语 [chéngyǔ] an idiom; an idiomatic phrase
成员 [chéngyuán] a member
成长 [chéngzhǎng] to grow up

盛 [chéng] (v) 把东西放进器皿里 to fetch with a utensil * 给我盛多一碗饭来。Fetch me one more bowl of rice.
另见 [shèng]

诚(誠) [chéng] 1 (adj)恳切 sincere * 我诚恳地希望你早日康复。 I sincerely hope you will soon recover. 2 (adj) 真实 true; honest * 这人有一副诚实的面孔。 This man has an honest face
诚敬 [chéngjìng] sincere and reverent
诚恳 [chéngkěn] cordial; hearty
诚然 [chéngran] indeed
诚实 [chéngshí] honest
诚心 [chéngxīn] sincerity
诚意 [chéngyì] sincerity ; cordiality; earnestness
诚挚 [chéngzhì] sincere

城 [chéng] 1 (n) 围绕一个地方的墙垣 city-walls 2 (n) 大市镇 a city; a town
城堡 [chéngbǎo] a bastian; a castle
城郊 [chéngjiāo] outskirts; suburbs
城楼 [chénglóu] a tower
城市 [chéngshì] a city
城乡 [chéngxiāng] city and country side
城下之盟 [chéngxià zhīméng] a capitulation; dictated peace
城镇 [chéngzhèn] city and town

呈 [chéng] 1 (v) 具有，显露 to show *在校庆日，学校呈现一片新气象。Our school campus showed a new atmosphere on the school anniversary day. 2 (v) 恭敬地送上去 to present; to submit; to offer * 让我们呈献一个节目给来宾吧。Let us present an item to the guests.
呈报 [chéngbào] submit a report
呈交 [chéngjiāo] tender ; deliver to ; present
呈上 [chèngshǎng] present to; hand in
呈现；呈露 [chéngxiàn ; chénglù] manifested ; disclosed
呈阅 [chéngyuè] submit for inspection; put forward

程 [chéng] 1 (n) 规章，法式 regulations ; formula 2 (n) 道路的远近距离 a journey 3 (n) 进度，顺序 procedure ; order; sequence * 课程 a course of study; curriculum * 议程 agenda 4 (n) 姓 a surname
程度 [chéngdù] degree; extent
程式 [chéngshì] a pattern; a formula; a grade
程序 [chéngxù] procedure; sequence; order

橙 [chéng] 1 (n) 常绿灌木，叶卵形，果圆果肉甘酸可食 the orange tree 2 (n) (adj) 红，黄合成的颜色 orange colour

澄 [chéng] (n) 水很清 clear
澄清 [chéngqīng] clear; to clarify
另见 [dèng]

承 [chéng] 1 (v) 接受，担当 to undertake ; to take a charge* 我承担起维持家计的责任。I undertake the responsibility of maintaining the family. 2 (adv) 受到，由于(别人的好处)

for; owing to; due to (somebody's good will) *承您殷勤招待，我很感激。Thank you very much for your hospitality 3 (v) 继续，连接 to continue; to succeed (somebody) *父亲一直希望儿子在他死后能继承他的事业。All along the father hoped that his son would be able to succeed him in his business after his death.

承办 [chéngbàn] to undertake ; to manage

承担 [chéngdān] to assume; to bear; to accept; to undertake

承当 [chéngdāng] to be responsible for

承接 [chéngjiē] to take in

承蒙 [chéngméng] for; owing to; due to

承诺 [chéngnuò] acceptance;consent ; assent

承认 [chéngrèn] to recognise ; to acknowledge; to admit; consent; acknowledgement

承上启下 [chéngshàngqǐxià] to continue; to carry forward

承受 [chéng shòu] to bear ; to stand; to withstand; to sustain

承袭 [chéngxí] to inherit; to succeed

承允 [chéngyǔn] to agree to; to promise

惩（懲）[chéng](v) 处分，责罚 to punish; to discipline *谋财害命的罪犯，应受严重的惩罚。A criminal who robs and kills should be punished heavily.

惩办 [chéngbàn] to punish

惩罚 [chéngfá] to punish

惩前毖后 [chéngqiánbìhòu] to learn from past mistakes to avoid future ones.

惩戒 [chéngjiè] to discipline ; to punish; to correct; to warn against

惩治 [chéngzhì] to govern strictly

乘 [chéng] 1 (v) 坐，骑 to ride; to mount *他乘巴士车上班。He goes to work by (mounting) bus. 2 (v) 利用 to make use of; to take advantage of; to seize(an opportunity) *老师还没来，我乘机上厕所。The teacher has not come yet, so I seize the opportunity to go to the tiolet. 3 (v) 求一个数的若干倍 to multiply *二乘以五等于十。Two multiplied by five is equal to ten .

乘法 [chéngfǎ] multiplication

乘方 [chéngfāng] square

乘风破浪 [chéngfēngpòlàng] forward in high ambition

乘机 [chéngjī] to sieze an opportunity

乘客 [chéngkè] passengers

乘凉 [chéngliáng] to enjoy cool air

乘人之危 [chéngrénzhīwēi] to take advantage of others' disaster

乘胜前进 [chéngshèngqiánjìn] to go forward ; to go forward in triumph

乘数 [chéngshù] a multiplier

乘务员 [chéngwùyuán] a crew

乘虚而入 [chéngxūérrù] to enter through a weak spot; to seize the opportunity ; to step in

另见 [shèng]

chěng

逞 [chěng] 1 (v) 炫耀，显示 to boast *他又在逞能，谁也不相信他。He is boasting of his own abilities again ; nobody will believe him. 2 (v) 放纵，施展 to do as one likes *人们英勇抵抗，不让敌人逞威。The people bravely resisted the enemies , disallowing them to do what they like.

逞能 [chěngnéng] to cut a dash ; to boast of one's ability

逞强 [chěngqiáng] to display one's ability or courage ;to demonstrate one's strength

逞威 [chěngwēi] to presume on power; to intimidate others

逞凶 [chěngxiōng] to be abusive; to act violently or with murderous intent

骋（騁）[chěng] 1 (v) 奔跑 to hasten; to run 2 (v) 放开，展开 to open up

chèng

秤 [chèng] (n) 衡量轻重的器具 a steelyard; scales

chī

嗤 [chī] (v) 讥笑 to laugh at; to jeer

嗤之以鼻 [chīzhīyǐbí] to treat with contempt; to sneer at

吃 [chī] 1 (v) 咀嚼吞咽食物 to eat 2(v) 消灭 to eradicate; to wipe out; to destroy 3 (v) 受 to receive; to get * 听了这消息后，大家都很吃惊。All of us got a shock after having heard the news

吃不开 [chībùkāi] to be unpopular

吃不消 [chībùxiāo] cannot bear

吃醋 [chīcù] to be jealous

吃得开 [chīdékāi] to be popular

吃得消 [chīdéxiāo] can bear

吃惊 [chījīng] to startle; to get a fright; to get a shock

吃苦 [chīkǔ] to suffer hardships

吃亏 [chīkuī] to suffer a loss ; to get the worst of

吃力 [chīlì] tiring

吃一堑，长一智 [chīyīqiàn,zhǎngyīzhī] a fall in a pit; a gain in wit

痴 [chī] (adj) 傻，呆笨 stupid; foolish; silly * 只有白痴才会相信他所编造的故事。 Only a fool will believe his story.

痴情 [chīqíng] passion of love ; lovesickness; infatuation

痴人 [chīrén] an idiot;

痴笑 [chīxiaò] to simper

痴心妄想 [chīxīnwàngxiǎng] wishful thinking; to hope vainly for

chí

池 [chí] (n) 水塘 a pond; a reservoir

池塘 [chítāng] a pool; a pond

池鱼之殃 [chīyúzhīyāng] unexpected calamity

持 [chí] 1 (v) 拿着，握住 to hold * 他手中持有一本书。He held a book in his hand. 2 (v) 扶助 to support * 墙壁支持屋顶。The walls support the roof. 3 (v) 主管，治理 to manage; to direct * 他有一位勤俭持家的好妻子。He has a good wife who manages the house with thrift. 4(v) 维系 to maintain * 小心护持你的名誉。Be careful to maintain your reputation.

持久 [chíjiǔ] lasting; enduring; durable; persistent

持久战 [chíjiǔzhàn] a protracted war

持票人 [chípiàorèn] the bearer of a cheque

持续 [chíxù] to last; to continue; to sustain; to carry on

持之以恒 [chízhīyǐhéng] in a persistent way

迟(遲) [chí] (adj) 晚 late; delayed * 今晚他又迟到了。He is late again tonight.

迟到 [chídào] behind time; be late in attending; to arrive late

迟钝 [chídùn] slow-witted; sluggish

迟缓 [chíhuǎn] slow and slack; tardy

迟暮 [chímù] old age

迟疑 [chíyí] to hesitate; to be in doubts

迟早 [chízǎo] sooner or later

踟 [chí] (adj) 〈踟蹰〉 犹豫不定，要走不走的样子 undecided; hesitating

弛 [chí] 1 (v) 弓卸下弦 to unstring a bow 2 (v) 解除，松懈，放松 to slacken; to relax; to loosen

驰(馳) [chí] 1 (v) 快跑 to run fast; to speed * 几辆车子在公路上飞驰。Several cars were speeding along the road. 2 (v) 传播 to spread

驰骋 [chíchěng] to gallop

驰马 [chímǎ] to gallop a horse

驰名 [chímíng] to become famous; to become celebrated

驰驱 [chíqū] to ride fast; to trot

驰送 [chísòng] send by mounted couriers

匙 [chí] (n) 舀汤用的小勺子 a spoon

chǐ

侈 [chǐ] 1 (adj) 浪费 extravagant; wasteful 2 (adj) 夸大 exaggerating

侈谈 [chǐtán] wild talk; exaggeration ; to engage in glib talk

尺 [chǐ] 1 (n) 长度单位 a foot (measurement) 2 (n) 量长度的器具 ruler

尺寸 [chǐcùn] feet and inches; dimension; measurements; size

尺度 [chǐdù] linear measure ; gauge ; scale; dimension

齿(齒) [chǐ] (n) 牙 tooth

齿长 [chǐcháng] elder; senior

齿垢 [chǐgòu] tartar (impurities) on the teeth

齿冷 [chǐlěng] ridicule; sneer

齿列 [chǐliè] in the same rank

齿轮 [chǐlún] a toothed wheel; a cogwheel; a gear

齿腔 [chǐqiāng] the pulp cavity of teeth

齿音 [chǐyīn] a sibilant

齿状 [chǐzhuàng] dentation

耻 [chǐ] (n) 羞愧 shame; disgrace ＊他的被捕使他家庭蒙受耻辱。His arrest has brought shame to his family

耻辱 [chǐrǔ] shame

耻笑 [chǐxiào] to scoff at; to ridicule; to sneer at

褫 [chǐ] (v) 剥去(衣服)引申为革除夺取 to strip (one) of (his clothes); to deprive of ;to discharge;to dismiss ＊ 上头不满他的工作表现，把他褫职了。His superiors are not satisfied with his work performance so they dismiss him.

褫夺 [chǐduó] to deprive of

褫衣 [chǐyī] to undress

褫职 [chǐzhí] to dismiss (one from one's office)

chì

敕 [chì] (n) 封建帝王的命令 an imperial edict or decree

翅 [chì] (n) 鸟类的翼 wings

翅膀 [chìbǎng] wings

叱 [chì] (v) 大声斥骂 to scold;to shout at; to hoot at

啻 [chì] (adj) 但，只 only

趩 [chì] (v) 一只脚走 to walk with one leg

斥 [chì] 1 (v) 责备 to blame;to reprove; to reprimand ＊做父亲的痛斥儿子把血汗钱乱花。 The father reprimands his son for squandering the hard-earned money. 2 (v) 排除 to exclude 3 (adj) 多，广 extensive; broad; wide 4 (v) 扩大，扩充 to extend; to enlarge

斥地 [chìdì] to extend the territory

斥候 [chìhòu] patrols; scouts; spies

斥退 [chìtuì] to dismiss ; to send away

斥责 [chìzé] to reprove; to reprimand; to rebuke ; to denounce

斥逐 [chìzhú] to drive away

斥资 [chìzī] to enlarge the funds

赤 [chì] 1 (adj) 红色 red 2 (adj) 露着 bare ; naked

赤膊上阵 [chìbóshàngzhèn] to step forward in person; to come out without any disguise;to come out into the open

赤诚 [chìchéng] sincerity; singleness of heart

赤胆忠心 [chìdǎn-zhōngxīn] a red heart with complete dedication

赤道 [chìdào] the equator

赤痢 [chìlì] dysentery

赤裸裸 [chìluǒluǒ] naked; bare; nude

赤手空拳 [chìshǒukōngquán] unarmed; with naked fists

赤心 [chìxīn] a true heart; sincerity

赤子 [chìzǐ] an infant; a baby; a newborn child

赤字 [chìzì] financial dificit

赤子之心 [chìzǐzhīxīn] innocence

饬(飭) [chì] (v) 整顿 to keep in order

炽(熾) [chì](n) 火焰，旺盛 flame; blaze

chōng

冲 [chōng] 1 (v) 浇 to water ＊走廊经过冲洗后很清洁。The corridor is very clean after having been watered. 2 (v) 迅速，推进 to rush; to dash; to charge 3 (n) 通行的大道 a highway; a public road

冲茶 [chōngchá] to infuse tea

冲淡 [chōngdàn] to dilute

冲动 [chōngdòng] excited

冲犯 [chōngfàn] to offend

冲锋 [chōngfēng] to charge forward

冲锋陷阵 [chōng fēng xiàn zhèn] to storm and shatter the enemy's position

冲昏头脑 [chōnghūntóunǎo] to be carried away (by success); to get dizzy (with success)

冲击 [chōngjī] to batter; to impact

冲击波 [chōngjībō] blast wave; shock wave

冲积土 [chōngjītǔ] alluvial soil; alluvium

冲破 [chōngpò] to break through; to breach; to burst open

冲散 [chōngsàn] to scatter; to rout

冲刷 [chōngshuā] to wash and brush clean

冲天 [chōngtiān] soaring; boundless (enthusiasm)

冲突 [chōngtū] to conflict

冲洗 [chōngxǐ] to flush ; to wash something down; to develope(film)

冲撞 [chōngzhuàng] to come in conflict with; to smash

忡 [chōng] 〈忡忡〉 (adj) 忧虑不安 grieved; distressed; sad

憧 [chōng] 〈憧憧〉 (adj) 摇晃不定 心意不定 irresolute

憧憬 [chōngchǐ] to fill up

充 [chōng] 1 (v) 填满，装满，使满 to fill; to satisfy; to fulfil 2 (v) 担任，当 to act as; to act in place of ＊他在法庭充当通译员。He acted as an interpreter in the court.

充斥 [chōngchì] to fill up

充当 [chōngdāng] to act as; to pose as

充电 [chōngdiàn] to charge with electricity

充耳不闻 [chōngěrbùwén] to turn a deaf ear to

充分 [chōngfèn] full; completely; thoroughly

充公 [chōnggōng] to confiscate; to forfeit

充饥 [chōngjī] to satisfy one's hunger

充军 [chōngjūn] to be sent into exile

充满 [chōngmǎn] to be full of ; to be filled with; to be crowded with

充沛 [chōngpèi] full of (energy)

充其量 [chōngqíliàng] at most

充实 [chōngshí] solid; replenish and rich; to reinforce;to fill..... with (new content); to substantiate

充数 [chōngshù] merely to take a part; nominally to make up the number

充溢 [chōngyì] be full of; be overflowing with

充裕 [chōngyù] well off; ample

充足 [chōngzú] abundant ; sufficient

舂 [chōng] (v) 捣 to pound

舂臼 [chōngjiù] a mortar

chóng

虫(蟲) [chóng] 1 (n) 动物的通称 an animal 2 (n) 无脊椎动物的通称 an invertebrate 3 (n) 节足动物及蠕体动物的通称 a worm; an insect

虫害 [chónghài] insect pest

虫胶 [chóngjiāo] shellac

虫蛆 [chóngqū] a maggot; a grub

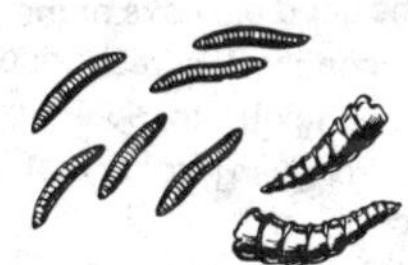

崇 [chóng] 1 (adj) 高 high; dignified; lofty 2 (v) 尊重 to honour; to respect; to worship *为什么有这么多青年崇拜电影明星？Why do so many young people worship movie stars?

崇拜 [chóngbài] to worship

崇高 [chónggāo] lofty; noble

崇敬 [chóngjìng] to respect; to look up to

崇尚 [chóngshàng] to hold in high esteem; to adore

崇山峻岭 [chóng shān jùn lǐng] high mountains and lofty hills

重 [chóng] 1 (adv) 再，又一次 repeatingly; reiterated; again *刚才我听不到你讲什么，请重说一遍。Please repeat; I could not hear what you said just now. 2 (n) 层 a layer *经过重重困难，他终於成功了。After having got over many difficulties, he finally succeeded.

另见 [zhòng]

重版 [chóngbǎn] a second edition

重重 [chóngchóng] layer upon layer; circle upon circle; heavily

重蹈覆辙 [chóngdǎofùzhé] to repeat the same mistake

重叠 [chóngdié] to reduplicate; to overlap

重复 [chóngfù] to repeat; to reiterate

重婚 [chónghūn] bigamy

重建 [chóngjiàn] to re-construct; to re-build

重聚 [chóngjù] re-assemble；re-unite reunion

重任 [chóngrèn] reappointment

重申 [chóngshēn] to reiterate; to re-affirm; to restate

重围 [chóngwéi] a close seige

重温旧梦 [chóngwēnjiùmèng] hoping for the good old days of the past

重新 [chóngxīn] a fresh; anew

重修 [chóngxiū] to repair; to revise

重演 [chóngyǎn] to repeat a perfor. mance

重整旗鼓 [chóngzhěngqígǔ] to begin all over again; to rally forces again

chǒng

宠（寵）[chǒng] (v) 偏爱，过分地爱 to love; to confer favours; to dote on; to pamper; to spoil，*别把孩子宠坏了。Don't pamper the child

宠爱 [chǒng'ài] dote on; love ardently

宠儿 [chǒng'ér] a favourite person; a pet

宠物 [chǒngwù] a pet

chòng

冲（衝）[chòng] 1 (adj) 强烈 strong; powerful; forceful; dynamic *这年青人做起事来很有冲劲。This young chap is very dynamic in doing his job. 2 (v) 撞压 to punch

冲床 [chòngchuáng] a punch; a punching machine

另见 [chōng]

铳（銃）[chòng] (n) 旧时指枪一类的火器 a blunderbuss; a gun

chōu

抽 [chōu] (v) 提，拔 to draw; to pump

抽查 [chōuchá] to make sample check

抽除 [chōuchú] pick out and reject; to subtract ; to deduct

抽出 [chōuchū] draw or take out from a lot

抽丁 [chōudīng] conscription

抽调 [chōudiào] to transfer

抽筋 [chōujīn] convulsion; spasms; cramp

抽空 [chōu kòng] to take advantage of any free time

抽泣 [chōuqì] to sob

抽签 [chōuqiān] to draw lots

抽气机 [chōuqìjī] an air pump

抽身 [chōushēn] to leave a place

抽水 [chōushuǐ] to draw up water

抽税 [chōushuì] to levy taxes

抽水机 [chōushuǐjī] a water pump

抽屉 [chōu·ti] a drawer (in desk or

table)

抽闲 [chōuxián] to take a little leisure

抽象 [chōuxiàng] to abstract

抽烟 [chōuyān] to smoke

瘳 [chōu] (v) 病愈 to convalesce; to recover

chóu

俦(儔) [chóu] (n) 同伴，伴侣 comrades; friends; companions

畴(疇) [chóu] 1 (n) 田地 cultivated field 2 (n) 类 class; category

踌(躊) [chóu] (v) 来回踱步--犹疑不决 to walk to and fro; to hesitate; to waver

踌躇 [chóuchú] to hesitate

筹(籌) [chóu] 1 (n) 计数的用具 a tally; a counter; a ticket 2 (v) 想办法，定计划 to plan out; to device

筹办 [chóubàn] to sponsor; to make preparation

筹备 [chóubèi] to prepare

筹划 [chóuhuà] to plan

筹集 [chóují] to collect and prepare (funds)

筹借 [chóujiè] to negotiate a loan

筹款 [chóukuǎn] to procure money; to raise funds

筹码 [chóumǎ] a counter; a medium of exchange

惆 [chóu] (adj) 愁闷，伤感 vexed; disappointed

惆怅 [chóuchàng] disappointed; sad; depressed

绸(綢) [chóu] (n) 软而薄的丝织品 light silk

稠 [chóu] (adj) 密 dense; crowded

仇 [chóu] 1 (n) 强烈的憎恨 hatred; animosity; enmity 2 (n) 敌人 a rival; an enemy

仇敌 [chóudí] an enemy; a foe

仇恨 [chóuhèn] to hate

仇人 [chóurén] an enemy

仇视 [chóushì] to hate; to be hostile to

雠(讎) [chóu] (v) 校对 to compare and revise (documents, etc)

愁 [chóu] (v) 忧虑 to worry

愁眉苦脸 [chóuméi kǔliǎn] to knit one's brows in despair; distressed looks

愁苦 [chóukǔ] distressed

愁闷 [chóumèn] melancholy

愁容 [chóuróng] a sad look; a mournful appearance

愁云 [chóuyún] an air of gloom

酬 [chóu] 1 (v) 敬酒招待 to pledge with wine; to entertain 2 (v) 报酬，报答 to repay; to return; to reward ＊你帮了我一个大忙，这点点东西是给你的报酬。This humble gift is to repay you for the great help you had given me.

酬金 [chóujīn] gratuity; renumeration earning

酬劳 [chóuláo] to renumerate

酬神 [chóushén] to thank the god

酬谢 [chóuxiè] to renumerate; to return thanks

chǒu

丑(醜) [chǒu] (adj) 难看 shameful ; ugly; disgraceful ＊那些闻人的丑行，已经是公开的秘密。 The ugly deeds of those well-known figures have already been an open secret.

丑恶 [chǒuè] loathsome; despicable; ugly

丑化 [chǒuhuà] to defame; to disfigure

丑剧 [chǒujù] a foul performance ; a farce

丑角 [chǒujué] a clown ;a comedian

丑陋 [chǒulòu] ugly; ill-looking

丑态 [chǒutài] a disgusting manner

丑态百出 [chǒutàibǎichū] to act like a buffoon; to act a ludicrous figure; utterly ridiculous

丑态毕露 [chǒutàibìlù] to expose

one's true character ; make a spectacle of oneself

丑闻 [chǒuwén] a scandal

丑行 [chǒuxíng] a shameful conduct; an ugly deed

瞅 [chǒu] (v) 看 to see; to look

chòu

臭 [chòu] (n)(气味)恶劣 stench; stink; smelly

另见 [xiù]

臭虫 [chòuchóng] bed bugs

臭架子 [chòujiàzi] the ugly mantle of pretentiousness

臭名 [chòumíng] a foul reputation ; an ill fame; infamy

臭名远扬 [chòumíng yuǎn yáng] notorious;infamous

臭味 [chòuwèi]discredited;foul smell

臭味相投 [chòuwèixiāngtóu] birds of a feather flock together

臭氧 [chòuyǎng] ozone

chū

出 [chū] 1 (v) 向外走,跟"进"相对 to go out 2 (v) 生长,产生to produce ; to generate *这个世纪出了许多大人物。The century produces many great men. 3 (v)发生 to occur ; to happen; to take place *假如他出了什么事,请立刻通知我。If anything happens to him, let me know at once.

出版 [chūbǎn] to publish

出版社 [chūbǎnshè]publishing house

出兵 [chūbīng] to march army for battle

出差 [chūchāi] to be out on duty; to be out on an official mission

出产 [chūchǎn] to produce; to make; to manufacture

出场 [chūchǎng] to appear

出超 [chūchāo] balance of trade surplus; export surplus

出岔子 [chūchà·zi] to run into trouble

出丑 [chūchǒu] to expose one's weak points; to be disgraced; to cut a poor figure

出处 [chūchǔ] source

出动 [chūdòng] to start out

出尔反尔 [chūěrfǎněr] inconsistent; to promise and then deny in succession

出发 [chūfā] to set out; to start off

出发点 [chūfādiǎn] starting point; point of departure

出凡 [chūfán] extraordinary

出风头 [chūfēngtóu] to cut a figure; to show off; to seek limelight

出轨 [chūguǐ] to derail

出海 [chūhǎi] to put to sea

出乎意料 [chūhūyìliào] unforeseen; beyond expectation

出击 [chūjī] to launch attack

出嫁 [chūjià] to be married (of girls)

出界 [chūjiè] outside (to hit wide; to be out of bound)

出境 [chūjìng] to leave a country; exit (visa)

出口 [chūkǒu] to export; exit; way out; outlet

出来 [chūlái] to come out

出类拔萃 [chūlèibácuì]the pick of the lot; to stand out among others; far above the average

出力 [chūlì] to make an effort; to do one's best; to contribute one's strength

出笼 [chūlóng] to come out into the open; to turn out; to emerge

出路 [chūlù] an outlet; a way out

出卖 [chūmài] to offer for sale; to betray

出门 [chūmén] to travel

出面 [chūmiàn] (to do something) in the name of...; in person

出名 [chūmíng] to become famous
出没 [chūmò] to infest; to haunt; to swarm around
出纳 [chūnǎ] the work of receiving and paying out money; a cashier
出品 [chūpǐn] an artistic or manufactured product; a produce; a make; a manufacture
出奇 [chūqí] strange; curious; peculiar; marvellous
出气 [chūqì] to vent one's anger
出其不意 [chūqíbùyì] to take
出勤 [chūqín] to attend work
出奇制胜 [chūqízhìshèng] to defeat... by surprise attack
出去 [chū·qù] to go out
出人头地 [chūréntóudì] to stand above others
出入 [chūrù] to come in and go out; difference; in conformity with (the fact, etc.)
出色 [chūsè] outstanding; remarkable; distinguished
出身 [chūshēn] to come from; class origin; family background
出神 [chūshén] to appear occupied in thought; deep in thought
出生 [chūshēng] to be born
出生入死 [chū sheng rù sǐ] to brave countless dangers; to go through thick and thin
出世 [chūshì] to be born
出示 [chūshì] to issue a proclamation; to notify; to show
出使 [chūshǐ] to be sent on a mission; to be appointed to a diplomatic post
出售 [chūshòu] to offer for sale
出庭 [chūtíng] to appear in court
出头 [chūtóu] to raise head (to be the head above others)
出土 [chūtǔ] to unearth; to be excavated
出席 [chūxí] to attend; to be present (at meeting)
出息 [chū·xi] to yield interest; promising
出现 [chūxiàn] to appear; to emerge; to arise
出血 [chūxuè] to bleed
出芽 [chūyá] to sprout; to germinate
出言不逊 [chūyánbùxùn] ill-mannered in speech
出洋 [chūyáng] to go abroad
出诊 [chūzhěn] to make a house call (of doctor)
出征 [chūzhēng] to go to the front; to go on active service
出租 [chūzū] for hire; to rent

初 [chū] 1 (n) 起头，刚开始 at first; beginning ＊初学游泳的人不应该在深水游泳。Those who begin to learn swimming should not swim in deep water. 2 (adj) 第一次 first ＊这是我初次到外国旅行，所以很兴奋。This is the first time I travel overseas so I am rather excited. 3 (adj) 较低的 junior ＊他目前正在一间初级中学就读。At present he has his schooling in a junior middle school.
初版 [chūbǎn] the first edition
初步 [chūbù] elementary; preliminary; initial
初出茅庐 [chūchūmáolú] a beginner; a debut
初等 [chūděng] elementary; preliminary
初犯 [chūfàn] the first offence
初稿 [chūgǎo] a draft
初交 [chūjiāo] newly formed acquaintance
初级 [chūjí] elementary
初期 [chūqī] initial stage
初生 [chūshēng] the first born
初试 [chūshì] the first trial; the first experience; the preliminary test

chú

刍（芻） [chú] (n) 喂牲口的草 hay; straw; fodder
刍秣 [chúmò] fodder
刍言 [chúyán] rustic speech
雏（雛） [chú] (n) 幼小的鸟 a young bird

雏形 [chúxíng] an embryo; fledgling; an embryonic form

除 [chú] 1 (v) 去掉 to remove; to get rid of; to do away with; to wipe out ＊你能清除这屋内的老鼠吗？ Can you rid this house of mice? 2 (v) 把一个数分成相等的若干份 to divide

除恶习 [chúèxí] to do away with evil practices; to get rid of bad habits

除法 [chúfǎ] division

除非 [chúfēi] unless; only if; with the exception of

除害 [chúhài] to get rid of danger; to remove evil

除旧布新 [chújiùbùxīn] to sweep away the old and bring in the new

除开 [chúkāi] except; besides; with the exception of

除去 [chúqù] to clear off; to blot out; to obliterate.

除数 [chúshù] divider

除外 [chúwài] except; apart from

除夕 [chúxī] the New Year's Eve

蜍 [chú] (n) "蟾蜍"，一种蛙 a toad

厨 [chú] (n) 做饭菜的地方 a kitchen

厨刀 [chúdāo] chopper

厨子 [chú·zi] a cook

橱 [chú] (n) 放東西的家具 a wardrobe; a case

橱窗 [chúchuāng] a show window; a display case

橱柜 [chúguì] a cupboard

锄(鋤) [chú] 1 (n) 一种松土，除草的农具，也叫锄头 a hoe 2 (v) 用锄头松土，除草 to hoe; to dig ; to weed 3 (v) 铲除 to get rid of

锄草 [chúcǎo] to root out; weed

锄地 [chúdì] to hoe the ground

锄强扶弱 [chúqiángfúruò] to eradicate the tyrant and assist the weak

chǔ

楚 [chǔ] 1 (adj) 清晰，整齐 distinct; clear; orderly＊我对那事件的经过已记得不清楚了。My memory on that event is not clear any more. 2 (n) 痛苦 pain ＊他受了十二鞭之后，痛楚不堪。He felt terribly painful after he had been given twelve lashes.

础(礎) [chǔ] (n) 建筑物柱子底下的石头 the foundation; the base

处(處) [chǔ] 1 (v) 居住 to live; to dwell; to stay; to get along with ＊新加坡是各族和谐共处的地方。Singapore is a place where all races get along with each other peacefully. 2 (v) 置身 to be in a position of ＊如果你处在她的地位，你就会明白她为什么要那样做了。If you are in her position you will understand why she should do so 3 (v) 对待，办理 to deal with; to manage; to handle ＊警方会处置这小偷的。The police will deal with this burglar.

处断 [chǔduàn] to decide; to judge

处罚 [chǔfá] to punish

处分 [chǔfèn] to be disciplined

处境 [chǔjìng] circumstances; conditions

处决 [chǔjué] to execute (criminals)

处理 [chǔlǐ] to treat; to deal with; to handle; to run affairs

处事 [chǔshì] to manage business; to deal with affairs; to handle

处世 [chǔshì] to deal with people and affairs

处死 [chǔsǐ] to sentence to death

处心积虑 [chǔxīnjīlù] to have all along nurtured schemes to

处刑 [chǔxíng] to condemn; to sentence; to punish

处于 [chǔyú] to find oneself in; to stand in

处置 [chǔzhì] to handle; to dispose

处之泰然 [chǔzhītàirán] to face a situation calmly

储(儲) [chǔ] (v) 积蓄，存放 to deposit; to store

储备 [chǔbèi] to reserve

储备粮 [chǔbèiliáng] grain reserves
储藏 [chǔcáng] to store
储藏处 [chǔcángchù] a store room
储存 [chǔcún] to accumulate
储君 [chǔjūn] the heir king; the crown prince
储蓄 [chǔxù] to save (money); to have a deposit

杵 [chǔ] (n) 舂米，捶衣或捣東西用的棒 a pestle; a pounder

chù

畜 [chù] (n) 受人饲养的兽 domestic animals
畜力 [chùlì] animal power
畜生 [chùsheng] a beast; a brute
另见 [xù]

触(觸) [chù] (v) 碰 to touch
触电 [chùdiàn] to get an electric shock
触动 [chùdòng] to touch ; to touch on
触犯 [chùfàn] to offend; to affront; to violate
触及 [chùjí] to touch; to touch on
触礁 [chùjiāo] to strike a hidden rock (under the sea)
触角 [chùjiǎo] an antenna; feelers of insects
触景生情 [chùjǐngshēngqíng] to see something which arouses one's deep feelings
触觉 [chùjué] the sense of touch; the tactile sense
触目 [chùmù] affect the eye in some particular manner; meet (greet) the eye
触目皆是 [chùmùjiēshì] it is everywhere; plenty
触目惊心 [chùmùjīngxīn] shocking; a startling fact; a ghastly sight
触怒 [chùnù] to provoke; to offend; to arouse wrath
触须 [chùxū] a palp; a feeler

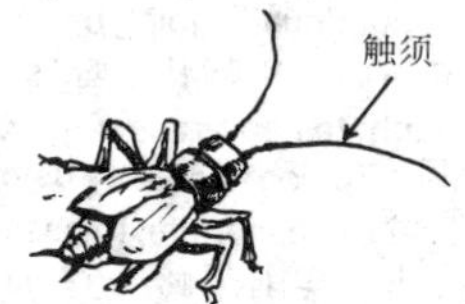

处(處) [chù] (n) 地方，地点 a place; a location; a spot; a point
另见 [chǔ]
处女 [chùnǚ] a virgin
处处 [chùchù] everywhere; here and there; in all places

绌(絀) [chù] (n) 不足，不够 deficiency

黜 [chù] (v) 免掉，革除 to dismiss; to expel

怵 [chù] (v) 害怕，畏缩 to fear

矗 [chù] (adj) 高耸向上的样子 upright
＊战士纪念碑矗立在广场上。The war memorial stands upright in the square.
矗立 [chùlì] to tower; to erect; to rise
矗然 [chùrán] straight; upright

chuāi

揣 [chuāi] (v) 放进 to put into
另见 [chuǎi]

chuǎi

揣 [chuǎi] (v) 估计，猜想 to estimate, to guess; to figure
另见 [chuāi]
揣度 [chuǎiduó] to conjecture ; to reckon
揣摩 [chuǎimó] to weigh and consider

chuài

踹 [chuài] (v) 踢，蹬，践踏 to tread ; to stamp; to trample

chuān

川 [chuān] 1 (n) 河流 a river; a creek 2 (n) 平地，平原 a plain: an area of level country

川流不息 [chūanlíubùxī] uninterrupted flow; continually going on

穿 [chūan] 1 (v) 刺孔，凿通 to bore through; to perforate *用锥子穿一个洞。To bore a hole by using a drill. 2(v)通过 to penetrate; to pass through *战士们穿山越岭，终于到达了西藏。The warriors passed through mountains after mountains and finally reached Tibet. 4(v) 着衣服 to dress; to put on; to wear

穿插 [chuānchā] to do alternately

穿戴 [chuāndài] what one wears (hat, hair, decorations and dress)

穿孔 [chuānkǒng] to punch; to pierce; to perforate

穿山甲 [chuānshānjiǎ] a scaly ant-eater

穿梭 [chuānsuō] to shuttle

穿透 [chuāntòu] to penetrate; to pierce through

穿针 [chuānzhēn] to thread a needle

穿针引线 [chuānzhēnyǐnxiàn] to play the role of bringing the two parties together

穿着 [chuānzhuó] what one wears

穿凿 [chuānzuò] a far-fetched explanation

chuán

船 [chuán] (n) 水上的交通工具 a boat; a vessel; a ship

船舶 [chuánbó] ships; vessels

船舱 [chuáncāng] a hold; a cabin (of ship)

船厂 [chuánchǎng] a dockyard

船舵 [chuánduò] the rudder

船帆 [chuánfān] a sail

船夫 [chuánfū] sailors; boatmen; crew

船腹 [chuánfù] ship space; cargo space; tonnage

船货 [chuánhuò] freight; load; cargo

船面 [chuánmiàn] the deck

船篷 [chuánpéng] the sail; the mat roofing to a boat

船身 [chuánshēn] the hull

船首 [chuánshǒu] the bow ; the prow

船桅 [chuánwéi] the mast

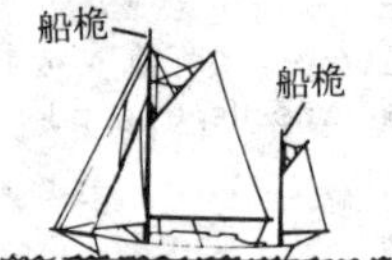

船尾 [chuánwěi] the stern of a ship

船坞 [chuánwù] a dock; a dockyard

船员 [chuányuán] mariners; the crew; seamen

船晕 [chuányūn] seasickness

船长 [chuánzhǎng] a captain ; a master mariner

传（傳）[chuán] (v) 转，转授，转递，转知，转达 to transfer; to pass from.....to.....; circulate; to pass on to *神话是代代相传的故事。 Most fairy tales are stories passed from generation to generation

传播 [chuánbō] to spread over; to propagate

传布 [chuánbù] to spread

传达 [chuándá] to transmit; to convey; to communicate

传达室 [chuándáshì] a reception office

传单 [chuándān] a handbill; a leaflet

传导 [chuándǎo] to conduct (heat, electricity)

传道 [chuándào] to spread a doctrine; to preach

传递 [chuándì] to hand round; to pass on

传供 [chuángòng] to interpret evidence

传呼 [chuánhū] to communicate; to inform; to send for

传家宝 [chuánjiābǎo] hereditary treasure

传教 [chuánjìao] to preach

传令 [chuánlìng] to issue orders

传名后世 [chuánmínghòushì] to hand down one's name to posterity
传票 [chuánpiào] summons; subpoena
传奇 [chuánqí] short stories; long plays; legends; legendary stories
传染 [chuánrǎn] to infect; to communicate (disease)
传热 [chuánrè] to transmit heat
传神 [chuánshén] vivid; graphic
传声筒 [chuánshēngtǒng] mouthpiece ;microphone
传示 [chuánshì] to send word; to communicate information; to give notice
传授 [chuánshòu] to teach; to hand down
传说 [chuánshuō] story that go around ; legend
传统 [chuántǒng] tradition ; conventions
传统观念 [chuántǒngguānniàn] traditional concepts
传闻 [chuánwén] a hearsay
传阅 [chuányuè] to circulate; to pass around (e.g. circular)
传真 [chuánzhēn] tele-autogram; telephotography
椽 [chuán] (n) 支架屋面瓦片的木条 the rafter

chuǎn

舛 [chuǎn] 1 (adj) 差错 mistaken; erroneous 2 (adj) 违背 contradictory
喘 [chuǎn] (v) 呼吸急促 to pant; to gasp; to breathe hard
喘气 [chuǎnqì] to gasp; to pant; short of breath; to take a break
喘息 [chuǎnxī] to gain a respite; to pause for a breath

chuàn

钏(釧) [chuàn](n) 镯子 an armlet; a bracelet
串 [chuàn] 1 (v) 连贯，相通 to string up; to connect 2 (n) 量词 a measure word; strain, string, bunch, etc
＊一串珠 a string of beads 一串锁匙 a bunch of keys.
串合 [chuànhé] to league together; to join as forces
串联 [chuànlián] to establish ties with; to contact
串谋 [chuànmóu] to plot or conspire together; collusion
串通 [chuàntōng] to collude with; to conspire with; to work hand in glove with

chuāng

创(創) [chuāng] (v) 伤 a wound; a cut; an injury ; a trauma
创口 [chuāngkǒu] a sore; a wound
另见 [chuàng]
疮(瘡) [chuāng] (n) 皮肤肿烂溃疡 a sore; a fester
疮疤;疮瘢 [chuāngbā;chuāngbān] the scabs of a sore
疮口 [chuāngkǒu] the opening of a sore
疮痍 [chuāngyí] calamity; plagues; distress
疮痍满目 [chuāngyímǎnmù] distress and suffering are seen on every side
窗 [chuāng] (n) 房屋通气透光的装置 window
窗户 [chuāng·hu] a window
窗帘 [chuānglián] window curtains; window screen
窗台 [chuāngtái] window sill
窗友 [chuāngyǒu] fellow students; schoolmates

chuáng

床 [chuang] (n) 睡觉的用具 a bed; a couch
床单 [chuángdān] bed sheet
床垫 [chuángdiàn] mattress
床架 [chuángjià] a bedstead
床铺 [chuángpù] bedding
床位 [chuángwèi] bed or berth (in hospital, hotel, ship, train, etc.)
床席 [chuángxí] the matting of a bed
床帐 [chuángzhàng] bed curtains; mosquito net

chuǎng

闯(闖) [chuǎng](v)冲，冲过，突破 to rush; to force one's way ; to break through＊他们闯进办事处，要找经理。They rushed into the office to look for the manager.

闯祸 [chuǎnghuò] to lead to trouble; to precipitate a disaster

闯入 [chuǎngrù] to burst in; to trespass on; to intrude into

chuàng

怆(愴) [chuàng] (adj) 悲伤 sad; grieved; mournful

创(創) [chuang] (v) 开始 to begin; to initiate; to inaugurate ＊他首创薪酬奖罚法，以改良行政。He initiated a merit and demerit scheme to improve the management.

创办 [chuàng bàn] to found; to sponsor

创见 [chuàngjiàn] a new idea or view-point

创建 [chuàngjiàn] to found; to create; to establish

创举 [chuàngjǔ] initiative; new creation ; pioneering undertaking

创刊 [chuàngkān] the first issue (of a magazine); the initial issue

创立 [chuànglì] to establish ; to set up; to originate

创设 [chuàngshè] to found; to open

创始 [chuàngshǐ] to begin; initiative; beginning

创新 [chuàngxīn] to create something new ; creative

创新记录 [chuàngxīnjìlù] to make a new record

创业 [chuàngyè] to start a business; to start a project; to pioneer

创造 [chuàngzào] to create

创造性 [chuàngzàoxìng] creativeness

创作 [chuàngzuò] to create; creation ; creative work

另见 [chuāng]

chuī

吹 [chuī] 1 (v) 合拢嘴唇，用力出气 to blow; to blast; to puff 2 (v) 说大话自夸 to boast; to brag ＊他什么也不会做，只会自吹自擂。He can do nothing but brag. 3 (v) 失败 to end up in failure ＊她的婚事吹了。Her marriage ended up with failure.

吹打 [chuīdǎ] to blow and beat—to play music

吹管 [chuīguǎn] a blowpipe

吹灰之力 [chuīhuīzhīlì] as easy as blowing away dust

吹毛求疵 [chuīmáoqiúcī] blowing aside the hair trying to discover a mole—to find fault with; hair-splitting

吹牛 [chuīniú] to brag; to boast

吹捧 [chuīpěng] to lavish praise on; to laud; to flatter

吹嘘 [chuīxū] to brag; to glibly profess; to boost up; to crack oneself up

炊 [chuī] (v) 烧火做饭菜 to cook food

炊饭 [chuīfàn] to cook rice

炊事员 [chuīshìyuán] a member of the kitchen staff; a cook

炊烟 [chuīyān] the smoke from kitchen

chuí

垂 [chuí] 1 (v) 从上到下 to hang ; to droop; to dangle; to bend downward; to hand down＊只有伟大的人物才永远名垂后世。Only the great men can hand down a name to posterity . 2 (adv) 将近 nearly; almost; to be on the verge of

垂钓 [chuídiào] to fish with a hook and line

垂老 [chuílǎo] growing old; in declining years

垂青 [chuíqīng] to cast a favourable glance upon

垂手而得 [chuíshǒuérdé] to gain something easily

垂死 [chuísǐ] at death's door

垂死挣扎 [chuísǐzhēngzhá] to give dying kicks; death-bed struggle; desperate struggle

垂头丧气 [chuítóusàngqì] dejected; downcast; crestfallen; in low spirit

垂危 [chuíwēi] close to death as a result of serious illness

垂涎 [chuíxián] to crave for; the mouth watering covcteously for; cannot hide one's greed

垂涎三尺 [chuí xián sān chǐ] with mouth watering copiously for (hankering after something)

垂直 [chuízhí] perpendicular

捶 [chuí] (v) 敲打 to beat with a staff; to cudgel

锤(鍾) [chuí] 1 (n) 一种敲打用的工具 a hammer 2 (v) 用锤子敲打 to hammer

锤炼 [chuíliàn] to steel and temper; to temper

锤子 [chuí·zi] a hammer

槌 [chuí] 1 (n) 一种敲打用的工具 a mallet; a pestle; a wooden hammer. 2 (v) 敲打 to beat; to strike

槌球 [chuíqiú] croquet (体育)

chūn

春 [chūn] 1 (n) 四季中的第一季 spring; springtime 2 (n) 比喻生机 gay; joyful; youthful

春播 [chūnbō] spring sowing

春风满面 [chūnfēngmǎnmiàn] face radiates happiness; face beaming with smiles

春耕 [chūngēng] spring ploughing

春光 [chunguāng] the splendour of spring

春季 [chūnjì] spring season

春节 [chūnjié] spring festival

春联 [chūnlián] New Year couplets

春秋 [chūnqiū] "Spring and Autumn Annals"; age

春色 [chūnsè] cheerful looking; delightful view; the beauty of spring

春天 [chūntiān] springtime

chún

淳 [chún] (adj) 朴实，敦厚 honest

淳厚 [chúnhòu] honest; devoted

淳朴 [chúnpǔ] simple and honest

鹑(鶉) [chún] 即"鹌鹑"[ānchún] 是一种小鸟和小鸡相像 a quail

醇 [chún] 1 (adj) 浓厚的，良好的(酒) rich, good (wine)

纯(純) [chún] (adj) 单一，没有夹杂 pure; simple; unmixed

纯粹 [chúncuì] pure; complete; sheer

纯洁 [chúnjié] fine; pure; chaste

纯洁性 [chúnjiéxìng] purity

纯朴 [chúnpǔ] plain; simple; honest

纯熟 [chúnshú] skilful; fluent

纯真 [chúnzhēn] pure; genuine; unsophisticated

纯正 [chúnzhèng] honest; pure

纯种 [chúnzhǒng] thorough bred

唇 [chún] (n) 口的边沿 the lips

唇齿相依 [chúnchǐxiāngyī] as closely related as the lips and the teeth; interdependent as lips and teeth

唇齿音 [chúnchǐyīn] labio-dental

唇枪舌剑 [chúnqiāng-shéjiàn] sharp statements in debate

唇舌 [chúnshé] lips and tongue; plausible speech; words; language

唇亡齿寒 [chúnwángchǐhán] without the lips, the teeth feel cold —— mutually dependent

chǔn

蠢 [chǔn] (adj) 愚笨 stupid; sluggish

蠢笨 [chǔnbèn] stupid; foolish; clumsy

蠢才 [chǔncái] blockhead

蠢蠢欲动 [chǔnchǔnyùdòng] evil; restless and about to start some

move; itch for action
蠢动 [chǔndòng] insidious move (on the part of the enemy or bad elements)

chuō

戳 [chuō] 1 (v) 用尖端触，刺 to poke; to pierce 2 (n) 图章 stamp; seal
戳穿 [chuōchuān] to lay bare; to expose

chuò

啜 [chuò] 1 (v) 喝，吃 drink; to taste 2 (v) 哭时抽噎的样子 to sob; to wail
辍(輟) [chuò] (v) 中止，停止 to stop; to cease; to suspend
辍学 [chuòxué] to stop schooling
绰(綽) [chuò] (adj) 宽裕，常叠用。generous; ample; wide *他花钱很宽绰。He is generous with his money.
绰绰 [chuòchuò] easy and free
绰绰有余 [chuòchuòyǒuyú] more than sufficient
绰号 [chuòhào] a nickname

cī

疵 [cī] (n) 毛病，缺点 a defect; a flaw

cí

磁 [cí] (n) 某些有吸铁，镍钴等属性的物质 a magnet
磁场 [cíchǎng] magnetic field
磁带 [cídài] magnetic tape
磁力 [cílì] magnetism; magnetic force
磁石 [císhí] a loadstone
磁铁 [cítiě] magnetic iron; magnet

磁性 [cíxìng] magnetic; of a magnetic nature
粢 [cí] (n) 糯米做的一种食品。 a pastry made of glutinous rice
慈 [cí] 爱怜，仁爱 merciful; kind; soft-hearted; humane
慈爱 [cí'ài] kindly
慈悲 [cíbēi] merciful
慈善 [císhàn] charitable; benevolent; philanthropic
慈祥 [cíxiáng] amiable; kindly
瓷 [cí] (n) 用粘土制坯入窑烧成的器皿 porcelain
瓷器 [cíqì] porcelain ware
瓷土 [cítǔ] porcelain clay
词(詞) [cí] 1 (n) 能自由运用的最小的语言单位 words; phrases 2 (n) 一种古体诗 a poem of classical Chinese
词不达意 [cíbùdáyì] the sentence does not fully convey the idea
词典 [cídiǎn] a dictionary of words and phrases
词汇 [cíhuì] vocabulary
词句 [cíjù] words and phrases
词类 [cílèi] part of speech
词头 [cítóu] prefix
词尾 [cíwěi] suffix
词性 [cíxìng] part of speech
词序 [cíxù] word order
词语 [cíyǔ] word; phrase
词藻 [cízǎo] ornate; phraseology (in pedantic writing)
词组 [cízǔ] word group
祠 [cí] (n) 供奉祖先的庙堂，庙。an ancestral temple; a temple
祠堂 [cítáng] the ancestral hall; a family temple
雌 [cí] (adj) 女性的（动，植物） female (animal or plant)
辞(辭) [cí] 1 (v) 告别 to bid farewell; to say goodbye; to take leave *我必须告辞了。I must say good-bye. 2 (v) 推却 to decline; to resign *因为老板太不讲理，雇员全体辞职。All the employees resign because the employer is too unreasonable. 3 same as 词[cí]
辞别 [cíbié] to take leave; to bid farewell

辞呈 [cíchéng] a letter of resignation; resignation
辞却 [cíquè] to dismiss; to decline
辞世 [císhì] to die; to pass away
辞退 [cítuì] to turn away; to discharge
辞行 [cíxíng] to say good-bye (before going on a long journey)
辞职 [cízhí] to resign

cǐ

此 [cǐ] (pron) (adj) 这，这个，这些 this; these
此地无银三百两 [cǐdìwúyínsānbǎiliǎng] a miser posts a marker saying "three hundred tahils of silver ingots are not buried here"—hiding and covering only to expose it
此后 [cǐhòu] here after; from now on; henceforth
此间；此外 [cǐjiān; cǐwài] this place; here
此刻 [cǐkè] this moment; now
此起彼伏 [cǐqǐbǐfú] constantly on the upsurge; ebb and flow; rising here and subsiding there
此生 [cǐshēng] this life
此时 [cǐshí] at present ; for the time being
此外 [cǐwài] besides; furthermore ; in addition

cì

刺 [cì] 1 (n) 尖锐象针的东西 a thorn; a sting; a prick 2 (v) 尖的东西穿过物体 to pierce; to thrust; to stab 3 (v) 暗杀 to assassinate; to murder
刺刀 [cìdāo] bayonet; dagger

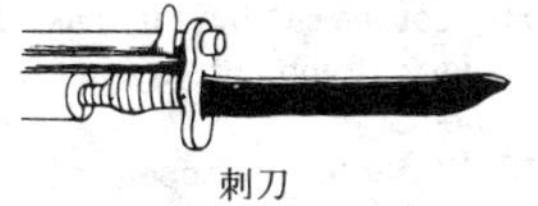

刺刀

刺耳 [cìěr] irritating or unpleasant to the ear
刺骨 [cìgǔ] to cut to the bones
刺激 [cìjī] to irritate; to stimulate; to excite; to be provoked
刺客 [cìkè] an assassin
刺杀 [cìshā] to assassinate; bayonet fighting
刺探 [cìtàn] to detect
刺蝟 [cìwèi] a hedgehog

刺绣 [cìxiù] embroidery
刺眼 [cìyǎn] dazzling; unpleasant to the eye

次 [cì] 1 (n) 顺序 order; position 2 (adj) 第二 second; next; secondary 3 (adj) 质量差的 inferior 4 (n) 量词 measure word: a time *他来过几次了。He has been here several times 5 (n) 地方 a place *旅次 a halting place; an inn; 客次 an inn; 席次 at the table; 途次 on the road
次等 [cìděng] second class
次品 [cìpǐn] shoddy products
次数 [cìshù] number of times
次序 [cìxù] order; series; sequence
次要 [cìyào] next in importance
次晨 [cì chén] the next morning
次长 [cìzhǎng] a vice-minister
次子 [cìzǐ] the second son

伺 [cì] 1 (v) 服侍 to wait upon; to serve 2 (v) 查察；查探 to examine; to spy
另见 [sì]
伺候 [cìhòu] to wait upon
伺探 [cìtàn] to spy

赐(賜) [cì] (v) 赏给 to confer upon an inferior; to bestow; to grant
赐覆 [cìfù] favour with a reply
赐予 [cìyǔ] to bestow.....on

cōng

囱 [cōng] 1 (n) 窗 a window 2 炉灶出烟的通路 a chimney
骢(驄) [cōng] (n) 青白色的马 a piebald horse

聪（聰）[cōng] 1 (adj) 听觉灵敏 quick at hearing 2 (adj) 灵巧，伶俐 wise; clever; sharpwitted; intelligent

聪慧 [cōnghui] intelligent; clever

聪明 [cōng·ming] intelligent; clever

匆 [cōng] (adj) 急，忙 hurried;hasty

匆匆 [cōngcōng] in a hurry; hurriedly

匆促 [cōngcù] hurriedly; in a rush

匆忙 [cōngmáng] hasty in; haste

葱 [cōng] 1 (n) 蔬菜名 an onion 2 (adj) 青绿色 green

葱葱 [cōngcōng] green

葱绿 [cōnglù] pale yellowish green

葱郁 [cōngyù] luxuriantly green

从（從）[cōng] (adj) 松弛，宽 lax; yielding

从容 [cōngróng] confident and without haste

从容不迫 [cōngróngbùpò] calm and leisurely; to take one's time in doing...

另见 [cóng]

cóng

从（從）[cóng] 1 (prep) 由，自 from ＊他从头到尾，没有说过一句话 He did not utter a word from beginning to end. 2 (v) 依顺，跟随 to obey; to observe; to follow ＊你从事那一种职业？ What profession do you follow?

从长计议 [cóngchángjìyì] to talk over at length; to take time to consider it

从此 [cóngcǐ] from now on

从…到… [cóng...dào] from...to...

从而 [cóng'ér] therefore

从犯 [cóngfàn] an accessory criminal

从古以来 [cónggǔyǐlái] since ancient times

从缓 [cónghuǎn] postpone

从…看来 [cóng...kànlái] judging from ; in view of

从宽 [cóngkuān] leniently

从来 [cónglái] at all times; always

从略 [cóngluè] to omit; in brief

从…起 [cóng...qǐ] from...on

从前 [cóngqián] formerly; before

从戎；从军 [cóngróng; cóngjūn] join the army; turn soldiers; go to the front

从事 [cóngshì] to engage in; to be taken up with

从属 [cóngshǔ] to be subordinate to

从头 [cóngtóu] from the beginning; once again

从未 [cóngwèi] never; at no time

从新 [cóngxīn] anew; begin afresh

从中 [cóngzhōng] thereby; therefrom

另见 [cōng]

丛（叢）[cóng] 1 (n) 聚集 a cluster; a collection 2 (n) 生长在一起的草木 a cluster of plants; shrubbery

丛刊 [cóngkān] a collection of periodicals

丛林 [cónglín] a thick wood; a grove; a forest

丛生 [cóngshēng] growing together; luxuriant; overgrow

丛书 [cóngshū] a collection of books; series

淙 [cóng] (n) 水声 noise of water

淙淙 [cóngcóng] the roaring of a river

琮 [cóng] (n) 古玉器名 a jade

còu

凑 [còu] 1 (v) 聚合 to assemble; to put together 2 (v) 迫近 to press near

凑合 [còu·he] to have to make do with ; fair to middling; to make shift; to assemble

凑巧 [còuqiǎo] to happen to; by chance ; accidentally

凑热闹 [còurènào] to take part in the fun

凑数 [còushù] to make up a number without active work

辏（輳）[còu] (n) 轮毂，车轮的中心 the hub of a wheel

腠 [còu] (n) 肌肤的纹理 the tissue between the skin and the flesh

cū

粗 [cū] 1 (adj) 不精细的（物体）coarse; thick; rough (objects) ＊粗面和幼面一样好。The thick noodle is as good as the fine one. 2 (adj) 疏略的（工作等）rough; unfinished (work, etc) ＊我粗略地读过一遍，把文章的要点找出来。Through rough reading I got the main points of the article. 3 (adj) 不雅的（行为，态度等）rough; vulgar; rude ＊这女售货员以粗鲁的态度对待顾客。This salesgirl serves the customers in a rude manner

粗暴 [cūbào] coarse; rude; outrageous

粗糙 [cūcāo] rough; crude

粗茶淡饭 [cūchá-dànfàn] eating and living simply

粗放 [cūfàng] forthright

粗工 [cūgōng] rough work; unskilled labour

粗犷 [cūguǎng] rash and boorish

粗话 [cūhuà] obscene language

粗粮 [cūliáng] coarse grain

粗劣 [cūliè] crude; coarse; inferior

粗鲁 [cū·lu] boorish; rude

粗略 [cūlüè] roughly; not detailed

粗浅 [cūqiǎn] superficial

粗人 [cūrén] a boor

粗食 [cūshí] coarse food; poor diet

粗手笨脚 [cūshǒubènjiǎo] awkward and clumsy

粗俗 [cūsú] vulgar; vile; rough; rustic

粗细 [cūxì] thickness; roughness

粗心 [cūxīn] careless

粗心大意 [cūxīndàyì] careless

粗野 [cūyě] rude

粗枝大叶 [cūzhī-dàyè] shoddy work style; crude and careless; crude and perfunctory

粗制滥造 [cūzhìlànzào] roughly made

粗壮 [cūzhuàng] stout; robust; strong

cù

簇 [cù] (1) (n) 聚集 to crowd; to gather foliage (2) (n) 量词 a measure word, bunch ＊一簇鲜花 a bouquet of flowers (3) 箭头 arrow-heads

簇聚 [cùjù] to crowd together

簇生 [cùshēng] to gather

簇新 [cùxīn] brand new

簇拥 [cùyōng] to escort

醋 [cù] (n) 酸的调味品 vinegar

醋酸 [cùsuān] acetic acid [化]

醋意 [cùyì] jealously

猝 [cù] (adj) 突然，出乎意外 abrupt; hurried

猝不及防 [cùbùjífáng] to put off one's guard

猝然 [cùrán] suddenly; abruptly; unexpectedly

蹙 [cù] 1 (adj) 急迫 urgent 2 (adj) 皱缩 wrinkled; contracted

蹴 [cù] (v) 踢，踩，踏 to kick; to tread on; to stamp

蹴踢 [cùtī] to trample on

促 [cù] 1 (adj) 赶快 to hurry ＊不必匆促，还有很多时间。Don't hurry, there is plenty of time. 2 (v) 催，推动 to promote; to spur ＊我深信这场足球赛能促进我们两国人民之间的友谊。I deeply believe that the football match will promote the friendship of the people between our two nations. 3 (adj) 靠近 near; close

促成 [cùchéng] to help materialize; to cause(somebody to do something

促进 [cùjìn] to promote

促迫 [cùpò] to urge; to press; to hurry on

促使 [cùshǐ] to precipitate; to cause

促膝谈心 [cùxītánxīn] to sit closely for a frank talk; to have a heart-to-heart talk

cuān

蹿（躥）[cuān] (v) 向上跳 to jump upwards

cuán

攒(攢) [cuán] (v) 聚，凑集 to bring together
另见 [zǎn]

cuàn

窜(竄) [cuàn] (v) 逃走，乱跑 to flee; to escape; to run away
窜犯 [cuànfàn] to raid; to make an inroad
窜匿 [cuànnì] to skulk off and conceal
窜窃 [cuànqiè] to steal; to pilfer
窜扰 [cuànrǎo] to harass
窜逃 [cuàntào] to flee and hide

篡 [cuàn] (v) 用非法手段夺取地位和权力 to usurp
篡夺 [cuànduó] to usurp; to arrogate
篡改 [cuàngǎi] to temper with; to alter; to revise (in derogatory sense)
篡逆 [cuànnì] to rebel against the government
篡位 [cuànwèi] to usurp the throne

cuī

崔 [cuī] (n) 姓 a surname

催 [cuī] (v) 促，使赶快行动 to urge; to press ＊他催她早点儿走。 He urged her to leave early.
催促 [cuīcù] to urge; to press for; to expedite; to quicken; to hasten
催化剂 [cuīhuàjì] a catalyst
催泪弹 [cuīlèidàn] a tear gas bomb; a lachrymatory gas shell
催眠 [cuīmián] to hypnotize
催眠曲 [cuīmiánqǔ] a lullaby
催眠术 [cuīmiánshù] hypnotism; mesmerism
催索 [cuīsuǒ] to demand urgently

摧 [cuī] (v) 折断，破坏 to break; to destroy; to devastate; to ravage ＊毒品能摧毁你的一生。 Drugs can destroy your life.
摧残 [cuīcán] to trample down; to tread under foot
摧毁 [cuīhuǐ] to smash into pieces; to destroy completely; to shatter
摧枯拉朽 [cuīkūlāxǐu] to smash easily like breaking dry branches; easily overcome
摧折 [cuīzhé] to break off; to snap

cuǐ

璀 [cuǐ] (n) 玉石的光泽 the lustre of gems
璀璨 [cuǐcàn] glittering

cuì

悴 [cuì] 忧伤，不振作 sad; downcast; distressed

啐 [cuì] (v) 用力吐出 to spit

淬 [cuì] 1 (v) 浸于水 to dip into water 2 (v) 锻炼 to temper
淬钢 [cuìgāng] to temper steel; tempered steel
淬水 [cuìshuǐ] to plunge (heated metal) into water and temper

粹 [cuì] 1 (adj) 纯，不杂 pure; unmixed 2 (adj) 精华 essence

萃 [cuì] 1 (adj) 草从生的样子 grassy; thick 2 (v) 聚集 to collect together; to assemble; to gather

翠 [cuì] (adj) 绿色 bluish-green
翠玉 [cuìyù] a variety of jade
翠竹 [cuìzhú] emerald bamboo

瘁 [cuì] (adj) 劳累 care-worn; to be distressed

脆 [cuì] 1 (adj) 容易断，容易碎 crisp; brittle 2 (adj) 声音清楚响亮 (voice) clear and loud
脆薄 [cuìbó] thin and brittle
脆弱 [cuìruò] weak ; friable

cūn

皴 [cūn] (adj) 干裂 chapped; cracked

村 [cūn] (n) 乡间许多人家聚住的处所 a village; a hamlet
村落 [cūnluò] a hamlet; a village
村塾 [cūnshú] a village school
村长 [cūnzhǎng] a village headman
村镇 [cūnzhèn] a village; a townlet
村庄 [cūnzhuāng] a village; a farmstead
村子 [cūn·zi] a village

cún

存 [cún] 1 (v) 在 to exist ＊她心底里存有很多的不满。There exists much discontent in her. 2 (v) 保留 to preserve; to retain 3 (v) 寄放 to deposit; to store; to keep ＊我把储蓄的钱都存放在银行里。 deposit all my savings in the bank.

存备 [cúnbèi] to keep in store

存放 [cúnfàng] to put aside for safekeeping

存根 [cúngēn] the counterfoil of a choque or a ticket

存货 [cúnhuò] goods kept in stock; stock

存款 [cúnkuǎn] deposit; savings

存亡 [cúnwáng] survival or extinction

存心 [cúnxīn] bent on; purposely; intentionally

存心不良 [cúnxīnbùliàng] to harbour evil intent

存在 [cúnzài] to exist

存摺 [cúnzhé] a bank pass book; a deposit book

cǔn

忖 [cǔn] (v) 细想，思量 to ponder over; to consider; to guess

忖度 [cǔnduó] to suppose; to guess

cùn

寸 [cùn] (n) 长度单位 a unit of length; inch

寸步不离 [cùnbùbùlí] not to move a step from; not to let out of one's sight

寸步难行 [cùnbùnánxíng] difficult even to move a step

寸草不留 [cùncǎobùliú] leaving not even an inch of grass (generally used to describe some savagery or brutality)

寸丝不挂 [cùnsībùguà] stark naked

寸土必争 [cùntǔbìzhēng] to fight for every inch of land

寸阴必惜 [cùnyīnbìxī] do not waste a single moment

cuō

搓 [cuō] (v) 擦，揉 to rub or roll between the hands or fingers

搓手 [cuōshǒu] to rub the hands together

搓线 [cuōxiàn] to twist thread

磋 [cuō] (v) 磨制 to polish

磋商 [cuōshāng] to negotiate; to confer with; to discuss; to consult

磋磨 [cuōmó] to discuss in order to learn; to polish; to rub

蹉 [cuō] (v) 差误 to miss; to err

蹉跎 [cuōtuó] to miss the time; to waste time

撮 [cuō] 1 (v) 聚拢，凑合 gather up; bring together 2 (v) 摘取 to pick; to hold between fingers

撮合 [cuō·he] to bring (two parties) together

撮要 [cuōyào] to make extracts; to pick out the important points; extracts; outlines; abstracts

另见 [zuǒ]

cuó

痤 [cuó] (n) 脸上的小疮，也叫"粉刺"或"酒刺" acnes

cuò

措 [cuò] 1 (v) 安排 to put or set in order; to arrange 2 (v) 筹划，筹办 to administer; to execute ＊由他去筹措这件事是最理想的。It is most ideal to let him execute this matter.

措办 [cuòbàn] to arrange; to raise

措词 [cuòcí] wording; phrasing; terms

措施 [cuòshī] measures; steps

措手不及 [cuòshǒubùjí] too late to do anything about

措置失当 [cuòzhìshīdāng] mismanaged; out of place

错 (錯) [cuò] 1 (n) 不正确，不对 a mistake, an error; mistaken; wrong 2 (adj) 交叉 cross

错别字 [cuòbiézì] wrongly written or

pronounced characters; wrong character
错处 [cuò·chu] fault; wrong; mistake; error in conduct
错愕 [cuòè] confused and amazed
错怪 [cuòguài] to blame somebody wrongly
错角 [cuòjiǎo] alternate angles
错觉 [cuòjué] an illusion
错误 [cuòwù] a mistake; an error
错综複杂 [cuòzōngfùzá] complicated

厝 [cuò] 1 (v) 葬 to bury 2 (v) 放置 place

挫 [cuò] 1 (v) 不顺利，失败 to be obstructed; to fail 2 (v) 压下去 to oppress; to repress 3 (v) 降低音调 to lower the tone
挫败 [cuòbài] to thwart; to frustrate; to foil
挫伤 [cuòshāng] to frustrate; to deflate
挫折 [cuòzhé] to suffer a set-back; to be frustrated; setbacks

锉(銼) [cuò] 1 (n) 磨东西的钢制工具，也叫锉刀 a file (tool) 2 (v) 用锉磨东西 to file

D

dā

搭 [da] 1 (v) 支起，架设 build ＊他们正在搭棚。 They are building up the tents now. 2 (v) 附挂，盖 hang ＊把衣服搭在竹竿上。Hang the clothes on the bamboo. 3 (v) 凑在一起 join ＊房租太贵了，要搭伙住才付得起。You have to join with some partners, otherwise you cannot afford to pay the high rent. 4 (v) 配合 match 5 (v) 乘 take a passage, as on a car or a boat. ＊搭车上班。 to take a car to office.

搭伴 [dābàn] travel with other; accompany another

搭救 [dājiù] rescue

搭客 [dā kè] passengers

答 [dā] (v) 回应，反响 echo ; respond

答理 [dālǐ] pay attention to

答应 [dāyìng] promise

另见 [dá]

dá

怛 [da] 1 (adj) 忧伤，痛苦 distressed; grieved 2 (adj) 惊讶 alarmed; shocked

答 [dá] 1 回復 (v) reply; answer (n) a reply; an answer 2 (v) 还，报 return; respond ＊为了答谢陈先生的帮助，她买一些水果送他。 To return thanks to Mr. Chen for his help, she bought some fruits for him.

答案 [dá an] an answer

答覆 [dáfū] answer; respond

另见 [da]

达(達) [dá] 1 (v) 畅通，到 pass through; reach ＊这火车将于下午五时抵达吉隆坡。This train will reach Kuala Lumpur by 5 p.m. 2 (v) 实现 realise ＊他不达到目的是决不罢休的。As long as he does not realise his objective, he will never give up. 3 (adj) 明白，透切 clear 4 (v) 告诉，表示 inform; notify ＊把这消息传达給所有的人知道。 Notify all the people of this news. 5 (adj) 显贵 of dignity; influential

达成 [dácheng] reach; accomplish.

达观 [dáguān] optimistic ; optimism

达意 [dáyì] make one's meaning clear; to the point

鞑(韃) [dá] [鞑靼] (n) Tartar, a tribe in China

打 [dá] (n) 量词，十二个叫"一打" a dozen

另见 [dǎ]

dǎ

打 [dǎ] 1 (v) 敲击 beat; strike＊警察用警棍打他的头。The policeman beat his head with a cudgel. 2 (v) 攻击，战斗 fight ＊军队已把敌人打败了。The troops have defeated the enemies. 3 (v) 取，收 to fetch＊到井边打水。to fetch water by the well. 4 (v) 制作

to make ＊他打刀很熟练。He is skilled in making knives. 5 (v) 捆扎 to tie up ＊打包裹。to tie a bundle. 6 (v) 发出 to issue ＊打个信号给总站。Issue a code to the main station 7 (v) 射击 to shoot ＊士兵在练习打靶。The soldiers are practising shooting at targets. 8 (v) 计算 calculate ＊他是个精打细算的商人。He is a calculating businessman. 9 (v) 立定 establish ＊把基础打好，事情就比较好办了。If the foundation is well established, the matter can be dealt with more easily. 10 (prep) 自，从 since ; from ＊打明天起，广告不用方言了。From tomorrow onwards, advertisements will not be in dialects.
另见 [dá]

打扮 [dǎ ban] dress up; make-up

打草惊蛇 [dǎ cǎo jing shé] not careful in movement, resulting in alerting the opponent

打倒 [dǎdǎo] knock (strike) down; overthrow

打稻 [dǎ dào] thrash

打官司 [dǎ guān·si] go to law; sue

打猎 [dǎ liè] hunting

打劫 [dǎ jie] plunder; rob

打扰 [dǎrǎo] trouble; bother

打胎 [dǎ tāi] abort ; abortion

打听 [dǎ ting] make inquiry; detect

打仗 [dǎ zhàng] fight; go to battle

打桩 [dǎ znuāng] drive piles

打主意 [dǎzhú yì] to plan

打字机 [dǎzìjī] typewriter

dà

大 [dà] 1 (adj) 跟"小"相对 big; huge ; great 2 (adj) 指范围广，程度深 wide ; deep ＊他进大公司工作，希望能大有作为。He goes to work in a big corporation, hoping that he may be able to use his talents widely. 3 (adj) 年长，排行第一 the oldest; eldest ＊大哥。eldest brother.

大便 [dàbiàn] excrement; faeces ; go to stool

大材小用 [dàcáixiǎoyòng] using a talented person in an insignificant position.

大肠 [dàcháng] the large intestines

大吹大擂 [dà chuī-dà léi] make a fanfare of oneself ; ostentation

大胆 [dàdǎn] courageous; daring; fearless

大刀阔斧 [dà dāo kuò fǔ] bold and decisive

大敌当前 [dà di dāng qián] in the face of a powerful enemy

大豆 [dàdòu] soya bean

大发雷霆 [dà fā léi tíng] extremely angry

大方 [dà fāng] generous

大纲 [dàgāng] chief point ; leading principles

大公无私 [dà gōng-wúsī] just and fair

大惑不解 [dà huò bù jiě] do not understand a certain thing

大将 [dàjiàng] a general; an admiral

大惊失色 [dà jīng shī sè] apprehensive

大惊小怪 [dà jīng-xiǎo guài] much fuss about nothing

大局 [dàjú] general situation; present condition

大快人心 [dà kuài rén xīn] to the satisfaction of everyone

大理石 [dàlǐshí] marble

大陆 [dàlù] a continent

大麻 [dàmá] hemp ; marijuana

大麦 [dàmài] barley

大名鼎鼎 [dàmíng dǐngdǐng] a grand reputation; renowned

大气层 [dàqìcéng] atmosphere

大器晚成 [dà qì wǎn chéng] grand talents mature slowly
大煞风景 [dà shà fēng jǐng] dampering one's spirits
大使 [dàshǐ] an ambassador; an envoy
大失所望 [dà shī suǒ wàng] greatly disappointed
大体 [dàtǐ] in general; on the whole
大庭广众 [dà tíng guǎng zhòng] public place with numerous people
大同小异 [dà tóng-xiǎo yì] almost similar, except slight differences
大无畏 [dàwúwèi] utterly fearless
大腿 [dàtuǐ] the thighs
大厦 [dàxià] a mansion; magnificent building
大写 [dàxiě] capital letters; block letters
大显身手 [dà xiǎn shēn shǒu] fully displaying one's capabilities
大小 [dàxiǎo] size; measurements
大学 [dàxué] a university.
大衣 [dà yī] a cloak; an overcoat
大意 [dàyì] general idea; careless
大众 [dàzhòng] the masses
大志 [dàzhì] high aims
大自然 [dàzìran] nature; mother nature
另见 [dài]

dāi

呆 [dāi] 1 (adj) 傻，不灵敏 foolish; stupid 2 (adj) 脸上表情死板 a still state of expression* 她对着死去的儿子发呆，却流不出眼泪。She looked at her dead son without any expression and had no tears to shed. 3 (v) 住，停留 stay * 他在这里呆了半年还找不到工作，所以回家乡去了。He had been staying here for half a year to look for a job; as he failed to find one, he returned to his homeland.

待 [dāi] (v) 停留，迟延 stay; delay * 大家好久不见，多待一会儿才走吧。I have not seen you for a long time. Please stay a bit longer before you leave.
另见 [dài]

dǎi

歹 [dǎi] (adj) 坏，恶 bad; wicked; evil

逮 [dǎi] (v) 捉拿 arrest; seize * 那强盗被警方逮捕了。That robber had been arrested by the police.
另见 [dài]

傣 [dǎi] (n) 傣族，中国少数民族名 a minority tribe in China

dài

殆 [dài] 1 危险 (adj) dangerous (v) endanger 2 (adv) 大概，恐怕 almost; probably 3 (adv) 仅，只 only

怠 [dài] (adj) 松劲，懒散不注意 idle; lazy; negligent; careless * 我们要爱惜光阴，不可怠惰。We should treasure our time and not be idle.
怠工 [dàigōng] go slow at work; slacking at work; slow down
怠慢 [dài màn] carelessly; impolitely; disrespectful; negligent

代 [dài] 1 (v) 替 substitue; replace; on behalf of * 你可以代我写一封信吗？Could you write a letter on my behalf? 2 (n) 同姓相传的辈次 a generation * 他辛苦地赚钱，希望后代有好日子过。He works hard to make money, hoping that the future generations will lead a good life. 3 (n) 历史上划分的时期 a dynasty 4 (n) 地质学的時期 geological eras
代办 [dàibàn] charge' d'affaires; agent; act or do for others
代表 [dàibiǎo] a representative
代表团 [dàibiǎotuán] delegation
代价 [dàijia] price; expense
代理 [dàilǐ] act for agent
代名词 [dàimíngcí] pronoun
代数学 [dàishùxué] algebra
代替 [dàtì] substitute for; instead of
代言人 [dàiyánrén] spokesman

贷(貸) [dài] 1 (v) 借出或借进 lend on interest; borrow; loan

*许多商人都向银行贷款做生意。Many businessmen borrow from the bank to operate their businesses. 2 (v) 推卸，推托 to make excuses 3 (v) 饶恕，宽免 pardon; forgive

贷借对照表 [dài jiè duì zhào biǎo] balance sheet

袋 [dài] (n) 用布，皮，紙等做成的有口盛器 a pouch; a bag; a sack; a pocket

袋鼠 [dài shǔ] the kangaroo

玳 [dài]〔玳瑁〕[dàimaò] (n) 一种海龟，甲可做装饰品 a turtle

黛 [dài] (n) 青黑色的颜料，画眉用。umber-black dye for painting eye-brow

逮 [dài] 到，及 (v) reach (conj) when; until

逮今 [dàijīn] until now

另见 [dǎi]

大 [dài]〔大夫〕就是医生 doctor

另见 [dà]

带（帶） [dài] 1 (n) 束衣物的条子，条状物 a belt; girdle; ribbon 2 (n) 地区 a zone; a region. *沿海一带都长了椰树。Coconut trees grow along the coastal regions. 3 (v) 佩挂，携带 wear; carry *无论去那里都得带你的登记。Carry your identity card with you wherever you go. 4 (v) 引导 lead; bring *带客人进屋里去吧。Lead the guests into the house. 5 (v) 含有，呈献 consists of; show *他心情愉快，面带笑容。He is happy with a smile on his face. 6 (conj) 和，连同 and; together *那个农人养猪带种菜。That farmer rears pigs and grows vegetables.

带兵 [dài bīng] lead troops

带动 [dàidòng] lead in action

带分数 [dàifēnshù] a mixed number (fraction)

带领 [dàilǐng] lead; take into one's charge

带路 [dàilù] lead the way; serve as a guide

带信 [dàixìn] carry letters; carry messages

戴 [dài] 1 (v) 把东西加在头，颈，胸，手等地方 wear; bear; put on (the body) *很多中学生都戴眼镜。Many secondary students wear spectacles. 2 (v) 尊敬，拥护 respect; support *他是个负责任的教师，受到学生们的爱戴。As a responsible teacher, he is respected by the students.

戴帽 [dài mào] put on a cap

待 [dài] 1 (v) 等候 wait *我在期待您的回覆。I am waiting for your reply. 2 (v) 应接 treat * 我們应该待人如己。We should treat others as we treat our selves. 3 (v) 需要 need *她本来就不喜欢出门，这次她不参加旅行团，更不待说。There is no need to explain why she does not join this tour because she actually dislikes outing. 4 (prep) 将要，打算 about; intending to do something. *我正待出门，有人来了。Just as I was about to go out, someone came.

待价而沽 [dài jiá ér gū] waiting to sell at a high price

待聘 [dàipìn] waiting for an employment

待遇 [dàiyù] treatment; dealing; pay

另见 [dāi]

dān

单（單） [dān] 1 (adj) 奇数的 odd (number) 2 (adj) 不复杂

plain; simple ＊那个学生衣着简单。The student is simply clothed. 3 (adj) 独，一个 single; alone＊这房子只租给单身的人。This room will only be rented to singles. 4 (adv) 只，仅 only; nothing but 5 (n) 记载账目的字据 a bill
单薄 [dānbò] thin; poor; weak
单程 [dānchéng] one way trip
单纯 [dānchún] simple; pure
单刀直入 [dān dāo zhì rù] straight to the point; straightforward; direct
单调 [dāndiáo] monotony; dullness; monotone
单独 [dāndú] alone; single; solitary
单方面 [dānfāngmiàn] onesided; unilateral
单价 [dānjià] unit price
单据 [dānjù] receipt; invoice; bill
单枪匹马 [dānqiāng-pǐmǎ] a lone ranger; solitary and unaided
单身汉 [dānshēnhàn] bachelor; single man
单位 [dānwèi] unit
单线 [dānxiàn] a single line (track)
单衣 [dānyī] clothes without lining
另见 [chàn]

禅(襌) [dān] (n) 单衣 clothes without lining

眈 [dān] 〔眈眈〕(adj) 注视的样子 staring at something

耽 [dān] 1 (v) 拖延 delay; impede ＊他因玩乐而耽误了工作。He delayed his work because of merry-making. 2 (v) 沉溺，入迷 be addicted to; indulge in＊她耽溺於赌博，别的事情一概不管。She indulges in gambling and ignores all other matters.

丹 [dān] 1 (n) 朱砂 cinnabar 2 (n) 红色 a carnation or cinnabar colour 3 (n) 配方制成的块状，颗粒状或粉末状的中药 medicinal pills or powder
丹青 [dānqīng] a painting

担(擔) [dān] 1 (v) 肩挑 carry on the shoulder.＊在码头上，不少的工人正担着一包包的货上船下船。At the harbour, many workers carry sacks of materials on their shoulders, loading and unloading a ship. 2 (v) 负责，承当 undertake; be responsible for＊父母亲去世后，一家人的生计由大哥担当。After our parents' death, my eldest brother was responsible for the livelihood of the whole family. 3 (adj) 心里牵挂 be anxious＊我们为他的安全而担心。We are anxious about his safety.
担保 [dānbǎo] be responsible for; guarantee
担搁 [dān·ge] delay
担荷 [dānhè] bear burden
担任 [dānrèn] undertake; take charge
担忧 [dānyōu] bear sorrow; be grieved
另见 [dàn]

dǎn

掸(撣) [dǎn] 1 (v) 拂去 brush away; dust ＊没有人愿意掸掉桌上的灰尘。None of them was willing to brush away the dust on the table. 2〔掸子〕(n) 扫拂灰尘的用具 a brush or duster

胆(膽) [dǎn] 1 (n) 腹内的器官，梨形，分泌绿色汁液，以助消化 the gall 2 (n) 勇气 courage
胆大包天 [dǎndàbāotiān] bold as a lion
胆大妄为 [dǎndàwàngwéi] undaunted and reckless
胆大心细 [dǎndàxīnxì] brave but cautious
胆敢 [dǎngǎn] dare; take liberties; venture
胆量 [dǎnliàng] courage; boldness
胆丧魂消 [dǎnsànghúnxiāo] frighten one out of one's wits
胆小；胆怯 [dǎnxiǎo; dǎnqiè] timid; cowardly; fearful
胆小如鼠 [dǎnxiǎorúshǔ] timid, chicken-hearted

胆战心惊 [dǎnzhànxīnjīng] in terror; terror-stricken
胆汁 [dǎnzhī] bile

dàn

旦 [dàn] 1 (n)天亮時，早晨 dawn; the morning; day-break 2 (n) 天，日 day ＊我的妹妹诞生于一九七〇年的元旦日。My younger sister was born on the first day of 1970.
旦旦 [dàndān] everyday; day by day
旦夕 [dànxī] morning and evening；a short period of time

但 [dàn] 1 (conj) 不过，可是 but; yet; however＊他个子小但是声音大。He has a small build but has a loud voice. 2 (adv) 仅，只 only; merely ＊打字不但要快，而且要准。Typing requires not only speed but also accuracy.
但愿如此 [dànyuànrúcǐ] I wish it to be so

担(擔) [dàn] 1 (n) 担子 burden; a load 2 (n) 比喻担负的责任 responsibility 3(n) 重量单位 a pikul
另见 [dān]

惮(憚) [dàn] (v) 怕 dread; fear; dislike

弹(彈) [dàn] (n) 弓弹，枪弹，炮弹等的统称 a crossball; bullet; a shot
弹坑 [dànkēng] crater
弹丸 [dànwàn] a shot; a ball; a bullet;
弹雨 [dànyǔ] a shower of bullets
另见 [tán]

啖 [dàn] 1 (v) 吃 eat; taste 2 (v)拿利益引诱人 entice with a bait

淡 [dàn] 1 (adj) 稀薄的液体 insipid; diluted; weak, (as of liquids) light in colour 2 (adj) 味道不浓 tasteless; fresh 3 (adj) 不热心 indifferent 4 (adj)颜色浅 light (in colour) 5 (adj) 生意不旺盛 dull in trade
淡薄 [dànbò] thin; profitless; poor; diluted
淡季 [dànjì] slack season
淡漠 [dànmò] calm; cool attitude
淡然处之 [dànránchǔzhì] attend to something unenthusiastically
淡色 [dànsè] a light colour
淡食粗衣 [dànshicūyī] simple living
淡水 [dànshǔi] fresh water
淡味 [dànwei] insipid taste
淡妆浓抹 [dànzhuāngnóngmò] either plainly dressed or richly attired，she looks well

澹 [dàn] 1 (adj) 安静 tranquil; quiet ＊他过着澹泊的生活。He lives a quiet life. 2〔澹澹〕(adj) 水波轻微动荡的样子 slight movement of ripples

诞(誕) [dàn] 1 (v) 出生 come into birth 2 (n) 生日 birthday 3 荒唐，欺骗 (adj) unfounded (v) brag; boast
诞辰 [dànchèn] a birthday
诞生 [dànshēng] be born; give birth to

石 [dàn] (n) 容量单位 a measure of weight ; a picul
另见 [shí]

蛋 [dàn] 1 (n) 鸟类或龟或蛇类所生带有硬壳的卵 the egg 2 (adj) 形状像蛋的 oval- shaped
蛋白 [dànbái] egg-white
蛋白质 [dànbáizhì] aebumen; protein
蛋糕 [dàngāo] cake
蛋黄 [dànhuáng] egg-yolk

dāng

当(當,噹) [dāng] 1 (v) 作，担任 to be; to act as ＊他要当航海家航行全世界。He wants to be a sailor sailing around the world. 2 (v) 掌管主持 manage ＊爸爸妈妈不在的时候，由大姐当家。When my parents are not at home, my eldest sister manages the household. 3 (v) 承担，承受 withstand 4 (conj) 正在那时候或那地方 when; at the time of; during ＊当貓不在，老鼠便游戏。When the cat is away, the mice will play. 5 (v) 应该 ought; should be＊当用就用，只要你不浪费就行了。Use what should be used as long as you don't waste any. 6 (v) 相等，相称 match equally 7 (v) 阻挡 obstruct; hinder; hold back 8 (n) 钟声 the ding-dong of a bell

当兵 [dāngbīng] be a soldier; in active military service

当场 [dāngchǎng] on the spot；at once

当初 [dāngchū] at first; at the beginning

当地 [dāngdì] on the spot; this place；at the place in question

当机立断 [dāng jī lì duàn] decide unhesitatingly in face of emergency

当局 [dāngjú] the authorities; the person responsible for that matter

当局者迷，旁观者清 [dang jú zhě mí, páng guān zhě qīng] the involved persons are confused，onlookers are clear

当面 [dāng miàn] face to face; in the presence of

当年 [dāngnián] in that year

当然 [dāngrán] naturally; as a matter of course

当心 [dāngxīn] beware; take care

当选 [dāngxuǎn] be elected

当之无愧 [dāng zhī wú kuì] deserving full merit

当中 [dānzhōng] in the midst

当众 [dāngzhòng] in the presence of all

另见 [dàng]

裆（襠）[dang] (n) 两裤腿相连的地方 seat of a pair of trousers

dǎng

党（黨）[dǎng] (n) 集团 party; association; club; society ＊政党 political party 私会党 secret society

党员 [dǎngyuán] a member of a party; a partisan; a factionist

挡（擋）[dǎng] 1 (v) 阻拦，抵挡 obstruct; hinder ＊一棵大树倒在路中央，挡住了车辆的往来。A big tree has fallen onto the middle of the road and obstructs the traffic. 2 (v) 遮蔽 cover; keep off 3 (n) 遮蔽的东西 a cover

挡风 [dǎngfēng] keep off the wind

另见 [dàng]

dàng

荡（蕩）[dàng] 1 (n) 湖沼 a pond；a pool 2 (v) 洗，冲刷 wash 3 (v) 清除，弄光 squander；sweep away 4 (v) 摇动，震动 move; shake 5 (adj) 行为放纵，不正派 extravagant behaviour；wild

荡产 [dàngchǎn] squander one's property

荡漾 [dangyàng] the ripplings of water

当（當）[dàng] 1 (adj) 合，适，合宜 suitable; adequate; fitting; proper＊对这件事，他处理得当。He deals with this matter in a proper manner. 2 (v) 抵作，顶 replace, represent ＊为了节省开销，工厂把一个工人当两个人用。To save expenditure, the factory replaces two workers with one. 3 (v) 用实物抵押钱款 pawn

当作 [dàngzuò] replace; regard or consider as

另见 [dāng]

挡（擋）[dàng]〔摒挡〕(v) 收拾；料理 arrange; put in order

另见 [dǎng]

档（檔）[dàng] 1 (n) 器物上的横木或分隔的木条 cross-piece 2 (n) 存放的案卷 official records 3 (n) 货物的等级 the grades of goods

dāo

刀 [dāo] (n) 切，割，削，砍，铡的工具 a knife

刀山火海 [dāo shān huǒ hǎi] the most hazardous place

dǎo

岛(島) [dǎo] (n) 四面环水的陆地 an island; an isle *半島 a peninsula 群岛 archipelago
岛屿 [dǎoyǔ] islands; islets

捣(擣) [dǎo] 1 (v) 用棍棒的一端撞击 pound; beat; hull 2 (v) 冲，攻击 attack 3 (v) 搅扰 disturb
捣臼 [dǎojìu] stone mortar
捣乱 [dǎo luàn] throw into confusion; disturb
捣米 [dǎo mǐ] hull rice in a mortar

祷(禱) [dǎo] 1 (n) 对神或上帝的恳求 prayer (v)pray; offer prayers 2 (v) 盼望，请求的敬词 supplication
祷告 [dǎogào] pray; offer prayer

导(導) [dǎo] 1 (v) 带领;指引 lead; guide; direct *教师们引导学生走向好的方面。 Teachers guide the students onto the correct path. 2 (v) 引，传 conduct *金属品会导电。Metals conduct heat.
导师 [dǎoshī] teacher, tutor, mentor
导线 [dǎoxiàn] a leading wire, fuse
导演 [dǎoyǎn] a director (film acting)

蹈 [dǎo] 1 (v) 用脚踏地;踩 tread on; stamp; trample 2 (v) 按照实行 fulfill

倒 [dǎo] 1 (v) 竖立的东西跌下去 fall; collapse *快跑开，树要倒了! Run away quickly, the tree is going to fall! 2 (v) (事业)失败，垮台 fail; bankrupt * 他的店生意不好，开了不久就倒闭了。His shop became bankrupt shortly after it had opened because of the poor business.
另见 [dào]

dào

到 [dào] 1 (v) 去，往 make way to; go to *我要到吉隆坡去旅行。I want to go to Kuala Lumpur for a tour. 2 (v) 抵达 reach; arrive *还差一个钟头就到目的地了。It takes an hour more to reach the destination 3 (adj) 周密 considerate; hospitable
到处 [dàochù] everywhere; in every place; far and wide
到底 [dàodǐ] after all; finally; in the end
到今 [dào jīn] up to the present; until now
到期 [dàgqī] in due time; expire
到手 [dào shǒu] receive; fall into one's hand; have it in possession
到头 [dàotóu] to the end

倒 [dào] 1 (v) 位置相反 upset; turn over 2 (v) 反转或倾斜容器，使里面东西出来 pour* 倒一杯茶给客人。 Pour a cup of tea for the guest. 3 (v) 往回去 to go back to the original homeland; to go home *我们的方向错了，该倒回头走 We are going in the wrong direction, let's turn back 4 (adv) 反而，相反地 on the contrary *这样倒是不好。 On the contrary, this is no good.
倒行逆施 [dào xíng nì shī] to act against the right principles of the time; act in a perverse manner
倒退 [dàotuì] recede; beat-a-retreat; withdraw
倒置 [dàozhì] put upside down

道 [dào] 1 (n) 路 direction; road *他朝着校门旁那条大道走去。He walked towards the road besides the school gate 2 (n) 方向，途径 path; way *有些人视勤俭为生财之道。Some people think that diligence is a way to riches 3 (n)正义 理由 principle; truth; reason 4 (n) 技术，方法，办法 skill; means; method 5 (v) 说 speak; tell 6 (n) 宗教名 taoist 7 (v) 用语言表示情意 express in words one's feelings 8 (n) 量词 a measure word *他的屋子和大路隔了一道墙。His house is separated from the main road by a wall.

道德 [dào dé] morality; virtue
道歉 [dào qiàn] apologize
道具 [dàojù] settings; scenes; lay-out
道理 [dào li] doctrine; reason; truth
道貌岸然 [dàomào ànrán] solemn and haughty in appearance
道听途说 [dàotīngtúshuō] hearsay
道义 [dàoyì] moral principle
道喜; 道贺 [dào xǐ, dàohè] congratulate upon
道学 [dào xuè] the study of rules; moral philosophy; ethics

盗 [dào] 1 (v) 偷 steal; rob; plunder ＊那些吸毒者想把盗取得来的东西换白粉。Those drug addicts intend to exchange what they rob for drugs. 2 (n) 抢劫财物的人 a robber; a thief; a bandit
盗寇; 盗匪 [dàokòu; dàofěi] rebels; bandits; brigands
盗窃 [dàoqiè] steal; rob; pilfer
盗贼 [dàozéi] a robber, a burglar

悼 [dào] (v) 怀念死者，表示哀痛 mourn; lament; express condolences ＊我们到殡仪馆去追悼死去的老师。We went to the funeral parlour to express condolences for the death of our teacher.
悼惜 [dàoxī] lament; feel great sorrow

稻 [dào] (n) 粮食作物 paddy; rice
稻草 [dàocǎo] rice straw, for fuel, etc
稻谷 [dàoké] unhusked rice

dé

得 [dé] 1 (v) 取到，受到 obtain; get; gain ＊他的做法，深得大家的支持。His action gains much support from all. 2 (adj) 适合 proper; suitable ＊我这本书生字很多，你送的字典非常得用。There are a lot of new words in my book. The dictionary you gave me is very suitable for it. 3 (adj) 得意，满意 proud; contented; self-complacent ＊他很得意於自己的表现。He is proud of his own performance. 4 (v) 可以，准许 allow; permit ＊不得大声说话。Talking loudly is not permitted.
得不偿失 [dé bù cháng shī] the gain cannot compensate the loss
得寸进尺 [dé cùn jìn chǐ] give him an inch and he will take a ell; insatiable; ever greater demands
得过且过 [dé guò qiě guò] living day by day; not caring about anything
得力 [dé lì] capable
得人心 [dérénxīn] be popular
得胜 [dé shèng] win; get a victory
得失 [déshī] success and failure; gain and loss
得势 [dé shì] in power
得手 [dé shǒu] have the upper hand of; success
得天独厚 [dé tiān dú hòu] excellent natural conditions
得益 [déyì] gain; benefit; profit
得意忘形 [dé yì wàng xíng] forgetting oneself in one's elation
得意洋洋 [dé yì yáng yáng] elated triumphant
得志 [dé zhì] realize the wishes; succeed
得罪 [dé·zui] offend; displease
另见 [děi] [·de]

锝(鍀) [dé] (n) 化学元素 an element, technetium, known as Tc

德 [dé] 1 (n) 多指好的思想品质 virtue; goodness 2 (n) 道德 morality; ethics 3 (n) 恩惠 kindness; favour
德才兼备 [dé cái jiān bèi] equipped with virtue and talent
德高望重 [dé gao wàng zhòng] highly respected for one's lofty conduct
德政 [dézhèng] good (benevolent) administration

·de

的 [·de] 1 (part) 用在名词后构成形容词 used after a noun or noun phrase to form an adjective or adjectival phrase ＊这是个真实的故事。This is a true story. 2 (part) 在名词或

代名词后表明属性used after a noun or pronoun to indicate possessive case * 我的 my; mine 谁的 whose 约翰的 John's 今天的 today's; of today 3 (part) 助词，用在句末，表示肯定语气 used at the end of a sentence to express a confirmation * 正义是不可战胜的。Righteousness is invincible.
另见 [dí]; [dì]

地 [·de] (part) 用在形容词后，构成副词 used after an adjective or adjectival phrase to form an adverb or adverbial phrase* 他对写作渐有兴趣起来。 He is gradually interested in writing.
另见 [dì]

得 [·de] (part) 用在动词或形容词后，表示可能性效果或程度 used after a verb or adjective to show either the possibility, or effect or degree * 这么重的箱子他竟拿得起。He can lift up such a heavy box. * 他跑得快。He runs very fast. * 天气热得很。The weather is very hot.
另见 [dé]; [děi]

děi

得 [děi] (v) 应该，必须 ought to; must * 你得想过才做。You must think before you act.
另见 [dè] [·de]

dēng

登 [dēng] 1 (v) 上，升 ascend; mount; go up * 爬山队正在登山。 The mountaineering team is ascending the hill. 2 (v) 记載 register; note * 父母亲带着孩子去登记入学。Parents bring along their children to register for school admission.

登岸;上岸 [dēngàn shàngàn] disembark; go ashore; to land

登报 [dēngbào] put it in the newspapers; insert an advertisement in the newspapers

登峯造极 [dēng fēng zào jì] reach the height of (good or bad)

登陆 [dēng lù] land; journey overland

登门 [dēngmén] call; enter the door

登位 [dēngwèi] ascend the throne; begin a reign

登账 [dēngzhàng] enter in the account books

蹬 [dēng] (v) 踩，踏 step upon; trample

灯 (燈) [dēng] (n) 发光照明的用具 a lamp; a lantern; a light

灯蛾 [dēngé] a moth

灯紅酒绿 [dēnghóng jǐu lù] life of extravagance and moral corruption

灯笼 [dēng lóng] a lantern

灯塔 [dēngtǎ] a lighthouse; a beacon

灯心 [dēngxīn] a lamp wick

灯心草 [dēngxīncǎo] a rush

děng

等 [děng] 1 (n) 品级，程度高低的分别 a class; a rank; a grade * 他的成绩是甲等。 His result is first grade. 2 (adj) 同，一样 equal to; same as * 这两间房子的面积相等。The area of these two houses is the same. 3 (v) 候，待 wait for; await 4 (part) 表示复数 to indicate that the noun is plural * 我等。 We 5 (part) 表示列举未完 et cetera; and others *热带水果有香蕉，山竹，榴梿等。 Tropical fruits include bananas, mangosteens, durians, etc.

等边三脚形 [děngbiān-sānjiǎoxíng] an equilateral triangle

等次 [děngcì] places in a series; rank; order

等待 [děngdài] wait for

等级 [děngjí] rank; grade; class; order

等闲视之 [děngxiánshìzhī] cannot regard it lightly

等于 [děngyú] be equal to

dèng

澄 [dèng] (v) 使液体里面的杂质沉下去 settle *把水澄清了再用。Settle the water before use. 另见 [chéng]

镫(鐙) [dèng] (n) 挂在马鞍子两旁给骑马的人踏脚用的东西 a stirrup

瞪 [dèng] (v) 睁大眼睛 stare at

瞪眼 [dèngyǎn] staring in anger

凳 [dèng] (n) 凳子，有脚没有靠背的坐具 a bench; a stool

邓(鄧) [dèng] (n) 姓氏 family name; a surname

dī

低 [dī] 1 (adj) 跟"高"相对 low*这本书不适合小学低年级的同学看。This book is not suitable for students of lower primary level. 2 (v) 俯，向下垂 incline; lower *她知错了，头也低下来。Knowing that she is in the wrong, she lowers her head.

低产 [dīchǎn] low yielding

低潮 [dīcháo] low tide; ebb-tide

低沉 [dīchén] deep and low

低垂 [dīchuí] hang down

低能 [dīnéng] mental deficiency; imbecility

低估 [dīgū] underestimate

低落 [dīluò] lower; on the ebb

低微 [dīwēi] low; lowly; low and mean

低音 [dīyīn] base (music)

堤 [dī] (n) 用土，石等材料修筑的挡水的高岸 a dike; a dam; an embankment

提 [dī]〔提防〕(v) 小心防备 guard against; take care of; take precaution 另见 [tí]

滴 [dī] 1 (n) 一点一点往下落的液体，也比喻为极少的东西 dripping; a drop; a trickle 2 (v) 液体一点一点地落下或使它落下 trickle; drip; ooze; drop *水从屋顶滴下来。Water drips from the roof.

滴管 [dīguǎn] a pipette

滴水成冰 [dīshui chéng bīng] freezingly cold weather

滴水穿石 [dīshui chuān shí] constant dropping denudes a rock

滴血 [dīxuè] drop blood - a test used to decide relationship

镝 [dī] (n) 化学元素 an element, dysprosium, symbol Dy

dí

嫡 [dí] (n) 家族中血统最近的，亲的 blood relatives

嫡室 [díshì] the legal wife

嫡堂兄弟 [dítáng xiōng dì] first cousins

敌(敵) [dí] 1 (n) 仇人 enemy; rival *猫和老鼠是敌人。Cats and rats are enemies. 2 (n) 相对的，相当的 opponent *这次比赛中，敌队表现优良。The opponent team has excellent performance in this match. 3 (v) 抵挡 withstand; oppose

敌对 [díduì] opposition; defiance

敌情 [díqíng] the condition (movement) of the enemy army

敌视 [díshì] be hostile to; regard with hostility

敌意 [díyì] hostile attitude

籴(糴) [dí] (v) 买粮食 buy grain

籴米 [dímǐ] purchase rice

迪 [dí] (v) 开导 to initiate *启迪 to direct in the right path

笛 [dí] 1 (n) 一种管乐器 a flute 2 (n) 响声尖锐的发音器 a whistle

笛子 [dí·zi] a flute

的 [dí] (adv) 实在 in fact; clearly; actually *他的确没说谎。In fact, he did not tell a lie.

的当 [dídàng] properly; satisfactorily 另见 [·de] [dì]

涤(滌) [dí] 1 (v) 洗 wash 2 (v) 清除 clear; cleanse

dǐ

邸 [dǐ] (n) 高级官员办事或居住的处所 the residence of senior officials

诋(詆) [dǐ] (v) 说别人的坏话 defame; slander *他们两人不合，彼此互相诋毁。The two men have fallen out and they now slander each other.

抵 [dǐ] 1 (v) 顶，当，代替 mortgage; give as equivalent *他用车子向银行抵款。He mortgaged his car for a loan from the bank. 2 (v) 到 arrive at ; reach *日本外长昨日抵新作三天访问。The foreign Minister of Japan arrived at Singapore yesterday for a three-day visit. 3 (v) 挡住 oppose; resist *许多人抵抗不了金钱的引诱，而干起坏事。Many people engage in wrong-doings because they cannot resist the temptation of money 4 (v)（牛羊等用角）顶，触 butt (by horned animals)

抵触 [dǐchù] butt; conflict (clash) with

抵抗力 [dǐ kànglì] resistance

抵消 [dǐxiāo] set-off; offset

抵押；抵质 [dǐyà dǐzhì] give something as a pledge or security

抵借 [dǐjiè] mortgage

抵制 [dǐzhì] boycott

底 [dǐ] 1 (n) 物体的最下部分 the bottom ; base;(prep) below ; under *那凶手将匕首抛落井底。The murderer threw the dagger to the bottom of the well. 2 (n) 尽头，末了 the end *他准备一到月底便向公司辞职。He prepared to resign from the company by the end of the month. 3 (n) 原样或草样 a rough draft 4 (n) 事件的內情，详情 details; the real story 5 (v) 达到 reach; come to

底本；底稿 [dǐběn dǐgǎo] a draft ; a first copy; manuscripts

底数 [dǐshù] a base〔算〕(Mathematics)

底细 [dǐ·xi] in details; the gist; the real story

底下 [dǐxià] under; below; low

dì

帝 [dì] 1 (n) 古时指最高的天神 god 2 (n) 皇帝的简称 the emperor

帝国 [dìguó] an empire ; imperialistic

帝国主义 [dìguózhǔyì] imperialism

帝王 [dìwáng] a sovereign; an emperor

缔(締) [dì] (v) 结合，订立 bind; join; contract

缔结 [dìjié] conclude; bethrothed; engaged

缔约 [dìyūe] contract a treaty

蒂 [dì] (n) 瓜，果跟茎枝相连的部分 a peduncle or footstalk of a flower or fruit

蒂固 [dìgù] firm support

弟 [dì] (n) 同父母的比自己年纪小的男子 a younger brother

弟妇；弟媳 [dìfùdìxí] sister-in-law ; a younger brother's wife

弟子 [dìzǐ] a pupil; a disciple

睇 [dì] (v) 斜着眼看 to look askance

第 [dì] 1 (n) 次序 a series; an order; a rank; a position *他是第二位报名的。He is second (in order) to register. 2 (n) 旧社会官僚的大住宅 a mansion; a residence 3 (adv) 但，只 merely; only (conj) but; however

第三者 [dìsānzhě] a bystander; the third party

第一 [dìyī] the first ; inferior or second to none; the best

第一代 [dìyī dài] the first generation

递(遞) [dì] 1 (v) 传送 transmit; pass over; forward; convey *把我们的问候递送给她。Convey our regards to her. 2 (adj) 顺着次序 successively

递补 [dìbǔ] fill a vacant position

递给；递与 [dìgěi; dìyǔ] give to; hand to

递算 [dìsuàn] calculate proportionately

的 [dì] (n) 箭靶或枪靶的中心 a mark; the bull's eye of a target

另见 [de]

地 [dì] 1 (n) 地球 the earth 2 (n) 指土地，田地，地面 field; ground; land; space 3 (n) 地方，区域 place; locality; territory 4 (n) 地位 place; situation 5 (n) 底子 foundation

地板 [dìbǎn] a floor

地步 [dìbù] a standpoint; one's stand (foothold, ground)

地层 [dìcéng] stratum

地产 [dìchǎn] estate

地带 [dìdài] a zone; a region; a belt

地大物博 [dìdàwùbó] vast land with abundant resources

地点 [dìdiǎn] location

地方新闻 [dìfāngxīnwén] local news ; a local press

地广人稀 [dìguǎngrénxī] vast land but thinly populated

地基 [dìjī] a foundation

地窖 [dìjiào] basement; cellar

地雷 [dìléi] mines

地理 [dìlǐ] geography

地利 [dìlì] advantages of position

地利人和 [dìlìrénhé] favourable geographical conditions and good human relationship

地面；地表 [dìmiàn; dìbiǎo] the surface of the earth

地盘 [dìpàn] the base; the ground

地平线 [dìpíngxiàn] horizon

地契 [dìqì] title deeds for land

地壳 [dìqiào] the earth's crust

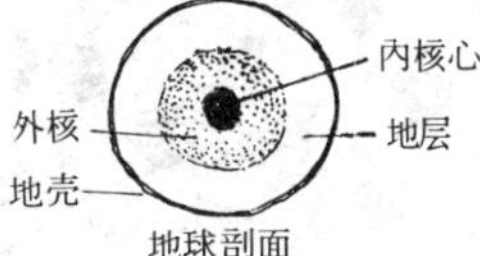

地球剖面

地势 [dìshì] physical features; topography

地图 [dìtú] a map; an atlas

地峡 [dìxià] an isthmus

地下 [dìxia] subterranean

地下铁道 [dìxia tiědào] a subway

地形 [dìxíng] configuration; geographical position

地形线 [dìxíngxiàn] contour

地心吸力 [dìxīn xīlì] gravitation

地狱 [dìyù] hell; Hades

地毡 [dìzhān] a carpet; a rug

地震 [dìzhèn] earthquake

地震学 [dìzhènxūe] seismology

地质 [dìzhì] geology

地址 [dìzhǐ] address

地中海 [dìzhōnghǎi] Mediterranean Sea

地主 [dìzhǔ] landlord; landowner

diān

颠（顛） [diān] 1 (n) 最高部分 the top 2 (n) 木，始 the beginning 3 (v) 摇动震荡 jolt

颠簸 [diānbǒ] joggle; jolt

颠倒 [diāndǎo] overturn; reverse; upset ; turn upside

颠倒黑白，颠倒是非 [diāndǎo hēibái, diāndǎo shìfēi] to distort or confuse

颠覆 [diānfù] subvert; overthrow; upset

颠末 [diānmò] from beginning to end ; the detail

颠扑不破 [diān pū bù pò] indestructible

颠三倒四 [diānsān-dǎosì] topsy turvy

巅（巔） [diān] (n) 山顶，山头 a summit

掂 [diān] (v) 把东西托在手上估量轻重 to assess the weight of an object by supporting it with the hands

diǎn

点（點） [diǎn] 1 (n) 细小的痕迹或物体 a speck; a dot; a spot 2 (v) 用笔加符号 punctuate 3 (n) 钟头 an hour; o'clock 4 (n) 一定的时间 a period 5 (n) 一定的地点或限度 a specified point or limit ＊水的沸点是100°C。 The boiling point of water is 100°C. 6 (v) 表示某种动作 indicate a certain action ＊点头 nod one's head 点火 Light a fire. 7 (v) 查对，检核 check; examine ＊

请你点验送到的货。Please tally and examine the goods sent to you. 8 (v) 指定，启示 point out ＊他是个聪明的人，一指点就明白了。Being an intelligent person, he will be clear once you point out. 9 (n) 点心 refreshment

点菜 [diǎncài] order the dishes; select the dishes; pastry

点名 [diǎn míng] a roll-call

点收 [diǎnshōu] check and receive

点缀 [diǎn·zhui] dot; embellish; adorn

踮 [diǎn] (v) 提起脚后跟，用脚尖着走 tip-toe

典 [diǎn] 1 (n) 标准，法则 rule; law; ordinances 2 (n) 作为依据或准则的书籍 book; records 3 (n) 郑重举行的仪式 ceremony; rite 4 (n) 典故 literary quotations; legends; allusions 5 (v) 典当 pawn; pledge; mortgage

典礼 [diǎnlǐ] ceremony; rite; celebration

典商 [diǎnshāng] pawn broker

典型 [diǎn xíng] an example; a pattern; a prototype

diàn

玷 [diàn] (n) 白玉上的斑点，也比喻人的缺点，过失 a stain; a defect

玷辱 [diánrǔ] bring discredit on; blot; disgrace

店 [diàn] 1 (n) 卖东西的单位 a shop; a store 2 (n) 旅店 an inn; a tavern

店夥；店员 [diànhuǒ; diànyuán] a shop assistant; a clerk

店主；店东 [diànzhū; diàndōng] a storekeeper; a shopkeeper

惦 [diàn] (v) 掛念 feel anxious; think of ＊他在外头工作，却老惦着家里的妻儿。Although he is working elsewhere, he always thinks of his wife and children back home.

惦念 [diànniàn] remember; miss

钿（鈿）[diàn] (n) 镶嵌器物 silver or gold filigree

淀（澱）[diàn] 1 (n) 水浅的湖泊 a shallow lake 2 (n) 液体里沉下来的渣滓或粉末 precipitation, sediment

淀粉 [diànfěn] starch

靛 [diàn] (n) 靛青 indigo

殿 [diàn] 1 (n) 高大的房屋 a hall; a palace 2 (n) 行军走在最后的 the rear of an army

殿廷 [diàntíng] the palace

电（電）[diàn] (n) 实物的一种属性 electricity

电报 [diànbào] telegram; cable

电表 [diànbiǎo] electrometer

电池；电槽 [diànchí; diàncáo] an electric battery (cell)

电光 [diànguāng] a flash of lightning

电话 [diànhuà] telephone

电缆 [diànlǎn] a telegraph cable

电流 [diànliú] electric current

电脑 [diànnǎo] computer

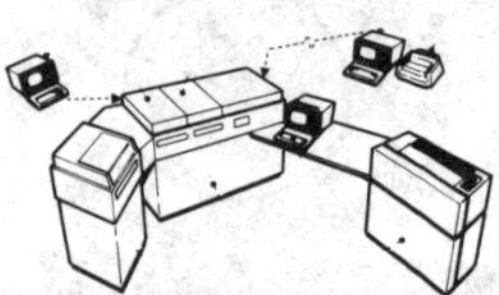

电视 [diànshì] television

电梯 [diàntī] lift

电筒 [diàntǒng] an electric torch

电刑 [diànxíng] electrocution

电影 [diànyǐng] a film; a movie

电子 [diànzǐ] an electron

垫(墊) [diàn] 1 (v) 代人暂时付钱 advance money for another person; pay another's debt ＊既然你的钱不夠，我们先替你垫还。Since you have not enough money, we help to pay for your debts first. 2 (v) 衬在下面 fill up

垫子 [diàn zǐ] cushion

奠 [diàn] 1 (v) 创立，定 determine; put down; settle 2 (v) 向死者致敬 pay respects to the dead ＊我们献鲜花，祭奠第二次世界大战蒙难者。We offered bouquets to pay our respects to the World War II victims.

奠定 [diàndìng] quiet; settled

奠基 [diànjī] lay foundation

奠仪;奠敬 [diànyí; diànjìng] an offering sent to mourners, usually of money

diāo

凋 [diāo] (adj) (v) (草木花叶)脱落 fading; withered; declined; fade; fall (leaves)

凋零 [diāolíng] dwindling; fading

凋落; 凋谢 [diāoluò, diāoxiè] fallen; withered; faded

凋萎 [diāowēi] fade; wither; decay

雕 [diāo] 1 (n) 一种凶猛的鸟 an eagle 2 (v) 刻 carve; engrave; cut＊小学生在肥皂上雕花。The primary students carve figures on pieces of soap. 3 (v) 用彩画装饰 decorate with painting

雕工 [diāogōng] an engraver; a carver

雕刻 [diāokè] engrave; cut out; carve; sculpture

雕像 [diāoxiàng] a carved statue; carve an idol; sculpture

雕琢 [diāozhuó] cut and polish gems

刁 [diāo] (adj) 狡猾，无赖 cunning; wicked; dishonest ＊他为人刁悍，你可别上他的当。He is a wicked and cunning person, don't be deceived by him.

刁难 [diāonàn] obstructive

刁野; 刁蛮 [diāoyě, diāomán] savage; barbarous; unruly

刁诈 [diāozhà] vicious; cunning

刁钻古怪 [diāozuāngǔguài] crafty and queer

貂 [diāo] (n) 哺乳动物 the sable; the marten

貂皮 [diāopí] sable skins; sable fur

diào

吊 [diào] 1 (v) 悬挂 suspend; hang ＊几个黑奴被主人吊着鞭打。Several negro slaves were hung up and flogged by their master. 2 (v) 提取 bring up; draw ＊到井边去吊一点水。Go to the well and draw some water. 3 (v) (n) 祭奠死者或慰问死者的家属 condole with; console; mourn ; condolence

吊床 [diàochuáng] hammock

吊儿郎当 [diào'erlángdāng] take a careless and casual attitude in everything

吊古 [diàogǔ] recall the past

吊桥 [diàogiáo] a suspension bridge

吊慰 [diàowèi] condole; express sympathetic sorrow with

吊孝;吊丧 [diào xiào diào sàng] mourn for the dead

吊唁 [diàoyàn] condole ; lament with another

钓(釣) [diào] 1 (v) 用饵诱鱼上钩 fish; fish with a hook and line 2 (v) 比喻用手段取得 bait; use something as a means

钓饵 [diào'ěr] a bait

钓竿 [diàogān] an angling rod; a fishing rod

钓钩 [diàogōu] a fish-hook; an angle

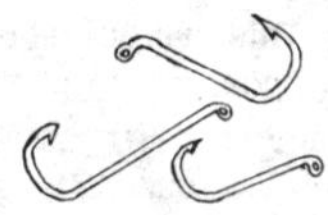

调(調) [diào] 1 (v) 更动，安排 transfer; move＊她跟同事不合，想调职。Unable to get along with her colleagues, she wishes to transfer job. 2 (n) 曲调，音乐的调

子 a tune; a note 3 (n) 声调 a tone 4 (n) 语调 pitch; tone (while talking)
调兵 [diàobīng] move troops
调兵遣将 [diàobīngqiǎnjiàng] arrangement of manpower
调查 [diàochá] investigate; examine; search; investigation
调动 [diàodòng] transfer
调换 [diàohuàn] exchange; change
调虎离山 [diào hǔ lí shān] to lure the tiger away from the mountain
调理 [diàolǐ] arrange as a business; repair; heal
调任 [diàorèn] transfer an official to another post
调转 [diàozhuǎn] change about; put end for end
另见 [tiáo]

掉 [diào] 1 (v) 落下 fall; drop ＊笔掉在地上了。The pen was dropped to the floor. 2 (v) 遗失 lose; miss＊我的钱包掉了。I have lost my purse. 3 (v) 减损，消失 decrease; fade ＊日子久了，衣服会掉色。The colour of the clothes will fade after a long time. 4 (v) 回转 turn back＊前面在修路，车子只好掉头了。Since there are roadworks ahead, cars have to turn back. 5 (v) 落在后头 lag; stay behind ＊你得努力点，才不会掉队。You will not be lagging behind if you work harder. 6 (v) 摇摆 shake ＊那隻狗一见主人就掉尾巴。That dog wags its tail once it sees its master. 7 (v) 对换 change; exchange ＊这双鞋子太大了，可掉换一双较小的吗？This pair of shoes is too large, is it possible to change for a smaller pair? 8 (part) 在动词后面，表示动作完成 used after a verb to show completion of action ＊你不该把好的都吃掉。You should not have eaten all the good ones.
掉队 [diàoduì] drop off; fall out
掉以轻心 [diào yǐ qīng xīn] to treat something lightly

diē

跌 [diē] 1 (v) 摔倒 stumble; slip; fall 2 (v) 下降 decline ＊树胶跌价。The price of rubber has fallen.
跌倒 [diēdǎo] fall down; tumble
跌价 [diējià] fall in price
跌跤 [diējiāo] fall down
跌落 [diēluò] drop
跌伤 [diēshēng] injured by a fall

爹 [diē] (n) 父亲 father; daddy
爹娘 [diēniáng] father and mother; parents

dié

谍(諜) [dié] 1 (v) 秘密刺探军事政治及经济等方面的情报 spy 2 (n) 为敌方探寻秘密情报的人 a traitor; a spy
谍报 [dié bào] spy upon enemies and report on their movements; intelligence; secret dispatches
谍探; 间谍 [dié tàn jiāndié] a spy; a secret agent

堞 [dié] (n) 城上如齿状的矮墙 a parapet; a battlement on a wall

喋 [dié] 1 〔喋喋〕(adj) 形容说话既多又烦琐 talkative 2 〔喋血〕(adj) 形容战争激烈 bloody (battle)
喋喋不休 [diédiébùxiū] to talk on endlessly

牒 [dié] (n) 文书或证件 document; record
牒书 [diéshū] a memorandum
牒文 [diéwén] an official dispatch

碟 [dié] (n) 小盘子 a small dish; a plate
碟子 [dié zǐ] a plate; a saucer

蹀 [dié] 〔蹀躞〕(v) 跨着小步走路的样子 step lightly

鲽(鰈) [dié] (n) 鱼类 a kind of flatfish

迭 [dié] 1 (v) (adv) 交换，轮流 change; alternate; by turns; alternately 2 (adv) 屡次 repeatedly; often; over and over again ＊他们迭挫强敌。They have repeatedly defeated their strong enemies. 3 (v) 重复或重复地堆积 to accumulate; to pile up; duplicate

迭次 [diécì] repeatedly; often, over and over again

dīng

丁 [dīng] 1 (n) 次序的第四 fourth in position; fourth in rank 2 (n) 成年的男子 a male adult ＊壮丁 a strong man. 3 (n) 人口 population 4 (n) 从事某种劳动的人 a servant ＊他是学校的园丁。He is the gardener of the school.

丁香 [dīngxiāng] cloves

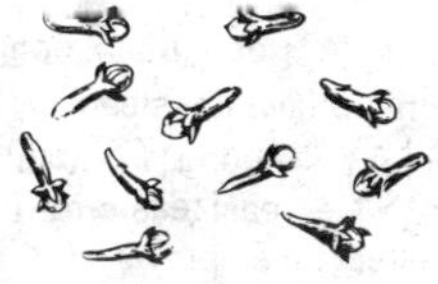

丁字尺 [dīngzìchǐ] T square

叮 [dīng] 1 (v) 追问 inquire into 2 (v) (蚊子等)虫类等用针形口器刺人 sting as a mosquito

叮咛 [dīngníng] instruct repeatedly

叮嘱 [dīngzhǔ] reiterate

盯 [dīng] 1 (v) 注视 observe closely; watch ＊大家眼睛直盯着他。All the eyes are fixed on him. 2 (v) 紧跟，不放松 watch closely ＊盯住他，别让他跑了。Watch him closely and don't let him escape.

钉 (釘) [dīng] 1 (n) 钉子 a nail, a spike 2 (v) 督促 press; urge 另见 [dìng]

dǐng

顶 (頂) [dǐng] 1 (n) 最上面的部份 the top; the crown of the head 2 (v) 用头支承 carry on the head; support with the head ＊那印度人把一篮面包顶在头上。The Indian man carried a basket of bread on top of his head. 3 (v) 支撑，抵住 to support; to hold on 4 (prep) 面对，迎着 against 5 (v) 反驳 rebuke; argue against; run against ＊因为他说话太没有道理了，所以我才顶他。I rebuke him because what he said is very unreasonable. 6 (v) 相当，等于 equal 7 (v) 担当 bear; assume responsibility ＊工作太重，他顶不了。The job is too heavy for him to bear. 8 (v) 代替 substitute for ＊他病了，找个人顶替他吧。He is sick, get someone to substitute for him. 9 (adj) 最，极 extreme; very; topmost ＊我顶喜欢唱歌。I like singing most. 10 (n) 量词 a numerical term ＊一顶帽子。a hat.

顶点 [dǐngdiǎn] the apex; the vertex; the climax

顶峯 [dǐngfēng] peak; top

顶替 [dǐngtì] substitute

顶天立地 [dǐng tiān lì dì] towering (used to describe heroes)

顶撞 [dǐngzhuàng] knock against; charge

鼎 [dǐng] 1 (n) 古代烹煮用的器物。a tripod with two ears; a cauldron 2 (v) 三方并立 take a triangular position 3 (prep) 正，当 during; while

鼎鼎大名 [dǐngdǐngdàmíng] illustrious

鼎立 [dǐnglì] form a triangle; stand in trio

鼎力；大力 [dǐnglì dàlì] great strength; your influence

鼎盛 [dǐngshèng] prosperous; flourishing

dìng

定 [dìng] 1 (adj) 平静，安稳，不动 tranquil; stable; fixed ＊现在局势已定，不能再改了。Now that the situation is fixed, it cannot be changed anymore. 2 (v) 决定，确定 determine; decide; fix ＊让我们事先定好计划。Let us decide on a plan before hand. 3 (adj) 已经确定的，不改变的 fixed; firm ＊这本书必须定期归还。This book must be returned on the fixed date. 4 (v) 事先约好 order; arrange ＊杂货店东让我们先定货，后付钱。The provision shop owner allowed us order goods first and pay later. 5 (adv) 必然 surely; certainly

定价 [dìngjià] fixed price

定居 [dìngjū] settle down

定局 [dìngjú] foregone conclusion

定理 [dìnglǐ] theorem; theory

定律 [dìnglǜ] theory; law

定率 [dìnglǜ] a fixed rate

定形 [dìng xíng] a fixed form; a regular shape

定义 [dìngyì] definition

定约 [dìngyuē] make an agreement; a contract or agreement

定罪 [dìngzuì] condemn; sentence; convict

锭(錠) [dìng] (n) 作成块状的金属或药物 ingot; a cake (medical preparation)

碇 [dìng] (n) 系船的石墩或铁锚 stone anchor; an anchor

碇泊 [dìngbó] anchoring; anchorage; mooring

订(訂) [dìng] 1 (v) 制定 fix; settle ＊按照所订的计划去做吧。Act according to the fixed plan. 2 (v) 约定 arrange ＊我们在放假前就订期去野餐。Before the holidays begin, we have already arranged a date to go for a picnic. 3 (v) 修改 adjust; revise ＊这课本不合时了，需要订正。This text-book is out of date; revision is necessary. 4 (v) 用线、丝等把书页或纸张连一起。to bind books or pieces of papers ＊把这些零散的纸订起来吧。Please bind these loose sheets of papers together.

订婚 [dìng hūn] engage; betroth; engagement; betrothal

订货单 [dìnghuòdān] order sheet; purchase order

订约 [dìngyuē] conclude a treaty

钉(釘) [dìng] 1 (v) 用钉子固定东西 nail 2 (v) 缝缀东西 sew one object onto another ＊衣扣掉了，我得钉一个新的。The button has come off; I have to sew on a new one. 另见 [dīng]

diū

丢 [diū] 1 (v) 失去，遗落 lose 2 (v) 放下，抛开 leave; cast away; throw away

丢下 [diūxià] lay it down; leave behind

dōng

冬(鼕) [dōng] 1 (n) 四季中的第四季 winter 2 (n) [冬冬] 鼓声 sound of the drum

冬瓜 [dōngguā] white gourd

冬眠；冬蛰 [dōngmián, dōngzhé] hibernation; winter sleep

东(東) [dōng] 1 (n)(adj) 方向 the east; eastern 2 (n) 主人 a master; an employer

东奔西跑 [dōngbēnxīpǎo] to bustle about

东道主 [dōngdàozhú] the employer; the host

东方 [dōng·fāng] the east; eastward

东方人 [dōngfāngrén] orientals; Eastern people

东拐西骗 [dōngguǎixīpiàn] swindling everywhere

东家 [dōng jia] the landlord; the host; the employer; the master

东鳞西爪 [dōnglín-xīzhǎo] scattered; incomplete record

东山再起 [dōngshānzaìqǐ] back in power after setbacks

东西 [dōng·xi] articles; things; east and west

dǒng

董 [dǒng] (v) 监督，管理 direct, govern

董事 [dǒngshì] a manager; a director

懂 [dǒng] (v) 明白，了解 understand; perceive the meaning clearly

懂得 [dǒng·de] understand

懂人意 [dǒngrényì] be able to read others' thoughts

dòng

峒 [dòng] (n) 山洞，石洞 a cave

恫 [dòng] (恫吓) (v) threaten; bully; scare ＊那个阿飞在学校附近恫吓学童给他钱。That rogue stays around the school and threatens students into giving him money.

洞 [dòng] 1 (n) 物体中间空着的部份 a hole; a cave 2 (v) 透彻，清楚 understand thoroughly; see through ＊你的一举一动，我都洞悉了。I know thoroughly every move you make.

洞察 [dòngchá] examine thoroughly; discern

胴 [dòng] 1 (n) 大肠 large intestines 2 (n) 躯干 trunk

冻 (凍) [dòng] 1 (v) 结冰 freeze 2 (adj) 受冷或感到冷 cold; icy; freezing; frozen

冻僵 [dongjiāng] benumbed with cold

冻结 [dòngjié] freeze; frozen

栋 (棟) [dòng] (n) 房屋的大樑 a beam; a pillar; a post

栋樑 [dòngliáng] pillars and beams; important people

动 (動) [dòng] 1 (v) 改变原来的位置和状态 move 2 (n) 动作，行动 motion; movement 3 (v) 使用，使起作用 stir; shake; take action; act ＊不要空口谈，得动手做。Don't just pay lip-service; take action. 4 (v) 感触 induce; influence; affect (n) agitation 5 (v) 开始 start ＊这项工程将在下个月动工。Works on the project will be started next month.

动兵 [dòng bīng] go to war; take up arms

动词 [dòngcí] a verb

动荡 [dòngdàng] vibrate; shake

动机 [dòngjī] motive; cause

动静 [dòng·jing] state; condition

动力 [dònglì] motive power; dynamic force

动脉 [dòngmài] artery

动怒 [dòngnù] become angry; enrage

动人 [dòngrén] charming; touching; moving

动身 [dòng shēn] set out; start

动听 [dòngtīng] convincing; pleasant to the ears.

动物 [dòng wù] animals

动武 [dòngwǔ] use force; resort to violence

动向 [dòngxiàng] a trend; movement

动议 [dòngyì] move; propose; motion (propose a motion)

动员 [dòngyuán] mobilize, mobilization

dōu

兜 [dōu] 1 (n) 口袋一类的东西 a sack; a bag 2 (v) 把东西包住，拢住 wrap up an object 3 (v) 围，绕 surround; wind; go round about ＊兜圈子。Go round in circles.

都 [dōu] 1 (adv) 全，表示总括某个范围 all; altogether ＊我们应该对所有功课差的同学都给予帮助。We should help all those classmates who are poor in their studies. 2 (part) 已经 already ＊都半夜了，还不睡？It's already midnight, why don't you sleep?

另见 [dū]

dǒu

斗 [dǒu] 1 (n) 容量单位，十升 peck; measure of 10 pint 2 (n) 量器 a peck measure

斗秤 [dǒuchèng] weights and measures

斗胆 [dǒudǎn] gall as big as a peck measure; be of great courage

斗笠 [dǒulì] a wide rain hat

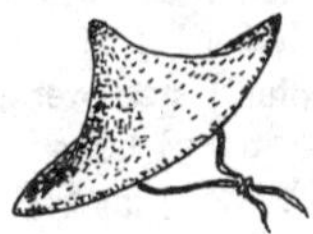

斗室 [dǒushì] a room as small as a peck measure; a small room

另见 [dòu]

抖 [dǒu] 1 (v) 哆嗦，战栗 tremble; shiver ✱ 天气冷得大家直发抖。The weather is so cold that all of us shiver. 2 (v) 振作 cheer; rouse ✱ 同学们抖擞精神，应付考试。The students aroused their spirits to prepare for the examination.

陡 [dǒu] 1 (adj.) 斜度很大 steep; high 2 (adv.) 突然 suddenly; unexpectedly ✱ 近来天气陡变无常，你最好备带雨伞。 The weather lately changes unexpectedly; you had better bring along an umbrella.

陡峭 [dǒuqiào] precipitous

陡然 [dǒurán] all at once; suddenly

dòu

豆 [dòu] 1 (n) 一种食用植物 beans; peas 2 (n) 古代祭器 a sacrificial vessel used in ancient days

豆饼 [dòubǐng] bean-cake

豆腐 [dòu·fu] bean curd

豆酱 [dòujiàng] bean sauce

豆浆 [dòujiāng] bean curd milk

豆蔻 [dòukòu] nutmegs; cardamoms

豆沙 [dòushā] bean cream

豆芽 [dòuyá] bean sprout

豆油 [dòuyóu] bean oil

痘 [dòu] 1 (n) 指全身发生豆子样脓疱的传染病 smallpox 2 (n) 牛痘的简称 cow pox

痘浆;痘苗 [dòujiang; dòumíao] vaccine

逗 [dòu] 1 (v) 停留 stay; delay ✱ 在这次旅途中，我在吉隆坡逗留了两天。During this trip, I stayed in Kuala Lumpur for two days. 2 (v) 引，惹 tempt; excite ✱ 他的动作将我们逗笑了。His action tempts us to laugh.

逗点 [dòudiǎn] a comma

逗留 [dòuliú] stop over for a time

逗弄 [dòu·nong] fidget; disturb; tease

窦 (竇) [dòu] (n) 洞孔 a hole; a burrow

斗 (鬥) [dòu] 1 (v) 冲突，对打 fight; conflict 2 (v) 比赛；竞争 contest; match ✱ 花園里万紫千红，争奇斗艳。In the garden, thousands of flowers in full bloom contest with one another for beauty.

斗技场 [dònjìchǎng] amphitheater

斗力 [dòulì] wrestling

斗牛 [dòuníu] a bull-fight

斗志 [dòuzhì] fighting spirit

另见 [dǒu]

dū

督 [dū] (v) 监管，察看 superintend; supervise; direct; watch ✱ 这份工作由你去督理。You will supervise this piece of work.

督促 [dūcù] press; urge; importune

督工 [dūgōng] supervise the workers

都 [dū] (n) 城市 city ✱ 首都 capital; a metropolis 大都会 a large city

另见 [dōu]

dú

读 (讀) [dú] 1 (v) 念 read 2 (v) 学习 study; learn 3 (v) 求学 study in school

读本 [dúběn] a reader; a reading-book

读物 [dúwù] reading matter; books

读音 [dúyīn] pronunciation

读者 [dúzhě] a reader

椟 (櫝) [dú] 1 (n) 木柜，木匣 a case; a box 2 (n) 棺材 a casket

牍 (牘) [dú] (n) 公文，书信 a note; a letter; a document

犊 (犢) [dú] (n) 小牛 a calf

黩 (黷) [dú] 1 (v) 玷，污，轻慢 defile; insult 2 (v) 滥用 abuse

黩武 [dúwǔ] disposed on war

黩武主义 [dúwǔzhǔyì] militarism

独(獨) [dú] 1 (adj) (adv) 单一，只有一个 solitary; single; alone 2(adv.) 只，唯有 only ✱大家都到了，独有他还没来。All have already arrived; only he is not here yet.

独裁 [dúcái] autocracy; dictatorship; despotism

独创 [dúchuàng] original; creative

独当一面 [dú dāng yī miàn] be solely responsible

独立 [dúlì] stand alone ; be independent; independence; self-support

独立自主 [dúlì zì zhǔ] independent and sovereign

独木舟 [dúmùzhōu] a canoe

独身 [dúshēn] bachelorhood; spinsterhood

独特 [dútè] special; unique

独子 [dúzǐ] an only son

独自 [dúzì] by oneself; one's own

独奏 [dúzòu] a solo

毒 [dú] 1 (n) 有害的东西 a poison; venom ✱色情影片是对观众思想的一种毒害。Blue films are a poison to the minds of the audience. 2 (v) 用毒物加害 posion ✱用药毒死老鼠。Posion rats with drugs. 3 (adj) 狠毒，凶恶 malicious; cruel; poisonous ✱他杀人放火，心肠毒得很。Being malicious, he killed people and set fire on houses.

毒害 [dúhaí] poison; infect

毒计 [dújì] a malicious project; a wicked plan

毒手 [dúshǒu] murderous means

毒刑 [dúxíng] cruel punishment; torture

dǔ

堵 [dǔ] 1 (v) 阻塞 obstruct; stop; block ✱堵住那洞口，水才不会流出去。Block that hole so that the water does not flow out. 2 (n) 墙壁 a low wall 3 (adj.) 闷，心中不快乐 sullen; unhappy 4 量词 a measure word ✱一堵墙。a wall.

堵塞 [dǔsè] block up

赌(賭) [dǔ] 1 (v) (n) 赌博 gamble; gambling 2 (v) (n) 争输赢 make a bet ; betting ✱我打赌今天不会下雨。 I bet that it will not rain today.

赌友 [dǔyǒu] a gambling companion

睹 [dǔ] (v) 看见 see; look at

睹物思人 [dǔwùsīrén] see the article and think of the owner

笃(篤) [dǔ] 1 (adj) 忠实 sincere; true; genuine ✱他对待朋友非常诚笃。 He is very sincere to all friends. 2 (adj) 病重 seriously ill

笃厚 [dǔhòu] honest; straightforward

笃实 [dǔshí] honesty; uprightness; sincerity

笃信 [dǔxìn] earnest belief; believe truly

笃行不倦 [dǔxíngbùjuàn] work diligently without weariness

笃学 [dǔxué] diligent at study; studiousness

肚 [dǔ] (n) 家畜的胃 the stomach of domesticated animals
另见 [dù]

dù

杜 [dù] 1 (n) 杜树，俗称"杜莉" a tree 2 (v) 阻塞 stop; restrict; shut out; keep off ✱我们应该杜绝不良的影响。We must keep off ill influence.

杜鹃 [dùjuān] a cuckoo

杜造;杜撰 [dùzào; dùzhuàn] fabricate; fabrication

肚 [dù] (n) 腹部，胸以下骨盆以上的部分 the belly; the abdomen

肚里 [dùlǐ] in one's mind

肚痛 [dùtòng] bellyache; have a pain in the bowels

肚泻 [dùxiè] diarrhoea
另见 [dǔ]

度 [dù] 1 (n) 计量长短的标准 a measure 2 (n) 按一定的计算标准规定的单位 a degree ✱水的冰点是摄氏零度。The freezing point of water is zero degree C. 3 (n) 限制 a limit 4 (n) 规则，标准 a rule 5 (n) 指人的器量 capacity of mind; generosity 6 (v) 计较，打算的意思 calculate; plan 7 (n) 回，次 times 8 (v) 渡过 spend ; pass

度量 [dùliàng] measure; capacity; capacity of mind

度量衡 [dùliànghéng] weights and measures

度日 [dùrì] spend or pass the day; make a living
另见 [duó]

渡 [dù] 1 (v) (adv) 横过水面，通过 cross; pass through ; across ✱我们的祖先远渡重洋去谋生。Our forefathers crossed seas to make a living. 2 (v) 载运(人，货) 过河 ferry ✱这只船只渡人不渡车。This launch ferries passengers only; it does not ferry cars 3 (n) 渡口 a ford; a ferry station

渡船 [dùchuán] a ferry boat; a passage boat

渡江；渡河 [dùjiāng; dùhé] cross a river

镀(鍍) [dù] (n) (v) 用电解或其他化学方法使一种金属附着到别的金属器物表面，形成一个薄层 overlay with metal; plate; gild

镀金 [dù jīn] plate with gold; gild

妒 [dù] (v) (adj) 忌，恨 be jealous of; be envious of ; jealous; envious

妒恨 [dùhèn] envy and hate

妒忌 [dùjì] envy; jealousy; grudge

duān

端 [duān] 1 (adj.) 正 proper; direct; decent✱老人家都认为女孩子应端坐。Most old folks think that girls should sit in a proper manner. 2 (n) 东西的一头 an end of an object 3 (n) 事情的开头 the beginning of an event 4 (n) 原因 a cause; reason 5 (n) 事情的件，项 a piece of work; a kind of event 6 (v) 平拿着东西 carry; bring

端倪可察 [duānníkěchá] the clue is traceable

端午；端阳 [duānwǔ ; duānyáng] the dragon-boat festival

端详 [duānxiáng] explicit ; in minute detail; giving full particulars

端正 [duānzhèng] orderly; neat; proper; just; upright; dignified

端庄 [duānzhuāng] grave; solemn; dignified

duǎn

短 [duǎn] 1 (adj) 跟"长"相反 short; brief 2 (adj) (v) 少，缺乏 lacking; deficient; be short of 3 (n) 缺点，不足 defect; short-coming ✱你的一个短处是缺乏耐性。One of your shortcomings is the lack of patience.

短兵相接 [duǎnbīngxiāngjiē] engage in a fierce struggle;hand-to-hand fight

短波 [duǎnbō] a short-wave-length

短处 [duǎn·chu]shortcoming

短促 [duǎncù] transient

短见 [duǎnjiàn] a short- sighted view; shallow knowledge; suicide

短跑 [duǎnpǎo] short-distance running

短期 [duǎnqī] a short-term; a short period

短缺 [duǎnquē] a deficiency; in defect

短文 [duǎnwén] short essay

短小精悍 [duǎnxiǎo-jīnghàn] (of writing a speech) concise and forceful

短暂 [duǎnzàn] momentary; twinkling

duàn

段 [duàn] (n) 事物或时间的一节 a piece; a section; a part; a portion; a paragraph

段落 [duànlào] a section; a paragraph; a conclusion; an end; a stage

缎(緞) [duàn] (n) 一种丝织品 heavy silk; satin

缎纱 [duànshā] glossy gauze

锻(鍛) [duàn] (v) 打铁 temper; forge

锻炼 [duànliàn] temper; train; perfect oneself

锻炼本领 [duànliànběnlǐng] improve one's art; train oneself

锻压 [duànyā] forging and pressing

锻造 [duànzào] forge

断(斷) [duàn] 1 (v) 从中间分开 sever; cut off; break off *绳子断了。The rope snaps. 2 (v)断绝，隔绝 discontinue; cut off *隔了几年，我们的旧同学都断了联系。After a lapse of a few years, the links among our old classmates have been discontinued. 3 (v)中止 discontinue * 这两个国家已经断交了。These two countries have cut off relations. 4 (adv) 一定，绝对 certainly; absolutely * 他想破坏我们的友谊，大家断不可信任他。Have no trust in him absoulutely for he intends to undermine our friendship. 5 (v) 决定，判定 decide; judge *在这紧急关头，我们要当机立断。We should take decisive action at this critical moment.

断肠 [duàncháng] heartbroken

断定 [duàndìng] decide; settle; give judgement; conclude

断绝 [duànjué] broken off; cut off; discontinued

断路 [duànlù] block up the way

断面图 [duànmiàntú] a side view; a sectional diagram

断气 [duàn qì] breathe one's last; expire

断然 [duànrán] surely; certainly; positively

断续 [duànxù] come off and on; be intermittent

断言 [duànyán] assertion; declaration; assert; affirm; say (state) positively

断章取义 [duàn zhāng qǔ yì] derive the meaning by extracting a sentence or a chapter in disregard of what preceeded or followed it

duī

堆 [duī] 1 (n) 累积，聚集成的东西 a heap; a mass; a pile 2 (v) 把东西积聚在一起 heap up; store

堆集 [duījī] accumulate; store up; pile up

堆塞 [duīsè] block up

duì

对(對) [duì] 1 (adj) 向着 opposite *我家对面有一间工厂。There is a factory situated opposite to my house. 2 (adj.) 是，正确 correct *星加坡是个发展中国家的说法是对的。It is correct to say that Singapore is a developing country. 3 (v) 回答 answer; respond; reply *关于他自已所犯的错误，他无言可对。He has nothing to reply regarding his own mistake. 4 (prep) 对于 for; towards *运动对身体有益。Sports is good for the body. 5 (v) 核实 check; examine * 记者把一切资料核对以后，才付印发表。The reporter checked all the data before releasing them to the press for publication. 6 (n) (adj) 互相矛盾的两方面 opposed *在国际足球赛中，我方代表遇到强大的对手。In the international soccer match, our national players met with strong opponents. 7 (n) (v) 双，成双的 a pair; a couple; correspond to; pair

对比；对照 [duìbi; duìzhào] contrast; comparison; check; counter view

对不起；对不住 [duì bùqǐ duìbùzhù] excuse me; I am sorry

对策 [duìcè] counter-measure

对待 [duìdài] deal with

对方 [duìfāng] the other side; the opposite party

对付 [duì·fu] deal with; match

对话 [duìhuà] dialogue

对换 [duìhuàn] exchange
对抗 [duìkàng] oppose; confront
对立 [duìlì] confrontaion; opposition; be opposed to
对牛弹琴 [duìníutánqín] it is all in vain
对数 [duìshù] logarithm
对外政策 [duìwàizhèngcè] a foreign policy
对象 [duìxiàng] object; partner; spouse
对照表 [duìzhàobiǎo] a synopsis
对证 [duìzhèng] check; verify
对症下药 [duì zhèng xiàyào] a disease with the right medicine
对峙 [duìzhì] face each other; stand opposite each other; stalemate

兑 [duì] (v) 兑换 ，换取 barter; exchange; give an equivalent
兑银 [duìyín] cash a draft

队(隊) [duì] 1 (n) 行列 a line; a squad; the ranks ＊大家排队出去。All line up in a row to go out 2 (n) 有组织的集体 a party; a company; a team
队伍 [duì·wu] the ranks; a line; a procession

dūn

惇 [dūn] (adj) 敦厚，忠实 sincere; honest; truthful

敦 [dūn] (adj) 诚恳，诚心诚意 sincere ＊我们在乡村里碰到不少敦厚的农家朋友。 We meet many sincere farmer friends in the countryside.
敦睦 [dūnmù] friendly
敦促 [dūncù] to hasten
敦请 [dūnqǐng] to invite sincerely

墩 [dūn] 1 (n) 土堆 a mound; a heap 2 (n) 大而厚的石头，木头等 a huge rock mass, log, etc

礅 [dūn] (n) 厚而粗的石头 a huge rock mass

吨(噸) [dūn] 1 (n) 重量单位，公制一吨等于一千公斤 ton 2 (n) 吨位 计算船只容积的单位。tonnage

蹲 [dūn] (v) 屈膝象坐，但身体不着地 crouch; squat

dǔn

盹 [dǔn] (v) 瞌睡 doze ＊昨晚睡不够，今早在上课时打盹。 Due to the lack of sleep last night, I dozed off in class this morning.

dùn

炖 [dun] (v) 用小火慢慢烧熟或隔水加温使热 stew; boil

钝 [dùn] 1 (adj.) 不锋利 blunt (as a blade) 2 (adj.) 不灵敏，笨拙 dull; stupid
钝角 [dùnjiǎo] obtuse angle

顿(頓) [dùn] 1 (v) 很短时间的停止 pause briefly; stop suddenly 2 (adv) 立刻 immediately; ＊听了我的话他顿时脸色苍白。His face turned pale immediately after he had listened to me 3 (v) 重新整理 rearrange 4 (v) 叩，碰 stamp ＊她一不高兴就顿脚。She stamps her feet whenever she is upset. 5 (n) 次数 a time; a turn ＊他得了胃溃疡之后，一天只吃一顿饭。 After he has suffered from gastric ulcer, he eats only a meal a day
顿号 [dùnhào] punctuation mark
顿时 [dùnshí] at once; immediately
顿首 [dùnshǒu] bow the head

囤 [dùn] (n) 用竹篾，荊条等编成的或用席箔等围成用以贮藏粮食的器物 a grain bin
另见 [tún]

盾 [dùn] (n) 古代打仗时用來防护身体，挡住敌人刀箭的牌 a buckler; a shield
盾牌 [dùnpái] a shield

遁 [dùn] (v) 逃走 hide away; escape
遁辞 [dùncí] an excuse; an evasive answer

duō

掇 [duō] (v) 拾取 pick

裰 [duō] (v) 缝补破衣 darn; patch * 妈妈在补裰破的衣服。My mother is darning the worn clothes.

咄 [duō] 表示斥责 scold

多 [duō] 1 (n) (adj) 数量大 plenty; a great number ; many; plentiful; much 2 (n) 有余 excess; surplus 3 (adj.) 数目在二以上的 more than two in number 4 (adj.) 表示提高或增强 much more; more * 服了药水之后，我感觉好了很多。After taking the medicine, I feel much better. 5 (part) 表示惊异，赞叹或疑问 to express a doubt or exclamation * 那怪物有多大？How large is that monster?

多半 [duōbàn] mostly; probably

多才多艺 [duōcáiduōyì] versatile

多产作家 [duōchǎnzuòjiā] a prolific (productive) writer

多愁善感 [duōchónshàngǎn] much worries and melancholy

多此一举 [duōcǐyījǔ] superfluous action

多多益善 [duō duō yì shàn] the more the better

多方 [duōfāng] by all means; in every way

多情 [duōqíng] passionate;affectionate

多少 [duōshǎo] how many? a certain quantity

多事之秋 [duōshìzìqīu] these eventful days; troublesome

多样 [duōyàng] various

多余 [duōyú] surplus; not necessary

哆 [duō] (v) 发抖，战栗 tremble ; shiver

duó

度 [duó] (v) 猜想，估计 guess; estimate * 别胡乱揣度朋友的用心。Don't simply guess the motives of your friends.
另见 [dù]

踱 [duó] (v) 慢步走 walk slowly; step

踱来踱去 [duó lái duó qú] walking to and fro

夺 (奪) [duó] 1 (v) 抢，强取 seize; take by force; snatch 2 (v) 争取得到的 seize; capture * 强盗从走在前面的妇人身上夺取了一个钱包。The robber seized a purse from the woman who was walking in front. 3 (v)决定取舍 to choose 4 (v) 冲 rush; break open * 犯人夺门而出。The prisoners broke the door and rushed out.

夺标 [duó biāo] win the prize

夺回 [duóhuí] get back by force; recover; recapture

夺目 [duómù] attractive

duǒ

朵 [duǒ] (n)量词 a measure word * 一朵花 a flower

躲 [duǒ] (v) 避开，隐藏 hide away; conceal

躲避 [duǒbì] avoid (meeting); evade

躲闪 [duǒshǎn] dodge out of sight

躲雨 [duǒyǔ] take shelter from the rain

duò

惰 [duò] 1 (adj.) (n) 懒 lazy; laziness 2 (adj)(n) 懈怠 idle ; idleness

堕 (墮) [duò] (v) 掉下，落下 sink; let fall * 飞机堕海。The plane fell into the sea.

堕落 [duòluò] sink; fall into decay ; lose reputation; degenerate

堕胎 [duò tāi] abort; cause abortion; miscarry

跺 [duò] (v) 用脚顿地 stamp

舵 [duò] (n) 控制船，飞机等运行方向的设备 a helm; a rudder

舵把；舵柄 [duòbǎ; duóbǐng] a tiller; a yoke

舵车；舵轮 [duòchē; duòlún] a steering-wheel

舵手 [duòshǒu] a helmsman; a steersman

驮（馱）[duò](n) 骡马等负载的成捆的货物 a load; a burden

驮负 [duòfú] carry a load

另见 [tuó]

E

ē

阿 [ē] 1 (v) 迎合，偏护 flatter; show partiality ＊他其实在阿谀我们，而不是说实话。He is in fact flattering us and not speaking the truth. 2 (n) 凹曲的地方 a depression

婀 [ē]〔婀娜〕[ēnáo] (adj) 柔软而美好的样子 elegant; graceful ＊ 年青的舞蹈家以婀娜舞姿走到台前向观众致谢。The dancer walked gracefully to the front of the stage and thanked the audience.

é

俄 [é] (adv) 不久，时间短促 instantly; presently

俄顷 [éqǐng] in a moment

哦 [é] (v) 吟哦，低声地唱 chant; hum

哦诗 [éshī] hum verses; poems

另见 [ó, ò]

峨 [é] (adj) 高峻 high, lofty; steep

娥 [é] 1 (adj) （女子姿态）美好 graceful; elegant 2 (n) 旧指美女 a beauty (terms used in olden days)

蛾 [é] (n) 昆虫 a moth ＊蛾子直飞向灯火而被烧死。The moth-fly flew directly to the lamp and killed itself.

蛾眉 [éméi] pretty (cresent) eyebrows

锇（鋨） [é] (n) 化学元素 an element; osmium; with symbol os

鹅（鵝） [é] (n) 家禽 the domestic goose; swan ＊ 鸭子和鹅都是会游水的。 Both the duck and the swan can swim.

鹅毛 [émáo] down of a goose; petty trifles

鹅绒 [éróng] velvet

讹（訛） [é] 1 (adj) 错误 false; erroneous ＊请把讹字改正。Please correct the wrong words. 2 (v) 敲诈，威胁 extort; blackmail ＊那群流氓到处讹诈索钱。Those rascals go everywhere to extort people for money.

讹言 [éyán] a lie; a false report

讹诈 [ézhà] extort; blackmail; swindle; cheat

额（額） [é] 1 (n) 眉毛以上和头发之间的部份 the forehead 2 (n) 规定的数量 a fixed number or quantity ＊ 支票上志明金额为二千三百元九角正。 On the cheque the amount was written clearly as "Two thousand three hundred dollars and ninety cents only". 3 (n) 匾 a board with an inscription

额面价值 [émiàn jiàzhí] face-value; par value

额角 [éjiǎo] the temples

额外 [éwài]beyond the stated quantity; excess; extra

ě

恶(惡) [ě]1〔恶心〕(v) 要呕吐 ill ; nauseous 2 (adj) 讨厌得难以忍受,如:可恶 abominable; detestable
另见 [è]
[wù]

è

谔(諤) [è]〔谔谔〕[èè] (adj) 说话正直的样子 outspoken; righteous

愕 [è] (adj) 吃惊,发楞 astonished ; startled ; amazed * 她对这意想不到的事情感到愕然。She is astonished at this unexpected happening.
愕然失色 [èránshīsè] turn pale at being surprised

腭 [è] (n) 口腔上的上膛 the palate

锷(鍔) [è] (n) 刀剑锋利的部分 the sharp edge of a knife or sword

鳄(鰐) [è] [鳄鱼] [èyú] (n) 一种体型大的爬虫类动物 crocodile * 鳄鱼最喜欢吃死的鸡和鸭。Crocodiles are fond of eating dead chickens and ducks.

鹗(鶚) [è] (n) 俗称"鱼鹰",鸟类 the fish hawk

萼 [è] (n) 花蕊在花瓣下部的一圈绿色小片 the calyx

厄 [è] 1 (n) 困苦,灾难 distress; difficulty (adj) distressed,difficult * 长期的干旱,使农民惨遭厄运。A long spell of drought causes the farmers to face difficulties. 2 (v) 阻塞 obstruct 3 (n) 险要的地方 a dangerous spot
厄运 [èyùn] miserable condition

扼 [è] 1 (v) 用力掐住,抓住 clutch; seize 2 (v) 把守,控制 hold; control * 英勇的士兵,扼守着小镇,不肯投降。Refusing to surrender, the brave soldiers held on to the control of the town.
扼要 [èyào] hold a strategical position , gist of a text
扼制 [èzhì] control ; hold

呃 [è] (v) 打嗝 hiccough; be affected with hiccup

遏 [è] (v) 阻止 stop ; check; prevent * 既然你知道他交上坏朋友,就应该遏止他跟那些人来往。Since you know that he befriends bad companies, you should stop him from mixing with such people.
遏禁 [èjìn] prevent ; prohibit
遏制 [èzhì] put down; repress

恶(惡) [è] 1 (adj) 坏的,不好 bad; wicked * 迟到是个恶习。Impunctuality is a bad habit. 2 (adj) 凶狠 malicious; fierce * 我们要提防他家门口的那只恶狗,它会咬伤人的。We must watch out for the fierce dog in front of his door ; it may bite and injure you. 3 (n) 极坏的事或犯罪行为 evil; wickedness * 他的恶行是不可原谅的。The evil he had done is unpardonable.
恶毒 [èdú] malignant ; malicious; vicious
恶感 [ègǎn] feeling of hatred; ill feeling
恶棍 [ègùn] bad characters
惡果 [èguǒ] evil results of evil doing
恶化 [èhuà] growing worse ; deteriorate
恶疾 [èjí] noxious disease
恶劣 [èliè] very bad
恶语中伤 [èyǔzhōngshāng] slander ;
恶习 [èxí] bad habits
恶心 [èxīn] evil intention; evil thoughts
恶性 [èxìng] malignant
恶意 [èyì] bad intentions; malice
恶运 [èyùn] bad fortune; ill luck; an evil fate

恶作剧 [ezuoju] mischievous tricks or practices; play pranks
另见 [wù]
[ě]

噩 [è] (adj) 惊人的,可怕的 startling; surprising
噩耗 [èhào] startling news (unlucky); as of death
噩梦 [èmèng] a dreadful nightmare

饿 (餓) [è] (n) (adj) (v) 肚子空,想吃东西 hunger; starvation; starved; hungry; suffer from hunger *孩子饿了,哭着要找妈妈。The child was hungry, and kept crying for his mother.
饿死 [èsǐ] be starved to death; die of hunger

ēi

欸 (誒) [ēi] (interj) 叹词,表示招呼 to acknowledge someone * 欸,你上哪儿去。Hi, where are you going?

éi

欸 (誒) [éi] (interj) 叹词,表示诧异 to express surprise *欸,他怎么这久还不回来?Why hasn't he returned after so long?

èi

欸 (誒) [èi] (interj) 叹词,表示答应或同意 to express approval or agreement *欸,就这么办。Alright, do it this way.

ēn

恩 [ēn] (n) 好处,深情厚谊 benevolence; affection; kindness *我们不要忘记父母亲给予我们的养育之恩。We must not forget the sincere love given us by our parents.
恩仇 [ēnchóu] love and hatred
恩惠 [ēnhuì] kindness; favour; grace
恩人;恩主 [ēnrén, ēnzhǔ] a benefactor

èn

摁 [èn] (v) 用手按 to press with the hand*要摁电钮门才会开。Press the button so that the door will open.

ér

而 [ér] 1 (conj) 连接同类的词…and *他是个聪明而勇敢的士兵。He is a clever and brave soldier. 2 (conj) 把表示时间的词连接到动词 to connect a phrase with a verb *一般上农人都是日出而作。Most farmers start work at sunrise. 3 (prep) 从…到 from… to *自小学而中学,她的功课一向很好。From primary school to secondary school her studies have been very good
而且 [érqiě] furthermore; moreover

儿 (兒) [ér] 1 (n) 小孩 a child; an infant *儿童们过着快快乐乐的日子。The children are passing their time happily. 2 (n) 男孩子 son 3 (n) 人 a person *他是运动健儿。He is a strongman in sports 4 (part) 用作词尾 used at the end of a phrase *花儿 flowers, *鱼儿 fishes.
儿女 [érnǚ] children; sons and daughters
儿孙 [érsūn] children and grandchildren; posterity
儿童 [értóng] children; child
儿戏 [érxì] child's play; trifling

ěr

耳 [ěr] 1 (n) 听声音的器官 the ear 2 (adv) 而已,罢了 that's all; only

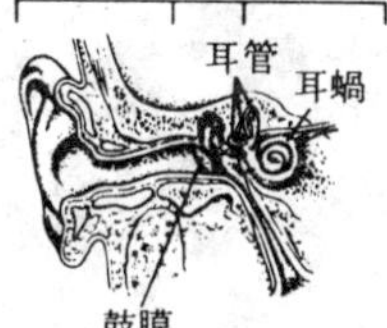

耳孔 [ěrkǒng] aperture of the ear
耳聋 [ěrlóng] deaf; hard of hearing
耳目一新 [ěr mù yī xīn] everything is new
耳濡目染 [ěr rú mù rǎn] influence of surroundings
耳闻目睹 [ěr wén mù dǔ] what one hears and sees

耳语 [ěryǔ] whisper

饵(餌) [ěr] 1 (n) 糕饼 cakes; meat dumpling 2 (n) 钓鱼用的鱼食 a bait 3 (n) 引诱 an enticement

饵敌 [ěrdí] entice the enemy

尔(爾) [ěr] 1 (pron) 你，你的 you; your ∗ 尔父 your father. 2 (pron) 那个(时间) that (referring to time) ∗ 尔时 that time. 3 (part) 用作词尾 used at the end of a phrase 4 (part) 那么样；有时 like that; like this ∗ 他的古典音乐造诣，也不过尔尔。His achievement in classical music is just like that.

尔等 [ěrděng] all of you

尔虞我诈 [ěryuwǒzhà] mutual cheating

迩(邇) [er] (pron) 近 near; close ∗ 他的名字遐迩皆知。His name is known everywhere - far and near.

èr

二 [èr] (n) 数词 two ∗ 二人在公园里游玩，把世上一切烦恼都忘到干干净净了。The two had fun in the public park and forgot all the troubles in the world.

二八年华 [èrbāniánhuá] in one's teens

二重人格 [èrchóngréngé] double personality

二者 [èrzhě] both

貳 [er] (n) "二"的大写 second

F

fā

发（發） [fā] 1 (v)射出 send forth; fire; shoot ＊印度发射了一颗人造卫星。India sent forth a satellite. 2 (v) 分给，付出，送出 give out; issue ＊校長发信通知同学在假期间回校。The headmaster issued letters to notify the students to come back to school. 3 (v) 产生，生出 happen; grow 4 (v) 揭露，暴露 disclose; reveal; expose ＊这部电影揭发了商界的黑暗。This movie exposes the corruptions of the commercial world. 5 (v) 显现 show ＊他见到警察就脸色发白。He shows paleness at the sight of police. 6 (v) 表达 express ＊他拒绝在会议上发表自己的意见。He refused to express his views in the meeting. 7 (v) 派遣 dispatch; discharge. ＊两国已发兵到边境备战。Both nations have dispatched their troops to the border in preparation for war.
另见 [fà]

发报机 [fābàojī] telegraph-transmitter

发表 [fābiǎo] reveal; publish; make public; announce

发布 [fābù] issue; announce

发愁 [fāchóu] become sad; sullen; worried

发达 [fādá] prosper; make progress

发呆 [fādāi] stunned

发电 [fā diàn] send a telegram; cable ;generate electricity

发动 [fadòng] start move; put in motion; set on foot

发动力 [fadònglì] motive power (force)

发抖 [fādǒu] shiver; shudder; tremble

发奋 [fāfèn] make great efforts; exert one's energy

发愤图强 [fāfèntúqiáng] resolve to be prosperous and strong

发疯 [fāfēng] lose one's senses; frantic;

发福 [fāfú] be in good health; grow fat

发光 [fāguāng] radiate; emit light ;luminous

发行 [fāháng] sell wholesale ;publish ;distribute ; put in circulation

发号施令 [fā hào shī lìng] issuing directives and orders

发慌 [fāhuāng] be flurried; be perturbed

发挥 [fāhuī] work out in full; display

发火；发怒 [fā huǒ fā nù] become angry

发掘 [fājué] excavate; unearth; dig

up

发觉 [fājué] disclose; discover; detect

发冷 [fālěng] shiver

发霉 [fāméi] mould

发明 [fā míng] invent; publish an original idea; invention

发难 [fānàn] be the first to start revolt

发脾气 [fāpíqì] fly into a rage

发起 [fāqǐ] promote; originate; start

发起人 [fāqǐrén] a founder; a promoter

发人深省 [fārénshēnxǐng] something to think deeply about

发热；发烧 [fārè; fā shāo] be feverish; have an attack of fever

发誓 [fāshì] take an oath; swear

发售 [fāshòu] offer for sale; put on sale

发问 [fāwèn] question

发现 [fāxiàn] come to light; manifest; appear; discover

发泄 [fāxiè] give free vent to

发炎 [fāyán] inflamed

发扬 [fāyáng] make known; raise; promote

发扬光大 [fā yángguāngdà] bring to light; glorify

发言人 [fāyánrén] a spokesman

发音 [fā yīn] pronunciation

发育 [fāyù] grow; develop

发展 [fāzhǎn] extend; develop

fá

伐 [fá] 1 (v) 砍 cut down 2 (v) 敲打 beat; strike 3 (v) 攻打 attack; invade. 4 (v) 自夸 brag; boast

伐木 [fámù] fell trees ; lumbering

垡 [fá] (v) 翻耕土地，也指翻耕过的土地 till the earth

筏 [fá] (n) 用竹子，兽皮等制成的水上交通工具 a bamboo raft

筏渡 [fádù] a ferryboat

阀(閥) [fá] (n) 由于握有势力而在某一方面有特殊支配地位的个人或集团 clique with influential powers ＊军阀统治的国家，时常会发生内战。Countries which are ruled by warlords are likely to have civil wars at times.

乏 [fá] 1 (adj) 缺少 defective; deficient; insufficient; short of ;poor; (prep) without; in want of ＊通晓两种语文的学生，不乏其人。We are not short of students who understand two languages. 2 (adj) 疲倦 weary; fatigued; tired; exhausted ＊ 工作了一整天，我感到很疲乏。After having worked for one whole day, I felt very tired.

乏术 [fáshù] at the end of one's wits

乏味 [fáwèi] monotony; insipid

罚(罰) [fá] (v) 对犯规，犯错误或犯罪的人进行处分 punish; fine; forfeit ＊他因驾快车而被罚款。 He was fined for speeding.

罚金 [fájīn] a fine; a penalty

罚款 [fákuǎn] fine; impose fine

fǎ

法 [fǎ] 1 (n) 国家的规制 law; statute. ＊新加坡目前正在实施禁止吸毒的法律。 The law against drug-taking is now in force in Singapore. 2 (n) 办事的道理 ways; methods; means 3 (n) 标准，样子，可以仿效的 precedent; model (v) imitate; take as an example

法案 [fǎ àn] law; bill; the act of congress

法定 [fǎdìng] legal; authorized; prescribed by law

法定年龄 [fǎ dìng nián líng] legal age

法官 [fǎguān] a judge; a judicial officer

法规 [fǎguī] a rule; a regulation

法郎 [fǎláng] the franc, unit of money in France, Belgium and Switzerland
法令 [fǎlíng] laws and ordinances
法庭 [fǎtíng] law court; court of justice
法网 [fǎwǎng] the meshes of law; justice
法西斯主义 [fǎxīsī zhǔyì] Fascism
法子;方法 [fǎ·zi ; fāng fǎ] means; ways; method

砝 [fǎ]〔砝码〕(n) 天平和磅秤上用作重量标准的金属片(块) metal weights used in a balance or weighing machine

fà

发(髮) [fà] (n) 头发 hair ＊学生不应该留长头发。Students should not keep long hair.
发妻 [fàqī] a wife
另见 [fā]

fān

番 [fān] 1 (n) 遍数,次数 a turn; a time ＊ 那么重要的事,你必须思考一番才做。You must take time to consider before you do such an important task. 2 (n) 旧时对外国或外族的通称 an archaic term for foreigners; aborigines; savages
番茄 [fānqié] the tomato
番石榴 [fān shí liú] guava
番薯 [fānshǔ] sweet potato

幡 [fān] (n) 古代用竹竿等挑起来直挂的长条形旗子 streamers hung before a shrine

翻 [fān] 1 (v) 反转 turn over; upset ＊ 車翻了。The car turned over. 2 (v) 越过 cross ＊走这条路必须翻山越岭很不容易。It is not easy to move along this route as it crosses mountain ranges. 3 (v) 翻译 translate
翻案 [fān àn] reverse a judgement
翻船 [fānchuán] capsize a boat
翻来复去 [fānláifùqù] toss and turn
翻脸 [fān liǎn] fall out
翻腾 [fānténg] upset; overturn everything
翻天覆地 [fān tiān fù dì] vast and thorough (changes)
翻印;翻版 [fānyìn, fānbǎn] reprint; infringe a copyright
翻阅 [fānyuè] turn over the leaves of a book and read it

蕃 [fān] (n) 指外国或外族 foreigners; aborigines
另见 [fán]

藩 [fān] 1 (n) 篱笆 a fence; a hedge 2 (n) 封建时代指属国 a feudal state; a vassal state
藩邦;藩属 [fānbāng; fānshǔ] an outlying dependent state
藩域 [fānyù] the frontier

帆 [fān] (n) 挂在船桅上,凭借风力使船行动的布篷 a sail; canvas
帆布 [fānbù] canvas ;sailcloth
帆船 [fānchuán] sailing vessels; a sail

fán

璠 [fán] (n) 美玉 a jade

燔 [fán] (v) 烧,炙 burn; roast meat for sacrifice

蹯 [fán] (n) 兽类的脚掌 paws

蕃 [fán] 1 (adj) 茂盛 luxuriant; flourishing ＊这里草木蕃盛,空气清新。There is luxuriant greenery here and the air is fresh. 2 (adj) 繁多 numerous; plentiful; plenty. (v) multiply; breed; produce ＊这样的环境,适合任何生物蕃殖。This environment is suitable for any living creatures to breed and multiply.
另见 [fān]

凡 [fán] 1 (adj) 不出奇,平常 common; usual ＊他立志做个平凡而有用的人。He aims to be a common but useful person. 2 (adj) 所有的；任何 all; every; any ＊凡事都得三思而后行。 Think before you leap when you deal with any problem.

凡士林 [fánshìlín] vaseline

凡人 [fánrén] mortals; mankind; human beings

凡事 [fán shì] everything ,all affairs

凡事预则立，不预则废 [fánshì yù ze lì, bùyù zéfèi] Things will be established with preparation but be ruined without it.

凡庸 [fán yōng] ordinary ; mediocre

钒(釩) [fán] (n) 化学元素 an element, vanadium, symbol V

繁 [fán] (adj) 多而复杂 many; numerous; abundant ＊百货公司的物品种类繁多，但价格并不便宜。In the emporium, there are great varieties of things, but the prices are in no way cheap.

繁华 [fánhuá] show; pomp; display; gaiety

繁忙 [fánmáng] busy; pressure of business

繁荣 [fán róng] abundant and flourishing, as of the growth of flowers; prosperity

繁盛 [fánshèng] prosperity ; flourish

繁文缛节 [fán wén rù jié] redtapism; multiplicity of formalities and ceremonies

繁杂 [fánzá] complexity; complication

繁殖 [fánzhí] breed; increase; multiply by reproduction

烦(煩) [fán] 1 (adj) 苦闷，急躁 troubled; distressed. (n) trouble; vexation ＊她很烦恼，想放声大哭。 She is distressed and wants to cry aloud. 2 (adj) 又多又乱 troublesome 3 (adj) 厌烦 annoyed; bothered 4 (part) 表示请，托的敬词 a polite form of requesting another person to do an errand ＊烦你替我买书。 Please buy books for me.

烦虑 [fánlǜ] anxious; concerned

烦闷 [fánmèn] perplexed; vexed; grieved; annoyed; depressed

烦恼 [fánnǎo] worries; vexation

烦碎；烦琐 [fánsuì, fánsuǒ] troublesome; trivial and vexing

樊 [fán] 1 (n) 笼子 cage 2 (n) 篱笆 fence

fǎn

反 [fǎn] 1 (adj) 跟"正"相对 contrary; opposite 2 (adv) 不赞成 against; oppose ＊有一个工友因为反对厂方的条例而被开除。 A worker was sacked because he opposed the rules of the factory. 3 (v) 翻转，倒过来 turn ＊在最后的一场比赛中，我队反败为胜。 In the last round of the match, our team turned defeat into victory. 4 (conj) 和原来的或预想的不同 but; on the contrary ＊他受了挫折，反而更努力工作。 He was frustrated but he worked harder.

反霸 [fǎnbà] anti-hegemony

反比例 [fǎnbǐlì] inverse proportion

反驳 [fǎnbó] retort; refute

反常 [fǎncháng] out of order; unusual

反动 [fǎndòng] reactionary

反对 [fǎnduì] oppose; object to

反而 [fǎn'er] on the contrary; instead

反覆 [fǎnfù] repeatedly; reiterate

反覆无常 [fǎn fù wú cháng] inconsistent

反戈一击 [fǎngēyījí] turn round and hit back

反话 [fǎnhuà] irony; ironical

反悔 [fǎnhuǐ] repent; retract

反击 [fǎnjī] a counter-attack; a

counter-charge
反抗 [fǎnkàng] defy; oppose; resist
反面 [fǎnmiàn] the opposite side; the other side; turn the cold shoulder
反面人物 [fǎn miàn rén wù] negative character
反目 [fǎnmù] squabble
反叛 [fǎnpàn] revolt; rebel
反射 [fǎnshè] reflect; reflection
反射作用 [fǎnshèzuòyòng] reflex action
反问 [fǎnwèn] interrogate
反响 [fǎnxiǎng] an echo; the reverberation of sound
反省 [fǎnxǐng] reflection; collect one's thought
反应 [fǎnyìng] reaction
反之 [fǎnzhī] on the other hand
反作用 [fǎnzuòyòng] reaction

返 [fǎn] (v) 回，回来 return; go back; come back ✱许多在外边工作的人都返家吃团圆饭。 Most people who work outside return home to take the reunion dinner.
返老还童 [fǎn lǎo huán tóng] rejuvenation; second childhood

fàn

饭(飯) [fàn] 1 (n) 煮熟的谷类食品 cooked rice ✱ 符先生的女儿太小，不会吃饭。Mr. Foo's daughter is very young, she does not know how to eat rice. 2 (n) 每日定时吃的食物 a meal

贩(販) [fàn] 1 (v) 出卖 buy and sell; trade; traffic ✱ 贩卖毒品是非法的。It is illegal to traffic drugs. 2 (n) 买卖货物的人 a peddlar ✱ 小贩。 a hawker.

范(範) [fàn] 1 (n) 模子 a pattern 2 (n) 榜样 a model; a standard ✱ 她那乐於助人的精神是我们的模范。 Her helpfulness sets a model for us.
范畴 [fànchóu] category
范围 [fànwéi] limit; scope; range

犯 [fàn] 1 (v) 违反，抵触 violate; offend ✱ 乱丢废物是犯法的。 Littering is violation of the laws. 2 (n) 犯罪的人 a criminal; an offender 3 (v) 侵犯 invade; infringe ✱把犯境的敌人赶走。 Chase off the enemies who have infringed into the frontiers. 4 (v) 发作，发生 commit ✱犯了错误要敢于承认。 One should be brave to admit the mistake one has committed.
犯规 [fàn guī] break through a rule or custom; violate regulations
犯罪 [fàn zuì] commit a crime

梵 [fàn] (n) 有关佛教的 Brahma
梵刹;梵宫 [fànshà; fàngōng] a Buddhist monastery
梵语 [fànyǔ] Sanskrit
梵咒 [fànzhoù] prayers and charms of Buddhists

泛 [fàn] 1 (v) 浮在水面上 float; drift ✱ 泛舟 Float a boat. 2 (v) 透出，露出 penetrate; expose ✱ 黑暗的天空泛出红光。 Red rays penetrate through the dark sky. 3 (adj) 普遍的，一般的 common; general ✱上地理课时，老师让我们对世界有个广泛的概念。 Our teacher let us have a general view of the world during geography lessons. 4 (adj) 不切实，不深 vague ;superficial
泛谈 [fàntán] a general talk
泛交 [fànjiāo] a superficial acquaintance
泛滥 [fànlàn] overflow; inundation; flood
泛论 [fànlùn] a general remark
泛言之 [fàn yán zhī] spoke of it in general terms
泛游 [fànyóu] wander aimlessly

fāng

方 [fāng] 1 (n) 四边形 a four-sided shape 2 (n) 向 direction 3 (n) 面；边 * 在这场比赛中，我方的水平比对方高。In this match, the standard of our side is higher than that of the opposite. 4 (n) 方法 a way; a plan *千方百计。all ways and means. 5 (n) 治病的药单 a prescription 6 (adv) 正，刚 just now; just then

方案 [fāng àn] a plan; a scheme; a device

方便 [fāngbiàn] convenient; beneficial; general advantage

方才 [fāngcái] a moment ago

方程式 [fāngchéngshì] an equation

方寸不乱 [fāngcùnbúluàn] presence of mind

方式 [fāngshì] an established form; a formula

方兴未艾 [fāng xīng wèi ài] rising and unabating

方言 [fāngyán] a dialect

方针 [fāngzhēn] a policy; the aim; an object in view

方正 [fāngzhèng] good; upright; just; righteous

方锥形 [fāng zhuīxíng] a pyramid

坊 [fāng] 1 (n) 街道的名称 a lane; an alley; a street 2 (n) 牌坊 a monument

坊市 [fāngshì] market place

另见 [fáng]

妨 [fāng] (v) 妨害 hinder; obstruct; interfere with; injure *你站在路中央，会妨碍交通。Standing in the middle of the road , you will obstruct the traffic.

妨害 [fānghài] hinder; disturb; obstruct one from doing

钫(鈁) [fāng] (n) 化学元素 an element, francium, fr

芳 [fāng] 1 (adj) 香，香味 fragrant; sweet-scented; aromatic * 那位小姐走过之后，空气中仍弥漫着浓郁的芳香。After that lady had passed by, there remained a strong fragrance in the air. 2 (adj) 比喻人的美好的德行 virtuous; good, said of reputation or morals * 万古流芳 The good reputation will live on with the time.

芳名 [fāngmíng] your honoured name

芳草 [fāngcǎo] fragrant plants

fáng

防 [fáng] 1 (v) 预先准备，避免损害 guard against; prevent; protect from *这些设备是防火的。These facilities are protections against fire. 2 (n) 关于守卫的设备或工作 defence; protection * 国防对每个国家都重要。National defence is important to every country. 3 (n) 堤，挡水的建筑物 a dyke

防不胜防 [fáng bú shèng fàng] impossible to take precaution against

防弹 [fángdàn] bullet-proof

防盗 [fángdào] guard against robbers

防腐剂 [fángfǔjì] antiseptic; a preservative

防空 [fáng kōng] air defence

防老 [fánglǎo] provide against old age

防守 [fángshǒu] guard; protect; defend

防水 [fángshuǐ] waterproof

防疫 [fángyì] prevention of epidemics

防御 [fángyù] defend; safeguard

防止 [fáng zhǐ] prevent; guard (take precautions) against; prohibit; check

坊 [fāng] (n) 某些小手工业的工作场所 a store; a workshop
另见 [fāng]

肪 [fáng] (n) 厚的脂膏。如：脂肪 fat

房 [fáng] 1 (n) 房屋的通称，也指房间 a house; an apartment; a room ＊ 房屋是用木材和钢骨水泥建成的。Houses are built with timber and reinforced concrete. 2 (n) 物体中分隔开的各个部分 a chamber

房东 [fángdōng] the owner of a house; landlord

房间 [fángjiān] room

房客 [fángkè] tenant

fǎng

仿 [fǎng] 1 (v) 照样子做 imitate; copy ＊这座大厦是仿照回教堂形式而建筑的。This building is built in imitation of the style of a mosque. 2 (adj) 相似 similar; resembling

仿办 [fǎngbàn] adopt similar measures

仿佛 [fǎngfú] similar; resembling

访(訪) [fǎng] 1(v) 探问，看望 call upon; visit; inquire ＊ 年初一的时候，大家都去拜访朋友。On the first day of the New Year, all of us went out to visit friends. 2 (v) 询问，调查 inquire about; search for ＊他登报访寻失散多年的弟弟。He published an advertisement in the newspapers to search for his long-lost brother.

访问 [fǎngwèn] inquire of ;pay a visit to; call on a person

访问团 [fǎng wèn tuán] a mission

访员 [fǎngyuán] a newspaper reporter or correspondent

纺(紡) [fǎng] 1 (v) 把棉，麻，毛，丝等纤维做成纱，线 reel; spin 2 (n) 一种绸子 reeled pongee

纺车 [fǎngchē] a spinning wheel

纺锤 [fǎngchuí] a spindle

纺织 [fǎngzhī] spinning and weaving ;textiles

纺织娘 [fǎngzhīniáng] a kind of grasshopper

昉 [fǎng] 1 (n) 曙光出现 dawn; twilight 2 (v) 开始 begin

舫 [fǎng] (n) 船 a boat; a vessel

fàng

放 [fàng] 1 (v) 驱逐，抛弃 expel; drive out; abandon ＊他经济情况不好，所以放弃留学的念头。His financial situation is not good so he abandons the idea of studying overseas. 2 (v) 解除束缚，不受限制 set free; release; let; go ＊ 匪徒要拿了钱后才肯放人。The robbers will not release their victim unless they receive the ransom .3(adj) 任意，随便 be disorderly and rude; licentious; wild ＊别放任孩子。Don't let the children go wild. 4 (v) 搁，置 place; put; lay down 5 (v) 放出，放射 send away; send forth; emit 6 (v) 扩展 extend; magnify; enlarge ＊最近我胖了，衣服要放宽才能穿。Having got fatter lately, I have to enlarge my clothes.

放大 [fàngdà] magnify; enlarge

放大镜 [fàngdàjìng] magnifying glass

放胆 [fàng dǎn] pluck up courage; be bold

放荡；放浪 [fàngdàng, fànglàng] wild; extravagant ;unstrained

放假 [fàng jiá] on holiday

放监 [fàngjiān] release the prisoners

放空炮 [fàngkōngpào] empty talk; boast

放牧 [fàngmǔ] graze; grazing

放炮 [fàng pào] fire a cannon

放任 [fàngrèn] do not interfere

放哨 [fàngshào] set up patrol; stand sentinel

放下屠刀，立地成佛 [fàng xìa tú dāo, lì dì chéng fó] a Buddhist saying advising people to relinquish vice and turn to virtue

放心 [fàng xīn] set heart at rest; make mind easy

放洋 [fàngyáng] go abroad; put to sea

放映 [fàngyìng] (of film) exhibit; show

放映机 [fàng yìng jī] projector

放债 [fàng zhài] lend money on interest

放账 [fàng zhàng] sell on credit

放逐 [fàngzhú] banish; exile; expel

放纵 [fàng zòng] all to run wild

fēi

非 [fēi] 1 (adv) 不，不是 not ＊这些是非卖品。These goods are not for sale. 2 (n) 错误，罪恶 wrong; error; evil ＊我们必须分清是非。We must distinguish what is right and what is wrong. 3 (adj) 不合于，越出 improper; beyond

非常 [fēicháng] unusual; uncommon; over and above; very

非但；非特 [fēi dàn fēitè] not only

非得 [fēidéi] must; it; is necessary that

非凡 [fēifán] uncommon; unusual; extraordinary

非礼 [fēilǐ] indecent; improper; impolite

非命 [fēimìng] die an unnatural death

非难 [fēinán] censure; blame; reprehend

非人待遇 [fēiréndàiyù] inhuman treatment

非同小可 [fēi tóng xiǎo kě] not a small matter

非议 [fēiyì] find fault with; criticize; vilify

绯（緋） [fēi] (n) (adj) 红色 dark red

绯衣 [fēiyī] high officials

菲 [fēi] 1 (adj) 花草茂盛的样子 luxuriant 2 (n) 花草的香味 fragrance (of plants)
另见 [fěi]

霏 [fēi]〔霏霏〕 (adj) 形容雨或雪下得很紧的样子 a description of how snow falls thick and fast

扉 [fēi] (n) 门 door

飞（飛） [fēi] 1 (v) 鸟类，虫类在空中拍翅往来活动 fly ＊在蓝色的天空中，三只小燕子在飞来飞去。In the blue sky, three little swallows were flying about. 2 (v) 物体在空中飘荡或行动 fly; move in the air; flit 3 (adj) 形容极快 quick; speedy (v) soar ＊听到有好吃的东西，他飞步而来。Once he hears of delicious food, he comes with quick steps.

飞驰 [fēi chí] go at express speed; run swiftly

飞黄腾达 [fēihuángténgdà] rise high; climb up the social ladder rapidly

飞机 [fēijī] aeroplane

飞机场 [fēijīchǎng] airport.

飞机库 [fēijīkù] hangar

飞骑 [fēi qí] light-horse; horsemen for scouting

飞禽 [fēiqín] birds.

飞禽走兽 [fēi qín zǒu shòu] birds and beasts

飞沙走石 [fēishazǒushī] a terrible storm (in which sand and dust fly; and rocks move)
飞速 [fēisù] quickly; swiftly
飞腾 [fēiténg] fly upwards; get rapidly promoted
飞舞 [fēiwǔ] fly about; flutter
飞翔 [fēixiáng] soar; fly
飞行 [fēixíng] aviation; flying; fly; make a flight
飞行员 [fēixíngyuán] a pilot
飞扬 [fēiyáng] float; sail; flutter
飞鱼 [fēiyú] flying fish

妃 [fēi] (n) 皇帝的小老婆或太子，亲王的妻子 an emperor's concubine; wife of a prince

féi

肥 [féi] 1 (adj) 跟“瘦”相对 fat; fleshy ＊他宰了一头肥鸡来宴客。He slaughtered a fat chicken to entertain his guests.
肥料 [féiliào] fertilizer; manure
肥胖；肥满 [féipàng féimǎn] corpulence; fatness
肥瘦 [féishòu] width of clothes
肥沃；肥饶 [féiwò, féiráo] fertile; productive; rich
肥皂 [féizào] soap
肥壮 [féizhuàng] stout; portly

腓 [féi] (n) 小腿后面鼓起的肉 the calf of the legs

fěi

诽（誹）[fěi] (v) 说别人的坏话 slander; defame; abuse ＊他因诽谤同事而失去了很多朋友。He has lost many friends because of defaming his own colleagues.
诽谤 [fěibàng] speak evil of; abuse; slander; defame
诽议 [fěiyì] malicious talk

蜚 [fěi] (n) 一种对稻有害的小飞虫 a hopper that feeds on padi

翡 [fěi] 〔翡翠〕 1 (n) 鸟类 a kingfisher 2 (n) 绿色的硬玉 green pyroxene ;jade

菲 [fěi] 1 (adj) 微薄 thin; poor; trifling 2 (n) 一种象芜菁的菜 a kind of plant having a turnip-like root
菲薄 [fěibó] poor; shabby; small and mean; trifling
另见 [fēi]

匪 [fěi] 1 (n) 强盗 robbers; scoundrels; bandits ＊那个匪徒在被捕之后，自杀身亡。After his arrest , the scoundrel committed suicide. 2 (adv) 不，不是 not; never
匪徒 [fěitú] vagabonds; robbers

fèi

沸 [fèi] (v) 液体受热到一定温度时，发泡化气 boil; bubble up
沸点 [fèidiǎn] the boiling point
沸腾 [fèiténg] boiling; excitement; unrest
沸溢 [fèiyì] boil over

费（費）[fèi] 1 (n) 费用，款项 expenses; expenditure; fees ＊到大学去念书，每个月费用要三百元左右。The monthly expenses for attending university is about $300.00. 2 (v) 花费 spend; use; consume; waste
费唇舌 [fèichúnshé] waste one's breath
费尽心机 [fèijìnxīnjī] spend much labour and care
费力 [fèi lì] difficult; laborious; use effort
费神 [fèi shén] causing mental fatigue
费事 [fèishì] troublesome; fussy

肺 [fèi] (n) 哺乳动物的呼吸器官 the lungs ＊那个妇人的肺部作痛，服了好多种药，还未治好。That woman is suffering from pains of the lungs ;she has taken many kinds of medicines, but is not cured yet.

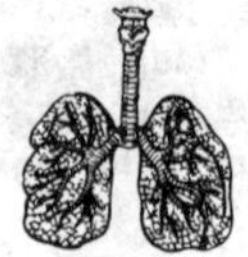

肺腑之言 [fèifǔzhīyán] confidential talk
肺炎 [fèiyán] pneumonia; inflammation of the lungs
肺叶 [fèiyè] lobe of the lungs

废(廢) [fèi] 1 (v) 取消，停止 cancel; discontinue; abandon ;abolish (adj)*一切的契约都废除了。All agreements are cancelled. 2 (adj) 破旧的，经过使用的 spoilt; worthless; waste *把废纸丢了。Throw away the waste papers.
废除 [fèichú] abolish; cancel; cast aside;
废票 [fèipiào] spoilt vote; cancelled ticket
废气 [fèiqì] exhaust steam; exhaust gas
废寝忘食 [fèi qǐn wàng shí] forgetful of sleep and food
废铁 [fèitiě] scrapped iron
废物 [fèiwù] junk; waste; rubbish
废墟 [fèixū] ruins; debris

吠 [fèi] (n) 狗叫声 the bark of a dog
吠形吠声 [fèi xíng fèi shēng] blindly parroting another man's words

fēn

分 [fēn] 1 (v) 离开 divide; separate; part *她们姐妹俩已分别廿年了。These two sisters have been separated for twenty years already. 2 (n) 支(机构或组织等) branch (of an establishment, or organisation) 3 (v) 配置；派遣 distribute *把工作分开来做才能早点完成。The work can be completed earlier if it is distributed to more people. 4 (v) 辨别，分开 distinguish; discriminate *凡事都要分辨好坏才去做。One should distinguish between good and bad before trying to do something. 5 (n) 成数，部分 portion; part *本厂的工友，有百分之五十为马来人。50 out of 100 of the workers in the factory are Malays. 6 (n) 长度名，等于十分之一寸 a length equals to 1/10 Chinese inch. 7(n) 重量名，等于百分之一両 a weight equals to 1/100 tahil
另见 [fèn]
分别 [fēnbié] classify; distinguish;
分布 [fēn bù] distribution; spread
分担 [fēndān] take charge of a portion of works; bear a part of
分道扬镖 [fēn dào yáng biāo] each going his own way because of the difference in interest and ideals
分店 [fēndiàn] a branch shop
分期支付 [fēnqī zhī fù] pay by installements
分工 [fēn gōng] division of labour
分毫 [fēnháo] the least part, a little bit
分化 [fēn huà] differentiation
分角器 [fēnjiǎoqì] a protractor
分解 [fēnjiě] decomposition ; disintegrate
分类 [fēn lèi] classify; assort
分量 [fēnliáng] measure; capacity; quantity
分裂 [fēnliè] split; divided; break;
分泌 [fēnmì] secretion
分娩 [fēnmiǎn] give birth to a child; delivery
分明 [fēn míng] clear
分母 [fēn mǔ] denominator
分派 [fēnpài] apportion duties; appoint
分散 [fēnsàn] disperse ; scatter
分手 [fēn shǒu] depart; take leave
分数 [fēnshù] marks; fraction
分庭抗礼 [fēntíngkànglǐ] to be equal in status by opposing another
分文不取 [fēn wén bù qǔ] free of

charge
分析 [fēnxī] analysis ;analyse
分心 [fēn xīn] distracted
分子 [fēnzǐ] molecule; numerator

吩 [fēn] 〔吩咐〕 (v) 口头的命令。指示 command ;order

纷 (紛) [fēn] (adj) 多；杂乱 numerous; a number of; profuse; confused; disorderly ＊公司生意失败，职员们已纷纷辞职他往！ As the Company's business has proved a failure, a considerable number of staff members tendered their resignation.
纷飞 [fēn fēi] flutter about
纷乱 [fēnluàn] be in disorder (confusion); be confused
纷歧 [fēnqí] a branch; side issues
纷纭 [fēn yún] numerous; prolific
纷争 [fēnzhēng] a dispute; a trouble

氛 [fēn] 1 (n) 气 vapour; fume 2 (n) 气象，情景 atmosphere ＊燃烧炮竹能增加节日的气氛。The firing of crackers can promote a festive atmosphere.

雰 [fēn] (n)雾气，早晨时，浮在空中的气体，能使人看不清楚东西 mist

芬 [fēn] (n) 香气 fragrance ＊她们都采用上等的香水和爽身粉，使到办公室发出芬芳的气味。The ladies are using quality cosmetics and talcum powder. This gives the office a fragrance.
芬芳 [fēnfāng] odoriferous; fragrant

fén

坟 (墳) [fén] (n) 埋死人的土堆 a grave ＊这坟里长眠着一位把生命献给教育的人。 In the grave lies a man who has dedicated his life to education.
坟场 [fénchǎng] a cemetry; a graveyard
坟墓 [fén mù] a grave

濆 (濆) [fén] (n) 沿河的高地 highland alongside a river

焚 [fén] (v) 烧 burn; set on fire ＊昨天的一场大火，焚毁了三间树胶厂，但无人受伤。 Yesterday's blaze had burnt down three rubber factories, but no one was injured.
焚毁 [fén huǐ] burn down
焚掠 [fénluè] burning and looting

fěn

粉 [fěn] 1 (n) 细末 flour; powder 2 (v) 涂饰 whitewash, white 3 (v) 使破碎，成为粉末 grind to powder;pulverize;smash completely 4 (n) 白色 white in colour 5 (n) 浅红色 pink colour 6 (n)化妆用的粉末 powder; cosmetic
粉笔 [fěnbǐ] chalk
粉末 [fěn mò] powder
粉墨登场 [fěn mò dēng chǎng] appear on stage after applying make-up
粉身碎骨 [fěn shēn suì gǔ] body and bones crushed to pieces
粉饰 [fěnshì] present pleasant appearance; cover up faults
粉刷 [fěnshuà] whitewash
粉碎 [fěnsuì] be ground to powder; crush ;smash completely (also used figuratively)

fèn

偾 (僨) [fèn] (v) 败坏，破坏 ruin; spoil ＊你这么不小心，一定偾事。 Being so careless, you will certainly spoil the matter.

愤 (憤) [fèn] (n) 生气，不满 resentment; anger ＊这官员的做法引起公愤。The action of this official causes resentment among the public.
愤愤 [fènfèn] angry

愤恨 [fènhèn] angry; indignant
愤怒 [fènnù] indignant; filled with anger and vexation
愤世 [fènshì] be pessimistic about the general order of things; look at life upon its dark side

分 [fèn] (n) 名位，责任和权利的限度 duty; function ;part of one duty ＊他连分内的工作也不管，太不负责任了。It is very irresponsible of him for not bothering about matters which are his duty.
另见 [fēn]

份 [fèn] 1 (n) 整体分成几部分，每一部分叫一份 a part; a portion 2 (n) 量词 a measure word ＊一份报纸。a copy of the newspapers.

忿 [fèn] (adj) 生气；恨 wrathful; angry. (n) anger; rage; hatred
忿恨 [fènhèn] bitter hatred
忿火 [fènhuǒ] fury; anger; hatred

粪(糞) [fèn] 1 (n) 屎，动物吃东西后，通过消化由体内排出体外的废物 dung; night-soil ＊在马来乡村，人们到处可以见到牛粪，农民用它来做肥料。In Malay villages cow-dung can be seen everywhere, the farmers use it as a kind of fertilizer. 2 (v) 施肥 apply fertilizer; manure
粪池 [fèn chí] a manure pit
粪夫 [fèn fū] a night-soil man

奋(奮) [fèn] (v) 精神振作，鼓起劲头 rouse; excite ＊战士们群起奋斗，把边境的敌军全部打死。The soldiers roused in crowds and killed all the enemy troops stationed at the border region. (adj) 热心的，热诚的 zealous
奋不顾身 [fèn bù gù shēn] braving forward in disregard of personal safety
奋斗 [fèndòu] fight hard; strive
奋发 [fèn fā] arouse; burst forth
奋勉 [fènmiǎn] ardent effort; exert strength
奋起直追 [fèn qǐ zhuī] work hard and catch up
奋勇 [fèn yǒng] ardent courage
奋志不懈 [fèn zhì bù xiè] unwearied; absolutely resolved

fēng

峯 [fēng] (n) 高山顶 a summit; the peak of a hill ＊我国的探险家光荣地把国旗升在高峯上！Our adventurers had proudly hoisted the national flag on the summit.

烽 [fēng] (n) 烽火，古代边防报警时所烧的烟火 a signal fire

蜂 [fēng] 1 (n) 一种昆虫 a bee; a wasp; a hornet ＊蜜蜂会制蜜糖，其味甜美可口。Bees make honey and honey tastes sweet. 2 (adj) 比喻众多 numerous; crowded
蜂窠 [fēng cháo] a beehive; a hornet's nest; the honey comb
蜂蜜 [fēng mì] honey
蜂鸟 [fēngniǎo] humming-bird
蜂拥 [fēngyōng] crowded

锋(鋒) [fēng] 1 (n) 刀，剑等兵器或其他器物的尖端 a sharp point; a blade ＊刀锋生锈了，不能用来切菜。The knife-blade is rusty; it cannot be used for cutting food. 2 (adj) 锐利 sharp; acute 3 (n) 队伍的前列 the front of a line or a troop
锋利 [fēnglì] acute; sharp
锋芒毕露 [fēng māng bìlù] revealing one's astuteness and talents

风(風) [fēng] 1 (n) 流动的空气 a wind; a gale; a breeze ＊一阵大风吹来，我们感到非常凉爽。A strong wind blew and we felt cool and comfortable. 2 (n) 時尚；习俗 style; custom 3 (n) 消息 news; rumour 4 (n)景象 scenery; a scene

5 (n) 态度 manner; style ＊他这种傲慢的作风要不得。Such proud manners of him is undesirable.

风暴 [fēngbào] storm

风标 [fēng biāo] vane

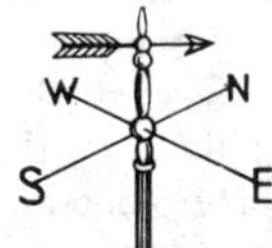

风波 [fēng bō] waves; a storm; disputes and quarrels

风采 [fēng cǎi] appearance; an air

风潮 [fēngcháo] campaign; storm and stress

风尘仆仆 [fēngchénpúpú]hard journey

风车 [fēngchē] a windmill

风吹草动 [fēng chuī cxǒ dòng] a slight movement from the breeze

风笛 [fēng dì] the bagpipes

风度 [fēng dù] bearing; graceful manner; behaviour

风格 [fēnggé] character; styles

风光 [fēngguāng] scenes

风化 [fēnghuà] reform by example; the influence of example or customs

风景 [fēngjǐng] scenery; a scene; a landscape; a view

风力表 [fēng lì biǎo] a wind-gauge; an anemometer

风马牛不相及 [fēng mà níu bù xiāng jí] unrelated

风靡一时 [fēngmǐyīshí] be popular for a time

风平浪静 [fēng píng làng jìng] peacefully quiet

风琴 [fēngqín] an organ

风扇 [fēngshàn] an electric fan

风声鹤唳，草木皆兵 [fēng shēng hè lì, cǎo mù jiē bīng] highly nervous and frightened

风湿[fēngshī] rheumatic ;rheumatism

风俗 [fēngsù] customs

风速表 [fēngsùbiǎo] an anemometer

风土 [fēngtǔ] climate; natural featurcs

风土人情 [fēng tǔ rén qíng] local manners and customs

风箱 [fēng xiāng] bellows

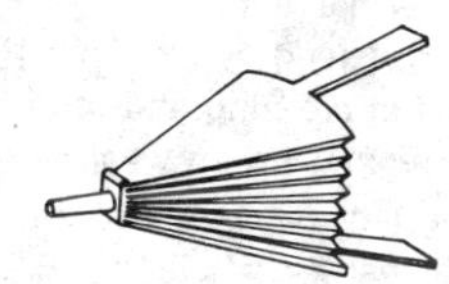

风行一时 [fēng xíng yīshí] very popular for a time

风云 [fēngyún] an approaching event

风云人物 [fēng yún rén wù] an active and influential person

风筝 [fēng zhēng] a kite

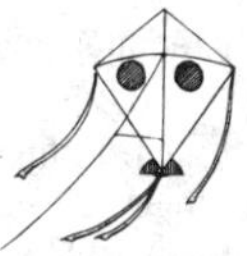

枫(楓) [fēng](n)也叫“枫香”，落叶乔木 the maple tree

疯(瘋) [fēng] (adj) (n) 神经错乱，精神失常 insane; lunatic ;mad ＊他因生意失败，想钱想到发疯。He had failed in the business, and was thinking hard about money until he became insane.

疯人院 [fēngrén yuàn] a lunatic asylum

疯瘫 [fēng tān] paralysis; palsy

丰(豐) [fēng] 1 (adj) 形容面貌，姿态美好 graceful; good-looking 2 (adj) 多，富足，如：丰富 abundant; plentiful * 她的父亲是个经验丰富的工程师。Her father is an experienced engineer.

丰采 [fēngcaǐ] fine manners

丰功伟绩 [fēng gōng wěi jī] meritorious deeds

丰满 [fēngmǎn] well-developed

丰年 [fēngnián] an abundant year; years of good crop

丰收 [fēngshōu] a good harvest; bumper harvest

丰衣足食 [fēng yī zú shí] abundance in clothing and food

丰裕 [fēngyù] rich; wealthy

封 [fēng] 1 (v) 盖密 close; blockade; seal * 封住洞口，别让老虎出来。Seal the entrance, don't let the tiger come out. * 她把药瓶封密，以防药水流出来。She corked the bottle tightly to avoid the lotion from spilling out. 2 (v) 限制 restrict; limit 3 (n) 量词 a measure word * 一封信 a letter.

封建制度 [fēngjiàn zhìdù] feudal system

封禁 [fēngjìn] prohibit; blockade

封面 [fēngmiàn] front cover

封锁 [fēngsuǒ] blockade; block up

féng

逢 [féng] (v) 遇到 meet; come across (upon); happen * 每逢假期，戏院便满座。The cinemas are always crowded during holidays.

逢场作戏 [féng chǎng zuò xì] to participate in something frivolous by chance

逢时过节 [féng shí guò jié] at holiday times

逢凶化吉 [féng xiōng huà jí] evil turned to good fortune

逢迎 [féngyíng] meet; curry favour with; cater to

缝(縫) [féng] (v) 用针线连缀 sew; stitch; mend; patch * 我的祖母在空闲时，喜欢缝衣服。My grand-mother is fond of sewing dresses when she is free.
另见 [fèng]

缝纫 [féngrèn] stitch

缝衣机 [féngyījī] sewing machine

冯(馮) [féng] 姓氏 a surname

fěng

讽(諷) [fěng] 1 (v) 用含蓄的话劝告或指责 satirize; ridicule (n) irony; satire * 帮忙朋友改过，应该用批评而非讽刺。To help a friend correct his mistakes, one should use criticism but not sarcasm. 2 (v) 背书，背着念 recite

讽刺画 [fěngcìhuà] a caricature; a cartoon

讽诵 [fěngsòng] recite in a singing tone; chant

fèng

凤(鳳) [fèng] 〔凤凰〕(n) 传说中的一种鸟 a fabulous bird; phoenix

凤梨 [fènglí] a pineapple

凤毛麟角 [fèng máo lin jiǎo] precious and rare

凤仙花 [fèngxiānhuā] a balsam

奉 [fèng] 1 (v) 恭敬地送上 deliver; offer 2 (v) 遵守，尊重 abide; obey * 他是个奉公守法的公民。He is a law-abiding citizen. 3 (v) 供养，伺候 serve * 皇帝有很多宫女侍奉。The emperor had many maids-of-honour to serve him.

奉承 [fèngchéng] flatter
奉告 [fènggào] have the honour to inform
奉公守法 [fènggōngshǒufǎ] law-abiding
奉命 [fèng mìng] receive a command or order
奉陪 [fèngpéi] company; together with
奉劝 [fèngquàn] give a piece of advice
奉行 [fèngxíng] carry out orders

俸 [fèng] (n) 旧时官吏等所得的薪金 salary; renumeration
俸给 [fèng jǐ] pay
俸金 [fèngjīn] salary

缝(縫) [fèng] (n) 裂开的窄长口子 a crack; a fissure * 她从门缝中看到房间里的一切布置。Through a small crack on the door, she saw the furnishings inside the bed-room.
另见 [féng]

fó

佛 [fó] (n) 释迦牟尼的尊称 Buddha * 每逢初一和十五，有很多妇人到佛庙去。On the first day and fifteenth day of each lunar month, many women go to the Buddhist temples.
佛教 [fójiáo] Buddhism
佛教徒 [fójiàotú] Buddhists
佛经 [fójīng] the religious books of Buddha scripture
佛塔 [fótǎ] a pagoda
佛像 [fóxiàng] Buddhist images

fǒu

否 [fǒu] (adv) 不 no; not *1956年间，在美国有两位华籍科学家否定了“宇称守恒定律”的学说。In 1956, two Chinese scientists disproved "The Law of Parity Conservation" in U.S.A. * 双方都否认自己有错。Both parties deny that they themselves were in the wrong.
否定 [fǒudìng] denial; negation; deny; reply in the negative
否决 [fǒujué] veto; decide against
否认 [fǒurèn] deny
否则 [fǒuzé] or else; otherwise

缶 [fǒu] (n) 一种肚大口小的瓦器 an earthenware; a wine jar

fū

夫 [fū] 1 (n) 女子的配偶 a husband * 公主的丈夫，是个出名的摄影师。The husband of the Princess is a well-known photographer. 2 (n) 旧社会对从事体力劳动的人或服劳役的人的称呼 a labourer; a coolie 3 (n) 古时成年男人的统称 a man
另见 [fú]
夫妇 [fū fù] husband and wife
夫妻 [fūqī] husband and wife
夫人 [fū rén] Mrs., Madame
夫婿 [fūxù] husband

肤(膚) [fū] 1 (n) 身体表面的皮 the skin; the surface * 非洲的土著，皮肤都是黑的。All aborigines of Africa have black skin. 2 (adj) 浅薄的 shallow; superficial * 我们认识才不久，所以对彼此间的了是解很肤浅的。Since we have not known each other for long, the understanding between us is very superficial.
肤浅 [fūqiǎn] superficial
肤色 [fūsè] complexion; colour

敷 [fū] 1 (v) 涂上 put on; apply * 在伤口上敷点药膏。Apply some ointment on the wound. 2 (v) 布置，铺开 arrange; lay; spread out 3 (adj) 够 sufficient; abundant * 他的薪水那么低，总是入不敷出。With such a low salary, he is seldom able to make the two ends meet.
敷衍 [fuyǎn] to neglect one's duties; to be careless and half-hearted in one's manner
敷衍了事 [fūyǎnliǎoshì] perfunctory

and irresponsible

孵 [fū] (v) 鸟类繁殖时伏在卵上，使卵内的胚胎发育成小鸟 hatch ＊ 十粒鸡蛋，只孵出八隻小鸡，其中两粒被母鸡弄破了。Out of ten eggs only eight chicks were hatched; two eggs had been broken by the hen.

跗 [fū] (n) 脚背 the top part of the foot

fú

弗 [fú] (adv) 不 not; neither; no

弗可 [fúkě] do not

弗如 [fúrú] not as good as

拂 [fú] 1 (v) 掸去 shake off; brush away; wipe ＊ 他用鸡毛扫去拂尘。He brushed away the dust with a feather duster. 2 (v) 轻轻擦过 brush gently ＊ 凉风拂面，使人感到舒服。It makes one feel comfortable when a cool breeze brushes gently against one's face. 3 (v) 违背 acts contrary to; go aginst ＊ 他立志不做拂逆自己心愿的事。He determines not to act contrary to his own will.

拂拭 [fúshì] dust; wipe away; brush away

拂袖而去 [fúxiuérqu] annoyed, and left

怫 [fú] (adj) 发怒的样子 angry; irritated

怫然作色 [fú rán zuò sè] flushed with anger

绋(紼) [fú] (n) 出殡牵引棺材进入墓穴时用的大绳。hearse rope ＊ 那位慈善家死后出殡那天，执绋者达一千人之众。On the funeral day of that philantropist, there were about one thousand people who took part in the procession.

孚 [fú] 1 (n) 信用 trust; confidence 2 (adj) 为人所信用 trustworthy

俘 [fú] 1 (v) 打战时捉住敌人 captivate; take prisoner; capture ＊ 在那场战斗中，我们俘获了七名敌兵。In that battle, we captured seven enemy soldiers. 2 (n) 俘虏，打战时被捉住的敌人 captives; prisoners of war ＊ 俘虏们被关在牢狱里，已达十年之久。The captives had been locked up in the prison for ten years.

浮 [fú] 1 (v) 漂在上面 float; drift ＊ 湖面上浮着很多落叶。Many fallen leaves were floating on the surface of the lake. 2 (adj) 表面的 surface; superficial 3 (adj) 暂时的 temporary 4 (adj) 不沉着，不沉静 hot-headed; rash; frivolous ＊ 他为人浮躁，做事情只凭一时冲动。Being a rash person, he does things out of impluse. 5 (adj) 空虚，不切实 empty; unsubstantial 6 (v) 超过，多余 overflow; exceed. (adj) excessive ＊ 这社会里人浮于事，找工作真不容易。In this society, it is not at all easy to look for a job because the number of job-seekers exceeds the number of jobs available.

浮标 [fúbiāo] a buoy

浮沉 [fúchén] ups and downs complete, unexpected changes of circumstances

浮秤；液体比重计 [fúchèng; yètǐbǐ zhòngjì] hydrometer

浮出 [fúchū] emerge; come to the surface

浮动 [fúdòng] float; be unsettled; fluctuate

浮光掠影 [fú guāng lüè yǐng] not a deep impression

浮华 [fúhuá] extravagant; showy

浮力 [fúlì] buoyancy

浮浅 [fúqiǎn] shallow; superficial

浮桥 [fúqiáo] a pontoon (floating)

浮现 [fúxiàn] appear (of memory; image)

bridge

浮游 [fúyóu] waft; float; drift

浮躁 [fú zào] impetuous; restless

莩 [fú] (n) 芦苇秆里面的薄膜 the culms of a water plant

符 [fú] 1 (n) 古代用来作凭证的东西 a seal; a tally 2 (n) 记号 a mark; a sign 3 (v) 相合，一致 correspond with; coincide; agree with * 证人的供证前后不符。The beginning of the evidence given by the witness did not correspond with its end. 4 (n) 指那些驱鬼治病而画在纸上的图形。a spell; a talisman * 那个妇女到寺庙去讨回来一张符贴在门口，她相信这会给家人带来好运。That woman got a piece of paper talisman from the temple and pasted it on the door. She believed that this would bring good luck to her family. 5 (n) 姓氏 a surname

符合 [fúhé] agree with; correspond with; coincide with; tally with

伏 [fú] 1 (v) 身体向前靠或向下跌 lie or fall prostrate *他伏在地上，使前面的人看不到他。He lay prostrate on the ground so that no one in front could see him. 2 (v) 使屈服 subject; suppress 3 (v) 认罪或受到制裁 confess; suffer punishment * 在众人面前，他不得不伏罪。Facing the crowd, he had to confess his crimes. 4 (v) 隐藏 conceal; hide; lie or place in ambush * 警察埋伏在山边捕捉匪徒。The police lie in ambush by the hillside to arrest the robbers.

伏兵 [fúbīng] soldiers in ambush; an ambush

伏倒 [fúdào] lay down on the ground

伏天 [fútiān] midsummer

伏罪 [fú zuì] confess one's guilt

袱 [fú] (n) 包东西用的布 a square cloth used for wrapping clothes

幅 [fú] 1 (n) 布帛等的宽度 the width of cloth 2 (n) 量词 a roll, as of paper * 一幅画。a scroll of painting; a piece of painting.

幅员 [fúyuán] the extent of a country; the territory of a country

辐（輻） [fú] (n) 车轮中连接轴心和轮圈的直条 the spokes of a wheel

辐射 [fúshè] radiate; radiation

福 [fú] (adj) 幸运 blessed; happy (n) happiness; good fortune; prosperity; luck

福份 [fú fèn] happiness; the allotted measure of happiness which man is said to have

福利 [fúlì] happiness and blessing; welfare

福禄寿 [fú lù shòu] happiness, wealth and longevity

福气 [fú qì] a man's allotted share of worldly happiness; lucky

福音 [fúyīn] happy tidings;the Gospel

夫 [fú] 1 (part) 助词。表示感叹 a particle, used to express interjection

另见 [fū]

扶 [fú] 1 (v) 用手支持人或物件使它不倒塌 support; uphold 2 (v) 帮助，支援 aid; assist * 我们必须扶危济困。We must assist those in difficulties and dangers.

扶持 [fúchí] uphold; support; sustain

扶老携幼 [fú lǎo xíe yòu] assisting the aged and leading the young

扶养 [fúyǎng] nourish; take care of; maintain; support

扶摇直上 [fú yáo zhí shàng] rising rapidly (commodity prices, personal status, etc.)

扶植 [fúzhí] implant; to assist

扶助 [fúzhù] aid; help; assist

扶助金 [fúzhùjīn] an allowance in aid

芙 [fú] 〔芙蓉〕 a hibiscus

服 [fú] 1 (n) 衣裳 clothes; dress; garment ＊他们所穿的衣服都是本地产品。The dresses which they are wearing are all local products. 2 (v) 遵从，顺从 submit; obey; subjugate ＊士兵得服从上司的命令。Soldiers must obey the orders of their superiors. 3 (v) 担任，做 serve; wait on 这间餐厅对顾客服务周到。This restaurant serves the customers well. 4 (v) 吃（药） take (medicine) ＊如果病人定时服药，一定会很快把疾病医好。If the patient took the medicine accordingly, the ailment could be cured quickly. 5 (v) 适应 be accustomed to ＊你到了日本，可能会不服水土。You may not be accustomed to the climate when you are in Japan.

服从 [fúcóng] obey; subordinate

服侍 [fú shì] serve; wait on

服役 [fú yì] render service to

服装 [fú zhuāng] costume; dressing

芾 [fú] (adj) 草木茂盛的样子 luxuriant

凫(鳧) [fú] (n) 俗称“野鸭”，鸟类 wild ducks

凫水 [fúshuǐ] swim

凫舟 [fúzhōu] duck-shaped boats

桴 [fú] (n) 打鼓的棒 a drum-stick; stick used for striking the drum

fǔ

拊 [fǔ] (v) 拍 beat; clap

拊掌 [fǔ zhǎng] clap one's hands

府 [fǔ] 1 (n) 旧时称官吏办理公事的地方，现在称国家政权机关 officialdom; government 2 (n) 旧时称贵族，官僚的住宅 a palace; a residence of officials 3 (n) 对别人住宅的尊称 a term of respect to refer to another person's residence

俯 [fǔ] (v) 向下，低头 stoop; condescend; bow

俯首听命 [fǔ shǒu tīng mìng] submissive

俯仰之间 [fǔ yǎng zhī jīan] in the briefest space of time

腐 [fǔ] (adj) 烂，变坏 rot; decay; rotten; corrupt; spoiled ＊警员在海边发现一具腐烂的尸体。The police-man found a decayed corpse by the sea-side.

腐败 [fǔ bài] spoilt; corrupt; decayed

腐烂 [fǔ làn] putrefy; rot; decompose

腐蚀 [fǔshì] corrode; rot; corrosion

腐朽 [fǔxiǔ] decayed; rotten.

甫 [fǔ] (adv) “刚”，“才”的意思 just now; a short time ago

甫初 [fǔchū] at first; a beginning

甫田 [fǔtiàn] a large-wide field

辅(輔) [fǔ] (v) 帮助，协助 aid; help; assist ＊他父母死后，同学辅助他把课程修完。After the death of his parents, his classmates support him to finish his course of study.

辅导 [fǔdǎo] lead; guide

辅颊 [fǔ jiá] the jawbone

脯 [fǔ] 1 (n) 肉干 dried meat; jerked meat 2 (n) 用糖浸渍以后再晾干的水果。sweetened dried fruits 另见 [pú]

釜 [fǔ] (n) 古代的一种锅 a pan; a cauldron, used in ancient times

釜底抽薪 [fǔ dǐ chōu xīn] to do something thoroughly

抚(撫) [fǔ] 1 (v) 安慰，慰问 comfort; pacify; quiet ＊各界人士不断到来抚慰火灾灾民。People from various circles came continuously to comfort the fire victims. 2 (v) 养育，照料 nurture; foster; rear; bring up ＊ 她是一个孤儿，由亲戚抚育成人。Being an orphan, she was brought up by her relatives. 3 (v) 轻轻地摸 pat; caress

抚爱 [fǔài] love; endear

抚琴 [fǔqín] strum the harp; play the piano or organ

抚慰 [fǔwèi] soothe; comfort

斧 [fǔ] (n) 用来砍柴的工具 an axe; hatchet ＊昨天，哥哥没有工作，便拿了一把斧头帮忙父亲砍柴。When my elder brother was free yesterday, he took an axe to help my father chop some fire-woods.

fù

付 [fù] (v) 交给 pay; give to; deliver over to another; hand over

付还 [fùhuán] pay back; repay

付清 [fùqīng] pay in full; clear off an account

付之一炬 [fù zhī yī jù] have it burnt

附 [fù] 1 (adj) 随带的，外加的 supplementary; additional 2 (v) 依靠，使附着，附着 subjoin; attach; adhere to; agree with ＊ 你太附和了，一点原则也没有。You are too agreeable to be of any principle. 3 (v) 靠近 be near to; be close to ＊他们附耳说话，不让别人听见。They speak close to each other's ears, so that others may not be able to listen.

附加 [fujiā] add; supplement; append

附件 [fùjiàn] an enclosure

附近 [fùjìn] near to; neighbouring; adjacent

附录 [fù lù] an appendix; a supplement

附属 [fùshǔ] dependent; tributary; belong to; be attached to

驸 (駙) [fù] (n) 几匹马共同拉车时，在旁边的马 an extra horse harnessed by the side of a team

驸马 [fùmǎ] an imperial son-in-law

复 (復) [fù] 1 (v) 再，又 repeat ; come back (adv) a second time; again ＊母亲老了，常常旧病复发。My mother is old. She often suffers from the comeback of her old sickness. 2 (v) 还原 restore ＊经过几天的休息，她的健康复元了。After a few days rest, her health has been restored. 3 (v) 回答，回报 answer; reply; respond ＊ 早点复信，免得家人挂念。Reply the letter earlier and don't let your family worry. 4 (v) 回，返 return; go back ＊为了工作，他往复新加坡和槟城之间。He comes and goes between Singapore and Penang for business.

复 (複) [fù] (v) 重复 repeat; reiterate; duplicate ＊请你把笔记复写一份给我。Please duplicate a copy of your notes for me.

复辟 [fùbì] stage a comeback; restoration

复查 [fùchá] recheck

复仇 [fù chóu] take revenge; retaliate

复古 [fùgǔ] revival of the ancient system

复合 [fùhé] reunite

复活节 [fù huó jíe] Easter

复句 [fùjù] a complex sentence

复决权 [fùjuéquán] referendum

复利 [fù lì] compound interest

复生 [fù shēng] revive; come to life

again; resurrection

复写纸 [fùxiězhǐ] carbon paper

复姓 [fù xìng] a surname consisting of two words

复兴 [fù xīng] revival; recover prosperity

复杂 [fùzá] complexity; complication

复职 [fù zhí] be reinstalled in office; resume office

覆 [fù] 1 (v) 遮盖 cover; shelter; screen 2 (v) 翻 overturn; upset; capsize 3 (v) 回答;回报 reply

覆盖 [fù gài] cover over

覆灭 [fùmiè] downfall; ruin; collapse

覆没 [fùmò] sunk; lost; routed

覆盆难照 [fù pén nán zhào] not easy to right unjust inflictions

覆水难收 [fù shuǐ nán shōu] what is done cannot be undone

覆土 [fùtǔ] cover with earth

覆舟 [fùzhōu] a shipwreck; capsize a boat

腹 [fù] (n) 体腔在横隔膜以下的部份，俗称"肚子" the belly; the abdomen ＊昨天他在工地上被机械撞伤腹部。Yesterday he was wounded by a knock at the belly by a machinery

腹背受敌 [fù bèi shòu dí] threatened by the enemy in both front and rear

腹饥 [fùjī] feel hungry

腹里藏刀 [fù lǐ cáng dāo] treacherous person

腹泻 [fùxiè] diarrhoea; have loose bowels.

腹心 [fùxīn] devoted; confidential; faithful; trustworthy

鳆(鰒) [fù] (n) 就是"鲍鱼" abalone

馥 [fù] (adj) 香气 fragrant. (n) a fragrant smell; odour

馥郁 [fùyù] fragrant; sweet-smelling

讣(訃) [fù] (v) 报丧 announce a death. (n) an obituary; a notice of death

讣告 [fùgào] obituary notice

赴 [fù] (v) 前往，去，奔 go, as to a place; proceed; attend as a meeting ＊我要赶着赴约，不能跟你多谈。I am in a hurry to go for an appointment so I cannot talk to you any longer.

赴任 [fùrèn] take up the duties of a post; leave for one's new post

赴汤蹈火 [fù tāng dǎo huǒ] fearless of sacrifice

阜 [fù] 1 (n) 土山 a mound; a small hill 2 (adj) 盛多，丰富 fat; fertile; abundant

富 [fù] (adj) 充裕，多，足 rich; wealthy; abundant; well-supplied. (n) wealth. ＊富有的人一般上很吝啬。The rich are usually stingy.

富贵 [fùguì] rich and noble; wealth and rank; prosperity.

富豪 [fùháo] a wealthy man; a millionaire.

富丽 [fùlì] splendid; luxurious.

富强 [fùqiáng] rich and powerful

富源 [fùyuán] sources of wealth; natural resources

富有 [fùyǒu] well off; rich in

副 [fù] 1 (adj) 第二的，次级的 second; vice. (n) an assistant ＊副总理已经出国了。The Deputy Prime Minister has already gone abroad. 2 (adj) 次要的，附带的 secondary; supplementary ＊他是个打字员，教补习是他的副业。He is a typist, and he gives tuition for supplementary income. 3 (v) 符合 assist; agree with; correspond with; fit ＊说巴厘岛的风景像图画，真是名副其实。To say that the scenery of Bali is like a painting is very appropriate.

副本 [fùběn] a duplicate copy.
副产物 [fù chǎn wù] by-product.
副手 [fùshǒu] an assistant.
副业 [fùyè] subsidiary business; a side job.
副主席 [fùzhǔxí] a vice-chairman; a deputy leader.
副作用 [fùzuòyòng] secondary reaction: by-effects.

负(負) [fù] 1 (v) 背，担任 carry on the back; bear ＊ 拿起这份工作就如负重担。Taking up this job is just like bearing a heavy burden. 2 (v) 仗恃，依靠 rely on; depend on 3 (v) 亏欠 be in debt ＊ 负债得还清 You must repay all debts you owe. 4 (n) 输，失败 loss; defeat ＊ 两国正打得胜负未分。Both nations are still at war and no victory or defeat can be distinguished. 5 (v) 背弃，违背 turn the back on; break; be ungrateful ＊ 你负约是不对的。It is wrong of you to break the agreement. 6 (v) 遭受 to bear; to suffer from ＊ 他错怪了朋友，于心负疚 After blaming his friend wrongly, he bears a guilty conscience. 7 (v) 具有 to bear; possess ＊ 赴宴的都是社会上负有名望的人。Those who attended the feast were people who posses high reputation in society. 8 (adj) 跟"正"相对 negative
负担 [fùdān] a burden; a charge; a responsibility
负荆请罪 [fùjīngqǐngzuì] to admit wrong and seek pardon
负咎 [fù jiù] bear the consequences of an offence; hold oneself responsible
负累 [fùlèi] be involved; involve
负屈 [fùqū] suffer a wrong
负伤 [fù shāng] sustain an injury; be injured; get hurt
负心 [fù xīn] ungrateful; heartless
负隅顽抗 [fùyúwánkàng] relying on certain conditions to resist stubbornly
负责 [fùzé] take the responsibility of; be under obligation; bear the blame for
负重致远 [fù zhòng zhìyuǎn] having patience and endurance

父 [fù] 1 (n) 父亲，爸爸 a father (adj) fatherly; paternal 2 (n) 对男性长辈的称呼 an elder (male)
父慈子孝 [fùcízǐxiào] a kind father makes a filial son
父老 [fùlǎo] village elders; seniors
父母 [fùmǔ] father and mother; parents

傅 [fù] 1 (v) 教导 guide; superintend 2 (n) 师傅，负责教导或传授技艺的人 a tutor; a teacher
傅训 [fùxùn] a teacher's instruction
傅油 [fùyóu] oil

缚(縛) [fù] (v) 捆起来，绑住 tie up; bind; fasten
缚紧 [fùjǐn] tie lightly

妇(婦) [fù] 1 (n) 已经结婚的女子 a married woman 2 (n) 儿媳 a daughter-in-law 3 (n) 妻子 wife 4 (n) 女性的通称 a female. (adj) female
妇产科 [fùchǎnkē] maternity department
妇女 [fùnǚ] ladies; women
妇女参政权 [fu nǚ cān zhèng quán] women (female) suffrage
妇女解放 [fù nǚ jiě fàng] emancipation of women
妇人 [fùrén] a woman; the fair sex

赋(賦) [fù] 1 (n) 旧时的田地税 land tax (in ancient times) 2 (v) 交给，给予 give; endow; bestow on ＊ 智慧是天赋的吗？Is wisdom bestowed upon one by nature? 3 (n) 中国古代文学中的一种文体 a kind of poetical composition in ancient Chinese literature 4 (v) 念诗或作诗 recite a poem; compose a poem

赋贡 [fùgòng] pay tribute

赋诗 [fùshī] write a poem

赋性 [fùxìng] natural abilities; one's natural powers and talents

赋予 [fùyǔ] give

G

gá

嘎 [ga] (n) 音译字 a transliterating word

gāi

该(該) [gāi] 1 (v) 应当；须 should; ought to * 政府应该处罚贩毒份子。The Government should punish the drug sellers. 2 (pron) 那个，特指前面说过的人或事物 that; the (person, organisation, etc.); the said (person, etc.) * 印尼的巴厘岛是该国的一个名胜。 Bali Island is a famous resort of the country Indonesia.

赅(賅) [gāi] (adj) 完备 provided for; prepared.

gǎi

改 [gǎi] (v) 变更，换过 change, correct; alter * 公司已改变一切行政方针，使生产工作能更顺利地进行。The company has changed its administration policy, in order to run the production jobs more smoothly.

改编 [gǎibiān] (of literary works) adapt; revise and rewrite; regroup; reorganise (troops)

改变 [gǎibiàn] change; alter

改朝换代 [gǎicháohuàndài] change of dynasty

改革 [gǎigé] reform; change, innovation

改观 [gǎiguān] present a new look; be quite different from

改过 [gǎi guò] repent; reform

改过自新 [gǎi guò zì xīn] correct one's errors and make a fresh start; turn over a new leaf

改行 [gǎi háng] change to new occupation; change to another trade

改换 [gǎi huàn] change; transform; turn over

改悔 [gǎihuǐ] repent; amend

改建 [gǎijiàn] reconstruction

改进 [gǎijìn] improve; improvement

改良 [gǎo liáng] reform; improve; mend

改良主义 [gǎiliángzhǔyì] reformism

改期 [gǎiqī] change the date

改善 [gǎi shàn] improve; better (the state of affairs)

改天换地 [gǎi tiān huàn dì] transforming nature; remoulding society

改头换面 [gǎi tóu huàn miàn] only changing in appearance but not in nature

改弦易辙 [gǎi xián yì zhè] alter the laws or change policy, plan, attitude, etc

改邪归正 [gǎi xié guī zhèng] give

up evil ways and return to the right; mend one's ways

改造 [gǎizào] transform; remould; reorganise

改正 [gǎizhèng] correct

改组 [gǎi zǔ] reorganise; reshuffle

改装 [gǎizhuāng] change the style of dress; change to a new packing

gài

丐 [gài] (v) 乞求、讨 beg; request; ask for alms * 一个可怜的老乞丐，天天流浪在街头。There is a poor old beggar who wanders about the streets everyday.

溉 [gài] (v) 浇灌 irrigate; water; wash * 为了要节省，我们可以拿用过的水来灌溉花草。In order to save water, we can resort to used water for watering flowers and grass.

概 [gài] 1 (adj) 大略，总括 (n) general; a summary; general outline *请你把这篇文章的概要说出来。Could you please give a summary of this article? 2 (n) 气节 bearing; attitude * 他演讲时表现出威严的气概。When he gives a speech, he adopts a stern and respectable attitude.

概观 [gàiguān] a general view

概况 [gàikuàng] general conditions; basic facts

概括 [gàikuò] generalize; summarize

概略 [gài lüe] brief outline; the gist

概论 [gài lùn] summary; outline

概念 [gàiniàn] concept; notion; idea

概念化 [gàiniànhuà] in abstract terms

概述 [gàishù] deal with......in general outline

概数 [gàishù] approximate number

概要 [gàiyāo] summary; outline

盖（蓋）[gài] 1 (n) 器物上部有遮蔽作用的东西。a cover; a lid * 他打破了杯子的盖。He broke the cup's cover. 2 (v) 遮掩 cover; hide; screen * 天气很冷，你睡时要盖好被。The weather is cold, you should blanket yourself when you sleep. 3 (v) 打上 seal; affix a seal; stamp * 经理忘了在支票上盖图章，带来了好多不便。The manager forgot to chop the cheque and caused a lot of inconveniences. 4 (v) 建造 build * 在市区中，工友们盖好了很多房子。In the urban area, the workers have built many houses.

盖棺定论 [gài guān dìng lùn] (fig.) only when a person is dead can he be finally judged

gān

干 [gān] 1 (v) 触犯，冒犯。interfere; oppose * 许多人都不喜欢别人干扰他们的家事。Many people do not like others to interfere with their family matters.

干扰 [gānrǎo] interfere with; jam (broadcasts); interference

干涉 [gānshè] interfere

干预 [gān yù] intervene; meddle in

干（乾）[gān] 1 (adj) 水份少或没有水份的 dry; dried *干的木材容易燃烧。Dry wood burns easily 2 (adj) 空虚 exhausted; empty * 他们一下子便把杯中的酒喝干了。They empty their cup at a draft.

另见 [gàn]

干杯 [gān bēi] drink a toast

干脆 [gān cuì] clear-cut; straightforward; frank

干电池 [gān diàn chí] dry battery or cell

干旱 [gān hàn] dry spells; drought

干涸 [gān hé] dried up

干枯 [gānkū] withered; dried up
干净 [gānjìng] clean; dried up
干粮 [gān liáng] ready-made food for journey
干扰 [gānrǎo] interfere with; jam (broadcasts); interference.
干涉 [gānshè] interfere
干燥 [gān zào] dry; parched

杆 [gān] (n) 棍子 a pole; a rod; a bar
另见 [gǎn]

肝 [gān] (n) 人类和某些动物体内的一种器官，能分泌胆汁 liver ＊猪肝是一种良好食品。Pig livers are fine food.
肝胆相照 [gān dǎn xiāng zhào] very sincerely
肝脑涂地 [gān nǎo tú dì] highest degree of loyalty and fearless of sacrifice
肝火 [gānhuǒ] irritability; irritation; fretfulness
肝炎 [gān yán] hepatitis
肝脏 [gānzàng] the liver

竿 [gān] (n) 长条，如：竹竿。pole; a bamboo stick, a rod; a cane ＊竹竿可用来晾晒衣服。Bamboo poles are used for hanging clothes to dry.
竿头日进 [gān tóu rì jìn] make still greater progress

甘 [gān] 1 (adj) 甜 sweet; delicious; pleasant ＊新鲜的菜心，味甘又鲜好。Fresh vegetables have a sweet taste. 2 (adj) 愿意；乐意。willing; voluntary ＊他对工作很认真，要做完才甘愿休息。Being very serious, he is not willing to rest until he has finished his task.
甘拜下风 [gānbàixiàfēng] willingly acknowledge defeat; willingly accept as being inferior
甘苦 [gānkǔ] joy and sorrow; sweet and bitter
甘霖 [gān lín] timely rains
甘泉 [gān quán] fresh spring
甘心 [gānxīn] be reconciled to; willing; contented; pleased
甘心情愿 [gānxīnqíngyuàn] willingly and galdly
甘休 [gānxiū] willing to let it go
甘愿 [gānyuàn] willing to
甘蔗 [gān·zhe] sugar-cane

柑 [gān] (n) 常绿灌木或小乔木，果实可吃 mandarin orange ＊目前，一箱柑值四十五元。At present, a crate of mandarin oranges costs $45.00.

尴（尷）[gān] [尴尬] [gāngà] 1 (adj) 神态不自然 embarrassed ＊老师告诉学生们不要赌博，却在赛马坊碰到自己的学生，一时感到万分尴尬。The teacher had told his students not to gamble, yet he was very embarrassed when he met his students at the Race Course. 2 (adj) 处境困难或事情棘手，不好处理 awkward ＊他们双方都不肯先承认錯误，情形很尴尬。The situation became awkward when neither of both parties would take the initial move to admit the wrong-doings.

gǎn

杆 [gǎn] (n) 器物上条形或管形的部分 stem of an article. ＊字要写得美，必须握紧笔杆。To write nicely, one should hold the stem of the pen tightly.

秆 [gǎn] (n) 稻，麦等植物的茎。stalk; stem (of padi, cereal plant, etc.)

赶（趕）[gǎn] 1 (v) 追上去。catch up; chase; pursue ＊你一个月没上学，要加倍用功才能赶得上其他同学。Since you have not come to school for a month, you must study doubly hard to catch up with the others. 2 (v) 加快 hurry; hasten ＊那几个长发青年一见警察就赶快躲

起来。Those few long-haired youths hastened to hide themselves once they saw the police. 3 (v) 驱，逐 chase; drive ＊快来赶掉苍蝇，不然食物会被弄脏了! Come and drive away the flies, or the food will become dirty!

赶紧 [gǎnjǐn] hurriedly

赶尽杀绝 [gǎn jìn shā jué] thorough extermination

赶快 [gǎnkuài] in a hurry; hurriedly; hurry up

赶路 [gǎn lù] hurry on one's way

赶忙 [gǎnmáng] haste; hurriedly

赶上 [gǎnshàng] overtake; catch up

敢 [gǎn] (v) 有勇气有胆量 dare; bold; daring ＊自已不懂的东西，要敢于请教别人，才会学到知识。In order to acquire some knowledge, one should be bold to enquire about anything he is ignorant of.

敢怒而不敢言 [gǎn nù ér bù gǎn yán] boiling with anger but dare not speak about it.

敢死队 [gǎnsǐduì] a suicide squad; a forlorn hope

敢言 [gǎnyán] dare to speak; speak boldly

敢作敢为 [gǎn zuo gǎn wéi] not afraid; daring

橄 [gǎn] [橄榄] [gǎnlǎn] (n) 常绿乔木，果实青、棕色，可生吃，也可榨油 the Chinese olive ＊在小时候，我很喜欢吃橄榄。When I was young, I liked to eat olive.

橄榄油 [gǎnlǎnyóu] olive oil.

感 [gǎn] 1 (v) 觉得 feel ＊母亲为儿子的好品行而感到骄傲。The mother feels proud of her son's good conduct. 2 (v) 内心受到触动 move; touch; affect (adj) affected; moved ＊安徒生所写的"卖火柴的小女孩"，很感动人。People are moved by "The Little Match Girl" written by Mr. Hans Christian Anderson. 3 (n) 情绪 sentiments; feeling ＊她是个和蔼可亲的人，大家都对她有好感。As she is kind and friendly, people have good feelings towards her.

感触 [gǎn chù] stirring of emotion; deep feeling; move

感到 [gǎn dào] feel; realize

感动 [gǎn dòng] move; touch; moved; touched

感恩图报 [gǎn ēn tú bào] grateful for kindness and seeking to recompense

感化 [gǎn huà] convert (a person); influence; reform

感激 [gǎn·ji] be grateful; be obliged; gratitude

感觉 [gǎn jué] sense; perceive; feel; sense of perception

感觉器官 [gǎnjué qìguān] sense organs

感概 [gǎn kǎi] deeply touched; deep emotions

感冒 [gǎnmào] catch cold; influenza

感情 [gǎnqíng] feelings; emotion; sentiment

感染 [gǎnrǎn] be infected by ; influence or be influenced by

感人 [gǎnrén] moving; touching

感人肺腑 [gǎn rén fèi fǔ] profound; touched

感受 [gǎnshòu] impression ; be affected by; be impressed with

感叹 [gǎntàn] mournful; feel melancholic; sorry

感叹词 [gǎntàncí] interjection

感叹号 [gǎn tàn hào] exclamation mark

感想 [gǎnxiǎng] impression; feeling; thoughts

感谢 [gǎnxiè] thanks; gratitude

感性 [gǎnxìng] the perceptual

感应 [gǎnyìng] induce · induction; sympathy

gàn

干（幹） [gàn] 1 (n) 事物的主体或重要部分 trunk; stem ＊热带森林里的树木有笔直的树干。The trees of tropical forests have straight trunks. 2 (v) 搞，做 do; make; work; manage ＊他是个公务员，在教育部干事。

He is a civil servant and works in the Ministry of Education. 3 (adj) 有才能的 skilful; able * 他是公司里干练的职员，所以公司派他管理吉隆坡的分行。Since he is an able and experienced employee of the firm, he is sent to manage the branch at Kuala Lumpur.

干部 [gànbù] cadre

干活 [gànhuó] work; labour

干劲 [gànjìn] vigour; energy; drive

干事 [gàn·shi] staff member; executive

干线 [gànxiàn] trunk line, main line

gāng

冈（岡）[gāng] (n) 山脊，也作"岗"。the ridge of a hill * 兵士们把国旗插在山冈上。The soldiers hoisted a flag on the ridge of a hill.

刚（剛）[gāng] 1(adj) 坚硬，坚强 solid; hard; stiff; firm; unyielding * 居礼夫人是个刚强的女性。Madam Curie was a firm and strong woman. 2 (adv) 才，时间过去不久 just; recently; only a moment ago * 我刚从学校毕业，没有工作经验。I graduated only recently so I have no working experience.

刚愎自用 [gānbìzìyòng] obstinate and self-opinionated; set in one's ways

刚才 [gāngcái] just now; a very short time ago

刚刚 [gānggāng] as soon as; just now; a short while ago; no sooner

刚劲 [gāngjīng] rigid; straight and powerful

刚强 [gānggíang] firm and uncompromising; wilful

刚毅 [gāngyì] resolute and firm; fortitude ; unyielding

刚直 [gāngzhí] upright; upright and tenacious

纲（綱）[gāng] 1(n)网上的主要绳索 the main rope of a net 2 (n) 事物最主要的部分。key link; subject matter; essential points * 电台的新闻报导只是个大纲，详细的情况还得参阅报章。The radio only gives the key points of the news, for details, we have to refer to the newspapers. 3 (n) 分类 categories or classification * "本草纲目"是一本古老的医学书籍。"Basic Classification of Herbs" is an antiquated book of medicine.

纲举目张 [gāngjǔmùzhāng] once the key link is grasped, everything falls into place

纲领 [gānglǐng] programme, general idea; essential points

纲目 [gāngmù] outline, programme; outline and detail

纲要 [gāngyào] summary; outline

钢（鋼）[gāng] (n) 铁基合金，非常坚硬，用来建筑及造桥 steel

钢笔 [gāngbǐ] pen; fountain pen

钢材 [gāngcái] rolled steel

钢管 [gāngguǎn] steel tube

钢筋 [gāngjīn] steel bar

钢盔 [gāngkuī] steel helmet

钢琴 [gāng qín] piano

钢丝 [gāngsī] steel wire

扛 [gāng] 1 (v) 用双手举重物 lift up with both hands 2 (v) 两人或两人以上共抬一物。carry by two or more persons * 冰箱太重了，需要四个人才扛得起。Such a heavy refrigerator requires four men to carry it away.

另见 [káng]

肛 [gāng] (n) 肛管和肛门的总称，是排泄废物的器官。the anus; the rectum

缸 [gāng] (n) 用陶，瓷或玻璃等制成的容器，底小口大。an earthen vessel; a jar * 父亲在马六甲买了一个古旧的缸，价值九千元。My father bought an old earthen ware vessel in Malacca for $9,000.

缸瓦 [gāng wǎ] earthen ware vessels; crockery

gǎng

岗（崗）［gǎng］1 (n) 高起的土堆。mound 2 (n) 守卫，工作的地方。 a post; a position 另见［gāng］
岗楼 ［gǎnglóu］ watch tower
岗哨 ［gǎng shào］ sentry; sentinel
岗位 ［gǎng wèi］ post; position

港 ［gǎng］1 (n) 江河的支流。tributary of a river 2 (n) 可以停泊大船的江海口岸 port; a harbour; entrance of a river ＊设备完善的新加坡海港，是全世界的第三大港。The well-equipped harbour of Singapore is the third biggest in the world.
港口 ［gǎngkǒu］ port; harbour
港湾 ［gǎngwān］ bay
港务 ［gǎng wù］ harbour (port) service

gàng

杠 ［gàng］(n) 粗的棍子 bar
杠杆［gànggǎn］ lever

gāo

高 ［gāo］ 1 (adj) 跟"低"相对。high; tall; elevated ＊ 在纽约有许多百多层的高楼大厦。There are many tall buildings with hundred over storeys in New York. 2 (adj) 响亮，尖锐 loud 3 (adj) 昂贵 expensive; dear ＊ 这些高价奢侈品，不是我们所买得起的。 All these expensive luxurious goods are not those which we can afford to buy.
高傲 ［gāoào］ arrogant; haughty; proud
高不可攀 ［gāo bù kěpan］ beyond reach
高超 ［gāochāo］ superb; exquisite
高潮 ［gāocháo］ high tide; upsurge; climax
高大 ［gāo dà］ lofty; high and noble; tall
高等 ［gāo děng］ high; advanced; high-degree; high-class
高低 ［gāo dī］ height; pitch; a state of being superior or inferior
高调 ［gāodiào］ high-pitch; bombastic words
高度 ［gāodù］ a high degree; highly; altitude
高峰 ［gāo fēng］ climax; peak; summit
高高在上 ［gāo gāo zàishàng］ hold oneself aloof; sit up on high
高山病 ［gāo shān bìng］ mountain-sickness
高官厚禄 ［gāo guānhoulu］ high position and handsome salary
高贵 ［gāo kuì］ noble; elated; exalted
高见 ［gāo jiàn］ wise ideas; farsight
高粱 ［gāo liáng］ kaoliang; sorghum
高明 ［gāomíng］ wise; brilliant; bright
高烧 ［gao shāo］ high fever
高尚 ［gāo shàng］ respectable; noble-minded; high-principled
高深 ［gāoshēn］ profound; advanced
高耸 ［gāosǒng］ lofty; high; towering
高速 ［gāo sù］ high speed; speedy
高抬贵手 ［gāo tái guì shǒu］ Raise your honourable hand-do not be too hard on me this time
高谈阔论 ［gāo tán kuò lùn］ loud and bombastic talk
高温 ［gāo wēn］ high temperature
高兴 ［gāo xìng glad; pleased; happy; elated
高压 ［gāo yā］ high pressure ; high-handedly
高音 ［gāo yīn］ a high pitch tone soprano
高原 ［gāo yuán］ plateau

高涨 [gāo zhàng] surge forward; run high

高瞻远瞩 [gāozhānyuǎnzhǔ] far-sighted; look far ahead and aim high

高枕无忧 [gāo zhěn wú yōu] retire or rest without worries; lack of alertness

膏 [gāo] 1 (n) 肥或肥肉 fat; fat meat 2 (n) 脂肪，油脂 fat; lard; oil 3 (n) 很稠的，糊状的，象脂膏的东西 plaster; ointment

膏药 [gāoyào] plaster (medicine)

膏腴 [gāoyú] rich soil

篙 [gāo] (n) 用竹竿或杉木等做成的撑船工具。a bamboo pole; a boat-pole

糕 [gāo] (n) 用米粉或面粉等煮成的食品。cakes; pastry ＊他的哥哥开一间咖啡店，店里有卖蛋糕和鸡饭。His elder brother has opened a coffee-shop where cakes and chicken-rice are sold.

糕点 [gàodiǎn] pastry and cakes

睾 [gāo] 〔睾丸〕[gāowán] (n) 人和动物的雄性生殖器官的一部分，能产生精虫 the testicles

gǎo

搞 [gǎo] (v)做，弄。do; work; make ＊他的朋友是专门搞出版事业的。His friend is a professional publisher.

搞鬼 [gǎo guǐ] play tricks

槁 [gǎo] (adj) 干枯 dry; rotten

稿 [gǎo] 1 (n) 稻，麦等谷类植物的秆子。the stalk of grain; straw 2 (n) 文字，图画的草稿。manuscript, a sketch

稿件 [gǎojiàn] manuscripts for publication

稿费 [gǎofèi] fee for writing an article for publication

稿纸 [gǎozhǐ] manuscript paper

gào

告 [gào] 1 (v) 用言语或文字让人知道。tell; inform ＊在课堂上，老师告诉我们要用功学习，以便长大后能为贫苦的大众服务。In the classroom, the teacher told us to work hard so that we would be able to serve to the masses when we grew up . 2 (v) 请求 for; seek ＊她生病了所以向老师告假两天。As she was sick, she sought for two days' leave from the teacher. 3 (v) 揭发，控诉。sue, indict ＊那个职员骗用了公司的钱，被公司控告。The employee was sued for having deceitfully used up the company's money 4 (v) 宣布事情成功或达到一定程度。announce ＊这座大厦的建筑已告完成。It is announced that the construction of this building has been completed.

告别 [gàobíe] take leave; bid farewell; say good-bye

告辞 [gàocí] take leave; say good-bye

告急 [gàojí] make an emergency request for help; report the danger

告捷 [gàojiè] announce a victory; win a victory

告诫 [gào jiè] warn; enjoin; counsel

告密 [gàomì] give secret information against somebody

告示 [gào shi] notice; notification; an official proclamation

告诉 [gào·su] tell; inform; make known

告知 [gàozhī] notify; inform; tell

告状 [gàozhuàng] sue; indict; bring a suit against, go to law; file a suit; bring an action against ;lodge complaints; complain of one's grievances

诰(誥) [gào] (n) 一种训诫勉励的文章 order; command

膏 [gào] (v) 在车轴，机器经常转动发生摩擦的部分加的润滑油 grease; oil
另见 [gāo]

郜 [gào] 姓 a surname

gē

咯 [gē] (n) 表示鸡只的叫声 a sound made by the hens.
另见 [kǎ]

胳 [gē] [胳膊] [gē bo](n) 手臂，肩膀以下手以上的部分 arm

搁(擱) [gē] 1 (v) 放，摆 lay by; put down * 把书包搁下才吃饭吧。Put down your bag before eating. 2 (v) 停顿 shelve; lay off; postpone; put aside * 垃圾堆起火了，快搁下工作过去帮忙救火吧。The heap of rubbish is on fire, let's put aside our work and go to help in putting off the blaze.
另见 [gè]

搁浅 [gē qiǎn] run aground; run ashore; be stranded

哥 [gē] (n) 兄 elder brother * 他的大哥是个律师，二哥是出版家，三哥是部长。His eldest brother is a lawyer; second elder , a publisher ; and the third elder , a minister.

哥哥 [gē·ge] elder brother

歌 [gē] 1 (n) 能唱的文词或散文 song; ballad 2 (v) 唱 sing

歌唱 [gēchàng] sing; chant

歌词 [gēcí] words of a song

歌功颂德 [gē gōng sòng dé] extolling meritorious deeds

歌剧 [gējù] opera

歌曲 [gēqǔ] song

歌手 [gēshǒu] singer; artiste.

歌颂 [gēsòng] eulogise; sing in praise of; extol

歌舞昇平 [gē wǔ shēng píng] peaceful days

歌谣 [gēyáo] ballads (songs)

歌咏 [gē yǒng] singing

戈 [gē] (n) 古时的一种兵器如矛形状 a lance; a spear; a javelin ; weapons

鸽 [gē] (n) 鸟类像鸡，常用它来象征和平。 dove; pigeon.

割 [ge] (v) 用刀截断 cut; sever; divide * 割鸡焉用牛刀？ why use an ox knife to kill a fowl?

割爱 [gē ài] give away or part with what one loves

割裂 [gēliè] sever; separate

割开 [gē kāi] rip open; cut asunder

割让 [gēràng] cession

gé

格 [gé] 1 (n) 正方或长方形的框子。square * 他们在纸上，画了许多小方格。They have constructed many small squares on the paper. 2 (v) 打 attack; resist; fight. * 刚才有两个人在格斗，所以地方很凌乱。Just now two persons fought with each other making the scene very messy.

格调 [gédiào] tune; rhythm; style

格格不人 [gé gé bùrù] incongruous;misfits

格局 [géjú] style; manner; arrangement; bearing

格杀勿论 [gé shā wù lùn] slay a man who is resisting will not be accounted murder.

格式 [gé shi] form; pattern; format

格外 [géwài] extraordinary

格言 [géyán] maxim; a wise saying

阁(閣) [gé] 1 (n) 一种宽阔的大建筑物 a chamber; a storied building; a pavilion 2 (n) 内阁的简称。 the cabinet

阁楼 [gé lóu] garret; mezzanine

阁下 [géxià] (Your, His) Excellency

搁(擱) [gé] (v) 承受，耐 hold up; preserve; keep ＊ 他虽然被老板无理责骂，却得搁住气以保饭碗。Although he was scolded unreasonably by the boss; he had to keep his temper to secure his job.
另见 [gē]

隔 [gé] 1 (v) 分开，阻隔 separate; part; cut off (n) partition; separation; division ＊ 马来半岛和新加坡只隔一道水。Peninsular Malaya and Singapore is separated by only a stretch of waters. 2 (adj) 距离 apart ＊ 你去了欧洲我们路隔千里，彼此很难互相照顾。When you are in Europe, we shall be thousands of miles apart and it will be difficult for us to take care of each other.

隔岸观火 [gé àn guān huǒ] indifferent to other people's plight

隔壁 [gébì] next door

隔绝 [géjúe] isolate; seal off; prevent ... from

隔离 [gélí] isolate; separate

隔膜 [gémò] estrangement; uncongenial; lack of understanding

隔靴搔痒 [gé xūe sāo yǎng] not touch the core of the matter

隔夜 [géyè] overnight

嗝 [gé] (n)胃里的气体从嘴里出來时发出的声音（多在吃饱后）belch; hiccup

蛤 [gé] [蛤蜊] [gé·lí] (n) 软体动物，壳分两半之贝类 a clam

葛 [gé] (n) 草本植物 creeping plant
另见 [gě]

革 [gé] 1 (n) 去毛并加工过的兽皮。leather; hides 2 (v) 改变 change; renew; reform ＊ 国会宣布今年的革新经济政策。The Parliament announced the reformed economic policy of the year. 3 (v) 撤除 dismiss; remove ＊ 他在工作上犯了一个很大的错误，所以被革职了。He was dismissed because he committed a major mistake in his job.

革命 [gé mìng] make revolution; revolution

革新 [géxīn] renovate; reform; innovation

革职 [gé zhí] dismiss; discharge

gě

舸 [gě] (n) 大船，也指一般的船。ship; boat

盖(蓋) [gě] 姓氏 surname
另见 [gài]

个(個) [gě] (pron) 自己 如：自个儿。oneself
另见 [gè]

合 [gě] (n)容量单位。a unit of measure
另见 [hé]

葛 [gě] 姓氏 surname
另见 [gé]

gè

各 [gè] (pron)每个，不同的 each; every (adv) separately; respectively ＊ 石油价格影响世界各国人民的生活。The price of oil affects the life of all people in every country of the world

各奔前程 [gèbēnqiánchéng] each goes his own way; each pursues his onward destiny

各持己见 [gèchíjǐjiàn] each persisting in his own opinion

各地 [gèdì] in every place; various districts

各个击破 [gègè jīpò] crush one by one

各尽所能 [gè jìn suǒ néng] each acts according to his abilities

各就各位 [gè jiù gè wèi] each to

his own position

各人自扫门前雪,莫管他人瓦上霜 [gè rén zi sào mén qián xuě, mò guǎn tā rén wǎ shàng shuāng]mind one's own business

各式各样 [gè shì gè yàng] all kinds of; various; in various ways

各行其是 [gèxíngquíshì] act as one pleases; each goes his own ways

各有千秋 [gèyǒuqiānqiū] each has its own advantages and characteristics

各自 [gèzì] by oneself

各自为政 [gèzì wéi zhèng] each goes his own way; lack of coordination

个(個) [gè] 1 量词 a measure word * 一个人。 a person. 2 (adj) 单独的 individual; isolated ; personal * 要把一部戏剧演得好,个别演员有责任把自己的角色搞好。 In order that a drama is well performed, individual actor has the responsibility to play his role well. 3 (n) 物体大小,身体高矮 如:个子。 size; a person's stature

个别 [gebie] individual; isolated; a few ; one by one

个人 [gèrén] individual; personal

个人主义 [gè rén zhǔ yì] individualism

个体 [gètǐ] individuality; individual

个性 [gèxìng] individuality; individual character

gěi

给(給) [gěi] 1 (v) 送,交 give; present; offer; provide; supply * 爸爸给我钱交学费 Father gives me money to pay school fees. 2 (prep) 替,为 for to * 快去给我买一些东西回来! Go and buy something for me! 3 (prep) 被 by * 几个吸毒青年给警察带走了。A few young drug-addicts were taken away by the police.

给与 [gěi yǔ] furnish; grant; supply

给还 [gěihúan] hand back; refund

给以 [gěiyǐ] give of; offer; deal with

另见 [jǐ]

gēn

根 [gēn] 1 (n) 植物的茎下蔓延在土中能固定植物全体的部份 roots * 树根除了支持树身之外,还能吸取水份和矿物质等。The roots, besides supporting the tree-trunk, suck up water and mineral matters. 2 (n) 物体的下部 base; foundation 3 量词 a measure word * 一根竹竿。 a piece of bamboo stick.

根本 [gēnběn] foundation; basic; fundamental ; radically; totally; entirely

根除 [gēnchú] uproot; exterminate; eradicate

根底 [gēndǐ] basis; foundation

根基 [gēnjī] foundation, basis

根据 [gēnjú] base on; in accordance with; in the light of; basis; ground

根深蒂固 [gēn shēn dì gù] have a firm foundation

根由 [gēnyóu] cause; origin

根源 [gēnyuán] source; origin; root

跟 [gēn] 1 (n) 脚,鞋,袜的后部 the heel * 现在,男人也穿起高跟鞋了! Now, men wear high-heel shoes too! 2 (prep) 对,向 to; from * 人家跟你说话,你要注意听。When people talk to you, you should listen attentively. 3(v) 随 follow; accompany * 很多年青人爱跟上潮流,只要是流行的东西他们都学。Many youngsters like to follow the fashion and learn anything that is popular 4 (conj) 同,和 with; and * 你跟我

到劳工部去好吗？Could you come along with me to the Ministry of Labour?

跟前 [gēnqián] in front of; nearby

跟随 [gēnsuí] follow; accompany

跟着 [gēn·zhe] follow; in the wake of; immediately; right away

跟踪 [gēnzōng] tail after; follow in the track of

gèn

亘 [gèn] (n) 连续不断（指时间或空间）continuance

亘古 [gèn gǔ] from ancient time; from time immorial

gēng

更 [gēng] (v) 改变，轮流，改换 alter; change ＊随着时代的需要，学校的课程常有更改。 To follow up with the needs of the time, syllabuses in the schools are always changing.

更动 [gēngdòng] modify; change

更改 [gēnggǎi] alter; change

更换 [gēnghuàn] replace; change

更深人静 [gēngshēnrénjìng] the quiet of the night

更替 [gēngtì] substitute

更新 [gēngxīn] renew; renovate; begin a new course of life

更衣室 [gēngyīshì] dressing room; toilet

更正 [gēngzhèng] make corrections; amend

另见 [gèng]

庚 [gēng] 1 (n) 天干的第七位，用作次序的第七 the seventh of the Ten Stems 2 (n) 年 age; year

赓 (賡) [gēng] (v) 継续 continue

耕 [gēng] (v) 用犁松土，翻土 plough; cultivate ＊在马来半岛可以看到农人用水牛来耕田。 In Peninsular Malaya farmers are seen using buffalos to plough the field.

耕地 [gēngdì] farmland; cultivated fields

耕种 [gēngzhòng] plough and sow; work on the farm

羹 [gēng] (n) 浓汤或糊状的食物 soup; broth

羹匙 [gēngchí] a spoon

gěng

哽 [gěng] 1 (v) 哭时声气阻塞 choke from grief ＊他听到叔叔突然逝世的消息，心里一酸，喉咙哽得一时说不出话来。 After the sudden death of his uncle, he felt very sad and choked so much so that he could not speak a word 2 (v) 喉咙被食物堵住 choke

哽咽 [gěngyè] utterance choked with sobs

绠 (綆) [gěng] (n) 汲水桶上的绳子 the rope attached to a bucket

梗 [gěng] 1 (n) 植物的茎秆 stem ; stalk 2 (v) 阻碍 impede; obstruct 3 (adj) 直爽 outspoken 4 (adj) 顽固 stubborn

梗概 [gěnggài] outline; a general idea; a summary

梗塞 [gěngsē] obstruct

梗阻 [gěngzǔ] impede; hinder; obstruct

鲠 (鯁) [gěng] (n) 鱼骨 bone of fish

耿 [gěng] 1 (adj) 光明 bright 2 (adj) 正直 upright; sincere; fair and just ＊传说包青天是个耿直的清官，处事公平。 Justice Pao was said to be an upright noble who dealt with matters fairly and justly.

耿直 [gěngzhí] fair and just; upright

耿耿于怀 [gěng gěng yú huái] stick at heart

gèng

更 [gèng] (adv) 越发，愈加 still; furthermore * 这房子里已挤满了人，再多几个人进来，情形更糟。The situation will further worsen when more people enter the already crowded room.

更加 [gèngjiā] to a higher degree; still further; even more

另见 [gēng]

gōng

工 [gōng] 1 (n) 劳动人们的简称 a workman; a labourer * 马来西亚的矿工在历史上多是中国的移民。The miners of Malaysia were historically immigrants from China. 2 (n) 工业 industry 3 (n) 工作，所做的事 work; a job 4 (n) 工作日 workday 5 (adj) 长于，善于 skilful in

工兵 [gōngbīng] engineering corps; a sapper

工厂 [gōngchǎng] factory; plant; mill; works

工潮 [gōngcháo] worker strike; industrial unrest

工程 [gōngchéng] construction work; job of work; project

工程师 [gōngchéngshī] engineer

工地 [gōngdì] work site; construction site

工夫 [gōngfū] labour; effort; time. ability; skill

工会 [gōnghùi] trade union

工具 [gōngjù] tool; instruments; means

工龄 [gōnglíng] working years; length of service

工人 [gōngrén] worker

工头 [gōngtóu] a foreman; an overseer

工业化 [gōngyèhùa] industrialize; industrialization

工艺 [gōngyì] technology; craftsmanship

工整 [gōng zhěng] neat and orderly

工资 [gōngzī] wage; salary

功 [gōng] 1 (n) 劳绩；成绩 merit; good deeds * 许多抗日战士都立下了卫国的大功。Many anti-Japanese warriors had performed meritorious services in defence of the country. 2 (n) 功效；成效 effect; achievement; virtue * 盘尼西林的功用是杀菌。The effect of penicillin is to kill germs.

功败垂成 [gōng bài chúi chéng] to fail only when nearing success

功德无量 [gōng dé wú liáng] boundless colossal deeds and benevolence

功夫 [gōng·fu] work; service

功绩 [gōngjī] merits; feat; achievement.

功课 [gōngkè] lessons ; work; task

功劳 [gōngláo] meritorious deeds; achievement; credit

功能 [gōngnéng] function

功效如神 [gōng xiào rú shén] divine like efficacy

功用 [gōngyòng] function; use

攻 [gōng] 1 (v) 进击 attack * 日本于1942年攻打马来半岛。Japan attacked Malay Peninsular in 1942. 2 (v)用功学习，从事研究 study hard * 他在外国攻读医科，现在已学成归国。He studied medicine abroad. Now he has successfully completed his study and returned home.

攻打 [gōngdǎ] attack (a place held by the enemy)

攻读 [gōngdú] study hard; take great pains in study

攻击 [gōngjī] attack; assault

攻克 [gōngkè] attack and capture, conquer

攻势 [gōngshì] offensive

攻无不克 [gōng wú bù kè] there is

none that cannot be captured when attacked

供 [gōng] (v)准备着东西给需要的人应用 supply; provide * 公用事业局供给全国所需要的水和电力。The Public Utilities Board supplies water and electricity for the whole country.
另见 [gòng]

供不应求 [gōngbùyìngqíu] supply falls short of demand
供给 [gōngjǐ] supply; provide, furnish
供求 [gōngqíu] supply and demand
供销 [gōngxiāo] supply and marketing
供养 [gōng yǎng] provide for the needs of one's parents or elders
供应 [gōng yìng] supply; provide

龚(龔) [gōng] 姓氏 a surname

弓 [gōng] (n) 射箭或发弹丸的器械 bow * 在很久以前，人们用弓和箭打猎。Very long ago, people used bows and arrows for hunting
弓箭 [gōng jiàn] bow and arrow
弓弦 [gōng xián] a bowstring; a chord

躬 [gōng] 1 (n) 身体 the body 2 (adv) 亲自 personally 3 (v) 弯下 bend

公 [gōng] 1 (adj) (n) 跟"私"相对 public * 本大学有开设公共关系课程。The University is offering a course in public relations. 2 (n) 雄性的 the male animals * 公鸡。the cock.
公报 [gōng bào] communique
公布 [gōng bù] issue; publish; announce
公尺 [gōngchǐ] metre
公道 [gōngdào] fair; just
公愤 [gōngfèn] public indignation
公告 [gōnggào] notice
公公 [gōnggōng] father - in - law (husband's father); grandfather
公函 [gōnghán] official document
公祭 [gōng jì] public sacrifices
公积金 [gōngjījīn] Central Provident Fund
公斤 [gōngjīn] kilogram
公开 [gōngkāi] open to the public; publicly
公款 [gōngkuǎn] public funds
公路 [gōnglù] high way
公论 [gōnglùn] public opinion
公民 [gōngmín] citizen
公平 [gōngpíng] fair; just
公然 [gōngrán] openly; undisguised
公认 [gōngrèn] universally acknowledged or recognised
公式 [gōngshì] formula
公事 [gōngshì] public affairs; official business
公司 [gōngsī] company
公文 [gōngwén] official document
公物 [gōngwù] public property; public asset
公演 [gōng yǎn] perform in public
公用 [gōngyòng] for public use ; for common use; communal
公寓 [gōngyù] apartment house
公园 [gōngyuán] park
公约 [gōng yuè] pact; convention; pledge
公债 [gōng zhài] government bonds
公正 [gōng zhèng] just; impartial
公正人 [gōng zhèng rén] referee; umpire
公转 [gōng zhuǎn] revolve (eg. round the sun)

恭 [gōng] (adj) 有礼貌，谦虚 reverent polite; courteous; respectful
恭敬 [gōngjìng] respectful; polite
恭维 [gōngwéi] flatter; praise
恭喜 [gōngxǐ] congratulate; wish one joy respectfully

宫 [gōng] (n) 帝王的住所 the palace; an ancestral temple * 她在宫里生活了四十年左右。She lived in the palace for about forty years.

宫殿 [gōngdiàn] a palace

肱 [gōng] (n) 手臂从肘到腕的部分 the arm

gǒng

拱 [gǒng] 1 (v) 两手相合，表示尊敬 salute by folding hands 2 (v) 环绕 encircle 3 (n) 建筑物成弧形的结构 an arch

拱桥 [gǒngqiáo] arched bridge.

巩（鞏） [gǒng] (v) 坚固，使牢固 consolidate; strengthen., (adj) consolidated; firm; stable * 每个国家都有军队和武器，以巩固国防。Every nation keeps its army and weapons to strengthen its national defence.

巩固 [gǒnggù] firm; solid; stable; consolidated ; consolidate; strengthen.

gòng

贡（貢） [gòng] (v) 奉献 to present as tribute

贡献 [gòngxiàn] contribute; render service; contribution; an offering

共 [gòng] 1 (v) 同，一齐 share; participate (adj) common; mutual * 去跑马场的人都有共同的愿望，那就是赢钱。People who go to the race course have a common wish; that is, to win money. 2 (adv) 总，合计 all; altogether; in all; totally; wholly * 我们一家的开销每月共计四百元。The monthly expenditure of our family is four hundred dollars altogether.

共产党 [gòngchǎndǎng] communist party

共产国际 [gòngchǎnguójì] Comintern; Communist International

共产党员 [gòngchǎn dǎngyuán] member of the communist party

共和国 [gònghé guó] republic

共鸣 [gòngmíng] accoustic resonance; resonance sympathy; applause

共事 [gòngshì] work together; be associated with

共同 [gòngtóng] common; joint; mutual

共同市场 [gòng tóng shì chǎng] Common Market

共性 [gòngxìng] common characteristics; general character

供 [gòng] 1 (n) 祭祀用的物品 offerings in worship 2 (v) 受审者的陈述 confess

供词 [gòngcí] confession. statement

供认 [gòngrèn] confess

另见 [gōng]

gōu

勾 [gōu] 1 (v) 除掉，取消 cancel; annul * 经过一番解释，他们以前的误会已一笔勾消。After some explanations,their previous misunderstandings are all forgotten (cancelled). 2 (v) 牵引，引起 hook on with; connect * 他跟几个流氓勾结去打抢路人。He hooked on with some rascals to rob passers-by.

勾搭 [gōu·da] ally oneself with; collude with

勾结 [gōujié] collude with; collaborate with; work hand in glove with; conspire with

勾销 [gōuxiāo] cancel; wipe out

勾心斗角 [gōuxīndòujiǎo] scheme against each other

勾引 [gōuyǐn] induce; entice; seduce

沟（溝） [gōu] 1 (n) 水道 a creek; a canal 2 (n) 人工修成的田间水道和壕沟 ditch; drain * 沟里的水不很清洁。The water in the ditch is not very clean. 3 (n) 平面上凹下去的长条痕迹。 a trench

沟壑 [gōuhè] gully; valley

沟渠 [gōu qú] ditch; irrigation canal

沟通 [gōu tōng] connect; communicate; understand each other

钩（鉤）[gōu] (n) 悬挂或探取东西用的器具，形状弯曲而头尖 hook; a clasp ＊他买的鱼钩太贵了，是日本制造的。The fishing hook which he bought was made in Japan.

钩针 [gōuzhēn] a hook; a crochet needle

钩深致远 [gōu shēn zhì yuǎn] to go doop into obocuro objects

钩心斗角 [gōu xīn dòu jiǎo] to conspire against each others

gǒu

狗 [gǒu] (n) 就是"犬"，家畜能帮助守门，性格友善 dog

狗急跳墙 [gǒu jí tiào qiàng] In desperation, a man will do anything rash; be driven to extremities

狗血喷头 [gǒu xùe pēn tóu] curse someone very thoroughly; pour out a torrent of abuses

狗仗人势 [gǒu zhàng rén shì] (term of abuse) bad elements rely on the forces of evil (to bully others)

枸 [gǒu] (n) 枸杞 [gǒujǐ] 落叶灌木，子，根，茎均可入药 matrimony ocve; lycium Chinense ; a Chinese herb
另见 [jǔ]

苟 [gǒu] 1 (adj) 随便，马虎 careless ＊他的工作态度认真，做什么都一丝不苟。With a serious attitude towards work, he is very careful in whatever he does.
2 (conj) 假使，如果的意思 If; at all ＊苟能坚持，必能胜利。If one can persist, one will surely succeed.

苟安 [gǒu ān] seek momentary ease

苟且 [gǒu qiě] careless; muddling along

苟且了事 [gǒu qiě liǎo shì] to do a thing carelessly, slovently

苟且偷安 [gǒu qiě tōu ān] to snatch a life of ease, thoughtless of the future.

苟延残喘 [gǒu yán cán chuǎn] eke out a meagre existence; barely manage to survive

笱 [gǒu] (n) 捕鱼时用的竹笼 a cage used for catching fish

gòu

勾 [gòu] (v) 伸直胳臂去拿 hook on (with one's arm)

勾当 [gòudàng] fraudulent deal
另见 [gōu]

构（構）[gòu] (v) 造，设计 build; construct; compose; make; plot ＊马来西亚是由十三个邦构成的。Malaysia is made up of thirteen states.

构成 [gòu chèng] consist of; constitute; form; formulate

构词法 [gòucífǎ] word formation; morphology

构思 [gòu sī] meditate; design

构图 [gòu tú] compose

构造 [gòu zào] structure; construction; construct

购（購）[gòu] (v) 买 buy ＊爸爸到农村去购买又新鲜又便宜的蔬菜。My father goes to the farms to buy cheap and fresh vegetables.

购买 [gòu mǎi] buy; purchase

购买力 [gòu mǎilì] purchasing power

购置 [gòu zhì] buy (big and durable items)

够 [gòu] (adj) 达到某种限度，充足 enough; sufficient; reach ＊他受够了老板的气，决定提出辞职。Having had enough from his boss, he decided to tender his resignation.

垢 [gòu] (n) 脏东西 dirt; filth; a stain 2 (adj) 污秽，肮脏 dirty; filthy 3 (n) 耻辱 disgrace

觏(覯) [gòu] (v) 遇见 see; meet

媾 [gòu] 1 (n) 交合 sexual intercourse 2 (v) 交好 make peace

媾和 [gòu hé] negotiate for peace; make peace with

gū

估 [gū] (v) 大约推算 estimate ＊科学家估计人类在地球已有好几百万年了。Scientists estimate that man has existed on earth for a few millions of years.

估计 [gūjì] estimate; calculate; appraise.

估价 [gū jià] evaluate; appraise

估量 [gū liáng] estimate; take it into account; appraise

另见 [gù]

咕 [gū] (n) 鸽子叫的声音 a sound made by pigeons

沽 [gū] 1 (v) 买 buy 2 (v) 卖 sell ＊股票市坊上的人常拿着股票，待价而沽。People in the stock market usually hold their shares and wait for a good price to sell.

沽名钓誉 [gū míng diào yù] fish for fame and reputation

姑 [gū] 1 (n) 父亲的姊妹 a paternal aunt ＊我有一个姑母，名叫玛莉。I have an aunt; her name is Mary. 2 (n) 丈夫的姊妹 sisters-in-law 3 (adv) 暂且 in the mean time; for the time being ＊我们姑且保留这建议，待下次会议再详细讨论。 We shall for the time being reserve this proposal for further discussion at the next meeting

姑且 [gū qiě] temporarily; for the time being; provisionally

姑妄听之 [gū wàng tīng zhī] listen casually to, not necessarily accepting what is said

酤 [gū] 1 (n) 酒 wine. 2 (v) 买酒，卖酒 buy or sell wine.

辜 [gū] (n) 罪过 a crime; a fault; guilt

辜负 [gū fù] fail to live up to; disappoint the hopes of; ungrateful

菇 [gū] (n) 同菰菌类植物 a mushroom; a fungus

骨 [gū] ⌊骨碌⌉ (v) 滚动 roll

另见 [gǔ]

呱 [gū] ⌊呱呱⌉ (n) 表示哭声，刚出世的婴儿的哭声 the cry of an infant.

另见 [guā]

孤 [gū] 1 (n) 父母双亡的小孩子 orphan ＊他是一个孤儿。He is an orphan. 2 (adj) 单独 alone; single ; lonesome; lonely ＊他是家里的独生子，所以常感到孤单。Being the only child in the family, he always feels lonely.

孤独 [gū dú] solitary; lonely

孤儿 [gū ér] orphan

孤芳自赏 [gū fāng zì shǎng] self-styled as being lofty

孤寂 [gū jì] lonely; lonesome

孤家寡人 [gū jiā guǎ rén] a man isolated from the masses ; totally isolated

孤军 [gū jūn] an army being isolated and cut off from help

孤苦伶仃 [gū kǔ líng dīng] lonely and miserable and destitute

孤立 [gū lì] isolate; isolated

孤零零 [gū līng līng] alone; helpless

孤立无援 [gū lì wú yuán] isolated and helpless

孤僻 [gūpì] eccentric; peculiar

孤树不成林 [gū shù bù chéng lín] a single tree does not make a forest

孤掌难鸣 [gū zhǎng nán míng] one

who stands alone has no power

孤注一掷 [gū zhù yī zhì] risk all on a single throw; make a last desperate effort

箍 [gū] 1 (v) 用竹篾或铁条等围住束紧 draw tight; hoop 2 (n) 束紧东西的圈 a hoop; a belt; a circlet

gǔ

古 [gǔ] (adj) 过去的，很久以前的 ancient; old ＊罗马帝国是一个文明古国。 The Roman Empire was an ancient civilised country

古板 [gǔ bǎn] old-fashioned; conservative

古典 [gǔ diǎn] classical; classic

古董 [gǔ dǒng] antiques; curios

古怪 [gǔ guài] strange; peculiar; quaint

古迹 [gǔ jì] historical sites; places of historical interests. relics

古人 [gǔ rén] the ancients; men of old

古色古香 [gǔ sè gǔ xiāng] mellowness of antiquity

古往今来 [gǔ wǎng jīn lái] from ancient to modern times

古为今用 [gǔ wéi jīn yóng] make the past to serve the present

古文 [gǔ wén] the classical style of writing; ancient literature

古物 [gǔ wù] historical relics; antiques

诂(詁) [gǔ] (v) 用通俗的话解释古文字义 explain classics or ancient literature in the common language

牯 [gǔ] (n) 母牛，也指阉割过的公牛 a cow (female); a castrated bull

骨 [gǔ] 1 (n) 人和脊椎动物体内支持身体的坚硬组织 bone 2 (n) 支撑物体起骨架作用的东西 a rib; frame (of umbrellas, etc.)

骨干 [gǔ gàn] mainstay; hard core; backbone

骨骼 [gǔ gé] skeleton

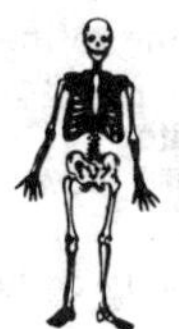

骨灰 [gǔhūi] ashes

骨架 [gǔ jià] framework

骨科 [gǔ kē] orthopedics

骨气 [gǔqì] moral integrity; loftiness

骨肉 [gǔ ròu] blood relationship; kinsmen

骨瘦如柴 [gǔ shòu rù chái] thin and emanciated like a stick

骨髓 [gǔsǔi] marrow

骨子里 [gǔ zǐlǐ] in one's heart; by nature

另见 [gú]

股 [gǔ] 1 (n) 大腿 thigh 2 (n) 集合资金的一分或均分财产的一分 a share in a concern or business 3 (n) 机关，企业，团体中的一个部门 a division 4 (a measure word) 量词 strand (for hair, rope), whiff (of fresh air), group (for persons, bandits, etc.) current (eg. a counter or adverse current). ＊一股冷气。a whiff of cold air.

股东 [gǔdōng] a share holder; a stockholder

股份 [gǔfén] a share in business

股份公司 [gǔfén gōngsī] a joint stock company

股票 [gǔ piào] shares; stocks; a share (stock) certificate

鼓 [gǔ] 1 (n) 打击乐器，木制，受击之平面用兽皮制成 drum ＊非洲土人击鼓传递消息。 The aborigines beat drums to pass on news. 2 (v) 发动，振奋 rouse; inspire ＊马可波罗游历中国激起了当时许多欧洲商人到远东来。 The visit of Marco Polo to China inspired many European traders of that time to come to the Far East. 3 (v) 凸出；高起 point; inflate (adj) inflated

鼓吹 [gǔ chuī] advocate; play up; agitate

鼓动 [gǔ dòng] agitate; instigate; urge

鼓励 [gǔ lì] encourage; inspire

鼓膜 [gǔ mó] the ear-drum; the tympanum

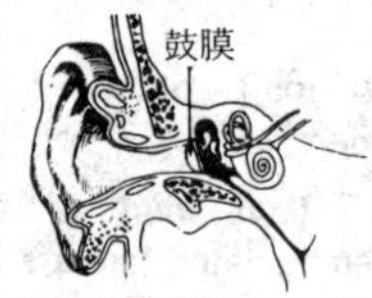

鼓舞 [gǔ wǔ] inspire; encourage; stimulate

鼓掌 [gǔ zhǎng] applaud

鼓足干劲 [gǔ zú gàn jìn] go all out; exert the utmost effort

臌 [gǔ]〔臌胀〕(n) 中医指腹内有水 dropsical swelling; bloated; bulging

瞽 [gǔ] (adj) 瞎 blind

蛊（蠱）[gǔ] (n) 旧时传说中一种由人工培养的毒虫 an insect in mythology

蛊惑人心 [gǔ huò rén xīn] confuse and poison people's minds

谷 [gǔ] 1 (n) 两山或两块高地之间的夹道或流水道 valley ＊ 在那遥远的山谷中，有一个小村庄，村民都是少数民族的人民。 In that far-away valley, there is a small village; the villagers are all of the minority races.

谷（穀）[gǔ] (n) 庄稼和粮食的总称。如：米，豆…… grain; cereals

谷仓 [gǔ cāng] a barn; a granary; a bin

谷物 [gǔwù] cereals

谷种 [gǔ zhǒng] seeds

谷子 [gǔ·zi] millet

贾（賈）[gǔ] 1 (n) 商人 a merchant 2 (v) 做买卖 to conduct business

鹄（鵠）[gǔ] (n) 射箭的目标，箭靶子 a target 另见 [hú]

gù

固 [gù] 1 (v) 使不动 make firm; fix 2 (adj) 结实，牢靠 strong; sturdy; firm ＊ 楼房要有坚固的基础，才不容易倒塌。 A building should be built on strong foundation so that it will not collapse easily. 3 (adv) 本来，已经。originally; already; inherent. ＊钢铁的固有性质就是坚硬耐用。 The inherent qualities of steel are strong, hard and durable.

固步自封 [gùbùzìfēng] contented with one's present condition and do not ask for improvement.

固定 [gù dìng] fix; fixed; stable; static

固然 [gù rán] although; though; of course; certainly

固体 [gù tǐ] solid

固有 [gù yǒu] inherent

固执 [gù zhí] stubborn; obstinate

固执己见 [gùzhíjǐjiàn] stick stubbornly to one's own opinion.

痼 [gù] (n) 时间长，不易治疗，不易克服的疾病或恶习 a deeply-rooted illness or habit

痼癖 [gù pǐ] a deep-rooted habit; a bad habit

梏 [gù] (n) 古代木制的手铐 handcuffs; manacles

估 [gù] 估衣 (n) 出售的旧衣服 second-hand clothes

估衣店 [gùyīdiàn] a second - hand clothes store
另见 [gū]

故 [gù] 1 (n) 意外事情 accidents; unexpected incidents or events. * 妹妹昨晚没有回家,不知是否在外面发生事故? Sister had not returned home last night, could some accidents have happened? 2 (n) 原因 cause; reason * 她本来有说有笑,不知何故突然间不出声。 Originally she was joking and talking, but for some unknown reasons, she suddenly became quiet. 3 (adv) 存心 intentionally; in pretext; purposely * 他遇到盗贼时,能故作镇定,使后者反而害怕起来。When he met the robber, he purposely showed a calm manner and made the latter frightened. 4 (conj) 所以,因此 because; for; as a consequence 5 (adj) 从前的 ancient; old; past * 他是我童年时期的伙伴,我们是故交。He is my childhood playmate; we are old friends. 6 (v) 死亡(指死人) die; pass away * 由於他父亲病故,一家的生计立刻发生困难。 That his father died of sickness had immediately made the family hard to find a living.

故步自封 [gù bù zì fēng] ultraconservative and self-satisfied; confining oneself to old conventions and refusing to change

故此 [gù cǐ] therefore; on this account

故都 [gù dū] ancient capital

故居 [gùjū] former residence

故弄玄虚 [gù nòng xuán xū] using intrigues and tricks

故事 [gù shì] story; tale

故乡 [gù xiāng] home town; native place; birthplace

故意 [gù yì] intentional; purposely; deliberately

故障 [gù zhāng] out of order; a hindrance: an obstacle

顾(顧) [gù] 1 (v) 转过头看 look around, look about * 他环顾周围,见没有人,才告诉我一个秘密。Having looked around to see that there is no one near by, he told me a secret. 2 (v) 照看,关心 care for; mind; attend to; look after * 工作这样繁重,你得照顾自己的健康,别熬坏了。Since the job is heavy, you must look after yourself and not spoil your health.

顾此失彼 [gùcǐshībǐ] take care of one matter while forgetting the other; unable to attend to everything at once

顾忌 [gù jì] be misgiven; misgivings

顾客 [gù kè] customer; client; shopper

顾虑 [gùlù] worry ; apprehensions; misgivings

顾名思义 [gù míng sī yì] from the name you know what it implies; understand the context by the name

顾全大局 [gù quán dà jú] take the interests of the whole into account; consideration for the general interests

顾问 [gù wèn] adviser; counsellor

雇 [gù] 1 (v) 请人帮忙,付给一定的酬劳 hire; employ; engage * 那间杂货店的老板雇用了两名童工。 The boss of that provision shop employs two child labourers 2 (v) 租赁交通工具 hire (a car, etc.)

雇工 [gù gōng] hired labour

雇农 [gù nóng] hired farm labourers; employed peasantry

雇佣 [gù yōng] hire

雇佣兵 [gù yōng bīng] a hired soldier; a mercenary

雇员 [gù yuán] employee
雇主 [gù zhǔ] employer; a master

guā

刮 [guā] 1 (v) 用刀具去掉物体表面的东西 scrape; raze; plane off; rub. * 他用刀刮平木块，使它光亮。He razed the piece of wood with a knife to make it smooth. 2 (v) 吹 blow * 刚才刮了一阵大风，把屋里的东西吹乱了。Just now a strong wind blew and messed up the things in the house.

刮脸 [guā liǎn] shave
刮脸刀 [guā liǎn dāo] razor

瓜 [guā] (n) 蔓生植物，果可食 gourds; cucumbers; melons
瓜熟蒂落 [guā shú di luò] when the melon is ripe, it falls at the right time — things are easily managed.
瓜子 [guā zǐ] watermelon seeds.

呱 [guā] (n) 青蛙，乌鸦等的叫声 quack; croak
另见 [gū]

guǎ

剐(剮) [guǎ] 1 (n) 封建时代最残酷的死刑，用刀把人体割碎 cutting the body into pieces, a punishment in ancient times 2 (v) 被尖锐的东西划破 hack

寡 [guǎ] 1 (adj) 少，缺少，跟"多"相对 few; single; rare 他本来就是个寡言的人，在大庭广众面前更不愿说话。As he is a reticent person in itself, he would not utter a word in public. 2 (n) 妇女死了丈夫叫"寡" a widow
寡不敌众 [guǎ bù dí zhòng] the few cannot withstand the horde
寡断 [guǎ duàn] lack of judgement
寡廉鲜耻 [guǎ lián xiān chǐ] dishonest and shameless
寡妇 [guǎfù] widow

guà

卦 [guà] (n) 巧妙的猜想或预测。如：八卦。divination

挂 [guà] 1 (v) 悬，使物体附着于高处的一点或几点，不落下来 hang up; suspend; put up * 老师把地图挂在黑板上让大家看。The teacher hanged the map on the blackboard for all to see. 2 (v) 牵记 think of; worry; anxious * 在外地的父亲写信告诉我们他很好，叫我们不必牵挂。Father, working abroad, writes to tell us not to worry about him as he is fine. 3 (v) 登记 note; record; register * 这封信很重要，必须挂号寄发。This letter is very important. It should be sent by registered mail.
挂彩 [guà cǎi] wounded (in battle)
挂念 [guà niàn] worry over (somebody); feel anxious about
挂帅 [guà shuài] put ... in command; take command
挂图 [guà tú] wall chart
挂羊头卖狗肉 [guà yáng tóu mài gǒu ròu] selling dog's meat under the label of a sheep's head; selling inferior goods under a better brand
挂一漏万 [guà yī lòu wàn] record one item while leaving out ten thousands; incomplete and full of omissions

褂 [guà] (n) 上身的衣服 an outer jacket; a coat

guāi

乖 [guāi] 1 (adj) 古怪，不和谐 odd; perverse; quaint; strange * 他的性情乖僻，常常做出非普通人所能料到的事。With an odd character, he always does things which are beyond the expectation of an ordinary man. 2 (adj) 机灵，警觉 quick-witted * 台上的司

仪很乖巧，能够应付当场的事变。The compere on stage is quick-witted enough to handle any changes at that occassion. 3 (adj) 指小孩子不淘气 obedient * 这小孩子很乖，父母亲谈话时不打扰。This child is very obedient, he does not interrupt his parents' conversation.

乖僻 [guāi pì] odd; crankey; perverse; queer

乖巧 [guāi qiǎo] clever, tricky; ingenious; artful

guǎi

拐 [guǎi] 1 (v) 转弯，改方向 turn * 这路牌写着「不准拐弯」。This road sign says that turning is not permitted. 2 (v) 用手段把人或财物骗去 deceive; swindle; entrap * 有些非法集团拐带乡村少女到城市去做坏事。Some illegal syndicates entrapped countryside girls to the city to do evil things. 3 (adj)腿或脚部有毛病走路不自然 lame

拐带 [guǎi dài] kidnap; seduce; decoy; abduct

拐棍 [guǎi gùn] walking stick; an old man's staff

拐弯 [guǎi wān] making turns; turn a corner

拐弯抹角 [guǎiwānmǒjiǎo] speak or write in a roundabout way

guài

怪 [guài] 1 (adj) 奇异的，不常见的 strange; abnormal * 大热天时，突然下雹，他觉得很奇怪。He feels strange that it hails suddenly in such a hot day. 2 (v) 埋怨，责备 blame; find fault with * 他自己迟到，却怪别人不等他。He was late and yet he blamed the others for not waiting for him. 4 (adv)很 unusually; very * 她唱的流行歌曲怪好听的。The pop songs she sings are very pleasant to the ears. 5 (n) 神怪传说中的妖魔 a monster; a prodigy

怪不得 [guàibù de] blamed; no wonder

怪话 [guàihuà] unprincipled complaints and remarks

怪模怪样 [guàimùguàiyàng] peculiar; queer; odd; strange

怪僻 [guàipì] (of persons) eccentric; odd; queer

怪物 [guài wù] monster

怪异 [guài yì] uncanny; supernatural; monstrous

guān

官 [guān] 1 (n) 指在国家机关，军队里充当各级部门人员 official; officer; the authorities * 汤美的父亲是一个视学官 Tommy's father is an inspector of schools. 2 (adj) 指属于国家的 official; governmental

官方 [guān fāng] official

官吏 [guān lì] government official in old society

官僚 [guān liáo] bureaucrat

官僚主义 [guānliáozhǔyì] bureaucracy

官司 [guān sī] law suits; case

官员 [guān yuán] government official; official

官样文章 [guān yàng wén zhāng] official formality; red tape; official jargon

官逼民反 [guān bì mín fǎn] the officials oppress, the people rebel

棺 [guān] (n) 棺材，装殓死人的器具 coffin * 棺材多数用木制成的。Most coffins are made of wood.

鳏（鰥）[guān] (n) 没有妻子的男子 an unmarried man; a widower * 我的邻居是个鳏夫，他已四十出头，为人彬彬有礼。My neighbour is a widower; he is over forty years old and well-mannered.

冠 [guān] 1 (n) 帽子 a cap; a hat; a crown 2 (n) 像帽子样的东西 things resembling a cap
另见 [guàn]

关(關) [guān] 1 (v) 闭，合拢 close; shut; cover ＊下雨了，小妹妹赶快把窗门关起来。It's raining, so little sister quickly closes the windows. 2 (n) 古代在险要的地方设立守卫的处所 a frontier gate; a post at strategic position; a pass 3 (n) 征收出口入口货税的机构 a customs station 4 (n) 在重要时机，转折点 crisis; a turning point; crucial moment ＊会考是学生必经的一关。The government examination is a crucial moment for students. 5 (v) 牵连 concern; involve; related to; have reference to ＊社会上的一切事物都关系到我们的日常生活。All that happens in the society is related to our daily life.

关闭 [guān bì] close down; shut
关怀 [guān huái] be concerned about
关键 [guān jiàn] pivot; key; crux; an important thing
关节 [guān jié] joint; links
关节炎 [guān jié yán] arthritis
关联 [guān lián] be related or interconnected; connections (of problems, etc.)
关门大吉 [guān mén dà jì] good luck for closing (sarcastic)
关卡 [guān qiǎ] a customs station
关切 [guān qiè] deeply concerned about
关税 [guān shuì] customs duties; tariffs
关头 [guān tóu] critical point; juncture
关系 [guān xi] relation; relationship; be related to; concern
关心 [guānxīn] show concern for; be concerned about
关于 [guān yú] about; concerning; regarding; on
关照 [guān zhào] take care of; take somethinig into account; inform
关注 [guān zhú] pay close attention to; be intensely concerned about

观(觀) [guān] 1 (v) 看 look at; see; view; inspect; display ＊许多人到体育馆去观看足球赛。Many people went to the Sports Stadium to watch the soccer match. 2 (n) 看到的景象 a view; a sight; an observatory ＊国庆日检阅典礼很壮观。The National Day Parade is a magnificent scene. 3 (n) 对事物的看法或认识 an opinion or view over things ＊ 人生观 a person's point of view towards life.
另见 [guàn]

观察 [guān chá] observe; view; examine
观点 [guān diǎn] point of view
观感 [guān gǎn] impression; view
观光 [guān guāng] make a sightseeing trip
观看 [guān kàn] watch; inspect; behold
观礼台 [guān lǐ taí] rostrum; reviewing stand
观摩 [guān mó] see the good in and learn from each other
观念 [guān niàn] idea; notion; concept
观赏 [guān shǎng] watch and enjoy
观望 [guān wàng] take a wait-and-see attitude
观众 [guān zhóng] audience; spectators

guǎn

馆(館) [guǎn] 1 (n) 供宾客或旅客住的宿舍 a hotel; a restaurant; an inn; a lodging 2 (n) 某种机关或某些政治文化场

所 a hall ＊展览馆。an exhibition hall. 3 (n) 某些服务性商店的名称 a commercial service centre ＊照相馆。a photo studio. 4 (n) 旧时指教学的地方。a schoolroom in the olden days

管 [guǎn] 1 (n) 园形成筒形的东西 a tube; a pipe 2 (n) 吹奏的乐器 a reed; a flute ＊双簧管 an oboe 3 (v) 负责办理 rule; govern; manage; take care of ＊他做事有条有理，把公司管理得很好。Being systematic in his work, he is managing the company very well. 4 (v) 约束 control; supervise ＊父母亲对子女管制得太严，有时会产生反效果。There may be adverse effect if parents control their children too tightly

管教 [guǎn jiào] teach; instruct; educate

管理 [guǎnlǐ] manage; administer; administration

管辖 [guǎn xiá] subject to the jurisdiction of; exercise control over; be under the rule of

管弦乐 [guǎn xián yuè] orchestral music; music from flutes and stringed instruments

管制 [guǎn zhì] control; put under surveillance

管子 [guǎn·zi] pipe; tube

guàn

灌 [guàn] (v) 浇，注入 pour in (liquid); irrigate; fill ＊不足够雨量的地方，需要有水供系统来灌溉农田。Places with inadequate rainfall require a water supply system to irrigate the farms.

灌溉 [guàn gài] irrigate

灌木 [guàn mù] shrubs, bush

灌输 [guàn shū] (of water) pour or pump into; imbue; instil into

灌注 [guàn zhù] pour into; fill

罐 [guàn] (n) 盛东西的器具通常用金属制成的 a can; pot; tin ＊我昨天买了两罐牛奶。Yesterday I bought two tins of condensed milk.

罐头 [guàn·tou] canned food; can

观(觀) [guàn] (n) 道教的庙宇 a Taoist temple 另见 [guān]

贯(貫) [guàn] 1 (v) 穿通 string; run through; connect; penetrate ＊一条新路把大山两边连贯起来，给居民带来不少方便。The new road penetrating a big hill facilitates the residents on both sides of the hill. 2 (n) 古代一千钱为一贯。a monetary unit (archaic) (n) 出生地，原籍 place of birth; domicile

贯穿 [guàn chuān] run through (all processes); continue through; be shot through and through with

贯通 [guàn tōng] have a thorough understanding; cover; interconnect be connected

贯注 [guàn zhù] concentrate; be imbued with; be absorbed in

惯(慣) [guàn] 1 (adj) 习以为常的 habitual; accustomed to; used to; familiar with; customary; usual ＊我惯于用左手工作，假如改用右手会不方便的。I am accustomed to working with left hand, so if I change to my right hand, it will be very inconvenient. 2 (v) 放任 pamper ＊让孩子娇生惯养，有害无益。More harm than good is done if children are pampered.

惯例 [guànlì] customary practice; convention

惯性 [guàn xìng] inertia

掼(摜) [guàn] 1 (v) 掷，扔 throw ＊他把废纸掼在一边。He threw aside the waste papers. 2 (v) 摔，跌

smash; fall ＊下雨后路上很滑，一位老太婆不小心掼了一交。The road was slippery after a shower and an old woman fell accidentally.

冠 [guàn] 1 (v) 戴上帽子 put on a cap 2 (adj) 表示第一的 first; champion ＊他在运动会上跑得最快，成为今年的冠军。Being the fastest runner in this sports meet, he becomes the champion of the year.

冠军 [guànjūn] champion (in games and sports)

另见 [guān]

盥 [guàn] (v) 洗手 wash hand

盥洗 [guanxǐ] wash hands and face

盥洗室 [guànxǐshì] toilet; washroom; lavatory

guāng

光 [guāng] 1 (n) 太阳，火，电等放射出来，使人感到明亮的東西 light 2 (adj) 荣誉 glorious; honorary (n) glory; honou ＊校长说今年会考成绩很好，同学们给学校带来了光荣。The principal said that due to the good examination results, the students had brought honour to the school. 3 (n) 景物 scenary; view; scene; sight ＊每年有不少旅客到新加坡来观光。Every year, there are many tourists who come to Singapore for sight-seeing. 4 (adj) 平滑 smooth ＊他花了一天的时间，把地板磨得很光滑。He spends one whole day to polish the floor until it is very smooth. 5 (adj) 完了，尽 finished; ended; thorough ＊月底未到，家里的米已吃光了。The stock of rice at home has been finished before the end of the month. 6 (adj) 单，只 solely; merely; only; alone ＊一个人要成功，光靠天赋是不夠的。It is not enough for one to rely merely on natural gifts on one's way to success. 7 (adj) 明亮 bright; luminous; lustrous; gleaming; radiant (n) brightness; illumination ＊她细心地把窗子抹得很光亮。She carefully polishes the window until it is very bright. 8 (adj) 裸露着 naked; bare ＊他只穿了短裤，光着上半身，在烈日下工作。Wearing only shorts and with the upper part of his body naked, he works under the hot sun.

光彩 [guāng cǎi] brilliance; splendour; glory; honour; bright; brilliant

光彩夺目 [guāng cǎiduó mù] colorful and dazzling

光辐射 [guāng fù shè] light radiation

光滑 [guāng·hua] smooth; sleek

光辉 [guāng huī] glory; splendour; radiance; splendid; glorious

光景 [guāng jǐng] landscape; view; scene; circumstances; situation; condition

光临 [guāng lín] come; arrive (polite form)

光芒 [guāng máng] brilliance

光明 [guāng míng] bright; brilliant

光明磊落 [guāng míng lěi luò] honest and open; above board

光芒万丈 [guāng máng wàn zhàng] radiant in brilliance

光明正大 [guāng míng zhèng dà] frank and straight forward; fair and square

光年 [guāng nián] light year

光谱 [guāng pǔ] spectrum

光天化日 [guāng tiān huàrì] in broad daylight

光秃秃 [guāng tū tū] barren; bald; bare

光线 [guāng xiàn] ray of light

光学 [guang xué] optics

光阴 [guāng yīn] time

光阴似箭 [guāng yīn sì jiàn] time flies like an arrow

光泽 [guāng zé] lustre

guǎng

广(廣) [guǎng] 1 (adj) 宽阔，大 wide; extensive; vast; ample; broad * 望着那广阔的海洋，我心里觉得非常舒畅。Looking at the vast sea, I feel very pleasant at heart. 2 (adj) 普遍，多 common; popular; many * 在五十年代初期，英文教育并不普遍。 In the early fifties, English education was not very common. 3 (v) 扩大，扩充 enlarge; popularize * 政府计划推广学习两种语文政策。The government plans to popularize bilingualism.

广播 [guǎng bō] broadcast

广场 [guǎng chǎng] square

广大 [guǎng dà] broad; wide; large

广泛 [guǎng fàn] extensive; widespread

广告 [guǎng qào] advertisement

广阔 [guǎng kuò] broad; wide

犷(獷) [guǎng] (adj) 粗野，凶悍 wild; fierce; ferocious * 豹是一种犷悍的动物。The panther is a ferocious animal.

guàng

逛 [guàng] (v) 闲游，游览 roam; wander; stroll; visit (a park) *很多有钱人的太太喜欢逛百货公司打发时间。Wives of many rich men like to roam about departmental stores to pass away the time.

guī

圭 [guī] 1 (n) 古代的一种玉器 a jade 2 (n) 古代测日影的器具 a sundial

闺(閨) [guī] 1 (n) 上园下方的小门 a small door 2 (n) 旧时指女子居住的内室 a woman's apartment

闺女 [guī·nü] girl;daughter

闺秀 [guī xiù] a lady writer;a literary woman;graceful girls

闺中 [guī zhōng] in a woman's apartment

规(規) [guī] 1 (n) 画园形的仪器 a pair of compasses 2(n) 章程，法则 law;rule;regulation * 校规禁止男同学留长头发。The school regulations forbid male students to spot long hair. 3 (n) 谋划 plan * 国家制订了一个农业发展规划。 The nation drew up an agricultural development plan. 4 (v) 劝告 advise;dissuade; admonish * 他犯错是因为年纪小不懂事，你应好好地规劝他。You should advise him properly as his mistakes are due to his young age and ignorance.

规程 [guī chéng] rules and regulations

规定 [guī dìng] formulate;define rules;regulations

规格 [guī gé] specifications

规划 [guī huà] work out a plan;project

规矩 [guī·ju] well-behaved;rules

规律 [gui lǜ] law

规模 [guī mó] scale

规劝 [guī quàn] admonished;persuade;offer advice to

规则 [guī zé] rules and regulations

规章 [guī zhāng] rules;regulations

瑰 [guī] (adj) 珍奇 extraordinary; admirable

瑰丽 [guīlì] very beautiful;elegant

归(歸) [guī] 1 (v) 返回 return;go back * 三年前他曾到外国深造，最近已学成归来。Three years ago he went abroad for further education. Recently he has graduated and returned home.

back;revert;restore ＊我已把借来用的相机归还给乔治。 I have already returned the borrowed camera to George. 3 (v) 属于；由 belong to; be due to

归队 [guī duì] rejoin one's unit;return to one's original occupation

归根结底 [guī gēn jié dǐ] in the final analysis

归功 [guī gōng] give the credit to.....;attribute.....to

归还 [guī huán] return(what is borrowed)

归咎 [guī jiu] lay the blame on;blame;attribute

归纳 [guī nà] infer by induction

归宿 [guī sù] the end results of

归心似箭 [guī xīn si jian] anxious to return home as soon as possible

归于 [guī yú] result in; ascribe to;be due to

龟（龜） [guī] (n) 爬虫类动物背有硬壳，是水陆两棲动物，可食 tortise

龟甲 [guī jiǎ] shell of the tortise

皈 [guī] 皈依 (n) 信仰佛教者的入教仪式 a ceremony in which devotees join in the religion

guǐ

诡（詭） [guǐ] 1 (adj) 欺诈，狡猾 cunning;crafty ＊商人以各种诡计谋利。To gain big profits, businessmen resort to all kinds of crafty means. 2 (adj) 怪异，出乎寻常 strange;outstanding;mysterious;secretive ＊看那个人行动诡秘，根本不像这里的居民，会不会是小偷？ That man acts strangely and does not look like a resident here at all, could he be a burglar?

诡辩 [guǐ biàn] sophisticated

诡诈 [guǐ zhà] crafty

轨（軌） [guǐ] 1 (n) 车子两轮之间的距离，也指车轮碾过的痕迹 the space between the two wheels of a cart 2 (n) 一定的路线，tracks; road; path; rail;orbit ＊地球是依一定的轨道绕着太阳运行的。The earth revolves along a definite orbit around the sun. 3 (n) 铁路上的钢条，the rails on the railroad.

轨道 [guǐ dào] track ;rail ;orbit

轨迹 [guǐ jì] locus

鬼 [guǐ] 1 (n)古代人们对自然现象不理解，认为人死后灵魂不灭，变为“鬼” a spirit; a ghost; a devil 2 (adj) 阴险，狡诈，不光明 cunning (n) trick ＊有两个青年每晚跑进一间小破庙里，不知搗什么鬼。The two youngsters go into a deserted temple every evening; we don't know what evil trick they are playing.

鬼鬼祟祟 [guǐ guǐ suì suì] stealthily

鬼话 [guǐ huà] utter nonsense; deception

鬼迷心窍 [guǐmíxīnqiao] possessed by ghosts

鬼蜮 [guǐyù] demon

鬼子 [guǐ · zi] devil

癸 [guǐ] (n) 天干的第十位，用作次序的第十 the last one of the Ten Stems ; tenth .

guì

贵（貴） [guì] 1 (adj) 价格高，价值大 dear; expensive; costly honorable ＊私人楼房比政府组屋贵。Private houses are more expensive than government flats. 2(n) 君主国家的封建皇族或地位高的人 noble; aristocrat

3 (adj) 敬词 (a term of respect) your * 请问贵姓 May I know your surname? 4 (adj) 值得珍惜或重视 precious * 前人所遗留下来的经验是后人宝贵的知识。Experiences passed down by the predecessors are valuable knowledge for later generations.

贵宾 [guì bīn] honoured guest
贵重 [guìzhòng] valuable; precious
贵族 [guì zú] aristocrat; noble

柜(櫃) [guì] 1(n) 收藏东西的家具 cupboard; wardrobe; drawer; cabinet * 他的父亲刚买了一个美国制造的铁柜。His father has just purchased an iron cabinet which is made in U.S.A. 2 (n) 商店营业的台子 counter

柜台 [guìtái] counter
柜子 [guì·zi] cupboard; wardrobe

刽(劊) [guì]〔刽子手][guì·zi shǒu] (n) 旧时专门执行斩刑的人，现在泛指杀害无辜者的人 executioner; killer; hangman; butcher

桂 [guì] (n) 一种常绿灌木或乔木 the cassia tree; the cinamon tree; laurel

跪 [guì] (v) 屈膝，使膝盖着地 kneel; drop (go down) on one's knees * 许多妇女跪在佛像前祈祷。Many women knelt down before the statue of Buddha and prayed.

gǔn

滚 [gǔn] 1 (v) 水流奔腾 rush (water); (adj) rushing; torrential * 马来半岛的东海岸面临白浪翻滚的南中国海。The east coast of Malay Peninsula faces the torrential South China Sea. 2 (v) 旋转着移动 roll; tumble * 皮球在草地上滚来滚去。The ball rolls here and there on the field. 3 (v) 走开（斥责的话）get away! get out! be off. * 王先生喝骂那考不及格的儿子,滚出去，别再回来!」 Mr. Wang shouted at his son, who flopped in the examination, "Don't come back!" 4 (v) 液体煮开，沸腾 boil (adj) boiling * 水要煮滚后才可以喝。Boil the water before you drink it.

滚动 [gǔn dòng] roll; tumble
滚滚 [gǔngǔn] rushing; torrential
滚瓜烂熟 [gǔnguā lànshú] (of reading and recitation) very fluent and well versed; well memorized by being able to repeat it fluently
滚珠 [gǔn zhū] ball (for ball bearing)

gùn

棍 [gùn] 1 (n) 木棒 stick; cudgel; a truncheon; a club * 警员用警棍和歹徒搏斗。The policeman used his baton to battle the rascal. 2 (n) 对人的贬称 a rascal

guō

锅(鍋) [guō] 1 (n) 煮饭菜的用具，用金属品制成 cooking pot; a caldron * 日本出产的电饭锅很耐用，有很多妇女喜欢采用。The Japanese electric cooking-pots are durable, many housewives love to use them. 2 (n) 形状象锅的东西 articles that look like a pan or a pot

鍋炉 [guōlú] boiler

过(過) [guō] (v) 超出 exceed pass; past

过费 [guōfèi] extravagant
过分 [guōfèn] excessive

另见 [guò]

聒 [guō] (adj) 声音噪杂 noisy; annoying (n) clamour; uproar * 早上的巴刹很聒噪。It is very noisy at the market in the morning.

郭 [guō] (n) 古代在城外再造的一道城 second wall of a city ＊城郭 the defences of a city

guó

国(國) [guó] 1 (n) 具有土地，人民，主权三要素的组织。a state;a country; a nation ＊世界上最古老的国家是：埃及，印度和中国。The oldest countries of the world are: Egypt, India and China. 2 (adj) 属于国家的 belonging to the nation; national ＊新加坡的国歌是「前进吧，新加坡」。 The national anthem of Singapore is 'Majulah Singapura'.

国宾 [guóbīn] state guest
国策 [guó cè] state policy
国都 [guó dū] the capital of a country
国度 [guó dù] country; nation
国防 [guó fáng] national defence
国歌 [guó gē] national anthem
国庆日 [guó jìng rì] national celebration; National Day
国画 [guó huà] traditional Chinese painting
国徽 [guó huī] national emblem
国会 [guó huì] national assembly; a parliament
国籍 [guó jí] nationality
国际 [guó jì] international
国境 [guójing] national boundaries
国计民生 [guó jì mín shēng] a country's finance and the livelihood of its people
国库 [guó kù] national treasury
国民 [guó mín] people of a country; nation
国民收人 [guó mín shōu rù] national income
国内 [guó neì] inside the country; domestic; internal; home (eg. home affairs); civil
国土 [guó tǔ] national territory
国外 [guó wài] abroad; overseas
国营 [guó yíng] state owned; government operated
国有化 [guò yǒu huà] nationalize; nationalization

掴(摑) [guó] (v) 用手掌打 slap; box ＊母亲很气恼儿子不听话，掴了他一个耳光。Being angry with her son for being disobedient, the mother slapped him in the face

guǒ

果 [guǒ] 1 (n) 某些植物花落后含有种子的部份a fruit ＊医生交代病人要多吃水果，才不致引起消化不良。The doctor advised his patient to take more fruits in order to avoid indigestion. 2 (n) 事情的最后结局 results; consequences; effect; outcome ＊你每天都不想温习功课，只顾游玩，得面对考不進大学的后果。Day after day you do not study hard but just fool around; you have to face the consequence of failing the matriculation examination 3 (adj) 坚决的 determined; resolute ＊对于一切错误的事物，我们应该果敢地去改正它。We must be determined to correct all the wrong things 4 (adv) 确实，真的 certainly; indeed; surely; really; in fact ＊他对歌唱很有兴趣，又肯虚心学习，果然，只经过两年的歌台经验，他便成名了。He was interested in singing and was willing to learn with an open mind. In fact, with the two years of stage experiences, he has become famous

果断 [guǒ duàn] resolute; decisive
果敢 [guǒ gǎn] resolute and daring; courageous
果酱 [guǒ jiàng] jam
果然 [guǒ rán] as expected; sure enough; certainly
果园 [guǒ yuán] orchard

果真 [guǒ zhēn] true to promise; as expected; really

果实 [guǒ shí] a fruit

裹 [guǒ] (v) 包，缠 wrap; pack up; bundle up; envelop * 快裹好伤口，别让它露出来。Wrap the wound quickly and don't let it be exposed.

裹脚 [guǒjiǎo] bind the feet.

裹头巾 [guǒ tóu jīn] a turban.

裹足不前 [guǒ zú bù qián] stop; not daring to advance.

guò

过(過) [guò] 1 (v) 从一个地点到另一个地点 pass; cross; go by. * 那个强壮的兵上曾经走过漫长的路。That strong soldier had already trekked a very long distance. 2 (part) 已经或曾经 a suffix used to express a completed action or past experience. * 我已经说过不可以去，你为什么还要去？I have already told you not to go, then why should you go? 3 (prep) 超出 over; above; beyond. * 全球有过半数的人口居住属于第三世界的国度里。Over half of the world's population lives in the Third World countries 4 (part) 跟"来"，"去"连用，表示趋向 used with "来" and "去" to indicate direction * 他在老远看到我，就立刻走过来跟我打招呼。On seeing me from afar, he immediately came to greet me. 5 (n) 错误 mistake; fault

过不去 [guò · bu qù] cannot pass through ; feel sorry for ... be hard on (somebody)

过程 [guò chéng] process; course.

过错 [guò cuò] error; fault

过得去 [guò · de qù] can pass through; passable

过度 [guò dù] excessive; over.

过渡 [guò dù] pass over; transition.

过分 [guò fèn] excessive

过关 [guó guān] go through a mountain pass; pass the test of

过活 [guò huó] making a living.

过火 [guò huǒ] excessive; carry things too far; overdo

过虑 [guò lǜ] be over-anxious; worry too much; worry needlessly

过滤 [guò lǜ] filter

过敏 [guò mǐn] allergic; over-sensitive

过目 [guò mù] go over; look over; read over; glance over

过期 [guò qī] overdue; out of date; expired

过去 [guò·qu] the past; previous; cross over; go over

过剩 [guò shèng] surplus

过失 [guò shī] error; fault; a blunder

过时 [guò shí] out-of-date; obsolete; outmoded

过世 [guò shì] deceased; dead

过问 [guò wèn] intervene; take action on; take an interest in

过于 [guò yú] too much; over; excessively

过意不去 [guò yì bú qù] feel ill at ease; sorry

过日子 [guò rì zǐ] make a living

另见 [guō]

H

hā

哈 [hā] 1 (v) 弯 bend * 奴才向主人哈腰作揖，表示恭顺。 The servant bent his back and bowed to his master to express obedience. 2 (v) 张口呼气 exhale 3 (n) 表示笑的声音 sound of laughter * 观众们看了小丑的表演，都「哈哈」大笑。"Ha, ha!" laughed the audience on watching the act of the clown.
另见 [hǎ]
哈雷慧星 [hāléihuìxīng] italley's comet
哈欠 [hāqiàn] yawn

há

蛤 [há]〔蛤蟆〕[há má] (n) 青蛙和蟾蜍的统称 frog
另见 [gé]

hǎ

哈 [hǎ] (n) 姓氏 a surname

哈巴狗 [hǎ·bagǒu] pekinese (dog)
另见 [hā]

hāi

咳 [hāi] (interj) 叹词，表示后悔或惊异 interjection expressing sorrow, regret or surprise* 咳！早知他是个骗子，我就不会把钱拿给他。Oh! If I had known that he was a swindler, I would not have given him the money.
另见 [ké]

嗨 [hāi] 1 (interj)叹词。表示惊异或惋惜 interjection expressing surprise or pity * 嗨！这孩子只十二岁，就学会吸毒了。 How pitiful! this child is only twelve years old but he already knows how to take drugs. 2 (interj)叹词，表示欢乐的感情 interjection expressing happiness* 嗨！不见那么久，你还是一样的强壮。 Hai! You are just as strong after such a long separation.

hái

孩 [hái] (n) 儿童，子女 child; children * 现在青年的夫妇们都不希望有太多的孩子。 Young couples nowadays do not wish to have too many children.
孩提之事 [háitízhīshì] puerile affairs
孩子气 [hái·ziqì] childishness
孩子头 [hái·zitóu] a person who likes to play with children

骸 [hái] 1 (n) 身体 body 2 (n)骨头，骨骼 bones; skeleton * 有人在

海滩上发现了一具已腐烂的尸骸。Someone found a decayed corpse on the beach.

还（還）[hái] 1 (adv) 更 still more; more ... than＊我的哥哥比爸爸还高。My elder brother is taller than my father. 2 (adv) 仍旧 still; yet＊夜已深了，他還在埋头温习功课。He still buries his head in his studies though it is already late in the night. 3 (adv) 又，再 furthermore; more＊我还有一个问题要先解决，才能去槟城旅行。I still have a problem to solve before travelling to Penang. 4 (conj) 或者 or＊你要去还是不去，由你自己决定。Whether you want to go or not, it is up to you.

还是 [hái·shi] still; or; it's better ...
还有 [hái yǒu] there is still; further
还在 [háizài] still in existence
还早 [háizǎo] still early
另见 [huán]

hǎi

海 [hǎi] 1 (n) 靠近大陆的大水 sea＊大海上有很多各国的船隻。On the boundless sea are many ships of various countries. 2 (n) 大湖 lake 3 (n) 比喻数量多的人或事物 to illustrate something great in number or dimension＊博览会里人山人海，非常热闹。The exposition bustled and stirred with mountains and seas of people.

海岸 [hǎi àn] coast; shore
海拔 [hǎibà] above sea-level
海报 [hǎibào] poster
海滨 [hǎibīn] seashore; beach
海潮 [hǎicháo] the tides
海盗 [hǎidào] pirate
海底捞月 [hǎi dǐ lāoyuè] (fig.) useless effort; a fruitless attempt.
海防 [hǎifáng] coastal defence
海港 [hǎigǎng] harbour; seaport
海关 [hǎiguān] customs house
海军 [hǎi jūn] Navy
海枯石烂 [hǎikū shí làn] (fig.) an oath of unchanging fidelity
海阔天空 [hǎikuòtiānkōng] (lit.) the vastness of nature; (fig.) at random and without direction
海洛英 [hǎi luò yīn] heroin
海马 [hǎi mǎ] a sea-horse

海绵 [hǎi mián] sponge
海內存知己，天涯若比邻 [hǎi nèi cún zhī jǐ, tiān yá ruò bǐ lín] if within the four seas are bosom friends, distant places are just like neighbouring lands
海鸥 [hǎi'ōu] sea-gull
海参 [hǎi shēn] sea slug ; sea cucumber

海市蜃楼 [hǎi shì shèn lóu] a mirage
海誓山盟 [hǎi shì shān méng] an oath taken by a man and a woman in ancient time to express their unchanging love which shall be like the mountain and the sea
海獭 [hǎi tǎ] beaver

海滩 [hǎi tān] beach
海外 [hǎiwài] overseas; abroad
海湾 [hǎi wān] gulf; bay
海味 [hǎi wèi] sea food
海峡 [hǎi xià] straits
海啸 [hǎi xiào] tidal waves
海员 [hǎi yán] sea-man; mariner
海洋 [hǎi yáng] ocean
海燕 [hǎiyàn] petrel
海域 [hǎiyù] marine area
海运 [hǎiyùn] sea transportation

hài

亥 [hài] (n) 地支的第十二位，用作次序的第十二 the last of the twelve branches; 12th
亥时 [hàishí] the time from 9 to 11 o'clock, in the evening

骇(駭) [hài] (v) 害怕，吃惊 startled; be frightened ＊两个强盗忽然将刀指住他的颈项，他惊骇得不知如何是好。When two robbers suddenly pointed a knife at his throat, he was so startled that he did not know what to do.
骇怕 [hàipà] be frightened ; scared
骇然 [hàirán] in astonishment
骇人听闻 [hàiréntīngwén] (of news, incident, etc.) shocking; terrifying
骇异 [hàiyì] strange; frightful

害 [hài] 1 (v) 损伤 injure; harm; damage ＊绑匪并没有伤害他。The kidnappers did him no harm. 2 (adj) 有坏处的 injurious; harmful ＊麻雀是稻田的害鸟。Sparrows are a kind of harmful birds to the padi fields. 3 (n) 灾害，灾祸 disaster; harm; danger; calamity ＊由於虫害，使到今年的稻谷收成大大减少。Due to the harm caused by pests, the padi harvest this year is greatly reduced.
害处 [hàichù] harm
害虫 [hàicháng] pest
害命 [haì mìng] murder; kill
害怕 [hài pà] be afraid of; scared
害群之马 [hài qún zhī mǎ] the black sheep (of the family, etc)
害人利己 [hài rén lì jǐ] to benefit oneself at the expense of others
害羞 [hài xīu] shy; bashful

hān

鼾 [hān] (n) 熟睡时的鼻息声 snoring; a snore＊由於他鼾声如雷，谁也不愿睡在他的房间。Nobody wishes to sleep in his room because his snores are like thunders.
鼾睡 [hānshuì] heavy sleep with snoring

酣 [hān] (adj) 酒喝得畅快 merry from drinking; rapturous; merry
酣睡 [hānshuì] sleep soundly
酣饮 [hānyǐn] drink to intoxication
酣醉 [hānzuì] drunk; intoxicated

憨 [hān] (adj) 呆，傻 foolish; silly ＊那白痴的憨笑使他母亲更伤心。The foolish laugh of the idiot saddens his mother further.
憨厚 [hān·hou] simple and honest

hán

含 [hán] 1 (v) 衔在嘴里 hold in the mouth ＊他含盐水以减轻齿龈的脓肿。He held salt water in his mouth to alleviate the boil on the gums. 2 (v) 里面存在着 contain; hold; be filled with ＊这句成语含有深奥的意义。This proverb contains profound meaning
含糊 [hán·hu] obscure; equivocal
含糊其辞 [hán·hu qí cì] ambiguous in speech
含泪 [hán lèi] restrained tears
含笑 [hán xiào] smile; chuckle
含蓄 [hán xiù] feel bashful or ashamed; blush; redden from a sense of shame

含沙射影 [hánshāshèyǐng] insinuate; insinuation
含羞 [hánxū] restrained but suggestive in speech or writing
含义 [hányì] content; significance; implication
含冤 [hán yuān] have grievances
含冤负屈 [hán yuān fù qū] to suffer an unjust wrong

晗 [hán] (adj) 天将亮的时候 dawn-time

韩(韓) [hán] 1 (n) 古代国名 name of an ancient state in China 2 (n) 姓氏 a surname

函 [hán] 1 (n) 匣子，套子 a case; an envelope 2 (n) 书信，文件 letter; document ＊书记小心地把公函存放在文件夹里。The clerk kept the official letter in the file carefully.
函覆 [hánfù] in reply
函授 [hánshòu] correspondence course; lessons by correspondence
函询 [hánxún] inquire by mail

涵 [hán] (v) 包含，包容 contain; bear
涵洞 [hándòng] tunnel; a sluice
涵养 [hányǎng] the virtue of patience

寒 [hán] 1 (adj) 冷 cold; chilly ＊一阵寒风使他打冷颤。A puff of cold wind made him shiver. 2 (adj)困穷 poor; needy ＊他来自贫寒的家庭。He came from a poor family.
寒潮 [hánchao] cold wave
寒带 [hándái] the frigid arctic zones
寒冷 [hánlěng] bitterly cold
寒暑表 [hán shǔ biǎo] thermometer
寒酸 [hánsuān] shabby
寒暄 [hánxuān] make small talk
寒战 [hánzhàn] the shivers, shivering with cold

hǎn

罕 [hǎn] (adj) 稀少 rare; uncommon; unusual ＊熊猫是一种罕见的动物。The panda is a rare species of animals.

喊 [hǎn] (v) 高声叫 shout; cry; call (n) a call; a cry ＊他已经走了那么远，你要大声喊他才能听到。He has gone quite far ; you should shout louder so that he can hear you.
喊叫 [hǎnjiào] shout; yell
喊救 [hǎnjiù] cry for help; call on to rescue

hàn

汗 [hàn] (n)皮肤表层的分泌物，有咸味 sweat; perspiration
汗流浃背 [hàn líu jiā bèi] full of perspiration
汗马功劳 [hàn mǎ gōng láo] achievements in war; laboriously achieved merits
汗衫 [hànshān] shirt; sweater
汗珠 [hànzhū] beads of sweat

旱 [hàn] 1 (n) 干燥，缺雨 drought; dry weather＊这整个月大旱，连一滴雨都没下过。Not a single raindrop falls during this whole month of drought. 2 (adj)陆地上的，没有水的 dry; arid. ＊旱田里种谷收成比较少。The yields of grains from dry fields are smaller.
旱涝保收 [hànlàobǎoshōu] sure to get high yields irrespective of drought or waterlogging
旱灾 [hànzaī] drought

捍 [hàn] (v) 保卫 defend; safeguard ＊捍卫国土，人人有责。It is everyone's duty to safeguard the territory of one's country.

悍 [hàn] 1 (adj) 勇猛 brave; fierce ＊古代的蒙古武士，以勇悍善戰著名。The ancient Mongolian warriors were famous for being brave and warlike. 2 (adj) 凶暴 fierce; violent

悍然 [hàn rán] brazenly; flagrantly

悍然不顾 [hàn rán bù gù] brutal and savage in disregard of anything

焊 [hàn] (v) 用高温熔化金属来连接金属器物 weld＊烧焊工人的生活是很辛苦的。 Life of a welder is very hard.

焊接 [hànjiē] connect by welding

颔(頷) [hàn] (n) 下巴 the chin; the jaws

翰 [hàn] 1 (n) 长而硬的羽毛，古代用来写字 a long and hard plumage used as writing-brush in ancient time 2 (n) 毛笔，泛指字或文章 a brush (adj) 文学的 literary

翰墨 [hànmò] writing materials; pen and ink

瀚 [hàn] (adj) 广大 vast; extensive＊轮船在浩瀚的大海中川行，好像一片浮叶。 A ship in the vast ocean is just like a floating piece of leaf.

撼 [hàn] (v) 摇动，震动 move; excite; stir up ＊他撼动那棵树，希望把果子摇下来。He shakes the tree, hoping that the fruits will drop.

憾 [hàn] (adj) 悔恨，不满 regretful; hateful; vexed; grievous. (n) vexation; regret ;enmity ＊他对于未能调解朋友之间的失和，一直觉得很遗憾。 All along he felt regretful for not being able to resolve the rift among his friends.

汉(漢) [hàn] 1 (n)中国民族名。占全国人口之九十巴仙以上 Chinese; the Han Race 2 (n) 朝代名 the Han Dynasty 3 (n) 成年男人 a male adult

汉奸 [hàn jiān] a traitor; a spy

汉学 [hànxué] sinology

汉字 [hàn zì] a Chinese character

háng

吭 [háng] (n) 喉咙，嗓子 throat; voice ＊我们终於爬上山顶，引吭高歌。Having climbed to the top of a hill, we raised our voice to sing a song.

另见 [kēng]

航 [háng] 1 (n) 船 a boat; a large vessel 2 (v) 在水上或空中行驶 sail; fly (a plane)＊轮船从此地航行到欧洲需要两个月的时间。 It takes two months for the ship to sail from here to Europe.

航程 [háng chéng] flying or sailing range

航道 [hángdào] channel; waterway

航海 [hánghǎi] navigation

航海家 [hánghǎijiā] navigator; mariner

航空 [hángkōng] aviation

航空公司 [hángkōnggōngsī] airline

航空母舰 [háng kōng mǔjiàn] aircraft carrier

航线 [hángxiàn] air or navigation line

航行 [hángxíng] sail; navigate

航运 [háng yùn] sea transportation

行 [háng] 1 (n) 排列 line; row＊学生们排成行列迎接来访的宾客。The students line up in rows to welcome the guests. 2 (n) 企业，商店 a branch of trade; a shop 3 (n) 职业 a vocation ; a trade; a line of business ＊他以前是教书的，最近已改行从商。 Previously he was a teacher, but recently he has changed his vocation and become a merchant. 4 (n) 量词 a measure word; used for row; column; line

行家 [háng·jia] expert; a person who is skilled in certain line

行列 [háng liè] ranks; columns

行情 [háng qíng] market prices

行业 [hángyè] a branch of trade; occupation

另见 [xíng]

háo

豪 [háo] 1 (n) 才能超过一般的人物 a hero ; a great man 2 (adj) 有气魄，不拘束 heroic; brave; generous＊他为人豪爽，不爱计较小节。 He is a generous person and does not like to be calculating on petty matters. 3 (adj) 强横，也指强横的人 violent; regardless of right; headstrong (n) violent people

豪放 [háofàng] gallant-minded
豪华 [háohuá] luxurious; sumptuous
豪杰 [háo jié] warrior; hero
豪迈 [háomài] gallant; magnificent
豪门 [háo mén] a wealthy and powerful family
豪情壮志 [háo qíng zhuàngzhì] lofty spirit and soaring determination
豪爽 [háo shuǎng] generous and broad-minded
豪猪 [háo zhū] a porcupine

壕 [háo] (n) 沟 trench; ditch ＊兵士躲在战壕里以避开敌人的炮火。 The soldiers hid in the trenches to avoid firings from the enemies.

壕沟 [háogōu] ditch; trench
壕堑战 [háoqiànzhàn] trench warfare

嚎 [háo] (v) 大声哭喊 to howl loudly; cry loudly ＊还没有打针，那孩子就嚎叫起来。 The boy cried loudly even before injection.

嗥 [háo] (n) 野兽叫声 howl of animals

号（號） [háo] 1 (v) 大声呼喊 shout loudly (n) shouting ＊他们一听到求救的呼号，便马上冲过去。 On hearing the shout for help, they immediately rushed to the spot. 2 (v) 大声哭 howl; wail ＊那群孤儿的哀号声，使人听了心酸。 The wailings of the orphans saddened us.

号啕大哭 [hàotáodàkū] wail loudly; cry loudly; utter a loud cry.

另见 [hào]

毫 [háo] 1 (n) 细毛 long, soft hair 2 (adj) 一点 minute: petty; tiny; trifling; slight. (n) bit ＊他夸口说，他能毫不费力地搬开大石头。 He boasts that without the slightest effort he can remove the boulder.

毫毛 [háo máo] hair
毫升 [háo shēng] millilitre
毫无 [háo wú] by no means; devoid of; without the least; not in the least; not the slightest

hǎo

好 [hǎo] 1 (adj) 善，优点多，跟“坏”相对 good; well; fine; excellent ＊她穿了这件衣服，特别好看。She is especially goodlooking with this dress on. 2 (adj) 友爱，亲切 friendly; intimate ＊他们虽然常有争论，却能保持友好的关系。In spite of frequent arguements, the friendly relation between them is well maintained. 3 (adj) 完成 well; completed ＊车修好，可以在路上跑了。The car is repaired well: it can run on the road again. 4 (adj) 容易 easy ＊这件事好办。 This task is easy to perform. 5 (adv) 很 very; quite; so ＊好多人来看这部电影，难怪买不到票。 So many people come to see this show : no wonder I cannot get a ticket.

好比 [hǎobǐ] be like; as; just like
好吃 [hǎochī] delicious; tasty.

好处 [hǎo·chu] benefit; goodness
好感 [hǎogǎn] good impression
好意 [hǎo gì] goodwill; well-intentioned
好汉 [hǎo hàn] wise man; hero
好景不长 [hǎo jǐng bù cháng] good times do not last.
好久 [hǎo jǐu] long time
好评 [hǎo píng] favourable comment (criticism)
好人好事 [hǎo rén hǎo shì] good personalities and good deeds
好人难做 [hǎo rén nán zuò] It is not easy to be a good man — there will always be those who criticize and are not satisfied with him
好容易 [hǎo róng yì] with much difficulty
好手 [hǎo shǒu] a very capable person
好似 [hǎo sì] look like; seem.
好听 [hǎo tīng] pleasant to the ear; fine sounding
好笑 [hǎo xiào] funny
好些 [hǎo xīe] a good many
好心 [hǎo xīn] good-willed; kindhearted; well-intentioned
好样的 [hǎoyàng·de] a fine person; a worthy man; a good sort
好意 [hǎoyì] goodwill; well-intentioned
好运 [hǎoyùn] good luck; good fortune
好在 [hǎozài] luckily; fortunately
好转 [hǎo zhuǎn] turn for the better
另见 [hào]

hào

浩 [hào] 1 (adj) 广大 extensive; vast; great; powerful ＊声势浩大的日军开进城里来。A powerful Japanese troop marched into the town. 2 (adj) 多 many; numerous ＊浩繁的星星在天上眨眼。Numerous stars twinkle in the sky.
浩大 [hàodà] great (eg. expense); gigantic; powerful
浩荡 [hàodàng] grand; mighty
浩翰 [hào hàn] expansive; limitless
浩浩荡荡 [hào hào dàng dàng] exceedingly great
浩然之气 [hào rán zhī qī] liberal mind; magnanimity

皓 [hào] (adj) 洁白，明亮 white; bright
皓月 [hào yuè] a brilliant moon
皓首 [hào shǒu] old age

耗 [hào] 1 (v) 消费，减损 waste; squander; spend; consume ＊马力强的车，耗油也多。Cars with a high horsepower usually consume more petrol. 2 (v) 拖延，等 delay; wait. 3 (n) 消息 news; tidings; information; messages. ＊她一听到丈夫在车祸中丧生的噩耗，便昏晕了。When she heard of her husband's death in a road accident, she fainted.
耗费 [hào fèi] consume; squander; waste; consumption
耗力 [hàolì] use strength
耗损 [hàosǔn] destroy; waste

号（號）[hào] 1 (n) 名称 name 2 (n) 标志 sign; mark 3 (n) 表示次第或等次 number ＊五号球员犯规。Player number 'five' plays foul. 4 (v) 号令，命令 order; command
号角 [hàojiǎo] clarion call; a bugle horn.
号码 [hào mǎ] number.
号召 [hào zhào] call upon; call.
另见 [háo]

好 [hào] (v) 喜欢 fond of; like; wish for＊她好讲话，上课时不专心。She likes talking and does not pay attention during lessons.
好吃懒做 [hào chì lǎn zuò] gluttonous and lazy — good for nothing

好高务远 [hào gāo wù yuǎn] crave for something high and out of reach
好客 [hàokè] hospitable
好奇 [hào qí] curious
好强 [hào qiáng] not willing to lag behind.
好色 [hào sè] sensual
好胜 [hào shèng] love of pre-eminence; ambitious of excelling
好逸恶劳 [hào yì wù láo] love leisure and dislike work
好战 [hào zhàn] war-like
好整以暇 [hào zhěngl yǐ xiá] to act steadily amidst busy task
另见 [hǎo]

hē

呵 [hē] 1 (v) 大声责骂 scold * 他太纵容孩子了，连他们做错也不忍呵斥。He pampers his children so much that he does not even scold them when they make a mistake. 2 (v) 张口呼气 exhale. 3 (interj) 叹词，表示惊讶 an interjection expressing surprise *呵！好一个漂亮的少女！Oh! what a beautiful, young girl. 4 (n) 笑声 (laughter) sound *老人家逗得孙子呵呵大笑。"Ha ha!" laughed the child heartily as he played with his grandfather
呵斥 [hēchì] reprimand; scold
呵欠 [hē qiàn] yawn
呵责 [hēzé] blame; scold

喝 [hē] (v) 饮，吸进液体以便止渴 drink; sip. *多喝开水，对身体有益。Drinking more water is good for health.
另见 [hè]

hé

曷 [hé] 1 (pron) 什么 what 2 (pron) 为什么 why

合 [hé] 1 (v) 闭上 close; fold up; shut *他合上眼睛，集中精神听音乐。He closes his eyes to concentrate on the music. 2 (v) 共同，跟"分"相对 combine; get together; unite; join *让我们合力把校园打扫乾净。Let us work together to sweep our school compound clean. 3 (v) 相符 coincide; match; meet; conform *你留长发，不合校规。In keeping your hair long, you have failed to conform to school regulations.
合并 [hébìng] merge; amalgamate
合不来 [hé·bu lái] not in harmony with; hard to get along together
合成 [hé chéng] synthesize; compose
合成橡胶 [hé chéng xiàng jiāo] synthetic rubber
合得来 [hé delái] be in harmony with; be on good terms
合法 [hé fǎ] legal; legitimate; lawful
合格 [hégé] qualified; up to the standard
合股 [hé gǔ] joint-stock; share
合伙 [hé huǒ] seek partnership with
合金 [hé jīn] alloy
合理 [hé lǐ] reasonable; rational
合情合理 [héqínghélǐ] reasonable and just
合适 [hé shì] suitable; fit
合算 [hé suàn] reasonable in price; worth
合同 [hé tóng] contract
合影 [hé yǐng] taking a group photo
合奏 [hé zòu] play a chorus; chorus
合作 [hé zuò] co-operate; collaborate
合作化 [hézuòhuá] collectivization (agriculture)
合作社 [hé zuò shè] co-operatives
另见 [gě]

盒 [hé] (n) 用木或铁制成的小箱子，底盖相合的盛器 a box; a carton; a casket ＊店员把金表放在精致的盒子里。 The shopkeeper placed the gold watch in a fine box.

何 [hé] 1 (pron) 什么 what; when; which; who ＊天下何时太平？When will there be peace on earth? 2 (pron) 为什么 why ＊既然你没做错，何以那么紧张？Since you have done nothing wrong, why are you so nervous? 3 (pron) 哪儿 where ＊你要到何处去呢？Where do you intend to go?

何必 [hé bì] why on earth; why should

何不 [hé bù] why not

何乐不为 [hé lè bù wéi] why are you not happy to do it

何妨 [hé fāng] why not

何苦 [hé kǔ] for what earthly reason; totally unnecessary

何况 [hé kuàng] besides; furthermore

何去何从 [hé qù hé cóng] a decision on questions of principle-to depart or follow

何谓 [hé wèi] what is meant by

何在 [hé zài] where is ...

河 [hé] (n) 水道的通称 a river; a canal; a stream; a brook ＊这小河给他带来好多美丽的回忆。 This streamlet has brought him many beautiful memories.

河床 [hé chuáng] river bed

河堤 [hédī] river embankment; dyke

荷 [hé] (n) 水生草本植物 lotus flower ; water lily

荷包 [hé bāo] a purse ; pouch

禾 [hé] 1 (n) 谷类植物的统称 grains; crops 2 (n) 稻 padi; rice

禾稼 [hé jià] crops in general

禾苗 [hé miao] grain seedling; rice-shoots

和 [hé] 1 (n) 相安，谐调 peace; harmony; union (adj) harmonious; peaceful; amiable ＊新加坡是个多元种族的社会，各族人民和睦共处。 Singapore is a multi-racial society where the different races live in harmony. 2 (adj) 平静，不猛烈 peaceful; mild; amiable ＊爷爷是个和蔼可亲的人，难得见他乱发脾气。 Being an amiable person, grand-pa rarely shows his temper 3 (n) 几个数目相加的结果 sum ＊三跟五的和是八。The sum of three and five is eight. 4 (conj) 同 and (prep) with＊我和弟弟都在星加坡出生。 My younger brother and I were both born in Singapore. 5 (prep) 向，对 to ＊请你和老师说我生病了，不能去上课。 Please tell the teacher that I have fallen ill and cannot attend class.

和蔼 [hé aǐ] peaceable; amiable; kindly

和风细雨 [hé fēng xì yǔ] gentle breeze and mild rain ; (fig) not be rough

和好 [hé hǎo] become reconciled with (somebody); peace

和缓 [hé huǎn] conciliatory; moderate; mild

和解 [hé jiě] reconcile; settle by mediation

和睦 [hé mù] friendly; harmonious

和平 [hé píng] peace

和气 [héqì] friendly; placid; agreeable

和尚 [hé·shang] a Buddhist priest; a monk

和谈 [hé tán] peace negotiations

和谐 [hé xié] harmonious

和约 [hé yuē] peace treaty

另见 [hè]
[huó]
[hù]

劾 [hé] (v) 揭发罪状 impeach; accuse; indict

核 [hé] 1 (n)果实或物质的中心部份 kernel; nucleus 2 (v) 仔细地对照检查 examine; inquire into *这件事在还没核查之前是不可轻易下判断的。 A judgement cannot be easily made on this matter before it is inquired into.

核保护伞 [hé bǎo hù sǎn] nuclear protective umbrella

核弹头 [hédàntóu] nuclear warhead

核定 [hé dìng] grant after due consideration

核对 [hé duì] verify; check; compare

核讹诈 [héézhà] nuclear blackmail

核垄断 [hé lǒng duàn] nuclear monopoly

核实 [hé shí] verify; check up

核算 [hé suàn] estimate; calculate; (economic) accounting

核桃 [hé tao] walnut

核武器 [hé wǔ qì] nuclear weapons

核心 [hé xīn] nucleus; hard core

核装置 [hé zhāng zhì] nuclear device

核子 [hé·zi] nucleus

阂(閡) [hé] (n) 阻隔 obstacle; barrier

盍 [hé] (adv) "何不","为什么不"的意思 why not

阖(闔) [hé] 1 (adv) 全，总共 all; whole; entire *请阖家前来观赏。 Please come to watch the show with your whole family. 2 (v) 关闭 shut; close *很冷了，把窗阖了。 It's cold, please close the windows.

翮 [hé] 1 (n) 翅膀 wings

貉 [hé] (n) 哺乳动物，形状像狸 the sable; the marten

涸 [hé] (adj) 水干 dried; exhaustted

hè

褐 [hè] 1 (n) 粗布或粗布衣服 coarse cloth; garment made of coarse cloth 2 (adj) 黑黄色 brown

喝 [hè] (v) 大声叫喊 shout *父亲大喝一声，孩子立刻不敢再哭了。 The father shouted and the child immediately stopped crying.

喝彩 [hè cǎi] applaud

另见 [hē]

壑 [hè] (n) 深山的 a valley; a pit

赫 [hè] (adj) 显耀，盛人 bright; luminious; glorious

赫然 [hè rán] to appear suddenly

赫赫有名 [hè hè yǒu míng] very well known; have a great reputation

赫然大怒 [hè rán dà nù] burst into a passion; fly into a rage

吓(嚇) [hè] (v) 威吓 scare; threaten; frighten *阿飞恐吓学生，要致他于死地。 The gangster threatens the student with death.

另见 [xià]

荷 [hè] 1 (v) 扛，揹在肩背上 carry on the shoulder *农夫荷锄开始一天的工作。 The farmer carries a hoe on his shoulder to begin the day's work. 2 (v) 负担 bear; sustain

另见 [hé]

鹤(鶴) [hè] (n) 鸟类，颈项很长 a crane; a stork

鹤发 [hèfà] white hair, old aged man

鹤立鸡群 [hè lì jī qún] very outstanding and prominent

和 [hè] (v) 呼应，声音相应 harmonize

另见 [hé]
[huó]
[hú]

贺(賀) [hè] (v) 庆祝 greet; congratulate; celebrate

* 他们结婚了，朋友都向他们贺喜。Friends congratulated them on their marriage.

贺词 [hè cí] speech of greeting

贺电 [hèdiàn] message of greeting

贺年片 [hè nián piān] a New-year's greeting card

贺喜 [hè xǐ] congratulate; felicitate

hēi

黑 [hēi] 1 (adj) 像墨或煤炭那样的颜色 black *他的朋友是个非洲人，皮肤是黑色的。His friend is an African whose skin is black in colour. 2 (adj) 暗 dark; obscure * 有一个人躲在黑暗的角落头，你要小心。Be careful, somebody is hiding in the dark corner. 3 (adj) 恶毒 sinister

黑板 [hēi bǎn] blackboard

黑洞洞 [hēidōngdōng] very dark;pitch-dark

黑名单 [hēimíngdān] black list

黑白分明 [hēi pái fēn míng] demarcation exceptionally clear-cut

黑市 [hēi shì] black market

黑夜 [hēi yè] night

黑云密布 [hēi yún mì bù] a gathering storm

嘿 [hēi] 1 (interj) 叹词。表示赞叹或惊异 interjection expressing surprise or praise *嘿，你长得那么高了。Hey, you've grown that tall. 2 (n) 冷笑声 sarcastic laugh

hén

痕 [hén] (n) 事物留下的印迹 a scar; a mark; a stain * 你只要看他的伤痕就知道他受伤不轻。Look at his scar and you will know his injury is serious.

痕迹 [hénjī] mark; trace; stamp

hěn

很 [hěn] (adv) 非常，表示程度高 very; quite *寡妇山很高，不容易爬上去。Mt. Kinabalu is very high. It is not easy to climb to the top.

狠 [hěn] 1 (adj) 凶恶 cruel; relentless *那些强盗真狠毒：他们抢了钱，还要杀人。How cruel those robbers are: they have not only robbed the money but also killed the person. 2 (adj) 厉害，严厉 firm; resolute * 对敌人要狠。Be firm against one's enemies.

狠毒 [hěn dú] malicious, cruel

狠心 [hěn xīn] cruel; ruthless

hèn

恨 [hèn] 1 (v) 怨仇 hate; dislike (n) hatred * 爸爸痛恨致使他家破人亡的战争。Father hated the war which had caused his family to break up. 2 (v) 懊悔 regret (adj) sorry (n) regret *他因为驾车不小心撞死人而遗恨终身。He feels sorry throughout his life for his having killed someone in his careless driving.

恨不得 [hèn bù dé] very anxious to; vexed at not being able to

hēng

亨 [hēng] (adj) 顺利 successful; prosperous; fortunate *他最近生意亨通，赚了大把钱。Lately, he earns a lot of money out of a prosperous business.

亨通 [hēng tōng] prosperous; successful

哼 [hēng] 1 (n) 表示痛苦的声音 moan; groan; grumble 2 (interj) 叹词。表示愤怒或不满 an interjection expressing distrust or dissatisfaction 3 (v) 轻声随口地唱 hum * 好多人喜欢一边冲凉，一边哼歌。Many people like to hum as they bathe.

héng

恒 [héng] 1 (adj) 长久不变 permanent; constant (adv) permanently;

perpetually; ever ＊钻石是永恒的。Diamond is for ever. 2 (adj) 经常的，普通的 regular; common (adv) continually

恒心 [héng xīn] persistence; constancy; perseverance

恒星 [héng xīng] fixed stars

衡 [héng] 1 (n) 称重量的器具，如磅秤，天平等 a weighing machine; a balance; a pair of scales 2 (v) 称东西的轻重 weigh 3 (v) 衡量，按标准来评定，比较事物的是非或轻重得失 measure; weigh; estimate; calculate; judge; consider ＊你得先衡量自己的能力才决定做多少。You must first judge your ability before deciding how much to do.

横 [héng] 1 (adj) 跟地平线平行的 horizontal; transverse (n) width ＊英文句子是横写的。English sentences are written in horizontal rows. 2 (v) 横放着 span; cross (adv) across ＊门口横放着一块板，使小孩子跑不出去。A piece of board is put across the door so that children cannot get out. 3 (adj) 不讲理 unreasonable; perverse ＊他不高兴时就打骂妻子，这种横行，应加以谴责。His unreasonable behaviour of beating up his wife whenever he is unhappy should be reprimanded.

横渡 [héng dù] cross; ferry or sail across; traverse

横贯 [héng guan] go through (from east to west)

横扫 [héng sǎo] sweep away or across

横冲直撞 [héng chōng zhì zhuàng] reckless action; colliding with (vehicles, etc.) in every direction 、

横征暴敛 [héng zhēng bào liǎn] exorbitant taxes and levies; ruthless taxation

横行霸道 [héngxíngbàdào] play the bully; arbitrary and lawless

横眉冷对千夫指，俯首甘为孺子牛 [héng méi lěng duì qiān fū zhǐ, fú shǒu gān wéi rú zǐ niú] This expression originated from writer, Mr Lu Hsun. Wrathfully defy the attacks of the enemy, but willingly submit to the wishes of the people

另见 [hèng]

hèng

横 [hěng] (adj) 粗暴，凶蛮 unreasonable; savage ＊那群私会党徒在这里专横了几个月，直到警察来扫清为止。That group of gangsters had been doing unreasonable acts here for several months until the police made a clean sweep on them.

横祸 [hěng-hòu] an unexpected misfortune or calamity

横暴 [hěng bào] brutal; tyrannical; high-handed

横财 [hěng cái] ill-gotten gains; underhand gains

另见 [héng]

hōng

哄 [hōng] (n) 许多人同时发出的杂乱声音 the hum of a crowd

哄动 [hōng dòng] cause a sensation; stir

哄堂大笑 [hōng táng dà xiào] the people of the whole house burst into laughter; fits of laughter

另见 [hǒng]
[hòng]

烘 [hōng] (v) 用火或烤熟取暖 dry at a fire; bake; roast

烘托 [hongtuò] set off in contrast; paint around an outline to make the object prominent

烘炉 [hōng lú] a furnace ; a

stove
烘烤 [hōng kǎo] roast; toast
轰(轟) [hōng] 1 (n) 指雷，炮等发出的巨大声响 bang; crash; roll; roar (of thunder, explosion,etc)＊雷声轰轰，快下雨了。The thunder roars continuously: it is going to rain very shortly. 2 (v) 用飞机，大炮等破坏 bomb; bombard ＊敌机已把城市轰炸成平地。The invading bombers had bombed the city into level ground. 3 (v) 赶走，驱逐 drive out
轰击 [hōng jī] bombard
轰炸 [hōngzhà] bomb
轰炸机 [hōng zhà jī] a bomber
轰轰烈烈 [hōng hōng liè liè] magnificent and grand; create a sensation

hóng

宏 [hóng] (adj) 广大 vast; wide; spacious; grand ＊这座宫殿很宏大。This palace is grand
宏亮 [hóng liàng] sonorous; loud
宏图 [hóng tú] far-reaching plans; grandiose plans
宏伟 [hóng wěi] magnificent; grand (prospects)
宏业 [hóng yè] an extensive business
闳(閎) [hóng] (adj) 大 great; large
虹 [hóng] (n) 雨后天晴，天空中小水珠经日光照射发生折射和反射，形成的彩色圆弧 rainbow ＊早晨的天空中出现了美丽的彩虹。A beautiful rainbow appeared in the morning sky.
鸿 [hóng] 1 (n) 野生鸟类，像鹅 a wild swan; a large wild goose 2 (adj) 大型，深远，久远 huge; great; vast; profound
鸿才 [hóngcái] great talents
鸿沟 [hónggōu] gap; chasm
鸿毛 [hóng máo] feather; the swan's down — very light; matter of no importance or value
洪 [hóng] 1 (n) 大水 flood; inundation; deluge ＊洪水给人们带来灾难。Floods bring disasters and hardship to the people. 2 (adj) 大 great; extensive.
洪量 [hóng liàng] magnanimity
洪亮 [hóng liàng] (of voice) loud and clear
洪流 [hóng liú] powerful current; tide.
洪炉 [hóng lú] crucible; a great furnace
洪水 [hóngshuǐ] flood; inundation
弘 [hóng] 1 (adj) 大 great; vast; expanded 2 (v) 扩充 to expand; enlarge; make great.
红(紅) [hóng] (adj) 血的颜色 red＊路边有一朵大红花。There is a big red flower on the road-side.
红宝石 [hóng bǎo shí] ruby
红茶 [hóng chá] black tea
红灯 [hóngdēng] red lantern; red light in traffic lights
红光满面 [hóngguāngmǎnmiàn] beaming with health; glowing with health
红军 [hóng jūn] the Red Army
红利 [hónglì] dividend ; bonus
红润 [hóngrùn] rosy (eg. cheeks)
红色 [hóngsè] red colour
红十字 [hóng shí zì] Red Cross
红糖 [hóngtáng] brown sugar
红血球 [hóng xuè qiú] red corpuscle
红枣 [hóng zǎo] red dates

hǒng

哄 [hǒng] 1 (v) 说假话，骗人 cheat; deceive; trick; tell lie ＊他哄骗父母要拿一百块钱买书。He told his parents a lie that he needed one hundred dollars to buy books. 2 (v) 用话或行动逗引人 coax; lull ＊ 你真行，把孩子哄得静静的。Very great of you to be

able to coax the child into silence.
另见 [hōng]
[hòng]
哄骗 [hǒngpiàn] to cheat by fine words

hòng

讧 [hòng] (v) 吵闹，扰乱 make an uproar (adj) noisy
另见 [hōng]
[hǒng]

讧(訌) [hòng] (v) 争吵，乱，溃散 quarrel; make trouble

hóu

侯 [hóu] (n) 封建制度五等爵位的第二等 a marquis
另见 [hòu]

喉 [hóu] (n) 颈的前部和气管相通的部分 throat; the gullet
喉咙 [hóu·lóng] throat; gullet
喉舌 [hóu shé] mouthpiece; spokesman

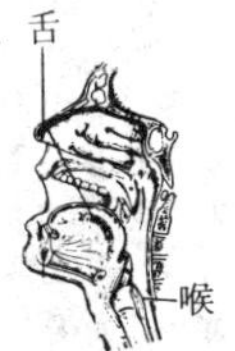

猴 [hóu] (n) 哺乳动物，像人，性情敏捷，活泼 monkey

hǒu

吼 [hǒu] 1 (n) 野兽大声叫 roar; bellow (of animals) 2 (v) 人在情绪激动时的大声呼喊 roar ; shout
吼叫 [hǒu jiào] roar

hòu

后 [hòu] (n) 封建帝王的妻子 a queen

后(後) [hòu] (adj) 跟"前"相对 hind; posterior; future; late; behind; rear *今后你要多努力，改过以前懒散的习惯。In future you must work harder to get rid of your laziness.
后盾 [hòu dùn] backing; support
后方 [hòu fāng] rear (area)
后顾前瞻 [hòu gù qián zhān] to look behind and ahead
后果 [hòu guǒ] consequence
后患无穷 [hòu huàn wú qióng] endless trouble ahead
后悔 [hòu huǐ] repent; regret ;remorseful
后会有期 [hòu huì yǒu qī] we shall meet again
后来 [hòu lái] afterwards; later on
后来居上 [hòu lái jū shàng] latecomers or new-comers have overtaken the old hands
后面 [hòu·mian] back ;behind
后母 [hòu mǔ] a step-mother
后起之秀 [hòuqǐ zhī xiù] the new talents that emerge afterwards
后生可畏 [hòu shēng kě wèi] the young should be respected, as they are capable of surpassing the elders
后台 [hòu tái] back-stage; behind-the scenes; supporters
后天 [hòu tiān] the day after tomorrow
后者 [hòu zhě] the latter

候 [hòu] 1 (v) 等待 wait; await; expect *上下班时的车站总是挤满了候车的人。At times before and after office, the bus-stop is always crowded with people who are waiting for buses. 2 (n) 时节 season; time 3 (v) 看望，问好 visit; inquire after *改天我到府上

拜候你父亲。 I shall visit your father

候命 [hòu mìng] await orders

候选人 [hòu xuǎn rén] candidate

厚 [hòu] 1 (n) 扁平物上下两面之间的距离 thickness 2 (adj) 粗肥，繁多，浓密，丰富 thick numerous ; abundant * 天气这样热，为什么你还穿厚的衣服？ Why do you wear thick clothing on such a hot day?

厚此薄彼 [hòu cǐ bó bǐ] discriminate against some and favour others

厚待 [hòudaì] treat well

厚道 [hòu daò] decent; sincere and considerate

厚度 [hòu dù] thickness

厚古薄今 [hòugǔbójīn] stress the past more than the present

厚惠 [hòu huì] high favours

厚今薄古 [hòujīnbógǔ] stress the present more than the past

厚礼 [hòu lǐ] handsome presents

厚颜无耻 [hòuyánwúchǐ] have the cheek to.......; have no sense of

厚意 [hòuyì] sincere feeling

hū

忽 [hū] 1 (v) 粗心，不注意 neglect; disregard (adj) careless; negligence *我一时疏忽，没关好门就上街，让小偷轻易入屋。 Due to my negligence in not locking the door properly before going out, the burglar easily got into the house. 2 (adj) 突然 sudden (adv) suddenly; unexpectedly *现在天气忽冷忽热，许多人都病倒。Many people fall sick in the present kind of weather which has sudden changes of temperatures.

忽略 [hū luè] neglect

忽然 [hū rán] suddenly; abruptly

忽视 [hū shì] overlook; neglect; disregard

乎 [hū] 1 (part) 表示疑问或感叹‥吗？…呀！a word placed at the end of a sentence to express doubt or exclaimation in classic Chinese 2 (prep) 放在动词或形容词后如“于”字之意 Used after a verb or adjective, similar to "to", "at", "through" *你的条件合乎工作的要求，所以你被录取了。 You are selected because your conditions meet the requirements of the job.

呼 [hū] 1 (v) 动物吐出气体，液体等，跟“吸”相对 exhale; breathe out 2 (v) 叫，喊 call; cry out; shout *妇人被抢劫时大声呼救，但路人全不理睬。When the woman was robbed, she cried out loudly for help but the passers-by took no notice at all. 3 (n) 表示声音 whistle; hiss (for sound of wind;flame, etc.) *风呼呼地吹着。The wind was whistling.

呼风唤雨 [hūfēng huàn yǔ] to summon wind and call for rain; the ability to harness nature

呼唤 [hū huàn] call to

呼啦啦 [hū lā lā] onomatopoeia (sound of flapping, sound of fluttering of flags, etc)

呼声 [hū shēng] voice; outcry

呼吸 [hū xī] respirate; breathe

呼啸 [hū xiào] scream

呼应 [hū yìng] respond to; echo

呼吁 [hūyù] appeal; call

糊 [hū] (v) 用粘的东西封缝子，窟窿等 paste up; stick together

另见 [hú]
[hù]

hú

胡 [hú] (adj) 随意乱来 reckless (adv) blindly *他每晚到酒吧去胡闹。Every evening he goes to the bar and acts recklessly.

胡 (鬍) [hú] (n) 须 the beard or moustache

胡姬 [hú jī] orchid

胡椒 [hú jiāo] pepper
胡闹 [hú naó] keep up one's wrong-doing
胡说八道 [hú shiō bā dào] talk nonsense
胡思乱想 [húsī luán xiǎng] day-dreaming; vain imaginations
胡桃 [hú tán] walnut
胡言乱语 [hú yàn luán yǔ] talk nonsense; babbling away
胡作非为 [hú zuò fēi wéi] doing all kinds of evil; criminal actions

湖 [hú] (n) 陆地上大面积的聚水处 lake

蝴 [hú]〔蝴蝶〕[húdié] (n)昆虫。会飞，有美丽的翅膀 butterfly

糊 [hú] (v) 粘贴 paste; gum

糊口 [hú kǒu] make a living
糊涂 [hú tū] blundering; foolish
另见 [hū]
[hù]

葫 [hú]〔葫芦〕(n) 草本植物，果壳可供药用 a gourd; a calabash

狐 [hú] (n) 哺乳动物，与狗同类，皮毛质地好，可做皮衣 fox; a vixen

狐狸 [hú lí] fox
狐群狗党 [hú qún gǔo dǎng] a gang of rascals
狐疑 [hú yí] suspicion; distrust

弧 [hú] (n) 圆周的一部分 arc

鹄（鵠）[hú] (n) 天鹅 a swan; the snow goose
另见 [gǔ]

囫 [hú] 囫囵 [húlún] (n) 整个儿 entire; the whole

囫囵吞枣 [hú lún tūn zǎo] (fig) gulp down without thought

壶（壺）[hú] (n) 有把有嘴盛液体的器具 a pot; a kettle

hǔ

虎 [hǔ] 1 (n) 哺乳动物，凶猛，会吃人 tiger; tigress 2 (adj) 比喻像虎的 tigerlike ＊ 威灵顿是英国历史上的一名虎将。Wellington was a tigerlike general in the British history.

虎口取食 [hǔ kǒu qǔ shí] to engage in hazardous occupation
虎口余生 [hǔ kǒu yú shēng] to escape from a dangerous situation; to escape from the jaws of death
虎头蛇尾 [hǔ tóu shé wěi] a magnificent beginning but a poor ending
虎穴龙潭 [hǔ xuèlóng ton] a very dangerous place

唬 [hǔ] (v) 吓 to scare; frighten ＊ 别扮鬼唬人！Don't act as a ghost to frighten people!

浒（滸）[hǔ] (n) 水边 the bank of a river; margin of a stretch of water

hù

户 [hù] 1 (n) 门 door 2 (n) 人家 family; household ＊家家户户在除夕晚上都一起吃团年饭。Every family takes a reunion dinner together on New Year's eve. 3 (n) 有账务关系的个人或单位 an account holder; a household ＊ 在银行开个储蓄户口吧。Go and open a savings account with the bank .

户外 [hù wài] in the open air; out-doors

护（護）[hù] (v) 保卫 protect; defend; guard; aid ＊一个好公民，应爱护公共财物。A good citizen should protect public property.

护士 [hù·shi] nurse
护送 [hù sòng] escort; convoy
护照 [hùzhào] passport

戽 [hù] (n) 戽斗，一种汲水灌田的工具 bailing ladle; bail

扈 [hù] (n) 随从 followers in procession

互 [hù] (pron) 彼此，互相 each other; one another (adj) mutual; reciprocal ＊我们鼓励国际贸易的互惠互利。We encourage mutual benefits in international trade.
互惠 [hù huì] reciprocal; mutually beneficial
互相 [hù xiàng] mutually; each other
互爱 [hù ài] to love each other
互助 [hù zhū] aid mutually; mutual help

怙 [hù] (v) 倚仗，凭持 rely on; depend on
怙恶不悛 [hù è bù quān] persist in evil doings; refusing to change
怙恶凌人 [hù è lǐng rēn] to intimidate and oppress others

糊 [hù] (n)有粘性的浆 paste; starch; gum
另见 [hū]
[hú]

huā

花 [huā] 1 (n) 植物的繁殖器官，有各种形状和颜色 flower; a blossom. 2 (adj) 各色的；种类复杂的 variegated; colourful; coloured ＊送殡时可别穿得花花绿绿。Don't put on a colourful attire to attend a funeral. 3 (adj)（视力）模糊 (of eye-sight) become dim, blurred or dizzy ＊她老人家眼花，看不清楚报纸上的新闻内容。The old lady is blurred in eyesight and she cannot read the contents of the newspapers clearly. 4 (v) 用；耗费 spend; use; expend ＊他花了一天的时间，才把工作完成。He spent one day to complete the job.
花边 [huā biān] lace
花朵 [huā duǒ] blossom; a cluster of flowers
花粉 [huā fěn] pollen
花费 [huā·fei] spend; use up
花岗岩 [huā gāng yán] granite
花花公子 [huā huā gōng zǐ] a profligate; a playboy
花花绿绿 [huā huā lǜ lǜ]multicoloured ; colourful
花花世界 [hua huā shì jiè] a world of self-indulgent luxury
花花絮絮 [huā huā xù xù] confused; muddle and ill-sorted
花卉 [huā huì] flowers; flowering plants
花街柳巷 [huā jiē liǔ xiàng] streets of ill-fame
花瓶 [huā pīng] flower vase
花圈 [huā qiān] wreath; garland
花生 [huā shēng] peanut; groundnut
花束 [huā shu] bouquet
花天酒地 [huā tiān jiǔ dì] gaiety and debauchery
花团锦簇 [huā tuán jǐn cù] colourful and gay bustle
花样 [huā yàng] pattern; design; style; variations ; tricks
花言巧语 [huā yán qiǎo yǔ] flowery words of flattery
花招 [huā zhāo] trick

哗（嘩）[huā] (n) 象声字 an onomatopoeia ; splash flowing water or chains, etc.) ＊小河哗拉哗拉地。The brook flows splashingly.
另见 [huá]

huá

华（華）[huá] 1 (n) 中华民族或中国的简称 China ; Chinese 2 (adj) 光彩；好看 splendid; elegant; gay; brilliant;

pompous; grand (n) glory; beauty ＊公主穿得很华丽地出席宴会。The Princess dressed up splendidly for the party.

华丽 [huá lì] showy; pompous; gorgeous; splendid; grand

华侨 [huá qiáo] overseas Chinese

华贵 [huá guì] honourable

华而不实 [huá ér bù shí] flashy without substance

哗（嘩）[huá] (adj) 人多声音杂乱 clamorous

哗然 [huá rán] clamorous

哗众取宠 [huá zhòng qǔ chǒng] impress people by claptrap; to win the good will and support of the people by words of flattery and acts of obsequiousness

另见 [huā]

滑 [huá] 1 (adj) 不粗涩；光溜 smooth; slippery; glossy ＊雨后路滑。The road is slippery after raining. 2 (v) 溜动 slip; skate; slide; glide ＊在寒带滑雪是最流行的运动。In frigid zones, skiing is one of the most popular sports. 3 (adj) 狡诈；不诚实 cunning; sly; dishonest ＊职员们都讨厌那位狡滑的上司。Most of the staff members dislike their cunning boss.

滑稽 [huá jī] ridiculous; ludicrous; comical

滑轮 [huá lún] pulley

滑润 [huá rùn] glossy; smooth

滑梯 [huá tī] slide for children to play on

滑头 [huátóu] cunning

滑翔 [huá xiáng] glide

滑翔机 [huáxiángjī] glider; gliding plane

滑雪 [huá xuě] ski

划 [huá] (v) 拨水前进 paddle; pole; oar ＊船夫把船划近岸边，让我们登陆。The boatman paddled the boat to the shore so that we could disembark.

划船 [huá chuán] paddle a boat; row

划（劃）[huá] (v) 擦 to rub; to strike; to scratch ＊划枝火柴来生火吧。Strike a match to start a fire, please.

另见 [huà]

huà

化 [huà] 1 (v) 改变 change; alter; transform ＊发电机把机械能化为电。A dynamo transforms mechanical energy into electricity. 2 (v) 融解；消散 dissolve; melt ＊春天一到，冰雪开始溶化。When spring comes, the snow will melt. 3 (suffix) 加在名词或形容词后；表示彻底转变性质或状态 -ize; -ization ＊许多发展中国家已渐渐工业化了。Many developing nations are gradually becoming industrialized. 4 (n) 化学的简称 Chemistry

化公为私 [huàgōngwéisī] appropriate public property

化合 [huà hé] combine in chemical process; chemical combination

化石 [huà shí] fossil

化为乌有 [huà wéi wū yǒu] to reduce to nothing

化险为夷 [huà xiǎn wéi yí] come

out safely from danger

化学元素 [huà xué yuán sù] chemical element

化验 [huà yàn] chemical examination

化妆 [huà zhuāng] make-up

桦(樺) [huà] (n) 落叶乔木，产于中国北部 a kind of birch found in Northern China

画(畫) [huà] 1 (n) 图 a drawing; a painting; a picture 2 (v) 绘，作出图形 draw; paint ∗ 那书记画了一张地图帮我们认路。The clerk drew a map to help us find our way. 3 (n) 汉字的一笔叫一画 a stroke of a Chinese character

画报 [huà bào] pictorial

画饼充饥 [huà bǐng chōng jī] draw a cake to satisfy one's hunger-using the imagination to console oneself

画家 [huà jiā] painter

画廊 [huà láng] gallery

画龙点睛 [huà lóng diǎn jīng] (fig) a critical touch; putting the finishing touches

画面 [huà mián] the general appearance of a work of art in respect of light, colour and composition ; picture (of film)

画蛇添足 [huà shé tiān zú] (fig) ruin the effect by adding what is superfluous

画室 [huà shì] a studio; an atelier

画像 [huà xiàng] portrait

画展 [huà zhǎn] art exhibition.

划(劃) [huà] 1 (v)分，区分 draw; classify; divide 两国经过商讨之后，重新划分国界。After some discussion, the two nations redraw their national boundaries. 2 (v) 预先打算；安排 plan; planning ∗经过长时间的筹划，这项工程即将开工。After a long period of planning, this project will be commenced soon.

划分 [huà fēn] divide; set apart; distinguish

划界 [huàjiè] draw a line ;demarcation

划清 [huàqīng] draw a clear line between

划时代 [huàshídài] epoh-making

另见 [huá]

话(話) [huà] 1 (n) 语言 speech; talk; words; conversation ∗ 谁也不相信他的话。Nobody believes in his words. 2 (v) 说，谈 talk; tell; speak; narrate ∗ 祖母爱坐在门外跟邻居话家常。Grand-ma loves to sit outside the house and have informal talks with the neighbours.

huái

怀(懷) [huái] 1 (n) 胸前 the breast; chest 2 (n) 心意，心胸 the affections; the bosom ∗ 在获晓自己考试及格后，他立刻满怀高兴地跑回家告诉妈妈。Filled with joy (in his bosom) on knowing that he has passed the examinations, he immediately ran home to inform his mother. 3 (v) 藏，思想上存有 cherish; harbour; think of; hold in mind ∗ 他曾经被李老师骂过，所以怀恨在心，毁坏李老师的车子。He harboured resentment againt the teacher Mr. Li who had scolded him and he damaged his car.

怀抱 [huái bào] embrace; (be in) the arms of …

怀恨 [huáihèn] have resentment in one's heart; nurse hatred against

怀念 [huái niàn] cherish the memory of; think of

怀疑 [huái yí] suspect; doubt ;suspicious

怀孕 [huài yùn] pregnancy ;become pregnant

槐 [huái] (n) 落叶乔木。木材坚硬有弹性；可以制造船舶 locust tree; acacia.

踝 [huái] 1 (n) 小腿与脚连接处两旁凸起的骨头，也叫"踝子骨"和"脚眼" the ankle 2 (n) 足跟 the heel

huài

坏（壞）[huài] 1 (adj) 不好；bad ＊电影中的坏人总是被好人打倒。 In the films, bad elements are always beaten by thc good ones. 2 (adj)东西受损害 wrecked; dilapidated; broken down. ＊巴士坏了，搭客得换另一辆。 As the bus engine has broken down, the passengers have to be transferred to another bus.

坏处 [huài·chu] harm; adverse effect

坏蛋 [huài dàn] a rascal; a villain

huān

欢（歡）[huān] (adj) 高兴；快乐 jolly; cheerful; merry; pleased. ＊父母亲看子女长大成人，感到欢喜。 Parents are pleased to see their children grow up and mature.

欢呼 [huānhū] cheer; acclaim; applaud; hail

欢聚一堂 [huān jù yì táng] a happy gathering; get together joyously

欢乐 [huān lè] happy; delighted; elated

欢送 [huān sòng] send off

欢天喜地 [huāntiān xǐ dì] extremely delighted; filled with joy

欢喜 [huāi xǐ] happy; like; be fond of.

欢心 [huān xīn] love; appreciation; (win one's) favour; goodwill

欢欣鼓舞 [huān xīng gǔ wǔ] very happy; elated.

欢迎 [huān yíng] welcome; greet

huán

缳（繯）[huán] 1 (n) 绳圈；绞索 noose 2 (v) 绞 fasten; tie; cord up

寰 [huán] (n) 广大的地域 domain

鬟 [huán] (n) 古代妇女梳的环形发结 a round knot of hair dressed by Chinese women in ancient days.

环（環）[huán] 1 (n) 圆圈形的东西 ring; a bracelet, a circlet 2 (v) 围绕 to encircle 3 (adv) 普遍地，周遭地 around; throughout ＊退休后，他们利用公积金去环游世界。 After retirement, they use their C. P. F. to travel round the world.

环抱 [huán bào] encircle; surround

环节 [huán jié] link; a segment

环境 [huan jìng] conditions; environment; circumstances

环球 [huán qiú] around the world; the whole world

环绕 [huán rǎo] go round; centre on; encircle; encompass

环虫 [huánchóng] ringed worms; annelida

环视 [huánshì] look round

还（還）[huán] 1 (v) 回；归 return＊他先打我，我才还手。He hit me first and then I returned a blow. 2 (v) 归还；偿付 repay; give back; recompense ＊借了别人的东西可别忘了归还。Don't forget to give back what you have borrowed.

还击 [huánjī] fight back; counterattack; deal counter blows

还礼 [huánlǐ] return the salute; return courtesy

还原 [huán yuán] reduce; restore; return to the original state; reduction; deoxidation

还债 [huán zhài] repay; pay a debt

另见 [hái]

huǎn

缓(緩) [huǎn] 1 (adj) 慢 slow; sluggish; loose (adv) gradually; slowly ＊学好一种语文是个缓慢的过程，绝对没有捷径。There is no short cut to the slow process of mastering a language. 2 (v) 推迟 postpone ＊由於下雨，今天的球赛缓期举行。Due to the rain, the match today is to be postponed.

缓兵之计 [huǎn bīng zhī jì] measures to stave off an attack; a scheme to gain time

缓步 [huǎn bù] walk slowly

缓冲地带 [huǎnchōngdìdài] a buffer zone

缓和 [huǎn hé] allay; moderate; mitigate; detente

缓慢 [huǎn màn] very slow

缓刑 [huǎnxíng] to suspend a sentence; to reprieve

huàn

奂 [huàn] 1 (adj) 文采鲜明 vivid 2 (adj) 盛 abundant; full; luxuriant

换 [huàn] 1 (v) 对调 exchange ; change ＊ 她牺牲荣誉以换取财富。 She exchanged honour for wealth.

换班 [huàn bān] relieve guard; change shifts

换句话说 [huànjùhuàshuō] in other words; that is to say

换汤不换药 [huàn tāng bù huàn yào] change the form but not the content

换新 [huàn xīn] renew; change for new

唤 [hàun] (v) 呼喊；叫 call; hail; summon ＊ 她那篇关於吸毒问题的文章已唤起了公众人士的注意。The attention of the public has been called forth by her article on drug addiction

唤醒 [huànxǐng] awaken

涣 [huàn] (adj) 消；散 scattered

涣散 [huàndsàn] dissipate; sap; dissipated

焕 [huàn] (adj) 光亮；光明 bright; brilliant; lustrous; resplendent

焕发 [huànfā] sparkling; sparkle; brim over with

焕然一新 [huàn rán yī xīn] brand new in appearance

患 [huàn] 1 (n) 祸害 evil; affliction; misery ; misfortune ＊ 青少年犯罪是社会的大患。 Juvenile delinquency is a great misfortune of the society. 2 (v) 遭受 suffer ＊ 他患了流行性感冒 。 He is suffering from influenza. 3 (v) 忧虑 grieve ; be distressed in mind

患病 [huànbìng] be afflicted with a disease; fall ill; suffer from illness

患得患失 [huàn dé huàn shī] worry about personal gain and loss

患难 [huàn nàn] adversity; hardship; misfortune

患难之交 [huàn nàn zhī jiāo] friendship made during adverse time

浣 [huàn] (v) 洗 wash; cleanse; bathe

豢 [huàn] (v) 喂养（牲口）；也比喻收买扶植爪牙 to feed (livestock); to cherish (henchmen)

豢养 [huànyǎng] nurture; groom; foster

幻 [huàn] 1 (adj)空虚的；不真实的 unreal ; imaginative; illusive 2 (v) 变化

change (adj) changeable ＊大自然的景象真是变化无穷。 The phenomena of nature are changeable.

幻灯 [huàn dēng] lantern slides; slides

幻觉 [huàn jué] hallucination

幻灭 [huàn miè] disillusion; shatter

幻想 [huàn xiǎng] illusion; imagination

宦 [huàn](n) 封建时代官吏的统称 an official (in ancient times)

huāng

荒 [huāng] 1 (n) 庄稼没有收成 famine 2 (n)没有开垦；无人耕种；野的 unexploited; uncultivated; wild ＊我们的祖先百多年前到这里来开荒。More than a hundred years ago, our forefathers came here to open up the wilderness. 3 (v) 废弃 be laid waste; neglect; put aside ＊勤劳的农夫是不会让田地荒芜的。An industrious farmer will never neglect his farmland.

荒地 [huāng dì] wasteland

荒废 [huāng fèi] fall into disuse; lay waste ;neglect and become unproficient

荒凉 [huāng liáng] desolate

荒谬；荒唐 [huāng miù]; [huāng tang] absurd; ridiculous

荒年 [huāng nián] crop failures; famine

荒芜 [huāng wú] (of land) overgrown with wild plants due to lack of management

荒野 [huāng yě] wilderness

慌 [huāng] 1 (adj) 急；忙乱 agitated; flurried ＊她慌忙穿好衣服，走出客厅开门。She put on her dress in a flurried manner and went out to the living room to open the door 2 (v) 害怕 scare; alarm (adj) nervous ; alarmed; apprehensive ＊人们因战争即将爆发而感到惊慌。The people become apprehensive because a war is about to break out.

慌乱 [huāng luàn] be alarmed and bewildered; in disorder

慌忙 [huāng máng] flustered; hurried

慌张 [huāng·zhang] helter-skelter; nervous;flurried

huáng

皇 [huáng] (n) 封建时代的君主 a sovereign, a ruler ; a king

惶 [huáng] (adj) 恐惧不安 scared; terrified; frightened

惶惶不可终日 [huáng huáng bù kě zhong rì] extremely afraid and uneasy

惶惑 [húang huò] perplexed and alarmed

惶恐 [huángkǒng] fear; alarmed

煌 [huáng] (adj) 明亮 bright; luminous; glittering

蝗 [huáng] (n) 一种昆虫。专吃庄稼，食量极大，常成灾祸 locust

遑 [huáng] 1 (n) 空闲 leisure. 2 (adj) 急 pressed; urged

黄 [huáng] (adj) 象金子那样的颜色 yellow＊ 花店里陈列着许多种花，有红色的，也有黄色的。Many kinds of flowers were shown in the flower-shop ;there were red ones, and also yellow ones.

黄疸病 [huáng dǎn bìng] jaundice

黄豆 [huáng dòu] soybean

黄蜂 [huáng fēng] a wasp

黄瓜 [huáng guā] cucumber

黄昏 [huánghūn] dusk

黄金 [huáng jīn] gold

黄金时代 [huáng jīn shí dài] golden

age

黄梨 [huánglí] a pineapple

簧 [huáng] (n) 有弹力的机件 the spring in a mechanical device

huǎng

恍 [huǎng] 1 (conj) 仿佛，好象 as if; like 2 (adj) 精神不集中，模模糊糊 absent-minded; confused; at a loss

恍然大悟 [hǔang rán dà wù] suddenly realize

晃 [huǎng] 1 (adj)明亮，常叠用 bright ; flashing * 他拿着明晃晃的军刀表演武术。He performs martial arts with a flashing sabre. 2 (v) 照耀 dazzle *她一身珠光宝气，非常晃眼。The jewellery on her dress is very dazzling. 3 (v) 闪过 flash past; flicker *一道银光一晃而过。A streak of silver light flashed past.

另见 [huàng]

幌 [huǎng] 1 (n) 帐幔，帘帷 curtain 2 〔幌子〕(n)旧时商店门外的布制招牌。常用来比喻装点门面，欺骗别人时假借的名义 signboard; under the guise of; pretext; smoke-screen

谎（謊）[huǎng] (n) 假话 lie; falsehood *一些小孩子因为做错事怕挨骂而说谎。Some children tell lies because they fear to be scolded for their wrong-doings.

huàng

晃 [huàng] (v) 摇动 sway; shake *晚上的树枝晃来晃去使人看了有点害怕。It makes one feel a little scared to see the tree branches swaying at night.

另见 [huǎng]

huī

辉（輝）[huī] 1 (n) 光彩 lustre; brilliance (adj) bright. 2 (v) 照耀 shine; illuminate; reflect *圣诞节前夕的灯火把街道辉映得象白昼一般。The lights in the Christmas Eve were so illuminative that the streets were as bright as in the daylight.

挥（揮）[huī] (v) 摇摆，舞动 wave; wag; sway *交通警察向车辆挥手示意表示可以前进。The traffic police waved to the cars asking them to go ahead.

挥动 [huī dòng] wave

挥霍 [huī huò] spend extravagantly; spend freely

挥金如土 [huī jīn rú tǔ] to squander gold as if it were dirt ;spend money foolishly

挥舞 [huī wǔ] wave; brandish

晖（暉）[huī] (n) 日光 a ray of the sun-light

灰 [huī] 1 (n) 东西燃烧后剩下来的粉末 ashes; cinder 2 (n) 尘土 dust; dirt 3 (adj) 黑色和白色之间的颜色 grey 4 (adj) 消沉，失望 disheartened; despaired *别因失败而灰心，应找出失败的原因。Don't be disheartened by failure; instead, find out the causes of the failure.

灰暗 [huī ' àn] obscure; dim; dismal

灰尘 [huīchén] dust

灰烬 [huī jìn] ashes; residue

恢 [huī] 1 (adj) 宽阔广大，有时叠用 great; liberal 2 (v) 还原 restore; recover; resume * 他在医院治疗了几个月，现在已恢复健康。After treatment in the hospital for a few months, he has already recovered.

诙（詼）[huī]〔诙谐〕(v) 开玩笑，说话有趣 humorous

徽 [huī] (n) 标志 emblem

徽章 [huī zhāng] badge

麾 [huī] (v) 指挥 beckon; call; make motion with the hand.

huí

回 [huí] 1 (n)还；归；返；转 return; go back; turn back ＊每天下了班后他就回家。Everyday, he goes home after office hours. 2 (n) 量词，次 a measure word : time ＊ 她每月受一回医药检验。She submitted herself to medical examination once a month. 3 (n) 章回小说的章节 a chapter in a story book

回拜 [huíbài] pay a return visit

回避 [huí bì] evade; avoid confrontation with

回答 [huídá] answer; reply

回电 [huídiàn] reply by telegram

回复 [huí fù] reply; restore

回顾 [huí gù] look back; retrospect

回归线 [huíguīxiàn] tropic

回合 [huí hè] rounds (eg. boxing)

回击 [huí jī] counter-attack; fight back

回教 [huí jiào] Islam

回教堂 [huíjiàotáng] a mosque

回敬 [huíjìng] reciprocate ; offer something in return

回绝 [huíjuè] turn down; reject

回升 [huí shēng] rise up again

回声 [huí shēng] echo

回头是岸 [huí tóu shìàn] repentance is salvation

回味 [huíwei] after taste; realize through recollection

回味无穷 [huíwèi wúqiong] endless pleasure in recollection

回想 [huí xiǎng] recall; reflect

回心转意 [huí xīn zhuàng yì] reconsider; repent; change one's mind

回旋 [huí xuán] go round and round. (room for) manoeuvre

回忆 [huí yì] recollect

回忆录 [huí yì lù] memoirs

回音 [huíyīn] letter of reply ;echo

茴 [huí]〔茴香〕(n) 草本植物果实可作调味香料；又供药用 fennel;anise

蛔 [huí]〔蛔虫〕(n) 一种寄生虫，在人、畜体内吸收养料和分泌毒素，损害人畜健康。 a round worm; an intestinal worm

huǐ

毁 [huǐ] 1 (v) 破坏 destroy; break to pieces ＊好好的一个大城市被地震毁了。Such a big city was destroyed by the earthquake. 2 (v) 说人坏话 slander; defame ＊毁谤是一些竞争者的手段。One of the tactics used by some competitors is to defame their opponents.

毁灭 [huǐ miè] wipe out; exterminate; destroy entirely

悔 [huǐ] (v) 认识到以前的事做错了 regret; repent (adj) repentent ＊他后悔求学时不肯用功，但是已太迟了。He repented too late of not having worked hard during school days.

悔改 [huǐ gǎi] mend one's ways; repent

悔过 [huǐ guò] repent

悔过自新 [huǐguò zì xīn] repent and turn over a new leaf

悔恨 [huǐ hèn] lament over
悔悟 [huǐ wù] awake to one's errors
悔之不及 [huǐ zhī bù jí] too late to repent; to cry over spilt milk (fig)

huì

彗 [huì] (n) 扫帚 a broom
彗星 [huì xīng] comet

慧 [huì] (adj) 聪明；有知识 bright; intelligent (n) wisdom; sagacity

会(會) [huì] 1 (v) 集合 assemble; meet together ＊要去郊游的同学们都得先在学校会合才出发。All those students who want to go to the picnic will first assemble in school before setting out. 2 (v) 见面 to meet 3 (n) 为一定的目的而成立的团体或组织 association; society ; union 4 (v) 能；可以做得到 ability to; be able ＊他会运用流利的英语与人交谈。He is able to converse in English fluently.
会餐 [huìcān] dine together
会场 [huì chǎng] place of meeting
会费 [huìfèi] membership dues (of a union, association, etc)
会合 [huìhé] meet; join
会话 [huì huà] conversation
会见 [huì jiàn] meet with; have an interview with
会客 [huì kè] see visitors
会客室 [huìkèshì] reception-room
会面 [huì miàn] meet each other
会谈 [huì tán] confer with; hold talks; negotiate
会晤 [huì wù] meet
会议 [huì yì] meeting; conference
会员 [huì yuán] member of an association, union, etc., membership
会战 [huìzhàn] engage in a decisive battle; general

另见 [kuài]

绘(繪) [huì] (v) 画；描画 draw; paint; make a picture
绘画 [huì huà] drawing; painting
绘影绘声 [huìyǐng huìshēng] vividly depicted
绘图 [huìtú] draw a design; draw a picture

惠 [huì] (v) 给人利益；好处 give in charity; be kind to ;kindness ; benefit; favour. ＊日后我一定重重地报答你的恩惠。One day, I will repay you well for your kindness.
惠赐 [huìcì] bestow graciously
惠赠 [huì zèng] give; present; gift

秽(穢) [huì] 1 (n) 乱草 weeds 2 (adj) 肮脏 dirty; filthy; mean ＊在污秽的沟渠旁边吃东西，是不卫生的。It is unhealthy to eat near the dirty drain. 3 (adj) 丑恶的 foul; dirty;indecent; detestable ＊那些阿飞的污言秽语，实在难听。It is really unbearable to listen to the foul language used by the hoodlums.

卉 [huì] (n) 草的总称 plants; herbs

晦 [huì] (adj) 暗；不明显 dark; obscure
晦涩 [huìsè] obscure in meaning

诲(誨) [huì] (v) 教育；劝导 teach; advise
诲人不倦 [huì rén bù juàn] teach with tireless zeal

汇(滙,彙) [huì] 1 (v) 会合在一起 to gather; to meet ＊山上的许多小川在山脚汇合成一条大河流向海洋。The small tributaries from the mountain gather at the foothill to form a big river which flows into the sea. 2 (v) 寄钱 remit (money) ＊他每月都汇钱回家给年老的爹娘。

He remitted a sum of money to his aged parents every month. 3 (v) 综合，集中 group together; collect ＊ 他汇集了各方面的资料，写成一本关於新加坡历史的书籍。 He collected materials of all aspects and wrote a book on the history of Singapore.

汇报 [huì bào] make a collective report; report

汇编 [huìbiān] assemble; collect and edit

汇合 [huì hé] concourse; merge with; confluence

汇集 [huìjí] pool; concourse (of rivers, people, etc.); come together

汇率 [huìlú] rate of exchange

讳(諱) [huì] 1 (v) 忌避 to avoid 2 (v) 隐蔽 to hide; to conceal ＊他在法庭里直言不讳。 He spoke plainly without concealing any fact in the court. 3 (n) 死者的名 name (of a deceased)

讳言 [huì yán] forbidden talk; not to be mentioned

贿(賄) [huì] (v) 贿赂，用财物收买 bribe ＊政府若是廉洁，公务员就不容易受人贿赂。In an incorrupt government, civil servants are not easily bribed.

hūn

昏 [hūn] 1 (n) 傍晚 evening; dusk ＊爸爸回到家里，已是黄昏时分。 It was already in the evening when father reached home. 2 (adj) 光线暗，不明朗 dark; dim; gloomy. ＊ 热带树林里的叶子遮着阳光，所以十分昏暗。It is dark inside the tropical forests because the sunlight is obscured by the thick leaves 3 (v)迷糊，神智不清楚 faint (adj) unconscious ＊房里空气不流通，一些人因支持不住而昏倒。 The ventilation in the room was so bad that some people could not bear it and fainted. 4 (adj) 思想糊涂，乱 confused ; at a loss ＊一连串不幸的事情发生在她身上，使她昏乱得不知怎么处理。 That a chain of misfortunes happened to her made her quite at a loss to know what to do.

昏沉 [hūn chén] dismal; dim; muddled

昏花 [hūn huā] dim-sighted

昏迷 [hūn mí] faint; unconscious; stupefied

昏天黑地 [hūn tiān hēi dì] in total darkness; social lawlessness and chaos

昏庸 [hūn yōng] stupid; idiotic

婚 [hūn] (n) 男女结合成为夫妻 marriage

婚姻 [hūn yīn] marriage; wedding

阍 [hūn] (n) 看门的人；如：司阍 gate-keeper; door-keeper

荤(葷) [hūn] 1 (n) 鱼，肉等食品 meat-dishes 2 (n) 葱 蒜等有特殊气味的蔬菜 vegetables with a spicy scent like onion garlic or leck

荤菜 [hūn cài] meat dishes

hún

浑(渾) [hún] 1 (adj) 水不清，污浊 turbid; dirty; polluted ＊ 浑浊的河水不能饮用。 The dirty water of a river is not potable. 2 (adj) 全，满 full; whole; entire; complete ＊ 运动场上个个运动员浑身是劲。Every sportsman on the field was filled with strength and vitality.

浑身是胆 [hún shēn shì dǎn] bold and courageous.

魂 [hún] 1 (n) 旧日不科学的说法，指能离开肉体而存在的精神 soul 2 (n) 人的精神思想方面活动的总称 spirit

魂不附体 [húnbùfùtǐ] scared out of one's wits.
魂飞魄散 [hún fēi pò sǎn] extremely frightened

hùn

混 [hùn] (v) 掺杂在一起 mix; mingle; blend * 把两件没有关联的事物混为一谈，一定谈不出结果的。 To mix up two unrelated matters in discussion will certainly bring no result.
混合 [hùn hé] mix; mingle
混合物 [hùnhé wù] a mixture
混乱 [hùnluàn] chaotic; disorderly
混凝土 [hùn níng tǔ] cement
混水摸鱼 [hùn shuǐ mō yú] fish in trouble waters
混为一谈 [hùn wéi yì tán] equate.... with....; mix the two together
混淆 [hùn xiáo] confuse; mix up
混淆是非 [hùn xiáo shì fēi] confuse right and wrong
混血儿 [hùn xuè ér] a hybrid
混浊 [hùn zhuó] muddy

huō

豁 [huō] 1 (v) 裂开；破缺 crack; break; spilt open *墙豁了一道口，不及时修补就会倒下来。 The wall has cracked and it will collapse if not repaired in time. 2 (v) 舍弃 forsake; abandon; give up
另见 [huò]
豁出去 [hūo chū qù] to go as one pleases ; stop at no sacrifices
豁唇 [hūo chún] hare-lipped

huó

活 [huó] 1 (v) 生存；跟"死"相对 live (n) life *活到老，学到老。 Live to old age, learn to old age. 2 (adj) 逼真 alive; lively; life-like * 他的风景画画得活生生的，使欣赏者有如身处其中。His scenery painting is so life-like that it makes one feel as if one is in the picture. 3 (adj) 不固定；可移动的 mobile; movable. * 活动图书馆把书载到乡村区鼓励孩子们阅读。 A mobile library carries books to the rural areas and encourages the children there to read them. 4 (n) 泛指工作 work; livelihood; abour living * 她身体虚弱，不宜干粗活。Being physically weak, she is unfit for rough labour.
活动 [húo dòng] act; activity; action; movable; mobile; active
活动家 [húo dòng jiā] protagonist; man of action
活该 [huógāi] it serves you (one) right
活力 [huólì] vitality
活龙活现 [huó lóng hóuxiàn] vividly portray; life-like
活路 [huó lù] a thoroughfare; a way out of the difficulty
活命 [huó mìng] survive; live on
活泼 [huó· po] lively; vigorous
活塞 [huó sāi] a piston ; a valve

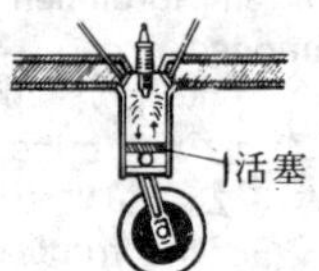

活生生 [huó shēng shēng] vivid; lively
活象 [huó xiàng] just like
活用 [huó yòng] put to practical use
活跃 [huó yuè] be active; lively; active
活字印刷 [huó zì yìn shuā] movable-type printing; block-printing

和 [huó] (v) 在粉状物中加水搅拌或揉弄使粘在一起 mix; compound (powdery substance with water)
另见 [hé]
[hè]

huǒ

火 [huǒ] 1 (n) 东西燃烧时发生的光和焰 fire; flame ＊ 无火不起烟，无风不起浪。 There is no smoke without fire, and there is no wave without wind. 2 (adj) 比喻发怒 fall into a rage; get angry ＊父亲见到儿子的成绩那么差，心头火起，把他打了一顿。On seeing that his son's results were so bad, the father became angry and gave his son a good walloping. 3 (n) 枪炮弹药 munitions; ammunitions

火柴 [huǒ chái] match

火车 [huǒ chē] train

火海刀山 [huǒ hǎi dāo shān] a sea of flames and a mountain of swords

火花 [huǒ huā] sparks

火箭 [huǒ jiàn] rocket

火警 [huǒ jǐng] an outbreak of fire; fire alarm

火酒 [huǒjiǔ] spirits; an alcoholic liquor

火坑 [huǒ kēng] a fiery pit; (fig) extremely miserable situation

火炉 [huǒ lú] stove; furnace

火山 [huǒ shān] volcano

火上加油 [huǒ shàng jiāo yóu] pour oil on the flames; make things worse

火烧眉毛 [huǒ shāo méi·máo] (fig) extremely urgent

火石 [huǒ shí] flint; flintstone

火速 [huǒ sù] very urgent; pressing

火腿 [huǒ tuǐ] ham

火星 [huǒxīng] sparks; the planet Mars

火焰 [huǒ yàn] flame; blaze

火药 [huǒ yào] gun powder; ammunition

火灾 [huǒ zāi] conflagration; fire-disaster

火葬 [huǒ zàng] cremate

火中取栗 [huǒ zhōng qǔ lì] pull chestnuts out of the fire

火种 [huǒ zhǒng] tinder

伙（夥）[huǒ] 1 (n) 结合在一块儿的人 group; a party 2 (n) 膳食 food ; food supply ＊ 宿舍里的学生是搭伙食的。The students in the hostel have their food catered for.

伙伴 [huǒ bàn] companion; partner

伙计 [huǒ·jì] shop assistant ;an employee

huò

镬（鑊）[huò] (n) 锅 a pot; a caldron

获（獲，穫）[huò] 1 (v) 得到，取得 get; aquire ; gain; obtain; catch; seize ＊ 猎人捕获了一只小老虎。The hunter has caught a tiger cub. 2 (n) 收割庄稼 reaping; harvest ＊由於风调雨顺，今年小麦的收获很好。Due to the favourable climatic conditions, the wheat harvest this year has been very good.

获得 [huò dé] get; attain

获胜 [huò shèng] win; victorious

获悉 [huò xī] learn (news, etc.)

霍 [huò] (adj) 快，迅速 quickly; suddenly ＊ 霍然病愈 He has recovered quickly.

霍乱 [huòluàn] cholera

或 [huò] (adv) (conj) 也许 perhaps; probably; or; whether ; either ∗今天来或是明天来。Come either today or tomorrow.

惑 [huò] 1 (v) 怀疑 doubt ; suspect 2 (v) 误导 deceive; lead to errors

惑乱 [huòluàn] be confused; be bewildered

货(貨) [huò] (n) 商品；物件 goods; merchandise; cargo; wares; commodities ∗这间店货真价实,吸引了许多顾客。The genuine goods and fair prices of the shop have attracted many customers.

货舱 [huò cāng] stowage; the hold (of a ship)

货车 [huò chē] freight car ; a truck

货船 [huò cháun] a cargo-boat; a freighter

货色 [huò sè] goods; rubbish (of person, things, or ideas); stuff

货栈 [huò zhàn] a warehouse; a godown

货真价实 [huò zhēn jìa shí] genuine quality and fair price

祸(禍) [huò] (n) 灾害，灾难 disaster; misfortune; calamity; evil; injury ∗他们记录了地震所造成的灾祸。They kept a record of earthquake disasters.

祸不单行 [huò bù dān xíng] disaster does not travel alone

祸国殃民 [huò guó yāng mín] harming the country and its people

祸患 [huò huàn] misfortune

祸首 [huò shǒu] principal criminal; cause of trouble

豁 [huò] (adj) 开通；开阔 open; broad-minded ∗她虽然年纪大，但是却很豁达，跟下一代很合得来。Although she is old, she is broadminded and can get along very well with the younger generation.

豁亮 [huò liàng] spacious and bright

豁免 [huò miǎn] exempt; release

豁然开朗 [huò rán kāi lǎng] suddenly broadened and brightened; suddenly understood

另见 [huō]

J

jī

几(幾) [jī] (adj) 几乎，差一点儿 almost; nearly; somewhat * 马来西亚的人口比新加坡的人口大了几乎五倍。 The population of Malaysia is almost five times bigger than that of Singapore.
另见 [jǐ]

讥(譏) [jī] (v) 讽刺；挖苦 ridicule; mock at; jeer; satirize; joke * 我们不应讥笑身体有缺陷的人。We should not ridicule people who have physical defects.

讥讽 [jīfěng] satirize; ridicule.

讥笑 [jīxiào] ridicule; jeer; make fun of; laugh at.

叽(嘰) [jī] (n) 表示杂乱的声音 a noise * 老师一踏出课室，班上的同学就叽叽喳喳地吵起来。Once the teacher stepped out of the classroom, the students began to chatter.

机(機) [jī] 1 (n) 机器 a machine. 2 (n) 飞机的简称 an abbreviation for aeroplane. * "协和"机的载量很大。The capacity of the 'Concorde' aeroplane is very large. 3 (n) 际会，合宜的时候 opportunity; chance * 他知道她急着要钱用，乘机向她索取高利息。Knowing full well that she needs money urgently he takes the opportunity to charge her a high interest rate. 4 (adj) 灵巧，能迅速适应事物的变化的 quick-witted; alert * 他是个机智的将军，在战场上常打胜仗。Being a quick-witted general, he was always victorious in the battlefield.

机场 [jīchǎng] airport

机床 [jīchuáng] machine tools

机构 [jīgòu] organisation; set-up; institution

机关 [jīguān] organisation; offices; institute

机关枪 [jīguānqiāng] machine gun

机警 [jījǐng] watchful

机灵 [jīling] quick-witted; clever

机敏 [jīmǐn] witty; dexterous; alert

机能 [jīnéng] function

机器人 [jīqìrén] a robot

机械化 [jīxièhuà] (mechanization) mechanize

机要 [jīyào] confidential; important; essential

机油 [jīyóu] lubricant

饥(饑) [jī] 1 (adj) 肚子饿 hungry; insufficient * 在印度，有好几百万人在饥寒交迫中生活。 In India, there are millions of people living in hunger and cold. 2 (n) 收成不好或没有收成 famine * 长期常年的饥荒，许多农民都离乡背井到城市去谋生。Due to the long period of famines,many farmers leave their homes for the cities to look for a living

饥不择食 [jī bù zé shí] any food will suffice in hunger

饥渴之际 [jī kě zhī jì] between hunger and thirst — at the last gasp

饥民 [jī mín] hunger-stricken people.

肌 [jī] (n) 肌肉；人或动物体内附着在骨头上或构成内脏的柔软物质，由许多纤维组成muscle

畿 [jī] (n) 古时称靠近国都的地方 land which pertained to the emperor (in the ancient time) or near the capital.

期 [jī] (n) 满一定的时间 a period of time
另见 [qī]

基 [jī] 1 (n) 建筑物的底脚 the foundation; a base (of a building) * 越高的层屋，地基就得打得越深。 The higher the building, is the deeper the foundation has to be made. 2 (adj) 根本的 basic; fundamental; base * 美国在日本的冲绳岛设有军事基地。The United States of America has installed military bases in Okinawa of Japan. 3 (adv) 根据 according to; based on * 公司基于他常迟到的原因，把他辞掉了。 Based on the reason that he was always late, the company dismissed him.

基本 [jīběn] basic; fundamental; essential

基本功 [jī běngōng] basic training; essential skill

基本上 [jī běn-shang] basically; fundamentally

基层 [jī céng] basic level or unit; grass roots

基础 [jīchǔ] base; foundation

基地 [jīdì] base; the base area

基点 [jīdiǎn] vital point; starting point; base

基督教 [jī dū jiao] Christianity

基金 [jījīn] fund

奇 [jī] (adj) 单的；不成双的 odd (in number)
另见 [qí]

畸 [jī] (adj) 不正常的 irregular; quaint; strange

畸人 [jīrēn] an extraordinary man; quaint, eccentric persons

畸形 [jīxíng] deformity; malformation

羁(羈) [jī] (v) 束缚；拘束 restrain; control; detain * 在案件还没审完之前，嫌疑犯须被羁留在警察所。 As the case has not been decided yet; the suspect had to be detained in the police headquarters.

羁绊 [jībàn] a yoke; fetters; bonds

羁留 [jīliú] detain; seize.

羁押 [jīyā] detain; keep in custody.

跻(躋) [jī] (v) 登；上升 to ascend; rise

绩(績) [jī] (n) 功业；成果 merit ; meritorious deeds; distinguished services

积(積) [jī] 1 (v) 聚集 accumulate; amass; collect; gather; assemble; hoard; store up (n) accumulation * 虽然你一天储蓄一角钱，可是积少成多，几年后就会有几百块了。 Although you save ten cents a day, yet when these are accumulated, there will be hundreds of dollars a few years later. 2 (n) 数目相乘的结果 the product of multiplication (in Mathematics) * 三乘五的积是十五。The product of three multiplied by five is fifteen.

积肥 [jī féi] stock up manure; collect fertilizer; manure accumulation

积分 [jīfēn] total marks; intergral calculus.

积极 [jī jí] active; positive; enthusiastic

积劳成疾 [jī láo chéng jí] sick from over-work

积累 [jīlěi] accumulate; cumulate

积少成多 [jīshǎo chéng duō] from small increments comes abundance

积蓄 [jīxù] save; accumulate; savings

迹 [jī] 1 (n) 事物留下的印象。foot mark; trace; a track; clue ＊那小孩子身上有被抽打的痕迹。There are traces of whippings on the body of that child. 2 (n) 前人遗留下的事物 a site (remains) ＊马六甲有葡萄牙殖民者的遗迹。There are remains of the Portuguese colonialists in Malacca.

迹象 [jī xiàng] trace; hint; indication

姬 [jī] (n) 古时对妇女的美称 charming woman

稽 [jī] 1 (v)查考；考核investigate; examine＊公司设立了一个委员会来稽查这次的意外事件。The company has formed a committee to investigate the accident. 2 (v) 停留 delay ＊他对什么都不紧张，做事总是稽延时日。Not excited over anything, he always delays time in whatever he does.

稽查 [jīchá] inspect; search for; examine

稽核 [jīhé] audit

屐 [jī] (n) 木底鞋，也泛指鞋 clog; wooden shoe

缉(緝) [jī] (v) 搜捕；捉拿 pursue; search; catch; come after＊警方在通缉一名逃走的歹徒。The police is searching for an escaped outlaw.

缉捕 [jībǔ] search and arrest

缉私 [jīsī] seize smuggled goods; preventive service

另见 [qī]

唧 [jī] (n) 表示声音；常叠用 a sound ＊她们俩在一个角落头唧咕，好像在谈秘密似的。They spoke softly in a corner as though they were talking secrets.

击(擊) [jī] 1 (v) 敲打 hit; knock; strike ＊在一场拳击赛中，拳王击败了对手。In a boxing match, the champion knocked out his opponent. 2 (v)攻打 strike; attack; kill ＊两名歹徒在抢劫银行时击毙了看守人。Two robbers killed a watchman while robbing the bank.

击败 [jībài] defeat; beat

击毙 [jībì] kill (in fighting)

击毁 [jīhuǐ] destroy

击剑 [jījiàn] sword-fighting; fencing

击落 [jī luò] shoot down; strike (knock) down

击破 [jīpò] rout; crush; frustrate; defeat

击杀 [jīshā] kill; beat one to death

击伤 [jī shāng] wound; injure

击退 [jī tuì] repulse; drive back; rebuff

乩 [jī] (n) 用木笔在沙盘上写字以占卜决疑。to divine by means of a willow stick writing upon sand

鸡(雞) [jī] (n) 一种家禽 fowls; hen or cock

鸡鸣狗盗 [jī míng gǒu dào] contemptible talent that's not worth mentioning

鸡鸣狗吠 [jī míng gǒu fèi] fowls crowing and dogs barking — a populous village

鸡犬不宁 [jī quǎn bù níng] even fowls and dogs are restless — turmoil

激 [jī] 1 (adj)急剧；强烈vexed; agitated; violent ＊堕胎合法化引起激烈的争论。The legalization of abortion gave rise to violent controversies. 2 (v) 使人感情冲

动 stir; arouse; excite. (adj) enraged; irritated; agitated ＊他无理地责骂女儿，激起了旁人的不满。 His act of reproaching his daughter unreasonably has aroused discontent among the bystanders.

激昂 [jī áng] fervent and excited; emotionally wrought up; spirited

激动 [jīdong] stir; agitate ; excited

激发 [ji fā] arouse

激愤 [jī fèn] irritated

激化 [jī huà] intensify; deepen

激进 [jījìn] radical; drastic

激烈 [jīliè] violent; drastic; intense

激流 [jī liú] torrent

激怒 [jīnù] annoy; irritate; enrage

激情 [jī qíng] strong emotions

激增 [jī zēng] increase greatly; a sudden (remarkable) increase

激战 [jī zhàn] fierce battle; wage an intensive struggle

jí

及 [jí] 1 (v)到；到达 reach; attain 2 (prep) 趁着 while ＊考期愈来愈近了，我们得及早复习功课。 Examination is drawing nearer and nearer, we should revise our lessons while it is still early. 3 (prep)够得上；比得上 to; up to; until; till ＊他已经及格，可当救生员了。He is up to the standard to be a lifeguard. 4 (conj)连接词 and; as well as; also ＊植物园里有胡姬花，玫瑰花及其他花卉。There are orchids, roses and other flowers in the botanic garden.

及格 [jígé] pass (an examination); up to the standard; qualified

及时 [jíshí] on time; in time

及早 [jízǎo] as early as possible; while it is early

汲 [jí] (v) 从下往上打水 draw; drag ＊从井里汲水。to draw water from a well.

级(級) [jí] 1 (n) 台阶 a step. 2 (n) 等第 a rank; grade; rung; class ＊领事是大使馆里的高级官员。A consulate is an official of high rank in the embassy. 3 (n)量词 a measure word ＊上吉隆坡的黑风洞得爬几百级石阶。 To go up to the Batu Caves in Kuala Lumpur, it is neccessary to climb hundreds of steps.

级别 [jíbié] rank; grade; class

级任 [jí rèn] the teacher in charge of a class; form teacher

级数 [jíshù] series (eg. arithmatical series)

笈 [jí] (n)书箱 a box for keeping books.

楫 [jí] (n)划船的短桨 a paddle; an oar

辑(輯) [jí] 1 (v)把分散的文章；文件等材料集中起来，作系统的整理和编选 compile; collect; compose＊一些学者把莎士比亚的作品编辑成书。 Some scholars compiled the works of Shakespeare into a book. 2 (n) 整套书籍，资料按内容或先后次序分成的各部分 abstract

辑录 [jílù] compile; edit

辑要 [jíyāo] an abstract; a synopsis; an outline

戢 [jí] 1 (v) 收敛；收藏 draw tight ; store up 2 (v) 停止 stop

戢兵 [jíbīng] to stop hostilities

戢怒 [jínù] stop being angry

籍 [jí] 1 (n) 书册 a book 2 (n)登记名册 a record; list; register 3 (n) 出生或久居的地方 native place; domicile of origin 4 (n) 个人对国家或组织的隶属关系 nationality; membership

瘠 [jí] 1 (adj) 瘦弱 lean; thin 2 (adj) 土地不肥沃 barren

meager (soil) ＊ 要把瘠土变成良田，必须施肥。Fertilizers must be applied to turn barren soils into fertile grounds.

吉 [jí] (adj) 吉祥；幸福 fortunate; lucky; auspicious ＊ 他的事业一开始即有吉兆。His career was begun under the fairest auspices.

吉普车 [jí pǔchē] jeep

吉日 [jírì] a lucky day; a red-letter day; an auspicious occasion

吉凶 [jíxiōng] the bright and black side of things; good and evil

即 [jí] 1(adv)立刻；当前 immediately; presently; at once ＊ 巫师告诉农民说他会造雨，召之即来。The wizard told the farmers that with his powers of making rain; he could call the rain to fall immediately. 2 (v) 就是 that is ＊ 斯里兰卡，即锡兰，盛产茶叶。 Sri Lanka, that is Ceylon, produces much tea. 3 (conj) 表示假定或就算是 even; though ＊ 由新加坡到香港即使你乘飞机，也得花上几个钟头的时间。 It will take a few hours from Singapore to Hong Kong even if you go by plane. 4 (v) 靠近 approach; reach

即便 [jíbiàn] even if

即或 [jíhuò] even though

即将 [jíjiāng] soon; in no time; nearly

即刻 [jíkè] immediately; at once; outright; as soon as

即日 [jírì] today; this day; the same day

即使 [jíshǐ] even if

即席 [jíxí] on-the-spot

极(極) [jí] (adv; adj) 最；最后；顶；非常 extremely; final; top most; very ＊ 她极端厌恶留长发的。She extremely disliked those who keep long hair 2 (n) 地球的南北两端，磁体的两端 the poles of the earth, magnet, etc 3 (v) 用尽 reach the end; exhaust ＊ 他为了送妻子到国外医病，极力地去筹足费用。He exhausts all efforts to gather enough funds to send his wife abroad for medical treatment.

极大 [jídà] maximum; greatest

极点 [jídiǎn] farthest point; climax; summit

极度 [jí dù] extreme

极端 [jíduān] extreme; radical

极力 [jí lì] spare no effort; do the utmost

极其 [jíqí] very; highly

极权主义 [jíquánzhǔyì] totalitarianism

极为 [jíwéi] extremely

极限 [jí xiàn] limit

极小 [jíxiǎo] minimum; smallest

殛 [jí] (v)杀死 kill ＊新闻报导说两名渔夫在海上的一场风暴里遭雷电殛毙。The news reported that two fishermen were killed by lightning in a tempest at sea.

疾 [jí] 1 (n)病 illness; disease; ailment; sickness 2 (n)痛苦 suffering; difficulty; misery 3 (v)恨 envy; hate; dislike; loath ＊ 他在贫苦的生活中成长，所以从小便疾恶如仇。 As he has grown up through various miseries, he hates wickedness ever since he was young. 4 (adj) 急速；猛烈 quick; hasty; rapid; fast ＊ 那汽车在高速公路上疾速飞驰。 That car drove along the expressway with a hasty speed.

疾病 [jíbìng] sickness; illness; ailment

疾驰 [jíchí] gallop away at full speed

疾恶如仇 [jí è rǔ chóu] abhor the wicked people

疾风劲草 [jí fēng jìng cǎo] only those who are firm and resolute can withstand severe trials (the strong wind reveals the strength of the grass; (fig.))

疾呼 [jíhū] calling out; shouting

疾苦 [jíkǔ] misery; suffering; difficulty

疾言厉色 [jí yán lìsè] harsh words and long face

嫉 [jí] 1 (v) 因别人比自己强；就忌恨人家 dislike; envy; to be jealous 2 (v) 仇恨；痛恨 dislike; hate

嫉妬 [jídù] jealous; envious

棘 [jí] (n) 泛指有刺的草木 a thorn; bramble; brier

棘手 [jíshǒu] difficult; thorny; knotty; troublesome

集 [jí] 1 (v) 聚拢；会合 assemble; gather together; collect; complete; accumulate ＊同学们先在学校集合，才出发到目的地郊游。The students first assembled in school before setting off for their picnic. 2 (n) 农村定期的市场 a fair; a market 3 (n) 把许多著作，作品编选成的书 literary works; collection of essays and poems

集合 [jíhé] assemble; muster; rally

集会 [jí huì] hold a meeting; assembly; mass rally

集聚 [jíjù] assemble in one place

集少成多 [jí shǎo chéng duō] little savings result in abundance

集市 [jíshì] (country) market

集体 [jítǐ] collective; a mass; a body

集团 [jítuán] group; clique; bloc

集腋成裘 [jí yè chéng qiú] gathering the little bits of fur from under the forelegs of animals to make a robe — do not despise small things

集中 [jízhōng] concentrate; centralized

急 [jí] 1 (adj) 急忙；迫切 urgent; quick; pressing; in a hurry ＊目前许多国家面对经济危机，就业问题急待解决。In face of the present economic crisis, many countries have to solve the pressing problem of employment populace. 2 (adj) 匆促 swift; rapid; abrupt ＊他急急忙忙地逃了。He got away rapidly. 3 (adj) 躁；没耐性 impatient; impetuous; quick in temper ＊他是个急性子的人，对事情还未详细了解就先下决定。Being an impatient person, he draws conclusion on matters without making any prior detailed understandings. 4 (adj) 紧要的；骤然的 urgent; quick; sudden; acute ＊他忽然得了急病，不久就逝世了。He suddenly contracted an acute disease and died not long after.

急促 [jícù] short and quick (eg. breaths); short time

急剧 [jíjù] abrupt; drastic

急救 [jíjiù] give first aids treatment

急流 [jíliú] rushing currents; a torrent; a rapid stream

急忙 [jímáng] in a great hurry; hurriedly

急迫 [jípò] hasty; urgent

急切 [jíqiè] pressing; instant; critical

急速 [jísù] speedy; at great speed; swift

急性 [jíxìng] acute; a hasty disposition; a quick temper

急需 [jíxū] be badly in need of

急用 [jí yòng] urgent need; pressing need

急于 [jíyú] eager (to do something)

急躁 [jízào] impetuous

急诊 [jízhěn] emergency case (med.)

急中生智 [jí zhòng sheng zhì] have quick wits in emergency

急转直下 [jízhuǎnzhíxià] a sudden turn; an abrupt change

jǐ

脊 [jǐ] 1 (n) 脊骨；背部中间的骨头 spine; the backbone 2 (n) 物体上形状象脊骨的地方 a ridge, as of a roof or of a mountain

脊背 [jǐběi] back

脊髓 [jǐsuí] the spinal cord (marrow)

脊椎 [jǐzhuī] the vertebrae

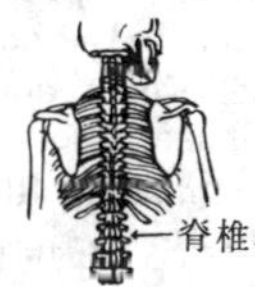

脊椎动物 [jǐzhuīdòng wù] the vertebrates

几(幾) [jǐ] 1 (adj) 数量多少 several; how many ＊你今年几岁了？ How old are you 2 (adj) 表示大约数目 a few; some; several ＊从星加坡到槟城有几百公里。 Penang is a few hundred from Singapore.
另见 [jī]

己 [jǐ] (pron) 自我 I; myself; self (n) private; self ＊舍己为人。to sacrifice oneself for others.

戟 [jǐ] (n) 古代的一种兵器 lance with two points

挤(擠) [jǐ] 1 (v) 榨；用力压(使排出) squeeze; extract ＊她挤出橙汁来制造果酱。 She squeezes juice from oranges to make jam. 2 (adj) 拥塞 crowded ＊十多个人住在一房式的屋子，实在太挤了。 It is really too crowded for over ten persons to stay in a one-room flat.

挤出 [jǐchū] screw out; elbow out

挤满 [jǐmǎn] overcrowded

济(濟) [jǐ] 河水名 a river's name in China

济济 [jǐ jǐ] many; numerous talents

济济一堂 [jǐ jǐ yī táng] many people crowded together
另见 [jì]

给(給) [jǐ] 1 (v) 供应 supply; provide 2 (adj) 富裕充足 sufficient; abundant

给养 [jǐ yǎng] provision; subsistence; supplies

给予 [jǐyǔ] present; supply; offer; give; render
另见 [gěi]

jì

剂(劑) [jì] (n) 配制成的药物 dose; prescription

济(濟) [jì] 1 (v) 救助 help; aid; relieve ＊当局发动了不少工作人员到地震灾区救济难民。 The authorities deployed many helpers to earth-quake striken regions to relieve the victims. 2 (v) 渡；过河 cross a river; ferry

济困扶危 [jì kùn fú wēi] help the distressed and relieve those in peril

济弱扶倾 [jì ruò fú qīng] to help the weak and raise the fallen

济善 [jìshàn] assist a good cause

济灾 [jìzāi] relieve a famine
另见 [jǐ]

既 [jì] 1 (adv) 已经 since; already ＊你考试既已不及格，那么你以后该更用功了。 Since you have already failed your examinations, you should be more hardworking in future. 2 (adj) 连词。常与"又"，"且"，"也"连用，表示两者并列。 as well as ＊用这个牌子的洗衣机，既快又清洁，值得买。This washing machine is worth buying as it washes clothes quick as well as clean. 3 (conj) 既然，后面常与"则"，"就"连用 since ＊既然你知道了，就不必再问。Since you have known, then there is no need to ask.

既定 [jìdìng] given; already committed; already decided

既然 [jìrán] since

暨 [jì] (conj) 和；与；及 and; also (prep) together with

记(記) [jì] 1 (v) 把印象保持在脑子里 remember; keep in mind; memorize ＊我们要牢记父母亲的教导。We should keep our parents' teachings in mind. 2 (v) 把事情写下来 record; note; write; register ＊请你把现场的一切记录下来，回去详细地讲给大家听。Please record whatever it is at the scene and come back to give us full details. 3 (n) 记叙事物的书册或文字 a record; a narration; a history ＊圣经是基督教的一部传记。The Bible is a record of the Christian religion.

记分 [jìfēn] keep the score

记功 [jìgōng] give credit for meritorious work

记过 [jìguò] give a demerit

记号 [jì·hao] sign; mark

记录 [jìlù] take notes; record; minutes (of meeting); record (sports)

记录片 [jìlùpiān] documentary film

记取 [jìqǔ] remember (advice); bear in mind; learn (eg. a lesson)

记叙 [jìxù] narrate

记忆 [jìyì] memorize; remember; memory

记忆犹新 [jì yì yóu xīn] the impression is still very vivid

记载 [jìzai] put down in writing; record

记账 [jìzhàng] charge it in account; keep account; make an entry in

记者 [jìzhě] newspaper reporter; journalist; correspondent

记住 [jìzhù] bear in mind; remember

纪(紀) [jì] (n) 纪律 rules; laws; discipline ＊军队里的纪律很严。The discipline in the army is very strict.

纪念 [jìniàn] commemorate; souvenir; commemoration

纪念碑 [jì niàn bēi] monument

纪念册 [jìniàncè] souvenir album

纪念品 [jìniànpǐn] souvenir

纪念日 [jìniànrì] anniversaries of important events; anniversary

纪念章 [jìniànzhāng] memorial badge; commemoration medal

纪录 [jìlù] a record; minutes; write down

纪元 [jìyuán] the beginning of a reign or an era; epoch

忌 [jì] 1 (v) 嫉妒 dislike; be jealous of. ＊她忌妒备受赞扬的姐姐。She is jealous of her elder sister who has recieved many praises. 2 (v) 顾虑；怕 fear; be afraid of 3 (v) 禁戒 avoid; abstain (from wine, smoking, etc.) ＊患高血压的人通常须忌酒。People with high blood pressure usually must abstain from alcohol.

忌妒 [jì·du] be jealous of; envy

忌讳 [jì·huì] taboo

伎 [jì] (n) 技巧；才能 skill; ability

技 [jì] (n) 技艺；本领 art; talent; skill; ability

技能 [jìnéng] ability; skill

技巧 [jìqiǎo] skill

技师 [jìshī] artists; experts; a mechanist

技术 [jìshù] technique

技术人员 [jìshùrényuán] technical personnel; technician

技艺 [jìyì] feat; skill; stunt

妓 [jì] (n) 妓女，在社会中被迫卖淫的女子 a whore; a prostitute

妓院 [jì yuàn] a brothel; a bawdyhouse

祭 [jì] 1 (n) 对死去的人举行追悼仪式 mourning 2 (n) 供奉天地鬼神 a sacrifice; an offering; (v) worship; sacrifice to the gods of ancestors

祭典 [jìdiǎn] sacred rites

祭品 [jìpǐn] sacrificial items or offerings

祭司 [jìsī] a priest; an overseer of sacrifices

祭坛 [jìtán] an altar for sacrifices

祭文 [jìwén] an address of consecration; a written prayer; a funeral address

际 (際) [jì] 1 (n) 交界或靠边界的地方 a border; limit 2 (conj) 时候 at the time when ＊正当获得胜利之际，我们更应当谦虚谨慎，不可骄傲。When we are just winning the battle, we should only be more modest and never become proud.

季 [jì] 1 (n) 弟兄中排行最小的 the youngest of brothers 2 (n) 三个月的气候期 a season

季节 [jìjié] season

季刊 [jìkān] a quarterly publication; quarterly

季风 [jìfēng] monsoon

寂 [jì] (adj) 静悄悄，没有声音 still; quiet; solitary; lonely; lonesome ＊这老妇人的子女都搬出外头住，所以她自己一个觉得很寂寞。Since her children have all moved out, the old woman feels very lonely on her own.

冀 [jì] 希望 hope; look forward to

骥 (驥) [jì] (n) 好马 a good horse; swift horse

继 (繼) [jì] (v) 连接，连续 continue; succeed ; follow after ＊皇帝死后，由他的儿子继位。The son of the Emperor succeeded to the throne after the Emperor died.

继承 [jìchéng] fall heir to; inherit; carry forward (the revolutionary tradition); take over

继而 [jì'ér] after this

继父 [jìfù] step-father

继母 [jìmǔ] step-mother

继任 [jìrèn] succeed somebody in office

继续 [jìxù] continue; go on with

继往开来 [jì wǎng kāilái] inheriting from the post and working for the future

髻 [jì] (n) 梳在头上的发结 tuft of a woman's hair

寄 [jì] 1 (v) 邮递 send by post; send ＊假如你经过邮政局，请把这信寄出去。If you pass by a post office, please send this letter. 2 (v) 托付 entrust to; place hopes on ＊他们的长子是个大学生，夫妇俩把一切希望都寄在这儿子身上。The couple place all hopes on their son who goes to the university. 3 (v)依靠，依附 live upon

寄存 [jìcún] hand over for safekeeping

寄居 [jìjū] put up at another person's house

寄人篱下 [jì rén lí xià] to sponge on another; relying on another person for a living

寄生 [jì shēng] on or within another organism; (of persons) depend on another for a living; be parasital

寄生虫 [jì shēng chóng] parasites

寄宿 [jìsù] have lodgings

寄托 [jìtuō] entrust to the care of; pin one's hopes on

寄望 [jì wàng] expect

寄予 [jì yú] place (hope or confidence) in

系 (繫) [jì] (v)结；扎 bind; tie 另见 [xì]

计(計) [jì] 1 (v) 算；计算 calculate; reckon; count 2 (n)策略；主意；计划 a plan; a scheme; a device ＊一年之计在于春。 Plan for the whole in spring. 3 (v) 作计划；打算 plan; devise ＊我要设计一个简单而又美观的图案做封面。I want to design a simple but beautiful pattern for the cover page.

计策 [jìcè] device; policy

计功受赏 [jì gōng shóu shǎng] to be rewarded according to merits

计划 [jìhuá] plan; devise

计较 [jìjiào] dispute; find fault with; be concerned for (eg. personal gain); bother about

计量 [jìliàng] measure; estimate

计谋 [jìmóu] scheme; plot; stratagem; take measure; plot

计上心来 [jì shàng xīn lái] an idea came across one's mind

计算尺 [jì suànchǐ] slide rule

计算机 [jì suànjī] computer; a calculator

鲫(鯽) [jì] (n) 也叫"鲋"，鱼类，生活在淡水里，可供食用 a kind of carp; golden carp

jiā

加 [jiā] 1 (v) 几个数合在一起 add; plus ＊二加三等于五。Two add three equals five. 2 (v) 使数量比原来多或程度比原来高 increase ＊要追上前面的车，你得加快速度。To catch up with the car in front, you must increase the speed. 3 (v) 添上去 add ＊要在句子后加标点符号，意思才能明确。Punctuation marks must be added to a sentence before the meaning is clear.

加班 [jiā bān] work overtime; work extra hours

加倍 [jiā bèi] double (an amount) redouble (efforts)

加工 [jiāgōng] process into a finished product; extra work

加紧 [jiājǐn] accelerate; intensify; step up

加剧 [jiā jù] intensify; heighten

加快 [jiā kuài] speed up

加强 [jiāqiáng] strengthen; consolidate

加热 [jiā rè] heat up

加入 [jiārù] join; enter

加深 [jiā shēn] deepen; intensify

加速 [jiā sù] speed up

加以 [jiā yǐ] give ...to; render; deal; besides; in addition to

加油 [jiā yóu] cheer (game player); refuel

加重 [jiā zhòng] increase (in weight, degree, etc.)

枷 [jiā] (n) 一种套在人脖子上的刑具，用木板或铁片制成 fetters; shackles

嘉 [jiā] 1 (adj) 美好的 good; excellent; fine; admirable 2 (v) 称赞夸奖 admire; commend; praise ＊学校因为她是个品学兼优的学生而嘉奖她。The school praises her because she is good in both personality and studies.

嘉宾 [jiā bīn] respected guests; guests of honour

嘉奖 [jiā jiǎng] praise; reward

嘉偶 [jiā ǒu] a happy couple

夹(夾) [jiā] 1 (v) 从两旁钳住 press; clip; hold with pincers or tweezers ＊ 用钳子夹出青蛙标本。Use the pincers to take the frog specimen out. 2 (v) 掺杂 mix with; insert between; contain ＊ 海滩的沙夹杂着各种大小不同的贝壳。 The sands on the beach are mixed with shells of different varieties and sizes. 3 (n) 夹东西的用具 instruments (pincers, tweezers, etc.) used to clip on to articles

夹攻 [jiā gōng] make a pincer

movement against (the enemy); pincer attacks; pincers around (eg. the enemy)

夹边 [jiābiān] included side (geom)

夹角 [jiā jiǎo] included angle (geom)

夹杂 [jiā zá] mix up; blend

夹子 [jiāzí] clips; tongs; pincers; pliers

另见 [jiá]

浃 [jiā] (adj) 湿透 soaked through

家 [jiā] 1 (n) 家庭 a household; a family; a home 2 (n) 学派 a school (of learning, thoughts, etc.) 3 (n) 从事某种专门工作或掌握某种专门知识，技能的人 a suffix to indicate a specialist in any branch, class or school: — ist, — lan, etc. ＊科学家。a scientist 画家 an artist. 4 (n) 量词 a measure word ＊ 两家工厂。two factories.

家常 [jiācháng] domestic affairs; home affairs; commonplace

家常便饭 [jiā cháng biàn fàn] ordinary meal

家丑不可外扬 [jiā chǒu bù kě wài yáng] do not wash dirty linen in public

家畜 [jiāchū] domestic animals

家伙 [jiā huǒ] tool or weapon; scoundrel

家家户户 [jiājiāhùhù] each and every family

家具 [jiā jù] furniture; household goods (utensils)

家眷 [jiā juàn] family (wife and children)

家破人亡 [jiāpòrénwáng] with the family broken up; family ruined and its members missing

家禽 [jiā qín] fowl

家属 [jiāshǔ] one's dependents; families

家徒四壁 [jiā tu sì bì] the family is so poor that it has only the four walls

家务 [jiāwú] family affairs; home affairs

家乡 [jiāxiāng] native place

家园 [jiāyuán] native place; home

家用 [jiā yòng] family expenditure

家喻户晓 [jiāyù hùxiǎo] known to every family

家长 [jiāzhǎng] parents of a child; head of a family

家政 [jiā zhèng] the management of domestic affairs; domestic science

家族 [jiāzú] clan

佳 [jiā] (adj) 美好的 beautiful; fine; splendid; excellent; good; fair; superior ＊ 对一个长期受战火蹂躏的国家来说， 和平确是个佳音。Peace is a very good news to a country that has spent years in war.

佳话 [jiā huà] matters of great interest; charming stories

佳节 [jiājié] a happy occasion; a joyful festival

佳丽 [jiālì] handsome; beautiful

佳人 [jiā rén] a beauty; a belle

jiá

夹(夾) [jiá] (n) 两层的衣物 a lined coat ; a doubled garment

另见 [jiā]

颊(頰) [jià] (n) 脸的两侧 the cheeks

jiǎ

甲 [jiǎ] 1 (n) 天干的第一位，用作次序的第一 the first of the Ten Stems; number one 2 (n) 用皮革或金属制成的 有保护作用的装备 an armour 3 (n) 动物身上具有保护作用的角质硬壳 shell (of animals) 5 (n) 手指或 脚趾上的角质硬壳 nails (of fingers, toes)

甲板 [jiǎ bǎn] the deck of a

ship

甲等 [jiǎ děng] first class ; first grade

甲骨文 [jiǎgǔwén] inscriptions on oracle bones

甲克 [jiǎ kè] jacket

甲壳 [jiǎ qiào] a shell ; a carapace

甲胄 [jiǎzhòu] armour

甲状腺 [jiǎ zhuàng xiàn] the thyroid gland

岬

[jiǎ] (n) 两山之间 side of a hill

假

[jiǎ] (adj)不真实的；虚伪的，跟"真"相对 false; pseudo; spurious; sham; unreal ＊他关心别人是假的，只是为了博取大家的信任。That he cares for others is false; he is only trying to win our confidence

假充 [jiǎchōng] pass oneself off as; pose as; pretend to be

假定 [jiǎdìng] assume; suppose; presume

假发 [jiǎfǎ] wig

假公济私 [jiǎgōngjìsī] promote one's private interests under the guise of serving the public

假借 [jiǎjiè] using various guises; (do something) in the name of

假冒 [jiǎ mào] counterfeit; sham

假面具 [jiǎ miànjù] mask; hypocrisy

假名 [jiǎ míng] a pseudonym: assumed name

假情 [jiǎqíng] pretended love

假仁假义 [jiǎ rén jiǎ yì] pretended kindness and goodness; hypocricy

假如 [jiǎrú] supposing that; if

假若 [jiǎruò] supposing that; if

假设 [jiǎ shè] assume; suppose; presume; hypothesis

假使 [jiǎ shǐ] if; in case

假想 [jiǎxiǎng] fancy

假象 [jiǎxiàng] feint; false appearance; false impression

假惺惺 [jiǎ xīng xīng] hypocritical

假造 [jiǎ zào] counterfeit; fake

假装 [jiǎzhuāng] feint; disguise; pretend; sham

另见 [jià]

jià

嫁

[jià] 1 (v)女子结婚 marry a husband ＊姐姐出嫁的那天，妈妈心里很难过。On the day when my elder sister got married, mother was very sad. 2 (v)把怨恨，祸害等推给别人 impute to; transfer; shift ＊他明明自已听错，却嫁怨别人说错。Simply it was he who mishear, but he shifted the blame for missaying on others.

嫁祸于人 [jià huò yú rén] put blame on others; transfer evil upon others through malice

嫁接 [jiàjiē] graft

嫁妆 [jià·zhuang] dowry

稼

[jià] 1 (v)种植 farm; plant; cultivate (n) farming 2 (n)谷物 grain

架

[jià] 1 (n) 用做搁置或支承的东西 a shelf; a framework; a stand; a rack ＊把书放回书架上。Place the book back on the shelf. 2 (v) 搭起 put up; prop up; support ＊自从架了一道桥之后，两岸的交通方便得多了。After a bridge has been put up (built) across the river, there is much convenience for the traffic on both sides. 3 (n) 殴打；争吵 fighting; quarrel; dispute. * 他们一言不合就打起来，同事们连忙去劝架。They started to fight once they cannot agree, so the other colleagues quickly help to stop them from fighting. 4 (n) 量词 a measure word, used for machine, T.V. set, aeroplane, etc. * 一架机器。a machine

架空 [jiàkōng] built or supported on stilts; aerial ; become nominal; render somebody powerless

架设 [jiàshè] put up; erect

架子 [jià·zi] a supporting framework; mantle; arrogance;haughtiness

驾 (駕) [jià] 1 (v) 把车套在牲口身上 yoke 2 (v) 操纵；使行驶 drive; ride; sail (a ship); fly (an aeroplane) * 他是个很谨慎的人，坐他驾驶的车很安全。He is a very cautious person. It is safe to take a ride in his car.

驾轻就熟 [jià qīng jiù shú] take the familiar path

驾驶 [jiàshǐ] drive; pilot

驾驭 [jiàyù] keep hold of the reins; dominate

假 [jià] (n) 按国家规定或经过批准的休息日 holiday; leave * 他们到中国去渡假了！They have gone to China for holiday!

假期 [jiàqí] holidays; vacation

假日 [jiàrì] holiday

另见 [jiǎ]

价 (價) [jià] (n) 货物所值的钱数 price; value; cost; worth * 近年来，物价一直高涨，同样数目的钱可以买到的东西越来越少。In the recent years, prices of things have been soaring, less and less can be bought out of the same amount of money.

价格 [jiàgé] price

价廉物美 [jià lián wù měi] fine wares at low prices; inexpensive and good

价值 [jiàzhí] value; worth; cost

jiān

笺 (箋) [jiān] 1 (n) 信纸 note paper; letter paper; writing pad 2 (n) 注释 notes; explanation

溅 (濺) [jiān] (n) 流水的声音 sound of flowing waters 小河流水溅溅，是一首大自然的音乐。The splashing of the river is a piece fo natural music.

另见 [jiàn]

兼 [jiān] 1 (conj) 同时作几件事或占有几样东西 and; as well as; combine; concurrent * 她的哥哥是副总理兼外交部长。Her elder brother is Deputy Premier and minster for Foreign Affairs.

兼备 [jiānbeì] be qualified for both or more

兼并 [jiān bìng] annex (territory, etc) absorb

兼程 [jiānchéng] to go by double statges; to go at double speed.

兼顾 [jiāngù] give consideration to both; give attention to both ... and ....

兼课 [jiākè] doing teaching work besides one's own work

兼任 [jiānrèn] hold concurrent post; concurrently

兼听 [jiāntīng] to hear both sides

兼职 [jiānzhí] (hold) concurrent jobs

煎 [jiān] (v) 煮 to boil 2 (v) 把食物放在少量的热 里煮熟 fry * 煎鱼火要慢。We should use slow fire to fry fish.

煎熬 [jiān áo] fry in oil or boil in water; (fig) endure long hardships and sufferings

煎饼 [jiān bing] fried cake

歼(殲) [jiān] (v) 消灭 destroy; kill

歼灭 [jiānmiè] exterminate; annihilate; destroy

歼击机 [jiān jì jī] fighter (aeroplane); bomber

奸 [jiān] 1 (adj) 邪恶；阴险；狡诈 treacherous; wicked; sinister; deceitful ＊中国历史上的曹操是个奸险的人。Tsao Tsao, in the history of China, was a treacherous person 2 (n) 出卖国家，民族利益或私通敌方的坏人 a spy; a traitor

奸商 [jiānshāng] profiteer; unscrupulous merchant

奸细 [jiān·xi] a spy; a secret agent; a traitor

奸险 [jiānxiǎn] crafty and dangerous

奸淫 [jiān yín] treacherous

奸诈 [jiānzhà] crafty

肩 [jiān] 1 (n) 肩膀；手臂和身体相连的地方 shoulder 2 (v) 担负 take upon; shoulder; assume (responsibility) ＊他因为肩负重担，所以很小心地行事。Because he bears a heavy responsibility, he therefore carries out his work with much care.

肩并肩 [jiān bìng jiān] side by side; to stand shoulder to shoulder with

肩负 [jiānfù] carry (a burden); shoulder; assume (responsibility for)

肩章 [jiān zhāng] a shoulder-strap

间(間) [jiān] 1 (prep) 两桩事物的当中或其相互的关系 between; in the midst; among ＊ 他们两人之间的仇恨不是外人所能了解的。The enmity between both of them is not comprehensible to outsiders. 2 (n) 一定的时间，地点或范围 a space; an interval ＊晚间的街道是静寂的。The streets during the night are quiet.
另见 [jiàn]

坚(堅) [jiān] 1 (adj) 牢固；硬 strong; hard; solid ＊这道墙坚如磐石， This wall is as solid as a rock. 2 (adj) 不动摇 determined; resolute ＊他坚决要登上这个山头。He was resolute in his attempt to climb to the top of the mountain.

坚持 [jiānchí] persist in; adhere to; hold fast to; insist on; uphold

坚持不懈 [jiān chí bú xiè] persistence

坚定 [jiāndìng] steady; firm; resolute; determined

坚定不移 [jiāndìngbùyí] firm and resolute; unswerving; persistently; fixed

坚固 [jiāngù] solid; firm; hard

坚决 [jiānjué] determined; resolute

坚苦卓绝 [jiān kǔ zhuō jué] overcome great difficulties with surpassing bravery; most arduous (struggle)

坚强 [jiānqiáng] staunch; firm; resolute

坚忍不拔 [jiān rěn bù bá] firm; stubbornly and unyieldingly

坚如磐石 [jiānrúpánshí] firm as rock; rock-firm; monolithic

坚守 [jiānshǒu] guard securely; hold fast (position)

坚信 [jiānxìn] firmly believe; convince

坚毅 [jiānyì] resolute; with firm determination

坚硬 [jiānyìng] hard ; strong and tough

坚贞不屈 [jiānzhēnbùqū] stand firm and unyielding; upright and unyielding

监(監) [jiān] 1 (v) 察看；督察 examine carefully ; supervise ＊为了赶工，工厂的老板亲自监督工人工作。 To speed up work, the boss of the factory comes personally to supervise the workers at work. 2 (n) 牢狱 a prison; a jail ＊他被法庭判定有罪，坐监三年。 He is found guilty by the court and sentenced to jail for three years.

另见 [jiàn]

监察 [jiānchá] supervise; control

监护 [jiānhù] serve as guardian for

监禁 [jiānjìn] put in prison; confine; imprisonment, detention

监考 [jiān kaǒ] expect, inspect; invigilate

监视 [jiān shì] keep a close watch over; keep an eye on

尖 [jiān] 1 (n) 物体锐利的末端或细小的部分 tip; point (of an object) 2 (adj) 声音高而细 sharp (voice) ＊小孩子的声音通常很尖。 The voice of a child is usually sharp. 3 (adj) 感觉灵敏 sharp (in senses) ＊她的耳朵很尖，一隻蚊子飞过也听得到。Her ears are so sharp that she can even hear a mosquito fly past.

尖兵 [jiānbīng] vanguard; trailblazer

尖端 [jiān dūan] the highest point; the pinnacle; the most advanced

尖利 [jiān lì] sharp; poignant

尖锐化 [jiānruì huà] become acute (intense)

尖锐 [jiān ruì] sharp; pointed; acute

艰（艱） [jiān] (adj) 困难 difficult; hard; distressful ＊以前我们的祖先是经过艰苦的航程，才来到南洋的。 Long ago, our ancestors took a difficult journey to sail to the South Seas.

艰巨 [jiān jù] extremely difficult; very tough; heavy

艰难 [jiānnán] difficult; hard; troublе; hardship

艰险 [jiānxiǎn] difficult and dangerous

艰辛 [jiānxīn] hard and arduous

缄（緘） [jiān] (v) 封闭 seal; seal up; bind up

缄口无言 [jiān kǒu wú yán] keep the mouth shut and say nothing

缄默 [jiān mò] keep silent and say nothing

jiǎn

剪 [jiǎn] 1 (n) 剪刀;铰切东西的工具 shears; scissors; clippers 2 (v) 用剪刀铰切 cut; clip; shear; cut off ＊天气太热了，把头发剪短较舒服。 The weather is so hot, it is more comfortable for one to have one's hair cut short.

剪彩 [jiǎncǎi] the ceremony of cutting the ribbon

剪贴 [jiǎntiē] paper cutting ; cut out and paste ; clipping

俭（儉） [jiǎn] (adj) 不浪费；节省 thrifty; economical; frugal

俭朴 [jiǎnpǔ] frugal and simple (eg. living a simple life)

俭约 [jiǎnyuē] economy; thrift; frugality

捡（撿） [jiǎn] (v) 拾取 pick up ＊捡到别人的东西，应还给失主。 You should return things you pick up to the owner.

检（檢） [jiǎn] (v) 查 check; examine＊医生说要先检查她的身体，才能诊断她的病症。The doctor said that he had to examine her body before he could diagnose her illness.

检查 [jiǎn chá] check; inspect; check up; investigate

检点 [jiǎndiǎn] keep watch over one's words or deeds

检讨 [jiǎn tao] examine one's own mistakes; self-criticism

检修 [jiǎn xiū] overhaul

检验 [jiǎn yàn] examine; inspect; test; verify

检阅 [jiǎnyuè] review (troops, parade, etc.); inspect

简(簡) [jiǎn] 1 (n) 古代用来写字的竹片 a slip of bamboo for writing on in the old ages 2 (n) 信件 a letter; a note 3 (adj) 单纯，不复杂 simple; brief; terse * 他的作品文字简洁，适合一般人阅读。The simple language in his writings suits most people.

简便 [jiǎnbiàn] simple and convenient; handy

简称 [jiǎnchēng] abbreviated term

简短 [jiǎnduǎn] short and brief

简化 [jiǎnhuà] simplify

简洁 [jiǎn jié] terse and concise; laconic

简练 [jiǎn liàn] succinct; terse; concise

简陋 [jiǎnlòu] rough (eg. accomodation); simple

简略 [jiǎn lüè] simple; brief; terse

简明 [jiǎn míng] concise; simple and clear

简明扼要 [jiǎn míng è yāo] concise and to the point

简体字 [jiǎntǐ zì] simplified characters

简要 [jiǎn yāo] concise; brief and to the point; a summary; a sketch

简易 [jiǎnyì] elementary; simple and easy

简直 [jiǎnzhí] absolutely; virtually; nothing less than

笕(筧) [jiǎn] (n) 连接起来引水用的竹管 bamboo pipes joined to carry water

减 [jiǎn] 1 (v) 由原有数量中去掉一部分deduct; take away; subtract *五减三等于二。Five take away three is equal to two. 2 (v) 减低；衰退 reduce; diminish; lessen; decrease *由於市场不乐观，工厂今年减低产量。Due to the poor prospects in the market the factory has reduced its production this year.

减价 [jiǎn jià] reduce the price

减轻 [jiǎn qīng] mitigate; lighten; reduce

减弱 [jiǎnruò] become weaker; wane

减少 [jiǎnshǎo] reduce; take away from a quantity; lessen

减缩 [jiǎn suō] reduce; decrease

减退 [jiǎntuì] diminish; reduce; drop (in temperature)

柬 [jiǎn] (n)信件；名片；帖子等的统称 a letter; an invitation card; a visiting card; a note

拣(揀) [jiǎn] 1 (v) 挑选；选择 choose; pick out; select 2 (v) 拾 pick up *把地上的糖果拣起来，不然会引来许多蚂蚁。Pick up the sweets on the floor; otherwise, it will attract a lot of ants.

拣货 [jiǎn huò] sort goods

拣取 [jiǎnqǔ] pick out by preference

拣选 [jiǎn xuǎn] select; choose; pick out

茧(繭) [jiǎn] (n)某些种类昆虫的幼虫在变成蛹之前吐丝或分泌其他物质形成的囊状外壳 the cocoon of a silkworm

趼 [jiǎn] (n) 手掌或脚底因经常劳动或走路而磨成的硬皮,也作"茧" blistered and rough skin; callous skin on the foot or hand *妈妈当了几十年的家庭女佣，如今手掌上长了一层厚厚的老趼。Having worked as a domestic servant for decades, mother's palms are filled with thick layers of rough skin.

jiàn

建 [jiàn] 1 (v)创立；成立 establish; found; set up; create *南洋大学是由星马的华人捐款建立的。The Nanyang University was set up with contributions made by Chinese in Singapore and Malaya. 2 (v) 修筑 build; construct; erect *他建筑了不少高楼大厦，自己却住在一简陋的亚答屋。He has built many edifices but he himself stays in a simple atap hut.

建国 [jiàn guó] create a new nation; reconstruct the nation

建交 [jiànjiāo] establish diplomatic relations with

建立 [jiàn lì] establish ; set up; build

建设 [jiànshè] build; construction

建议 [jiànyì] suggestion; propose

建筑师 [jiàn zhù shī] a builder; an architect

建筑物 [jiànzhù wù] building; edifice structure

健 [jiàn] 1 (adj) 强壮；身体好 strong; healthy; stout *他每天运动所以很健壮。He exercises every; day, therefore he is very healthy. 2 (v) 使强壮 strengthen; invigorate *许多老年人学打太极拳来健身。Many old folks learn "taichi" to strengthen themselves.

健步 [jiàn bù] walk with firm strides; vigorous steps

健康 [jiàn kāng] healthy; health

健全 [jiàn quán] sound and hale perfect

健谈 [jiàntán] talkative; loquacious

健忘 [jiànwàng] forgetful; oblivious

健在 [jiàn zài] still alive and in good health (referring to elderly people); still going strong

键（鍵） [jiàn] 1 (n) 机器上使轴与齿轮，皮带轮等连接并固定在一起的零件 the linchpin on the nave 2 (n) 琴，打字机或其他机器上可按动的部分 the keys of an organ, piano, type-writer, etc 3 (n) 门闩 the bolt of a door

毽 [jiàn] (n) 毽子，一种文娱体育用品 shuttle-cock

间（間） [jiàn] 1 (n) 空隙 an opening ; a partition; an interspace 2 (v) 不连接；隔开 separate; set apart; interrupt; divide *这间房子大得可以间隔成三个小房间。This room is big enough to be divided into three small rooms.

间谍 [jiàndié] spy; espionage; a secret agent

间断 [jiànduàn] interrupt; intermission

间隔 [jiàngé] divide; interval; gap; space; separate

间接 [jiànjiē] indirect

间歇 [jiànxiē] intermittence; pause

另见 [jiān]

涧（澗） [jiàn] (n) 两山间的流水 a brooklet; a torrent

涧流 [jiàn liú] a rapid; a torrent; a stream in valley

涧水 [jiàn shuǐ] brook water

饯（餞） [jiàn] (v) 备酒食送行 give a farewell party *我班上的一个同学要到外国深造，我们为他饯行。A classmate of ours is going abroad for further studies, so we give him a farewell party.

践（踐） [jiàn] (v) 踩 walk; step; trample on *我刚践踏在泥浆里，所以弄得一身污泥。I have just trampled on a pool of mud, therefore my body is very muddy.

贱（賤） [jiàn] 1 (adj) 价格低质地不好 cheap; low; worthless *价钱低的东西未必就是贱货。Things which are cheap are not necessarily low in quality. 2 (adj) 指地位低下 base; humble; mean

贱鄙 [jiànbǐ] base; low

贱骨头 [jiàn gú tóu] a loafer; a worthless fellow

贱价 [jiànjià] low priced; cheap

溅(濺) [jiàn] (v) 液体受冲激向四面飞射 splash; spatter ✱ 一粒石块掉进平静的湖面，立刻引起水花四溅。A piece of stone fell into the motionless pool and immediately the water spattered in all directions.
另见 [jiān]

见(見) [jiàn] 1 (v) 看 see; view; look ✱ 见到了离别多年的母亲，我忍不住流出热泪。I could not control my tears when I saw my mother whom I had parted from many years ago. 2 (v) 显出 show ; manifest ; come out ✱ 他不停的下苦功，学业日见进步。Having kept working hard constantly, he shows steady progress in his study. 3 (v) 会面 meet with an interview 4 (n) 对事物的看法，意见 an opinion; a view ✱ 依我之见，你最好参加这场篮球比赛。In my opinion, you had better join the coming basket-ball match.

见风使舵 [jiàn fēng shǐ duò] to change with the wind; opportunism

见个高低 [jiàn gè gāo dī] to see who is superior

见怪 [jiànguài] blame; take offence

见解 [jiànjiě] understanding; opinion

见机行事 [jiàn jī xíng shì] take cue and act accordingly; act according to circumstances

见面 [jiàn miàn] come face to face with; meet

见识 [jiàn shí] general knowledge; insight

见闻 [jiàn wén] what one sees and hears; general knowledge; experience

见习 [jiàn xí] learn through practice

见效 [jiànxiào] obtain results; effective; fruitful

见异思迁 [jiànyìsīqiān] whis to change one's mind the moment one sees something different

见证 [jiànzhèng] evidence; proof

舰(艦) [jiàn] (n) 军舰；战船 naval vessels; a warship

舰队 [jiàn duì] fleet; a squadron

舰艇 [jiàn tǐng] naval vessels

荐(薦) [jiàn] 1 (v) 推举；介绍 introduce; recommend ✱ 由於他的语文基础很好，老师推荐他参加全国作文比赛。As he has a very good foundation in language, his teacher recommends him for the national essay competition. 2 (n) 草；草荐 the feeding grass; a straw mat

监(監) [jiàn] (n) 封建时代的官名或官署名 a eunuch
另见 [jiān]

槛(檻) [jiàn] 1 (n) 栏杆 a railing; bars 2 (n) 关野兽的笼子 a cage
另见 [kǎn]

鉴(鑑) [jiàn] 1 (n) 古时的镜子 a mirror 2 (v) 照 reflect ✱山上的小溪水清可鉴。The water in the mountain streams is so clear that it reflects the scenery above clearly. 3 (v) 仔细看；审察 scrutinize; inspect; examine ✱ 要鉴别古瓷器的真伪，可不容易。It is not easy to scrutinize and distinguish a piece of genuine porcelain from the fake. 4 (v) 可作为警戒或引为教训的事 look into; take warning from an occurrence

鉴别 [jiànbié] distinguish

鉴定 [jiàn dìng] evaluate; appraisal; differentiate

鉴赏 [jiǎnshǎng] discern and appreciate

鉴于 [jiànyū] in consideration; in

view of

渐（漸）[jiàn] (adv) 慢慢地，一步一步地 gradually; step by step; slowly ＊黄昏时分，太阳渐渐消失在地平线下。In the evening, the sun disappears slowly under the horizon.

箭 [jiàn] (n) 借弓上弦线的弹力发射到远处的兵器，用金属做头 arrow

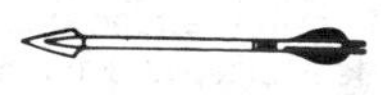

箭步 [jiànbù] quick strides
箭猪 [jiànzhū] the porcupine

僭 [jiàn] (v) 超越本分，旧时下级冒用上级名义或器物等 overpass one's duty; usurp; arrogate to oneself

件 [jiàn] 1 (n) 量词 a measure word; piece; item ＊一件事。A matter; 两件衣服。two pieces of dresses 2 (n) 指可以一一计算的事物 an article; an item; a case ＊每天报纸所刊登的车祸事件有好几宗。Everyday there are several cases of accidents published in the newspapers.

剑（劍）[jiàn] (n) 古代的一种兵器，两面有刃 sword; a dagger

剑击 [jiàn jì] fencing
剑客 [jiànkè] a knight; a fencer
剑鞘 [jiàn qiào] a scabbard
剑术 [jiàn shù] the art of fencing; swordsmanship
剑鱼 [jiàn yú] swordfish

谏（諫）[jiàn] (v) 直言规劝，使改正错误。一般用于下对上 advise; admonish; expostulate (by a lower rank to a higher rank) ＊参议院议员谏劝总统重新考虑他的新外交措施。The senators advised the president to reconsider his new diplomatic policies.

jiāng

僵 [jiāng] (adj) 生硬；不能活动 stiff; still; rigid ＊要是我们这些热带地区的人跑去北极居住，一定会冻僵的。If people like us from the tropical region go to live in the North Pole, we will surely be frozen stiff.

僵局 [jiāngjú] dead-lock; impasse.
僵尸 [jiāngshī] corpse; an indecomposed corpse.
僵硬 [jiāngyìng] numb and rigid; inflexible.

缰（繮）[jiāng] (n) 牵牲口的绳子 a bridle; reins; halter

疆 [jiāng] (n) 界限；边界；境界 a limit; a boundary; frontier; border ＊两国为了领土的问题而在边疆发生冲突。The two countries have conflicts at the border because of the territorial issue.

姜（薑）[jiāng] (n) 草本植物，可供调味和药用 ginger

将（將）[jiāng] 1 (v) (adv) 就要；快要 shall; will; be ready to ; soon; presently ＊新年将要到来，妇人们都忙着筹备庆祝。The New Year is coming soon, the housewives are busy preparing for the festival. 2 (v) 把；用 get ; use.

将错就错 [jiāng cuò jiù cuò] leaving the error unchanged
将近 [jiāngjìn] near; be on the verge; almost; nearly
将就 [jiāngjiù] have to make do

with

将军 [jiāng jūn] general (military)

将来 [jiānglái] in the future; in time to come

另见 [jiàng]

浆 (漿) [jiāng] 1 (n) 汁液，一般指较浓的液体 a thick fluid; sirup 2 (v) 用米汤或粉浆浸纱布或使衣服发硬发挺 starch

另见 [jiàng]

江 [jiāng] (n) 大河 large river

江河 [jiāng hé] rivers

江河日下 [jiān hérìxià] deteriora-ting day by day going from bad to worse

江口 [jiāng koǔ] an estuary ; the mouth of a river

江米 [jiāngmǐ] glutinous rice

江山 [jiāngshān] national territory

江山如画 [jiāng shān rú huà] the majestic rivers and mountains; scenery like a picture

jiǎng

蒋 (蔣) [jiǎng] (n) 姓氏 a surname

奖 (獎) [jiǎng] 1 (v) 鼓励；表扬 praise; reward; encourage * 孩子做对了，应嘉奖他，鼓励他。When a child has done right, we should praise and encourage him. 2 (n) 为了勉励或表扬而给的物品 reward; prize 3 (n) 彩金 lottery

奖金 [jiǎngjīn] a prize; a reward

奖励 [jiǎng lì] commend; reward; award; commendation

奖品 [jiǎngpǐn] award; prize

奖卷 [jiǎng quàn] gift coupon

奖赏 [jiǎng shǎng] commend and reward

奖学金 [jiǎngzuéjīn] scholarship

奖章 [jiǎngzhāng] medal

奖状 [jiǎngzhuàng] citation

桨 (槳) [jiǎng] 1 (n) 划船的用具 an oar; a paddle

讲 (講) [jiǎng] 1 (v) 说 talk over; speak *他把事情的经过讲得很详细，使听的人都了解那是什么一回事。He spoke in details the happenings of the matter so that those who listened knew what it was about. 2 (v) 解释；说明 explain * 李老师讲课很生动，同学们上他的课时决不会打瞌睡。Mr. Li explains his lessons in such an interesting manner that all students who attend his class do not feel sleepy. 3 (v) 商议 discuss; discourse on; converse *他们要讲清楚条件，才肯合股。They want to discuss clearly the conditions before they consent to co-partnership.

讲话 [jiǎnghuà] talk; give a speech; speak

讲解 [jiǎng jiě] explain

讲究 [jiǎngjiū] be particular about; pay attention to

讲理 [jiǎng lǐ] be reasonable

讲授 [jiǎng shòu] teach; lecture

讲述 [jiǎngshù] describe; recount

讲师 [jiǎngshī] a lecturer

讲坛 [jiǎngtán] rostrum; podium

讲义 [jiǎngyì] lecture notes; teaching materials

jiàng

降 [jiàng] (v) 落下 drop; descend; fall; come down

降低 [jiàngdī] reduce; lower; descend

降级 [jiàngjí] reduce in rank; demote ; degradation

降临 [jiànglín] condescend; visit; coming down

降落 [jiàngluò] alight; land (of airplanes); descend; fall from

降落伞 [jiàng luò sǎn] parachute

另见 [xiáng]

绛 (絳) [jiàng] (adj) 赤色；大红色 red

将 (將) [jiàng] (n) 军衔名；在校之上 commander
将军 [jiàng jūn] a military commander; a general
将领 [jiànglǐng] generals
另见 [jiāng]

浆 (漿) [jiāng] (n) 用面粉等做成的可以粘贴东西的糊状物 paste ; gum
另见 [jiàng]

酱 (醬) [jiàng] 1 (n) 用发酵后的豆、麦和盐制成的糊状调味品 sauce; soy 2 (n) 浓稠象酱一样的食品 jelly; jams
酱菜 [jiàngcài] pickled vegetables; vegetables seasoned in soy
酱油 [jiàng yóu] soy sauce

强 [jiàng] (adj) 固执任性 stubborn; crabbed
另见 [qiáng]
[qiǎng]

匠 [jiàng] (n) 指有专门技术的工人 a maker; a mechanic; a craftsman.

jiāo

交 [jiāo] 1 (v) 付给，托给 deliver; turn over; handover to *两个钟头后，每个考生得把考卷交给监考员。Two hours later, every candidate must hand in their answer sheets to the invigilators. 2 (v) 结识 to acquaint; to make friends with *交友要小心。Be careful in making friends. 3 (v) 相切 intersect *AB线交CD线于E点。The line AB intersects the line CD at the point E.
交叉 [jiāo chā] intersect; intercross; cross
交错 [jiāo cuò] overlap; inter-lace
交代 [jiāodài] hand over; explain; give an account of ...
交锋 [jiāofēng] engage each other (in a battle or ball game).
交换 [jiāohuàn] exchange
交际 [jiāojì] social functions
交接 [jiāojiē] contact; hand over and take over
交界 [jiāojiè] boundary; border; frontier
交流 [jiāoliú] exchange (eg. cultural exchange)
交情 [jiāoqíng] friendship; mutual affection
交涉 [jiāoshè] negotiate; discuss terms; deal with
交谈 [jiāotán] talk with
交通 [jiāotōng] communication
交往 [jiao wǎng] associate with; have dealings with
交响乐 [jiāoxiǎng yuè] symphony
交易 [jiāo yì] transaction; business deal; trade

姣 [jiāo] (adj) 美好 handsome; pretty

胶 (膠) [jiāo] 1 (n) 能粘合东西的物质 glue 2 (v) 粘合 stick; adhere; glue *胶住信封，别让他人看到里面的信。 Glue up the envelope and don't let anyone read the letter inside. 3 (n) 橡胶 rubber
胶布 [jiāobù] adhesive plaster
胶鞋 [jiāoxié] rainshoes; rubber shoes
胶卷 [jiāojuǎn] film (undeveloped)

郊 [jiāo] (n) 城市周围的地区 suburban areas; country; outskirts
郊外 [jiāowài] outskirts; suburbs
郊游 [jiāoyóu] outing; excursion

礁 [jiāo] (n) 江海里距水面很近的岩石 hidden or sunken rocks

焦 [jiāo] 1 (adj) 火力过猛，使东西烧黄或烧黑 scorched; burnt *饭烧焦了，真浪费！ The rice is burnt, what a waste! 2 (adj) 着急 anxious; harassed *母亲因为女儿半夜三更还未归来而焦急。The mother becomes anxious about her daughter who has not returned home yet when it is already midnight.
焦点 [jiāodiǎn] focal point; focus;

heart of the matter
焦急 [jiāojí] very anxious and restless; worried; pressing
焦炭 [jiāotàn] coke
焦土 [jiāotǔ] scorched earth
焦躁 [jiāozào] anxious and fretful; impatient; worried

娇(嬌) [jiāo] 1 (adj) 美好 beautiful; lovely 2 (adj) 畏难怕苦，感情脆弱的 delicate
娇嫩 [jiāo·nen] young and delicate; frail
娇生惯养 [jiāo shēng guàn yǎng] spoilt; brought up in comfortable circumstances

骄(驕) [jiao] 1 (adj) 不驯服；不受控制 ungovernable 2 (adj) 自高自大 arrogant; proud; haughty ＊ 他自以为成绩好而骄傲，看不起其他同学。Thinking that his results are good, he becomes proud and despises all other classmates.
骄气 [jiāo qì] arrogant; proud; unbearably conceited
骄阳 [jiāoyáng] scorching sun

浇(澆) [jiāo] (v) 洒；灌溉 water; sprinkle with water; irrigate ＊ 园丁一天浇花两次。The gardener waters the plants twice a day
浇灌 [jiāo guàn] irrigate; water

教 [jiāo] 1 (v) 传授 teach; instruct ＊ 做父母的常教导孩子要孝顺。Parents often teach their children to be filial. 2 (v) 使；令 order; command
教书 [jiāoshū] teach
教学 [jiāoxué] teaching
另见 [jiào]

jiáo

嚼 [jiáo] (v)用牙齿磨碎食物 masticate; chew
另见 [jué]
[jiào]

jiǎo

狡 [jiǎo] (adj) 狡猾；诡诈 crafty; cunning; sly ＊许多寓言都把狐狸形容为狡猾的动物。Many fables describe the fox as a cunning animal.
狡辩 [jiǎobiàn] quibble about; use specious arguments to defend oneself
狡猾 [jiǎohuá] sly; cunning; crafty
狡诈 [jiǎo zhà] deceitful; cunning; swindling

饺(餃) [jiǎo] (n) 饺子，半圆形的有馅儿的面食 (meat) dumplings

绞(絞) [jiǎo] 1 (v) 拧；扭紧 wring; twist ＊ 把衣服绞干才晒出去，就不会弄湿楼下的衣服。If clothes are wringed dry before hanging out, they will not wet the clothings hanging downstairs. 2 (n) 一种死刑，用绞索把人勒死 hanging
绞尽脑汁 [jiǎo jìn nǎo zhí] rack one's brain
绞死 [jiǎo sǐ] strangle one to death
绞索 [jiǎo suǒ] noose
绞刑架 [jiǎo xíng jiá] the scaffold

皎 [jiǎo] (adj) 清洁，清秀雅丽 clear; splendid; pure

矫(矯) [jiǎo] 1 (v) 改正；扭转；把弯的弄直 correct; revise; straighten; reform; rectify ＊大家帮他矫正吸毒的恶习，使他重新过健康的生活。We help him to rectify his drug addicting habits and make him lead a healthy life again. 2 (adj) 强壮，勇敢 strong; robust; vigorous ＊每日的辛勤劳动使农夫的体格矫健。The daily hard labour has made the farmer physically strong.
矫捷 [jiǎojíe] agile; nimble
矫揉造作 [jiǎoróu zào zuò] artificial; unnatural; made-up

矫枉过正 [jiǎo wǎng guò zhèng] (fig) exceeding the proper limits in righting a wrong; go beyond the proper limits in righting a wrong

剿 [jiǎo] (v) 追迫；用武力消灭 annihilate; wipe out (the enemy); suppress; destroy

剿捕 [jiǎobǔ] arrest; suppress

剿匪 [jiǎofěi] put down bandits

缴(繳) [jiǎo] (v) 交纳；交付 pay (tax); hand over; deliver ＊我们必须準时缴纳每个月的水电费，否则水电供应将被停止的。We must pay the monthly electricity and water bill in time, otherwise, the supply will be stopped

缴还 [jiǎohuán] return; repay

缴交 [jiǎojiāo] deliver up; hand over

缴纳 [jiǎo nà] pay (tax, duties, fees, dues, etc.)

缴械 [jiǎo xiè] disarm; lay down one's weapons

侥(僥) [jiǎo] [侥幸] [jiǎo xìng] (adj) 由于偶然的机会得到成功，或避免不幸 through good luck; by chance ＊他在贫困中，很侥幸的拾到了一张头奖彩票。Through good luck, he picked up a first prize lottery ticket in the midst of his poverty.

搅(攪) [jiǎo] 1 (v) 拌和 stir; mix 2 (v) 打扰；扰乱 disturb; annoy; confuse; trouble ＊一些人的打斗搅乱了整个博览会的场面。The fight of some people confused the whole scene at the exposition.

搅拌 [jiǎobàn] mix; stir; beat up

搅动 [jiǎodóng] stir

搅乱 [jiǎo luàn] confuse; throw into disorder

搅扰 [jiǎo rǎo] disturb; harrass; stir up; make trouble

脚 [jiǎo] 1 (n) 人或动物身体最下部接触地面的肢体 legs; the foot 2 (n) 物体的最下部 base or bottom; the leg or base on which a thing rests or stands

脚步 [jiǎobù] footstep; pace

脚跟 [jiǎogēn] the heel

脚镣 [jiǎo liào] shackles; ankle chains

脚气病 [jiǎo qì bìng] beri beri

脚踏车 [jiǎotàchē] bicycles

脚踏实地 [jiǎotàshídì] do solid work down-to-earth

脚印 [jiǎoyìn] footprints

脚趾 [jiǎozhǐ] toe

角 [jiǎo] 1 (n) 牛；羊；鹿等头上长的坚硬的东西 horn 2 (n) 由一点引出两条直线所成的形状 an angle 3 (n) 物体边沿相接的地方 corner 4 (n) 古时候军用的乐器 a trumpet 5 (n) 指货币的辅助单位，十角等于一元 coins; a unit of currency

角度 [jiǎo dù] angular magnitude; an angle (of view)

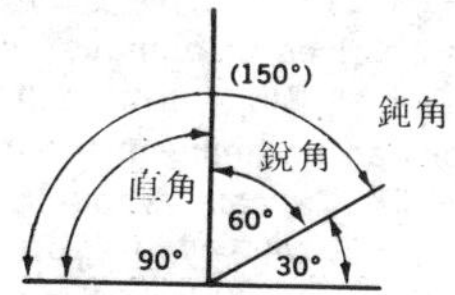

角落 [jiǎoluò] corner

另见 [jué]

jiào

噍 [jiào] (v) 嚼；吃东西 chew; eat

醮 [jiào] 1 (n) 古代人们结婚时用酒祭神的一种礼节 an offer of drink or a sacrifice made during a marriage ceremony 2 (v) 妇女再嫁 re-marry (referring to women)

校 [jiào] 1 (v) 比较 compare; contest 2 (v) 订正 correct; proof-reading ＊稿件要经过校对，才可正式出版。The scripts must be proof-read before they can be published.

另见 [xiào]

较(較) [jiào] (v) (adv) 比较compare; comparatively; rather *太平洋较大西洋阔。The Pacific Ocean is comparatively wider than the Atlantic Ocean.

较量 [jiàoliang] match; compare (eg. strength, skill); contest

较早 [jiàozǎo] earlier; sooner

峤(嶠) [jiào] (n) 山道 a passageway in the mountains

另见 [qiào]

轿(轎) [jiào] (n) 轿子，旧时用人抬着走的交通工具 sedan-chair

轿车 [jiào chē] car; saloon (car)

窖 [jiào] 1 (n) 收藏东西的地洞 a vault; a cellar; pit 2 (v) 把东西收藏到地窖里 store in a cellar *防空洞里窖藏了许多粮食。 A lot of provisions are stored in the air-raid tunnels.

叫 [jiào] 1 (v) 动物发出声音 call; cries; voices of animals *天亮时就会听到鸡叫。The call of the cock can be heard in the morning. 2 (v) 呼喊 call ; shout ; cry out * 在深海处有人正高声叫救命。Someone is shouting for help in the deep of the sea. 3 (v) 称呼，称为 name * 他们把新出世的儿子叫做汤米。They named their new-born son Tommy.

叫喊 [jiàohǎn] cry; shout; call out; yell

叫苦连天 [jiào kǔ lián tiān] constantly complain; endless groaning and moaning

叫门 [jiàomén] call at the door; knock at the door

叫嚷 [jiàorǎng] bluster; clamour; yell

叫嚣 [jiàoxiāo] clamour

觉(覺) [jiào] (n)睡眠sleep; nap *他每天总得睡一个午觉才能继续工作。 Everyday he must take an afternoon nap (sleep) before continuing with his work.

另见 [jué]

教 [jiào] 1 (n) 指导，训诲 education; teaching 2 (n) 宗教 religion

教材 [jiàocái] teaching materials (textbook, etc.); text

教导 [jiào dǎo] teach; instruct; teaching; instruction

教具 [jiáojù] teaching aids

教练 [jiàoliàn] coach; teach; instruct ; a rainer

教派 [jiào pài] sect; denomination

教师 [jiàoshī] teacher

教室 [jiàoshì] classroom

教授 [jiàoshòu] professor ; teach; instruct; coach; lecture

教堂 [jiàotáng] a church; a chapel; a cathedral

教条 [jiàotiáo] dogmas

教徒 [jàio tú] follower of a religion; believer

教学 [jiào xué] teaching

教训 [jiào·xun] teach; educate (learn) a lesson; teach (somebody) a lesson; reproach; rebuke

教养 [jiàoyǎng] bring up; upbringing

教育 [jiàoyù] educate ; education; instruction

另见 [jiāo]

酵 [jiào] (n) 发酵，有机物由于酶的作用而分解 yeast; barm

酵饼 [jiàobǐng] yeast cakes

酵粉 [jiàofěn] enzyme

酵母 [jiàomǔ] yeast; ferment

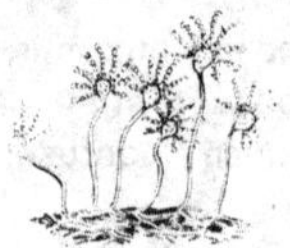

jiē

皆 [jiē] (adj) 全 all; altogether *人人皆知太阳是从东方升起来的。

Everybody knows that the sun rises from the east.

皆大欢喜 [jiē dà huān xǐ] everybody is happy (pleased)

阶 (階) [jiē] (n) 台阶 a step; stairs ＊ 登吉隆坡的黑风洞需要走几百级石阶。To go into the Batu Caves in Kuala Lumpur, one has to walk through a few hundred stone steps.

阶层 [jiē céng] social strata

阶段 [jiē duàn] period; stage; phase

阶级 [jiē jí] class

阶梯 [jiē tī] steps; ladder

结 (結) [jiē] (v) 植物长出果实或种子 bear (fruit) ＊木瓜树在一两年内就可开花结果了。The papaya tree can flower and bear fruits within one or two years.

结实 [jiēshí] strong; stout; robust; sturdy

另见 [jié]

接 [jiē] 1 (v) 收；收受 receive; accept ＊ 他接到家信后就立刻回覆。He replied immediately after he had received a letter from home. 2 (adv) 连续；继续 continuously; one after another＊顾客一个接一个的前来买东西，店员忙得不可开交。Customers came one after another to buy goods, and the shop assistant became very busy. 3 (v) 迎 receive＊一个朋友从外国回来渡假，我得到码头去接他。I have to go to the harbour to receive a friend who has come from abroad for holiday here. 4 (v) 连结；接合 connect

接班 [jiēbān] take over (eg. shift)

接班人 [jiēbànrén] successor

接触 [jiēchù] contact; get in touch with

接触點 [jiē chù diǎn] point of contact

接待 [jiēdài] receive; accommodate; reception; attend

接骨 [jiēgǔ] bone-setting

接管 [jiēguǎn] take over

接济 [jie jì] support; help; supply

接见 [jiējiàn] receive somebody; allow one an interview

接近 [jiējìn] come closer to; approach; draw near

接力 [jiēlì] relay (eg. relay race)

接纳 [jiēnà] accept; take up; admit

接洽 [jiēqià] contact (someone) to discuss something; deal with

接任 [jiērèn] take up duty

接生 [jiēshēng] assist with childbirth; act as midwife

接受 [jiēshòu] accept; succumb; receive

接替 [jiē tì] take someone's place; replace somebody

接头语 [jiē tóu yǔ] prefix

接尾语 [jiēwěiyǔ] suffix

接吻 [jiēwěn] kiss

嗟 [jiē] (interj) 叹词。表示失望或疲倦 a sigh

另见 [juē]

揭 [jiē] 1 (v) 掀起；掀开 lift up; take off; uncover＊ 鱼蒸了那么久，可以揭开锅盖了。You can uncover the pan now since the fish has been steamed for so long. 2 (v) 使显露出来 lay bare; expose; disclose＊ 那个大慈善家背地里干了许多坏事，我们要揭穿他的假面具。That "great pilanthropist" has done many evils deeds under cover, we must expose his hypocrisy.

揭发 [jiēfā] bring to light; expose; lay bare

揭露 [jiē lù] expose; unmask; uncover (a plot)

揭幕 [jiē mù] raise the curtain; inaugurate

揭晓 [jiē xiǎo] announce the results

街 [jiē] (n) 城镇中的大道 a street; an avenue; a road

街道 [jiēdào] street

街头巷尾 [jiētóuxiàngwěi] all over the city; in all parts of the city

jié

诘(詰) [jié] (v) 追问 interrogate; ask; examine * 警方把嫌犯带回警察局盘诘。The police brought the suspect back to the police station for interrogation.

诘问 [jiéwèn] cross-question (examine); question closely; inquire authoritatively

洁(潔) [jié] (adj) 干净 clear;clean ; neat

洁白 [jiébái] pure white; clean

洁净 [jiéjìng] clean; pure, neat

洁身自好 [jié shēn zì hào] keeping oneself clean by refusing to associate with the vulgar

结(結) [jié] 1 (v) (n) 用绳;线或布条等相联或编织,也指联成的节knot ; tie ; a tie ; a knife* 古代的人在一条绳子上打几个结来记事。People of olden times tied knots on a string to help remember things. 2 (v) 组织;订立 unite; connect; allied* 不结盟国家的人民努力工作, 希望在短期内把自己的国家经济搞好起来。The people of non-allied nations have been working hard, hoping to better their national economies within a short period of time.

结伴 [jié bàn] form companionships

结冰 [jiébīng] freeze

结构 [jiégòu] construction; structure; framework

结果 [jiégǒu] result; consequence

结合 [jié hè] combine; integrate with; in co-ordination with

结婚 [jiéhūn] marry; wedding

结交 [jiéjiāo] associate with; make acquaintance with; make friend

结晶 [jiéjīng] crystallization; crystallize

结局 [jiéjú] end; result; outcome; finale

结论 [jiélùn] conclusion

结盟 [jiéméng] ally with; alliance

结识 [jiéshí] become acquainted

结束 [jiéshù] finish; terminate; wind up

结算 [jiésuàn] balance account

结拜兄弟 [jié yì xiōng dì] sworn brothers

结尾 [jiéwěi] end; finals

结账 [jié zhàng] pay bills; clearing (of account); settle one's account

另见 [jiē]

拮 [jié] [拮据] [jiéjū] (adj) 经济状况不好;困难 money is running short; lack of funds; poverty

碣 [jié] (n) 稍带圆形的石碑 stone plate

竭 [jié] (v) 尽;用尽 deplete; exhaust; use up (adj) exhausted. * 他乐於助人,答应帮别人做的事,一定竭力去办。Keen on helping people, he will exhaust all means in carrying out what he has promised others to do.

竭尽 [jiéjìn] energy quite gone; exhausted

竭尽全力 [jié jìn quán lì] using every bit of strength

竭力 [jiélì] do one's best

捷 [jíe] 1 (n) 胜利victory* 士兵在接到捷报后大事庆祝。 After receiving news of victory, the soldiers celebrated grandly. 2 (adj) 快;灵活quick; swift; fast; active * 猫的行动比猪敏捷得多了。The movement of a cat is much faster than that of a pig

捷径 [jiéjìng] shortcut path; short-cut

捷足先登 [jiézùxiāndēng] the fastest reaches the goal first

睫 [jié] (n)眼睫毛 the eyelashes

节(節) [jié] 1 (n) 物体各段之间相连的地方 a knot; a joint. 2 (n)段落 a section; a paragraph. 3(n)纪念日 a season; a festival. 4 (v) 限制 restrict; economize. * 许多国家都在设法节制人口的增长率。 Many countries are making attempts to restrict the rate of population growth. 5 (n) 量词 a measure word. * 一天得上七节课。There are seven periods of lessons in one day.

节俭 [jiéjiǎn] economical; frugal; thrifty

节目 [jiémù] programme; item

节日 [jié rì] festival

节省 [jiéshěng] save; use something sparingly

节食 [jié shí] cut one's normal diet; fastening

节外生枝 [jiéwàishēng zhī] raise side issues; new problems arising

节衣缩食 [jiéyīsāoshí] sparing foods and clothings

节育 [jié yù] birth control

节约 [jié yuē] practise economy; economize

节制 [jiézhì] limit; regulate; control; restrict

节奏 [jié zòu] rhythm

劫 [jié] (v)用强力夺取rob; snatch; plunder 海盗常常劫掠渔民，使渔民们生活更加贫苦。Pirates used to rob the fishermen, and so made them live a harder and poorer life

劫案 [jié àn] a case of robbery.

劫夺 [jiéduó] rob; plunder; loot.

劫富济貧 [jié fù jì pín] robbing the wealthy to relieve the poor.

截 [jié] 1 (v) 切断；割断 cut * 他把甘蔗截成几节。He cut the sugar cane into several pieces. 2 (v) 阻拦 intercept; stop. *警察在路上截住交通以搜查可疑的车辆。Police intercept the traffic on the roads to examine vehicles under suspicion.

截断 [jié duàn] cut into pieces; cut off; block.

截面 [jiémiàn] cross-section.

截然 [jiérán] abruptly; obviously; entirely

截止 [jiézhǐ] stop; close; cut off

截阻 [jié zǔ] obstruct.

杰 [jié] 1 (n) 才能突出的人 a hero; outstanding person. 2 (adj) 出色的 famous; distinguished; eminent.* 萧伯纳是英国一位杰出的剧作家。Bernard Shaw was a distinguished dramatist of England.

杰出 [jiéchū] excellent; outstanding; distinguished.

杰作 [jiézuò] masterpiece.

桀 [jié] (adj) 凶暴 cruel; savage; tyrannical; harsh. *历史上的罗马帝王，有些是十分桀黠的。in history, some of the Roman emperors were cruel men.

孑 [jié] (adj)单独；孤独only; single; solitary; alone. *这老人被儿女们所遗弃，落得孑然一身。Having been deserted by his children, this old man remained a lonesome self.

孑孓 [jiéjué] the larvae of mosquito.

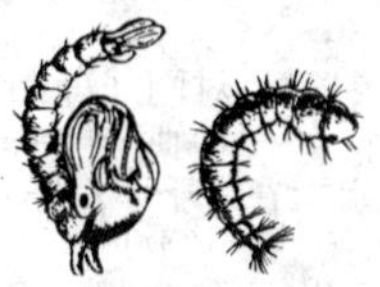

讦(訐) [jié] (v) 揭发别人的短处或阴私 to disclose another's secrets; charge one with faults; incriminate.

讦发 [jiéfā] to reveal.

jiě

解 [jiě] 1 (v)剖开；分开break up; disperse; cut apart ∗医生把老鼠解剖了，发觉它的体内有毒菌。The doctor dissected the rat, and found out a type of virus in its body. 2 (v)松开 loosen; untie take off ∗他热得晕了过去，快解开他的衣服吧。He has fainted because of the extreme heat; loosen his clothes quickly. 3 (v) 消除；解除 get rid of; relieve of ∗喝杯柠檬汁解渴吧。Drink a glass of lemonade to relieve of your thirst. 4 (v) 说明 explain; understand; comprehend ∗林老师把这一课文解释得很清楚。 Mr. Lin explains this lesson very clearly.

解除 [jiěchú] relieve of; get rid of; remove

解答 [jiě dá] answer; reply

解放 [jiěfàng] liberate; emancipate; emancipation; liberation

解雇 [jiěgù] dismiss; sack; fire

解救 [jiějiù] give relief to; save

解决 [jiějué] settle; solve

解渴 [jiě kě] quench

解闷 [jiě mèn] kill time; find distraction

解剖 [jiěpōu] dissect; analyse

解说 [jiě shuō] explain

解脱 [jiětuō] free from; extricate ... from

解散 [jiě zàn] dismiss; scatter; disperse

姐 [jiě] (n) 对同父母而年纪比自己大的女子的称呼elder sister ∗她的姐姐在饼干厂工作。Her elder sister is working in a biscuit factory.

姐夫 [jiě·fu] brother-in-law (husband of one's elder sister)

姐妹 [jiě mei] sisters

jiè

介 [jiè] 1 (v)在两者中间lie between ∗他们兄弟俩争吵，父母亲介於两者之间，不知如何处理。 As the two brothers were having a serious dispute, their parents stood between them and did not know what to do. 2 (n) 动物身上的甲壳 shells 3 (v)介绍 introduce;recommend (n) introduction ∗这是作者的简介。This is a brief introduction of the writer.

介词 [jiè cí] preposition

介入 [jiè rù] take sides in;intervene

介绍 [jiè shào] introduce; recommend

介意 [jiè yì] care;mind

芥 [jiè] (n)芥菜；草木植物。种子可榨油或制芥辣粉 the mustard plant

疥 [jiè] (n)疥疮，俗称“癞疥病”，一种容易传染的皮肤病，非常刺痒 itch;skin-itch；scabies

借 [jiè] (v) 暂时使用他人的物品或金钱，或暂时把物品，金钱给别人使用 lend to;borrow from ∗借了别人的东西一定要还。Things borrowed from others must be returned.

借(藉) [jiè] (v)假托 take ... as a pretext;excuse∗他不喜欢上历史课，所以借口肚子疼就在厕所躲了半个钟头。He disliked history lesson so he took the excuse of having a stomach ache and hid in the toilet for half an hour.

借刀杀人 [jiè dāo sha rén] use other people to cause harm to somebody;to make the third party the instrument of crime

借题发挥 [jiè tí fā huī] utilizing a certain incident to express one's view

借助 [jiè zhǔ] presume on;ask assistance for;by the help of

藉 [jiè] (n) 垫在下面的东西 a soft pad;a cushion
另见 [jí]

戒 [jiè] 1 (v) 防备；警惕；避免 take precaution; warn; watch; guard against;keep a watchful eye on … ✱ 你们家里常常没有人在，得戒备窃贼进入 Since your house is usually empty, you must take precautions against burgulars robbing your house 2 (v) 革除（嗜好）give up (a habit);get rid of (a habit) ✱ 为了健康和金钱，我劝你还是戒烟吧。 For the sake of health and money, I would advise you to give up smoking.

戒备 [jiè bèi] watchfulness; guard against;be on the alert against
戒禁 [jiè jìn] exhort;forbid
戒律 [jié lǜ] a commandment
戒食 [jiè shí] fast
戒心 [jiè xīn] be on guard against; wary
戒严 [jiè yán] proclaim martial law; curfew;place guards around
戒指 [jiè·zhi] (finger) ring

诫(誡) [jiè] (v)警告；规劝 warn; caution against;prohibit ✱ 警方告 诫公众人士不得乱丢垃圾。 The police caution of the public against littering

界 [jiè] 1 (n)相交的地方 boundary; a limit;a frontier ✱ 在马、泰边界地区，住了很多少数民族的农民。 In the Thai-Malaysian border region live many farmers of minority races.2(n)范围 horizon;range;extent ✱ 出国旅行能扩大我们的眼界。Travelling abroad can widen our horizon. 3 (n) 按社会职业、信仰 性别等划分的范围 a world;a field ✱ 教师，校长等都是教育界人士。 Teachers and principals are people of the educational field.

界限 [jiè xiàn] limit;confine;demarcation line
界线 [jiè xiàn] boundary line;demarcation line

届 [jiè]量词 a measure word;time; term;session;etc ✱ 在南大第十届的毕业典礼上，教育部长发表了重要的演讲。At the tenth Graduation Ceremony of Nanyang University, the Minister of Education delivered an important speech.

届时 [jiè shú] when the time comes;in due course

jīn

今 [jīn] (adj.) 现在 present;modern; (adv.)now;at present;nowadays.

今非昔比 [jīn fēi xí bǐ]the past is incomparable to the present.
今后 [jīn hòu] from now on;future; henceforth; hereafter
今天 [jīn tiān] today
今昔 [jīn xī] present and past;modern and ancient

衿 [jīn] (n) 襟 lapel of a coat

衿兄弟 [jīn xīong dì]brothers-in-law

矜 [jīn] 1 (v) 同情；怜悯 pity;have sympathy with ✱ 公众人士都矜恤那几个孤儿，所以纷纷捐款。 The public pity the several orphans. They donate money one after another 2 (adj.) 自夸；自大 conceited 3 (adj) 拘谨；莊重 careful

矜持 [jīn chí]behave awkwardly;solemn;austere
矜惜 [jīn xí]pity;sympathize.
矜恤 [jīn xù]sympathize;have pity on

斤 [jīn] (n) 重量单位 chinese measure of weight

斤斤计较 [jīn jīn jì jiào]think about narrow personal gains and losses;

paying attention to trifling amounts

金 [jīn] 1 (n) 化学元素 Au, a chemical element 2 (n) 金属的通称 metal 3 (n) 钱 money

金碧辉煌 [jīn bì huī huáng]magnificient;splendid

金钢石 [jīn gāng shū] diamond

金科玉律 [jīn ke yǜ lù] infallible law;golden rules

金牌 [jīn paí] a gold metal

金钱 [jīn qián]money

金融 [jīn róng]finance

金星 [jīn xīng] (planet) Venus

金鱼 [jīn yú] goldfish

金玉良言 [jīn yù liàng yan]sound and good advice

金字塔 [jín zì tǎ] pyramid

禁 [jīn] (v) 忍住 be able to withstand or endure ✱ 那伙计禁不起老板的无理指责而辞去工作。Having been unable to endure the unreasonable censure of his boss anymore, the shop assistant resigned.

禁不住 [jīn·bu zhù] cannot withstand;be unable to help (doing something)

襟 [jīn] (n) 衣服胸前的部分 the lapel of a coat

襟怀坦白 [jīn huái tǎn bái]open and frank

襟兄弟 [jīn xiong dì]brothers-in-law;the husband of wife's sister

巾 [jīn] (n) 用来擦身体或裹身体的纺织品 a towel;a handkerchief;a neckcloth

巾帼英雄 [jīn quó yīng xíong] a heroine;a brave woman

筋 [jīn](n) 俗称肌腱或骨头上的韧带 a sinew;a muscle;a tendon

筋疲力尽 [jīn pí lì jìn]exhausted

津 [jīn] 1 (n) 渡口 a ferry;a ford 2 (n) 唾液 saliva. 3 (n) 汗 sweat

津津有味 [jīn jīn yǒu wèi] very interesting;do something with zest or relish.

津贴 [jīn tiē] allowance; subsidy; subsidize

jǐn

谨(謹) [jǐn] (adj) 小心 careful; cautious; prudent; discreet ✱ 那边治安不好，你身上带了那么多钱，得谨慎点。The security over there is not good, you had better be careful when you carry such a large sum of money.

谨防 [jǐn fáng] be on one's guard against.

谨守 [jǐn shǒu] guard carefully; watch over

谨小慎微 [jǐnxiǎoshènwēı] cautious and meticulous

谨言慎行 [jǐn yán shèn xíng] cautious in words and actions.

馑(饉) [jǐn] 荒年 a dearth; a scarcity

馑赠 [jǐn zèng] to offer (as a present)

仅(僅) [jǐn] (adv) 只；不过 only; merely;scarely ✱ 参考室的资料仅供室内阅读，不得借出。The materials in the reference room is only for reading inside the room and not for lending out.

另见 [jìn]

尽(儘) [jǐn] (v) (adv) 力求达到最大限度 to exert the utmost; to do the best; with all the strength; at full speed ✱ 这项工程要尽快在半年内完成。The work must be completed at full speed in half a year's time.

尽管 [jǐn guǎn] inspite;despite; even though;nonetheless

尽快 [jǐn kuài] as soon as possible

尽量 [jǐn liàng] the best of one's ability;as full as possible
另见 [jìn]

紧(緊) [jǐn] 1 (adj) 密切合拢，跟"松"相对 tight;closely * 那时候，警员紧紧地跟在我后面。At that time the policeman was following closely behind me. 2 (adj) 迫切；急 urgent;pressing * 你家乡打来了一封紧急的电报说你父亲病危。There is an urgent telegram from your hometown saying that your father is dangerously ill.

紧凑 [jǐn còu] concise and to the point;tightly packed or arranged

紧急 [jǐnjí] emergency; urgent; critical

紧密 [jǐn mì] close;tight

紧缩 [jǐnsuō] to reduce

紧握 [jǐnwò] grip; clench

紧要 [jǐnyào] important; essential; critical

紧张 [jǐn zhāng] critical;tense;nervous

锦(錦) [jǐn] 1 (n) 有彩色花纹的丝织品 tapestry; embroidered silk 2 (adj) 色彩鲜明美丽 ornamented;flowered

锦标 [jǐn biao] championship; a trophy

锦上添花 [jǐn shàng tiān huā] add flowers to embroidery-superfluous; add good to excellence.

锦绣前程 [jǐn xiù qián chéng] brilliant future

锦绣山河 [jǐn xiù shān hé] beautiful land

jìn

殣 [jìn] (v) 饿死starve to death

尽(盡) [jìn] 1 (adj) 完 completed;finished; exhausted (n) the utmost;the last;end * 生活所提供的写作题材，真是取之不尽。The subject matters for writings provided by life are inexhaustible. 2 (v) 达到极点 fulfill; come to an end;finish * 他把一天的工资全都捐献给火灾灾民，已尽其所能了。To donate all of his day's wage to the fire victims , he has done his best.

尽力 [jìn lì] with might and main; with all one's strength;do the utmost;do one's best

尽情 [jìn qíng] clatcdly

尽人皆知 [jìn rén jiē zhī] it is widely known;known to all

尽善尽美 [jìn shàn jin mei] to the zenith of perfection;try one's best (to do something) to perfection

尽头 [jìn tóu] the very end;the extremity

尽心 [jìn xīn] with all one's heart

尽职 [jìn zhí] faithfully carry out one's duties

尽忠报国 [jìn zhōng bào quò] loyalty and patriotism
另见 [jǐn]

烬(燼) [jìn](n) 火烧后剩下还没熄灭的东西 ashes;remains; burning residues

赆(贐) [jìn] (n) 临离别时赠送的礼物 present to a friend when going on a journey

赆仪 [jìn yí]parting gift

仅(僅) [jìn] (adv) 将近；几乎的意思 almost; nearly
另见 [jǐn]

妗 [jìn] 1 (n) 舅母 an aunt; wife of mother's brother 2(n) 妻兄；妻弟的妻子 wife of wife's brother

妗子 [jìn zi] auntie

浸 [jìn](v) 泡在水里，被水渗入 soak; immerse;sink into * 浸过水的棉花比干的时候重得多。Soaked cotton is very much heavier than the dry one.

浸湿 [jìn shī] wet;drenched;saoked

浸蚀作用 [jìn shí zuò yòng]erosion ;erosive action

浸水 [jìn shui] be flooded;be inundated

浸死 [jìn sǐ] drowned

浸透 [jìn toù] saturated through and through with

晋 [jìn] (v) 升 promote

禁 [jìn] 1 (v)不准；制止 forbid;prohibit; prevent ＊戏院里禁止抽烟。Smoking is prohibited in the cinema. 2 (v) 法律或习惯上制止的事 prohibition 3 (v) 拘押；看管 take into custody;lock up;imprison ＊警方把几个嫌疑犯监禁起来。The police take into custody several suspects.

禁闭 [jìnbì] imprision; detain; lock up

禁锢 [jìngù] jail; lock up; put under custody

禁忌 [jìn jì] taboo

禁绝 [jìnjué] absolutely prohibit

禁令 [jìn lìng] legal restriction;forbidden;prohibition law;a ban.

禁区 [jìn quí] forbidden area;off limits.

禁运 [jìn yùn] embargo

禁止 [jìnzhǐ] forbid; prohibit; ban

另见 [jīn]

噤 [jìn] (v) 闭口不作声 shut the mouth; unable to speak

噤口 [jìn kǒu] seal the lip;hold one's tongue

噤若寒蝉 [jìn ruò hán chán] dare not say a word

近 [jìn] 1 (adj) 空间或时间的距离短 near; recent (adv) recently; soon; nearby ＊近年来，越来越多的购物中心已在各地区建立。More and more shopping complexes are set up in the different districts during the recent years.

近代 [jìn dài] modern (times,etc.)

近郊 [jìn jiāo] suburbs;outskirts

近况 [jìn kuàng] the current situation

近来 [jìn lái] recently;not long ago; of late

近邻 [jìn lín] the neighbourhood

近亲 [jìn qīn] a near relation (relative);kinsmen

近日 [jìn rì] recent days; recently

近似 [jìnshì] approximation

近视 [jìn·shi] short-sighted

近水楼台 [jìn shǐu lóu tái] benefitting because of the favourable position

近朱者赤，近墨者黑 [jìn zhū zhě chì, jìn mò zhě hēi] influence of companionship—He who touches pitch shall be defiled therewith

进（進）[jìn] 1 (v)向前移动，跟"退"相对 go ahead;move forward; advance; proceed; make progress ＊士兵们唱着歌曲，阔步前进。The soldiers were singing and marching forward in big strides 2 (v) 从外面到里面，跟"出"相对 enter; come in;make way into ＊进入别人的屋子要脱鞋。Take off your shoes when you enter other peoples' house.

进步 [jìn bù] progressive;make progress;progress.

进程 [jìnchéng] developments; course; progress

进度 [jìn dù] progress.

进攻 [jìn gōng] attack;assault

进化 [jìn huà] evolve;evolution

进军 [jìn jūn] march on;advance; push on (to an area)

进口 [jìn kǒu] import;trade in

进退两难 [jìn tuì liǎng nan] in a dilemma

进退维谷 [jìn tuì wéi gǔ] find oneself in a dilemma

进行 [jìn xíng] proceed with;go ahead;carry on.

进行曲 [jìn xíng qǔ] march (music)

进修 [jìn xīu] pursue furthur studies
进一步 [jìn yī bù] furthur
进展 [jìn zhǎn] advance;improve;progress;make headway;develop.

劲(勁) [jìn] 1 (n) 力气 strength effort * 渔人使劲的把那满是鱼儿的网拉起来。The fishermen exerted strength to drag the fully loaded fish-net. 2 (n) 精神;情绪 spirit; mood * 同学们都为即将来临的校庆而感到兴奋,干劲很高。 Excited by the coming of the anniversary of the school, the students are high-spirited
另见 [jìng]

jīng

睛 [jīng] (n) 眼珠 the eye-ball;the pupil of the eye

精 [jīng] 1 (adj)经过提炼的 refined *精制的白糖目前又涨价了。At present there is another price hike for refined white sugar. 2 (adj) 完美的;最好的 best;exquisite;excellent * 这些手工艺品都很精美,难怪那么贵。It is no wonder that these handicrafts are so expensive since they are really exquisite. 3 (n)提炼出来的纯净物质 essence 4 (adj) 细密fine * 手表里的机件很精细。The movements of a watch are very fine 5 (adj) 机灵心细 clever; smart *他办事精明。He is smart in running affairs 6(n)气魄,魄力mental strength;spirit;energy * 年青人精力旺盛,可以干许多好事。Full of spirit and energy, young people can do a lot of good deeds 7 (adj) 用功深;擅长 skilful;skilled;versed; expert * 那中医精于针灸,许多人都找他诊治。 The Chinese physician is expert in acupuncture, many people approch him for treatment 8 (n)妖怪 spirit; devil
精彩 [jīng cǎi] excellent (eg. show) brillant
精打细算 [jīng dǎ xì suàn]calculate meticulously
精悍 [jīng hàn] capable;sharp;dauntless
精华 [jīng huá] fine essence;the cream (of the nation)
精简 [jīng jiǎn] cut down (the number of the personnel);simplify
精练 [jīng liàng] at the highest grade or the best quality
精密 [jīng mì] exact;precise;comprehensive
精明 [jīng míng] smart;bright;brilliant;clever
精明强干 [jīng míng qiáng gàn] ingenious and capable
精疲力竭 [jīng pí lì jíe] completely exhausted;tired out;mentally and physically exhausted
精巧 [jīng qiǎo] skilful;delicate
精神 [jīng shén] spirit; spiritual ;vigorous
精通 [jīng tōng] proficient in;be versed in;
精心 [jīng xīn] careful;meticulous
精选 [jīng xuǎn] careful selection
精液 [jīng yè] semen,sperm
精益求精 [jīng yì qíu jīng] perfect one's skill constantly; seeking further improvements in one's own fields
精湛 [jīng zhàn] exquisite ;skilful; deep;profound
精致 [jīng zhì] of fine workmanship;fine
精装 [jīng zhuàng] deluxe or high quality edition; hard-cover book.

经(經) [jīng] 1 (n) 织布时的直纱或直线 The warp of a web in the loom 2 (n)地球赤道圆周所匹分的 360 度 the longtitude 3 (n) 中医称人体内的脉络 the unseen veins in our body as described in Chinese medicine 4 (n)月经,女子的周期性

子宫出血的现象 menses;monthly courses;menstruation 5 (v) 经营；治理 manage; control;regulate ＊公司里的财务是由他经营的。The financial matters of the company is managed by him 6 (v)经过；经历；经受 go or pass through;experience (adv.) already;then ＊他小时候经历过贫苦的日子，所以对穷人有很深厚的同情心。As he had gone through hardship in his younger days,he has strong compassion for the poor 7 (n)宗教中称教义的书 classics;canon

经常 [jīng cháng] often;consistent; usual

经典 jīng diǎn] classics;classical

经度 [jīng dù] longtitude;the meridian

经费 [jīng fèi] expenditure;expenses;fund

经过 [jīng guó] pass through;process

经济 [jing jì] economy;economical

经纪 [jīng jì] a broker;an agent

经济学 [jīng jì xué] economics

经理 [jīng lǐ] manager

经商 [jīng hang] trade;carry on business

经手 [jīng shǒu] responsible for; pass through one's hands

经受 [jīng shòu]undergo;suffer;go through

经验 [jīng yan] experience

经营 [jīng yíng] manage;run

茎（莖） [jīng] (n) 植物的一部分，介于根和叶之间 stem; stalk of a plant

京 [jīng] (n) 国家的首都 capital city

惊（驚） [jīng] 1 (v) 害怕，由于突然来的刺激而引起精神紧张不安 terrify;surprise;frighten;startle (adj) alarmed;frightened; surprised; astonished ＊许多国家的环境污化问题非常惊人。The environmental pollution problems in many countries are very astonishing 2 (adj.) 震动 shaking; shocking

惊动 [jīng dòng] trouble;disturb; startle;shock

惊慌 [jīng huāng] alarmed;startled; frightened

惊慌失措 [jīng huāng shī cuò]state of panic and confusion.

惊恐万状 [jīng kǒng wàn zhuàng] extremely frightened;panic-stricken

惊奇 [jīng qí] surprised;astonished

惊人 [jīng rén] astonishing;surprising

惊天动地 [jīng tiān dòng dì] earth-shaking;highly significant

惊叹号 [jīng tàn hào]exclamation mark (!)

惊涛骇浪 [jīng tāo hài làng]tempestuous storm; turbulent waves (often referred to sharp struggles)

惊喜 [jīng xǐ]pleasantly surprised

惊险 [jīng xiǎn] thrilling

惊心动魄 [jīng xīn dòng pò] extra power of influence over others;be seized with a panic;breath-taking

惊讶 [jīng yà] surprised;alarmed

惊异 [jīng yì] astonished

鲸（鯨） [jīng] (n) 生长在海里，形状象鱼，用肺呼吸的一种哺乳动物 whale

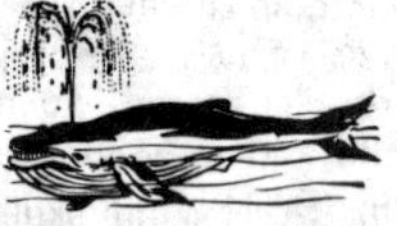

鲸吞 [jīng tūn] annex;swallow up; devour

鲸油 [jīng yóu] whale-oil

旌 [jīng] (n) 泛指一般的旗子 flags; bannerettes

晶 [jīng] 1 (adj) 形容光亮 bright; shining ＊早晨的露珠晶莹剔透像是草丛上的珍珠。The morning dew is shining like pearls among the green 2 (n)水晶和晶体的简称 crystal

晶体 [jīng tǐ] crystal

晶体管 [jīng tǐ guǎn] transistor

荆 [jīng] 1 (n)落叶灌木 a thorn; a bramble 2 (n) 指古代用荆条做成的刑杖 a whip made of bramble

荆棘 [jīng jí] brambles

粳 [jīng](n) 粳稻；稻的一种 a kind of padi or rice;unglutinous rice

兢 [jīng] (adj) 小心谨慎 cautious; anxious

兢惧 [jīng jù] dreading;afraid

jǐng

景 [jǐng] 1 (n)风光 a view;sight;scenery;scene＊这海滩的景色多美！How beautiful is the scenery on the beach! 2 (n) 情况 ；情形 circumstances;situation;condition ＊他看到这般情景，不由得不灰心了。Seeing such a situation, he felt disheartened. 3 (v) 尊敬；佩服 regard kindly;admire;respect ＊她是个众人所景仰的名作家。She is an eminent writer whom many people respect

景气 [jǐng qì] economic prosperity; boom

景物 [jǐng wù] lovely prospects; spectacle

景象 [jǐng xiàng] prospects;aspect

景致 [jǐng·zhi] beautiful scenery or scene

憬 [jǐng] (v) 觉悟 awaken

井 [jǐng] 1 (n) 在地上挖成用来取水的深洞 well;a deep pit 2 (adj) 整齐；有条理 orderly;well regulated＊军队里秩序井然。Everything in the army is in order.

井底之蛙 [jǐng dǐ zhī wā] a person of limited knowledge and experience.

井井有条 [jǐng jǐng yǒu tiáo]arranged in good order

井水不犯河水 [jǐng shuǐ bú fàn hé shuǐ] each minding his own business.

阱 [jǐng] (n) 捕捉野兽或杀伤敌人用的陷坑 a trap; a pitfall ＊很多时候，赌场是个陷阱。 Many a time, the gambling den is a pitfall.

儆 [jǐng] (v) 使人觉悟而不敢重犯错误 warn

警 [jǐng] 1 (v) 注意可能发生的危险 notify;caution;warn ＊交通警察警告他以后不得驾快车。The traffic police warn him not to speed in future 2 (n) 警察的简称 police 3 (n)危险紧急的情况或事情dangerous matters or circumstances; alarm:emergency ＊船上起了火警，搭客们都十分惊慌。 When the ship raised a fire alarm, the passengers became panicky.

警报 [jǐng bào] combat alert;alarm.

警告 [jǐnggào] warn; warning ; put on guard· caution (punishment)

警戒 [jǐng jiè] be vigilant;guard against;warn;counsel

警句 [jǐngjù] a brilliant sentence; epigram

警觉 [jǐngjúe] alert

警惕 [jing tì] maintain vigilance;be on the look out

警卫队 [jǐng wèi duì] a guard; a vigilance corp

警钟 [jǐng zhōng] an alarm bell; warning

刭（剄） [jǐng] (v)用刀割脖子 cut throat

颈（頸） [jǐng] (n)脖子，头和躯干相连接的部分 neck

颈巾 [jǐngjīn] a neckerchief

颈椎 [jǐngzhuī] cervical vertebrae

jìng

径(徑) [jìng] 1(n) 狭路，小路 a byway;a pass ✱要爬上这座山，得走许多曲折的小径。To climb this hill one must go through many winding passes. 2 (n) 直径的简称 diameter 3 (adj) 直截了当 direct;straight forward

径直 [jìng zhí] directly;straightforward

径自 [jìng zì] direct personal action (eg. without permission)

胫(脛) [jìng] (n) 小腿，从膝到踝的一段 the shank;the shin

劲(勁) [jìng] (adj) 坚强有力 strong; powerful; muscular ✱那外国拳王是我国拳王的劲敌。That foreign boxing champion is a powerful rival for our national boxing champion.

劲敌 [jìngdí] redoutable enemy

劲旅 [jìng lǚ] crack troops

劲松 [jìngsōng] a sturdy pine

靖 [jìng] 1 (adj) 安定 calm,peaceful 2 (v) 使秩序平定 pacify;suppress ✱ 不少兵队被派出靖乱。 Many troops are despatched to suppress the rebellions.

静 [jìng] 1 (adj) 安定不动 still,peaceful;calm;motionless ✱ 心急也没用，你就安静地等一会儿吧。It's no point being impatient, you just sit still and wait for a while 2 (adj) 没有声响 silent;quiet;noiseless ✱ 这里远离热闹的市区，环境清静。The environment here is quiet since it is far away from the noisy city.

静电 [jìng diàn] electrostatic;static electricity

静脉 [jìng mài] veins

静默 [jìng mò] silence;hold one's peace;stillness

静悄悄 [jìng qiāo qiāo] quietly;silently

静养 [jìng yǎng] rest;recuperation; keep quiet and take care of oneself.

静止 [jìng zhǐ] static;statoinary; motionless

竞(競) [jìng] (v) 比赛，互相争胜 complete;contend; struggle; strive

竞赛 [jìng sài] compete;contest; competition

竞选 [jìng xuǎn] campaign;run for (eg.office);election

竞争 [jìngzhēng] compete; contend; struggle for; competition

竟 [jìng] 1 (v) 完成；完毕 finish ✱继承先辈未竟的事业。To carry on the work which had not been finished by ancestors. 2 (adv) 终于 finally;at last; ultimately ✱ 有志者事竟成。Those with determination will ultimately succeed. 3 (adv) 从头到尾 go to the end; examine thoroughly; from beginning to the end ✱ 他为了准备明天的考试而竟夜赶读。To prepare for the examinatons tomorrow, he studied throughout the night. 4 (adv) 表示出乎意料之外 unexpectedly;surprisingly ✱这样大的工程，竟在短短的两年间内完成了，真了不起。 It is really wonderful that such a large project can surprisingly be completed within a short period of two years.

竟然 [jìng rán] even;go to the length of;go so far as to

境 [jìng] 1 (n) 疆界；边界 a limit; a boundary ✱ 这货币只可以在本国境内通用。 This currency can only be used within the national boundary. 2 (n) 地方；处所 a place; region;a district; a locality ✱ 这里有山有水， 真是佳境。It is a lovely place here, with mountains and rivers. 3 (n) 境况；

境地 situation;condition; circumstances state ＊ 事情到了今天这个境地，你得快设法挽救才行。As things have come to such a bad state today,you had better be quick to think of a means to remedy it.

境内 [jìng nèi] within the territory or area; within the national boundary

境遇 [jìng yù] circumstance;situation

镜(鏡) [jìng] 1 (n) 有光滑的平面，能反映物体的形象 a looking glass;a mirror ＊ 在理发室里，一定能看到镜子。We are sure to see mirrors in a barber-shop 2 (n) 利用光学原理制成的器具 lens; optical lens ＊ 望远镜 telescope

镜头 [jìng tóu] a camera lens

敬 [jìng] 1 (v) 尊敬 respect;hold in veneration ＊ 大家都很敬佩战士们的勇敢。All the people respect the warriors for their bravery 2 (v) 有礼貌地送上 offer something respectfully; present with respect ＊ 这件礼物是敬献给我们那将退休的校长的。This humble gift is to be presented to our retiring principal.

敬爱 [jìng ài] love and respect;esteem

敬而远之 [jìng ér yuǎn zhī] to respect a person, but to stay afar from him; keep someone at a respectable distance

敬礼 [jìng lǐ] salute

敬仰 [jìng yǎng] have the highest admiration for

敬意 [jìng yì] salute; regards; esteem; respects

敬启者 [jìng qǐ zhě] I have the honour to inform you

净 [jìng] 1 (adj) 清洁 clean;undefiled ＊ 他把地方收拾得很乾净。He keeps the place very clean. 2 (adj) 没有剩余 no remainder;finish ＊ 他饿到把盘上的东西吃得一干二净。He is so hungry that he eats until there is no remainder on the plate.3 (adv) 全部；都 all;completely ＊ 满仓净是一袋袋的白米。The godown is completely filled with sacks of rice.4 (adj) 纯 pure; net ＊这罐牛油净重120克。The net weight of this can of butter is 120 grams.

净化 [jìng huà] purify

jiǒng

迥 [jiǒng] 1 (adj) 远 far off;distant, remote ＊ 你要从新加坡驾车到欧洲，山高路迥，可不容易啊。It is not easy for you to drive from Singapore to Europe in the face of highlands and remote roads. 2 (adj) 形容差别很大 different;very different ＊ 当海员与当救生员的工作环境迥然不同。The working conditions between a sailor and a life guard are entirely different.

迥然 [jiǒng rán] utterly ; entirely

迥然不同 [jiǒng rán bù tóng] remarkably different

窘 [jiǒng] 1 (adj) 穷困 poor;pressed ＊那失业汉生活窘迫，孩子们也停学了。That unemployed man leads a poor life and his children have stopped schooling already. 2 (adj)为难；难住 embarrassed;distressed;afflicted;awkward ＊ 新郎新娘被亲友们闹得窘极了。The bridegroom and the bride were disturbed by friends and relatives into an awkward situation.

jiū

啾 [jiū] (n) 虫，小鸟的叫声 sound with a pause,onomatopoeia (as a bird,an insect,etc)

揪 [jiū] (v)抓住；扭住 hold fast;grasp;catch ＊ 店员及时揪住那偷货物的顾客。The shop attendent caught hold of the shoplifter in time.

纠(糾) [jiū] 1 (adj) 缠绕 mutually involved;complicated ＊ 她整天被情情爱爱的问题纠缠得不能安心读书。Her mind is always complicated by love problems so much, so she cannot study in peace. 2 (v) 纠正 correct (a mistake) ＊ 朋友之间应该互相纠正彼此的错误才是真正的互相帮忙。To actually help one another, friends should correct each other's mistakes.

纠察 [jiū chá] examine;investigate

纠缠 [jiū chán] entangle;pester

纠纷 [jiū fēn] quarrel;dispute

纠葛 [jiū gé] entanglement;dispute; complication

赳 [jiū] [赳赳] [jiū jiū] 威武雄壮的样子 valiant

鸠(鳩) [jiū] 1 (n) 鸟类，种类很多 the turtle-dove;the pigeon;the cuckoo 2(v)聚集 assemble ;collect;call together(derog) ＊ 外面有一群阿飞鸠聚，大概不会是为了好事。A group of gangsters assemble outside;it is likely to be something bad.

究 [jiū] 1 (v) 仔细推求，追查 examine;investigate;search out ＊公司经过一番追究查询后，发现会计主任曾亏空公款。After much investigation, the company found that the chief accountant has embezzled the company's funds. 2 (adv)到底；究竟 after all;at last; finally ＊你说了那么久，究竟有完没完？You keep talking for so long. Is there an end after all?

究竟 [jiū jìng] the whys and wherefores;the reasons for something; after all;anyway

jiǔ

久 [jiǔ] (adj) 时间长 long(in time, period); lasting;for a long time ＊ 儿子要到外国工作三年，他父母亲都舍不得他离开那么久。When the son wanted to work abroad for three years, his parents were unwilling to part with him for such a long time.

久经 [jiǔjīng] have gone through... a long time;long standing

灸 [jiǔ] (n) 中医的一种治疗方法，用燃烧的艾绒烧灼人体的某些穴位 moxibustion

九 [jiǔ] 1 (n) 数词 the numeral nine 9 2 (adj) 表示多数或多次 many; plenty;frequent

九牛二虎之力 [jiǔ niú èr hǔ zhī lì] tremendous effort;great strength

九牛一毛 [jiǔ niú yì máo] a drop in the ocean

九泉之下 [jiǔ quán zhī xià] the underworld; under the earth

九死一生 [jiǔ sǐ yì shēng] (lit) nine chances to die and one chance to live (fig) a narrow escape (of one's life);a close shave

九霄云外 [jiǔ xiāo yún wài] far distant place, so far that there is no sign of it

九月 [jiǔ yuè] September

韭 [jiǔ] (n)韭菜，草本植物是一种蔬菜 leeks;Chinese chive

酒 [jiǔ] (n) 用高粱，米麦或葡萄等发酵制成的含乙醇的饮料，有刺激性，多喝对身体有害 liquor;wine; spirit

酒会 [jiǔ huì] cocktail party

酒精 [jiǔ jīng] alcohol;spirit

酒肉朋友 [jiǔ ròu péng yǒu] those who are friends while invitations last

酒色 [jiǔ sè] woman and wine

酒徒；酒鬼；酒仙 [jiǔ tú; jiǔ guǐ; jiǔ

xiān] a heavy (hard) drinker;a drunkard;a guzzler of liquor

酒席 [jiǔ xí] a formal banquet

jiù

臼 [jiù] 1 (n) 舂米的器具,多半用石头制成 a mortar 2 (adj) 象臼的东西the shape of a mortar

臼杵 [jiù gǎn] mortar and pestle

舅 [jiù] 1 (n) 舅父，母亲的弟兄 maternal uncles 2 (n) 舅子，妻的弟兄brothers-in-law (of a man)

舅母 [jiù mǔ] aunt (wife of mother's brother)

旧(舊) [jiù] 1 (adj)过去的，过时的 old; ancient; past ; out of date ＊「婚姻应由父母作主」这种想法，已经是旧思想了。That parents should decide on children's marriage is already an out-dated concept. 2 (adj) 因经过长时间或经过使用而损耗的 worn;second hand ＊ 他驾驶一辆日德士，以维持生活。He drove an old taxi to earn a living.

旧调重弹 [jiù diào chóng tán] harping on the same old tune

旧居 [jiù jū] the former dwelling place;former residence

旧例 [jiù lì] old custom;a usage

旧历 [jiù lì] lunar calendar

旧瓶装新酒 [jiù píng zhuāng xīn jiǔ] new wine in an old bottle;employing the old form to express the new content (mainly in literature)

旧事 [jiù shì] past events;things past

旧式 [jiù shì] old fashioned;obsolete;old-styled

就 [jiù] 1 (prep) 凑近；靠近 nearby; by 2 (prep) 表示肯定的语气 an auxilliary word,used to emphasize the conclusion, eg that is; must; will ＊ 要成功，就得努力。To be successful, one must work hard. 3(adv)立刻 immediately;forthwith; then;soon ＊ 你不舒服，吃一片药丸就好了。If you don't feel well, you just have to take a tablet and you'll soon be better. 4 (v) 开始担任 be appointed ＊ 他就任为公会的财政。He was appointed the Treasurer of the Association. 5 (adv) 单；只；仅 just; only; merely ＊ 他什么也不爱吃，就是喜欢吃鱼。He just like to eat fish and nothing else.

就此 [jiù cǐ] then;just then

就地取材 [jiù dì qǔ cái] seeking material and talent in the local area

就来 [jiùlái] come at once; coming

就寝 [jiu qiǔ] go to bed;sleep

就任 [jiùrèn] to take up a post, to come into office; to be appointed

就是 [jiù shì] even if;simply;just

就事论事 [jiù shì lùn shì] take the matter on its merit;be pragmatic

就业 [jiù yè] take up empolyment ; begin a job

就职 [jiùzhí] to take up one's office; inauguration

鹫(鷲) [jiù] (n) 鸟类；性凶猛；食鸟；兽类等尸体 a vulture;an eagle;a hawk

疚 [jiù] 1 (adj) 久病sick for a long time 2 (n) 内心痛苦regret remorse ＊他因为曾出卖朋友而一直感到内疚。All along he was filled with remorse for the betrayal he had done to his friends.

柩 [jiù] (n) 装着尸体的棺材 a coffin with a corpse in it

厩 [jiù] (n) 马棚，泛指牲口棚 stable;a shed (for animals)

咎 [jiù] 1 (n)过失；罪过fault;blunder;error; blame ＊他常不肯认错，却爱归咎于人。He often denies his mistakes and lays the blame on others. 2 (v) 责备；处分 blame; repraoch;chide

救 [jiù] (v) 帮助摆脱困难或危险 save;relieve;rescue;assist ＊那排店屋着火了，大家都赶去救火。All the people rushed to relieve the fire which affects that row of shops.

救国 [jiù guó] rescue the country; national salvation

救护 [jiù hù] give first aid to;come to the rescue of;save and protect

救火 [jiù huǒ] put out fire

救火车 [jiù huǒ chē] fire engine

救火队 [jiù huǒ duì] fire brigade

救济 [jiù jì] give relief to;provide relief for

救济金 [jiù jì jīn] a relief-fund

救命 [jiù mìng] save a person's life;life-saving

救伤车 [jiù shāng chē] an ambulance

救生圈 jiù shēng quān] life buoy

救世主 [jiù shì zhǔ] the Saviour

救星 [jiù xīng] liberator ; saviour

救灾 [jiù zāi] give relief aid

jū

狙 [jū] (n) 古书里指一种猴子 a monkey

狙击 [jū jī] raid;a surprise attack

疽 [jū] 一种毒疮，因细菌感染局部血行阻滞而形成 a carbuncle;an abscess

居 [jū] 1 (v)住 live;inhabit; stay; lodge 2 (n) 住处 dwellings;abode; residence ＊我父亲在新加坡住了三十多年。My father has been staying in Singapore for more than thirty years. 3(v)处於；站在 station at;position at ＊我们在山上居高临下，可眺望山谷的迷人风景。Positioned at the top of the hill, we could overlook the charming scenery of the valley. 3 (v) 存 have; keep;maintain ; intend; mean ＊我并没有居心得罪人。 I have no intention to offend anyone.

居高临下 [jūgāolínxià] commanding height

居功 [jūgōng] claim credit (for oneself)

居留 [jū liú] reside;stay

居民 [jū mín] resident;inhabitant

居然 [jū rán] even;go as far as

居心 [jūxīn] intend (to do something); bent on

居心叵测 [jūxīnpǒcè] with ulterior motives; harbour evil intent towards

居中 [jū zhōng] in the middle

拘 [jū] 1 (v) 逮捕；扣押 arrest;lay hold of＊那个逃掉的杀人凶手终於被拘捕归案了。 That murderer who had earlier escaped was finally arrested. 2 (v)限制 constrain restrain; pestrict 本图书馆只开放给会员，借书多少不拘。 This library is open to members only , and there is no restriction to the number of books to be borrowed. 3 (adj) 固执；死板 stick to; bigoted ＊他常拘泥于旧说， 是个思想古旧的人。He is an old-fashioned man who always sticks to the old thoughts .

拘谨 [jū jǐn] cautious;over reserved

拘留 [jū liú] detain;hold in custody

拘票 [jūpiào] warrant of arrest

拘束 [jū shù] restrained;inhibited

驹(駒) [jū] (n) 少壮的骏马 a colt;a young horse

掬 [jū] (v)两手捧东西hold or grasp with both hands

鞠 [jū] 1 (v) 养育；抚养 nourish; rear; bring up 2 (v) 弯曲 bend, as the body

鞠躬 [jū gōng] bow (in respect)

鞠躬尽瘁，死而后已 [jū gōng jìn cuì, sǐ ér hòu yǐ] I will do my best,unto death I stop; give one's all (to the service of the people)

车(車) [jū] (n) 象棋棋子的一种 one of the pieces in Chinese chess
另见 [chē]

jú

局 [jú] 1 (n) 机关，单位的名称 an office;a bureau;a board;a department;club;depot ＊ 去邮政局买张邮票吧。Go to the Post Office to buy a stamp,please 2 (n) 形势 situation;aspect;condition ＊ 那个国家正发生内战，局势很不平静。The situation in that country which is having a civil war is very unpeaceful.3 (n) 圈套 a trap;a farce ＊ 当骗子溜走之后，他才晓得那是个骗局。Only when the swindlers had slipped away did he realize that it was a trap.4 (n)量词 a unit of measure(for chess game table-tennis,etc) ＊ 来一局象棋好吗？How about playing a game of Chinese Chess?

局部 [jú bù] partial;in part;local

局促 [jú cù] narrow and small;short (of time),stand on ceremony

局促不安 [jú cù bù ān] uneasy and unnatural

局面 [jú miàn] condition;situation

局势 [jú shì] situation;state of affairs

局限 [jiú xiàn] be limited to

菊 [jú] (n) 菊花，草本植物 the chrysanthemum

橘 [jú] (n)常绿乔木。果实叫"橘子"，果皮可供药用 mandarin orange ＊在新年期间，很多人买橘子送给亲戚朋友。During the new Year time, many people buy oranges and give them to friends and relatives.

jǔ

咀 [jǔ] (v)用牙齿细嚼，辨别滋味 chew;munch ＊ 马来人很爱咀嚼槟榔。The Malays like to chew the betel-nuts.

矩 [jǔ] (n)法则；规则 a rule;a law;a pattern

矩形 [jǔ xíng] rectangular

沮 [jǔ] 1 (v) 阻止 stop;prohibit 2(adj) (气色)败坏 dispirited;depressed;in low spirits;dejected ＊ 一个女学生因会考不及格而沮丧得去自杀。A female student was so depressed over her failure in the certificate exams that she committed suicide.

举(舉) [jǔ] 1 (v)向上抬；向上托 raise;lift up;hold up ＊ 要发问的先举手。Raise your hands first if you want to ask any question. 2 (v) 推选 praise;recommend ＊因为他是个好学生，同学们都推举他做班长。Because he is a good student, all his classmates recommend him to be the monitor. 3 (n)动作；行为 matter; affair;behaviour;conduct ＊老师站在课室后面，学生的一举一动她都看得很清楚。Standing at the back of the classroom,the teacher can see clearly the conduct of all the students. 4 (v) 发起 begin;inaugurate;hold;open ＊ 学校每年都举办一次「用手劳动运动」。The school holds a 'Use Your Hands' campaign every year. 5 (v)提出 bring up (an opinion,a topic,etc);cite ＊大家都不明白你的理论，请你举些例子说明吧。We are not clear about your theory, please cite some examples to illustrate it. 6 (adv) 整个；全 all; whole;entire ＊在五月一日，举国

工人都庆祝劳动节。On May 1st, workers in the whole country celebrated Labour Day.

举办 [jǔ bàn] sponsor;hold;conduct

举动 [jǔ dòng] behavior ;conduct

举世闻名 [jǔ shì wén míng] be known to all the world;world renowned

举国 [jǔguó] the whole country

举目 [jǔmù] look up

举世瞩目 [jǔ shì zhǔ mù] the whole world is watching

举行 [jǔ xíng] take place;stage

举一反三 [jǔyīfǎnsān] derive or infer other things from one fact; make inferences by analogy

举重 [jǔ zhòng] weight-lifting

举足轻重 [jǔ zú qīng zhòng] be in an important position;every move has a huge impact on the situation

龃(齟) [jǔ] (adj) 〔龃龉〕[jǔ yǔ] 牙齿上下对不上。比喻意见不合，发生争执 irregular;discordant (teeth) (v) (figuratively) quarrel ; disagree

jù

巨 [jù] (adj)非常大 large;huge;giant (size);great;vast ＊一条小舟在海洋中是不能抵挡巨浪的。A small boat in the middle of the ocean is unable withstand the huge waves

巨大 [jù dà] huge;immense;gigantic

巨额 [jù é] a huge sum of(money); a large amount

巨型 [jù xíng] large (model);giant

巨头 [jù tóu] a leader;a prominent figure

炬 [jù] (n) 火把 a torch

讵(詎) [jù] (conj)岂;怎 but; however(pron) why;how?

拒 [jù] 1 (v)抵挡；抵抗 ward off with the hand;resist;oppose ＊那个大盗拒捕，並且跟警察发生枪战。That robber resisted the arrest and had a gun fight with the police 2 (v)不接受，不答应 reject; refuse; prevent; decline ＊她拒绝了我的帮忙。She refused my offer of help .

拒人於千里之外 [jù rén yū qiān lǐ zhī wài] unapproachable;no grounds for discussion

距 [jù] 1 (n) 两者间的长度 distance; discrepancy (conj) in ; between ＊新加坡和吉隆坡之间的距离是394 公里。The distance between Singapore and Kuala Lumpur is 394 kilometres. 2 (n) 雄鸟腿后面突出象脚趾的部分 a cock's spur

倨 [jù] (adj) 傲慢；自大 haughty; overbearing;proud

据(據) [jù] 1 (adv) 按照；依照 according (v)depend;rely ＊据报导，每天报纸的销路是三万份。According to the information ,the daily sales of newspapers is thirty thousand copies. 2 (n) 可以作证明的事物 evidence;proof ＊你没有证据，是不能提控任何人的。You cannot sue anyone without evidence. 3 (v) 占 occupy;take over;take possession of ＊封建地主常把贫农的田地据为已有。Feudal landlords used to take possession of land belonging to poor farmers.

据点 [jù diǎn] stronghold;foothold; fortified points

据理力争 [jù lǐ lì zhēng] to argue forcefully in accordance to reason

据说 [jù shuō] allegedly;be said to;it is said that

锯(鋸) [jù] 1 (n) 用来切削木料，石料，钢材等的刀具 saw ＊他在锯木厂已经工作了五个年头了。For the past five years, he has been working in the saw-mill.2 (v)用锯拉 to saw

踞 [jù] (v)蹲；坐 crouch;squat

剧(劇) [jù] 1 (n)午台表演戏 a play;an act;a theatrical performance ＊他们在路边观看广东戏剧。They were watching Cantonese opera by the road-side. 2 (adj) 厉害；很 violent;severe; strong＊两派的私会党徒博斗得很剧烈，造成五个人死亡。The two parties of gangsters were involved in a violent fight causing the death of five persons.

剧本 [jù běn] a play;script

剧场 [jù chǎng] theatre

剧情 [jù qíng] dramatic plot

剧团 [jù tuán] theatrical troupe;ensemble

剧院 [jù yuàn] theatre

遽 [jù] 1 (adj)急；仓猝 quick;rash; hasty ＊案情太复杂了，没有人敢遽下断言。Nobody dares to make a rash judgement as the whole case is too complicated.2 (adj) 害怕frightened ＊ 大火的突然发生，使到木屋居民很惶遽。The sudden occurence of fire makes the residents dwelling in plank houses very frightened.

具 [jù] 1 (n) 使用的器物。如：工具器具utensil;implements;apparatus; tools;instruments ＊ 试电笔是电器工人的一个重要工具。The testing pen(of electricity) is an important tool to the electrician.2 (v) 备；备有prepare;possess (adj) prepared; ready ＊美国具备着最先进的军事武器。The United States possesses the most advanced military weapons.3 (n) 量词a measure word ＊ 一具尸体 。a corpse

具体 [jù tǐ] concrete ;specific

具有 [jù yǒu] be provide with;possess

俱 [jù] (adv) 全；都altogether;wholly (adj) all;whole;both ＊购物中心里设有几百间店铺，可说是万物俱备。With the existence of hundreds of stalls in the shopping complex, it can be said that all goods are available.

俱乐部 [jù lè bù] club

惧(懼) [jù] (v) 害怕fear;dread; be afraid of (adj) afraid; (n) fear;apprehension ＊父母常吓孩子有鬼，造成他们惧怕黑暗。The parents often frighten their children of ghosts. This causes them to be afraid of the dark.

惧怯 [jù qie] timid;nervous;cowardly

惧色 [jù sè] appearance of being scared

飓(颶) [jù] (n)发生在大西洲西部和西印度群岛一带热带海洋上的大风暴 typhoon; hurricane

屦(屨) [jù] (n) 古代一种用麻，葛等制成的鞋 a kind of sandals made of hemp, used in olden days

聚 [jù] 1 (v)会集；集合assemble; gather together＊校长叫学生们聚集到讲堂内，准备报告一项重要的消息。The principal assembled all the students in the hall, intending to announce an important piece of news. 2 (v) 积聚 gather;collect; accumulate ＊ 他积聚了大量邮票。He has accumulated a large number of stamps.

聚餐 [jù cān] dine (lunch) together

聚会 [jù huì] gather together; meet

聚精会神 [jù jīng huì shén] concentrating one's attention

聚居 [jù jū] live closely together;live in a compact community

句 [jù] (n) 由词或单字组成的能表示一个完整意思的语言单位sentence;a clause;a phrase

句法 [jù fǎ] syntax;sentence cons-

truction
句号 [jù hào] a full stop (。)
句型 [jù xìng] sentence pattern

juān

圈 [juān] (v)用栏栅把家禽，家畜围起来 to encircle;surround (fowls, poultry) with fences ✱ 把鸡圈起来，以免它们跑到别处去。Surround the hens with fences so that they could not go to other places. 另见 [quān] [juàn]

捐 [juān] 1 (v) 舍弃 forsake; give up ✱ 在第二次世界大战时，无数的英勇战士在战场上为国捐躯。 In the Second World War, innumerable courageous warriors had given up their lives for their country on the battlefield. 2 (v) 捐助 contribute; donate ✱ 公众人士捐款救济火灾灾民。 Members of the public contributed money to help the fire victims
捐献 [juàn xiàn] contribute
捐赠 [juān zèng] donation

涓 [juān] (n)细小的流水a brook;a rivulet

娟 [juān] (adj)秀丽；美好beautiful; graceful

juǎn

卷(捲) [juǎn] 1 (v) 把东西弯成圆筒形 roll up ✱ 为了避免地上的水弄湿了裤脚，他把它卷起来小心地走。To prevent the bottom of his pants from being dampened by the water on the floor, he rolled up his pants and then walked cautiously. 2 (v) 掀起 raise up ✱ 在干旱天时，汽车跑在沙路上会卷起尘土。On dry days, cars running on sand roads will raise the dust and dirt up. 3 (n) 量词 a measure word; roll ✱ 一卷纸。 a roll of paper
卷发 [juǎn fā] curly hair
卷入 [juǎn rù] be drawn into
卷土重来 [juǎn tǔ chang lái] stage a comeback

juàn

倦 [juàn] 1 (adj) 疲乏；劳累tired;-fatigued;worn out;exhausted ✱ 经过一天的繁重工作后，他感到非常疲倦。After a day's heavy work, he became very tired. 2 (v) 厌烦 be tired of;annoyed ✱ 他的一切遭遇都不如意，使他对人生感到厌倦。 Most of his experiences in life had not been successful: this made him tired of life.

卷 [juàn] 1 (n) 书本 a book;a volume 2 (n) 考试用纸 test paper 3 (n) 量词 a measure word;a volume 另见 [juǎn]

眷 [juàn] 1 (n) 亲属 family;relatives 2 (v)关心；怀念 care for;look back-ward ✱ 那孤苦伶仃的老公公常常眷念他年青时快乐的日子。That lonely old man always looks back to those happy days in his youth.
眷属 [juàn shǔ] family

圈 [juàn] (n) 养猪羊等牲畜的栅栏 a pen (for cattle,sheep,etc) 另见 [juān] [quān]

绢 [juàn] (n) 一种很薄的丝织品 plain silk;silk taffeta

juē

撅 [juē] 1 (v) 翘起 to lift;to raise;stick up 2 (v) 折 break off (a branch)

嗟 [juē] (v) 叹息 sigh;deplore ✱ 那妇人常为自己的不幸遭遇而嗟叹。That woman often sighs over her misfortune 另见 [jiē]

jué

厥 [jué](v)气闭；昏倒faint (n)swoon; fainting fit ✱ 地下矿井的一名工人热得昏厥过去。 A worker in the underground mine fainted due to the extreme heat. 2 (pron)他的，那个 his;her;its;that;this

决 [jué] 1 (v) 决定determine;decide; resolve upon ✱经过这次的教训，我决定以后要谨慎处事。After this lesson, I have decided to be careful in handling matters in future. 2 (v)执行死刑pass sentence by;execute ✱那政治犯已被枪决。The political detainee was sentenced to death by shooting. 3 (adv) 一定 certainly;absolutely;no doubt;surely ✱一个平时好好的人，突然跑去自杀，决不会没有原因的。That a normal person should suddenly commit suicide is certainly not without reason.

决策 [jué cè] decide on (a plan, etc);decision;policy-making

决定权 [jué dìng quán] the decisive power;the casting-vote

决定性 [jué dìng xìng] decisive;crucial

决断 [jué duàn] make a firm decision

决裂 [jué liè] break with;rupture; sever friendly relation

决赛 [jué sài] (sports) finals;final contest

决心 [jué xīn] determination; resolve ;make up one's mind

决议 [jué yì] resolution;decision;resolve;decide

诀(訣) [jué] 1 (v) 分别（多指不易再见的离别）bid farewell;take leave (usually separation which is difficult to meet again) 2 (n)解决问题的好方法a craft;secret;key to success ✱那名作家说他成功的秘诀是辛勤苦干。That famous writer said that his key to success is industry and hard work.

诀窍 [jué qiào] secret to success; key to success;the knack of a thing

抉 [jué] (v)剔出；剜出to pick;rake; dig

抉择 [jué zé] select;to pick;choose

倔 [jué]〔倔强〕[jué jiàng] (adj)（性情）强硬，固执 obstinate; stubborn;resolute ✱他是个倔强的人，没有充份的理由是不容易说服他的。He is an obstinate person who cannot be convinced without sufficient reason.

另见 [juè]

掘 [jué] (v)挖；刨dig;excavate;hollow out ✱在郊外远足时，我们通常掘坑来埋垃圾。While hiking in the country,we usually dig a pit to bury the garbage.

掘出 [jué chū] dig out;unearth;excavate

掘穿 [jué chuān] dig through

掘壕 [jué háo] entrench;tunnel

掘金 [jué jīn] dig gold

掘井 [jué jǐng] dig a well

掘土机 [jué tǔ jī] a bulldozer

掘凿机 [jué zào jī] land dredge

崛 [jué] (adj)突起；兴起eminent; towering

攫 [jué] (v) 抓；引申为夺取 seize; grasp;snatch ✱在马六甲海峡常有海盗攫取渔人的财物。On the straits of Malacca, pirates often seize the properties of fishermen.

谲(譎) [jué] (adj) 欺诈，玩弄手段 crafty;cunning;treacherous ✱他在朋友之间挑拨离间，是个很诡谲的人。Sowing discord among friends, he is a very treacherous person.

角 [jué] 1 (v)竞争；争胜compete; contest;vie with ✱两国的足球队将在决赛中角逐今年的世界杯冠军。The soccer teams of both countries will contest for this year's World Cup championship. 2 (n) 角色 role (in drama or cinema ＊珍妮是罗密欧与朱丽叶这部影片中的女主角。 Jeanie plays the female role in 'Romeo and Juliet'.

角逐 [jué zhú] tussle;contend with; compete with...mastery;rivalry 另见 [jiǎo]

爵 [jué] 1 (n) 古代的酒器 a wine cup 2 (n) 爵位，君主国家封贵族的等级 peerage and court rank;noble

爵士 [jué shì] knight

爵士音乐 [jué shì yīn yuè] jazz music

嚼 [jué] (v) 咬碎食物 chew 另见 [jiǎo]

绝(絕) [jué] 1 (v) 断 discontinue; cease;become extinct ＊目前,白象已经绝种了！ At present white elephants are extinct. 2 (adj) 尽；完 run out of;exhaust 3 (adj) 精湛的，特别出色的 exquisite ＊中国杂技团在国家剧场表演绝技。 The Chinese Acrobatic troupe performed exquisite tricks in the National Theatre. 4 (adv) 极端 very; definitely; absolutely; extremely ＊ 师长们绝不允许少年吸毒。 Parents and teachers will definitely forbid young people to take drugs.

绝对 [jué duì] absolute;pure;positive

绝技 [jué jì] a superb skill

绝迹 [juéjì] completely disappear

绝交 [jué jiāo] break off relations with;sever relations with

绝路 [jué lù] heading or doom;doom;dead end

绝食 [jué shí] hunger strike

绝望 [jué wàng] have no hope for;despair;lose all hope for

绝无仅有 [jué wú jǐn yǒu] the one and only one

绝育 [jué yù] sterilization;sterilized; be sterilizied

绝种 [jué zhǒng] become extinct; exterminate a species

觉(覺) [jué] 1 (n) (人的器官)对外界刺激的感受和辨别 sense;(v) feel;perceive ＊盲人因为眼睛看不见，所以听觉变得很敏锐。 Unable to see with their eyes, the blind have developed a very sharp sense of hearing. 2 (v) 醒悟，清醒过来 be aware;understand;awake;enlighten;be conscious of;realize ＊经过一场风波之后,大家才觉悟到团结就是力量。 After the crisis, all the people became aware that unity is strength.

觉察 [jué chá] sense;discern;discover

觉醒 [jué xǐng] consciousness;awareness;awakening

jué

倔 [jué] (adj) 性情粗直，态度生硬 hard to please 另见 [juè]

jūn

均 [jūn] 1 (adj) 平等；相等 equal; average ; even;balanced ＊在本国,一个文员的薪水平均每月三百八十元。 In our country the average monthly pay of a clerk is $380. 2 (adj) 全；都 all ＊这座大厦的各项工程均已及时完成，下星期二可举行落成典礼。All the different phases of construction of the building have been completed and the inauguration ceremony can be held next Tuesday.

均等 [jūn děng] on an equal footing;equality

均衡 [jūn héng] balance

均势 [jūn shì] balance of power;relative equilibrium of forces

均匀 [jūn yún] even;uniform;uniformity

钧(鈞) [jūn] (n) 古代重量单位，合三十斤 a weight of thirty catties

君 [jūn] 1 (n) 封建帝王king;emperor a ruler 一般人的尊称 you (archaic); honorable

君主国 [jun zhǔ gnó] a monarchy

菌 [jūn] 1(n) 细菌，寄生微生物 teria;germs 2 (n) 隐花植物之一 mushrom
另见 [jun]

军(軍) [jūn] 1 (n)武装部队an army; troops; soldiers; corps ＊一个国家须要军队以防卫外来的侵犯。A nation needs to have an army to defend itself against external aggression.

军备 [jūn bèi] armaments

军队 [jūn duì] troops;army;forces (mil.)

军阀 [jūn fá] warlord

军费 [jūn fèi] military expenses

军国主义 [jūn guó zhǔ yì] militarism

军官 [jūn guān] officer; military officers

军火 [jūn huǒ] munitions

军舰 [jūn jiàn] warship;a man-of-war

军人 [jūn rén] military man;serviceman;military personnel

军事 [jūn shì] military affairs

军事基地 [jūn shì jī dì] military bases

军事家 [jūn shì jiā] military strategist

军衔 [jūn xián] military rank

军训 [jūn xùn] military training

军乐 [jūn yuè] military band (music)

军装 [jūn zhuāng] military uniform

jùn

俊 [jùn] 1 (adj)容貌美丽good-looking;handsome ＊电影上的男明星通常都很英俊。Most of the male stars in movie are handsome. 2 (adj)才智出众的bright;eminent;talented;distinguished ＊爱迪生是科学界中的一名俊才。Edison is a distinguished figure in the field of Science.

峻 [jùn] 1 (adj)高大 lofty;high;steep ＊要越过高山峻岭的喜马拉雅山脉很不容易。It is not easy to cross the Himalayas. 2 (adj)严厉；苛刻 stern;severe ＊古代的罗马帝王对奴隶强施严刑峻法。 Emperors of ancient Rome imposed severe penalties and laws upon their slaves.

峻峭 [jùn qiào] (of mountain,cliff) precipitous

骏(駿) [jùn] 好马a fine horse; a noble steed

骏才 [jùn cái] a man of talent

骏速 [jùn sù] swift;rapid

竣 [jùn] (v) 完毕 finish;complete;end (adj)complete ＊这部作品只差最后一章就可告竣。 Except for the last chapter, this book will be completed.

郡 [jùn] (n) 中国古代的行政区划单位，比县大 an administrative district;a country (archaic)

郡王 [jùn wáng] the grandson of an emperor

郡城 [jùn chéng] a prefectural city; a country town

K

kā

咖 [kā] (n) 译 音 字 a word used in transliterating

咖啡 [kāfēi] coffee

咖啡馆 [kā fēi guǎn] a coffee-house; a cafe

kǎ

卡 [kǎ] 1 (v) 梗塞 to choke; to stick * 她的拉链拉到一半便卡住了。Her zipper stuck half way up. 2 (n) 译音字 a word used in transliterating

卡车 [kǎchē] a car (for heavy load); a truck; a lorry

卡迭儿 [kǎdiéěr] cartel

卡路里 [kǎlù lǐ] calorie

卡片 [kǎpiàn] cards

卡通 [kǎtōng] cartoon

咯 [kǎ] (v) 呕，吐 to cough; to spit out * 他被阿飞打得咯出血来。He had been beaten so hard by the hoodlums that he spit out blood

另见 [gē]

kāi

开（開）[kāi] 1 (v) 张启 to open * 小陈开门迎接客人。Small Chen opened the door to receive the visitor 2 (v) 发起 to start. * 火车按时开行。The train started on time.

开办 [kāibàn] to set up; to start; to establish; to open up

开标 [kāi biāo] to open the tenders

开采 [kāi cǎi] to mine; to extract; to exploit

开彩 [kāi cǎi] to draw a lottery

开场 [kāi chǎng] the opening of a show

开场白 [kāi chǎngbái] opening speech or remarks; prologue

开车 [kāichē] to drive a vehicle

开诚布公 [kāi chéng bù gōng] to maintain mutual sincerity; to lay all the cards on the table; frank and straightforward

开除 [kāi chú] to dismiss; to expel; to discharge; to fire; to sack

开创 [kāi chuàng] to found; to start; to establish; to usher in

开单 [kāidān] to make a bill or a list

开刀 [kāi dāo] kill; to operate; operation (surgical)

开导 [kāidǎo] to enlighten; to explain and convince

开倒车 [kāi dǎochē] to turn the clock back; to turn back the wheel of history; to turn it in the opposite direction

开动 [kāi dòng] to start; to operate; to set into motion; to supply the

motivating power
开端 [kāi duān] the beginning; the inauguration (of affairs, selections, etc.)
开发 [kāi fā] to open up; to exploit; to tap
开饭 [kāi fàn] to have meal served
开方 [kāi fāng] to extract a root of a number
开放 [kāi fàng] to blossom; to be open
开赴 [kāifù] to set out for; to be on the way to; to move to
开工 [kāi gōng] to set to work; to go into operation
开关 [kāiguān] an electric switch; a mechanical control button
开国 [kāiguó] the founding of a new state power
开航 [kāi háng] to open up a sea route or airline; to set sail; to cast off (ship)
开花 [kāi huā] to blossom; to crack; to pop (e.g. pop-corn)
开化 [kāi huà] civilized; modernized
开怀 [kāihuāi] to relax the mind; to be at ease
开荒 [kāi huāng] to reclaim land; to open up waste land
开会 [kāi huì] to hold a meeting; to attend a meeting
开火 [kāi huǒ] to open fire
开价 [kāijià] to quote a price
开禁 [kāijìn] to cancel an existing prohibition; to relax restrictions
开垦 [kāi kěn] to reclaim land; to bring wasteland under cultivation
开矿 [kāi kuàng] to open mines
开阔 [kāi kuò] wide; broad
开朗 [kāi lǎng] open-minded
开路 [kāi lù] to open a new road; to lead the way; to pave the way
开路先锋 [kāi lù xiān fēng] the vanguard; a pioneer
开门 [kāi mén] open door
开门见山 [kāi mén jiàn shān] the door opens on a view of mountains — to put it bluntly; no beating about the bush; to come straight to the point
开门揖盗 [kāi mén yī dào] to invite trouble to oneself
开明 [kāi míng] enlightened
开幕 [kāi mù] inauguration; opening (ceremony)
开炮 [kāi pào] to open fire with guns; shelling; gunfire
开辟 [kāi pì] to open up; to usher in; to create; to break new ground; to pave (the way); to blaze the trail
开窍 [kāi qiào] to come to understand; to be enlightened
开山 [kāi shān] to quarry stones; to build roads by blasting mountains
开设 [kāi shè] to establish; to found; to start (shop, hospital, etc)
开始 [kaishǐ] to begin; to start; to begin with
开释 [kāi shì] to relax; to set free
开水 [kāishuǐ] boiled water
开通 [kāitōng] enlightened
开头 [kāi tóu] beginning; start; at the outset of
开脱 [kāi tuò] to extricate (oneself) from .....; to absolve (somebody of his responsibility)
开拓 [kāi tuò] to carve out; to open up
开挖 [kāiwā] to excavate; to clear out; to dig; to dredge
开外 [kāiwài] beyond; over (usually referring to a person's age)
开玩笑 [kāi wán xiào] to make a joke
开胃 [kāi wèi] to relish; to excite an appetite
开销 [kāi xiāo] to pay out; expen-

ses

开小差 [kāi xiǎo chāi] to desert (post); absent-minded

开心 [kāi xīn] merry; happy; joyous; pleasant

开学 [kāi xué] opening of a school term

开演 [kāiyǎn] to start a perform-ance

开眼界 [kāi yǎn jiè] to enlarge the field of vision; new experiences

开夜车 [kāi yè chē] to work late into the night

开源节流 [kāi yuán jié liú] to open up the source and regulate the flow; to develop resources and be economical

开凿 [kāi záo] to dig; to cut (a canal, etc.); to tunnel

开展 [kāizhǎn] to carry out; to develop; to launch; to promote

开张 [kāi zhāng] to open for business; to start

开支 [kāizhī] to spend; cost; expenditure; expenses

揩 [kāi] (v)擦，抹 to rub; to brush; to wipe; to clean. *校工在揩桌子。The school servant is wiping the tables

揩油 [kāiyóu] to wipe oil — to gain some advantage

kǎi

凯(凱) [kǎi] (n)胜利 triumph

凯歌 [kǎigē] song of victory

凯旋 [kǎixuán] to return in triumph

恺(愷) [kǎi] (adj) 快乐 joyful; contented

铠(鎧) [kǎi] (n) *古时战士所穿的铁甲 armour; coat of mail

楷 [kǎi] 1 (n)正体书法 a regular style of writing chinese 2 (n)法式，典范 a model; a pattern

楷模 [kǎi mó] a model; a pattern

慨 [kǎi] 1 (adj) 悲哀 sad; regretful 2 (adj) 慷慨；愤激 angry * 他对不合理的待遇感到愤慨。 He felt angry at the unreasonable treatment. 3 (adj) 大方 generous; large-minded

kān

堪 [kān] 1 (adj)可以，能够 able to 2 (v)忍受 sustain; bear * 他当众受到无理的责骂，心里很难堪。He finds it hard to bear being scolded unreasonably in public

勘 [kān] 1 (v)校对 to compare; to collate 2(v)调查 to investigate

勘测 [kāncè] to survey

勘察 [kānchá] to prospect

勘估 [kāngū] estimate

勘究 [kānjīu] investigate thoroughly

勘探 [kāntàn] to prospect; to survey; to examine on the spot; to investigate

勘误 [kān wù] corrigendum; to correct printing error

勘验 [kānyàn] investigate; examine by comparison

戡 [kān] 1 (v) 平定 to suppress; to subdue; to put down 2(v) 诛戮 to kill

戡乱 [kān luàn] to suppress a rebellion or riot; to put down an insurrection

刊 [kān] 1 (n) 排版印刷 to print 2 (n) 出版物 publications; journal

刊登 [kān dēng] to publish (news, story)

刊物 [kān wú] a periodical; a magazine; a journal; publications

刊行 [kānxíng] to publish; to issue; to bring out

刊印 [kān yìn] to print

刊载 [kān zài] to publish; to print

看 [kān] 1 (v) 守护,照料 to guard; to take care of; to look after *我们都出街，只剩妈妈在家看门。 We all go out leaving mother to look after the house. 2(v) 监视 to observe; to keep watch

看管 [kānguǎn] to take care of; to look after

看护 [kānhù] a nurse; to tend; to take care of

看守 [kāng shǒu] to guard; to watch; to keep a lookout

看守人 [kān shǒurén] a keeper; a warden

另见 [kàn]

龛（龕） [kān] (n) 供奉佛像，神位等的石室或小柜子 a shrine

kǎn

坎 [kǎn] (n) 低陷不平的地方，坑穴 a pit

坎坷 [kǎn kě] uneven; irksome; difficulties of the way; ups and downs

砍 [kǎn] (v) 用刀，斧等猛劈 to hew to chop; to cut off ＊ 他到山上去砍柴。He goes to the hill to hew wood for fire.

槛（檻） [kǎn] (n) 门限 door-sill

另见 [jiàn]

kàn

瞰 [kàn] (v) 俯视，向下看 to look down; to watch; to command a view

看 [kàn] 1 (v) 用眼观察 to look at; to see; to watch 2 (v) 阅读 to read

看病 [kàn bìng] to receive a patient; to consult a doctor

看不起 [kàn·bu qǐ] to look down upon; to despise; to belittle

看出 [kànchū] to find out

看穿 [kàn chuān] to see through; to be disillusioned

看待 [kàndài] to view; to assess; to look at; to treat

看得起 [kàn dé qǐ] to look up to; to attach great importance to; to hold in high esteem

看法 [kàn fǎ] a view; an opinion; the way one looks at something; an approach

看风使舵 [kàn fēng shǐ duó] flexible; react or respond according to circumstances; to trim the sails to the wind

看见 [kàn jiàn] to see (actually); can see

看来 [kàn lái] to appear; to take in the appearance of; to seem; to look like

看破 [kànpò] to see through; to detect; to discover (trick, falseness)

看齐 [kànqí] to keep abreast of; to keep pace with; to follow the example

看轻 [kàn qīng] to look down upon; to take no account of

看中 [kàn zhòng] to pick out; to select; to take a liking to

看重 [kànzhòng] to think highly of; to value (of person)

kāng

康 [kāng] (adj) 安宁，平安 peaceful; healthy

康乐 [kāng lè] happiness; delight.

康宁 [kāng níng] in good health; healthy

康庄大道 [kāng zhuāng dà dào] a broad path; a broad road

慷 [kāng] 〔慷慨〕 1 (adj) 情绪激昂 high-spirited; noble 2(adj) 大方，肯帮助人 generous; public-spirited ＊他对穷人的慷慨，为人所熟知。His generosity to the poor is well-known

慷慨激昂 [kāng kǎi jiáng] in lofty and energetic spirit; out of the fullness of one's heart

糠 [kāng] (n) 谷的皮 husk; chaff

káng

扛 [káng] (v) 用肩承担，承担 to carry; to shoulder; to undertake ＊ ＊ 他扛着担子到街上叫卖。He

shoulders the load and goes hawking on the street
另见 [gāng]

kàng

亢 [kàng] 1 (adj) 高傲 proud 2(adv) 过度 excessively; extremely ＊ 天气亢旱，草木快枯死了。 The weather is extremely hot and the plants are going to wither

伉 [kàng] (n) 配偶 spouse

伉俪 [kànglì] a pair; husband and wife

抗 [kàng] (v) 对敌 to resist; to oppose; to struggle against ＊ 那银行职员勇敢地抵抗强盗。 The bank clerk bravely resisted the robbers.

抗暴 [kàng bào] to struggle against tyranny

抗毒素 [kàng dú sù] antitoxin

抗旱 [kàng hàn] to fight against drought

抗击 [kàng jī] to resist

抗拒 [kàng jù] to resist; to oppose; to frustrate

抗生素 [kàng shēng sù] antibiotics

抗体 [kàng tǐ] anti-body

抗议 [kàng yì] to protest

抗战 [kàng zhàn] to offer resistance

抗争 [kàng zhēng] to dispute; to contend; to take issue

炕 [kǎng] 1 (v) 烘焙 to dry at a fire 2 (n) 烘暖的砖床 heated brick bed

kǎo

考 [kǎo] 1 (v) 测验 to test 2(v) 检查，检验 to examine 3 (v) 调查 to investigate ＊ 他考学生的英文 He examined the students in English.

考查 [kàochá] to investigate; to study (facts, conditions); to subject (somebody) to a good test; to examine; to judge

考察 [kǎo chá] to investigate; to study

考官 [kàoguān] examiners

考古学 [kǎogǔxué] archaeology

考核 [kǎo hé] to check up

考究 [kǎo jìu] closely examine; thoroughly study; to be particular about; to pay attention to

考据 [kǎojù] a comparative study of the text of a work

考卷 [kǎojuàn] examination papers

考虑 [kǎolǜ] to consider; to think over; to ponder over

考期 [kǎoqī] date of examination

考勤 [kǎo qín] (of work, study) to check attendance

考试 [kǎo shì] to sit for an examination; test

考验 [kǎoyàn] to make trial of; to test; an ordeal

考证 [kǎo zhèng] to research; a study of data

拷 [kǎo] (v) 打 to beat; to flog

拷贝 [kǎo beì] a copy or print (of film)

拷打 [kǎodǎ] to beat and extort a confession

拷问 [kǎowèn] to examine by torture; to try by torture

烤 [kǎo] 1 (v) 用火烘干，烘熟或取暖 to roast; to bake

kào

铐（銬）[kào] (n) 手械 handcuffs for prisoners

靠 [kào] (adv) 倚，依赖，信赖 to lean; to depend; to rely on ＊小孩的衣食都靠父母。 Children depend on their parents for food and clothing.

靠岸 [kàoàn] along the shore

靠边 [kào biān] keep to one side

靠不住 [kào bù zhù] undependable; unreliable

靠得住 [kào dé zhù] reliable; dependable; trustworthy

靠近 [kàojìn] to be near by; to be

close to
靠拢 [kàolǒng] alongside; to be drawn to; to come close to
靠山 [kàoshān] a patron; a stand by; a supporter; a protector;mainstays ; a protector; near to a hill

kē

珂 [kē] (n)象玉的石 an inferior kind of jade
柯 [kē] 1 (n)草木的枝茎a stalk; a branch 2 (n)斧头的柄the handle of an axe 3 (n) 姓氏 surname
苛 [kē] 1 (adj)刻薄，过分cruel; harsh 2 (adj)繁重，使人难于忍受 heavy; troublesome; unbearable * 苛政猛于虎。 The harsh system of government is fiercer than a tiger.
苛待 [kedaì] to treat with harshness and severity
苛捐杂税 [kējuān-záshuì] multifarious takes; exorbitant taxes and miscellaneous levies
苛刻 [kē kè] stern; harsh
苛酷 [kē kù] severe; harsh; cruel
苛求 [kē qìu] to ask too much; to be too exacting
苛税 [kēshuì] heavy taxation
苛责 [kēzé] to rebuke; to reprove
疴 [kē] (n) 病 disease; ailment; sickness
疴痢 [kēlì] dysentry
疴吐 [kētǔ] diarrhoea and vomitting
颗(顆) [kē] 量词，用于计算粒状的东西 a measure word for grains, kernels, etc.
窠 [kē] (n) 鸟兽住的巢穴 a nest; a den
磕 [kē] (v) 碰撞，敲击 to knock; to bump
磕头 [kētóu] kow tow
瞌 [kē] (v) 倦时合眼坐睡 to doze; to mod
瞌睡 [kēshui] to drowse; to doze, to nod
科 [kē] 1(n)类别，部门a classification; a department; a class; a category * 文科 The Faculty of arts. 理科 The Faculty of Science. 卫生科 The Department of Health. 2定罪 to sentence * 法官科以五年监禁予这强盗。 The judge sentenced the robber to five years in prison. 3 (v) 征抽 (税) to levy (taxes) * 政府为了支付国家的费用而科税。The government levies taxes for national expenses.
科技 [kējì] science and technology
科目 [kē mù] oubject branch of a study
科税 [kē shuì] to levy a tax
科学 [kē xue] science
科学家 [kēxuéjiā] scientists
科学试验 [kēxuéshíyàn] scientific experiment
科学性 [kēxuéxìng] scientific spirit
科学仪器 [kēxuéyígì] scientific instruments
科长 [kē zhǎng] head of a department; chief of a section
科罪 [kē zuì] to deal with a crime

ké

颏(頦) [ké] (n)下巴；在口部的下面 the chin
壳(殼) [ké] (n) 坚硬的外皮 husk; shell; crust
另见 [qiào]
咳 [ké] (v)喉间发声吐出痰或空气 to cough
咳血 [kéxuě] haemoptysis
另见 [hāi]

kě

可 [kě] 1 (aux v)应许 can; may; able * 妈妈，我可以出去吗？ Mother, may I go out? 2 (adv) 到底，究竟 ever * 你可有问过她？Have you ever asked her? * 你可别忘了！Don't you ever forget.
可爱 [kěai] lovable; lovely; charming

可悲 [kěbēi] deplorable; pitiable

可不是 [kěbúshì] that's right; that's it

可乘之机 [kě chéng zhī jī] (to give somebody) an opening to exploit; avail oneself of the opportunity to ...

可耻 [kě chǐ] shameful; ignominous; despicable

可歌可泣 [kě gē kě gì] worthy of praise and emotional tears; heroic and moving; laudable

可观 [kěguān] appreciable; considerable.

可贵 [kěguì] valuable; worth; precious; fine

可恨 [kě hèn] hateful

可嘉 [kějiā] worthy of praise; praiseworthy

可见 [kě jiàn] it is obvious that; it can be seen that; it is apparent that

可敬 [kě jìng] worthy of respect; respectable

可靠 [kě kào] reliable; trustworthy; dependable

可可 [kě kě] cocoa.

可控硅 [kě kòng guì] controlable silicon

可口 [kě kǒu] palatable; delicious; tasty

可兰经 [kě lán jīng] the Koran

可怜 [kělián] pitiable; pitiful

可恼 [kěnáo] irritating

可能 [kě néng] possible; possibility; maybe

可能性 [kěnéngxìng] possibility; potentiality

可怕 [kě pài] terrible; dreadful; horrible; awful

可巧 [kě qiǎo] happen to; as it happens

可亲 [kěqīn] amiable; agreeable

可取 [kě qǔ] worth having; useful

可溶性 [kě róng xìng] solubility

可塑性 [kě sùìng] plasticity

可是 [kě shì] but

可望而不可即 [kě wàng ér bù kějí] beyond reach; within sight but beyond reach

可恶 [kěwù] hateful; wicked; disgusting

可惜 [kě xī] unfortunately; pitiful

可笑 [kě xiào] ridiculous; absurd

可心 [kěxīn] nice; pleasing; admirable; just as one would like

可疑 [kèyí] suspicious; doubtful; questionable; dubious

可以 [kě yǐ] may; can; will do; good enough; passable

渴 [kě] (adj) 口干想喝水 thirsty; thirst * 那马在河中痛饮解渴。The horse satisfied its thirst at the river.

渴望 [kě wàng] to yearn; to eagerly hope for; to long for; to thirst for

kè

恪 [kè] (v) 恭敬 to respect. (adj) respectful; faithful

恪守 [kèshǒu] to follow faithfully

恪遵 [kèzūn] to obey respectfully

客 [kè] 1 (n) 主人的对面 guest 2 (n) 到外地的人 a visitor 3 (n)人的泛称 a person * 政客 a politician; 搭客 a passenger; 顾客 a customer.

客车 [kèchē] a passenger train

客串 [kèchuàn] amateur player

客船 [kèchuán] passenger ship

客观 [kèguān] objective; objectivity; objective

客观主义 [kè guān zhǔyì] objectivism

客气 [kè qì] polite; civil

客人 [kè rén] a guest; a visitor

客套 [kètào] formality; politeness; conventional greetings
客厅 [kètīng] a sitting-room; a drawing-room
客栈 [kè zhàn] an inn; a lodging; a hotel
课 [kè] 1 (n)学业 lesson; classwork 2 量词 a measure word (e.g. lesson) 3 征抽（捐税）to impose (taxes)
课本 [kè běn] a text-book
课程 [kèchéng] a course of study; a ourriculum
课程表 [kè chéng biǎo] schedule
课期 [kèqī] oooolon
课室 [kè shì] classroom
课税 [kèshuì] taxation
课题 [kètí] a subject; a theme; main topic
课外活动 [kè wàihuódòng] extra-curricular activities
课文 [kèwén] lessons in a text-book
克 [kè] 1 (v) 能 can; able to 2 (v) 制胜 to surmount; to subdue; to overcome ＊以柔克刚。to overcome the stronger side with soft methods 3 (n) 量词；公制重量单位 gram
克敌制胜 [kè dí zhì shèng] to defeat the enemy and win victory
克分子 [kè fēn zǐ] gram molecule; mole
克服 [kèfú] to surmount; to over-come
克己 [kèjǐ] have one's passions or emotions under control
克己奉公 [kèjǐ féng gōng] restrain oneself but devoted to the public
克制 [kè zhì] to restrain; to restrict; to control (oneself)
刻 [kè] 1 (v)用刀子等工具挖，划 to carve; to engrave; to sculpture 2 量词，十五分钟的时间 measure word: a quarter of an hour 3 (adj) 苛虐 harsh＊因为老板娘太刻薄，女佣辞工不做了。The maid-servant resigned from her work because the mistress had been too harsh to her.
刻板 [kèbǎn] mechanical; inflexible; dogmatic
刻薄 [kè bó] acrimonious; acrid; harsh
刻不容缓 [kè bùróng huǎn] not a minute to lose, very critical; pressing
刻骨铭心 [kè gǔ míng xīn] well ingrained, unforgettable
刻画 [kèhuà] to portray; to depict
刻苦 [kèkǔ] painstaking; industrious
刻下 [kèxià] at present; now
刻舟求剑 [kè zhōu qíu jiàn] using the same old approach and overlooking the changed situation

kěn

垦（墾）[kěn] (v) 耕地 to plough; to open new soil; to reclaim land＊百多年前，许多华人和印度人来南洋垦荒。More than a hundred years ago, many Chinese and Indians came to South-east Asia to reclaim barren lands.
垦荒 [kěnhuāng] to open up barren lands; to reclaim wasteland
垦种 [kěnzhòng] to plough and sow
恳（懇）[kěn] (adj) 真诚 sincere; frank.＊我诚恳地盼望你不久即告康复。I sincerely hope you will soon recover.
恳切 [kěngiè] sincere
恳请 [kěngǐng] to entreat; to implore; to beg earnestly
恳亲会 [kěngīnhuì] a friendly gathering; a social meeting
恳求 [kěngíu] to implore; to entreat
恳商 [kěn shāng] to consult
肯 [kěn] (v) 愿意 to consent to; to agree to; be willing to (adj) willing ＊他肯接受意见，所以工

作做得好。As he is willing to accept suggestions, he does his work well.

肯定 [kěndìng] to affirm; to approve; to assert; affirmative; positive; determined

啃 [kěn] (v)咬嚼 to bite; to chew

kēng

坑 [kēng] (n) 地面陷下处 a pit; a sunken hole in ground

坑道 [kēngdòw] a gallery; a tunnel; an underground passage

坑害 [kēnghài] to make false accusation; to frame up

坑渠 [kēngqú] a sewer; to entrap a drain

吭 [kēng] (v)出声 to utter; to speak 另见 [háng]

铿(鏗) [kēng] (n) 金石声；响亮的声音 the jingling of metals; jingling

铿锵 [kēngqiāng] jingling

kōng

空 [kōng] 1(n)天空 the sky; the air; heaven 2(adj) 虚 empty; vacant; vain * 火灾发生时那屋子是空的。The house was empty when the fire broke out.*我们的一切努力都落空了。All our efforts were in vain. 3 不切实际的 unreal; unrealistic *他沉迷于广告艺术的空想世界里。He drowned himself in the unreal world of advertising art.

空洞 [kōngdòng] devoid of content

空话 [kōng huà] empty or meaningless talk

空欢喜 [kōng huānxǐ] baseless rejoicings

空间 [kōngjiān] space

空军 [kōng jùn] an air force; a flying corps

空口无凭 [kōng kǒu wú píng] to speak without evidence; oral evidence is no proof

空旷 [kōng kuàng] open; wide; spacious

空气 [kōng qì] air; atmosphere

空前 [kōng qián] never before; unprecedented

空前绝后 [kōng qián jué hoù] without parallel in history; without either precedent or sequel

空前未有 [kōng gián wěi yǒu] it has not been known before; without precedent

空谈 [kōngtán] mere words; empty (idle) talk; gossip

空投 [kōng tóu] airdrop

空头 [kōng tóu] phoney (writer, etc.)

空头支票 [kōng tóu zhī piào] a dishonoured cheque, an empty promise; lip service

空望 [kōng wàng] an empty hope;

空袭 [kōng xí] an air-raid

空想 [kōng xiǎng] to be under illusion; illusion; fantasy

空心 [kōng xīn] hollow; tubular

空虚 [kōng xū] vacant; empty; void of content

空中 [kōng zhōng] in the air

空中楼阁 [kōng zhōng lóu gé] castles in the air; ivory towers

另见 [kòng]

kǒng

孔 [kǒng] 1 (n)小洞，窟窿 a hole; an opening; an aperture

孔道 [kǒngdào] a thoroughfare; important roads

孔雀 [kǒng què] the peacock

孔穴 [kǒngxuè] a hole; an opening; an aperture

孔子 [kǒng zǐ] Confucius

恐 [kǒng] (v) 害怕；畏惧 to fear; to apprehend; be afraid of

恐怖 [kǒng bú] horror; terror

恐吓 [kǒng hè] to terrify; to frighten; to intimidate

恐慌 [kǒng huāng] panicky; panic-stricken

恐惧 [kǒng jù] to frighten; to fear; to dread

恐怕 [kǒngpà] perhaps; (I am) afraid...

kòng

空 [kòng] 1 (v) 腾出来 to leave blank; to empty 2 (n) 闲暇 leisure; free

空白 [kòng bái] blank space; unfilled space

空额 [kòngé] vacancy

空隙 [kòngxì] an empty space; a gap; a loophole

空闲 [kòngxián] free time; leisure; not busy

空余 [kòngyú] leisure; unoccupied

空子 [kòngzǐ] an occupied space; an opening

控 [kòng] 1 (v) 操纵，控制 to sue; to charge; to accuse *那官员被控贪污罪。That official is accused of corruption. 2 (v) 告发，揭发 to control; to check; to rein in; to overrule

控告 [kòng qào] to charge; to accuse; to proceed against; to impeach

控诉 [kòng sù] to appeal; an appeal to a higher authority

控制 [kòng zhì] to control; to dominate; to contain

kǒu

口 [kǒu] 1 (n) 嘴 the mouth 2 (n) 出入经过的地方 an entrance; the mouth (as of river); a gorge; a pass 3 (n) 破裂的地方 slit; crack; an opening 4 量词 a measure word (for person, pig, well, etc.)

口才 [kǒucái] eloquence; the ability to talk

口吃 [kǒuchī] falter; to stammer; to stutter

口齿 [kǒuchǐ] the ability to talk

口袋 [kǒudài] a bag; a coat pocket

口风琴 [kǒufeng qín] harmonica

口供 [kǒugòng] confession; testimony; deposition

口号 [kǒu hào] a slogan; catchword

口红 [kǒu hóng] rouge; a lip-stick

口惠而实不至 [kǒu huier shíbú zhì] lip service only

口技 [kǒujì] mimicry; an entertainment by vocal imitation

口角 [kǒu jué] quarrel; dispute

口径 [kǒujìng] calibre; gauge; aperture

口诀 [kǒujué] rhyme for a formula; mnemonic

口口声声 [kǒu kǒu shēng shēng] glibly (profess, say, announce); to keep on proclaiming; to say something repeatedly

口粮 [kǒuliáng] rations; provisions; food grain

口令 [kǒulìng] password; word of command

口蜜腹剑 [kǒu mì fú jiàn] honey words with malicious intent

口沫 [kǒumò] saliva; spit

口气 [kǒu qì] expression; tone; a manner of speaking

口腔 [kǒugiāng] oral cavity

口若悬河 [kǒu ruò xuàn hé] eloquence in speech

口哨儿 [kǒu shà ǒr] whistle; whistling

口实 [kǒushí] basis or material (for gossip)

口试 [kǒushì] oral examination

口是心非 [kǒu shí xīn fēi] double faced; hypocrisy

口述 [kǒushù] to dictate

口头 [kǒutóu] verbal; oral
口头禅 [kǒu tóu chán] cant; common saying
口头语 [kǒutóuyǔ] common place sayings; conventional or habitual expressions
口味 [kǒuwèi] taste; flavour
口吻 [kǒu wěn] tone of speech
口信 [kǒuxìn] a verbal message
口译 [kǒu yì] interpretation; to interprete
口音 [kǒuyīn] accent; enunciation
口语 [kǒu yǔ] spoken language
口罩 [kǒuzhào] mouth-mask
口诛笔伐 [kǒu zhū bǐ fá] criticize in words and in writing
口子 [kǒu zǐ] a crack

kòu

寇 [kòu] 1 (n) 盗匪；侵略者 highway men; an enemy; an invader 2 (v)侵略，进犯 to invade; to rob; to plunder
叩 [kòu] (v)敲；打 to knock; to strike lightly; to tap
叩拜 [kòu bài] to worship; to pay respects to
叩辞 [kòucí] to take one's leave of a superior
叩见 [kòujiàn] to visit a superior
叩头 [kòutóu] to kowtow
扣 [kòu] 1 (v)套住；拢住，盖住 to hook on; to fasten 2 (n) 钮子；绳结；钩搭 a button; a knot; a hook 3 (v) 从中减除 to discount; to rebate; to reduce
扣除 [kòuchú] to deduct; to take off
扣留 [kòu líu] to detain
扣帽子 [kòumàozǐ] to tag (somebody) with a label; to be branded as
扣门 [kòu mén] knock at the door
扣人心弦 [kòu ren xīn xián] stirring; moving; gripping
扣押 [kòu yā] detain; put in jail
扣子 [kòu zǐ] a knot: a button

kū

枯 [kū] (adj)失去水分 dried; dried up; withered
枯黄 [kū huáng] withered; wilted
枯脊 [kūjí] to grow thin
枯竭 [kū jié] to dry up (spring of water; of thought, etc.); to exhaust
枯渴 [kū kě] be parched dry; be dried up; be exhausted (drained)
枯木逢春 [kū mù féng chūn] a withered tree comes to life again in spring
枯萎 [kū weǐ] to decay; to rot
枯朽 [kū xǐu] to decay; to wither and die
枯燥 [kūzào] monotonous; uninteresting; dry and dull
骷 [kū] (n) 没有皮肉毛发的尸首或头骨 a skeleton; skull of the dead
窟 [kū] 1 (n)洞穴 a hole; a cave; a furrow. *在怡保附近有许多石窟。There are many stone caves near Ipoh.
窟窿 [kūlóng] a hole; an opening
窟室 [kū shì] a cave-dwelling
哭 [kū] (v) 因悲痛或激动而流泪发声 to cry; to wail; to weep
哭哭啼啼 [kū kū tí tí] to wail and whine; to keep on weeping
哭泣 [kūqí] to cry; to weep; to sob
哭丧着脸 [kū·sang·zhe liǎn] to show a melancholic face
哭诉 [kū sù] tell with tears

kǔ

苦 [kǔ] 1 (adj) 苦味；跟“甜”相对 bitter 2 (adj)难受；痛苦 painful; painstaking (n) suffering; pains
苦处 [kǔchù] a hardship; difficulty; suffering; plight; distress
苦斗 [kǔ dòu] fight desperately; to struggle
苦功 [kǔ gōng] painstaking effort.
苦工 [kǔgōng] hard toil (labour); penal servitude; drudgery

苦瓜 [kǔguā] bitter gourd

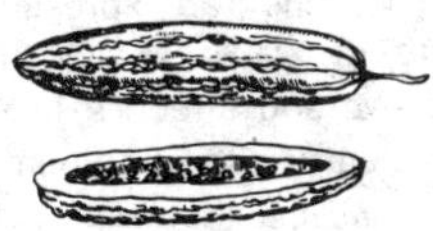

苦海 [kǔhǎi] the miserable world
苦尽甘来 [kǔjìngānlái] after bitterness comes sweetness
苦口婆心 [kǔ kǒu-póxīn] advice in earnest words and with good intention
苦乐 [kǔlè] joys and sorrows; pain and pleasure
苦力 [kǔlì] a coolie; a labourer
苦闷 [kǔ mèn] gloomy
苦难 [kǔnàn] hardships; calamity; sufferings
苦恼 [kǔnǎo] trouble; annoyance; suffering; worried; vexed
苦求 [kǔ qíu] implore earnestly
苦水 [kǔshuǐ] bitter water; untold sufferings
苦头 [kǔtóu] bitterness; sufferings
苦心 [kǔxīn] taking great pains; painstaking
苦刑 [kǔxíng] severe punishment; torture
苦心孤诣 [kǔxīngūyì] unequalled by others in study and research
苦学 [kǔxué] study hard
苦战 [kǔzhàn] to engage in hard battle
苦衷 [kǔzhōng] difficulty; embarrassment

kù

酷 [kù] 1 (adj) 残暴狠毒 cruel; oppressive; harsh; violent *割掉犯人的耳朵是一种酷刑。 Cutting off the ears of a criminal is a cruel punishment. 2 (adv) 很，极 very; extremely
酷爱 [kùài] to have an ardent love for
酷法 [kùfǎ] harsh or cruel laws
酷烈 [kù liè] severe; harsh; intense
酷疟 [kù nuè] tyrannical; harsh; cruel; oppressive
酷热 [kùrè] exceedingly hot
酷暑 [kù shǐn] torrid summer heat
酷肖;酷似 [kùxiāo, kùsì] very similar; a close resemblance; resemble closely
酷刑 [kùxíng] torture; severe punishment

库（庫）[kù] (n)贮存东西的房屋或地方 a storehouse; a depot; a magazine
库存 [kù cún] stocks; stores; to store up
库房 [kù fáng] a treasury; a vault; bursary
库项 [kùxiàng] stores in a treasury.

裤（褲）[kù] (n)衣服的下身部分 trousers; pants
裤衩 [kù chǎ] underpants
裤腿 [kù tuǐ] trouser legs
裤子 [kùzi] trousers

kuā

夸（誇）[kuā] 1 (v) 表扬，称赞 take pride in; praise; extol * 大家夸他学习刻苦认真。 All the people praise him for being hardworking and serious in learning. 2 (v)言过於实，说空话 to exaggerate; to boast; to brag * 有不少人爱夸耀自己的才干。 Many people love to boast of their own abilities.
夸大 [kuādà] to exaggerate; to magnify; to overstate
夸大狂 [kuādà kuáng] megalomana; a megalomaniac
夸奖 [kuā jiǎng] to praise
夸口 [kuā kǒu] to boast; to brag
夸夸其谈 [kuā kuā qí tán] flippantly boastful
夸耀 [kuā yào] to display; to show off; to brag about
夸张 [kuā zhāng] brag; to exaggerate

kuā

胯 [kuā] (n)两股之间 the thigh; the legs

胯下 [kuāxià] the crotch between the legs

跨 [kuā] 1 (v)迈步 to stride; to step over 2 (v)骑 to bestride; to ride ＊那将军跨在马上多威风。How grand the general looks as he rides a horse. 3 (v) 越过 cross; to encroach upon; to pass over

跨步 [kuābù] to straddle

跨国公司 [kuāguógōngsī] a multinational corporation

跨越 [kuā yuè] pass over; excel; surpass

kuài

会（會）[kuài]清算账目 to balance an account

会计 [kuàijì] accounting

会计员 [kuài jì yuán] an accountant

另见 [huì]

侩（儈）[kuài] (n) 指社会里介绍买卖从中取利的人：市侩 a broker; an agent

狯（獪）[kuài] (adj)狡狯，狡猾 sly; cunning

脍（膾）[kuài] (n)切细的肉 minced meat or fish

脍炙人口 [kuài zhì rén kǒu] on everybody's lips; popular

块（塊）[kuài] 1 (n) 成件的东西 a lump; a mass; a piece. 2 量词 a measure word: piece, lump.＊一块布 a piece of cloth.＊一块肥皂 a cake of soap

块茎 [kuàijìng] tuber

块状 [kuài zhuàng] lumpy; massive

快 [kuài] 1 (adj) 速度大，跟“慢”相对quick; swift; fast; rapid 2 (adj)锋利 sharp. ＊快刀 a sharp knife 3 (adj) 高兴，喜欢 glad; happy; joyful

快报 [kuài bào] quick news bulletin; newsflash

快畅 [kuàichàng] refreshing; pleasant

快车 [kuàichē] an express train

快刀斩乱麻 [kuài dāo zhǎn luàn má] decisive and effective like a sharp knife cutting through hemp

快感 [kuàigǎn] pleasant sensation; agreeable feeling

快活 [kuài huó] delight; pleased; pleasure; gay; cheerful; happy

快捷 [kuàijié] promptly; quickly; in a brief time; hasty

快乐 [kuàilè] happy

快利 [kuàilí] sharp; keen

快马加鞭 [kuài mǎ jiā biān] to apply the whip to the galloping horse; with the greatest urgency

快慢 [kuàimàn] rate of speed

快事 [kuàishì] a gratifying event

快速 [kuàisù] fast; high-speed

快慰 [kuài wèi] elated

筷 [kuài] (n) 筷子 chopsticks

kuān

宽（寬）[kuān] 1 (adj) 阔，跟“窄”相对 spacious; broad 2 (v) 放宽，使松缓 to relax; to be lenient; to enlarge; to extend 3 (adj) 容忍 lenient; tolerant

宽敞 [kuān chǎng] spacious

宽绰 [kuān chuò] well-off; spacious

宽大 [kuān dà] generous; to be lenient

宽大为怀 [kuān dà wéi huái] magnanimous towards others

宽广 [kuān guǎng] wide; spacious

宽宏大量 [kuān hóng dà liàng] liberal-minded; magnanimous; broad-minded and generous

宽厚 [kuān hòu] generous; kind

宽怀 [kuān huái] take things easy; easy in mind; light-hearted

宽阔 [kuān kuò] broad; extensive; wide

宽猛并济 [kuān měng bìng jì] severity coupled with gentleness

宽仁 [kuānrén] generosity; magnanimity
宽容 [kuān róng] to tolerate; to be lenient to
宽恕 [kuān shù] to forgive; to tolerate
宽慰 [kuān wéi] comforting
宽心 [kuānxīn] be easy in mind; pleased
宽裕 [kuān yù] in good financial standing; well-to-do
宽窄 [kuā zhǎi] width.

kuǎn

款 [kuǎn] 1 (n) 钱，经费 monoy ＊五百元是一笔不小的款项。Five hundred dollars is a big sum of money. 2 (n) 法令，规章等分条列举的项目 an article or clause (in the orders, rules and regulations, agreements, etc.) 3 (adj) 殷勤，诚挚 sincere; real; true ＊他以佳肴美酒款待嘉宾。He sincerely treated the guests to a good dinner.
款待 [kuǎndài] to entertain
款款 [kuǎnkuǎn] slowly and quietly
款式 [kuǎn shì] a style; a fashion; a pattern; a sample
款项 [kuǎnxiàng] money.

kuāng

匡 [kuāng] 1 (v) 纠正 to correct 2 (v) 帮助 to assist; to help; to aid
诓（誆）[kuāng] (v) 欺骗，哄骗 to deceive; to cheat
筐 [kuāng] (n) 篮子 a basket
筐子 [kuāngzi] a basket

kuáng

狂 [kuáng] 1 (adj) 发疯，精神失常 mad; eccentric; crazy; insane 2 (adj) 任情，任意 wild; unrestrained 3 (adj) 猛烈 violent; outrageous; excited
狂放 [kuáng fàng] wild; unrestrained
狂吠 [kuáng fèi] to bark
狂风 [kuáng fēng] gale
狂喊 [kuáng hǎn] to bawl
狂欢 [kuáng huān] to hold carnival; to have a lively celebration
狂澜 [kuáng lán] roaring waves
狂热 [kuáng rè] frantic; feverish; frenzied
狂人 [kuángrén] a madman; a maniac
狂妄 [kuáng wàng] rowdy; disorderly; ill-behaved; arrogant
狂妄自大 [kuáng wàng zìdà] to be arrogant and conceited
狂喜 [kuáng xǐ] frantic with joy; extreme (wild) joy; be overjoyed
狂想 [kuáng xiǎng] extravagant thoughts
狂言 [kuáng yán] crazy remarks
诳（誑）[kuáng] (v) 欺骗，哄骗 to deceive; to lie; to cheat; to mislead
诳言 [kuáng yú] lies; falsehood
诳骗 [kuáng piàn] to deceive; to impose upon; to cheat; to defraud

kuàng

旷（曠）[kuàng] 1 (adj) 空阔 spacious ＊婆罗洲地旷人稀。Borneo has spacious land space but a small population. 2 (v) 使空缺 to desert; to skip 3 (v) 荒废，耽搁 leave empty; neglect ＊老板说他旷工，要辞退他。The boss said he neglected his work, so he will be sacked.
旷工 [kuàng gōng] to skip work
旷课 [kuàng kè] to skip school
旷日持久 [kuàng rì chí jiǔ] procrastination; laid waste for too long; a long drawn-out; to drag on
旷野 [kuàng yě] a widlerness; a vast plain
矿（礦）[kuàng] 1 (n) 生于地中，须采掘而得的材物

minerals 2 (n) 开采矿物的场所 a mine

矿藏 [kuàngcáng] deposit; mineral reserves; mine

矿产 [kuàng chǎn] mineral products; mine

矿工 [kuàng gōng] a miner; a mine-worker

矿井 [kuàng jǐng] a mine pit; the shaft of the mine

矿苗 [kuàng miáo] out crop of mineral or ore

矿山 [kuàng shān] mining area; mining

矿石 [kuàng shī] ore

矿水 [kuàng shuǐ] mineral water

矿物 [kuàng wù] mineral

矿业 [kuàng yè] mining indusrtry

况 [kuàng] (n)情形 condition; circumstance; situation ＊近况如何？How's your condition lately? 2 (adv)而且，甚且（更深一层的意思）moreover; furthermore; in addition; besides ＊我不喜欢这房子，况且它的价钱也太高 I did not like the house; moreover, it was too high-priced.

框 [kuàng] (n)门窗，器物四边的架子 a frame; a framework

眶 [kuàng] (n)眼睛的四周 surroundings of the eye; the socket of the eye

kūi

亏(虧) [kuī] 1 (v)损失 to lose ＊他将房屋亏本出售。He sold his house at a loss 2 (adj) 欠缺，短少 to wane; deficient; short of ＊总额还亏十元。The sum comes short by ten dollars. 3 (v) 由于，幸而 owing to; thanks to

亏得 [kuī dé] fortunately; it is fortunate that

亏耗 [kuīhào] to lose money

亏空 [kuī kōng] deficit; bankruptcy; a total failure; embezzle

亏欠 [kuī qiàn] in debt; in arrears; deficiency

亏蚀 [kuī shì] wane; to be on the wane; to suffer loss

亏损 [kuīsùn] to lose money; loss; deficit

亏心 [kuī xīn] discreditable; ungrateful; a bad conscience

窥(窺) [kuī] (v)偷看 to peep; to pry ＊贼人从门缝窥看屋内的动静。The thief peeped through the door slit at the happenings in the house.

窥测 [kuīcè] to make observations; to conjecture; to spy out

窥察 [kuīchà] to ferret out; to look into; to pry into

窥见 [kuījiàn] spy; observe

窥伺 [kuīsì] to spy into; to peep

窥探 [kuītàn] to detect; to pry; to spy over

窥听 [kuītīng] to listen stealthily

窥占 [kuīzhān] to encroach on

盔 [kuī] (n) 用来保护头的帽子 a helmet ＊摩托单车骑士须戴头盔。A motor-cyclist should wear a helmet.

盔甲 [kuī jiǎ] armour.

kúi

揆 [kuí] 1 (v)揣测，估量 to calculate; to estimate; to guess; consider 2 (v)掌管，管理 to administer; to manage; to govern

暌 [kuí] (adj)分离 separated; apart

睽 [kuí] (v) 张大眼睛 to stare at ＊众目睽睽 stared at by everyone; everybody staring

葵 [kuí] (n) 蔬类植物，如葵菜，葵花等 the mallow; the sunflower

葵菜 [kuícaì] the edible mallow

葵花 [kuí huā] the sunflower

葵倾 [kuíqǐng] lean towards — as the sunflower to the sun — longing affection

葵扇 [kuíshǎn] palm-leaf fan

魁 [kuí] 1 (n) 为首的，头子 the head; the chief 2 (adj) 高大 great; eminent; stalwart; gigantic
魁伟 [kuíwěi] well built; stately
魁梧 [kuíwú] well built (of a person)

逵 [kuí] (n) 通各方的道路 cross-roads; a thorough-fare

kuǐ

傀 [kuǐ] (adj) 伟大，怪异 great; gigantic; monstrous
傀儡政府 [kuǐlěizhèngfǔ] a puppet government
傀儡 [kuǐlěi] a puppet-doll

kuì

馈（饋）[kuì] (v) 赠送 to present as gift

愦（憒）[kuì] (adj) 昏乱，糊涂 troubled; confused

溃（潰）[kuì] 1 (v) 大水冲开堤岸 to overflow; to rush as a stream 2 (adj) 散乱 confused; defeated; dispersed 3 (n) 腐烂 ulcer; sore
溃败 [kuì bài] defeat
溃不成军 [kuì bù chéng jún] badly routed; disastrous defeat
溃烂 [kuìlàn] to fester; to ulcerate
溃灭 [kuìmiè] collapse; extinction
溃散 [kuìsàn] to disperse; to fall apart
溃疡 [kuìyáng] ulcer

聩（聵）[kuì] (adj) 耳聋 deaf

篑（簣）[kuì] (n) 盛土的竹筐 a basket for carrying earth

喟 [kuì] (v) 叹气 to sigh; to moan; to lament

愧 [kuì] (adj) 羞惭，惭愧 ashamed; bashful; conscience-stricken ＊他对他做过的事感到羞愧。He is ashamed of what he did.
愧忿 [kuìfèn] shame and anger
愧汗 [kuìhàn] pespiring on account of deep mortification
愧色 [kuìsè] shame

kūn

昆 [kūn] 1 (adj) 众多 many; numerous 2 (n) 哥哥 an older brother 3 (n) 后嗣 a descendent; posterity
昆虫 [kūnchóng] insects
昆虫学 [kūnchóng xué] entomology
昆裔 [kūnyī] future generations; posterity
昆仲 [kūnzhòng] brothers

坤 [kūn] (n) 八卦之一，代表地，妇人 one of the Eight Diagrams which conveys the meaning of the earth, female, faminince

kǔn

捆 [kǔn] 1 (v) 用绳等缠紧打结 to bind; to plait; to tie up. 2 量词 a measure word: a bundle; package. ＊一捆报纸 a bundle of newspapers

kùn

困（睏）[kùn] 1 (v) 艰难 distress; confused 2 (adj) 穷苦 poor; needy 3 (v) 被围 besiege; surrounded by 4 (adj) 疲倦 weary; tired
困惑 [kùnhuò] perplexed; bewildered; puzzled
困境 [kùnjìng] dilemma; difficult position
困苦 [kùnkǔ] poverty-striken; in distress
困难 [kùn nán] perplexity; difficulty; distress; hard pressed
困恼 [kùnnǎo] vexation
困守 [kùn shǒu] be hemmed in
困兽犹斗 [kùn shòu yóu dòu] cornered animals fight back; even a trapped beast trys to struggle

kùo

括 [kùo] 1 (v) 扎，束 to tie up; to bind into bundles 2 (v) 包含 to contain; to include; to embrace.

括号 [kuòhào] brackets

阔 [kuò] 1 (adj) 宽广 broad; wide 2 (adj) 时间长，距离远 long (time period); distant (distance) 3 (adj) 有财有势，生活奢侈豪华的 rich; well off ＊ 有的女孩子梦想嫁个阔少 Some girls dream of marrying rich young men.

阔别 [kuòbié] be parted for a long time

阔步 [kuò bù] take big strides; walk long steps

阔绰 [kuò chuò] luxurious

阔大 [kuòdà] capacious; liberal

阔度 [kuò dù] width

阔气 [kuò qì] luxurious; extravagant

阔狭 [kuòxiá] wide and narrow

廓 [kuò] 1 (n) 物体的周围：轮廓 profile 2 (adj) 空阔 wide; spacious; empty; open; great 3 (v) 清除 sweep away; get rid of

扩（擴）[kuò] (v) 放大，张大 to enlarge; to expand; to extend; to widen

扩充 [kuòchōng] to expand; to extend; to enlarge

扩大 [kuòdà] magnification; to magnify; to enlarge; to increase

扩建 [kuò jiàn] to enlarge; to expand

扩军 [kuòjūn] arms expansion

扩军备战 [kuòjūnbèi zhàn] arms expansion and war preparations

扩散 [kuòsàn] to spread; to proliferate (nuclear weapons)

扩音机 [kuòyīnjī] a micro-phone

扩展 [kuòzhǎn] to expand; to dilate

扩张 [kuòzhāng] to extend; to dilate; to expand; to develop

扩张主义 [kuò zhāng shǔyì] expansionism

L

lā

垃 [lā]〔垃圾〕[lājī] (n) 尘土或扔掉的破烂的东西 rubbish; garbage
 垃圾箱 [lājīxiāng] a dust-bin

拉 [lā] 1 (v) 牵引 pull; draw 2 (v) 使延长 drag; prolong; lengthen ＊跟上他们，不要拉开距离。Catch up with them, don't lengthen the gap.
 拉倒 [lādǎo] forget about it
 拉丁文 [lādīngwén] Latin language
 拉肚子 [lā dù·zǐ] suffer from diarrhoea; have loose bowels; purge
 拉拉扯扯 [lālāchě chě] (literally) tug; (figuratively) exchange favours and flattery
 拉力 [lālì] tensile force; pull; drawing force
 拉链 [lāliàn] zipper; zip fastener
 拉拢 [lā lǒng] draw ... in; pull (somebody) over to (one's side); be roped in (by ...)
 拉杂 [lāzá] disconnected; rambling; disorganised
 拉住 [lāzhù] hold fast
 另见 [lǎ]

啦 [lā] (n) 表示水向下落的声音 a sound; sound of rain-drops ＊雨哗啦哗啦地落下來。The rain falls with pattering sound.
 另见 [lá]

邋 [lā]〔邋遢〕[lātā] (adj) 肮脏，不整洁 dirty; untidy; filthy

lá

拉 [lá] 1 (v) 割划 cut 2 (v)〔闲谈〕talk casually ＊妈妈常跟邻居的妇人拉扯家常。Mother always talks casually about family matters with the women in the neighbourhood.
 另见 [là]

lǎ

喇 [lǎ]〔喇叭〕1 (n) 一种管乐器 musical instrument; a trumpet or a horn 2 (n) 象喇叭的东西 objects resembling a trumpet or a horn

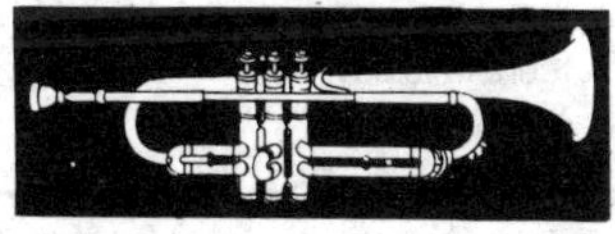

 喇嘛 [lǎ·má] a Buddhist monk in Tibet or Mongolia

là

辣 [là] 1 (adj) 带刺激性的味道 acrid; pungent; hot. (of taste or smell); peppery 2 (adj) 凶、狠、恶毒 cruel; violent ＊凶手真是心狠手辣。The murderer was really heartless and cruel.
 辣词 [là cí] sharp words
 辣椒 [làjiāo] hot pepper; chilli
 辣口 [làkǒu] pungent remark
 辣手 [làshǒu] cruel; hard to be handled; rough handling

瘌 [là]〔瘌痢〕(n) 又作"秃疮" bald from skin disease; scald-headed

腊(臘) [là] 1 (n) 阴历十二月 December in the lunar calender, the 12th month 2 (n) 把魚、肉等用盐腌后再熏制，使可以保藏 preserving meat and fish by adding salt

腊月 [làyuè] the 12th lunar month

蜡(蠟) [là] (n) 由蜂，蜡虫分泌的，从栌树，漆树等果实中榨取而得的，或从矿物中提炼的物质 wax; paraffin; bees-wax

蜡笔 [làbǐ] crayon

蜡像 [làxiàng] a waxen statute; wax-work

蜡烛 [làzhú] candle

落 [là] (v) 遗漏 miss; omit ＊这里落了几个字要补写上去。A few words are missing here, they must be filled in.

另见 [luò]

·la

啦 [·la] 助词，表示决定並兼有感叹或劝止的语气 (a modal particle) ＊有什么话快说吧，他要走啦。He must leave; speak quickly whatever there is to say.

另见 [là]

lái

来(來) [lái] 1 (v) 从别的地方走到这里 come; arrive; be here ＊朋友常来我家坐。Friends often come to my house for a visit. 2 (v) 发生 happen; effect; come ＊暴风雨快来了，渔夫们都趕回港口。A storm is coming and the fishermen hurried back to the port. 3 (adj) 未来的 future; coming ＊你今年成绩不好，希望来年会有进步。Your result this year is no good; I hope that in the coming year there will be improvement. 4 (adj) 表示约略估计的数目 about; around ＊有十来个青年围在门口。About over ten young people crowded at the gate.

来宾 [láibīn] visitor; guest

来福枪 [láifúqiāng] rifle

来回 [láihuí] go to (a place) and come back; make a round trip; to and fro; back and forth

来历 [láilì] background; origin

来临 [láilín] approach; come; arrive

来龙去脉 [lái lóng-qù mài] the cause and effect of something

来头 [lái·tóu] (of person) background; backing; source

来往 [láiwǎng] come and go; intercourse; dealings

来信; 来函 [láixìn; láihán] letter that has arrived; letter received

来由 [láiyóu] cause; reason

来源 [láiyuán] cause; reason; source

来自 [láizì] come from

lài

徕(徠) [lài] (v)〔招徕〕设法把人招来 call; invite

睐(睞) [lài] (v) 看，向旁边看 look (at the side)

赖(賴) [lài] 1 (v) 依偎，依靠 depend on; trust in; rely on ＊这件事的成功，有赖你的帮忙。The success of this matter depends on your help. 2 (v) 抵赖，推脱，不承认 disclaim; deny; ignore; disavow ＊他犯了错还想赖。He intends to deny the mistake he made. 3 (v) 诬赖，嫁罪 shift the blame onto someone else ＊自己错了，不能诬赖别人。If one has committed a mistake, one should not shift the blame onto others. 4 (v) 留在某处不肯走开 hold on (to a place); hang on (in a place) ＊孩子要玩水，赖着在海边不肯走。The child wants to play with water, so he hangs on in the beach, not willing to move.

赖债 [làizhài] repudiate a debt; to refuse to pay a debt

赖仗 [làizhàng] rely on; trust in

濑(瀨) [lài] (n) 从沙石上流过很急的水 a brook

癞(癩) [lài] (n) 一种皮肤病 skin disease; leprosy; scabies

癞狗 [làigǒu] a mangy dog

癞蛤蟆想吃天鹅肉 [lài há·má xiǎng chī tiān é ròu] vain hopes; foolish imaginings; hopeless wishes

癞癣 [làixuǎn] ringworm; a spreading scab

癞者 [làizhě] a leper

lán

兰(蘭) [lán] (n) 胡姬花 an orchid

兰摧玉折 [lán cuī yù zhé] death of a virtuous man

兰交 [lánjiāo] an intimate friend

兰心 [lánxīn] a refined nature

兰质蕙心 [lánzhì huì xīn] a refined nature

拦(攔) [lán] (v) 阻止,阻挡 block; bar; hold back * 警员拦住他的去路,不让他前进。The policeman stood on his way, refusing to let him walk forward.

拦洪坝 [lánhóngbà] flood-control dam; dam

拦截 [lánjié] intercept

拦路 [lánlù] block the way

拦阻 [lánzǔ] block; obstruct; hinder; intercept

栏(欄) [lán] 1 (n) 栏杆 a railing; a balustrade 2 (n) 养家畜的圈 a pen or enclosure for animals 3 (n) 报章分类的部份 a column in a newspaper 4 (n) 集中张贴墙报,公告,报纸等的场所 notice-board

阑(闌) [lán] 1 (n) 栏杆 railing 2 (v) 阻挡 block 3 (adj) 将尽,将完 nearly finished or completed * 她做完夜班回到家里,已是夜阑人静。 It was already in the dead of night when she had fulfilled her night shift and returned home.

阑人 [lánrù] go in abruptly; enter without a permission

阑尾炎 [lánwěiyán] appendicitis

谰(讕) [lán]〔谰言〕(n) 诬赖的话,没有根据的话 slander; baseless accusation

澜(瀾) [lán] (n) 大波浪 strong waves; huge storm

褴(襤) [lán] (adj) 衣服破烂 ragged; shabby; slovenly

蓝(藍) [lán] (n) 象晴天天空的颜色 blue

蓝本 [lánběn] original script

蓝图 [lántú] blue-print

篮(籃) [lán] 1 (n) 用藤,竹,柳条等编成的器具 basket 2 (n) 篮球架上的铁圈 basket-ball net

篮球 [lánqíu] basket ball

婪 [lán] (adj) 贪得无厌 covetous; greedy * 他为人贪婪,没有人信任他。He is a covetous person and no one trusts him.

岚(嵐) [lán] (n) 山里象雾似的水蒸气 vapour; mist

lǎn

览(覽) [lǎn] (v) 看,阅 see; read; view

览胜 [lǎnshēng] visit scenic places

揽(攬) [lǎn] 1 (v) 掌握 monopolize; grasp; hold control * 古代的帝王常常独揽大权。Kings in olden days always held control of the powers by himself. 2 (v) 拉到自己这方面或自己身上来 grasp; hug; clutch; undertake

揽利 [lǎnlì] monopolize

揽取 [lǎnqǔ] seize up; grasp

揽权 [lǎnquán] grasp at authority; get the ascendancy; hold of power

缆(纜) [lǎn] (n) 粗绳或铁索 rope; cable; cord

缆车 [lǎnchē] cable-car

懒(懶) [lǎn] (adj) 怠惰,不勤快 lazy; slothful; sluggish

懒得 [lǎn·dé] reluctant to

懒惰 [lǎnduò] lazy
懒散 [lǎnsàn] slothful; sluggish; negligent
懒洋洋 [lǎnyāngyāng] listless; languid

làn

烂(爛) [làn] 1 (adj) 东西因煮太久而酥软 overcooked 2 (adj) 东西腐坏 rotten; decayed; gone bad 3 (adj) 破碎 worn out; torn
烂漫 [lànmàn] bright-coloured; brilliant; luxuriant
烂衣 [lànyī] ragged garments

滥(濫) [làn] (adj) 过度,没有限制 extravagant; excessive; lawless＊滥伐林木会造成土壤被侵蚀。The excessive felling of trees will cause soil erosion.
滥交 [lànjiāo] form undesirable companionship
滥竽充数 [lànyú chōngshù] hold a position without proper qualification
滥用 [lànyòng] abuse; use indiscriminately; misuse
滥支 [lànzhī] extravagant expenditure

lāng

啷 [lāng] (n) 形容撞击或破碎的声音 metal sound

láng

狼 [láng] (n) 哺乳动物,像狗,性格狡猾。wolf

狼狈不堪 [lángbèi bù kān] highly embarrassed
狼狈为奸 [lángbèi wéijiān] work hand in glove with; co-operate with people in evil doing
狼藉 [lángjí] messy; chaotic; in utter disorder
狼戾无亲 [lánglì wú qīn] merciless; cruel; without affection
狼吞虎咽 [láng tūn-hǔyàn] gobble up; devour
狼心狗肺 [lángxīngǒufèi] ungrateful; brutal and cruel

琅 [láng] 1〔琅琅〕(n) 常指响亮的读书声 sound of reading aloud 2 [琅玕] (n) 象珠子的美石 a kind of jade

郎 [láng] (n) 年轻男子 young man; gentleman
郎君; 才郎 [lángjūn; cáiláng] a husband

榔 [láng] [榔头] (n) 就是"铁锤" hammer

锒 [láng] [锒头] (n) 就是"铁锤" a hammer

廊 [láng] (n) 有顶的过道 a verandah; a corridor; a gallery

lǎng

朗 [lǎng] 1 (adj) 明亮 clear; bright＊下了一场大雨后,天气晴朗。After a heavy rain, the day is bright and the air fresh. 2 (adj) 声音清脆响亮 clear and distinct (sound)
朗读 [lǎngdú] read aloud
朗诵 [lǎngsòng] recite; read with expression
朗吟 [lǎngyín] recite; recitation

làng

浪 [làng] 1 (n) 水波 waves; billows; surges 2 (adj) 没有节制,放纵 profligate; dissolute; wasteful＊父亲叫他不要浪费金钱买玩具,要努力学习功课。Father asked him not to waste money on toys, but to study his school-work diligently.
浪潮 [làngcháo] tide; wave
浪费 [làngfèi] waste; be extravagant; squander
浪漫主义 [làngmànzhǔyì] romanticism
浪游 [làng yóu] roaming; wandering
浪子 [làngzǐ] a dissolute person; tramp

lāo

捞(撈) [lāo] 1 (v) 从液体中取出(东西) dredge for; drag out

of water; scoop up (from water) *这艘船准备在大海中打捞宝藏。The ship is intended for dredging treasure in the sea. 2 (v) 用不正当的方法取得 gain; acquire (through improper means) *他利用自己的职位，捞了不少金钱。He used his position to gain a lot of money.

捞起 [lāoqǐ] drag or pull out of water; raise up by grappling

捞取 [lāoqǔ] reap; gain

捞一把 [lāo yī bǎ] make some profit; profiteering

láo

劳(勞) [láo] 1 (v) (n) 出大力工作 labour; work; labour; manual labour *经过一天的劳作，他觉得很疲倦。After a day of labour, he feels very tired. 2 (adj) (n) 辛苦，疲乏 care-worn; fatigued; fatigue *他为大家的事忙了几个星期，十分劳累。Having been busy in public matters for weeks, he becomes worn out. 3 (part) 烦劳，请人做事的客气话 an excuse for putting others to the trouble of doing a favour *劳驾你代我向大家问好。Would you mind sending my regards to all the people? 4 (n) 功劳 merits

劳动 [làodòng] work; labour; physical labour; manual labour

劳动节 [láodòngjié] May Day; Labour Day. (1st May)

劳而无功 [láoérwúgōng] time and energy spent but fruitless

劳工 [láogōng] labour

劳苦 [láokǔ] toilsome

劳苦患难 [láo kǔ huàn nán] distress and difficulties

劳累 [láolèi] tired; exhausted; fatigue

劳力 [láolì] labour; manpower; capacity for work

劳碌 [láolù] burdensome; toilsome

劳民伤财 [láo mín shāng cái] burdening the people and wasting money

劳神 [láo shén] take the trouble to; overtax or exert (oneself)

劳役 [láoyì] forced labour

唠(嘮) [láo]〔唠叨〕(v) 说话罗嗦 nag; keep repeating the same thing
另见 [lào]

痨(癆) [láo] (n) 结核病 consumption; tuberculosis

痨咳 [láoké] consumptive cough

牢 [láo] 1 (n) 养牲畜的圈 a stable for cattle 2 (n) 监狱 a jail; prison 3 (adj) 坚固 strong; firm; secure; solid

牢不可破 [láo bù kě pò] solid; indestructible

牢固 [láogù] firm; solid

牢骚 [láosāo] discontent; complaint

醪 [láo] 1 (n) 汁滓混合的酒 mixture of juice and wine 2 (n) 浓厚的酒 strong wine

lǎo

老 [lǎo] 1 (adj) 年龄大 aged; old 2 (adj) 经历长，有经验 experienced; skilled; expert *他在这里做了几十年，是个老手了。Having worked here for several decades, he is an experienced old hand. 3 (adj) 关係久 long-timed or old (in relationship) *在一起工作了几年，大家算是老同事了。Working together for a few years, we can be regarded as old colleagues. 4 (adj) 过去的，原来的 old; past; original *我们别只依老方法做，要多创新。Instead of merely follow old methods,we should be more creative. 5 (adv) 很，极 very *我从老远赶来，却得不到大家的欢迎。I come from very far away, yet I am not welcomed by the people. 6 (adv) 总，常 often *他老是不听别人的劝告，所以常常犯错。He often turns a deaf ear to others' advice, so he is used to making mistakes.

老板 [lǎo bǎn] shop-owner; boss

老百姓 [lǎobǎixìng] common people;

civilians

老本 [lǎo běn] capital (first investment)

老成持重 [lǎochéngchízhòng] experienced and steady

老当益壮 [lǎodāng yì zhuàng] the older one is, the stronger one will be (in determination)

老调 [lǎo diào] worn-out theme; same old story

老虎 [lǎo hǔ] tiger

老奸巨滑 [lǎojiānjùhuá] experienced and very crafty; an old rogue

老练 [lǎoliàn] experienced; seasoned; veteran

老马识途 [lǎomǎshítú] an experienced person

老前辈 [lǎoqiánbèi] senior; elder; predecessor

老气横秋 [lǎoqìhéngqīu] lacking in youthful vigour, but conceited and boastful in seniority

老人家 [lǎo·rén·jiā] a term of respect for an old man or woman

老少 [lǎoshào] the old and the young

老实 [lǎo·shí] honest; well-behaved

老鼠 [lǎo shǔ] mouse; rat

老鼠过街,人人喊打 [lǎo shǔ guò jiē, rén rén hǎn dǎ] a pest that is hated by everyone

老态龙钟 [lǎotàilóngzhōng] old and decrepit

老羞成怒 [lǎoxīuchéngnù] enraged at having been embarrassed

老一套 [lǎoyītào] old ways; old practice; the same old story

老子 [lǎo zǐ] father; regard oneself as the number one authority; the name of a philosopher in ancient China

佬 [lǎo] (n) 对人轻视的称呼 a disrespectful term to address people

姥 [lǎo]〔姥姥〕(n) 外祖母 maternal grandmother

潦 [lǎo] 1 (n) 路上的流水,积水 a puddle left by rain 2 (adj) 雨大的样子 raining heavily
另见 [liǎo]

lào

络(絡) [lào][络子](n) 线,绳结成的网状袋子 bag sewn of thread or hemp
另见 [luò]

烙 [lào] 1 (v) 烤熟 bake; burn 2 (v) 熨,烫 iron (clothes, etc.)
另见 [luò]

烙饼 [làobǐng] pancake

烙铁 [lào tiě] iron (for ironing clothes, etc.); welding iron

烙印 [làoyìn] brand (with hot iron)

酪 [lào] (n) 用鲜奶或羊奶制成的半凝固食品 cream; cheese

酪酥 [làosū] cheese

唠(嘮) [lào] (v) 说话,闲谈 talk casually
另见 [láo]

涝(澇) [lào] (adj) 雨水过多,水淹 waterlogging; flooded

lè

勒 [lè] 1 (n) 带嚼子的牲口笼头 a hurdle; the rein 2 (v) 收紧结绳使牲口不再前进 tighten the rein 3 (v) 强制,逼迫 force; compel
另见 [lēi]

勒令 [lèlìng] order sb. to do one's bidding; force compliance; insist on

勒索 [lèsuǒ] extort (money, food, etc.)

乐(樂) [lè] (adj) (n) 喜悦,愉快 happy; glad; joyful; delightful happiness; joy; delight.

另见 [yuè]
乐不可言 [lè bù kě yán] inexpressible pleasure; profound enjoyment
乐不思蜀 [lè bù sī shù] too happy to think of one's home
乐极生悲 [lè jí shēng bēi] excessive joy ends in sadness
乐观 [lèguān] optimistic; hopeful
乐观主义 [lèguān zhǔ yì] optimism
乐趣 [lèqù] delight; pleasure; joy
乐意 [lèyì] be willing to; ready to ... ; want
乐于 [lèyú] be glad or happy to
乐园 [lèyuán]paradiso; land of promise

·le

了 [·le] 1 助词，放在动词或形容词后，表示动作或变化已经完成 particle, expression of completion or change of an action ＊天亮了，起床吧。Wake up, it's already daybreak. 2 助词，用在句末表示肯定语气 particle, to express a confirmative attitude ＊十二月一开头，雨季就来了。The rainy season had come since the beginning of December.
另见 [liǎo]
[liào]

lēi

勒 [lēi] (v) 用绳子等捆住或套住，再拉紧 strap something tight; tighten; strangle ＊既然你没钱吃饭，那就勒紧腰带吧。Tighten your belt since you have no money for food.
另见 [lé]

擂 [lēi] (v) 打 hit; beat＊ 我气得擂了他一拳。 I was so angry that I hit him a blow with my fist.
另见 [léi]
[lèi]

léi

累 [léi] [累赘] (adj) 使人感到多余或麻烦 troublesome; unmanageable. worrying; harassing
另见 [lěi]
[lèi]

雷 [léi] 1 (n) 一种自然现象，随着闪电发出的声响 thunder 2 (n) 一种爆炸性的武器 mine
雷达 [léidá] radar
雷管 [léiguǎn] detonator
雷厉风行 [léilì fēngxíng] strict and swift in doing something
雷鸣 [léimíng] thunder clap; a loud sound like thunder clap
雷同 [léitóng] identical (copy or echo what others have said); follow another person blindly
雷霆万钧 [léi tíng wàn jūn] exceptional might
雷霆之怒 [léitíng zhī nù] wrathful as the thunder
雷雨 [léiyǔ] thunderstorm

擂 [léi] (v) 研磨 pound
另见 [lēi]
[lèi]
擂钵 [léibō] a mortar
擂锤 [léichuí] a pestle

礌 [léi] (n) 礌石，自高处往下击的滚石 rolling stones falling from a height

羸 [léi] (adj) 瘦，弱 thin; weak ＊羸弱的人才会常生病。Only thin and weak people often fall ill.

lěi

累 (纍) [lěi] 1 (v) 重叠，堆积 accumulate; pile up; heap up ＊你经验丰富，一定累积了不少知识。 You are experienced, I am sure you have accumulated much knowledge. 2 (adv) 连接，屡次 continuous ＊你累次犯同样的错误，到底要不要改？You have made the same mistake several times; are you going to correct it? 3 (v) 连累，麻烦 involve; trouble; entangle; implicate ＊父亲犯错，连累孩子到处被人瞧不起。The mistake made by the father involved the child in the trouble of being despised everywhere.
另见 [lèi]

累积 [lěijī] accumulate
累进 [lěijìn] progress; build up gradually
累及无辜 [lěijí wú gū] to involve the innocent
累累 [lěilěi] cluster; heap; innumerable
累月经年 [lěiyuèjīng nián] month after month and year after year
累战皆捷 [lěizhànjiē jié] victorious in successive battles

垒(壘) [lěi] 1 (n) 古代军队中作防守用的墙壁或建筑 a rampart; a fort; a fortress 2 (v) 把砖，石及土块砌起来 build by piling up (as bricks.)
垒球 [lěiqíu] base-ball

耒 [lěi] (n)古代犁上的木把 the handle of a plough

蕾 [lěi] (n) 将要开出来的小花 a flower bud

磊 [lěi] (adj) 石头多的样子 rocky
磊落 [lěiluò] open and above-board

lèi

类(類) [lèi] 1 (n) 种类 kind; class; category 2 (adj)类似，相象 like; alike; similar *画虎类犬 draw a tiger but it looks like a dog.
类别 [lèibié] classification; category
类似 [lèisì] similar; resembling; analogous
类推 [lèituī] analogize
类型 [lèixíng] type; class

累 [lèi] (adj) 疲乏，过劳 tired; fatigued; overwork; exhausted *你忙了一整天，现在应该是很累吧。You must be very tired now after having been busy for the whole day.
另见 [léi]

擂 [lèi] (v) 敲，打 beat; hit; knock *古代开战时总是擂鼓。In ancient days, the drums were always beaten when a battle began.
另见 [lěi]

[lèi]
肋 [lèi] (n) 胸膛的两侧 the ribs

泪(淚) [lèi] (n) 人在哭的时候，从双眼流出来的液体 tears; teardrops

léng

棱 [léng] (n) 角边 edge; corner
棱镜 [léngjìng] prism

lěng

冷 [lěng] 1 (adj) 温度低，跟"热"相对 cold; chilly; frigid; icy *天气冷，我得穿上外套。The weather is cold, I must put a coat on. 2 (adj) 不热闹 quiet; lonesome; solitary *半夜三更时街边是冷冷清清的。At midnight, the street is very quiet. 3 (adj) 不热情，不温和 cold-hearted; indifferent *自从上回生意失败后，他对一切事物都很冷淡。He became indifferent to everything since his previous failure in business. 4 (adv) 突然的，暗中的 suddenly; secretly; off guard *肯尼迪总统被人以冷枪杀害。President Kennedy was killed by someone who sniped at him with a rifle. 5 (adv) 表示轻蔑的意思 expressing despise *老板对于工友们的建议竟报以冷笑。The employer laughed scornfully at the suggestion made by the workers.
冷藏 [lěngcáng] keep in cold storage; refrigeration
冷场 [lěng chǎng] an embarrassing pause, awkward silence (at a meeting, etc.)
冷嘲热讽 [lěngcháorèfěng] sarcasm
冷箭 [lěngjiàn] (fig.) a stab in the back
冷静 [lěngjìng] calm; sober
冷酷 [lěngkù] grim; unfeeling; hard-hearted
冷落 [lěngluò] cold-shouldered; treated indifferently

冷气 [lěngqì] cold air; air conditioning
冷清 [lěngqīng] quiet and dreary; desolate; quiet and isolated
冷若冰霜 [lěng ruò bīng shuāng] as cold as ice or frost; stern and difficult to get close to
冷食 [lěngshí] cold drinks and snacks
冷笑 [lěngxiào] sneer; laugh scornfully
冷血动物 [lěng xuě-dòng wù] cold-blooded animal
冷眼旁观 [lěng yǎn páng guān] to observe coolly and objectively from aside
冷遇 [lěngyù] cold shoulder; cold reception
冷战 [lěngzhàn] cold war

lèng

楞 [lèng] 1 (adj) 呆，失神 become dazed; become stupefied ＊她对着向她要钱的儿子发楞。 She was dazed at her son who asked her for money. 2 (adj) 鲁莽 rude; reckless; foolhardy

lí

离(離) [lí] 1 (v) 分开，分别 separate; part; leave; depart; take leave of ＊不要为了别离而伤心，我们会再见的。 Don't feel sad to part, we will meet again. 2 (adv) 相距，相隔 far --- from ＊马来西亚离英国很远。 Malaysia is very far from England. 3 (v) 缺少 be short of; lack; be without (something) ＊鱼离开水便不能活。 A fish cannot live without water.
离别 [líbié] part; leave
离合 [lí hè] parting and meeting
离婚 [lí hūn] get a divorce
离间 [líjiān] set one person against another
离开 [lí kāi] leave; depart; deviate from
离经叛道 [líjīng pàn dào] wayward and rebellious
离奇 [líqí] fantastic; odd; strange; extraordinary
离散 [lísàn] disperse; be separated from one another
离题万里 [lí tí wàn lǐ] far off the subject
离乡背井 [líxiāng bèijǐng] leave one's native place; be away from home

缡(縭) [lí] (n) 古时女子出嫁时所系的佩巾 ornamental girdle worn by a bride in olden days

篱(籬) [lí] (n) 用竹，木或芦苇等编成的围墙 a fence; hedge (of bamboo)

梨 [lí] (n) 落叶乔木，果实也叫"梨" pear

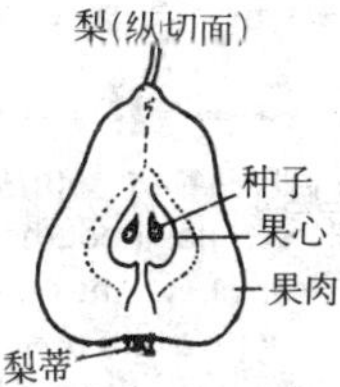

犁 [lí] 1 (n) 耕地用的农具 a plough 2 (v) 用犁耕地 to plough

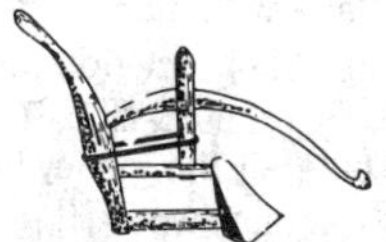

犁刀 [lídāo] a coulter

黎 [lí] (adj) 众多 many
黎民 [límín] the people; the masses
黎明 [límíng] early dawn; daybreak

黧 [lí] (n) 黑黑带黄的颜色 a black, yellowish colour; a dark colour

藜 [lí] (n) 草本植物，嫩叶可供食用 pigweed

骊(驪) [lí] (n) 纯黑色的马 a black horse

狸 [lí] (n) 一种比狐小的兽 the wild cat; the fox; the racoon; a striped cat

厘 [lí] 1 (n) 长度，重量，地积单位。 a unit of measure for length, weight and land area 2 (n) 计算利息用

的百分率 percent; percentage 3 (n) 表示很小的数量 smallness in quantity

厘定 [lídìng] regulate; adjust; settle

蠡 [lí] (n) 贝壳做的瓢 a calabash; a gourd

蠡测 [lícè] measure the sea with a calabash — (fig) a man of limited experience

罹 [lí] 1 (v) 遭遇困难或不幸 undergo; suffer; incur; be a victim of an accident *这次飞机失事，罹难者共达一百人。The number of victims of this plane crash was 100 in total. 2 (n) 忧患，苦难 sorrow; grief

lǐ

里(裏) [lǐ] 1 (n) 家乡，街坊 a neighbourhood; a village; a lane; an alley; the native town 2 (n) 长度单位 a unit of measure. (length) *奔跑了三里路之后，我们终于到达了火车站。After having run for three miles, we finally reached the Railway Station. 3 (n) 内部，跟"外"相对 interior; (prep) inside *她把所有的钱都放在手提袋里。She puts all the money in the handbag. 4 (aux. word) 附在"这"，"那"等字后边表示地点 to indicate location

里程碑 [lǐchéngbēi] milestone

里面 [lǐmiàn] interior; inside

里通外国 [lǐtōngwàiguó] have illicit or treacherous relations with a foreign country

里头 [lǐtóu] inside; interior

里应外合 [lǐyìngwàihé] co-ordinated attack from without and within

俚 [lǐ] (adj) 民间的，通俗的 rustic; rude; rough

俚歌 [lǐgē] rustic songs and ditties

俚谚 [lǐyàn] proverb; common saying

理 [lǐ] 1 (n) 物质组织的条纹 the structure of material 2 (n) 道理 law; doctrine; principle; reason 3 (v) 管理，办 manage; undertake *他是个细心的人，由他理财最适当。He is a careful person, so it is appropriate to let him manage financial matters. 4 (v) 弄整齐 arrange; regulate; manage; tidy; put in order *花园的草长得很乱，去理一理它吧。The weeds in the garden are growing disorderly, go and tidy them up. 5 (v) 对别人的言语行动表示态度 respond; acknowledge; pay attention to; take notice of; heed *她生气时，对谁都不理睬。When she is angry, she takes no notice of anybody.

理发 [lǐfà] hair-cut; have a hair-cut

理发员；理发师 [lǐfàyuán; lǐfàshī] barber; hairdresser

理会 [lǐhuì] comprehend; understand; take notice of

理解 [lǐjiě] understand; comprehend; grasp

理科 [lǐkē] science

理亏 [lǐkuī] unjustifiable; in the wrong

理论 [lǐlùn] theory; thesis

理屈词穷 [lǐqù cí qíong] insufficient grounds and lack of reasoning

理所当然 [lǐ suǒ dāng rán] it is rightly so; obviously

理想 [lǐxiǎng] ideal; aspiration

理性 [lǐxìng] reason (in philosophy)

理由 [lǐyóu] reason; ground; argument

理智 [lǐzhì] intellect; reason

理直气壮 [lǐ zhí qì zhuàng] right and confident

鲤(鯉) [lǐ] (n) 淡水鱼类 a fresh water fish; the carp

醴 [lǐ] (n) 甜酒 sweet wine; sweet spring

礼(禮) [lǐ] 1 (n) 根据一定社会的道德观念和风俗习惯形成的表示庆贺，尊敬，哀悼等的仪式 ceremony 2 (n) 表示尊敬的态度或动作 ritual politeness; propriety; etiquette; courtesy; manners *如果大家都以礼待人，许多不必要的冲突就可以避免了。If all the people treat others with courtesy, many unnecessary conflicts will not occur. 3 (n) 礼物 gifts; presents

礼服 [lǐfú] ceremonial dress; formal attire

礼节 [lǐjié] formality; courtesy; etiquette; protocol

礼貌 [lǐmào] politeness; manners; courtesy

礼让 [lǐràng] give precedence to somebody out of courtesy or thoughtfulness

礼尚往来 [lǐshàngwǎnglái] propriety demands reciprocity

礼堂 [lǐtáng] auditorium, assembly hall; hall

李 [lǐ] 1 (n) 落叶乔木，果实叫"李子"，可吃 a plum; a prune 2 (n) 姓 surname

lì

历(歷,曆) [lì] 1 (n) 过去的事件，经过 undergo; go through; experience 2 (adj) 过去的各（个） successive ＊他是历届运动会的冠军。He is a champion of the successive annual sports meet. 3 (n) 历法，推算年，月，日和节气等的方法 the system of determining the systems and solar terms of a year 4 (n) 记载年，月，日和气候等的书，表等日历 calendar

历次 [lìcì] various (occassions, events, etc.)

历代 [lìdài] successive dynasties; past dynasties

历来 [lìlái] always;all along;all through the ages

历历可数 [lìlìkéshǔ] you can count one by one

历历在目 [lìlìzàimù] vividly before one's eyes (of past events and so on)

历年 [lìnián] over the years; in past years

历史 [lìshǐ] history; historical

呖(嚦) [lì] (n) 形容清脆流利的鸟声 chirping sounds of birds

沥(瀝) [lì] 1 (v) 液体一滴一滴地落下 trickle; drop; drain out ＊许多战士都在战场上沥血。Many warriors shed (drop) blood in the battlefield. 2 (n) 液体的点滴 a drop 3 (v) 过滤 filter

沥陈 [lìchén] represent in detail

沥沥 [lìlì] the sound of blowing wind

沥恳 [lìkěn] implore earnestly

沥青 [lìqīng] pitch; asphalt; bitumen

厉(厲) [lì] 1 (n) 磨刀石 a whetstone 2 (v) 引中为磨砺 (fig.) sharpen; grind ＊厉兵 sharpen weapons. 3 (adj) 严格，严肃 stern; severe ＊校长是个严厉的人，学生们都不敢不听话。The principal is a stern person; all the students dare not be disobedient. 4 (adj) 凶猛，狠恶 cruel; harsh; oppressive

厉风 [lìfēng] a violent wind; severe air

厉害 [lìhài] fierce; terrible; formidable; serious

厉疾 [lìjí] a serious illness

厉禁 [lìjìn] a stringent prohibition

厉色 [lìsè] a stern countenance

厉声 [lìshēng] speak sternly; harsh tone

厉行 [lìxíng] strictly carry out; practise

厉行节约 [lìxíngjiéyuē] strict implementation of economy

励(勵) [lì] (v) 勤勉 stimulate; encourage; urge; animate; spur

励民 [lìmín] encourage the people

励志 [lìzhì] intent upon; bend the mind to

蛎(蠣) [lì] 〔牡蛎〕(n) 软体的动物，也叫"蚝" an oyster

蛎塘 [lìtáng] an oyster bed

粝 [lì] (n) 粗糙的米 coarse rice

疠(癘) [lì] 1 (n) 指流行性急性传染病 a pestilence; a plague 2 (n) 恶疮 a malignant sore

戾 [lì] 1 (adj) 凶恶，残暴 rebellious; oppressive; perverse; cruel ∗历史上的秦始皇是个暴戾的执政者。In history, Shih Huang Ti was a cruel ruler. 2 (n) 罪过 crime; sin

唳 [lì] (n) 鸩叫声 the crying of a crane

利 [lì] 1 (adj)(n) 好处 advantageous; beneficial; useful advantages; benefits; gain ∗做个有利于社会的人才会有生活意义。There is meaning in life only if one becomes useful to society. 2 (v) 使得到好处 benefit ∗贬低别人，提高自己是损人利己的事。To degrade others and value oneself is an act in which one benefits oneself at the expense of others. 3 (adj) 顺利，与愿望相合 smooth-going ∗这次考试不很顺利，有几科的题目都很难。The examination this time is not smooth-going because the questions in several subjects are very difficult. 4 (adj) 锋利 sharp; acute ∗他的言语像把利刀似地刺伤别人的心。His words are like a sharp knife which hurts the hearts of others. 5 (n) 利润，利息 gains; profits; advantages; interest ∗做生意的人时时刻刻都在找有利可图的生意做。Businessmen are always looking for business with good profits.

利弊 [lìbì] advantages and disadvantages

利害 [lì hài] gains and losses; interest

利害 [lì-hài] fierce; powerful; terrible; formidable

利令智昏 [lìlìngzhìhūn] self-interest blinds the eyes; greed blinds or tends to make one do foolish things

利益 [lìyì] interest; benefit; gain; profit

利用 [lì yòng] use; make use of; take advantage of; exploit; utilize

利诱 [lìyòu] lure by promise of gain

利欲熏心 [lìyùxūnxīn] blinded by avarice; obsessed with the desire for gain

痢 [lì] (n) 痢疾，一种肠道传染病 dysentry; diarrhoea

立 [lì] 1 (v) 站 stand ∗升国旗时要立正。Stand still when the flag rises. 2 (v) 建立，制定 erect; set up; fix; establish ∗学校订立了校规让学生遵从。The school has set up school rules for students to follow. 3 (adv) 即刻，马上 immediately; instantly; at once ∗他一听说在远地的母亲去世，立刻请假前往追丧。Once he heard that his mother who stayed in a distant place had passed away, he immediately asked for leave to attend the funeral.

立场 [lìchǎng] stand; position; standpoint

立法 [lì fǎ] legislation; legislative; legislate; make laws

立方 [lìfāng] cube; cubic measurement

立功 [lì gōng] perform deeds of merit; render meritorious service

立功赎罪 [lì gōng shú zuì] earn merits to offset wrongs

立即 [lìjí] at once; immediately; promptly

立身处世 [lì shēn chǔ shì] one's behaviour in society and attitude towards life

立体 [lìtǐ] solid; three-dimensioned

立志 [lì zhì] be determined; aim (at doing something); aim to do (something); make a resolution

立足 [lìzú] gain a foothold; be on a .... footing; base oneself on

粒 [lì] 1 (n) 果子或谷类的单位及数量 a grain ∗当知盘中餐，粒粒皆辛苦。We should understand that every grain in the dish is the product of tough labour. 2 (n) 成颗的东西 granule; kernal 量词(a measure word) grain ∗我吃了一粒萍果。I have eaten an apple.

粒子 [lìzǐ] particle

笠 [lì] (n) 斗笠，用竹或棕皮等编成的帽子，也叫"笠帽" a basket-shaped hat; a rain hat made of bamboo splinters

涖 [lì] (v) 到（有尊敬的意思）attend honourably
涖臨 [lìlín] attend ------ for a visit

栗 [lì] 1 (n) 落叶乔木，果实叫"栗子" the chestnut 2 (v) 发抖 shiver; shudder; tremble ∗那只貓在雨中战栗。That cat shivers in the rain.

砾(礫) [lì] (n) 碎石，碎瓦 small stones; gravels ∗瓦砾 broken pieces of tiles.

丽(麗) [lì] (adj) 好看，美 nice looking; beautiful; handsome; splendid; magnificently ornamented

俪(儷) [lì] (n) 相并，配偶 a pair; a couple

郦(酈) [lì] (n) 姓氏 a surname

力 [lì] 1 (n) 气能 physical strength; power; force ∗成人的体力一定比小孩大。The strength of an adult is certainly greater than that of a child. 2 (n) 物质之间的互相作用 force 3 (n) 力量 strength; power; force ∗人多力量强。A great number of people makes tremendous strength. 4 (n) 能力，效能 ability; efficiency ∗他想帮忙那小乞丐，但口袋里却只有一毛钱，真是力不从心。His ability falls behind his wishes when he intends to help that small beggar, for he has only ten cents in his pockets.
力不能胜任 [lì bù néng shěng rèn] unable to shoulder (anything important)
力求 [lìqíu] do one's best strength to; strive to
力所能及 [lì suǒ néng jì] within one's power or ability
力图 [lìtú] try hard to; strive to
力挽狂澜 [lìwǎnkuánglàn] using tremendous effort to retrieve a critical situation
力争上游 [lìzhēngshàngyóu] strive for the best; aim high

荔 [lì] (n) 常绿乔木，果实可食 the lichee

例 [lì] 1 (n) 可以做依据示范的事物 example; instance ∗要把字的涵义解释得清楚，最好举个例子。To explain clearly the meaning of a word, it is best to give an example. 2 (n) 规定，标准 rules; regulations; by law; custom ∗回教徒的惯例是进屋前必须脱鞋。It is a custom of Muslims to take off one's shoes before entering the house. 3 (v) 按条例规定的，照成规进行的 follow the regulation ∗小职员只是例行公事，真正做决定的是老板。The clerk only follows regulations to carry out his work, the actual decision comes from the boss.
例会 [lìhuì] regular meeting
例假 [lìjià] official holidays; legal holidays
例如 [lìrú] for instance; such as; for example; e.g.
例外 [lìwài] exceptional; make an exception of
例证 [lìzhèng] proof; evidence; example; case in point; demonstration

吏 [lì] (n) 旧社会的官员 bureaucrats; officials. (in ancient China)

隶(隸) [lì] 1 (n) 古代对奴隶，差役统称为"隶" slaves; servants; subordinates 2 (v) 附属，属于 belong to; subordinate to ∗全部学校都隶属于教育部。All schools are subordinate to the Ministry of Education. 3 (n) 封建时代的衙役 officials; servants (in feudal age)

·li

哩 [·li] 助词。用在句子末尾，相当于"呢""啦" (a modal particle) ∗别收拾，我还没吃完哩。Don't clear up yet, I haven't finished eating.

liǎ

俩(倆) [liǎ] (n) (numeral) 两个 two; both; couple ✱他们夫妇俩都出去工作。Both of the couple went to work.

lián

廉 [lián] 1 (adj) (价钱)低，便宜 cheap ✱廉价物美的东西，一定值得买。It is worthwhile to buy things which are cheap in price and good in quality. 2 (adj) 不贪污 honest; pure; incorrupt ✱历史上的帝王很少有廉政。The kings in history seldom had incorrupt government.

廉耻 [liánchǐ] modest; bashful

廉耻心 [liánchǐxīn] a sense of shame (honour)

廉洁 [liánjié] honest; not corrupt; morally clean

镰(鐮) [lián] (n) 镰刀 a sickle; a scythe; a reaping hook

帘(簾) [lián] (n) 用布，竹，芦苇等做的遮蔽门，窗的东西 a screen; a bamboo-blind

帘幕 [liánmù] a curtain; a hanging-screen

帘内帘外 [liánnèi lián wài] within and without the screen-private and public

连(連) [lián] 1 (v) 相接，连续 link; join; connect; continue 2 (v) 包括在内 include ✱我们这边已经有五个人，连你在内就有六个。Here there are five persons in us, and there will be six including you. 3 (n) 军队的编制单位。a military unit-a company ✱连长 a company commander. 4 (adj) 表示强调，含有"甚至于"的意思and; even; also ✱他的话谁也不信，连小孩子都骗不过。His words are so unbelievable that they cannot coax even a child.

连带 [liándài] connect; in relation with

连贯 [lián guàn] link up; piece together; hang together; coherent; consistent (of writing)

连环 [lián huán] chain of rings

连环画 [lián huán huá] series of pictures telling a story; picture story book

连接 [lián jiè] join; link

连累 [lián lěi] implicate; involve; get somebody into trouble

连忙 [liánmáng] without delay; hastily; promptly; at once

连绵不断 [lián mián bú duàn] continuous; unbroken

连年 [lián nián] successive years; consecutive years; year after year

连篇累牍 [lián piān lěi dú] keep on repeating; lengthy

连阡累陌 [lián qiān lěi mò] in every direction

连日 [liánrì] for days on end; day after day

连锁反应 [liánsuofǎngíng] chain reaction. (physics)

连同 [liántóng] together with; along with

连系 [liánxì] linking; connection

连载 [liánzài] linking; connection

涟(漣) [lián] (n) 水面被风吹起的波纹 a ripple on water ✱春风轻拂湖面，泛起圈圈涟漪。Once and again the spring breeze ripples the quiet water of the lake.

怜(憐) [lián] 1 (v) (n) 冈情 sympathise; pity; have charity for;

pity; compassion; sympathy ✱这个小孤儿得到公众人士垂怜。This orphan gains the sympathies of the public. 2 (v) 宠爱，爱惜 pamper; be fond of ✱ 怜孤惜寡。Have compassion on the orphans and widows.

怜悯 [liánmǐn] take pity on; have compassion for

怜惜 [liánxī] take pity on; have pity for

奁(奩) [lián] (n) 旧时女子梳妆时用的镜匣 a lady's dressing case; a bridal trousseau or dowry

奁仪 [liányì] money given to a bride

联 [lián] 1 (v) 相合在一起，接合 unite; join; ally oneself with; combine; connect ✱在第二次世界大战中，德国，意大利和日本 联合在世界各地进行侵略行动。In the Second World War, Germany, Italy and Japan allied with one another to make invasions in different parts of the world. 2 (n) 对联 a couplet; a scroll

联邦 [liánbāng] federation; union

联欢 [lián huān] have a get-together; have a gathering

联络 [lián luò] establish contact; liaison

联盟 [liánméng] alliance; coalition; league

联系 [liánxì] contact; get in touch with; connect; (have) ties (with)

联想 [liánxiǎng] associate something with; an association of ideas

liǎn

脸(臉) [liǎn] 1 (n) 面部 the face; the cheeks ✱那演员在演出之前，脸上涂上许多脂粉。Just before the performances; the actress applied plenty of powder onto her face. 2 (n) 指面部表情 expression; look

脸皮 [liǎnpí] face- saving; personal consideration

脸皮薄 [liǎnpí bó] bashful; thin-skinned

脸皮厚 [liǎnpíhòu] shameless; brazen-faced

脸色 [liǎnsè] complexion; expression ; look

敛(斂) [liǎn] 1 (v) 收缩，聚集 collect back; shrink 2 (v) 收束，约束 control; concentrate 3 (v) 征收 increase collection of taxes; fees, etc.

敛翅 [liǎnchì] fold back the wings - scared; frighten

敛容 [liǎnróng] assume a serious countenance

敛身 [liǎnshēn] control conduct; control temperament

liàn

琏(璉) [liàn] (n) 古代帝王祭祖先时盛黍稷等食品用的木盘子 wooden disc; plate

殓(殮) [liàn] (v) 把死尸装进棺材 dress a corpse for burial; encoffin; layout

殓衣 [liànyī] the clothing for a corpse; shroud

潋(瀲) [liàn] 〔潋滟〕(n) 水波相连的样子 wavy

炼(煉) [liàn] 1 (v) 用火烧制 refine; purify; smelt 2 (v) 用心琢磨使词句精简 refine a sentence to be precise

炼丹术 [liàndānshù] alchemy

炼钢 [liàn gāng] steel-making; steel-smelting

炼油 [liàn yóu] oil refining; refining of petroleum

练(練) [liàn] 1 (n) 白绢 a peice of silk 2 (v) 反复地温习 practise; train; drill ✱ 我们要多练习，才能学好数学。 We must practise Mathematics constantly in order to do them well. 3 (adj) 经验多，熟悉 experienced ✱ 他在这个部门工作了十多年，是个老练的技术人员。 Having worked in this department for over ten years, he is an experienced technician.

练兵 [liàn bīng] train troops; training

练习 [liànxí] practise; exercise

链 [liàn] (n) 用金属环连接而成的长条 a metal chain

恋（戀）[liàn] 1 (v) (n) 爱情 love. romance; love 2 (v) 感情深，想念不忘 love deeply; feel strong attachment for

恋爱 [liàn'ài] love; be in love

恋恋不舍 [liàn liàn bùshě] reluctant to part

恋人 [liànrén] lovers; sweetheart

liáng

良 [liáng] 1 (adj) 好 good; virtuous; kind ＊他是个善良的人，很乐于帮助人家。He is a good person, and is happy to help others. 2 (adv) 很 very; quite; indeed; really

良好 [liánghǎo] good; fine

良师益友 [liáng shī yì yǒu] a good teacher and friend

良田 [liángtián] fertile farmland

良心 [liángxīn] conscience

良心有愧 [liángxīnyǒukuì] conscience-stricken

良药苦口 [liáng yào kǔ kǒu] good medicine is usually bitter

良缘 [liángyuán] a happy union; a good match

良种 [liángzhǒng] picked seed; high-quality seed; fine strain; fine breed

粮（糧）[liáng] 1 (n) 食物，用来吃的农产物 grain; provisions; foods 2 (n) 农业税 taxes

粮草；粮秣 [liángcǎo][liángmò] food and fodder; rations and forage

粮食 [liáng·shi] grain; cereals; staple food

粮饷；军粮 [liáng xiǎng; jūn liáng] food supplies or rations for the army

踉 [liáng] [跳踉] (v) 跳跃 jump 另见 [liàng]

凉 [liáng] 1 (adj) 微寒，不热 cool; cold; refreshing＊早上下了一场雨，使到下午天气很凉。The rain in the morning contributes to the coolness in the afternoon. 2 (adj) 比喻失望灰心 disappointed; disillusioned ＊他重考好几次都不及格，心都凉了。After he had failed in several re-examinations, he became disappointed. 另见 [liàng]

凉快 [liáng·kuai] nice and cool; delightfully cool

凉爽 [liángshuǎng] pleasantly cool

凉鞋 [liángxié] sandals

梁 [liáng] 1 (n) 架在墙或柱上支撑房顶的横木 a beam 2 (n) 桥 a bridge 3 (n) 物体中间高起长条的部分 an elevation ＊山梁 a ridge

粱 [liáng] 1 (n)[高粱] 草本植物 kaoliang 2 (n) 品种特别好的栗 millet

量 [liáng] 1 (v) 用工具计算东西的多少，长短，大小 measure＊弟弟買新鞋子时，先把自已的脚量好。Before buying his new shoes, my younger brother measured his feet. 2 (v) 估量 estimate

量角器 [liángjiǎoqì] protractor

量具 [liángjù] measuring tools 另见 [liàng]

liǎng

两（兩）[liǎng] 1 (numeral) 数词 two; double; couple ＊我有两本字典。I have two dictionaries. 2 (adj) 双方 both 3 (n) 表示不定的数目 an arbitrary number; a few; some ＊他所说的话只有两三个人相信。Only two or three persons believe in what he said. 4 (n) 重量单位，十钱为一两 a tail; an ounce (weight)

两败俱伤 [liǎngbàijùshāng] neither side wins; both sides suffer

两不相照 [liǎng bù xiāng zhào] ignoring one another

两重性 [liǎngchongxìng] duality; dual character

两极分化 [liǎngjífēnhuà] polarization

两面派 [liǎngmiànpài] double-dealer; double-faced

两方 [liǎngfāng] both sides; the two

parties
两可 [liǎngkě] alternative; optional
两棲动物 [liǎng qīdòng wù] amphibian
两全其美 [liǎng quán qì měi] satisfy both demands; both sides were taken care of
两面三刀 [liǎng miàn sāndāo] double-dealing; vicious

liàng

凉 [liàng] (v) 把东西放在通风或阴凉的地方 to cool something
另见 [liáng]

谅(諒) [liàng] 1 (v) 不计较 excuse; pardon; believe ✱ 如果学生不用功读书，老师不应该原谅他们。If the pupils are not serious in studies, the teacher should not pardon them. 2 (v) 料想 suppose; guess ✱ 上週寄去的信，谅已收悉。I guess you have received my letter which was sent to you a week ago.
谅必如此 [liàngbìrúcǐ] I think it must be so; most probably it is so
谅解 [liàngjiě] be tolerant and understanding; understand; come to an agreement

晾 [liàng] (v) 在太阳底下晒干或通风处吹干 to air ✱ 她把湿衣服掛在屋外。**She hanged the clothes outside the house to dry.**

辆(輛) [liàng] (a measure word) 量词，用于计算车的数目 a number-word for wheeled vehicles ✱ 一辆气车 a motor-car

踉 [liàng]〔踉跄〕(adj) 脚步不稳的样子 stagger; totter
另见 [liáng]

亮 [liàng] 1 (adj) 明，光明 bright; brilliant; clear; luminous; lustrous ✱ 灯光不亮，我看不清楚。**I cannot see clearly because the light is not bright.** 2 (v) 发光 elucidate; illuminate ✱ 黎明来临了，太阳慢慢地升上来，照亮了大地。**The dawn had approached, and the sun rose slowly to illuminate the earth.** 3 (adj) (声音) 强，响 loud, clear (sounds)
亮光 [liàngguāng] light
亮晶晶 [liàng jīng jīng] sparkling; glistening

量 [liàng] 1 (n) 计算东西体积的器具的总称 a measure: quantity 2 (n) 容纳的限度 capacity ✱ 你的酒量很好，但是不可喝了太多。**You have a good capacity for wine, but you should not drink too much** 3 (n) 数限 quantity; amount; volume; output ✱ 雨量多的地方，每年生产较多白米。Places with abundant rainfall yield more rice annually. 4 (v) 估计 estimate; think ✱ 你的胆子这么小，量你不敢接受他们的挑战。**You are so timid that I think you dare not accept their challenge.**
量变 [liàngbiàn] quantitative change
量才录用 [liàng cái lù yòng] assigning work according to ability
量大;量广 [liàngdà; liàngguǎng] broad-minded; liberal; of wide capacity
量力 [liànglì] according to one's ability and strength
量力而行 [liàng lìérxíng] act according to one's ability
量入为出 [liàng rù wéi chù] budget according to income
量体裁衣 [liàng tǐ cái yı] cut the garment according to the figure
另见 [liáng]

liāo

撩 [liāo] (v) 提，掀起 raise; lift up
另见 [liao]

liáo

僚 [liáo] 1 (n) 旧社会的官史 officer; official 2 (n) 指定在一起做官的人 official
僚属 [liáoshǔ] staff; subordinates
僚友 [liáoyǒu] a comrade; a colleague

撩 [liáo] (v) 挑弄，引逗 disturb
另见 [liāo]

嘹 [liáo]〔嘹亮〕[liáoliàng] (adj) 声音清晰，响亮 (person's voice) clear; resonant; reverberant ＊学生们以嘹亮的歌声，唱出了一首优美动听的歌曲。The students raised their voice loud and clear, to sing a beautiful song.

缭（繚）[liáo] 1 (v) 缠绕 encircle; linger in the air ＊在工业区里到处可看到烟雾缭绕。In the industrial estate, heavy smokes could be seen lingering in the sky. 2 (v) 用针缝缀 sew

缭乱 [liáoluàn] confused; confounded

缭绕 [liáorǎo] encircle; linger in the air

燎 [liáo] (v) 火绕（原野）blaze up; set fire to (the wild)

燎原 [liáo yuán] start a prairie fire; prairie on fire

寮 [liáo] (n) 小屋 hut; shed

疗（療）[liáo] (v) 医治 heal; cure; treat; remedy

疗养 [liáoyǎng] recuperate; convalesce

疗养院 [liáoyǎngyuàn] sanatorium

辽（遼）[liáo] (adj) 远 far; distant ＊科学家们计划把北极的冰山运到辽远的中東干燥区。The scientists planned to drag the Arctic icebergs over a great distance to the arid regions in the middle East.

辽阔 [liáokuò] vast expanses; very extensive; boundless

辽落 [liáo luò] distant, remote

辽远 [liáoyuǎn] far away; remote

寥 [liǎo] 1 (adj) 稀少 scarce; scanty; a few ＊半夜三更，街道上的行人寥寥无几。There are few passers-by on the street at mid-night. 2 (adj) 空虚，静寂 solitary ; vacant; empty ＊她一个人关在一间大屋，又沒有亲友到访，感到十分寂寥。Staying in a big house alone and with no relatives or friends visiting her, she feels solitary and lonely.

寥廓 [liáokuò] broad and far-reaching; immensity

寥寥无几 [liáo liáo wú jǐ] very few

寥落 [liáo luò] deserted; desolate

聊 [liáo] 1 (adv) 姑且，略微 carelessly; merely; anyhow 2 (v) 依赖 depend on; rest on ＊在经济危机的严重打击下，物价飞涨，民不聊生。Seriously affected by economic crisis and in the face of soaring of prices, the people have nothing to depend on for a living. 3 (v) 闲谈 chat; talk freely ＊如果你有时间请到我家来聊聊。If you are free , please come over to my house and have a chat.

聊且粗略 [liáo qiě cū luè] careless; indifferent

聊胜于无 [liáoshèngyūwú] a little bit is better than none

聊天 [liáo tiān] chat; have a free and easy talk

聊以自慰 [liáo yǐ zì wèi] merely to console oneself

liǎo

潦 [liǎo] 1〔潦草〕(adj) (v) 马虎，草率 rough;careless;scrawl negligently; scribble over 2〔潦倒〕(adj) 颓废失意的样子 unlucky; never getting a chance of good life; having a bad time 另见 [lǎo]

了（瞭）[liǎo] 1 (v) 明白 understand; apprehend ＊他不了解基本的数学，所以无法把物理学搞好。He does not know basic Mathematics, and so has no means to do well in Physics. 2 (v) 完 complete; finish; end up ＊他们之间的冲突早已了結，因为他们已经不是同事了。The conflict between them was over long ago, because they were no more colleagues. 3 (adv) 完全（不）一点（也不）very; fully ＊面对重重困难，他却了无惧色，冷静地去处理。In face of difficulties, he is not frightened at all; instead, he handles them calmly. 4 (part) 放在动词后，表示完結 a particle used after a verb toindicate the completion of an action ＊他已经离开新加坡了。 He had already left Singapore.

了不得 [liǎo·bu·de] something serious; grave; wonderful; marvellous

了不起 [liǎo·bu qǐ] swell with pride; far from common

了解 [liǎojiě] understand; know; grasp

了结 [liǎojié] have completed; be through with; have done with

了然 [liǎorán] clearly; plainly

了如指掌 [liǎo rú zhǐ zhǎng] a thorough understanding; insight

了事 [liǎo shì] make an end of; end up (eg. end up in nothing definite)

另见 [liào]
[·le]

liào

了(瞭) [liào] (v) 登高远望 look from afar

了望 [liàowàng] observe; take a distant view; look from afar

另见 [·le]
[liǎo]

镣(鐐) [liào] (n) 加在脚上使行动不自由的刑具 shackles

镣铐 [liàokào] shackles

料 [liào] 1 (n) 材物，東西 materials; raw materials ＊要有足夠的材料，才能造出既壮丽又牢固的房子。Adequate supply of materials is necessary for the construction of a splendid and solid house. 2 (n) 喂牲口的食物 provender;grain 3 (v) 猜想，估計 suppose; guess; expect ＊小偷没料到有便衣警员跟在后面，竟在店面拿走了一个手表。 The thief did not expect to be followed by a policeman in plain clothes and lifted a watch from the shop.

料理 [liàolǐ] look after; arrange; set in order

料想 [liàoxiǎng] imagine; conceive; consider

廖 [liào] (n) 姓 a surname

liē

咧 [liē] (v) 嘴张开，嘴角向两边伸展 to open one's mouth slightly

liè

列 [liè] 1 (v)摆出来line up; enumerate ＊博物院里陈列了很多历史古物。Many historical relics were displayed in the museum. 2 (v) 安排，归类 arrange, name ＊出入口公司的职员把一切要买的物件列入訂货单里，然后连同支票寄給卖力。The clerk of the import-export company named all the items to be purchased on the Purchase Order, and then sent it to the seller, together with a cheque. 3 (n) 排 a rank; a file; a row; a line

列表 [lièbiǎo] list

列队 [lièduì] line up

列举 [lièjǔ] list; enumerate; bring up one by one

列强 [lièqiáng] the big powers; industrialised nations

列位 [lièwèi] ladies and gentlemen

列席 [liè xí] be an observer at a conference

列传 [lièzhuàn] biography; story of one's life

冽 [liè] (adj) (n) 寒冷 very cold; chilly ; cold air; chill

冽风 [lièfēng] a cold wind

烈 [liè] 1 (adj) 猛烈，强烈 fiery; energetic; fierce; furious; raging ＊经过一场烈火后，这地方变成一个死城。 After a raging fire, this place had become a dead city 2 (n) 事业，功业 merit 3 (adj) 正直，刚毅 high principled; meritorious＊他是个刚烈的英雄。He was a high principled hero

烈火 [lièhuǒ] raging flames

烈火见真金 [liè huǒ jiàn zhēn jīn]from amidst blazing fires one can see genuine gold

烈日 [lièrì] scorching sun

烈士 [lièshì] martyr; a hero

烈性 [lièxìng] violent temper;strong (wine.)

烈焰 [lièyàn] a big blaze

裂 [liè] (v) 破开，分 crack; split; break; rip open; tear ＊ 在工作的工友们，衣服破裂不堪。The clothes of the labouring workers were badly torn.

裂缝 [liè fèng] a crack; an opening; a small gap

裂痕 [liè hén] split; crack; fissure

裂开 [lièkāi] split open; burst

裂口 [liè kǒu]an opening made by force (eg. gash, crack); a slit

裂纹 [liè wén] small surface cracks; cleavage

趔 [liè]〔趔趄〕(v) 脚步歪斜，站不稳，要摔倒的样子 stumble

躐 [liè] (v) 超越，跳 skip over; overstep

躐等 [lièděng] overstep the order

鬣 [liè] (n)马，狮子等兽类颈上的长毛 fur

猎（獵） [liè] (v) (n) 捕捉禽兽 hunt wild animals;hunting; field sports

猎场 [lièchǎng] hunting place

猎户 [lièhù] foresters; huntsmen

猎奇 [lièqí] hunt for novelty; hunting after grotesqueries

猎取 [lièqǔ] gained by hunting; seize

猎犬，猎狗 [lièquǎn; liègǒu] a pointer; a hunting dog; a hound

猎人 [lièrén] hunter

猎食 [lièshí] hunt for food

捩 [liè] (v) 扭转 to twist; wrest; wrench

劣 [liè] (adj) 坏，不好 bad; inferior; poor ＊你买了劣等货，却付了那么多的钱，实在不值得。It is indeed not worthwhile for you to pay so much for such inferior goods.

劣德 [lièdé] little virtue; of low virtue

劣迹 [lièjì] a bad reputation; proof of misconduct

劣品 [lièpǐn] inferior quality;a black guard; a bad character

劣行 [lièxíng]misconduct;ill behaviour

·lie

咧 [·lie] (part) 助词，意思相当于“了”“啦”。 similar in meaning to “了”“啦”＊开门吧，我回来咧！Please open the door, I'm back!

lín

粦 [lín] (adj) 形容流水清澈 clear; lucid (water)

嶙 [lín] 〔嶙峋〕1 (adj)山石重叠的样子 abrupt and craggy, (of mountains) 2 (adj) 身体消瘦的样子 skinny; thin (physique)

璘 [lín] (n) 玉的光彩 the lustre of jade

鳞（鱗） [lín] (n) 鱼类，爬行动物等身体表面长的角质或骨质的透明薄片 scale (of fish, reptile, etc.)

鳞集 [línjí] herd together

鳞介 [línjiè] fishes and shells; marine products

鳞爪 [lín zhǎo] trifles

麟 [lín] 〔麟角〕(n) 比喻某些罕得的东西 rare; few; scarce

遴 [lín] (v) 挑选 choose; select for appointment ＊本校要遴选代表去参加全国的中学演讲比赛。 Our school will select representatives to enter the nation-wide secondary school oratorical contest.

邻（鄰） [lín] 1 (n) 住处接近的人家 neighbour; neighbourhood 2 (adj) 靠近的 near; next; neighbouring; close by ＊印尼是星加坡的邻国。Indonesia is a neighbouring country of Singapore.

邻邦 [línbāng] neighbouring country

邻境 [línjìng] vicinity; neighbourhood

邻居 [línjū] a neighbouring house; neighbour

林 [lín] 1 (n) 成片的树木 a forest; a wood; a grove; a thicket 2 (n) 聚集在一起同类的人或事物 crowd; group; multitude ＊图书馆的小说部是著作之林。The novel section of the library is a multitude of classics. 3 (n) 林业 forestry

林立 [línlì](fig.) standing like a forest; a forest of ...; numerous

林林总总 [línlínzǒngzǒng]together; as crowded trees growing in a forest

淋 [lín] (v) 浇 take a shower; be caught (in the rain); sprinkle ＊她身体很弱，被雨淋了便会生病。She is so weak that her being caught in rain will make her suffer from sickness.

淋漓 [línlí] vivid and moving; roundly

淋漓尽致 [lín lí jìn zhì]deep and vivid; thoroughly; fully (portrayed or expressed)

淋浴 [lín yù] shower bath

另见 [lìn]

琳 [lín] (n) 美玉 a gem

琳琅 [línláng] valuables

琳琅满目 [línlángmǎnmù] an array of beautiful things

霖 [lín] (n) 久下不停的雨，也称干旱时所需的大雨 a continuous shower; rain; the rain which comes after a dry spell

霖霖 [lín lín] continuous rains

霖雨 [línyǔ] a long spell of rain

临(臨) [lín] 1 (v) 到 come about; befall; reach; approach＊总理亲临乡村地区去了解农民生活。The Prime Minister reached the rural area in person in order to understand more about the life of the peasants. 2 (prep) 靠近，对着 near to; on the point of; at ＊那老财迷临死的時候，还想着赚钱。That old miser still thinks of making money at the point of death. 3 (v) 照着字或画模彷 copy

临别 [línbié] at parting; when leaving

临床 [línchuáng] clinical treatment

临海 [línhǎi] seaside

临机应变 [línjīchùzhì] do what is appropriate at the hour

临近 [línjìn] approach; close by

临渴掘井 [lín kě jué jǐng] to dig a well when thirsty (fig)—do a thing at the last minute

临盆 [lín pén] child-brith

临时 [lín shí] provisional; temporary

临危不惧 [lín wēi bùjù] fearless in face of danger

临阵退缩 [lín zhèn tuì sù] to skulk when going into battle

临终，临死 [línzhōng línsǐ] about to die; at death's doors; at the point of death

lǐn

凛 [lǐn] 1 (adj) 寒冷 cold 2 (adj) 严肃可敬，威严的样子 stern; severe

凛冽 [lǐnliè] biting cold; freezing cold

凛凛 [lǐnlǐn] stern and severe; biting cold

凛然 [lǐnrán] awe-inspiring

懔 [lǐn] (v) (n) 畏惧 fear; be afraid of; fear; awe

懔懔 [lǐnlǐn] trembling from fear

懔栗 [lǐnlì] shivering with cold

懔然 [lǐnrán] awe-struck; startled

檩 [lǐn] (n) 也叫"桁" purlines of a roof

廪 [lǐn] (n) 粮仓 a public granary

lìn

蔺(藺) [lìn] (n) 草本植物。可作蓆用 a kind of rush used for making mats

吝 [lìn] (adj) 应该用的不舍得用 stingy; miserly

吝啬 [lìnsè] miserly; stingy

吝惜 [lìnxī] stint; save or spare (effort, etc.)

赁 [lìn] (v) 租 hire; rent

淋 [lìn] (n) 一种性病 gonorrhea 另见 [lín]

líng

伶 [líng] (n) 戏剧演员 an actor; actress

伶丁 [língdīng] lonely; isolated; desolate

伶俐 [líng·lì] clear headed; intelligent

伶牙俐齿 [língyálìchǐ] fluent; eloquent

玲 [líng] (n) 玉石相碰的声音 tinkling sound of gem-pendants

玲珑 [línglóng] cleverly carved; intricate (carving); elegant

铃(鈴) [líng] 1 (n) 打击乐器 a bell (music) 2 (n) 响器 a bell (eg. door-bell; hand-bell) 3 (n) 铃状的东西 bell-like articles

铃鸣；铃响 [lingmíng; língxiǎng] a bell rings (tinkles); ring (push, press) the bell

聆 [líng] (v) 听 hear; pay attention to ＊他虚心地聆听别人的意见 。He humbly hears the opinions of others.

聆教 [língjiāo] hear one's instruction

羚 [líng]〔羚羊〕(n) 哺乳动物，羊类，其角可作药材 antelope; a gazelle

羚羊角 [língyángjiǎo] the horns of the antelope, used as medicine for relief of heat in the body

龄(齡) [líng] 1 (n) 岁数 one's age ＊这小孩子已是十岁，进入一年级 算是超龄。 This child, being ten years old, is over aged in primary one 2 (n) 年数，时期 number of year; period ＊这老工人有十年的工龄 。The old worker has experienced ten work years.

翎 [líng] (n) 鸟翅膀或尾巴上的长羽毛 a plume; a feather

翎毛 [língmáo] feather

零 [líng] 1 (v) 下雨，比喻象雨一样的落下 rain; (fig) fall 2 (v) 草木凋落 fall(plant, leaves); be stripp ed of leaves 3 (adj) (n) 部分，零碎，不成整数的 fractional; broken-up a fraction; a remainder 4 (n) 数学上把数字符号"〇"读作零 zero; naught

零活儿 [línghuór] odd jobs

零件 [língjiàn] spare parts; accessory

零乱 [língluàn] disorderly; messy; disordered

零七八碎 [língqībāsuì] odd pieces; small separate pieces ; odds and ends

零钱 [língqián] small change

零散 [líng·san] incomplete in a set

零食 [língshí] tit-bits (eating between meals)

零售 [língshòu] retail; sell in small quantities

零碎 [língsuì] remnants; odd pieces; left over; fragmentary

零星 [língxīng] sporadic; in pieces; in fragments; odds and ends,; miscellaneous

零用钱 [língyòngqián] pocket money

囹 [líng]〔囹圄〕(n) 监狱 a prison; a jail

凌 [líng] 1 (n) 冰 ice 2 (v) 侵犯，欺侮 treat badly; ill-treat. ＊以前的帝王常常凌辱人民。Kings of ancient days always ill-treated the people. 3 (v) 逼近 advance; approach ＊凌晨

approaching dawn; daybreak 4 (v) 升高 rise; soar ∗ 军机快速地凌空飞去。 The military planes swiftly soared in the sky.

凌驾 [língjià] override; exceed; surpass

凌空 [língkōng] soar; fly high

凌厉 [línglì] quick and forceful

凌乱 [língluàn] in great disorder; in a mess

凌辱 [língrǔ] humiliate; insult; disgrace; put to shame; abuse

凌云 [língyún] reach the clouds; pre-eminent

陵 [líng] 1 (n) 大土山 a high mound; a hill 2 (n) 坟墓 a tomb; a grave

陵谷变迁 [línggǔ biànqiān] mounds and valleys change - the changes of the times

陵墓 [língmù] mausoleum; tomb; grave

绫(綾) [líng] (n) 一种很薄的丝织品 silk damask

菱 [líng] (n) 草本植物 water chestnut

菱形 [língxíng] rhombus

灵(靈) [líng] 1 (adj) 聪明，机敏 intelligent; clever ∗ 他是个精灵的小孩子，不论学什么都很快。 Being an intelligent child, he is quick in learning anything. 2 (adj) 有效验 effective ∗ 有人说这药品很灵，头痛时吃一粒就立刻见效。 Some people say that this medicine is effective, one tablet will cure any headache. 3 (adj) 精神的，神圣的，超自然的 spiritual; divine; supernatural

灵便 [líng·bian] light and convenient

灵感 [línggǎn] inspiration

灵魂 [línghún] soul; spirit

灵活 [línghuó] flexible; agile; active and intelligent

灵柩 [língjiù] hearse

灵机一动 [língjīyīdòng] a bright idea occurs; hit upon a good idea

灵敏 [língmǐn] intelligent; quick-witted; smart

灵巧 [língqiǎo] clever; dexterous; skilful; ingenious

灵通 [língtōng] well-informed

灵验 [língyàn] efficacious; effective

lǐng

岭(嶺) [lǐng] 1 (n) 山顶 a peak 2 (n) 山脉 a ridge; a mountain range

领(領) [lǐng] 1 (n) 颈部 the neck 2 (n) 衣领 the collar 3 (n) 大纲，要点 outline; main point 4 (v) 带，引 guide; lead; direct ∗ 大将军领兵打战。 The general led his troops to war. 5 (v) 接受，取得 receive ∗ 父親见儿子到台上领奖时，感到十分高兴。 The father saw his son receiving the prize on stage, he felt extremely happy.

领带 [lǐngdài] necktie; tie

领导 [lǐngdǎo] lead; leader; leadership

领海 [lǐnghǎi] territorial inland sea; territorial waters

领会 [lǐnghuì] grasp; understand; comprehend

领教 [lǐngjiào] have enough experience of ... ; have the pleasure of seeing .. ; seek advice

领空 [lǐngkōng] air space; territorial inland air

领略 [lǐnglüè] comprehend; catch the idea

领命 [lǐngmìng] receive commands

领取 [lǐngqǔ] receive what is due

领事 [lǐngshì] consul

领事馆 [lǐngshìguǎn] consulate

领土 [lǐngtǔ] territory

领悟 [lǐng wù] comprehend; realise

领袖 [lǐngxiù] leader

领域 [lǐngyù] domain; sphere; national territory

lìng

令 [lìng] 1 (v) (n) 指示 order; instruct; command; order 2 (v) 使得 cause; make ∗ 全球性的空气污化令人担忧。 The world-wide air pollution causes worries among people.

令名 [lìngmíng] a good name; reputation; honour

令人发指 [lìngrénfāzhǐ] make one's hair stand on end with anger; makes one highly annoyed

令人作呕 [lìngrénzuō oǔ] make one sick; disgusting

令闻广誉 [lìngwénguǎng yù] a good reputation and widespread praises

令尊 [lìngzūn] your father

另 [lìng] (adj) 别的 another; separate; other; extra ＊这件事还没谈完又谈起另一件，太乱了。It is very confusing to talk about another thing without first completing this matter.

另起炉灶 [lìngqǐlúzào] make a fresh start

另外 [lìngwài] separate; apart from; separately; other; besides

另眼相看 [lìng yǎn xiāng kàn] regard somebody favourably; see something in the new light

另议 [lìng yì] discuss separately

liū

溜 [liu] 1 (v) 滑行 glide 2 (adj) 光滑，平滑 smooth; glossy 3 (v) 偷偷地走开 slink off; slip away; sneak away＊小偷在混乱中溜走了。The thief slipped away amidst the confusion.

溜冰 [līubīng] ice skating

溜达 [līu dá] stroll; go for a walk

另见 [liù]

liú

留 [líu] 1 (v) 停在某一个地方或地位上不离开 stay; remain; detain; keep ＊瑪利因听写不及格，放学后被老師留在校里，达半小时之久。Mary failed in her Spelling test and was detained by the teacher for half-an-hour after school. 2 (v)把注意力放在某方面 pay attention to＊姐姐要找工作，所以很留心报纸上的广告。My elder sister is looking for a job so she pays much attention to the advertisements in the papers. 3 (v) 保留 retain; reserve; keep ＊文件有留底稿，以后查起来就会很方便。The duplicate copies of the documents are kept for easy reference in future.

留恋 [líuliàn] reluctant to part with; long for

留连忘返 [líu lián wàng fǎn] have much enjoyment and forget to go back home

留念 [líuniàn] give something on parting as a souvenir

留情 [líu qíng] show consideration; or mercy

留任 [líu rèn] remain (continue) in office

留神 [líu shén] be on the look-out; be wary

留宿 [líusù] lodge a person; ask one to lodge over the night

留心 [líu xīn] be careful; pay attention

留学 [líuxué] study abroad; be abroad for further studies

留意 [líu yì] take precaution; be careful; keep in mind

留有余地 [líu yǒu yú dì] leave room for; make allowance for

榴 [líu]〔石榴〕(n) 落叶灌木或小乔木，果可吃 the pomegranate

榴梿 [líulián] durian

瘤 [líu] (n) 动物身体组织增殖生成的肉疙瘩 a tumour; a swelling

流 [líu] 1 (v) 液体移动 flow; drift ＊山上的水不停地流入山下的河里。Water flows from the hill-top continuously into the river below. 2 (n) 水道

江河 a water way; a stream, a river ＊我国有多少河流？ How many rivers are there in our country? 3 (v) 流传，传布 circulate; spread; hand down ＊许多古代民间故事流传到今天。Many old folktales are handed down till today. 4 (v) 往来无定或转运不停 circulate; pass ＊通过卖买和物件的交换，货币在社会上流通。Through trade and exchange of things, money circulates in the society 5 (n) 派别 a class; a kind ＊第一流的餐馆不是普通受薪者有能力光顾的。First class restaurants are not what ordinary wage-earners can afford to patronize.

流弊 [liúbì] malpractice; weak point; short-coming

流产 [liú chěn] miscarriage

流畅 [liúchàng] fluent

流动 [liúdòng] float; fluid; mobile; circulate

流毒 [liú dú] poision; of evil effect

流芳百世 [liú fāng bǎi shì] leaving behind a good reputation for posterity

流汗 [liúhàn] perspire; sweat

流浪 [liú làng] wander about; rove

流利 [liú lì] fluent; glib; smooth

流连忘返 [liú lián wàng fǎn] lingering on; forgetting to return

流离失所 [liú lí shì suǒ] wandering about; homeless

流露 [liú lù] show unintentionally

流落 [liúluò] become destitute and drift about

流氓 [liúmáng] vagabond; loafers; rascals

流民 [liúmín] vagrants; wandering people; tramps

流亡 [liú wáng] live in exile abroad; exile; flee

流行 [liúxíng] prevail; be wide-spread; popularity; fashion

流星 [liúxīng] meteor

流言蜚语 [liú yán fēi yǔ] rumours and slanders

流转 [liúzhuǎn] circulate

琉 [liú]〔琉璃〕(n)用铝和钠的硅酸化合物烧制成的釉料 an opaque, pottery-like substance; a kind of pottery-ware found near Peking, China

刘（劉）[liú] (n) 姓 a surname

镠（鏐）[liú] (n) 纯美的金子 pure gold

liǔ

绺（綹）[liǔ] 量词(a measure word) 一绺丝线 a skein of silk thread

柳 [liǔ] (n)落叶乔木，树不很高，枝作弯状，統称"杨柳"the willow tree

柳条布 [liǔtíobù] stripped cotton cloth

柳巷 [liǔxiàng] brothels; places of dissipation

liù

溜 [liù] (v) 水流 flow of water
另见 [liū]

馏（餾）[liù] (v) 把凉了的熟食品蒸热 to heat the food which is already cold

六 [liù] 数词 (numeral) six (6)

六角形 [liùjiǎoxíng] hexagon; a six-sided figure (geometry)

六书 [liùshū] the six principles of formation of Chinese script

六月 [liùyuè] June. the 6th month in Chinese calender

陆（陸）[liù] 数词 (numeral) "六"的正楷写法，和"六"同义 another written form of the word "six"
另见 [lù]

lóng

龙（龍）[lóng] 1 (n) 传说中的一种动物。体大有鳞，能吐火球，代表吉祥事物 the dragon

2 (n) 古生物学上指一些巨大的有脚有尾的爬行类动物 a dinosaur

龙飞凤舞 [lóng fēi fèng wǔ] a description of excellent calligraphy
龙骨 [lónggǔ] the keel
龙马精神 [lóng mǎ jīng shén] vigorous ; persistence in working
龙潭虎穴 [lóngtánhǔxué] exceptionally dangerous places
龙头蛇尾 [lóng tóu shé wěi] dwindling away to nothing after an initial display of greatness
龙虾 [lóngxiā] lobster
龙涎香 [lóngxiánxiang] ambergris
龙争虎斗 [lóng zhēng hǔ dou] fierce battle or competition; a close fight
龙钟之年 [lóng zhōng zhī nián] the age of senility; old age

栊(櫳) [lóng] 1 (n) 窗 window 2 (n) 养兽的栏槛 cages used to keep animals

茏(蘢) [lóng] (adj) 也作"葱茏"，草木青翠茂盛的样子 luxuriant growth of vegetation

笼(籠) [lóng] 1 (n) 用竹，木或铁丝等制成用来捕鸟兽或养鸟兽的器具 a cage 2 (n) 用竹，木等制成，用以盛东西或罩东西的器具 a basket
笼头 [lóng tóu] a halter
另见 [lǒng]

聋(聾) [lóng] (adj) (n) 耳朵失灵听不见声音 deaf; hard of hearing ; deafness
聋人; 聋子 [lóngrén; lóng·zi] a deaf man; the deaf
聋哑者 [lóngyǎzhě] a deaf-mute

隆 [lóng] 1 (adj) 盛大 grand; solemn 2 (adj) 兴盛 prosperous; flourishing ＊他所经营的餐馆，目前生意十分兴隆。 Presently, the restaurant he is running enjoys prosperous business. 3 (n) 形容剧烈震动的声音 a peal (roar, crack) of thunder ＊雷声隆隆 peals of thunder
隆冬 [lóngdōng] the depth of winter
隆厚 [lónghòu] substantial; wealthy; generous
隆起 [lóngqǐ] upheave; rise; bulge
隆盛 [lóngshèng] booming; prosperous ; flourishing
隆重 [lóngzhòng] honour

lǒng

拢(攏) [lǒng] 1 (v) 集合起来，总合 collect; assemble; gather ＊他聚拢资料后，才动笔写文章。He assembled the data and then started to write his essay. 2 (v) 靠近 draw near ＊轮船一靠拢海港，工友们便开始卸货了。Once the steamer drew near the port, the workers began to unload the cargoes. 3 (v) 收缩使不松散 tie things together
拢岸 [lǒng àn] reach shore; lie along ashore
拢总 [lǒng zǒng] all; the sum total

垄(壟) [lǒng] 1 (n) 田埂 rice-field 2 (n) 农作物的行或行与行之间的空地 lines between plots of rice-fields
垄断 [lǒngduàn] monopolize; the exclusive control of something, especially some commercial products or a service that may be sold

笼(籠) [lǒng] (v) 遮盖，罩住 rest on; cover ＊早晨的雾笼罩着大地。 Heavy morning fog covers the good earth .
笼括 [lǒngkuò] contain; embody
笼统 [lǒngtǒng] general
笼罩 [lǒng zhào] hover over; be enveloped by
另见 [lóng]

弄 [lòng] (n) 小巷，胡同，弄堂 an alley
另见 [nong]

lōu

搂（摟） [lōu] (v) 用手或工具把东西聚集起来hold fast in the arms ＊他搂着几本书就往学校跑。 Holding a few books fast in his arms, he ran to school quickly.
另见 [lǒu]
[lǒu]

lóu

喽（嘍） [lóu] 〔喽罗〕 (n) 强盗的部下，大恶霸的爪牙，帮凶 the followers or men under a chief bandit; gangsters
另见 [·lou]

楼（樓） [lóu] 1 (n) 两层或多层以上的房屋 a house with one or more storeys 2 (n) 楼房的一层 an upper floor or storey; a tower 3 (n) 建筑物的上层部分或有上层结构的 the upper portion of a building structure

楼顶 [lóudǐng] attic
楼阁 [lóngé] an upper chamber; a terrace
楼上 [lóushàng] upstairs
楼台 [lóutái] a stage for the theatrical exhibitions; tower
楼梯 [lóutı] a staircase
楼下 [lóuxià] downstairs: ground-floor
楼厢 [lóuxiāng] gallery

蝼（螻） [lóu] 〔蝼蛄〕 (n) 昆虫 a mole-cricket
蝼蚁 [lóuyǐ] ants

lǒu

搂（摟） [lǒu] (v) 牵引，拉拢 drag or pull
另见 [lōu]
[lǒu]

搂（摟） [lǒu] (v) 两臂合抱 hug; embrace ＊剧终时，男女主角热情的搂抱在一起。 At the end of the film, the two main actor and actress embraced each other passionately.
另见 [lōu]
[lǒu]

篓（簍） [lǒu] (n) 用竹子，荊等编成用来盛东西的器具 a basket; a hamper ＊他买了一个木制的掷纸篓，只费一元八角。 He bought a new wooden waste paper basket just for $1.80.

lòu

镂（鏤） [lòu] (v) 雕刻 engrave;carve
镂刻 [lòukè] engrave; carve

陋 [lòu] 1 (adj) 丑的，粗劣的 vulgar; low; rustic; simple ＊他因为住在一间简陋无华的房子，所以不喜欢让同事们到他家去。 He shuns visiting by colleagues because of his simply—furnished house. 2 (adj) 狭小，简略 mean; humble; rustic ＊这间陋室的租金很低。 The monthly rent of this small room is low. 3 (adj) 不文明，不合理 uncivilized; unreasonable ＊陪葬这一陋习已被人们扬弃。The vulgar practice of burying the living with the dead has been abandoned by the people. 4 (adj) 见闻少 low; inexperienced in knowledge ＊关于哲学，我只有浅陋的认识。 As to philosophy, I have but a little knowledge.

陋劣 [lòuliè] despicable; base; mean; vile
陋巷 [lòuxiàng] humble quarters; slum; a narrow and dirty alley
陋习 [lòu xì] vulgar habits
陋於见闻 [lòu yu jiàn wén] solitary and inexperienced

漏 [lòu] 1 (v) (n) 从孔或缝中滴落或透过 leak; drip; a leak; leakage ＊袋子已被老鼠咬破，米慢慢的漏出來。 The sack was bitten by the rats, and rice leaked out little by little. 2 (v) 泄露 leak out; let out; let slip; disclose ＊一个公务员因走漏消息而被革职。 A civil servant was dismissed because he had leaked out information

漏斗 [lòudǒu] a funnel; a hopper

漏勺；酒漏 [lòusháo; jiǔlòu] a strainer; a colander

漏网 [lòu wǎng] escape the net; evade punishment

漏泄 [lòuxiè] leak out; be divulged; transpire

漏夜 [lòuyè] late in the night

露 [lòu] (v) 显现出来，如露面，露马脚 disclose; expose; manifest

露出 [lòu chù] disclose; let out; bare; expose; come out

露锋芒 [lòu fēng máng] show signs of one's astuteness; make one's shrewdness felt

露骨 [lòugǔ] candid; plainly spoken; frank

露光 [lòu guāng] exposure

露马脚 [lòu mǎ jiǎo] reveal one's evil character

露面 [lòu miàn] appear in public; show the face

loú

喽（嘍）[loú] (part) 助词。用于句末，同"啦" particle ＊走快点，要到喽！ Walk faster, we're reaching the place soon.
另见 [·lou]

lū

噜（嚕）[lū] (v) 说空话太多 to talk too much (adj) talkative; loquacious

lú

卢（盧）[lú] (n) 姓 a surname

鲈（鱸）[lú] (n) 鱼类 a perch

鸬（鸕）[lú]〔鸬鹚〕(n) 鸟类 the fishing cormorant

颅（顱）[lú] (n) 头盖骨，也指头部 the skull; the head

炉（爐）[lú] (n) 盛火的器具，多以土制 a stove; a fireplace; a furnace; an oven

炉格 [lúgé] fire gate; furnace bar; grate of a stove

炉火纯青 [lú huǒ chún qīng] one's training has reached perfection; well-trained

炉灶 [lúzào] a kitchen stove; a cook-stove

庐（廬）[lú] (n) 简陋的房屋 a hut; a cottage

庐舍 [lúshè] a hut; a cottage; a hovel

庐山真面目 [lú shān zhēn miàn] the real appearance of a person or thing

芦（蘆）[lú] (n) 草本植物生于水中 common reed; rushes

芦席 [lúxí] rush mats

鲁（魯）[lú] 1 (adj) 迟钝，笨 dull; stupid; mentally subnormal ＊一些老师不喜欢鲁钝的学生。Some teachers do not like dull students. 2 (adj) 莽撞，粗野 rude; blunt; rough ＊你不应以为工人们都是粗鲁的，他们也有智慧和经验。 You should not think that all workers are ill-mannered, they too possess knowledge and experiences.

鲁犷 [lú guǎng] crude; rough

鲁莽 [lú mǎng] rash; careless; rude; rough

lǔ

橹（櫓）[lǔ] (n) 用来摇摆，使小船前进的木制器具 a long oar

镥（鑥）[lǔ] (n) 化学元素 lutecium, an element, symbol Lu

虏（虜）[lǔ] 1 (v) 俘获 capture prisoners; seized ＊战事中，双方都俘虏了不少敌军。

During the battle, both parties captured many enemy soldiers. 2 (n) 捉住的敌人 a prisoner of war; a captive

虏掠 [lǔlüè] capture; take captive; plunder; seize

掳(擄) [lǔ] (v) 抢劫 plunder; seize

掳禁 [lǔjìn] carry off and keep prisoner

掳掠 [lǔlüè] plunder; carry off

卤(鹵，滷) [lǔ] 1(n) 盐卤 salt marsh; salt 2 (n) 浓汁 a kind of sauce

卤莽 [lǔmǎng] rash; careless; abrupt; rude

lù

录(錄) [lù] 1 (v) 记下来，抄写 record; note; write down; copy; transcribe * 一切供词已被庭内的书记录下来了。All that were said had been recorded down by the clerk in the court. 2 (n) 记载言行或事物的书刊，表册等 a record; annals; a document 3 (v) 采纳，任用 accept; select; employ * 老板喜欢录用听话的职员。Bosses like to employ obedient staff.

录供 [lùgòng] take down evidence

录请 [lù qǐng] send a copy with request

录取 [lùqǔ] select

录音 [lù yīn] sound-recording; record on the disc

录音广播 [lùyīnguǎngbō] broadcasting of a recorded speech

绿(綠) [lù] (adj) 青色 green

绿林好汉 [lùlínhǎohàn] people who band together in the forest to fight against the feudal ruling class

碌(磟) [lù] 1 (adj) 形容辛苦，繁忙 toilsome; laborious; busy * 政治家在大选之前便忙碌起来，到处访问选民，了解民情。Before the election, politicians became busy, visiting the voters everywhere so as to get better understanding about them. 2 (adj) 平凡，没有什么作为 ordinary; common * 你只想过着庸碌的一生吗？ Do you want merely to lead an ordinary life?

碌碌 [lùlù] ordinary; common

禄 [lù] (n) 古时称官吏的俸给 salary; official pay

禄俸 [lùfèng] official pay

禄位日隆 [lù wèi rì lóng] rise in rank and emolument

鹿 [lù] (n) 哺乳动物，比马小，性温柔 a deer; a stag (male); a hind (female deer); a fawn (young deer)

鹿角 [lùjiǎo] deer's horn

鹿茸 [lùróng] catilaginous part of root of antler

鹿肉 [lùròu] venison

鹿死谁手 [lù sǐ shuí shǒu] (fig.) it is still unknown that who will become the winner

漉 [lù] 1 (v) 滤去水分或渣滓 filter; drain 2 (adj) 渗出，润湿 dripping; wet * 湿漉漉 dripping wet

辘(轆) [lù] 1〔辘轳〕(n) (1) 装在井上吊水的器具 a pulley; wheel and axle (2) 机器上的绞盘 a roller; a pulley; a windlass 2〔辘辘〕(n) 形容车轮声 the rumbling of carriages

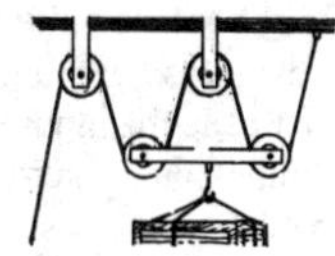

麓 [lù] (n) 山脚 foothill

路 [lù] 1 (n) 街道 a road; a path; a route; a street *从远处我们看见几个女孩在路上玩耍。From a distance, we saw a few girls playing on the road. 2 (n) 思想或行动的方向 way; direction; line (as of thoughts, action, etc.) *许多年青人从乡下到城市找生路。Many young people from the countryside went to cities to find a living. 3 (n) 种类 kinds; types

路不通行 [lù bù tōng xíng] close to traffic; no thoroughfare

路程 [lù chéng] a journey; a distance to be covered

路过 [lùguò] pass by or through a place; en route

路径 [lù jìng] path; route; way

路人 [lùrén] a traveller; a passer-by

路上 [lù·shang] on the road; on the way; on a journey

路遥知馬力,日久见人心 [lù yáo zhī mǎ lì, rì jiǔ jiàn rén xīn] distance reveals the stamina of a horse, and time shows up a man's true character

鹭(鷺) [lù] (n) 鸟类 an egret; a paddy bird; a snowy heron

鹭鸶 [lùsī] a chinese egret

露 [lù] 1 (n) 在大清早，留在草上和树叶上的水珠 dew 2 (v)(adj) 没有遮蔽或在屋子外面 exposed; bare; expose; outdoors *在露天地方集会，下雨时是很麻烦的。It is quite troublesome to hold an outdoor meeting when it is raining. 3 (v) 显出来，现出来 discloses; show through, manifest *他脸上露出惊讶之色。Surprise is manifested on his face.

露骨 [lùgǔ] become quite open; bareface; undisguisedly; bluntly

露宿 [lùsù] pass the night in the open

露天矿 [lùtiānkuàng] surface mining; an open mine

露营 [lù yíng] camping; camp out

另见 [lòu]

戮 [lù] (v) 杀 kill; stab; slaughter; put to death

戮力同心 [lù lì tóng xīn] concerted in effort and united in mind

戮囚 [lùqíu] kill prisoners

陆(陸) [lù] 1 (n) 陆地，高出水面的土地 the shore 2 (n) 地面上的 land; continent

陆地 [lùdì] land

陆路 [lùlù] by land; a land journey (route)

陆军 [lùjūn] army; the land force

陆续 [lù xù] in succession; one after the other; continually

另见 [liù]

辂(輅) [lù] (n) 古代的大车 a state carriage

lú

闾(閭) [lú] (n) 里巷的门，也指里巷 a lane or alley

闾巷 [lú xiàng] a lane; an alley

驴(驢) [lú] (n) 家畜，帮农人劳作的动物 donkey

lǔ

侣 [lǔ] (n) 同伴 a companion; a mate; a comrade

偻(僂) [lǔ](adj)(身体)弯曲 hunch-backed; bentbacked

偻佝 [lǔgōu] deformed; short and ugly

缕(縷) [lǔ] 1 (n) 线 hempen or silken threads 2 (adj) 一条一条地，有条理地 in detail *请你缕述失火的经过。Please tell us in detail how the fire broke out.

屡(屢) [lǔ] (adv) 多次 repeatedly; often; frequently

屡次 [lǔcì] repeatedly; time and again;

one after another

屡次三番 [lǚcì sānfān] repeatedly; again and again

屡见不鲜 [lǚjiànbùxiān] often seen; common place

屡教不改 [lǚjiàobùgǎi] refuse to mend one's way despite repeat rectification

屡易 [lǚ yì] frequent changes

旅 [lǚ] 1 (v) 在外，在外作客，到外国去观光 travel 2 (n) 军队的一种编制单位 a brigade 3 (n) 泛指军队 forces

旅程 [lǚchéng] journey

旅费 [lǚfèi] travelling expenses

旅馆 [lǚguǎn] hotel; an inn

旅客 [lǚkè] traveller

旅途 [lǚtú] journey

旅行 [lǚxíng] travel; journey; take a trip; make a tour

旅行支票 [lǚxíngzhīpiào] traveller's cheque

膂 [lǚ] (n) 脊梁骨 the back-bone

膂力 [lǚlì] strength

履 [lǚ] 1 (n) 鞋 shoes 2 (v) 踩走过 walk; tread ∗这里的土族，翻山越岭，如履平地。To the tribes people here, mountaineering is just like walking on level ground. 3 (v) 实行，执行 fulfil; perform; carry out ∗我们有责任履行合约中所立的规定。We have the responsibility to carry out all the requirements provided in the contract.

履历 [lǚlì] resume; record of working experience

履行 [lǚlíng] carry out; perform (eg. duty); put into effect

lǜ

虑(慮) [lǜ] 1 (v) (n) 思考 think upon anxiously; consider; thought; consideration ∗ 婚姻大事，你要好好地考虑才作决定。 Marriage is a serious matter; you must consider carefully before making a decision. 2 (v) 担忧，发愁 be anxious; suspicion; doubt ∗他顾虑孩子们的学业，决定为他们聘请一名家庭教师。Having been concerned about the children's study, he decided to employ a tutor for them.

虑及 [lǜjí] have anticipated

虑深 [lǜshēn] having forethought

虑远 [lǜyuǎn] long foresight

滤(濾) [lǜ] (v) 使液体通过纱布，木炭，沙或纸等，除去杂质，变为纯净 filter; strain; purify

滤清 [lǜqīng] filter; strain through cloth; percolate; leach

滤渣 [lǜzhá] strain off the sediment

绿(綠) [lǜ] (adj) 象草和树叶茂盛时的颜色，由藍，黄合成的颜色 green colour

绿豆 [lǜdòu] green lentils

绿化 [lǜhuà] clothe with greenery; make green; beautify

绿林 [lǜlín] greenwood; forest

绿野 [lǜyě] grassy plains

绿洲 [lǜzhōu] oasis

另见 [lù]

率 [lǜ] (n) 两个相关的物件在一定条件下的比值 a rate ∗这班的出席率每年都是全校最高的。The attendance rate of this class is the highest in the school every year.

另见 [shuài]

律 [lǜ] 1 (n) 规章，法则 rule; discipline; law ∗校长训示学生们遵守学校的纪律。The headmaster ordered that all students must observe school discipline. 2 (n) 音律，乐律 standard tunes in music

律典 [lǜdiǎn] a code

律师 [lǜshī] a solicitor; an attorney; lawyer

luán

峦(巒) [luán] 1 (n) 小而尖的山 low hills 2 (n) 连着的山 ridges

娈(孌) [luán] (adj) 美好 beautiful; pretty

孪(孿) [luán] (adj) 双生 twins * 占美和通美是一对孪生兄弟。 Jimmy and Tommy are twin brothers

鸾(鸞) [luán] (n) 传说中凤凰一类的鸟 a fabulous bird phoenix

鸾凤和鸣 [luán fèng hé míng] living in harmony-of marriage

鸾笺 [luánjiǎn] coloured letter-paper

脔(臠) [luán] (n) 切成小块的肉 meat in slices

脔分 [luán fēn] slice; cut to pieces

脔割 [luángē] dismemberment

luǎn

卵 [luǎn] (n) 成熟的雌性生殖细胞 egg

卵白 [luǎnbái] the albumen; the white portion of an egg

卵形 [luǎnxíng] oval; egg-shaped

luàn

乱(亂) [luàn] 1 (adj)(n)(adv)没有秩序 confused; disorderly; disorder; confusion; in a mess; out of order * 你的房间那么乱，收拾一下吧。Your room is in a mess, please tidy it. 2 (adj) 混杂，混淆 ravelled; perplexed: confused * 那个歹徒捣乱本地区的治安，终于被警方逮捕了。 The rogue had upset the security of this region; he was arrested by Police eventually. 3 (n) 战争；武装骚扰，叛乱 insurrection; revolt * 中国历史上的叛乱事件很多。 There were many revolts in Chinese history.

乱七八糟 [luàn qī bā zāo] topsy-turvy ; at sixes and sevens

乱世 [luàn shì] a stirring period; a chaotic period

lüè

掠 [lüè] 1 (v) 抢夺 rob; plunder; ravage * 敌兵入侵后，掠夺百姓的财物。After their invasion, the enemy forces plundered the properties of thepeople 2 (v) 轻轻擦过或拂过 flash; sweep, flit * 一架飞机在空中掠过。 An aeroplane swept across the sky.

掠夺品 [lüè duó pìn] prey; loot

掠过 [lüèguò] sweep

略 [lüè] 1 (adv) 简单，稍微 slightly; rather * 你略微大声一点，后座的人才能听到。 You speak slightly louder and those seated at the back will be able to hear. 2 (n) 简要的叙述 an outline; a sketch * 史书上有各国的史略。History books contain an outline of the history of every country. 3 (v) 省去，简化 leave out; omit; summarize * 略去不必要的细节。Omit unnecessary details. 4 (v) (n) 计划，计谋 plan; strategy; plan * 要打胜战，必须注意战略。To win a battle, one must attend to strategy. 5 (v) 夺取 seize; plunder; capture

略地 [lüèdì] seize territory

略可 [lüèkě] perhaps it will do; slightly possible

略知一二 [lüè zhī yì è] understand a little

略取 [lüèqǔ] take by force; capture

略胜一筹 [lüè shèng yì chóu] slightly better

略图 [lüètú] sketch

lūn

抡 [lūn] (v) 手臂用力挥动 swing 另见 [lún]

lún

伦(倫) [lún] 1 (n)同类，同等 relationships 2 (n) 人与人之间的道德关系 moral principles 3 (n) [伦次] degrees of comparison ; a series

伦理 [lúnlǐ] ethics

论(論) [lún]〔论语〕(n) 古书名 the Analects of Confucius 另见 [lùn]

抡(掄) [lún] (v) 选择 choose; select

另见 [lūn]

沦(淪) [lún] 1 (v) (adj) 淹没 submerge, submerged; sunk ＊有一艘油槽船在暴风雨中沉沦。A tanker submerged in the sea during the tempest. 2 (v) (adj) 没落，陷落 lost; ruin; lost; ruined ＊战争过后，海港沦为死市。 After the war, the sea-port was ruined and reduced to a dead city.

沦落 [lúnluò] ruin; degeneration; sink into vicious courses; fall into misery

沦亡 [lúnwáng] (of a country) perish

沦陷 [lúnxiàn] be occupied (territory); be fallen (into enemy's hand)

纶(綸) [lún] 1 (n) 钓鱼用的线 fishing-line 2 (n) 現用作合成纤维的名称 silken threads

轮(輪) [lún] 1 (n) 为使车前进走动，装在它下面的圆形物件 a wheel 2 (n) 机器上样子象车轮，能转动的零件 a gear 3 (v) (n) 按次序替换 take turns ;by turns ＊下个星期二，才轮到我做夜班。 It will be my turn to work on night shift next Tuesday 4 量词 a measure word ＊一轮明月。a bright moon

轮班 [lún bān] shift; rotation; in turn

轮船 [lúnchuán] steamer; steamship; ship

轮渡 [lúndù] ferry

轮廓 [lúnkuò] outline; contour; rough sketch; frame

轮流 [lúnliú] in turn; take turns; by shifts

轮值 [lúnzhí] take turns of duty

轮作，轮种 [lúnzuò; lúnzhòng] rotation of crops

lùn

论(論) [lùn] 1 (v) (n) 檢讨，分析，说明事理 discourse; talk about; discuss; debate; consider a discussion; an argument ＊对方的论点不强，所以在辩论会上败给我方。 The points raised by the opponents were weak, hence they lost to us in the debate. 2(n)分析和说明事理的话或文章 a composition; an essay 3 (n) 学说，有系统的理论 a thesis; a treatise 4 (v) 说，看待 consider; regard as 5 (v) 评定 judge; conclude 6 (prep) 按照 according to

另见 [lún]

论调 [lùndiao] argument; view; tone.

论断 [lùnduàn] infer; conclude

论功行赏 [lùngong xíngshǎng] reward according to merits

论及 [lùnji] with reference to; in regard to

论据 [lunjù] basis of argument

论理学 [lùnlǐxué] logic

论述 [lùnshù] deal with; elaborate; speak or write in detail; expound

论坛 [lùntán] comment; review; forum

论文 [lùnwén] essay; thesis

论月；按月 [lùnyuè; ànyuè] monthly; by months

论证 [lùnzhèng] expound and prove; demonstrate

论著 [lùnzhù] published works

luō

罗(囉) [luō] [罗嗦] 1 (v) 说话繁复，絮絮叨叨 talk too much; talkative ＊他罗嗦了一天，还是没有把问题说清楚。He has been talking so much the whole day, yet he is not able to clarify the problem. 2 (adj) 麻煩，琐碎 annoying; vexatious; troublesome ＊他们的事真罗嗦，不容易处理。It is not easy to handle their matter which is very annoying.

另见 [luó] [·lou]

luó

罗(羅) [luó] 1 (n) 捕鸟的网 a net to catch birds 2 (v) 张网捕捉 snare; catch with a net or trap ＊门

可罗雀 birds may be snared at the door of a deserted house. 3 (v) 排列，分布 list; arrange; spread out ∗他把这次旅行所拍的照片罗列给大家看。 He lists the photographs taken during this trip to show everybody. 4 (n) 一种丝织品 a kind of light silk; gauze 5 量词 (a measure word) a gross

另见 [luō]

[luó]

罗汉 [luóhàn] the disciples of Buddha

罗列 [luó liè] list (phonomenon, etc)

罗马教皇 [luó mǎjiàohuáng] the pope; the supreme pontiff

罗曼蒂克 [luómàndìkè] romantic

罗盘 [luópán] a compass

罗纱 [luóshā] gauze

罗网 [luówǎng] a net; snare; trammels

罗致 [luózhì] to collect

猡(玀) [luó] 〔猪猡〕(n) 猪 pig

锣(鑼) [luó] (n) 一种打击乐器，用铜制成 a gong

锣槌 [luóchuí] a stick used to beat gong

锣鼓 [luó gǔ] gong and drum

萝(蘿) [luó] 1 (n) 通常指某些能爬蔓的植物 creeping plant, vine 2〔萝卜〕(n) 草本植物，可食用 the garden radish; turnip 3〔萝芙木〕(n) 常绿小灌木 ivy

萝卜糖 [luó·bo táng] beet sugar

箩(籮) [luó] (n) 用竹子或柳条编制的装粮食或货物的器具 deep and open basket without a cover, made of bamboo

逻(邏) [luó] (v) 巡察，到处观看 patrol; inspect; watch ∗由于私会党蠢蠢欲动，警車经常巡逻这地区。 Due to the frequency of secret society activities, the police cars patrolled this area regularly.

逻辑 [luójí] logic

逻卒 [luózù] a patrolman

骡(騾) [luó] (n) 家畜 mule

螺 [luó] (n) 也叫"螺蛳"，软体动物 a spiral univalve shell; a conch

螺丝钉 [luósīdīng] screw

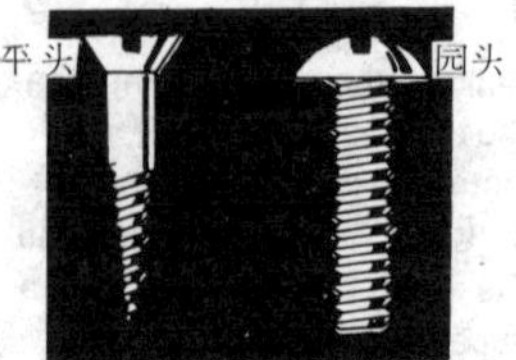

螺丝钻 [lusizuan] an auger

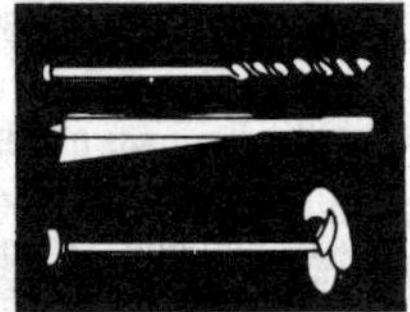

螺旋 [luóxuán] spiral

螺旋起重机 [luó xuán qǐ zhòngjī] a lifting-screw; a screw-jack

luǒ

裸 [luǒ] 1 (adj) 光着身子 naked; bare; unclothed; nude 2 (adj) 没有东西包着的 uncovered; unprotected

裸露 [luǒ lù] be exposed

裸体 [luǒ tǐ] a naked body; nudity

裸足 [luǒzù] barefooted; undressed

瘰 [luǒ] 〔瘰疬〕(n) 结核菌侵入人体的淋巴腺，局部发生硬块，多生在脖子上 scrofula; scrofulous swellings

luò

络(絡) [luò] 1 (v) 缠绕（纱线等）spin; bind; coil ∗目前，许多工厂已采用机器络纱。 At present, yarn spinning has been mechanised in most factories. 2 (v) 用网状物兜住 to protect materials with a net

另见 [lào]

络纬 [luòwěi] a cricket

络绎不绝 [luòyìbùjué] keep coming or going, uninterruptedly

骆(駱) [luò] (n) 骆驼 a camel

烙 [luò] (n) 古代的一种酷刑，把烧红的铜器印在人体上 punishment of putting one around a heated bronze pillar
另见 [lào]

硌 [luò] (n) 山上的大石 huge rocks on the mountains

落 [luò] 1 (v) (adj) 降失下来，下降 fall; drop; shed ＊那老人家的不幸遭遇使人落泪。The misfortune sufferod by that aged man could make one shed tears. 2 (v) (adj) 衰败，飘零 decline; fail; come down; descending＊清代早在十八世记时便开始没落。The Ching Dynasty began to decline in the eighteenth century. 3 (n) 人聚居的地方 a gathering place; a community ＊别以为在深山里就没有村落。Don't suppose that there is no village in the remote hills. 4 (v) 归 settle upon; be placed on ＊繁重的工作总是落在我身上。Heavy tasks are always placed upon me.

落魄 [luò pò] be in reduced circumstances; spiritless; lose energy; living in poverty

落成 [luòchéng] complete; finish (e,g, construciton)

落地 [luò dì] fall to the ground; be born

落后 [luò hòu] fall behind; backward; lag behind

落户 [luò hù] settle down

落花流水 [luòhuālíushuǐ] utterly routed in battle

落荒而逃 [luò huāng ér táo] scamping away in the open country(after suffering a defeat in battle)

落脚 [luò jiǎo] stop for a rest

落井下石 [luò jǐng xià shí] to take mean advantage

落空 [luò kōng] nothing comes of it; comes to nothing

落雷 [luò léi] a thunderbolt

落落大方 [luòluòdàfāng] poised and unstrained

落难 [luò nàn] fall into distress; in misery

落网 [luò wǎng] (of criminal) be arrested

落伍 [luò wǔ] (fall) behind the ranks; lag behind

落选 [luò xuǎn] fail to be elected
另见 [là]

摞 [luò] (v) 把东西一个一个往上堆 pile up materials

荦(犖) [luò] [荦荦] (adj) 明显，清楚 clear

·luo

罗(囉) [luo] (part) 助词，表示决定的语气(口语) to express that a decision is already made
另见 [luō], [luó]

M

ḿ

呣 [ḿ] (interj) 叹词，表示答应 an expression before a positive reply ＊呣，知道了。Mn, I know.

mā

妈(媽) [mā] (n) 对母亲的称呼 an address to mother ＊妈妈，我回来了。Mummy, I'm back. 2 (n) 对长辈或年长已婚妇女的称呼 an address to an elder woman ＊姑妈，姨妈。aunt or auntie. ＊姑妈，新年快乐。Happy New Year, auntie.

抹 [mā] (v) 揩，擦 to wipe; to rub ＊请你抹一下这玻璃。Please wipe the glass.
另见 [mǒ]
另见 [mò]

摩 [mā] (v) 〔摩娑〕用手轻轻按着一下一下地移动 to massage lightly
另见 [mó]

má

麻 [má] 1 (n) 草本植物，纤维可制绳索，及供纺织工业用途 hemp; jute ＊菲律宾的马尼拉麻很著名。Philippines is famous for its Manila hemp. 2 (adj) 感觉不灵 numb ＊他的手脚冻麻了。His limbs are numb with cold. 3 (adj) 表面粗糙的 rough in the surface 4 (adj) 起斑点的 pocky; pock

麻痹 [mábì] paralysed; benumbed; to go numb
麻布 [mábù] linen
麻烦 [má·fan] troublesome; to trouble
麻疯 [máfēng] leprosy
麻将 [májiàng] mahjong
麻利 [málì] quick-witted; clever
麻木 [mámù] without sensation of feeling
麻木不仁 [mámù bùrén] benumbed; indifferent; apathetic
麻雀 [máquè] a sparrow
麻药 [máyào] an anaesthetic
麻疹 [mázhěn] measles
麻子 [mázǐ] hamp; seed; pock-mark; a person with pocky face
麻醉 [mázuì] to anaesthetize; to narcotize; to render insensible

mǎ

马(馬) [mǎ] (n) 家畜 a horse

马齿苋 [mǎchǐxiàn] portulaca, a vegetable, also used as a herb
马到成功 [mǎ dào chénggōng] to accomplish a quick success
马粪紙 [mǎfènzhǐ] strawboard
马虎 [mǎhū] perfunctory; careless; sloppy
马会 [mǎhuì] a turf club; a jockey club; a horse-race club
马克 [mǎkè] mark, a German coin
马克思主义 [mǎkèsī zhǔyì] Marxism
马口铁 [mǎkǒutiě] tinplates

马拉松赛跑 [mǎlāsōng sàipǎo] a marathon race; a long-distance race
马力 [mǎlì] horse-power
马铃薯 [mǎlíngshǔ] potato
马路 [mǎlù] road; street; avenue
马匹 [mǎpì] horses
马票 [mǎpiào] a pool ticket; a lottery ticket
马尔萨斯主义 [mǎ ěr sà sī zhǔ yì] Malthusianism
马赛克 [mǎsàikè] mosaic
马上 [mǎshàng] instantly; at once
马蹄铁 [mǎtítiě] horseshoe
马蹄形 [mǎtíxíng] hoof-shape; U-shape
马桶 [mǎtǒng] a night stool
马戏 [mǎxì] a circus

吗(嗎) [mǎ] (n) 〔吗啡〕[mǎfēi] 一种有毒的麻醉药，用鸦片制成 morphine; morphia; a poisonous anaesthesia made from opium ＊他因走私吗啡而被捕。He was arrested for smuggling morphine.

玛(瑪) [mǎ] (n) 〔玛瑙〕[mǎnǎo] agate

码(碼) [mǎ] 1 (n) 表示数目的符号或用具 a symbol or article for numerals 2 英美制长度单位 yard, an English measure
码头 [matou] a jetty; a wharf

蚂(螞) [mǎ] (n) 〔蚂蚁〕[mǎyǐ] ants

mà

骂(罵) [mà] (v) 指用话斥责人，或用粗野，恶意的话侮辱人 scold; abuse; curse; rebuke ＊不要骂他，这不是他的错。Don't scold him; it is not his fault.

·ma

嘛 [·ma] (n) 助词，表示道理显而易见。modal particle

吗(嗎) [ma] (part) 助词 表示疑问，用于句末 an interrogative particle used at the end of a question ＊你难道不懂吗？Don't you know it?
另见 [mǎ]

mái

埋 [mái] 1 (v) 把东西放在坑里用土盖上 to bury ＊一名工友在土崩时被活埋。A worker was buried alive during the landslide. 2 隐藏，不让人知道 conceal ＊他被逼隐姓埋名。He was forced to conceal his name and hide himself from being known.
埋藏 [máicáng] to bury; to conceal underneath
埋伏 [mái·fu] to ambush
埋没 [máimò] to hide; to fail to bring up
埋头苦干 [máitóu kǔgàn] to bury (one's) head in and work hard; to work hard; to be industrious
埋怨 [máiyuàn] to grumble; to complain; to blame

mǎi

买(買) [mǎi] 1 (v) 拿钱换东西，跟"卖"相对 to buy; to purchase ＊我买了一个照相机。I bought a camera. 2 (v) 用金钱拉拢 to influence someone with money ＊他以为金钱和地位可以收买一个人。He thought he could buy a person over with wealth and status.
买办 [mǎibàn] a compradore
买办资产阶级 [mǎi bàn zī chǎn jiē jí] comprador bourgeoisie
买卖 [mǎimài] trade; business
买通 [mǎitōng] to bribe
买主 [mǎizhǔ] a buyer or purchaser; a customer

mài

脉(脈) [mài] 1 (n) 血管 blood vessels 2 (n) 脉搏，动脉的跳动 pulse; pulsation ✱ 他的脉搏每分钟一百次。 His pulse is at a hundred. 3 (n) 象血管那样分布的东西 veins; ranges; things that run in the pattern of blood vessels ✱ 不同的叶子有不同的叶脉。 Different kinds of leaves have different veins.

脉络 [màiluò] veins and arteries; line of thoughts

脉门 [màimén] the pulse at the wrist

另见 [mò]

迈(邁) [mài] 1 (v) 提起脚向前走 to walk forward with great strides ✱ 我们迈着步前进。 We are making a stride forward. 2 (adj) 老 old; aged ✱ 李伯伯年纪老迈，还得做粗重的工作。 Although uncle Lee was at an old age, he had to do the rough works.

麦(麥) [mài] (n) 粮食作物。有大麦，小麦，燕麦等多种，统称麦子 a common name for crops like barley, wheat and oat; wheat

麦精 [màijīng] maltose

麦克风 [màikéfēng] a microphone

麦芽糖 [màiyátáng] maltose ; malt-sugar

卖(賣) [mài] 1 (v) 拿东西换钱，跟"买"相对 to sell ✱ 你们卖笔记本吗？Do you sell note books? 2 (v) 出卖 to betray ✱ 我们不能出卖朋友。We cannot betray our friends. 3 (v) 尽量使出 to do the utmost; to work hard ✱ 你何必替这种人卖力。 . Why should you work so hard for these people? 4 (v) 表现自己，显示自己 to show off; to make a show of ✱ 不踏实的人总喜欢卖弄本领。 Generally an im-practical person likes to show off his ability.

卖国贼 [màiguózéi] a traitor

卖命 [màimìng] to sweat one's guts out ; to sweat blood; to throw away one's life.

卖身契 [màishēnqì] an indenture by which one sells oneself or family

卖身投靠 [màishēn tóukào] to sell oneself for personal gains

卖艺者 [màiyì zhě] a performer ; an acrobat

mān

颟(顢) [mān] 〔颟顸〕[mānhān] (adj) 糊涂而马虎，不明事理 foolish; inept

mán

谩(謾) [mán] (v) 欺骗，蒙蔽 to deceive; to mislead

另见 [màn]

馒(饅) [mán] (n) 〔馒头〕[mán·tou] 一种用发酵的面蒸成的食品 steamed bread

鳗(鰻) [mán] (n) 鱼类。体长，呈圆柱形，身体表面有粘液，可供食用 an eel

蔓 [mán] (n) 〔蔓菁〕 [mánjīng] 二年生草本植物，块根可做蔬菜。也叫芜菁。 the rape turnip

另见 [wàn]

[màn]

瞒(瞞) [mán] (v) 隐瞒实情，不让别人知道 to deceive; to hoodwink; to conceal the truth ✱ 这件事你想瞒是瞒不住的。 Don't think you can conceal the truth.

瞒上欺下 [mánshàngqīxià] to deceive those above and bully those below

瞒天过海 [mán tiān guò hǎi] to cross the sea under camouflage (to get a-way with it under false pretences)

蛮(蠻) [mán] (adj) 1 粗野，不通情理 savage ; wild ; barba-rous ; rude ✱ 这些兵士吃了东西不还钱还要打人，真是蛮不讲理。 The soldiers were really savage and rude, they refused to pay for their meal and threatened to beat someone up. 2

强悍 strong; rugged ＊不要看他年纪小，倒有不小的蛮劲。 Don't see that he is young, he is not in the short of rugged energy.

mǎn

满（滿） [mǎn] (adj) (adv) 全部充实，完全 full; complete; fully; completely ＊ 这个货仓放满粮食。The warehouse was fully stocked with foodstuffs. 2 (v) 达到一定的程度 to expire; to fill up; to reach a certain state ＊ 他在这儿工作三年期满。 His three years' term of working has expired. 3 (n) 骄傲 pride; complacency; haughtiness ＊ 满招损，谦受益。Haughtiness invites disaster, modesty deserves advantage. 4 (n) 满族，中国少数民族名 the Manchus, a minority in China.

满不在乎 [mǎn bù zài·hu] to take it for nothing; not to care a fig

满城风雨 [mǎnchéng fēngyǔ] like a storm over the whole city; (news) spread all over

满面春风 [mǎn miàn chūn fēng] face beaming with delight; smiling all over

满腔热情 [mǎngiāng rèqíng] full of enthusiasm

满意 [mǎnyì] satisfied; contented

满载而归 [mǎnzài ér guī] come home fully loaded

满足 [mǎnzù] satisfy; content

满座 [mǎnzuò] full house

màn

曼 [màn] 1 (adj) 柔和；美好 graceful; fine; handsome ＊ 观众们都給芭蕾舞演员的曼姿妙舞吸引住了。The audience were much attracted by the graceful gestures of the ballerina. 2 (v) 长 long; prolonged ＊曼声高歌，山谷响应。 She sang highly in a long tone and the valley echoes.

谩（謾） [màn] (v) 轻蔑；没有礼貌 insulting; contemptuous; rude

谩骂 [mànmà] to abuse; to vilify; to rail at; to swear at
另见 [mán]

漫 [màn] 1 (v) 水涨而向外流 to overflow; to flood; to spread over ＊ 河水漫出路上来了。The river has overflowed the road. 2 (adj) 满，全部 entire, complete; whole; all over ＊ 漫山遍野都是鲜红色的枫叶。 All over the mountains and wilderness are red maple leaves. 3 (adj) 随便，没有限制，不受拘束 free without restriction; carefree ＊ 他在街上漫无目的的走着。 He walked freely and aimlessly on the streets.

漫步 [mànbù] to stroll; to ramble

漫不经心 [màn bù jīng xīn] careless; inattentive

漫画 [mànhuà] cartoon

漫长 [mànchǎng] long; lengthy

漫漫 [mànmàn] vast; boundless; long

漫谈 [màntán] to have a casual conversation

漫游 [mànyóu] to travel; to have a pleasure trip

慢 [màn] 1 (adj) 迟缓，速度小，跟"快"相对 slow; sluggish ＊ 他做事情总是慢吞吞。 He is always slow at work. 2 (adj) 态度冷淡，没有礼貌 indifferent; rude ＊ 他对穷亲戚很是傲慢。He is very rude to his poor relatives.

慢性病 [manxìng bìng] a chronic disease

慢手慢脚 [màn shǒu màn jiǎo] slow in movements

慢条斯理 [màn tiáo sī lǐ] in an easy manner

幔 [màn] (n) 挂在屋里的帳幕 a curtain; a screen

蔓 [màn] (adj) 蔓草，田野生的杂草 a creeping plant which grows wildly in the field ＊ 在荒废了的花园里，蔓草丛生 The creepers spread densely over the deserted garden.

蔓延 [mànyán] to spread; to diffuse
另见 [wàn]
[mán]

máng

忙 [máng] 1 (adj) 事情、工作繁多 busy; occupied with work ∗ 他是一个大忙人。 He is a very busy man. 2 (adj) 急，速 quick; hurried; hasty ∗ 一听到喊救火声，大家都慌忙逃命。 Everybody ran hastily for life when the shouting of fire was heard.

忙碌 [mánglù] busy; bustling

忙乱 [mángluàn] in haste and confusion

氓 [máng] (n) 〔流氓〕[liúmáng]不务正业，为非作歹，扰乱社会治安的坏人 rascals, loafers, vagabonds ∗ 他竟敢雇用流氓打人。He even dared to hire rascals to beat up the people.

芒 [máng] 1 (n) 一种叶边锋利的草 a sharp-edged grass 2 (n) 麦粒，禾粒等外壳顶端的针状物 the awn or beard of grains 3 (n) 像芒的尖锋、光线， 锋芒，光芒 an awn-like point or ray ∗ 光芒。 a ray of light ∗ 锋芒。 a sharp point or edge

芒刺在背 [máng cì zài bèi] having prickles down the back-of a man who sits stiffly and ill at ease.

芒果 [mángguǒ] the mango

芒鞋 [mángxié] straw sandals

芒种 [mángzhǒng] a solar term; grain in ear; about June 6th-20th

盲 [máng] 1 (adj) 眼睛看不见东西 blind 2 (adj) 不能辨认某种事物 blind in heart; unable to distinguish a certain thing ∗他是一个文盲。 He is a literacy blind; an illiterate. 3 (adj) 无主见，无计划，无目的 undecided, acting without a plan or aim

盲肠 [mánchǎng] the coecum

盲肠炎 [máng cháng yán] appendicitis

盲动 [mángdòng] to act recklessly

盲从 [mángcóng] to follow blindly; blind adherence

盲目 [mángmù] blindly

盲人瞎马 [mángrén xiāmà] a blind man riding a blind horse-very dangerous

茫 [máng] 1 (adj) 形容水或其他事物没有边际，看不清楚 boundless; vast; vague ∗ 船在茫茫大海中飘流。 The boat is drifting in the boundless ocean. 2 (adj) 对事理一点也不知晓 ignorant; bewildered ∗我们对过去的历史不能茫无所知。 We should not be ignorant of the past history.

茫然 [mángrán] be puzzled or perplexed; at a loss

茫无头绪 [máng wú tóu xù] not knowing what to do

mǎng

莽 [mǎng] 1 (n) 密生的草 clusters of grass 2 (adj) 粗鲁，冒失 rough; rash ∗他是个鲁莽的小伙子。He is a rash young man.

蟒 [mǎng] (n) 一种热带无毒大蛇 a python

māo

猫 [māo] (n) a cat

猫头鹰 [māotóuyīng] an owl

máo

毛 [máo] 1 (n) 动植物皮上所生的丝状物 hair; fur 2 (adj) 粗糙，半制成的 rough coarse 3 (adj) 总的 gross 4 (adj) 做事粗心，不细致 careless;

rough handed 5 (n) 角；一元的十分之一 ten cents; one tenth of a dollar ＊ 他身上只剩下二毛钱。 He has only twenty cents left.

毛笔 [máobǐ] a writing brush

毛病 [máobìng] a fault; a flaw; a defect; disease

毛骨悚然 [máogǔ sǒngrán] hair standing on end; horror-stricken

毛巾 [máojīn] towel

毛孔 [máokǒng] pores of the skin

毛毛雨 [máomáoyǔ] drizzle

毛皮 [máopí] fur

毛坯 [máopī] the coarse unburnt models of bricks, tiles, or porcelain

毛茸茸 [máorōngrōng] soft like fur

毛手毛脚 [máoshǒu máojiǎo] flurried in movement; rough-handed

毛线 [máoxiàn] woolen yarn; knitting wool

毛细管 [máoxìguǎn] capillary

毛泽东 [máozètōng] the founder of the Chinese Communist Party

毛织品 [máozhìpǐn] woolen fabrics

毛重 [máozhòng] gross weight

牦 [máo] (n) 〔牦牛〕[máoniú] 西藏高原一带的家畜 a yak

矛 [máo] (n) 古代的兵器，在长杆的一端装有金属枪头 a spear; a lance

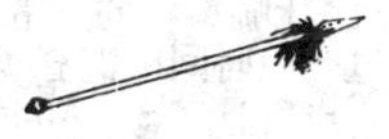

矛盾 [maodùn] contradiction; conflict ; contradictory

矛盾百出 [máodùn bǎichù] full of contradictions

矛头 [máotóu] spearhead

茅 [máo] (n) 一种草 a grass

茅塞顿开 [máosè dùn kāi] to become enlightened all of a sudden

茅台酒 [máotáijiǔ] Maotai (a famous Chinese wine)

茅屋 [máowō] a thatched hut; a cottage

蝥 [máo] (n) 吃苗根的害虫 cantharides; a pest

蝥贼 [máozéi] the pests that eat grains-the pernicious enemies of the people

锚（錨） [máo] (n) 铁制的停船用具 an anchor

mǎo

卯 [mǎo] 1 (adj) 地支的第四位，用作次序的第四 the fourth of the Earthly Branches; the fourth 2 (adj) 卯时，指五点到七点 the period from 5 to 7 a.m. 3 (n) 器物接榫的地方凹入的部份，榫眼 a mortise ＊ 他在木的一端凿个卯儿。 He cut a mortise at the end of a piece of wood.

mào

冒 [mào] 1 (v) 升起，透出 to rise up; to ooze out; to emerge ＊ 烟囱冒出浓烟。Thick smoke emerges from the chimney. 2 (v) 不顾一切，顶着 to venture; to run the risk ＊ 他冒着生命的危险把孩子救出来。He ran the risk of his life to save the child. 3 (v) 不加小心，鲁莽，冲撞 to take no care; to rush 4 (v) 假充 to disguise; to pretend; to forge; to falsify ; to imitate ＊ 小心冒牌货。 Beware of goods with imitation trade mark.

冒充 [màochōng] pretend to be

冒犯 [màofàng] to offend ; to violate openly; to insult

冒汗 [màohàn] to sweat

冒昧 [màomèi] take the liberty of; presumptuous

冒名 [màomíng] toact under false name

冒牌 [màopái] to forge a trade mark(of

goods)

冒死 [màosǐ] to risk one's life; to brave death

冒失 [mào·shi] rash; thoughtless

冒险 [màoxiǎn] to run the risk; to lay oneself open to danger

冒雨 [màoyǔ] to brave the rain

帽 [mào] (n) 帽子 a hat; a cap

貌 [mào] 1 (n) 面容 face ＊其貌不扬。His face is ugly. 2 (n) 外表，样子 look; appearance; view ＊从这里可看到工厂全貌。We can get a complete view of the factory from here.

貌合神离 [mào hé shén lí] one in appearance but each going his own way

贸(貿) [mào] 1 (n) 贸易，商品交换 trade; exchange of commodities ＊两国的树胶贸易每年都有增加。There is an increase of rubber trade between the two countries every year. 2 (adj) 轻率 rash ＊这事要深入调查研究，不要贸然下结论。This matter requires a thorough investigation; we should not jump into conclusion rashly.

贸然 [màorán] rashly

贸易 [mào yì] trade; commerce

贸易差额 [màoyì chāé] the balance of trade

贸易中心 [màoyì chōngxīn] commercial centre

贸易公司 [màoyì gōngsī] trading company

茂 [mào] 1 (adj) 草木旺盛，长得密 luxuriant; flourishing ＊热带森林非常茂盛。The tropical forests are luxuriant. 2 (adj) 丰富，精美 abundant; fine ＊这本书图文並茂，值得一读。This book being abundant of illustrations and explanations is worth reading.

·me

么(麼) [·me] 1 (part) 这么（长，高，难，容易，……）this (long, tall, difficult, easy........) 那么（久；迟；臭；……）that (long, late, smelly, ...) 什么（事？名？时候？）What (is the matter? is the name? is the time? ....) 2 (part.) used at the end of the first part of a sentence ＊要去么，又没工夫。I wanted to go but I am not free.

méi

湄 [méi] (n) 水边 edge of water

楣 [méi] (n) 门框上的横木 the lintel of a door

镅(鋂) [méi] (n) 放射性元素 Americium-am

梅 [méi] (n) 落叶乔木。果实叫"梅子"，味酸可吃 plum; prune

梅毒 [méidú] syphilis a venereal disease

梅花 [méihuā] the plum blossoms

梅花鹿 [méihuālù] the spotted deer

酶 [méi] (n) 酵素 yeast

酶制剂 [měizhìjì] yeast extract

眉 [méi] (n) 眉毛，眼上额下的毛 the eye-brows〔眉目〕1 (n) 指面貌 the eye-brows and the eyes-the face ＊他眉目之间流露出兴奋和喜悦。An expression of excitement and gladness was shown on his face. 2 (n) 比喻事物的头绪 a clue ＊经过一段时间的调查，事情已经有一点眉目了。After a period of investigation, we have found a clue to the matter.

眉飞色舞 [méi fēi sì wǔ] excited and cheerful

眉开眼笑 [méi kāi yǎn xiào] a beaming countenance

眉来眼去 [méi lái yǎn qù] exchanging glances

眉清目秀 [méi qīng mù xiù] beautiful; handsome

莓 [méi] (n) 一种小浆果 berry; a small seedy fruit

霉（黴）[méi] 1 (v) 衣物、食品等因生菌而变质 to mould; mouldy; be mildewed ✽ 这面包已经发霉了。The bread has moulded. 2 (n) 霉菌（蕈）低等植物，形状象细丝，有毛霉和青霉等多种 mould

霉烂 [méilàn] mouldy and rotten

媒 [méi] 1 (n) 旧时撮合男女婚事的人 a go-between; a match-maker ✽ 现在男女找对象很少通过媒人了。Men and women nowadays seldom require a match-maker. 2 (n) 媒介，介绍或引导两方发生关系的 a medium; an intermediary ✽ 昆虫是传播花粉的媒介。Insects are media for the pollination of flowers.

媒人 [méi·ren] a match-maker

煤 [méi] (n) 古代植物压埋在地底下，年久变成黑色或黑褐色坚硬矿物 coal ✽ 煤是很重要的燃料和化工原料。Coal is a very important fuel and raw material in most industries.

煤坑 [méikēng] a coal pit

煤矿 [méikuàng] a coal mine

煤矿工人 [méikuàng gōngrén] a collier; a coal mine worker

煤气炉 [méiqìlú] a gas stove

没 [méi] (adv) 未，没有 never; not; no; without ✽ 我没见过他。I have never seen him before. ✽ 我没穿鞋也可以跑。I can run without shoes.

没办法 [méibànfǎ] cannot do anything

没出息 [méichūxì] good for nothing

没精打采 [měijīng dá cǎi] dispirited and discouraged

没头没脑 [méi tóu méi nǎo] stupid; thoughtlessly, heedlessly

没用 [meíyòng] useless

另见 [mò]

玫 [méi]〔玫瑰〕[méiguì] rose

枚 [méi] 量词 a measure words ✽ 一枚针。a needle.

枚举 [méijǔ] to enumerate

měi

每 [měi] 1 (adj) 指全体中的任何一个或一组 each; every ✽ 每一个人都有机会。Everyone has a chance. ✽他每三天就要去报到。He has to report for duty every three days. 2 (adv) 常常 always; constantly ✽ 虽然我们分隔很远，但我每每会想起你。Although we are separated far away, I always think of you.

每到 [měidào] every time; whenever

每况愈下 [měi kuàngyù xià] from bad to worse

每每 [měiměi] often; all the time

美 [měi] 1 (adj) 色、声、味好 nice in colour sound or taste ✽ 这套傢俬很美观。This set of furniture has a nice look. 2 (adj) 质量好 good in quality ✽ 这里的东西价廉物美。These goods here are cheap and excellent in quality. 3 (adj) 好、善 good; fine ✽ 多为别人着想是新社会的美德。To care more for others is a fine virtue in the new society. 4 (v) 称赞 praise; commend ✽ 我们赞美他那无私的精神。We commended him for his selfless spirit.

美不胜收 [měi bù shèng shōu] too many nice things, cannot see them all

美中不足 [měi chōng bù zhú] a flaw in the perfection; happiness incomplete.

美化 [měihuà] to beautify

美妙 [měimiào] admirable; pleasant

美术家 [měishùjiā] an artist

美味 [měiwèi] delicious; tasty

镁（鎂）[měi] (n) 化学元素 magnesium

mèi

妹 [mèi] (n) 对同父母而年纪比自己小的女子的称呼 younger sister's

妹夫 [mèifū] younger sister's husband;

brother-in-law

昧 [mèi] 1 (a) 糊涂，不明事理 stupid, blunt ＊只有愚昧无知的人才会受骗。Only the stupid and ignorant ones will be decieved. 2 (v) 隐藏 hide ; conceal ＊他拾金不昧。He did not conceal the valuable he found.

昧着良心 [mèi zhè liáng xīn] against one's conscience.

魅 [mèi] (n) 鬼怪 a demon

魅力 [mèilì] enchantment; charm

寐 [mèi] (v) 睡觉 sleep ; doze

媚 [mèi] 1 (v) 巴结，讨好 flatter ; fawn on; coax ＊他很会向其主子谄媚。He is good at flattering his boss. 2 (adj) 美好 charming ; fascinating ＊这里的风光明媚。The scenery here is charming.

媚权势 [mèi quánshì] truckle (cringe) to men of influence

mēn

闷（悶）[mēn] 1 (adj) 气压低或空气不流通所引起的不舒服的感觉 stuffy ＊这间房比较闷热。This room is quite stuffy. 2 (v) 使密闭 to close tightly; to cover ＊把沏好的茶再闷一会儿。Cover the infused tea for a while

mén

门（門）[mén] 1 (n) 建筑物的出入口，又指安全出入口上能开关的装置 an entrance; a door; a gate 2 (n) 门径，诀窍 a way; a means ＊我模不着门儿。I cannot find the way to solve it. 3 (n) 学派，宗教派别 a school of thought; a religious sect ＊孔门弟子五谷不分。The students of Confucianism could not recognise the cereals. 4 (n) 一般事物的分类 types or class of things ＊陈列馆里的东西必须分门别类。Things in the show house must be classified. 5 量词 a quantity word ＊两门大炮。two cannons ＊一门功课。a subject of study

门户 [ménhù] the door; a family; a sect

门户之见 [ménhù zhī jiàn] sectarian bias

门槛 [ménkǎn] threshold

门可罗雀 [ménkě lố què] have only a few customers ; deserted.

门市 [ménshì] selling in a shop; retail

门庭若市 [méntíng rò shì] crowded with visitors; having a good business

门外汉 [ménwàihàn] an outsider; not in the trade or profession

门牙 [ményá] incisor ; front teeth

扪（捫）[mén] (v) 按，摸 lay the hand on; touch

扪心自问 [ménxīn zìwèn] 反省 introspection; to ask oneself

钔（鍆）[mén] (n) 放射性化学元素 mendelevuim - Md, a radioactive chemical element

mèn

闷（悶）[mèn] 1 (adj) 心里烦，不痛快 frustrated ; unhappy ＊他觉得很苦闷。He was very frustrated and unhappy. 2 (adj) 密闭，不透气 closed ; air-tight ＊他闷胡芦里不知卖什么药。What does he sell from his closed jar? (I wonder what he is up to)

闷闷不乐 [mènmèn bù lè] in distress ; be much worried

另见 [mēn]

焖（燜）[mèn] (v) 盖紧锅盖，用微火把食物煮熟 to stew

懑（懣）[mèn] (adj) 烦闷 sorrowful ; melancholy; depressed＊看到正义不能伸张，他感到愤懑。He felt angry and depressed when he saw justice being undone.

·men

们（們）[·men] (n) 表示人的多数 a word added to I, you, he, she and it to express the plural

＊我们 we ＊你们 you ＊同胞们 fellow countrymen

mēng

蒙（矇）[mēng] 1 (v) 欺骗 deceive ; cheat ＊谁也蒙不了他。Nobody can deceive him. 2 (adj) 昏迷 fainted ＊ 他被球打得昏蒙过去。He fainted after being hit by the ball. 3 (v) 胡乱猜测 guess blindly 另见 [méng]

蒙蒙亮 [mēngmēngliàng] at dawn

méng

蒙 [méng] 1 (v) 遮盖 to cover ＊ 他被蒙上眼睛。 He was blind folded. 2 (adj) 幼稚，无知 ignorant ＊皇帝蒙昧无知。 The king was stupid and ignorant. 3 (v) 受 to receive; to get ＊ 承蒙热情招待，感激不尽。Thank you very much for your warm reception.

蒙蔽 [méngbì] to hide; to hoodwink; to befuddle; to mislead

蒙古 [ménggǔ] Mongolia

蒙汉 [ménghùn] to slip by

蒙昧 [méngmèi] ignorant

蒙受 [méngshòu] be favoured; suffer (eg. humiliation; losses)

蒙受损失 [méngshòu sǔnshì] sustain (suffer) a loss

另见 [mēng]

獴 [méng] (n) 哺乳动物。体长，脚短，头小，口尖 ，耳朵小，捕食蛇，蛙，鼠，魚，蟹等 a mongoose

檬 [méng]〔柠檬〕[níngméng] lemon

朦 [méng]〔朦胧〕[ménglóng] (a) 不清楚，模糊 dim; misty; hazy ＊ 月色朦胧 。It is a dim moon-light.

虻 [méng] (n) 昆虫，比苍蝇稍大生活在田野杂草中。种类很多，最常见的是牛虻。雌虫刺吸人畜的血 an insect e.g. the gadfly and the house-fly

萌 [méng] 1 (n) 植物的芽 a shoot ; a sprout 2 (v) 植物生芽 budding ; germinating 3 (v) 开始，发生 start ; occur ＊ 他又故态复萌了。His old temper recurred.

萌芽 [méng yá] germinate, bud; sprout

萌芽时代 [méng yáshídài] initial stages of growth or development.

盟 [méng] 1 (n) 国家和国家之間立誓缔约 an oath; a pledge ＊ 二国有盟约在先，共同对付齐国。The two countries had earlier made a pledge to confront the kingdom of Chi jointly. 2 (n) 现在指集团和集团或国家之间的联合 union among groups or nations; a confederation; a leaque ＊ 世界上许多小国已经组成许多联盟来对抗霸权主义。Many small countries in the world have formed leagues and confedera - tions to fight hegemonism.

盟书 [méngshū] the form of an oath; a written agreement

盟国 [méngguó] states bound to one another by treaties; allied nations

另见 [míng]

měng

懵 [měng] (adj) 无知 ignorant

猛 [měng] 1 (adj) 力量大，气势壮 strong ; violent ＊ 他用力过猛，球被踢出界。 He kicked too hard that the ball went outside. 2 (adj) 勇猛的 brave ＊不是猛龙 不过江。Only the brave (dragon) will dare to venture (cross the river) 3 (adj) 凶狠的 fierce ＊ 山上有只猛虎。There is a fierce tiger in the mountain. 4 (adj) 忽然，突然 sudden ＊ 他从睡梦中猛然惊醒。He woke up suddenly.

猛攻 [mèng gōng] to make a desperate a ack; a furious assault

猛火 [měnghuǒ] a blazing fire; raging flames

猛将 [měngjiàng] a brave general

猛兽 [měngshòu] a fierce (wild) beast; a beast of prey

懵 [měng] 〔懵懂〕 [měngtǒng] (adj) 糊里糊涂，不明事理 stupid

mèng

梦(夢) [mèng] (n) 人在睡眠时，大脑皮层的一部分没有完全停止活动或受到其他刺激，就产生梦 dream *她从恶梦中醒来。She awakes from a nightmare.

梦话 [mènghuà] talking in a dream; nonsense

梦幻 [mènghuàn] a dream; a fantasy

梦寐以求 [mèngmèi yǐ qiú] to try to get even in a dream; to hanker after

梦游症 [mèng yóu bìng] sleep-walking; somnambulism

梦想 [mèngxiǎng] to dream of; to hope in vain; illusion

孟 [mèng] (adj) 称秩序在第一的 first in order

孟春 [mèngchūn] the first month of spring; the first month

孟浪 [mènglàng] reckless

mī

咪 [mī] 1 (adj) 微笑的样子，叠用 smilingly *他笑咪咪地说：「欢迎你」。He said smilingly, "Welcome to you." 2 (n) 貓叫的声音。呼唤猫的声音 the mewing of cat; calling to the cat

眯 [mī] (v) 眼皮将合未合 narrowing one's eyes *他眯起一只眼睛，瞄准靶心。He narrows one of his eyes while aiming at the bulls-eye.

mí

糜 [mí] 1 (n) 粥 porridge 2 (adj) 糜烂不堪（烂到不可收拾）rotten; corrupted; decadent*他生活糜烂。He is leading a decadent life

靡 [mí] (adj) 浪费 extravagant

糜烂 [mílàn] rotten; decadent

麋 [mí] (n) 俗称"四不像"，也叫"麋鹿"，哺乳动物。头似马，身似驴，蹄似牛，角似鹿。是一种珍贵的兽类 a tailed deer

迷 [mí] 1 (v) 分辨不清 cannot differentiate; be at a loss *这个孩子迷了路。The child has lost his way. 2 (adj) 昏昏沉沉 infatuated; bewildered *他吃了这药，整个人就迷迷糊糊。He became infatuated after taking this medicine. 3 (adj) 对某一事物发生特殊爱好 mad about *他迷恋舞台生活。He was mad about the stage. 4 (n) 沉醉于某种事物的人 a fan *他是个足球迷。He is a football fan.

迷惑 [míhuò] bewildered; fascinating; puzzling

迷离 [mílí] confusing; bewitching

迷人 [mírén] charming; enchanting

迷信 [míxìn] superstitions

谜(謎) [mí] 1 (n) 叫人猜的隐语 riddle *我们来猜谜。Let's play riddle guessing. 2 (n) 比喻还没有弄明白的或难以理解的事物 a puzzle; an enigma *这对我来说是一个谜。It is an enigma to me.

醚 [mí] (n) 有机化合物的一类。乙醚是医药上常用的痲醉剂 ether

弥(彌，瀰) [mí] 1 (adj) 满 full; whole *做母亲的在婴儿弥月后就可恢复劳动。The mother can resume work one month after the baby's birth. 2 (v) 填补 to make up; to amend; to redeem *他以为念经拜佛可以弥补他以往的过失。He thought he can redeem his past faults by praying to the Buddha. 3 (adj) 越，更加 more *坏人做事，欲盖弥彰。The more a bad person tries to cover up his evil deeds, the more exposed they become.

弥漫 [mímàn] widespread; boundless

弥天大谎 [mítiān dàhuǎng] a big lie

猕(獼) [mí] 〔猕猴〕 [míhóu] (n) 毛褐色，有颊囊，臀疣显

著 a macacus monkey; a macaque

mǐ

米 [mǐ] 1 (n) 稻谷或其他植物的种子去掉外壳叫"米" rice ＊吉打州盛产稻米。 Kedah produces a lot of rice. 2 (n) 公制长度单位。即"公尺" a measure word metre ＊他参加一百米赛跑。 He takes part in the hundred metre race.

米仓 [mǐcāng] a rice-granary
米尺 [mǐchǐ] metre-rule
米虫 [míchóng] rice weevil
米粉 [mǐfěn] rice flour
米黄 [mǐhuáng] dull yellow
米糠 [mǐkāng] paddy chaff; rice bran
米粮 [mǐliáng] provisions
米商 [mǐshāng] a rice dealer

敉 [mǐ] (v) 安抚，安定 to pacify

敉平 [mǐpíng] to pacify; to appease

弭 [mǐ] (v) 止，息 to stop; to check

弭兵 [mǐbīng] an armistice

mì

泌 [mì] (v) 分泌，从生物体里产生某种液体物质 secrete ＊汗是汗腺的分泌物。 Sweat is a secretion from the sweat gland.

泌尿系统 [mì niàoxìtǒng] urinary system

秘 [mì] 1 (adj) 不公开的，不让大家知道的，难以预测的 secret; mysterious ＊他装出一副神秘的样子。 He puts on a mysterious look. 2 (v) 守密 to keep secret; hide; conceal ＊大家秘而不宣。 We are keeping it a secret.

秘方 [mìfāng] a prescription of medicine kept secret
秘诀 [mìjié] a secret solution to a problem
秘密警察 [mìmìjǐng chá] secret police
秘密投票 [mìmìtóupiào] secret ballot
秘书 [mìshū] secretary

另见 [bì]

谧（謐） [mì] (adj) 安静 quiet

密 [mì] 1 (adj) 靠得近，距离小 close together; dense ＊东京人烟稠密。Tokyo is densely populated. 2 (adj) 关系近，切近 closely related; intimate ＊他们二人很亲密。 These two persons are very intimate. 3 (adj) 秘密 secret ＊你必须保密。 You must make it a secret. 4 (adj) 不公开的 secret; confidential ＊这是一封密函。 This is a secret letter. 5 (adj) 精致，细致 precise ＊手表里的零件都是非常精密的。 The parts inside a watch are very precise.

密度 [mìdù] density
密集 [mìjí] be highly concentrated; closely concentrated
密件 [mìjiàn] a secret document
密码电报 [mìmǎ diànbào] coded telegram
密谋 [mìmóu] plot
密切 [mìqiè] close; frequent
密室 [mìshì] a secret cell
密谈 [mì tán] a secret conversation
密友 [mìyǒu] intimate friend

蜜 [mì] 1 (n) 蜂蜜，蜜蜂采取花的甜汁酿成的东西 honey 2 (adj) 甜美 sweet ＊不要给他的甜言蜜语骗了。 Don't be deceived by his sweet talk.

蜜饯 [mìjiàn] sugar-preserved fruit
蜜糖 [mìtáng] honey
蜜月 [mìyuè] honey-moon

觅（覓） [mì] (v) 寻，找 seek; look for; search for ＊蝙蝠夜里才出来觅食。The bats will come out to look for its food at night.

mián

绵（綿） [mián] 1 (n) 丝绵，蚕茧加工成的絮片 floss silk 2 (adj) 软弱 soft and weak 3 (adj) 连续不断 continuous; unbroken;

uninterrupted ＊这里的羣山绵延不绝。The mountains here stretched continuously.

绵薄 [miánbó] weak in strength

绵绸 [miánchóu] cotton pongee

绵亘 [miángèn] to extend

绵绵 [miánmián] continuous; uninterrupted

绵羊 [miányáng] a sheep

棉 [mián] 1 (n) 草棉，是一种重要经济作物。种子外面的纤维就是纺纱用的棉花。种子可榨油 the cotton plant; cotton ＊美国南部盛产棉花。The southern part of America produces a lot of cotton. 2 (n) [木棉] [mùmián] 落叶大乔木。果实内的纤维不能纺，可作救生圈填料或枕芯 kapok

棉袄 [mián'áo] a wadded garment

棉布 [miánbù] cotton cloth

棉花 [miánhuā] cotton

棉纱 [miánshā] cotton yarn

棉线 [miánxiàn] cotton thread

棉织品 [miánzhīpǐn] cotton fabric

棉子油 [mián·ziyóu] cotton-seed oil

眠 [mián] (v) 睡觉 sleep ＊他睡眠不足。He did not have enough sleep.

眠卧 [mián wò] lie down to sleep

miǎn

免 [miǎn] (v) 去掉，除掉 to get rid of; to remove ＊入场免费。Admission is free. 2 (v) 防止 to avoid; to dodge; to stop; to prevent ＊要先做好准备，以免到时手忙脚乱。We must get ready first in order to avoid confusion when the moment comes. 3 (v) 勿，不可 not to; not allowed to ＊闲人免进。no admission except on business.

免不了 [miǎn·buliǎo] unavoidable

免除 [miǎnchú] to dismiss; to remove; to avoid

免费 [miǎnfèi] free of charge

免试 [miǎnshì] exempted from taking examinations

免税 [miǎnshuì] duty-free; free of taxes

免役 [miǎnyì] exemption from military service

免疫力 [miǎn yìlì] immunity from disease

免职 [miǎnzhí] to dismiss from service; to discharge

娩 [miǎn] (v) 分娩，生孩子 to give birth to a baby

冕 [miǎn] (n) 古代士大夫以上的官所戴的礼帽。后专指帝王的礼帽 a crown; a coronet

勉 [miǎn] 1 (v) 努力 to strive; to work hard; to endeavour ＊他奋勉求学。He endeavours to study. 2 (v) 鼓励，使人努力 to encourage; to stimulate ＊老师勉励我们用功学习。The teacher encourages us to study diligently.

勉力 [miǎnlì] to strive; to work diligently

勉励 [miǎnlì] to inspire; to encourage

勉强 [miǎnqiǎng] to force; to compel; to do something unwillingly; reluctant

勉为其难 [miǎn wéi qí nán] to manage to do what is beyond one's power

湎 [miǎn] (v) 沉迷（多指喝酒。）to indulge in (e.g. drinking)

缅（緬）[miǎn] (adj) 遥远 far and away ＊不要缅怀过去。Don't think far (recall) of the past.

腼 [miǎn] [腼腆] [miǎn·tiǎn] (adj) 害羞，不大方 shy; bashful ＊这小孩太腼腆了。This kid is very shy.

miàn

面 [miàn] 1 (n) 脸 the face ＊他面带笑容。He is having a smiling face. 2 (n) 事物的外表 the surface ＊水面上有一层油。There is a layer of oil on the surface of water. 3 (v) 向着 to face something ＊这间别墅背山面海。The bungalow is on a hill slope facing the sea. 4 量词，

特指扁形的物体 piece ; a measure word (for flat things) ＊ 一面镜子。 a piece of mirror; 二面旗。 two pieces of flags.

面（麵） [miàn] 1 (n) 粮食磨成的粉，特指小麦磨成的粉 flour ; wheat flour ＊这面包是由上等白粉制成的。This bread is made from top quality white flour. 2 (n) 面条 noodles ＊我喜欢吃炒面。I like to eat fried noodles.

面包 [miànbāo] bread
面红耳赤 [miàohóngěrchì] blush to the roots; crimson with shame
面黄肌瘦 [miànhuángjīshòu] sallow and thin
面积 [miànjī] area
面具 [miànjù] mask

面临 [miànlín] to encounter; to be confronted with
面貌[miànmào]appearance;countenance
面面俱到 [miàn miàn jùdào] all parties (or aspects) attended to; in every way
面面相觑 [miànmiànxiāngqù] looking at each other in astonishment
面目全非 [miàn mù quán fēi] totally different from the original appearance ; beyond recognition
面前 [miànqián] front; in the face of
面色 [mànsè] complexion
面生 [mànshēng] unfamiliar
面试 [mian shì] interview (for a job) ; oral examination
面熟 [miànshú] familiar
面子 [mian zi] face; surface; face-sa ving; prestige; social standing

miāo

喵 [miāo] (n) 貓叫的声音 mewing of a cat

miáo

苗 [miáo] 1 (n) 一般指幼小的植株 seedings; sprouts; saplings ＊果树苗要小心照料。The sapling of a fruit tree must be looked after carefully. 2 (n) 初生的饲养动物 small fry ＊他放了一些鱼苗在鱼塘里。He puts some fish fry into the pond.

苗床 [miáochuáng] a nursery; a seed-bed
苗条 [miáo·tiao] slender ; slim
苗头 [miáo· tou]sign ; indication
苗裔 [miáoyì] descendants ; progeny
苗族 [miáozú] Miao tribe

描 [miáo] (v) 照原样摹写或绘画 to trace; to draw; to sketch ＊他在布上描了一条龙的轮廓。He sketched the figure of a dragon on a cloth.

描画 [miáohuà] to portray
描绘 [miáohuì] to depict by words or painting
描摹 [miáo mó] to trace (painting or design)
描写 [miáoxiě] to describe; to portray; to depict

瞄 [miáo] (v) 目标、视力集中在一点上 to take aim ＊他瞄准目标后一连开了几枪。 After having taken the aim, he fired a few shots.

miǎo

秒 [miǎo] 1 (n) 谷物种子壳上的芒 the awn of grains 2 (n) 计算时间单位 second (of time) 3 (n) 计算弧或圆角的单位 second (of degree of arc or angle)

秒针 [miǎozhēn] the second hand (of clock or watch)

眇 [miǎo] 1 (adj)瞎了一只眼睛 blind in one eye 2 (adj) 细小 minute

渺 [miǎo] 1 (adj) 微小 tiny ; negligible ＊个人的力量是渺小的。 The strength of an individual is negligible. 2 (adj) 辽远而模糊 remote and dim

渺茫 [miǎománg] indistinct ; hazy; uncertain
渺小 [miǎo xiǎo] tiny, negligible; paltry

缈(緲) [miǎo] (adj) 模糊不清 indistinct

藐 [miǎo] 1 (adj) 小 small; petty; insignificant ∗不要藐视别人。Do not look down upon others. 2 (v) 轻视 to slight

藐视 [mǐaoshì] to treat with contempt; to look down upon; disdain

miào

妙 [miào] 1 (adj) 美、好 fine; excellent; wonderful ∗妙不可言。It is so fine that it cannot be described in words. 2 (adj) 奇巧，奥秘 wonderful; mysterious; subtle ∗这个东西妙用无穷。This object has many wonderful uses.

妙计 [miàojì] wonderful plan

妙龄 [miào líng] teenage (girl)

妙品 miàopǐn] a fine thing; a rare thing

妙趣横生 [miàoqù héng shēng] wonderful and interesting throughout

妙手回春 [miào shǒu huí chūn] people with excellent medical skills

庙(廟) [miào] (n) 用来供奉祖宗、神佛或历史人物的地方 temples; a place for worshipping ∗泰国有许多佛庙。There are many Buddhist temples in Thailand.

庙堂 [miào táng] a temple; a shrine

庙祝 [miào zhù] a temple curate or sexton

缪(繆) [miào] (n) 姓 a surname

另见 [móu; miù]

miē

乜 [miē] 〔乜斜〕 [miē xié] (v) 略眯着眼斜看，多表示不满或看不起 to squint

咩 [miē] (n) 羊叫的声音 bleating of sheep

miè

蔑(衊) [miè] 1 (adj) 无，没有 nothing 2 (v) 诬，毁 to slander; to defame ∗你不要污蔑好人。Don't you slander a good person.

蔑视 [mièshì] to look down upon; to disdain; to despise

篾 [miè] (n) 竹子劈成的长条薄片 bamboo splints

篾匠 [mièjiàng] a worker on bamboo

篾篓 [mièlǒu] bamboo splint basket

篾席 [miè xí] bamboo split mat

灭(滅) [miè] 1 (v) 熄灭 to extinguish ∗火灭了。The fire has gone out. 2 (v) 消灭 to exterminate; to destroy ∗这种药可以消灭许多害虫。This chemical can destroy many pests.

灭顶 [mièdǐng] to be drowned

灭火器 [mièhuǒqì] fire extinguisher

灭迹 [miè jī] to obliterate traces

灭绝 [mièjué] to destroy completely; to annihilate

灭口 [mièkǒu] to silence; a witness

灭亡 [mièwáng] to fall; to go out of existence; to perish; to doom

mín

民 [mín] 1 (n) 人 the people; the mass ∗民有，民治，民享。of the people, by the people, for the people. 2 (n) 指人或人群 the populace; the folks; the inhabitants; the citizens; the residents ∗木屋居民。the inhabitants of wooden houses (the squatters) 3 人民大众的 of the folks ∗这是一首民歌。This is a folk-song.

民办 [mínbàn] run by the local people

民变 [mínbiàn] insurrection

民兵 [mínbīng] people's militia

民不聊生 [mín bù liáo shēng] people have no ways of living

民愤 [mínfèn] indignation among the people; wrath of the masses

民歌 [míngē] folk song

民间 [mínjiān] folk (e.g. story, song, dance); among the people

民间文学 [mínjiānwénxué] folk literature

民间艺术 [mín jiān yì shù] folk arts

民权 [mínquán] human rights; the people's rights
民谣 [mínyiáo] ballads; folk songs
民意调查 [mínyì diào chá] survey of public opinions
民用 [mín yòng] civilian; civil
民怨沸腾 [mín yuàn fèi téng] people's resentment seething
民乐 [mín yuè] folk music
民脂民膏 [mín zhī míngāo] the wealth acquired through blood and sweat by the people
民众 [mínzhòng] the people; the populace
民主 [mínzhǔ] democracy
民主党派 [mínzhúdǎng pài] democratic parties
民主改革 [mínzhǔgǎigó] democratic reforms
民族 [mínzú] the race, the nation
民族革命 [mínzú gémìng] national revolution
民族英雄 [mín zú yīng xíong] national heroes
民族主义 [mínzú zhǔ yì] nationalism
民族自决 [mín zú zì jué] national self-determination
民族自治 [mínzú zì zhì] national autonomy

mǐn

抿 [mǐn] 1 (v) 刷，抹 to brush * 抿头发。 to brush the hair. 2 (v) 闭住，合拢 to shut * 她抿着嘴偷笑。She smiles stealthily with her lips pursed up.

泯 [mǐn] (v) 消灭 to destroy; to put an end to * 英雄人物给我们留下了不可泯灭的印象。 The heroes have given us an undestroyable impression

敏 [mǐn] 1 (adj) 迅速，灵活 prompt; ingenious; active; adroit * 猴子爬树身手敏捷。 Monkeys are adroit in climbing trees. 2 (adj) 奋勉 earnest ; hardworking * 这孩子聪敏而好学。This child is earnest and fond of study.
敏捷 [mǐnjié] quick response to; agile ; adroit
敏感 [mǐnkǎn] sensitive; keen feeling
敏锐 [mǐnruì] acute; sharp; keen

鳘（鰵）[mǐn] (n) 就是"鳕鱼" cod-fish

黾（黽）[mǐn] (v) 努力 to put forth an effort
黾勉 [mǐnmiǎn] to urge to effort

闵（閔）[mǐn] (n) 姓 a surname

悯（憫）[mǐn] 1 (v) 哀怜 to pity ; to sympathise with * 我们决不怜悯这个恶棍。 We will never pity this scoundrel. 2 (v) 忧愁 to grieve

皿 [mǐn] (n) 器皿，碗、碟、杯、盘等一类用器的总称。 utensils

闽（閩）[mǐn] (n) 福建省的简称 simpler name for the Hokkien Province
闽语 [mǐn yǔ] the Hokkien dialect

míng

冥 [míng] 1 (adj) 昏暗 gloomy ; dim * 洞内一片晦冥。 It was very dim in the cave. 2 (adj) 深沉 in deep * 他冥思苦想也想不出个道理来。He did not arrive at anything concrete after a deep contemplation. 3 (adj) 愚昧，昏庸 stupid; ignorant * 这个母亲强逼生病的孩子喝符水，真是冥顽不灵。 The mother is so ignorant and stupid as to force her ailing son to drink water with burnt charm paper. 4 (n) 迷信说法称人死后进入的世界; 地狱。the Hades; the unseen world
冥钱 [míng jián] paper money burnt for the dead
冥间 [míngqiān] the Hades
冥顽 [míngwán] stubborn; stupid
冥物 [míng wù] paper articles burnt at funeral
冥想 [míngxiǎng] to contemplate

瞑 [míng] (v) 闭上眼睛 to close the eyes ＊ 他死不瞑目。He could not close his eyes to die (could not die in peace).

螟 [míng] (n) 螟虫，螟蛾的幼虫，种类很多。蛀食水稻、玉米等农作物的茎，害处很大 various kinds of caterpillars which feed on the roots and stems of padi and maize plant

螟蛉 [mínglíng] a caterpillar

螟蛉子 [mínglíngzǐ] a caterpillar taken (adopted) by a wasp as food for its larvae (as its son); an adopted son

名 [míng] 1 (n) 人或事物的称呼 name; appellation; title 2 (v) 叫，说出 to name; to call ＊ 无以名之。 not knowing how to name it. 3 (n) 名气，声望 fame; reputation ＊ 他不为名利而工作。 He works not for his personal fame and gain. 4 (adj) 有名的 famous; well-known ＊ 吉隆坡的黑风洞是一个名胜。 The Batu Cave in Kuala Lumpur is a famous resort. 5 量词 a measure word for number of persons ＊ 评判员有三名。The judges are three in number.

名不副实 [míngbùfúshí] more in name than is reality

名不虚传 [míng bùxiū chuán] true to the reputation

名册 [míng cè] personnel roster; record of names

名产 [míngchǎn] famous product

名正言顺 [míngchèngyángshùn] proper and reasonable

名词 [míngcí] nouns; terms; words

名次 [míngcì] order of selection

名存实亡 [míngcán shí wáng] existing in name only

名单 [míng dān] name list

名额 [míng'é] the given number (of persons)

名副其实 [míng fù qí shí] worthy of the name

名贵 [míng guí] valuable

名列前茅 [míng liè qián máo] name ranking in the fore

名目 [míngmù] name ; title

名胜 [míng shēng] places of historic interest

名言 [míngyán] epigram; famous saying; proverb

名义 [míng yì] under the name of; nominal

名誉 [míng yù] reputation; honour

名誉会长 [míng yù huì zhǎng] an honorary president

名著 [míngzhù] a fine work; a famous novel

名字 [míngzì] persons' names

铭(銘) [míng] (v) 在器物上刻字，比喻深刻记住 to carve; to inscribe; to engrave; to remember ＊ 你的恩情我永远铭记在心头。 I will remember your kindness forever.

铭感 [míng gǎn] deeply grateful

铭记不忘 [míngjì bú wàng] will never forget

铭文 [míngwén] engraved inscription

茗 [míng] 1 (n) 茶树的嫩芽 the young shoot of tea plant 2 (n) 茶 tea ＊ 他们在月下品茗。 They are sipping tea under the moonlight.

明 [míng] 1 (adj) 亮 bright ＊ 礼堂内灯火通明。The hall is brightly lit. 2 (v) 明白，清楚 to understand; to make clear; to know＊我们要爱憎分明。We must know definitely what to love and what to hate. 3 (adj) 公开，清楚 open; clear ＊ 有话明说。 speak up openly 4 (n) 视觉 eyesight ＊ 他因车祸而失明。He lost his eye-sight as a result of an accident. 5 (n) 次 the next (day, month or year) ＊ 明天是劳动节。 Tomorrow (the next day) will be Labour Day. 6 (n) 朝代名 the Ming Dynasty

明白 [míngbǎi] apparent; clear; to understand

明辨是非 [míng biàn shì fēi] to distinguish right from wrong

明查暗访 [míng chá àn fǎng] to investigate in the open and to visit in the quiet

明澈 [míngchè] crystal clear

明朗 [mínglǎng] bright; forthright

明了 [mínliǎo] clear ; to understand; distinct

明媚 [míngméi] bright and beautiful

明目张胆 [míngmù zhāng dǎn] in a bare-faced way; brazenly; openly

明确 [míngquè] clear ; accurate; explicit; definite

明晰 [míngxī] perspicuous ; clear-cut

明显 [míngxiǎn] obvious ; evident

明眼人 [míng yǎn réh] a clear-sighted man

明哲保身 [míngzhébǎoshēn] to be wordly wise and playsafe

明争暗斗 [míng zhēng àn dǒu] overt and covert struggle

明智 [míngzhì] wise ; sagacious

明知故犯 [míng zhīgù fàn] deliberate violation; to commit mistakes deliberately

鸣(鳴) [míng] 1(v) 鸟兽、昆虫叫 the cry of a bird, an animal or an insect＊许多人爱听鸟鸣。Many people like to hear the chirping of birds. 2 (v) 发出声响 to sound ＊警笛大鸣。The siren sounds noisily. 3 (v) 用语言、文字发表意见 to sound literarily ＊ 百家争鸣。Let a hundred schools of thought contend (sound competitively)

鸣鼓 [mínggǔ] to beat a drum

鸣谢 [míngxiè] to express thanks

mǐng

酩 [mǐng] (酩酊) [mǐngdǐng] (adj) 喝酒过量，醉得迷迷糊糊的样子 drunk ＊ 他喝得酩酊大醉。He drank until he was completely drunk .

mìng

命 [mìng] 1 (n) 生命。表示动物、植物的生活能力 life ＊生命不息，战斗不止。Keep on struggling so long as there is life. 2 (n) 指示 order; command; instruct ＊他奉命行事。He acts by order . 3 (v) 给予，名称 to give a name ＊这艘刚完成的客轮被命名为"东风"。The newly completed ship is christened "East Wind". 4 (n) 人的贫富、寿数等；发展变化的趋向或规律。fate ;destiny;the tendency or law of development and change ＊ 贫富並不是命中注定。It is not fated to be rich or poor.

命根子 [mìng gēn·zi] lifeline ; one's very life

命令 [mìng lìng] to order; to command

命脉 [mìng mài] life -blood

命运 [mìngyún] fate ; destiny ; fortune

miù

谬(謬) [miù] (adj) 错误的，不符合客观规律和实际情况的 erroneous; fallacious; untrue; misleading ＊不要聽他的谬论。 Don't listen to his fallacious talk.

谬论 [miù lùn] fallacy

谬误 [miù wù] falsehood

谬种流传 [miù zhǒng liú chuán] absurdity passed on from generation to generation

mō

摸 [mō] 1 (v) 用手接触或轻轻抚摩 touch ; feel ＊这孩子想摸一摸那兔子。 This child wanted to touch the rabbit. 2 (v) 用手探取 feel for ; grope ＊他从衣袋里摸出一个银角来。He felt for a coin from his pocket. 3 (v) 通过试探而了解 to understand something by groping and testing ＊我们还没有摸清楚他的底细。 We have not understood clearly his background.

摸索 [mō suo] to grope for

摩 [mō] 1 (v) 摩擦，接触 to rub; to feel ＊ 他们个个摩拳擦掌，准备和来犯者拼过。 Rubbing fists and palms together,every one of them was ready to fight with the intruders. 2 (v)

研究切磋 to see the good and learn from each other; to study and discuss mutually * 各文娱小组将呈献一个观摩会。 The cultural groups will jointly present a show for mutual discussion and criticisms.

摩擦 [mócā] to rub together; conflict

摩擦力 [mó cā lì] friction

摩登 [módēng] modern

摩肩接踵 [mójiān jiēzhǒng] rubbing shoulders and joining heels (very crowded)

摩托车 [mó tuō chē] a motorcycle

磨 [mó] 1 (v) 以硬物摩擦 to grind; to rub; to sharpen * 刀是越磨越利。The more you grind a knife, the sharper it becomes. 2 (n) 阻碍，波折 hardships; sufferings * 我们要经得起磨炼。 We must be able to stand hardships and sufferings. 3 (v) 拖延 to delay; to consume * 这作法是很磨工夫的。This method is very time-consuming.

磨蹭 [mó cèng] rubbing; idle at work; to pester

磨床 [móchuáng] a grinder

磨砺 [mólì] to sharpen a knife; to toughen oneself under difficult conditions

磨炼 [mó liàn] to discipline oneself diligently; to steel; to temper

磨灭 [mó miè] to dull; to blunt; to paralyse

磨损 [mósǔn] to fray; to breakdown due to friction

魔 [mó] 1 (n) 恶鬼 a devil; an evil spirit; a demon 2 (adj) 神奇，使人入迷 bewitching; fascinating

魔力 [mólì] fascination; magical power

魔术 [móshì] juggling

魔术家 [móshùjiā] a magician

魔爪 [mózhǎo] claws

蘑 [mó] 〔蘑菇〕 [mógū] (n) 一种食用真菌 mushroom

馍(饃) [mó] (n) 通常指馒头，叫"馍馍" dumplings

模 [mó] 1 (n) 制造器物的模型 a mould; a pattern *这是制造塑胶杯的模型。This is a mould for making plastic cups. 2 (n) 标准，规范 a standard; a model 3 (v) 仿效 imitate; copy * 孩子们在模仿演员的动作。The children are imitating the actors.

模范 [mófàn] a model; an example to be learned

模糊 [mó hú] obscure; vague; blurred

模稜两可 [mó léng liáng kě] ambiguous; in an equivocal way; to shift and hedge

模拟 [mónǐ] to imitate; to copy

模特儿 [mótèr] a model

模型 [mó xíng] model; pattern

另见 [mú]

膜 [mó] 1 (n) 生物体内象薄皮的组织 a membrane * 小心不要挖穿耳膜。Beware of puncturing the tympanic membrane. 2 (n) 象膜一样的东西 things which look like a membrane; film

摹 [mó] (v) 仿效，照着样子做 imitate; follow a pattern * 他在临摹中国字帖中的书法。He is imitating the strokes of model chinese calligraphy.

摹本 [móběn] a copy; a facsimile

mǒ

抹 [mǒ] 1 (v) 涂，搽 to apply; to rub *她在替演员抹粉。She is applying powder on the face of the actor. 2 (v) 揩，擦 wipe *她在抹眼泪。She is wiping her tears.

抹杀 [mǒshā] to ignore; to negate; to deny; to write off

另见 [mò]

[mā]

mò

末 [mò] 1 (n) 东西的梢，尖端 the tip of something * 秋毫之末。 the

tip of the fine hair of a bird or animal; very minute thing. 2 (n) 不是根本的，重要的部分 unimportant part *我们不可以本末倒置。We can not misplace the important and the unimportant; the essential and the non-essential. 3 (adj) 终，最后 the end; the last *她周末很忙。She is very busy this weekend. 4 (n) 碎屑 powder; dust *他把药片研成粉末。He grinds the tablets into powder.

末路 [mò lù] doom; the end

末叶 [mòyè] last part of century or dynasty

沫

[mò] (n) 液体形成的许多细泡 foam; bubbles *这瓶洗发水泡沫很多。This shampoo produces a lot of bubbles.

秣

[mò] 1 (n) 牲口的饲料 fodder 2 (v) 喂牲口 to feed the animals

秣马厉兵 [mò mǎ lì bīng] to mobilise; to prepare horses and troops for battles

抹

[mò] 1 (v) 把泥灰涂上再弄平 to plaster; to smear; to brush off; to wipe clean *她是个抹泥灰工人。She is a plaster. 2 (v) 紧挨着绕过 to go round *请别拐弯抹角了。Please don't go round the corner (beat about the bush).

另见 [mǒ]
[mā]

茉

[mò]「茉莉」[mò lì] (n) 常绿灌木。花白色，有香气，可以提取芳香油 jasmine

莫

[mò] (adv) 不 not

莫不 [mò bù] might it not be...; perhaps; probably

莫大 [mòdà] most important

莫非 [mòfēi] could it be.....?

莫名其妙 [mòmíngqímiào] unaccountably mysterious; inexplicable

莫逆 [mònì] very intimate

莫如 [mò rú] it would be better

莫衷一是 [mòzhōngyīshì] cannot decide which is right

漠

[mò] 1 (n) 面积广阔的沙石地带 a desert 2 (adj) 冷淡，不经心 indifferent; cool *我们不能只顾读书而对周围发生的事漠不关心。We should not be concerned only with our study and be indifferent to things happening around us.

漠视 [mòshì] indifferent; apathetic

漠然 [mòrán] ignore; disregard

貘

[mò] (n) 哺乳动物。皮厚毛短，颈粗眼小。吃树叶、嫩芽、果实等 a tapir

寞

[mò] (adj) 清静，冷落 still; silent

蓦(驀)

[mò] (adj) 突然 sudden *他蓦地站了起来。He stood up suddenly.

蓦地 [mòdì] suddenly

蓦然 [mòrán] carelesslv

瘼

[mò] (n) 疾苦 sufferings *他很关心民瘼 He was very concerned about the people's sufferings.

默

[mò] (adj) 不出声，不说话 silent *他沉默了一阵子。He kept silent for a while.

默哀 [mò āi] to silence (mourning)

默读 [mò dú] read silently

默默无闻 [mò mò wú wén] unknown to public

默契 [mòqì] a tacit understanding (agreement)

默然 [mò rán] speechless

默认 [mòrèn] to recognize tacitly

默写 [mòxiě] to dictate

默许 [mòxǔ] to approve tacitly

墨

[mò] (n) 写字绘画用的黑色颜料 blank ink

墨迹 [mòjī] original copy of writings
墨守成规 [mòshǒuchéngguī] conservative in ideas, sticking to old values and refusing to change
墨水 [mòshuǐ] fluid ink

陌 [mò] (n) 小路 a path
陌生 [mòshēng] strange

没 [mò] 1 (v) 沉下 to sink; to submerge ＊潜水员很快就没入水中。The diver submerges into the water within a short time. 2 (v) 漫过，高过 to cover; to overflow ＊水深没顶。The water is deep enough to cover the head.
没落 [mòluò] degenerate; perish
没收 [mòshōu] to confiscate
另见 [méi]

殁 [mò] (v) 死 die; perish

磨 [mò] 1 (n) 弄碎粮食或其他物品的工具 a mill; grinding equipment ＊这个石磨很笨重。This grindstone is very heavy. 2 (v) 用磨把粮食或其他物品弄碎 to grind, ＊你看过人家磨大豆来制豆腐吗？Have you seen people grinding soya beans to make bean curds?
磨坊 [mòfáng] a mill
另见 [mó]

脉 [mò] 〔脉脉〕(n) 形容用眼神表达爱慕的情意 an eye expression of love
另见 [mài]

móu

牟 [móu] 1 (v) 谋取 to encroach on; to take
牟利 [móulì] to make profit
另见 [mù]

眸 [móu] (n) 眼珠 the pupil of the eye; the eye

谋(謀) [móu] 1 (n) 主意，计策 plan; device; strategy ＊他有勇无谋 。He has the courage but not strategy. 2 (v) 设法求得 to contrive ＊我们都想为人民谋幸福。We all wish to contrive for the happiness of the people. 3 (v) 商议 to consult; to discuss ＊我们的想法不谋而合。Our ideas correspond without previous discussion.
谋害 [móuhài] to plot; to injure
谋杀 [móushà] to attempt murder; to try to kill
谋生 [móushēng] to contrive to earn a living

mǒu

某 [mǒu] (adj) 代替不明确指出的人、事物、时、地和单位等 a certain (person, thing, place etc.) ＊我在歐洲某地见过这个人。I have seen this person at a certain place (somewhere) in Europe.

mú

模 [mú] (n) 模子 mould ＊这銅模是用来制糕饼的。This copper mould is for making cakes and cookies.
另见 [mó]
模样 [múyàng] pattern; model

mǔ

母 [mǔ] 1 (n) 妈妈 mother ＊他的母亲是一名厂工。His mother is a factory worker. 2 (adj) 象母亲能产生其他事物的 able to reproduce like a mother ＊航空母舰。an aircraft carrier (an aircraft mother ship) ＊工作母机 a machine tool (a mother machine for work)
母系 [mǔxì] the maternal line
母音 [mǔyīn] vowel

拇 [mǔ] (n) 手、脚的大指 the thumb; the great toe ＊他在一次工业意外中丧失了一只拇指。He lost a thumb during an industrial accident.
拇指印 [mǔzhǐyìn] thumb-print

姆 [mǔ] (n) 代别人负责照顾孩子的妇女为"保姆" nanny; baby-sitter ＊当有钱人家的保姆并不容易。To work as a nanny for a rich family is not easy.

亩(畝) [mǔ] (n) 地积单位 mou, a chinese land-measure of area *这个地主拥有几千亩良田。This landlord owned a few thousands "mou" of fertile land.

牡 [mǔ] (adj) 雄性的(鸟、兽),跟"牝"相对 male (birds; animal)

牡丹花 [mǔdanhuā] a peony

牡蛎 [mǔlì] oyster

mù

募 [mù] (v) 广泛征求 to solicit; to raise; to canvass *学生们到处筹募建校基金。The students went everywhere to solicit for building funds.

募兵 [mùbīng] to raise troops

募款 [mùkuǎn] to raise fund

墓 [mù] (n) 埋死人的地方 a burial ground; a grave; a tomb *同学们在他的墓前献花。The fellow students present flowers before his grave.

墓碑 [mùbēi] a gravestone; a tombstone

墓志铭 [mùzhìmíng] an epitaph; the inscriptions on a grave-stone

幕 [mù] 1 (n) 帐蓬 a tent *我们在空地上搭起一个帐幕。We built a tent on the open ground. 2 (n) 舞台上用的大块的布、绸、丝绒等 the curtain or screen used on the stage *幕徐徐而下。The curtain drops gradually. 3 (n) 银幕:放映电影用的银白色屏帐。the screen used in film shows 4 (n) 戏剧的大段落 act (of a play) *这部三幕剧演出十分成功。This three-act play has proved a great success.

暮 [mù] 1 (n) 傍晚 dusk; sunset; evening. *暮色苍茫。in the boundless and indistinct view of the evening. 2 (adj) 晚,(时间)将尽 late; the close of a period of time *他暮景凄凉。The later period of his life is miserable.

暮景 [mùjǐng] the sunset view; the later period of one's life

暮年 [mùnián] the declining years

暮气 [mùqì] spirit of decline

慕 [mù] 1 (v) 想念 to think of affectionately *她无时不思慕远离了她的爱人。She is all the time thinking of her lover who is away from her. 2 (v) 羡慕,仰慕 to envy; to admire; to long for; to esteem *我们都很敬慕他。We have a great esteem for him.

目 [mù] 1 (n) 眼 eye *这个国家的建设和发展是有目共睹的。The construction and development of this country are witnessed by all (who have eyes). 2 (n) 看 a look; a glance *这些图片和说明使人们对锡的生产过程一目了然。These pictures and illustrations enable people to understand the process of tin mining just by a glance. 3 (n) 大项中再分的小项 a detailed item *这分章程共有三十条细目。This constitution consists of thirty items. 4 (n) 条目,目录 an index; a catalogue *我在书店拿到了一分书目。I have got a catalogue from the book shop.

目标 [mùbiāo] the target; the aim; the objective

目不识丁 [mù bu shí dīng] an illiterate

目不转睛 [mùbùzhuǎnjīng] to stare continuously

目瞪口呆 [mùdèngkǒudāi] stunned; dumbfounded

目的 [mùdì] the aim; the object; the goal

目的地 [mùdìdè] the destination

目睹 [mùdǔ] to witness

目光如豆 [mùguāng rú dòu] very short-sighted

目击 [mùjī] to witness

目击者 [mùjīzhě] an eye-witness

目空一切 [mù kōng yíqiè] to look down upon all

目录 [mùlù] contents (of books), the catalogue

目前 [mùqián] the present
目中无人 [mùzhōngwúrén] to look down on everyone

木 [mù] 1 (n) 有枝干的植物；树 a plant with branches; a tree; wood ＊独木不成林。 A single tree will not grow into a jungle. 2 (adj) 没有知觉 insensitive; numb ＊我的手脚冻得麻木了。My limbs are numb with cold.
木板 [mùbǎn] wooden board
木材 [mùcái] timber
木筏 [mùfá] a wooden raft

木工 [mùgōng] wood work; carpenter
木架 [mùjiá] wooden framework
木刻 [mùkè] woodcut; wood engraving
木讷 [mùnè] stupid and inarticulate
木偶 [muou] a wooden figure; a puppet
木排 [mùpái] a raft
木器 [mùqì] wooden furniture
木然 [mùrán] benumbed
木薯 [mùchú] tapioca

木炭 [mùtàn] charcoal
木头 [mùtóu] a wood; a wood block
木屑 [mùxiè] saw dust
木星 [mùxīng] the Jupiter (planet)
木已成舟 [mùyǐchéngzhōu] the wood has been made into a boat— something has been done

沐 [mù] (v) 洗 to watch; to bathe
沐猴而冠 [mùhóu ér guān] a monkey dressed up — no sort of a man
沐浴 [mùyù] to bathe
沐雨栉风 [mùyǔzhìfēng] bathed by the rain and combed by the wind — the hardship of toil and travel

穆 [mù] 1 (n) 肃静 solemn silence ＊会场一片肃穆。The meeting place was in a state of solemn silence. 2 (n) 姓 a surname
穆罕默德 [mùhǎnmòdé] Mohammed
穆斯林教 [mùsīlínjiào] Mohammedanism
穆斯林教徒 [mùsīlínjiàotú] a muslim

牧 [mù] (v) 放养牲口 to pasture; to tend cattle (sheep) ＊苏武被放逐到北海边牧羊。 Su Wu was exiled to the coast of North Sea to tend sheep.
牧场 [mùchǎng] herding ground; pasture
牧人 [mùrén] herdsmen
牧师 [mù shī] a pastor
牧童 [mùtóng] a shepherd; a cowherd

睦 [mù] (adj) 关系友好，亲近 friendly; affectionate; harmonious ＊这儿的各民族人民和睦共处。 The different races here live together in harmony.
睦邻 [mùlín] to harmonise with one's neighbour

N

ná

拿 [ná] 1 (v) 用手取，握在手里 to hold; to carry; to take ＊他手里拿着枪。He is holding a gun. 2 (v) 捕捉 to catch; to arrest ＊朝廷要捉拿起义军首领。The government wanted to arrest the leader of the revolutionary army.

拿定主意 [nádìngzhǔ-yī] to make up one's mind

拿手 [náshoǔ] expert; to be good at

nǎ

哪 [nǎ] (part) 表示疑问的词 which……? ＊你在哪儿？Where are you? ＊你要哪个？Which one do you want?

另见 [nà]

哪个 [nǎ-gē] which one?

哪里 [nǎ-li] where? whenever

哪怕 [nǎpà] even if; even though

哪儿 [nǎr] where?

哪些 [nǎxiē] which?

哪样 [nǎyàng] what kind?

nà

呐 [nà]〔呐喊〕(v) [nàhǎn] 大声叫喊 to shout

纳 (納) [nà] 1 (v) 接受 to accept; to take in; to adopt ＊我们将采纳他的建议。We shall adopt his proposal. 2 (v) 交付 to pay ＊这项政策只有增加纳税人的负担。This policy would only increase the burden of tax payers.

纳粹主义 [nàcuìzhǔyì] Nazism

纳罕 [nàhǎn] to be surprised

纳闷 [nàměn] to be baffled; to be in doubt and confused

纳入 [nàrù] to bring within; to fit into

纳税 [nànshuì] to pay a tax

衲 [nà] 1 (v) 缝补，补缀 mend; patch. 2 (n) 和尚穿的衣服，也指和尚 monk's garment; a monk; a priest

那 [nà] (adj) 指较远的时间、地点事物、跟"这"相对 that; which

那个 [nà-gē] that one

那里 [nà-lī] over there

那么 [nà-mē] such

那么点儿 [nà-mēdiǎnr] so little; so few

那么些 [nà-mēxiē] so much; so many

那么着 [nà-mē-zhē] like that; in that way

那儿 [nàr] there

那样 [nàyàng] so; in such a manner

捺 [nà] 1 (v) 用手按 to press with the hand 2 (v) 抑制 to control ＊他捺着性子不作声。He controlled his temper and did not say anything.

•na

哪 [•na] (part) 助词，用于句末 a particle used at the end of a sentence ＊大家加油干哪！Let's do it to the

best of our ability!
另见 [nǎ]

nǎi

乃 [nǎi] (v) 是,就是 to be *失败乃成功之母 Failure is the mother of success.

乃至 [nǎizhì] even

奶 [nǎi] 1 (n) 乳房，分泌乳汁的器官 a woman's breast. 2 (n) 乳汁 milk. 3 (v) 用自己的乳汁喂孩子 to breast feed *她正在奶孩子。She is breast feeding her baby.

奶粉 [nǎifěn] milk powder

奶奶 [nǎi-nǎi] grandmother; a respectful term of address used by young people to a woman of about their grandmothers' age

nài

奈 [nài] (v) 对付 to tackle; to deal with

奈何 [nài-hé] how to deal with it? what to do?

耐 [nài] (v) 受得住，禁得起 to endure; to bear *我们的祖先刻苦耐劳。Our fore-fathers were very hardworking and could endure hardship.

耐烦 [nàifán] patient

耐火材料 [nàihuǒ-cáiliào] heat-resistant material; refractory material

耐久 [nàijiǔ] durable

耐劳 [nàiláo] can endure hardships; good stamina

耐热 [nàirè] heat-resisting; heat-proof

耐人寻味 [nàirénxúnwèi] intensely interesting; pregnant with meaning which needs careful tasting

耐心 [nàixīn] patient; patience

耐性 [nàixìng] patience

耐用 [nàiyòng] durable; lasting

nán

南 [nán] (n) 方向，跟"北"相对 south

南边 [nán-biān] the south

南瓜 [nángua] pumpkin

南极 [nánjí] the South Pole

南极圈 [nánjíquān] antarctic circle

南极洲 [nánjízhōu] antarctic

南美洲 [Nánměizhōu] South America or Latin America

南腔北调 [nánqiāng-běidiào] to talk with a strong local accent

南辕北辙 [nán yuánběi zhé] to go south by driving the chariot north-diametrically opposite; heading in wrong direction

南征北战 [nánzhēng běi zhèn] to fight north and south (all over the country)

喃 [nán] (v)〔喃喃〕低低说话的声音 to gabble; to chatter

楠 [nán] (n) 常绿乔木，木质坚硬，是建筑的优良木料 a kind of fine grained hard wood, commonly known as cedar

难(難) [nán] (a) 不容易 difficult; not easy *这个题目很难。This question is very difficult.

难产 [nánchǎn] difficult labour (in child birth); difficult to get result

难处 [nánchù] difficulties; hard to get along with

难道 [nán dào] is it possible.....? does it mean....?

难得 [nándé] hard to get; rare

难度 [nándù] extent of difficulty; difficulty

难分难解 [nánfēnnánjiě] stalemate, (in argument or fighting); highly intimate, difficult to part also

难怪 [nánguài] no wonder; that's why

难关 [nánguān] difficult position; impasse; predicament; barrier

难过 [nánguò] to feel miserable; to feel sorry; hard up; uncomfortable

难堪 [nánkān] intolerable;embarassing; hard to endure

难看 [nánkàn] ugly

难免 [nánmiǎn] unavoidable; cannot help

难能可贵 [nánnéngkěguì] praiseworthy for one who has achieved something difficult

难受 [nánshòu] unbearable; distressed

难说 [nánshuō] hard to say; not sure
难题 [nǎntí] a knotty problem; a baffling problem; a hard nut to crack
难听 [nántīng] unpleasant to hear
难为 [nán-wéi] to make it difficult for; to embarass; to trouble
难为情 [nánwéiqíng] embarassing
难闻 [nánwén] ill-smelling; stinking
难言之隐 [nányánzhīyǐn] things and causes difficult to talk of
难以置信 [nányǐzhìxìn] unbelievable; incredible
另见 [nàn]

男 [nán] 1 (n) "女"的反义字 male; men 2 (n) 儿子 son ＊他是长男。He is the eldest son
男爵 [nánjué] the rank of baron
男女平等 [nánnǔpíngděng] equality for both sexes
男女同校 [nánnǔtóngxiào] co-education
男人 [nánrén] a husband; a man
男性 [nánxìng] masculine sex; male

nàn

难（難） [nàn] 1 (n) 灾祸，不幸的遭遇 calamity; disaster ＊许多人在这次地震中遭难。Many people met disaster (died) during this earthquake. 2 (v) 诘责 to find fault with; to reprove ＊这个管工常常非难新来的工人。 This supervisor always finds fault with the new workers.
难民 [nànmín] refugees
难兄难弟 [nànxīong-nàndì] fellow sufferers; one as bad as the other
另见 [nán]

náng

囊 [náng] (n) 口袋或象口袋的东西 a bag; a sack; ＊他把工具放在布囊里。 He put his tools into a canvas bag.
囊括 [nángkuò] to envelope all; to include everything
囊中物 [nángzhōngwù](fig) things which can be obtained easily

náo

挠（撓） [náo] 1 (v) 扰乱 to disturb; to interrupt; to throw into confusion ＊学生队伍受到大雨阻挠。The troops of students were interrupted by the heavy rain. 2(v)弯曲，比喻屈服 to bend

蛲（蟯） [náo] 蛲虫 [nàochǒng] (n) 寄生在人体肠内的一种白色针状小虫 a kind of human round worm

nǎo

恼（惱） [nǎo] (adj) 发怒，愤恨 angry; annoyed; worried ＊别为这些小事而烦恼。 Don't worry ovor such trifles.
恼恨 [nǎohèn] to be irritated and filled with hatred
恼火 [nǎohuǒ] to be enraged; to lose patience; to be annoyed
恼怒 [nǎonù] to be irritated and angry
恼羞成怒 [nǎo xīu chéng nù] to fly into a rage with shame

脑（腦） [nǎo] (n) 高等动物头腔内主持知觉运动的器官 the brain
脑袋 [nǎo·dai] the head
脑海 [nǎohǎi] the brain; the mind
脑筋 [nǎojīn] brains; mental ability
脑壳 [nǎoké] the skull
脑力劳动 [nǎolì láodòng] mental labour; brain work
脑膜 [nǎomó] the covering membranes of the brain
脑膜炎 [nǎomóyán] meningitis
脑炎 [nǎoyán] encephalitis
脑溢血 [nǎoyì xuè] cerebral haemorrhage; celebral apoplexy
脑子 [nǎo•zi] the brain; mental power

nào

闹（鬧） [nào] 1 (adj) 不安静，喧哗 noisy; bustling ＊这条街道很热闹。 This street is very busy. 2 (v) 吵，扰乱 to get very noisy; to create disturbance

*这个孩子又哭又闹。This kid cries and creates disturbances. 3 (v) 发生（灾害或疾病），发泄 to befall; to suffer from; to vent one's feelings *她很会闹情绪。 She gives in to her emotion very easily.

闹别扭 [nào biè·niu] to be at odds

闹病 [nào bìng] to be ill

闹肚子 [nào dù·zi] to suffer from diarrhoea

闹革命 [nàogémìng] to make revolution

闹哄哄 [nàohōnghōng] noisy; boisterous

闹脾气 [nào pí qì] to show ill temper; to lose temper

闹情绪 [nào qíng xù] to be ill-tempered

闹市 [nào shì] downtown area; busy streets

闹事 [nào shì] to cause trouble

闹意见 [nào yìjiàn] to quarrel; to dispute

闹着玩儿 [nào·zhe wánr] to do something for fun

闹钟 [nào zhōng] an alarm clock

·ne

呢 [·ne] (part) 助词，用于句末，表示疑问或肯定的语气，或表示动作正在进行 particle at the end of a sentence to show doubt or affirmation or to show that an action is still in progress *怎么办呢？ What to do? *还早呢。It's still early. *他在看报呢。He is reading the newspaper. 另见 [ní]

něi

馁(餒) [něi] 1 (adj) 饥饿 hungry 2 (v) 失去勇气 to lose one's courage; to be discouraged *胜不骄，败不馁。 Not to be conceited when one wins and not to be discouraged when one loses.

nèi

内 [nèi] (n);(a) 里头（跟"外"相对） inside; inner part; internal; interior

内部 [nèi bù] internal parts; within; inner

内定 [nèidìng] private (unofficial) decision

内阁 [nèigé] the cabinet

内海 [nèihǎi] inland sea

内行 [nèiháng] one who knows how, skilful

内河 [nèihé] inland river

内讧 [nèihòng] internal conflicts

内奸 [nèijiān] a hidden traitor

内角 [nèijiǎo] an interior angle

内疚 [nèijiù] prickings

内科病房 [nèikēbìngfáng] a medical ward

内乱 [nèiluàn] civil conflicts; internal trouble

内幕消息 [nèimùxiāo xì] inside facts

内勤 [nèiqín] office personnel

内情 [nèiqíng] the ins and outs of the matter

内燃机 [nèiránjī] a diesel engine

内容 [nèróng] content

内外交困 [nèiwàijiāokùn] beset with difficulties both at home and abroad

内线 [nèixiàn] interior lines; extension line (of telephone)

内衣 [nèiyī] underwear

内因 [nèiyīn] internal cause

内应 [nèiyìng] uprising from inside; support from inside

内在 [nèizài] inside; internal

内脏 [nèizàng] internal organs of the body

内战 [nèizhàn] civil war

内政 [nèizhèng] interior affairs

内子，内人 [nèizǐ] [nèirén] wife

nèn

嫩 [nèn] 1 (adj) 初生而柔弱的 tender: weak; young *地上长出许多木瓜的嫩芽。There are many tender papaya shoots coming out of the soil. 2 (adj) 不老练 inexperienced; unseasoned *这小子初入行，还嫩得很。This chap has just learned the ABC of the trade;he is still very inexperienced. 3 (adj) 淡，浅 of a light colour*嫩黄。 light yellow

néng

能 [néng] 1 (n) 才干 capability; talent; and skill ＊他有能力担当这个任。He has the capability to shoulder this task. 2 (a) 可以胜任的 capable ＊他是美术设计的能手。He is an expert (capable man) in art design. 3 (v) 胜任 can; be able ＊她能歌善舞。She can sing and dance. 4 (n) 物体做功的力 energy ＊原子能。atomic energy. ＊能源 source of energy.

能动 [néngdòng] consciously active; active
能干 [nénggàn] capable; able
能够 [nénggòu] can; be able to
能力 [nénglì] ability; capability
能量 [néngliàng] capacity; energy
能耐 [néng nài] capability; ableness
能手 [néngshǒu] an expert; a good hand at ...
能源 [néngyuán] energy source
能者多劳 [néngzhěduōláo] the able ones will do more
能文能武 [nénwénnénwǔ] skilled both in literary talents and military arts; able to do both mental and manual labour

nī

妮 [nī] (n) 女孩子 a girl

ní

尼 [ní] (n) 尼姑，出家修行以宗教为职业的女佛教徒 a buddhist nun

尼罗河 [níluóhé] the Nile River

呢 [ní] (n) 一种毛织品 kind of woolen fabric ＊呢绒线。woolen yarn.

呢喃 [nínán] twittering of swallows; to whisper; to murmur
呢绒 [níróng] woolen textiles
另见 [·ne]

怩 [ní] (v) 脸红，羞愧 to blush; to look ashamed
另见 [nǐuní]

泥 [ní] (n) 土和水合成的东西 mud; soil; earth

泥垢 [nígòu] mud and dirt
泥鳗 [nímán] eel

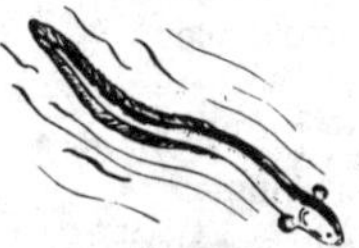

泥泞 [nínìng] muddiness; mud
泥牛入海 [ní niú rù hǎi] a clay-ox enters the sea - never to return
泥炭 [nítàn] peat
泥塑木雕 [ní sù mù diāo] a clay or wooden figure —dull expression and sluggish movement of a person
另见 [nì]

倪 [ní] 1 (n) 起始，边际 a beginning; a limit, a bound 2 (n) 姓 a surname

霓 [ní] (n) 虹的一种，也叫"副虹" a rainbow

霓虹灯 [níhóngdēng] neon lights

nǐ

旎 [nǐ] (n) 旎旗的飘扬 fluttering of flags

你 [nǐ] (pron) 代词，指称谈话的对方 you (singular number)

你们 [nǐ mén] you (plural number)
你死我活 [nǐ sǐ wǒ huó] life and death.(struggle)
你自己 [nǐzijǐ] you yourself

拟（擬） [nǐ] 1 (v) 起草 to draft ＊我们必须拟订一个计划。We have to draft a plan. 2 (v) 打算，想要 to intend to; to plan to ＊我拟于下月去槟城。I plan to go to Penang next month. 3 (v) 模仿 to imitate; to mimic ＊他在摹拟差利卓别麟的动作。He is mimicking the actions of Charlie Chaplain.

拟订 [nǐdìng] to draw up; to work out; to map out

nì

泥 [nì] (v) 涂抹 to apply; to spread; to plaster ＊工人正在泥墙。 The

worker is plastering the wall. 2 (v) 固执 to stick stubbornly to
泥古不化 [nìgǔbúhuà] to stick stubbornly to old rules
另见 [ní]

昵(暱) [nì] (adj) 亲热，亲近close; intimate

睨 [nì] (adj) 斜着眼睛看，有藐视的意思 glancing sideway in a contemptuous manner

匿 [nì] (v) 隐藏，躲避 to hide; to conceal ∗那个大盗最近销声匿迹了。That robber has vanished in hiding recently.
匿名 [nìmíng] anonymous

溺 [nì] 1 (v) 淹没 to be drowned ∗善泳者溺于水。A good swimmer may possibly be drowned in water. 2 (adj) 过分 excessive
溺爱 [nì ài] to love excessively; to spoil (a child)

逆 [nì] 1 (v) 违背 to disobey; to rebel; to go against ∗逆水行舟。 to sail against the current. 2 (adj) 抵触，不顺从 adverse; disobedient ∗忠言逆耳。Sincere advice is adverse (unpleasant) to the ear. 3 (adv) 预先 in advance ∗逆料。 to anticipate.
逆差 [nìchā] deficit
逆境 [nìjìng] adverse circumstances
逆来顺受 [nì lái shùn shòu] tolerating all the adversities tacitly
逆流 [nì liú] a counter current
逆时针方向 [nìshízhēnfāngxiàng] anti-clockwise

腻(膩) [nì] 1 (adj) 食物油脂过多 greasy; oily 2 (adj) 因过多而厌烦 disgusted; sick of; tired of ∗这些话我都听腻了。I am sick of what he says. 3 (adj) 滑泽 smooth; glossy ∗细腻。 fine and smooth.

nīan

拈 [niān] (v) 用两三个手指捏 to hold with the fingers; to pick up ∗只要我们留心观察，很多东西信手拈来就是写作的材料了。 Many things can be picked up readily as writing materials if only we were to observe with care.
拈轻怕重 [niān qīng pà zhòng] to select the easier task and avoiding the difficult ones; to prefer the light and shirk the heavy

nián

粘(黏) [nián] (adj) 有浆糊或胶的性质的 sticky; glutinous; adhesive ∗这胶水很粘。 The gum is very sticky.
另见 [zhān]
粘合剂 [niánhéjì] chemical adhesives
粘土 [niántǔ] clay
粘液 [niányè] mucus; viscous liquid

年 [nián] 1 (n) 地球绕太阳一周的时间 year 2 (n) 人的岁数 a person's age
年表 [niánbiǎo] a chronology
年产量 [niánchǎnliàng] annual output
年成 [niàn chéng] the result of a year's harvest
年初 [nián chū] the beginning of a year
年代 [niándài] an age; years
年底 [niándǐ] the end of a year
年度 [niándù] year; annual
年分 [niánfèn] a particular year; age; vintage
年俸 [niánfèng] annual salary
年糕 [nián gāo] new year cake made of glutinous rice flour
年级 [niánjǐ] grade or class in a school
年纪 [niánjǐ] a person's age
年景 [niánjǐng] harvest condition
年龄 [niánlíng] age
年迈 [niánmài] advanced in age;old-aged
年轻 [niánqīng] young
年头 [niántóu] condition of the times
年限 [niánxiàn] a fixed number of years
年幼 [niányòu] young; tender years
年月 [nián yuè] conidtion of the times; years
年终 [niánzhōng] the end of a year

niǎn

捻(撚) [niǎn] (v) 用手指搓转 to twist something with the

fingers; to twist; to pinch ＊她在把细纱捻成线。She is twisting the yarn into a thread.

碾 [niǎn] (v) 轧 to roll; to grind; to crush; to polish; to husk ＊工人在碾米。The worker is husking the rice grain.

碾坊 [niǎnfáng] a mill for husking grain

碾米 [niǎnmǐchǎng] a rice-hulling mill

碾子 [niǎn·zi] a mill for husking grain

撵(攆) [niǎn] (v) 赶走，驱逐 to drive away; to expel ＊我们一定要把坏人撵出去。We must drive the bad man away.

niàn

念 [niàn] 1 (v) 常常想 to long; to yearn ＊我们很想念远方的亲人。We long for our distant relatives. 2 (n) 念头 thought ＊他觉得自己总有许多私心杂念。He felt that he had always had a lot of private and confused thoughts in himself. 3 (v) 诵读 to recite; to read ＊请你把这段念出来。Please read this paragraph.

念经 [niànjīng] to chant prayers

念念不忘 [niàn niàn bú wàng] to bear in mind constantly

念书 [niàn shū] to study; to read; to receive an education

念头 [niàn tóu] an idea; a thought; a motion

廿 [niàn] (n) 数词，二十 twenty

niáng

娘 [niáng] (n) 母亲 mother

娘家 [niángjiū] a married women's maiden home

娘子军 [niáng zijǔn] women's detachmen

niàng

酿(釀) [niàng] 1 (v) 利用发酵作用制造(酒、醋、酱油等) to ferment; to brew (wine; vinegars; sauce, etc.) ＊米可用来酿酒。Rice can be brewed into spirits. 2 (v) 使逐渐形成 to cause something to mature gradually; to brew ＊想不到一件小事会酿成大祸。It is never expected that a smallmatter will brew into a big trouble. 3 (n) 酒 wine ＊佳酿。good wine.

酿酒 [niàngjiǔ] to distil wine

酿造 [niàngzào] to make by fermentation

niǎo

鸟(鳥) [niǎo] (n) 飞禽的通称 bird

鸟瞰 [niǎokàn] a bird's eye view

鸟枪 [niǎoqiāng] a gun used for killing birds; an air-rifle; a shot-gun

袅(裊) [niǎo] 1 (adj) 缭绕的样子 curling upward 2 (adj) 温柔优雅的样子 delicate and graceful

袅袅 [niǎo niǎo] curling upward; delicate and graceful; (melody) floating like gossamer

袅袅婷婷 [niǎoniǎotíng tíng] slim or slender (figure of a woman)

袅娜 [niǎonuó] sweet and charming

niào

溺 [niào] (n) 同"尿" urine 另见 [nì]

尿 [niào] 1 (n) 小便，肾脏的分泌液 urine ＊人尿是优质肥料。Human urine is a high quality fertilizer. 2 (v) 排泄小便 to urinate

尿布 [niàobù] baby's napkin

尿素 [niàosù] urea

niē

捏 [niē] 1 (v) 用姆指和其他手指夹住 to grip; to hold ＊捏住这支笔。Hold this pen. 2 (v) 用手指把东西做成一定的形状 to knead ＊他在捏制面包。He is kneading the flour in order to make bread. 3 (v) 虚构，假造 to fabricate; to frame up ＊他们捏造罪名来陷害人。They frame up a person with false accusations.

捏报 [niēbào] to make a false report

捏一把汗 [niē yī bǎ hàn] to be seized with fear or deep concern

捏造 [niēzào] to fabricate; to trump up; to concoct

niè

聂（聶）[niè] (n) 姓 a surname

镊（鑷）[niè] (n) 夹取毛发，细刺或细小物件的器具 forceps; nippers; tweezers

蹑（躡）[niè] 1 (v) 放轻（脚步）to walk softly ＊他轻轻地站起来，蹑着脚走过去。He stood up quietly and walked across softly. 2 (v) 追随 to follow ＊蹑踪。to pursue.

蹑手蹑脚 [niè shǒu niè jiǎo] to move very softly and quietly

啮（嚙）[niè] (v) 咬 to bite ＊这包米给鼠啮虫咬了。This sack of rice was destroyed (bit) by rats and insects.

啮齿动物 [nièchǐ dòngwù] rodents e.g. rats; rabbits etc

孽 [niè] 1 (n) 恶事，罪恶 evil deeds ＊他会有今天也是自己造的孽。It is his evil deeds that land him in the present condition. 2 (n) 灾殃 misfortune

nín

您 [nín] (pron) "你"的敬称 a polite address of "you"

níng

宁（寧）[níng] (adj) 安宁 peaceful; tranquil ＊这孩子很顽皮，使你不得安宁。This child is so naughty that he will not let you remain peaceful.

宁静 [níngjìng] quiet; tranquil

另见 [nìng]

拧（擰）[níng] (v) 握住物体的两端向相反方向扭绞 to twist; to wring; to pinch

另见 [nǐng]

狞（獰）[níng] (adj) 凶恶的样子 fierce ＊他面目狰狞。He has a fierce look.

狞笑 [níngxiào] hyena laugh; to smile hideously and hypocritically

柠（檸）[níng] (n) 木名，树皮可入药 a tree

柠檬 [níngméng] lemon

凝 [níng] 1 (v) 气体因温度降低或压力增加变成液体，液体遇冷变成固体 to liquify (vapour to liquid); to solidify; (liquid to solid) 2 (v) 注意力集中 to concentrate ＊他在凝想。He is concentrating his thoughts.

凝固 [nínggù] to solidify; to coagulate

凝固点 [nínggùdiǎn] freezing point; solidification point

凝结 [níngjié] to condense; to stalemate; to cement

凝神 [níngshén] fully concentrating

凝视 [níngshì] to stare at

凝思 [níngsī] to meditate

拧（擰）[nǐng] (v) 扭转，控制住东西的一部分而绞转 to screw; to turn ＊他把盖子拧开。He turned off the lid.

另见 [níng]

nìng

宁（寧）[nìng] (v) 情愿 would rather; better ＊宁为玉碎，不为瓦全。Rather be a smashed piece of precious jade than an unbroken tile.

宁可 [nìngkě] would rather; have rather; to prefer ..... to ....

宁缺毋滥 [nìng quē wú làn] rather be short than excessive; rather leave the vacant post than have it filled with by anybody unqualified for it

宁死不屈 [nìngsǐbúqù] rather die than surrender

宁愿 [nìngyuàn] would rather to; to prefer

泞（濘）[nìng] (n) 泥浆，烂泥 mud; mire ＊他的脚沾满了泥泞。His legs are covered with mud.

nīu

妞 [niū] (n) 女孩子 a girl

níu

牛 [niú] (n) 家畜 cattle

牛痘 [niúdòu] vaccine; vaccination
牛犊 [niúdú] a calf
牛鬼蛇神 [niúguǐ shé shén] monsters and ghosts; bad elements
牛劲 [niújìn] the strength of an ox; stubborness
牛奶 [niúnǎi] cow's milk
牛排 [niúpái] beef-steak
牛皮 [niúpí] ox hide; leather
牛皮胶 [niúpíjiāo] cow-glue
牛脾气 [niúpí qì] the temperament of an ox - stubborness
牛肉 [niúròu] beef
牛头不对马嘴 [niú tóu bú duì mǎ zuǐ] the answer given does not reply the question
牛油 [niúyóu] butter

nǐu

扭 [niǔ] 1 (v) 掉转 turn around * 把头扭过来。Turn your head round. 2 (v) 用力拧 twist with force * 他把树枝扭断。He twists the branch into two. 3 (v) 因猛然用力使筋骨受伤 sprain * 他在踢足球时扭伤了脚趾。He sprained his ankle when playing football. 4 (v) 揪住 grapple * 两个青年在互相扭打。Two youths are grappling at one another.

扭扭捏捏 [niǔniǔ nièniè] not dignified enough in speech; bashful
扭转 [niǔzhuǎn] to reverse; to turn back (the tide, etc.)

忸 [niǔ] (a) 羞愧 bashful

忸怩 [niǔní] to be bashful; to be shy

纽(紐) [niǔ] 1 (n) 器物上手提的部分 a handle; a handling loop * 秤纽 The handling loop on a steelyard. 2 (n) 附在衣服或器物上的小圆块 a button; a knot; a fastening * 一粒衣纽掉了。A button has come off. 3 (v) 连结，联系 to tie; to connect

纽带 [niǔdài] ties (e.g. of friendship)
纽扣 [niǔkòu] a button
纽门 [niǔmén] a buttonhole

钮(鈕) [niǔ] (n) 同"纽" 2, 3

nìu

拗 [niù] (adj) 固执，任性 stubborn; having one's own way * 他脾气很拗。He has a stubborn character.

拗不过 [niu bú guò] unable to change one's idea
另见 [ǎo]

nóng

农(農) [nóng] 1 (n) 耕种事业 agriculture * 青年们下乡务农。The youths go to the countryside to cultivate the soil (to deal with agriculture). 2 (n) 农民 peasants; farmers * 工农一家亲。The workers and peasants are one family.

农场 [nóngchǎng] a farm
农产品 [nóngchǎnpǐn] farm products; agriculture products
农村 [nóngcūn] countryside; rural district
农会 [nónghuì] peasants' association
农活 [nónghuó] farm work
农具 [nóngjú] farm implements
农忙 [nóngmáng] busy farming season
农民 [nóngmín] peasants
农民起义 [nóngmín qǐyì] an agrarian uprising; a peasants' uprising
农奴 [nóngnú] a serf
农田 [nóngtián] farm land
农田水利 [nóntián shuǐlì] water conservancy
农闲 [nóngxián] slack farming season
农药 [nóngyào] insecticides
农业 [nóngyè] agriculture; farming
农业合作社 [nóngyè hézùshè] Agricul-

tural Co-operative Society

农业信用 [nóngyèxìnyòng] agricultural credit

农作物 [nóngzuòwù] the agricultural produce (crop; plant; fruit; etc.)

浓(濃) [nóng] (adj) 厚 strong; thick; dense ＊我对美术有浓厚的兴趣。I have a strong liking for art.

浓度 [nóngdù] density of concentration

浓厚 [nónghòu] thick and heavy; deep (e.g. emotion)

浓密 [nóngmì] dense

浓情厚意 [nóng qíng hòu yì] affectionate regard

浓缩 [nóngsuō] to condense; concentrated (liquid)

浓郁 [nóngyù] rich and fragrant

浓重 [nóngzhòng] thick and heavy

浓粧 [nóngzhuāng] a rich attire

脓(膿) [nóng] (n) 皮肉或内脏发炎腐烂所生的黄白色粘液 pus; purulent matter ＊他脚上的疮出脓。The sore on his leg is giving a purulent discharge.

脓包 [nóngbāo] pustules filled with pus; a useless person

脓溃 [nóngkuì] suppurating freely

脓肿 [nóngzhǒng] an abscess

nòng

弄 [nòng] 1 (v) 耍，玩 to play or trifle with; to tease ＊他在戏弄那只猴子。He is teasing the monkey. 2 (v) 做，搞 to handle; to do ＊不要把机器弄坏了。Do not spoil (do harm to) the machine.
另见 [lòng]

弄假成真 [nòng jiǎ chéng zhēn] pretence has become reality; to fulfil what was promised in a joke

弄巧成拙 [nòng qiǎo chéng zhuó] to try to be clever but turn out the contrary cunning outwits itself

弄权 [nòngquán] to abuse one's power

弄瓦 [nòngwǎ] to bear a baby girl

弄璋 [hòngzhāng] to bear a baby-boy

nú

奴 [nú] (n) 过去封建社会时，那些受压迫、剥削、役使而丧失自由的人 a slave; a serf; a bondman ＊农奴为地主做牛马。The serf worked like an animal for the landlord.

奴才 [nú cái] a vassal; a stooge; a flunkey

奴化 [núhuà] to enslave

奴隶 [núlì] a slave

奴仆 [núpú] a servant

奴颜婢膝 [nú yán bì xī] submissive and servile

奴役 [núyì] to enslave; to bondage

驽(駑) [nú] (n) 不好的、跑不快的马 an inferior horse

驽钝 [núdùn] a bad horse and a blunt knife — not of much use

nǔ

努 [nǔ] 1 (v) 尽量地使出（力量）to exert; to strive ＊我们要努力学习。We must study very hard (exert our capability to study). 2 (v) 突出，鼓起 to bulge ＊他努起嘴巴走了。He bulged his mouth and went away.

弩 [nǔ] (n) 古代一种利用机械力射箭的弓 a crossbow

nù

怒 [nù] 1 (adj) 生气 angry; furious; wrathful ＊老板无理开除职工，使到大众非常愤怒。We are very angry that the boss sacks the workers without good reasons. 2 (adj) 强盛的，奋发的 raging; flourishing ＊百花怒放。The flowers are flourishing in full bloom. ＊怒海汹涌。a raging sea.

怒不可遏 [nùbùkěè] anger knows no bound

怒潮 [nùcháo] angry waves; raging tide

怒冲冲 [nùchōngchōng] in a great rage

怒发冲冠 [nù fǎ chōng guān] extremely wrathful

怒号 [nùháo] roar

怒火中烧 [nǔhuǒzhōngshāo] smoul-

dering anger
怒目相视 [nùmùxiāngshì] glaring at each other angrily
怒气 [nùqì] anger; fury; wrath
怒视 [nùshì] to look at with angry eyes
怒涛 [nùtāo] raging waves

nǚ

女 [nǚ] (n) "男"的反面 female; girl; daughter ＊她是一名女工。 She is a factory girl.
女儿 [nǚ ér] a daughter; a girl
女高音 [nǚ gāo yīn] a soprano
女工 [nǚgōng] women workers
女人 [nǚrén] a woman
女声 [nǚshēng] woman's (solo or chorus)
女生 [nǚshēng] a school girl
女士 [nǚshì] lady; miss
女童 [nǚtóng] a young girl
女婿 [nǚ xù] a son-in-law
女佣人 [nǚ yòng rén] a maid-servant
女招待员 [nǚzhāodàiyuán] a waitress
女子 [nǚzǐ] a girl; a woman

nǜ

衄 [nǜ] (v) 鼻孔出血 to bleed at the nose
衄鼻 [nǜbí] to bleed at the nose

nuǎn

暖 [nuǎn] 1 (adj.) 暖和 warm; genial ＊春暖花开。 Flowers bloom during the warm spring. 2 (v) 使温暖 to warm ＊让我暖一暖手。 Let me warm my hands
暖风 [nuǎnfēng] a warm, gentle wind
暖烘烘 [nuǎnhōnghōng] comfortably warm
暖壶 [nuǎnhú] a thermos bottle
暖和 [nuǎn huǒ] warm
暖流 [nuǎnlíu] a warm current

nuè

虐 [nuè] (adj) 残暴 harsh; cruel; tyrannical
虐打 [nuèdǎ] to beat someone cruelly
虐待 [nuèdài] to maltreat; to ill-treat; to bear a heavy hand on
虐政 [nuèzhèng] oppressive government; tyranny
疟(瘧) [nuè] (n) 疟疾，又叫"冷热病"，是由疟蚊将疟原虫传染到人的血液里 malaria
疟蚊 [nuèwén] anopheles mosquitio

nuó

挪 [nuó] (v) 搬动，移动 to move, to remove
挪动 [nuó dòng] to move; to remove
挪借 [nuójiè] to borrow from
挪用 [nuóyòng] to embezzle; to misappropriate
娜 [nuó] (adj) 美貌; 柔婉 fascinating; elegant; courteous

nuò

懦 [nuò] (adj) 软弱，没有勇气 cowardly; timid; weak ＊自杀是懦弱的行为。 Suicide is a cowardly behaviour.
懦夫 [nuòfū] a coward
懦弱 [nuòruò] weak (in character)
糯 [nuò] (adj) 富于粘性的 glutinous; sticky
糯米 [nuòmǐ] glutinous rice
诺(諾) [nuò] (v) 答应，允许 to promise; to consent
诺言 [nuòyan] a promise

O

ō

喔 [ō] (part) 叹词,表示了解或省悟 particle used to express understanding or realization ＊喔,原来是你。Oh, it's you.

喔唷 [ōyō] particle to express surprise or painfulness
另見 [wō]

噢 [ō] (part) 叹词,表示了解或省悟 particle to express understanding ＊噢,我知道了。Oh, I know it.

ó

哦 [ó] (part) 叹词,表示疑问或惊讶 particle to express doubt or surprise ＊哦,是真的吗? Oh, is it true?
另見 [ò] [é]

ò

哦 [ò] (part) 叹词,表示省悟 particle to express realization ＊哦,原来是那样。Oh, that's it.
另見 [ó] [é]

ōu

区(區) [ōu] (n) 姓 surname
另見 [qu]

讴(謳) [ōu] (v) 歌唱 sing

讴歌 [ōugē] to sing in praise

欧(歐) [ōu] 姓 surname

殴(毆) [ōu] (v) 打 beat; strike; fight ＊他被殴打至死。He was beaten to death.

鸥(鷗) [ōu] (n) 鸟类 a gull

ǒu

偶 [ǒu] 1 [n]用木头或泥土等制成的人形 idol; puppet ＊孩子们爱看木偶戏。The kids like to watch the puppet show. 2 (n) 双 pair; couple ＊偶数 even number. 3 (adv.) 偶然 accidentally; by chance ＊这是偶然发生的事件。This matter occurs accidentally.

偶尔 [ǒu'ěr] occasionally; now and then

偶然 [ǒurán] occasional; casual; accidental; by chance; by coincidence

偶数 [ǒushù] even number

偶象 [ǒuxiàng] idol

偶遇 [ǒuyù] to meet by chance

藕 [ǒu] (n) 荷的地下茎 the root stock of the lotus; arrowroot

藕断丝连 [ǒu duàn sī lián] not thoroughly severed, there are still lingering threads

呕 [ǒu] (v) 吐 to vomit; to spit out ＊病人不停的呕吐 The patient vomited continuously.

呕心沥血 [ǒu xīn lì xuè] to make painstaking efforts

P

pā

趴 [pā] (v) 伏下 to lie forward;to bend forward ∗ 兵士们趴下放枪。The soldiers lie forward to shoot

啪 [pā] (n)放枪、拍掌、东西撞击等的声音 the noise made by shooting,clapping or knocking

葩 [pā] (n) 花 flower ∗奇葩异草。wonderful flowers and rare herbs.

pá

耙 [pá] 1 (n) 聚拢和散开谷物、柴草或平整土地用的农具 a rake ;a harrow 2 (v) 用耙操作 to rake;to harrow ∗ 他把土耙平。He raked the soil level.

爬 [pá] 1 (v) 以身体伏地行走 to crawl∗一条蜈蚣从裂缝里爬出来。A centipede is crawling out of a crack. 2 (v)攀登 to climb ∗ 猴子正在爬树。The monkey is climbing a tree.

爬虫类 [pá chóng lèi] reptile

爬山队 [pá shān duì]mountaineering team

扒 [pa] 1 (v)把东西聚拢或散开 to rake∗ 园丁正在扒草。The gardener is raking the grass. 2 (v) 煨，煨 to stew

扒窃 [pá qiè] steal; purloin

扒手 [pá shǒu] a pickpocket

另见 [bā]

pà

怕 [pà] 1 (v) 畏惧 to fear;to dread;to be afraid of ∗ 我们不怕任何困难。We are not afraid of any hardship. 2 (adv) 恐怕，也许，表示估计或疑虑 perhaps∗事情怕没那么简单。The matter perhaps is not that simple

怕事 [pà shì] afraid of getting involved

怕羞 [pà xiū] shy;bashful

帕 [pà] (n)包头或擦手脸用的巾 a turban;a handkerchief

pāi

拍 [pāi] 1 (v)轻打 to hit lightly;to pat;to clap ∗ 观众们拍手叫好。The audience clap their hands in applause. 2 (n) 打小型球类的用具 a bar;a racket ∗他买了一个羽毛球拍。He bought a badminton racket. 3 (n)乐曲的节奏 beat;timing of musical note ∗音乐老师教我打拍子。The music teacher teaches me how to count the beats.

拍电报 [pāi diàn bào] to tap the telegraph instruments—to send a wire

拍卖 [pāi mài] to sell by auction

拍马屁 [pāi mǎpì] to flatter obsequiously

拍摄 [pāi shè] to take photo;to photograph

拍手 [pāi shǒu] to clap hands
拍手称快 [pāi shǒu chēng kuài] to clap hands to express one's satisfaction;to hail gleefully
拍照 [pāi zhào] to have photograph taken
拍子 [pāi·zi] a bat or racket;a(fly) swatter;a baton (music) ;beats (music)

pái

排 [pái]1 (v) 摆成行列 to line up ＊很多人排队买票。Many people line up to buy tickets. 2 (n) 行列 row ＊他站在后排。He stands in the back row. 3 (n) 军队的编制单位，是班的上一级，连的下一级 platoon ＊他是排长。He is a platoon leader. 4 (v) 除去 to drain off;to reject; to exclude;to expel ＊ 我们希望农村里有更好的排水系统。 We hope the village will have a better drainage system. 5 (n) 量词 a measure word(a volley of shots,row of houses,etc.)
排版 [pái bǎn]to compose type
排比 [pái bǐ] parallel construction or form
排场 [pái · chang] display of splendour ;impressive rights(e.g. gatherings)
排斥 [pái chì] to shut out; to exclude;to eject;to discriminate against
排除 [pái chú] to exclude;to dispel; to overcome;to surmount
排除异己 [pái chú yì jǐ]purge those who differ with us in belief, outlook etc
排队 [pai duì]to line up; to queue up
排骨 [pái gǔ]pork ribs
排灌 [pái guàn] to drain and irrigate
排挤 [pái jǐ] to squeeze out;to edge out;to exclude;to push out
排涝 [pái lào] to drain waterlogged farmland
排练 [pái liàn]to rehearse
排列 [pái liè] to arrange in order
排难解纷 [pái nàn jiě fēn] to arbitrate;to mediate
排球 [pái qíu] volley ball
排山倒海 [pái shān dǎo hǎi] overturning mountains and emptying out seas;irresistible force
排水 [pái shuǐ] drainage;to drain; to pump
排水量 [pái shǔ liàng] displacement
排外 [pái wài]anti-foreign
排泄 [pái xiè] to excrete;to let off
排泄器官 [pái xiè qì guān] excretary organ
排演 [pái yǎn] to rehearse
排印 [pái yìn] to set up and print from type
排字 [pái zi] to set up type
徘 [pái]〔徘徊〕1 (v) 流连不前进 to hover;to linger 2 (adj) 犹豫不决 to hesitate
徘徊歧路 [pái huái qí lù] to hesitate at the crossroads
牌 [pái] (n) 宣传、标志、告示用的板或片 board; tablet or card(for advertisement; signs, notices,etc.) ＊招牌。a signboard ＊灵牌。an ancestral ; tablet ＊纸牌。playing cards
牌坊 [pái fāng] arch
牌价 [pái jià] fixed price;market quotation;market price
牌楼 [pái·lou] arch or gateway for celebration purposes
牌照 [pái zhào]license
牌子 [pái·zi]brand; label; trademark

pài

派 [pài] 1 (n) 水的支流 a tributary 2 (n) 事物、思想的流别 a clan;a party or school of thought ＊学派 a school of thought ＊党派 a party ＊教派 a sect 3 (n) 分配，派遣 to assign;to dispatch;to send ＊我们将派代表出席会议。We shall send representative to attend the meeting. 4 (n) 量词 measure word (for faction, school, etc)

派别 [pài bié] (of thought or beliefs) categories;schools;clique; faction

派遣 [pài qiǎn] to send someone on mission;to dispatch

派生词 [pài shēn cí] a derivative

派生 [pài shēng] to derive from; derivative

派系 [pài xì] a faction;a clique

pān

潘 [pān] (n) 姓氏 a surname

攀 [pān] 1 (v) 往上爬 to clamber;to climb up ＊他想攀登大汉山。He hopes to climb Gunong Tahan. 2 (v) 拉扰 to implicate;to relate 3 (v) 拦扯，抓住，往下拉 to pull;to grape;to drag down

攀扯 [pān chě] to implicate;to drag into an affair

攀登 [pān dēng] to climb up;to scale

攀折 [pān zhé] to break(branches)

pán

磐 [pán]〔磐石〕(n) 厚而大的石头 a huge rock ＊安如磐石。steady as a rock.

盘（盤） [pán] 1 (n) 盛放东西的扁而浅的用具 a plate; a dish;a tray 2 环绕，卷曲 to circle around;to wind;to coil up ＊飞机在头顶盘旋。The plane is hovering(circling around)overhead. 3 详细，严密 in detail;thoroughly;closely ＊他被移民厅官员盘问了很久。He was qustioned in detail by the immigration officers for quite a long time. 4 费用，市价 expenses; costs;the market rate 5 市场，交易，事务 the market;the transaction; the business ＊开盘 to open the market; ＊收盘 to wind up the business; ＊头盘商 first transactor (the importer) ＊二盘商 the second transactor(the wholesaler) ＊三盘商 the third transactor(the retailer)

盘剥 [pán bō] to exploit;usurious

盘查 [pán chá] to examine thoroughly;to interrogate

盘点 [pán diǎn] to make an inventory;to take stock

盘费 [pán fèi] travelling expenses

盘根错节 [pán gēn cuò jié] with twisted roots and intercrossing branohos -complicated and difficult ; entangled

盘桓 [pán huán] to loitor about;to stroll about

盘货 [pán huò] to take stock;stock-taking

盘据 [pán jù] to occupy;to entrench

盘算 [pán·suan] to calculate;to plan;to premeditate

盘问 [pán wèn] to interrogate;to question

盘旋 [pán xuán] to hover;to circle around;to linger

盘子 [pán·zi] a plate;a saucer

蟠 [pán] (v) 屈曲，环绕 to curl round;to coil

蟠据 [pán jù] to encroach upon;to occupy

蹒（蹣） [pán] 蹒跚 [pán shān] : 跛行的样子 (to walk) with a limp; to limp

pàn

畔 [pàn] (n) 旁边 side;bank;boundary ＊他在河畔拍了一张照。He took a photo at the river bank.

判 [pàn] 1 (v) 分开，分辨 to divide ; to differentiate ;to distinguish ＊你能判别真假吗？ Can you differentiate the genuine from the fake? 2 (v) 评定，决心 to judge; to decide * 我不能判定他是对是错。I can't judge whether he was right or wrong.

判断 [pàn duàn] to judge;to determine;to ascertain

判决 [pàn jué] to bring in a verdict; judgement;verdict

判刑 [pàn xíng] to pass sentence;to sentence(a person)

叛 [pàn] (v) 背离 to betray * 他们背叛自己的国家。 They betrayed their own country.

叛变 [pànbiàn] to betray;to turn traitor

叛国 [pàn guó] to turn traitor to one's country

叛乱 [pàn luàn] to revolt;to rebel;to mutiny

叛卖 [pàn mài] to commit acts of treachery;to betray

叛逆 [pàn nì] treason;betrayal;rebel

叛徒 [pàn tú] a traitor;a renegade

盼 [pàn] 想望 to hope;to long for;to look forward to * 他盼望亲人早回家。She longs for the early return of her beloved.

pāng

滂 [pāng] (n) 水涌的样子 gushing of water

滂沱 [pāng tuó] torrential;pouring

乓 [pāng] (n) 表示声音 used for the sound

páng

旁 [páng] 1 (prep.) 侧边 by the side of * 不可停放车辆在路旁。Parking of vehicles by the road side is prohibited. 2 (n) 其他，另外 other * 这件事由我负责，跟旁人不相干。 I am responsible over this matter which does not concern other persons

旁边 [páng biān] nearby position; right by

旁观 [páng guān] to observe from the sidelines;to look on with folded arms

旁观态度 [páng guān tài dù] look on with indifference; stand by; ramain a spectator

旁观者清 [páng guān zhě qīng] the onlooker is always clear-minded;an onlooker sees most

旁门 [páng mén] a sidegate

旁门左道 [páng mén-zuǒ dào] not orthodox paths and ways

旁敲侧击 [páng qiāo-cè jī] to extract information indirectly; to beat about the bush;to attack by innuendo

旁若无人 [páng ruò wú rén] as if no one was nearby—expression of pride—haughtiness; overweening; to behave in a natural way

旁征博引 [páng shēng bó yǐn] quoting numerous sources and substantial material as reference

旁听 [páng tīng] to attend (a lecture) in the capacity of an associate student;to be present (at a conference) as an observer

旁听生 [páng tīng shēng] an external student;a listener

旁听席 [páng tīng xì] visitor's seats

旁证 [páng zhèng] circumstantial evidence;side witness

膀 [páng] 膀胱 [páng guāng] (n) 人或其他高等动物体内储存尿的器官 the urinary bladder
另见 [bǎng]

磅 [páng] 磅礴 充塞弥满 extensive ; filling everywhere ; grand
另见 [bàng]

螃 [páng] 螃蟹的一种 a crab

彷 [páng] 彷徨 [páng huáng] (v) 意志不定 to hesitate uncertain * 他彷徨在十字路口。He hesitated at the crossroads

庞（龐）[páng] 1 (adj) 大 large; great 2 (adj) 杂乱 confused;disorderly

庞大 [páng dá] colossal;huge;massive

庞然大物 [páng rán dà wù] a colossus ;formidable giant; a large monster

庞杂 [páng zá] disorderly and motley

pàng

胖 [pàng] (adj)肥大 fat;plump

胖子 [pàng zi] fatty;a fat person

pāo

抛 [pāo] (v)扔，投掷 to throw;to fling;to cast ＊ 他把球抛给我。He throws the ball to me.

抛开 [pāo kāi] to fling off; to throw off

抛锚 [pāo máo] to cast an anchor; (of cans) to get stuck midway

抛弃 [pāo qì] to throw away;to discard;to get rid of

抛售 [pāo shòu] to undersell;to dump;to sell at low prices

头露面 [pāo tóu lù miàn] to appear in the open

抛物线 [pāo wù xiàn] parabola

抛砖引玉 [pāo zhuān yǐn yù] to pass out the brick to attract a jadestone;to throw a sprat to catch a whale

泡 [pāo] 1 (n) 鼓起的或松软的圆团 the bulb;the puff 2 (adj) 松软 soft＊ 面团发得泡起来了。The dough is raised and becomes soft

páo

咆 [páo] 咆哮 [páo xiāo] (v) 猛兽怒吼，也比喻人的怒吼 to roar

炮 [páo] (v) 把生药烘炒加工 to process crude drugs by baking or roasting

炮制 [páo zhì] to process crude drugs;to dish up;to cook up
另见 [pào]
[bāo]

袍 [páo] (n) 长衣服的通称 a robe;a gown

刨 [páo] (v) 挖掘 dig ＊ 他在刨土 He is digging the soil.
另见 [bào]

pǎo

跑 [pǎo] (v) 疾走 to run

跑步 [pǎo bù] double time march

跑道 [pǎo dào] athletic track;runway

跑龙套 [pǎo lóng tào] utility man;a general handiman

跑腿儿 [pǎo tuǐr] a foot-man;a messenger;to run an errand

pào

泡 [pào] 1 (n) 液体上的浮沫 bubble ; foam 2 (n) 表皮因伤病而成的凸起形状 blister 3 (v) 用水冲注或浸渍 to dip;to soak;to steep ＊ 她用沸水泡茶。She steeped the tea in boi ing water

泡沫 [pào mò] foam;bubbles;froth

泡影 [pào yǐng] bubble;an illusion
另见 [pāo]

炮 [pào] 1 (n) 发射药弹的重型武器 artillery 2 (n) 爆竹 firecrackers ＊ 鞭炮。strings of firecrackers
另见 [páo] | [bāo]

炮兵 [pào bīng] an artillery man;artillery

炮弹 [pào dàn] a shell

炮轰 [pào hōng] to bombard

炮火 [pào huǒ] artillery fire;gunfire

炮灰 [pào huī] cannon fodder

炮舰 [pào jiàr] a gunboat

炮舰政策 [pào jiàn zhèng cè] gunboat policy

炮楼 [pào lóu] gun turret

炮台 [pào tái] a fortress;fortification

pēi

呸 [pēi] 叹词，表示唾弃，鄙薄或斥责 an exclamation to show contempt or reproach

胚 [pēi] (n) 发育初期的生物体 a germ;an embryo

胚胎 [pēi tāi] an embryo;origin of matter

胚珠 [pēi zhū] an ovule

péi

陪 [péi] (v) 伴随 to accompany; to keep company with ＊我陪他去看病。I accompany him to see the doctor.

陪伴 [péi bàn] to accompany;to keep company with

陪从 [péi cóng] to follow

陪衬 [péi chèn] a contract;to serve as a contract

陪审团 [péi shěn tuán] the jury

陪同 [péi tóng] to accompany;to keep company with

培 [péi] (v) 以土壤保养植物 to cultivate; to bring up＊这种药草不容易栽培。It is not easy to cultivate this kind of herb.

培土 [péi tǔ] to bank up with earth

培训 [péi xùn] to train;to cultivate

培养 [péi yǎng] to cultivate;to nourish;to foster ;to bring up

培育 [péi yù] to nurture;to grow;to breed

培植 [péi zhí] to grow

赔(賠) [péi] 1 (v) 偿还损失 to compensate ＊玻璃是我打破的，应该由我来赔。I broke the glass so let me compensate for it. 2 (v) 亏损 to suffer a lose;at a loss ＊他赔本出售房屋，以清债务。He sold his house at a loss to settle the debts.

赔不是 [péi bù shi] o apologise for a fault

赔本 [péi běn] to run at a loss

赔偿 [péi cháng] to compensate;to make compensation

赔偿名誉 [péi cháng míng yù] indemnity for defamation

赔偿协定 [péi cháng xié dìng] reparations agreement

赔款 [péi kuǎn] to pay indemnity; indemnities

赔礼 [péi lǐ] to apologise

赔罪 [péi zuì] to apologise;to make an apology

pèi

沛 [pèi] (adj) 盛大，旺盛 abundant; plentiful;full of ＊他精力充沛。He is full of energy.

配 [pèi] 1 (v) 匹对 to match;to pair＊他将女儿许配给一个富人。He betrothed his daughter to a rich man. 2 (v) 调和，混合，安排，拼凑 to compose;to blend;to arrange ; to match ＊他懂得配各种不同的饲料 He knows how to blend different kinds of feeds. 3 (v) 相当 worth;fit

配备 [pèi bèi] to equip;to furnish with

配不上 [pèi bù shang] unworthy; undeserving;unsuitable

配搭 [pèi dā] to adjust;to arrange; supplement;to add to

配方 [pèi fāng] prescription;formula

配给 [pèi jǐ] to ration out;to put on rations

配件 [pèi jiàn] parts;accessories

配给制 [pèi jǐ zhì] ration system

配角 [pèi jué] minor roles;supporting actors

配合 [pèi le] to coordinate;to be in harmony with

配偶 [pèi ǒu] to mate;to make a pair;spouse;couple

配色 [pèi sè] to match colours

配上 [pèi shàng] to be harnessed

to;to be joined to;to be afraid to

配套 [pèi tào] to serialize

配药 [pèi yào] to compound medicine

配音 [pèi yīn] dubbing (e.g. motion picture)

配种 [pèi zhǒng] breeding;artificial insemination

佩 [pèi] 1 (v) 挂在身上 to wear;to grid on ＊ 这军官身上佩带着许多勋章。This army officer wears many medals on his uniform 2 (v) 尊敬，铭记 to respect;to remember ＊ 我敬佩他那舍己为人的精神。I respect his willingness in sacrificing himself for others

辔（轡） [pèi] (n) 驾驭牲口用的嚼子和缰绳 the birdle

pēn

喷（噴） [pēn] (v) (液体、气体、粉末等) 受压力而射出 to spurt; to squirt; to spray; to sprinkle ; to spit out

喷壶 [pēn hú] a sprinkler;a watering-can

喷漆 [pēn qī] to spray paint;spray-pain

喷气式飞机 [pēn qì shì fēi jī] a jet plane

喷泉 [pēn quán] a geyser; a fountain

喷洒 [pēn sǎ] to spray;to sprinkle

喷射 [pēn shè] to jet

喷嚏 [pēn tì] sneeze

喷雾器 [pēn wù qì] a sprayer

另见 [pèn]

pén

盆 [pén] (n) 阔而浅的盛物或洗物器皿 a basin;a pot;a tub ＊ 花盆 a flower-pot; ＊浴盆 a bath tub; ＊脸盆 a face-basin

盆地 [pén dì] basin (geographical feature)

盆栽 [pén zāi] potted plants

pèn

喷（噴） [pèn] (v) (光、热、烟雾、气味等) 自然射出，发出，冒出，流出 to emit

喷香 [pèn xiāng] to emit fragrance; rich and fragrant

pēng

抨 [pēng] (v) 斥责 to rebuke; to denounce

抨劾 [pēng hé] to impeach

抨击 [pēng jī] to play;to attack vigorously;to censure

怦 [pēng] (adj) 心动 ardent; impulsive

砰 [pēng] (n) 重物撞击或落地的声音 the crash or fall of hoavy matters

澎 [pēng] (n) 浪涛 the sound of waves

澎湃 [pēng pài] the roaring of breakers

烹 [pēng] (v) 烧煮 to cook;to boil

烹调 [pēng tiáo] cooking

烹饪 [pēng rèn] cookery;to cook

péng

朋 [péng] 1 (n) 彼此友好的人 a friend;an acquaintance;a companion 2 (n) 党类 a cabal;a clique 3 (v) 比 to match;to compare ＊ 硕大无朋 so big that nothing can compare with

朋比为奸 [pěng bǐ wéi jiān] to associate for treasonable purposes

朋党 [péng dǎng] a cabal;a clique

朋友 [péng yǒu] friends

鹏（鵬） [péng] (n) 传说中的一种大鸟 a fabulous bird of enormous size-the roc

鹏程万里 [péng chéng wàn lǐ] the roc's journey of 10,000 miles-prospects ahead

棚 [péng] (n) 遮蔽太阳或风雨的架子 a shed;an awning;a tent;a booth

＊我们在凉棚休息一会儿吧。Let us rest for a while in the shed

膨 [péng] (v) 膨大 fat; bloated; swollen; inflated

膨胀 [péng zhàng] expansion;inflation

蓬 [péng] 1(n) 草本植物，覆盆子的一种 a herb;a specie of raspberry 2 (adj) 散乱 dishevelled;untidy ＊诗人蓬头垢面行吟江畔。The poet with dishevelled hair and grimy face,wandered humming poems along the riverbank. 3 (adj) 茂盛 overgrown;luxuriant

蓬勃 [péng bó] thriving;prosperous; vigorous;surging

蓬莱仙境 [péng lái xiān jìn] fairyland

蓬松 [péng sōng] fluffy ;dishevelled

篷 [péng] 1(n) 遮蔽风雨和日光的设备 a shelter;an awning;a covering 2 (n) ＊船帆 a sail＊扯篷 to hoist the sail ＊落篷 to drop the sail

篷车 [péng chē] a covered truck or wagon;a van;a caravan

篷船 [pēng chuán] a sailing vessel

彭 [péng] (n) 姓氏 a surname

pěng

捧 [pěng] 1 (v) 两手托着 to hold up in both hands＊他捧着一碗面。He is holding up a bowl of mee in both of his hands 2(v) 奉承，吹嘘 to flatter;to fawn on;to lavish praise on ＊许多亲戚朋友都捧那老富翁。Many relatives and friends fawned on the rich old man.

捧场 [pěng chǎng] to lavish praise on;to flatter;to sing praise to

捧腹大笑 [pěng fù dà xiào] to split one's sides with laughter

pèng

碰 [pèng] 1 (v) 撞击 to run against; to hit against;to collide ＊孩子的额头在桌子的角上碰了一下。The child hit his forehead against the corner of a desk 2 (v) 相遇 to meet;to come across ＊我在路上碰到一位旧同学。I met an old classmate on the road 3 (v) 试探 to try;to probe ＊他买了张马票想碰运气。He bought a lottery ticket to try his luck

碰杯 [pèng bēi] to clink glasses with

碰壁 [pèng bì] to run one's head against a stone wall;to meet with a rebuff

碰钉子 [pèng dīng . zi] to receive serious rebuff;to run into snags

碰见 [pèng jiàn] to meet;to run into;to chance upon

碰礁 [pèng jiǎo] to strike a rock;to meet with a rebuff

碰机会 [pèng jī huì] to meet with an opportunity;to take a chance

碰巧 [peng suǒ] to happen by chance;coincidentally

碰头 [pèng tóu] to meet (to discuss something);to put (our)heads together

碰运气 [pèng yùn qī] to depend upon one's luck

pī

坯 [pī] 1 (n) 没有烧过的砖瓦、陶器 unburnt brick;tile or earthenware 2 (n) 半制成品 semi-finished products

披 [pī] 1 (v) 穿上 to wear;to put on ＊他披上大衣就走了。He puts on a coat and walks off 2 (v) 打开 to open;to unroll;to spread out ＊他披读家书，心情沉重。After he had opened and read the letter from home,his heart became heavy

披肩 [pī jiān] a shawl

披荊斩棘 [pī jīng zhǎn jí] clearing away brambles and bushes (or difficulties) along the road of progress

披沥 [pī lì] to speak without reserve

披露 [pī lù] to announce;to publish ; to disclose

披靡 [pī mǐ] blown down by the wind;scattered,as troops

披星戴月 [pī xīng dài yuè] to soak oneself with the stars and wear the moon—to travel by night;to start work in the morning and continue till late at night

批 [pī] 1 (n)量词 a measure word (batch,lot,group,shipment,etc) ＊一批旅客刚到。A group of tourists has just arrived. 2 (v)断定 to ascertain;to criticize ＊谁能批判他人？Who can judge another? ＊他的政策受到严厉的批评。His policies were severely criticized.

批驳 [pī bó] to refuse,to rebut

批发 [pī fā] to wholesale;wholesale

批改 [pī gǎi] to correct

批评 [pī píng] to criticize;to repudiate;criticism;repudiation

批判 [pī pàn] to criticize;criticism

批示 [pī shì] to write an official comment;official comments

批语 [pī yǔ] comments

批阅 [pī yuè] to read or see official document with remarks

批准 [pī zhǔn] to approve;to endorse;to sanction

批注 [pī zhù] to annotate with comments;annotation

霹 [pī] 急雷 the crash of thunder

霹雳 [pī lì] sound of thunder;a rumbling noise;lightning flash

砒 [pī] (n) 矿物，又名信石，就是化学原质的砷，有剧毒 arsenic

砒霜 [pī shuāng] arsenic

劈 [pī] 1 (v)破开 to split;to chop;to slice ＊他在劈柴。He is splitting firewood 2 (v)面对着 facing;in front of ＊他踏进家门，一见到妻子，劈面就骂。Once he had stepped into his house and saw his wife,he scolded her face to face.

pí

枇 [pí]〔枇杷〕[pí·pá] (n) 常绿乔木果实也叫"枇杷"，味甜，可吃。叶可供药用 the loquat

毗 [pí] (adj) 接连 adjoining ＊大火波及毗邻的屋子。The fire has spread to the neighbouring houses

毗连 [pí lián] to be adjacent;to adjoin

毗邻 [pí lín] to adjoin;neighbouring

琵 [pí] 琵琶 (n)一种弦乐器 pipa,a Chinese guitar

啤 [pí] 啤酒 [pí jǔ] (n) 用大麦作主要原料制成的一种酒 beer

脾 [pí] (n) 人体内的器官，在胃的左下侧，赤褐色，能制造新血球，破坏老血球 the spleen

脾气 [pí·qi] temper;disposition; nature

皮 [pí] 1 (n)动植物体表面的一层组织 skin;hide;leather;fur;peel＊生皮 raw hides;undressed leather ; 表皮 the epidermis 2 (n) 表面 wrapping;covering ＊书皮 book cover

皮袄 [pí ǎo] leather jacket

皮包 [pí bāo] a leather bag

皮包骨 [pí bāo gǔ] very thin;emaciated

皮带 [pí dài] a leather belt;a leather girdle

皮带轮 [pí dài lún] pulley

皮蛋 [pí dàn] eggs preserved in lime

皮肤 [pi fū] skin

皮肤病 [pí fū bìng] skin disease

皮革 [pí gé] hides;leather

皮货 [pí huò] hide;fur goods

皮毛 [pí máo] hide;leather;fur;superficiality;outward look

皮球 [pí qíu] leather ball

皮靴 [pí xuē] leather boots

皮影戏 [pí yǐng xì] puppet shadow ; show

疲 [pí] (adj)困倦，劳累 tired;weary; worn out * 他工作了一整天，回到家已是精疲力倦。He has been working for the whole day and is completely worn out on reaching home.

疲惫 [pí bèi] tired;weary
疲乏 [pí fá] worn out;exhausted
疲倦 [pí juàn] weary;fatigued
疲劳 [pí láo] fatigued;tired;weary
疲塌 [pí·ta] inertia
疲于奔命 [pí yú bēn mìng] to be fully occupied;to be kept constantly on the run

pǐ

痞 [pǐ] 1 (n) 肚子里生的硬块 a swelling of the abdomen 2 (n) 流氓 hooligan ;rascal;riff-raff *地痞。rascal; *喜痞士 hippie

痞棍 [pǐ gùn] scoundrel

癖 [pǐ] (n)对某些事物特别嗜好 a vicious appetite;a craving;a strong liking * 他对酒有很深的癖好。He has a strong liking for liquor.

癖好 [pǐ hào] to take special liking to something;special hobby;favourite hobby

匹 [pǐ] 1 (v) 比得上,相称 to match; to pair * 法国的美酒佳酿，举世无匹。Nothing in the world can match the good wine of France. 2 (adj) 单独 single;individual * 国家兴亡，匹夫有责。An individual has the responsibility for the rise or fall of a country 3 (n)量词 a measure word *一匹布。 a bale of cloth.

pì

辟(闢) [pì] 1 (v)开发 to open up * 农民自辟园地。The farmers open up the land themselves 2 (v)驳斥或排除 to refute * 我们应该帮他辟谣。 We should help her to refute the rumours.

另见 [bì]

僻 [pì] (adj) 离开中心地区的；远的 remote

僻静 [pì jìng] quiet and out-of-the-way
僻壤 [pì rǎng] an obscure country; a remote place
僻巷 [pì xiàng] a side lane;a private alley

譬 [pì] (v)打比方 to compare;to illustrate

譬如 [pì rú] to take for example

屁 [pì] (n) 由肛门排出的臭气 fart; wind (from bowels)

屁股 [pì·gu] buttocks

媲 [pì] (adj) 比並 to compare; to match * 他画的马可以和名家的媲美。The horse he drew compares favourably with that of an artist

媲美 [pì měi] to be on a par with;to compare favourably with

piān

扁 [piān] (n) 扁舟小船 small boat
另见 [biǎn]

偏 [piān] 1 (adj)歪斜，不正 slanting; to be inclined to;to deviate from * 他的行为偏离常轨。 His action deviated from the ordinary rules 2 (adj) 不公正，不全面 prejudiced: partial * 考官偏袒漂亮的女生。The examiner was partial to pretty women students

偏爱 [piān 'ài] to be partial to;to favour
偏差 [piān chā] deviation;errors
偏方 [piān fāng] local folk prescri-

ption

偏废 [piān fèi] over-emphasize one thing to the neglect of the other

偏激 [piān jì] to go to the extreme

偏见 [piān jiàn] prejudice;bias

偏旁 [piān páng] the side of a Chinese character

偏僻 [piān pì] out-of-the-way

偏偏 [piān piān] deliberately;against expectation;by coincidence

偏袒 [piān tǎn] to take sides with; to be partial to

偏听偏信 [piān tīng piān xìn] to be partial to;to believe in one-sided story

偏向 [piān xiàng] deviation

偏斜 [piān xié] oblique;slanting;inclining

偏邪 [piān xié] depraved

偏心 [piān xīn] to be partial to

偏重 [piān zhòng] to have a bias towards;to be inclined to;to tend to

翩 [piān] (v) 飞腾 to flutter;to fly ＊姑娘们象彩蝶般翩翩起舞。 The girls are dancing about like butterflies

翩翩 [piān pian] gracefully moving; flying;dancing

篇 [piān] (n) 量词 a measure word (for an article,etc) ＊这是一篇好文章。 This is a good essay

篇幅 [piān fù] the length of an article;the spaces of an article

篇目 [piān mù] chapter;heading

篇章 [piān zhāng] literary piece; writing in general

片 [piān] (n) 扁平的薄块 card; film; sheet piece ＊名片。 a name card; 唱片。 a (piece of)record
另见 [piàn]

pián

胼 [pián] (n) 手上生的厚皮 callosities on the hands

胼手胝足 [pián shǒu zhī zù] with hands and feet becoming callous-hardworking

便 [pián] 1 (adj)适当,平允 suitable; reasonable 2 (adj) 丰满 plump;full and round
另见 [bián]

便便大腹 [pián pián dà fù] barrel-belled

便宜 [pián· yi] suitable;reasonable; cheap;unrightful advantages;to get away with

便宜行事 [pián·yi xíng shì] to act as circumstances may require

piàn

骗(騙) [piàn] (v) 欺诈 to cheat; to swindle ＊他用卑鄙的手段骗了她。 He cheated her by using vulgar means.

骗局 [piàn jú] fraud;swindling;double dealing;trickery

骗取 [piàn qǔ] to gain something by cheating

骗子 [piàn·zi] swindler;a deceiver;a juggler;a charlatan

片 [piàn] 1 (n) 扁平的块 sheet;slice 2 量词 a measure word ＊一片茫茫。 a piece of obscure prospect ＊一片好意 a piece of goodwill

片段 [piàn duàn] chapter;section; fragment;part

片刻 [piàn kè] a short moment

片面 [piàn miàn] one-sided;unilateral
另见 [piān]

piāo

漂 [piāo] (v) 浮在水面 to float; to drift ＊树叶在水上漂浮。 The leaf is drifting on the water.

漂泊 [piāo bó] to wander about

漂浮 [piāo fú] to float about

漂流 [piāo líu] to drift about

漂洋过海 [piāo yāng guò hǎi] to cross the ocean
另见 [piǎo] [piào]

剽 [piāo] 1 (v)抢劫to rob 2 (adj) 轻捷prompt

剽悍 [piāo hàn] brave and prompt in action

剽窃 [piāo qiè] to plagiarize

飘（飄） [piāo] 1 (v)随风飞动to flutter;to fly＊旗子迎风飘扬。The flag flutters with the wind. 2 (v) 在水上浮动 to float about;to flow about

飘泊 [piāo bó] to drift aimlessly;to have no fixed abode

飘荡 [piāo dàng] to drift about ;to flutter

飘浮 [piāo fú] to float about

飘忽 [piāo hū] swift,as the wind

飘零 [piāo líng] fallen as leaves in autumn;ruined,as family fortunes

飘渺 [piāo miǎo] misty;unrealistic; obscure

飘飘然 [piāo piāo rán] to be carried away with one's own importance; light;airy

飘摇 [piāo yáo] to drift about

飘扬 [piāo yáng] to flutter;to fly in the wind

piáo

嫖 [piáo] (n)宿娼 whoring;prostitu-tion

瓢 [piáo](n)舀水用具,把瓢葫芦剖开做成 a ladle made of a gourd

piǎo

漂 [piǎo] 1 (v) 用水或药品使东西退去颜色或变白 to leach 2 (v)用水冲洗 to wash;to rinse＊把衣服放在水里漂一漂。Rinse the clothes in the water

另见 [piāo]
[piào]

瞟 [piǎo] (v)斜着眼睛看to wink at; to cast a glance at

殍 [piǎo] (n)饿死的人people who die of hunger＊郊野有饿殍。The femished lay dead in the wilder-ness

piào

票 [piào] 1 (n) 当凭证用的纸卡 a tic-ket;a bill;a certificate;a permit;a bank note;a document 2 (n) 被绑架勒赎的人 a kidnapped person;a person used as a ransom

票房 [piào fáng] ticket office;book-ing office

票根 [piào gēn] the counterfoil of a ticket

票据 [piào jù] certificate;bill

票友 [piào yǒu] theatrical amateurs

漂 [piào]〔漂亮〕[piào liàng] 1 (adj)好看 good-looking;beautiful＊她的样子很漂亮。She has a beautiful look. 2 (adj) 出色 excellent＊这一战打得真漂亮。This battle is fought very smartly.

另见 [piāo]
[piǎo]

骠（驃） [piào] (adj) 勇猛 brave; valiant＊他是一个骠勇的斗士。He is a brave fighter

另见 [biāo]

piē

撇 [piē] (v)丢开，抛弃cast away;to leave behind;to abandon;to desert＊他不能撇下妻儿就走。He cannot abandon his wife and children and leaves just like that

撇开 [piē kāi] to cast off;to set aside;to pay no attention to

撇脱 [piē tuō] cast aside

另见 [piě]

瞥 [piē] (v)眼光掠过，匆匆一看 to catch a glimpse of;to glance at

瞥见 [piē jian] to catch a glimpse of

piě

撇 [piě] 1 (v) 扔出去 to throw;to hurl 2 (n) 汉字向左下斜写的一种笔形 a down stroke to the left in Chinese calligraphy

另见 [piē]

pīn

拼 [pīn] 1 (v) 合在一起，连合 to join ; to assemble;to put together ＊ 她把零碎的布拼凑成大块的布。She joined pieces of cloth together to form a bigger piece. 2 (v)豁出去，不顾一切地干 to do something desperately ＊ 要是敌人再来，我们就和他们拼到底。If the enemy come again, we will desperately fight them till the end

拼凑 [pīn còu] to scrape together; to patch up;to piece together;to join

拼命 [pīn mìng] to risk one's life for;to do something desperately

拼盘 [pīn pán] cold hors d'oeuvre

拼写 [pīn xiě] spelling

拼音 [pīn yīn] phonetic transcriptions

拼死 [pīn sǐ] desperately;frantically

拼音文字 [pīn yīn wén zì] phonetic language

拼音字母 [pīn yīn zì mǔ] phonetic alphabet

姘 [pīn] (n) 男女私通 illicit intercourse

姘头 [pīn tóu] a lover;a sweetheart

pín

频（頻） [pín] (adv) 连续多次 incessantly;frequently ＊ 捷报频传。News of victory comes in incessantly

频繁 [pín fán] continuous;frequent

频率 [pín lǜ] frequency

频频 [pín pín] continuously

贫（貧） [pín] (adj) 穷，收入少，生活困难 poor; destitute;impoverished ＊ 他家境贫苦。His family is in a destitute condition

贫病交迫 [pín bìng jiāo pò]scissored by poverty and sickness

贫乏 [pín fá] needy;meagre;thin

贫富悬殊 [pín fù xiàn shū] wide gap between the poor and the rich

贫寒 [pín hán] poor

贫瘠 [pín jí] poor;arid

贫苦 [pín kǔ] poor;poverty

贫困 [pín kùn] poor and hard-up; impoverished

贫民 [pín mín] poor people

贫民窟 [pín mín kū] slums

贫农 [pín nóng] poor peasant

贫穷 [pín qiong] poor;poverty;privation

贫血 [pín xuě] anaemia

pǐn

品 [pǐn] 1 (n) 物件 goods;articles; things ＊货品到达时完好无损 The goods arrived in good order. 2 (n) 等级，种类 grade;class;variety ＊ 品质好的咖啡价钱很贵。The first grade coffee is highly priced. 3 (n) 性质 quality;character (of persons) ＊ 他的人品不错。 He has a good character. 4 (v) 体察出好坏 to test the quality ＊他的父亲深知品茶之道。His father knows now to test the quality of tea.

品德 [pǐn dé] quality (of person)

品格 [pǐn gé] character (of person)

品头论足 [pǐn fóu lùn zú] to find faults with

品性 [pǐn xìng] temper;disposition; nature

品行 [pǐn xíng] conduct;behaviour

品质 [pǐn zhì] quality;character

品种 [pǐn zhǒng] variety;sort;grade

pìn

牝 [pìn] (adj) 雌性的（鸟、兽），跟“牡”相对female (of bird or animal) ＊ 牝鸡 a hen

聘 [pìn] 1 (v) 请人担任职务 to employ ＊他被解聘了。He is suspended from employment 2 (v) 订婚 to betroth;to espouse

聘金 [pìn jīn] money paid at a betrothal

聘礼 [pìn lǐ] the presents for engagement

聘请 [pìn qǐng] to employ; to engage; to invite

聘任 [pìn rèn] to employ somebody to hold a post

聘书 [pìn shū] letter of employment

pīng

乒 [pīng] (n) 表示声音a sound

乒乓 [pīng pāng] the sounds of hail

乒乓球 [pīng pāng qíu] a table tennis game;a ping-pong ball

píng

瓶 [píng] (n) 口小腹大，用来盛液体的器皿bottle;jar;pitcher;jug;vase

瓶塞 [píng sè] a cork;a stopper

屏 [píng] (n) 用来挡风或隔断视线的用具a screen

屏风 [píng fēng] a screen

屏障 [píng zhàng] frontier defence; outpost;mountain range

另见 [bǐng]

平 [píng] 1 (adj) 不倾斜，没有高低 flat;level;even;plain;smooth ✱ 这路很平。 The road is level. 2 (v) 使平 to level ✱ 农民垦平了三亩地。 The peasants have levelled three acres of land. 3 (adj) 均等 equitable;fair 4 (adj) 安静 peaceful;calm ✱ 海上风平浪静。The sea is peaceful. 5 (v) 使安定，使恢复正常 to pacify;to restore to normal ✱ 政府无法平定内乱。The government is unable to pacify the internal conflicts. 6 (adj) 经常的，普通的 usual;ordinary;general;common ✱ 他平时很爱打球。He likes to play games at ordinary times.

平安 [píng'ān] safe; well; fine: peaceful

平白无故 [píng bái wǘ gù] without any reason

平常 [píng cháng] common;general;ordinary;usual

平淡 [píng dàn] uninteresting;dull

平等 [píng děng] equality;equal

平等互利 [píng děng hù lì] reciprocity based on equality; equality and mutual benefit

平地 [píng dì] flat ground; level ground

平定 [píng dìng] to put down; to quell;to pacify

平地一声雷 [píng dì yī shēng léi] a sudden important upheaval (usually one for the good)

平凡 [píng fán] common;ordinary; undistinguished

平方 [píng fāng] square

平房 [píng fáng] one-storied house

平分 [píng fēn] to divide equally

平分秋色 [píng fēn qīu sè] to divide equally between two

平衡 [píng héng] to balance;equilibrium

平衡木 [píng héng mù] a bean (gymnastics)

平滑 [píng huá] smooth

平静 [píng jìng] quiet;tranquil

平均 [píng jūn] average;to equalize

平均主义 [píng jūn zhǔ yì] equalitarianism

平炉 [píng lú] open hearth furnace

平面 [píng miàn] flat surface; plain

平面几何 [píng miàn jǐ hé] plane geometry

平面图 [píng miàn tú] a plane chart;a plan

平铺直叙 [píng pū zhí xù] speaking or writing simply and plainly; monotonous; uninteresting; flat; dull

平起平坐 [píng qǐ píng zuò] an equal footing

平日 [píng rì] at ordinary times;normal days

平生 [píng shēng] life time;has

never before....;never have...
平时 [píng shí] usually;in peace time;in normal times
平素 [píng sù] in normal days
平坦 [píng tǎn] flat;level
平稳 [píng wěnn] steady;safe;even; smooth
平息 [píng xī] to put down; to stamp out
平行 [píng xiáng] parallel;on equal footing
平信 [píng xìn] ordinary mail
平行四边形 [píng xíng si biān xíng] a parallelogram
平行线 [píng xíng xian] parallel line
平易近人 [píng yì jìn rén] easy to get along with, amiable;well-disposed
平原 [píng yuán] plain;level land
平整 [píng zhěng] neat;level
平装 [píng zhuāng] ordinary packing

坪 [píng] (n) 平坦的地方 a level ground;a plain

评(評) [píng] 1 (v)议论 to discuss;to comment;to criticize ＊由大家来评理吧，看看谁是谁非。Let everybody discuss and see who is in the right. 2 (v) 判断 to judge ＊我不能评定他是对是错。I cannot judge whether he was right or wrong.
评比 [píng bǐ] to compare; to appraise
评定 [píng dìng] to judge;to decide ; to evaluate
评断 [píng duàn] decide;judge
评分 [píng fēn] evaluation of work points or marks
评价 [píng jià] appraisal;evaluation; to appraise;to evaluate;to assess
评奖 [píng jiǎng] the granting of awards through discussion
评工记分 [píng gōng jì fēn evaluation of work and allotment of points
评理 [píng lǐ] to reason out something
评论 [píng lùn] comment;commentary
评论员 [píng lùn yuán] a commentator
评判 [píng pàn] to pass judgement ; to decide
评选 [píng xuǎn] to appraise and elect
评议 [píng yì] to appraise;to discuss
评语 [píng yǔ] comment
评判员 [píng pàn yuán] an umpire
评注 [píng zhù] edition with comments

苹(蘋) [píng] 苹果(n) 落叶亚乔木。果实扁圆形，味甘美。 the apple

萍 [píng] (n) 浮生在浅水上的小植物 duckweed
萍水相逢 [píng shui xiāng feng] patches of duckweed meeting-unexpected meeting of friends abroad

凭(憑) [píng] 1 (v)身子靠着to lean against ＊我们凭栏远望。We lean against the railings to look afar. 2 (v) 依靠，倚仗，借口 to depend on;to rely on;by means of ＊我们祖先只凭双手改造自然。Our ancestors merely made use of their hands to change nature. 3 (v) 根据 confide in;according to ＊我们将凭单付款 We shall pay according to the bill. 4 (n)证据 evidence ＊他们拿不出真凭实据来。They cannot show any true evidence.
凭吊 [píng diao] to pay respect at the grave or at a memorial place
凭借 [píng jiè] to rely on;to resort to
凭据 [píng jù] evidence;basis for belief
凭空 [píng kǒng] without evidence;

groundlessly
凭眺 [píng tiào] to look from top
凭证 [píng zhèng] evidence

pō

坡 [pō] (n)倾斜的地方a slope∗牛儿在山坡上吃草The cows are gazing on the hill slopes.

颇 [po] (adv)很，相当地fairly;rather; somewhat;pretty∗他讲得颇有道理What he said was rather reasonable.

泼（潑） [pō] 1 (v) 用力倒酒或液体，使散开 to splash;to sprinkle;to pour out ∗孩子们喜欢在浴盆里泼水。 The children like to splash in their tub. 2 (adj)蛮不讲理的 arrogant and unreasonable ∗杨太太泼辣起来，杨先生只好让步。 When Mrs. Yang turned arrogant and unreasonable, Mr. Yang had to give way to her. 3 (adj)有魄力，有生气 vigorous;lively

泼溅 [pō jiàn] dash;spatter
泼辣 [pō là] pungent;clear-cut;having a lot of drive
泼冷水 [pō lěng shuǐ] to pour cold water;to discourage;to dampen one's spirit

泊 [pō] (n) 湖 a lake
另见 [bó]

pó

婆 [pó] 1 (n)年老的妇女an old woman 2 (n)丈夫的母亲husband's mother

婆罗门教 [pó luó mén jiào] Brahmanism
婆娑 [pó suō] to circle around
婆婆妈妈 [pó · po mā mā] slow and talkative;sentimental

pǒ

叵 [pǒ](adj)不可cannot;unable∗他居心叵测 What he is up to is unfathomable.

pò

魄 [pò] 1 (n)附在人体内的精神 the soul;the spirit 2 (n) 指人的气质和精力disposition and vitality∗他办事有政治家的气魄。 In the running of affairs he has the disposition and vitality of a statesman

魄力 [pò·li] courage;vigour

迫 [pò] 1 (v)用强力压制，硬逼 to compel;to force ∗村民被迫迁出家园 The villagers are forced to evict from their homes. 2 (adj) 紧急 pressing;urgent;imminent∗我们迫切的需要人手 We need helpers urgently. 3 (v) 接近 to draw near;to approach∗我们的先头部队已迫近敌营 Our advance detachment had drawn near the enemy's camp.

迫不及待 [pò bù jí dài] hurriedly;in haste;to brook no delay
迫害 [pòhài] to persecute; to oppress
迫近 [pò jìu] close; near; to get close to
迫切 [pò qiè] urgent; imminent; pressing
迫使 [pò shǐ] to compel;to enforce; to coerce;to oblige
迫在眉睫 [pò zài méi jiè]imminently urgent;approaching

破 [pò] 1 (adj)碎裂的，损坏的 broken;ruined ∗他住在一间破烂的亚答屋里。He lives in a broken attap hut. 2 (v)劈开 to split open ∗他破开门儿。He splits open the door . 3 (v)冲开，打败to defeat; destroy∗我们必须攻破敌人的防线。 We must destroy the enemy's line of defence. 4(v)打倒，废除 to do away with;to abolish∗我们应该破除迷信。 We should abolish superstitions 5 (v)使真相露出，揭穿 to expose; to discover; to lay bare∗我们已经识破敌人的诡计了。 We have discovered the enemy's trick. 6 (v) 使损坏 to break ; to damage *贼打破了窗，但没有进屋。The thief broke the window but did not get into the house.

破案 [pò àn] to clear up a case;to solve a case;to bring a case to book

破产 [pò chǎn] bankruptcy;ruin;to be wrecked

破除 [pò chú] to do away with;to abolish

破费 [pò fèi] to waste money

破釜沉舟 [pò fǔ chén zhōu] to smash the cooking vessels and sink the boats-to cut off all retreat; to be determined to succeed

破格 [pò gé] to make an exception for

破坏 [pò huài] to destroy;to undermine;to wreck;to sabotage

破获 [pò huò] to unearth;to uncover

破旧立新 [pò jiù lì xīn] to destroy the old and establish the new

破烂 [pò làn] torn-down;ragged; tumble-down;rags;rubbish

破例 [pò lì] as an exception

破裂 [pò liè] to split;to break

破落户 [pò luò hù] a family on the decline economically

破灭 [pò miè] to vanish

破碎 [pò suì] to break into pieces

破天荒 [pò tiān huāng] unprecedented;epoch-making;for the first time

破绽 [pò·zhàn] loopholes;weak point

破折号 [pò zhé hào] a dash (——)

pōu

剖 [pōu] (v) 破开，解析 dissect;to cut open;to analyze *医生在解剖尸体。The doctor is dissecting the corpse. *教师设法剖析我们失败的原因。The teacher tried to analyze the cause of our failure.

剖析 [pōu xī] to analyse

pū

仆 [pū] (v) 向前跌倒 to fall to the ground;to tumble down

另见 [pú]

扑(撲) [pū] 1 (v) 向前冲 to rush on*孩子高兴得一下子扑到我怀里来。The kid is so happy that he rushes to my bosom suddenly 2 (v) 攻打 to attack;to strike;to rush *我军猛扑敌人的战壕。Our troops rushed to the enemy's trench. 3 (v) 轻打，拍 pat *他扑去衣服上的灰尘。He pat off the dust on his clothes.

扑克 [pū kè] playing cards

扑空 [pū kōng] to miss a punch;to fail to get what one wants

扑灭 [pū miè] to put down;to stamp out;to extinguish

扑通 [pū tōng] plop(for sound of something dropping into water)

铺 [pū] (v) 展开，敷设 to spread;to pave* 他把草席铺在地上。He spreads the straw mat on the floor.

铺床 [pū chuáng] to make the bed

铺盖 [pū·gai] bedding

铺路 [pū lù] to build a road;to pave the way

铺设 [pū shè] to spread out;to lay in order

铺张 [pū zhāng] extravagant

另见 [pù]

pú

璞 [pú] (n) 没有雕琢过的玉 an unpolished gem

脯 [pú] (n) 胸前的肉 the breast * 胸脯。the breast;the chest

另见 [fú]

蒲 [pú] (n) 草本植物。生长在浅水里。叶子可以制席，袋，扇等 a kind of rush from which mats, bags are made

匍 [pú] 匍匐 [pú fú] (v) 爬行 to crawl on hands and knees

匍 [pú] 匍匐 [pú táo] (n)藤本植物，果实也叫"匍匐"，是常见的水果 grapes;vine

仆(僕) [pú] (n) 身为奴隶或受雇用而任人役使的人 a servant;a menial ∗ 主人在大声斥责女仆。The master is scolding his servant loudly.

仆仆 [pú pú] wearied;tired
仆从 [pú cóng] servant;hangers-on
另见 [pū]

菩 [pú] (n) 草本植物 a herb

菩萨 [pú sà] a Buddhist of very high rank;an idol for worship;a very kind person
菩提树 [pú tí shù] the Ficus religiosa;the linden tree
菩提子 [pú tí·zi] linden seeds;beads of a rosary

pǔ

浦 [pǔ] (n)水边，河流入海的地区 a river bank;the rivermouth area

圃 [pǔ] (n)菜园，花园 a vegetable garden;a nursery

普 [pǔ] (adj) 全面 general;common; all;universal;everywhere ∗ 阳光普照。The sun shines everywhere.

普遍 [pǔ biàn] universal
普遍性 [pǔ biàn xìng] universality; universal nature
普及 [pǔ jí] to popularize;to reach all;widely difused;universal
普及教育 [pǔ jí jiào yù] universal education for all
普天同庆 [pǔ tiān tóng qìng] universal celebration;rejoiced by all
普天之下 [pǔ tiān zhī xià] all over the world
普通 [pǔ tong] common;ordinary
普选 [pǔ xuǎn] general election
普照 [pǔ zhào] to illuminate

谱(譜) [pǔ] 1(n)按照事物的类别或系统编成的表册 a register;a record;a table ∗ 年谱。2 (n) 可以用来指导练习的图书样本 a guide book ∗ 棋谱。a guide book for chess play ∗曲谱 a song book 3 (v) 按歌词作曲 to write melody for ∗ 他为一首著名的唐诗谱曲。He wrote melody for a famous poem of the Tang Dynasty.

朴(樸) [pǔ] (adj) 不加修饰的 plain;simple ∗ 她穿得很朴素。She dressed up plainly.

朴实 [pǔ shí] simple;direct;honest
朴素 [pǔ sù] simple;plain

蹼 [pǔ] (n) 鸭、蛙等动物脚趾间的一层膜 web (of ducks,frogs,etc)

pù

曝(暴) [pù] (adj) 晒 to sun; to expose; to dry; to air ∗ 赵姨把洗过的衣服挂在外边去曝晒。Auntie Zhao hung the washing out to dry in the sun.
另见 [bào]

曝光 [pù guāng] exposure (photography)

瀑 [pù] (n) 瀑布，从山壁上急流下来的水 a waterfall

铺(鋪) [pù] (n) 商店，摊子 a shop;a store;a stall
另见 [pū]

Q

qī

欺 [qī] 1 (v) 欺骗 cheat; deceive; fool. ∗ 不要自欺欺人。Do not deceive yourself to deceive others. 2 (v) 欺负；侮辱 bully; insult; abuse. ∗ 这些傢伙欺人太甚。Those fellows abuse people too much.

欺凌 [qīlíng] to bully.
欺压 [qīyā] to insult and oppress.
欺诈 [qīzhà] to swindle.
欺善怕恶 [qīshánpàè] to bully the good-natured and to fear the hostile ones.

期 [qī] 1 (n) 规定的时间或一段时间 period. ∗我们如期完成任务。We completed our work within the required period. 2(v) 盼望；希望 long for; hope; expect. ∗ 我们期望早日见到亲人。We hope to see our beloved soon 3 (v) 约定；约会 make appointment. ∗ 我们不期而遇 We met each other without prior appointment. 4 (n) 量词 numeral. ∗ 这个刊物已经出版了三期。This periodical has published three issues already.

期待 [qīdài] wait; expect; look forward to.
期刊 [qīkān] periodical.
期限 [qīxiàn] a limited time; period.

另见 [jī]

戚 [qī] 1 (n) 亲戚，因婚姻联成的关系 relatives. ∗ 我有一个亲戚住在北海。I have a relative who lives in Butterworth. 2 (adj) 忧愁；悲伤 sad ∗ 他和我休戚相关。He shares happiness and sadness with me.

蹊 [qī] (adj) 奇怪，可疑 如〔蹊跷〕也作"跷蹊"。strange. ∗ 这件事有点蹊跷。This incident is a bit strange.

妻 [qī] (n) 男子的配偶 wife

妻离子散 [qīlízǐsàn] broken up family; break up family

凄 [qī] 1 (adj) 寒冷 cold; chilly ∗ 在一个凄风苦雨的夜晚她走了。She left in a cold and rainy night. 2 (adj) 形容冷落萧条 grievous; sorrowful; grim. ∗ 这个老人的身世凄凉。This old man's life is sorrowful.

凄惨 [qīcǎn] sorrowful; distressing.
凄厉 [qīlì] very sad and sharp (tone, cry).

萋 [qī] (adj) 草长得很茂盛的样子 如〔萋萋〕 luxuriant growth of grass.

栖 (棲) [qī] 1 (v) 居住，停留 stay; rest; perch ∗ 许多燕子栖息在电线上。Many sparrows perch on the wire.

栖身之所 [qìshēnzhīsuǒ] place of stay; a shelter

七 [qī] (n) 数词 seven 7

七零八落 [qīlīngbāluò] scattered here and there; in confusion ; in ruins

七拼八凑 [qīpīnbācòu] improvise desperately; scrape together

七上八下 [qīshàngbāxià] in a mental flurry of in decision

七手八脚 [qīshǒu bā jiǎo] great confusion

漆 [qī] 1 (n) 一种树皮里的粘汁或其他树脂制成的涂料 paint; varnish; lacquer 2 (v) 涂 paint ＊我正在漆家俱。 I am painting the furniture.

漆黑 [qīhēi] pitch dark

漆黑一团 [qīhēiyītuán] be completely in the dark; be quite hopeless

漆匠 [qī·jiang] painter

缉(緝) [qī] (v) 缝 to stitch

另见 [ji]

qí

其 [qí] 1 (pron) 他的；她的；它的；他们的 his; her; its; their ＊鸟之将死，其鸣也哀； 人之将死，其言也善。 When a bird is dying, its cry is mournful; when a man is dying, his words are sage . 2 (adj) 这个；这些；那个；那些 this; these; that those ＊能够担任这项工作的不乏其人。 Those who can take up this job are many. 3 词尾，用在副词后 suffix after an adverb (resembling "-ly") ＊他的舞步极其优美。His dancing postures are extremely graceful.

其次 [qícì] the next; moreover

其乐无穷 [qílèwúqióng] endless joy and happiness

其实 [qíshí] in fact; in truth; in reality

其他 [qítā] others

其余 [qíyú] the rest; the remainder

其中 [qízhōng] among them; in the midst of

骐(騏) [qí] (n) 有青黑色纹理的马 horses with green and black stripes

棋 [qí] (n) 文娱用品。通常为木制，可供二人或多人作智力游戏。 chess ＊象棋 Chinese chess.

棋逢对手 [qíféng duìshǒu] a good chess player meets his match

琪 [qí] (n) 美玉 beautiful jade

祺 [qí] (adj) 吉祥 fortunate; auspicious

麒 [qí]〔麒麟〕[qílín] (n) 古代传说里的一种动物 fabulous animal of good omen

旗 [qí] (n) 用布、绸、纸等做成的标识，多半为长方形或方形 flag ＊他们手持国旗，朝向市区走去。With a flag in their hands, and they marched towards the city.

旗杆 [qígān] a flagstaff

旗鼓相当 [qí gǔ xiāng dāng] be a match for; to be equal to

旗开得胜 [qíkaīdéshèng] win victory as soon as one's banner is displayed ; triumphantly .....at one stroke

旗手 [qíshǒu] a flag-bearer

旗帜鲜明 [qízhìxīanmíng] to make one's standpoint clear

奇 [qí] 1 (adj) 特殊的；不常见的；不平凡的 strange; unusual; uncommon ＊昨晚我作了一个奇怪的梦。I had a strange dream last night. 2(adj) 出人意料的，令人不测的 unexpected; surprise 3 (adj) 惊异 surprise ＊这事情不足为奇。This matter is not surprising at all. 4 (adj) 非常 extraordinary; exceptional. ＊把国土奉送给敌人是一项奇耻大辱。It is an exceptional humiliation to surrender one's country to the enemy.

奇观 [qíguān] spectacle

奇迹 [qíjì] miracle; wonders

奇闻 [qíwén] strange news

奇形怪状 [qíxíng-guàizhuàng] funny shapes; unusual shapes

奇异 [qíyí] peculiar; extraordinary

崎 [qí] (adj) 山路高低不平的样子。如:崎岖rugged (mountain path); uneven ✱ 在吉隆坡有许多街道是崎岖不平的。In Kuala Lumpur, there are many streets with rugged surface.

骑（騎） [qí] (v) 两腿分开跨坐 ride ✱ 他在骑脚车。He is riding a bicycle.

骑墙派 [qíqiángpài] fence sitters; neutral

骑师 [qíshī] a rider; a jockey

琦 [qí] (n) 美玉 beautiful jade

祈 [qí] 1 (v) 向神求福 pray; worship ✱ 王嫂祈求观音赐她儿子聪明和健康。Madam Wang prayed the goddess, Kuan Yin, to bestow wisdom and health on her son. 2 (v) 请求 beg; request ✱ 敬祈指导 I humbly request you for guidance.

颀（頎） [qí] (adj) (身材) 高 tall ✱ 他身材颀长。He is tall in build.

歧 [qí] 1 (adj) 岔路；大路分出的小路diverging road; forked road

歧见 [qíjiàn] different ideas

歧视 [qíshì] discrimination

歧途 [qítú] a fork in the road; the wrong path

歧异 [qíyì] conflicting; discrepancies

齐（齊） [qí] 1 (adj) 端正 in order 2 (adj) 一起；同 together; alike ✱ 我们齐心协力搞演出。We work together for the performance. 3 (adj) 全；完备 complete; all ✱ 客人都到齐了。The guests have all arrived. 4 (adj) 相同 to be the same ✱ 水深齐腰。The depth of the water is the same as the height of the waist.

齐备 [qíbeì] all ready

齐集 [qí jì] all assembled

齐名 [qímíng] of the same fame

齐全 [qíquán] complete

脐（臍） [qí] (n) 胎儿出生后，脐带脱落的地方叫“脐”，在人的腹部 the navel ✱ 脐带 。umbilical cord.

鳍（鰭） [qí] (n) 鱼类的运动器官 fins of fish

qǐ

杞 [qǐ] (n) 姓氏 a surname.

杞人忧天 [qǐ rén yōu tiān] unnecessary and groundless anxieties

起 [qǐ] 1 (v) 立 get up; stand up 那时候，太阳已经升起来了。At that time, the sun had already risen. 2 (v) 开始 begin; start; commence ✱ 从今天起，我要 好好 的学习。I will study hard starting from today. 3 (v) 取出 to take out ✱ 明天我们就要起货了。We will unload the goods to-morrow. 4 (v) 发生 occur; happen. ✱ 又起风了。The wind blows again. 5 (v) 发动 start ✱ 农民起义了。The peasants had started an uprising. 6 (v) 建造 build ✱ 高楼平地起。The tall building is built from the ground. 7(v) 拟写 draft. ✱ 我们在起草章程。We are drafting the constitution. 8 (part) 用在动 词后，表示 力量够得上或够不上 used after a verb to show ability ✱ 他经得起考验。He is able to stand the trial.

起初 [qǐchū] in the beginning; at first

起点 [qǐdiǎn] a starting point

起伏 [qǐfú] up and down; to undulate

起居 [qǐjū] one's daily life

起诉人 [qǐsùren] suitor
起因 [qǐyīn] cause; origin
起重机 [qǐzhòngjī] a crane; a derrick

企 [qǐ] 1 (v) 踮起脚跟站着 stand erect 2 (v) 仰望；盼望 look up; hope for ＊ 她企望丈夫在深海捕鱼后安全归来。 She hoped that her husband would come home safely from deep-sea fishing.
企图 [qǐtú] intention; endeavour
企业 [qǐyè] enterprise

绮（綺）[qǐ] 1 (n) 有花纹或图案的丝织品 silk with designs 2 (adj) 美好 fine; beautiful ＊ 这里风景绮丽迷人。The scenery here is beautiful and enchanting.

岂（豈）[qǐ] (part) 助词。表示反问，“怎么”、“哪里”、“难道”等意思 an interrogative particle. How? ＊ 岂有此理。 How can it be!

启（啓）[qǐ] 1 (v) 打开 open ＊ 启封 to open a letter 2 (v) 开始 start; begin ＊ 代表团还没启程。The delegation has not begun their journey yet. 3 (v) 开导 enlighten; make clear; teach ＊ 老师应启发学生的创造能力。The teacher should enlighten the creativity of his students.
启蒙 [qǐméng] to enlighten the young
启事 [qǐshì] a notice; an announcement
启行 [qǐxíng] to set out a journey

乞 [qǐ] (v) 讨取，求 beg; ask for ＊ 他拿着饭钵，到处乞食。 He took a bowl and went everywhere to beg for food.
乞丐 [qǐgài] beggar
乞命 [qǐ mìng] beg for life
乞求 [qǐqiú] beg
乞援 [qǐyuán] to beg for aids

qì

契 [qì] 1 (n) 证明买卖、抵押、租赁等关系的合同、或字据。a bond; a certificate; an agreement 2 (n) 符合，一致 tally; agreement ＊ 他们之间似乎有个默契。 They seem to have an unwritten agreement.
契约 [qìyuē] a written contract; an agreement; a bond

讫（訖）[qì] (v) 完结 finish; settle ＊ 我已经把账款付讫。I have already settled the accounts

迄 [qì] 1 (prep) 到；还 till; yet; up to ＊ 他迄今还没回信。He has not replied the letter till today. 2 (adv) 始终；一直 （用于“未”或“无”前）up to the present ＊ 他的尝试迄未成功。Up till now he has not succeeded in his endeavour.

汽 [qì] (n) 液体或固体受热而变成的气体。特指水蒸气 vapour; steam; gas ＊ 汽管爆炸了。 The steam pipe has burst.
汽车 [qìchē] motor car
汽船 [qìchuán] a steamship
汽水 [qìshuǐ] aerated water

泣 [qì] 1 (v) 小声哭 sob ＊ 她泣述她兒子惨死的故事。 She sobbed out the story of the disastrous dead of her son.

葺 [qì] (v) 用茅草覆盖房顶，现在指修理房屋 repair a house ＊ 这间屋子很多年没有修葺了。 This house has not been repaired for many years.

砌 [qì] (v) 建筑时垒砖石，用泥灰粘合 to lay (bricks) ＊ 工友们正在砌墙。 The workers are laying bricks for a wall.

器 [qì] 1 (n) 用具 a tool; a utensil ＊ 瓷器。Porcelain wares. 2 (n) 生物的器官 organs of living things ＊ 生殖

器。 reproductive organs. 3 (n)度量；才能 capacity；ability. ＊他的器量很大。He is broad minded. 4 (v)器重 have a high opinion of. ＊他很受上司的器重。He received a high consideration from his superior.

器材 [qìcái] equipment; materials; stuff.

器具 [qìjù] tools; implements.

器皿 [qìmǐn] plates; dishes; crockery.

气（氣） [qì] 1 (n) 物体的一种形态，没有一定的形状和体积，能自由散佈。 gas；air 2 (n)呼吸 breath. ＊他在喘气。He is panting. 3 (n)指自然界冷热阴晴等现象 weather ＊今天的天气很好。The weather is fine today. 4 (n) 精神状态 mentality; spirit. ＊他勇气百倍的跳过去。He jumped across with great courage. 5 (v)恼怒 anger ＊他生气了。He is angry. 6 (n) 嗅觉上的味道 smell ＊厕所里臭气熏天。 The toilet is filled with foul smell. 7 (n) 中医指人体内能使各器官正常地发挥机能的原动力 a term used in Chinese medicine, it refers to the power within the human body which can regulate the functioning of various organs. ＊人参可以补元气。Ginseng can replenish the vitality of a person.

气昂昂 [qì áng áng] high morale; high spirits

气冲冲 [qì chōng chōng] enraged; angry

气喘 [qìchuǎn] asthma.

气氛 [qìfèn] atmosphere; mood.

气愤 [qìfèn] angry; indignant

气概 [qìgài] spirit; strength.

气管 [qìguǎn] the windpipe.

气候 [qìhòu] climate; weather

气恼 [qìnǎo] angry; upset.

气势汹汹 [qìshìxīong xīong] menacing in attitude.

气味 [qìwèi] odour; scent.

气温 [qìwēn] atmospheric temperature.

气象台 [qìxiàngtái] meteorological station.

气象万千 [qìxiàng wànqiān] many splendid scenes.

气息奄奄 [qìxìyānyān] feeble in breathing; at one's last gasp.

气压计 [qì yà jì] a barometer

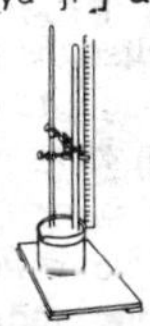

气质 [qìzhì] temperament; disposition.

弃（棄） [qì] (v)扔掉；舍去 to throw; to discard. ＊我们要弃旧图新。 We should discard the old and search for the new.

弃权 [qì quán] to abstain from voting; to disclaim one's right.

弃置 [qìzhì] to cast away; to throw aside.

憩 [qì] (v) 休息 rest. ＊我们在树下小。We take a short rest under tne tree.

qiā

掐 [qiā] 1 (v) 用手指使劲夹、按或用指甲刻入、截断 grip; nib. ＊他两手掐住敌人的脖子。He used both hands to grip the enemy's neck. 2 (v)割断；截去cut; sever. ＊他掐断电线。He severs the wire. 3 (n) 量词。一只手或两只手指尖相对握着的数量 numeral for a handful

qiǎ

卡 [qiǎ] 1 (n) 关卡，在交通要道所设的检查所a custom check-point. ＊他在关卡被捕。He was arrested at the custom check-point.

2 (v) 夹在中间，堵塞 stick in the middle ＊ 鱼刺卡在他的喉里。He was stuck by a fish bone to the throat.
另见 [kǎ]

qià

洽 [qià] 1 (adj) 和睦，合得来 harmonious ＊ 他们谈得很融洽。They talk in a harmonious manner. 2 (v) 接头，商量 contact; discuss ＊ 他约我面洽。He invited me to discuss personally.

洽商 [qiàshāng] to discuss.

恰 [qià] 1 (adj) 适当 suitable ＊ 你用的一些字眼不大恰当。Some of your wordings are not very suitable. 2 (adv) 刚刚，正 just; in good time; exactly ＊ 他的想法和我的恰恰相反。His idea is exactly the opposite of mine.

恰到好处 [qiàdàohǎochù] very appropriate; just right (in words and deeds)

恰巧 [qiàqiǎ] in the right time

qiān

千 [qiān] 1 (n) 数词。百的十倍 a thousand ＊ 二千元。two thousand dollars. 2 (adj) 表示极多，常与"万"或"百"连用 numerous ＊ 他千方百计想夺取政权。He tried to grab political power by all ways and means.

千钧一发 [qiān jūn yī fà] very dangerous; precarious

千篇一律 [qiān piān yīlǜ] monotonous

千山万水 [qiān shān wàn shuǐ] thousands of mountains and rivers; arduous journey

千变万化 [qiān biàn wàn huà] ever changing

千辛万苦 [qiān xīn wàn kǔ] all kinds of difficulties and hardships

千载难逢 [qiān zài nán féng] once in a life time; a very rare opportunity

千真万确 [qiān zhēn wàn què] absolutely true

阡 [qiān] (n) 田地里纵横交错的小路 footpath between fields

钎（釬） [qiān] (n) 一头尖的长钢棍，多用来在矿石上打洞 steel rod pointed at one end, used for the drilling of holes in mines

芊 [qiān] (adj) 草木茂盛的样子 exuberant; luxuriant

迁（遷） [qiān] 1 (v) 搬移 shift; move ＊ 木屋居民被逼迁。The squatters were forced to move out. 2 (n) 变动 change. ＊ 他去外国留学十年，回来后发现本国的环境已变迁了不少。After having studied overseas for ten years, he returned to find that local society had changed a lot.

迁就 [qiān jiù] to make a compromise; to accomodate

迁居 [qiānjū] to shift house

搴 [qiān] (v) 拔起 pull up ＊ 搴旗 to grab the flag.

签（簽，籤） [qiān] 1 (v) 亲自写姓名，表示负责 sign; endorse ＊ 我还没签名。I have not signed. 2 (v) 简单地写出意见 endorse ＊ 请你签注意见。Please endorse your remark. 3 (n) 作为标志的纸片或其他的物名 slip; label ＊ 书签 book mark. 4 (n) 用竹木等制成的细棍或薄片 a bamboo slip or stick ＊ 牙签。toothpicks

签到 [qiāndào] sign in on arrival at meeting or office

签订 [qiāndìng] to sign an agreement

签发 [qiānfā] authorize and despatch (documents, etc)

签署 [qiānshǔ] to sign; to endorse

签证 [qiānzhèng] visa

谦（謙） [qiān] (adj) 虚心，不自满 modest; humble ＊ 他不够谦逊。He is not modest enough.

谦让 [qiānràn] to give way to others; be courteous

谦虚 [qiānxū] humble

悭(慳) [qiān] (adj)吝啬 stingy

铅(鉛) [qiān] (n) 化学元素。lead; a metal

牵(牽) [qiān] 1 (v) 拉 pull; drag; haul ✱ 农夫牵着一头牛。The farmer is pulling a cow. 2 (v)连带;连累connect; involve; implicate ✱ 这贪污案牵涉许多人。Many people were involved in the corruption case.

牵挂 [qiānguà] remember fondly; be concerned;worry over

牵累 [qiān lěi] be entangled with

牵制 [qiānzhì] check; restrain; hamper

愆 [qiān] 1 (n) 过失 wrong ✱ 他罪深愆重。His crime is serious. 2 (v) 错过;失误 miss

qián

钳(鉗、拑) [qián] 1 (n)用来夹持小物件、弯曲或切断金属丝的一种工具 pincers; pliers ✱ 老虎钳。pliers. 2 (v)夹住;限制clasp; check; restrain ✱ 我军从后方钳制敌人的兵力。Our troops had restrained the enemy's force from the rear. 3 (v)用钳夹东西 to grip with pincers

黔 [qián] 1 (adj) 黑色 black 2 (n) 贵州省的简称 a simplified name for Kweichow, a province in China

钱(錢) [qián] (n) 货币 money; cash ✱ 你有足够的现钱吗? Do you have enough cash?

潜(潛) [qián] 1 (v) 隐在水面下活动 hide under water; dive ✱ 他潜入水底找寻尸首。He dived into the water to look for the dead body. 2 (adj) 隐藏的,不露在表面的 hidden; potential ✱ 我们应该充份发挥一切潜力。We should bring all potentialities into full play. 3 (adv) 秘密地 secretly ✱ 防止犯罪分子潜逃。Stop the criminals from running away secretly.

潜伏 [qián fù] concealed; lie hidden

潜热 [qiánrè] latent heat

潜水员 [qíshuǐyuán] a diver

潜意识 [qián yì shí] subconsciousness

潜在 [qiánzài] potential; hidden

前 [qián] 1 (adj) 在正面的,跟"后"相对。front ✱ 前门。Front door. 2 (v) 往前走 advance; go forward; proceed ✱ 他一遇到困难就畏缩不前。He was afraid to go forward once he encountered difficulty. 3 (adj) 过去的,较早的 former; previous ✱ 我们要学习前辈们艰苦奋斗的精神。We should learn the spirit of persistent struggle of our forerunners. 4 (adj) 次序在先的 first in order; front ✱ 他坐在前排。He sits in the front row.

前车之鉴 [qián chē zhī jiàn] learning from the follies of predecessors

前功尽废 [qián gōng jìn fèi] all the previous effort wasted.

前进 [qiánjìn] march; advance; proceed.

前任 [qiánrèn] former incumbent; predecessor.

前提 [qián tí] a logical premise.

前途 [qiántú] the future; prospect.

虔 [qián] (adj) 恭敬 respectful; pious; devout ＊ 他是一个虔诚的教徒。He is a devout follower.

掮 [qián] (v) 用肩扛 bear on the shoulder ＊ 工友掮了一袋百多斤重的米。The worker carried on his shoulder a sack of rice weighing more than a hundred katis.

qiǎn

遣 [qiǎn] 1 (v) 打发；派 send; dispatch ＊ 他因为触犯移民条例，所以被遣送回国。He was sent back to his home country for having offended the immigration rule. 2 (v) 排解；消除 drive away; remove ＊ 他打扑克牌是为了消遣。He plays poker for amusement.

遣返 [qiǎnfǎn] to send back

遣散 [qiǎnsàn] to dismiss; to discharge

谴（譴） [qiǎn] (v) 责备；申斥 reprimand; scold ＊ 我们谴责南非白人政权的种族隔离政策。We reprimand the apartheid policy of the South African white regime.

浅（淺） [qiǎn] 1 (adj) 从上到下或从外到里的距离小 shallow ＊ 这里河水浅。The river here is shallow. 2 (adj) 简明易懂 easy to understand; simple ＊ 这本课本的内容比较浅。The contents of this text-book are simpler. 3 (adj) 交情不深 superficial ＊ 你我交浅言深。Though the friendship between you and me is superficial we can have profound discussion. 4 (adj) 不久；时间短。short (time) ＊ 我和他相处的日子还浅。The period in which I have been staying with him is still short. 5 (adj) 颜色淡 light in colour ＊ 他穿了一件浅蓝色的上衣。He wore a light blue shirt.

浅见 [qiǎnjiàn] modest view

浅陋 [qiǎnlòu] poor (in knowledge)

qiàn

欠 [qiàn] 1 (v) 借别人的财物没有还 owe ＊ 我欠他十元。I owe him ten dollars. 2 (adj) 不够；缺少 lacking; deficient ＊ 这部电影欠佳。This film is not very good. 3 (v) 呵欠；疲倦时张口出气 yawn ＊ 他在打呵欠。He is yawning.

欠妥 [qiàntuǒ] not good enough

欠债 [qiànzhài] debts; obligation; liability

欠账 [qiànzhàng] outstanding accounts

歉 [qiàn] 1 (adj) 收成不理想 bad harvest ＊ 今年是歉年。This year is a year of bad harvest. 2 (adj) 觉得对不住人 sorry; regretful ＊ 我错怪了你，现在向你道歉。Now I apologise for putting the blame on you.

歉收 [qiánshou] a bad harvest; failure of crops.

歉意 [qiànyì] apology

慊 [qiàn] (adj) 不满；恨 dissatisfied; hateful

倩 [qiàn] (adj) 美好 beautiful

堑（塹） [qiàn] (n) 隔断交通的沟 a trench; a ditch ＊ 兵士们在挖堑壕。The soldiers are digging a trench.

纤（縴） [qiàn] (n) 拉船前进的绳索 a rope for dragging the boat
另见 [xīạn]

茜 [qiàn] 茜草；草本植物。其根可作红色染料，也可供药用 rubia, a plant whose roots can be used as red dye or medicine

嵌 [qiàn] (v) 把东西镶在空隙里 inlay; set in; insert ＊ 她的金手镯嵌了一些玉。Her gold bangle is inlaid with some jade pieces.

嵌工 [qiàngōng] mosaic

qiāng

哈（嗆）[qiāng] (v) 水或食物进入气管引起咳嗽，把东西喷出来 cough ＊ 他吃饭时，给饭粒哈住喉咙。When he was having dinner, an irritation in the throat by a grain of rice made him cough violently.
另见 [qiàng]

枪（槍）[qiāng] 1 (n) 刺杀用的长矛，以木制成 spear; a lance 2(n) 发射子弹的武器 gun; rifle＊机关枪。machine gun. 3 (n) 形状象枪的工具 tool which looks like a gun ＊电焊枪 welding tool.

枪法 [qiāngfǎ] shooting skill

枪杆 [qiāng gǎn] weapon; military strength

枪林弹雨 [qiāng lín-dànyǔ] forest of rifles and hails of bullets (describing the fierceness of a battle)

枪手 [qiāng shǒu] a gunman; a spearman

腔 [qiāng] 1 (n)身体或器物中空的部分 cavity ＊ 我们要注意口腔清洁。We must look after the cleanliness of our mouth cavity. 2 (n) 歌曲或戏曲的曲调 tone of a song 3 (n) 话；说话的声音；语气等 accent ＊ 他说的华语有湖南腔。He spoke Mandarin with a Hunan accent.

腔调 [qiāng diào] tune; accent

锵（鏘）[qiāng] (n) 金属器物相撞时的响声 tinkling sound of metal objects ＊ 锣声铿锵。The gong tinkles and jingles.

羌 [qiāng] (n) 羌族，中国少数民族名 the chiay Tribe, a minority race in China

戕 [qiāng] (v) 杀害；伤害 kill; wound ＊ 侵略军残酷地戕杀平民。The invading army killed the civilians savagely.

镪（鏹）[qiāng] (n) 具有强烈腐蚀性的浓硝酸、浓盐酸，俗称"镪水" strongly corrosive liquid e.g. concentrated nitric acid and concentrated hydrochloric acid

qiáng

墙（墻;牆）[qiáng] (n) 用砖石等砌成承架房顶或隔开内外的建筑物 wall

樯（檣）[qiáng] (n) 桅杆 mast. ＊ 帆樯如林。The numerous sailmasts look like a forest.

强 [qiáng] 1 (adj) 健壮有力 strong in health ＊ 父亲身强力壮。My father is healthy and strong. 2 (adj) 好，优越 strong; good ＊ 我的儿子记性强。My son has a very good memory. 3 (adj) ……还多一点 more than....;.... or more ＊ 十万强 more than 100,000. 4 (adv) 暴烈地，以武力 violently; by force ＊ 日本人强占了我们的土地。The Japanese occupied our land by force. 5 (adj) 强横 violent; atrocious ＊ 他们抗议警察的强暴行为。They protest against the violent act of the police. 6 (adj) 感情或意志所要求达到的程度高 strong in emotion or will ＊ 他意志很坚强。He is very firm. 7 (adj) 接在数字后面，表示略多 used at the back of numeral to mean more ＊ 今年的产量比去年 增加 三分之一强。This year's production is one third more than that of last year.

强调 [qiángdiào] to emphasize

强姦 [qiángjiān] to rape

强姦民意 [qiáng jiān mín yì] imposing will on the people

强硬 [qiángyìng] strong; rigorous

强佔 [qiáng zhàn] take by force; usurp

强制公债 [qián zhì gōng zhài] compulsory bonds

另见 [qiáng]
[jiàng]

qiǎng

强 [qiǎng] (v) 勉力 compel; force ＊我们不要强人所难。 We should not force a person to do something he doesn't like.

强辩 [qiǎngbiàn] to argue without good reasons

强词夺理 [qiǎng cí duó lǐ] to argue forcefully when lacking reason or validity

另见 [qiáng] [jiàng]

襁 [qiǎng]〔襁褓〕(n)包婴儿的被、毯等 blankets, cloth for baby; swaddling clothes ＊母亲历尽千辛万苦，把他从襁褓中抚育成人。 Mother had experienced many difficulties in bringing him up.

抢（搶）[qiǎng] 1 (v) 争夺 snatch; struggle for ＊球员们正在抢球。 The players are snatching the ball. 2 (v) 硬拿 rob; take away by force ＊他们计划抢劫银行。They plan to rob the bank. 3 (v) 赶紧；赶快 rush ＊村民在抢救河堤。The villagers are rushing to repair the river dam.

抢夺 [qiǎngduó] to take away by force; to plunder

抢救 [qiǎng jiù] rush to save

抢先 [qiǎng xiān] struggle to become the first

qiàng

呛（嗆）[qiàng] (v) 有刺激性的气味使人的鼻子、嗓子感到难受 to irritate (the throat and the nose) ＊炒辣椒的味儿呛得我直咳嗽。 The smell of frying chilli irritated me so much that I coughed violently.

另见 [qiāng]

qiāo

跷（蹺）[qiāo] 1 (v) 抬起(肢体的一部分)。raise; lift ＊他跷起腿来。He lifts up his leg.

跷跷板 [qiāoqiāobǎn] seesaw

跷蹊 [qiāo·qi] strange; dubious

悄 [qiāo]〔悄悄〕(adv) 没有声音；不动声色 quietly ＊他悄悄地溜走了。He slipped away quietly.

另见 [qiǎo]

敲 [qiāo] (v) 打；击 strike; hit ＊有人敲门。Somebody is knocking at the door.

敲打 [qiāo·da] beating; knocking

敲诈 [qiāozhà] to extort; to blackmail

锹（鍬）[qiāo] (n) 一种挖土的工具 a spade; a shovel

qiáo

憔 [qiáo] (adj) 身体瘦弱，脸色不好看的样子 becoming thin and haggard ＊他受了许多折磨，样子很憔悴。 He looks haggard after undergoing many tortures.

樵 [qiáo] 1 (n) 柴 firewood 2 (v) 打柴 cut firewood

瞧 [qiáo] (v) 看 look; see ＊让我瞧一瞧。Let me have a look.

乔（喬）[qiáo] 1 (adj) 高 tall; lofty ＊松树是一种乔木。 The pine tree is a lofty tree. 2 (v) 假（扮）disguise ＊他乔装成一个老人。He disguised himself as an old man.

侨（僑）[qiáo] 1 (v) 寄住在国外 living in a foreign country ＊他们侨居在英国。They stay in England as foreigners 2 (n) 寄住在国外的人 people who stay in a foreign land. ＊华侨。 overseas Chinese.

侨胞 [qiáobāo] fellow countrymen who stay overseas

桥（橋）[qiáo] (n) 架在江、河等水上以便通行的建筑物 bridge ＊麻河有一座木桥。

There is a wooden bridge over the Muar River.

桥梁 [qiáoliáng] the beams of a bridge

桥牌 [qiáopái] bridge; a card game.

荞（蕎）[qiáo] (n) 草本植物。生长期短。种子磨成粉供食用。茎叶可作饲料或绿粉 buckwheat.

翘（翹）[qiáo] (v) 抬起 lift up ＊ 他翘首四望。He lifts up his head to look around.

另见 [qiào]

qiǎo

悄 [qiǎo] 1 (adj) 声音很低 soft; quiet ＊ 他低声悄语。He talks softly 2 (adj) 忧愁的样子 sad; grieved ＊ 她悄然落泪。She cried sadly.

愀 [qiǎo] (adj) 形容神色变得严肃或不愉快 melancholic ; sorrowful ＊ 他愀然不乐。He turned sorrowful.

巧 [qiǎo] 1 (adj) 灵敏；机灵 skilful; ingenious 2 (adv) 恰好；正好 just; in the right time ＊ 你来得真巧。You come at the right time. 3 (adj) 虚伪；欺诈 cunning; artful ＊ 他用花言巧语来欺骗一个少女。He used sweet talks to deceive a girl.

巧夺天工 [qiǎo duó tiān gōng] the skill of workmanship surpasses that of nature

巧合 [qiǎohé] coincidence.

巧计 [qiǎojì] an ingenious plan; a clever trick

巧妙 [qiǎo miào] clever; wonderful; ingenious

qiào

诮（誚）[qiào] (v) 讽刺 satirize; mock

俏 [qiào] 1(adj) 美丽;英俊 handsome ＊ 他长得俊俏。He is handsome. 2 (adj) 商品销路好 popular (goods)

俏皮 [qiào· pi] lively and jovial in talking

峭 [qiào] 1 (adj) 山势高又陡 precipitous; steep ; abrupt ＊ 这里是悬崖峭壁。Here we have an overhanging cliff and a steep precipice. 2 (adj) 比喻严峻 strict; stern

鞘 [qiào] (n) 刀剑的套子 a sheath; a scabbard ＊ 他把刀放回刀鞘里。He put the knife back into its sheath.

另见 [shāo]

壳（殼）[qiào] (n) 坚硬的外皮 shell; crust ＊ 她喜欢在海滩拾贝壳。she likes to collect shells on the beach.

另见 [ké]

窍（竅）[qiào] 1 (n) 洞 an opening; a hole. ＊七窍。the seven openings (ears, eyes, nose and mouth). 2 (n) 事情的关键 key to a matter; gist of a matter. ＊ 他还没找到解决这个问题的诀窍。He has not found the key to the problem yet.

窍门 [qiào mén] solution; channel.

翘（翹）[qiào] (v) 抬起，昂起 to elevate; to raise ＊ 你一踏上木板的一头，另一头就会翘起来了。If you step on one end of a plank, the other end will be lifted up.

另见 [qiáo]

撬 [qiào] (v) 用棍；棒等把东西挑开或抬起 to force open ; to lift with a stick or rod. ＊ 他用一根铁棒把大石撬起。He lifted the big rock with an iron rod.

qiē

切 [qiē] (v) 割开 cut; chop. ＊ 妈妈在切菜。My mother is chopping the vegetable.

切断 [qiēduàn] to sever; to cut off

切片 [qiē piàn] to slice
另见 [qiè]

qié

茄 [qié] (n) 草本植物。果实可供烹食 egg-plant

qiě

且 [qiě] 1 (adv) 暂时 for the time being. ✱ 且慢。Hold on for the time being. 2 (adv) in addition; as well as. ✱ 这建筑物既高且大。This building is lofty as well as magnificent. 3 (conj)尚且；相当于"连………都"。also; yet.✱ 死且不避，困难何足惧！ I am ready to face death , so why should I dread difficulty. 4 (conj) 表示同时进行的两种行动 a conjunction to show two actions occuring at the same time. ✱ 她且弹且唱。She sings while playing the piano.
另见 [jū]

qiè

切 [qiè] 1 (v) 符合 agree with; correspond. ✱ 这篇文章不切题。This passage does not agree with its title. 2 (adj) 贴近；亲近 close; intimate; immediate. ✱ 这件事关系到大家的切身利益。This matter concerns everybody's immediate interest. 3 (adj) 紧急 urgent ✱ 我们迫切需要援助。We need help urgently. 4 (adv) 表示强调或提醒 with emphasis. ✱ 你要多注意身体健康。 Remember to heed more about your physical health.

切齿 [qièchǐ] gnashing the teeth in deep rage or hatred

切肤之痛 [qiè fū zhī tòng] bodily pain; fully experienced

切合 [qièhé] coincide; agree with
另见 [qiē]

窃（竊）[qiè] 1 (v) 偷；用欺诈的手段取得 steal; usurp. ✱ 这是一宗窃案。This is a case of theft. 2 (adv) 暗中；偷偷地 secretly; stealthily. ✱ 他们在窃窃私语。They are talking behind secretly.

窃取 [qièqǔ] steal; take without permission

窃听 [qiètīng] eavesdrop

窃笑 [qièxiào] feel silent contempt for; laugh secretly

挈 [qiè] 1 (v) 举；提 raise; carry. ✱ 提纲挈领。to raise the important topics. 2 (v) 带领 lead. ✱ 他挈眷离开。He leads the family members in retreat.

锲（鍥）[qiè] (v) 用刀刻 carve; cut. ✱ 锲而不舍 to carve something without abandoning it; to work persistently.

惬（愜）[qiè] (adj) 满足；畅快 contented; pleasant. ✱ 他在这里呆得很惬意。He feels satisfied and pleased staying here.

箧（篋）[qiè] (n) 小箱子 a trunk ;a case. ✱ 旅客提着一个行箧。The tourist is holding a luggage.

妾 [qiè] (n) 旧社会男子在妻子以外娶的女人 a concubine ✱ 这个地主硬逼穷人家的女儿嫁给他做妾。The landlord forced the daughter of a poor family to be his concubine.

怯 [qiè] (adj) 胆小；没有勇气 timid; cowardly. ✱ 他很胆怯。He is very timid.

怯场 [qiè chǎng] to get uneasy and nervous at a public gathering

怯懦 [qiènuò] show sign of fear; be a coward

qīn

侵 [qīn] (v) 攻击；进犯 aggress; invade ＊敌人正在侵略我们的领土。The enemy is invading our territory.

侵略 [qīnluè] aggression; to invade

侵蚀 [qīnshí] to erode; erosion

侵吞公款 [qīn tūn gōng kuǎn] to misappropriate funds for personal use

钦（欽） [qīn] (v) 恭敬 respect ＊我们钦佩他那舍己为人的精神。We respect his selfless spirit.

钦仰 [qīnyǎn] to look upon with respect

亲 [qīn] 1 (n) 父母 parents.＊他的双亲都还健在。His parents are still alive. 2 (adj) 有血统或婚姻关系的 with blood relation; related by marriage ＊ 他是我的亲弟弟。He is my brother. 3 (n)婚姻关系 relation by marriage ＊ 他们还没成亲。They are not married to each other yet. 4 (adj) 本人的 own; personal; self ＊他想亲身体验下层人民的痛苦。He intends to experience personally the miseries of the lower class. 5 (adj)感情好；关系深 close; dear; intimate ＊ 他们关系亲密。They are close in relationship. 6 (v) 吻 kiss ＊妈妈亲了亲孩子。The mother kisses her child.

亲爱 [qīn aì] dear

亲近 [qīnjìn] close; intimate

亲口 [qīnkǒu] with one's own mouth

亲戚 [qīnqì] relatives

亲切 [qīnqiè] kindly; affectionate

亲情 [qīn qíng] warm affection; love

亲生 [qīnshēng] of one's own begetting, as children

亲信 [qīnxìn] trusted

亲友 [qīnyǒu] relatives and friends

亲自 [qīnzì] personally; in person

亲嘴 [qīnzuǐ] to kiss.

另见 [qìng]

衾 [qīn] (n) 被子 a large quilt; a cover cloth

qín

勤 [qín] 1 (adj) 做事尽力；不偷懒 hardworking; diligent; industrious ＊他是一个勤劳的孩子。He is a diligent child. 2 (adv) 常常 always; often ＊他勤于看报。He always reads newspapers. 3 (n) 勤务；分派的工作 duty ＊他是个外勤记者。He is a reporter assigned with outdoor duties.

勤工奖 [qíngōngjiǎng] a reward for the most diligent worker, aimed to promote production and increase productivity.

勤恳 [qínkěn] painstaking; in good earnest.

勤劳 [qínláo] toilsome; laborious.

勤力 [qín lì] diligent.

勤勉 [qínmiǎn] industrious; hardworking.

勤务员 [qínwùyuán] staff on duty.

琴 [qín] 1 (n) 弦乐器 a string instrument ; a lute 2 (n) 某些乐器的统称 a general name for some musical instruments ＊钢琴。piano. ＊手风琴。accordian. ＊ 口琴。harmonica.

禽 [qín] (n) 鸟类的统称 a general name for birds. ＊ 森林里有各种各样的飞禽。There are many kinds of birds in the forest.

禽兽 [qínshòu] birds and beasts

禽兽不如 [qínshòubùrú] worse than beasts; inhuman

噙 [qín] (v)（嘴或眼里）含 hold tears in the eyes or water in the mouth. ＊ 孩子噙着眼泪说有人欺侮他。The child said with tears in his eyes that somebody bullied him.

擒 [qín] (v)捉拿 arrest; capture.＊他生擒一隻狐狸。He captured a

fox alive.

qǐn

寝(寢) [qǐn] (v) 睡觉 sleep *他们废寝忘食地工作。They work so hard that they forget to sleep and eat.

寝室 [qǐnshì] a bedroom

寝食不安 [qǐnshíbùān] no peace either in sleep or eating; without peace of mind.

qìn

沁 [qìn] (v) 渗入 penetrate *沁人心脾。penetrate into one's heart. (in reference to the beauty of literary works)

揿(撳) [qìn] (v) 按 press

qīng

青 [qīng] 1 (n) 一般指蓝色；绿色 dark green; blue * 青菜。green vegetables. 2 (n) 没有成熟的庄稼 green crop 3 (adj) 比喻年少 young *他是一个有希望的青年。He is a prospective young man.

青春 [qīngchūn] youth; the prime (springtime) of life; the bloom of youth

青出於蓝 [qīng chū yú lán] to surpass one's master or forerunner

青翠 [qīngcuì] fresh and green

青黄不接 [qīng huáng bù jié] bad years or a difficult period

青苔 [qīngtá] green moss (lichen]

青蛙 [qīng wā] a green frog; a tree-frog

清 [qīng] 1 (n) 纯净；没有混杂的东西(液体或气体) pure; clean; clear *这里的水很清。The water here is very clear and clean. 2 (adj) 安静 quiet *这间店冷冷清清的，没什么生意。This shop is very quiet; not much business is done. 3 (adv) 彻底；一点不留 completely; thoroughly *他还没还清账目。He has not settled his account completely. 4 (adj) 不贪污 incorruptible 5 (adv) 明白 clearly; distinctly *他没说清楚。He did not say it clearly. 6 (n) 朝代名 name of a dynasty in China — The Ching Dynasty (1644—1911) or Manchu Dynasty

清白 [qīngbái] innocent; pure

清洁 [qīngjié] clean

清理 [qīnglǐ] to clear; clearance

清贫 [qīngpín] honest poverty

清闲 [qīngxián] free; at ease

清香 [qīngxiāng] fragrant

清新 [qīngxīn] fresh; new

清醒 [qīngxǐng] get sober; to come to one's senses

清秀 [qīngxiù] handsome

清早 [qīngzǎo] at dawn; very early

蜻 [qīng] 〔蜻蜓〕俗称"蚂螂"；昆虫。有翅两对，腹部细长，复眼发达。常在水边捕食小飞虫是益虫 dragonfly, useful insect

氢(氫) [qīng] (n) 化学元素；符号 H。是最轻的气体 hydrogen, the lightest gas

氢弹 [qīngdàn] hydrogen bomb, a nuclear weapon

轻 [qīng] 1 (adj) 分量小；不重 light *油比水轻。Oil is lighter than water. 2 (adj) 程度浅 slight; minor; little *他只受了轻伤。He sustained only a slight injury. 3 (adv) 用力小；不费力 lightly; easily *这件事轻而易举。This job can be done easily. 4 (v) 轻视；不注意 look down upon; pay little attention *我们不可轻敌。We should not pay little heed to the enemy. 5 (adj) 轻率 rash; heedless; careless; hasty ＊千万不可轻举妄动。You should never act rashly.

轻工业 [qīnggōngyè] light industry. e.g. food, textile industry

轻快 [qīngkuài] light; cheerful; swift

轻描淡写 [qīngmáo-dànxiě] to gloss over lightly; to describe without giving details

轻生 [qīngshēng] to commit suicide

轻松 [qīngsōng] relaxed

轻微 [qīngwēi] slight;light

轻信 [qīngxìn] to believe readily

倾(傾) [qīng] 1 (v) 向一边偏过去；歪斜 incline; lean towards ＊那根灯柱有点倾斜。The lamp post is inclined to one side. 2 (n)偏向 inclination ＊这个右倾的军人政府逮捕很多学生。This rightist military government arrested many students. 3 (v) 倒塌 collapse ＊这座旧楼有倾覆的危险。This old building has a danger of collapsing. 4 (v) 倒出 pour ; dump ＊日本和美国竞相在东南亚国家倾销他们的剩馀产品。Japan and America compete with each other in dumping their surplus products in South-east Asian countries. 5 (v) 尽力 exert ＊我们将倾全力把工作做好。We shall exert all our efforts in making the job a success.

倾倒 [qīngdǎo] overturn

倾家荡产 [qīngjiā-dàngchǎn] to squander the entire family fortune

倾泻 [qīngxiè] (mud) tumble down

qíng

情 [qíng] 1 (n)感想；心绪 emotions; feelings; mood ＊她的心情不好。She was in a bad mood. 2 (n) 好意 influence; favour; personal esteem ＊你去和他讲情吧。Go and ask for his favour. 3 (n) 爱意 love; passion ＊这是一首马来情歌。This is a Malay love song. 4 (n) 状况 condition ＊他的病情严重。His sickness is in a serious condition.

情报 [qíngbào] information; intelligence

情操 [qíngcào] sentiments

情调 [qíngdiào] mood; atmosphere

情妇 [qíngfù] a mistress

情节 [qíngjié] details of a story

情投意合 [qíng tóu yì hé] perfectly suited to each other

情形 [qíng xíng] state of affairs (things); situation; condition

情谊 [qíng yí] friendship kindness

情愿 [qíngyuàn] willingly; voluntarily

晴 [qíng] (n) 天空无云的景色 fine weather; a cloudless sky ＊今天是晴天。 Today is a fine day

擎 [qíng] (v)往上托；举 lift up ＊众擎易举。with concerted effort, it is easily raised.

黥 [qíng] (v) 古代的一种刑罚，在犯人脸上刺字，再涂上黑色 brand criminals on the face, as a measure of punishment

qǐng

顷(頃) [qǐng] 1 (n) 地积单位；一百亩为一顷 unit for the area of land — a hectare 2 (adv) 短时间 for a short while ＊洪水在顷刻之间就淹满了全村。The flood water has overflowed the whole village within a short time. 3 (adv)刚才 just now ＊顷接来信。I have just received your letter.

请(請) [qǐng] 1 (v)要求 request; ask for ＊我想请假。I want to request for a leave.

2 (v) 邀 invite ＊ 我请他来我家吃饭。I invite him to my house for dinner. 3 (adv) 敬词；用在动词前面 a word for courtesy—please ＊ 请坐。Please take your seat.

请柬 [qǐngjiǎn] an invitation card; a letter of invitation

请教 [qǐngjiào] to request for instruction or help

请客 [qiǎn kè] to invite guests; to give a feast

请问 [gǐnguèn] may I ask you?

请愿 [qǐng yuàn] to petition to those in authority

qìng

罄 [qìng] (adj) 完；尽 finished; exhausted. ＊ 货品已经售罄。All the goods have been sold out.

庆（慶）[qìng] 1 (v) 祝贺 celebrate; congratulate ＊ 让我们欢庆一堂。Let us celebrate joyously together. 2 (n) 可庆祝的事 celebration. ＊ 国庆。National day celebration.

庆典 [qìngdiǎn] official rites of congratulation; a joyous occasion or festival; a ceremony

庆功 [qìnggong] triumph

庆贺 [qìnghè] to congratulate

庆幸 [qìngxìng] be favoured by luck

庆祝 [qìngzhù] to celebrate

亲（親）[qìng]〔亲家〕(n) 夫妻双方的父母相互的称呼 an address used by the parents of both husband and wife calling each other.

另见 [qīn]

qíong

穷 [qíong] 1 (adj) 没有钱；贫寒 poor ＊ 在这个社会里，穷人越来越穷。In this society, the poor people are getting poorer and poorer. 2 (adj) 完；尽 exhausted ＊ 他理屈词穷。He cannot find any more good reasons to support his argument. 3 (adj) 达到极点 extreme ＊ 这大地主一家穷奢极侈。The family of this big land-lord is extremely extravagant.

穷苦 [qíong kǔ] poverty-stricken; in distress

穷困 [qíongkùn] poor; without resource

穷奢极欲 [qíong shē jí yù] the fat have every luxury; live off of the land

穷途末路 [qíongtúmòlù] no way out (in a desperate situation)

穷乡僻壤 [qíongxiāng pìrǎng] poor or remote villages; places in obscurity

穷凶极恶 [qíongxīongjí è] exceptionally violent and wicked

穷追 [qíongzhuī] a hot pursuit; to push to the extreme

琼（瓊）[qióng] (n) 美玉，泛指精美的东西 beautiful jade; excellent things ＊ 琼楼玉宇。beautiful and expensive houses.

qīu

秋 [qiū] 1 (n) 四季中的第三季 autumn ＊ 秋收。the autumn harvest. 2 (n) 庄稼成熟的时期 harvest time ＊ 麦秋 harvest time for wheat. 3 (n) 年 year ＊ 我们的事业是一项千秋大业。Our undertaking is one which will go on for many generations. 4 (n) 日子；时期 time; period ＊ 多事之秋。eventful years; the country's troubled hours.

秋波 [qiūbō] bewitching eyes

秋千 [qiūqiān] swing

丘 [qiū] 1 (n) 小土山 hill; a mound ＊ 孩子们在沙滩上堆沙丘。The kids are building up sand hills on the beach. 2 (n) 坟墓 grave 3 (n) 量

词 numeral word ＊一丘田。a plot of land.

丘八 [qiūbā] soldier (a colloquial word)

丘陵 [qiūlıng] mounds

邱 [qiū] (n)姓氏 a surname

蚯 [qiú]〔蚯蚓〕(n) 也叫〔蛐蟮〕，环节动物。体形园长，由许多环节构成。能翻松土壤，对农作物有益。也可供药用 。earthworm

qíu

求 [qiú] 1 (v)寻取；探索；设法得到 seek; look for ＊我们一定要实事求是 。We must seek truth by verifying facts. 2 (n)需要 demand ＊供过于求。supply exceeds demand. 3 (v) 请求 request; beg ＊那艘船曾发出求救的讯号。 The ship had given a signal for help.

求助 [qiú qìng] to ask a favour

求学 [qiúxué] to study

求情 [qiúzhuó] to ask for help

球 [qiú] 1 (n) 由中心到表面各点距离都相等的园形立体 sphere; ball 2 (n) 球形或接近球形的东西 spherical or near spherical object ＊羊毛线球。a ball of wool. 3 (n)指某些球形的体育用品 sports equipment in the shape of a ball; ball ＊乒乓球。ping-pong ball.

球场 [qiúchǎng] a tennis court; a basketball court etc

球拍 [qiúpāi] racket

球心 [qiúxīn] the centre of a sphere

裘 [qiú] (n)皮毛制成的衣服 garment made of fur ＊狐裘 garment made of fox fur.

逑 [qiú] (n)匹配；配偶 male

酋 [qiú] 1 (n) 酋长；部落的首领 the chief of a tribe; a headman; a chieftain 2 (n) 盗贼或敌人的头子 the head of robbers or enemies

遒 [qiú] (adj)强劲；有力 strong; powerful

囚 [qiú] 1 (v)拘禁；关押 imprison; put in jail ＊犯人被囚在岛上。The prisoners were jailed on an island. 2 (n) 被拘禁的犯人 a prisoner; a criminal; a convict ＊囚犯企图逃跑。 The prisoner tried to escape.

囚禁 [qiújìn] to lock up someone in a prison

泅 [qiú] (v)浮行水上 swim ＊兵士们泅水而过。 The soldiers swam across the river

qū

祛 [qū] (v) 除去 drive off; expel ＊这个药可祛痰。 This medicine can drive the phlegm off the respiratory tract.

区(區) [qū] 1 (v) 分别；划分 discriminate; classify; distinguish ＊你能区分鸡蛋的好坏吗？Can you discriminate the fresh eggs from the bad ones? 2 (n)地区；区域 district; region ＊裕廊是个工业区。 Jurong is an industrial district. 3 (n) 行政区划 an administrative district; territory

区别 [qūbié] to discriminate; to distinguish; differ; distinct

区分 [qūfēn] differentiate between

区划 [qūhuà] seperate into classes or categories; the division of regions

区区 [qūqū] small (in amount); petty; trifling

区域 [qūxù] region; location

另见 [ōu]

驱(驅) [qū] 1 (v) 赶 to urge; to drive ＊他在驱马前进。 He is urging the horse to advance. 2 (v) 赶走 expel; to drive away ＊他被驱逐出境。He was deported.

驱虫剂 [qūchóngjì] an insecticide

驱除 [qūchú] to get rid of; to

stamp out

驱散 [qūsàn] to scatter; to disperse

驱使 [qūshǐ] to urge on by force

躯(軀) [qū](n) 身体 the body * 血肉之躯。human body; blood and flesh.

躯干 [qūgàn] the trunk

躯体 [qūtǐ] the physical body

蛆 [qū] (n) 蝇类的幼虫 maggots * 灭蝇要注意灭蛆。 In exterminating the flies we should get rid of the maggots also.

曲 [qū] 1 (adj) 弯曲 crooked; curved * 画一条曲线。Draw a curved line. 2 (adj) 不公正;不合理 unjust; wrong * 我们要分清是非曲直。 We must distinguish clearly between the right and wrong or the just from the unjust. 3 (n) 弯曲的地方 a bend

曲尺 [qūchǐ] a carpenter's square

曲解 [qūjiě] to misinterpret

曲折 [qūzhé] circuitous; intricate; ups and downs

另见 [qǔ]

屈 [qū] 1 (v) 弯曲 bend *他屈膝投降了。He bends his knees and surrenders. 2 (v) 屈服 submit; subdue * 他宁死不屈。He would rather die than to submit. 3 (v) 冤枉 to wrong; to feel unhappy * 我们都替你叫屈。We all feel that you have been wronged. 4 (adj) 理亏 without good reasons * 他知道自己 理屈词穷了。 He knows that he is losing grounds and lack of good reasons.

屈从 [qūcóng] yield to; submit to

屈就 [qūjiù] condescend to take

屈指可数 [qū zhǐ kě shǔ] you could count them on your fingers

趋(趨) [qū] 1 (v) 快步走 walk quickly *他趋前一看。He hastened forward to have a look. 2 (n) 倾向;朝着某个方向发展 tendency; trend of development * 这种趋势越来越明显。The trend is getting more and more significant.

趋向 [qūxiàng] a trend; a tendency

趋炎附势 [qūyánfùshì] to fawn and rely on those with power and influence

趋之若鹜 [qū zhī ruò wù] to chase after something e.g. wealth, benefits

qú

渠 [qú] 1 (n) 水道;特指人工开凿的水道 a drain, a ditch *沟渠。drain. 2 (pron) 他 he; she; him; her; it *渠等。they

qǔ

取 [qǔ] 1 (v) 拿 take; get * 他上台去领取奖品。He went up the stage to get the prize. 2 (v) 得到 receive; obtain * 在这场战役中,我军取得了巨大的胜利。In this battle, our troops obtained a great victory. 3 (v) 选用;采用 choose; select; use * 他被录取了。He has been selected.

取长补短 [qǔchángbǔduǎn] supplementing one's weakness with the strong points of others

取代 [qǔdài] to replace; to supplant

取缔 [qǔdì] to control; to prohibit

取之不尽 [qǔ zhī bù jìn] inexhaustible; abundant

取消 [qǔxiāo] to cancel; to call off; to revoke

取笑 [qǔxiào] to ridicule; to laugh at

娶 [qǔ] (v) 男子结婚 marry (a wife) * 他还没娶妻。 He is not married yet.

曲 [qǔ] 1 (n) 歌 song 2 (n) 歌谱;乐调 lyrics; song *这是聂耳作的曲。This song was composed by Nie Er. 3 (n) 古代韵文的一种 a

rhymed literature in classical chinese
另见[qū]

qù

觑(覷) [qù] (v) 看；窥探 look at; steal a look＊你可别小觑残废的人。You should not look down upon the disabled.

去 [qù] 1 (v) 离开到别处 go; depart. ＊ 她要去买菜。She wants to go to buy some vegetables 2 (v) 距离；差别 to be apart; to be different ＊ 两地相去不远。The two places are not far apart. 3 (adj) 已过的 past; provious ＊去年。last year. 4 (v) 除掉 remove; discard ＊ 我们要懂得去伪存真。We should know how to discard the false and retain the genuine. 5 (v) 离开 leave ＊ 他已经去世了。He had passed away. 6 (adv) 在动词后，表示趋向 used after the verbs to show tendency. ＊你敢爬上去吗？Do you dare to climb up? 7 (adv) 在动词后；表示持续 placed after the verbs to show continuation of the actions. ＊ 让他说下去。Let him speak on.

去处 [qùchù] a place to go.
去向 [qùxiàng] whereabout.

趣 [qù] 1 (n) 趋向 inclination. ＊ 他们的志趣相同。Their ambitions and inclinations are the same. 2 (n) 兴味 interest. ＊ 这个故事很有趣。This story is very interesting. 3 (adj) 有趣味的 amusing; interesting.

quān

圈 [quān] 1 (n) 环形；环形的东西 ring; ring-shaped articles. 2 (n) 一定的地区或活动范围 range; sphere; scope; circle. ＊ 他的生活圈子很小。His circle of activities is very small. 3 (v) 围 encircle; surround ＊ 地主用篱笆把地圈起来。The landlord enclosed the plot of land with fences. 4 (v) 画圈作记号 to mark with a circle ＊ 他把错字圈出来。He circled the wrong words.

圈内 [quānnèi] within the sphere (circle, range)
圈去 [quānqù] cancel; erase
另见 [juān]
[juàn]

悛 [quān] (v) 悔改 alter; repent ＊ 他怙恶不悛。He sticks to his bad habits.

quán

全 [quán] 1 (adv) 完备；完整 fully; wholly 2 (adj) 整个 whole; entire ＊ 全世界人民团结起来。People all over the world unite together. 3 (adj) 完全 complete ; full; whole ＊ 我们获得全胜。We have secured a complete victory. 4 (v) 保存 keep; to preserve ＊你有没有两全其美的办法？Do you have any plan to keep the both sides satisfied?

全长 [quán cháng] the total length
全权代表 [quán quán dài biǎo] a plenipotentiary
全集 [quánjí] a complete collection
全景 [quán jǐng] the whole view; a panorama.
全军覆没 [quán jūn fù mò] the entire army being totally wiped out.
全力以赴 [quán lì yǐ fù] putting in all one's effort.
全面 [quánmiàn] overall; thorough-going; comprehensive.
全神贯注 [quán shén guàn zhù] with full attention.
全心全意 [quán xīn quán yì] whole-heartedly.

诠（詮）[quán] 1 (v)解释；说明 explain; note 2 (n) 事理；真理facts; truth

痊 [quán] (v)病后复原；恢复健康 to recover from sickness

蜷 [quán] (v)（身体）弯曲 curl up ＊一隻猫蜷缩在草地上。A cat curled up on the grass.

鬈 [quán] (n) 卷曲的头发 curly hair; hair in curls ＊林先生有满头的卷发。Mr. Lim has curly hair.

拳 [quán] 1 (n) 屈指卷握起来的手 fist ＊他握紧拳头。He clenched his fist. 2 (n)拳术；一种体育运动 pugilistic art ＊太极拳。Tai-ji.

颧（顴）[quán] (n) 颧骨；眼睛下面两颊 上面突出的部分the cheek bones ＊他瘦得颧骨高耸。He is so thin that his cheek bones stand out prominently.

权（權）[quán] 1 (n)古代指秤锤 a weight used in the olden days 2 (n) 权力；职责范围内支配和指挥的力量 power; authority ＊他阴谋夺权。He is plotting to grab power. 3 (n)依法享受的利益 rights as given by the constitution or acts; privileges ＊每个公民都应该有选举权。Every citizen should have the right to vote. 4 (v)比较；衡量weigh; balance ＊他不懂得权衡轻重。He does not know how to weigh the importance of things.

权力 [quán lì] power and authority; power

权势 [quán shì] influence; authority

权能 [quánnéng] power; function; authority

权威 [quánwēi] authority; authoritative

权限 [quánxiàn] legal capacity

权益 [quányì] rights and interests

泉 [quán] (n) 地下涌出来的水 spring water

quǎn

犬 [quǎn] (n) 狗dog

犬马之劳 [quǎn mǎ zhī láo] render whatever service one can

犬牙交错 [quǎn yá jiāo cuò] intricate and interwoven

quàn

劝（勸）[quàn] 1 (v) 讲明道理，使人听从advise; persuade ＊我劝他不要赌博。I advise him not to gamble. 2 (v) 鼓励 encourage ＊我们常互相劝勉。We always encourage one another.

劝导 [quàn dǎo] exhort；induce；persuade

劝告 [quàngào] advise; advice

劝解 [quànjiě] exhort to peace

券 [quàn] 1 (n)票证 ticket;a bond＊入场券。admission ticket. 2 (n)比喻保证 a guarantee ＊他稳操胜券。His victory is guaranteed. 另见[xuàn]

quē

缺 [quē] 1 (adj)短少，不够short of; deficient; insufficient; lack of ＊我们缺乏土地。We are short of land 2 (adj) 破损imperfect; chipped ＊碗边有个缺口。The rim of the bowl is chipped. 3 (n) 空额 a vacancy ＊这个部门有几个缺额。There are a few vacancies in this department. 4 (adj)当到而不到absent ＊他这学期没有缺课。He did not absent from school this term.

缺点 [quēdiǎn] a defect; a flaw; a shortcoming

缺陷 [quēxiàn] defect; an imperfection

què

确（確） [què] 1 (adj)真实，实在 true; real ＊这篇报导不确实。This report is not true. 2 (adv)坚定 firmly ＊ 我们确信能够战胜一切困难。We firmly believe that we can overcome all difficulties.

确保 [quèbǎo] to guarantee; to ensure

确定 [quèdìng] decide; fix; settle

确立 [quèlì] to establish; fix; secure

确切 [quèqiè] true to fact; exact

榷 [què] (v)商量，讨论 to discuss ＊ 这件事没有商榷的余地。There is no more room for discussion on this matter.

阙（闕） [què] 1 (n)古代皇宫门前两边的楼，也用作宫门的代称 a gate tower of an imperial palace 2 (n) 古代墓道外所立的石碑坊 an epitaph of tomb in the olden days

另见 [quē]

阕（闋） [què] 1 (v) 终止 the end 2 (n) ＊ 量词。歌曲或词一首叫一阕 a tune

却 [què] 1 (v)往后退 regress; move backwards. ＊ 他望而却步。He moved back on seeing it. 2 (v)推辞，不接受 reject. 3 (adv)去，掉 away. ＊ 他忘却了一切烦恼。He has forgotten all worries. 4 (conj) 表示语气转折，跟"倒"、"可是"差不多 but; yet; however. ＊ 这件事大家都懂了，他却不知道。Everybody has learned about this matter yet he is ignorant of it.

雀 [què] (n) 鸟类。体小，翅膀长，雌雄的羽毛颜色多不相同。吃植物的果实或种子，也吃昆虫。特指麻雀 泛指小鸟 sparrow; small birds in general.

雀跃 [quèyuè] dance (leap) for joy.

qún

裙 [qún] (n)一种围在下身的服装 a skirt.

裙带关系 [qúndàiguānxì] relation by marriages which has been made used of for getting a high post; nepotism.

群 [qún] 1 (n) 相聚成伙的人或物 a crowd; a group. 如：人群越来越多The crowd is getting bigger and bigger. 2 (adj)聚在一起的 in a group; flocking together. 3 (n) 众人 all the people; everyone. ＊ 我们群而攻之。All of us rise up and attack him.

群策群力 [qúncèqúnlì] concerted wisdom and strength.

群集 [qúnjí] to gather in great numbers; to throng.

群众 [qúnzhòng] the masses; the people.

群众运动 [qúnzhòngyùndòng] mass movement.

麇 [qún] (v) 成群 band together; collect in crowds.

R

rán

髯 [rán] (n) 两颊上的胡子。泛指胡子 the beard; the whiskers

然 [rán] (adv) 是，对 yes;right ＊我不以为然。I do not think it is right. 2 (adv)如此，这样 so;thus＊知其然，不知其所以然。 One knows it is so,but does not know why it is so. 3 (conj) 但是，可是，不过，却 but;however;nevertheless;yet ＊我们热爱和平，然而我们不应乞求它，而应争取它。We love peace, but we have to fight for it, not beg for it.4 (part) 放在字或词之后而组成副词或形容词 to be placed after a word or a pharse to make adverb or adjective＊你请我做这事,然而我怕不能胜任。You ask me to do the work;I am afraid,however, that I am not able to do it. ＊忽然 sudden;suddenly ＊显然 apparent; apparently ＊欣然 happy;happily ＊自然 natural; naturally

然而 [rán'ér] but;however;nevertheless

然后 [rán hòu] then;afterwards

燃 [rán] (v) 烧 to burn;to set on fire＊干柴很容易燃烧。 Dry wood burns easily.

燃料 [rán liào] fuel

燃眉之急 [rán méi zhī jí] as urgent as if the eyebrows were burning

rǎn

染 [rǎn]1 (v) 上颜色to dye ＊他把白布染成红色。He dye the white cloth red. 2 (v) 沾上，一般指不良的嗜好、症病等 to contract;to get infected with;to catch(e.g. illness) ＊他染上了性病。He got infected with venereal disease.

染料 [rǎn liào] dye;dyestuff

染色 [rǎn sè] dye;to dye

染指 [rǎn zhǐ] to have a hand in;to meddle in(for gain)

ráng

瓤 [ráng] (n)瓜、果等里面包着种子的肉、瓣 the pulp;the pith＊西瓜瓤 the pulp of water-melon.＊橘瓤 。the pith of an orange.

rǎng

壤 [rǎng] 1 (n)松软的土。泛指土地 soil; earth＊ 土壤是由各种化学物质构成的。Soil consists of various chemical substances 2 (n) 地

方；地区；地 a place; a region; land

攘 [rǎng] 1 (v) 排斥 to reject; to expel; to drive out 2 (v) 侵夺 to seize; to clutch 3 (v) 伸出，举出 to stretch; to bare

攘臂 [rǎngbì] to bare the arms — for a fight

攘夺 [rǎng duó] to seize; to snatch

攘灾 [rǎng zāi] to drive off evil; to ward off calamity

嚷 [rǎng] (v) 喊；叫 to shout; to yell; to hail ＊主队中锋踢进一球，观众高兴得嚷起来。 The centre-forward of the home team kicked a goal and the spectators shouted for joy.

ràng

让（讓） [ràng] 1 (v) 给别人方便或好处 to concede; to make way for; to offer hospitatlity ＊所有行人车辆都应该让路给救火车。 All traffic has to make way for a fire engine. 2 (v) 索取一定的代价，把东西转给别人所有 to transfer; to cede ＊他把屋子转让给一个朋友。 He transferred the house to a friend. 3 (v) 使；容许 to let; to allow ＊别让他进来。 Don't let him in.

让步 [ràng bù] to make concession; to compromise

让路 [ràng lù] to make way (for somebody)

让位 [ràng wèi] to give up a seat; to abdicate

让与 [ràng yǔ] to transfer; to cede to

ráo

娆（嬈） [ráo] (adj) 优雅的；娇媚的 graceful; fascinating

饶（饒） [ráo] 1 (adj) 富足；多 abundant; plentiful; resourceful ＊马来西亚是一个物产富饶的国家。Malaysia is a resourceful country. 2 (v) 宽容 to spare; to excuse; to forgive ＊他饶恕了敌人。 He spared his enemy.

饶舌 [ráo shé] talkative

饶恕 [ráo shù] to forgive; to pardon; to excuse

rǎo

扰（擾） [rǎo] (v) 搅乱 to disturb; to trouble; to throw into disorder; confuse ＊他想扰乱人心。 He intended to cause confusion among the people.

扰乱 [rǎo luàn] to cause havoc with; to mess up; to perturb; to disturb

rào

绕（繞） [rào] 1 (v) 缠 to coil; to entwine; to intertwine ＊我在绕线圈。 I am coiling the thread. 2 (v) 围着转 to revolve round ＊地球绕太阳运转。 The earth revolves round the sun. 3 (v) 走弯路 to make a detour; to steer clear of ＊大路阻塞了，我们只好绕道而行。The main road was blocked so we had to make a detour.

绕圈子 [rào quān ·zi] to take a round-about(wag); to beat about the bush

rě

喏 [rě] (n) 古代回答别人表示敬意的呼喊 a respectful reply of accent others in the old ages

另见 [nuò]

惹 [rě] (v) 挑起；招引 to provoke; to rouse; to stir; to attract ＊她的装扮惹人注意。The way she dresses and makes up attracts people's attention.

惹不起 [rě bù qǐ] dare not provoke

惹祸 [rě huò] to incur mischief; to induce calamities; to court troubles

惹事 [rě shì] to create trouble; provoke

惹是生非 [rě shì shēng fēi] to provoke mischief

rè

热(熱) [rè] 1(n) 物体内部分子不规则运动放出的一种能heat ＊植物因酷热而渐趋枯干。The plants are suffering from the heat. 2 (adj)温度高，跟“冷”相对 hot ＊天气很热。The weather is very hot. 3 (v)使温度升高to heat＊他把饭菜热一热，才端出来。He heated the rice and dishes a little and then brought them out.4 (adj)感情强烈、深厚 earnest; enthusiastic ＊我们受到热烈的欢迎。We were received with great enthusiasm. 5 (n) 生病引起的高体温fever ＊他发高热。He has a high fever. 6 (adj)受很多人的欢迎的 popular ＊万字票早已成为一种热门赌博。The four digit game has long been a popular gambly

热爱 [rè'ài] to love fervently;to love ardently;to love heartily

热潮 [rè cháo] an upsurge

热忱 [rè chén] enthusiasm;zeal

热带 [rè dài] the tropics;the torrid zone

热电厂 [rè diàn chǎng] thermo-electric plant

热核反应 [rè hé fǎn yìng] thermonuclear reaction

热烘烘 [rè hōng hōng] stirring;nice and warm;affectionate

热火 [rè·huo] deeply attached to; seething

热火朝天 [rè huǒ cháo tiān] burning with ardour;stirring and seething with activity

热量 [rè liàng] heat capacity;warmth

热烈 [rè liè] fervent;earnest; arduous ;enthusiastic;heartily

热力学 [rè lì xué] thermodynamics

热泪盈眶 [rè lè yǐng kuāng] one's eyes brim over with warm,excited tears

热闹 [rè nào] bustle and astir; noisy; boisterous; bustling; lively; jolly; animated; exciting

热能 [rè néng] termal engery

热切 [rè qiè] warm and cordial; ardent; earnest

热情 [rè qíng] enthusiastic; fervent spirit; devotion; warmth

热水瓶 [rè shuǐ píng] a thermos flask

热望 [rè wàng] to hope fervently; to long for earnestly

热心 [rè xīn] enthusiasm ardor; zeal

热血 [rè xuě] hot blood

热源 [rè yuán] heat source

热衷 [rè zhōng] to hanker for; to be bent on; to be intent on

rén

人 [rén] 1 (n)有最高灵性，能制造工具并能使用工具进行劳动的动物 man; human beings; mankind ＊科学家应为人类福利而工作。A Scientist should work for the benefit of mankind. 2 (n) 人的个体。个人；人身 person; individual ＊昨天有四个人看见飞碟。Four persons saw a flying saucer yesterday. 3 (n) 人的群体。民众；众人；人民 people ＊街上挤满了人。The streets were crowded with people.

人才 [rén cái] men of talent; men of ability

人称 [rén chēng] the first; second or third person

人次 [rén cì] men-times

人道主义 [rén dào zhǔ yì] humanism

人定胜天 [rén dìng shèng tiān] it is man's will, not heaven that decide

人浮於事 [rén fú yú shì] superfluous staff; overstaffed

人格 [rén gé] personality;character

人格化 [rén gé huà] to personify

人工 [rén gōng] artifical; a calculating unit of the amount of work

done (e.g. man hours)
人工降雨 [rén gōng jiàng yǔ] artificial rain
人家 [rén jiā] household people; persons;someone else
人间 [rén jiān]the world of men
人口 [rén kǒu]population
人口调查 [rén kǒu tiào chá] population census
人类 [rén lèi]mankind
人类学 [rén lèi xué] anthropology
人力 [rén lì] manpower; manual labour
人们 [tén mén]people ;the others
人民 [rén mín] people
人情 [rén qíng] human relationship; a favour
人权 [rén quán]human right
人人 [rén rén]everybody
人山人海 [rén shān rén hǎi] a huge crowd of people
人身 [rén shēn] the human body; person
人参 [rén shēn]ginseng
人生 [rén shēng]the life of man
人生观 [rén shēng guān] one's outlook on life; philosophy of life
人士 [rén shì] personages;public figures
人事 [rén shì] human affairs; personnel affairs
人所共知 [rén suǒ gòng zhī] it is common knowledge that..., it is widely known that.....
人为 [rén wéi]artificial ;man-made
人物 [rén wù] personages ;a notable figure; characters
人心 [rén xīn] the feelings of the people
人心所向 [rén xīn suǒ xiàng] the feelings of the people are for
人性 [rén xìng] humanity; human nature
人行道 [rén xíng dào] pavement; sidewalk
人选 [rén xuǎn] candidate
人烟 [rén yān] men and smoke-human habitation;population
人烟稠密 [rén yān chóu mì] densely-populated
人员 [rén yuán]personnel
人云亦云 [rén yún yì yún] to repeat word for word what others say;to parrot others
人造地球卫星 [rén zào dì qiú wèi xīng] man-made earth satellite
人造丝 [rén zào sī] artificial silk; rayon
人造橡胶 [rén zào xiàng jiāo] synthetic rubber
人造胰岛素 [rén zào yí dǎo sù] artificial insulin
人证 [rén zhèng] testimony given by a witness
人质 [rén zhì] hostage
人之常情 [rén zhī cháng qíng] the normal human nature
人种 [rén zhǒng] the human species;a person;race

仁 [rén] 1 (adj) 友爱；同情 kind; benevolent ; merciful ＊那仁慈的老人帮我找到一份工作。 The kind old man helped me get a job. 2 (n) 果核或果壳中最里面的较柔软部分 kernal ＊杏仁 the almond kernel. ＊ 桃仁。 the walnut kernel
仁慈 [rén cí] kind; benevolent; mericiful
仁政 [rén zhèng] the policy of benevolence
仁至义尽 [rén zhì yì jìn] to exercise great restraint and exert one's utmost effort; magnanimous

rěn

忍 [rěn]1 (v) 抵受；宽容 to endure; to bear; to suffer; to tolerate ＊我们忍受蚊虫的叮咬。 We tolerate the bites of mosquitoes . 2 (adj) 心肠硬；无

情 hard-hearted ; cruel ＊他对待犯人非常残忍。 He is very cruel to the prisoners.
忍不住 [rěn bú zhù] unable to restrain (oneself) ; unbearable
忍得住 [rěn dé zhù] endurable; bearable ; to put up with
忍耐 [rěn nài] to be tolerant of; to endure; to put up with
忍气吞声 [rěn qì tūn shēng] to restrain one's temper and say nothing; to swallow insults in meek submission
忍辱 [rěn rǔ] to endure contempt
忍受 [rěn shòu] to suffer; to endure; to undergo; to bear
忍痛 [rěn tòng] bear the pain
忍无可忍 [rěn wú kě rěn] to be driven past the limits of forbearance ; to come to the end of one's patience
忍心 [rěn xīn] pitiless ; hard-hearted

稔 [rěn] 1 (n) 庄稼成熟，收获 ripe gain; a harvest ＊丰稔之年。 a year of abundant harvest. 2 (adj) 熟悉 familiar
稔熟 [rěn shú] a ripe and abundant harvest; to be familiar with

荏 [rěn] 1 (n) 草本植物。种子可榨油 a plant, the seeds of which produce oil (perilla ocimoides) 2 (adj) 软弱 weak; feeble; timid ＊色厉内荏。 tough-looking outside but really timid within.
荏苒 [rěn rǎn] in the course of time

rèn

刃 [rèn] 1 (n) 刀剑的锋利部分或刀口 the blade of a knife or sword 2 (v) 用刀杀 to put to blade ＊他手刃仇人。He put his enemy to blade with his own hand.

纫（紉） [rèn] 1 (v) 引线穿针 thread a needle 2 (v) 缝缀 to sew; to stitch ＊她每天学缝纫。She learns sewing every day.

韧（韌） [rèn] (adj) 又柔软又坚固，不容易折断 soft but strong; pilable but tough; pliable; flexible ＊这种人造纤维很韧。This synthetic fibre is flexible.
韧性 [rèn xìng] an obstinate disposition ; tenacity ; flexibility

轫 [rèn] (n) 停车时支住车轮不使转动的木头 a wooden brake; a brake

认（認） [rèn] 1 (v) 分辨；识别 to understand ; to recognise; to realise ＊他改变得太多，我几乎认不得他。He had changed so much that I could hardly recognise him. 2 (v) 表示同意 to acknowledge; to confess; to admit ＊他已供认谋杀那女子。He confessed that he had murdered the girl.
认得 [rèn dé] to know (e.g somebody) ; to recognise
认定 [rèn dìng] to affirm
认可 [rèn kě] to approve ; to give legal force to
认领 [rèn lǐng] to claim (something) one has lost and is found by others
认生 [rèn shēng] (of a child) feeling shy (before a stranger)
认识 [rèn shì] to understand ; to comprehend with; to be aware of; cognition; knowledge
认识论 [rèn shì lùn] theory of knowledge
认输 [rèn shū] to admit defeat
认为 [rèn wéi] to consider; to think; to take for; to regard as
认贼作父 [rèn zéi zuò fù] to take enemies for benefactors
认帐 [rèn zhàng] to acknowledge an account or debt; to confess what one has done or said
认真 [rèn zhēn] earnest ; serious (e.g. attitude)

认罪 [rèn zuì] to confess a crime; to acknowledge one's guilt; to plead gulity

妊 [rèn] (v) 怀孕 to conceive ; to become pregnant

妊娠 [rèn shēn] pregnancy ; to conceive ; to be with child

妊妇 [rèn fù] a pregnant woman

饪(飪) [rèn] (v) 煮熟 to cook

衽(袵) [rèn] 1 (n) 衣襟 the lapels; the breast of a coat 2 (n) 睡觉用的席子 a sleeping mat

任 [rèn] 1(v)委派；使用 to appoint ; to employ; to put in office ＊董事部委任他作校长。 The directors have appointed him as the headmacter 2 (v) 担当 to undertake ; to be responsible for, to hold office ＊他连任二年大使。 He took up office as an ambassador for two years continuously 3 (n) 职位；职责 an official position ; an office ＊他升任为校长。 He was raised to the position of headmaster. 4 (v) 由着；听凭 to allow; to let; to tolerate ＊我们的国土绝不能任由他人宰割。 We could never allow other people to encroach upon our land.

任何 [rèn hé] whatever ; any

任劳任怨 [rèn láo rèn yuàn] to work hard without complaint

任免 [rèn miǎn] to appoint and dismiss

任命 [rèn mìng] to appoint; to nominate

任凭 [rèn píng] let one take his own course; no matter what; despite

任期 [rèn qī] term of office; term of service

任人摆布 [rèn rén bǎi bù] to be at the mercy of; under someone's thumb

任人唯亲 [rèn rén wéi qīn] to appoint people by favouritism

任人唯贤 [rèn rén wéi xián] to appoint people on their merits

任务 [rèn wù] duties ; an assigned task; a role

任性 [rèn xìng] to have one's own way; capricious ; unrestrained ; intractable

任意 [rèn yì] just as one wishes; wilfully ; arbitrarily; at will

任用 [rèn yòng] to appoint; to assign

任职 [rèn zhí] to take office

任重道远 [rèn zhòng dào yuǎn] to shoulder a heavy burden for a long way

rēng

扔 [rēng] (v) 抛，投 to throw; to cast; to hurl ＊他把旧鞋扔掉了。He throws away the old shoes.

réng

仍 [réng] (adv) 依然；还 as before; still; yet ＊你仍须努力。You still have to work diligently. ＊我同意你的看法，但是仍不能答允。I agree with you, but yet I cannot consent.

仍旧 [réng jiù] as before; still; yet

仍然 [réng rán] as usual; as before

rì

日 [rì] 1 (n) 太阳 the sun 2 (n) 白天；昼；跟"夜"相对 day; daytime ＊日有所思，夜有所梦。 What you think about in the daytime, will dream of it at night. 3 (n) 一天；一昼夜 a day ＊一星期有七日。 There are seven days in a week. ＊大多数报纸每日出版。Most newspapers appear daily.

日报 [rì bào] a daily newspaper

日薄西山 [rì bó xī shān] the sun

is pressing on the western hills — one's days are rapidly declining ; in one's later days

日常 [rì cháng] day-to-day; usual ; daily; everyday

日程 [rì chéng] a daily schedule ; agenda for the day

日光 [rì guāng]sunshine ; sunlight ; rays of the sun

日光灯 [rì guāng dēng] flourescent light ; daylight lamp

日光浴 [rì guāng yù]sun bath

日记 [rì jì] diary

日积月累 [rì jī yuè lěi] by gradual accumulation ; day's and month's multiplying

日历 [rì lì] a calendar

日暮途穷 [rì mù tú qíong]in one's decline ; on one's last legs to head for doom

日期 [rì qī] a date

日上三竿 [rì shàng sān gān] the day is getting late

日蚀 [rì shí] eclipse of the sun ; solar eclipse constant changes

日薪工友 [rì xīn gōng yǒu]waged worker

日新月异 [rì xīn yuè yí] to change rapidly; to bring about new changes day after day

日夜 [rì yè]day and night

日益 [rì yì] more and more; with each passing day; day by day

日以继夜 [rì yǐ jì yè] night and day

日用品 [rì yòng pǐn] articles for daily use; daily necessities

日子 [rì zǐ] day; date; a particular day; life; living condition

róng

容 [róng] 1 (v) 包含；盛载 to hold;to contain ✱ 这房间可容纳五十人。The room could hold fifty persons. 2 (v)让；允许 to permit;to allow of;to tolerate ✱ 主权领土不容侵犯。Sovereignty and land allowed no encroachments upon. 3 (n)相貌；外貌 appearance;look ✱ 他的脸上带着笑容。A smiling look comes to his face.

容光焕发 [róng guāng huàn fā] glowing with health and in high spirits

容积 [róng jī] volume

容量 [róng liàng] capacity

容貌 [róng mào] (a person's) facial appearance and expression

容纳 [róng nà] to contain;to accomodate;to hold

容器 [róng qì] container

容忍 [róng ren] to endure;to tolerate;to stand

容许 [róng xǔ] to permit;to allow

容易 [róng yì] easy; to be liable to;likely

溶 [róng] 1 (v) 物质在水或其他液体中化开 to dissolve ✱ 盐溶解在水中。Salt dissolves in water. 2 (v) 固体化为液体 to melt;to thaw

溶化 [róng huà] to melt;to thaw;to dissolve

溶济 [róng jì] a solvent

溶解 [róng jiě] to dissolve;to thaw; to melt;to disintegrate

熔(鎔) [róng] (v) 固体金属；使变成液体 to fuse; to smelt

熔炉 [róng lú] smelting rurnace

熔点 [róng diǎn] the smelting point

熔化 [róng huà] to smelt;to fuse

熔线 [róng xiàn] fuse

榕 [róng] (n)常绿乔木有气根。生长在热带和亚热带。木材供制器具、薪炭等用 the banyan tree

蓉 [róng] [芙蓉] [fú róng] (n) 花名 a flower; the hibiscus mulabilis

戎 [róng] (n) 军事；军队 military; army 投笔从戎 to give up secretaryship and join the army.

戎马 [róng mǎ] warfare; the army

戎装 [róng zhuāng] martial array; in military dress

绒(絨) [róng] 1 (n) 细软的毛 velvet; wool; floss; nap; down 2 (n) 毛织品 woollen cloth ∗ 法兰绒。flannels ∗ 火绒 tinder ∗ 天鹅绒 velvets ∗ 斜绒 twills

绒线 [róng xiàn] woollen yarn; floss for embroidering

荣(榮) [róng] 1 (adj) 茂盛；兴旺 prosperity; prosperous; flourishing; thriving 2 (adj) 有好名声；受人敬重 glorious; honourable; glory; honour ∗ 和平带来繁荣。Peace brings prosperity. ∗ 承蒙您的邀请；我觉得很荣幸。I deem it an honour to accept your invitation.

荣幸 [róng xìng] honoured; honourable

荣华 [róng huá] glory and prosperity

荣耀 [róng yào] glorious; splendid; honour

荣誉 [róng yù] honour; an honourable reputation

融 [róng] 1 (v) 溶化 to melt; to dissolve; to thaw ∗ 春天到来了，冰雪开始融化。When spring comes, the snow begins to thaw 2 (v) 调和 to blend; to harmonize; to compromise ∗ 这个新设计融合了中西式的优点。The new design compromises the merits of Chinese and Western styles.

融合 [róng hé] to reconcile; to harmonize; to compromise; to blend; to amalgamate

融化 [róng huà] to melt; to thaw

融会贯通 [róng huì guan tōng] to be well versed in; to understand thoroughly

融解 [róng jiě] to melt; to fuse; to liquefy; to dissolve

融洽 [róng qià] harmonious

融融 [róng róng] happy; joyful; cheerful

茸 [róng] 1 (adj) 草初生时细小柔软的样子 soft and downy (of young grass) 2 (n) 鹿的带细毛的幼角 young antler of the deer

rǒng

冗 [rǒng] 1 (adj) 多余的 extra; superfluous 2 (adj) 繁忙 busy ∗ 他事务烦冗。He is very busy with business

冗长 [rǒng cháng] lengthy; tediously long; cumbersome (e.g. writings; speeches)

冗员 [rǒng yuán] extra officials; officials out of office

冗杂 [rǒng zá] confused; mixed

róu

柔 [róu] 1 (adj) 软弱 soft; tender; delicate; feeble ∗ 他的声音柔弱。His voice sounded feeble. 2 (adj) 和顺 mild; tame; gentle; submissive ∗ 这鹦鹉很柔顺。This parrot is very tame.

柔道 [róu dào] judo

柔和 [róu hé] mild; gentle; soft

柔软体操 [róu ruǎn tǐ cāo] physical fitness exercise

柔软 [róu ruǎn] soft; flexible

柔术 [róu shù] jujetsu

柔顺 [róu shùn] submissive; meek; tame

揉 [róu] 1 (v) 来回地摩擦、搓弄 to rub; to massage ∗ 孩子在揉眼睛。The kid is rubbing his eyes. 2 (v) 把直的弄弯 to bend

揉目 [róu mù] rub the eyes

糅 [róu] (v) 混杂 to mix; to mingle

蹂 [róu] (v)踩；践踏 to tread;to trample on
蹂躏 [róulìn] to trample on; ravage; crush under one's feet
鞣 [róu] (v) 生皮加工使其变软 to tan (the leather)
鞣料 [róu iào] tan
鞣酸 [róu suān] tanin

ròu

肉 [ròu] 1 (n) 人或动物体内附在骨骼上的软物质 flesh;meat 2 (n) 果实中可以吃的部分 the edible part of fruits
肉搏 [ròu bó] hand-to-hand fighting;to come to close quarters
肉瘤 [ròu liú] a tumor
肉麻 [ròu má] disgusting;nauseating;sickening
肉票 [ròu piào] captives held for ransom
肉松 [ròu sōng] dried fluffy meat
肉体 [ròu tǐ] the body
肉眼 [ròu yǎn] the naked eye

rú

儒 [rú](n)孔子的学派 Confucianism; confunianist
儒家 [rú jiā] Confucianists;confucian school
儒生 [rú shāng] Confucian scholars
孺 [rú] (n) 幼儿；小孩子 child;baby 妇孺 women and children
濡 [rú] 1 (v)沾湿 to moisten;to wet; to soak in
襦 [rú] (n)短衣 a short coat;a jacket
蠕 [rú] (adj) 象虫那样慢慢地爬行的样子 wriggling
蠕动 [rú dòng] to wriggle
如 [rú] 1 (adv) 依照 according to;as * 会议如期召开。The meeting is held as scheduled.2 (adj)象；同 like; similar to * 筹募基金运动如火如荼地展开。The fund raising campaign flared like a fire set to dry tinder. 3(v)比得上；及 to compare favourably; to be as.....as * 我们的意志坚如钢。Our will is as strong as steel. 4 (conj)假使 if * 你如不努力学习，就要落后了。If you do not study diligently, you will lag behind.
如常 [rú cháng] common place;ordinary;as usual
如出一辙 [rú chūyī zhé] one and the same;identical;originate from the same source
如此 [rú cǐ] so;thus;such;like this
如法炮制 [rú fǎ pào zhì] to follow suit;to be modelled on
如故 [rú gù] as usual;as before;to be like old friends
如果 [rúguǒ] if;suppose;provided
如何 [rú hé] how? what?
如火如荼 [rú huǒ rú tú] flaring like a fire set to dry tinder;momentous; imposing;grand;roaring
如虎添翼 [rú hǔ tiān yì] just like adding wings to a tiger
如获至宝 [rú huò zhǐ bǎo] as if one has gained treasured possessions
如今 [rú jīn] now;nowadays;these days
如饥似渴 [rú jī sì kě] thirst for
如期 [rú qī] in time;as scheduled
如丧考妣 [rú sāng kǎo bǐ] as bereaved as at the loss of one's parents
如上 [rú shàng] as above
如释重负 [rú shì zhòng fù] just like a big load has been taken off one's mind
如下 [rú xià] as follows
如意 [rú yì] as one wishes;as one likes it
如愿以偿 [rú yuàn yǐ cháng] to obtain what is desired;to achieve what one wishes
如鱼得水 [rú yú dé shuǐ] like fish getting into water;readily pleased; one's desire is gratified
茹 [rú] (v) 吃 to eat

茹苦含辛 [rú kǔ hán xīn] to eat bitterness;to suffer
茹毛饮血 [rú máo yǐn xué] to eat the hairy flesh and drink the blood

rǔ

汝 [rǔ] (pron) 你 you;thou

辱 [rǔ] 1 (n) 耻羞；丑；不体面；不名誉可耻的事 to disgrace;a disgrace,disgraceful *贫而无欺则不为辱。Honest poverty is no disgrace. *守军宁死不辱。The garrison chose death before disgrace.
辱骂 [rǔ mà] to vilify;to abuse;to revile
辱命 [rǔ mìng] to dishonour one's commission

乳 [rǔ] 1 (n) 人和动物的哺乳器官 breasts 2 (n) 奶汁 milk 3 (adj) 幼小的或初生的（鸟兽） baby or young(birds or animals);(chick; cub)
乳房 [rǔ fáng] the breasts
乳鸽 [rǔ gē] the chicks of pigeons
乳牛 [rǔ niú] milk cow
乳燕 [rǔ yán] the chicks of swallows
乳汁 [rǔ zhī] milk
乳猪 [rǔ zhū] piglings

rù

缛（縟）[rù] (adj) 繁多；繁重 complex and elaborate *我们不要繁文缛节。We do not want elaborate ceremonies.

蓐 [rù] (n) 草席；草垫子 mat

褥 [rù] (n)装绵絮的或用兽皮制成的铺垫物 a mattress;a cushion

入 [rù] (v) 进 to enter;to go into;to come in(into) *这些货物不准入口。These goods are not allowed to be imported.
入不敷出 [rù bù fú chū] the income falls short of expenditure
入场券 [rù chǎng juàn] entrance ticket;admission ticket
入超 [rù chāo] adverse trade balance;trade deficit;import excess
入籍 [rù jí] be naturalised
入境 [rù jìng] to enter country;entry(e.g. visa)
入口 [rù kǒu] entrance;import
入手 [rù shǒu] to begin;to start;to get under way
入睡 [rù shuì] to fall asleep
入伍 [rù wǔ] to enlist;to enroll;to join the army
入席 [rù xí] to take one's seat
入息 [rù xí] income
入狱 [rù yù] be sent to prison
入学 [rù xué] to enrol(for school)
入乡随俗 [rù xiāng suí sú] in Rome, do as the Romans do

ruǎn

软(軟,輭) [ruǎn] (adj) 柔弱；跟"强硬"相对 soft;yielding ;pliable;weak
软骨头 [ruǎn gú tóu] a cowardice
软化 [ruǎn huà] to soften up;to become conciliatory;to attenuate
软禁 [ruǎn jìn] to detain a person
软片 [ruǎn piàn] film;negatives
软和 [ruǎn huo] soft and tender
软绵绵 [ruǎn mián mián] velvety; feathery
软弱 [ruǎn ruò] weak; feeble
软弱性 [ruǎn ruò xìng] weakness; flabbiness
软席 [ruǎn xí] soft(cushioned)seats
软体动物 [ruǎn tǐ dòng wù] mollusc e.g. snail
软硬兼施 [ruǎn yìng jiān shī] to apply the soft and hard tactics at the same time; to couple persuasion with force

ruǐ

蕊（蘂）[ruǐ] 1 (n) 花心，种子植物的生殖器官，分雄蕊，雌蕊两种 stamen or pistil of a flower 2 (n) 未开的花 unopened flowers;buds

ruì

蚋(蜹) [ruì] (n) 昆虫。体形象苍蝇，刺吸牛、羊等牲畜血液 a gnat

锐(鋭) [ruì] (adj) 锋利 sharp

锐不可当 [ruì bù kě dāng] a keenness that cannot be stopped;high spirits that cannot be dampened

锐角 [ruì jiǎo] an acute angle

锐利 [ruì lì] keen;sharp;pointed

锐气 [ruì qì] (man with)brains and drive;elan

睿(叡) [ruì] (adj)看得清楚，看得深远 far-sighted and clear

睿智 [ruì zhì] intelligent and far-sighted

瑞 [ruì] (n) 吉祥；好预兆 a good omen

瑞兽 [ruì sòu] auspicious animal

瑞色 [ruì sè] a lovely colour

rùn

闰(閏) [rùn] (adj) *历法上把年月中余下来的时间积成一月或一日。 intercalary;extra; leap

闰年 [rùn nián] a leap year

闰日 [rùn rì] the intercalary day in leap year; February 29th

闰月 [rùn yuè] an intercalary month for the lunar calendar

润(潤) [rùn] 1 (adj)不干燥；干湿适当 moist *雨露滋润禾苗壮。The plants grow sturdy with the moist from the rain and dew. 2 (v) 加油或加水，使不干枯 to moisten;to lubricate

润滑 [rùn huá] lubricating

润滑油 [rùn huá yóu] lubricating oil;lubricating grease

润色 [rùn sè] larded with;to give the final polish to

润泽 [rùn zé] glossy;agreeable; enrich by favours

ruò

若 [ruò] 1 (conj)假如；如果 if;suppose;in case *知识分子若不把理论和实践相结合必将一事无成。The intellectuals will accomplish nothing if they do not intergrate their theories with practices. 2 (conj)似；好象 as if *他装出若无其事的样子。 He pretends as if nothing has occurred.

若干 [ruò gān] a certain amount; how many?how much?

若然 [ruò rán] if so;if this is the case

若即若离 [ruò jí ruò lí] far away; seemingly attached to each other

偌 [ruò] (adv)那么；这样 that;this *李叔偌大年纪了，还要出卖劳力。Uncle Lee still has to sell his own labour at this old age.

箬 [ruò] (n) 竹皮；笋壳 bamboo sheath

弱 [ruò] 1 (adj)气力小，势力差，跟“强”相对 weak;feeble *他的身体很弱。 He is physically weak. 2 (v)差；不足 less by ;short of *五分之一弱。less by one fifth

弱点 [ruò diǎn] weak point;weakness

弱不禁风 [ruò bù jīn fēng] the body is so weak that it cannot stand the wind

弱国 [ruò guó] weak countries

弱肉强食 [ruò ròu qiáng shí] the weak will stand an easy prey to the strong; jungle law

弱小 [ruò xiǎo] small and weak

弱者 [ruò zhě] the weak

S

sā

撒 [sā] (v) 放开 set loose; cast ＊渔夫在撒网。 The fisherman is casting a net.

撒哈拉沙漠 [sāhālāshāmò] sahara Desert

撒野 [sāyě] to act impudently

撒谎 [sā huǎng] to tell a lie

撒手 [sāshǒu] let go the hand; relinquish one's hold on ; wash one's hands off the matter; give it up; refuse to take any further interest in

另见 [sǎ]

sǎ

洒（灑） [sǎ] (v) 撒布水或液体 to sprinkle water or liquid on the ground ＊ 为了不使尘土飘扬,他在地上洒了一些水。In order to stop the dust from flying about ,he sprinkles some water on the ground.

撒 [sǎ] (v) 散布 to scatter ＊稻农在撒种。The padi planter is sowing the seeds.

撒娇 [sǎjiāo] to act pettishly ; to tease

另见 [sā]

sà

萨（薩） [sà] (n) 姓 surname

卅 [sà] (n) 三十 thirty

飒（颯） [sà] (adj) 形容风吹动树木枝叶等的声音the sound of wind blowing at the leaves of trees ＊秋风飒飒。The autumn wind is soughing.

飒爽 [sàshuǎng] lively

sāi

腮 [sāi] (n) 脸的两侧的下半部 the cheek

鳃（鰓） [sāi] (n) 鱼类的器官，在头部两边 the gills of fish

塞 [sāi] 1 (v) 堵，填满 to block; to fill up; stuff ＊房子里面塞满了东西。The room is stuffed with many things.
2 (n) 堵住瓶口和器物的东西 a stopper ＊瓶塞。bottle stopper. ＊软木塞。 cork.

另见 [sài]
[sè]

sài

塞 [sài] (n) 边界上险要的地方 a strategic spot at the frontier ＊要塞。an important pass at the frontier.

塞翁失马 [sài wēng shī mǎ] a blessing in disguise

另见 [se]

赛（賽）[sài] 1 (v) 比赛 compete; contest 2 (n) 比赛项目 a tournament; a race; a contest; a competition 3 (v) 胜过，比得上 excel; surpass

赛车 [sài chē] car-racing ; a car race

赛船 [sàichuán] a regatta; a boat race

赛马 [sài mǎ] horse racing ; a horse race

sān

三 [sān] 1 (n) 数词 three 2 (adj) 表示多数或多次 many times ∗我一而再，再而三的劝告他。I have advised him many times.

三八国际妇女节 [Sān Bā Guójì Fù Nǔ Jié] the International Women's Day (March 8th)

三倍 [sānbèi] treble; triple; threefold

三次 [sāncì] thrice; three times

三等 [sānděng] third class

三国 [Sān Guò] the three kingdoms - Wei, Shu, Wu in ancient China (222 - 265 A.D.)

三合土 [sānhétǔ] concrete

三夹板 [sānjiábǎn] plywood

三角形 [sānjiǎoxíng] triangle

三角洲 [sānjiǎozhōu] a delta

三K党 [sānkèidǎng] the Ku Klux Klan

三棱镜 [sānléngjìng] a prism

三轮车 [sānlùnchē] a trishaw

三文治 [sānwénzhì] sandwiches

三心两意 [sānxīn-liǎngyì] half-hearted; hesitant

三月 [sānyuè] March

叁 [sān] (n) "三"的大写 the second form of "三", used in accounts to present fraud

sǎn

散 [sǎn] 1 (v) 松开 loosen; come off ∗绳子没绑好，都散了。The string was not properly tied and it came off. 2 (adj) 没有约束 without restraint ∗我们应该防止自由散漫的作风。We should avoid the liberal and undisciplined style of work. 3 (v) 分裂，组织解体 break up; disperse; disband ∗戏班散了。 The troupe is broken up. 4 (adj) 零碎的，不集中的 odd; scattered ∗他是一名散工。He is an odd job labourer. 5 (n) 药末 medicine in powder form

散兵 [sǎnbīng] disbanded soldiers

散光 [sǎnguāng] astigmatism

散乱 [sǎnluàn] be strewn in disorder

散文 [sǎnwén] a short essay; prose

散装 [sǎnzhuāng] packed in small quantities

另见 [sàn]

伞（傘）[sǎn] 1 (n) 挡雨或遮太阳的用具，可張可收 umbrella 2 (n) 象伞的东西 things shaped like an umbrella ∗降落伞。parachute.

sàn

三 [sàn] thrice; to treble

三思而行 [sànsīérxíng] think thrice before you act

散 [sàn] 1 (v) 分开，由聚集而分离 disperse; dismiss ∗主席宣佈散会。The chairman dismissed the meeting 2 (v) 分发，分给 distribute ∗我帮他散发传单。I helped him to distribute the pamphlets. 3 (v) 排遣；放松 to take off; to loosen; to relax

散播 [sànbō] to spread

散步 [sàn bù] to take a stroll

散布 [sànbù] scatter; disperse

散场 [sàn chǎng] the show has ended and the audience leaves

散会 [sànhuì] dismiss a meeting

另见 [sǎn]

sāng

桑 [sāng] (n) 落叶乔木，树叶可以喂蚕。树皮可以造纸。果实可吃。叶、果、枝、根、皮可供药用 the mulberry tree

丧 (喪) [sāng](n) 有关人死亡的事 mourning; things related to a dead person * 治丧委员会。 a funeral committee

丧服 [sāngfú] mourning clothes
丧家 [sāngjiā] the bereaved family
丧事 [sāngshì] funeral rites
另见 [sàng]

sǎng

嗓 [sǎng] 1 (n) 嗓子，喉咙 the throat * 他的嗓子疼。He had a sore throat. 2 (n) 发出的声音 voice * 他的嗓音洪亮。His voice is loud.

sàng

丧 (喪) [sàng] (v) 丢掉，失去 lose; miss * 在战争中，他丧失了两个儿了。 He lost two sons in the war.

丧胆 [sàndǎn] to lose heart; to be discouraged
丧尽天良 [sàng jìn tiān liáng] lost all conscience; vicious and brutal to the extreme
丧命 [sàng mìng] dead
丧气 [sàng qì] in low spirits; melancholy
另见 [sāng]

sāo

搔 [sāo] (v) 用指甲轻轻地抓 scratch

搔头 [sāotóu] to scratch the head — in perplexity

骚 (騷) [sāo] (v) 扰乱 to disturb; to annoy ; to stir * 足球迷因争购门票而骚动起来。 The football fans were stirred up by the rush for admission tickets.

骚动 [sāodòng] disturb; harass; ferment; riots
骚乱 [sāoluàn] trouble; commotion
骚扰 [sāorǎo] disturb; trouble; vex

臊 [sāo] (n)腥臭 rank ; rancid ; frowzy ; fetid * 狐 臊。 body odour .
另见 [sào]

缫 (繅) [sāo] (v) 从茧抽丝 to reel silk from cocoons

sǎo

扫 (掃) [sǎo] 1 (v) 抹除； 清除 to sweep; to clear away * 清道夫每天扫净街道。The scavenger sweeps the road clean every day. 2 (v) 消灭 to exterminate * 政府致力扫除文盲。 The government spares no effort to exterminate illiteracy. 3 (v) 迅速地横掠过去 sweep across very fast. * 几只军用飞机在长空里一扫而过。 A few military planes sped across the sky.

扫除 [sǎochú] erase ; eliminate; sweep out
扫荡 [sǎodàng] to clear; to wipe out; to annihilate with force
扫雷艇 [sǎoléitǐng] a mine-sweeper
扫墓 [sǎo mù] to visit the grave and clear the grass grown around it
扫射 [sǎoshè] to strafe
扫兴 [sǎo xìng] disappointing
扫帚 [sǎozhǒu] a broom
扫帚星 [sǎozhǒuxīng] a comet
另见 [sào]

嫂 [sǎo] 1 (n)哥哥的妻子 an elder brother's wife; sister-in-law 2 (n) 称呼一般年纪不大的已婚的妇女 young married woman

sào

臊 [sào] (adj) 羞 shy * 他很害臊。 He is very shy.
另见 [sāo]

扫 (掃) [sào] (n) 清除拉圾的工具 a broom

sè

啬(嗇) [sè] (adj) 应当用的财物舍不得用 stingy ＊他很吝啬。He is very stingy.

穑(穡) [sè] (v) 收割 to crop; to reap ＊须知稼穑之艰难。You should know how difficult it is to harvest the crop.

涩(澀) [sè] 1 (adj) 粗糙不光滑 rough＊轮轴已发涩生锈，该上油了。The axle is rough and rusty; it should be lubricated. 2 (adj) 味道生硬而不甘美 harsh; astringent ＊这果子还不熟、有涩味。This fruit is unripe and tastes harsh 3 (adj) 语文生硬难懂 abstruse; intractable; obscure (as of language) ＊这古文词句晦涩。The phrases of this old essay are obscure and difficult to understand.

色 [sè] 1 (n) 颜色 colour ＊红色 red 2 (n) 脸色 countenance; expression on the face ＊他喜形于色。His happiness shows on his face. 3 (n) 情景 scene ＊这里的景色很美丽。The scenery here is very beautiful. 4 (n)种类 kind; sort ＊货色齐全。Different kinds of goods are available. 5 (n) 物品的质量 the quality of things 6 (n) 情欲 lust; sexual desire＊ 色情文化。pornography

色彩 [sècǎi] colour

色调 [sèdiào] tone

色厉内荏 [sèlìnèirěn] tough-looking outside but really timid within; strong looking outside but brittle within; fierce of visage but faint of heart

色盲 [sèmáng] colour blind

色泽 [sèzé] lustre

瑟 [sè] (n) 古弦乐器 a kind of harp or lute

瑟瑟 [sèsè] the sound of wind

塞 [sè] (v) 阻隔不通 to block; to stop up; to hinder; to fill up.

塞责 [sèzé] to evade responsibility; perfuntory performance of duties

塞职 [sèzhí] to shirk one's duties

另见 [sài]

sēn

森 [sēn] 1 (adj) 树木多而密 overgrown with trees. 2 (adj) 茂密 luxuriant; abundant 3 (adj) 阴暗的 sombre; dark. 4 (adj) 严厉的 severe; strict

森林 [sēnlín] a forest; a jungle

森森 [sēnsēn] luxuriant; abundant

森严 [sēnyán] solemn; severe; strict

sēng

僧 [sēng] (n) 和尚 a buddhist monk

僧侣 [sēnglǚ] monks; ecclesiastics

shā

纱(紗) [shā] 1 (n) 用棉花、麻纺成的细缕 yarn ＊ 棉纱。cotton yarn 2 (n) 经纬稀疏的布或类似物 gauze ＊ 纱布 gauze 薄纱 muslin 玻璃纱 organdie 铁纱 wire gauze

纱厂 [shāchǎng] a cotton mill

纱窗 [shāchuāng] screen window

纱锭 [shādìng] (cotton) spindles

纱线 [shāxiàn] yarn; thread

砂 [shā] 1 (n) 矿物和岩石的碎屑 gravel sand ＊锡砂。tin gravel; tin ore. 2 (n) 细碎象砂的物质 material in granulated form ＊砂糖。granulated sugar

砂砾 [shālì] gravel; sand

砂岩 [shāyán] sandstone

砂纸 [shāzhǐ] emery paper; sand paper

沙 [shā] 1 (n) 细碎的石粒 sand ＊沙土。sandy soil 2 (n) 象沙一样的东西 things like sand in small particles ＊ 豆沙。peas ground into particle form. 3 (adj) 嗓音不清脆，不响亮 hoarse in voice ＊他的喉咙疼，所以声音沙哑。 His voice is hoarse because he has a sore throat

沙蚕 [shācán] sea-centipede

沙丁鱼 [shādīngyú] sardine

沙皇 [shāhuáng] czar; tzar

沙漠 [shāmò] a desert

沙丘 [shāqiū] sand hill; dune

沙石 [shāshí] sand-stone; pebbles

沙滩 [shātān] a sand bank

沙文主义 [shāwénzhǔyì] chauvinism

沙眼 [shāyǎn] trachoma

沙子 [shāzi] sand

鲨(鯊) [shā] (n) 也叫"沙鱼""鲛"鱼类，生活在海洋中，种类很多，性凶猛，捕食其他鱼类。鳍叫鱼翅，是珍贵的食品，肉可食用，皮可制革 shark

痧 [shā] (n) 中医指中暑霍乱等急性病 a sun-stroke; cholera or other acute diseases ＊他突然间得了痧症。 He had cholera suddenly.

杀(殺) [shā] 1 (v) 弄死，使失去生命 kill; slaughter ＊他杀人不见血。 He kills people without leaving any sign. 2 (v) 战斗 fight ＊我们已经杀出重围。 We have fought out of the encirclement. 3 (v) 消减 reduce; diminish ＊那个孩子在影片上映时哭闹。真是杀风景。 The child cried in the midst of the show. How disenchanting it was! 4 (v) 止住；制动 to stop; to brake ＊司机在转弯时杀车。 The driver braked around the curves. 5 (adv) 到了极点；很；非常 to the extreme; very; exceedingly ＊气杀 very angry 急杀 worried to death

杀车 [shāchē] to brake

杀虫剂 [shāchóngjì] insecticide pesticide

杀风景 [shāfēngjǐng] spoil the landscape;(fig.)dampen one's enthusiasm

杀害 [shāhài] to kill a person

杀价 [shājià] to force down prices; to slash prices

杀菌剂 [shājùnjì] a sterilizer; a germicide; a fungicide

杀戮 [shālù] slaughter

杀气腾腾 [shāqìténgténg] menacingly, murderously

杀人犯 [shārénfàn] homicide, murder

杀生 [shāshēng] to slaughter the animals

煞 [shā] 1 (v) 消减 reduce 2 (v) 止住 stop

shǎ

傻 [shǎ] 1 (adj) 愚蠢不聪明 stupid; foolish; silly ＊他一点儿也不傻。 He is not stupid at all. 2 (adj) 楞呆 stunned ＊他听到消息後，吓得傻傻地楞在那儿。 He was stunned after hearing the news.

shà

霎 [shà] 1 (n) 小雨 a slight shower 2 (n) 极短的时间，一会儿 an instant ＊一声巨响，霎时天空出现了千万朵美丽的火花。 After a loud noise, a multitude of flame-sparks instantly bloomed like flowers in the sky.

厦 [shà] (n) 高大的房子 a lofty building ＊高楼大厦。 high rise buildings

煞 [shà] 1 (n) 迷信说法，指凶神 demon ＊凶神恶煞。demons 2 (adj) 极，很 very＊为了把书店办好，他们煞费苦心。In order to make the book shop a success, they have spent much effort.

煞白 [shàbái] deadly pale

煞费苦心 [shàfèikǔxīn] cudgel or rack one's brains; painstakingly

煞气 [shàqì] the active spirit of death

煞有介事 [shàyǒujièshì] pull a sanctimonious face; pretend to be serious

另见 [shā]

shāi

筛(篩) [shāi] 1 (n) 有孔器具，用以分别物质的粗细。a sieve 2 (v) 用筛分隔东西 to sift; to strain ＊马来妇女在筛米。The Malay woman is sifting the rice 3 (v) 敲打 beat ＊他筛了二下锣。He beats the gong twice.

筛骨 [shāigǔ] the ethmoid bone

筛酒 [shāijuǐ] to strain wine; to pour out liquor

shài

晒(曬) [shài] (v) 放在阳光下使干燥 to dry in the sun ＊晒衣服。to dry the clothes in the sun. ＊晒谷。to dry the rice grains in the sun.

shān

删 [shān] (v) 去掉 to cancel ＊这一段可以删去。This passage can be cancelled.

删除 [shānchú] to efface; to erase

删繁就简 [shānfánjìujiǎn] to simplify

删改 [shāngǎi] to correct; to revise

删节 [shānjé] abridge; chop out

删节号 [shānjiéhào] abridgement mark

删去 [shānqù] delete; cut; to strike out; blot out; write off; erase; cancel; obliterate

姗 [shān]〔姗姗〕(adj) 走路缓慢从容的样子 walking slowly ＊一对新人姗姗来迟。The newly-wed walked slowly and came late.

珊 [shān]〔珊瑚〕(n) 暖海产的一种虫类群体所分泌的石灰质的骨骼有红白等色形状象树枝，可做装饰品 coral

磨菇珊瑚 鹿角珊瑚

玫瑰珊瑚 脑珊瑚

苫 [shān] (n) 草席 a straw mat

苫次 [shāncı] in mourning

另见 [shàn]

杉 [shān] (n) 也叫"沙木"，常绿乔木树干又高又直，可供建筑和制器具用 fir tree

衫 [shān] (n) 衣 clothes; garments

扇 [shān] (v) 摇动物体使空气流动生风 to fan ＊她扇走食物上的苍蝇。She fanned away the flies from her food.

扇动 [shāndòng] to incite

扇风点火 [shanfēngdiǎnhuǒ] fan up the fire; stir up; make trouble

扇惑 [shānhuó] to agitate; to deceive

扇乱 [shānluàn] to stir up revolt

另见 [shàn]

揙 [shān] 1(v) 扇凉 to fan 2(v) 批打 to strike

煽 [shān] 1(v) 扇火 to fan into a flame 2(v)鼓动 to incite; to instigate

山 [shān] (n) 陆地上隆起的部份。mountain ; hill ; range ＊ 高山峻岭。tall and steep mountain ranges

山隘 [shānài] a mountain pass
山崩 [shānbēng] a land-slide
山洞 [shāndòng] a cave
山峰 [shānfēng] mountain peaks
山歌 [shāngē] folk song
山谷 [shāngǔ] valley ; ravine

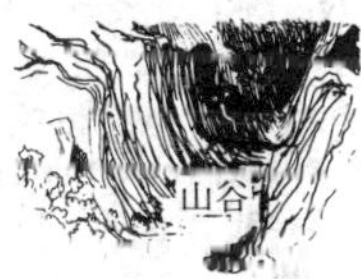

山河 [shānhé] mountains and rivers ; the country
山脊 [shānjǐ] mountain ridge
山鸡 [shānjī] pheasant
山脉 [shānmái] mountain range
山盟海誓 [shān méng hǎi shì] a solemn pledge
山炮 [shānpào] mountain gun; pack howitzer
山坡 [shānpō] a hill slope
山穷水尽 [shānqíongshuǐjìn] at the end of one's rope
山水 [shānshuǐ] landscape
山兔 [shāntù] hare
山羊 [shānyáng] a goat

山楂 [hānzhā] the hill haw
山珍海味 (本作"山珍海错") [shānzhēnhǎiwèi] from the hills and seas delicacies

山竹 [shānzhú] mangosteen

舢 [shān] (n) 舢舨，一种小船 a sampan

膻 [shān] (n) 羊臭 rank ordour of sheep or goat

芟 [shān] (v) 割草 to cut down; to mow

shǎn

睒 [shǎn] (v) 眨眼，眼睛很快地开闭 to wink

陕(陜) [shǎn] (n) 陕西省的简称 the province of Shensi

闪(閃) 1 (n)突然发出的光 a flash of light ＊ 2(v) 光亮突然一现 flash ＊ 闪电闪过天空。 The lightning flashed over the sky. 3 (v) 侧身避开 dodge ; evade ; shun ; avoid ＊ 那工人来不及闪避那根掉下来的木棒。 The worker failed to dodge the peice of falling rod. 4 (v) 扭伤 to sprain ＊ 他闪了腰。 He sprained his hip.

闪避 [shǎnbì] dodge
闪电 [shǎndiàn] lightning
闪电战 [shǎndiànzhàn] a lightning war
闪光 [shǎnguāng] to glitter; to sparkle
闪光摄影 [shǎnguāngshèyǐng] flash-light photography
闪烁 [shǎnshuó] flash ; glitter
闪烁其词 [shǎnshuòqící] to dodge about; to evade issues
闪耀 [shǎnyào] to twinkle

shàn

善 [shàn] 1 (adj) 好，优秀，品质或言行好 good ; virtuous ＊ 善欲人知，不为真善。good deeds done for mere show are not really good. 2 (adv) 很会，擅长 good at ; skilful in ＊这支军队勇敢善战。This troop is brave and skilful in fighting. 3 (adv) 容易 easily＊他很善忘。He is very forgetful. 4 (adj) 熟悉 familiar ＊他很面善。He looks familiar

善本 [shànběn] rare editions

善恶 [shànè] good and evil

善后 [shànhòu] rehabilitate

善男信女 [shànnán xìnnǔ] pious people

善事 [shànshì] charity

善意 [shànyì] good-will; well-meant

善于 [shànyú] good at; expert at; skilled in

善终 [shànzhōng] a natural death

缮(繕) [shàn] 1 (v) 整理，修补 arrange; repair 2(v) 抄写 copy ＊他帮忙缮写一分议定书。He helps to write out a copy of the Agreement.

膳 [shàn] (n) 饭食 lunch or dinner ＊膳宿费。fees for food and lodging.

蟮 [shàn] (n) 蚓蚯 the earth worm

鳝(鱔) [shàn] (n) 一种鱼类也叫"黄鳝"；体黄褐色有黑斑，无鳞；生活在池塘、小河、稻田等处可供食用 the yellow eel

禅(禪) [shàn] 1(v) 帝王让位 to abdicate 2 (v) 祭山川 to fice to the hills and rivers.
另见 [chán]

擅 [shàn] 1 (v) 自作主张，独断独行 act without permission ＊未经批准不得擅自离开。You cannot leave without permission. 2 (v) 善于，专长 skilled in; well-versed in; expert in ＊他擅长画人物。He is skilled in painting portraits.

擅长 [shàncháng] be good at; be expert at

擅自 [shànzì] arbitrarily; take the liberty; take it upon oneself to; without permission; on one's own

讪(訕) [shàn] (v) 毁谤 to abuse; to revile; to speak evil of

讪笑 [shànxiáo] to mock at; to laugh at

讪言 [shànyán] to slander; backbiting

疝 [shàn] (n) 内脏脱出体腔的病症 rupture; hernia; stricture; swelling of the testicles

扇 [shàn] 1 (n) 一种纸或丝布作的生风取凉的用具 fan 2 (n) 量词用来计算门窗 numeral for doors and windows ＊一扇门 a door.
另见 [shān]

骟 [shàn] (v) 阉割（禽畜）to geld (a domestic animal)

赡(贍) [shàn] 1 (v) 供给，供养 supply; maintain ＊赡养 alimony. 2(adj) 丰富，充足 abundant; sufficient

苫 [shàn] (v) 用草席，布等遮盖 to cover with straw mat or cloth ＊要下雨了，快把水泥袋苫上。It is going to rain, quickly cover the cement bag.
另见 [shān]

shāng

伤(傷) [shāng] 1 (n) 身体受损坏 injury; wound＊他受了重伤。He sustained a serious injury. 2 (v) 损害 harm; impair; hurt ＊烟酒伤身。Cigarettes and liquors are harmful to the body.

伤风 [shānfēng] to catch cold

伤害 [shānghài] to harm

伤痕 [shānghén] scar

伤口 [shāngkǒu] wound

伤逝 [shāngshì] to mourn a dead person

伤脑筋 [shāng nǎojīn] to wreck one's brain

伤天害理 [shāng tiān hài lǐ] brutal; without conscience

伤亡 [shāng wáng] casualty
伤心 [shāngxīn] sad; grievous; heart-broken

商 [shāng] 1 (v) 交换意见 discuss ∗有事面商。 something to be discussed personally 2 (n) 生意买卖 trade; commerce; business ∗他的父亲经商。 His father is in business. 3 (n) 专指做买卖的人 textile; merchant; dealer ∗ 布商。 textile merchant 4 (n) 一个数除以另一个数所得的结果 quotient (arith)
商标 [shāngbiāo] trade mark
商船 [shāngchuán] a trading vessel; a merchant ship
商店 [shāngdiàn] shop; firm
商会 [shāng huì] chamber of commerce
商量 [shāng·liang] consult; confer
商品 [shāngpǐn] commodity
商品经济 [shāngpǐnjīngjì] commodity economy
商榷 [shāngquè] counsel; consult; confer with
商人 [shāngrèn] merchant; trader; business man
商讨 [shāng tǎo] consult and discuss
商业 [shāng yè] commerce; trade
商业机构 [shāngyèjīgòu] business organization; commercial undertaking
商业税 [shāngyèsuì] tax on commerce; business tax
商业资本 [shāng yè zī běn] commercial capital
商议 [shāngyì] consult each other; discuss

shǎng

晌 [shǎng] 1 (n) 中午 noon 2(n) 一会儿 a while

上 [shǎng] (n) 汉语四声之第三声，符号作 "V" the third of the 4 tones
另见 [shàng]

赏 (賞) [shǎng] 1 (v) 赐给 bestow; grant ∗主人赏他一两银子。His master granted him a tahil of silver. 2 (v) 奖励 reward ∗ 赏善罚恶 To reward the good and punish the evil. 3(v) 因爱好而把玩 to enjoy; to appreciate ∗ 他在赏花。 He is enjoying the flowers.
赏赐 [shǎng cì] a reward; to bestow gifts; to reward
赏格 [shǎnggé] a reward; price offered; sum offered
赏脸 [shǎngliǎn] to favour with one's presence; to give face to
赏识 [shǎngshí] to appreciate
赏心悦目 [shǎng xīn yuè mù] pleasant to the heart and eyes

shàng

上 [shàng]1 (prep) 位置在高处 on top; above∗ 山上有一面旗。 There is a flag on top of the mountain. 2 (adj) 时间、次序在前的 previous; last ∗ 他是上一届的学生会会长。He was the chairman of the student union for the previous year. 3 (adj) 等级高的 superior; high ranking ∗ 下级应服从上级。 officers in the lower rank should obey those in the higher rank. 4(v) 由低处到高处 ascend; go up ∗ 他上山去砍柴。 He went up the hill to chop woods. 5 (v) 到，去 go ∗他没吃早餐，便上学了。 He went to school without any breakfast. 6 (v) 向上级进呈 appeal ∗ 被告可以上诉。The accused may appeal to a higher court. 7 (v) 增添，安装 fix; install ∗ 他在上螺丝。 He is fixing a screw. 8 (prep) (抽象名词)在、里、中、间、方面。in, at (abstract noun) ∗晚上 at night ∗早上 in the morning ∗ 历史上 in history; historically

*会上。at the meeting. *经济上 in economy. 9 (adv) 放在动词后表示动作的完成或趋向 placed at the back of a verb to show a completed act or a tendency *他把门锁上。He locked up the door. *他爱上了农村。He loved the rural area.

上策 [shàngcè] an excellent idea
上层 [shàngcéng] the top; the upper layer
上当 [shàng dàng] to be cheated
上帝 [shàngdì] God; the lord
上工 [shàng gōng] to begin work
上将 [shàngjiàng] General
上卷 [shàng juǎn] the first volume
上列 [shàngliè] the above-stated; the above mentioned
上流社会 [shàngliúshèhuì] rank and fashion
上任 [shàng rèn] to assume office
上升 [shàngshēng] to rise; ascend
上市 [shàngshì] to enter the market; on sale
上述 [shàngshù] the above-mentioned
上尉 [shàngwèi] captain
上校 [shàngxiào] colonel
上演 [shàngyǎn] give a public performance; on show
上瘾 [shàng yǐn] to get addicted
上映 [shàngyìng] (film) on show
上游 [shàngyóu] the upper course of a river
另见 [shǎng]

尚 [shàng] 1 (v) 推崇，注重 honour; respect; reckon; esteem highly *他崇尚有军事才华的人。He esteemed highly those with military skills. 2 (adv) 还；尤 still; yet; however 他年纪尚小。He is still young. 3〔尚且〕(adv) 表示进一层的意思跟"何况"连用 what is more*这么冷的天气，大人尚且受不住，何况是孩子。The adult cannot stand such a cold weather, what is more with children.

尚且 [shàngqiě] still; however; for all that
尚待 [shàngdài] to have still to; to remain to be

shāo

捎 [shāo] (v) 带；拿；寄 to carry; to take
捎信 [shāoxìn] to send a letter.

梢 [shāo] (n) 树枝的顶端，条状物较细的一头 the tip of a branch; a twig *小鸟在树梢歌唱。The birds are singing at the tree top.

稍 [shāo] (adj) 略微 a little *今天的生意稍有起色。The business is slightly better today.
稍等 [shāoděng] to wait for a while
稍微 [shāowēi] slightly; somewhat
稍有更动 [shāoyǒugèngdòng] little change

艄 [shāo] (n) 船尾 the stern of a boat *船艄。stern

鞘 [shāo] (n) 鞭鞘，拴在鞭子头上的细皮条 the leather part at the head of a whip
另见 [qiào]

筲 [shāo] (n) 水桶，多用竹子或木头制成 water pail made of bamboo or wood *一筲水。a pail of water.
筲箕 [shāojī] a bamboo basket for washing rice

烧(燒) [shāo] 1 (v) 使东西着火 burn *他的屋子被烧毁了。His house has been burnt down. 2 (v) 煮熟或加热使物体起变化 cook or heat something *我在烧饭。I am cooking the rice. 3 (n) 烹调方法，就是烤 roast; bake *烧鸡 roast chicken *烧肉。roast pork. 4 (n) 因病而体温增高 fever *他現在烧得相当厉害。He is having high fever.
烧饼 [shāo bǐng] baked cake
烧焊 [shāohàn] welding
烧焦 [shāojiāo] scorch; sear
烧伤 [shāoshāng] a burn

sháo

勺 [sháo] (n) 一种有柄可以舀东西的用具 a ladle ∗ 汤勺 soup ladle.

芍 [sháo]〔芍药〕(n) 草本植物。花象牡丹。块根可制成药材，叫"白芍"或"赤芍" peony

韶 [sháo] (adj) 美好；和谐 beautiful; excellent; harmonious

韶光 [sháoguāng] spring time, one's young days

韶华 [sháohuá] the beauties of spring; one's youth

shǎo

少 [shǎo] 1 (adj) 数量小，跟"多"相对 little; few ∗ 观众很少。There are very few spectators. 2 (v) 缺，不夠 deficient; lack ∗ 还少一双筷子。We still lack a pair of chopsticks. 3 (v) 丢失 lose ∗ 他屋里少了东西。He had lost something in his house. 4 (adv) 短时间 for a short while

少不得 [shǎo·bu dè] indispensably; essential

少见多怪 [shǎo jiàn duō guài] things seldom seen are strange

少数 [shǎoshù] a minority; a small number

少数民族 [shǎoshùmìnzù] national minorities; minority nationalities

少说废话 [shǎo shuō fèihuà] talk less

少许 [shǎoxǔ] a little

少有 [shǎoyǒu] rare

另见 [shào]

shào

绍 (紹) [shào] (v) 接续，继续 continue ∗ 绍箕裘。to carry on the father's profession

邵 [shào] (n) 姓 surname

哨 [shao] 1 (n) 警戒防守的岗位 an outpost; a guard post ∗ 哨兵 a sentry 2 (v) 巡逻 patrol 3 (n) 哨子，一种小笛 a whistle ∗ 我们將吹哨集合。We shall assemble by blowing the whistle.

少 [shào] 1 (adj) 年轻 young ∗ 少女 young girl 2 (n) 年轻人 young people ∗ 男女老少。men and women, old and young.

少妇 [shàofù] a young married woman

少将 [shàojiàng] Major General

少年 [shàonián] a youth

少尉 [shàowèi] Second Lieutenant

少校 [shàoxiào] Major

少壮 [shàozhuàng] young and strong

少壮不努力，老大徒伤悲 [shào zhuàngbùnǔlì, lǎodàtúshāngbēi] not working hard when young, it is useless to lament when old

另见 [shǎo]

shē

赊 (賒) [shē] (v) 买卖东西时延期付款或收款 trade on credit ∗ 这些货物可以赊账。These goods can be obtained on credit.

赊购 [shēgòu] to buy on credit

赊卖 [shēmài] credit sale

赊账交易 [shēzhàngjiāoyì] transaction on credit basis

奢 [shē] 1 (adj) 大量挥霍钱财 extravagant; lavish ∗ 官僚和大地主生活奢侈。The bureaucrats and big landlords are extravagant. 2 (adj) 过分的 excessive ∗ 他的收入有限，不能满足妻子的奢望。His salary is too small to satisfy his wife's excessive wishes.

奢侈品 [shēchǐpǐn] luxuries

奢华 [shēhuá] showy; extravagant

shé

折 [shé] (v) 亏损 lose

折本 [shéběn] to foul in business

折秤 [shé chèng] decrease in weight due to loss of part of the material

折耗 [shéhào] loss or wastage in-

curred during the manufacturing process, transportation and storage
另见 [zhé]

蛇 [shé] (n) 爬虫类，身体圆而细长，有鳞，没有四肢。有毒和无毒之分。捕食青蛙等小动物 snake, ＊眼镜蛇 cobra ＊蟒蛇 python

舌 [shé] (n) 舌头，辨别味道，帮助咀嚼和发音的器官 tongue
舌战 [shézhàn] a heated argument

什(甚) [shé] (pron) 何，表示疑问 what
什么 [shé·me] what
另见 [shí]

shě

舍(捨) [shě] (v) 不要，不顾 part with; let go; abandon ＊他舍弃了老家，定居美国。He abandoned his old home to settle in the United States.
舍本逐末 [shěběnzhùmò] grasp the shadow instead of the essence; penny wise, pound foolish
舍不得 [shě bu dé] not willing to part with; not ready to use something; not willing to give up
舍己为人 [shějǐwèirén] to give up one's interests for others
舍生取义 [shěshēngqǔyì] to sacrifice one's life for justice
舍生忘死 [shěshēngwàngsǐ] lay down one's life for
另见 [shè]

shè

摄(攝) [shè] 1 (v) 吸收 take; absorb ＊摄取养料 to absorb the nutrients 2 (v) 摄影，照相 to make a film; to take a photograph ＊他们在参观影片的摄制过程。They are watching the film making processes.
摄氏寒暑表 [shèshìhánshǔbiǎo] a Celsius thermometer
摄影机 [shèyǐngjī] camera
摄影室 [shèyǐngshì] studio

慑(懾) [shè] 1 (v) 威胁；威吓 to frighten; to intimidate; to coerce 2 (adj) 恐惧 frightened; afraid
慑服 [shèfù] to subdue ; to awe into submission
慑于 [shèyú] fear

舍 [shè] 1 (n) 房屋，住所 house; residence ＊宿舍 hostel ; dormitory 2 (adj) 旧时谦词 a word used in the olden days to mean "humble" ＊寒舍 my humble home ＊舍弟 my younger brother
另见 [shě]

设(設) [shè] (v) 建立，布置，安排 set up; found; form; establish; arrange ＊联合国的总部设在纽约。The United Nation headquarter was set up in New York.
设备 [shèbèi] facilities ; equipment
设法 [shèfǎ] devise; means; scheme or plan
设防 [shèfáng] set up patrol or defense
设计 [shèjì] design; to plan ; to project
设立 [shèlì] to establish ; set up
设身处地 [shèshēnchǔdì] place oneself in other's position
设施 [shè shī] facilities; buildings system and organisation
设想 [shèxiǎng] suppose; imagine
设置 [shèzhì] arrange; place(e.g. obstacles)

射 [shè] 1 (v) 以力使某固体向一定方向推进 shoot; project; dart ＊警察开枪射击示威群众。The police shot at the demonstrators. 2 (v) 喷注 spurt; inject ＊医生把葡萄糖注射入病人

的静脉。The doctor injects glucose into the veins of the patient. 3 (v) 放出光、热等 to radiate light or heat ∗太陽放射出光和热。The sun radiates light and heat.

射程 [shèchéng] range

射击 [shèjì] firing; shooting

射击场 [shèjìchǎng] range

射击术 [shèjìshù] marksmanship

麝 [shè] (n) 哺乳动物，比鹿小，没有角，雄的脐部有香腺，能分泌麝香，麝香可以做香料或药材 the musk deer

社 [shè] 1 (n) 团体；集团；机构 a society; an organisation; an association ∗ 合作社 co-operative ∗出版社 publishing firm ∗ 通讯社 news agency ∗ 旅行社 travel agency 2(n) 土地的神 the god of the soil

社会 [shèhuì] society

社会存在 [shèhuìcúnzài] social existence; social being

社会分工 [shèhuìfēngōng] social division of labour

社会服务 [shèhuì fú wù] social service

社会工作 [shè huì gōng zuò] social work

社会活动 [shèhuì huó dong] community activities

社会科学 [shè huì kē xué] social science such as law, economics, political science, etc

社会制度 shèhuìzhìdù] social system

社会主义 [shèhuìzhǔyì] socialism

社会主义革命 [shèhuì zhǔyì gémìng] socialist revolution

社会主义国家 [shè huì zhúyì guó jiā] socialist country

社交 [shèjiāo] social intercourse

社论 [shèlùn] editorial of a newspaper

社团 [shètuan] association; society

社员 [shèyuán] member; member of a commune

涉 [shè] 1 (v) 徒步渡水 wade through water ∗ 战士们涉水而过，穷追敌军。The soldiers waded through the water to chase after the enemy. 2 (v) 经历 to experience ∗他涉世不深。He is inexperienced. 3 (v) 牵连 involve ∗他涉嫌贪污事件。He was suspected of corruption.

涉及 [shèjí] concern; in regard to

涉猎 [shèliè] to study in general, not going into detail

涉讼 [shèsòng] to get involved in a legal case

涉足 [shèzú] to enter a certain environment

赦 [shè] (v) 对罪犯免除刑罚 pardon; forgive ∗他们请求元首的赦免。They appeal to the king for a pardon.

赦罪 [shèzuì] to forgive a crime

shēn

申 [shen] 1 (n) 地文的第九位，用作次序的第九 the ninth of the twelve branches; ninth in order 2 (n) 申时；指下午三时至五时 from 3 p.m. to 5 p.m. 3 (v) 陈述，说明 explain; state

申辩 [shēnbiàn] to defend

申斥 [shēnchì] to reprimand; to scold

申明 [shēnmìng] try to clear the matter up; avow; make a statement

申请 [shēnqǐng] to redress a grievance

申请人 [shēnqǐngrén] an applicant

申诉 [shēnsù] to appeal; to plead; to complain

申冤 [shēnyuān] to request; to apply

伸 [shēn] 1 (v) 舒展开 stretch; extend ∗孩子伸手拿糖。The child stretched out his hands to take the sweets.

伸长 [shēncháng] to lengthen

伸懒腰 [shēn lǎnyāo] to stretch the body and yawn

伸性 [shēnxìng] flexibility; elasticity

伸张正义 [shēnzhāngzhèngyì] to get justice done

呻 [shēn]〔呻吟〕(v) 病痛时发出的哼声 groan;moan * 病人在床上呻吟。The patient groaned in his bed.

绅(紳) [shēn] (n) 地方上有势力的人 the gentry, 乡绅 village gentry. * 太平局绅 justice of the peace

绅士 [shēnshì] a gentry; a gentleman

砷 [shēn] (n) 化学元素;符号 AS 旧名"砒" arsenic, a chemical element

参(參) [shēn](n)〔人参〕草本植物一种贵重的药材 ginseng 另见 [cān] [cēn]

深 [shēn] 1 (n) 从上到下或从外到里的长度 depth * 池水有二米深。The pool has a depth of two metres. 2 (adj) 从上到下或从外到里的长度大 deep * 富在深山有远亲。A rich man though living deep in the mountain attracts visitors. 3 (adj) 奥妙的 profound * 苏格拉底是一名深奥的思想家。Socrates was a profound thinker. 4 (adj) 浓厚。dark; thick * 她穿着一件深红色的上衣。She puts on a dark red blouse. 5 (adj) 久;迟 long; late * 他读书直到深夜。He read till late at night 6 (adj) 极甚 strongly; extremely; very much * 我深信他不会背叛我们。I firmly believe that he will not betray us.

深奥 [shēnào] profound; deep

深表同情 [shēnbiǎotóngqíng] show the deepest sympathy

深长 [shēncháng] profound and far-reaching; penetrating

深仇大恨 [shēnchóudàhén] implacable hatred

深沉 [shēnchén] profound; deep

深度 [shēndù] depth

深更半夜 [shēngēngbànyè] in the dead hour of the night; late at night

深究 [shēnjiū] go deeply into the matter

深厚 [shēnhǒu] deep (in feelings)

深刻 [shēnkè] profound; deep; penetrating

深谋远虑 [shēnmóu yuǎnlù] plan well and think far ahead

深切 [shēnqiè] intensely; earnestly; friendly

深入 [shēnrù] enter at great depth; to go deep into

深渊 [shēnyuān] an abyss; a ravine

深造 [shēnzào] deepened or higher studies; mastery

深重 [shēnzhòng] heavy; grave; severe

莘 [shēn] (adj) 众多 numerous 莘莘学子。[shēnshēnxuézì] a great number of students.

身 [shēn] 1 (n) 躯体 the body * 他身强力壮。He has a strong body. 2 (n) 生命 life * 无数的英雄烈士舍身为国。Many heroes and martyrs had sacrificed their lives for the country. 3 (n) 自己,本人,亲自 the person; oneself * 钱财身外物 Money should not be connected intimately with oneself. 4 (n) 指人的社会地位 one's social status * 他出身贫寒。He is poor in social status. 5 (n) 孕 pregnancy * 她有了身孕。She is pregnant. 6 (n) 物体的主要部分 the main part of an object * 船身 hull; (飞机)机身 fuselage; 树身 trunk

身败名裂 [shēn bài míng liè] status lost and reputation stained

身材 [shēncái] stature; height

身段 [shēnduàn] figure

身份 [shēn·fen] status; rank; position

身份证 [shēnfènzhèng] identity card

身故 [shēngù] die

身后萧条 [shēnhòuxiāotiáo] die without any money left

身体 [shēntǐ] the body

身价百倍 [shēn jià bǎi bèi] status and reputation greatly enhanced

身体力行 [shěntǐlìxíng] to put into practice

娠 [shēn] (adj) 怀孕 pregnant; conceived

shén

神 [shén] 1 (n) 具有超自然的能力，能统治天地万物者，也指某些有权力的人死后的精灵 God ; divine spirits 2 (adj) 不平凡的，异乎寻常的 unusual;extraordinary * 他进步神速。He improves at an extraordinary rate. 3 (adj) 奇妙的，不可思议的 mysterious ; miraculous * 许多自然现象是可以解释的，它们并不神祕。 Many natural phenomena can be explained ; they are not mysterious at all. 4 (n) 心力 ; 注意力 ; 精力 attention; energy * 这件事很费神。 This matter needs much attention. 5 (n) 表情 expression ; appearance * 他神色匆忙。He appears to be in a hurry.

神出鬼没 [shén chū-guǐ mò] sudden appearance and disappearance

神采奕奕 [shéncǎiyìyì] hale and ruddy looking

神话 [shénhuà] myths ; fairy tales

神魂颠倒 [shénhúndiāndǎo] mentally unbalanced; abnormal

神经 [shén jīng] nerves ; insane

神经病 [shénjīngbìng] nervous disease

神经衰弱 [shénjīngshuāiruò] nervous debility; neurasthenia

神明 [shénmíng] Gods

神奇 [shénqí] miraculous ; wonderful

神气 [shén qì] appearance ; air ; look

神情 [shénqíng] appearance ; bearing

神圣 [shénshèng] holy ; sacred

神通广大 [shéntōngguǎngdà] capable of performing anything

神象 [shénxiàng] images ; idols

神效 [shénxiào] wonderful , effective ; efficacious

什 [shén]〔什么〕 1 (pron) 代词，表示疑问 what? * 你说什么？What did you say? 2 (Pron) 代词，指不确定的事物 pronoun for indefinite things * 他什么都不讲。He would not tell any thing.

另见 [shí]

甚 [shén]〔甚么〕(pron) 同"什么" what?

另见 [shèn]

shěn

审（審） [shěn] 1 (adj) 详细，周密 in detail; careful * 他审慎地考虑整个计划。He has thought carefully over the whole plan. 2 (v) 仔细分析，考究 analyse carefully; investigate in detail; examine * 他在审查一篇报告。He is examining a report. 3 (v) 讯问案件 try; investigate * 他因犯罪而受审。He was tried for a crime.

审察 [shěnchá] to investigate

审定 [shěndìng] to examine and decide (a plan or scheme)

审度 [shěndù] deliberate upon

审供 [shěngòng] hear evidence

审核 [shěhé] examine and pass on

审理 [shěnlǐ] try; examine a case

审美观 [shěnměiguān] aesthetic view

审判 [shěnpàn] to pass sentence ; examine and decide cases

审批 [shěpī] examine and endorse; check and approve

审视 [shěnshì] to scrutinize

审问 [shěnwèn] to interrogate a person ; to investigate

审讯 [shěnxùn] to interrogate a person

审阅 [shěnyè] to examine a written material

婶（嬸） [shěn] 1 (n) 婶婶，叔父的妻子 aunt , a father's younger brother's wife 2(n) 小婶，称丈夫的弟媳 sister-in-law 3 (n) 大婶，对年长已婚妇女的尊称 aunty , an honorary address to an elderly married woman

哂 [shěn] (v) 微笑 smile

哂纳 [shěnnà] to receive with a smile—please accept my present

shèn

甚 [shèn] 1 (adv) 很，极 very; extremely ＊他进步甚快。 He improves very fast. 2 (adv) 超过，胜过 more than ＊他关心别人甚于自已。He is more concerned about others than himself. 3 (adv) 过度 excessively;too ＊不要欺人太甚。Do not bully others excessively.

蜃 [shèn] 1 (n) 蛤类通称 clam 2 (n) 海中怪物 a marine monster

蜃楼 [shènlóu] buildings in a mirage

蜃气 [shènqì] a mirage

蜃市 [shènshì] a mirage

肾（腎） [shèn] (n) 分泌尿液的器官 kidney,

肾炎 [shènyán] nephritis

肾脏病 [shènzàngbìng] kidney disease

渗（滲） [shèn] (v) 液体慢慢地透过或漏出 permeate; soak; leak ＊包扎伤口的绷带上渗出了血。Blood permeates from the bandage on the wound.

渗透性 [shèntòuxìng] osmose; osmosis

渗透 [shèntòu] to permeate; percolation

渗透压 [shèntòuyà] osmotic pressure

渗透作用 [shèntòuzuòyòng] osmotic action

慎 [shèn] (adj) 小心，仔细 cautious; careful; prudent ＊他做事谨慎。He is cautious in his undertaking.

慎重 [shènzhòng] prudent

shēng

生 [shēng] 1 (v) 产出，发出 give rise to; produce; effect ＊这項条例將於五月生效。 This rule will come into effect in May. 2 (v) 产育 give birth to ; bear children ＊她在昨天生了一个男孩。 She gave birth to a baby-boy yesterday. 3 (v) 生长 grow ＊种子已经生根发芽了。The seed has grown roots and sprouts.4 (v) 活 live; exist survive＊只有十名船员在海难中生还。Only ten of the crew survived the shipwreck. 5 (n) 人员 a person; a member ＊学生 a student ＊书生 a literary man ＊小生 an actor ＊医生 a doctor ＊接线生 a telephone operator 6 (n) 生命 life ＊ 她的儿子在一次工业意外中丧生。 Her son lost his life in an industrial accident. 7 (adj) 活的 live;living ＊动物和植物都是生物。Animals and plants are living things. 8 (adj) 没煮熟，没成熟，没经锻炼，不熟悉。uncooked; unripe; unsmelt; unfamiliar ＊生米 uncooked rice 生木瓜 unripe papaya 生铁. pig iron 9 (adv) 勉强 forcedly; constrainedly ＊我们不能生搬硬套别人的经验。We should not forcedly apply others' experiences

生病 [shēngbìng] fall ill; get ill; be taken ill

生搬硬套 [shēngbānyìngtào] apply mechanically; mechanical application

生产 [shēngchǎn] to create various materials for subsistence and production with the aid of tools ; to give birth to

生产方式 [shēng chǎn fāngshì] mode of production

生产力 [shēngchǎnlì] productivity

生存 [shēngcún] exist ; survive; live; existence

生动 [shēng dòng] lively; life-like

生活 [shēnghuó] living; well-being ; live; everyday matters; livelihood ; life

生活费 [shēng huó fèi] cost of living

生力军 [shēnglì jūn] fresh troops ; reinforcement

生龙活虎 [shēnglóng huóhǔ] vigorous and active

生离死别 [shēng lí sǐ bié] a sad farewell

生平 [shēngpíng] the whole life; life-long

生气 [shēng qì] angry; vitality; vigour

生擒 [shēngqín] to catch alive

生日 [shēng·ri] birthday

生事 [shēng shì] to bring disturbances ; to cause trouble

生手 [shēngshǒu] inexperienced worker ; a beginner; a greenhorn
生疏 [shēngshū] unfamiliar
生锈 [shēng xìu] to get rusty
生涯 [shēngyá] occupation; living
生意 [shēng yì] business
生殖器 [shēngzhíqì] reproductive organs

牲 [shēng] 1 (n) 家畜 domesticated animals 2 (n) 古代祭神用的牛、羊、猪等 animal sacrifice
牲畜 [shēngchú] livestock; cattle
牲口 [shēngkǒu] domesticated animals

甥 [shēng] (n) 姊妹的儿子 the children of a sister
甥儿 [shēngér] son of a sister
甥女 [shēngnǚ] daughter of a sister

笙 [shēng] (n) 一种管乐器，通常用竹制成，用口吹奏 a Chinese wind musical instrument
笙歌 [shēnggē] music and singing

升 [shēng] 1 (n) 中国旧容量单位，等于1.0355公升 a Chinese old measure 1 sheng = 1.0355 litres 2 (v) 向上移动 ascend; rise up ＊太阳升起来了。The sun has risen. 3 (v) (等级) 提高 promote; rise in rank ＊他升级了。He was promoted.
升班 [shēng biān] be promoted to a higher standard
升华 [shēnghuá] to sublime
升降机 [shēngjìangjī] an elevator; lift
升旗 [shēng qí] to hoist a flag
升学 [shēng xué] be promoted to a higher school

昇 [shēng] (v) "升"的异体字 another written form of the word "升"

声(聲) [shēng] 1 (n) 音响，物体振动时所产生的能够引起听觉的波 sound; voice; noise ＊你有听到脚步声吗？ Did you hear the sound of foot-steps? 2 (n) 音调 tone ＊四声。the four tones in Chinese pronunciation. 3 (v) 发话；扬言，宣称 announce; declare ; publicise ＊请不要把事情声张出去。Please do not publicise the matter. 4(n) 名誉 reputation ＊他因为挪用公款而弄得声名狼藉。He makes an evil reputation for himself because he misappropriated the public fund.
声波 [shēngbō] sound waves
声称 [shēngchēng] to state verbally; to declare
声调 [shēngdiào] tone
声东击西 [shēng dōng jī xī] to make a noise in the east, while attacking in the west
声母 [shēngmǔ] "sheng"—initial
声明 [shēng míng] declaration ; announcement ; to declare ; to annouce; to make a statement
声泪俱下 [shēnglèijùxià] pour oneself out in tears
声色俱厉 [shēngsèjùlì] harsh in words and expression
声色犬马 [shēngsèquǎnmǎ] music, women, dog and horse — a way of life of the rich
声势浩大 [shengshìhàoda] powerful; influential
声讨 [shēngtǎo] to reproach someone's crime in the open; to denounce
声望 [shēngwàng] reputation, renown
声援 [shēngyuán] to encourage ; to shout encouragement; to support
声乐家 [shēng yuè jiā] a vocalist

shéng

绳(繩) [shéng] 1 (n) 用棉、麻、棕、草、金属丝等绞成的条状物 rope; cord; string ＊绳索。a thick rope. 2(v) 约束，制裁 restrain＊这些坏人应该绳之以法。These bad hats should be restrained by law.
绳床 [shéngchuáng] a hammock
绳梯 [shéngtī] a rope ladder

shěng

省 [sheng] 1 (n) 地方最大的行政区域 a province ＊湖南省。the Hunan Province 2 (v) 节约

save＊他不懂得省钱。He does not know how to save money. 3 (v) 免掉，减去 omit ＊你可以省略这篇文章的第二段。You may omit the second paragraph in the article.

省城 [shěngchéng] the provincial capital

省吃俭用 [shěng chī jiǎn yòng] thrifty; frugal

省力 [shěnglì] save energy

省时 [shěng shí] save time

省事 [shěng shì] save trouble

另见 [xǐng]

shèng

乘 [shèng] 1 (n) 车辆的量词 numeral for vehicles ＊ 一乘车 a car, cart or carriage ＊一乘轿子 a sedan chair 2 (n) 记载 records ＊ 史乘 historical records

另见 [chéng]

剩 [shèng] 1 (n) 多余 surplus; leftover; remainder; remnant; residue ＊他把剩饭倒进桶里。He throws the remains of the meal into a container. 2 (v) 余下 remain ＊ 整座大厦，只剩下他一个人。He alone remained in the big building.

剩货 [shènghuó] remnants of goods

剩钱 [shèngqián] balance; money left over

剩余 [shèngyú] surplus; remainder

剩余产品 [shèngyǔ chǎnpǐn] surplus products

剩余价值 [shèngyú jiàzhí] surplus value

盛 [shèng] 1 (adj) 茂密，繁荣 luxuriant; prosperous; flourishing ＊这个国家繁荣昌盛。 This country is prosperous and flourishing. 2 (adj) 强烈，旺 strong ＊火势很盛。The flame is very strong. 3 (adj) 隆重 grand; splendid ＊东主国设了一个盛大的宴会以招待外国来宾。The host country gave a grand banquet in honour of the foreign visitors. 4(adv) 广泛地 widely; to a great extent ＊盛传他已经逃跑了。 It is widely rumoured that he has escaped.

盛大 [shèngdà] grand; gala

盛典 [shèngdiǎn] grand ceremony

盛会 [shènghuì] a splendid meet

盛极一时 [shèng jí yì shí] very popular for a time

盛举 [shèngjǔ] a grand occasion; a festivity; a gala

盛开 [shèngkāi] in full bloom or blossom, as flowers

盛况 [shèng kuàng] a splendid occasion

盛怒 [shèngnù] in great passion; enraged

盛气凌人 [shèng qì líng rén] arrogant and insulting

盛情 [shèngqíng] courtesy; hospitality; kindness

盛行 [shèngxíng] prevailing; popular; prevalent; become current· be in vogue

盛意 [shèngyì] good intentions

盛赞 [shèngzàn] to commend highly of ; to be loud in one's praise of

盛装 [shèngzhuāng] festival clothes

胜(勝) [shèng] 1 (n) 估优势，跟"败"相对 win; overcome ＊在这场比赛中，我方得胜。We have won in this match. 2 (v) 优于，超过 surpass; excel; outshine ＊事实胜于雄辩。The facts outshine allegation. 3 (adj) 优美的（指景色）beautiful (scenery) ＊圣陶沙是个旅游胜地。Sentosa is a tourist resort. 4 (adj) 能担任，能承受 competent; capable ＊这项工作我不能胜任。 I am not competent for this task.

胜负 [shèngfù] victory and defeat

胜利 [shènglì] win; victory; triumph

胜任 [shèngrèn] competent; be well qualified to do something; capable

胜诉 [shèngsù] to win in a law suit

胜仗 [shèng zhàng] a victorious battie

圣(聖) [shèng] 1 (adj) 人格最高尚、智慧最高超的 holy ＊圣人 a holy man; a sage ＊诗圣杜甫 the sage of the poets—Tu Fu 2 (adj) 对皇帝的尊称 an address to a king ＊圣旨 an imperiai decree. 3 (adj) 神的 sacred; holy; divine

圣诞节 [Shèngdàn Jié] Christmas

圣地 [shèngdì] a sacred ground; a holy place

圣母 [shèngmǔ] the Holy Mother

圣贤 [shèngxián] sages; wise men

shī

师(師) [shī] 1 (n) 教给人知识·技术的人 teacher; instructor; tutor 2 (n) 榜样;教训 example;lesson ＊前事不忘，後事之师。An antecedent event unforgotten could be an example to be followed. 3 (v) 效法 imitate ＊师法。to do the same 4 (n) 对从事某种专业的人的称呼 persons in certain profession ＊工程师 engineer 讲师 lecturer 律师 lawyer 5 (n) 军队 army ＊百万雄师。a huge army. 6 (n) 军队的编制单位，是团的上一级 a division of the army

师出无名 [shīchūwúmíng] there is no excuse for the campaign; carry out a campaign without any justifiable reason.

师傅 [shī·fu] a master; an expert

师范学院 [shīfàn xuéyuàn] teachers' training college

师母 [shīmǔ] teacher's wife

师兄 [shī xiōng] an older fellow workman

师心自用 [shīxīnzìyòng] self-opinionated

师长 [shīzhǎng] divisional comandor; teacher

师资 [shīzī] people who can be trained (up) as teachers

狮(獅) [shī] (n) 哺乳动物，毛通常黄褐或暗褐色，雄狮从头到颈有宗毛，力大凶猛，常夜间活动，捕食其他动物，多产于非洲及印度西北部 lion

狮吼 [shīhǒu] the roar of a lion

狮身人面象 [shī shēn rénmiàn xiàng] the sphinx

狮子狗 [shī·zigǒu] a dog with long fur

施 [shī] 1 (v) 实行 carry out; enforce; implement ＊政府将实施新的劳工法令。The government will enforce the new Labour Act soon. 2 (v) 用上，加上 use; apply; put; add ＊菜农正在施肥。The farmer is applying manure. 3 (v) 给 to give

施肥 [shīféi] apply fertilizer or manure

施工 [shī gōng] to build houses, roads or bridges according to the plan

施加 [shījiā] bring or exert; exercise .... over

施舍 [shīshě] to bestow in charity

施手术 [shīshǒushù] to perform an operation

施行 [shīxíng] to carry into effect; to put into force

施展 [shīzhǎn] to show one's talent or ability

施诊 [shī zhěn] to provide free medical aid to the poor

施政 [shī zhèng] implementation of policy

尸 [shī] (n) 尸体，人或动物死后的躯体 the corpse ＊死者的尸首已经腐烂。The corpse has decomposed.

尸骸 [shīhái] corpse

尸位素餐 [shīwèisùcān] to neglect the duties of an office while taking the pay

诗 (詩) [shī] (n) 一种文体，形式很多，大多用韵，可以歌詠朗诵 poetry; poem; verse
诗经 [shījīng] the Book of Odes
诗篇 [shīpiān] the Psalms
诗人 [shīrén] poet
诗圣 [shīshèng] the sage of the poets
诗选 [shīxuǎn] an anthology
诗韵 [shīyùn] a rythm of the verse in a poem

虱 [shī] (n) 昆虫。体小，背腹扁，无翅。寄生在人或牲畜身上，能传染疾病 a flea; a louse; a bug

失 [shī] 1 (v) 丢掉；遗漏；忽略 to lose; to slip; to neglect ＊他遗失了一些文件。 He lost some documents. 2 (n) 错 a fault ; a mistake; an error ＊智者千虑，必有一失。 Even a clever person may miss out something or make an error after numerous deliberations. 3 (v) 没有掌握住 fail to; miss ＊他失足从高空跌了下来。 He lost his footing and fell down from a height.
失策 [shīcè] to commit a blunder
失常 [shīcháng] abnormal
失传 [shīchuán] be lost through the generations
失当 [shīdàng] inapropriate; improper
失道寡助 [shīdàoguǎzhù] an unjust cause finds meagre support
失魂落魄 [shīhúnluòpò] be scared out of one's wits
失火 [shīhuǒ] catch fire; aflame ; fire breaks out
失利 [shīlì] suffer setback; lose ground
失眠 [shī mián] cannot sleep; insomnia
失明 [shī míng] blind ; lose one's eyesight
失色 [shīsè] frightened; turn pale
失守 [shīshǒu] fall into the hands of enemy; to lose the control of a territory
失笑 [shīxiào] to burst into laughter
失学 [shī xué] to lose the chance of education
失言 [shī yán] to say the wrong thing; make a slip of the tongue
失业 [shī yè] to become unemployed; jobless
失意 [shī yì] unhappy
失约 [shī yuē] to miss an appointment
失踪 [shī zōng] disappear

湿 (濕) [shī] (adj) 沾了水或含的水分多 wet; damp ＊他的衣服都给雨淋湿了。 He was all drenched in the rain.
湿度 [shīdù] humidity
湿透 [shītòu] wet through

shí

时 (時) [shí] 1 (n) 持续存在的过程 time ＊时势大好 Times are favourable 2 (n) 季节 season＊春夏秋冬四时。 the four seasons, spring, summer, autumn and winter. 3 (n) 一日的十二分之一 a unit for measuring time used in ancient China, equivalent to a period of two hours; ＊ 丑时 chou time, 1 a.m. to 3 a.m. 4 (n) 一日的二十四分之一 hour 5 (adj) 当前的，现代的 current ＊时事 current affairs. 6 (adv) 常常 always; often; constantly ; from time to time ＊他时常来探我。 He often visits me. 7 (adv) 偶然的 sometimes ; occasionally
时代 [shídài] age; period; epoch ; era
时候 [shí hou] time
时间性 [shíjiānxìng] limited to a period only; period of time suitable for a certain event
时节 [shíjié] occasion; time
时机 [shíjī] opportunity
时髦 [shímáo] fashionable
时期 [shíqī] time; period
时时刻刻 [shíshíkèkè] constantly; al-

ways; from time to time

时事问题 [shíshìwèntí] current issues

时宜 [shiyi] appropriate to the occasion ; at an appropriate time

鲥(鰣) [shí] (n) 鱼类，身体扁长，背黑绿色，腹银白色，鳞下的脂肪很多，肉味甜美 ilisha elongata, an edible fish

石 [shí] (n) 构成地壳的坚硬物质，是由矿物集合而成的 stone; rock＊大理石。marble.

石斑鱼 [shíbānyú] spotted grouper, a type of fish

石沉大海 [shí chén dà hǎi] no news here after

石膏 [shígāo] gypsum; plaster-of Paris

石膏象 [shígāoxiàng] a statue made of plaster- of Paris

石灰 [shíhuī] calcium oxide; lime

石灰岩 [shíhuīyán] limestone

石块 [shíkuài] stone; boulder

石榴 [shí·liu] pomegranate

石棉 [shímián] asbestos

石墨 [shímò] graphite

石器时代 [shígì shídài] the stone age

石笋 [shísǔn] stalagmite, a feature in limestone cave

石英 [shíyīng] quartz

石油 [shíyóu] petroleum

另见 [dàn]

十 [shí] 1 (n) 数目 ten; 10 2(adj)完全，极 complete; to the extreme＊他十分满意你的工作。He is very satisfied with your work.

十进制 [shíjìnzhì] denary system

十全十美 [shíquán shí měi] faultless; perfect

十万 [shíwàn] a hundred thousands (10 0,000)

十亿 [shíyì] a billion (1,000,000,000)

十字路口 [shízìlùkǒn] crossroad

十足 [shízú] complete; pure

什 [shí] 1 (n) 十 ten 2 (adj) 多种的，杂样的 miscellaneous; sundry

什货 [shíhuò] sundries; miscellaneous goods

什锦菜 [shíjǐncài] a dish made up of various items of food

什物 [shíwù] miscellaneous articles

另见 [shén]

食 [shí] 1 (v) 吃 eat ＊食肉。 to eat the meat. 2 (n) 人吃的东西 food ＊人民都丰衣足食。The people have enough clothes to wear and food to eat. 3(adj)可供人吃的edible ＊食油。 edible oil.

食道 [shí dào] food canal , the gullet; the oesophagus

食饵 [shíèr] a bait

食粮 [shíliáng] food ; foodstuff; grain

食谱 [shípǔ] food recipe ; cook book

食堂 [shítáng] canteen; tuckshop

食物:食品 [shíwù]:[shípǐn] food

食物中毒 [shí wù zhòng dú] food poisoning

食言 [shíyán] to break one's promise

食盐 [shíyán] table salt

食蚁兽 [shiyǐshòu] an ant-eater

食欲 [shíyù] appetite

食斋 [shízhāi] to abstain from meat for religious reasons

食指 [shízhǐ] the index finger; the fore-finger

另见 [sì]

蚀(蝕) [shí] 1 (v) 损伤 damage; corrode ＊铁很容易受到海水腐蚀。Iron can be easily corroded by sea water. 2 (v) 亏损 lose ＊他做生意蚀本了。 He has failed in his business. 3 (n) 日月的亏损 eclipse

实(實) [shí] 1 (adj) 充满，和"空"，"虚"相对 compact; solid; full *实心的铁球。solid iron ball. 2 (adj)真的，real; actual; factual *这是一篇真实的故事。This is a story of real life 3(n) 种子，果实 seed; fruit *木瓜树已经开花结实了。The papaya tree has bloomed and borne fruits.

实话 [shíhuà] the truth
实践 [shíjiàn] to practise; to put into practice
实际 [shíjì] practice; real; actual; practical
实况 [shíkuàng] the actual state; the real condition
实权 [shíquán] real power
实事求是 [shí shì qiú shì] to act pragmatically
实物 [shíwù] real object; actual object
实习 [shíxí] practise; practical training; drill
实行 [shíxíng] to put into practice; to carry out; to enforce
实验室 [shíyanshì] laboratory
实用主义 [shíyǒng zhǔyì] pragmatism
实在 [shízài] really; truly; in fact; in reality

识(識) [shí] 1 (v) 认得，知道，辨别 recognise; know; distinguish *他教村民们识字。He teaches the villagers to recognise words. 2 (n) 知识，所知道的道理 knowledge *他学识丰富。He is full of knowledge. 3 (n) 见解 opinion; view *他有卓越的见识。He has an outstanding view.

识别 [shí bié] to distinguish; to discern
识货 [shí huò] know the quality of goods
识破 [shípò] to detect; to see through; to be fully aware of; to find out
识相 [shíxiàng] to adapt oneself looking at the expression of people
另见 [zhì]

拾 [shí] 1 (v) 从地上拿起来，捡 pick up *园丁拾起地上的果子 The gardener picked up the fruits on the ground. 2 (n) "十"的大写 another version of ten

拾掇 [shíduō] tidy up; repair
拾金不昧 [shíjīnbùmèi] not taking the gold picked up
拾荒 [shíhuāng] to pick up throwaways
拾取 [shíqǔ] pick up

shǐ

史 [shǐ] (n) 历史，自然或社会以往发展的进程 history *人类社会的发展史。a history of the development of human society

史册 [shǐcè] history books; historical works
史籍 [shǐjí] historical writings; annals
史迹 [shǐjī] historical remains
史诗 [shǐshī] historical epic
史实 [shǐ shì] historical data
史书 [shǐshū] history books
史无前例 [shǐ wú qián lì] unprecedented
史学 [shǐ xuè] historiology

驶(駛) [shǐ] 1 (v) 泛指车马快跑 run swiftly as a horse; to speed. *汽车疾驶而过。The car speeds past. 2 (v)开动 drive; steer(ship, boat) *他的驾驶技术很好。He is skilled in driving.

使 [shǐ] 1 (v) 派 send;order *他使人前去打听消息。He sent a person there to gather information. 2 (v) 用 use; utilize *农民们开始使用机器来耕田。The peasants begin to use machines for ploughing. 3 (v) 叫，让 let *不要使他失望。Do not let him feel disappointed. 4 (n) 派驻外国的外交官 envoy *大使。ambassador. 5 (conj)假如 if *假使。

If
使馆 [shǐguǎn] embassy
使唤 [shǐ·huan] call (usually a servant) to do things for you
使节 [shǐjié] envoy; ambassador
使命 [shǐmìng] mission; errand
使眼色 [shǐ yǎn·se] to hint at some body with the movement of the eyes
使用 [shǐyòng] use; apply; employ; exercise
使用价值 [shǐyòng jiàzhí] utility value
使者 [shǐzhě] emissary; messenger; envoy

矢 [shǐ] 1 (n) 箭 arrow ＊无的放矢。shooting an arrow aimlessly. 2 (v) 发誓 vow; swear ＊他矢口否认。He flatly denies.

豕 [shǐ] (n) 猪 pig

屎 [shǐ] 1(n) 大便，粪 feces ＊屎桶。a container for feces; commode. 2 (n) 眼、耳分泌的东西 discharge from eyes or ears

始 [shǐ] 1 (n) 开头，起头，最初 beginning; commencement; start ＊他自始至终不说一句话。He did not say anything from the beginning till the end. 2 (conj) 才 then only ＊坚持学习，始能进步。Persist in your study, then only can you progress.
始末：始终 [shǐmò]:[shǐzhōng] from beginning to the end
始终不渝 [shǐzhōngbùyú] unswervingly; consistently
始终如一 [shǐ zhōng rú yī] consistent from the start to the end.
始祖 [shǐzǔ] founder; first ancestor

shì

式 [shì] 1 (n) 特定的规格 format; standard; example ＊写信的格式 format of letter writing. 2 (n) 仪式，典礼 ceremony ＊开幕式。opening ceremony
式样 [shìyàng] pattern
式子 [shì·zi] posture; formula; equation

试（試）[shì] 1 (v) 尝试，做一做 try; attempt ＊我们在试用这辆新车。We are trying the new car. 2 (n) 考查，测验 trial; test ＊口试。oral test.
试工 [shì gōng] to try somebody for a job
试管 [shìguǎn] test-tube
试剂 [shìjì] a chemical reagent
试金石 [shìjīnshí] a touchstone
试探 [shì·tan] to probe
试题 [shìtí] test questions
试图 [shìtú] attempt to
试想 [shìxiǎng] imagine; think
试行 [shìxíng] try; make a try
试验 [shìyàn] test; make an experiment
试用 [shìyòng] try out; test; on probation
试用期 [shì yòng qī] probation period for an employee

拭 [shì] (v) 抹，擦 wipe; rub ＊孩子在拭泪。The child is wiping his tears.
拭目以待 [shì mù yǐ dài] to anticipate; to wait earnestly for something to happen

轼（軾）[shì] (n) 古代车厢前供乘者做扶手的横木 leaning board before a carriage in the ancient time

弑 [shì] (v) 杀害尊长。to kill one's elder
弑父 [shìfù] to kill one's father
弑君 [shìjūn] parricide
弑亲罪 [shìqīnzuì] regicide

侍 [shì] (v) 照顾，陪伴 accompany; look after ＊卫生人员在服侍病人。The hospital attendants are looking after the patient.
侍候 [shìhòu] to attend to somebody
侍从 [shìcóng] an attendant; a servant

恃 [shì] (v) 依赖，依仗 rely upon; depend; fall upon ＊这些爪牙有恃无恐，常常欺压百姓。These henchmen are bold because they have good backing and they often bully the people.

恃才傲物 [shì cái ào wù] showing contempt for one's fellow men because of one's talent

噬 [shì] (v) 咬 bite; gnaw ＊那条蛇吞噬了一只青蛙。 The snake has swallowed up a frog.

噬脐莫及 [shìqímòjí] too late to repent

氏 [shì] 1 (n) 姓 family name 2(n) 旧时对已婚妇女的称呼 an address to a married woman ＊ 黄氏 a woman surnamed Huang; Madam Huang 3 (n) 对男士的称呼 an address to a gentleman ＊摄氏温度表。 the Celsius thermometer

氏族 [shizú] gens, clan

舐 [shì] (v) 舔 lick ＊ 老牛舐犊（比喻父母爱子女）The old cow is licking its calf (parental love for children)

舐犊情深 [shìdú jíngshēn] deep parental love for children

市 [shì] 1 (n) 做买卖东西的地方 trade ; market ＊ 夜市。 night market 2 (n) 人口密集的行政中心和工商业较发达的地方 city; town ＊城市。town ＊都市 city

市场 [shíchǎng] market

市价 [shìjià] market price

市郊 [shìjiāo] the outskirt of a city; the suburb

市侩 [shìkuài] gigman; philistine

市侩主义 [shìkuàizhǔyì] philistinism

市立 [shì lì] municipal

市面萧条 [shì miàn xiāo tiáo] stagnation of industrial and business activities ; depression

市民 [shìmín] town or city dwellers

市区 [shìqū] the centre of a city

市容 [shìróng] appearance of the city

市委 [shìwěi] municipal party committee

市镇 [shìzhèn] town; small town

市政 [shìzhèng] municipal administration

市长 [shìzhǎng] a mayor

市政局 [shìzhèng jú] the municipal council

市政厅 [shìzhèngtīng] the city hall; the town hall; the municipal office

柿 [shì] (n) 落叶乔木。果实叫"柿子"，味甜可吃 the persimmon

释（釋）[shì] 1 (v) 说明，解说 explain ＊請你解释这难题。 Please explain this problem. 2 (v) 消散，解除 dissipate ; remove; resolve ＊ 他们的误会已冰释。 They have resolved the misunderstandings between them. 3 (v) 放，release, ＊犯人已被保释出来。The convict has been released on bail. 4 (n) 佛教创始人［释迦牟尼］的简称，泛指有关佛教的事物 a short form for Sakyamuni, the Buddha; things buddhist in general ＊ 释子 buddhist monk.

释放 [shìfàng] set free; release

释教 [shìjiào] buddhism

释然 [shìrán] be relieved; doubt dispelled

释义 [shìyì] to explain the meaning of a word or phrase

释疑 [shìyí] to remove a doubt

士 [shì] 1 (n) 研究学问的人，或从事某种职业的人 scholar ＊ 学士 Bachelor 硕士 Master 博士 Doctor 教士 a clergyman 护士 a nurse 2 (n) 古代男子的通称；以后对女子也尊称为"女士" an address to men in the olden days , now it is used for women also ＊陈女士收。 to madam Chen 3 (n) 对人的尊称 an address to a person to show one's respect ＊ 烈士。matyr 4 (n) 泛指

军人 soldiers in general

士敏土 [shìmǐntǔ] cement

士气 [shìqì] morale

仕 [shì] (n) 做官的人 an official

仕进 [shìjìn] to become an official

世 [shì] 1 (n) 古代以三十年为一世。现指一辈子 one's whole life time ＊我今生今世不会忘记您的恩惠。I will not forget your kindness throughout my life. 2 (n) 世世代代 from generation to generation ＊中医针灸世代相传。The Chinese acupuncture was passed from generation to generation. 3 (n) 时代 age ＊唐山地震是近世所罕见的天灾。The earthquake at Tangshan is quite a rare natural disaster at this age. 4 (n) 世界 the world ＊世上无难事。There is nothing difficult in the world

世代 [shìdài] generations

世故 [shìgù] the ways of the world; worldly-wise; sophisticated

世纪 [shìjǐ] century; a period of one hundred years

世交 [shìjiāo] a friendship of many generations

世界 [shìjiè] world; earth; global

世界观 [shìjièguān] view of the world

世面 [shìmiàn] world affairs; the world (e.g. see much of the world)

世人 [shìrén] people in the world; people in general

世事 [shìshì] world affairs

世世代代 [shìshìdàidài] generation after generation ; age after age

世态炎凉 [shìtài yánliáng] the ways of the world — the rich look down upon the poor

世外桃源 [shì wài táo yuán] secluded utopia

世袭 [shìxí] hereditary

是 [shì] 1 (adj) 这，这个 this; that ＊是日天气很好。The weather was very fine on that day. 2 (adj) 对，正确 right; positive; correct ＊他自以为是。He claimed that he is right. 3 (adv) 然;对的 yes; agree 甲：你准备好了吗？A: Are you ready? 乙：是，准备好了。B: Yes, I am ready. 4 (v) 係tobe 首要的财富是健康 The first wealth is health.5 (v) 表示存在 to show existence ＊前面正是我们的学校。Our school is right in front. 6 (inter) 加重语气 interjection to emphasize something said ＊是谁告诉你的？Who did tell you so? 7 (v) (inter)用在名词前面，含有"凡是"的意思 interjection used before a noun to mean "any", "all", "every" ＊是人都应该勤劳。Everyone should labour. 8 (v) 表示适合 verb-to-be,to show " at the right time" ＊这一场雨下的正是时候。The rain comes at the right time. 9 (v) 表示让步，含有"虽然"的意思 verb -to -be to show concession and imply "although" ＊东西旧是旧，可真耐用 Although the article is old, it is very lasting. 10 (inter) 用于问句 interjection used in a question＊你是要吃饭还是吃面？Do you take rice or noodles? 11 (conj) (谁……是……) 表示"只这样做"的意思 conjunction to show "acting in this manner only" ＊他是一个唯利是图的书商。He is a book trader selling books for profit only.

是否 [shìfǒu] whether or not

嗜 [shì] (v) 喜爱，爱好 to take delight in; to be fond of; to indulge in ＊他嗜酒如命。He is very much addicted to liquor.

嗜好 [shìhào] hobby; interest

适(適) [shì] 1 (adj) 切合，适合 suitable; fitting; agreeable＊这本书适合孩子们看。This book is suitable for children. 2 (adj) 舒服 comfortable; feeling well ＊我感觉不适。I am not feeling well. 3 (adv) 恰好 just * 我去曼谷时，适值学生示威。 I went to Bangkok just at the time of student demonstration 4 (v) 去，往 go to; proceed *无所适从。do not know who to follow. 5 (v) 旧称女子出嫁 marry (of women) *她已适人 She was married to somebody

适当 [shìdàng] appropriate ; proper; well; suitable

适得其反 [shì dé qí fǎn] got exactly the opposite; very disappointed ; on the contrary

适度 [shì dù] appropriate; proper

适合 [shìhè] suit; fit in with; accommodate to; conform with

适可而止 [shì kě ér zhǐ] stop at the right time ; avoid over doing

适口 [shìkǒu] palatable

适量 [shìliàng] suitable amount

适龄 [shìlíng] of the right age

适时 [shìshí] opportune; timely; well-timed; in good time

适宜 [shìyí] suitable; agreeable

适应 [shìyìng] adapt; adjust; fit

适用 [shìyòng] suitable for; applicable

适者生存 [shì zhě shēng cún] survival of the fittest

适中 [shìzhōng] central (of location); mild

逝 [shì] 1 (v) 失去，过去 lose; pass *光阴易逝。Time passes easily. 2 (v) 死 die *他病逝了。He died of illness.

逝世 [shìshì] to pass away

势(勢) [shì] 1 (n) 力量，势力power ; strength ; force ; influence *双方势均力敌（双方势力相等，不分上下）。Both sides are evenly matched in strength ; of equal strength. 2 (n) 冲击力 impact ; force *洪水来势凶猛。The flood is rushing at a formidable speed. 3(n) 人和动物的睾丸 the testicles of man and animal *去势。 to remove the testicles.

势必 [shìbì] will definitely ; compelled by circumstances

势不两立 [shì bù liǎng lì] incompatible with one another

势均力敌 [shìjūnlìdì] all square; be in equilibrium ; balance of forces

势利 [shì lì] devoted to the pursuit of wealth

势利眼 [shì·liyǎn] to treat people differently according to their wealth and status

势力 [shìlì] force; power; influence

势力范围 [shìlìfànwéi] spheres of influence

势如破竹 [shì rú pò zhú] as smooth as chopping through a bamboo ; irresistible

誓 [shì] 1 (v) 表示决心，依照说的话去实行 swear; vow; pledge;make an oath *他们宣誓就职。They were sworn into office. 2 (n) 表示决心的话pledge; a vow; an oath *他誓为伟大的理想终身奋斗。He pledged struggle for the great ideals throughout his whole life.

誓不反悔 [shìbùfǎnhuǐ] to swear not to break one' promise

誓师 [shìshī] to deliver a speech before an army and make a vow

誓死不降 [shìsǐbùxiáng] to vow not to surrender even till death

誓言 [shì yán] an oath; a vow; a pledge

誓约 [shìyuē] bound by an oath ; contract; words of honour

示 [shì] (v) 表明，把事物指出来或摆出来使人知道 make known ; show; manifest; direct *请出示你的居民证。Please show me your identity card

示范 [shì fàn] to demonstrate how something is done

示弱 [shìruò] to show one's weakness

示意 [shì yì] to make known one's wishes by facial expression, actions or words

示众 [shìzhòng] to make known to the

public

视(視) [shì] 1 (v) 看待 regard; consider ＊校长很重视语文的学习。The headmaster placed much emphasis on the study of languages. 2 (v) 看，观 see; look; inspect; examine ＊他在厂內巡视了一番。He made an inspection of the factory.

视察 [shìchá] inspect

视而不见 [shì'érbùjiàn] look at but not see; turn a blind eye to; shut one's eyes to

视力 [shìlì] eyesight; visual power; vision

视觉 [shìjué] the sense of vision

视若无睹 [shìruòwúdǔ] nonchalance

视死如归 [shì sǐ rú guī] fearless of death; courageous

视听教具 [shìtīngjiào jù] audio-visual aid

视爲畏途 [shìwéiwèitú] regard it as a frightening and dangerous road; scared

视线 [shìxiàn] line of vision; sight

视学官 [shìxuéguān] school inspector

视野 [shìyě] the field (range) of vision

饰(飾) [shì] 1 (v) 打扮，化装，使美观 decorate ＊他在装饰橱窗。He is decorating the showcase. 2 (n) 装饰品 ornament; decorative article ＊玉饰 jade ornament. 3 (v) 扮演 to play a role in a drama ＊她在剧中饰演皇后。She acts as a queen in the play. 4 (v) 遮掩 gloss over ＊文过饰非。to gloss over faults.

室 [shì] 1 (n) 屋子，房间 house; room ＊教室。classroom. 2 (n) 机关，团体的办事单位 office; room ＊实验室。laboratory. 3 (n) 指饮食的地方 place where food or drinks are served and sold ＊餐室。restaurant.

室內运动 [shì nèi yùn dòng] indoor sport

室內装修 [shì nèi zhuāng xiū] indoor decoration and renovation

谥(謚) [shì] (n) 中国封建时代，帝王和有地位的人死后所追加的称号；有文德的谥为［文］，如周文王；有武功的谥为［武］，如岳武穆。a posthumous title for the emperors or the influential people in ancient China

事 [shì] 1 (n) 发生的东西 affairs; matter ＊我们要关心国家和世界大事。We must concern ourselves with national and world affairs. 2 (n) 职业，工作 occupation; job ＊他已经离开学校出来谋事了。He has left school and is now looking for a job. 3 (v) 做，进行 to do; to carry on; to engage in; to work at ＊乞丐是个不事生产的人。The beggar is a person who does not engage in production.

事变 [shìbiàn] event; incident

事半功倍 [shìbàngōngbèi] more efficiency with less labour; very efficient; effective

事倍功半 [shìbèigōngbà] inefficient

事故 [shìgù] accident; trouble

事过境迁 [shìguòjìngqiān] When the event is over the circumstances are different

事迹 [shìjì] record of events; deed

事件 [shìjiàn] matter; affair; occurrence; incident

事例 [shìlì] case; example

事实 [shìshí] a matter of fact; the facts

事态 [shìtài] situation

事务 [shìwù] affairs; matters; work

事物 [shìwù] objects; things; phenomena

事项 [shìxiàng] item of business

事业 [shìyè] undertaking; career

事由 [shìyóu] reason; cause

事与愿违 [shìyǔyuànwéi] things don't turn out the way one wishes

事在人为 [shì zài rén wéi] events are determined by man

事主 [shìzhǔ] a client; the principal person concerned in any matter

shōu

收 [shōu] 1 (v) 把东西集起来 collect; gather＊他喜欢收集邮票。He likes to collect stamps. 2 (v) 合拢 close＊他的疮已收口了。His wound has been healed. 3 (v) 接到，接受 receive; accept ＊你的信我已经收到了。I have received your letter 4 (v) 把本来属於自己的东西要回来，招回 claim back; get back; retrieve ＊屋主决定收回这间屋子了。The house owner decided to claim back his house. 5 (v) 已割取的成熟农作物 harvest ＊秋收。autumn harvest . 6 (v) 结束，完结 finish ＊新年快到时，很多人都提早收工。When the New Year was approaching, many people stopped their work in advance.

收兵 [shōubīng] to withdraw troops

收藏 [shōucáng] to keep; to hide

收场 [shōuchǎng] to come to an end ; to conclude

收成 [shōu·chěng] harvest ; yield

收购 [shōugòu] to purchase in bulks

收归国有 [shōu guī guó yǒu] to nationalise

收回成命 [shōu huí chéng mìng] to withdraw an order

收获 [shōuhuò] to reap a crop; things gained; results achieved

收殓 [shōuliàn] to put a corpse into the coffin

收留 [shōulíu] to accept people in difficulties

收罗 [shōu luó] to gather people or materials

收据 [shōujù] receipts

收买 [shōumǎi] to purchase ;. to bribe a person

收盘 [shōupán] the end of a market ; to cease a business activity

收容 [shōuróng] to give shelter ; to accept

收入 [shōurù] income

收拾 [shōu·shi] to put (things) in order

收缩 [shōusuō] to contract

收条 [shōutiáo] receipts

收听 [shōutīng] to listen to the radio

收效 [shōuxào] have results ; reap; bear fruit

收养 [shōuyǎng] to adopt

收音机 [shōuyīnjī] radio

收账 [shōuzhàng] to collect accounts due

收支 [shōuzhī] income and expenditure

收租 [shōuzū] to collect rents

shǒu

手 [shǒu] 1 (n) 人使用工具、拿东西的肢体 hand 2 (v) 拿着 hold ＊人手一册。Everybody holds a copy. 3 (n) 作某种工作或有某种技能的本领 engage in some specific work or with some specific skill ＊运动选手。sportsmen. 4 (adv) 亲自的 personally ＊手稿。original drafts of a writer. 5 (v) 表示动作的开始或结束 to show the beginning or end of an action＊他已经着手编那本字典了。He has started to edit the dictionary 6 (n) 量词；用于技能和本领 numeral for skills ＊她最拿手的就是煮咖哩鱼。She is really good at preparing curry fish.

手臂 [shǒubì] the arm

手表 [shǒubiǎo] watch

手册 [shǒucè] a handbook

手抄 [shǒuchāo] handwritten; copied by hand

手电筒 [shǒudiàntóng] electric torch

手段 [shǒuduàn] means; vicious steps ; measures

手法 [shǒufǎ] technique; skills

手巾 [shǒujīn] towel

手风琴 [shǒufēngqín] accordion

手工 [shǒu gōng] handicraft ; handwork
手工业 [shǒu gōng yè] handicraft industry
手工艺品 [shǒugōngyìpǐn] handicraft
手巾 [shǒu jin] handkerchief
手榴弹 [shǒuliúdàn] a hand-grenade
手枪 [shǒuqiāng] pistol; revolver
手势 [shǒushì] gestures
手术 [shǒushù] surgical operations
手套 [shǒutào] gloves
手提包 [shǒutíbāo] a handbag
手腕 [shǒuwàn] wrist
手无寸铁 [shǒuwúcùntiě] unarmed
手下 [shǒuxià] adherent; follower; under one's order
手续 [shǒuxù] procedures
手杖 [shǒuzhàng] a walking stick
手掌 [shǒuzhǎng] palm
手指 [shǒuzhǐ] fingers
手制 [shǒuzhì] hand-made
手中 [shǒuzhōng] fall into one's hand ; be in one's possession
手足 [shǒuzú] brothers; the limbs
手足无措 [shǒu zú wú cuò] frightened and helpless

首 [shǒu] 1 (n) 头 head ＊首相。Prime Minister 2 (n) 领导者，带头的 chief; leader ＊各国首长。leaders of the various countries. 3 (adj) 第一，最高的 first; highest ＊首要任务。the first important task. 4 (adj) 开始，最先 the founder; the original manufacturer ＊这间书店是他首创的。This book shop was founded by him. 5 (n) 量词，诗、词、歌曲的篇数 numerals for poems, songs etc ＊一首歌。a song. 6 (v) 出头，告发 to inform ＊他已向当局自首了。He had given himself up to the authority.

首当其冲 [shǒudāngqíchōng] first to bear the brunt
首都 [shǒudū] capital of a country
首恶 [shǒuè] chief criminal ; ringleader
首府 [shǒufǔ] capital of a province or state
首领 [shǒulǐng] the leader; the chief
首名 [shǒumíng] first in position
首脑 [shǒunǎo] the head
首屈一指 [shǒuqūyìzhǐ] outstanding
首饰 [shǒushì] ornaments
首尾相应 [shǒuwěixiāngyìng] the beginning and the end correspond with each other
首先 [shǒuxiān] first; in the first place
首席代表 [shǒuxídàibiǎo] chief representative

守 [shǒu] 1 (v)保卫 to guard; to defend ＊以攻为守。defend by attacking. 2 (v) 遵照着做 to abide by; to follow ＊他们都是守法的公民。They are law-abiding citizens. 4 (v) 等待 wait ＊我们已经守候多时了。We have waited for a long time.

守财奴 [shǒucáinú] a miser
守寡 [shǒuguǎ] to remain a widow
守护 [shǒuhù] to protect ; to defend; to watch over
守纪律 [shǒujìlù] to keep to the rules and regulation ; well disciplined
守旧 [shǒujiù] conservative
守口如瓶 [shǒukǒurúpíng] refuse to reveal a secret ; to be secretive
守门 [shǒumén] to guard the door
守秘密 [shǒumímí] to keep a secret
守时 [shǒushí] to be punctual
守望相助 [shǒu wang xiāng zhù] to help one another
守卫 [shǒuwèi] to keep guard; to defend
守信 [shǒuxìn] true to one's words; keep one's promise

守株待兔 [shǒuzhūdàitù] lazy, trying to get something for free, without working for it; wishful thinking of obtaining some thing without an effort

shòu

受 [shòu] 1 (v) 动词的被动式 showing passive voice ＊天天下雨，街边小贩的生意大受损失。The street vendors suffer great losses because it rains everyday. 2(v) 忍受 bear; endure ＊他受不了敌人的严刑拷打。He could not bear the enemy's tortures. 3 (adj)适合 suitable ＊他的话很受用。His words benefit me a lot

受宠若惊 [shòu chǒng ruò jīng] startled by the favour bestowed

受害 [shòuhài] killed; be injured

受惊 [shòujīng] frightened; shocked

受精 [shòujīng] be fertilized; fertilization

受累 [shòulèi] word of thanks to a person who has done something for you ; be involved

受苦 [shòukǔ] to suffer from hardship

受困 [shòukún] be trapped

受骗 [shòupiàn] be deceived

受聘 [shòupìn] be employed

受屈 [shòu qù] be wronged

受辱 [shòurǔ] be insulted or disgraced

受托人 [shòutuòrén] trustee

受益人 [shòuyìrén] beneficiary

受用 [shòuyòng] comfortable; at ease

受罪 [shòuzùi] suffer

授 [shòu] 1 (v) 交给 give; grant; confer; authorise ＊政府授权他买了一些新机器。The Government authorised him tc buy some new machineries. 2 (v) 传，教 instruct; teach ＊他每天授课三小时。He teaches for three hours everyday

授命 [shòumìng] to give order

授意 [shòuyì] to hint; to intimate

授予 [shòuyǔ] to confer a medal, a rank or a title to a person during a ceremony

绶(綬) [shòu]〔绶带〕(n) 一种丝质的带子，用来系印或勋章 a ribbon attached on a medal or a seal

狩 [shòu](v)打猎 hunt＊本地区禁止狩猎 Hunting is forbidden in this area.

寿(壽) [shòu] 1 (n) 生命，年岁 life; age ＊人寿保险。life insurance. 2 (adj) (n) 年岁长久 long(life); longevity ＊仁者寿。Those who are kind live long. 3 (n) 生日 birthday ＊做寿。to celebrate the birthday 4 (adj)属于待葬死者的 things for the dead during burial ＊寿衣。a burial dress. 寿木 coffin

寿比南山 [shòubǐnánshān] longevity like Nan San

寿命 [shòumìng] age; life

寿终正寝 [shòuzhōngzhèngqǐn] dying of old age at home; dying a natural death in peace

售 [shòu] (v) 卖出 sell ＊今天开始售票。Tickets will be sold from today.

售货员 [shòu huò yuán] salesman

售价 [shòujià] selling price

售卖 [shòumài] to sell

售票房 [shòupiàofáng] booking office ; ticket office

售票员 [shòupiàoyuán] ticket seller; conductor (e.g. bus)

售完 [shòuwàn] sold out

兽(獸) [shòu] 1 (n) 一般指四条腿全身生毛的哺乳动物 an animal; a beast ＊野兽。wild beasts. 2 (adj) 比喻野蛮，下流 brutish ; beastly and base ＊兽行。beastly act e.g. rape.

兽心 [shòuxīn] cruel; inhuman

兽行 [shòuxìng] brutality

兽性 [shòuxìng] bestial nature

兽医 [shòuyī] a veterinary surgeon

兽欲 [shòuyù] beastly lust; desire

瘦 [shòu] 1 (adj) 脂肪少 thin; lean ＊那个病人经过一场病后，身体变得瘦弱。After the illness, the patient had become thin and weak

瘦弱 [shòuruò] thin and weak
瘦小 [shòuxiǎo] thin and small
瘦削 [shòuxuē] thin; lean

shū

抒 [shū] (v) 表达 express (emotion)

抒发 [shūfā] to express (one's sentiments)
抒情诗 [shūqìngshī] a lyric
抒写 [shūxiě] to express and describe through writing

舒 [shū] (v) 伸展，张开 spread out ; stretch

舒畅 [shūchàng] in good spirit; cheerful; pleasant
舒服 [shūfú] comfortable
舒适 [shū shì] at ease ; comfortable; cosy
舒心 [shuxin] feel happy
舒展 [shūzhǎn] stretch; comfortable

梳 [shū] 1 (n) 理发的用具。 comb 2 (v) 用梳子理头发 to comb ＊我每天早上洗脸梳头。Every morning I wash my face and comb my hair.

疏 [shū] 1 (v) 清除阻塞，使通畅 to clear away obstacles ; to ease the flow; to make the going smooth＊农民在疏通水田间的排沟。The farmers are clearing the irrigation canals in the padi field. 2 (adj) 稀，不密，少 sparse＊晨星疏落。The morning stars are few and sparsely distributed. 3 (adj) 关系远，不亲近，不熟悉 distant in relationship; unfamiliar＊他是刚从印尼来的，所以人地生疏。He had just arrived from Indonesia so he found the people and place unfamiliar. 4 (adj) 不细密，粗心 careless; negligent ＊他的疏忽造成了一些不必要的损失。His negligence has brought about some unnecessary damages. 5 (v) 分开 separate; disperse＊村民们在敌军来袭击之前赶快疏散。The villagers dispersed quickly before the enemy attacked.

疏忽 [shūhù] negligent; relax vigilance against; overlook
疏懒 [shūlǎn] idle; indolent; lazy
疏林 [shūlín] a thinly-grown grove of trees
疏漏 [shūlòu] negligent ; careless ; heedless; miss
疏散 [shūsàn] disperse; spread out
疏通 [shūtōng] dredge
疏远 [shūyuǎn] alienated; estranged ; at arm's length; to turn a cold shoulder
疏于防范 [shūyúfángfàn] heedless at taking due precautions ; not well guarded

蔬 [shū] (n) 食用植物 vegetables

叔 [shū] 1 (n) 父亲的弟弟 father's younger brother; uncle 2 (n) 丈夫的弟弟 husband's younger brother 3 (n) 对父亲的同辈而年纪较轻的男子的尊称 an address for a father's male friend who is younger than father but of the same generation ＊李叔叔。Uncle Lee.

淑 [shū] (adj) 善良，美好 virtuous ; fine ＊淑女。 a virtuous woman.

菽 [shū] (n) 豆类的总称 a collective name for beans; peas etc ＊ 菽麦。bean and wheat.

输（輸） [shū] 1 (v) 运送 transport ; convey ＊泰国每年输出大量的白米。 Thailand exports big quantities of rice yearly. 2 (v) 败，失去 lose; defeat ＊他赌输了很多钱。 He lost a lot of money in gambling.

输出 [shūchū] export
输卵管 [shūluǎnguǎn] oviduct in the female reproductive system
输尿管 [shū niào guǎn] ureter in the urinary system
输送 [shūsòng] to transport
输送带 [shūsòngdài] conveyor belt
输赢 [shūyíng] gain and loss

输油管 [shū yóu guǎn] oil pipe-line
输血 [shūxuè] transfusion of blood ; to transfuse blood

姝 [shū] (n) 美女 a pretty girl

殊 [shū] 1 (adj) 不同，差异 different ; unlike 人人可以看出贫富之间的悬殊。Everyone could see the tremendous differences between the poor and the rich. 2 (adj) 特别，不同一般 special ; distinguished ＊他屡建殊功。He has made many fine achievements. 3 (adv) 很，极 very; extremely ＊他的学业成织殊佳。His results in study are very good.

殊功 [shūgōng] distinguished services; special merits
殊可钦敬 [shū kě qīn jìng] worthy of being respected
殊死战 [shūsǐzhàn] fight to the death
殊途同归 [shū tú tóng guī] arriving at the same destination from different routes
殊效 [shūxiào] special effects

书(書) [shū] 1 (n) 装订成册的著作 book ＊教科书。text book. 2 (v) 写字，记录 write; copy ＊书法。calligraphy; the art of penmanship. 3 (n) 字体 writing ＊楷书。standard chinese calligraphy. 4 (n) 文件 document ＊证明书。certificate＊协议书。agreement. 5 (n) 信件 letter ＊家书。letter from home

书报 [shūbào] books and newspapers
书包 [shūbāo] school-bag
书橱 [shūchú] a bookcase
书呆子 [shūdāizǐ] a bookworm
书店 [shūdiàn] book shop; book store
书法 [shūfǎ] handwriting; calligraphy
书房 [shūfáng] a study
书局 [shūjú] book shop; a book store
书记 [shūjì] a clerk
书籍 [shūjí] books
书架 [shūjià] a book shelf
书刊 [shūkān] books and publications ; magazine
书库 [shūkù] room for storing books
书面 [shūmiàn] written form
书面申请 [shūmiànshēnqıng] to apply in writing
书面语 [shūmiànyǔ] written language
书名号 [shūmínghào] editorial marks for books or articles 《》 or 〈 〉
书目 [shūmù] catalogue of books
书评 [shūpíng] book review
书签 [shūqiān] book mark
书写 [shūxiě] write
书信 [shūxìn] letter
书桌 [shūzhuō] desk

枢(樞) [shū] (n) 套在门和墙之转轴 an axis; the centre of motion; a pivot; a hinge ＊脊髓是神经中枢。The spinal cord is the centre of nervous system.

枢纽 [shūnǐu] cardinal point; a hinge; a pivot
枢密院 [shūmìyuàn] the privy council

倏 [shū] (adv) 极快地，忽然地 suddenly＊松鼠倏地不见了。The squirrel disappeared suddenly.

shú

孰 [shú] (pron) 谁；什么 who? what? which? ＊孰是孰非？who is in the right and who in the wrong?

塾 [shú] (n) 学校 a school ＊私塾 a family school; ＊村塾 a village school.

熟 [shú] 1 (adj) 煮过的 cooked ＊熟食。cooked food 2 (adj) (果实或种子)长成 ripe ＊番茄熟了。The tomatoes are ripe. 3 (adj) 常见的；知道清楚的 familiar ＊这个地方我不熟。I do not know this place well. 4 (adj) 程度深 deep ; fast ＊他睡熟了。He is fast asleep. 5 (adj) 经过加工炼制的 processed; wrought ＊熟铁。wrought iron.

熟客 [shúkè] a well-acquainted guest; an old customer

熟练 [shúliàn] skilled; experienced
熟路 [shúlù] familiar route
熟能生巧 [shúnéngshēngqiǎo] practice makes perfect
熟人 [shúrén] a familiar person ; an acquaintance
熟识 [shúshì] acquaint oneself with ; be familiar with
熟视无睹 [shúshìwúdǔ] heedless
熟手 [shúshǒu] an old hand ; an experienced worker
熟思 [shúsī] to think in depth
熟习 [shúxí] have full and deep knowledge of ; to know a subject at one's finger-tips
熟悉 [shúxī] well versed in ; familiar with
熟语 [shúyǔ] idiom
熟字 [shúzì] familiar word

赎(贖) [shú] (v) 换回；抵销 to redeem; to ransom ＊他去当舖把手表赎回。He went to the pawnshop to redeem his watch.
赎金 [shújīn] ransom
赎买政策 [shúmǎizhèngcé] policy of redemption ; buyout policy
赎罪 [shúzuì] to expiate; to redeem from sin
赎身 [shúshēn] redeem oneself ; ransom oneself

shǔ

署 [shǔ] 1 (n) 办公的处所或机关 an office; a government office ＊警署。police station. 2 (v) 布置 arrange ＊将领们开会讨论军事部署计划。The generals held a meeting to discuss about military plans. 3 (v) 签名 sign ＊双方签署了这份联合公报。Both parties have signed this joint communique.
署名 [shǔmíng] signature; sign one's name

曙 [shǔ] (n) 天刚亮 dawn
曙光 [shǔguāng] the first streak of light; dawn.
曙色 [shǔsè] dawning ; the gray of the morning

薯 [shǔ] (n) 块根，含大量淀粉，可作粮食或可供制淀粉等。tuber ＊木薯；树薯 cassava; tapioca

薯粉 [shǔfěn] starch powder
薯蓣 [shǔyù] the Chinese yam

暑 [shǔ] (n) 炎热，炎热的季节 the summer heat; hot weather ＊暑天。hot days in summer.
暑假 [shǔjià] summer vacation
暑气 [shǔqì] the heat on hot days
暑期学校 [shǔ qī xué xiào] summer school
暑天 [shǔtiān] the hot summer

蜀 [shǔ] 1 (n) 古代国名 name of a kingdom in ancient China 2 (n) 四川省的简称 Szechuan province in China

鼠 [shǔ] (n) 一种小哺乳动物。门齿很发达，无齿根，终生继续生长，常借啮物以磨短，是偷吃粮食，咬坏衣物，传染疾病的有害动物 rat; mouse
鼠目寸光 [shǔmùcùnguāng] cannot see far (fig).—short-sightedness
鼠疫 [shǔyì] the bubonic plague; the black plague (death)

属(屬) [shǔ] 1 (n) 类别; 门类 a class; a category ＊金属 metal 家属 one's family members 2(v) 归从；附从 belong ＊这问题属化学范围。The question belongs to the field of chemistry.
属地 [shǔdì] annexed territory; colony
属国 [shǔguó] vassal state
属实 [shǔshí] turn out true; be verified

属下 [shǔxià] subordinates; under the jurisdiction of
属性 [shǔxìng] an attribute
属于 [shǔyú] belong to

黍 [shǔ] (n) 一年生草本植物，果实叫黍子，性粘，可酿酒。the glutinous millet

数(數) [shǔ] (v) 计算 count ＊我来数一数 Let me count. ＊全班数他成绩最好。We count him the best in results in the whole class.

数词 [shùcí] numeral
数典忘祖 [shǔdiǎnwàngzǔ] to forget one's origin or ancestors
数额 [shù'é] number; quota
数量 [shùliàng] quantity
数目 [shùmù] number
数学 [shùxué] mathematics
数一数二 [shǔ yī shǔ èr] among the best; outstanding; count at the top
数值 [shùzhí] number; numerical value
另见 [shù]
[shuò]

shù

术(術) [shù] (n) 技艺; 方法 art; skills; method ＊他的医术高明 He is good in the art of healing

术语 [shùyǔ] technical term

述 [shù] (v) 说，讲 narrate; tell ＊他要我陈述整个事件的经过。He wants me to narrate the whole story again.

述评 [shùpíng] narrate; comment
述说 [shùshuō] describe; tell; narrate; detail
述语 [shùyǔ] predicate
述职 [shùzhí] (of an ambassador) report work

束 [shù] 1 (v) 捆住、系住 bind; tie ＊他腰束皮带。He tied a leather belt around his waist. 2 (n) 成扎，成捆的东西 a bundle; a cluster; ＊花束。a bouquet 3 (v) 加以限制或受限制 restrain; restrict ＊父母不要太过约束孩子们的行动。Parents should not restrict their children too much.

束缚 [shùfù] to chain; restrict
束手待毙 [shùshǒudàibì] waiting death with bound hands; not doing anything positive to avoid disaster or failure
束手就擒 [shǔ shòu jiù qín] to offer no resistance and be caught
束手束脚 [shù shǒu shù jiǎo] undue caution; over-cautiousness
束手无策 [shùshǒuwucè] helpless
束之高阁 [shǔzhigàogé] have it tied and placed on high shelf; left unused

漱 [shù] (v) 含水洗口腔 rinse out ＊吃完饭後要漱口。We should rinse out our mouths after dinner.

树(樹) [shù] 1 (n) 木本植物的总称 tree 2 (v) 种植，栽培，培养。to plant; to grow ＊十年树木，百年树人。It takes ten years to grow a tree, but it requires hundred years to educate a person. 3 (v) 建立，确立 establish; found; set up ＊他给我们树立了一个很好的榜样 He has set up a very fine example for us.

树丛 [shùcóng] groves
树碑立传 [shùbēilìzhuàn] glorify somebody by singing the praises of his life
树倒猢狲散 [shùdǎohúsūnsàn] Once the tree falls, the monkeys on it will flee helter-skelter; rats leave a sinking ship
树敌 [shùdí] incur enmity

树干 [shùgàn] tree trunk
树胶 [shùjiào] rubber
树林 [shùlín] forests; woods
树皮 [shùpí] tree bark
树荫 [shùyīn] the shade under a tree
树脂 [shùzhī] resin from the tree
树枝 [shùzhī] branches

数(數) [shù] 1 (n) 记量的名目 number 2 (adj) 几个;少许 few; several *在昨天的骚乱中,有数十人被拘捕。In the commotion yesterday, several people were arrested. 3 (n) 命运 fate; destiny *在数难逃。It is fate and cannot be avoided

数词 [shucí] numerals
数滴 [shùdī] a few drops
数量 [shùliàng] amount; quantity
数日 [shùrì] several days in succession
数学 [shùxue] mathematics
数字 [shùzì] figures; numerals
另见 [shǔ]
[shuò]

戍 [shù] (v) 军队驻守 to guard 戍边 to guard the border region

竖(豎) [shù] (adj) 跟地平线垂直的;直立的 vertical; erect *铁塔竖在山上。The steel tower stands erect on the hill.

竖井 [shùjǐng] a vertical shaft in mining
竖旗 [shù qí] to hoist a flag

庶 [shù] 1(adj) 众多 numerous; various; all;我们会成为一个富庶的国家。In the future our country will become a land of abundance and wealth. 2 (adv) 将近;差不多;大概 nearly; about; thus; it may be; so that 庶不致误 so that one may not blunder 3 (adj) 妾的;旁支的 of concubine *庶出 children of the concubine

庶民 [shùmín] the people;the masses
庶务 [shùwù] general affairs; miscellaneous matters
庶子 [shùzǐ] a concubine's son

恕 [shù] (v) 原谅 forgive; pardon; excuse *恕我不能奉陪。Forgive me for not being able to accompany you.

恕难从命 [shùnáncóngmìng] pardon me for not being able to accept the order
恕罪 [shùzuì] to pardon a crime

墅 [shù] 1 (n) 田野中的草房 a cottage 2 (n) 住宅以外的供游玩休养的园林房屋 a villa; a bungalow; a summer house

shuā

刷 [shuā] 1 (n) 清洁或涂抹东西的用具,用毛棕制成。brush* 牙刷 tooth-brush 2 (v) 用刷子除去脏东西 to brush *工人用灰水刷墙壁。The worker brushed the wall with slaked lime.

刷洗 [shuāxǐ] to brush and clean; scrub
刷新 [shuāxīn] to renovate
刷子 [shuāzi] brush

shuǎ

耍 [shuǎ] 1 (v) 游戏 play *妈妈劝告孩子们不要常常到海边去玩耍。Mother advised her children not to play at the sea-side often. 2 (v) 玩弄捉弄;舞弄 trifle; play

耍花招 [shuǎhuāzhāo] to play tricks
耍赖 [shuǎlài] be deliberatery dishonest
耍弄 [shuǎnòng] make a fool of; play
耍拳脚 [shuǎquánjiǎo] to do gymnastics
耍手腕 [shuǎshǒuwàn] play a trick; manoeuvre; juggle with

shuāi

衰 [shuāi] (adj) 人或事物由强变弱 growing weak *她的父亲年老力衰。Her father is old and weak.

衰败 [shuāibài] be in a state of decline

and decay
衰老 [shuāilǎo] old and feeble
衰弱 [shuāiruò] weak ; feeble
衰退 [shuāituì] decline;decay; fall off

摔 [shuāi] 1 (v) 跌交跌倒 fall down ∗他从树上摔了下来。He fell down from the tree-top. 2 (v) 用力扔，抛 throw; cast ∗把那双旧鞋摔掉。Throw away that pair of old shoes. 3 (v) 使落下而破损 break ∗妹妹把碗摔了。Our younger sister has broken the bowl.
摔打 [shuāidǎ] give hard knocks; treat roughly
摔交 [shuāijiāo] wrestling

shuǎi

甩 [shuǎi] 1 (v) 抡，摆动 flip; shake; swing ∗他在做甩手运动。He is doing arm-swinging exercise. 2 (v) 扔 throw;cast ∗他甩了一枚手榴弹。He has hurled a hand grenade.

shuài

率 [shuài] 1 (v) 带领 lead ∗他率队出击。He led the army to attack. 2 (adj) 爽直;坦白 frank and honest; straight ∗他很直率。He is straight and frank. 3 (adj) 轻易，不仔细，不慎重 careless; not cautious; rash ∗他做事很草率。He is rash in his work.
率领 [shuàilǐng] lead; conduct
率众 [shuài zòng] to lead the group
另见 [lù]

帅(帥) [shuài] 1 (n) 军队中最高指挥官 commander-in-chief ∗元帅 marshall∗统帅commander-in-chief 2 (adj) 漂亮，好看 smart; handsome . ∗他长得很帅。He is very handsome.

shuān

拴 [shuān] (v)用绳子系上 tie with a rope ∗他把马拴在树桩上。He tied the horse to the tree stump.

栓 [shuān] (n) 器物上可以开关的机件 a control gadget ∗枪栓。trigger on a gun

闩(閂) [shuān] 1 (n) 插在门後使门推不开的棍或铁条 a bolt behind the door 2 (v) 插上门闩 bolt ∗把门闩上。Bolt the door.

shuàn

涮 [shuàn] 1 (v) 把东西放在水里摆动洗清洁 to rinse with water ∗把衣服涮一涮。Rinse the clothes. 2 (v) 以火锅快煮 to quick-boil in a chafing dish ∗涮羊肉 lamb chafing dish

shuāng

双(雙) [shuāng] 1 (adj) 偶数的，跟"单"相对，如二、四、六、八等都是双数 even (of number, opposite of odd) 2 (n) 量词 numeral ∗一双鞋。a pair of shoes. 3 (adj) 加倍 double ; two ∗我要做双倍的工作。I have to do twice as much work.
双边 [shuāngbiān] bilateral
双重 [shuāngchóng] double
双层重床 [shuāngchéngchóngchuáng] double decker
双重间谍 [shuāngchóng jiàndié] double spy
双重人格 [shuāngchóng réngé] double character
双唇音 [shuāngchúnyīn] labial
双打 [shuāngdǎ] double (as in table tennis, badminton)
双方 [shuāngfāng] both sides ; both parties
双杠 [shuānggàng] horizontal bars
双关 [shuāngguān] a word or phrase with double meanings
双管齐下 [shuāngguǎnqíxià] to undertake two things simultaneously for a similar purpose

双轨 [shuāngguǐ] double track

双季稻 [shuāngjìdào] double cropping padi

双亲 [shuāngqīn] parents

双拳难敌四手 [shuāng quán nán dí sì shǒu] two fists can not be equal to four hands

双日 [shuāngrì] date with an even number

双数 [shuāngshù] even number

霜 [shuāng] 1 (n)附着在地面或物体上面的白色微细结晶，是接近地面的水蒸气冷至摄氏零度以下凝结而成的，一般产生于晴朗无风的夜间或清晨。frost ＊ 早霜 morning frost 2 (adj) 比喻白色 grizzled ; hoar ＊ 霜鬓。grizzled hair on both sides of the face

孀 [shuāng] (n) 死了丈夫的妇人 a widow ＊ 遗孀 widow

shuǎng

爽 [shuǎng] 1 (adj) 明朗，清亮 clear; bright ＊秋高气爽。The atmosphere in the very Autumn is fresh and clear 2 (adj) 痛快，直率 cheerful; delighted; happy ＊他为人豪爽。He is dauntless and cheerful. 3 (adj) 舒服 comfortable; well

爽快 [shuǎng kuai] pleasant; light-hearted; refreshing

爽朗 [shuǎnglǎng] cheerful; open-minded; delighted

爽身粉 [shuǎng shēn fěn] talcum powder

爽直 [shuǎngzhí] straight and cheerful

shuí

谁(誰) [shuí] 1 (pron) 什么人？who?＊谁在敲门啦？Who is that knocking at the door? 2 (pron) 任何人，无论什么人 anybody ＊ 大家抢着干，谁都不肯落后。All strive to work hard ; nobody likes to lag behind.

shuǐ

水 [shuǐ] 1 (n) 一种无色、无臭、透明的液体。water 2 (n) 江、河、湖、海的通称 the general term for river, stream, lake and sea ＊ 水陆交通 water and land transport 3 (n) 汁液 fluid; liquid ＊ 药水 liquid medicine. a lotion ＊ 墨水 ink

水泵 [shuǐbèng] water pump

水彩 [shuǐcǎi] water colour

水产 [shuǐchǎn] marine products ; aquatic products

水池 [shuǐchí] a water tank; a pool

水道 [shuǐdào] water course; a channel ; a canal

水稻 [shuǐdào] wet padi

水底 [shuǐdǐ] at the bottom of a pond of water

水分 [shuǐfèn] moisture

水缸 [shuǐgāng] earthen jar

水沟 [shuǐgōu] drain

水管子 [shuǐguǎnzi] water tube

水果 [shuǐguǒ] fruit

水壶 [shuǐhú] kettle

水火不相容 [shuǐ huǒ bú xīng róng] treat each other like enemies

水库 [shuǐkù] reservoir

水利 [shuǐlì] water conservancy

水力 [shuǐlì] water-power ;hydraulic power

水力发电厂 [shuǐ lì fā diàn zhǎn] a hydro - electric power station

水利工程 [shuǐlìgōngchéng] water conservancy project

水力学 [shuǐlìxué] hydraulics

水落石出 [shuǐluòshíchu] truth fully revealed

水面 [shuǐmiàn] the surface of water

水母 [shuǐmǔ] a jelly-fish

水平 [shuǐpíng] water level; standard
水渠 [shuǐqú] canal; irrigation ditch
水上人家 [shuǐ shàng rénjiā] people who live in boats on water
水深火热 [shuǐshēnhuǒrè] intolerable living condition; in extreme difficulty
水手 [shuǐshǒu] sailor; seamen; crew on a ship
水乳交融 [shuǐrǔjiāoróng] to get on very well
水位 [shǔiwèi] water level
水仙花 [shuǐxiānhuā] narcissus
水泄不通 [shuǐ xiè bù tōng] crowded with many people
水银 [shuǐyín] mercury
水域 [shǔiyù] body of water
水源 [shuǐyuán] the source of a river
水灾 [shuǐzaī] flood
水闸 [shuǐzhá] a dam; a flood gate
水涨船高 [shuǐzhǎngchuángāo] as the water swells, the boat rises
水蒸气 [shuǐzhēngqì] water vapour
水蛭 [shuǐzhì] leech

水准 [shuǐzhǔn] standard

shuì

说(說) [shuì] (v) 用言语劝告，使别人听从自己的意见 persuade ∗孔子到许多国家游说，劝各国的君主接受他的政治思想。Confucius went to many countries to persuade the feudal lords to accept his political thoughts
说客 [shuìké] persuasive politicians; intriguing persons
另见 [shuō]

税 [shuì] (n) 国家向组织或个人征收的钱或实物. tax; duty; toll ∗所得税。 income tax
税额 [shuì'é] the amount of tax to be paid
税率 [shuìlù] rate of duty; tariff rates
税收 [shuìshōu] tax revenue

睡 [shuì] (v) 闭目安息，大脑皮层处于休息状态 sleep ∗他正睡在地板上。 He is sleeping on the floor now.
睡觉 [shuìjiào] to sleep
睡眠 [shuìmián] sleep
睡衣 [shuìyī] nightdress; pyjamas

shǔn

吮 [shǔn] (v) 用嘴吸取 suck ∗婴儿在吮乳。 The baby is sucking the breast.

shùn

舜 [shùn] (n) 传说中国古代部落联盟的首领，后来作为勤劳、勇敢和智慧的象征 chief of a tribal community in ancient China; symbol for diligence, courage and wisdom

瞬 [shùn] (v) 一眨眼，转眼，极短的时间 blink; wink ∗瞬息之间，那颗卫星就消失了。 The satellite disappeared in a wink.
瞬息万变 [shùnxīwànbiàn] myriad of changes in a blink

顺(順) [shùn] 1 (adj) 趋向同一个方向 in the same direction ∗木筏顺流而下。 The raft flows down in the same direction as the current. 2 (v) 沿，循 follow ∗他顺着大街走。 He follows the main road. 3 (adv) 随，趁便 at one's convenience; by the way ∗你如果要去邮政局，顺便给我买几张五分的邮票。If you happen to go to the Post Office, please buy for me a few five-cent stamps by the way. 4 (v) 整理，使有条理 arrange; to make something reasonable; justifiable ∗当工友们的生产力已提高的时候，增加薪水是顺理成章的。Now that the productivity of workers has been raised, it is justifiable to increase their salaries. 5 (v) 服从，不违背 obey; yield to ＊他顺从父母的意思。 He obeys what his parents say. 6 (adv) 次序，按次序 in regular order ＊他顺次数下去。 He counts according to the order of arrangement. 7 (v) 适合 favourable; suitable＊他的行为叫人看了很不顺眼。His behaviour is quite disagreeable to the eye

顺次 [shuncì] in regular order; by turns

顺风 [shùnfēng] with the wind; favourable winds; fair wind

顺口 [shùnkǒu] fluent ; to say without thinking

顺利 [shùnlì] smooth going ; favourable

顺路 [shùnlù] by the way; convenient; on the route

顺其自然 [shùnqízìrán] in accordance with its natural tendencies

顺手牵羊 [shùnshǒuqiānyáng] to take possession of something when the opportunity avails itself

顺我者昌;逆我者亡 [shùnwǒzhěchāng nìwǒzhěwáng] those who follow me will prosper and those who oppose, perish

shuō

说(說) [shuō] 1 (v) 用话来表达自己的思想 to say;to speak; to talk; to tell; to narrate; ＊我有话要说。I have something to say. 2 (v) 解释 explain ＊经他一说，我就明白了。 I understand after his explanation. 3 (n) 言论，主张 sayings; theory＊黑格尔学说 Hegel's theory (on philosophy) 4 (v) 责备，批评 reproach; criticize ＊我说了他一顿。I criticized him. 另见 [shuì]

说不过去 [shuōbùguòqù] not reasonable; difficult to explain

说服 [shuōfú] to convince

说谎 [shuōhuǎng] to tell lies

说教 [shuōjiào] to preach; to expound something mechanically

说来话长 [shuōlaíhuàcháng] it is a long story to tell

说梦话 [shuōmènghuà] to talk in one's dream

说明 [shuōmíng] explanation; to show ; to illustrate

说明书 [shuōmíngshū] an explanatory booklet ; leaflet

说项 [shuōxiàng] to mention favourably: to say something good for somebody

shuò

朔 [shuò] 1 (n) 阴历的每月初一 the first day of the lunar month 2 (adj) 北 north ＊朔风。north wind

铄(鑠) [shuò] 1 (v) 熔化金属 melt (a metal)＊铄金。to melt gold 2 (v) 消毁，消损 destroy damage ; 3 (adj) 光明貌 bright

数(數) [shuò] (adv) 屡次 for many times; frequently ＊车祸数见不鲜。Road accidents occur frequently 另见 [shǔ] [shù]

硕(碩) [shuò] (adj) 大 huge＊整个地球可以想象为一个硕大无朋的磁石。 The whole earth can be imagined as one huge magnet.＊硕果。big and ripe fruits.

硕果仅存 [shuòguǒjǐncún] the only good one left

硕士 [shuòshì] Master of Arts or Science

sī

斯 [sī] (adj) 这个，这样，这里 this; here ＊如斯。like this manner; ＊斯人。this person ＊生于斯 born here

斯大林 [sīdàlín] Stalin

斯德哥尔摩 [sīdegérmò] Stockholm

斯时 [sīshí] this time; presently
斯文 [sīwén] gentlemanly; scholarly
斯文败类 [sī wén bài lèi] polished scoundrels

撕 [sī] (v) 扯破 tear * 他把布撕成两块。 He tears the cloth into two.
撕毁 [sīhuǐ] to destroy by tearing
撕开 [sīkaī] to rip open
撕票 [sīpiào] to tear the ticket ; to kill one who is held for ransom
撕碎 [sīsuì] to tear into pieces

嘶 [sī] 1 (v) 马叫声 neigh (of horse) * 我听见人喊马嘶声。I heard people shouting and the horse neighing. 2 (adj) 声音沙哑 hoarse (in voice) * 她哭得声嘶力竭。She cried until she lost her voice and strength.

厮 [sī] 1 (n) 服杂役的人 a menial; a servant * 小厮。an errand-boy 2 (n) 旧时对人的轻慢称呼 an unpolite address of someone * 这厮。this fellow .
厮杀 [sīshà] to fight or kill each other

思 [sī] 1 (v) 想，考虑，动脑筋 think * 人是会思考的动物。 Man is an animal that can think. 2 (v) 想念，掛念 think constantly of a person * 她思念着好久不曾见面的母亲。She is thinking of her mother whom she had not seen for years. 3 (n) 思路，想法 line of thought; thought * 他的文思敏捷。He is quick in literary thought
思潮 [sīcháo] the trend of thought; a continuous thought
思考 [sīkǎo] think carefully; meditate; ruminate
思量 [sīliàng] weigh and consider
思慕 [sīmù] to think of somebody whom one respects
思念 [sīniàn] remember fondly; feel the absence of
思前想后 [sīqiánxiǎnghòu] to recall what has happened and to think about the future
思索 [sīsuǒ] ponder; to speculate
思维 [sīwéi] thought ; thinking ; to think
思想 [sīxiǎng] thought — a reflection of the world
思想斗争 [sī xiǎng dòu zhēng] ideological struggle; struggle in mind
思想家 [sīxiǎngjīa] a thinker
思绪 [sīxù] train of thought

丝(絲) [sī] 1 (n) 绸缎等的纤维原料 silk 2 (adj) 形容极少，细微 little; small amount * 他的工作丝毫没有进展。 There is little progress in his work
丝绸 [sīchóu] silk
丝瓜 [sīguā] the loofah gourd
丝毫 [sīháo] the slightest; in the least ; at all
丝绵 [sīmián] silk floss; silk-wadding
丝袜 [sīwà] silk stockings
丝织品 [sīzhīpǐn] silks; silk fabrics

司 [sī] 1 (v) 主管 manage * 司炉。boiler attendant 2 (n) 中央各部中所设立的分工办事单位 a bureau; a department; an office * 外交部礼宾司。 protocol of the ministry of Foreign Affairs
司法部门 [sīfǎbùmén] judiciary departments
司空见惯 [sīkōngjiànguàn] normally seen; nothing unusual
司机 [sījī] driver; chauffeur
司仪 [sīyí] master of ceremony; compere
司账 [sīzhàng] book keeper

私 [sī] 1 (adj) 只顾自己的，跟"公"相对 selfish * 他很自私。 He is very selfish. 2 (adj) 属于个人的 personal; private * 这是他的私事。This is his personal affair. 3 (adj) 秘密的，不公开的，不合法的 secret; illegal * 他们在窃窃私语。 They are whispering secretly.
私奔 [sībēn] to elope; to run away
私邸 [sīdǐ] private home of an official
私立学校 [sīlìxuéxiào] private school
私立银行 [sīlìyínháng] private bank

私情 [sīqíng] private feelings ; illicit love
私人秘书 [sīrénmìshū] private secretary
私人企业 [sīrénqìyē] private enterprise
私生活 [sīshēnghuó] private life
私生子 [sīshēngzǐ] an illegitimate child ; bastard
私有制社会 [sīyǒuzhìshèhuì] a society with private ownerships
私运∶私带 [sīyùn] :[sīdài] to smuggle
私心 [sīxīn] selfish motive
私信 [sīxìn] a private letter
私自 [sīzì] privately; arbitrarily

sǐ

死 [sǐ] 1 (v) 失去生命，跟"活"相对 die ✱他生得伟大，死得光荣。He led a great life, and died a glorious death. 2 (adv) 不顾生命，拼命 desperately to the last ✱他们死守阵地。They defended their battle ground to the last. 3 (adv) 形容达到极点 extremely ✱他高兴死了。He is extremely happy. 4 (adj) 不能通过 blocked ✱那是一条死路(喻)。It is a blind alley 5 (adj) 固定，不灵活，不活动，没有朝气 still; non-versatile; inactive; not lively ✱做事情不能死板。We should not be rigid in our dealings. 6 (adj) 不可调和的 uncompromising ✱他们是死对头。They are at loggerheads.
死灰復燃 [sǐhuīfùrán] re-emergence of something that was quelled or banished
死火山 [sǐhuǒshān] an extinct volcano
死结 [sǐjié] a hard knot
死气沉沉 [sǐqìchénchén] dull ; not lively ; quiet
死尸 [sǐshī] dead body
死水 [sǐshuǐ] stagnant water
死亡 [sǐwáng] death; to die
死亡率 [sǐwánglù] mortality rate; death rate
死刑 [sǐxíng] death sentence
死讯 [sǐxùn] news of somebody's death
死硬派 [sǐyìngpài] the diehards
死有余辜 [sǐyǒuyúgū] even death cannot recompensate his crimes
死战 [sǐzhàn] a desperate fight
死者 [sǐzhě] dead person
死罪 [sǐzuì] a capital crime; penalty of death

sì

伺 [sì] 1 (v) 守候 wait ✱我军伺机进攻。Our troops waited for the opportunity to attack. 2 (v) 侦察 to watch; to detect
另见 [cì]
饲(飼) [sì] (v) 喂食，喂养 feed; roar ✱饲料 fodder; feed
饲蚕 [sìcán] to rear silk worms
饲鸡 [sìjí] to rear chickens
饲养 [sìyǎng] to rear; raise; breed
嗣 [sì] 1 (v) 接续，继承 to succeed; to inherit ✱嗣位 to succeed to the throne 2 (n) 子孙 descendants ✱后嗣。descendants; posterity
嗣后 [sìhòu] hereafter; henceforth
嗣子 [sìzǐ] heir
四 [sì] (n) 排在三和五之间的数字 four 4
四边形 [sìbiānxíng] a quadrilateral four-sided figure
四方 [sìfāng] square; all corners; everywhere
四分五裂 [sìfēn- wǔliè] fragmented ; disunited
四分之一 [sìfēn-zhīyì] a quarter
四海 [sìhǎi] the whole world ; everywhere
四海之內皆兄弟 [sì hǎi zhī nèi jiē xiōng dì] all men are brothers
四季 [sìjì] the four seasons, spring, summer, autumn and winter
四面 [sìmiàn] the four sides ; on all sides

四面八方 [sìmiànbāfāng] on every side; everywhere

四面楚歌 [sìmiànchǔgē] surrounded by enemy's troops; hopeless

四散 [sìsàn] dispersed ; scattered in all directions

四体不劳，五谷不分 [sì tǐ bù láo, wǔgǔbúfēn] lack of labour and practical knowledge

四通八达 [sìtōngbādá] highly convenient (of a place well served with communication routes).

四肢 [sìzhī] the limbs, legs and arms

四周 [sìzhōu] on all sides; all around

泗 [sì] (n) 鼻涕 mucus; snivel

泗水 [sìshuǐ] Surabaya, a port in Indonesia

驷(駟) [sì] (n) 套四匹马的车，也泛指马 a chariot drawn by four horses; horse in general ＊一言既出，驷马难追。 What is said cannot be retracted.

巳 [sì] (n) 地支的第六位，用作次序的第六 the sixth of the Twelve Branches; sixth in order

巳时 [sìshí] 9.00 to 11.00 a.m.

祀 [sì] (v) 拜祭 to offer sacrifices to gods ＊祀祖。to offer sacrifices to one's ancestors

似 [sì] 1 (adj) 象，如同 like; similar; resembling ＊她们姊妹长得很相似。The sisters look very much alike. 2 (v) 好象 seem; appear to; look as though ＊这计划似属可行。This plan seems feasible. 3 (conj) 比较 than ＊人民生活一年强似一年。The life of the people this year is better than that of last year.

似乎 [sìhū] to look like; appear; seem; to seem like

似是而非 [sìshìérfēi] paradoxical

sì

肆 [sì] (adj) 不顾一切，任性 reckless; unrestrained ＊他越来越放肆。He is getting more and more unscrupulous.

肆无忌惮 [sìwújìdàn] reckless in total disregard to anything

肆意 [sìyì] recklessly; unscrupulously

肆意攻击 [sìyìgōngjī] to attack unscrupulously

俟 [sì] (v) 等待 wait for ＊他们俟机出击。They waited for an opportunity to attack.

寺 [sì] 1 (n)中国古代官署名 name of a government office in ancient China ＊大理寺（最高司法机关）。 the highest judiciary 2 (n) 寺院，宗教徒供奉神佛、举行宗教仪式或居住的地方 a monastery; a temple ＊佛寺 buddhist temple

食 [sì] (v) 拿东西给人吃 to feed somebody with food 另见 [shí]

·si

厕(厠) [si] (n) 洗手间 a toilet

sōng

松 [sōng] (n) 常绿或落叶乔木，种类很多，木材用途很广，种子可榨油和供食用。树脂是重要工业原料 the pine tree

松节油：松油 [sōng jié yóu]: [sōng yóu] turpentine

松明 [sōngmíng] resin; pine splints

松鼠 [sōngshǔ] squirrel

松子 [sōngzǐ] pine seeds; fir cones

松(鬆) [sōng] 1 (adj) 不紧密，稀散，跟"紧"相对 loose, opposite of tight ＊我的腰带很松。My waist-band is very loose. 2 (v) 放开 loosen ＊他要松一松腰带。

He wants to loosen his waist-band a little. 4 (adj) 不紧张，不严格 relaxed; lenient ＊在学习上，我们决不可松懈。We should never slacken in our study 5 (n) 用鱼、瘦肉等做成的绒状或碎末状食品 meat floss made of fish or lean port＊肉松。meat floss

松弛 [sōngchí] relax; slacken; lenient; not severe

松软 [sōngruǎn] porous and soft (of soil); loose and soft

松散 [sōngsǎn] loose and scattered; to put oneself at ease

松手 [sōngshǒu] to let go; to release

松爽 [sōngshuǎng] elated ; refreshed in high spirit

sǒng

怂(慫) [sǒng] (adj) 惊怂 frightened

怂恿 [sǒngyǒng] to incite people or to lure people to do something evil

悚 [sǒng] 1 (adj) 恐惧，怕 afraid; terrified＊他听了这个鬼故事不禁毛骨悚然。He got frightened after hearing the ghost story.

耸(聳) [sǒng] 1 (adj) 高起，直立 high; towering; lofty ＊烟囱高耸人云霄。The chimney is towering into the sky. 2 (v) 惊动 excite; startle; shock＊你不要危言耸听。Don't you deliberately exaggerate the story to shock people.

耸立 [sǒng lì] stand erect

耸肩 [sǒngjiān] to shrug one's shoulders

耸人听闻 [sǒng rén tīng wén] to exaggerate something deliberately so as to shock people; to create a sensation

sòng

宋 [sòng] 1 (n) 古代国名 name of an ancient state in China 2 (n) 朝代名 name of a dynasty ＊宋朝 the Song Dynasty (960—960 A.D.)

宋体字 [sòngtǐzì] a form of Chinese characters where the horizontal strokes are finer than the vertical strokes ; Song Calligraphy

送 [sòng] 1 (v) 把东西运去或拿去给人 send; despatch; transport ; deliver ＊他要去送货。He has to send the goods to the purchasers. 2 (v) 陪着走 accompany ; escort ＊我要送他去火车站。I will accompany him to the railway station. 3 (v) 赠给 present; give ＊我送他一支钢笔。I gave him a pen as a present. 4 (v) 丧失 lose ＊他差一点就送命。He nearly lost his life.

送别 [sòngbié] send off

送殡 [sòngbìn] to attend a funeral

送旧迎新 [sòngjiùyíngxīn] to speed the old and welcome the new

送客 [sòngkè] to escort a visitor to the door or gate

送礼 [sònglǐ] to send a present

送命 [sòngmìng] lose one's life worthlessly

送信 [sòngxìn] to send message

送行 [sòngxíng] to see a person off—as for a friend on a journey ; farewell ; send-off

送终 [sòngzhōng] to gather round a death-bed

颂(頌) [sòng] 1 (v) 赞美，称赞别人的好处 praise; commend; admire＊这首曲子是歌颂劳动工人的。This song is in praise of the labourers 2 (n) 赞美诗 psalm 黄河颂。the Psalm of Yellow River.

颂词 [sòngcí] commendatory odes

颂歌 [sònggē] ballads; odes

颂古非今 [sònggǔfēijīn] eulogize the past at the expense of the present

颂扬 [sòngyáng] laud; praise

诵(誦) [sòng] 1 (v) 读出声音来 recite; read out aloud＊诗歌朗诵。poem recitation 2 (v) 称说 praise ＊民间传诵着英雄的事迹。The common people are praising in

turns the deeds of the heroes.
诵读 [sòngdú] to recite; to read aloud

讼（訟） [sòng] 1 (v) 在法庭上争辩是非曲直，打官司 to bring a complaint or a law suit against somebody ＊民事（刑事）诉讼。 civil (criminal) suit 2 (v) 争辩是非 contend ; argue ＊人们聚讼纷纭。Many people start to argue about right and wrong.
讼案 [sòngàn] a case at law
讼词 [sòngcí] an indictment
讼事 [sòngshì] a law suit

sōu

搜 [sōu] 1 (v) 寻求，寻找 search; find; inquire ＊我们在搜集材料。We are looking for materials. 2 (v) 检查，搜查 examine; search ＊海关人员要搜查你们所有的行李。Customs officers will check all your luggage
搜捕 [sōubǔ] to hunt for somebody wanted by police
搜查 [sōuchá] to search and examine (for something prohibited)
搜刮 [sōuguā] take away by force; loot; plunder
搜罗 [sōuluó] to look for things or people everywhere and then group them together
搜索 [sōusuǒ] to search thoroughly for something or somebody hidden
搜索枯肠 [sōusuǒkūcháng] to wrack one's brain (in search of something to write about); an exhaustive search for some data
搜寻 [sōuxún] to search; to seek for

艘 [sōu] (n) 量词 numeral for ships and vessels ＊一艘军舰 an army vessel.

嗖（颼） [sōu] (n) 象声词，形容很快通过的声音 a word to describe a fast sound or the sound of wind ＊那辆汽车象一阵风似的嗖的一声开过去了。 That car passed by like the whirl-wind

sǒu

叟 [sǒu] (n) 老年的男人 an old man ＊童叟无欺。We are fair to all people, young and old.

sòu

嗽 [sòu] (v) 咳 cough

sū

酥 [sū] 1 (adj) 食物松脆 crispy; short; flaky 2 (adj) 食物软烂 soft; tender (of food) 3(n)松脆的点心 crispy or short snack 花生酥 short peanut cake 4 (n) 牛羊乳制成的油或酪 butter; cheese 5 (adj)（肢体）软弱无力 weak (of limb) ＊工作了一整天，他的四肢酥麻。His limbs became numb and weak after a full day's work.

苏（蘇） [sū] 1 (n) 草本植物，花紫色，叶和种子可供药用 a Chinese herb with purple flowers 2 (v) 从昏迷状态中醒过来 revive from unconsciousness ＊他苏醒过来了。He has gained consciousness. 3 (n) 江苏省的简称 abbreviation for the Province of Kiangsu
苏打 [sūdǎ] soda
苏丹 [sūdān] Sudan
苏格兰 [sūgelán] Scotland
苏联 [sūlián] U.S.S.R.
苏门答腊 [sūméndálà] Sumatra
苏彝士运河 [sūyíshìyǔnhé] Suez Canal
苏醒 [sūxǐng] wake up ; come round

sú

俗 [sú] 1 (n) 习惯 customs; conventions; habits ＊各民族有自己的风俗习惯。Every race has its own customs and habits. 2 (adj) 大众的，普通流行的 popular; common ＊俗语 colloquial language; a common saying 3 (adj) 趣味不高，使人讨厌

的。vulgar;unrefined＊这个人俗不可耐。This person is unbearably vulgar.

俗不可耐 [sū bù kě nài] unbearably vulgar

俗话 [súhuà] a colloquial expression

俗名 [súmīng] common name

俗气 [súqì] vulgar (of tastes, style, in terests)

俗人 [súrén] layman

俗套 [sútào] old (in style); inelegant

俗字 [súzì] popular form of a character

sù

速 [sù] 1 (adj) 快 quick; fast; speedy; rapid ＊这件事要速战速决。This matter must be dealt with and settled as fast as possible. 2 (v) 邀请 invite ＊他是一名不速之客。He is an uninvited guest.

速成班 [sùchéngbān] a short course

速度 [sùdù] speed; rate velocity

速度表 [sùdùbiǎo] a speed indicator; a speedometer; a Rapid Course

速记 [sùjì] short-hand; stenography

速写 [sùxiě] a quick sketch; sketching

速战速决 [sùzhànsùjué] prompt action and quick decision; quickly decided battle

簌 [sù] [簌簌] (adj) 象声词 1 形容风吹叶子等的声音 sound made by wind blowing against the leaves 2 纷纷落下的样子 streaming down (of tears) ＊她的眼泪簌簌而下。Her tears flowed down in streams.

素 [sù] 1 (n) 白色 white ＊素服 white clotnes; mourning garments 2 (adj) 颜色单纯，不艳丽 plain ＊她穿了一件朴素的衣服。She wears a plain dress 3 (n) 本质 predisposition; nature; element ＊ 化学原素 chemical elements; 因素 factors; causes 4 (adj) 本来的，原始的 original; primitive ＊写作的素材可以从现实生活中寻取。Source materials for literary writings could be obtained from real life incidents. 5 (adv) 平日，向来 usually; all along; since ＊我和他素不相识。I have never known him before. 6 (n) 蔬菜类的食物，与"荤"相对 vegetable diet ＊ 素食。vegetable diet; herbivourous

素菜 [sùcài] diet for a vegetarian

素昧平生 [sùmèipíngshēng] never acquainted with (a person)

素描 [sùmiáo] a rough sketch

素养 [sùyǎng] cultivation of learning; cultivated manners

素质 [sùzhì] basic quality; original nature

宿 [sù] 1 (v) 住，过夜 stay; sojourn; lodge ＊我昨晚露宿街头。I slept on the street last night. 2 (adj) 一向有的，旧有的 former; old; long cherished ＊ 他宿愿得偿。His long cherished dreams were realised. 3 (adj) 年老的，有经验的 old; experienced ＊他是体坛上的宿将。He is a veteran player in the sports activities.

另见 [xǐu] [xìu]

宿疾 [sùjí] a chronic disease

宿命论 [sùmìnglùn] a belief in fate, that the world phenomena are predetermined

宿舍 [sùshè] hostel; dormitory

宿志 [sùzhì] long-standing ambition; long cherished will

肃(肅) [sù] 1 (adj) 恭敬，庄重 respectful; solemn ＊全体肃立。Everybody stands solemnly at attention 2 (adj) 严正，认真 stern; majestic; serious ＊我们要严肃地对待这个问题。We must treat this matter seriously.

肃静 [sùjìng] silence

肃穆 [sùmù] solemn and respectful

肃清 [sùqīng] to get rid of; to remove

肃然起敬 [sùránqǐjìng] respect and veneration suddenly emerge

粟 [sù] 1 (n) 草本植物。粟粒去壳后叫"小米"，是中国北方重要的粮食作物 millet 2 (adj) 比喻极小的 minute ; extremely small ＊沧海一粟。a grain in the boundless ocean —very minute.

溯 [sù] 1 (v) 逆着水流的方向走 to go against the current. ＊汽船溯流而上。The steam boat advances against the current. 2(v) 回想过去，追求根源 ＊ 推本溯源 。 to recall the past and trace for the historical origin.

塑 [sù] (v) 用泥土等作成人物的形象 to model in clay ＊塑象 clay figure.

塑胶 [sùjiāo] plastics
塑料 [sùliào] plastic material
塑像 [sùxiàng] statue; figure
塑造 [sùzào] to mould a figure; to describe a personality in writing

诉(訴) [sù] 1(v) 说，告示 ＊告诉我你住在那儿。Tell me where you live. 2 (v) 控告 sue; plead accuse; ＊他要起诉这间公司的老板。He wants to sue the boss of the company.

诉苦 [sùkǔ] to tell of one's grievances
诉说 [sùshuō] to tell with emotion
诉讼 [sùsòng] legal proceeding; a lawsuit; a case; to sue a person
诉讼人 [sùsòngrén] a plaintiff; a suitor
诉状 [sùzhuàng] a petition; a written complaint

suān

酸 [suān] 1 (n) 化学上称能在水溶液中产生氢离子的物质，有酸味，分无机酸、有机酸两大类 acids ＊盐酸 hydrochloric acid 2 (adj) 象醋的气味 a pungent smell like vinegar; a sour taste ＊酸菜 pickled vegetable 3 (adj) 悲痛，伤心 grieved; sad ; sorrowful ＊她的遭遇真是令人心酸。We were sorry for her misfortune. 4 (n) 因疲劳或疾病而引起的微痛无力感觉 ache from over-fatigue or sickness ＊他腰酸背痛。He has an ache in the back

酸楚 [suānchǔ] sad; grieved
酸醋 [suāncù] vinegar
酸梅 [suānméi] sour prune
酸性 [suānxìng] acidic
酸味 [suānwèi] sour in taste

suàn

蒜 [suàn] (n) 大蒜，草本植物，地下茎叫"蒜头"，分瓣，味辣，可供调味用，蒜苗可作蔬菜 garlic; garlic bulb ＊蒜瓣儿。segments of a garlic bulb

算 [suàn] 1 (v) 核计，计数 count; calculate; compute ＊他在算钱。He is counting the money. 2 (v) 谋划，计划 plan; contrive ＊我打算今晚就走。I plan to leave tonight. 3 (v) 推测 reckon ＊我算着他今天该到了。I reckon that he would arrive today. 4 (v) 认作，称得上 consider ＊他肯学肯干，可算是一个好工友。He is willing to learn and work, so he should be considered a good worker. 5 (v) 作数，承认有效力 to mean something; to admit something to be effective ＊我讲话是算数的。I mean what I say.

算命 [suànmìng] to tell fortunes
算盘 [suàn·pan] abacus

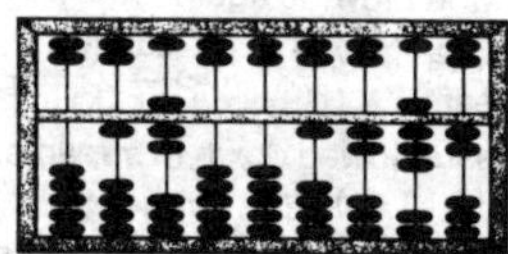

算术 [suànshù] arithmetic
算帐 [suànzhàng] to make up accounts ; to argue and compete after a defeat or a loss

suī

虽(雖) [suī] (conj) 连词，虽然，即使，表示语气转折 although; though; even though ＊工作虽然忙，可是学习决不能放松。

Although we are busy in our work, we should not slacken in our study.

虽然如此 [suīránrúcǐ] be that as it may; even though

虽说 [suīshuō] although; though; not-withstanding

虽则 [suīzé] nevertheless

suí

隋 [suí] (n) 朝代名 Dynasty (589–618 A.D.)

随(隨) [suí] 1 (v) 跟 follow ＊他随着队伍到德国去。He followed the troop to Germany. 2 (adv) 任凭 as one pleases ＊随你的便。Do at your own free will. 3 (adv) 顺便 at one's convenience ＊他随手把门关上。He shut the door after him.

随笔 [suíbǐ] brief notes; miscellaneous writings

随便 [suíbiàn] at your convenience; at pleasure; anyhow

随波逐流 [suíbōzhúliú] to follow the crowd

随处 [suíchù] in all places; everywhere

随从 [suícóng] attendants

随地 [suídì] everywhere; in every place; here and there

随风转舵 [suífēngzhuǎnduò] to sail with the wind,— to follow the line of least resistance (figurative)

随感 [suígǎn] occasional thoughts

随和 [suí·he] agreeable; act as others do

随后 [suíhòu] later on; soon after

随机应变 [suíjīyìngbiàn] adapt oneself to circumstances; do as the circumstances dictate;

随即 [suíjí] immediately

随口 [súikǒu] (promise) freely; without consideration; without hesitation

随身 [suíshēn] carry something (always) on body

随声附和 [suíshēngfùhè] to echo what others say

随时随地 [suíshísuídì] at all times and all places; any time and anywhere

随同 [suítóng] accompany; attend to

随心所欲 [suíxīnsuǒyù] to do as one pleases

随行 [suíxíng] accompany; follow

随意 [suíyì] freely; at one's pleasure; of one's own accord; as one pleases

绥(綏) [suí] (v) 安抚 pacify ＊这是政府的绥靖政策。This is the government's policy of pacification

suǐ

髓 [suǐ] 1 (n) 骨头里象脂肪的东西 marrow ＊骨髓。bone marrow ＊脊髓。spinal cord; pith 2 (n) 植物茎的中心部分 the pith of a stem 3 (n) 精华部份 pith ＊一篇演说的精髓。the pith of a speech

suì

遂 [suì] 1 (v) 顺，如意；成功 be as one wishes; succeed ＊他自杀未遂。He did not succeed in committing suicide. 2 (adv) 就，于是 thereupon; then; subsequently ＊他服药后腹痛遂止。His stomach – ache stops after he has taken the medicine.

遂心 [suìxīn] be as one like it; fulfil one's desire

隧 [suì] (n) 凿穿山石或挖通地下而成的通路 a tunnel; an underground passage; a vault; a subway ＊隧道 a tunnel

隧洞 [suìdòng] underground passage

碎 [suì] (adj) 破裂成散块的 broken; fragmented; cracked ＊不要让碎玻璃伤到你的手。Don't let the broken glasses hurt your hand.

碎裂 [suìliè] to break into pieces

碎石机 [suìshíjī] stone breaker

碎屑 [suìxìe] fragments; splinters; chips

穗 [suì] 1 (n) 谷类植物聚生在一起的花或果实 a ear or spike of grains; a spike of flowers ＊沉甸甸的稻穗。drooping ears of rice. 2 (n) 中国广州市的别称 another name for Kwangchow.

岁(歲) [suì] 1 (n) 年 year ＊岁月不留人。Time and tide wait for no man. 2 (n) 计算年龄的单位 years for age ＊我今年十八岁。I am eighteen years old.

岁末 [suìmò] end of a year

岁收 [suìshōu] the annual financial income for a country

岁数 [suì·shù] age

岁月 [suìyùe] times and seasons; time and tide

祟 [suì] 1 (n) 鬼怪 evil spirits ;calamities ＊作祟 make mischief 鬼祟 evil spirits 鬼鬼祟祟 mischievous; develish.

sūn

孙(孫) [sūn] 1 (n) 儿女辈的儿子 grandchild ＊孙女 grand-daughter 2 (n) 姓 a surname; a family name in China

孙子 [sūnzǐ]

sǔn

损(損) [sǔn] 1 (n)减少 lessening; loss ＊损益相抵。Profit and loss cancel each other out. 2 (v) 害，伤害 harm; injure: spoil; damage＊学会掌握一种语文是有益无损的。Learning to master a language is beneficial and not harmful 3 (v) 用刻薄话挖苦人 criticize with sarcastic remarks

损害 [sǔnhài] injure; damage; harm

损坏 [sǔnhuài] to spoil; to impair: to damage

损耗 [sǔnháo] lose; wear out; loss

损害主权 [sǔnhàizhǔquán] to impair one's sovereignty

损人利己 [sǔnrénlìjǐ] harming others to benefit oneself

损伤 [sǔnshāng] injure; harm; wound

损失 [sǔnshī] damage; loss

榫 [sǔn] (n) 木器两部分接合处 a tenon

榫头 [sǔntòu] tenon; dove-tail

榫眼 [sǔnyǎn] mortise

笋(筍) [sǔn] (n) 竹子的地下茎所生的嫩茎、芽、可供食用 bamboo shoot; bamboo sprout

suō

唆 [suō] (v) 指使，挑动别人做坏事 to instigate or incite others to do something evil ＊地主唆使我放火烧毁这些木屋。The landlord instigated me to set fire on tnese wooden houses.

梭 [suō] (n) 织布机上穿引纬纱(横线)的工具，两头尖，中间粗，象枣核形，俗称"梭子" a shuttle for weaving

梭鱼 [suōyú] barracuda

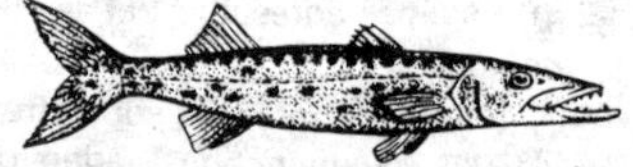

蓑 [suō] (n)用草或棕制成的雨衣 rain coat made of straw or dried palm leaves

缩(縮) [suō] 1 (v) 后退 to draw back; to withdraw ＊许多人碰到困难就畏缩不前了。Many people become afraid and draw back when confronted with difficulties. 2 (v) 由大变小或由长变短 shrink;

contract; shrivel; curl up; shorten ✱ 炎热的阳光使树叶枯乾缩萎了。The leaves have shrivelled in the hot sun.

缩成一团 [suōchéngyītuán] to huddle oneself up; to curl oneself up

缩短 [suōduǎn] to shorten

缩回 [suōhuí] to draw back; to retract

缩减 [suōjiǎn] to reduce; to diminish

缩手缩脚 [suōshǒu suōjiǎo] timid, not daring to do anything; scared

缩小 [suōxiǎo] to reduce; to cut down

缩写 [suōxiě] abbreviation;condensed form (of long article or novel)

缩影 [suōyǐng] drawing of something on a reduced scale

suǒ

唢(嗩) [suǒ] (n) [唢呐] 一种吹奏乐器 a Chinese trumpet)

锁(鎖) [suǒ] 1 (n) 加在门、箱等上面使人不能随便开的器具 lock ✱ 弹簧锁 a spring lock 2 (v) 封闭 to lock ✱记得锁门。Remember to lock the door. 3 (n) 链子 chain; fetter ✱ 枷锁 fetter

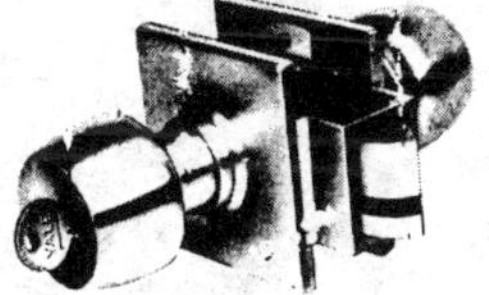

锁链 [suǒliàn] chain; fetter

锁匙 [suǒshí] a key

琐(瑣) [suǒ] (adj) 细小、零碎 trifling; minute; insignificant ;trivial ✱家庭中总有许多烦琐的事情。 There are many trivial matters in the family.

琐事 [suǒshì] trivial matter

琐碎 [suǒsuì] trifling

索 [suǒ] 1 (n) 粗绳子 rope ✱ 铁索。iron rope 2 (v) 寻找 search; look for ✱警方人员在搜索屋子。The police are searching the house. 3 (v) 要，讨取 ask for; demand ✱他索取十万元。He asked for one hundred thousand dollars 4 (adj) 寂寞；没有意味 lonely ; not interesting ✱ 我觉得这个节目索然无味。I feel that this programme is not interesting at all. 5 (adj) 单独 isolated✱ 他为什么离羣索居？ Why does he isolate himself from the folk ?

索价 [suǒjià] to state the price in a bargain

索取 [suǒqǔ] to ask from people ; to get

索性 [suǒxìng] courageously; to make up one's mind

索引 [suǒyǐn] an index

所 [suǒ] 1 (n) 地方 a place ✱我们还没找到适当的场所。 We have not found a suitable place 2 (n) 机关或其他办事的地方 an office; a place for various purposes; institute; centre ✱ 诊疗所。 clinic ✱ 研究所 research department 3 (n) 量词 numeral for buildings ✱ 一所学校。 a school 4 (pron) what; that; which 所食 what we eat; 所求 that which we ask for; 所见 what we see 5 (adv) 此；因此 whereby; therefore 所以然 for this reason

所得 [suǒdé] earnings; wages;

所得税 [suǒdéshuì] income tax

所属 [suǒshǔ] belong; possess; all one's subordinates

所谓 [suǒwèi] as it is said; that which is called; so-called

所向披靡 [suǒxiàngpīmǐ] ever triumphant; ever victorious

所向无敌 [suǒxiàngwúdì] no adversaries in whatever direction

所有主 [suǒyǒuzhǔ] owner;possessor ; holder; proprietor

所作所为 [suǒzuòsuǒwéi] all one's actions; one's deeds; what one does

it drives

所以 [suǒyǐ] therefore; wherefore

所有 [suǒyǒu] own; possess

所有权 [suǒ yǒu quán] ownership;

所在 [suǒzài] whereabouts; the location; the site

所长 [suǒzhǎng] the head of a department

T

tā

它 [tā] (pron) 代词，专指动物和事物 it ＊它有很长的尾巴。It has a very long tail.

它们 [tā·men] they (neuter gender)

他 [tā] 1 (pron) 代词，称你,我以外的第三位男性 he ＊他是我哥哥。He is my brother. 2 (adj) 别的，另外的 other; another ＊他乡遇故知。meet an acquaintance in another country.

他们 [tā·men] they (common gender)

他人 [tā rén] the other; other person or persons

他日 [tā rì] another day

她 [tā] (pron) 代词，称你、我以外的第三位女性 she ＊她是工厂女工。She is a factory worker.

她们 [tā·men] they (faminine gender)

塌 [tā] (v) 倒下，下陷 to collapse; to fall in; to cave in ＊墙塌了。The wall has collapsed.

塌台 [tā tái] to collapse; to fail

塌陷 [tāxiàn] to cave in; to sink downward; to fall in; to give way (under pressure)

tǎ

塔 [tǎ] (n) 一种高而尖的建筑物 a tower; a pagoda ＊ 宝塔，灯塔，水塔。 a pagoda; a light house; a water tower.

獭（獺） [tǎ] (n) 哺乳动物，常见的有水獭，山獭，海獭 an otter

tà

踏 [tà] 1 (v) to tread; to stamp on; to trample ＊不要残踏花草。 Do not trample on the plants 2 (v) 步行 to walk

踏板 [tàbǎn] a treadle (of a sewing-machine); a tread (of a stair); a pedal

踏步 [tàbù] to mark time (at drill)

踏歌 [tàgē] to beat time with the feet to a song

踏勘 [tàkān] to make a personal investigation on the spot

踏青 [tàqīng] to walk on the green grass; to hike

踏实 [tàshí] in a thorough going manner; on a firm footing

榻 [tà] (n) 床 a bed; a couch ＊下榻。to lodge at.

蹋 [tà] (v) 踏 to tread; to stamp

拓 [tà] (v) 把石碑或器物上的字画摹印在纸上 to take an impression of a writing or drawing from a stone tablet

另见 [tuò]

挞（撻） [tà] (v) 打 to flog; to strike ; to beat; to slash ＊他们用籐杖鞭挞犯人。They flogged the criminals with canes.

tāi

胎 [tāi] 1 (n) 人或其他哺乳动物在母体内的幼体 an embryo; a fetus; a pregnant womb 2 (n) 象胎的东西 things like a pregnant womb *轮胎。a tyre. 3 (n) 根源 the origine *祸胎。the origin of disaster.

胎儿 [tāiér] an embryo

胎生 [tāishēng] viviparity

胎死腹中 [tāisǐfùzhōng] the embryo dies in womb-the plan turns invalid before implementation

胎盘 [tāipán] the placenta

苔 [tāi][舌苔][shétāi] (n) 舌头上衰死的上皮细胞和粘液形成的垢腻 fur on the tongue

另见 [tái]

tái

台(臺) [tái] 1 (n) 高平面 a flat raised surface *午台 stage. *乐队指挥台。padium. *讲台。dais. *月台。platform 2(n) 量词 a measure word (for machine) *一台拖拉机。a tractor.

台秤 [táichèng] platform scales

台阶 [táijiē] steps of a staircase

抬 [tái] (v) 举，提起 to lift up; to carry *他抬起头来一看。He lifts up his head to have a look.

抬举 [táijǔ] to think highly of somebody and praise or promote him

苔 [tái] (n) 普通叫"青苔"，在阴湿的地方生长，有叶绿素，是低等植物中的一大类 moss; lichen

苔藓植物 [táixiǎn zhíwù] bryophyta

台(檯) [tái] (n) 桌 a table

台(颱) [tái] (n) 台风 typhoon

tài

太 [tài] (adv) 最，极 too; over; excessively

太多 [tài duō] too much; too many

太极拳 [tài jí quán] one kind of traditional Chinese callisthenics (for physical training)

太空 [tàikōng] outer space; sky; firmament

太空人 [tài kōng rén] spaceman; astronaut

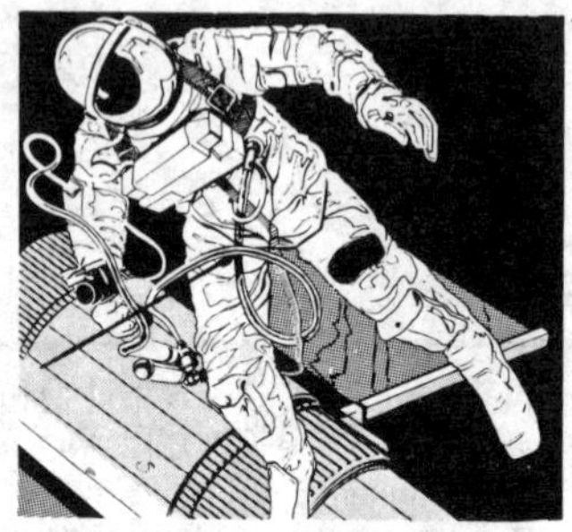

太平 [tàipíng] peaceful

太平门 [tàipíng mén] emergency exit; safety exit

太平天国运动 [tài píng tiān guó yùn dòng] the Movement of the Taiping Heavenly Kingdom (1851-1864)

太阳 [tài yáng] the sun

太阳能 [tài yáng néng] solar energy

太阳系 [tài yáng xì] the solar system

汰 [tài] (v) 洗去没有用的部份 to wash out; to clean *淘汰。to wash out and reduce-natural selection.

态(態) [tài] (n) 事物的形状，样子，情况 manner; attitude; approach; position; form

态度 [tàidù] attitude; manner; position; stand

泰 [tài] (adj) 平安，安定 peaceful; calm; stable *国泰民安。The country is stable and the people lead a peaceful life

泰斗 [tàidǒu] a leading authority

泰然 [tài rán] calm; cool; collected; composed

泰山 [tài shān] a famous mountain in Shantung Province of China

泰丝 [tàisī] Thai silk

泰运 [tài yùn] a good luck

tān

摊(攤) [tān] 1 (v) 展开，揭示 to set up; to put on display; to spread out 2 (v) 分担，分配 to share; to divide up; to share out ＊五人决定分摊那四百万元。 The five persons decided to share out that four million dollars among themselves. 3 (n) 小型简单的售货处 a stall ＊书摊，鱼摊 a book stall ; a fish stall.

摊贩 [tānfàn] a stall-keeper; a hawker

摊分 [tānfēn] to pay a share; to divide up money

摊还 [tānhuán] to pay by instalments

摊牌 [tān pái] to have a show-down; to put the cards on the table

摊位 [tanwèi] a street stall

摊子 [tān·zi] a booth; a stall

滩(灘) [tān] 1 (n) 海边泥沙淤积成的地方：海滩 a beach 2 (n) 海中海床接近海面的地方：浅滩 a sand bank 3 (n) 江河中水水浅多石而水流很急的地方：急滩 a rapid

瘫(癱) [tān] (v) 神经机能发生障碍，肢体麻木不能活动 to paralyse

瘫痪 [tānhuàn] to paralyse

贪(貪) [tān] (v) 不知足，求多 to covet; to be greedy for

贪得无厌 [tāndéwúyàn] covetous for gain; avaricious; insatiable greed

贪官污吏 [tānguānwūlì] corrupt officials

贪婪 [tān lán] voracious; rapacious; greedy for; covetous

贪生怕死 [tānshēnpàsǐ] coward; afraid of death; to cling to life notwithstanding dishononour

贪天之功 [tāntiānzhīgōng] to credit other people's meritorious service to oneself; to arrogate service to oneself

贪图 [tāntú] to covet; to desire eagerly ; to hanker after (e.g. a life of ease)

贪玩 [tānwán] be fond of play

贪污 [tānwū] corrupt; embezzle; corruption and graft

贪心 [tānxīn] greedy

坍 [tān] (v) 岸、建筑物或堆起的东西从基部崩坏 to collapse ＊墙坍了。The wall has collapsed.

坍塌 [tāntā] to collapse; to crumble; to fall down

tán

谈(談) [tán] 1 (v) 说，谈话 to talk; to speak; to converse ＊他希望和我面谈。He wishes to talk to me personally. 2 (n) 话 talk; speech; conversation; gossip ＊这是无稽之谈。 This is a baseless gossip.

谈何容易 [tánhéróngyì] how easy to talk about it!-how difficult to achieve

谈虎色变 [tánhǔsèbiàn] speaking of tiger makes one pale-nervous fears make things seem real

谈话 [tánhuà] to talk together; to engage in conversation

谈论 [tánlùn] to discuss; to talk about

谈判 [tán pàn] to negotiate; to conference

谈天 [tántiān] to chat about things in general

谈天说地 [tántiānshuōdì] to talk on all kinds of subjects

谈吐 [tántù] to discuss; to talk

谈笑风生 [tán xiào fēng shēng] lighthearted and interesting in talking

谈心 [tán xīn] to have a heart-to-heart talk

痰 [tán] (n) 气管或支气管分泌出来的粘液 phlegm; spit

痰盂 [tányú] a spittoon

谭(譚) [tán] 1 (n) 同"谈" [tan]. 2 (n) 姓 a surname

潭 [tán] (n) 深水坑 a deep pool; a big pond

坛(壇) [tán] 1 (n) 台，祭台 a platform; an altar ＊天坛，花坛。the Altar to Heaven ; a flower bed. 2 (n) 指文艺界、体育界或舆论阵地 field; circle ＊文坛，体坛，时事论坛。 cultural circle; sports circle ; news forum.

坛(罎) [tán] (n) 一种口小肚大，用来盛东西的陶器 an earthenware jar; a jug

昙(曇) [tán] (adj) 云彩密布，多云 cloudy

昙花一现 [tánhuā yí xiàn] like the night -blooming cereus- a flash of brilliance ; short lived

弹(彈) [tán] 1 (v) 轻击 to fillip ; to flick; to flip＊他弹去衣上的尘土。 He flicks away the dust on his clothes. ＊他在弹吉他。 He is playing (fillipping) the guitar. 2 (v) 射击 to shoot; to snap ＊他用橡皮和石子来弹鸟儿。He made use of the rubber bands and stones to shoot the birds. 3 (v) 跳 to spring; to bounce ＊皮球反弹回来。The ball bounces back.

弹劾 [tán hé] to impeach

弹簧 [tánhuáng] a spring (metal)

弹力 [tánlì] elasticity

弹性 [tánxìng] elasticity

弹性限度 [tánxìngxiàndù] limit of elasticity

弹指之间 [tán zhǐ zhī jiān] within a very short time

另见 [dàn]

檀 [tán] 1 (n) 落叶乔木，果实有翅，木质坚硬 a kind of hard wood like rosewood 2 (n) 常绿乔木，产于热带和亚热带。木材香气浓郁，可作香料，供药用，也可制用具 sandal wood

檀香木 [tánxiāngmù] sandal wood

檀香山 [tánxiāngshān] Honolulu

tǎn

毯 [tǎn] (n) 一种供铺设用的较厚的毛，棉织品 blanket; rug; carpet ＊地毯 carpet

坦 [tǎn] (adj) 宽平；开朗 level , smooth; open ; easy＊他坦然承认是凶手。 He confessed frankly that he himself was the murderer.

坦白 [tǎn bái] frank; candid to confess; to make a clean breast of

坦克 [tǎn kè] tank for military purpose

坦克车 [tǎn kè chē] a tank; an armoured motor-car

坦然 [tǎn rán] calm; cool (e.g. headed); composedly

坦率 [tǎn shuài] open; straightforward; frank

袒 [tǎn] 1 (v) 裸露 to lay bare＊这个女人袒露肩背。 This woman lays bare her shoulders and back. 2 (v) 庇护 to screen; to give improper protection to ＊母亲总会偏袒自己的孩子的。 A mother usually gives improper protection to her children.

袒护 [tǎnhù] to be partial to; to screen (somebody from blame)

忐 [tǎn] (adj) 心虚，心神不定 timorous; nervous

tàn

碳 [tàn] (n) 一种非金属元素 carbon

碳酸 [tànsuān] carbonic acid

碳水化合物 [tànshǔy-huàhéwù] carbohydrate

炭 [tàn] 1 (n) 木炭，由木材燃烧而成的黑色燃料 charcoal 2 (n) 煤炭，煤块 coal

探 [tàn] 1 (v) 寻找 to search; to detect; to find out; to explore ＊他们来这里勘探石油。 They come here to explore oil. 2 (v) 侦察 to investigate; to examine; to pry＊他想探听消息。He wants to pry for information. 3 (v) 看望，访问 to visit ＊他去太平探亲。 He went to Taiping to visit his relatives. 4 (v) 伸出 to stretch forward; stretch out ＊车行时不要探身车外。 Do not stretch your body out when the vehicle is moving.

探测 [tàncè] to prospect ; to explore; to probe into

探索 [tànsuǒ] to explore; to probe into

探讨 [tàntǎo] to study; to investigate ; to look into

探听 [tàntīng] to find out; to make inquiry; to pry.

探望 [tànwàng] to visit

探险 [tànxiǎn] to go on an adventure; to explore

探询 [tànxún] to make inquiries, to find out

探照灯 [tànzhàodēng] search light

叹(嘆) [tan] (v)叹气，因忧闷或悲痛而呼气出声 to sigh ＊他叹了一口气。He heaved a sigh.

叹词 [tàncí] exclamation; interjection

叹气 [tànqì] to give a sigh; to sigh over

叹息 [tànxì] to sigh; to sigh audibly

tāng

汤(湯) [tāng] 1 (n) 热水 hot water; soup; broth＊羊肉汤 mutton soup＊鸡汤 chicken soup 2 (n) 姓 a surname

汤匙 [tāngchí] a soup spoon; a tablespoon

汤药 [tāngyào] concocted medicinal herbs; concoctions (medicinal herbs)

táng

唐 [táng] (n) 朝代名 Tang Dynasty (618—905 A.D.)

唐诗 [táng shī] poems of Tang Dynasty

唐突 [tángtū] rude; abrupt

塘 [táng] 1 (n) 堤防，堤岸 an embankment; a bank ＊海塘。 a sea wall ; a sea embankment 2 (n) 水池 a pond; a pool ＊魚塘。a fish pond

搪 [táng] (v) 抵挡 to ward off; to keep out; to block ＊搪风。 to keep out the wind.

搪瓷 [tángcí] enamel

搪塞 [táng sè] to perform one's duty perfunctorily

糖 [táng] 1 (n) 从甘蔗，甜菜，米，麦等提制出来的有甜味的东西 sugar 2 (n) 糖果 sweets; candies

糖精 [tángjīng] saccharin

糖尿病 [tángniàobìng] diabetes

糖衣炮弹 [tángyī pàodàn] sugar-coated bullets

糖汁 [tángzhì] molasses; syrup

溏 [táng] (n) 池 a pond 2(a) 不凝结的，半流动的 not congeal , semi-fluid

棠 [táng] (n) 果树名 the crab apple; the wild plum

堂 [táng] 1 (n) 宽敞的大厅 a hall; a meeting place; a court of justice＊礼堂 an assembly hall 公堂 a court of justice 讲堂 a lecture hall 教堂 a church 2 (adj)同宗异支的（亲属）(relatives) of same forefather but different family branch

堂皇 [táng huáng] majestic; grand; magnificent

堂堂 [táng táng] in a dignified manner; with great dignity; magnificently

堂兄弟 [tángxiōngdì] male first cousins on the father's side

堂姊妹 [tángzǐmài] female first cousins on the father's side

膛 [táng](n) 器物中空的部分 the hollow part of a thing ＊枪膛。gun barrel ＊ 胸膛 the breast

螳 [táng] (n) 昆虫 the mantis

螳臂当车 [tángbìdāngchē] a mantis tries to stop a carriage with its legs—overrate one's own strength
螳螂 [tángláng] the praying mantis

tǎng

傥(儻) [tǎng] (conj) 假如 if

倘 [tǎng] (conj) 如果，假使 if; supposing ＊倘若你有困难，我一定帮忙你。If you have difficulty, I will surely help you.
倘然 [tǎngrán] if
倘使 [tǎngshǐ] if

淌 [tǎng] (v) 流 to flow; to drip＊因为天气太热，我一直在淌汗。Because of the hot weather I continue to drip sweat.

躺 [tǎng] (v) 身体卧倒 to lie down＊他躺在床上。He is lying on the bed.
躺椅 [tǎngyǐ] a deck chair; a lounge

tàng

烫(燙) [tàng] 1 (adj) 温度高 not; scalding. ＊这杯水很烫。This glass of water is very hot. 2 (v) 加热 to heat; to scald 3 (v) 以热物推压使滑 to iron ＊我在烫衣服。I am ironing clothes.
烫斗 [tàngdǒu] an iron
烫伤 [tàngshāng] scald

趟 [tàng] (n) 次，回 a measure word (e.g. one trip) ＊司机每天要走三趟车。The driver has to make three trips everyday.

tāo

滔 [tāo] (adj) 漫，水势大的样子 overflowing; torrential
滔滔 [tāotāo] overflowing; exuberant; incessantly
滔滔不绝 [tāo tāo bù jué] talking incessantly
滔天 [tāotiān] rolling; billowy (e.g. waves); towering(e.g. crimes)

掏 [tāo] (v) 用手探取东西 to take out; to pull out; to clean out ＊他从裤袋里掏出钱来。He took out some cash from his trouser pocket.

涛(濤) [tāo] (n) 大波浪 billows; great waves ＊惊涛骇浪。huge and formidable waves.

táo

桃 [táo] (n) 落叶亚乔木。高丈余，叶长椭园形，果甘酸可食 peach
桃花 [táo huā] peach blossom
桃色事件 [táosèshìjiàn] love affairs; romantic affairs
桃子 [táo·z] peach

逃 [táo] (v) 跑开，躲避 to run away; to flee; to escape ＊他想逃出集中营。He intended to escape from the detention camp
逃避 [táobì] a evade; to shun; to shirk
逃兵 [táobing] a deserter
逃窜 [táo chuan] to flee; to run away
逃犯 [táofàn] an escaped criminal
逃荒 [taohuāng] to flee from famine area
逃难 [táo nàn] to flee for one's life; to seek refuge
逃跑 [táo pǎo] to run away; to flee; to desert
逃生 [táoshēng] to escape with one's life; to flee for life
逃脱 [táotuò] to succeed in escaping
逃亡 [táo wáng] to seek safety in flight; to flee from home or country
逃学 [táoxué] to play truant
逃之夭夭 [táo zīyāoyāo] escaped; to make a getaway; to take to one's heel; to run away

陶 [táo] 1 (n) 瓦器 earthenware; pottery; ceramics 2 (v) 造就培养 to cultivate; to nurture ＊在新思想的熏陶下，他逐渐成熟了。Under the influence of new thoughts, he gradually matured. 3 (adj) 喜欢，快乐 pleased: happy; joyful
陶器 [táoqì] pottery; earthenware; ceramics
陶陶 [táotáo] happily
陶冶 [táoyě] to mould; to influence through contact

陶醉 [táo zuì] to become intoxicated with ; to be infatuated with ; to be indulged in

淘 [táo] 1 (v) 洗去杂质 to rinse;to wash ＊一位妇人在淘洗锡米。A woman is washing the tin ore. 2 (v) 消除泥沙、渣滓等，挖浚 to clean ＊他在淘井。 He is cleaning out a well.

淘气 [táoqì] naughty; mischievous

淘汰 [táotài] to eliminate; to sift out

tǎo

讨（討） [tǎo] 1 (v) 征伐 to take punitive action ＊我们准备讨伐犯境的敌人。 We are ready to take punitive action against the enemies who cross the border . 2 (v) 索取，请求 to ask for ; to seek for ; to beg ＊他是来讨债的。He comes here to ask for debt payment. ＊乞丐在讨钱。 The beggar is begging for money.

讨伐 [tǎofá] to take punitive action against

讨饭 [tǎofàn] to beg; to go begging

讨好 [tǎohǎo] to curry favour with; to ingratiate; to flatter; to fawn on

讨价还价 [tǎojiàhuánjià] to bargain; to haggle (e.g. about terms)

讨教 [tǎojiào] to seek advice from; to consult

讨论 [tǎolùn] to discuss; to talk over

讨嫌 [tǎoxián] to excite dislike ; to detest; detestable; disgusting; irritating

讨厌 [tǎoyàn] to be disgusted at; detestable ; to be annoyed about; to be sick of

tào

套 [tào] 1 (n) (v) 罩 a covering ; to cover; to slip over; to put on ＊手套。gloves＊他套上一件毛衣。He puts on a sweater. 2 (v)(n) 拴，系 to tie; to harness; to hitch;put(nooses)around; a tie; a noose 3(n) 成组的同类事物 a measure word: set ＊一套家私。a set of furniture; a suite ＊一套农具。a set of agriculture tools ＊一套理论。 a set of theories

套房 [tàofáng] a suite (of rooms in a hotel)

套购 [tàogòu] to transact illegally

套绳 [tàoshéng] a noose; a lasso

套索 [tàosuō] a lasso

套语 [tàoyǔ] courteous sayings; conventional phrases

套子 [tào zi] a covering; a loop; a noose; a snare

tè

特 [tè] (adj) 不寻常，超出一般 unusual; special; extraordinary ＊他享有特权。He enjoys special rights .

特别 [tèbié] special; exceptional; particular

特产 [tèchǎn] local products ; special products (peculiar to a particular place)

特长 [tècháng] speciality ; special aptitudes; strong points

特等 [tèděng] specially high grade or class; deluxe quality ; top class or highest class

特地 [tèdì] specially; purposely; on purpose

特点 [tèdiǎn] distinguishing characteristics ; special features or traits ; salient features

特定 [tèdìng] specific; peculiar; particular; designated

特技 [tèjī] special technique; special skill; trick photography (cinema)

特价 [tè jià] special prices; special offers

特刊 [tèkān] special issue

特权 [tèquán]prerogatives'; privileges; special right

特色 [tèsè] characteristics; distinctive feature

特赦 [tèshè] amnesty ; pardon by special decree

特使 [tèshǐ] special envoy
特殊 [tèshú] special; particular; extraordinary; exceptional; specific
特殊化 [tèshúhuà] to hanker after special privileges; to specialize
特殊性 [tèshúxìng] particularity; speciality; specific characteristics
特务 [tèwù] a secret agent; a spy
特效 [tèxiào] (medicine) specificity; specific
特写 [tèxiě] special article ; feature; close-up
特性 [tèxìng] speciality; feature; character
特邀 [tèyāo] specially invite
特意 [tèyì] purposely; characteristic
特约 [tèyuē] by special invitation or appointment ; specially invite or appoint
特征 [tèzhēng] specific feature; characteristic
特种 [tèzhǒng] special (e.g. kind, brand, troops)

téng

誊(謄) [téng] (v) 抄写 to copy; to transcribe
誊清 [téngqīng] to make a fair copy; to copy up (notes)
誊写 [téngxiě] to copy up

腾(騰) [téng] 1 (v) 升 to ascend; to mount; to soar ＊物价因通货膨胀而腾涨。 Prices soared as a result of inflation. 2 (v) 跳跃 to jump ＊万众欢腾。Millions of people jump with joy. 3 (v) 空出来，移让 to vacate; to make place for; to empty..........for ＊他腾出一个房间来安置客人。 He vacates a room for the guests.

疼 [téng] 1 (n) 痛 pain; ache 2 (v)爱 to love
疼爱 [téngài] to love dearly
疼痛 [téngtòng] painful

藤 [téng] 1 (n) 蔓生木本植物 rattan; cane ＊藤球。 rattan ball. 2 (n) 泛指植物的蔓 creeping plants; climbers; tendrils ＊瓜藤 tendrils on the gourd plant.

tī

梯 [tī](n)登高用的器具或设备 a ladder; stairs ＊楼梯。staircase.
梯田 [tītián] terraced fields
梯形 [tīxíng] trapezoid; trapezium
梯子 [tīzi] a ladder

剔 [tī] 1 (v) 刮 to scrape ＊我把骨头剔干净。I scrape the bone of its meat. 2 (v) 挑，从缝隙里往外挑 to pick (from the crevices) ＊他在剔牙。He is picking his teeth.
剔除 [tīchú] to reject; to get rid of what is bad or undesirable

踢 [tī] (v) 用脚触动 to kick ＊他在踢足球。He is kicking the football.

tí

提 [tí] 1 (v)拿起；举高 to lift; to carry; to raise; to elevate; to enhance; to heighten ＊他提着一桶水。He is carrying a pail of water.＊我们要提高警惕。We must heighten our vigilance. 2 (v) 倡议，谈起 to propose; to mention; to put forward; to suggest＊请大家多提意见。 Everyone of you please give more suggestions. 3 (v) 取出 to take out; to draw
提案 [tíàn] a motion; a proposition; a resolution
提拔 [tíbá] to promote (e.g. rank or position)
提倡 [tíchàng] to advocate; to encourage; to promote; initiate
提纲 [tígāng] an outline; a thesis; a general sketch
提纲挈领 [tígāngqièlǐng] to give an outline; to put forward the main points
提高 [tígāo] to improve; to raise; to heighten; to enhance

提供 [tígōng] to present; to provide; to offer; to render
提交 [tíjiāo] to hand over; to submit; to deliver
提炼 [tíliàn] to purify; to refine; to sift
提名 [tímíng] to nominate; nomination
提前 [tíqián] to advance; to bring ahead of schedule
提琴 [tíqín] a cello; a double-bass; a violin; a viola
提取 [tíqǔ] to take delivery of; to take out; to extract
提审 [tíshěn] to bring up for trial; to bring (a criminal) before the court
提升 [tíshēng] to promote (in rank or position)
提示 [tíshì] to point out; to draw (somebody's) attention (to something)
提心吊胆 [tíxīndiàodǎn] sick with fear or terror
提醒 [tíxǐng] to remind; bring to mind; alert (somebody) to
提要 [tíyào] a brief summary; chief points
提议 [tíyì] to propose; to put forward; to recommend; to bring up; proposal
提早 [tízǎo] earlier than usual; to bring forward
另见 [dī]

题（題） [tí] (n) 标目；标识 a subject; a topic; a theme.
题材 [tícái] subject matter; subject
题词 [tící] instructive; encouraging or complimentary remarks; inscription
题解 [tíjiě] explanation; solution to problem
题名 [tímíng] inscription
题目 [tímù] title; topic
题字 [tízì] inscription

啼 [tí] 1 (v) 哭 to cry; to weep; to whimper ＊那个妇人为什么哭哭啼啼的？Why does that woman keep crying? 2 (n) 鸟兽叫 cry of birds or animals ＊鸡啼。cock's crow
啼笑皆非 [tíxiàojiēfēi] one can neither laugh nor cry

蹄 [tí] (n) 兽足 hooves; trotters; ＊蹄 trotters ＊马蹄。horse's hooves

tǐ

体（體） [tǐ] 1 (n) 身躯，躯干 the body; the trunk 2 (n) 事物的本质 the substance; the essentials; the essence ＊中学为体，西学为用。Chinese learnings as essentials and western learnings as purposes. 3 (n) 状态 the state (of things) ＊固体 solid ＊液体 liquid 4 (n) 形式；制度；系统 the style; the form; the system ＊文体。literary style. ＊政体。political system
体裁 [tǐcái] form or style of an article
体操 [tǐcāo] gymnastics; gymnastic exercises
体格 [tǐgé] physical constitution (of person)
体会 [tǐhuì] to appreciate; to understand; to realize; to size up (a situation)
体积 [tǐjí] volume
体例 [tǐ lì] form; style
体力 [tǐlì] physical strength; manual (labour)
体力劳动 [tǐlìláodóng] physical labour; manual work
体谅 [tǐliàng] to make allowance for; to excuse
体面 [tǐmiàn] honourable; dignified; prestigious; good-looking
体贴 [tǐtiē] to be considerate of (others); to be thoughtful
体统 [tǐtǒng] propriety; decorum
体温 [tǐwēn] (bodily) temperature
体无完肤 [tǐwúwánfū] the body is covered with wounds all over; to be refuted down to the last point
体系 [tǐxì] system
体现 [tǐxiàn] to find expression in....; to embody.......in; to manifest
体验 [tǐyàn] to experience; to go

through
体育场[tǐyùchǎng] a stadium
体制[tǐzhì] system; system of organisation
体重[tǐzhòng] weight (of a person)

tì

惕 [tì] (adj) 谨慎小心 cautious; vigilant ∗我们不可放松警惕。We should not relax our vigilance.

剃 [tì] (v) 用刀子刮去(头发，胡须) to shave ∗他在剃胡子。He is shaving his whiskers
剃刀 [tìdāo] a razor
剃头 [tìtóu] to cut the hair.

涕 [tì] (1) (n) 眼泪 tears ∗ 他痛哭流涕。He cried sadly with tears dripping down. (2) (n) 鼻的粘液 mucus from the nose ∗ 流鼻涕。to snivel.

屉 [tì] (n) 器物上的隔层 a drawer; a tray ∗桌子的抽屉。the drawer of a desk.

倜 [tì] 倜傥 [tì tǎng] (adj) 洒脱，不拘束的样子 free and easy (of manner); unrestrained; unoccupied

嚏 [tì] (v) (n) to sneeze; a running at the nose
嚏喷 [tì·pen] to sneeze

替 [tì] 1 (v) 代，代理 to substitute; to replace; on behalf of; in place of; instead of; for ∗我替他写信。I write letters for him.
替代 [tìdài] to substitute; to change; to replace
替工 [tìgōng] a substitute workman
替换 [tì·huan] to change; to exchange; to replace (somebody)
替身 [tìshēn] a substitute
替死鬼 [tìsǐguǐ] a scapegoat

tiān

天 [tiān] 1 (n) 地球周围的空间 the sky 2(n) 一昼夜的时间 a day∗ 我忙了一整天。I have been very busy for the whole day. 3 (n) 气候 weather; climate ∗ 天晴。The weather is fine. 4 (n) 时节 season ∗ 春天。spring 5 (adj) 自然的，生成的 natural ∗ 天灾。natural disaster
天才 [tiāncái] genius
天才论 [tiāncáilùn] the (idealist) theory of innate genius
天窗 [tiānchuāng] a skylight
天地 [tiāndì] the universe; heaven and earth
天鹅 [tiān'é] the swan
天鹅绒 [tiān'éróng] velvet
天翻地覆 [tiānfāndìfù] the sky and earth turning upside down; earth-shaking (changes)
天赋 [tiānfù] natural ability; gift; talent
天花 [tiānhuā] smallpox
天花板 [tiānhuābǎn] ceiling
天花乱坠 [tiānhuāluànzhuì] to speak in superlatives; laud something to the skies; extravagantly laud
天经地义 [tiānjīng-dìyì] universally accepted principle; unalterable principle; it stands to reason
天空 [tiānkōng] the sky
天伦 [tiānlún] the natural relationships of mankind
天罗地网 [tiānluó dìwǎng] a dragnet; nets above and snares below; an escapeproof net
天南地北 [tiānnán] far apart; poles apart
天平 [tiānpíng] (weighing) scales
天气 [tiānqì] weather
天堑 [tiānqiàn] natural barrier; a deep chasm
天桥 [tiānqiáo] an overpass; an overhead bridge
天气预报 [tiānqìyùbào] weather forecast
天然 [tiānrán] natural (not artificial)
天然气 [tiānránqì] natural gas
天色 [tiānsè] time or weather of the day as judged by the colour of the sky
天生 [tiānshēng] naturally; born to be
天使 [tiānshǐ] the angel
天堂 [tiāntáng] paradise; heaven
天体 [tiāntǐ] heavenly body; celestial body

天文 [tiānwén] astronomy
天文台[tiānwéntái] observatory
天下大乱 [tiānxiàdàluàn] there is great disorder under heaven; the whole world (country, place) is in great chaos.
天险 [tiānxiǎn] natural defence; natural fortifications
天线 [tiānxiàn] antenne
天涯海角[tiānyá-hǎijiǎo]the remote regions of the earth
天灾 [tiānzāi] natural calamities; natural disasters; natural catastrophe
天灾人祸 [tiānzāi-rénhuò] natural and man-made calamities
天真 [tiānzhēn] naive; innocent
天诛地灭 [tiānzhūdìmiè] to be executed by heaven and destroyed by earth; absolutely and utterly destroyed
天主教 [tiān zhǔ jiào] Roman Catholicism
天资 [tiānzī] talent; (a man of) natural endowment

添 [tiān] (v) 增加 to add; to increase; to replenish ∗我去油站添油。 I go to the petrol kiosk to replenish petrol.
添补 [tiān·bu]to supplement; to make up; to replenish (goods, tools etc)
添丁 [tiāndīng] to have an increase in one's family
添置 [tiānzhì] to buy more (e.g. furniture)

tián

田 [tián] (n) 种植农作物的土地 a farm ; a farmland; a field ∗这个地主拥有很多亩田。The landlord owns many acres of farm land.
田地 [tiándì] farm land; situation (usually bad)
田赋 [tiánfù] land tax
田埂 [tiángěng] ridge (of the furrowed field)
田鸡 [tiánjī] the edible frog
田径赛 [tiánjìngsài] track and field competition
田野 [tiányě] open country

填 [tián] 1 (v) 把凹陷或空缺的地方垫平或塞满 to fill up (hole; ditch etc) ∗工人在填路上的洞。The workers are filling up the holes on the road. 2 (v) 在表格上按照项目写 to fill in (forms) ∗我在填申请表格。 I am filling in the application form.
填表 [tiánbiǎo] to fill in a blank form
填补 [tiánbǔ] to make up; to replenish
填充 [tiánchōng] fill in the blanks
填空 [tiánkòng] to fill up the gap
填写 [tiánxiě] to fill in (a form)
填鸭 [tiányā] stuffed and fattened ducks
填鸭式 [tián yā shì] cramming; cram

甜 [tián] (adj) 象糖和蜜的味道，並引伸为愉快，可爱等，跟"苦"相对 agreeable; pleasant ∗这梨子很甜。This pear is very sweet. ∗他睡得很甜。He sleeps sweetly.
甜美 [tiánměi] sweet, sweet and comfortable
甜蜜 [tiánmì] sweet; loving; comfortable
甜头 [tián·tou]sweet taste; benefit
甜言蜜语 [tiányán - mìyǔ] honeyed words; honey-lipped

恬 [tián] (adj) 宁静，安闲quiet; calm; tranquil
恬不知耻 [tiánbùzhīchǐ] shameless; calm and devoid of any sense of shame
恬静 [tiánjìng] tranquil; calm

tiǎn

舔 [tiǎn] (v) 用舌头接触东西 to lick ∗猫在舔它的尾巴。 The cat is licking its tail.

殄 [tiǎn] (v) 尽，天绝 to terminate; to exterminate∗暴殄天物(不爱惜和糟蹋上天给予的东西)。to waste and misuse God's gift.

tiāo

佻 [tiāo] (adj) 不庄重 frivolous

挑 [tiāo] 1 (v) 用肩担着 to carry with a pole on the shoulder ∗她挑着两

篮菜。She carries with a pole on the shoulder two baskets of vegetable 2 (v)拣 to choose; to select; to pick out ＊我挑了三粒榴梿给他。I selected three durians for him.

挑剔 [tiāo·ti] be critical (toward); to carp (at others)

挑选 [tiāoxuǎn] choose; select

tiáo

迢 [tiáo] (adj) 远。叠用 far away (of journey); long ＊我千里迢迢来探望亲人。I have travelled thousands of miles to visit my relatives.

条(條) [tiáo] 1 (n) 狭长的东西 strip; bar; slip ＊布条。a banner. ＊面条。noodles ＊收条。a receipt. ＊便条 a short note; a memo 2 (n) 量词 a measure word (for long, thin things) ＊一条河。a river. ＊二条腿。two legs ＊一条蛇。a snake. ＊一条街。a street.

条件 [tiáojiàn] conditions; terms

条件反射 [tiáojiàn fǎnshè] conditioned reflex

条款 [tiáokuǎn] clause (e.g.agreement)

条理 [tiáolǐ] orderly; systematically

条例 [tiáolì] regulations; statutes; ordinances

条目 [tiáomù] articles; items

条文 [tiáowén] articles; the text (of a treaty)

条纹 [tiáowén] stripes; streaks

条约 [tiáoyuē] a treaty; a pact

条子 [tiáo·zi] a slip of paper; a short note

调(調) [tiáo] 1 (v) 配合均匀 to blend ＊我在调色。I am blending the colour. 2 (v) 使和谐 to harmonize; to reconcile; to mediate ＊我将出面调解他们的纠纷。I personally shall mediate their disputes. 3 (v) 挑逗 to provoke; to stir up

调羹 [tiáogēng] a spoon; to season soup

调和 [tiáo·he] harmonising; agreeable; to compromise to mediate; to reconcile

调剂 [tiáojì] to regulate; to adjust; to put right

调节 [tiáojié] to adjust; to regulate

调解 [tiáojiě] to mediate; to reconcile

调理 [tiáo·li] to look after; to recuperate

调皮 [tiáopí] naughty; cheeky

调情 [tiáoqíng] to dally with

调停 [tiáo·ting] to mediate

调味 [tiáowèi] to season; to blend flavours

调戏 [tiáo·xi] lewd defiance; to flirt

调养 [tiáoyǎng] to recuperate; to harmonize; to tune

调整 [tiáozhěng] to readjust; to reorganise

另见 [diào]

tiǎo

挑 [tiǎo] 1 (v) to poke up (e.g. the fire); to pick ＊我在挑在手指上的刺。I am picking a thorn from my finger. 2 (v) 拨弄，引动 to stir up; to incite

挑拨 [tiǎobō] to foment (disunity and dissention); to stir up

挑拨离间 [tiǎobōlíjiān] to foment dissention; to sow discord; to poison the relation between; to create dissention

挑动 [tiǎodòng] to instigate; to provoke; to stir up

挑花 [tiǎohuā] needle point (e.g. lace, embroidery)

挑起 [tiǎoqǐ] to instigate; to stir up; to provoke

挑唆 [tiǎo·suo] to instigate; to incite

挑衅 [tiǎoxìn] to provoke

挑战 [tiǎozhàn] to challenge; to issue a challenge; to throw down the glove

另见 [tiāo]

窕 [tiǎo] 隐逸的; 高洁的; 文雅的 secluded; elegant; refined

tiào

眺 [tiào] (v) 远望 to gaze;

眺望 [tiàowàng] to look far into the distance

跳 [tiào] 1 (v) 跃 to jump; to leap 2 (v) 一起一伏地运动 to palpitate; to twitch; to beat * 他心跳得很厉害。His heart beats very fast.

跳板 [tiàobǎn] a spring board; a diving board

跳槽 [tiàocáo] to go from one job to another; to throw up a situation

跳动 [tiàodòng] to jump about; to palpitate; to twitch

跳高 [tiàogāo] the high jump

跳级 [tiàojí] to be skipped to one grade higher

跳梁小丑 [tiàoliángxiǎochǒu] a clown; a buffon (a silly and contemptible person)

跳伞 [tiàosǎn] to land by parachute; to parachute

跳绳 [tiàoshéng] to skip rope

跳水 [tiàoshuǐ] to dive

跳舞 [tiàowǔ] to dance

跳远 [tiàoyuǎn] the long jump

跳跃 [tiàoyuè] to jump; to hop

tiē

贴（貼）[tiē] 1 (v) 粘 to paste; to stick on * 我忘了贴邮票在信封上。I forgot to paste the stamp on the envelope * 孩子把头贴在母亲胸前。The child sticks his head on his mother's chest. 2 (v) 补助 to subsidize * 津贴。allowance

贴切 [tiēqiè] pertinent; very much to the point

贴金 [tiējīn] to gild; to beautify; to embellish

贴心 [tiēxīn] intimate (e.g. friend or talk)

帖 [tiē] (n) 量词 a measure word; dose * 一帖药。a dose of herbs.
另见 [tiě] [tiè]

tiě

帖 [tiě] (n) 邀请或通知的便条 invitation card or notice * 请帖。invitation card.
另见 [tiē] [tiè]

铁（鐵）[tiě] (n) 一种金属元素 iron

铁板 [tiěbǎn] iron plate

铁饼 [tiěbǐng] discus

铁窗风味 [tiěchuāngfēngwèi] the flavour of prison bars

铁钉 [tiědīng] iron nail

铁轨 [tiěguǐ] the rails (of railway)

铁汉 [tiěhàn] an iron man — a determined and strong man

铁匠 [tiě·jiang] blacksmith

铁路 [tiělù] railway

铁面无私 [tiěmiànwúsī] (a person of) unbending principles or firm integrity

铁器 [tiěqì] iron ware

铁锹 [tiěqiāo] a shovel; a spade

铁器时代 [tiěqìshídài] iron age

铁拳 [tiěquán] an iron fist

铁石心肠 [tiěshíxīncháng] flint-hearted; hard as steel; unmoved by emotions

铁水 [tiěshuǐ] melted iron

铁树开花 [tiěshùkāihuā] an iron tree blossoms — rarity

铁丝 [tiěsī] wire; steel wire

铁丝网 [tiěsīwǎng] wire net

铁蹄 [tiětí] iron heel

铁锨 [tiěxiān] a spade; a shovel

铁砧 [tiězhēn] an anvil

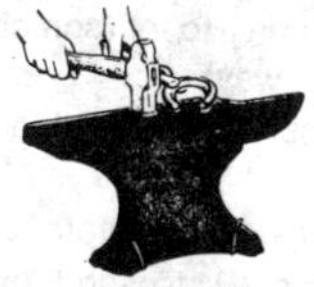

铁证 [tiězhèng] an iron-clad evidence; an iron-clad proof

铁证如山 [tiězhèngrúshān] irrefutable proof; a mass of cast iron proof

tiè

帖 [tiè] (n) 写字、画图的样本 a copy-book for writing or drawing * 字帖。calligraphy copybook
另见 [tiē] [tiě]

tīng

厅（廳）[tīng] (n) 广大的房间 a hall ✱客厅。a living room; a parlour; a saloon. ✱ 餐厅。a canteen; a dining-saloon. ✱ 舞厅。a dancing-saloon

听（聽）[tīng] 1 (v)用耳朵接受声音 to listen; to hear ✱我在听广播。I am listening to the radio. 2 (v)服从，接受，照着办 to obey ✱这孩子很听话。This child is very obedient. 3 (v) 任凭 to leave; to allow; to let

听从 [tīngcóng] to obey

听而不闻 [tīngérbùwén] to pay no attention; to turn a deaf ear to

听候 [tīnghòu] to wait for decision, etc); to be prepared for; pending (e.g. further instructions)

听话[tīnghuà] to be obedient; to be docile

听见 [tīng·jiàn] to hear

听讲 [tīngjiǎng] to attend lectures

听觉 [tīngjué] sense of hearing

听力 [tīnglì] hearing; perception of sound

听其自然 [tīngqízìrán] to let matters take their own course; to let things drift

听取 [tīngqǔ] to listen to; to hear (opinion)

听任[tīngrèn] to let (somebody to have his own way)

听说[tīngshuō]it is said that; to be told that

听写 [tīngxiě] to dictate; dictation

听信 [tīngxìn] to lend oneself to; to listen to and believe

听诊器 [tīngzhěnqì] stethoscope

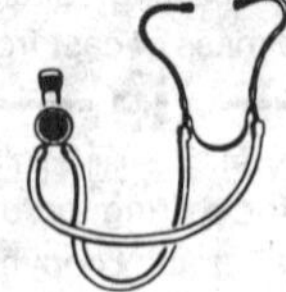

听众 [tīngzhong] audience

tíng

廷 [tíng] (n) 封建帝王接受朝见 和办理政事的地方 the imperial court ✱朝廷。the imperial court.

蜓 [tíng] (n) 一种头大腹细长的昆虫 a dragon fly 也叫"蜻蜓" (qingting)

霆 [tíng] (n) 响雷 a loud crash of thunder

庭 [tíng] 1 (n) 院子 a courtyard ✱庭前有一棵树。There is a tree in the courtyard. 2 (n) 审判案件的地方 a court of justice ✱ 法庭 court of justice

亭 [tíng] (n) 有顶无墙，供休息用的建筑物 a pavilion; a kiosk; a shed; an arbour ✱凉亭。a pavilion; an arbour ✱候车亭。bus stop shed

停 [tíng] (v) 止住，不动 to stop; to halt; to discontinue ✱雨停了。The rain has stopped.

停泊 [tíngbó] to anchor; to moor

停车 [tíngchē] stop a vehicle ; parking

停当 [tíng·dang] all set; all arranged

停顿 [tíngdùn] to be at a standstill

停工 [tínggōng] to stop work

停火 [tínghuǒ] to cease fire

停刊 [tíngkān] to suspend publication

停留 [tínglíu] to stop over (e.g. during journey); to remain (stagnant)

停用 [tíngyòng] to lay down

停战 [tíngzhàn] armistice; truce; cessation of hostilities

停止 [tíngzhǐ] to stop; to halt

停滞[tíngzhì] to standstill; to cease; to be tied up; to hold back

停滞不前 [tíngzhìbùqián] to be at a standstill; to remain stagnant; to cease to make progress; to remain at the stage of

婷 [tíng] (adj) 美好的样子 graceful; elegant

tǐng

挺 [tǐng] 1 (v) 直立 to stand erect; to stick up ✱红树林挺立在水中。

The mangroves stick up in the water. 2 (v) 突出；伸出 to thrust out; to stick out *他挺起胸膛，接受挑战。He, with his chest thrust out, accepted the challenge. 3 (adv) 很 very *他是挺和气的。He is very friendly 4 (n) 量词*一挺机关枪。a piece of machine-gun

挺拔 [tǐngbá] straight and towering; firm and powerful

挺进 [tǐngjìn] forward; to make a deep thrust into (e.g. enemy position); to advance

挺立 [tǐnglì] to stand erect, to straighten up

挺身而出 [tǐngshēnérchū] to step forward courageously; to come out boldly

铤(鋌) [tǐng] (adj) 急走的样子 in a hurry

铤而走险 [tǐngérzǒuxiǎn] to risk danger in desperation

艇 [ting] (n) 小船 a boat; a canoe; a punt; a barge *快艇；游艇 a yacht *汽艇。a steam boat *潜艇。a submarine

tōng

通 [tōng] 1 (adv) (v) 没有阻碍；穿过 through; passable; to go through *这两间房是相通的。These two rooms are passable to one another. 2 (v) 懂得，彻底明白。to be well-versed in; to understand *他精通马来文。He is well-versed in Malay. 3 (adj) 一般 general; ordinary; common (4) (adj) 普遍的，全部的 all; whole *我们一定要有个通盘计划。We must have an all round plan.

通报 [tōngbào] notification for general information; circular

通病 [tōngbìng] common failing; common illness

通常 [tōngcháng] usual; ordinary;

通畅 [tōngchàng] fluent

通称 [tōngchēng] generally known as

通道 [tōngdào] a thoroughfare

通敌 [tōngdí] to conspire with the enemy

通电 [tōngdiàn] to make electric connection; to open telegram; circular telegram

通风 [tōngfēng] airy; well ventilated; to provide somebody with information; to reveal; to disclose

通告 [tōnggào] to notify the public; official public notice

通观全局 [tōngguānquánjú] to take an overall view of the situation

通过 [tōngguò] to pass through; to pass (a resolution, etc); to approve

通航 [tōngháng] to be open to navigation

通红 [tōnghóng] burning red; glowing red

通货 [tōnghuò] currency

通货紧缩 [tōnghuòjǐnsù] deflation

通货膨胀 [tōnghuòpéngzhàng] inflation (e.g. financial)

通缉 [tōngjī] to issue a wanted notice; to order the arrest of somebody

通令 [tōnglìng] to issue an order (e.g. to the whole country); an order

通明 [tōngmíng] lit up; brightly lit; ablaze with light

通盘 [tōngpán] all round

通情达理 [tōngqíngdálǐ] to be reasonable; to be sensible

通融 [tōng rong] to be accomodating or flexible

通商 [tōngshāng] to trade with (e.g. other country)

通史 [tōngshǐ] general history; comprehensive history

通顺 [tōngshùn] fluent; flowing (e.g. writing)

通俗 [tōngsú] popular; simple (e.g. language)

通俗化 [tōngsúhuà] to popularize

通通 [tōngtōng] all; altogether; entirely

通统 [tōngtǒng] all; altogether; entirely

通宵 [tōngxiāo] all night; through the night

通晓 [tōngxiǎo] to be well-versed in; to understand thoroughly
通信 [tōngxìn] to correspond
通行 [tōngxíng] to be current (e.g. language; customs); to be open to traffic
通行证 [tōngxíngzhèng] a pass
通讯 [tōngxùn] communications
通讯处 [tōng xùn chù] address
通讯社 [tōngxùnshè] news agency
通讯员 [tōngxùnyuán] a correspondent
通用 [tōngyòng] to be current; to apply universally
通知 [tōngzhī] to notify; to inform; a notice

tóng

同 [tóng] 1 (adj) 一样 same; equal * 男女应同工同酬。Men and women should have equal pay for equal work 2 (adj) 一起 together * 我们同甘共苦。We share our joy and sorrow together. 3 (prep) 介词，与"跟"相同 with 4 (conj) 连词，与"和"相同 and; as well as; with * 房里有一张桌子同四把椅子。There is a table and four chairs in the room.
同班 [tóngbān] in the same class (e.g. school)
同伴 [tóngbàn] a companion; a mate
同胞 [tóngbāo] compatriots; fellow-countrymen
同病相怜 [tóngbìngxiānglián] fellow sufferers sympathise with one another; those who have the same complaint sympathise with each other
同仇敌忾 [tóngchóudíkài] to fight shoulder to shoulder with; to bear common hatred for the enemy
同床异梦 [tóngchuángyìmèng] to sleep in same bed but dream different dreams
同等 [tóngděng] equivalent; the same level or standard
同调 [tóngdiào] in concert
同感 [tónggǎn] common feelings; same feelings
同甘共苦 [tóng gān gòng kǔ] to share joys and sorrows; to share weal and woe
同工同酬 [tónggōng tóngchóu] equal pay for equal work
同归于尽 [tóngguīyújìn] both sides are doomed; to end in common ruin
同行 [tóngháng] persons of same profession
同化 [tónghuà] to assimilate.
同化作用 [tónghuà zuòyòng] assimilation
同伙 [tónghuǒ] a copartner
同流合污 [tóngliúhéwū] to join in the evil doings
同盟 [tóngméng] alliance; ally
同盟军 [tóngméngjūn] allied forces; allies
同谋 [tóngmóu] to conspire; to form a conspiracy
同情 [tóngqíng] to sympathise; sympathy
同时 [tóngshí] at the same time; simultaneously
同事 [tóngshì] a colleague
同位素 [tóngwèisù] isotope
同位语 [tóngwèiyǔ] appositive
同乡 [tóngxiāng] persons of the same village; country or province; fellow townsmen
同性 [tóngxìng] same sex; similar quality
同心同德 [tóngxīn-tóngdé] with one heart and one mind; to unite (for the same course)
同心协力 [tóngxīnxiélì] to unite in a concerted effort
同心圆 [tóngxīnyuán] concentric circles
同学 [tóngxué] classmates; schoolmates
同样 [tóngyàng] same; likewise
同意 [tóngyì] to agree; to approve
同义词 [tóngyìcí] synonyms
同音词 [tóngyīncí] homonym

同一性 [tóngyīxìng] identity
同志 [tóngzhì] a comrade
同舟共济 [tóngzhōugòngjì] to come together rain or shine; to be together through thick and thin; to be in the same boat; to help each other in distress

桐 [tóng](n)落叶乔木，有油桐、梧桐、泡桐等数种 tung tree
桐油 [tóngyóu] tung oil; wood oil

铜(銅)[tóng](n)化学元素，是淡红色的金属 copper; brass; bronze
铜版 [tóngbǎn] plates for printing
铜板[tóngbǎn]copper coins;bar copper
铜匠 [tóng·jang]a coppersmith; a brass finisher
铜皮铁骨 [tóngpítiěgǔ] a brass and iron constitution —a strong man
铜器 [tóngqì] copperware; brassware
铜墙铁壁 [tóngqiáng tiěbì] wall of bronze and iron; bastion of iron
铜像 [tóngxiàng] bronze statues; brazen images
铜印 [tóngyìn] brass seals
铜乐队 [tóngyuèduì] a brass band

童 [tóng] (n) 小孩 kid; child; lad
童工 [tónggōng] child labourer
童话 [tónghuà] fairy tales
童年 [tóngnáin] childhood
童谣 [tóngyáo] children's song; a nursery rhyme

僮 [tóng] (n) 僮仆 a young servant

瞳 [tóng] (n) 眼球中的圆孔，可以随着光线的强弱而扩大或缩小 pupil of the eye

彤 [tóng] (adj) 朱红色 dark red

筒 [tóng] (n)硬管状器物 a hard tube-shaped container ＊笔筒。a brush cover; a pen cover ＊邮筒 post pillar

tǒng

桶 [tǒng] 1 (n)盛东西的器具，圆形，有的有提梁 a bucket; a barrel; a casket ＊水桶。water bucket 2 (n) 量词 a measure word: bucket ＊一桶水。a bucket of water

捅 [tǒng] (v) 戳，刺 to poke

统(統)[tǒng] 1 (v) 总合 to gather into one; to unify ＊南韩和北韩还没统一 North and South Korea have not been unified. 2 (n)事物彼此间的连续关系；头绪 order; system ＊血统。blood heritage. ＊体统。propriety; decorum ＊传统。traditions ＊系统。system
统称 [tǒngchēng] generally known as; to be generally named
统筹 [tǒngchóu] to plan as a whole
统筹兼顾 [tǒngchóujiāngù] overall planning and all round considerations
统计 [tǒngjì] (compile) statistics
统计表 [tǒng lì biǎo] table of figures; statistical returns
统率 [tǒngshuài] to command
统帅 [tǒngshuài] the commander
统统 [tǒngtǒng] entirely; all; together
统一 [tǒngyī] to unify; unity
统一体 [tǒngyītǐ] entity
统一战线 [tǒngyīzhànxiàn] united front
统制 [tǒngzhì] to control
统治 [tǒngzhì] to rule; to govern; to dominate
统治阶级 [tǒngzhìjiēji] ruling class

tòng

痛 [tòng] 1 (n) 苦楚 pain; ache ＊头痛。headache 2 (adj) 悲伤 agonizing; agonized; bitter ＊听到他的死讯，我感到十分悲痛。On learning his death I felt much agonized. 3 (adv) 极度地，尽情地 to the extreme; thoroughly; deeply
痛斥[tòngchì]thoroughly refute;bitterly denounce; to rebut severely
痛处 [tòngchù] sensible spot; tender subject; the quick
痛打 [tòngdǎ] to give a severe thrashing
痛定思痛[tòngdìngsītòng]to recall past pains

痛改前非 [tònggǎiqiánfēi] to reform earnestly one's misdeeds; to mend one's ways
痛感 [tònggàn] to feel keenly
痛恨 [tònghèn] to hate bitterly
痛哭 [tòngkù] to cry bitterly
痛苦 [tòngkǔ] painful; bitter
痛快 [tòngkuài] to one's heart content, outspoken; straight forward; thrilled with gladness
痛哭流涕 [tòngkùlíutì] to cry and shed bitter tears
痛骂 [tòngmà] to scold severely
痛心 [tòngxīn] heart rending; heart-stricken
痛心疾首 [tòngxīn-jíshǒu] with deep hatred
痛痒[tòngyǎng] pain and itch; concern
痛饮 [tòngyǐn] to drink deeply

恸(慟) [tòng] (n,v,a,) 悲伤 grief; sadness; to mourn; moved; affected

tōu

偷 [tōu] 1 (v) 窃取，暗中拿别人的东西 to steal; to pilfer ＊他被控偷窃。He was accused of pilfering. 2 (adv) 暗中瞒着人(做事)有时叠用 stealthily; secretly
偷安[tōuān] to take one's ease ; to shirk work
偷盗 [tōudào] to steal; to rob
偷渡 [tōudù] to stow away
偷渡者 [tōudùzhě] a stowaway
偷工减料 [tōugōngjiǎnliào] to cheat in work and cut down material; to do shoddy work and use inferior materials;
偷看 [tōukàn] to peep at; to steal a glance
偷懒 [tōulǎn] idle; negligent
偷梁换柱 [tōuliánghuànzhù] stealing the beams and pillars and replace them with rott en timbers;to resort to fraudulence
偷窃 [tōuqiè] to steal; to pilfer
偷听 [tōutīng] to listen secretly; to eavesdrop
偷偷 [tōutōu] stealthily; secretly
偷偷摸摸 [tōutōumōmō] stealthily; quietly and secretly.
偷袭 [tōuxí] to make a surprise attack; to raid
偷运 [tōuyùn] to smuggle

tóu

投 [tóu] 1 (v) 抛，掷，扔(多指有目标的) to throw; to hurl; to cast 2 (v) 进入 to jump into; to throw (oneself) into ＊他投身于工业生产的行列。He throws himself into the column of industrial production. 3 (v) 放入，送进 to submit; to send in; to deliver ＊他常常投稿。He always submits manuscripts for publication.
投奔 [tóubēn] to go to join.....; to fly to .....for support
投标 [tóubiāo] to tender for a contract
投产 [tóuchǎn] to put into production; to begin production
投诚 [tóuchéng] to come over to brightness;to surrender to the people
投弹[tóudàn] hand-grenade throwing
投敌 [tóudí] to surrender to enemy
投递 [tóudì] to deliver
投稿 [tóugǎo] to submit manuscripts (for publication)
投合 [tóuhè] to be suitable to; to suit; to cater; to cater for the taste
投机 [tóujī] to speculate; harmonious; agreeing; suiting
投机倒把 [tóujīdǎobǎ] to speculate; profiteering
投机取巧 [tóujīqúqiǎo] to gain something by fraud
投靠[tóukào] to become retainer of;to throw oneself into the arms of
投票 [tóupiào] to cast vote
投其所好 [tóuqísuóhào] to feed a man on what he relishes
投入[tóurù]to plunge;to throw(oneself) into
投身 [tóushēn] to plunge into ; to

participate in; to throw oneself into

投降 [tóuxiáng] to surrender; to capitulate

投降主义 [tóuxiángzhǔyì] capitulationism

投影 [tóuyǐng] a projection

投掷 [tóuzhì] to throw; to cast

投资 [tóuzī] investment; to subscribe capital; to invest

骰 [tóu] (n) 一种正立方粒形的骨制赌具也读 "shǎi" 或 "gǔ" a dice

头(頭) [tóu] 1 (n) 人或物的最上或最前部分 the head; the top ＊头颅。the skull; the head 2 (n) 端 the edge; the end; ends ＊针头。the point of a needle ＊棍头 the ends of a rod 3 (n) 零碎物件 odd pieces ＊烟头 cigarette butts ＊石头 stones 骨头 bones 4 (adj) 最上的 first; the most important; the best ＊他旅行坐头等车厢。He travelled in a first class coach 5 (adj) 最初的 。the first ＊头两年 the first two years. 6 (n) 首领 the chief ＊工头 foreman 7 (n) 量词 a measure word (e.g. for farm animals) ＊一头牛 a cow.

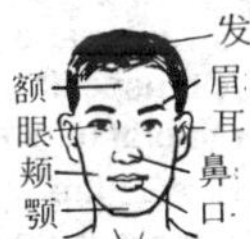

头等 [tóuděng] first class; paramount; prime (e.g. importance)

头发 [tóu·fa] hair on human head

头号 [tóuhào] the biggest; no. 1.

头奖 [tóujiǎng] first prize

头巾 [tóujīn] a headscarf

头盔 [tóukuī] a helmet

头目 [tóumù] a head; a boss; a chieftain; a chief

头脑 [tóunǎo] head; brains; the human mind

头破血流 [tóupòxuèlíu] head broken and blood flowing; to be badly battered; a disastrous defeat

头痛 [tóutòng] headache

头头是道 [tóutóushìdào] clear and convincing; systematically and methodically

头衔 [tóuxián] rank; title

头屑 [tóuxiè] dandruff

头绪 [tóuxù] in order; (in good) working order

头子 [tóu·zi] chief; boss; head

tòu

透 [tòu] 1 (v) 通，穿过。to pass through ;to penetrate ＊阳光透过玻璃照进来。The sunlight passes through the glass. 2 (adv) 彻底 thoroughly ＊浸透。soaked through 熟透 thoroughly ripe ＊他把道理说得透彻。He reasoned out the matter very thoroughly.

透彻 [tòuchè] thorough; profound; penetrating; incisive

透风 [tòufēng] well ventilated

透光 [tòuguāng] transparent

透汗 [tòuhàn] a very heavy perspiration

透镜 [tòujìng] lens

透亮 [tòu·liang] transparent; clear

透漏 [tòulòu] to divulge

透露 [tòulù] to reveal; to disclose; to bring to light

透明 [tòumíng] transparent

透辟 [tòupì] deep; thorough; profound

透视 [tòushì] to sea through;clairvoyance; perspective

透视 [tòushì] to have an X-ray examination; perspective

透视图 [tòushìtú] perspective

透印版 [tòuyìnbǎn] an offset

透印版印刷机 [tòuyìnbǎnyìnshuàjī] an offset press

透支 [tòuzhī] to overdraw (from bank)

tū

突 [tū] 1 (adv) 忽然。suddenly; all of a sudden; abruptly ＊风云突变。The wind and clouds suddenly change — The situation suddenly changes. 2 (v) 隆起，伸出 to protrude; to project; to bulge ＊峯峦突起。 The mountain peaks project into the sky. 3 (v) 冲出 to rush out; to break through ＊我们已经突围 We have broken through the encirclement. 4 (v) 相触犯 to offend＊冲突 to conflict 5 (n) 烟窗，灶窗 chimney ＊曲突徙薪 to bend the chimney and remove the fuel — to guard against danger.

突变 [tūbiàn] to change suddenly; a sudden change; a sudden leap takes place

突出 [tūchū] to be outstanding; striking

突飞猛进 [tūfēiměngjìn] to advance by leaps and bounds

突击 [tūjī] to make surprise attack; to rush (work)

突击队 [tūjīduì] storm troops; shock brigade; assault force

突破 [tūpò] to make a breakthrough; to breach (e.g. enemy's line)

突起 [tūqǐ] suddenly arise; to bulge

突然 [tūrán] sudden; abrupt

突如其来 [tūrúqílái] suddenly; abruptly

突围 [tūwéi] to break through encirclement

凸 [tū] (adj) 周围低中间高，跟"凹"相对 convex; bulging; protruding

凸透镜 [tūtòujìng] convex lens

秃 [tū] 1 (adj) 没有毛发的 bald; bare

tú

涂（塗） [tú] (v) 抹上 to apply; to rub on; to smear 2 (v) 抹去 to erase; to cross out ＊一些字給涂掉了。Some words have been crossed out

涂改 [túgǎi] to alter; to make correction

涂沫 [túmǒ] to smear over

涂墙 [túqiáng] to plaster a wall

涂炭生灵 [útànshēnglíng] to oppress the masses

涂鸦 [túyā] to write badly; to scribble

涂脂沫粉 [túzhīmǒfěn] to apply rouge and powder-to beautify; to whitewash

荼 [tú] (n) 苦菜 a bitter edible plant; the sow-thistle

荼毒 [túdú] bitter and poisonous; calamities; sorrows

途 [tú] (n) 道路 a road; a path; a journey; a career; a pursuit ＊前途。the road ahead-the future ＊长途。a long journey; a long distance ＊用途。 uses

途径 [tújìng] path way

途中 [túzhōng] on the way

图（圖） [tú] 1 (n) 画出来的形象 a drawing; a picture; an illustration ＊书里面有許多插图 There are many illustrations in the book. 2 (v) 计谋 to plan; to plot ＊他图谋不轨。 He is planning for something evil.

图案 [tú àn] a design; a pattern

图饱私囊 [túbǎosīnáng] planning to fill one's own pockets

图表 [túbiǎo] a chart; a graph; a diagram; a blue-print

图钉 [túdīng] thumb-tacks

图画 [túhuà] a painting; a drawing

图解 [tújiě] an illustration; a graph

图景 [tújǐng] prospects

图谋 [túmóu] to plot (e.g. a conspiracy)

图片 [túpiàn] a picture

图书 [túshū] books in general

图书馆 [túshūguǎn] a library

图像 [túxiàng] a painted picture; a portrait; a graph

图形 [túxíng] a sketch; a figure; a graph

图样 [túyàng] a sketch; a design

图章 [túzhāng] (official or personal) seal; stamp

徒 [tú] 1 (v) 步行 to walk; to go on foot ＊他们计划徒步旅行。 They plan to travel on foot. 2 (adj) 空的，白白的 empty; bare; only; merely; in vain 3 (n) 跟师傅学习的人 apprentice ＊他是一名学徒。He is an apprentice

4 (n) 参加者 participants ＊ 教徒。religious disciples ＊ 党徒。gangsters ＊ 暴徒。rioters ＊ 赌徒。gamblers ＊ 匪徒 bandits ＊ 叛徒。traitors

徒步 [túbù] on foot

徒弟 [tú · di] an apprentice; a disciple

徒劳 [túláo] futile; of no avail; fruitless labour; to try in vain

徒手 [túshǒu] bare-handed

徒然 [túrán] in vain

徒子徒孙 [túzǐtúsūn] disciples and followers (derogatory)

徒刑 [túxíng] legal sentence (e.g. life sentence) ; penal servitude

屠 [tú] 1 (v) 宰杀 to butcher; to kill and dress animals 2 (v) 残杀 to slaughter; to kill

屠城 [túchéng] to slaughter the inhabitants of a captured city

屠刀 [túdāo] butcher's knife

屠夫 [túfū] a butcher

屠杀 [túshā] to kill; to massacre

屠宰 [túzǎi] to slaughter animals (esp. for food)

屠宰场 [túzǎichǎng] an abattoir; a slaughter house

tǔ

土 [tǔ] 1 (n)地面上的泥、沙等混合物 soil; earth ＊ 黄土。yellow soil. 2 (n) 地 land ; ground; territory ＊ 领土。territory. 3 (adj) 本地的，本国的 native; local ＊ 土产。 ocal products ＊ 土人 natives; aborigines

土崩 [tǔbēng] a cataclysm

土崩瓦解 [tǔbēng-wǎjiě] to disintegrate and collapse; to crumble and perish; to fall apart

土产 [tǔchǎn] local products

土地 [tǔdì] land

土地改革 [tǔdìgǎigé] land reform

土豆 [tǔdòu] potato

土匪 [tǔfěi] bandits

土风 [tǔfēng] local customs

土风舞 [tǔfēngwǔ] folk dances

土豪劣绅 [tǔháolièshēn] local tyrants and evil gentry; local bullies and bad gentry

土话 [tǔhuà] local dialects

土沥专 [tǔlìzhuān] bitumen;asphattum

土木工程 [tǔmùgōngchéng] civil engineering

土气 [tǔ·qi] exhalations of the ground; miasma ; vulgar; rustic

土埌 [tǔrǎng] soil

土生土长 [tǔshēng tǔzhǎng] indigenous; locally born and brought up

土头土脑 [tǔtóutǔnǎo] rustic; countrified

土星 [tǔxīng] Saturn

土质 [tǔzhì] properties of soil

土著 [tǔzhù] natives; aborigines; indigenous people

吐 [tǔ] 1 (v) 从口里随意放出 to spit out ＊ 不要随地吐痰。 Do not spit on the floor. 2 (v) 泄露 to disclose, to reveal ＊ 他不愿意吐露实情。 He is not willing to disclose the real story.

吐故纳新 [tǔgùnàxīn] to exhale the old and inhale the new

吐露 [tǔlù] to disclose; to reveal

吐气扬眉 [tǔqìyángméi]to get over one's temper and smooth out one's frown 另见 [tù]

tù

兔 [tù] (n) 一种尾短耳大的小兽 a hare; a rabbit

兔唇 [tùchún] hare-lipped

兔死狐悲 [tùsǐhúbēi] the fox mourns over the death of the hare; like mourns over the death of like

兔脱 [tùtuō] to run away like an escaping hare

吐 [tù] 1 (v) 从口里不随意放出 to vomit; to throw up 2 (v) 退还（侵佔的东西）return (things robbed)

吐血 [tùxiě] to vomit blood; to spit blood

吐泻 [tùxiè] vomiting and purging

吐赃 [tùzāng] to return the stolen goods

另见 [tǔ]

tuān

湍 [tuān] (n) 急流的水 a rapid flow of water
湍急 [tuānjí] (of river) flowing rapidly
湍流 [tuānliú] a swift flow (stream, river, etc)

tuán

团(團) [tuán] 1 (n) 球形物 a roundish mass; a ball ∗线团 a thread ball 2 (n) 因工作或活动而组织的集体 a body; an organisation; delegation∗旅行团 tour group 代表团 delegation ∗艺术团 arts troupe. 3 (n) 军队编制单位，是师的下一级，营的上一级 a regiment of soldiers 4 量词 a measure word (for round things) ∗一团毛线 a ball of knitting wool
团结 [tuánjié] to unite
团聚 [tuánjù] to have a reunion;to rally
团体 [tuántǐ] a body; a group; an organisation
团体操 [tuántǐcāo] group calisthenics
团圆 [tuányuán] to have a family reunion.
团员 [tuányuán] members of a group or organisation or body; members of a delegation
团长 [tuánzhǎng] head of a delegation; regimental commander
团(糰) [tuán] (n)一种粉制球形食品 dumplings; donghnuts ∗汤团 dumplings of rice flour in soup

tuī

推 [tuī] 1 (v) 用力使东西向前移动 to push; to push forward ∗我们帮他推车。We help him to push the car. 2 (v) 根据已知事实断定其余 to infer; to deduce; 3 (v) 辞让，脱卸 to decline; to shirk; to evade ∗我们不应该推卸责任。 We should not evade responsibilities.
推波助澜 [tuībōzhùlán]to help intensify the billows and waves; to fan the fire; to add fuel to the fire(usuallynegative)
推测 [tuīcè] to infer; to speculate; to draw an inference; to fathom out
推陈出新 [tuīchénchūxīn] to weed through the old to let the new grow; the new emerging out of the old
推迟 [tuīchí] to postpone; to put back
推辞 [tuīcí] to reject; to decline (e.g. invitation; offer etc)
推倒 [tuīdǎo] to overthrow; to push down
推动 [tuīdòng] to spur...... into action; to push forward;to propel;to promote
推断 [tuīduàn] to infer; to draw an inference; to deduce
推翻 [tuīfān] to overthrow
推广 [tuīguǎng]to popularize;to spread; to extend; to promote
推荐 [tuījiàn] to recommend
推己及人 [tuījǐjìrén]to put oneself in the place of another
推进 [tuījìn] to propel; to advance; to push ahead
推进机 [tuījìnjī] a propeller
推举 [tuījǔ] to nominate; to recommend
推理 [tuīlǐ] inference; deduction; deduce; to infer
推论 [tuīlùn] inference; reasoning; to infer; to conclude; to deduce
推敲 [tuīqiāo] to weigh and consider; to fathom out; to work out in detail
推却 [tuīqiè] to reject; to shirk (e.g. responsibility)
推让 [tuīràng] courteously decline in favour of another
推三阻四 [tuīsānzǔsì] to make lame excuses
推算 [tuīsuàn] to calculate; to deduce; to work out
推土机 [tuītǔjī] a bull dozer
推托 [tuītuō] to make an excuse; to find a pretext for
推脱 [tuītuō] to shirk
推委 [tuīwěi]to shift (e.g.responsibility);

evade by excuse
推想 [tuīxiǎng] to reason out; to speculate;conjecture; infer inference; calculation
推销 [tuīxiāo] to peddle; to promote the sale of……
推卸 [tuīxie] to evade; to shove off(e.g. duty); to shirk
推行 [tuīxíng] to promote; to carry through
推心置腹 [tuīxīnzhìfù] to deal honestly and sincerely with others
推选 [tuīxuǎn] to choose; to elect
推移 [tuīyí] to progress ; (as time) goes on

tuí

颓(頽) [tuí] 1 (v) 坍塌 to collapse; to fall ＊颓垣断壁 ruined walls 2 (adj) 衰败 decaying; declining; decadent ＊美国的"嬉皮士"是颓废派的代表。The hippies of America are one representative of the decadent.
颓败 [tuíbài] decadent
颓废 [tuífèi] decadent; dispirited
颓丧 [tuísàng] drooping; decadent; disconcerted
颓唐 [tuítáng] dispirited; disconsolate; decadent

tuǐ

腿 [tuǐ] (n) 胫(小腿)和股(大腿)的总称 the whole leg; the leg; the thigh

tuì

蜕 [tuì] 1 (n) 蛇或虫类脱下的皮 the skin or moult cast off by snakes or insects during moulting ＊蛇蜕 the moult of snake 2 (v) 蛇或虫类脱去皮壳 to moult; to shed the skin or covering
蜕变 [tuìbiàn] degenerate
蜕化 [tuìhuà] degenerate
蜕化变质 [tuìhuàbiànzhì] degenerate; degeneration

退 [tuì] 1 (v) 向后移动，跟"进"相对 to retreat; to fall back; to retrograde; to subside ＊我们迫退敌人。We force the enemy to retreat. ＊潮水退了。The tide has subsided 2 (v) 离开 to leave; to resign; to withdraw ＊他已经退出这个团体了。He has left this organisation. 3 (v) 送还，不接受 to return (e.g. goods; things etc) 4 (v) 脱落，减除 to reduce; to fade; to drop ＊他的烧已经退了。His fever has dropped.
退避三舍 [tuìbìsānshè] to compromise and avoid a conflict
退步 [tuìbù] to retrograde; to degenerate; to fall behind; retrogression; degeneration
退潮 [tuìcháo] ebb tide
退出 [tuìchū] to withdraw from
退化 [tuìhuà] to fall behind in development; to become decadent
退还 [tuìhuán] to send back; to return
退回 [tuìhuí] to return; to send back
退婚 [tuìhūn] to break off a betrothal engagement
退路 [tuìlù] a way out; room for retreat
退票 [tuìpiào] to return tickets
退却 [tuìquè] to step back; to retreat; to back down
退让 [tuìràng] to make concessions to; to compromise
退色 [tuìsè] to fade in colour
退烧 [tuìshāo] to reduce fever
退缩 [tuìsuō] to shrink back
退伍 [tuìwǔ] to be demobilised
退席 [tuìxí] to leave the meeting or dinner party half way; to walk out (e.g. in protest)
退休 [tuìxiū] to retire (stop work in old age)
退学 [tuìxué] to give up study; to give up attendance at school

tūn

吞 [tūn] 1 (v) 咽下 to swallow 2 (v) 兼并 to annex ＊这个大国想并吞

邻近的小国。 This bigger country tries to annex the neighbouring smaller countries.

吞没 [tūnmò] to swallow up; to gobble up; to devour

吞噬 [tūnshì] to gobble up; to eat up in large mouthfuls

吞吐量 [tūntǔliàng] loading and unloading capicity (of harbour; port; station etc)

吞吞吐吐 [tūntūntǔtǔ] mince words; to mutter and mumble; to hum and haw

tún

屯 [tún](v) 聚积，储存 to accumulate; to hoard; to pile up＊农民忙着屯粮。The peasants are busy piling up the crop.

屯田 [túntián] to station soldiers on borders making them raise their own food

囤 [tún](v) 积存 to hoard; to stock up

囤货 [túnhuò] to stock up the goods

囤积 [túnjī] to hoard; to stockpile (goods for sale at a higher price)

囤积居奇 [túnjījūqí] hoarding and speculation

另见 [dùn]

豚 [tún] (n) 小猪，也泛指猪 a piglet or a pig

豚鼠 [túnshǔ] a guinea pig

臀 [tún] (n) 屁股 the buttocks

tuō

托 [tuō] 1 (n)用手掌承着 to carry on the palm; to support with hands＊他两手托着下巴 He supports his chin with his hands. 2 (v) 衬着 to serve as contrast or as background＊绿叶把红花衬托得更好看了 The green leaves serve as a good contrast for the red flower. 3 (n) 承托器物的东西 a support; a stand＊茶托 tea set tray. 4 (v) 请人代办 to entrust (somebody to do something)＊我托你买本书 I entrust you to buy me a book. 5 (v) 推委 to shift (e.g. responsibility); to evade by excuse＊他托故不来。He declined to come with an excuse.

托词 [tuōcí] a pretext; an excuse

托儿所 [tuō'érsuǒ] a nursery

托福 [tuōfú] thanks to

托付 [tuōfù] to entrust

托管 [tuōguǎn] to put under trusteeship

托辣斯 [tuōlàsī] trust; a monopoly organisation

托运 [tuōyùn] to send by freight or in the goods van (of a train)

脱 [tuō] 1 (v) 剥落 to peel; to fall out (e.g. skin; hair; paint)＊他的头发很容易脱落。His hair falls off very easily. 2 (v) 解下，除掉 to take off (e.g. shoes, clothes)＊进门之前要脱鞋。Take off your shoes before you enter.

脱轨 [tuōguǐ] to derail

脱节 [tuōjié] out of keeping with; lack of coordination; out of gear

脱口而出 [tuōkǒuérchū] to speak without any consideration; to speak rashly

脱离 [tuōlí] to separate from; to detach from; to divorce from; to keep aloof from; to isolate.... from; to alienate from

脱粒机 [tuō lì jī] a thresher

脱落 [tuōluò] to drop; to fall

脱毛 [tuōmáo] to moult

脱身 [tuōshēn] to get away; to disengage

脱手 [tuōshǒu] sold out (of goods during speculation or pawn)

脱水 [tuōshuǐ] to dehydrate; dehydrated

脱胎换骨 [tuōtāihuàngǔ] to make a thoroughgoing change; completely remoulded

脱险 [tuōxiǎn] to escape from danger

拖 [tuō] 1 (v) 拉，牵 to drag; to pull 2 (v) 拉长时间 to prolong; to delay＊要抓紧时间，不能再拖。 Seize the time; do not delay anymore.

拖把 [tuōbǎ] a mop
拖车 [tuōchē] a trailer
拖船 [tuōchuán] a tugboat
拖拉机 [tuōlājī] a tractor

拖累 [tuōlěi] to involve; to embroil;
拖泥带水 [tuōnídàishuǐ] to be dragged through the mud; not snappy about things; messy
拖网渔船 [tuōwǎngyúchuán] trawler
拖鞋 [tuōxié] slippers
拖延 [tuōyán] to delay; to procrastinate

tuó

陀 [tuó] 〔陀螺〕(n) 一种儿童玩具 a top

驼 (駝) [tuó] 1 (n) 骆驼的简称 a camel *驼峯（骆驼背部突出的肉峯）the hump of a camel. 2 (adj)（脊骨）弯曲 hunchbacked *公公年纪老了，背有点驼。Grandfather is quite old and he is a bit hunchback.
驼子 [tuó zi] a hunchback

鸵 (鴕) [tuó] (n) 现代生存的最大鸟类，头小，颈长，足具二趾和肉垫，强而善走，但翅膀退化，不能飞，生活在沙漠里。an ostrich

鸵鸟政策 [tuóniǎozhèngcè] ostrich policy; behaving like an ostrich which buries its head in the sand when faced with danger— not able to face reality

驮 (馱) [tuó] (v) 用背部（多指牲口）载负（人或物）to carry on the back *这匹马能驮四袋粮食。This horse can carry four bags of crop on its back.
另见 [duò]

tuǒ

椭 (橢) [tuǒ](adj) 长园形 oval-shaped; elliptical *鸡蛋是椭园形的。The egg is oval in shape.
椭园 [tuǒyuán] ellipse
椭园体 [tuǒyuántǐ] ellipsoid

妥 [tuǒ] (adj) 适当，合适 good; well-arranged; sound; proper
妥当 [tuǒdàng] well-thought out; sound; good; solid; safe
妥善 [tuǒshàn] well-thought out; proper
妥帖 [tuǒtiē] proper; appropriate
妥协 [tuǒxié] to compromise

tuò

拓 [tuò] (v) 开辟，扩充 to open up; to clear up; to extend *村民开拓了一片森林地。The villagers have opened up a forest land.
拓荒 [tuòhuāng] to reclaim waste land
拓荒者 [tuòhuāngzhě] the pioneers
拓扑学 [tuòpūxué] topology (as in mathematics)

唾 [tuò] 1 (n) 口水 spit; spittle; saliva *病人的唾沫能够危害健康。Spittle from the patients can be a health hazard. 2 (v) 用力吐唾沫，表示轻视、鄙视 to spit hard to show one's contempt or despite
唾骂 [tuòmà] to abuse; to rebuke coarsely
唾沫 [tuò·mo] spittle
唾弃 [tuòqì] to cast aside; to renounce; to repudiate
唾手可得 [tuòshǒukědé] can be easily gained
唾液 [tuòyè] saliva

W

wā

哇 [wā] (n) 哭、喊、呕吐等声音 the sound made when a person cries, shouts or vomits ＊孩子哇的一声哭了起来。"Wa...." the child bursts into cries.
另见 [•wa]

洼(窪) [wā] 1 (adj) 凹下去，低凹 low; hollow; depressed 2 (n) 低凹的地方 pit; hollow; swamp; bog

蛙 [wā] (n) 两栖动物，卵孵化后为蝌蚪，逐渐变化成蛙，捕食昆虫，对农业有好处，种类很多，常见的有青蛙 frog

蛙人 [wārén] frog-man; a diver

蛙泳 [wāyǒng] breast stroke; (swimming style)

挖 [wā] (v) 掘，发掘 dig; excavate ＊村民在挖渠道。The villagers are digging a drain.

挖掘 [wājué] dig out; excavate; tap (e.g. potentialities)

挖空心思 [wākōngxīnsī] rack one's brain; think hard

挖苦 [wākǔ] ridicule; hurt others by sarcastic remarks

挖墙脚 [wāqiángjiǎo] subvert; undermine the foundation

挖泥机 [wāníjì] dredge ; excavator

娲(媧) [wā] [女娲] (n) 神话里的人物，传说她曾经炼石补天 a goddess in Chinese mythology , she was known to have refined rocks to mend the sky.

wá

娃 [wá] 1 (n) 小孩 baby ＊女娃 baby girl 2 (n) 称美女 a beautiful woman ＊娇娃 noted beauty

wǎ

瓦 [wǎ] 1 (n) 铺屋顶用的建筑材料，用陶土烧制而成 tile for the roof ＊瓦房 a tile-roofed house 2 (n) 用陶土烧制的（器物）earthen wares＊瓦缸 earthen jar 3 (n) 电的功率单位"瓦特"的简称 unit of electrical power-watt
另见 [wà]

瓦工 [wǎgōng] tile-layer; brick-layer; mason

瓦解 [wǎjiě] break up; disintegrate; cause to collapse; undermine

瓦砾 [wǎlì] broken pieces of tile, brick and stone; rubbles

瓦特 [wǎtè] watt

wà

袜(襪) [wà] (n) 足的套子 socks; stockings

瓦 [wà] (v) 把瓦盖在屋顶上 to cover the roof with tiles ＊屋顶可以瓦瓦了。The roof is ready to be tiled.
另见 [wǎ]
瓦刀 [wàdāo] trowel

·wa

哇 [·wa] (Inter) 助词。同于句末 an interjection used at the end of a sentence
另见 [wā]

wāi

歪 [wāi] 1 (adj) 不正，偏 not straight; crooked; awry; slanted ＊那间亚答屋有点歪了，恐怕吹大风時便会倒塌下来。That atap house is a little slanting; it may collapse amidst a heavy wind-storm. 2 (adj) 不正当的 crooked; immoral; indecent; bad; evil ＊青年们的吸毒和犯罪行为，可能是受西方国家的歪风所影响。Drug taking and criminal activities among the younger people could be the influence of evil trends from western countries.
歪曲 [wāiqū] distort; misrepresent; twist
歪歪扭扭 [wāi wāi niǔ niǔ] twisting; twisted
歪斜 [wāixié] slanting; oblique

wài

外 [wài] 1 (adj) 不是內部或里面，跟"內"，"里"相对 external; out; outside ＊我们不能单从外表判断一个人。We should not judge a person from his external appearance only. 2 (adj) 指自己所在地以外的 foreign ＊他是从外国来的。He came from a foreign country. 3 (adj) 指外国 foreign ＊外援 foreign aid. 4 (adj) 称母亲、姐妹、女儿方面的亲戚 relatives of one's mother, sisters or daughter ＊外祖母。maternal grandmother. 5 (Prep) 不在分內的 beyond; besides; without ＊林医生除了是个外交家之外，同时也是个教育家。Besides being a diplomat, Dr. Lim is also an educationist.
外观 [wài guān] appearance; aspect
外国 [wàiguó] foreign country; abroad
外行 [wàiháng] inexperienced; out of one's normal line
外号 [wàihào] nickname
外汇 [wàihuì] foreign exchange
外交 [wàijiāo] diplomacy
外交部 [wàijiāobù] the ministry of Foreign Affairs
外界 [wàijiè] outside world
外科 [wàikē] surgery; surgical department
外流 [wàiliú] outflow (of talents, capital etc.)
外面 [wàimiàn] outside; exterior
外强中干 [wài qiáng zhōng gān] strong in appearance but weak inside
外勤 [wàiqín] field (outside) work
外甥 [wàishēng] nephew (sister's son)
外围 [wàiwéi] outer circles; periphery; outer-ring (e.g. organisation)
外文系 [wài wén xì] department of foreign languages
外衣 [wài yī] coat; overcoat; camouflage; (under) the cloak of
外因 [wài yīn] external causes
外资 [wàizī] foreign capital

wān

剜 [wān] (v) 用刀挖 cut out; scoop out ＊剜肉补疮 cutting out flesh to patch up the wound — a makeshift to tide over present difficulty.

蜿 [wān] 1 (n) 蛇类爬行的样子。又称蜿蜒 crawling of a snake 2 (adj) (山脉，河流，道路等) 弯弯曲曲的样子 winding (of road); undulation (of mountain ranges); meandering (of river) ＊江水从高山流经森林地区，再蜿蜒注入海中。The river water meanders through forest regions, and finally flows into the sea.

弯 (彎) [wān] 1 (v) 开弓 draw a bow 2 (adj) 屈曲不直 bent; curved; arched ＊学生们在做弯腰

动作。 The students are bending their bodies. 3 (n) 弯曲的部分 bend; turn; twist ＊汽车转了一个大弯。The car makes a big turn. 4 (v) 使弯曲 to bend ＊她弯下了身体，把地上的手巾拾起来。 She bent down her body and picked up the handkerchief lying on the floor.

湾(灣) [wān] 1 (n) 水流弯曲的地方 a bay 2 (n) 海岸向陆地凹入的地方 a gulf; bay ＊近来，很多废物污染了孟加拉湾。The Bay of Bengal has been polluted with a lot of waste materials lately.

wán

玩 [wán] 1 (v) 游戏，工作之后的一种活动 play; have fun with ＊他们常常到海边去玩耍。They go to play at the sea-side often. 2 (v) 欣赏 admire ＊ 他在闲暇时玩花赏鱼。He admires flowers and fishes at his leisure. 3 (n) 供观赏的东西 things for admiration＊古玩 antiques 4 (v) 轻视，不严肃地对待 treat with contempt; take things lightly ＊这个富家子一向玩世不恭。This rich man's son assumes a frivolous attitude towards life. 5 (v) 耍弄，使用(不正当的方法，手段等) trifle; make use of certain means or deceptions＊这个人很会玩弄手段。This man is good at playing tricks and deceptions.

玩火自焚 [wánhuǒzìfén] he who plays with fire gets burnt

玩忽职守 [wán hū zhí shǒu] neglect one's duty

玩具 [wánjù] toys

玩弄 [wánnòng] play with; flirt with; practise tricks and deceptions

玩物丧志 [wán wù sàng zhì] too much play wears down the will to work hard

玩笑 [wánxiào] joke; jest

顽(頑) [wán] 1 (adj) 愚蠢无知 stupid and ignorant ＊痴顽 foolish 2 (adj) 固执，坚持自己的意见 stubborn; obstinate ＊这个老妇人很顽固，她不愿让媳妇出外工作。This old lady is very stubborn; she does not want her daughter-in-law to work outside. 3 (adj) 淘气，顽皮 naughty; cheeky; mischievous ＊李老师受了顽皮学生的气，吃不下饭。 Having been angered by the naughty students, teacher Mr Lee could not eat at meal.

顽敌 [wán dí] diehard enemy

顽固不化 [wán gù bù huà] incorrigible; headstrong; diehard

顽强 [wánqiáng] tenacious; staunch; indomitable

完 [wán] 1 (adj) 齐全，没有缺损 complete; whole; perfect ＊学校的一切设备很完善。The school facilities are complete and excellent. 2 (v) 做成 complete; finish ＊填海工程计划在年底完竣。The land reclamation project is scheduled to be completed at the end of this year. 3 (adj) 尽，没有了 finished; gone; use up＊煤气已经用完了。The gas has been used up.

完毕 [wán bì] come to an end; be finished; be completed

完成 [wán chéng] accomplish; fulfill; complete

完工 [wán gōng] complete work; finish a job or work

完好 [wán hǎo] not broken; in good condition

完结 [wán jié] conclude; be completed; end

完美 [wán měi] beautiful (e.g. work of art); fine and complete; perfect

完全 [wán quán] complete; absolutely; full

完整 [wán zhěng] intact and complete; not broken; comprehensive; integrity

丸 [wán] (n) 球形的细小东西 pill; small ball ＊药丸 pills; tablets ＊她

对医生说，避孕药丸的效力并不可靠。She told the doctor the effect of the birth control pill is not at all reliable.

纨(紈) [wán] (n) 细绢，很细的丝织品 a very fine silk

纨袴子弟 [wánkù zǐdì] a fop; children from a rich family; play-boy

wǎn

宛 [wǎn] 1 (adj) 曲折 winding 2 (adv) 相象，仿佛 as if; very similar to ＊欢腾的人群，宛如大海上的波涛。The mass of joyous people looks like the waves of the mighty sea.

惋 [wǎn] (v) 惊叹，叹惜 feel sorry for; pity; lament ＊他虽然进了大学，但不肯用功，年年考不及格，实在令人惋惜。Although given a chance to enter university, he refused to work hard at studies and failed in examinations every year; we really feel sorry for him.

婉 [wǎn] (adj) 温和，和顺 mild and obliging; courteous ＊我们婉言相劝，他却不听。We advise him in a mild and obliging tone but he will just not listen.

婉求 [wǎnqiú] to entreat

婉顺 [wanshùn] yielding; accommodating; agreeable

婉言谢绝 [wǎnyán xièjué] refuse (an offer) tactfully and mildly; refuse politely

碗 [wǎn] (n) 一种盛食物的器皿，用陶土或金属品制成 a bowl ＊饭碗。rice bowl; means of living (fig)

挽 [wǎn] 1 (v) 拉 pull ＊他们手挽着手沿着小巷漫步。They were strolling along the lane, hand in hand. 2 (v) 设法使情况好转或恢复原状 retrieve a situation; save; rescue; avert ＊就算有才华的经济学者也不能把目前的不景气挽救过来。Even a talented economist cannot save the present depression.

挽回 [wǎnhuí] retrieve (a situation); avert; save (a situation)

挽留 [wǎnliú] persuade or ask somebody to stay

晚 [wǎn] 1 (n) 日落以后到深夜以前的时间，也泛指夜间 night ＊我的父亲每晚要到八点半才回到家。Every night my father comes home as late as half past eight. 2 (n) 时间接近终结时 late ＊老医生在寂寞中渡过晚年。The old doctor spends the later years of his life in loneliness. 3 (adj) 迟 late ＊人们应该提倡晚婚。People should encourage late marriages. 4 (adj) 后来的 coming later ＊晚辈。coming generation.

晚报 [wǎnbào] evening papers

晚会 [wǎn huì] (evening) gathering; evening party

晚景 [wǎnjǐng] evening scene

晚上 [wǎnshàng] in the evening; at night

晚霞 [wǎn xiá] sunset glow; colourful sky at sunset

绾(綰) [wǎn] 1 (v) 把长条形的东西盘绕起来打个结 tie something long into a knot ＊妇女用棉布条绾个扣儿。The lady ties the cotton tape into a knot. 2 (v) 向上卷 to roll up ＊他绾起袖子。He rolls up his sleeves.

腕 [wàn] (n) 手臂和手掌相连的部分 wrist ＊手腕。wrist

腕表 [wàn biǎo] wrist watch

腕关节 [wàn guān jié] wrist joints

wàn

蔓 [wàn] (n) 草本植物，能攀延、缠绕的茎 tendrils of plants for support or climbing ＊瓜蔓。tendrils of gourds.

另见 [mán]
[màn]

万(萬) [wàn] 1 (n) 数词:十千 numeral word for ten thousand

＊昨天，大约有一万个学生集合在草场上操练。Yesterday, about 10,000 students grouped together and did physical exercises at the padang. 2 (adj) 比喻众多 many; all; numerous ＊排除万难去争取胜利。Sweep away all the difficulties and strive for victories. 3 (adv) 极，很，绝对 very; extremely; absolutely ＊敌人惶恐万分。 The enemy is extremely frightened.

万般 [wàn bān] various kinds

万恶 [wàn è] thoroughly wicked; evil; completely atrocious; diabolical

万古长青 [wàngǔcháng qīng] be evergreen; evernew; flourishing forever

万籁 [wàn lài] various kinds of sound

万里长城 [wànlǐ cháng chéng] the Great Wall of China

万里长征 [wàlǐchángzhēng] a long march of ten thousand "li"; the long march

万马奔腾 [wàn mǎ bēn téng] surging forward

万能 [wàn néng]universal; all-purpose; all powerful

万千 [wànqiān] innumerable

万寿无疆 [wànshòuwújiāng] a long life to....; boundless life span

万水千山 [wànshuǐqiānshān] a long and arduous journey

万岁 [wàn suì] longevity (in ancient times) addressing a king

万万 [wàn wàn] one hundred million; absolutely; never

万无一失 [wàn wú yī shī] utterly sure; absolutely certain

万幸 [wàn xìng] unusually lucky

万一 [wàn yī] in case; in the event of

万有引力 [wàn yǒu yǐnlì] the force of gravity

万众一心 [wànzhòng yīxīn] all of one heart and one mind; united like one man

万紫千红 [wàn zǐ qiān hóng] a profusion of colours; innumerable flowers of purple and red

wāng

汪 [wāng] 1 (adj) 水深而广 deep and vast (of ocean) ＊汪洋大海。a vast ocean; a boundless ocean. ＊水手们天天在汪洋大海上过日子，却不觉得寂寞。The mariners while away the time on the mighty oceans everyday, yet they do not feel lonely 2 (n) 狗吠的声音 the barking of dogs 3 (n) 姓氏 a surname

汪汪 [wāng wāng] filled with tears

汪洋 [wānyáng] a vast expanse of water

汪洋大海 [wānyángdàhǎi] a vast ocean; a boundless ocean

wáng

亡 [wáng] 1 (v) 逃跑 flee; escape ＊很多难民逃亡到美国去谋生。Many refugees escaped to America to find a living 2 (v) 失去，丢失 lose ＊亡羊补牢 Mend the fold after losing the sheep —— never too late to mend. (fig)3 (v) 死 die ＊他的儿子阵亡了。His son died in a battle. 4 (v) 毁灭 subjugate; subdue＊没有人愿意做亡国奴。Nobody wants to become a slave under foreign subjugation.

亡国 [wáng quó] national subjugation; ruin of a country; national disaster

亡命 [wángmìng] flee; escape

亡命之徒 [wáng mìng zhī tù] desperado; wild ruffian

王 [wáng] 1 (n) 君主 king; ruler ＊泰国的国王年青有为。The king of Thailand is young and capable. 2 (n) 封建时代的最高爵位 the highest rank in a feudal society ＊王爷。a person with the highest title conferred upon him; lord. 3 (n) 头子 head; chief ＊擒贼先擒王。In capturing the rebels, first take their chief. 4 (n) 同类中最特出或最大的 the best or the strongest of a kind of animal or insect ＊蜂王 the queen bee

王朝 [wáng cháo] dynasty

王法 [wángfǎ] the royal laws

王冠 [wángguān] a crown

王国 [wáng guó]kingdom; monarchy

王宫 [wáng gōng] the royal palace

王牌 [wáng pái] trump card

王子 [wáng zǐ] prince

wǎng

网(網) [wǎng] 1 (n) 用绳、线等结成的捕捉鱼、鸟的器具 net for catching fish or birds 2 (n) 象网的东西 thing which looks like a net ＊蜘蛛网 spider web ＊铁丝网 wire mesh; wire gauze ＊他买的羽毛球网，是用尼龙造成的。The badminton net which he bought is made of nylon. 3 (n) 象网一样分布四处互相联系的组织或系统 net work; a system ＊通讯网 communication network.＊铁路网 a network of railways. 4 (v) 用网捕捉 to catch with a net ＊他网了很多大鱼。He has netted many big fishes.

网罗[wǎngluó] gather; seek and collect

网球[wǎngqiú] tennis

往 [wǎng] 1 (v) 去 go ＊街上有很多车辆来来往往。There are many vehicles travelling to and fro on the road. 2 (v) 向（某处去）leave for; head toward ＊火车正要开往吉隆坡。The train is leaving for Kuala Lumpur 3 (adj) 过去，从前 previous; former ＊由於严旱，今年的收成比往年差。Owing to a serious drought, this year's harvest is worse than that of previous years.

往常 [wǎng cháng] usually; as usual

往返 [wǎng fǎn] go and come back; to and fro; back; and forth

往来 [wǎng lái] go and come back; have dealings with each other; (friendly) intercourse

往年 [wǎngnián] former years; previous years

往日 [wǎngrì] former days; past

往事 [wǎngshì] things of the past

往往 [wǎng wǎng] often; usually

枉 [wǎng] 1 (adj) 曲，不直 crooked; bent ＊矫枉 to straighten the crooked. 2 (v) 使歪曲 to distort; act crookedly ＊官僚们贪污枉法。The bureaucrats are corrupt and they abuse the law. 3 (v) (n) 冤屈 wrong; injustice ; grievance ＊不要冤枉好人。Do not wrong on a good person. 4(adj) 白白地，徒然 in vain: to no purpose ＊他屡试不成，真是枉费心机。He fails after many attempts, it is really a waste of effort.

枉费 [wǎngfèi] spend to no purpose; in vain

枉费唇舌 [wǎng fèichúnshé]try in vain to persuade somebody

枉费心机 [wǎngfèixīnjī] rack one's brains in vain; waste one's efforts

惘 [wǎng] (adj) 失意的样子 at a loss; unhappy; disappointed ＊好朋友一个一个离开了，他惘然若失。He was quite at a loss when his good friends had gone away one by one.

罔 [wǎng] 1 (v) 蒙蔽 deceive ＊欺罔 to deceive 2 (adj) 没有 nothing; none ＊朋友的劝告他置若罔闻。He paid no heed to his friends' advice.

魍 [wǎng] 〔魍魉〕(n) 传说中的一种怪物 a demon.(mythology)

wàng

旺 [wàng] (adj) 盛，兴盛 prosperous; vigorous * 兵士们士气旺盛。The soldiers are in high spirits.

旺季 [wàng jì] doing much business; flourishing or prosperous season; in season

旺月 [wàngyuè] the best month of a year in terms of business done

望 [wàng] 1 (v) 往远处看 oversee; look afar * 我们登高远望。We ascend to look afar; 2 (v) 探访 visit; pay a visit * 我常常去探望他的祖母。I always pay visits to his grandmother. 3 (v) 心所愿 hope; expect * 看到儿子的成绩时，他大失所望。He is greatly disappointed on seeing his son's results in study. 4 (n) 声誉 reputation * 他的医术高明，在这里很有名望。Being good in medical skills, he has won a high reputation in this locality. 5 (n) 阴历每月十五 the fifteenth day of a lunar month.

望尘莫及 [wàng chén mò jí] lag a long way behind; unequal to; incomparable

望而生畏 [wàng'ér shēng wèi] be filled with fear at the sight of (e.g. person.)

望风披靡 [wàng fēng pī mǐ] flee after witnessing from a distance the high morale of the opposing army

望梅止渴 [wàngmèizhǐkě] an imagination to console oneself

望眼欲穿 [wàng yǎn yù chuān] gaze anxiously till one's eyes are overstrained; look forward eagerly

望洋兴叹 [wàng yáng xīng tàn] gaze at the sea and sigh, feeling helpless

望远镜 [wàng yuǎn jìng] field glasses; telescope

妄 [wàng] (adj) 荒谬，不合理，过分 absurd; irrational; overdone * 他妄图以一张假支票去向银行领取巨款。He made an absurd attempt to get a big sum of money from the bank with a dud cheque.

妄动 [wàngdòng] act recklessly; act irrationally; arrogant

妄想 [wàng xiǎng] try in vain; vain attempt; indulge in vain hopes

妄自菲薄 [wàng zì fěi bó] underestimate one's achievement; belittle; demean oneself; have an inferiority complex

妄自尊大 [wàngzìzūndà] conceited; over bearing; arrogant

忘 [wàng] (v) 不记得，忘记 forget * 他到戏院以后才发觉忘记将门票带来。He only became aware that he had forgotten to bring along the ticket on reaching the cinema.

忘本 [wàng běn] forget one's origin

忘掉 [wàng diào] forget

忘恩负义 [wàng'ēn fùyì] be ungrateful; devoid of all gratitude

忘怀 [wànghuái] forget

忘却 [wàng què] forget

忘我 [wàng wǒ] selfless

往 [wàng] (prep) 朝向 toward * 往前看 look forward * 水往低流 Water flows towards a lower level

往后 [wànghòu] from now on; hereafter

另见 [wǎng]

wēi

偎 [wēi] (v) 亲热地互相靠着 together; cuddle together; lean close * 孩子依偎在母亲的怀里。The child clings close to her mother's bosom.

煨 [wēi] 1 (v) 把食物用微火慢慢地煮 stew; simmer * 煨鸡。to stew chicken. 2 (v) 把食物埋在火烬里烤熟 bake in half-burnt charcoal * 煨番薯 to bake sweet potatoes

委 [wēi]〔委蛇〕(v) 随便应付 perform one's duty perfunctorily; be half-hearted about ∗虚与委蛇 ∘pretending to be interested and sympathetic. 另见 [wěi]

萎 [wēi] (adj) 衰落 declining; be on the wane ∗气萎∘ weak in breathing; lack of strength.

威 [wēi] 1 (n) 强大的声势，使人敬畏的气魄 intimidating power; might; majesty ∗学生示威，反对军人政权 ∘ Students demonstrate against the military regime. 2 (v)凭借力量或势力 threaten; intimidate; coerce ∗骑劫者威胁政府释放他们的同志∘ The hijackers threaten the government to release their comrades.

威风 [wēifēng] dignity; majesty; grandeur, prestige, majestic; splendid; grand

威风凛凛 [wēi fēng lǐn lǐn] awful air; with great dignity

威吓 [wēihè] threaten; terrify by threats, intimidate

威力 [wēilì] might; power; force

威迫利诱 [wēipòlìyòu] to coerce and to tempt; temptation with threats

威望 [wēi wàng] high reputation; high prestige

威信 [wēixìn] prestige; credit; high repute; dignity

威信扫地 [wēixìn sàodì] be thoroughly discredited; disgraced; forfeited prestige

威严 [wēi yán] august; commanding; dignity

微 [wēi] 1 (adj) 细小 fine; tiny; minute; small ∗微细的病菌已侵入病人血管∘ The minute viruses have already reached the blood vessel of the patient. 2 (adj) 少，稍 little; a little ∗微笑∘ smile. 3 (adj) 衰弱 on the wane; declining ∗这个家族逐渐的衰微了∘ This family is slowly on the decline. 4 (adj) 精深奥妙 profound; subtle; delicate ∗这个问题很微妙∘ This problem is quite delicate. 5 (n) 主单位的万分之一 ten thousandth of a unit

微薄 [wēibó] meagre; feeble

微不足道 [wēibùzúdào] not worth mentioning; insignificant; trivial

微乎其微 [wēihūqíwēi] very small; very little

微积分 [wēijīfēn] differential and integral calculus. (maths)

微弱 [wēiruò] weak; feeble

微生物 [wēishēngwù] microbes

微小 [wēixiǎo] very small; little; tiny

危 [wēi] 1 (adj) 不安全 dangerous; unsafe; harmful ∗建筑工友在没有安全设施的地方工作是很危险的∘ It is very dangerous for construction workers to work at places without safety measures. 2 (v) 损害，伤害 harm; endanger ∗抽烟可以危害身体健康∘ Smoking can be harmful to health. 3 (adj) 指人快要死 dying ∗祖母病危∘ Grandmother is suffering from an acute disease and is on the verge of dying. 4 (adj) 高而陡 high and steep ∗危崖∘ steep cliff; precipice. 5 (adj) 端正 upright ∗他正襟危坐∘ He sits upright in a serious manner.

危害 [wēihài] endanger

危机 [wēijī] crisis

危急 [wēijí] urgent; critical; in peril; at stake

危惧 [wēijù] be in fear

危难 [wēinàn] danger and disaster; at stake

危亡 [wēiwáng] (the fate of a nation is) at stake; in imminent danger of being conquered

危险性 [wēixiǎnxìng] danger

危在旦夕 [wēizàidànxī] death is expected at any moment; in imminent danger of death

巍 [wēi] (adj) 高大的样子 high and great; lofty ∗巍峨的群山已出现在眼前∘ High mountain ranges could been seen right infront.

巍然 [wēirán] stand firmly and majestically

wéi

韦(韋) [wéi] 1 (n) 去毛加工制成的皮革 hide; leather 2 (n) 姓 surname

帏(幃) [wéi] (n) 帳子，幕 a tent; a curtain; a screen

违(違) [wéi] 1 (v) 背，反，不遵守 defy; violate; disobey * 他因为违反了交通规则而被罚款。He was fined for violating traffic rules. 2 (adj) 不见面，离别 not seeing each other; separated * 久违了。I have not seen you for a long time.

违背 [wéibèi] violate; act contrary to; run counter to

违法 [wéifǎ] break the law

违法乱纪 [wéifǎ luàn ji]breach of law and discipline; break the laws and violate discipline

违约 [wéiyuè] breach of promise(contract)

围(圍) [wéi] 1 (v) 四面拦住，环绕 surround; encircle * 军警已包围了整个校园。The army and police have surrounded the whole campus. 2 (adj) 四周 surrounding; around * 他很关心周围发生的事情。 He is very concerned about things happening around him.

围攻 [wéigōng] attack and encirclement; converging attack; attack from all sides

围剿 [wéijiǎo] launch a campaign of encirclement and annihilation; encircle and suppress

围巾 [wéijīn] muffler; scarf

围困 [wéikùn] besiege; confine

围棋 [wéiqí] a kind of Chinese chess

围裙 [wéiqún] apron、

围绕 [wéirǎo] surround; encircle; revolve around

惟 [wéi] 1 (adv) 只，单单 only; solely * 这是惟一可行的办法。This is the only way out. 2 (adv) 只有 except * 大家都同意了，惟有你不同意。We all agreed except you. 3 (conj) 但是 but * 他病虽已治愈，惟身体仍衰弱。 His sickness is cured but his health is still poor. 4 (v) 想 think * 思惟 to think, thought.

惟独 [wéidú] only; solely; alone

惟恐 [wéikǒng] only fear; for fear

惟利是图 [wéilìshìtú] making profit as one's only aim

惟妙惟肖 [wéimiàowéixiào] life-like; strikingly true to life

惟命是听 [wéi mìng shì tīng] very obedient

惟我独尊 [wéiwǒdúzūn] overlordship; behaving like an overlord

唯 [wéi] (adv) 单单，只是 only; solely

唯生产力论 [wéishēngchǎnlìlùn] the (revisionist) theory that productive forces decide everything

唯物辩证法 [wéiwùbiànzhèngfǎ] dialectical materialism

唯物论 [wéiwùlùn] materialism

唯武器论 [wéiwǔqìlùn] theory that weapon decides everything

唯物史观 [wéiwùshǐguān] historical materialism

唯心论 [wéixīnlùn] idealism

帷 [wéi] (n) 围起来遮挡用的帐幕 tent; curtain * 帷幕 curtain for screen

维(維) [wéi] 1 (v) 连结 connect; join; hold together * 他们以共同的理想来维系彼此之间的感情。They preserve their friendship through common ideals. 2 (v) 想 think * 人的思维是从实际的工作中产生的。The thinking of mankind arises from actual practice in working.

维持 [wéichí]maintain; keep; preserve

维护 [wéihù] uphold; safeguard

维生素 [wéishēnsù] vitamins

维修 [wéixīu] maintain ; maintenance

(e.g. of machinery)

为(爲) [wéi] 1 (v) 做，作为 do ✱事在人为。Man is the determining factor in doing things. 2 (v) 作，充当 take as ✱他被选为代表。He is being elected as a representative. 3 (v) 成为，成 become ✱他的希望已化为泡影。His hope has come to nothing. 4 (v) 是 make; be ✱十六两为一斤。Sixteen tahils makes a kati. 5(adv) 被（跟"所"字连用）by; for ✱艺术形式必须为广大群众所喜闻乐见。The various forms of art should be welcomed and loved by the general masses.

为非作歹 [wéifēi-zuòdǎi] committing evil

为难 [wéinán] embarass; put obstacles in the way; make things hard (for somebody)

为期不远 [wéiqībùyuǎn] not far from the appointed date

为人 [wéirén] behaviour; manner in dealing with others

为首 [wéishǒu] headed by; led by

为所欲为 [wéisuǒ yù wéi] do as one pleases; do whatever one likes

为伍 [wéiwǔ] as a partner

桅 [wéi] (n) 桅杆，船上挂帆用的杆子 ship's mast

wěi

伟(偉) [wěi] (adj) 大，高大 great; magnificent ✱我们来到了雄伟的天安门广场。We have arrived at the magnificent Tian An Men Square.

伟大 [wěidà] great

伟绩 [wěijī] meritorious service; deeds; great service

伟人 [wěirén] a great man; a distinguished person

纬(緯) [wěi] 1 (n) 针织品上横的纱或线 the weft or cross thread of knitted materials 2 (n) 地理学上所假定的跟赤道平行的线 parallels of latitude ✱纬度。degrees of latitude.

纬线 [wěixiàn] weft; parallels of latitude

委 [wěi] 1 (v) 任，派，把事情交给人办 appoint; despatch; entrust ✱总统委任他出任驻泰国大使。The president appointed him as ambassador to Thailand. 2 (v) 抛弃，舍弃 discard; abandon ✱委弃。abandon. 3 (v) 推托，推卸 evade by excuse; shift (responsibility) ✱他想委过于人。He tries to shift his responsibility to other people. 4 (adj) 婉转，曲折 winding; not straight forward ✱他说话委婉动听。He speaks in an intriguing and persuasive tone. 5 (n) 末尾 end; result ✱我一定要弄清事情的原委。I must find out the whole affair from the beginning to the end. 6 (adv) 确实 truly; actually, really ✱他委实不错。He is really a nice person.

另见 [wēi]

委靡不振 [wěimǐbùzhěn] be low in spirits; dispirited; dejected

委派 [wěipài] appoint

委屈 [wěi·qu] suffer from injustice; be wrongly accused

委曲求全 [wěiqūqíuquán] to make compromises to achieve one's final aim

委托 [wěituō] entrust; appoint; put in charge

委员 [wěiyuán] committee member

委员会 [wěi yuán huì] commission; committee; board

委员长 [wěiyuánzhǎng] chairman of a committee

诿(諉) [wěi] (v) 推却 shirk; evade; lay blame on others

萎 [wěi] (v) 枯干 wither ✱由于没有浇水，花草已经枯萎了。The plants have withered because there was no watering.

另见 [wēi]

萎靡 [wěimǐ] low in spirits; downhearted; dejected

萎缩 [wěisuō] shrivel; wither; diminish

萎谢 [wěixiè] fade; droop away; wither

痿 [wěi] (n) 身体某一部分萎缩，丧失运动机能的病 paralysis; weakness

猥 [wěi] 1 (adj) 卑鄙，下流 morally low; base; despicable ＊猥琐。vulgar; philistine. 2 (adj) 杂，多 mixed and plentiful ＊猥杂 mixed

猥亵 [wěixiè] obscene; indecent

伪(僞) [wěi] 1 (adj) 假的 forged; false; counterfeit; bogus ＊歹徒利用伪造的证件混过关口。The rogue made use of forged documents to sneak through the custom check-point. 2 (adj) 非法的 illegal; illegitimate; puppet ＊伪政权。puppet government.

伪钞 [wěichāo] counterfeit note

伪君子 [wěijūnzǐ] a hypocrite

伪善 [wěishàn] hypocritical

伪装 [wěizhuāng] conceal; disguise; camouflage

尾 [wěi] 1 (n) 动物外体末端，如一条小绳子，如猴子尾，猪尾 tail ＊我家的小猫有一条长长的尾巴。In my house I have a kitten with a very long tail. 2 (adj) 末端，最后 ending; last ＊会谈已接近尾声了。The conference is coming to an end. 3 (v) 跟在后面 follow behind 4 (n) 量词 a measure word ＊一尾鱼 a fish

尾随 [wěisuí] to follow at behind

娓 [wěi] 〔娓娓〕(adj)（说话）不疲倦的样子 untiring ＊他们娓娓而谈。They talk on without signs of tiredness.

娓娓动听 [wěiwěidòngtīng] eloquent and charming in speaking

唯 [wěi] (n) 答应的声音 answering in the affirmative; uttering yes ＊他对其主子总是唯唯诺诺的。He always utters "yes, sir, yes sir" to his master.

另见 [wéi]

wèi

尉 [wèi] 1 (n) 古代官名 an official in ancient China 2 (n) 军衔名，是校的下一级，士的上一级 a rank in the armed forces ＊他在那场战役中英勇作战，立下大功，被擢升为中尉。He was appointed a lieutenant as he fought courageously and render meritorious service in that battle.

蔚 [wèi] 1 (adj) 草木茂盛的样子 luxuriant 2 (adj) 兴盛，盛大 prosper; flourish ＊展出的中外名画，蔚为大观。The famous foreign and local paintings exhibited form a splendid panorama.

蔚蓝 [wèilán] sky blue

蔚然成风 [wèirànchèngfēng] become a common practice which prevails; become a popular practice

慰 [wèi] 1 (v) 安慰 console; comfort ＊朋友们去慰问受伤的工友。Friends visited the wounded worker to comfort him. 2 (adj) 心安 having no anxiety about; pleased ＊知道你已考及格了，我很感欣慰。Knowing that you have passed your test, I feel very pleased.

慰劳 [wèiláo] extend (one's) best wishes to; express regards and concern for

慰唁 [wèiyàn] to console (the relatives of a dead person)

胃 [wèi] (n) 消化器官的一部分，能分泌胃液，消化食物 stomach, a digestive organ in the body ＊医生说有胃病的人，不可吃太多的牛肉。The doctor said people with stomach disorder must not take too much beef.

谓(謂) [wèi] 1 (v) 告诉 tell 2 (v) 说 say ＊他的进步可谓神速。His progress can be said to be amazingly fast. 3 (v) 称呼，叫作 mean; call ＊何谓人造卫星？ What is meant by an artificial satellite? 4 (n)

意义 meaning ＊不要说这些无谓的话。Do not say these meaningless things.

猬 [wèi] (n) 小哺乳动物，身上长着硬刺，嘴很尖，捕食昆虫和小动物 porcupine

畏 [wèi] (v) 害怕 fear; frighten ＊他做事畏首畏尾的。 He is always timid and over-cautious in his undertakings.

畏惧 [wèijù] fear

畏缩 [wèisuō] flinch; recoil in fear

畏罪 [wèizuì] fear punishment for one's crime

喂 [wèi] 1 (Inter) 叹词，表示招呼 interjection used when one calls out for somebody ＊喂，你是谁？ Hello, who are you? 2 (v) 给人或牲口吃东西，饲养 feed ＊她在喂孩子吃奶。She is feeding her child with milk.

喂养 [wèiyǎng] feed; raise (animals)

未 [wèi] 1 (adj) 没有 not; not yet ＊他的健康尚未恢复。 His health has not yet recovered. 2 (adv) 不 not ＊这消息未必可靠。 This piece of news may not be reliable. 3 (n) 地支的第八位，用作次序的第八 the eighth place of the earthly branches; the eighth in order 4 (n) 未时，指十三点至十五点 from 1.00 p.m. to 3 p.m.; from 13.00 Hrs. to 15.00 Hrs

未必 [wèibì] not necessarily so; perhaps not; not necessarily

未卜先知 [wèibǔxiānzhī] having foresight

未曾 [wèicéng] unprecedented ; never; not yet

未尝 [wèicháng] never; there is no...

未婚夫 [wèihūnfū] fiance

未婚妻 [wèihūnqī] fiancee

未來 [wèilái] future

未老先衰 [wèilǎoxiānshuāi] young but looks rather old

未免 [wèimiǎn] can't say that it isn't; it really is

未遂 [wèisuì] not realised; not fulfilled; not attained

未完 [wèiwán] unfinished; incomplete

未详 [wèixiáng] not clear; not known

未雨绸缪 [wèiyǔchóumóu] to undertake repairs before it rains

未知数 [wèizhīshù] an unknown quantity or number

味 [wèi] 1 (n) 舌头尝东西时所得到的感受 taste; flavour ＊这碗鸡汤味道甜美。 This bowl of chicken soup has a good flavour. 2 (n) 鼻子闻东西时所得到的感受 smell ＊我闻到一阵臭味。 smell something foul. 3 (n) 兴趣，意味 enjoyment; interest ＊他看小说看得津津有味。He enjoyed reading the novel. 4 (v) 体会 appreciate; understand ＊他的话耐人寻味。His words need careful thinking and appreciation. 5 (n) 量词，中药方上的一种药叫"一味"药 a measure word for a type of Chinese medicine or herb in a prescription ＊这个方子共有九味药。 There are nine types of Chinese herbs in this prescription.

味精 [wèijīng] sodium glutamate, a flavour extract

味美 [wèiměi] delicious

味香 [wèixiāng] of a fragrant smell

卫(衞) [wèi] (v) 保护 protect ＊我们要坚决捍卫祖国领土的完整。We must protect resolutely the territorial integrity of our mother country.

卫兵 [wèibīng] guards

卫道士 [wèidàoshì] apologist

卫生 [wèishēng] hygiene

卫生设备 [wèishēng shèbèi] health facilities ; sanitation

卫生员 [wèishēngyuán] medical personnel

卫生所 [wèishēngsuǒ] clinic

卫生院 [wèishēngyuàn] public health centre

卫生站 [wèishēngzhàn] clinic; health station

卫戍 [wèishù] guard; garrison

为(爲) [wèi] 1 (adv) 替，给，因，由于 for; for the sake of; because of; on account of ＊我们要为理想而奋斗。We want to strive for our ideals.

另见 [wéi]

为…而… [wèi....ér.....] for; for the sake of

为丛驱雀 [wèicóngqūquè] chasing the birds into the bush

为何 [wèi hé] why

为虎傅翼 [wèihǔfùyì] adding wings to a tiger; assisting the villain

为虎作伥 [wèihǔzuòchāng] act as a cat's paw; be an accomplice; be a lackey

为了 [wèi le] for the sake of

为…起见 [wèi....qǐjiàn] for the sake of

为人作嫁 [wèirénzuòjià] to sew the wedding attirements of others; to labour for others

为渊驱鱼 [wèiyuānqūyú] chasing the fish into the pool——chasing your own people into enemy camps

为什么 [weishén·me] why

位 [wèi] 1 (n) 所在或所占的地方 seat; position ＊星加坡位于东南亚的中心，是个非常美丽的花园城市。Singapore, situated at the centre of South-east Asia, is an extremely beautiful garden-city. 2 (n) 量词 a measure word for person ＊家里来了五位客人。Five visitors had come to our house.

位于 [wèiyú] situate

位置 [wèi·zhi] position

位子 [wèi·zi] seat; post

魏 [wèi] 1 (n) 古代国名 name of a country in ancient China 2 (n) 朝代名 name of a dynasty 3 (n) 姓氏 a surname

wēn

温 [wēn] 1 (adj) 不冷不热 lukewarm ＊小妹妹生了病，妈妈用温水给她冲凉。My younger sister is ill, so motner uses lukewarm water to bathe her. 2 (adj) 平和 mild; moderate; gentle ＊他的性情温和，很少见他发脾气。He has a gentle nature for we seldom find him in a hot temper. 3 (v) 稍微加热 warm ＊把药温一温才喝。Warm the medicine before you drink it. 4 (v) 复习 revise ＊温故知新。to acquire new understanding from revising the old

温饱 [wēnbǎo] warmly clothed and well-fed

温床 [wēnchuáng] hot bed

温带 [wēndài] temperate zone

温度 [wēndù] temperature

温度计 [wēndùjì] thermometer

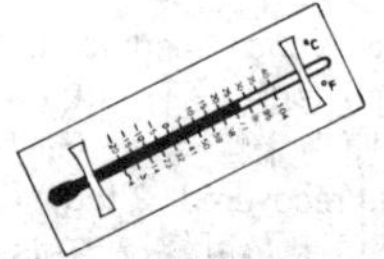

温厚 [wēnhòu] kind and generous

温暖 [wēnnuǎn] warm

温情 [wēnqíng] warm feeling; warmth

温情主义 [wēnqíngzhǔyì] paternalism

温泉 [wēnquán] a hot spring

温柔 [wēn róu] pleasingly affectionate; gentle; meek

温室 [wēnshì] greenhouse; a warm and cosy room

温习 [wēnxí] review (e.g. lessons)

瘟 [wēn] (n) 瘟疫，流行性急性传染病的总称 plague; epidemic ＊黑死病是一种可怕的瘟疫。The bubonic plague is a terrible epidemic.

wén

文 [wén] 1 (n) 字，文字 word; writing; written language * 文字和语言只是传达思想的工具。 Writings and languages are merely tools for communicating ideas. 2 (n) 用文字写成的作品 literary work * 作文 composition; essay. 3 (adj) 柔和，不猛烈 gentle * 他谈吐文雅。 He is gentle and refined in his manner and talk. 4 (adj) 非军事的，跟"武"相对 literary * 他能文能武。 He is skilled both in literary talents and military arts. 5 (n) 自然界的某些现象 some of the natural phenomena * 天文 astronomy. 6 (v) 掩饰 cover * 文过饰非 gloss over one's fault; cover up one's error by excuses. 7 (n) 旧时指礼节、仪式 customs or ceremony * 繁文缛节 the multiplicity of formalities and ceremonies; red-tapism. 8 (n) 量词，用于旧时的铜钱 a measure word for coins in the olden days * 一文钱 a coin.

文不对题 [wénbùduìtí] go off the subject; wide of the mark

文采 [wéncǎi] beauty of style of writing; literary embellishment

文风 [wénfēng] literary fashion; style of writing

文工团 [wéngōngtuán] art troupe; ensemble

文豪 [wénháo] a famous writer

文化 [wénhuà] culture

文化遗产 [wén huà yí chǎn] cultural heritage

文件 [wénjiàn] document; programme

文教 [wénjiào] culture and education

文具 [wénjù] stationery

文盲 [wénmáng] illiterate; illiteracy

文明 [wénmíng] civilization; civilised

文凭 [wénpíng] certificate; diploma

文人相轻 [wénrénxiàngqīng] scholars scorn each other

文书 [wénshū] secretary

文坛 [wéntán] literary world of circles

文体 [wéntǐ] literary style

文物 [wénwù] historical relics

文献 [wénxiàn] literary record; historical document

文选 [wénxuǎn] selected works

文学 [wénxué] literature

文学家 [wénxuéjiā] writers; man of letters

文学史 [wénxuéshǐ] history of literature

文雅 [wényǎ] refined;elegant

文言 [wényán] classical literary language

文艺 [wényì] literature and arts

文艺理论 [wényìlǐlùn] theory of literature and art

文娱 [wényú] recreation

文质彬彬 [wénzhìbīnbīn] with elegant manners

文章 [wénzhāng] literary composition; essay;article

纹（紋） [wén] (n) 皮肤上皱起的痕跡 stripes; lines; streaks; wrinkles * 老人的脸上有许多皱纹。 There are many wrinkles on the old man's face.

蚊 [wén] (n) 昆虫。幼虫叫"孑孓"生活在水中。雄蚊吸食植物液汁。雌蚊吸血，能传播疾病。 mosquito * 好多蚊子在小池面飞来飞去。A lot of mosquitoes are flying about above the small pond .

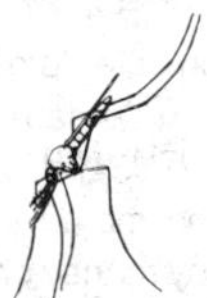

雯 [wén] (n) 成花纹的云彩 cloud in beautiful patterns

闻（聞） [wén] 1 (v) 听见 hear * 敌人闻风丧胆。 The enemy loses courage at hearing it. 2 (n) 消息，听见的事情 news * 新闻稿通常都要经过编辑檢查。 News scripts usually need to be checked by the trained editor. 3 (v) 嗅 smell; take a smell; scent ＊他闻一闻洗剂。 He takes a smell at the lotion. 4 (n) 名气 fame ＊他是个工人画家，但是寂寂无闻。 He is a worker-artist but remains unknown all the time.

闻风而动 [wénfēngérdòng] get into action as soon as one gets to know some information

闻名 [wénmíng] famous: well known

闻人 [wénrén] a famous person; a well-known person

闻所未闻 [wénsuǒwèiwén] unheard of; unprecedented

wěn

紊 [wěn] (adj) 杂乱 in a mess ＊他做事有条不紊。He works in an orderly manner.

紊乱 [wěnluàn] disorderly; confused

刎 [wěn] (v) 割脖子 to slit the throat ＊他自刎了。He comitted suicide by slitting his own throat.

吻 [wěn] 1 (n) 嘴唇 lips 2 (v) 用嘴唇接触，表示喜爱 kiss ＊工作后回家，他先吻那美丽的小女儿。Having come home from office, he kissed his little pretty daughter.

吻合 [wěnhé] agree; in conformity with

稳(穩) [wěn] 1 (adj) 安定，不动摇 stable; steady ＊中东的政治局势很不稳定。 The political situation in Middle East is not stable. 2 (adj) 可靠 safe and reliable ＊钱以汇票方式寄出去比较稳当。It is safer and more reliable to send the money by money order.

稳步 [wěnbù] by steady steps; steadily

稳定性 [wěndìngxìng] stability

稳固 [wěngù] strong (e.g. foundation); solid; stable

稳健 [wenjiàn] solid; steady

稳扎稳打 [wěnzhā wěndǎ] go ahead steadily and strike at the right time; wage steady and sure struggles

稳重 [wěnzhòng] steady; solidly

wèn

问(問) [wèn] 1 (v) 请人解答事情 ask; inquire; question ＊他问我一些有关经济和政治的事情。He asked me some questions on economics and politics. 2 (v) 慰问 ask about one's health ＊请代我问候他。 Please send my regards to him. 3 (v) 审讯，追究 interrogate; investigate ＊法官正在审问那名嫌疑犯。The judge is interrogating the suspect. 4 (v) 过问，管 care; bother; manage

问长问短 [wèncháng wènduǎn] ask all sort of questions; bombard somebody with questions

问答 [wèndá] questions and answers

问暖嘘寒 [wènnuǎnxūhán] ask after one's needs; express concern for

问号 [wènhào] question mark

问好 [wènhǎo] give (one's) regards to

问候 [wènhòu] inquire about a person's health; to give one's regards

问世 [wènshì] be presented to the public

问题 [wèntí] question; problem

wēng

翁 [wēng] 1 (n) 老年男子 old man ＊再过十五年后，他就变成一个孤苦零丁的老翁了。 In another fifteen years he will become a lonely old man. 2 (n) 父亲 father 3 (n) 丈夫或妻子的父亲 father-in-law ＊家翁。 father of one's husband.

嗡 [wēng] [嗡嗡] (v) 昆虫发出的声音，听不清楚的声音 the sound of bees and other insects ＊蜜蜂嗡嗡地飞来飞去。The bee is humming and flying about.

wèng

瓮(甕) [wèng] (n) 一种口小腹大的陶器，通常用来盛液体 earthen jar; big pottery jar

wō

涡(渦) [wō] (n) 大水急流旋转的中心。如漩涡 a whirlpool; an eddy ✱ 她为了避免被卷入政治漩涡之中，便到美国去念书。In order to avoid the political whirlpool, she went to the United States for further study.
另见 [guō]

蜗(蝸) [wō] (n) 软体动物名叫蜗牛。有螺旋形扁圆硬壳，头部有两对触角，后一对顶端有眼，吃植物的嫩叶，对农作物有害，但某些种类可供食用 snail

窝(窩) [wō] 1 (n) 禽兽鸟类和昆虫住的地方 den; nest; lair ✱ 鸟窝。birds nest. ✱鸽子找了树枝和干草，做成一个温暖的小窝。The pigeons have found some branches and dried grass with which they made into a warm rest. 2 (n) 比喻坏人藏匿的地方 hideout ✱ 匪窝 bandits hideout 3 (v) 藏匿坏人或赃物 hide; shelter; conceal a fugitive ✱ 他被控窝藏逃犯。He was accused of sheltering a fugitive. 4 (n) 凹进去的地方 a hollow part of place ✱胳肢窝 armpit 5 (n) 量词，用于一胎所生或一次孵出的动物 a quantity denoting for new-born animals or birds ✱ 一窝小猪。a lot of new-born piglings .

窝棚 [wō·peng] a mat shed
窝头 [wōtóu] corn bread
窝主 [wōzhǔ] a receiver of stolen goods; one who harbours thieves

倭 [wō] (n) 古代称日本 Japan (an ancient name)

喔 [wō]〔喔喔〕(n) 公鸡叫的声音 the crow of a cock✱住在组屋区，我们不曾在清晨时分听到公鸡喔喔的啼叫。Living in a housing estate, we have never heard the crow of a rooster at daybreak.
另见 [ō]

wǒ

我 [wǒ] (pron) 自称，自己 I; my ✱ 我是新加坡公民。I am a Singapore citizen.

我军 [wǒjūn] our army; our troop
我们 [wǒ·men] we
我行我素 [wǒxíngwǒsù] I do as I used to do, regardless of what people say

wò

握 [wò] (v) 捏，拿住 grasp; take by the hand ✱我们紧握手中枪，保卫祖国神圣的领土。We grasp tightly our rifles to defend our sacred motherland.

握别 [wobie] shake hands at departure; good-bye
握手 [wòshǒu] shake hands

幄 [wò] (n) 帐幕 tent; curtain ✱帷幄 tent

龌(齷) [wò] 1 (adj) 脏，不干净 dirty ✱她住的地方太龌龊了，孩子们时常生病。She lives in a very filthy place and her children get sick often. 2 (adj) 卑鄙 mean filthy base

沃 [wò] 1 (v) 灌溉，浇 irrigate; water ✱沃田 to irrigate the padi farm 2 (adj)（土地）肥，肥沃 fertile ✱ 沃土 fertile soil

卧 [wò] 1 (v) 睡倒，躺下 lie down ✱ 病人卧在床上，等待医生来。The patient is lying on the bed, awaiting the doctor . 2 (adj) 睡觉用的 for sleeping purpose ✱ 卧铺 berth

卧倒 [wòdǎo] lie down; lie on one's stomach
卧室 [wòshì] bedroom
卧薪尝胆 [wò xīn cháng dǎn] endure hardship to achieve one's purpose

斡 [wò] 1 (v) 转，旋 turn around; move around 2 (v) 调解 to settle a dispute; to mediate ✱他从中斡旋，希望能解决两方的争端。He mediates between the two parties hoping that their dispute can be solved.

wū

乌(烏) [wū] 1 (n) 乌鸦 crow 2 (adj) 黑色 black in colour ＊乌云满天，快下雨了。 The sky is filled with dark clouds, the rain is imminent.

乌合之众 [wūhézhīzhòng] an unorganised group of people
乌亮 [wūliàng] dark and shiny
乌纱帽 [wūshāmào] official post
乌托邦 [wūtuōbāng] utopia
乌烟瘴气 [wū yān-zhàng qì] vicious practices; create a foul atmosphere
乌有 [wūyǒu] nothingness ; a loss ; emptiness

呜(鳴) [wū] (adj) 表示声音 sound of honk ＊火车呜呜地叫。 The train gives a whistling sound.
呜呼 [wūhū] alas! alack!
呜咽 [wūyē] sob

污 [wū] 1 (n) 停滞不流动的水 stagnant water 2 (adj) 脏 dirty; filthy ＊污水。 filthy water 3 (v) 侮辱 insult; stain ＊她被日军污辱了之后，就一直想要离乡背井，到外国去工作。 After she was insulted by Japanese army, she had decided to leave her homeland and go abroad to work. 4 (adj) 诬谤 to defame; to abuse slanderously ＊公务员有时会被敌对者污蔑。 Public officers are sometimes defamed by opponents. 5 (v) 沾染 stain; pollute ＊我们要防止空气污染。 We must stop air pollution.
污点 [wū diǎn] stain (on clothing); stain on a character
污垢 [wūgòu] dirt; filth; stain
污秽 [wūhuì] disreputable (conduct); filthy
污泥浊水 [wūnízhuóshuǐ] mud and filthy water
污辱 [wūrǔ] stain; insult

屋 [wū] (n) 房子 house ＊这屋子是他们自己建的。 They built this house themselves.

巫 [wū] 1 (n) 专以装神弄鬼骗取财物的人，如巫婆 witch ＊在一个马来乡村里，有个巫婆会替小孩子医病。 In a Malay Kampong, there lives a witch who is able to cure sickness of children.
巫术 [wūshù] witchcraft
巫医 [wūyī] wizards or quack doctors

诬(誣) [wū] (v) 无中生有，硬说别人做了坏事 accuse falsely; slander ＊他诬赖我偷了他的东西。 He accused me falsely of stealing his things.
诬告 [wūgào] accuse falsely
诬蔑 [wūmiè] vilify; smear; slander
诬陷 [wūxiàn] implicate falsely; injure by false accusation

wú

吾 [wú] (pron) 我，我的，我们的 ; my; our ＊吾子。 my son

梧 [wú] (n) 落叶乔木，树干直亦称梧桐。木材可制器具，树皮可作造纸原料，叶可供药用 the phoenix tree

鼯 [wú] (n) "大飞鼠"，哺乳动物。前、后肢之间有宽而多毛的皮膜，借此在树间滑翔; 尾长，住在树洞中，夜里出来活动。以果实、甲虫为食。毛皮柔软，可制衣物 flying squirrel

无(無) [wú] (adj) (adv) (prep) 没有 no; none; not ; without ＊他无缘无故地发脾气。 He lost his temper without reason. ＊这件事无论如何你都要保守秘密。You must keep this matter a secret under whatever circumstances.
无比 [wúbǐ] matchless
无病呻吟 [wubingshenyin] to complain about something imaginary

无偿 [wúcháng] gratis; free of charge
无产阶级 [wúchǎnjiējí] proletariat
无产者 [wúchǎnzhě] proletarian, the have-nots
无耻 [wúchǐ] shameless; unscrupulous
无从 [wú cóng] having no way (to do something)
无敌 [wúdí] matchless; unmatched
无动于衷 [wúdòngyúzhōng] aloof and indifferent; untouched
无恶不作 [wú è bù zuò] commit all manner of crimes; be as wicked as possible
无妨 [wúfāng] it's no harm to do so
无法无天 [wúfǎ-wútiān] lawless; unruly
无非 [wúfēi] it's only; nothing but
无辜 [wúgū] innocent, innocence
无故 [wúgù] for no reason
无关 [wúguān] has nothing to do with
无坚不摧 [wújiānbùcuī] all conquering; invincible
无价之宝 [wújiàzhībǎo] priceless treasure
无济于事 [wújìyúshì] of no help; of no avail
无稽之谈 [wú jī zhī tán] baseless gossips
无可争辩 [wúkězhēngbiàn] indisputable
无孔不入 [wú kǒng bù rù] lose no chance; poke into every nook and corner
无愧 [wúkuì] be worthy of
无赖 [wúlài] rogue; rascal
无聊 [wúliáo] nonsense; boring
无理取闹 [wúlǐqǔnào] unreasonable quarrelling; mischief-making
无奈 [wú nài] have no alternative but; but
无能 [wú néng] incapable; impotent
无能为力 [wúnéngwéilì] powerless; incapable; can do nothing about it
无奇不有 [wúqíbùyǒu] strange things of every description
无情 [wú qíng] merciless; heartless; ruthless
无穷无尽 [wúqíongwújìn] inexhaustible; infinity
无期徒刑 [wúqītúxíng] jailed for an indefinite period
无伤大雅 [wú shāng dà yǎ] nothing serious
无神论 [wúshénlùn] atheism
无事生非 [wú shì-shēng fēi] make trouble out of nothing
无时无刻 [wúshi-wúkè] at any moment; all the time
无数 [wúshù] innumerable; countless; no end of
无私 [wúsī] selfless
无所事事 [wúsuǒshìshì] idle; loating; jobless
无所谓 [wùsuǒwèi] it does not matter if... ; cannot be taken as; cannot be regarded as
无条件 [wútiáojiàn] unconditional
无往不胜 [wú wǎng bù shèng] invincible; all-conquering
无畏 [wúwèi] fearless; daring; bold
无微不至 [wú wēi bù zhì] lavish every care
无效 [wúxiào] invalid; null and void
无限 [wúxiàn] infinite; boundless
无线电 [wúxiàndiàn] wireless; radio
无懈可击 [wú xiè kě jī] invulnerable; perfect
无隙可乘 [wúxìkěchéng] no crack to get in by; water-tight (e.g. plan)
无心 [wú xīn] without any intention; have no mind to
无形中 [wúxíngzhōng] invisibly
无疑 [wúyí] doubtless
无意 [wúyì] unintentional
无影无踪 [wúyíngwúzōng] not a trace left; gone
无依无靠 [wúyīwúkào] have no dependents and no-one to depend upon; be alone in the world
无用 [wúyòng] useless
无政府主义 [wúzhèngfǔzhǔyì] anarchism
无知 [wú zhī] ignorant; lacking know-

ledge

无中生有[wúzhōngshēngyǒu]unfounded; groundless; sheer fabrication

芜(蕪) [wú] 1 (adj) 田地荒废，长满乱草 weeded (land); uncultivated *田地荒芜了。The farm land is left uncultivated. 2 (adj) 比喻杂乱 confused; mixed up *芜杂。mixed. 3 (n) 杂乱的东西 impurities *去芜存菁。discarding the impurities and retaining the fine essence.

芜菁 [wújīng] turnip

吴 [wú] 1 (n) 古代国名 name of a country in ancient China 2 (n) 姓氏 a Chinese surname or family name

蜈 [wú] [蜈蚣] [wúgōng] (n) 节肢动物，全身分二十一节，每节有脚一对.头后一对叫"唇足"，有毒腺，能捕食小动物，也能螫人。晒干处理后可供药用。a centipede

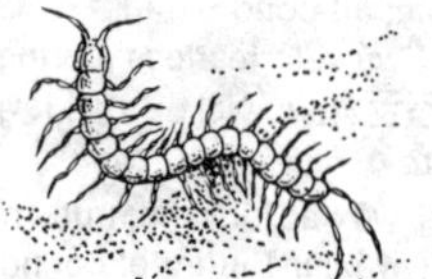

毋 [wú] (v) 不要，不可以 do not *毋中奸计。Do not fall into the treacherous plot.

wǔ

午 [wǔ] 1 (n) 地支的第七位，用作次序的第七 the seventh place of the Earth Branches; seventh in order 2 (n) 指早上十一点到下午一点的一段时间 11 a.m. to 1.00 p.m 3 (n) 正午，指十二点 noon; twelve o'clock in daytime

午饭 [wǔfàn] lunch

午睡 [wǔshuì] nap after lunch

午夜 [wǔyè] midnight

武 [wǔ] 1 (adj) 关于军事的，跟"文"相对 military; armed *武装力量。military power. 2 (adj) 关于战斗技术的 martial *中国武术。Chinese traditional martial art. 3 (adj) 勇猛 brave; chivalrous

武断 [wǔduàn] arbitrary

武官 [wǔguān] military attache

武力 [wǔlì] force of arms; military force

武艺 [wǔyì] martial arts

妩(嫵) [wǔ] (adj) 姿态美好 beautiful; charming; fascinating

舞 [wǔ] 1 (n) 人们在欢乐时表演的动作。dance *红绸舞。the red sash dance. 2 (v) 挥动，舞动 flutter about; brandish *舞剑。to brandish a sword. 3 (v) 耍，玩弄 play with *他只会舞文弄墨。He knows only how to play with words.

舞弊 [wǔbì] juggle with the law; indulge in malpractices; irregularity

舞剧 [wǔjù] dance drama

舞台 [wǔtái] stage; platform

五 [wǔ] (n) 数词 five; 5 *五线谱。musical notation.

五彩缤纷 [wǔcǎibīnfēn]full of colours; multicoloured

五谷 [wǔgǔ] grains

五光十色[wǔguāng-shísè] a great variety; kaleidoscopic

五湖四海[wǔhú-sìhǎi] all corners of the country

五花八门[wǔhuā-bāmén] kaleidoscopic; manifold

五金 [wǔjīn] the five metals (gold, silver, iron, copper and tin); metals

五体投地 [wǔtǐtóudì] kneel at the feet of someone; treat with respect

五颜六色 [wǔyánliùsè]colourful; filled with various colours

五一国际劳动节 [wǔyīguójì láodòng jiè] May 1st,International Labour Day

五脏 [wǔzàng]the five internal organs (the heart, livers, spleen, lungs and kidneys)

伍 [wǔ] 1 (n) 军队或集体 army troop; a group *弟弟被征召入伍了。Our brother is being called up for national service. 2 (n) 伙伴 companior. *他的所作所为使大家羞与

为伍。We feel shameful to be in his company because of his bad deeds. 3 (n) "五"的大写 five (in complicate form) ＊支票上清楚志明：伍仟伍佰圆另叁角正。On the cheque is clearly written: Five thousand five hundred dollars and thirty cents only.

捂 [wǔ] (v) 遮盖，密封 cover up tightly; seal ＊他用手捂着我的嘴巴，不让我喊。He covered my mouth with his palm so that I could not shout.

侮 [wǔ] (v) 欺负，轻慢 bully; humiliate; insult; despise ＊非洲的黑人被少数的白人统治者侮辱了好多年。For many years, African Negroes have been humiliated by a few white rulers.

侮蔑 [wǔmiè] despise; hold one in contempt; scorn

侮弄 [wǔnòng] make fun of; mock at

wù

悟 [wù] (v) 明白，领会，觉醒 understand; perceive; awake ＊听了他的解释以后，我才恍然大悟。I begin to understand only after having listened to his explanation.

晤 [wù] (v) 见面 meet each other ＊家长们和校长晤面，讨论问题学生的事情。The parents met the Headmaster and had a discussion about problem pupils.

骛（騖） [wù] 1 (v) 马乱跑，快跑 the swift gallops of a horse 2 (v) 从事，追求 crave for

务（務） [wù] 1 (n) 事情 matter; affair ＊他的父亲是个出版家，其业务非常繁忙。His father is a publisher who is very busy with his business. 2 (v) 从事某项工作 undertake or do a job ＊他的父亲务农。His father is working as a farmer. 3 (v) 追求 crave for ＊他做事好高务远，不求脚踏实地。He craves for something high and beyond reach and never works on a firm footing.

务必 [wùbì] must; should

雾（霧） [wù] (n) 接近地面的水蒸气遇冷时，附着在尘埃上面，凝结成大量小水滴，飘浮在空气中称为雾 mist; fog ＊云雾。fog; mist

勿 [wù] (v) 不要 do not ＊请勿吸烟。Please do not smoke.

物 [wù] 1 (n) 东西 things; objects ＊百货公司里陈列着各种各样的物品。A great variety of things are displayed in the emporium. 2 (n) 内容，实质 content; substance ＊文章必须言之有物。All articles must have contents.

物产 [wùchǎn] produce or manufactured products

物极必反 [wùjíbìfǎn] when an idea reaches its limit, opposition will emerge

物价 [wùjià] prices of commodities

物理 [wùlǐ] physics

物力 [wù lì] economic or material strength

物体 [wùtǐ] form and state of matter; substance; things

物以类聚 [wùyǐlèijù] birds of the same feather flock together

物证 [wùzhèng] material evidence

物质 [wùzhì] material; matter

物质不灭定律 [wùzhìbúmièdìnglǜ] law of conservation of matter

物资 [wùzī] goods; materials

坞（塢） [wù] (n) 在水边建筑的修造船只的地方或工场 a ship-yard; dock ＊她的弟弟在一间船坞当烧焊工人。Her younger brother works in a shipyard as a welder.

误（誤） [wù] 1 (n) 做错事情 mistake; error; blunder ＊他承认轰炸北越是一项错误的决定。He admits that it was a wrong decision to bomb North Vietnam. 2

(v) 使人受害 to make somebody suffer ∗ 他粗心大意，误人不浅。He makes people suffer owing to his carelessness. (v) 赶不及 fail ∗ 那天他因为迟起身，结果误了班车。He got up late that day and consequently he failed to make the train

误差 [wùchā] an error

误会 [wùhuì] misunderstanding

误解 [wùjiě] misinterpretation; misunderstanding; misinterpret

误事 [wushi] spoil an affair

误印 [wùyìn] a misprint

恶(惡) [wù] (v) 讨厌，憎恨 hate; loathe ∗ 有些老板非常可恶，他们常常讲骗话，欺侮工友。Some employers are horrible. They always tell lies and bully the workers.

戊 [wù] (n) 天干的第五位，用作次序的第五 the fifth of the ten celestial items

xī

希 [xī] 1 (v)心愿 hope ＊ 希准时出席。Hope you will be punctual. 2 (adj)很少的 rare ＊ 物以希为贵。What is rare is precious.

希罕 [xī·han] rare;uncommon;appreciate something for its rareness

希奇 [xī qí] rare and curious

希望 [xī wàng] hope

稀 [xī] 1 (adj)空隙大，不紧密 loose; thin; sparse ＊这个国家地广人稀。This country is big in land area but sparsely populated. 2 (adj)很少的 rare 3 (adj)不浓厚，含水份多的 dilute

稀薄 [xī bó] thin and diluted; rarefied

稀少 [xī shǎo] rare;few;sparse

稀有金属 [xī yǒu jīn shǔ] rare metals

奚 [xī] (n)姓氏 a surname

奚落 [xī luò] ridicule;mock;jeer

溪 [xī] (n)山间的小河沟 brook; stream

嘻 [xī] (n)笑的声音或样子 laughing voice or look ＊孩子们嘻嘻哈哈的不知道在笑什么。I do not know what the children are laughing at.

嬉 [xī] (v)玩耍，游戏 play;amuse ＊孩子们在沙滩上嬉戏。The children were having fun on the beach.

嬉笑 [xī xiào] laugh merrily

嬉皮笑脸 [xī pí xiào liǎn] grinning

熹 [xī] (n)天亮，天明 daybreak; brightness

西 [xī] (n)方向，太阳落的一边 the west

西半球 [xī bàn qiú] western hemisphere

西北 [xīběi] northwest

西边 [xī bian] west side

西餐 [xīcān] European food

西方 [xī fāng] the west;the western world

西服 [xīfù] western style dress

西瓜 [xī guā] water melon

西南 [xīnán] southwest

西医 [xī yī] western doctor ; western medicine

牺(犧) [xī] [牺牲] [xī shēng] 1(n) 古代祭祀用的牲畜的通称 animal sacrifice 2 (v) 舍弃、捐弃 sacrifice ＊他已为国牺牲。He sacrificed his life for the country.

析 [xī] 1 (v)分开，散开 divide;split 2 (v)解释，辨别 explain;discriminate ＊总理在记者招待会上分析了我国目前的经济发展情况。At the press conference, the Prime Minister had explained the present economic development situation of our country.

析疑 [xī yí] to explain one's doubt; to clarify

晰 [xī] (adj)清楚，明白 clear *画面不很清晰。The picture is not very clear.

蜥 [xī]〔蜥蜴〕[xī yì] (n) 爬行动物。身体表面有细小鳞片,有四肢,尾巴细长。生活在草丛中，捕食昆虫和其他小动物，种类很多，有草蜥、壁虎等 lizards

息 [xi] 1 (n) 呼吸 breath 2 (v) 停止 stop * 掌声经久不息。The applause lasted long and did not stop. 3 (v)休息 rest 4 (n) 音信 news *你有听到关於他的消息吗？Do you have any news about him? 5 (n) 利息 interest

息事宁人 [xī shì níng rèn] settle the dispute and pacify the people

息息相关 [xī xī xiāng guān] closely interrelated;be linked with each other closely

息息相同 [xīxīxiǎngtóng] exactly similar

熄 [xī] (v) 灭火 extinguish;go out;die out

熄灭 [xī miè] extinguish;stop; destroy

夕 [xī] (n) 傍晚，晚上 evening; sunset

夕阳 [xī yáng]the setting sun

汐 [xī] (n) 晚潮 the evening tide

吸 [xī] 1 (v) 把气体从鼻或口引入体内 breathe in *他呼吸发生困难。He has difficulty in breathing. 2 (v)吸取，吸引 suck;draw in;absorb

吸尘器 [xī chén qì] vaccum cleaner

吸干 [xīgān] to suck dry

吸取 [xī qǔ] assimilate;draw;accept

吸收 [xī shōu] absorb;take in;assimilate;draw in

吸血鬼 [xī xuè guǐ] blood sucker; an exploiter

吸烟 [xī yān] smoke;smoking

吸引 [xī yǐn] attract;be drawn into; pin down

昔 [xī] (n)从前；过去 the past *今非昔比。The past is incomparable to the present.

昔日 [xī rì] former days; early days

惜 [xī] 1 (v) 表示遗憾、悲伤 pity; feel sad for *本来很纯洁的一位少女,一踏入社会后竟变得爱慕虚荣，实在可惜。It is a pity that an originally innocent girl becomes vain after stepping into society. 2(v) 重视,不随便丢弃 hold something dear;treasure;love and care *我们要爱惜光阴。We must treasure time. 3 (v) 舍不得 not willing to give up * 他不惜牺牲自己的生命去营救受困在坑底的工友。He was willing to give up his life in order to save the worker trapped in the pit.

惜别 [xī bié] be reluctant to part with somebody

悉 [xī] 1 (v) 知道，明白 know*他很熟悉这一带的街道。He knows the streets in this area very well. 2 (adj)尽，全 all;entire;total * 医生很悉心的照料这位病人。The doctor looks after this patient with his entire attention.

锡(錫) [xī] (n) 化学元素。符号 sn 常见的白锡是一种银白色金属，可制家用器皿 tin

锡匠 [xī·jiang] tinsmith

锡矿 [xī kuàng] tin mine

曦 [xī] (n) 太阳光 sunlight

兮 [xī] (n)文言助词。相当于"啊"或"呀"。an interjection of admiration;doubt or inquiry used in the old Chinese language

熙 [xī] (adj)光明，和乐 bright; harmonious

膝 [xī] (n)大腿和小腿相连的关节的前部 knee

蟋 [xī] 蟋蟀 [xī shuài] (n)也叫"促织"，"蛐蛐"，小昆虫。身体黑褐色，触角长，后腿粗大，善于跳跃，雄的前翅能摩擦发声。生活在阴湿的地方，吃植物的根和茎，对农作物有害 a cricket

犀 [xī] (n) 犀牛，哺乳动物。体粗大，鼻上有一角或二角，毛极稀少，皮肤厚而韧。产在亚洲和非洲的森林里，其角可供药用 rhinoceros

犀利 [xī lì] sharp

xí

习(習) [xí] 1 (v)学过后再反复地学，使能熟练 practise; revise *我练习吹口琴。I practise playing the harmonica. 2 (n) 惯常的行为 habit *他有迟到的恶习。He has the bad habit of being not punctual. 3 (adj) 惯于 used to; accustomed to *他在吵杂的环境下做功课已经习以为常了。He is used to studying in a noisy environment.

习惯势力 [xíguànshìlì] the force of habit

习气 [xí qì] bad habit; mannerism

习俗 [xí sú] customs; secular

习题 [xí tí] an exercise

习性 [xí xìng] a habit; propensity

媳 [xí] (n) 儿子的妻子，一般也用来称孙或侄的妻子 the wife of a son, grandson or nephew

席 [xí] 1 (n)用草、芦苇、竹篾等编成的铺垫用具 mat made of straw or bamboo splints 2 (n)座，座位，席位 a seat;place 3(n)成桌饭菜 a table of dishes in a feast or banquet * 男方摆了十桌酒席。The bridegroom has given a wedding feast with ten tables.

席卷 [xíjuǎn] to sweep through; engulf; rage over

席位 [xí wèi] place or seating during dinner,meeting or assembly; seat (membership of international organisatons and parliament)

席子 [xí·zi] mat

袭(襲) [xí] 1 (v) 攻击 raid;assault;attack * 美军空袭河内。The American army air-raided Hanoi 2 (v) 照样做，继承 follow suit;inherit;succeed * 不要因袭陈规。Do not follow the old rules.

袭击 [xí jī] to attack; to assault; to storm; to raid

袭用 [xí yòng] to adopt what has been used

檄 [xí] (n) 征召晓谕的文书 a manifesto; a proclamation

檄文 [xí wén] a declaration ; a manifesto

xǐ

徙 [xǐ] (v)迁移 move;remove

喜 [xǐ] 1 (adj) 高兴；快乐 happy; delightful *他喜形于色。A happy expression is shown on his face. 2 (v)爱好 love ; like ; prefer * 他喜爱游泳。He likes swimming

喜报 [xǐbào] happy news; good tidings; glad tidings

喜欢 [xǐ·huan] like;be partial to;delight;enjoy

喜剧 [xǐ jù] comedy

喜气洋洋 [xǐ qì yáng yáng] overwhelmed with joy;outburst of joy

喜鹊 [xǐ·que] magpie

喜事 [xǐshì] a happy event ; a joyous occassion; marriage

喜闻乐见 [xǐwēnlèjiàn] happy to hear and see; something that is welcome

喜笑颜开 [xǐxiàoyánkāi] beaming with smiles

喜形于色 [xǐ xíng yú sè] happiness shown on the face

喜讯 [xǐ xùn] happy news;pleasant news;good news

喜悦 [xǐ yuè] happy;joyful;delightful

禧 [xǐ] 1 (n)吉祥，幸福blessings; good luck;joy 2 (n)喜庆a happy occasion

洗 [xǐ] (v) 用水去掉脏东西 wash; clean

洗尘 [xǐ chén] entertain a friend who had returned from overseas

洗涤 [xǐ dí] wash;cleanse

洗耳恭听 [xǐ ěr gōng tīng] to listen with reverent attention

洗劫 [xǐjiè] to loot; to rob

洗礼 [xǐ lǐ] baptism

洗衣机 [xǐyījī] a washing machine

洗手不干 [xǐshǒubùgàn] to wash one's hands of; to be through with

洗刷 [xǐ shuā] wash and brush; wash away;be cleared of;cleanse

洗心革面 [xǐ xīn gé miàn] change one's thought and appearance

洗澡 [xǐ zǎo] take a bath

玺(璽) [xǐ] (n) 皇帝的印 the royal seal of the emperor

xì

隙 [xì] 1 (n)裂缝 a crack;a fissure;a crevice * 蟑螂钻进墙隙里。 The cockroach has slipped into a crack on the wall. 2 (n) 空闲free time * 冬季是农隙时分。Winter is a free time for the farmers. 3 (n) 怨恨 resentment; hatred

细(細) [xì] 1 (adj) 小的 fine; thin ; slender ; minute ; small ; 2 (adj) 声音 轻微 soft (of voice) * 他的声音很细小。His voice is soft. 3 (adj) 精致 delicate; fine;polished * 这两件象牙雕刻很精细 。These two pieces of ivory carvings are very fine. 4 (adj) 周密，小心 careful * 做这项侦察工作要胆大心细。 One must be bold and careful in carrying out this investigation task. 5 (adj) 详尽 detailed * 我们先讨论主要的几个问题，其他细节可以迟些再谈。We shall discuss the few main problems before going into the details.

细胞 [xì bao] cell

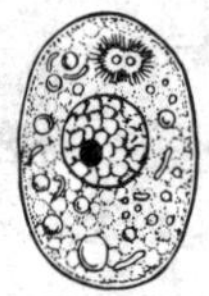

细节 [xìjiè] details

细菌 [xì jūn] bacteria;germ

细菌肥料 [xì jún féi liào] bacterial [bacteriological] fertilizer

细粮 [xìliáng] refined grain

细密 [xì mì] fine;delicate;careful

细腻 [xì nì] dainty;fine;detailed

细水长流 [xì shuǐ cháng liú] continuously do something bit by

bit;plan on a long term basis

细微 [xì wēi] small; minute

细小 [xì xiǎo] small;trivial;minute

细心 [xì xīn] careful;patient;

细则 [xì zé] detailed rules

细致 [xìzhì] meticulous; fine; delicate ; dainty; polished

戏(戲) [xì] 1 (n)玩耍 play; game * 不要把生命当儿戏。Do not regard your life as a child's game. 2 (v) 开玩笑;嘲弄 make fun of;mock * 这些学生真顽皮,竟敢戏弄老师。These students are very naughty ; they even make fun of the teacher. 3(n) 戏剧,也指杂技 theatrical show ; drama;play;acrobatic show

戏法 [xìfǎ] trick; hocus-pocus

戏剧家 [xìjùjiā] a stage artist

戏剧节目 [xìjùjiémù] repertoire

戏剧性 [xì jù xìng] dramatic;dramatization

戏曲 [xì qǔ] theatrical performance

戏院 [xì yuàn] theatre;cinema

系 [xì] 1 (n) 联属 connection 2 (n) 高等学校按学科分的教学单位 departments in institutions of higher learning *化学系 Department of Chemistry

系统 [xì tǒng] system;systematic

系统性 [xì tǒng xìng] systematization

系主任 [xì zhǔ rèn] head of a college department

系(係) [xì] 1 (v) 联属;拘束 to connect with; to attach to; to bind 2 (v) 是 to be

系数 [xì shù] coefficient

系(繫) [xì] (v)缚;拴 tie up ; fasten

阋(鬩) [xì] (v)争吵 quarrel

xiā

虾(蝦) [xiā] (n)甲壳动物。体分头胸部和腹部,外被甲壳,步足五对,腹部发达。种类很多,生活在水里。大都可供食用 prawn;shrimp

虾米 [xiā·mi] dried shrimps

虾仁儿 [xiā rén r] shelled shrimp meat

瞎 [xiā] (adj)眼睛失明,不能看见东西blind

瞎忙 [xiā máng] to busy oneself without achieving anything

xiá

瑕 [xiá] 1 (n) 玉上面的红色斑点 the red stain on a jade 2 (n) 比喻缺点 defect;a weak point;a flaw

瑕不掩瑜 [xiá bù yǎn yǔ] one's defects do not obscure one's virtues

暇 [xiá] (n) 空闲 leisure;spare time* 父亲在公余之暇去湖滨公园散步。Father takes a walk in the Lake Garden during his spare time.

霞 [xiá] (n) 日出或日落前后,接近地平线的阳光经大气中灰尘 水汽等的散射, 在天空和云层中出现的彩色景象 rosy clouds

遐 [xiá] 1 (adj) 远 distant;remote * 这里卖的咖啡粉遐迩闻名。The coffee powder sold here is famous far and near. 2 (adj) 长久 advanced in years

侠(俠) [xiá] (n) 扶弱抑强、见义勇为的人 hero; a chivalry; a knight; a chivalrous man

狭(狹) [xiá] (adj) 窄;不宽阔 narrow * 他生活在狭小的朋友圈子中。He moves in a narrow circle of friends

狭隘 [xiá' a] narrow;small;narrow-minded

狭路相逢 [xiá lù xiāng féng] (the two enemies) meeting in a narrow path

狭义 [xiá yì] in a narrow or strict

sense of the word

狭窄 [xiá zhǎi] narrow;narrow-minded

峡(峽) [xiá] 1 (n) 两山夹着的水道a gorge;a sharp ravine 2(n)两旁有陆地夹着形状狭长的海 straits ＊ 马六甲海峡。The Straits of Malacca. 3 (n) 连接两块大陆的狭窄地带 Isthmus ＊克拉地峡。The Kra Isthmus

狎 [xiá] (n) 亲近而态度轻浮 to be intimate in a frivolous manner

匣 [xiá] (v) 装东西的用具，通常指小型的，有盖子可以开合 box; a chest

辖(轄) [xiá] 1 (n) 轮轴头上的零件，可使车轮不掉下来 the linchpin of a wheel 2 (v) 管理 govern; regulate: rule; control ＊吉隆坡受中央政府直接管辖。Kuala Lumpur is directly controlled by the Central Government.

黠 [xiá] (adj)聪明；诡诈crafty;cunning ＊他为人狡黠。He is very cunning.

xià

下 [xià] 1 (prep)在低处below;beneath;under;down ＊他在楼下。He is downstairs.2 (adj)次序或等级在后的 next;inferior (of grade) ＊ 下星期。next week 3 (v)到；去go to ＊青年们下乡劳动。The young people go to the countryside to labour. 4 (v) 卸掉unload ＊码头工人在忙着下货。The port workers are busily unloading the goods. 5 (v)用 use up;devote ＊ 你要学好华文就得下一番功夫。You have to devote some time and effort in order to master the Chinese language. 6 (v) 作出 to fix; to make ＊我不了解情况，所以很难下结论。As I do not understand the situation, it is hard for me to draw a conclusion from it. 7 (v) 投递；发出 submit;send; issue ＊我们向敌人下战书。We sent a Declaration of War to the enemy. 8 (v)攻克 capture ＊我军连下数城。Our army capture several cities successively. 9 (v)退让 to give in ＊两兄弟你争我夺；相持不下。The two brothers; contending with one another were unwilling to give in. 10 (v) 结束; 完结 to end; to be over ＊下课了 The lesson is over. 11 (v)(鸟类)产(蛋)to lay (egg) ＊母鸡下蛋了。The hen has laid an egg.

下巴 [xià·ba] the chin

下班 [xiàbān] go off duty;be off duty

下边 [xiàbiān] the underneath; the following

下笔成章 [xià bǐ chéng zhāng] great facility in composition

下不为例 [xiàbùwéilì] should not take such an action next time

下策 [xiàcè] ill-advised policy; an unwise policy

下层 [xià céng] lower strata;lower level;subordinate level

下场 [xià·chǎng] end;fate; shamful end of a person's career

下等 [xià děng] inferior;low;mean; vulgar

下放 [xià fàng] transfer cadres to work at the grass root levels (e.g. countryside,factories); go to the countryside;factories and mines

下工夫 [xiàgōngfū] exert great effort; devote time and effort

下级 [xià jí] subordinate;lower levels

下降 [xià jiàng] descend;reduce;go down;decrease;decline

下课 [xiàkè] the class is over

下列 [xià liè] the following

下令 [xià lìng] issue a decree or order;give instruction

下流 [xià liú] lower reaches of river; downstream; despicable; scurrilous;vulgar
下落 [xiàluò] whereabouts
下棋 [xià qí] play chess
下去 [xiàqù] go down; descend
下身 [xià shēn] the lower part of the body
下手 [xià shǒu] start doing something; an assistant
下台 [xià tái] exit (of actors or players);be relieved of office;step down;removed from power;get out of embarrassing situation
下文 [xià wén] the next part;the following; the continuation or the end of something
下午 [xià wǔ] afternoon
下旬 [xià xún] the last ten days of a month
下议院 [xià yì yuàn] House of Commons;House of Representatives
下游 [xià yóu] lower reaches of river;lower river valley;downstream
下葬 [xià zàng] inter; bury

吓(嚇) [xià] (v) 害怕 frighten; scare; shock ＊他看到一具尸体，吓了一跳。He was shocked at the sight of a corpse.
另见 [hè]

夏 [xià] 1 (n)四季中的第二季 summer 2 (n) 朝代名 name of a dynasty in ancient China
夏历 [xià lì] the Chinese calendar
夏令营 [xià lìng yíng] summer camp
夏收 [xiàshōu] summer harvest
夏种 [xià zhǒng] summer planting

xiān

先 [xiān] 1 (adj) 时间或次序在前 first;ahead;early ＊先到先得。first come,first served. 2 (adj) 对死去的人的尊称 late;deceased 3 (n)祖上；上代 ancestors;forefathers
先辈 [xiān bèi] the elder generation; forefathers
先导 [xiān dǎo] pioneer;guide;precursor
先睹为快 [xiān dǔ wéi kuài] the greatest happiness is being the first to see
先发制人 [xiān fā zhì rén] strike first to pin down your opponent;he who makes the first move rules others
先锋 [xiān fēng] pioneer;vanguard
先后 [xiān hòu] first and last;in order of precedence; successively; one after the other
先见之明 [xiān jiàn zhī míng] foresight;able to predict
先进 [xiān jìn] outstanding;advanced;progressive
先决条件 [xiān jué tiaó jiàn] prerequisite
先例 [xiān lì] precedent
先前 [xiān qián] previous;in earlier times;former
先遣队 [xiān qiǎn duì] vanguard; advance detachments
先驱 [xiān qū] forerunner;pioneer; vanguard
先生 [xiān sheng] teacher; gentleman;mister
先天不足 [xiān tiān bù zú] prenatal deficiency

纤(纖) [xiān] (adj) 细小 minute ; fine
纤维 [xiān weí] fibre

纤维素 [xiān wéi sù] cellulose
纤细 [xiān xì] fine;minute;thin
另见 [qiàn]

仙 [xiān] (n) 长生不老的人 a fairy; an immortal person
仙女 [xiān nǚ] a fairy;an angel

仙人掌 [xiān rén zhǎng] cactus

掀

[xiān] 1 (v) 揭起；打开 open ＊我掀起锅盖看看鱼熟了没有。lifted up the cover of the pot to see whether the fish is cooked. 2 (v) 激起，激腾 stir; arouse; surge ＊大海掀起了波涛。Huge waves surge high on the ocean.

鲜（鮮）

[xiān] 1 (adj) 新的，不干枯的 fresh 2 (adj) 有光彩的 bright; colourful ＊舞蹈员穿着鲜艳的服装。The dancers were in colourful costumes. 3 (adj) 滋味好 tasty; delicious ＊这碗鸡汤真鲜美。This bowl of chicken soup is really delicious.

鲜红 [xiān hóng] bright red
鲜花 [xiān huā] fresh flower
鲜明 [xiān míng] crystal clear; clear-cut; vivid
鲜血 [xiān xuè] fresh blood
鲜艳夺目 [xiān yàn duó mù] splendour blinding the eyes

另见 [xiǎn]

xián

闲（閑）

[xián] 1 (adj) 没有事做，有空 unoccupied; free 2 (adj)（东西）放着不用 left unused (of thing) ＊别让机器闲着。Do not leave the machine unused. 3 (adj) 同正事无关的 (things or people) not concerned ＊闲人免进。No admittance except on business.

闲逛 [xián guàng] take a stroll; loiter
闲话 [xián huà] gossip; chitchat; idle talk
闲聊 [xián liáo] talk at random; idle talk; chat
闲情逸致 [xián qíng yì zhì] carefree
闲事 [xián shì] private affairs; matters that do not concern

娴（嫻）

[xián] 1 (adj) 熟练 skilled ＊他娴于辞令。He is eloquent. 2 (adj) 安静；文雅 quiet and refined ＊那少女举止娴雅。The girl has a quiet and refined bearing.

弦

[xián] 1 (n) 弓背两端之间系着的绳状物，有弹性，能发箭 the elastic cord on a bow 2 (n) 乐器上能振动发声的线 the cord or string on musical instruments; musical chord 3 (n) 月亮半圆 a moon in crescent ＊上弦月 a waxing moon; 下弦月 a waning moon

弦外之音 [xián wài zhī yīn] between the lines; indirect reference

舷

[xián] (n) 船的左右两侧 the side of a ship; the bulwarks; the gunwale

咸

[xián] (adj) 都，全 all; whole; together ＊这部戏老少咸宜。This film is suitable for both young and old.

咸（鹹）

[xián] (adj) 象盐的味道，也指含盐分过多的 saltish; salty ＊这菜太咸了。This dish is too salty. 3 (adj) 用盐或酱等腌制的 salted; pickled

咸蛋 [xián dàn] salted egg
咸肉 [xián ròu] salted meat; bacon

嫌

[xián] 1 (n) 可疑 suspicion ＊他涉嫌偷窃。He was suspected of theft. 2 (v) 厌恶；不满意 dislike; detest; complain ＊他常常嫌菜不好吃。He always complains of the food. 3 (n) 怨恨 grudge; ＊经过这次事件后，他们前嫌尽释。After this incident, they gave up their former grudge against one another.

嫌弃 [xián qì] dislike and avoid somebody
嫌恶 [xián wù] be sick of; dislike; detest

嫌隙 [xián xì] detest due to dissatisfaction or suspicion
嫌疑犯 [xián yí fàn] a suspected criminal;a suspect

涎 [xián] (n)唾沫，口水saliva

衔（銜） [xián] 1 (v)用嘴含着 hold in the mouth ＊他嘴里衔着一个烟斗。He is having a pipe in his mouth.2 (v)怀在心里 feel in one's heart;contain ＊他衔恨在心。He has a hatred in his heart. 3 (v) 连接 connect ;link up ＊这个计划的前后阶段必须衔接。The initial and final stages of this plan must be linked up. 4 (n) 区分级别或职务的名称 rank;title＊他领有上校军衔。He holds the rank of a colonel.
衔头 [xián·tou] title

贤（賢） [xián] (n)指有才德的人 an able and virtuous man ＊ 任人唯贤 employ those with ability and virtue
贤明 [xián míng] wise;intelligent; judicious
贤能 [xián néng] an able person
贤人 [xiánrén] sage; wise man

xiǎn

冼 [xiǎn] (n) 姓氏 a surname

险（險） [xiǎn] 1 (n)可能发生或遭受的灾难 danger;risk; hazard ＊我不想冒险。I do not intend to take the risk. 2 (adj)可能发生灾难的 dangerous;risky 3 (adv) 几乎，差一点儿 nearly;almost ＊他险些给车撞倒。He was nearly knocked down by a vehicle.
险隘 [xiǎnài] a dengerous pass
险恶 [xiǎn è] wicked;treacherous; sinister;precarious
险峻 [xiǎn jùn] steep;precipitous
险些 [xiǎnxīe] nearly; almost
险要 [xiǎn yào] strategic points;strong natural defence position
险阻 [xiǎnzǔ] difficult to cross; danger

鲜（鮮） [xiǎn] (adj)少 rare ＊这是鲜有的怪事。This is a very rare and strange affair. 另见 [xiān]

藓（蘚） [xiǎn] (n) 隐花植物，草本，丛生于湿地腐木岩石上。moss;lichen

显（顯） [xiǎn] 1 (adj) 明白的; 清楚的; 突出的 manifest; evident; clear; illustrious; conspicuous ＊这段新闻应该登在最显著的版位上。This piece of news should be put in the most conspicuous column in the newspaper. 2 (v)表现，露出show,display;appear ＊这次由你做厨师，你可以大显身手了。This time you will be the cook and you can fully display your skill. 3 (n) 上流社会中有名声地位者 a reputed or prominent person in the rank and fashion
显得 [xiǎn·de] appear to be
显而易见 [xiǎn ér yì jiàn] clearly shows;obvious;evident
显露 [xiǎn lù] reveal;manifest
显然 [xiǎn rán] clearly;evidently; obviously;apparently
显示 [xiǎn shì] show;reveal;display
显示力量 [xiǎnshìlìliàng] to display one's strength; to show one's muscles
显微镜 [xiǎn wēi jìng] microscope
显现 [xiǎnxiàn] appear; reveal
显眼 [xiǎn yǎn] attractive ; striking; arresting
显要 [xiǎn yào] a high and powerful position;high ranking and powerful;prominent
显著 [xiǎnzhù] remarkable; conspicuous; note-worthy; outstanding

蚬（蜆） [xiǎn] (n) 软体动物贝壳呈园形或心脏形，青黑色，有环纹。生活在水泥里

肉可供食用 clam;mussel

xiàn

现（現） [xiàn] 1 (v)显露；露出 appear;reveal ＊狡猾的狼外婆现出了原形。The cunning wolf in disguise as an old woman revealed its true feature.2 (adj) 目前，此刻present ＊现任校长原是教务主任。The present principal was the former supervisor. 3 (n)现款 cash

现场 [xiàn chǎng] on-the-spot
现成 [xiàn chéng] ready-made;off the peg
现代 [xiàn dài] modern age;contemporary era;modern
现代化 [xiàn dài huà] modernise
现代修正主义 [xiàn dài xiū zhèng zhǔ yì] modern revisionism
现金 [xiàn jīn] cash; money in coins or notes
现实 [xiàn shí] reality; realistic; practical
现实主义 xiàn shí zhu yì] realism, pragmatism
现象 [xiàn xiàng] phenomenon
现行 [xiàn xíng] current;active;present
现在 [xiàn zài] now;at present
现状 [xiàn zhuàng] present conditions; existing state; status quo

苋（莧） [xiàn] (n)苋菜，草本植物。可作蔬菜 amaranth , a green vegetable

宪（憲） [xiàn] 1 (n)法令 law 2 (n)宪法，国家的根本法 constitution

宪兵 [xiàn bīng] military police
宪章 [xiàn zhāng] charter

羡 [xiàn] (v)因喜爱而希望得到。envy; adore;admire

羡慕 [xiànmù] admire

限 [xiàn] 1 (n) 指定的范围limit;within a fixed time or region ＊我们必须规定旅行费用的限度。We must set allimit to the expenses of the trip. 2(v)指定范围，不许超过 to limit ;define ＊会员限于妇女。Membership is limited to women.

限定 [xiàn dìng] limit;set limit to; define
限度 [xiàn dū] limits;extent
限额 [xiàn é] quota;ration;norm
限量 [xiàn liàng] limited capacity; fixed quantity
限期 [xiànqí] within a set time; within a definite time
限于 [xiàn yù] confine to;restrict to;be bound to;be limited to
限制 [xiàn zhì] limit;restrict;be restrained;constrain

陷 [xiàn] 1 (v) 掉进去，沉下去 fall into;sink into ＊车轮陷在泥里了。The wheels have sunk into the mud. 2被攻破，被占领 to capture ; to occupy ＊ 许多城市失陷了。Many cities were captured.

陷害 [xiànhài] to frame up; to make false accusation
陷阱 [xiàn jiňg] trap;pitfall
陷落 [xiàn luò] sink into;sink down ; fall
陷入 [xiàn rù] fall into;sink into;get bogged down in
陷入圈套 [xiánrújuāntào] to get trapped into; to fall into the clutches of
陷入僵局 [xiànrùjiāngjú] to reach an impasse

县（縣） [xiàn] (n) 省、自治区或直辖市领导下的一级政区划单位 county ; prefecture

线(綫) [xiàn] 1 (n) 丝、棉、麻、毛或其他物质制成的细长而软的东西 thread;filament; wire 2 (n) 两个面的交界 line 3 (adj)比喻细微 slim ＊他们抱着一线希望等待失踪的渔船归来。They hang onto a slim hope for the return of the missing fishing boat.

线路 [xiàn lù] line of communication;circuit

线圈 [xiàn quān] coil of thread or wire

线索 [xiàn suǒ] clue;line of (story); indication

线条 [xiàn tiáo] the line in drawing contour

馅(餡) [xiàn] (n) 装填在另一种食品内的食品 stuffing (food)

腺 [xiàn] (n)生物体内具有分泌功能的组织 gland

献(獻) [xiàn] 1 (v)恭敬地送上 present;offer;give politely ＊我把花束献给敬爱的导师。I present a bouquet to my respected teacher. 2 (v) 表现出来 show ＊他向其上司大献殷勤。He curries much favour to his boss.

献策 [xiàn cè] present a plan or strategy;submit schemes for

献丑 [xiàn chǒu] expose one's defects

献词 [xiàn cí] greeting messages

献花 [xiànhua] present bouquets or flowers

献计 [xiàn jì] suggest ways and means;offer (plans) for

献礼 [xiàn lǐ] a contribution;make contributions

献媚 [xiàn mèi] curry favour;fawn upon

献身 [xiàn shēn] devote oneself to;dedicate oneself to

献殷勤 [xiànyīngqín] to pay (one's) court to; to curry favour with; to be at someone's beck and call

xiāng

襄 [xiāng] (v)帮助 help

襄理 [xiāng lǐ] an assistant manager

镶(鑲) [xiāng] (v)把东西嵌进去，或在外围加边 inset with; inlay; fill; border ＊他去牙医处镶了一隻门牙。He went to the dentist for inlaying an incisor.

镶边 [xiāng biān] to border

相 [xiāng] 1 (adj)交互，表示事物的相互关连或比较 mutual;correlative; reciprocal 2 (adv) 表示一方对另一方的动作 mutually;reciprocally

相比 [xiāng bǐ] compare with each other; contrast

相差 [xiāng chā] differ,deviate

相称 [xiāng chèn] fit;correspond; match;well-balanced;worthy

相乘 [xiāng chéng] multiply

相处 [xiāng chǔ] live or work together

相当 [xiāng dāng] .....equal.....; appropriate; fairly; in a certain degree;to a certain extent

相等 [xiāng děng] be equal to;equivalent

相对 [xiāng duì] opposite;relative; comparative

相反 [xiāng fǎn] contrary to;counter;opposite;converse

相仿 [xiāng fǎng] alike;similar

相逢 [xiāng féng] meet;come face to face with

相符 [xiāng fù] agree with; correspond with

相干 [xiāng gān] have to do with; relate with;relate to;concern

相关 [xiāng guān] have something to do with;be relevant to;be related to

相继 [xiāng jì] follow one another; successive

相交 [xiāng jiāo] (lines) cross each other;intersect;make friends with each other

相似 [xiāng sì] similar;analogous; resemble each other

相同 [xiāng tóng] be alike;be the same

相提并论 [xiāng tí bìng lùn] mention in the same breath;regard in the same category;put something on par with

相信 [xiāng xìn] to believe

相应 [xiāng·yìng] correspond; accordingly;proper;corresponding

相依为命 [xiāng yī wéi mìng] share life together;depend on each other

另见 [xiàng]

湘 [xiāng] (n) 湖南省的简称 another name for the Province of Hunan

箱 [xiāng] (n) 收藏衣物的方形器具 a box;a trunk

厢 [xiāng] 1 (n) 正屋两旁的房屋 a side-room 2 (n) 边；方面 side 3 (n) 靠近城的地区，如城厢 a suburb 4 (n) 间隔 a compartment * 车厢 a compartment (of a train); 厢座 a box seat

乡（鄉） [xiāng] 1(n) 农村 village ;countryside * 许多破产的农民从乡村涌向城市。Many bankrupt peasants move from the countryside to big towns. 3 (n) 生长居住的地方 native place ; home town

乡村 [xiāngcūn] village; countryside

乡亲 [xiāngqīn] fellow citizen of the same district; villager

乡绅 [xiāng shēn] village gentry

乡土 [xiāngtǔ] native place or district

乡下 [xiāng xià] the countryside; village

香 [xiāng] 1 (adj) 气味好闻（跟“臭”相对）fragrant; sweet ; scented ;aromatic * 这花很香。 This flower smells sweat. 2 (adj) 睡得熟 fast (asleep) * 孩子睡得正香呢。This child is fast asleep. 3 (adj) 比喻受欢迎 popular * 这货很吃香。This article is very popular. 4 (n) 用来燃点生烟祭神的东西。incense

香蕉 [xiāng jiāo] banana

香料 [xiāng liáo] condiment;spice; perfume

香炉 [xiānglú] incense burner

香喷喷 [xiāngpènpèn] rich in fragrance; fragrant

香水 [xiāng shuǐ] perfume;eau-de-cologne

香甜 [xiāng tián] sweet and nice smelling

香烟 [xiāng yān] cigarettes

香皂 [xiāng zào] toilet soap

xiáng

详（詳） [xiáng] (adj) 周密 in detail; detailed; comprehensive * 我们见面时再详谈。We shall discuss in detail when we meet again.

详尽 [xiáng jìn] with complete detail;in full detail

详情 [xiáng qíng] details

详细 [xiáng xì] detailed,at length

祥 [xiáng] (n) 吉利 felicity;good luck

翔 [xiáng] (v) 盘旋地飞 soar;hover over * 鸟儿在天空中飞翔。 The bird is hovering over in the sky.

降 [xiáng] 1 (v) 屈服；顺从 surrender;yield;give in * 他宁死不降。He would rather die than surrender. 2 (v) 制服 subdue

另见 [jiàng]

降龙伏虎 [xiáng lóng fú hǔ] subduing the dragon and taming the tiger;capable of defeating a formidable force

降服 [xiáng fú] subdue;overpower; put down

xiǎng

响(響) [xiǎng] 1 (n)声音 sound;ring 2 (v)发声 to give a sound * 大炮响了。The gun has sounded. 3 (adj)声音大 loud 他的歌声响亮。He is singing in a loud and clear voice.

响彻云霄 [xiǎng chè yún xiāo] resound through the skies;echoing to the skies

响亮 [xiǎngliàng] loud and clear ; resounding

响声 [xiǎng shēng] a sound

响应 [xiǎngyìng] to respond ; to echo

饷(餉) [xiǎng] 1 (n)军粮 rations for the army 2 (n) 薪给 pay ; salary ; remuneration

享 [xiǎng] (v) 受惠得到利益 enjoy * 劳动的果实大家享。We share the fruits of our labour.

享乐 [xiǎng lè] enjoy material comforts;seek pleasure;indulge in luxuries

享有 [xiǎng yǒu] possess;have ; in possession of

想 [xiǎng] 1 (v) 动脑筋 ; 思索 think * 有困难时一定要想办法解决。If there is any difficulty, we must think of a way to solve it. 2 (v)愿望 ; 打算 hope;intend * 他想当一名海员。He hopes to become a sailor. 3 (v)估计 ; 推测 suppose * 我想他今天不回来。I suppose he will not come back today. 4 (v)怀念 ; 思念 think affectionately of * 我很想家。I am homesick.

想必 [xiǎngbì] surely;likely

想不到 [xiǎng· bu dǎo] unexpectedly ; never thought of

想不开 [xiǎng·bu kāi] take things too hard;keep on worrying;be upset

想当然 [xiǎngdāngrán] take for granted; jump to conclusion without proof; assumption

想得开 [xiǎng de kāi] make light of worries;take things easy

想法 [xiǎng fǎ] ideas;thinking

想念 [xiǎng niàn] miss;cherish the memory of;yearn

想入非非 [xiǎng rù fēi fēi] having fantastic ideas;indulge in dreams or undesirable thinking

想望 [xiǎng wàng] hope;expect

想象 [xiǎng xiàng] imagine

想象力 [xiǎng xiàng lì] imagination ;fancy

xiàng

象 [xiàng] 1 (n)哺乳动物，体高约三米，皮厚毛少，肢粗如柱。鼻与上唇愈合成圆筒状长鼻。上颌有一对长牙 elephant

象棋 [xiàng qí] Chinese chess

象牙 [xiàng yá] ivory;elephant tusks

象牙之塔 [xiàng yá zhī tǎ] ivory tower ;the intellectuals' restricted haven which is divorced from reality

象(像) [xiàng] 1 (n) 事物的形状 ; 样子 shape ; appearance ; image ; impression *他的演说给听众一个深刻的印象。His speech made a strong impression on the audience. 2 (v) 相似 resemble;look like * 她长象她的母亲。She looks like her mother.

象征 [xiàng zhēng] symbol;symbolize;signify

象片 [xiàng piān] photograph;picture
象样儿 [xiàng yàng ŕ] decent;pretty good;proper

橡 [xiàng] (n) 落叶亚乔木，叶狭长有锯齿，花黄褐色。果有壳斗，球形，可食。 oak
橡胶 [xiàng jiāo] rubber
橡胶树 [xiàngjiāoshù] a rubber tree
橡皮 [xiàng pí] rubber;eraser
橡实 [xiángshì] acorn

向(嚮) [xiàng] 1 (n) 方向 direction 2 (v) 对着 face;turn towards ✱ 葵花向着太阳。 The sunflowers are facing the sun. 3 (adv) 从来 hitherto ; all along ✱ 我们向无此例。 We never have such rules.
向导 [xiàng dǎo] guide;person who shows others the way
向来 [xiànglái] usually; so far
向上 [xiàng shàng] upward;advance;progress
向往 [xiàng wǎng] aspire to;long for
向心力 [xiàng xīn lì] centripetal force
向阳 [xiàng yáng] facing the sun

相 [xiàng] 1 (n)形状；样子appearance;look ✱他装出一副可怜相。He puts up a pitiful look. 2 (v)察看 examine ✱ 我们要相机行事。We should act according to opportunity.
另见 [xiāng]
相机 [xiàng jī] camera
相貌 [xiàng mào] appearance;look
相片 [xiàng piàn] photograph
相声 [xiàng shēng] comic monologue

项(項) [xiàng] 1 (n)颈的后部 the nape of the neck 2 (n)事物的种类sort;kind;item ✱ 看看这些出口项目。Look at these export items. 3 (n) 量词，用于分项目的事物 a measure word for things;item ✱ 这是一项重要议程。This is an important item on the agenda.

巷 [xiáng] (n) 大街两旁较窄的街道 alley;lane ✱ 在过去三十年间，他们一直住在大成巷。They have been living at Lorong Tai Seng for the last thirty years.
巷战 [xiang zhàn] street fighting; house-to-house fighting

xiāo

削 [xiāo] (v)用刀切去物体表面的一层 peel;cut;sharpen ✱我正在削铅笔。I am sharpening the pencil.
另见 [xuē]

消 [xiāo] 1 (v)除掉；灭掉eliminate; destroy;extinguish ✱ 消灭蚊蝇。Destroy the mosquitoes and flies. 2 (v)溶化；散失melt; vanish;disappear ✱ 飞机慢慢的消失在云层里。The aeroplane slowly disappeared into the clouds. 3 (v) 需要 need ✱不消说，他是去赌博了。Needless to say, he has gone gambling.
消沉 [xiāo chén] down-hearted
消除 [xiāo chú] eliminate;remove; abolish;do away with
消毒 [xiāo dú] disinfection;sterilization
消费 [xiāo fèi] consume;spend
消耗 [xiāo hào] deplete;diminish; eat up;exhaust;drain;wear down; consume
消化 [xiāo huā] digest;absorb
消极 [xiāo jí] passive;dispirited;negative
消灭 [xiāo miè] eradicate ; wipe out ; destroy ; abolish ; exterminate
消遣 [xiāo qiǎn] spend spare time
消失 [xiāo shī] vanish;disappear; fade away
消逝 [xiāo shì] wither away;vanish
消瘦 [xiāo shòu] become thinner

and thinner

消息 [xiāo·xi] news;information

销(銷) [xiāo] 1 (v)熔化金属 melt;fuse metal 2 (v) 去掉 remove;do away with 3 (v)出售 sell * 他每天要出外推销电视机。He has to go out to sell the television sets everyday.

销毁 [xiāohuǐ] destroy; ruin

销路 [xiāo lù] range of sale;area of consumption;saleability

销声匿迹 [xiāoshēngnìjì] draw in one's horns

销售 [xiāo shòu] sell;sales

硝 [xiāo] (n) 某些矿物盐的泛称，如硝石 nitre;saltpetre

硝酸 [xiāo suān] nitric acid

硝烟 [xiāo yān] smoke of gunpowder

宵 [xiāo] (n)夜 night;evening * 他们打了一个通宵麻将。They played mah-jong throughout the whole night.

宵禁 [xiāo jìn] night curfew

宵小 [xiāo xiǎo] thief;bad hats

霄 [xiāo] 1 (n)云 clouds 2 (n)天空 sky * 山岭高入云霄。The mountain towers into the sky.

逍 [xiāo] (adj) 自由自在、无拘无束的样子。如：逍遥 at ease;free and unrestrained * 我紧张死了，他却一副逍遥自在的样子。I was very excited but he still looked free and unrestrained.

逍遥法外 [xiāo yáo fǎ wài] be at large (from law); not yet arrested

萧(蕭) [xiāo] (adj) 冷落 lonely; desolate * 荒山老树，景色萧索。The scene of a barren hill and an old tree is desolate enough.

萧瑟 [xiāo sè] bleak;dreary;gloomy

萧条 [xiāo tiáo] desolate;economic depression;slump

箫(簫) [xiāo] (n)一种管乐器 a flute

潇(瀟) [xiāo] (adj)水清而深 clear and deep(of water)

潇洒 [xiāo sǎ] elegant and unconventional

骁(驍) [xiāo] 1 (n) 好马 a good horse 2 (adj) 勇猛 brave

嚣(囂) [xiāo] (v)大声说话，吵闹 to shout and make a lot of noise * 他们不懂在叫嚣什么？What are they shouting for?

嚣张 [xiāo zhāng] unscrupulous and rampant

哮 [xiāo] (v) 吼,叫 roar;howl * 风在咆哮。The wind is howling.

枭(梟) [xiāo] 1 (n)鸟类，俗称「猫头鹰」。owl 2 (adj) 勇猛 valiant;brave

枭雄 [xiāo xióng] a powerful and aggressive man

xiáo

淆 [xiáo] (v)搞乱；混杂 confuse;mix up;jumble up * 不要混淆是非。Do not mix up the right and the wrong.

xiǎo

晓(曉) [xiǎo] 1 (n) 天刚亮 dawn;daybreak * 他们拂晓出发。They set out at dawn. 2 (v) 知道 know;understand * 他通晓英文。He knows English well.

晓得 [xiǎo·de] know;understand

小 [xiǎo] 1 (adv) 不大 small ; little * 他还是个小孩子，不懂得礼貌。He is still a small child and does not know about manners. 2 (adj)时间短 short in time * 我在他家小住几天。I stayed in his house for a few days.

小半 [xiǎobàn] less than a half

小便 [xiǎo biàn] urine;urinate

小产 [xiǎochǎn] premature birth ; abortion; miscarriage

小吃 [xiǎochī] snacks

小丑 [xiǎo chǒu] clown

小恩小惠 [xiǎo ēn xiǎo huì] paltry charity ; sops ; a small economic bait

小儿科 [xiǎo ér kē] division of pediatrics

小贩 [xiǎn fàn] hawker

小鬼 [xiǎo guǐ] little devils;little ones;kiddy

小孩儿 [xiǎo hái ér] child

小伙子 [xiǎo huǒ zi] young fellow; young man

小节 [xiǎo jié] minor points of conduct

小麦 [xiǎo mài] wheat

小米 [xiǎo mǐ] millet

小脑 [xiǎonǎo] cerebellum

小品文 [xiǎo pǐn wén] short essay; sketch

小器 [xiǎo qì] pettiness;mean;narrow-minded

小巧玲珑 [xiǎo qiǎo líng lóng] pretty;cleverly made;cute

小商品 [xiǎo shāng pǐn] small-scale commodity;petty commodities

小生产 [xiǎo shēng chǎn] small-scale production

小时 [xiǎo shí] hour

小数点 [xiǎo shù diǎn] decimal point

小说 [xiǎo shuō] novel;short story

小题大作 [xiǎo tí dà zuò] make a fuss about the trifling matter;make a mountain out of a mole-hill.

小偷 [xiǎo tōu] petty thief;pilferer

小巫见大巫 [xiǎo wū jiàn dà wū] pale into insignificance in comparison with

小写 [xiǎo xiě] small letter

小心 [xiǎo·xīn] take care;careful

小型 [xiǎo xìng] small type;small scale

小心翼翼 [xiǎo xīn yì yì] extremely careful

小学 [xiǎoxué] primary school; elementary school

小资产阶级 [xiǎo zī chǎn jiē jì] petty-bourgeoisie

小组 [xiǎo zǔ] team;section;group; division

xiào

肖 [xiào] (v) 像；相似 resemble;be like ＊孩子扮演的老人维妙维肖。The old man played by the child was excellent and vivid.

肖像 [xiào xiàng] portrait

校 [xiào] 1 (n) 学校；读书学习的地方或场所 school ; college ; academy 2 (n)军衔名，是将的下一级，尉的上一级 a colonel; a lieutenant

校规 [xiào guī] school regulations

校庆 [xiào qìng] school anniversary

校园 [xiào yuán] school campus

校长 [xiào zhǎng] head of a school principal

另见 [jiào]

效 [xiào] 1 (v) 摹仿 imitate;follow the example ＊这种勇于承认错误的德行值得效法 This spirit of readily admitting one's mistake is worth following 2 (v) 献出 contribute;work for ;serve the ends of ＊你怎么为这种自私自利的人效劳？Why do you work for this selfish person? 3 (n) 功用 effect ＊这药很有效。This medicine is very effective.

效果 [xiào guǒ] effect;result

效力 [xiào lì] efficacy;render one's service to

效率 [xiào lǜ] efficiency

效能 [xiào néng] efficacy;function; capacity

啸（嘯） [xiào] (v) 人或动物发出长而高的声音 a sharp and dragging sound made by man or animals

孝 [xìao] 1 (n)子女顺从及照顾父母的美德 filial piety 2 (adj) 居丧的 funeral ＊孝服 funeral costume

笑 [xìao]1 (v) 脸部露出快乐的表情，发出高兴的声音 laugh; grin ＊他哈哈大笑。He hee hawed. 2 (v) 讥讽 tease; ridicule; mock at; jeer ＊不要讥笑别人。 Do not tease others.

笑柄 [xiào bǐng] laughing-stalk
笑话 [xiào·huà] joke;laugh at
笑里藏刀 [xiào lǐ cáng dāo] murderous intent behind one's smile;cover the dagger with a smile.
笑脸 [xiào liǎn] smiling face
笑眯眯 [xiào mī mī] smiling
笑容 [xiào róng] a happy,smiling expression
笑嘻嘻 [xiàoxīxī] smile happily
笑逐颜开 [xiàozhùyánkāi] beam with smiles ; beaming ; covered with smiles

xiē

歇 [xīe] 1 (v)休息 rest＊我走得很累了，让我歇一会儿吧。 I am very tired after walking ; let me rest for a while. 2 (v)停止 stop＊工厂今天歇工。The factory stops work today.

歇后语 [xīehòuyǔ] a popular phrase with its latter part understood or not spoken
歇脚 [xiē jiǎo] stop for a rest after a walk.
歇斯底里 [xiē sī dǐ lǐ] hysteria
歇业 [xiē yè] stop business

些 [xiē] 1 (adj) 少许 some; few; a few ＊ 我要买些东西。I want to buy something. 2 (adv) 一点 a bit ＊走快些。walk faster. (walk fast a bit)

蝎 [xiē] (n)蛛形动物。有一对发达的钳状足，腹部长，有一尾刺，内有毒腺。捕食昆虫等，晒干可供药用 scorpion

xié

协（協）[xié]1 (adv) 共同 together ＊让我们同心协力搞好这个演出。Lot us work hard together to make this show a success. 2(v) 协助；帮助 help;assist ＊他协助我办理出国手续。He helps me deal with documentation for going abroad.

协定 [xié dìng] agreement;convention
协会 [xié huì] association;league
协商 [xiè shāng] consult and discuss with each other
协调 [xié tiáo] adjust to each other ; readjust;coordinate
协同 [xié tóng] work together;cooperate
协同一致 [xiètóngyīzhì] coordination ; concerted ; to bring into line ; combined
协同作战 [xiétóngzuòzhàn] combined action
协议 [xiè yì] agreement;understanding
协奏曲 [xié zòu qǔ] concerto

胁（脅） [xié] 1 (n)从腋下到肋骨尽处的部分 the ribs 2 (v) 逼迫；恐吓 threaten; intimidate ＊ 他威胁我们离开此地。 He threatens us to leave the place.

胁从 [xié cóng] person forced into wrong doing; those who are coerced into joining vice
胁迫 [xié pò] coerce; intimidate; force

偕 [xié] (adv) 一同，在一块 together;jointly

偕同 [xié tóng] accompany with; together with

谐(諧) [xié] 1 (adj) 协调；配合得适当 harmonious;agreeable ＊ 各民族人民和谐相处。People of various races live in harmony. 2 (adj) 滑稽 funny; ridiculous

挟(挾) [xié] 1 (v) 夹在胳臂底下 clamp under the arm ＊他挟着书走了过来。He comes forward with a book under his arm. 2 (v) 心里怀着 bear in one's heart ＊ 他挟恨报复。He bears the grudge to revenge. 3(v) 倚仗势力或抓住人的弱点强迫人 force somebody to submit;threaten ＊ 我撞死了富人的一条狗，那富人就要挟我赔他八百元。I knocked down a dog of a rich man who then forced me to pay him eight hundred dollars as compensation.

挟持 [xié chí] force to do one's bidding;force others to submit to one's will

携 [xié] (v) 带着 carry;bring;to take along with ＊ 他携眷回国。He brought his family back to his homeland.

携手 [xiéshǒu] hand in hand; side by side

邪 [xié] (adj) 不正当；不正派 evil; vicious;wicked;crooked ＊ 他要改邪归正 He wishes to return to the correct course from the past wrongful deeds.

邪路 [xiélù] immoral or illegal doing

邪气 [xiéqì] sinister trend;noxious influence of

斜 [xié] (adj)不正；歪 slanting; inclining;sloping;oblique

斜边 [xié biān] hypotenuse

斜面 [xié miàn] inclined plane

斜坡 [xié pō] slope

斜线 [xié xiàn] oblique line

xiě

写(寫) [xiě] 1 (v) 用笔在纸上或其他物体上作出文字 write ＊ 他正在写信。He is writing a letter. 2(v) 描绘；作画 sketch; draw; portray ＊ 他去户外写生。He went outdoor to sketch the landscape.

写实主义 [xiě shí zhǔ yì] realism

写作 [xiě zuò] essay-writing;write (essay,story,novel,etc)

xiè

懈 [xiè] 1 (adj) 不紧张；放松 relax; slacken;remit ＊ 我们要坚持不懈的学习。We must study unremittingly. 2 (n) 漏洞；破绽 loop-holes; weak point ＊ 他把事情办得很好，实在是无懈可击。He has managed the affair very well; there is really no weak spot for criticism.

懈怠 [xiè dài] slack;sluggish;idle

蟹 [xiè] (n) 甲壳动物。全身有甲壳。种类很多，可供食用的有螃蟹、梭子蟹等 crab

泄 [xiè] 1 (v) 从里面排出来 drain out;excrete ＊ 皮肤排泄汗液。The skin excretes sweat. 2 (v) 漏 let out;disclose;leak out ＊ 一定是有人泄密，敌人才会知道我们在那里。Somebody must have leaked out the secret;otherwise the enemy would not have known our whereabout. 3 (v) 发散 vent ＊ 他时常以打骂儿女来泄愤。He always vents his spite upon his kids.

泄露 [xiè lú] disclose;reveal

泄气 [xiè qì] lose one's spirit;disappointing

泄劲 [xiè jìn] lose one's confidence and relax one's efforts

屑 [xiè] 1 (n) 碎末 bits and pieces; fragments;scraps 2 (adj) 细小 minute;trifling;petty;trivial

泻(瀉) [xiè] 1 (v)很快地流 flow rapidly ✱河水奔腾，一泻千里。The river water surges forward and flows rapidly for thousands of miles. 2 (v)排泄 to drain out; to excrete

泻肚 [xiè dù] to have loose bowels

泻药 [xiè yào] a purgative;a laxative;a cathartic

泻盐 [xiè yán] Epsom salt

械 [xiè] 1 (n)机器；用具instrument; tools 2 (n)武器 arms;weapons

械斗 [xiè dǒu] fight with weapons

谢(謝) [xiè] 1 (v)表示感激 express gratitude; thank 2 (v)认错；道歉admit one's fault; apologise 3 (v)辞去；拒绝decline; refuse;reject ✱谢绝参观。No visitors are allowed. 4 (v)凋落；衰弱 wither;fade ✱花谢了。The flower has withered.

谢幕 [xièmù] (performers appear on stage) thank audience for curtain calls

谢意 [xiè yì] gratitude

亵(褻) [xiè] 1 (n)内衣 underwear 2 (adj)轻慢；不敬 behaving irreverently 3 (adj)淫秽 indecent;obscene;filthy

卸 [xiè] 1 (v) 把东西从车上、船上搬下来unload ✱码头工友正在卸货。The dock workers are unloading the goods. 2 (v) 拆开；拆除 dismantle;dismount ✱把机器上的零件卸下来。Dismantle the parts from the machine 3 (v)解脱get rid of;put off;shove off ✱他想推卸责任。He intends to shove off his duty.

卸任 [xiè rèn] to go off an official post;to resign

xīn

欣 [xīn] (adj)喜欢；高兴merry;happy;delightful;glad ✱听到这个消息后，大家欣喜若狂。Everybody goes wild with joy after hearing the news.

欣然 [xīn rán] happily;gladly;readily

欣赏 [xīn shǎng] take pleasure in; appreciate;enjoy

欣慰 [xīn wèi] pleased;satisfied

欣羡 [xīn xiàn] envy

欣欣向荣 [xīn xīn xiàng róng] thriving;flourishing

欣喜若狂 [xīn xǐ ruò kuáng] leap with joy; go wild with joy; rejoice

辛 [xīn] 1 (adj)辣 hot 2 (adj)劳苦 hard;toilsome ✱农人在田里辛勤的劳作。The farmers toil very hard in the field. 3 (adj)悲伤；痛苦sad ;bitter ✱他不愿谈起那辛酸的往事。He does not want to talk about the bitter sufferings he has had.

辛亥革命 [xīn hài gé mìng] the Revolution of 1911 in China

辛苦 [xīn kǔ] hard;exhausting with much toil;industrious

辛劳 [xīn láo] laborious;industrious ;painstaking

心 [xīn] 1 (n)人或动物体内推动血液循环的器官 heart 2 (n) 情绪；感情；意志emotion;feeling;mood ✱他心情不好。He is in a bad mood 3 (n) 事物的中间地位或重要部分 centre

心爱 [xīn ài] love;favour;hold...dear

心安理得 [xīn ān lǐ dé] have an easy conscience;one's conscience is void of offence;feel at ease

心不在焉 [xīn bù zài yān] absent-minded; preoccupied; with one's mind wandering

心肠 [xīn cháng] intention;heart; mood

心潮 [xīn cháo] state of mind;emotion

心潮澎湃 [xīn cháo pēng pài] be

full of excitement
心得 [xīn dé] personal insight;individual understanding or experience
心烦 [xīn fán] annoyed;vexed
心甘情愿 [xīn gān qíng yuàn] willingly;content oneself with
心怀鬼胎 [xīn huái guǐ tai] with misgivings in one's heart;have evil intention
心慌 [xīn huāng] mentally confused;nervous
心花怒放 [xīn huā nù fàng] one's heart bursts into bloom
心惊胆战 [xīn jīng dǎn zhán] be deeply alarmed;tremble with fright
心急如火 [xīn jí rú huǒ] with a confused and worried mind
心坎 [xīn kǎn] chest;bosom; the bottom of one's heart
心理 [xīn lǐ] psychology
心里 [xīn li] in one's heart;mind
心领神会 [xīn lǐng shén huì] appreciate thoroughly;understand fully
心乱如麻 [xīn luàn rú ma] mind confused like entangled hemp
心满意足 [xīn mǎn yì zú] satisfied ;satisfaction
心平气和 [xīn píng qì hé] be in a calm mood;in one's sober senses
心如刀割 [xīn rú dāo gē] heart-rending;agonising
心事 [xīn•shi] things that weigh on one's mind;worries in mind;cares
心思 [xīn•si] thinking;motive;mood
心疼 [xīn téng] love;be fond of;be reluctant to part with
心头 [xīn tóu] heart
心心相印 [xīn xīn xiāng yìn] a tacit understanding;alike in thoughts
心胸 [xīn xiōng] breadth of mind; ambition
心虚 [xīnxū] afraid of being found out; lack of confidence
心血 [xīn xuè] heart-felt labour; energy;effort
心血来潮 [xīn xuè lái cháo] suddenly hit upon an idea
心意 [xīn yì] intention; purpose;
心脏 [xīn zàng] heart

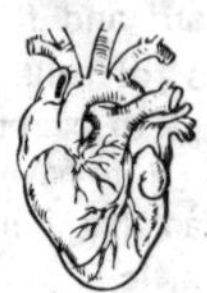

心直口快 [xīn zhí kǒu kuài] open hearted and out-spoken
心中有数 [xīn zhōng yǒu shù] understand the situation;be concerned and know what to do next

新 [xīn] (adj) 刚出现的;刚经验到的;现行的; 最近的 new; fresh; recent ; modern 新年快乐! Happy New Year! 2 (v) 更新;改掉旧的 to change from the old to the new ✱他决定改过自新 。He decided to turn over a new leaf.3 (adv)刚;才 just ✱我是新来的。 I am a new comer. 4 (adj) 经历较短的 inexperienced ✱他是一名新手。He is a greenhorn (a new- hand). 5 (adj)相识不久的 known recently
新陈代谢 [xīn chén dài xiè] the transition from the old order of things to the new;metabolism; the new displacing the old;the old being superseded by the new
新纪元 [xīn jì yuán] new epoch; new era
新年 [xīn nián] New Year
新奇 [xīn qí] interesting; novel; strange;surprising
新生 [xīn shēng] new born (e.g. force,things);new students
新式 [xīn shì] new type; modern type;new style
新闻 [xīn wén] press;news
新闻公报 [xīn wén gōng bào] press communique
新鲜 [xīn xiān] fresh

新兴 [xīn xīng] newly rising;newly emerging;newly established;new-born

新型 [xīn xíng] new type;new pattern

新颖 [xīn yǐng] novel (e.g. ideas); new

新殖民主义 [xīn zhí mín zhǔ yì] neo-colonialism

薪 [xīn] 1 (n) 柴火 firewood 2 (n) 工资 wage;salary;pay

薪俸 [xīn fèng] salary

薪水 [xīn shuǐ] salary

馨 [xīn] (n) 很远闻到的香气 fragrant odour;sweet

xìn

衅(釁) [xìn] 1 (v)古代祭神时用牲畜的血涂钟鼓等祭器的缝隙 to smear the cracks of sacrificial instruments such as bells and drums with animal blood (in ancient worship) 2(n) 缺陷；破绽 defect; flaw 3 (n) 争端 cause of a quarrel; subject of dispute

芯 [xìn] (n)指物体的中心部分 the central part of an object

信 [xìn] 1 (adj) 诚实；不欺骗 honest;sincere *他很守信。He keeps to his promise. 2 (v) 相信；不怀疑 believe;trust *我们相信他的话。We believe in what he said. 3 (v) 信仰 believe in a religion;worssip *他信仰基督教。He believes in Christianity. 4 (n) 消息 news;information *有人向敌人通风报信。Somebody has disclosed the information to the enemy. 5 (n) 书函letter *我收到你的信了。I have received your letter. 6 (adv)随便 at discretion: at ease

信封 [xìn fēng] envelope

信服 [xìn fú] believed and be convinced

信号 [xìn hào] signal

信件 [xìn jiàn] letters and other printed matters

信赖 [xìn lài] trust;rely on

信念 [xìn niàn] faith;belief;creed

信任 [xìn rèn] trust;place confidence in;have confidence in

信徒 [xìn tú] disciple;follower;adherent

信托 [xìn tuō] trust;entrust

信息 [xìnxī] letter; news

信箱 [xìn xiāng] post box; letter box

信心 [xìn xīn] confidence;conviction ;belief

信义 [xìn yì] faith;honesty

信用 [xìn yòng] trustworthiness; credit

信纸 [xìnzhǐ] letter paper

xīng

星 [xīng] 1 (n)天空中发光的或反射光的天体，如太阳、地球、北斗星等。通常指在夜间闪闪发光的天体planet;celestial body;star 2(n)细小的东西 minute things

星罗棋布 [xīng luó qí bù] scattered about like the pieces on a chessboard;dotted around like stars in the sky;scattered about in every direction

星期 [xīng qī] week

星星之火，可以燎原 [xīng xīng zhī huǒ kě yǐ liáo yuán] a single spark can start a prairie fire

猩 [xīng] (n)猩猩，猿类，哺乳动物。体大，额部突出，耳壳小，前肢长，能在地上直立行走 chimpanzee

猩红 [xīng hóng] red like the blood of chimpanzee; scarlet

猩红热 [xīng hóng rè] scarlet fever

惺 [xīng] (adj)清醒；聪明 intelligent

惺松 [xīng sōng] flickering (of eyes when one just wakes up)

惺惺作态 [xīng xīng zuò tài] hypocritical

腥 [xīng] 1 (n) 生肉 flesh 2 (adj) 鱼|臭 fishy

腥臭 [xīng chòu] rancid; rank; stinking (of smell)

兴(興) [xīng] (v) 发动；举办；提倡；开始 launch; found ; promote; start ＊ 政府准备兴建一座桥梁。The government plans to build a bridge.

另见 [xìng]

兴办 [xīng bàn] establish;build

兴奋 [xīng fèn] excited;elated

兴风作浪 [xīng fèng zuò làng] stir up trouble;incite and create trouble

兴建 [xīnjiàn] build

兴起 [xīn qǐ] spring up;rise in prominence

兴盛 [xīngshèng]prosperous;flourishing

兴师动众 [xīngshī dòngzhòng] mobilise a lot of people to do something

兴亡 [xīng wáng] the rise and fall

兴旺 [xīng wàng] be vigorous and flourishing

xíng

刑 [xíng] (n) 对犯人实行各种处罚的总称 punishment imposed on convicts ＊他被判五年徒刑。 He was sentenced to five years imprisonment.

刑罚 [xíng fá] punishment

刑事 [xíng shì] matters pertaining to crimes and laws (e.g. criminal case,criminal code)

刑事犯 [xíng shì fàn] criminal

刑事法庭 [xíng shì fǎ tíng] criminal court

形 [xíng] 1(n) 样子，状态 appearance ; shape 2 (v) 显露；表现 show; appear ＊ 他喜形於色。Happiness is shown on his face. 3 (v) 比较；对照 compare ; contrast

形成 [xíng chéng] take shape;become;form

形而上学 [xíng ér shàng xué] metaphysics

形迹可疑 [xíng jī kě yí] suspicious behaviour or conduct

形容 [xíng róng] describe;express by words or looks;modify

形容词 [xíng róng cí] adjective

形式 [xíng shì] pattern;form

形势 [xíng shì] geographical outlay ;situation; conditions; circumstances

形势逼人 [xíng shì bī rén] reality is a compressing force; the situation is pressing

形态 [xíng tài] shape ; form ; outlook

形象 [xíng xiáng] image;figure; form

形形色色 [xíng xíng sè sè] of all shades; of various forms; of all kinds

形影不离 [xíng yíng bù lí] (two people) inseparable; follow each other like form and shadow

形状 [xíng zhùang] shape;form

型 [xíng] 1 (n) 模子 mould 2 (n)样式 type;pattern; model

行 [xíng] 1 (v)走 walk;go 2 (v)传布；流通 distribute;circulate ＊ 中央银行将发行新的硬币。The Central Bank will put the new coins into circulation. 3 (v)做、办 act;conduct;practise ＊ 他们正在进行一项调查。They are conducting the survey. 4 (adj) 能干 able;competent ＊老陈，你真行。 Tan, you are marvellous. 5 (adj) 可以 all right;(that) will do ＊行，就这样办吧。All right, we shall do it

this way 6 (adv) 不久 soon; before long ＊ 那个老狐狸行将就木了。 That cunning old man is going to die soon.
另见 [háng] [xìng]

行程 [xíng cheng] route or distance of travel;itinerary

行刺 [xíng cì] to assasinate (an important person)

行动 [xíng dong] walk;go;move;act; do;deed;action;operation

行贿 [xíng huì] bribe

行径 [xíng jìng] action;conduct;behaviour

行军 [xíngjūn] march

行李 [xínglǐ] baggage; luggage;

行人 [xíng rén] pedestrian

行驶 [xíng shǐ] sail;drive

行使 [xíng shǐ] exercise;carry out; perform

行尸走肉 [xíng shī zǒu ròu] a walking corpse;a person without a soul

行为 [xíngwéi] action; behaviour; conduct; deed

行星 [xíng xīng] planet

行凶 [xíng xiōng] commit assault or murder

行政 [xíng zhèng] administration

行装 [xíng zhuāng] clothes and bedding needed for travel

行踪 [xíng zōng] person's whereabouts

xǐng

省 [xǐng] 1 (v) 检查 to examine ＊ 我们要常常反省。 We must always examine our own conduct. 2 (v) 知道 know ＊他跌下去后，就不省人事了。 He became unconscious after falling onto the floor. 3 (v) 探望 visit ＊他回中国省亲。He went to China to visit his relatives.
另见 [shěng]

省悟 [xǐng wù] come to realize; awaken

省视 [xǐng shì] visit;pay a visit

醒 [xǐng] 1 (v) 从睡眠、酒醉或昏迷状态中恢复知觉，也指还没有睡着awake ; sober 2 (v) 觉悟 awaken; come to realize ＊ 他的话提醒了我。 His words have reminded me.

醒目 [xǐng mù] refreshing to the eye;attractive looking;attract attention

醒悟 [xǐng wù] come to realize;awaken

xìng

幸 [xìng] 1 (n)(adj) 快乐；好运 happy; furtune; ;happiness 2 (v) 认为幸福而高兴 feel happy;feel fortunate ＊ 他庆幸自己在这次意外中没有受伤。He felt fortunate that he was not injured in the accident. 3 (adv) 意外地得到成功或免除困难 fortunately;luckily ＊幸亏在我们动身前雨停了。 Fortunately the rain stopped before we started. 4 (v) 希望 hope ＊ 幸勿推却。I hope you will not refuse.

幸好 [xìng hǎo] luckily;fortunately

幸免 [xìng miǎn] escape through good luck;narrow escape

幸运 [xìng yùn] lucky

幸灾乐祸 [xìng zāi lè hùo] gloat over disaster of others;take pleasure in the calamity of others; be glad when other people are in difficulties

悻 [xìng 〔 悻悻〕[xìng xìng] (adv) 不满、怨恨的样子 resentfully ＊他听了之后 悻悻而去。 He walked off resentfully after hearing it.

性 [xìng 1 (n) 人或事物所具有的特质、能力、作用等 property; characteristic;nature;quality ＊铁的化学性质 the chemical properties of iron 2 (n) 脾气 nature;temperament; character ＊ 他们姐妹俩的个性完全不一样。The two sisters have completely different personalities.

3 (n) 男女或雌雄的分别 sex

性病 [xìng bìng] venereal disease

性格 [xìng gé] character;temperament;quality;nature

性急 [xìng jí] impatient;quick-tempered

性命 [xìng mìng] life

性能 [xìng néng] properties;function;performance;working capacity

性情 [xìng·qing] temperament;character;nature

性器官 [xìng qì guān] sex organ

性质 [xìng zhì] properties;essence;character;nature;quality

性状 [xìngzhùang] nature and appearance; characteristics

姓 [xìng] (n) 表明家族系统的名 surname;family name ＊他姓王。His surname is Wang.

杏 [xìng] (n) 落叶乔木果实叫“杏子”，种子叫“杏仁”可供食用和药用 apricot

杏黄 [xìnghúang] apricot yellow

兴(興) [xìng] (n) 对事物感觉喜爱的情绪 interest ＊我对下棋不感兴趣。I have no interest in playing chess.
另见 [xīng]

兴高采烈 [xìng gāo cǎi lié] exhilaration;in high spirits;jubilant

兴亡 [xìng wáng] rise and fall of a nation

兴旺 [xìngwàng] prosper ; flourish; to be getting on very well

兴味 [xìngwèi] keen interest

兴味索然 [xìng wèi sūo rán] uninteresting

兴致 [xìng zhì] interest;mood

兴致勃勃 [xìng zhì bó bó] in high spirits

xīong

凶 [xīong] 1 (adj)不吉的unfortunate ;bad;evil; calamitous 2 (adj)残暴，恶 cruel;savage; fierce;ferocious ＊虎豹都是凶猛的野兽。The tiger and leopard are fierce beasts. 3 (adv) 利害 furiously; to the extreme ＊他们两个吵得很凶。 The two men quarrelled furiously.

凶暴 [xīong bào] cruel;brutal

凶残 [xiōngcán] ferocious ; brutal ; ruthless; savage

凶多吉少 [xīong duo jí shǎo] more misfortune;less blessings

凶恶 [xīong è] ferocious; cruel; vicious;brutal

凶耗 [xīonghào] bad tidings

凶狠 [xīong hěn] brutal;cruel

凶器 [xīong qì] the weapon used for killing or wounding a person

凶猛 [xiōngměng] ferocious; fierce

凶险 [xīong xiǎn] extremely hazardous;dangerous

凶相毕露 [xīong xiàng bì lù] reveal the atrocious features;bare one's fangs

汹 [xiōng] 1 (n) 水的声势。the rush of water 2 (n) 人众鼓噪的情形 excitement; clamour; uproar

汹汹 [xīong xīong] ferociously ; clamourously

汹涌 [xīongyǒng] tempestuous;surging

胸 [xīong] 1 (n) 身体前面，颈项与腹部之间的部分chest;thorax 2 (n) 指心里（跟思想、见识、气量等有关）mind;outlook;heart ＊他心胸狭窄。He is narrow-minded.

胸怀 [xīong huái] mind; outlook; cherish;show concern

胸怀祖国 [xīong huái zǔ guó] keep the interests of the country at heart;have one's motherland at heart

胸襟 [xīong jīn] breadth of mind; breadth of vision

胸有成竹 [xīong yǒu chéng zhú] have a preconceived idea before doing something

兄 [xīong] 1 (n) 哥哥 elder brother 2 (n) 对年岁差不多的人的尊称 a polite address to persons almost of the same age ✱ 老兄，你好吗？Dear friend,how do you do?

兄弟国家 [xīong dì guó jiā] fraternal countries;countries on friendly terms with each other

xíong

雄 [xíong] 1 (adj) 阳性的；牡的 male 2 (n) 强有力的人 a strong and powerful person ✱英雄 a hero 3 (adj) 宏伟，充足，有气魄的 grand;majestic;tremendous;magnificent;splendid ✱ 雄伟的五十层银行大厦座落于市中心。The magnificent 50-story bank building is situated at the centre of the city.

雄辩 [xíong biàn] persuasive argument;eloquent;incontrovertibly

雄才大略 [xíong cái dà lüè] a man with clever strategy

雄厚 [xíong hòu] tremendous;solid

雄赳赳 [xíong jiū jiū] strong;strong and valiant

雄心壮志 [xíong xīn zhuàng zhì] lofty aspirations and high aims;a high aspiring mind

雄鹰 [xíong yīng] strong and brave eagle

雄壮 [xíong zhuàng] full of grandeur;stalwart;magnificent; majestic

熊 [xíong] (n) 兽名。种类很多、能用两只后脚直立而行走，也能爬树bear

熊貓 [xíong māo] panda

熊熊 [xíong xíong] flaming;raging (of fire)

熊掌 [xíong zhǎng] a bear's paw

xiū

休 [xiū] 1 (v) 歇息 rest;retire ✱ 他今天休假。He is on leave today. 2 (v) 停止stop;cease;give up ✱ 他们一直争论不休。They argue unceasingly . 3 (adv) 不必；不要 do not think;never expect ✱ 你休想逃脱。Don't you try to escape.

休会 [xiū huì] adjourn (meeting); stand adjourned;recess

休戚相关 [xiū qī xiāng guān] be of close concern to each other

休息 [xiū xi] rest;relax;repose

休养 [xiū yǎng] rest;recuperate; convalesce ; rehabilitation

休战 [xiū zhàn] ceasefire;armistice

休止 [xiū zhǐ] stop;cease

羞 [xiū] 1 (v)感到耻辱 feel ashamed ✱ 我羞与他为伍。I feel ashamed to be in his company. 2 (n) 耻 shame 3 (adj) 难为情，害臊 shy; bashful ✱ 他羞得满脸通红。 He feels so shy that his face blushes.

羞答答 [xiū dā dā] bashful;shy;timid

羞愧 [xiū kuì] feel ashamed;shame; disgrace

羞怯 [xiū qiè] bashful and nervous

羞辱 [xiū rǔ] insult;disgrace;cause shame

修 [xiū] 1 (v) 使完整，使损坏的东西恢复原来的形状或作用 mend;repair ✱ 他在修理脚车。He is repairing the bicycle. 2 (v) 建造 build; erect ✱ 工人正在修建铁路。The workers are building a railway-track. 3 (v) 编；写 edit;write 4 (v) 学习study ✱ 他的学问全靠自修而来。 His knowledge is acquired completely through self-study. 5 (v) 剪或削；使整齐 cut even; trim ✱ 他在修指甲。He is clipping his nails. 6 (v) 改正；重订 revise ; amend;modify;correct ✱ 他们准备修改章程。They are prepared to amend constitution.

修补 [xiū bǔ] mend

修辞 [xiū cí] rhetoric;the skill of using words effectively

修订 [xiū dìng] revise;re-edit

修饰 [xiū shì] make up;beautify;decorate

修养 [xiū yǎng] learning or skill of art and literature;cultivate

修造 [xiū zào] build;construct

修整 [xiū zhěng] keep in good condition; cut even; level (e.g. ground)

修正 [xiū zhèng] revise;amend;correct

修正主义 [xiū zhèng zhǔ yì] revisionism

xiǔ

朽 [xiǔ] 1 (adj)腐烂 rotten;decayed 2 (v)磨灭；消散 wear out;be defaced;be effaced ＊永垂不朽。imperishable

朽木不可雕 [xiǔ mù bù kě diāo] decayed wood cannot be carved — a useless man

宿 [xiǔ] (n) 夜 night＊我在那儿住了一宿。I stayed there for one night.
另见 [sù] [xiù]

xiù

臭 [xiù] (n)气味 odour ＊空气是无色无臭的流体。Air is a colourless and odourless fluid.
另见 [chòu]

嗅 [xiù] (v)用鼻子辨别气味，闻 smell;sniff ＊嗅嗅看，这是什么。Just smell it,see what it is.

嗅觉 [xiù jué] sense of smell

秀 [xiù] 1 (adj)美丽 beautiful ＊那里山明水秀。The mountains there were clear, and the water exquisite. 2 (adj) 优异 outstanding; excellent

秀才 [xiù cái] a graduate from the old examination system

秀丽 [xiù lì] delicate;graceful;beautiful (of landscape)

秀气 [xiù·qi] refined;delicate;elegant;exquisite

绣(綉) [xiù] (v) 用彩色的线在绸或布上刺成花纹、图像或文字 embroider ＊她在枕头套上绣花。She embroidered some flowers on the pillow case.

锈(銹) [xiù] (n) 金属表面所生的氧化物 rust

袖 [xiù] 1 (n)衣袖 sleeve ＊这袖子太长了。The sleeve is too long. 2 (v)藏入袖内 to hide inside the sleeve

袖手旁观 [xiù shǒu páng guān] look on with folded arms;stand by with indifference

袖章 [xiù zhāng] armband;insignia

袖珍 [xiù zhēn] pocket(edition); small-format (edition);pocketsized

宿 [xiù] (n) 星座 constellation
另见 [sù] [xiǔ]

xū

吁 [xū] 1 (v) 叹气 sigh ＊老人家不知为什么长吁短叹？Why is the old man sighing? 2 (inter)叹词。表示惊奇 interjection to show surprise
另见 [yù]

虚 [xū] 1 (adj)空 empty;vacant ＊敌人乘虚而入。The enemy seizes the opportunity to step in. 2(adj)假;不真实 false;sham;fictitious ＊这个人很虚伪。This person is a hypocrite. 3 (adj) 忧虑；恐惧 apprehensive ＊做贼心虚。An evildoer is always apprehensive. 4 (adj) 衰弱 weak;feeble ＊她身体虚弱。She is weak in health. 5 (adj) 不自满；不骄傲 modest; humble ＊他很谦虚。He is modest.

虚报 [xū bào] give a false report

虚词 [xūcí] grammatical particle; functional word and form word
虚构 [xū gòu] imagine;fabricate
虚假 [xūjiǎ] false; sham; unreal; fictitions
虚惊 [xūjīng] cause a false alarm; get alarmed for nothing
虚名 [xū míng] a reputation without the facts to support it;undeserved reputation;unwarranted reputation
虚荣 [xū róng] vanity;vain glory
虚设 [xū shè] nominal ;in name; symbolic;titular
虚实 [xū shí] hollow and solid;truth and deceit
虚数 [xū shú] imaginary number;imaginary quantity
虚脱 [xūtùo] physical collapse from general debility
虚无飘渺 [xū wú piāo miào] utterly visionary; with no reality; whatever vague with nothing in it; nothing to hold on.
虚无主义 [xū wú zhǔ yì] nihilism
虚线 [xū xìan] dotted line
虚心 [xū xīn] modest;ready to take advice;open-minded
虚有其表 [xūyǒuqìbiǎo] a mere form or appearance
虚张声势 [xū zhāng shēng shì] make pompous but empty show of (power and influence)

墟 [xū] 1 (n)土丘 a mound 2(n) 集市 a market; a bazaar ＊ 村民们在赶墟。 The villagers are rushing to the market place.

嘘 [xū] (v) 慢慢地吐气，呵气 breathe;puff
嘘寒问暖 [xū hán wèn nuǎn] show great concern in the livelihood of others

须(須) [xū] 1 (v) 应当；必要 ought;should; must;have to ＊ 你必须准时到达学校。 You must reach shool in time. 2 (v) 等待 wait
須要 [xū yào] must; absolutely necessary
須知 [xū zhī] take note;necessary to be known

须(鬚) [xū] 面毛；胡子 beard
须根 [xūgēn] rootlets
须眉 [xūméi] beard and eyebrows —a man

需 [xū] 1 (v) 要求 need;want ＊你需要钱吗？Do you need any money? 2 (n) 用品 necessity;need ;requirement
需求 [xū qíu] demand
需要 [xū yāo] nced

xú

徐 [xú] (adv)慢慢地 slowly;gradually ＊ 幕徐徐而下。 The screen moved down gradually.

xǔ

许(許) [xǔ] 1 (v)同意;答应 agree; approve;permit ＊允许我说几句话。 Allow me to say a few words. 2 (v)称赞 praise ＊他的善举获得了许多人的嘉许。His generous act receives many praises. 3 (adv) 或者；可能 may be;perhaps ＊ 他也许不来开会。 He may not come for the meeting. 4 (part) 约莫；大概 about ＊只要加少许糖就够了。To add a little sugar is enough. 5 (part) 很 very 6 (part) 多 more; excess; surplus ＊三十许 thirty odd; over thirty
许多 [xǔ duō] a great many;a lot of;numerous;plenty of
许久 [xǔ jiǔ] a long time; such a long time
许可 [xǔ kě] permit;consent;approval
许可证 [xǔ kě zhèng] permit;pass

许诺 [xǔ nuò] promise; give one's consent
许愿 [xǔ yuán] make promise
栩 [xǔ] (n) 一种橡树 a species of oak
栩栩 [xǔxǔ] lively; happily
诩 [xǔ (v) 说大话，夸耀 boast * 他自诩为天才。He boasts that he is a genius.

xù

序 [xù] 1 (n) 顺次 order;sequence * 名字是按字母次序排列。The names are arranged in alphabetical order. 2 (n) 引言 introduction; foreword
序幕 [xù mù] prologue;prelude
序曲 [xùqǔ] prelude; overture
序数 [xùshù] ordinal number
恤 [xù] 1 (v) 怜悯；同情 pity; sympathize with * 我们要多体恤他老人家。We should sympathize more with the old man. 2(v) 救济 relieve;give alms to
畜 [xù] (v) 饲养禽兽 rear animals; breed livestocks
另见 [chù]
蓄 [xù] 1 (v) 积聚；储藏 accumulate; store up;save * 他储蓄了五千元。He has saved five thousand dollars. 2(v) 保存 store up * 运动员正在养精蓄锐。The sportsmen are building up their strength. 3 (v) 心里藏着 harbour * 他蓄谋已久。He has harboured the conspiracy for a long time.
蓄电池 [xù diàn chī] storage battery;accumulator;storage cell
蓄谋 [xùmóu] conceive a plot in secret ; harbour a long-intended conspiracy
蓄水池 [xù shuǐ chí] reservoir
蓄意 [xù yì] be calculated;deliberate
叙 [xù] 1(v) 谈话 chat;talk * 他们在叙旧 They are talking over old times. 2 (v) 叙述；述说 narrate; describe * 他在叙述一个实验的过程。He is narrating the process of an experiment.
叙别会 [xù bié huì] farewell party
叙事诗 [xù shì shī] an epic; a narrative poem
叙说 [xù shuō] narrate; relate; account
煦 [xù] (adj) 温暖 warm
续(續) [xù] (v) 接下去；连接 continue; connect; keep on;follow 他继续订阅新闻周报。He continued the subscription to the Newsweek.
续稿 [xù gǎo] next (remaining) manuscripts
续假 [xù jià] to extend leave
续弦 [xù xián] to rejoin the guitar string— to marry a second wife after the death of the first
续约 [xù yuē] to continue a contract
酗 [xù] (v) 喝醉 to get drunk * 他常酗酒滋事。He often gets drunk and becomes disorderly.
旭 [xù] (n) 太阳出来时光明的样子 dawn
旭日 [xùrì] the morning sun; the rising sun
绪(緒) [xù] 1 (n) 丝线的头尾 the end of a ball of silk or thread 2 (n) 事物的开头 the beginning * 事情千头万绪，不知从何做起。The matter is so complicated that I do not know where to start. 3 (n) 思路 thread of thoughts or emotion * 她的情绪很容易波动。Her emotion varies easily.
绪论 [xù lùn] introduction;preliminary remarks;preface
絮 [xù] 1(n) 粗棉 cotton 2(n) 绵柔而飘扬的花 catkins 3 (adj) 话多；罗嗦 talkative;naggy
絮叨 [xù·dào] unending and tedious talk; chatter

絮烦 [xù fán] getting fed up of repeated talks

絮絮不休 [xù xú bù xiū]nagging non-stop

婿 [xù] 1 (n) 女婿，女儿的丈夫 son-in-law ✱ 她的女婿在华校教书。His son-in-law is teaching in a Chinese school. 2(n) 夫婿，丈夫 husband

xuān

宣 [xuān] (v)公开发表；传扬开去 proclaim;announce;make known; publish; declare; publicise; propagate ✱ 我们应该大力宣扬好人好事。We must publicise earnestly about good personalities and good deeds.

宣布 [xuān bù]declare;announce; proclaim

宣称 [xuān chēng]make known;declare;announce

宣传 [xuān chuán] propagate;advertise;publicize;propaganda

宣读 [xuān dú] read out

宣告 [xuān gào] proclaim;declare; make an arrangement

宣判 [xuān pàn] give decision in a state;pass sentence;pass judgement

宣誓 [xuān shì]swear; take an oath

宣泄 [xuānxiè] to drain; to leak away; to divulge

宣言 [xuān yán] declaration;manifesto

宣扬 [xuānyáng] advocate; advertise; praise; play up

宣战 [xuān zhàn] declaration of war

喧 [xuān] (v) 大声说话，闹 talk loudly;clamour ✱ 请勿喧哗。Please do not talk loudly.

喧宾夺主 [xuānbìnduózhǔ] (lit) the guest takes precedence over the host; (fig.) minor takes precedence over a major issue

喧嚷 [xuān rǎng]shouting (many people)

喧嚣 [xuān xiāo] clamour;disturbingly noisy;bluster

暄 [xuān] (adj) 温暖 warm

萱 [xuān] (n) 多年生草，晒干称金针菜。 a day lily

轩(軒) [xuān] 1(n)古代一种有围棚的车 a kind of carriage with curtain (in ancient China) 2 (n) 有窗的长廊或小屋 a porch;a balcony;a small house

轩昂 [xuān áng] high-spirited; grand;dignified

轩然大波 [xuān rán dà bō] a massive dispute;a serious quarrel

xuán

旋 [xuán] 1 (v) 转动 rotate;revolve; spin ✱ 行星绕太阳旋转。The planets revolve round the sun. 2 (v) 归来 return ✱ 军队凯旋归来。The troops return in triumph. 3 (adj)不久；很快地 within some time;soon ✱ 入场券旋即卖完。The admission tickets were sold out soon.

旋风 [xuánfēng] whirlwind

旋律 [xuán lǜ] melody; rhythm; tunefulness

旋涡 [xuán wō] a whirlpool;an eddy;vortex

另见 [xuàn]

漩 [xuán] (n)旋转的水流，如：漩涡 whirlpool;eddy

玄 [xuán] 1 (adj) 黑色 black;dark 2 (adj) 深奥不易理解的 profound; miraculous;mysterious;occult ✱ 哲学并不玄虚。Philosophy is not mysterious or occult. 3 (adj) 虚伪的，不可信的 false

玄化 [xuán huà] incorporeal

玄虚 [xuán xu] deceitful means to confuse others so as to cover up the truth

悬(懸) [xuán] 1(v)挂 hang;suspend ＊罢工工人在厂外悬挂布条和标语。The workers on strike hang up banners and placards outside the factory. 2 (adj)没有结果 pending;unsettled 3 (adj)相差很远 differing widely ＊他们二人的地位悬殊。There is a wide disparity in the social status of the two persons.

悬案 [xuánàn] a pending question

悬挂 [xuánguà] hang

悬梁 [xuán liáng] to commit suicide by hanging oneself

悬赏 [xuán shǎng] offer a reward; promise a reward

悬崖 [xuán yá] cliff;precipice

悬崖勒马 [xuān yá lè mǎ] ward off disaster at the critical moment; stop in time

悬崖峭壁 [xuán yá qiào bì] high and steep cliff

悬殊 [xuánshú]disparity; unevenness; great difference between; poles apart; distant

xuǎn

烜 [xuǎn] (adj)盛大 grand ＊ 这个军官曾经烜赫一时。This army official had been grand and powerful for some time.

癣(癬) [xuǎn] (n) 一种传染性皮肤病，患处发痒 ringworm

选(選) [xuǎn] (v) 挑；拣 select;choose ＊ 他被选为代表。 He was chosen as a representative.

选拔 [xuǎn bá] select;choose;recommend

选购 [xuǎngòu] selective purchasing

选辑 [xuǎn jí] compile;edit

选举 [xuǎnjǔ] to elect; election

选举权 [xuǎn jǔ quán]the right to vote (elect)

选派 [xuǎn pài]select and appoint

选票 [xuan piào] ballot paper;ballot

选手 [xuǎn shǒu] player (of sport, contest);contestant;competitor

选修 [xuǎn xīu] take an optional subject

选择 [xuǎn zé]pick and choose; make the choice;make one's preference

选种 [xuǎn zhǒng]seed selection

xuàn

炫 [xuàn] 1(v)照耀 dazzle 2(v)夸耀 make a show; brag ＊他自炫其能。 He brags about his own capabilities

炫耀 [xuàn yào] make a display; show off;boast;cut a dash

眩 [xuàn] 1(adj) 眼花 dizzy ＊孩子转圆圈转得头晕目眩。 The child feels dizzy after making many circular turns. 2 (adj) 迷乱 confused;possessed ＊他眩于名利。 He is possessed by fame and wealth.

眩惑 [xuàn huò] be at a loss; be perplexed (puzzled)

券 [xuàn] (n) 门窗、桥梁等建筑成弧形的部分 arch of buildings or bridges
另见 [quàn]

旋(鏇) [xuàn] 1(adj) 打转的 rotary 2(v) 用车床转动 to turn in a lathe
另见 [xuán]

绚(絢) [xuàn] (adj)有文彩 brilliant in colours ＊姑娘们穿着绚丽的民族服装。 Young girls are wearing their colourful national costumes.

绚丽 [xuànlì] brilliant with colours

绚烂 [xuàn làn] flashing;brilliant with lighting and colours

渲 [xuàn] (v) 把水墨淋在纸上 to splash black ink on a paper

渲染 [xuàn rǎn] play up ; exaggerate;add (touches) of colour

xuē

削 [xuē] (v) 刮；夺除 cut; shave; scrape off
另见 [xiāo]
削减 [xuē jiǎn] cut down;reduce
削弱 [xuē ruò] weaken;impair;curtail
削足适履 [xuē zú shì lǚ] cut the feet to fit the shoes—to do a senseless thing

靴 [xuē] (n) 连胫部包裹着的鞋 boots

xué

学(學) [xué] 1 (v) 受教；研究 learn, study ＊我在学华文。I am learning Chinese. 2 (n) 受教的所在 school ＊小学 primary school; 中学 secondary school; 大学 university 3(n) 研究的科目 subject of study; branch of learning ＊经济学 economics; 政治学 politics; 文学 literature; 化学 chemistry; 物理学 physics; 科学 science 4 (n) 知识 knowledge; learning ＊他博学多才。He is learned and capable. 5 (v) 模仿 imitate ＊弟弟学老人走路的样子。My younger brother imitates the gait of an old man.
学潮 [xué cháo] tide of student movement
学费 [xué fèi] school fees;tuition
学府 [xué fǔ] institute;college;university
学会 [xué huì] society
学籍 [xué jí] record of registration as qualifications for study in schools or colleges
学科 [xuékē] subject of study
学历 [xué lì] record of schooling
学龄 [xué líng] schooling age
学年 [xué nián] academic year
学派 [xué pài] school of thought; schools
学期 [xué qī] semester;academic term
学生 [xué·sheng] student;pupil
学识 [xué shí] knowledge;learning
学术 [xué shù] academic knowledge
学说 [xué shuō] theory;teachings; doctrine
学徒 [xué tú] apprentice
学位 [xué wèi] academic degree
学问 [xué·wèn] learning, knowledge
学校 [xuéxiào] school
学业 [xué yè] studies;lessons and school assignments
学以致用 [xué yǐ zhì yòng] put to use whatever one has studied
学员 [xué yuán] trainee;participant of training course or institution as different from regular student
学院 [xué yuàn] academy;institute; college
学者 [xué zhě] scholar
学制 [xué zhì] educational system; school system;arrangements for schooling

xuě

穴 [xué] 1 (n) 洞；窟窿 hole;cave; den 2(n) 针灸的部位 acupuncture points on human body 3 (n) 坟墓 grave

噱 [xué] (v) 笑 laugh ＊丑角的动作令人发噱。The actions of the clown make you laugh.
另见 [jué]

雪 [xuě] 1 (n) 在寒带气温低于摄氏零度时，云中水蒸气直接凝成白色晶体（主要是六角形），成团地飘下来，就是雪 snow 2(v)洗刷；除去 clean;wipe away;avenge ＊他发誓要雪耻。He swore to avenge the insult.
雪白 [xuě bái] snow-white
雪花 [xuě huā] snow-flakes

雪茄 [xuě jiā] cigar

雪亮 [xuě liàng] bright as snow
雪橇 [xuě qiāo] sledge
雪人 [xuě rén] snowman
雪冤 [xuě yuān] to clear a person from a false charge
雪中送炭 [xuě zhōng sòng tàn] to send fuel in cold weather—timely assistance

xuè

血 [xuè] (n) 人和其他高等动物的血管和心脏里流动的红色液体 blood
血管 [xuè guǎn] blood vessels; arteries and veins
血海深仇 [xuè hǎi shēn chóu] huge debt in blood; immense and deep-seated hatred
血汗 [xuè hàn] blood and sweat—the hardest toil
血迹 [xuè jī]bloodstain
血浆 [xuèjiǎng] plasma
血库 [xuèkù] blood bank
血泪 [xuè lèi] tears of blood—extreme grief
血清 [xuèqīng] serum
血球 [xuèqiú] blood cells; corpuscles
血肉 [xuè ròu]flesh and blood
血统 [xuètòng] blood relationship; a family line
血腥 [xuè xīng] bloody;blood-stained;sanguinary
血型 [xuèxíng] blood type
血性 [xuèxìng] violent temperament; resolute disposition
血性男儿 [xuèxìngnánér] a rough-tempered man; a manly man
血压 [xuéyā] blood pressure;
血液 [xuèyè] the blood
血缘 [xuè yuán] blood relationship; consanguinity
血债 [xuè zhài] debt in blood;blood debt
血战 [xuè zhàn] a bloody battle

xūn

熏 [xūn] 1 (v) 以烟烘物 to scent; to smoke; to fumigate ＊烟把墙熏黑了。The wall was smoked black 2 (adj) 温暖 warm
熏染 [xūn rǎn] have slow but deep-going influence upon somebody
熏陶 [xūn táo] have gradual good influence over somebody;thinking or learning from people or environment constantly contacted; be nurtured by
熏鱼 [xūnyú] smoked fish; bloaters
醺 [xūn] (adj) 酒醉 drunk;intoxicated ＊他喝得醉醺醺的。He kept on drinking until he was helplessly drunk.
勋(勳) [xūn] (n) 功劳 merit; service ＊他屡建奇勋。He has repeatedly secured marvellous merits.
勋爵 [xūn júe] lord, a title in the British aristocracy
勋业 [xūn yè]merit and achievement
勋章 [xūn zhāng] decoration; medal;order of merit

xún

旬 [xún] 1 (n) 十天 ten days 2 (n) 十年 a period of ten years; a decade
旬刊 [xún kān] a magazine published three times a month
询(詢) [xún] (v) 问 inquire;ask ＊他写信去探询详细情况。He wrote a letter to inquire about the details.

询问 [xún wèn] inquire;enquire;ask

寻(尋) [xún] (v) 找;求find; seek;search;look for * 他要寻访失去联系的哥哥。 He wants to look for his brother with whom he has lost contact.

寻常 [xún cháng] ordinary;usual

寻觅 [xún mì] look for;search;find

寻求 [xún qiú] seek;look for

寻找 [xún zhǎo] look for;find; search;hunt for

浔(潯) [xún] (n) 英制测量水深单位 fathom

驯(馴) [xún] (adj)顺从;服从 tame ;docile ;subdue ; obedient * 猫是很驯服的。 The cat is very docile. 2 (v) 使驯服 to tame; domesticate

驯化 [xún huà] domesticated

驯良 [xún liáng] tame;obedient; tractable;docile;mild

驯兽师 [xún shì rēn] an animal-tamer

驯养 [xún yǎng] domesticate

循 [xún] (v) 依照;顺着 follow; accord * 他没有遵循条例办事。 He did not work according to the rules

循环 [xún huán] move in cycles; circulate;recur

循规蹈矩 [xún guī dǎo jǔ] stick to convention;observe due rules;follow the custom or law

循途守辙 [xúntúshǒuzhè] to follow the tracks and keep to the rut—to keep to the beaten path; to follow precedent

循序渐进 [xún xù jiàn jìn] progress step by step;advance by regular steps;develop by gradations;follow in proper sequence and make steady progress

循循善诱 [xún xún shan yòu] lead one gradually into good deeds

巡 [xún] (v)来回察看 patrol;go on circuit and inspect *门外有卫兵巡逻。There are guards on patrol outside 2(n)量词,用于斟酒的次数 round (of toasting) * 酒过三巡。 after three rounds of toasting

巡回 [xún huí] go on circuit; make the circuit of

巡回医疗 [xún huí yi liāo] mobile medical service

巡回法庭 [xún húi fǎ tíng] circuit court

巡视 [xún shì]make one's rounds of;supervise;inspect

巡洋舰 [xún yáng jiàn] a cruiser

xùn

殉 [xùn] 1 (v) 为一定目的舍弃自己的生命 die for; lay down one's life for * 这位消防员为扑灭这场大火不幸以身殉职。 The fireman died a martyr at his post when he tried to put out the fire. 2 (v) 随着死人埋葬 be buried with the dead.

殉难 [xùn nàn] to suffer martyrdom; to sacrifice one's life to

殉情 [xùn qíng] to commit suicide for love ; to die for love

殉葬品 [xùn zàng pǐn] a funerary object;a sacrificial object

殉职 [xùnzhì] die a martyr at one's post

讯(訊) [xùn]1(v) 问 interrogate; try 2 (n) 消息;信息 news;information

讯问 [xùn wèn] try at court;inquire after information

汛 [xùn] (n) 河流涨水 high water 春汛 spring flood ; 秋汛 autumn flood

迅 [xùn] (adj) 快 fast;swift;quick;rapid;speedy * 新的科学技术正在迅速发展。Modern technology is developing rapidly.

迅速 [xùn sù] speedy ;fast rapidly

训(訓) [xùn] (v)教导;教育 teach;educate;train * 我们要训练一批新的接

班人。We should train up a new batch of successors 2 (n) 法则 principle;rule＊他的话不足为训。His words should not be taken as an example

训斥 [xùn chì] scold;rebuke;reprimand

训词 [xùn cí] advice;words of advice

训话 [xùn huà] lecture;sermon;admonition

训令 [xùn lìng] an official order;an instruction

训育 [xùn yù] discipline; moral education

逊(遜) [xùn]1 (v) 让出 give up 2 (adj) 谦虚；恭敬 modest 3(adj) 不如，差 inferior ＊他的画不逊名家的。His paintings compare favourably to those of noted artists.

蕈 [xùn] (n) 伞菌一类的植物，种类很多，无毒的可供食用如香蕈、蘑茹等 toadstool (poisonous); mushroom

yā

押 [yā] 1 (v) 把财物交给人作担保 pawn;mortgage;deposit;pledge ＊他把车押给金融公司。He mortgaged his car to a finance company. 2 (v) 在文件或契约上签字或画记号 sign ; stamp a seal ＊他在借据上画押。He signed on the loan certificate. 3 (v) 拘留 detain ＊他被海关局人员扣押。He was detained by the custom officers. 4 (v) 监督 guard;escort; convoy ＊他把货物押运到目的地。He convoys the goods to the destination.

押款 [yā kuǎn] deposit money; a mortgage loan

押柜 [yā guì] deposit money

押解 [yā jiě] to send in custody to; to escort

押金 [yā jīn] deposit

押韵 [yā yùn] rhyme

鸭(鴨) [yā] (n) 家禽。嘴扁，腿短，脚有蹼，会游泳 duck

呀 [yā] (inter) 叹词。表示惊奇 exclamation to show surprise ＊呀，这猴子会采椰子。Hey, this monkey can pluck coconuts.

鸦(鴉) [yā] (n) 乌鸦，鸟类。身体黑色。杂食谷类、果实、昆虫。种类很多 the crow

鸦片战争 [yā piàn zhàn zhēng] the Opium War (1840)

鸦雀无声 [yā què wú shēng] very quiet ; cannot hear the punos made by the crows and the sparrows

压(壓) [yā] 1 (v) 从上往下加重力 exert pressure on ; bear down on; press; crush 2 (v) 用暴力 to overpower with force ; suppress; repress; subdue ＊统治者企图镇压农民起义。The rulers attempted to suppress peasant uprising. 3 (v) 制止，抑制 control ; hold......back ; restrain ＊他再也压不住心中的怒火。He could no longer hold back his anger. 4 (v) 逼近 draw near ; close in ＊强敌压境。The strong enemy forces have closed in at the border.

压倒 [yā dǎo] overwhelm ; overcome; overpower; prevail over

压力 [yā lì] pressure ; force of pressure

压服 [yā fú] domineer ; vanquish; subdue; coerce into submission ; suppress; overwhelm

压路机 [yālùjī] steam-roller
压迫 [yā pò] subdue;oppress;press hard on;bear down upon
压迫者 [yā pò zhě] oppressor
压缩 [yāsuō] compact; reduce; cut down
压抑 [yāyì] suppress; keep down; be constricted
压韵 [yā yùn] rhyme
压榨 [yā zhà] squash; squeeze; bleed;oppress and exploit;fleece
压榨机 [yā zhà jī] a press; a compressor
压制 [yā zhì] suppress;stifle;smother; hold down; muzzle; clamp down

yá

牙 [yá] 1 (n) 齿 tooth
牙床 [yá chúng] jaw;alveolus;ivory-in laid bed
牙雕 [yá diāo] ivory carving
牙膏 [yá gāo] tooth paste;dental cream
牙科 [yá kē] dentistry
牙签 [yá qiān] tooth pick
牙刷 [yá shuā] toothbrush

蚜 [yá] (n) 蚜虫，也叫“腻虫”，昆虫。能分泌“蜜露”。种类很多。危害粮食、棉花、蔬菜等植物 aphis

芽 [yá] (n) 植物体上尚未发育成长的茎、叶或花 sprout; shoot; bud
芽孢 [yá bāo] spores
芽眼 [yá yǎn] buds on a tuber

涯 [yá] 1 (n) 水边 bank; shore; water-line 2 (n) 边际；边缘 boundary;limit

崖 [yá] (n) 山边，高地的边沿 a cliff;a precipice;a steep slope

衙 [yá] (n) 官署 a government office; a court; yamen ＊ 衙门八字开，有理无钱莫进来。Though the door of the court opens widely, those who have reasons but have no money rather not to go in.

yǎ

雅 [yǎ] 1 (n) 正的，合乎规范的 standard 2(adj)优美，高尚，不庸俗 elegant; graceful; dignified; refined ＊书房里的陈设很雅致。The arrangement of the study is elegant.
雅观 [yǎ guān] nice looking;nice appearance
雅俗共赏 [yǎ sú gòng shǎng] to be enjoyed by the refined and vulgar alike
雅致 [yāzhì] refined; elegant; beautiful

哑(啞) [yǎ] 1 (adj) 不能说话 dumb;mute ＊ 他又聋又哑。He is both deaf and dumb. 2 (adj) 嗓子干涩，发音不清楚 hoarse ＊他喊得太多，声音都沙哑了。He shouted so much that his voice turned hoarse. 3 (adj) 无声的 silent 4 (n) 笑声 laughing voice
哑巴 [yǎ ba] a mute; a dumb person
哑然失笑 [yǎránshīxiào] laughed out involuntarily
哑剧 [yǎjù] pantomine; dumb show; mummery
哑口无言 [yǎ kǒu wú yán] dumbfounded; to be silent
哑铃 [yǎ líng] dumb-bell

yà

轧(軋) [yà] 1(v) 圆轴或轮子等在东西上面滚压 grind; crush; press 2 (n) 机器开动时的声音 the noise made by a

working machine * 工厂里机声轧轧。 The machines are giving a lot of noise in the factory.
另见 [zhá]

讶(訝) [yà] (v) 诧异；惊奇 express surprise;wonder at; suspect;doubt *他的到来使我们感到惊讶。 His coming here surprises us.

迓 [yà] (v) 迎接 welcome *总理在印尼受到热烈的迎迓。The Prime Minister had a warm welcome in Indonesia.

亚(亞) [yà] 1 (adj) 次等的 second ;next to; inferior * 他在游泳比赛中得到亚军。He is the runner-up in the swimming contest. 2 (n) 亚洲，全名"亚细亚洲"，世界七大洲之一 Asia *亚非拉人民团结紧。The Afro-Asian and Latin-American people are in deep solidarity.

亚热带 [yà rè dài] subtropics;subtropical regions

揠 [yà] (v) 拔 pull up

揠苗助长 [yàmiàozhùzhǎng] to pull up the seedlings hoping that they will grow faster — to make things worse by doing something contradictory to their development

yān

淹 [yān] (v) 沈在水中 submerge ; immerse ; drown ; soak * 洪水淹没了整个村庄。The flood submerged the whole village.

腌 [yān] (v) 用盐浸渍食品 to soak food in salt; to preserve food by putting plenty of salt on it .
另见 [ā]

焉 [yān] 1 (adv) 相当于"此" here *他心不在焉。 (His heart is not here) He is not paying attention 2 (adv) 相当于"怎么" how *不入虎穴，焉得虎子。How can one acquire the cub without going into the lair? (Nothing ventured, nothing gained)

阉(閹) [yān] (v) 割去动物的生殖腺 castrate

嫣 [yān] (adj) 美好 beautiful; charming * 她回头嫣然一笑。 She turned her head around and gave a charming smile.

咽 [yān] (n) 消化和呼吸的共同通道，位于鼻腔、口腔的后方，喉的上方 the throat; the pharynx * 他咽喉疼。 He has a sorethroat.

咽喉要道 [yān hóu yào dào]a vital communication line
另见 [yàn]

烟 [yān] 1 (n) 物质燃烧时冒出的气体 smoke ; fume 2 (n) 烟草和它的制成品 tobacco ; cigarette * 他买了一包香烟。He bought a packet of cigarettes.

烟草 [yān cǎo] tobacco
烟窗 [yān cōng] chimney
烟袋 [yāndài] tobacco pipe
烟斗 [yān dǒu] a pipe
烟花 [yān huā] fireworks
烟灰 [yān huī] cigarette ashes
烟灰缸 [yān huī gāng] ash tray
烟火 [yānhuǒ] fireworks
烟煤 [yānmèi] soft coal; bituminous coal
烟幕弹 [yān mù dàn] smoke-bomb; smoke screen
烟幕 [yān mù] smoke screen; smoke;smoke cloud
烟丝 [yān sī] prepared tobacco
烟筒 [yān · tong] stove pipe;chimney
烟雾 [yān wù]mist;haze
烟叶 [yān yè]tobacco leaves
烟消云散 [yān xiāo yún sàn] vanish

without a trace; disappear in a flash

烟嘴 [yān zuǐ] cigarette holder

胭 [yān] (n) 胭脂，一种红色的颜料，可作化妆品 rouge; cosmetics ＊她在两颊搽上了胭脂。She applied rouge on her cheeks.

湮 [yān] (v) 埋没 fall into water ;sink; disappear ＊那寺院湮没无闻了。The temple no longer existed.

湮灭 [yān miè] destroyed;lost

殷 [yān] (adj) 黑红色 dark red ＊他发觉地上有殷红的血迹。He discovered dark red blood stains on the floor.

另见 [yīn]

yán

延 [yán] 1 (v) 引长，伸展 extend; lengthen; prolong ＊工作时间延长了。The working hours have been extended. 2 (v)（时间）向后推移 postponed;defer;delay;put off ＊会议延期至下星期举行。The meeting is postponed until next week. 3 (v) 聘请 invite;employ; engage ＊被告没有延聘律师代辩。The accused did not engage any lawyer for defence.

延长线 [yán cháng xiàn] prolong line;prolongation of a line

延迟 [yán chí] postpone;delay

延搁 [yán gē] postpone ; shelved ; delay

延缓 [yánhuǎn] postphone; be postponed; retard; delay

延年益寿 [yán nián yì shòu] aid and prolong life

延伸 [yán shēn] extend; spread to;stretch

延续 [yán xù] continue

延展性 [yán zhǎn xìng]ductility;extensibility

筵 [yán] 1 (n) 竹席 mat 2 (n) 酒席 a feast; a dinner; a banquet ＊他们在酒楼设喜筵。They have their wedding feast in a restaurant.

筵席 [yán xí] a banquet;full dinner; feast

阎（閻）[yán] 1 (n) 巷门，里巷 the gate to a lane 2 (n) 姓氏 a surname

阎罗 [yán luó] the chinese Pluto: the king of Hades

阎王 [yán·wang]the king of Hades; a very fierce person

阎王帐 [yán·wang zhàng] usury

妍（姸）[yán] (adj) 美丽 beautiful ＊百花争妍。Hundreds of flowers strive for beauty.

研（硏）[yán] 1(v) 细磨 to grind ＊我把药丸研成粉末。I grind the medicine into fine powder 2 (v) 探索，深究 study;investigate;research ＊我们在研究社会发展史。We are studying the history of social development.

研究生 [yán jiū shēng] a research fellow

研究院 [yán jiū yuàn] a research institute attached to a university

研讨 [yán tǎo] study and discuss

言 [yán] 1 (n) 话 speech ;words; saying ＊我们必须有言论自由。We must have the freedom of speech. 2 (v) 说 say ;talk ＊我们应该知无不言，言无不尽。We should say all that we know and say them without reserve.

言不由衷 [yán bù yóu zhōng] one's words belie one's mind;insincere in one's words;hypocritical

言多必失 [yánduōbìshī] much talk leads to error

言归于好 [yán guī yú hǎo] to reconcile

言归正传 [yán guī zhèng zhuàn] getting back to the topic

言过其实 [yán guò qí shí] to exaggerate;to be bombastic

言论 [yánlùn] speach; public opinion
言外之意 [yán wài zhī yì] insinuation;implication ;meaning between lines
言行 [yán xíng] words and deeds
言行不一 [yán xíng bù yī] say one thing and do another ;one's words and deeds are at complete variance;one's acts belie one's words
言语 [yán yǔ] spoken language; words
言之无物 [yán zhī wú wù] contentless in what is said ;a talk of no cubstance

簷 [yán] (n) 屋顶下边伸出的部分 the eaves of a house ＊燕子在屋簷下筑巢。 The swallows build their nests under the eaves.

沿 [yán] 1 (v) 顺着 follow;go along 2 (adv) (prep) 靠近 near; along ＊沿岸有许多树木。 There are many trees along the shore.
沿革 [yángé] course of development and changes
沿海 [yán hǎi] along the coast;inshore;off-shore
沿途 [yán tú]along the road;on the way
沿袭 [yánxì] follow the old conventions
沿用 [yányòng] continue to use
沿着 [yánzhe] along

严(嚴) [yán] 1(adj) 有威可畏的; 可敬的; stately; majestic; respectable; dignified 2 (adj) 不放松，要求高，认真 strict;stern; serious;solemn ＊ 我们将严格遵守纪律。 We shall strictly abide by the rules. 3 (adv) 厉害 very; extremely ＊ 天气严寒。 The weather is extremely cold.
严冬 [yán dōng]severe winter
严防 [yán fáng] be on sharp guard against; take strict precautions against;maintain high vigilance
严格 [yángé] strict; exact; be strict with
严寒 [yánhán] severely cold
严紧 [yán jǐn] rigid;carefully guarded;tightly organised
严谨 [yán jǐn] conscientious and careful;strict and cautious
严禁 [yán jìn] strictly forbidden; strict prohibition
严峻 [yán jùn] severe; vigorous; stern
严酷 [yán kù] strict; stern; severe; cruel;ruthless;unrelenting
严厉 [yán lì] harsh;severe;stern
严密 [yánmí] close-knit; tight; close
严明 [yán míng] stern and impartial;strict and just
严守 [yán shǒu] strictly observe; strictly abide by;maintain strictly
严肃 [yán sù] strict ;earnest; conscientious ; serious;stern
严正 [yán zhèng] solemn;impartial; strict;serious
严阵以待 [yánzhènyǐdài] stand ready in battle array; vemain in combat readiness
严重 [yán zhòng] severe;serious; stern;grave

岩(巖) [yán] 1(n) 高峻的山崖 a precipice 2(n) 石 a rock
岩浆 [yánjiāng] magma
岩石 [yánshí] rocks
岩穴 [yánxué] a cave; a grotto

炎 [yán] 1 (adj) 热 hot; burning; blazing ＊天气炎热。The weather is extremely hot. 2 (n) 发热膨胀而痛的病症 inflammation ＊ 他皮肤发炎。 He has inflammation of the skin.
炎暑 [yán shǔ] hot summer

盐(鹽) [yán] 1(n) 食盐，咸味的原料，主要的成份是氯化钠，有海盐、池盐、井盐、岩盐等。table salt 2(n) 化学盐，酸类中的氢根被金属元素置换而成的化合物 chemical salt formed by the replacement of hydrogen ion in an acid with metal ion
盐场 [yán chǎng] salt field
盐酸 [yán suān] hydrochloric acid

颜(顏) [yán] 1 (n) 脸，脸色 the face;the countenance *他和颜悦色的向我解释。He explains to me with a benign countenance 2 (n) 体面，面子 prestige; face * 她无颜见人。She had no face to meet the people. (n) 颜色 colour *橱窗里挂着五颜六色的灯泡 Light bulbs of various colours hanging in the show case.
颜料 [yán liào] dye-stuff
颜色 [yán sè] colour; countenance; facial expression

yǎn

偃 [yǎn] 1 (v) 仰面倒下 to lie on the back 2 (v) 停止 stop
偃旗息鼓 [yǎn qí xī gǔ] to roll up the banners and silence the drums—on a secret expedition

鼹 [yǎn] (n) 鼹鼠，也叫"田老鼠"、"地爬子"，哺乳动物。毛黑褐色，咀尖，眼小，耳小，能爬土。对农作物有害 mole

奄 [yǎn] 1 (v) 覆盖；包括 cover 。2 (adv) 突然 suddenly 3 (adj) 呼吸微弱的样子 gasping for breath *当受伤的工友被送进医院时，他已经奄奄一息了。When the injured worker was sent to the hospital, he had scarcely a breath left.

掩 [yǎn] 1 (v) 遮盖 to cover; to shelter; to screen; to shut; to close * 谎言掩不住事实 Lies will not cover up the fact. 2 (adv) 乘人不备地；暗中 by surprise; stealthily
掩蔽 [yǎn bì] cover up;shelter
掩耳盗铃 [yǎn ěr dào líng] stuff one's ear when stealing a bell-self deceit
掩盖 [yǎngài] to cover up
掩护 [yǎn hù] provide cover; cover of ;camouflage
掩埋 [yǎn mái] bury
掩人 [yǎnrù] to enter stealthily
掩杀 [yǎnshā] to fall upon and slay
掩饰 [yǎn shì] cover up; conceal; mask; under the cloak of

演 [yǎn] 1 (v) 引申；发展 develop; extend * 宇宙间一切事物都是不断演变的。Everything in the universe develops and evolves continuously 2(v) 表现技艺 perform;act;play * 我们将表演「竹竿舞」。We shall perform the Bamboo Dance.
演变 [yǎnbiàn] to evolve; progressive
演唱 [yǎn chàng] sing for the audience
演出 [yǎn chū] present;perform;put on performance;play;show
演技 [yǎn jì] acting skill;acting change
演讲 [yǎnjiǎng] speak; to lecture
演说 [yǎnshuō] to give an address; to lecture; a lecture
演算 [yǎn suàn] do exercise in mathematics;operate
演习 [yǎnxí] to exercise; to practice; to rehearse; manoeuvre
演义 [yǎn yì] historical novel
演员 [yǎn yuán] actor;performer
演奏 [yǎn zòu] play or perform on musical instrument

俨(儼) [yǎn] 1 (adj) 恭敬；庄严 solemn 2 (adj) 好象；相似 look like *日光灯下俨如白昼。It looks like day-time under the white fluorescent tube.
俨然 [yǎn rán] impressive;solemn; look like;as if

衍 [yǎn] 1 (v) 开展；发挥 spread out;extend 2 (adj) 多余的 superfluous

眼 [yǎn] 1 (n) 目，视觉器官 eye * 打乒乓要眼明手快。One has to

be quick with the eyes and dexterous with the hands in playing table-tennis. 2 (n) 洞孔；窟窿 hole;eye 3 (n)关节；要点an important point 4 (n) 音乐的节拍 musical beat

眼高手低 [yǎn gāo shǒu dī] have high aim but no real ability

眼光 [yǎn guāng] vision;eyesight; insight;judgement

眼红 [yǎn hóng] envious;jealous; angry look

眼花缭乱 [yǎn huā liáo luàn] dazzling

眼界 [yǎn jiè] field of vision;range of experience

眼镜 [yǎn jìng] spectacles;glasses

眼镜蛇 [yǎn jìng shé] cobra

眼看 [yǎnkàn] at once; immediately; give way see.....with one's own eyes

眼科 [yǎn kē] ophthalmic department;opthalmology

眼泪 [yǎn lèi] tears

眼力 [yǎn lì] vision;power of discrimination

眼明手快 [yǎnmìngshǒukuai] quick of eye and deft of hand

眼前 [yǎn qián] in the present moment;immediate; under one's nose

眼球 [yǎn qiú] eyeball

眼色 [yǎn sè] look;glance

眼神 [yǎn shén] look;expression in one's eyes

yàn

燕 [yàn] (n) 燕子，鸟类，候鸟翅膀长，尾象剪刀形，捕食昆虫。swallow

燕尾服 [yàn weǐ fú] an evening dress for man;a swallow-tailed coat

燕窝 [yàn wō] a sea-bird's nest

咽 [yàn] (v)吞下 swallow;gulp *他咽下了一口水。He swallows a gulp of water
另见 [yān]

咽气 [yàn qì] stop breathing;die

宴 [yàn] 1 (n) 酒席 a feast;a banquet * 他不准备赴宴。He is not going to attend the banquet. 2 (v) 用酒席招待客人to give a feast;to entertain *主人在大会堂内宴客。The host gives a dinner at the great hall. 3 (adj) 安；乐at ease; enjoyable

宴会 [yàn huì] dinner party;banquet

宴请 [yàn qǐng] invite to dinner; give a dinner

谚（諺）[yàn] (n) 在民间流传的俗语 proverb; common saying ; maxim

厌（厭）[yàn] (v) 不喜欢；不满；嫌恶 dislike; dissatisfied; loathe; be fed up * 他厌恶这种寄生虫式的生活。He hates this parasitic way of life.

厌烦 [yàn fán] annoyed;be tired of

厌倦 [yàn juàn] be wearied of;fatigued;grow tired of

厌恶 [yànwù] detest; loathe; hate; dislike

厌战 [yànzhàn] be loath to continue fighting battles; war-weariness; battle fatigue

艳（艷）[yàn] 1 (adj) 色彩光泽鲜明好看 beautiful; lovely;gorgeous;attractive *舞蹈员穿着艳丽夺目的服装。The dancers were wearing beautiful and attractive costumes 2 (adj)关于爱情的;浪漫的 affectionate;romantic

艳丽 [yànlì] beautiful; glorious
艳阳天 [yàn yáng tiān] fine, bright weather

焰 [yàn] (n)火苗 flame;blaze;flare

堰 [yàn] (n)挡水的堤坝 a dike;an embankment;a levee

雁 [yàn] (n) 鸟类，形状象鹅，群居在水边，秋天往南飞，春天向北飞，飞行时排列成行。wild goose

赝(贋) [yàn] (adj) 假的；伪造的 counterfeit;false; fake * 那古董是一件赝品。That antique object is a fake.

砚(硯) [yàn] (n) 砚台，写毛笔字研墨用的文具 an ink-slab;an ink-stone

唁 [yàn] (v)慰问死者的家属 to console the family of the dead * 我们拍了一封唁电给死者的遗孀。We have sent a telegram of condolence to the widow of the dead.

验(驗) [yàn] 1 (v)察看；查考 inspect;examine;test * 病人需要验血。The patient needs a blood test. 2 (adj) 有效果effective * 这个方法果然灵验。 This method is indeed effective.
验方 [yàn fāng] an effective prescription
验尿 [yàn niào] to test the urine
验尸 [yàn shī] autopsy
验尸官 [yàn shī guān] a coroner
验收 [yàn shōu] to check before receiving

yāng

央 [yāng] 1 (n)当中 centre;middle * 不要站在路中央。Do not stand in the middle of the road. 2 (v)恳求；请求 beg;request * 我再三央求，他才答应。He consented only after I had begged him several times.

殃 [yāng] 1 (n) 灾难；祸害 misfortune;calamity 2 (v)损害 injure; harm

秧 yāng] (n) 水稻的幼苗 seedlings of padi plants * 农人在田里插秧。The farmers are planting padi seedlings in the field.
秧歌 [yāngge] yangko dance; Yangko opera ; song accompanied by dance
秧苗 [yāng miáo] seedlings of any plant nursery
秧田 [yāngtián] paddy field; a field where rice seedlings are raised

yáng

羊 [yáng] (n) 家畜。有山羊、绵羊等。毛、皮、骨都可作工业上的原料，肉和乳可供食用goat;sheep
羊肠小道 [yáng cháng xiǎo dào] small winding path
羊毛 [yáng máo] sheep's wool; fleece
羊肉 [yáng ròu] mutton

佯 [yáng] (v)假装 pretend;make believe * 他佯死。He pretends to be dead.

洋 [yáng] 1 (n) 地球表面上特别广大的水域 ocean * 那是一艘远洋轮船。 That is an ocean liner. 2 (adj)盛大；多 abundant * 联欢会上大伙儿热情洋溢。People were filled with enthusiasm at the party. 3 (adj)外国的 foreign;western * 这些洋人对本地的风俗很感兴趣。These westerners are very interested in the local customs. 4 (adj) 现代化的 modern
洋服 [yáng fú] western clothes
洋行 [yáng háng] firms opened by foreign capitalists
洋灰 [yáng huī] cement
洋货 [yáng huò] imported goods; foreign goods
洋洋 [yáng yáng] numerous;joyful
洋洋得意 [yáng yáng dé yì] be

come wild with joy

扬(揚) [yáng] 1 (v) 向上升；高举 raise; lift; hoist 2 (v) 在空中飘动 flutter; soar ＊国旗在空中飘扬。The national flag is fluttering in the sky. 3 (v)传布 make known;publish ＊ 他以卓越的成就扬名海外。He became famous overseas for his distinguished achievement.

扬长而去 [yáng cháng ér qù] shake the sleeves and go away haughtily.

扬场 [yáng cháng] winnow

扬眉吐气 [yáng méi tǔ qì] be elated;feel proud;hold one's head high

扬弃 [yáng qì] discard;abandon

扬水站 [yángshuǐzhàn] water raising station

扬言 [yáng yán] clamour; make known;claim;announce openly

扬扬得意 [yáng yáng dé yì] self-satisfied; conceited

杨(楊) [yáng] (n) 落叶乔木。种类很多，有白杨、大叶杨等。木材可以做器物 aspen; poplar

杨梅 [yáng méi] the arbutus

杨桃 [yáng táo] sweet carambola; star-fruit

疡(瘍) [yáng] (n) 疮 tumour

阳(陽) [yáng] 1 (n) 日 the sun 2 (adj) 明亮的 bright; clear 3 (adj) 人世的 pertaining to this world 4 (adj) 男性的；正面的 masculine; positive

阳电 [yángdiàn] positive electricity

阳奉阴违 [yáng fèng yīn wéi] comply in public but oppose in private

阳光 [yáng guāng] sunshine;sunlight

阳历 [yáng lì] solar calender

阳台 [yáng tái] balcony

阳性 [yáng xìng] the male sex; masculinity ; positive

yǎng

氧 [yǎng] (n) 化学元素，无色、无臭、无味气体。oxygen

氧化 [yǎng huà] oxidize

氧化物 [yǎng huà wù] oxides

痒(癢) [yǎng] (adj)皮肤受刺激，需要搔擦的感觉 itchy;itching ＊我的手脚给蚊子咬得发痒。My limbs become itchy after being bitten by mosquitoes.

养(養) [yǎng] 1 (v) 抚育 to bring up ＊她养了一个儿子。She brought her son up. 2 (v) 维持,供给生活品 support; sustain; maintain ＊ 父亲要赚钱来养家。Father has to earn money to support the family. 3 (v) 饲；喂 feed;rear;raise ＊ 我们在屋子后面养鸡。We rear chickens at the back of the house. 4 (v)使身心得到滋补和休息 convalesce;recuperate;nourish;refresh;care for ＊受伤的工友获准在医院里养伤。The injured worker is allowed to recuperate from his wounds in the hospital. 5 (v)保护；修补 protect; maintain ＊ 他的部门负责保养电梯。His department is responsible for maintaining the feasibility of lifts. 6 (v) 培育 cultivate ＊他从小就养成了好劳动的习惯。He had been cultivated with the love for labour since he was young. 7 (adj) 领养的，非亲生的 adopted ＊ 她是我的养母。She is my foster-mother.

养病 [yǎng bìng] convalesce;recuperate from illness through rest and medical treatment

养精蓄锐 [yǎng jīng xù ruì] build up one's strength;conserve strength and store up energy

养料 [yǎng liào] nutrition;nourishment

养伤[yǎngshāng]on leave to recuperate from one's wounds
养神 [yǎng shén] refresh one's spirit by keeping quiet(for a while)
养育 [yǎng yù] bring up;foster
养尊处优 [yǎng zūn chǔ yōu] revel in a high position and indulge in comfort

仰 [yǎng] 1(v)抬头向上 face upward; look up * 他仰望着苍穹。He looks up into the sky.2 (v)尊敬;佩服 admire * 他的丰功伟绩令人敬仰。His marvellous achievement is much admired by the people. 3 (v)依赖 rely on;depend on * 只要你有一技之长，就不用仰仗别人了。You do not have to rely on others if you acquire a skill.
仰而思之 [yǎngérsīzhī] puzzled ; in a brown study
仰给 [yǎng jǐ] depend on the supply from others
仰慕 [yǎng mù] admire and respect
仰取俯拾[yǎngqǔfǔshì] in one way or another-gained competency
仰人鼻息[yǎngrénbíxì] act according to the likes and dislikes of others
仰泳 [yǎng yǒng]back stroke (in swimming)

yàng

样(樣)[yàng] 1 (n) 形状 shape; appearance; pattern;model; form * 她把衣服的图样画在黑板上。She drew the dress pattern on the blackboard 2(n)种类kind*商店里摆着各种各样的物品。There are many kinds of things on display in the shop. 3 (n) 作为标准的东西 sample * 推销员给我们看布料的样本。The salesman shows us the cloth sample.
样板 [yàng bǎn] templets ; model
样品 [yàng pǐn] sample; specimen
样式 [yàng shì] style;form;pattern
样子 [yàng·zǐ] pattern; sample; shape;manner;figure;feature

恙 [yàng] (n) 疾病;伤害 disease; illness;harm * 他安然无恙。He is fine.

漾 [yàng] 1 (v)水面动荡ripple;wobble * 湖水荡漾。The lake water is rippling. 2 (v) 液体太多而向外流 overflow * 河水漾到岸上来了。The river water has overflowed its banks.

怏 [yàng] (adj)因不服气、不满意而不高兴的样子 disappointed; dissatisfied;unhappy *他拿不到奖品，心里怏怏不乐。He is disappointed for not getting the prize.

yāo

要 [yāo] (v) 求 to ask for ; to claim; to require; to want
另见 [yào]
要求[yāoqiú] to request; to demand
要挟[yāoxié] to coerce; to force; to extort

腰 [yāo] (n) 身体中部，胯骨以上、肋骨以下的部分 waist; loin*他的腰很粗。He has a large waist.
腰包 [yāo bāo] purse
腰带 [yāo dài] belt;girdle
腰围 [yāowéi] apron
腰子 [yāo zǐ] kidney

夭 [yāo] (v) 尚未成年就死去 die young * 她的孩子不到一岁就夭折了。Her son died when he was less than a year old.

妖 [yāo] 1 (v) 反常怪异 evil spirit ;monster * 这部小说里有许多妖怪的故事。There are many tales of monsters in the novel. 2 (adj) * 不正派的，邪恶的 evil; vicious ; heretical * 她想妖言惑众。She tried to incite the people with heresies.
妖风 [yāo fēng] evil winds;evil blast;vicious blast
妖魔鬼怪[yāo mó guǐ guài]monsters

of every description; demons; ghosts;demons and monsters

妖娆 [yāo ráo] charming;enchanting

吆 [yāo] (v) 大声喊，如吆喝 shout loudly;yell * 我们都不能忍受工头的吆喝。We cannot tolerate the abusive shouts from the foreman

邀 [yāo] 1 (v) 约请 invite * 他邀请我参加他的婚宴。He invited me to his wedding dinner. 2 (v) 得到 obtain

邀功 [yāo gōng] to beg for merit;to take the meritorious deeds of others as one's own

邀请 [yāoqǐng] invite; invitation

yáo

谣（謠） [yáo] 1 (n) 反映生活的歌曲 folk song;ballad; rhymes * "凤阳花鼓"是一首民谣。The Flower Drum of Feng Yang is a folk song. 2 (n) 没有事实根据的不可相信的话 rumour ;heresy * 他被捕的消息，不过是谣言而已。The information about his arrest is nothing but a rumour.

徭（傜） [yáo] (n) 强迫劳动 forced labour

摇（搖） [yáo] (v) 摆动 shake;quake; flutter; wag * 大风吹来，树枝摇个不停。The branches of the trees flutter in strong wind.

摇摆 [yào bǎi] stagger;move to and fro;waver

摇晃 [yáo·huàng] tremble;flutter; sway

摇篮 [yáo lán] cradle

摇旗呐喊 [yáo qí nà hǎn] wave the flag and shout;functioning as followers or supporters;clamour

摇头 [yáo taó] shake one's head

摇头摆尾[yàotòubǎiwěi] nodding the head and wagging the tail—well contented; pleased

摇尾乞怜 [yáo wěi qǐ lián] wag the tail and flatter;fawn on

摇摇摆摆 [yáoyáobǎibǎi] swagger.

摇摇欲坠 [yáo yaó yù zhuì] totter; shaky;crumble

瑶（瑤） [yáo] (n) 美玉 beautiful jade

瑶池 [yáo chí] residence of the god mother in a fairy tale

瑶族 [yáo zú] The Yao, a minority race in China,

遥 [yáo] (adj) 远 distant;remote;far away

遥控 [yáo kòng] remote control

遥望 [yáo wàng] look to the distance;take a distant view

遥相呼应 [yáo xiāng hū yīng] action in cooperation with each other across a long distance

遥遥 [yáo yáo] faraway,remote

窑 [yáo] 1 (n) 烧制陶器、瓷器、砖、瓦、石灰等物的建筑物 kiln;furnace 2 (n) 泛指硅酸盐工业常用的高温处理设备 equipment for high temperature process in silicate industry. 3 (n) 采煤时开凿的洞 mine pit

窑洞 [yáo dòng] cave residence; cave dwelling

窑姐儿 [yáo jiěr] a prostitute

窑子 [yáo·zi] a brothel

尧（堯） [yáo] (n) 传说中国古代部落联盟的首领，后来作为勤劳、勇敢和智慧的象征 name of a legendary chief of federated tribes in ancient China—a symbol of industriousness, bravery and wisdom.

肴（餚） [yáo] (n) 烧熟的鱼肉等荤菜 dishes; food; delicacies; feast

yǎo

咬 [yǎo] (v) 上下牙齿对着夹住或弄碎东西 bite; gnaw;chew * 狗咬他的腿。The dog bit him in the leg.

咬定 [yǎodìng] to bite and hold on—to stick to what one has said.

咬紧牙关 [yǎojǐnyáguān] to set the teeth firmly—determined

咬文嚼字 [yǎo wén jiáo zì] pedantry; mince words in speech or writing; talk pedantically

咬牙切齿 [yǎo yá qiè chǐ] gnash one's teeth—show deep seated hatred

窈 [yǎo] (adj) 深远 deep; profound

窈窕 [yǎo tiǎo] modest and refined; attractive(of girl)

舀 [yǎo] (v) 用瓢、杓等取水 to bale out water; to dip

yào

耀 [yào] 1 (v) 光线强烈地照射 shine brightly; dazzle *阳光照耀着大地。The sun shines brightly on the earth. 2 (v) 显示 show off * 真正有才能的人，从来不在人面前夸耀自己。A person with real talents never shows off himself in front of others.

耀武扬威 [yào wǔ yáng wēi] make a big show of one's power; swashbuckling

耀眼 [yào yǎn] dazzling to the eyes

药(藥) [yào] 1 (n) 治病的物质 medicine 2 (v) 治疗 cure; remedy *他的病已无可救药。His illness is incurable. 3 (n) 有某种化学作用的物质 chemicals

药材 [yào cái] medical herbs; medicinal crops

药方 [yào fāng] prescription; medical recipe

药房 [yào fáng] pharmacy; drugstore; dispensary

药费 [yào fèi] medical fees; fees for medicine

药膏 [yào gāo] medical ointment

药棉 [yào mián] antiseptic cotton

药片 [yào piàn] tablet of medicine

药品 [yào pǐn] medicine

药水 [yào shuǐ] liquid medicine; lotion mixture

药丸 [yào wán] pills(medicine)

要 [yào] 1 (v) 索取，需求 want; need; desire; demand; require *他要一个口琴。He wanted a harmonica. 2 (adj) 重大的；迫切的；必需的 important; essential; main *我们记录谈话的要点。We note down the main points of the talk.
另见 [yāo]

要不 [yàobù] otherwise; if not

要不得 [yào bu·de] intolerable; unacceptable; no good

要不是 [yàobùshì] important place; strategic position; key area

要道 [yào dào] strategic pass; main route; main line

要地 [yàodì] important place; strategic position.

要点 [yàodiǎn] main point; essentials

要饭 [yào fàn] beg for food; go begging

要害 [yào hài] vital part of body; key point; vital issue; vital area of defence; key military point

要紧 [yào jǐn] important

要领 [yào lǐng] main themes; main point; essential element

要命 [yào mìng] fatal; extremely; exceedingly

要强 [yàoqiáng] want to forge ahead;

unwilling to lag behind
要塞 [yàosài] stronghold; fortress
要是 [yào shì] if
要素 [yào sù] vital factor;essential element

钥(鑰) [yào] (n) 开锁用的东西 key ＊我没有钥匙开门。I do not have the key to the room.
另见 [yuè]
钥匙 [yàoshi] a key

yē

噎 [yē] (v) 食物塞住喉咙 choke ＊这孩子吃得太快，噎着了。This child ate too fast and he choked himself.

yé

椰 [yé] (n) 常绿乔木，产在热带地区，果实叫"椰子"，果肉可榨油和食用,果汁可作饮料，也可酿酒。coconut tree;coconut

椰梗 [yègěng] rib or rein of a coconut palm leaf

椰壳 [yékè] coconut shell
椰油 [yéyoú] coconut oil
椰汁 [yézhì] coconut milk

耶 [yé] 1. (n) 爺；父亲 a father ＊耶娘 father and mother; parents 2. (n)译音字 a transliterating word
耶和华 [yéhénuá] Jehovah
耶卡达 [yékǎdà] Jakarta
耶路撒冷 [yélùsālěng] Jerusalem
耶稣 [yésū] Jesus

爷(爺) [yé] 1 (n) 父亲 a father 2 (n) 对年长男性的尊称 a gentleman
爷爷 [yéye] grandpa; grandfather

yě

也 [yě] (adv) 亦；同样地 also;too; as well as ＊你不去，我也不去。If you don't go, I won't go also.
也罢 [yě bà] might as well;all right; let it be
也许 [yě xǔ] perhaps

冶 [yě] (v) 熔炼金属 smelt;melt;fuse
冶金工业 [yě jīn gōng yè] metallurgical industry
冶炼 [yě liàn] forge;smelt

野 [yě] 1 (n) 郊外 country-side; a moor;wilderness ＊他到野外去打猎了。He went for hunting in the country side. 2 (n) 界限；范围 limit;field;region ＊旅行可以扩大我们的视野。Travelling can widen our field of vision. 3 (adj) 蛮横；粗鲁savage;uncivil;rough;rude ＊这个少年举止粗野，没有人要接近他。This youth is very rude, nobody likes to be with him.
野菜 [yěcài] wild vegetable
野餐 [yě cān] picnic
野地 [yědì] open country; wilderness
野蛮 [yě mán] uncivilized;brute;savage ; barbarous
野兽 [yě shòu] beast;wild animal
野外 [yěwài] open field
野味 [yěwèi] savoury dishes
野心 [yě xīn] vaulting ambition;covetous desire;
野心勃勃[yěxīnbóbó] highly ambitious
野心家 [yě xīn jiā] careerist;social climber
野战军 [yězhànjūn] field army
野猪 [yě zhū] boar

yè

夜 [yè] (n) 从天黑到天亮的一段时间 night * 船厂工友日夜不停的在赶工。 The shipyard workers have to work day and night to finish the job in time.

夜班 [yè bān] night shift

夜不闭户 [yèbùbìhù] no need to lock the door at night

夜长梦多 [yè chángmèng duō] when dragged on, many unfavourable changes are possible

夜车 [yè chē] night train;night bus

夜间 [yè jiān]during the night

夜校 [yè xiào] evening school or class

夜以继日 [yè yǐ jì rì] day and night

夜莺 [yè yīng]nightingale

夜总会 [yè zǒng huì] night clubs

掖 [yè] (v) 扶持 to support;to lend a hand; to uphold

液 [yè] (n) 液体，能流动、有一定的体积而没有一定形状的 物质 liquid;fluid; juice; sap

液态 [yè taì] liquid state

液体燃料 [yè tǐ rán liào] liquid fuel

液压 [yèyā] fluid pressure

腋 [yè] (n) 腋窝，就是"胳肢窝"胳膊和肩膀连接处的凹窝 armpit

腋下 [yè xià] under the armpit

谒(謁) [yè] (v) 进见 see or visit a superior; call upon * 他谒见了元首及元首后。 He visited the emperor and the empress.

业(業) [yè] 1 (n) 事务 business ; profession ; work * 事业 career;职业 occupation;employment; profession; 专业 profession; 行业 line of business 企业 enterprise; 工业 industry;商业 commerce;农业 agriculture; 林业 forestry; 渔业 fishery; 学业 education;studies 2 (n) 财产; 房屋田地 property; estate 产业 property ; estate 3 (v) 从事 to do; to engage in; to pursue * 李家世代业农。Le's family has engaged in agriculture for generations. 4 (adv) 既；已 already * 成绩业已公布。The results have been published.

业绩 [yèjì] outstanding accomplishment; great achievement

业务 [yè wù] business

业务挂帅 [yèwùguàshài] put vocational work in command

业余 [yè yú] spare time;off-duty hour;after-working hours;amateur

业余时间 [yèyúshíjiān] spare time

业主 [yèzhǔ] property owner

曳 [yè] (v) 拉；牵引 drag;draw;pull * 两匹马曳一辆车。Two horses drag a carriage.

叶(葉) [yè] 1 (n) 植物的营养器官，多呈片状，绿色，长在茎上 leaf *橡胶树落叶了。The rubber trees shed leaves. 2 (n) 较长时期的分段 a period * 十三世纪初叶。the initial period of the thirteenth century.

叶柄 [yè bǐng] leaf stalk

叶绿素 [yè lǜ sù] chlorophyll

叶落归根 [yèluòguīgēn] the leaves fall and return to the roots—everythings reverts to its original source

叶落知秋 [yèluòzhīqiū] leaves fall, autumn approaches

叶子 [yèzǐ] leaf

页(頁) [yè] 1 (n) 单篇，单张（指书、纸等） a leaf;a sheet(of paper) 2 (n) 量词，指书本一张纸的一面 a page in a book * 这本书总共有二百页。There are altogether two hundred pages in this book.

yī

医(醫) [yī] 1 (v) 治病 cure;heal; give medical treatment

病向浅中医 Treat your trouble early. 2 (n) 增进健康、预防和治疗疾病的科学 medical science; medicine ＊ 我在学中医。I am learning Chinese medicine. 3 (n) 以治病为职业的人 doctor ;physician ＊ 他是一名牙医。He is a dentist.

医疗 [yī liáo] medical care;medical treatment

医务 [yī wù] medical service

医院 [yī yuàn] hospital

医治 [yī zhì] cure;treat;give medical treatment;heal

衣 [yī] 1 (n) 用布缝成遮蔽身体的东西 clothes; coat, dress; apparel ; garment; attire ＊妈妈替孩子穿衣。The mother puts on the clothes for the child. 2 (n) 物件的皮、膜 husk;skin;membrane

衣钵 [yī bō] mantle;legacy(of ideology, technology and learning etc.)

衣食住行 [yī shí zhù xíng] clothing; food; lodging and travel—necessities and means of life

依 [yī] 1 (v) 靠 depend on;rely on＊我们两国唇齿相依。Our two countries rely on each other as lips and teeth. 2 (adv) 按照 according to;in accordance with;in conformity to＊违例者将依法惩处。The offenders will be punished according to the law. 3 (v)顺从 obey;follow;adhere to ＊ 他对妻子总是千依百顺的。He adheres very much to what his wife says and does.

依次 [yī cì] in proper order;in turn;in order of

依存 [yīcún] interdepend; depend upon sb. or sth. (for existence) ; (mutual) dependence for existence

依旧 [yī jiù] as it used to be;still as usual

依据 [yī jù] based on;adhere to;basis

依靠 [yī kào] rely on;depend on

依赖 [yī lài] rely on;place total reliance on;depend on

依然 [yī rán] still;yet

依依不舍 [yī yī bù shě] unwilling to part with;reluctance to part from

依照 [yī zhào] according to;adhere to;as; in the light

漪 [yī] (n)水波纹 ripples ＊ 风一吹，湖水泛起了涟漪。Ripples spread over the lake when it breezes.

伊 [yī]1(pron)他;牠;它;那;某 he; she; it; that; one 2 音译字 a transliterating word

伊拉克 [yīlākè] Iraq

伊朗 [yīlǎng] Iran

伊斯兰教 [yīsīlánjiào] Islam

伊索寓言 [yīsùoyùyán] Aesop's fable

一 [yī] 1 (n) 数词 a numeral 2 (adj) 相同 similar;identical ＊ 他们兄弟俩长得一样高。The two brothers are of the same height. 3 (adj) 纯；专 sincere;whole-hearted ＊他一心一意为人民服务。He served the people with all his heart and mind. 4 (adj) 全；满 all;whole ＊ 鲁迅的一生是战斗的一生。The whole life of Lu Hsun was one of struggle. 5 (adv) 跟"就"呼应，表示两事时间紧接 as soon as;no sooner than ＊ 他一接到消息，就赶回家去。He hurried home as soon as he received the news.

一败涂地 [yī bài tú dì] a thorough defeat;a total loss

一般 [yī bān] alike;just as in general;ordinary;usual

一半 [yī bàn] half

一本正经 [yī běn zhěng jīng] serious;grave(mostly sarcastic)

一笔勾销 [yī bí gōu xiāo] wipe out the gains;write off at one stroke

一笔抹杀 [yībǐmǒshā] obliterate; be written off at one stroke; completely deny

一边 [yībiān] (1) side; edge; end (2) by the side; beside; aside

一不做，二不休 [yī bùzuò,è bù xiū]

once it is started, go through with it;a thing once begun will not be put off until done

一唱一和 [yī chàng yī hè] sing in chorus with;chime in with;echo each other

一尘不染 [yī chén bù rǎn] not to be stained with a particle of dust;pure-minded

一成不变 [yī chén bù biàn] hard and fast;unchangeable;invariable;unalterable

一筹莫展 [yī chóu mò zhǎn] could do nothing with it

一触即发 [yī chù jí fā] to an explosive point;touch and go

一代 [yī dài] one generation;of one age

一带 [yī dài]area;surroundings

一旦 [yī dàn] once;whenever;as soon as;one day

一刀两断 [yī dāo liǎng duàn] break with.....once and for all;make a clear break with

一点儿 [yī diǎn] just a little;a small amount;just a tiny bit

一定 [yī dìng] certain;definite; bound to;certainly;definitely;firmly

一度 [yī dù] once;for a time

一发千钧 [yī fà qiān jūn] an impending situation

一帆风顺 [yī fān fēng shùn] smooth sailing;plain sailing

一概 [yī gài] all;without exception; altogether

一概而论 [yī gài ér lùn] lump people or things under one head;lump together

一干二净 [yī gān èr jìng] nothing left

一共 [yī gòng] altogether;in total;in all;wholly;entirely

一贯 [yī guàn] consistent;invariable; all along;always

一鼓作气 [yī gǔ zuò qì] make one vigorous effort;with one effort

一哄而散 [yī hǒng ér sǎn] disperse in a rush

一会儿 [yī huì r] in a while;at one time;in a short moment

一伙 [yī huǒ] a group of; a gang of

一见如故 [yī jiàn rú gù] like old friends at the first meeting

一箭双雕 [yī jiàn shuāng diāo] kill two birds with one stone;achieve two things at one stroke

一技之长 [yī jì zhī cháng] a single skill;capable of one specific job; useful in some kind of work

一举两得 [yī jǔ liǎng dé] achieve two things at one stroke; double gain

一口气 [yī kǒu qì] in one breathe;at one go

一块儿 [yī kuài r] together, at the same place

一来……二来…… [yī lái.........èr lái...] on the one hand.....on the other hand;firstly....secondly..

一劳永逸 [yīláoyǒngyì] solution that holds good for all time;once and for all

一连 [yī lián] serially;successively; continuously

一连串 [yī lián chuàn] serial;a series of;a succession of;a whole string of

一律 [yī lǜ] undiscriminatingly; without exception;all;without distinction

一落千丈 [yī luò qiān zhàng] sudden decline;disastrous drop

一路平安 [yī lù píng ān] a pleasant journey

一马当先 [yī mǎ dāng xiān] taking the lead

一毛不拔 [yī máo bù bá]very sparing in spending

一鸣惊人 [yī míng jīng rén] achieve overnight success

一目了然 [yī mù liǎo rán] understand fully at a glance

一年半载 [yī nián bàn zāi] round

about a year
一年到头 [yī nián dào tóu] all the year round;in season and out of season
一旁 [yī páng] by the side of
一盘散沙 [yī pán sǎn shā] a plate of loose sand-utterly lacking cohesion
一片 [yī piàn] sheet;a sheet of;a stretch of
一起 [yī qǐ] together;together with; jointly
一文不值 [yī wén bù zhí] not worth a rap;completely insignificant
一窍不通 [yī qiào bù tōng] be utterly ignorant of;know nothing of
一切 [yī qiè] all;everything;every kind of;whole;entire
一气呵成 [yī qì hē chéng] complete something at a stretch
一清二楚 [yī qīng èr chǔ] perfectly clear;as clear as daylight
一丘之貂 [yī qīu zhī hé] jackals of the same lair;birds of a feather
一去不复返 [yī qù bù fù fǎn] once gone, never to return
一日千里 [yī rì qiān lǐ] a tremendous pace
一扫而光 [yī sǎo ér guāng] make a clean sweep of;a clean sweep
一生 [yī shēng] all one's life;lifetime;in one's whole life
一声不响 [yī shēng bù xiǎng] keep silent;say nothing at all
一时 [yī shí] momentary; at a given moment;for a while
一视同仁 [yī shì tóng rén] be treated the same; treat equally without discrimination
一事无成 [yī shì wú chéng] nothing accomplished;achieve nothing
一手 [yī shǒu] skill;trick;by oneself
一手包办 [yī shǒu bāo bàn] control exclusively;be stagemanaged by
一手遮天 [yī shǒu zhē tiān] attempt to hoodwink public opinion
一丝一毫 [yī sī yī háo] the slightest; the least;a shred of
一塌糊涂 [yī tā hú tú] in a great mess;in the worst state;in utter disorder
一天到晚 [yī tiān dào wǎn] from morning to night;all day long
一条心 [yī tiáo xīn] be of one mind with;all of one mind
一同 [yī tóng] together;together with
一网打尽 [yī wǎng dǎ jìn] all captured at once;captured in a dragnet
一往无前 [yī wǎng wú qián] go straight boldly;go straight with an indomitable spirit;go right on; indomitable
一味 [yī wèi] obsessively; persistently;doggedly
一无是处 [yī wú shì chù] nothing is right;without a single virtue;not a single merit
一无所有 [yī wú suó yǒu] have nothing at all;penniless;destitute
一向 [yī xiàng] consistently;always
一小撮 [yī xiǎo cuō] a handful of;a small number;a bunch of
一些 [yī xiē] some;a little;a few; several
一系列 [yī xì liè] a train of(e.g. events) a series of;a number of ; a great
一心 [yī xīn] set one's mind on;heart and soul;with one heart and one mind
一行 [yī xíng] company;party;suite
一心一意 [yī xīn yī yì] with all one's heart and mind;heart and soul
一言不发 [yī yán bù fā] keep silent; say nothing
一样 [yī yàng] same;of one size;like
一言一行 [yī yán yī xíng] each word and deed;every word and action
一意孤行 [yī yì gū xíng] have everything one's own way;act arbitrarily; act in disregard of other people's opinions

一元化 [yī yuán huà] unity
一元化领导 [yī yuán huà lǐng dǎo] unified leadership ; centralized leadership
一语道破 [yī yǔ dào pò] pin point; hit upon the truth
一月 [yī yuè] January
一再 [yī zài] again and again;once and again;repeatedly;many times
一张一弛 [yīzhāngyīchí] tense and relax alternatively
一朝一夕 [yī zhāo yī xī] overnight;a short duration of time
一整套 [yī zhěng tào] a whole set of;the whole range of
一针见血 [yī zhēn jiàn xiě] hit the nail on the head;make a pointed remark
一阵风 [yīzhènfēng] a gust of wind
一针一线 [yīzhēnyīxiàn] a single needle or a piece of thread
一阵雨 [yīzhènyǔ] shower; flurry of rain
一阵子 [yī zhèn zi] for a short time
一直 [yī zhí] all the time;all the while;always
一致 [yī zhí] unanimous; unified; identical
一知半解 [yī zhī bàn jiě] scant knowledge;the scantiness of knowledge;half-baked knowledge
一掷千金 [yīzhìqiānjīn] one splash is a thousand taels of gold ; throwing away gold
一致同意 [yīzhìtóngyì] to agree on; to endorse unanimously
一紙空文 [yī zhǐ kōng wén] a mere scrap of paper;empty words on a sheet of paper
一字不漏 [yīzìbùlòu] not omit a single word

壹 [yī] (n) "一"的大写 another version for the numeral "one"

揖 [yī] (n) 拱手礼 a greeting by holding the hands together near thechin

yí

夷 [yí] 1 (n)平安；平坦 safety 2 (v) 削平 flatten;level ✱铲泥机横冲直撞最后把简陋的木屋夷为平地。The bull-dozer charged and knocked in every direction ; finally it turned the simple and make-shift squatter houses into a level ground. 3 (v) 杀尽 kill all 4 (n) 中国古代称东部野蛮民族，后泛称野蛮民族及非汉族 eastern barbarian tribes ; barbarians ; non - Hans ; foreigners

咦 [yí] (inter) 惊怪的声音 hey, to show surprise ✱咦！这是怎么一回事？Hey,what's the matter?

姨 [yí] 1 (n)母亲的姊妹 maternal aunt 2 (n)妻子的姊妹 wife's sister ✱她是我的小姨。She is the younger sister of my wife.

姨父 [yí fù] maternal aunt's husband
姨太太 [yí tài·tài] concubine;a second wife

胰 [yí] (n) 人体内脏之一，在胃的下方，分泌消化液。the pancreas

胰岛素 [yí dǎo sù] insulin

痍 [yí] (n)创伤；伤痕 wounds;injuries ✱战火过后，这个市镇满目疮痍。After the war, we could see the devastation the war had brought to the town.

饴(飴) [yí] (n) 糖浆 syrup

怡 [yí] (adj) 愉快 happy;delighted; pleased ✱ 金马仑高原气候温和，景色优美，令人心旷神怡。The cool weather and beautiful scenery in Cameron Highlands make people feel delighted.

怡然 [yí rán] happy

贻 [yí] 1 (v) 赠送 give; present; confer 2 (v) 遗留 leave; bequeath; hand down ✱ 有些人认为孔子的儒家思想贻害无穷。Some say the thoughts of Confucianism had caused endless damage to the people.

贻害无穷 [yíhàiwúqióng] leaving behind endless trouble

贻人口实 [yí rén kǒu shí] to give occasion for scandal

贻误 [yí wù] cause delay;throw hindrance;mislead

贻笑大方 [yíxiàodàfàng] to become a laughing stock by showing inability before the specialists

移 [yí] 1 (v) 挪 move ; shift ; remove ＊我把桌子移到旁边去。I moved the table to the side. 2 (v) 改变；变动change;transfer ＊他的立场坚定不移。His stand is steadfast.

移动 [yí dòng] move;shift;change of place

移交 [yí jiāo] turn over;hand over

移居 [yí jū] change residence;emigrate

移民 [yímín] immigrate;emigrate; immigrant; emigrant

移山倒海 [yí shān dǎo hǎi] remove mountains and drain seas (in reference to man's mighty strength in conquering nature)

移植 [yí zhí] transplant;graft

颐(頤) [yí] 1 (n) 面颊 the cheek;the chin 2 (v) 休养；保养 recuperate;convalesce

疑 [yí] (v) 不相信 suspect;doubt ＊我怀疑他有上课。I doubt that he has gone to school.

疑案 [yíàn] a disputed case at court; an unsolved question

疑惑 [yí huò] doubt

疑虑 [yílǜ] worry;trouble;concern

疑难 [yí nàn] difficulty, doubt

疑神疑鬼 [yíshènyígǔi] suspecting everyone

疑团冰解 [yítuánbīngjiě] doubts and suspicion cleared away

疑问 [yí wèn] problem; question; doubt

疑心 [yí xīn] doubt;suspicion

疑义 [yí yì] doubtful point

仪(儀) [yí] 1 (n) 容貌；外表 appearance;bearing＊他仪容俊秀。He is handsome in appearance. 2 (n) 按规定程式进行的礼节 form of ceremony ＊他们的结婚仪式很简单。Their wedding ceremony was very simple. 3 (n) 礼物 present

仪表 [yí biǎo] a person's appearance

仪器 [yiqì] instruments; apparatus

仪式 [yíshì] form of ceremony

仪仗队 [yí zhàng duì] guard of honour

宜 [yí] 1 (adv) 应当；应该 should ＊事不宜迟。The matter should not be delayed. 2 (adj) 合适 fit; suitable;proper ＊她身体虚弱，不适宜做粗重的工作。She is not suitable for hard job as she is weak.

宜人 [yí rén] pleasant to one's mind

遗(遺) [yí] 1 (v) 丢失 lost; miss ; left ＊我遗失了一个钱包。I lost a purse. 2 (n) 丢失的东西 things lost ＊路不拾遗。Things left at the roadside are not picked by the passers-by ——a utopian society. 3 (v) 余；留 leave behind; remain

遗产 [yí chǎn] heritage;inheritance; legacy

遗臭万年 [yí chòu wàn nián] leave a bad name for thousands of years to come;everlasting shame;leave a bad name forever

遗传 [yí chuán] heredity;inheritance;inherit;carry over

遗憾 [yí hàn] sorry;regretful;regrettable

遗迹 [yí jī] remnants;relics;trace

遗留 [yí liú] leave behind;hand

down
遗弃 [yí qì] desert;abandon ;forsake
遗容 [yí róng] portrait of a dead person ; countenance of a deceased person
遗书 [yí shū] writings of a deceased author ; dying testament
遗体 [yí tǐ] a dead body
遗忘 [yí wàng] forget
遗象 [yí xiàng] portrait of a deceased person
遗志 [yí zhì] person's last will
遗著 [yí zhù] writings of a dead author
遗嘱 [yízhǔ] a will

yǐ

倚 [yǐ] 1 (v)靠；凭着；仗着 rely on; depend upon;lean on * 他倚势欺压善良的人民。 Relying upon the backing power, he oppressed the innocent people. 2 (adj) 偏 bias , partial * 在这场激烈的辩论中，要想不偏不倚，是不可能的。 In this heated debate , it is impossible to be impartial.
倚官仗势 [yǐguānzhàngshì] relying on those with power and influence
倚靠 [yǐ kào] depend on;rely on
倚赖 [yǐ lài] solely rely on;place reliance on
倚老卖老 [yǐ laǒ mài laǒ] displaying one's seniority
倚势欺人 [yǐshìqīrén] to presume on authority ; to browbeat others
倚仗 [yǐ zhàng] rely on;hang on somebody's coat-tails

椅 [yǐ] (n) 有靠背的坐具 chair

旖 [yǐ] (adj) 柔和美丽的样子 beautiful * 多峇湖风光旖旎。Lake Toba is a scenic place.

迤 [yǐ] 1 (adj) 地势斜着延长 extending;sloping 2 (adv) 往；向 toward
迤逦 [yǐ lǐ] wind;circle about
迤迤 [yǐ yǐ] continuous; extending

蚁(蟻) [yǐ] (n) 蚁，昆虫。多在地下做窠，成群生活，种类很多。ant
蚁酸 [yǐ suān] formic acid

乙 [yǐ] (n)天干的第二位，用作次序的第二 the second of the ten stems;second;2nd

以 [yǐ] 1 (v) 用；拿；把 use.....as..... * 我军的战略是以攻为守。It is the strategy of our army to use an attacking posture as a method of defence. 2 (prep) 依 according to * 排名以姓的笔画为序。The names are arranged according to the number of strokes of surnames. 3 (prep) 因 because of;on account of; for * 他不以此自满。 He is not self-conceited for this
以德报怨 [yǐdébàoyuàn] recompense injury with kindness
以毒攻毒 [yǐ dú gōng dú] to attack poison with poison
以讹传讹 [yǐéchúané] to transmit errors to perpetuate mistakes
以攻为守 [yǐgōngwèishsǔ] to defend by attacking
以己度人 [yǐjǐdùorén] judging others by our own standard
以及 [yǐ jí] and;as well as
以理服人 [yǐ lǐ fù rén] persuade through reasoning;convince people by reasoning
以卵击石 [yǐ luǎn jì shí] to hit a rock with egg — grossly overestimate one's strength
以貌取人 [yǐ mào qǔ rèn] judging a person by his appearance
以免 [yǐ miǎn] lest;in order to prevent
以前 [yǐ qián] before;previously; prior to;in the past
以上 [yǐ shàng] above;above-mentioned
以身殉职 [yǐ shēn xùn zhí] die a martyr at one's post
以身作则 [yǐ shēn zùo zé] make

oneself serve as an example to others;set an example with one's own conduct
以外 [yǐ wài] beyond ;excluding; outside
以往 [yǐ wǎng] the past;bygone days
以下 [yǐ xià] below;what follows
以牙还牙 [yǐ yá huán yá] a tooth for a tooth ; tit for tat
以致 [yǐzhì] with the result that; resulting in
以逸待劳 [yǐ yì dài láo] wait on one's ease for the fatigued enemy

已 [yǐ] 1 (v) 停止 stop;cease 2 (adv) 经过 already *办公时间已过。Office hours are already over.
已经 [yǐ·jīng] already
已知数 [yǐ zhī shù] known number

矣 [yǐ] 文言助词。多用在句末，相当于"了"、"啦"、"啊" a modal particle in classic Chinese to denote perfect tense

yì

意 [yì] (n) 见地; 心思 idea; opinion; view
意见 [yì jiàn] opinion;idea;view
意境 [yì jìng] mood and atmosphere
意料 [yìliào] expectation
意气 [yì qì] spirit; enthusiasm; impulse
意气风发 [yì qì fēng fǎ] boundless enthusiasm;heroism in display
意识 [yì shì] consciousness;ideology;outlook;be conscious of
意识形态 [yì shí xíng tài] ideology; ideological form
意思 [yìsì] meaning
意图 [yì tú] beyond expectation;unexpected accident;unforseen
意外 [yì wài] beyond expectation ; unexpected accident; unforseen
意味 [yì wèi] intention ; plan ; aim
意味着 [yìwèizhe] mean; suggest; imply; signify
意义 [yì yì] meaning;significance; purport
意译 [yìyì] liberal translation; free translation
意愿 [yì yuàn] will and wishes;desires
意志 [yì zhì] will;ambition

臆 [yì] 1 (n) 胸chest;breast 2 (adj)主观的 subjective *他的说法纯属臆造。What he says is nothing but a subjective conclusion.
臆测 [yì cè] conjecture;make baseless assumption
臆断 [yì duàn] make arbitrary decision;guess;make groundless conclusion

译(譯) [yì] (v) 翻译，把一种语言文字依照原意翻成另一种语言文字 translate ;interpret *这篇文章译自法文。This article is translated from French.
译名 [yì míng] translated name
译文 [yì wén] translation

驿(驛) [yì] (n) 旧时传送公文或官员来往中途休息、换马的地方 a station;a stop

益 [yì] 1 (v) 增加 increase *人参可以延年益寿。Ginseng can prolong one's life. 2 (adv) 更多 more *我们的队伍日益壮大。Our team becomes bigger day after day. 3 (n)好处 benefit;advantage;profit *每天做早操对我们有益。We benefit from daily morning exercises.4 (adj) 有好处的 beneficial;useful *燕子是益鸟。The swallow is a bird beneficial to man.
益虫 [yì chóng] beneficial(useful)insects
益处 [yì·chù] advantage;benefit
益友 [yì yǒu] beneficial friends

溢 [yì] (v) 充满了流出来 overflow *河水溢出堤岸。The river water overflows its banks.

缢(縊) [yì] (v) 用绳子勒死，吊死 strangle;hang ＊被逼退位的国王已经自缢。 The king who was forced to abdicate hanged himself.

亿(億) [yì] (n) 一万万 a hundred million；100,000,000 ＊中国有八亿人口。 China has a population of eight hundred million

亿万 [yì wàn] hundreds of millions

亿万富翁 [yìwànfùyēng] multi-millionaire

忆(憶) [yì] 1 (v) 回想 recall;recollect; think over ＊她回忆起辛酸的往事，不觉泪下。 She shed tears involuntarily when she recalled her bitter past. 2 (v) 记住;不忘 remember ＊他的记忆力很差。 His memory is very poor.

艺(藝) [yì] 1 (n) 技能；技术 skill;craft ＊这位裁缝的手艺很好。 This tailor is highly skilled in his work. 2 (n) 美术与技能，如图所画、雕刻、音乐、戏剧等 art ＊他是一名文艺工作者。 He is a worker of literary art.

艺人 [yì rén] professional player(artiste,acrobat,etc.)

艺术 [yì shù] art;skill

艺术标准 [yì shù biāo zhǔn] artistic criteria

艺术发展 [yìshùfàzhǎn] flourishing of the arts.

艺术家 [yì shù jiā] artist

艺术品 [yì shù pǐn] works of art

艺术性 [yì shù xìng] artistic level; artistry

呓(囈) [yì] (v) 说梦话 mutter in one's dream ＊他在梦呓。 He is muttering in a dream.

邑 [yì] (n) 城市；都城 town;city

悒 [yì] (adj) 愁闷；不安 distressed; worried ＊他因为找不到职业，非常忧悒。 He is very worried for being unable to get a job.

悒悒 [yìyì] sorrowful; sad; grieve

亦 [yì] (adv) 也 also, too

亦步亦趋 [yì bù yì qū] imitating every movement of the master

亦工亦农 [yì gōng yì nóng] take part both in industry and agriculture

亦孔之昭 [yìkǒngzhīshāo] it is clearly seen

奕 [yì] (adj) 精神饱满 in full spirit ＊他老人家和我们谈话时，神采奕奕。The old man was in full spirit when he talked to us.

役 [yì] 1 (n) 事务 event; service; business ＊兵役 military service; 劳役 compulsory labour；战役 battle. 2(n) 受使令的人 one who carries out order ＊奴役 slave-labourers; 校役 a school care-taker 杂役 errand boy 什役 servant 3(v) 使唤；驱使 to employ; press into service; to drive; to compel 南非白人政权继续奴役黑人。 The white regime in South Africa continues to enslave the negroes.

役然决然 [yìrǎnjuèrǎn] resolute

役使 [yì shǐ] employ;force someone to work

毅 [yí] (adv) 果断地；坚决地 resolutely; firmly ＊他毅然挑起了这个任务。He resolutely accepted the task

毅力 [yí lì] stamina;fortitude;will power

疫 [yì] (n) 流行性急性传染病的总称 an epidemic;a prevalent disease;a plague ＊农村人民要讲究卫生，积极防疫。 The village people should pay attention to hygiene and actively guard against epidemic.

疫苗 [yì miáo] vaccine

翼 [yí] (n) 翅膀 wings ＊工党的左翼人士反对工资冻结。 The left wingers in the Labour Party oppose the freezing of wages.

异（異）[yì] 1 (adj) 不同different ＊如果没有异议，这项议案就算通过了。If there is no disagreement, the motion will be passed. 2 (adj) 特别的，突出的 extraordinary; outstanding ＊ 他的考试成绩优异。His examination results were excellent. 3 (v) 奇怪 surprised ＊ 听到他要辞职的消息，大家都感到惊异。 All of us were surprised to hear that he wanted to resign. 4 (adj) 另外的，别的 other;foreign ＊ 他身处异地。He is in a foreign land.5 (v) 分开 separate ＊ 他们两人已经离异了。The couple has separated.

异常 [yì cháng] extraordinary;unusual;exceptional

异己 [yì jǐ] dissidents;alien(e.g. element)

异口同声 [yì kǒu tóng shēng] cry out in one voice; with one voice; with one accord

异曲同工 [yì qǔ tóng gōng] play the same tune on different instruments the same result achieved by different methods

异体字 [yì tǐ zì] different forms of a same character or letter

异想天开 [yì xiǎng tiān kāi] wishful thinking;fanciful ideas

异性 [yì xìng] opposite sex;different qualities(of matter);different in properties

异议 [yìyì] disagreement; objection; dissension; dissent

屹 [yì] (adj) 形容山势挺拔高耸，比喻坚定不可动摇 lofty (of mountains);towering;firm;determined ＊ 任他怎样威迫利诱，我屹然不动。I stand resolutely no matter how he tries to coerce and tempt me

屹立 [yì lì] stand firmly

裔 [yì] (n)后代；子孙descendants, off-springs ＊ 据说中国人是黄帝的后裔。It is said that the Chinese are the descendants of the Yellow Emperor.

翌 [yì] (adj) 次（指日或年） next

易 [yì] 1 (adj) 便当；不费力 easy; simple ＊这件衣服的制作简易。The making of this dress is simple and easy. 2 (adj) 和气 amiable;friendly ＊他平易近人，从来不摆架子。 He is friendly and amiable and he never puts on airs. 3 (v) 改变；变换 change ＊村里的年青人在推行一个移风易俗的运动。The youths in the village are launching a campaign to change existing habits and customs. 4 (v) 交换 barter;exchange;trade ＊我国将和世界各国进行贸易。Our country will trade with all countries in the world.

易燃 [yì rán] easy to kindle;inflammable;combustible

易燃品 [yì rání] highly inflammable materials

易如反掌 [yì rú fǎn zhǎng] as easy as turning one's palm

义（義）[yì] 1 (n) 公正合理的思想或行为 righteousness; justice 见义勇为 to act bravely for righteousness 2 (adj)公正的;合理的 just; right; ＊捐钱帮助水灾灾民是一项义举。Donating money to the flood victims is a just cause. 3 (n) 道德 morality ＊他为了金钱竟然抛弃妻儿和另一女人结婚，可谓无情无义He deserted his wife and children to marry another woman for her money;what a merciless and immoral man! 4 (adj) 人工制造的 artificial(of parts of the human body) ＊他需要一条义腿来代替那在车祸中失去的腿。He needs an artificial leg to replace the leg he lost in a road accident.

义不容辞 [yì bù róng cí] act from a strong sense of duty;inescapable duty

义愤 [yìfèn] righteous indignation
义气 [yì · qi] sense of justice (honour);self-sacrificing spirit;chivalry
义和团运动 [yìhétuányùndòng] the Yi Ho Tuan Movement
义务 [yì wù] voluntary duty;voluntary service; responsibility; obligation
义演 [yì yǎn] charity show
义正词严 [yìzhèngcíyan] just and severe terms

议(議) [yì] 1 (v) 言论；意见 suggestion; proposal; idea ＊我建议成立一个调查团。I make a proposal for the formation of an investigation team. 2 (v)商量；讨论 discuss ＊ 亚细安首长在商议工业计划问题。The Asean heads-of-states are discussing the problems of industrial projects.
议案 [yì àn] proposal;bill
义程 [yì chéng] agenda
议定书 [yì dìng shū] protocol
议会 [yì huì] parliament
议会道路 [yì huì dào lù] parliamentary road
议决 [yì jué] resolve;pass a vote of;decide
议论 [yì lùn] discuss;discussion
议题 [yì tí] a subject of discussions
议员 [yì yuán] members-of-parliament
议院 [yì yuàn] the Chamber;the Parliament;the Congress

诣 [yì] (n)学问或技术所达到的程度 the standard of achievement in study or techniques ＊他的音乐造诣很高。He has achieved a high standard in music.

抑 [yì] (v) 向下压；压制 repress;restrain;curb;stop;keep back;control ＊ 看到他的爱人来了，他抑制不住心中的喜悦。He could not control his happy feelings when he saw his lover.
抑扬顿挫 [yì yǎng dùn cuò] rising and falling of tones; rhythmical

谊(誼) [yì] (n) 交情；情意 friendship;relations ＊我们忘不了当地人民的深情厚谊。We cannot forget the deep friendship shown to us by the local people.

逸 [yì] 1 (v) 奔跑；逃跑run;get away; get off;escape ＊当官兵来抓人时，街上的市民四处逃逸。The people on the street ran away when the soldiers came to arrest someone. 2 (adj) 散失了的 lost;scattered 3 (adj) 安乐；安闲ease;free;leisure 4)v) 超过一般 exceed;excel
逸民 [yì mín] a hermit
逸事 [yì shì] a story(about a person)not recorded down in history

肄 [yì] (v) 学习study;learn ＊他曾在星大工程系肄业二年。He has studied for two years in the engineering faculty of the University of Singapore.

yīn

因 [yīn] 1(n) 缘故;理由 cause;reason ＊他想弄清楚这事件的前因后果。He wished to make clear about the cause and effect of this incident. 2 (conj) 由于 because;as;for; due to ＊ 我们因下雨而呆在家里 We stayed at home because of the rain. 3 (adv)依照；根据according to;as
因此 [yīn cǐ] so that;hence;thus
因地制宜 [yīn dì zhì yí] to be guided by circumstances.
因而 [yīn ér] therefore;because of
因果 [yīn guǒ] the causes and effects
因陋就简 [yīn lòu jiù jiǎn] make use of whatever is available
因式 [yīn shì] factor
因式分解 [yīn shì fēn jiě] factorisation; resolution into factors
因素 [yīn sù] factor;element

因势利导 [yīnshìlìdǎo] guide it along its course of development;
因时制宜 [yīnshízhìyí] to do what is suitable to the occasion.
因循 [yīnxún] to follow suit; to fall in with; to let matters drift

姻 [yīn] 1 (v) 结婚男女两家的关系 relationship by marriage 2 (n) 姻亲，由婚姻而结成的亲戚。 relation by marriage;a wife's relatives
姻亲 [yīngqīn] a wife's relatives
姻缘 [yīnyuán] marriage affinity
姻族关系 [yīnzúguānxì] relationship by affinity

茵 [yin] (n) 席毯褥 mat; a carpet; a cushion ✱ 公园里绿草如茵。The grass in the park looks like a carpet.

音 [yīn] 1 (n) 声 a sound;a musical note;a tone;voice ✱ 这音乐很优美。This piece of music is beautiful. 2 (n) 消息 news;tidings ✱ 我们静候佳音。 We are waiting quietly for the good news.
音节 [yīn jié] syllable;key or pitch in music
音量] yīn liàng] volume of sound
音信 [yīn xìn] news;tidings
音译 [yīn yì] transliterate by sound
音乐会 [yīn yuè hùi] concert

阴(陰) [yīn] 1 (n) 太阴；即月亮 the moon 2 (adj) 凹进的；不显露的 indented; obscured 3 (adj) 属于死人和死后的 of the dead 4 (adj) 天空被云遮住 cloudy;gloomy 5 (n) 不见阳光的地方 shade ✱ 我们在树阴底下休息。 We rested in the shade of a tree. 6 (adj)秘密；奸诈 mysterious;secret ✱ 严防阴险的敌人。Be on sharp guard against the insidious enemy. 7 (adj) 带负电的 carrying negative charges
阴暗 [yīn àn] dark;dull;gloomy;dim
阴历 [yīn lì] the lunar year;the lunar calendar
阴谋 [yīn móu] ill-intended scheme; sinister plot;conspiracy
阴极 [yīnjì] cathode
阴险 [yīnxiǎn] cunning; wily; crafty; treacherous ; subtle
阴性 [yīn xìng] feminine character; feminine gender; negative
阴影 [yīn yǐng] shadow

殷 [yīn] 1 (adj) 大；多；富足 great; many; abundant; prosperous 2(adj) 深厚 profound;deep ✱ 我们殷切地期望他早日归来。We waited earnestly for his early return.
另见 [yān]
殷勤 [yīn qín] attentive;solicitous; obliging
殷商 [yīn shāng] prominent merchant
殷实 [yīnshí] rich,substantial;well-to-do

yín

银(銀) [yín] (n)化学元素。符号 Ag白色金属 silver,a white metal
银行 [yín háng] bank
银河 [yín hé] the Milky Way
银幕 [yín mù] screen

龈(齦) [yín] (n) 牙龈；牙根上的肉 gum ✱ 他的齿龈脓肿 He has gum-boil.

寅 [yín] 1 (n)地支的第三位，用作次序的第三 Third in order;3rd 2 (n) 寅时，指早晨三点到五点 from 3.00 a.m.to 5.00 a.m. 3 (n) 职员；同事 a fellow officer; a colleague

淫 [yín] 1 (adj)过多；过甚 excessive ✱ 连绵不绝的淫雨造成严重的水灾。The long and continuous rain has caused serious floods. 2 (n) 放纵 self-indulgence ; extravagance ; wildness ✱ 这些皇族过着骄奢淫逸的生活。The royal family is leading a life of luxury and self-indulgence. 3 (n) 不正当的男女关系；色情 adultery; fornication ; lust ; lewdness ; debauchery ✱ 这些妇女被控卖

淫。These women are charged for prostitution. (selling lewdness)

霪 [yín] (n) 久雨 long and continuous rain

吟 [yín] (v) 用高低快慢的声调读 recite;hum;intone * 他在吟诗。He is reciting a poem.

yǐn

隐(隱) [yǐn] 1 (v) 遮掩；不显露 cover up;conceal * 他想隐瞒实情。He tried to conceal the facts. 2 (adj) 内里的，暗藏的 hidden;obscured * 他好象有什么隐痛似的。He seems to have some untold bitterness.

隐蔽 [yǐn bì] cover up;hide;conceal

隐藏 [yǐn cáng] conceal;hide;cover up

隐约 [yǐn yuē] indistinctly visible or audible

瘾(癮) [yǐn] (n) 特别深的嗜好 craving;addiction * 他吸毒成瘾。He has become addicted to drugs.

引 [yǐn] 1 (v) 拉弓 draw(a bow) 2 (v) 拉长；伸 stretch * 他引颈而望。He stretched his neck to gaze. 3 (v) 带领 guide;lead;conduct * 主人引导我们参观了几个生产部门。The host guided us to various production units. 4 (v) 参考 to refer to * 辩论者引述大纲。The debater referred to his notes.

引吭高歌 [yǐn háng gāo gē] singing sonorously

引号 [yǐn hào] quotation mark

引经据典 [yǐnjīngjùdiǎn] quoting authorities and classic

引狼人室 [yǐn láng rú shì] allow rogues to enter one's premises

引力 [yǐn lì] attraction;gravitation

引起 [yǐn qǐ] arouse;give rise to;lead to

引人人胜 [yǐn rén rù shèng] interesting and absorbing;fascinating

引文 [yǐn wén] quotations from other writings

引言 [yǐn yán] introduction;preface

引以为戒 [yǐn yǐ wéi jiè] take warning;serve as a grave warning

引用 [yǐn yòng] quote;cite

引诱 [yǐn yòu] lure;seduce;entice

饮(飲) [yǐn] (v) 喝 drink

饮恨以终 [yǐnhènyǐzhōng] to die in hatred

饮料 [yǐnliào] drinks; beverages

饮食 [yǐn shí] food and drink;food

yìn

印 [yìn] 1 (n) 图章 a seal;a rubber-stamp * 秘书在公函上盖印。The secretary affixes his seal to the official letter. 2(n) 痕迹 trace * 沙滩上有许多脚印。There are many footprints on the beach. 3 (v) 复制文书图画 print * 这本书是由我们公司印刷的。This book was printed by our company. 4 (v) 符合 tally with * 材料已印证过了。The material has been corroborated.

印发 [yìn fā] print and publish; issue

印染 [yìn rǎn] print and dye

印刷品 [yìn shuā pǐn] printed matter

印象 [yìn xiàng] impression

荫(蔭) [yìn] (v) 庇护；遮蔽 shelter

另见 [yīn]

yīng

婴(嬰) [yīng] (n) 刚出生的孩子 baby;infant * 我在假期中代人照顾婴孩。I worked as a baby-sitter during the holidays.

缨(纓) [yīng] (n) 器物上穗状的彩色装饰品 a coloured

tassel on an object

樱（樱） [yīng] 1 (n) 落叶乔木，花淡红色，日本产最多 cherry-blossom trees. ✱ 日本的樱花节吸引了许多旅客。The cherry-blossom season in Japan attracted many tourists. 2 (n) 樱桃，落叶乔木，果实园球形，色红，味甜，可吃。 cherry

鹦（鸚） [yīng] (n) 鹦鹉，鸟类，羽毛颜色美丽，种类很多，产在热带，能学人说话。 parrot

罂（罌） [yīng] (n) 大腹小口的瓶子 a jar; a vase

罂粟 [yīngsù] poppy

英 [yīng] 1 (adj) 杰出的 superior; outstanding 2 (n) 杰出的人 genius; outstanding people ✱ 体育总会最近举办了一个体坛群英会。 The Sports Association recently organised a mass gathering for sports talents.

英里 [yīnglǐ] mile

英俊 [yīng jùn] brilliant and handsome

英明 [yīng míng] wise; brilliant

英镑 [yīngpáng] sterling; pound

英镑集团 [yīngpángjítuan] sterling bloc

英雄 [yīng xióng] hero

英雄主义 [yīngxiòngzhǔyì] heroism struggle

英勇 [yīng yǒng] brave; valiant; courageous

英勇奋斗 [yīngyǒngfèndoù] heroism

英勇就义 [yīngyǒng jiùyì] to die with one's head high

英勇无双 [yīngyǒng wúshuāng] unrivalled bravery; unequalled heroism

英语字幕 [yīngyǔzìmù] English titles

英姿 [yīng zī] heroic figure; bright and brave; valiant and fine-looking

英姿焕发 [yīngzīhuànfa] heroic and dignified in appearance

英姿飒爽 [yīngzīsàshuǎng] dignified and spirited looking

莺（鶯） [yīng] (n) 也叫“黄鹂”、“黄莺”，鸟类。通体几乎都是鲜黄色，叫声清脆。主食昆虫 oriole; a yellow bird

膺 [yīng] 1 (n) 胸 chest; breast 2 (v) 承受 bear; sustain; receive; undertake ✱ 他膺选为代表。He was elected as a representative.

鹰（鷹） [yīng] (n) 鸟类。嘴弯曲而尖，足趾有长而锐利的爪。性凶猛。捕食鼠类和其他鸟类 eagle; falcon; hawk.

应（應） [yīng] (v) 该；当 ought; should ✱ 一旦发现错误，应马上纠正。Once you spotted your mistake, you should correct it immediately.
另见 [yìng]

应当 [yīng dāng] must; should; ought

应该 [yīng gāi] should; need; ought

应届 [yīngjie] graduating

yíng

莹（瑩） [yíng] 1 (n) 象玉的石头 a jade-like stone 2 (adj) 光洁透明 shining and transparent

萤(螢) [yíng] (n) 也叫"萤火虫"，昆虫、尾部具发光器，能发光 a firefly

萤光屏 [yíngguangping] fluorescent screen; television screen
萤石 [yíngshí] fluorspare; fluorite

营(營) [yíng] 1(n)军队驻扎的地方 army camp;an encampment ＊他在营地守哨。He stood sentry over the camp 2 (n) 军队的编制单位，是团的下一级，连的上一级 a battalion 3 (v) 图谋；筹划；办理 plan; deal in; run ＊他经营一家五金公司 He is running a hardware firm.
营房 [yíng fáng] barracks;quarters
营火会 [yíng hǔo huì] camp-fire
营救 [yíng jiù] save;rescue
营垒 [yíng lěi] camp
营私舞币 [yíng sī wǔ bì] malpractices;embezzlement
营养 [yíng yǎng] nourishment;nutrition
营业 [yíng yè] do business;trade; commercial
营业主任 [yíng yè zhǔ rèn] sales manager
营造 [yíngzào] build; building; construct; to lay out; erect
营长 [yíng zhǎng] battalion commander

赢(贏) [yíng] (v) 胜利 win; score ＊这局棋我赢了。I have won this round of chess.
赢得 [yíngdé] win over ; gain ; score
赢利 [yíng lì] gain;profit

盈 [yíng] 1 (v)充满 fill ＊她一想起死去的孩子就热泪盈眶。Tears filled her eyes when she thought of her deceased child 2 (adj) 多出来；多余 surplus;excess ＊本公司今年有九千元的盈余。The company enjoys a surplus of nine thousand dollars this year.
盈亏 [yíng kuī] gain and loss;waxing and waning(of the moon)
盈余 [yíng yúı] surplus;profit

迎 [yíng] 1 (v) 接待 welcome ; receive ＊欢迎你们到槟城来。Welcome to Penang. 2 (v) 朝着；向着 face;meet ＊我们迎着困难勇敢前进。Facing difficulties, we advance courageously.
迎风招展 [yíng fēng zhāo zhǎn] wave in the wind
迎合 [yíng hé] cater to;fawn upon; accomodation to serve the purposes of
迎接 [yíng jiē] meet;welcome
迎面 [yíng miàn] meet face to face
迎刃而解 [yíng rèn ér jiě] once the main problem is grasped,all the other problems can easily be solved
迎头赶上 [yíngtóugǎnshàng] to catchup
迎头痛击 [yíng tóu tòng jì] deal head-on blows
迎新 [yíng xīn] welcome the newcomers

蝇(蠅) [yíng] (n) 昆虫，幼虫叫"蛆"，传播霍乱、伤寒等症病，害处很大 fly
蝇头小利 [yíngtóuxiǎolì] meagre profits

yǐng

颖(穎) [yǐng] 1 (n)东西末端的尖锐部分 the pointed end of an object 2(adj) 聪明 intelligent ; distinguished; clever ＊他的弟弟聪颖过人。His younger brother is intelligent. 3 (adj) 光鲜 bright; sharp ＊她穿上新颖的晚礼服。She puts on a stylish evening dress.
穎慧 [yǐng huì] clever; sharp

影 [yǐng] 1 (n) 物体挡住光线后，映在地面或其他物体上较四周暗些的形象 shadow;image *他害怕自己的影子。 He is afraid of his own shadow.

影片 [yǐng piàn] film

影射 [yǐng shè] insinuate;hint at (something else)

影响 [yǐng xiǎng] have an effect on;affect;influence;impact

影印 [yǐng yìn] photoprint;photostat

影子 [yǐng·zi] shadow

yìng

应 (應) [yìng] 1 (v) 回答，随声相和 answer ; respond ; echo *当他唱歌时，山谷响应 The valley echoed as he sang. 2(v) 接受 accept * 他应邀访问中国。 He accepted the invitation to visit China. 3 (adj) 适合；配合suitable;appropriate * 本店售卖各种应时货品。 Our shop sells various kinds of goods suitable for the festive season. 4 (v)对付;对待 deal with ;attend to * 我们要学会恰当地应付各种复杂的局面。 We should learn to deal properly with all kinds of complicated situations.

另见 [yīng]

应承 [yìng chéng] promise;comply with

应酬 [yìng·chou] engage in social activities;have sócial intercourse

应得 [yìngdé] deserve; to be worthy of ; merit ; due ; ought to receive ; entitled to

应付 [yìng·fu] cope with;deal with; contend with;manage

应接不暇 [yìng jiē bù xiá] too busy to attend to ; have no time to tend to

应声虫 [yìng shēng chóng] echoer; mouthpiece;yes-man

应邀 [yìngyāo] in response to an invitation; answer the invitation of; at the invitation of

应用 [yìng yòng] apply;put to use

应用文 [yìng yòng wén] practical writings (such as letters, notices, invitations etc.)

应允 [yìngyǔn] to comply with ; to agree to; to assent to

应战 [yìng zhàn] accept battle;accept combat;engage.....in battle; accept a challenge

应征 [yìng zhēng] enlist;join the army;essay-writing in response to the editor's arrangements

映 [yìng] 1 (v) 照 shine;illuminate * 炉火把他的脸映得通红。 His face was shone red by the stove fire.

硬 [yìng] 1 (adj) 坚；跟“软”相对 hard * 柚木非常坚硬。Teak wood is very hard and strong. 2(adj)刚强；坚强 unyielding;firm * 他态度强硬，敌人拿他没办法。 He is firm and unyielding. The enemy can do nothing about him. 3 (adv) 执拗。insistently * 他不顾大雨，硬要外出。 In spite of the heavy rain, he insisted on going out. 4 (adj) 勉强；不自然；生硬。 uneasy ; unnatural *演员的台词念得很生硬。 The actors recited the dialogues in an uneasy manner.

硬币 [yìng bì] hard currency;coin

硬度 [yìng dù] hardness

硬骨头 [yìn gú·tou] spirit of unyielding integrity;steel-willed person

硬化 [yìn huà] cemented;vulcanize; hardening;stiffening

yō

唷 [yō] (inter) 叹词。表示惊奇或疑问 oh, to show surprise or doubt * 唷，你还没上学！ Oh, you haven't gone to school yet!

哟(喲) [yō] (inter) 叹词。表示惊奇 oh; oho

yōng

雍 [yōng] 1 (adj) 和谐 harmonious 2 (adj) 大方；从容不迫的样子 dignified ✱ 我看到一位雍容华贵的妇人走了过来。 I saw a dignified lady in gorgeous attire walking towards me slowly.

臃 [yōng] (adj) 身体过分肥胖或衣服穿得太多，转动不灵 fat and clumsy; swollen ✱他的老板拖着臃肿的身体走过去。His boss dragged his fat body and walked past.

壅 [yōng] (v) 堵塞 block up ✱ 水道壅塞不通。The waterway is blocked up and the flow of water impeded.

庸 [yōng] 1 (adj) 平常 ordinary; common ✱ 他不想庸庸碌碌的渡过一生。He does not wish to spend his life like any ordinary man with no achievement. 2 (adj) 低；劣 inferior; mediocre ✱ 市面上有许多庸医，大家要小心。 There are many quack doctors around ; beware of them.

庸才 [yōngcài] ordinary talents; mediocre ability

庸民 [yōngmín] the masses; the simple ordinary people

庸人多福 [yōngrénduōfú] ignorance is bliss; the sweetest life is in knowing nothing

庸人自扰 [yōngrénzìrǎo] ignorant persons only disturb themselves

庸俗 [yōng sù] vulgar; philistine

庸俗化 [yōng sù huà] vulgarisation; debase

庸庸禄禄 [yōngyōnglùlù] with no achievement

庸禄之相 [yōnglùzhixiàng] common-looking

慵 [yōng] (adj) 困倦；懒 tired; lazy

佣(傭) [yōng] (n) 指为了薪给供人役使的人，仆人 hired labour; servant ✱ 她为了生活，不得不在有钱人家里当女佣。 In order to earn a living she has to work as a servant in a rich man's house.
另见 [yòng]

佣工 [yōng gōng] hired labourer

佣人 [yōng rén] servant

拥(擁) [yōng] 1 (v) 抱 hug; embrace ✱ 他们高兴得拥抱在一起。 They embraced for joy. 2(v) 围绕 to gather round ✱ 当那位演讲者步下讲坛时，人们前呼后拥 When the speaker stepped down the stage, the people cheered and gathered round him.

拥护 [yōnghù] to support

拥挤 [yōng jǐ] crowded; packed; pressed together

拥塞 [yōng sè] crowded; packed (of people, vehicles or boats)

拥有 [yōngyǒu] to own; to possess

拥政爱民 [yōngzhèng'àimín] support the government and cherish the people

痈(癰) [yōng] (n) 一种毒疮，因细菌感染局部血行阻滞而形成，红肿热痛，根部大而浅 a carbuncle; an abscess

痈疽 [yōng jū] a carbuncle

yóng

喁 [yóng] (v) 低声细语 talk softly; whisper ✱ 两人在一旁喁喁私语。 They whispered quietly at one side.

yǒng

甬 [yǒng] 1 (n) 房屋前面居中的小路 a straight path leading to the front of a building 2 (n) 建筑物内部走廊 gallery ; hallway ; covered corridor; passageway

俑 [yǒng] (n) 古代贵族们用作陪葬的木或陶土做的偶象 a wooden or earthen puppet used as an attendant to be buried with the deceased noble.

涌 [yǒng] 1 (v) 水向上冒 bubble up; gush forth ＊清澈的泉水从地下涌了出来。Clear spring water gushed out from below the ground. 2 (v) 冒出 emerge ＊东山上涌出一轮明月。A bright moon emerges from the hills in the east. 3 (v) 冲；流 to rush; to surge; to flow ＊人群从体育场里涌了出来。Big crowds rushed out from the stadium.

涌出 [yǒngchū] gush; spout; outpouring; to burst out; to burst through

涌现 [yǒngxiàn] come to the fore; come forward in great numbers

蛹 [yǒng] (n) 完全变态的昆虫从幼虫发育成虫时的一种形态。在这个期间不食，外皮变硬，体内原有的幼虫组织器官改组，新的成虫组织器官逐渐形成 a pupa; a chrysalis

踊 (踴) [yǒng] (v) 跳 jump

踊跃 [yǒngyuè] eagerly; happily; enthusiastically

勇 [yǒng] (adj) 有胆量，不怕危险和困难 brave; valiant; courageous; bold; daring ＊. 他生擒鳄鱼，真是勇敢。It was brave of him to catch a crocodile alive

勇敢 [yǒng gǎn] bold; courageous; brave

勇猛 [yǒng měng] valiant; militant; fearless

勇气 [yǒng qì] courage; dauntless spirit

勇士 [yǒng shì] brave man; valiant fighter

勇往直前 [yǒng wǎng zhí qián] march dauntlessly; stride bravely forward; advance courageously

勇于 [yǒngyú] dare to; have the courage to

永 [yǒng] (adv) 长久，久远 forever; always; eternally ＊我将永远记住您的教导。I will remember your teaching forever.

永别 [yǒng bíe] parting forever

永垂不朽 [yǒng chuí bù xǐu] eternal glory to; immortal; live for ever in the hearts of

永恒 [yǒng héng] eternal; everlasting

永久 [yǒng jǐu] perpetual; everlasting; forever

永久性 [yǒng jǐu xìng] eternity; perpetuity

永生 [yǒng shēng] eternal life

永盛不衰 [yǒngshèngbúshuāi] to blossom forever; to be forever green

泳 [yǒng] (v) 游泳，在水里游动 swim

泳池 [yǒngchí] swimming pool

泳衣 [yǒngyī] swimming costume

咏 [yǒng] (v) 唱 sing; hum; chant

咏诗 [yǒngsī] hum verses

yòng

用 [yòng] 1 (v) 使物动作 use; employ; make use of; resort to; apply ＊农民已经学会使用动力机器耕田。The peasants have learned to use machines to plough the field. 2 (n) 用处；效果 use; effect ＊这本词典对我非常有用。This dictionary is of great use to me 3 (v) 需要 need; have to ＊你不用替他担心。You do not have to worry for him.

用不着 [yòng bù zhao] there is no need to;needless
用处 [yòng chu] use;application; function
用得着 [yòngdezháo] of use; needful; necessary
用功 [yòng gōng] study hard;work hard
用劲 [yòngjìn] exert ; with all one's energy
用具 [yòng jù] appliance;instrument;tool
用力 [yòng lì] exert one's strength; devote greater efforts
用品 [yòng pǐn] usable things (matters) ; necessities
用途 [yòng tú] use;application
用心 [yòng xīn] with concentration; set one's mind upon;intention;purpose
用以 [yòngyǐ] serve as; in order to; for
用意 [yòng yì] intention;purpose; meaning;attempt
用语 [yòngyǔ] phrases; phraseology
佣 [yòng] (n) 也叫"佣金"一种居间买卖，现指社会里交易、买卖中介绍人在成交时从中所得的钱财 commission ＊保险代理人将在每笔生意中抽取百分之十的佣金。The insurance agent will draw a commission of 10% on each sale. 另见 [yōng]

yōu

忧(憂) [yōu] 1 (v) 发愁；担心 worry; grieve; concern; be anxious ＊我们忧虑他的安全 We are anxious about his safety. 2 (n) 使人发愁的事 distress; grief ＊这几年来他饱经忧患，所以人显得苍老。He seems to have grown old because he has undergone many difficulties and distress in these few years.
忧愁 [yōu chóu] sorrowful;worried; anxious;sad
忧伤 [yōu shāng] sad;grieved;sorrowful
忧心忡忡 [yōuxīnchōngchōng] look dismal and unhappy. ; gloomy ; grieved
忧心如焚 [yōuxīnrúfén] worried as if on fire; very worried
忧郁 [yōu yù] melancholy;sad;depressed
优(優) [yōu] 1 (adj)好 excellent; superior;fine;outstanding ＊我们选出几篇优秀的作品来朗读。We select a few excellent essays for recitation. 2 (n) 戏剧演员 drama actor;opera actor ＊名优。a famous opera actor.
优待 [yōu dài] give preferential treatment;lenient treatment
优点 [yōu diǎn] merit;strong point; advantage
优等 [yōu děng] special grade;excellent grade
优厚 [yōu hòu] (of treatment)favourable;generous;good
优良 [yōu liáng] excellent;good;fine
优美 [yōu měi] elegant;beautiful; graceful
优胜 [yōu shèng] outstanding;superior
优势 [yōu shì] have the upper hand; dominant position;superiority
优先 [yōu xiān] priority;precedence; preference
优异 [yōu yì] excellent ;outstanding
优越 [yōu yuè] superior;advantageous
优越性 [yōu yuè xìng] superiority; advantage;supremacy
悠 [yōu] 1 (adj) 久；远 distant;far; long ＊这座建筑物历史悠久。This building has a long-standing history. 2 (adj) 闲适 carefree;leisurely free ＊他态度悠闲的坐在那儿。He sat there in a leisurely manner.
悠扬 [yōu yáng] melodic ; melodious

幽 [yōu] 1 (adj)僻静；暗 quiet and secluded;gloomy 2 (adj) 隐藏的，不公开的 hidden; secret 3 (adj) 沉静；深远 tranquil;deep 4 (adj) 阴间 hell ; hades

幽谷 [yōugǔ] a dark ravine; a dark gorge

幽会 [yōuhùi] a stolen (secret) interview

幽魂 [yōuhùn] the soul

幽静 [yōu jìng] quiet;tranquil;secluded

幽灵 [yōulìng] spirit; phantom; apparition; spectre; ghost

幽默 [yōu mò] humour; humorous

幽思 [yōusī] contemplation

幽雅 [yōu yǎ] tranquil and enjoyable;quiet and in good taste

yóu

尤 [yóu] 1 (adv) 突出地；特别地 extraordinarily;especially ＊ 此地盛产水果，尤以榴梿著称。 This place produces a lot of fruits especially durains. 3 (v) 埋怨 blame ＊ 你自己没把事办好却要怨天尤人。You yourself fail to do it properly, yet you murmur against the Heaven and blame other people.

尤其 [yóu qí] extraordinarily;especially;particularly

尤物 [yóuwù] a beautiful woman

犹（猶） [yóu] 1 (adv) 好象；如同 like;as if ＊ 灯烛辉煌，犹如白昼。The lights shine brightly as if it is in daylight. 2 (adv) 还 still ＊ 他记忆犹新。He still remembers.

犹可 [yóukě] it is probably to be so.

犹太教 [yóutàijiào] Judaism

犹太人 [yóu tài rén] Jews

犹有 [yóu yǒu] there are still some more

犹豫 [yóu yù] hesitate; uncertain

犹豫不决 [yóu yù bù jué] indecisive; hesitate to act;not able to make up one's mind

鱿（魷） [yóu] (n) 软体动物，头象乌贼，身体白色，有淡褐色斑点，尾鳍呈菱形，海产，可供食用。cuttle-fish

由 [yóu] 1 (n) 原因，来历 reason; cause ＊ 把你改变计划的理由讲一下。 Give your reason for changing the plan. 2 (conj) 因为 because of;owing to; due to ＊ 由于我们的共同努力，任务提前完成了。Owing to our joint efforts, the task was fulfilled ahead of schedule 3 (v) 归；让 let; leave ＊ 这事由他负责。 Let him be responsible for this matter. 4 (prep) 自；从 from ＊ 我们分析问题，要由表及里 When we analyse a problem, we should go from the surface to the core.

由不得 [yóu·bu·de] cannot help

由此及彼 [yóu cǐ jí bǐ] proceed from one to the other;proceed from one point to another

由此可见 [yóucǐkějiàn] from this, it can be seen

由简而繁 [yóujiǎnérfáng] from the simple to the complex

由近及远 [yóu jìn jí yuǎn] from the close-by examples to those far off

由来 [yóu lái] origin of occurrence; reason;cause

由浅入深 [yóu qiǎn rù shēn] from the shallower to the deeper;proceed from the simple to the more complex;from the superficial to the deep

由天而降 [yóutiānérjiàng] came down from heaven

由衷之言 [yóu zhōng zhī yán] words from the bottom of one's heart;sincere words

邮（郵） [yóu] (n) 递送书信的机关。 a post office.

邮差 [yóuchī] a postman
邮购 yóugòu] to purchase by post.
邮递员 [yóu dì yuán] postman
邮费 [yóu fèi]postage;postal charges
邮寄 [yóujì] to send by post
邮件 [yóu jiàn] postal matter;letters and parcels
邮筒 [yóu tǒng] pillar box
邮箱 [yóu xiāng] post box
邮政 [yóu zhèng] postal service
邮政局 [yóu zhèng jú] post office

油 [yóu] 1 (n) 含有脂质或类似脂质的液体或半液体 fat;oil;grease ＊石油是一种重要的工业原料。Petroleum is an important raw material for industries. 2 (v)涂抹 paint ＊这间屋子每三年油漆一次。This house is painted once in three years.
油布 [yóu bù] water-proof material
油画 [yóu huà] oil painting
油井 [yóu jǐng] oil well
油料作物 [yóu liào zuò wù] oil-bearing crops
油漆匠 [yóu qī jiáng] painter
油棕 [yóu zōng] oil-palm
油腔滑调 [yóuqiānghúadiào] flippant and insincere speech
油腻 [yóunì] greasy; oily
油漆 [yóuqì] varnish; oil paint
油水 [yóushùi] oil or fat in meal
油田 [yóutián] oil-field
油汪汪 [yóuwāngwāng] very shiny; oily
油印 [yóuyìn] mimeograph
油毡 [yóuzhān] asphaltic rug; linoleum

柚 [yóu] (n) 柚木，落叶大乔木。木质坚硬耐用，适于制造船、车、家具等 teak;a type of hard wood 另见 [yòu]

铀(鈾) [yóu] (n) 化学元素可作核子炸弹，符号U Uranium

游 [yóu] 1 (v)在水里行动 swim ＊鱼在水里游来游去。The fish swim about in the water. 2 (adj) 不固定的，经常移动的 wandering;moving all the time ＊草原上有许多游牧部落。There are many nomadic tribes on the grassland.3(n)河流的一段 part of a stream ＊河的上游有许多急流。There are many rapids in the upper course of the river. 4 (v) 从容地行走，玩 walk without haste;enjoy oneself;roam; tour ＊我们在泰国游览了许多名胜古迹。We toured many places of historical interest in Thailand.
游船 [yóu chuán] yacht;pleasure boat
游逛 [yóu guàng] wonder;roam;take a stroll
游记 [yóu jì] travels;a travel sketch;travelogue
游击队 [yóu jī duì] guerillas;partisans
游击战 [yóu jī zhàn] guerilla warfare
游客 [yóu kè] tourist; traveller; sight-seer
游手好闲 [yóu shǒu hào xián] loaf; idle
游玩 [yóu wán] play;amuse (oneself)
游戏 [yóu xì] (play) game
游行 [yóu xíng] parade;demonstration;march
游泳 [yóu yǒng] swim
游泳池 [yóu yǒng chí] swimming pool

yǒu

黝 [yǒu] (adj) 黑色 black;dark ＊他的脸晒得黑黝黝的。He has a tanned face

有 [yǒu] 1 (v) 表示所属 have;posses; own ＊他有一辆脚车。He has a bicycle. 2 (v) 表示存在 to exist; there is; there are; there was; there were ＊屋子里有很多人。There are many people in the house. 3 (adj) 丰足 rich; plentiful; abundant 他愈富有，愈不知足。 The more he is rich, the more he desires

有备无患 [yǒu bèi wú huàn] preparedness prevents calamity

有待 [yǒu dài] wait for;have still to be;remain to be seen

有的 [yǒude] some; certain

有的是 [yǒudeshi] a lot of; many; be abundant in

有的放矢 [yǒudìfàngshǐ] shoot the arrow at the target; with a definite object in view

有点儿 [yǒudiǎnr] a few; a little

有关 [yǒu guān] relativo;relevant; concerned;have.....to do with

有过之而无不及 [yǒu guò zhī ér wú bù jí] rather overdone than underdone; overdone

有害 [yǒu hài] harmful;pernicious; detrimental; do harm to; impair; damage

有机 [yǒu jī] organic

有机肥料 [yǒujīféiliào] organic fertilizer

有机化学 [yǒu jī huà xué] organic chemistry

有机物 [yǒu jī wù] organic matter

有口皆碑 [yǒukǒujiēbēi] be praised by all; universal praise

有赖 [yǒu lài] depend on;rely on; place hope upon;rest with

有理 [yǒu lǐ] reasonable;be in the right; with good reason;on just ground

有力 [yǒulì] weighty; convincing; powerful; effective

有利 [yǒu lì] favourable;with advantage;advantageous

有名 [yǒumíng] famous; well-known

有名无实 [yǒu míng wú shí] titular; in name but not in reality;symbolic;merely nominal

有目共睹 [yǒu mù gòng dǔ] obvious to all;clear to all

有气无力 [yǒu qì wú lì] lifeless;feebly

有趣 [yǒu qù] interesting;amusing; pleasant

有色金属 [yǒu sè jīn shǔ] nonferrous metals

有声有色 [yǒu shēng yǒu sè] vivid; alive;full of sound and colour

有时 [yǒu shí] sometimes;at times; occasionally;now and then; from time to time

有始有终 [yǒu shǐ yǒu zhōng] finish what is started;do something well from beginning to end; prosecute to the end

有说有笑 [yǒu shuō yǒu xiào] talking and joking

有条不紊 [yǒu tiáo bù wěn] systematic; in perfcot order;orderly; (everything) in good order

有条有理 [yǒu tiáo yǒu lǐ] methodical;well-organised and clearly stated

有限 [yǒu xiàn] limited;restricted

有效 [yǒu xiào] efficient;effective; valid;remain in effect;in force

有些 [yǒu xiē] some;a part of;a bit of;there is a few;have a little;several

有心 [yǒu xīn] having the intention to;set one's mind to; deliberately; purposely

有血有肉 [yǒu xuè yǒu ròu] vivid; life-like

有益 [yǒu yì] beneficial;useful;helpful;good for

有意 [yǒu yì] want to;intentionally; purposely;deliberately

有意识 [yǒuyìshì] consciously; deliberately

有意思 [yǒu yì sì] significant;meaningful

有则改之，无则加勉 [yǒu zé gǎi zhī, wú zé jiā miǎn] correct mistakes if you have commited them and guard against them if you have not

有增无减 [yǒu zēng wú jiǎn] never reduce but increase

有朝一日 [yǒu zhāo yí rì] some day;there will be a day

有志者事竟成 [yǒu zhì zhě shì jìng chéng]where there is a will,there is a way; strong will leads to success

酉 [yǒu] 1 (n) 地支的第十位，用作次序的第十 the tenth of the twelve branches ; tenth in order ; 10th 2 (n) 酉时，指下午五时至七时。5.00 p.m. to 7.00 p.m.

友 [yǒu] 1 (n) 朋友 friend ＊患难之交才是真朋友。A friend in need is a friend indeed. 2 (adj) 亲密；要好 friendly;cordial ＊两国关系友好。The two countries have a friendly relation.

友爱 [yǒu aì] befriend;amiable

友邦 [yǒu bāng] friendly country

友好 [yǒuhǎo] friendly ; amiable ; cordial ; good will

友情 [yǒu qíng] friendship;cordial feelings

友人 [yǒurén] friend

友善 [yǒu shàn] kind;friendly

友谊 [yǒu yì] friendship

友谊第一，比赛第二 [yǒu yì dì yi bǐ saì dì eì] friendship first, competition second

莠 [yǒu] (n) 田间杂草的总称，也用来比喻坏人 weeds;bad persons

yòu

宥 [yòu] (v) 原谅；饶恕 forgive; pardon

右 [yòu] 1 (adj) 面向南时靠西的一边 right 2 (adj) 政治上保守的 rightist ＊右派反对和中国建交。The rightists objected to the establishment of diplomatic relations with China.

右边 [yòu·bian] the right side;right hand side

右派 [yòu pài] rightists

右倾机会主义 [yòu qīng jī huì zhǔ yì] right opportunism

右翼 [yòu yì] right wing;right flank

幼 [yòu] 1 (adj) 年纪小，还没长成的 young ＊ 孩子年幼无知。The child is young and ignorant. 2 (n) 小孩 child ＊屋子里有男女老幼二十人。There are twenty persons in the house , men and women, young and old.

幼儿 [yòu ér] young child;baby;infant

幼儿园 [yòu ér yuán] kindergarten

幼苗 [yòu miáo] sprout ; young shoot

幼小 [yòu xiǎo] infantile;young

幼稚 [yòu zhì] childish;naïve;immature

佑(祐) [yòu] (v) 保护；帮助 protect;help ＊上帝会保佑你。God will help you.

柚 [yòu] (n) 常绿乔木，果实叫“柚子”，可吃、花、叶、果皮可提炼芳香油. pomelo
另见 [yǒu]

釉 [yòu] (n) 涂在陶瓷表面有光彩的薄层 glazing for porcelain and earthenwares

鼬 [yòu] (n) 也叫“黄鼠狼”，哺乳动物，毛黄褐色，捕食鼠类，是有经济价值的毛皮兽。 weasel

诱(誘) [yòu] 1 (v) 教导；劝导 teach;guide;induce ＊循循善诱。to teach methodically (v) 2 引人做坏事 lure; entice;seduce ＊他企图诱骗无知的少女。He tried to entice innocent girls.

诱导 [yòu dǎo] guide and instruct;

induce

诱饵 [yòuěr] bait; entice

诱拐 [yòu guǎi] lure;abduct;kidnap (woman or girl)

诱惑 [yòu huò] lure;induce;incite

诱奸 [yòu jiān] entice into adultery;seduce

诱骗 [yòupiàn] lure; entice; inveigle ....into the trap

又 [yòu] 1 (adv) 再；更 again;further ＊他又迟到了。He is late again. 2 (conj) 而且 but ; also＊这架缝衣机既便宜又好用。This sewing machine is not only cheap but also good. 3 (adv) 和；同 and

yū

迂 [yū] 1 (adj)曲折；绕弯 winding; circuitous ＊ 山路迂回曲折。The mountain path is circuitous and tortuous. 2 (adj) 拘泥守旧，固执成见，不切实际的 conservative ; obstinate and unpractical

迂道 [yūdào] a round about road

迂腐 [yūyǔ] doltish; inapt

迂缓 [yūhuǎn] slow; dilatory

迂阔 [yūkuò] impracticable ; wild of the mark

淤 [yū] 1 (n) 水道中沉积的泥沙 silt ＊工人在清除河淤。The workers are clearing away the river silt. 2 (v) 阻塞；不流通 block up; be clogged up ＊水道淤塞。The waterway is clogged up with silt.

淤积 [yū jī] silt up

淤泥 [yū ní] filth;mud

淤塞 [yūsè] silk; block up; be clogged up; full of sediment

淤血 [yūxuè] having blood clot

瘀 [yū] (v) 血液凝积 have blood clot ＊ 他的大腿因重物击中而瘀血。He has blood clot on his thigh which has been hit by a heavy object.

瘀脓 [yūnóng] effuse pus

瘀血 [yūxuè] the effuse blood

yú

俞 [yú] (n) 姓氏 a surname

愉 [yú] (adj) 快乐；喜欢 happy;merry;delightful ＊她去西马旅行回来后，心情愉快。She is in a happy mood after a tour to West Malaysia.

渝 [yú] (v) 改变(多指态度或感情) change (in attitude or feelings) ＊他对林小姐的爱始终不渝。 His love for Miss Lim will never change.

瑜 [yú] 1 (n) 美玉 beautiful jade 2 (n) 玉的光彩；比喻优点 lustre of jade;virtues

瑜加 [yú jiā] yoga

榆 [yú] (n) 落叶乔木，木材结实细致，可供建筑和制器具、嫩叶、嫩果 可吃、树皮纤维可代麻用，叶煎汁可杀虫。 the elm tree

逾 [yú] (v) 超过；越过 exceed; go beyond ; pass over ＊ 这张支票逾期将作废。This cheque for drawings having exceeded the time limited is considered invalid.

逾越 [yú yuè] go beyond;exceed

隅 [yú] (n) 角落 corner ＊欲购从速，以免向隅。 Those who want to buy please come early to avoid being kept waiting at the corner.

愚 [yú] (adj)蠢；傻 stupid;foolish; silly;dull-witted＊只有愚蠢无知的人才会上当。Only a stupid person will be taken in.

愚笨 [yú bèn] dull-witted;silly; blockhead

愚蠢 [yuchǔn] blockhead; foolish; stupid

愚弄 [yúnòng] to fool

愚公移山 [yú gōng yí shān] The Foolish Old Man Who Removed the Mountain(the story of how an old man removed the mountain)

愚昧 [yú mèi] ignorant
愚民政策 [yú mín zhèng cè] a policy to keep the people in an ignorant and secluded state

于(於) [yú] 1 (prep) 在 in; at * 孙中山先生生于1866年。Dr. Sun Yat Sen was born in 1866. 2 (adv) 给 to * 为了自己不受任何损失，他企图嫁祸于人。He attempts to transfer the evil upon others so that he himself would not suffer any losses. 3 (adv) 对；对于 to * 他忠于人民。He is loyal to the people. 4 (adv)自；从 from;out of * 他说他所作的都是出于自愿。He said what he did was out of his own free will. 5 (adv) 向 to * 我们学会了华文后，就不用求教于人了。After we have mastered the Chinese language we will not have to ask others for assistance. 6 (adv) 表示比较 for comparison * 这个数目大于一百。This number is greater than one hundred. 7 (adv) 表示被动（用于动词后面）to show passive voice
于是 [yú shì] therefore;hence;also; then;accordingly;consequently

盂 [yú] (n) 盛液体的圆口用器 a large cup; a basin

舆(輿) [yú] 1 (n) 地；疆域 land 2 (adj) 众人的 public (opinions;critics) * 政府的新文化政策获得舆论的支持。The new cultural policy of the government has gained the support of public opinion.

谀(諛) [yú] (v) 谄媚；奉承 flatter;praise * 为了升级，他努力阿谀老板。In order to get promotion, he tried hard to flatter his boss.

腴 [yú] (adj) 肥；丰满 fat; plump * 她体态丰腴。She has a plump figure

余(餘) [yú] 1 (adj) 剩下的，多出来的 remainder ; extra ; surplus * 家家有余粮。Every family has surplus food. 2 (adv) 以外；以后 beyond; after * 他工余常爱去打羽毛球。He used to play badminton after work. 3 (pron) 我 I
余地 [yú dì] room(for);extra space (for):(enough) place (for)
余额 [yú'é] available sum unused; vacancies not taken up ; balance;
余数 [yúshù] left-over number; remainder after subtracition
余暇 [yú xiá] leisure;spare time

鱼(魚) [yú] (n) 水生脊椎动物，通常体侧扁，有鳞和鳍，用鳃呼吸。fish

鱼翅 [yú chì] shark's fins
鱼饵 [yú ěr] fish bait
鱼肝油 [yú gān yóu] cod-liver oil
鱼贯而进 [yúguànérjìn] coming in succession, one after another like fishes
鱼米之乡 [yú mǐ zhī xiāng] district where fish and rice are abundant; region teeming with fish and rice
鱼目混珠 [yú mù hūn zhū] mix the genuine with the faked objects
鱼网 [yú wǎng] a fishing net
鱼雁往来 [yúyànwǎnglái] epistolary correspondence to and fro—from the legends of letters being found in the bellies of fish; and the story of a letter attached to the leg of a goose by Su Wu.

渔(漁) [yú] 1 (adj) 捕鱼的 of fishing 2 (v) 捕鱼 to fish
渔村 [yú cūn] fishing village
渔民 [yú mín] fisherman
渔业 [yú yè] fishery;fishing-industry

虞(虞) [yú] 1 (v) 预料 expect * 以备不虞。prepare for unexpectedness. 2 (v) 欺骗 cheat; deceive

娱(娛) [yú] 1 (adj) 快乐 happy 2 (v) 使快乐 amuse; rejoice;delight

娱乐 [yú lè] amusement; entertainment; recreation

娱乐场所 [yúlèchángsǔo] place of amusement

娱乐税 [yúlèshì] an entertainment tax

yǔ

语(語) [yǔ] 1 (n) 话 language; words * 汉语其实不难学。Actually it is not difficult to learn Chinese. 2 (v) 说 say;speak * 他站在一旁默默不语。He stands at one side without saying a word.

语病 [yǔ bìng] mistakes in the use of words ; a rhetorical error

语调 [yǔ diào] intonation

语法 [yǔ fǎ] grammar

语汇 [yǔhuì] vocabulary

语句 [yǔ jù] sentence

语录 [yǔlù] quotation

语气 [yǔ qì] tone of one's words

语态 [yǔtài] articulation

语文 [yǔ wén] language and its written form

语无伦次 [yǔwúlúncì] ramble in one's statement.

语言 [yǔ yán] language

语言学 [yǔyánxúe] Linguistics

语音 [yǔ yīn] phonetics

语重心长 [yǔ zhòng xīn cháng] words of sincerity and affection

语助词 [yǔ zhù cì] particle

宇 [yǔ] 1 (n) 屋边，泛指房屋 house 2 (n) 上下四方，所有的空间 space

宇宙 [yǔ zhòu] universe

伛(傴) [yǔ] (adj) 弯腰；驼背 humpbacked; hunchbacked

伛偻 [yǔlóu] humpbacked ; hunchbacked

与(與) [yǔ] 1 (conj) 和 and * 2 (prep) 同；跟 with * 农民必须与自然灾害斗争。The peasants must fight with natural disasters. 3 (v) 给 give 4 (v) 帮助 help 5 (adj) 交好 friendly; intimate; familiar

与虎谋皮 [yǔ hǔ mów pí] to ask the tiger for the skin—an impossible undertaking

与国 [yǔguó] allied states

与此同时 [yǔcǐtóngshí] together with this ; simultaneously ; in the meantime ; coincident ; concurrent ; at the same time ; meanwhile

与日俱增 [yǔ rì jù zēng] increase with each passing day; multiply daily;grow with time

与世隔绝 [yǔ shì gē jué] seclude from the world

另见 [yú]

屿(嶼) [yǔ] (n) 小岛 a small island; an islet

予 [yǔ] (v) 给 give;present;confer; grant; bestow * 校长授奖状予模范生。The principal presents a medal to the model student.

予以 [yǔ yǐ] give

羽 [yǔ] (n) 鸟类的毛 feather

羽毛球 [yǔ máo qíu] badminton shuttlecock

羽毛球拍 [yǔ máo qíu pāi] badminton rackets

羽翼未丰 [yǔ yì wèi fēng] not grown up;still young and immature

羽翼 [yǔ yì] wings; assistance

雨 [yǔ] (n) 云中小水滴结成大滴，落在地上 rain

雨过天晴 [yǔ guó tiān qíng] sunny spell after rain ; difficult period gives way to bright future

雨后春笋 [yǔ hòu chūn sǔn] (spring up like) bamboo shoots after spring rain

雨季 [yǔ jì] rainy reason

雨量 [yǔ liàng] rainfall

雨伞 [yǔ sǎn] umbrella

雨衣 [yǔ yī] raincoat

yù

域 [yù] (n) 在一定疆界以内的地方 region;land ＊亚细安国家举行了一连串的区域性工业计划会议。The Asean countries had held a series of regional conferences regarding regional industrial projects.

鹬(鷸) [yù] (n) 鸟类，羽毛茶褐色，嘴、腿很长，常在水边或田野吃小鱼、小虫和贝类。snipe, a wading bird

鹬蚌相争，渔翁得利 [yùbàngxiāng zhēngyúwēngdélì] Contention between a snipe and a clam only benefits the fisherman.

浴 [yù] (v) 洗澡 bathe

浴血奋战 [yù xuè fèn zhàn] fighting a brave and bloody battle; fierce battle

裕 [yù] 1 (adj)富足；宽绰 rich;wealthy;generous ＊他来自富裕的家庭。He comes from a wealthy family. 2 (adv) 从容；不费力 easily ; with ease ; with little effort ＊他对外交事务应付裕如。He managed foreign affairs with ease.

欲 [yù] 1 (n) 要求 desire ＊他想办法满足自己的欲望。He tries to satisfy his own desire. 2 (v) 想要；希望 wish; desire; hope ＊他觉得很苦闷，因为他不能畅所欲言。He feels very frustrated for he cannot say what he wishes to say. 3 (v) 需要 need ＊胆欲大而心欲细 One needs to be bold but attentive. (4)adv 将要 going to ; likely to ＊山雨欲来风满楼。The room is filled with breezes just before the coming of a storm.

欲盖弥彰 [yùgàimízhāng] the more one tries to hide, the more one is exposed; the more it is concealed, the more conspicuous it becomes

欲加之罪，何患无辞 [yù jiā zhī zuì, hé huàn wù cí] if you wish to prosecute, there is never any lack of charges

欲念 [yù niàn] desire;longing;hankering

欲速则不达 [yù sù zè bù dá] haste brings no success

欲望 [yùwàng] hankering ; longing ; desire

谕(諭) [yù] (v) 告诉；吩咐 to instruct; to tell

喻 [yù] 1 (n)比方 metaphor; analogy 2 (v) 明白 understand ＊他完成了任务，心里高兴是不言而喻的。It goes without saying that he feels happy after accomplishing his duty. 3 (v) 说明 to reason ＊他性情暴躁，发脾气时，简直不可理喻。He is short-tempered; when he losses his temper, it is impossible to reason with him.

愈 [yù] 1 (adv)更；越 the more...... the more;more and more ＊山路愈走愈陡。The more we go the steeper is the mountain path. 2 (v)(病)好了 recover from an illness ＊他病愈后就可以开始工作了。He can begin work after recovering from his illness.

愈合 [yù hé] heal up

愈加 [yù jiān] increasingly; all the more

预(預) [yú] (adv)事前 in advance ＊如果你不能出席会议，请预先通知我。If you cannot attend the meeting, please inform me in advance.

预报 [yù bào] forecast (e.g. weather)

预备 [yù bèi] prepare;get ready; arrange for

预订 [yù dìng] place an order for; book;subscribe

预定 [yù dìng] prearrange;preconcert;predefine;predetermine

预防 [yù fáng] prevent;provide against;guard against

预防为主 [yùfángwéizhǔ] put prevention first

预感 [yù gǎn] have premonitions of

预告 [yù gào] predict;foretell;forecast;prediction

预计 [yùjì] expect; envisage; reckon in advance

预见 [yù jiàn] foresee;prediction; foresight

预料 [yù liào] predict;expect;foresee;anticipate

预期 [yù qī] expect;anticipate

预赛 [yúsài] preliminary contest

预示 [yù shì] portend;predict;foretell

预算 [yù suàn] budget;an estimate

预习 [yùxí] prepare lessons

预想 [yù xiǎng] expect;anticipate; previously formulate

预言 [yù yán] predict;presage;foretell;prophesy

预演 [yùyǎn] rehearsal; rehearse

预约 [yù yuē] pre-engage; make an appointment.....before hand

预展 [yùzhǎn] exhibit in advance

预兆 [yù zhào] omen;presage;foreshadow

育 [yù] 1 (v)生;扶养 give birth ＊许多妇女生儿育女后 就给家庭事务缠住了。Many women are totally occupied with family matters after having given birth to children 2 (v) 培养 cultivate ; bring up ＊我们要好好的养育下一代。We must bring up the new generation properly. 3 (v) 养活；养护 breed; cultivate;nourish ＊菜农在小心培育幼苗。The vegetable farmer is cultivating the seedlings with care.

育婴 [yù yīng] to nourish and bring up the baby

育种 [yù zhǒng] breeding of seeds

寓 [yù] 1 (v) 居住 live;stay 2 (n) 住的地方 residence 3 (v) 寄托；含蓄 carry; cover (a meaning) ＊这句话的寓意很深。This saying carries a deep meaning.

寓言 [yù yán] fable;parable

遇 [yù] 1 (v)碰到 meet ＊他们在街上相遇。They met on the street. 2 (v) 对待；接待 treat 3 (n) 机会 opportunity ＊他的际遇比他的弟弟好得多了。He has a better opportunity than his brother.

遇到 [yù dào] meet;meet with;encounter;run into (e.g. difficulties)

遇害 [yù hài] be murdered; be killed

遇见 [yù jiàn] meet;encounter

遇救 [yù jiù] be rescued

遇难 [yù nàn] die in an accident or as a result of persecution

遇险 [yù xiǎn] meet with danger

妪(嫗) [yù] (n)年老的妇女 old woman

芋 [yù] (n) 俗称“芋头”，草本植物，地下茎可供食用 ，叶柄可作饲料。taro;an edible tuber

吁（籲）[yù] (v) 为某种要求而呼喊appeal ＊小商人呼吁政府减低捐税 The petty traders appeal to the government for the reduction of tax payment.

吁请 [yù qǐng] appeal

另见[xū]

玉 [yù] 1 (n) 一种有光泽、略透明、质地坚硬的矿物，可用作装饰品或雕刻的原料 jade;gem 2 (n) 敬词，称对方的身体或行动 a word of courtesy for a person's body or actions.

玉米 [yù mǐ] maize;corn

玉石俱焚 [yù shí jù fén] the good and bad being destroyed altogether

玉蜀黍 [yù shǔ shǔ] maize;corn

玉簪 [yù zān] jade hair-pin

御（禦）[yù] 1 (v) 驾驶车马drive a chariot 2 (v) 抵挡 withstand;resist;keep out ＊喝酒可以御寒。One can keep out the cold by drinking wine. 3 (adj) 与皇帝有关的 imperial

御用文人 [yù yòng wén rén] a person who writes in the interests of the ruler

与（與）[yù] (v) 参加 take part; attend

另见[yǔ]

誉（譽）[yù] 1 (n) 名声 reputation 他很重视名誉地位。He pays great attention to reputation and status. 2 (v) 称赞 praise

誉满全国 [yù mǎn quán gúo] well-reputed throughout the country

郁（鬱）[yù] 1 (adj) 树木丛生，很茂盛的样子 dense and flourishing ＊草木郁郁葱葱。The trees and plants are dense and flourishing in growth. 2 (adj) 形容香气浓 fragrant ; strong (of odour) ＊他闻到浓郁的香水味。He smells the strong odour of perfume. 3 (adj) 苦闷，心情不舒畅 frustrated;depressed ＊他因为考试不及格，神情非常忧郁。He is highly depressed because he failed in the examination.

郁闷 [yù mèn] depressed;melancholy

郁郁不乐 [yù yǘ bù lè] frustrated and unhappy

郁郁寡欢 [yù yù kuǎ huān] unhappy

驭 [yú] 1 (v) 驾驶车马 drive;ride 2 (v) 统率；控制 rule;lead;control

狱（獄）[yù] 1 (n) 监狱，监禁犯人的地方，prison ; jail ; gaol ＊他被判入狱三年。He was sentenced to jail for three years. 2 (n) 指官司，罪案 law suit;criminal case

狱卒 [yù zú] prison warden

yuān

鸳（鴛）[yuān] (n) 鸟类，雄的叫"鸳"，雌的叫"鸯"，形状象野鸭，雄的羽毛美丽，雌雄常在一起。a male mandarin duck

鸳鸯枕 [yuān yāng zhěn] a double pillow for married couples.

渊（淵）[yuān] 1 (n) 深水，潭 deep water; deep pool 2 (adj) 深 profound ＊他是一位知识渊博的学者。He is a scholar with profound knowledge.

渊博 [yuānbó] profound

渊深 [yuān shēn] deep(e.g. learning)

渊源 [yuān yuán] the source;the origin

冤 [yuān] 1 (v) 受屈 be wronged;be falsely accused;be falsely implicated ＊那个被抓的人大喊冤枉。 The person who had been caught cried that he had been falsely implicated. 2 (n)冤仇；冤屈 injustice;unfairness;false charge;wrong charge ＊穷人有冤没处诉。 The poor have nowhere to voice the injustice done on them. 3 (n)仇恨 enmity;hatred

冤家路窄 [yuān jiā lù zhǎi] the street for the foes is narrow

冤狱 [yuān yù] a case where the accused had been wronged or falsely implicated

yuán

原 [yuán] 1 (adj) 起初的，本来的 initial;orginal ＊他没有说明原意。 He did not explain his original intention. 2 (adj) 没有经过加工的 crude; raw 3 (n) 宽广平坦的地方 a plain

原封不动 [yuán fēng bù dòng] be kept intact;remain unchanged;in its original state

原稿 [yuán gǎo] original manuscript;original copy

原告 [yuán gào] plaintiff;accuser

原籍 [yuán jí] native home;native place

原来 [yuán lái] at first;at the beginning;originally;it turns out that...; as a matter of fact

原理 [yuán lǐ] principle;fundamental theory; axiom

原谅 [yuán liàng] pardon;excuse

原料 [yuán liào] raw materials

原始 [yuán shǐ] primitive;virgin;primeval;initial;first hand

原始社会 [yuán shǐ shè huì] primitive society

原先 [yuán xiān] original;at first

原形毕露 [yuán xíng bì lù] reveal one's true nature;show one's true colours(derogatory)

原野 [yuán yě] open country;wilderness

原因 [yuán yīn] cause ; reason ; grounds

原原本本 [yuán yuán běn běn] from the beginning to the end

原则 [yuán zé] principle;fundamental rule

原则性 [yuán zé xìng] in principle; highly principled

原著 [yuán zhú] original; original copy

原子 [yuán zǐ] atom

原子弹 [yuán zǐ dàn] atomic bomb

原子核 [yuánzǐhé] atomic nucleus

原子结构 [yuánzǐjiégòu] atomic structure

原子量 [yuánzǐliàng] atomic weight

原子能 [yuánzǐnéng] atomic energy

原子序数 [yuán zǐ xù shù] atomic number

援 [yuán] 1 (v) 支持；帮助 support; help;assist;aid ＊我们以金钱援助他 We assisted him with money. 2 (v) 引用 quote;cite ＊当局援用移民法令驱逐他出境 。The authority cited the Immigration Act and deported him.

援救 [yuán jiù] rescue;extricate from danger;save

援军 [yuán jūn] rescue troops;reinforcement

援助 [yuán zhù] aid;assistance 、

猿 [yuán] (n) 哺乳动物，与猴同类，没有尾巴，如猩猩，长臂猿等 ape;gibbon

猿人 [yuán rén] anthropoid ape;ape man

元 [yuán] 1 (adj) 开始的，第一的;为首的 beginning;first 2 (adj) chief; st ＊国家元首 the head of a state. 3 (n) 单位。 unit 4 (n) 货币单位，十角为一元，也作“圆” dollar a unit of currency

元老 [yuán lǎo] veteran

元帅 [yuán shuài] marshal

元素 [yuán sù] (chemical) element

元素周期表 [yuán sù zhōu qī biǎo] the periodic table (of chemical element)

元月 [yuán yuè] January

源 [yuán] 1 (n) 水流起头的地方 source of water ＊长江发源于何处？Where does the Yangtse River take its source? 2 (n) 事情的来由 origin;source ＊ 他们收入的主要来源是渔业。Their chief sources of revenue are their fisheries.

源泉 [yuán quán] spring;fountain; source

源头 [yuán tóu] waterhead

源源不绝 [yuán yuán bù jué] perpetual;endless

源远流长 [yuán yuǎn líu chàng] the flow is long and the source distant

园（園） [yuán] 1 (n)种蔬菜花果的地方 a garden; an orchard;a yard 2 (n)供人休息和娱乐的地方a park ＊ 公园里有许多凉亭。There are many pavilions for shelter in the park.

园地 [yuán dì] a general term for vegetable plot,fruit orchard,flower garden etc

园丁 [yuán dīng] gardener

园林 [yuán lín] tree garden;landscape garden

园艺 [yuán yì] art of gardening;horticulture

辕（轅） [yuán] (n)车前驾牲口的两条长木 the shafts of a cart or carriage

员（員） [yuán] 1 (n)组织或团体中的人 member ＊ 他是工会会员。He is a member of the trade union. 2 (n) 工作或学习的人 student or professional ＊差利卓别灵是一位著名的演员。Charlie Chaplain was a famous film star. 3 (n) 量词，用于武将 a measure word for a general ＊他是我手下的一员大将。He is a great general under me.

员工 [yuán gōng] officer and worker

圆（圓） [yuán] 1 (n) (adj) 从中心点到周边任何一点距离都相等的体形 circle;circular; round 2 (adj)完整；周全full;perfect;complete＊人权大会圆满地结束了。The Human Rights Conference ended satisfactorily as planned. 3 (v) 使周全，多指掩饰矛盾 to make something perfect by covering up the contradictions ＊ 他很会自圆其说。He is able to present his view well without creating any loopholes.

圆规 [yuán guī] compasses

圆滑 [yuán huá] oily;cunning;slippery

圆心 [yuán xīn] centre of a circle

圆形 [yuán xíng] circular;round

圆柱 [yuán zhù] cylinder;column; pillar

圆锥 [yuán zhuī] cone

缘（緣） [yuán] 1(n) 原因 reason; cause 他无缘无故发脾气。He loses his temper for no reason. 2 (n)边缘 border;boundary;side ＊ 在马路边缘玩耍是危险的。It is dangerous to play at the roadside. 3 (n)关系 relation

缘分 [yuán fén] affinity; chance meeting

缘故 [yuán gù] reason;cause

yuǎn

远（遠） [yuǎn] 1 (adj) 距离大 far;distant ＊我的家离开市区很远。My home is very far away from the urban district. 2 (adj)时间长久 long; distant (in time) ＊这是一些年代久远的出土文物。These are unearthed historical relics of a distant past. 3 (adj) （差别）程度大great(in difference) ＊ 美国的生活费和这里的相差很远 There is a great difference between the cost of living in America and here.

远方 [yuǎn fang] distant;remote

远见 [yuǎn jiàn] far-sighted view; far-sightedness;foresight

远景 [yuǎn jǐng] distant prospect; outlook;long-range prospect

远亲不如近邻 [yuǎnqīnbùrújìnlín] a near neighbour is better than a distant cousin

远涉重洋 [yuǎnshèchóngyáng] travelling across oceans and seas

远视眼 [yuǎnshìyǎn] Hypermetropia; long-sightedness.

远洋 [yuǎn yáng] the distant seas; ocean-going (e.g. vessel)

远征 [yuǎn zhēng] expedition;military expedition;long march

远走高飞 [yuǎn zǒu gāo fēi] go away to a distant place

远足 [yuǎnzú] excursion;trip

yuàn

苑 [yuàn] 1 (n)养鸟兽和种植树木的地方。 a garden; a park 2 (n)（学术、文艺）聚集的地方 a centre for academic studies and literature

怨 [yuàn] 1 (n)仇恨 hatred;spite;resentment;grudge* 他的儿子为非作歹，到处结怨。His son commits evil at will and thus invite spite everywhere. 2 (v)责怪 grumble;blame * 他不辞劳苦，为群体任劳任怨的工作。He fears no difficulty and can tolerate hardships and grumblings in working for the masses.

怨不得 [yuàn·bu·de] cannot blame; not to be blamed

怨恨 [yuàn hèn] hatred;grudge;bear resentment against

怨气 [yuàn qì] grudge;resentment; complaint

怨声载道 [yuànshēngzàidào] complaints ringing everywhere.

怨天尤人 [yuàn tiān yóu rén] blame Heaven and others

怨言 [yuàn yán] grumble ; complaints

院 [yuàn] 1 (n)围墙以内的空地，有时也指房屋 a courtyard* 院子里种了一些花。Some flowers are planted in the courtyard. 2 (n)机关、单位和公共场所的名称。 institution;public building*工艺学院。the institute of Polytechnic.

院长 [yuàn zhǎn] the dean of a college;the director of a hospital

愿（願） [yuàn] 1 (v) 乐意；肯 be willing;would like * 他愿意帮忙我。He is willing to help me. 2 (n) 希望 wish;desire;aspiration;hope * 他如愿以偿了。His wishes came true.

愿望 [yuàn wàng] wish;desire;aspiration;hope;expectation

媛 [yuàn] (n)美女 beautiful girl

yuē

曰 [yuē] (v)说 say

约（約） [yuē] 1 (v)限制 restrain; restrict; keep under control * 他虽被释放了，但行动却受到约束。 Although he has been released, his movement is restricted. 2 (n) 共同议定的条文 treaty;agreement;bond * 两国签署了一项和约。 The two countries have signed a peace treaty. 3 (v)事先说定 make an appointment * 我已经和他约好今天去看戏。 I have already made an appointment with him to go for a show. 4 (adj)大概 about * 观众约三百人。 There are about three hundred spectators. 5 (v)节省 save;economize * 我们要尽可能节约开支。 We should try our best to economize in our expenditure

约会 [yuē huì] appointment;engagement

约数 [yuē shù] approximate number

yuè

月 [yuè] 1 (n) 地球的卫星 the moon 2 (n) 一年的十二分之一 month ＊他这个月的收入减少了。His income is reduced this month.

月初 [yuè chū] the beginning of a month

月底 [yuè dǐ] the end of a month

月份牌 [yuè fèn pái] the monthly calendar

月经 [yuè jīng] menstruation;menses

月刊 [yuè kān] monthly publication;magazine

月色 [yuè sè] moonlight

月薪 [yuè xīn] monthly salary

月中 [yuè zhōng] the middle of a month

钥(鑰) [yuè] (n) 锁 lock

悦 [yuè] 1 (adj)欢喜；高兴 pleased; delighted;gratified ＊他脸露不悦之色。He appears to be displeased. 2 (v)使愉快 be pleasing＊这首曲子悦耳动听。This piece of music is pleasant to the ear.

悦目 [yuè mù] pleasant to the eye; please the eye

阅(閱) [yuè] 1 (v) 看；查看 see; read; go over; examine ＊他只能阅读通俗书报。He can only read simplified popular books and newspaper. 2 (v) 经历；经过 go through; experience ＊他应该出去阅历一番。He should go out to experience something new.

阅兵 [yuè bīng] review troops;a military review;an inspection of troops

阅读 [yuèdú] read

阅览 [yuè lǎn] read

阅览室 [yuè lǎn shì] reading room

越 [yuè] 1 (v) 度过(障碍) overcome;pass over;climb over ＊军队在征途中翻山越岭。The troops climbed over many mountains and hills in their military expedition. 2 (v) ＊不按照一般的次序，超出范围 transgress;deviate from;depart from : rules, principles etc ＊他有越权之嫌。He is suspected of transgression of power. (adv) 越……越……，表示程度加深 the more.....the more..... ＊脑子越用越灵。The more you use your brain,the cleverer you become.

越发 [yuèfa]more and more; increasingly

越轨 [yuè guǐ] beyond bounds;derail;deviate;departure(from rules; principles etc)

越过 [yuè guò] surpass;pass over; cross;pass by

越境 [yuè jìng] illegally cross over a boundary

越狱 [yuè yù] escape from prison; break prison

越…越 yuè...yuè...] the more....the more

乐(樂) [yùe] (n) 音乐；五声八音的总称 music ＊他喜欢华乐。He likes Chinese music. 另见 [lè]

乐队 [yuè duì] orchestra;band

乐理 [yuè lǐ] musical theory

乐谱 [yuè pǔ] musical score;score sheets

乐器 [yuè qì] musical instruments

乐曲 [yuè qǔ] melody;musical composition

乐团 [yuè tuán] musical troupe

跃(躍) [yuè] 1 (v) 跳 jump ＊人们高兴得欢呼跳跃。The people are so happy that they jump for joy. 2 (adv) 生动地呈现出来的样子 vividly exposed ＊义愤之情跃然纸上。The feelings of anger for justice being undone were vividly described in the book.

跃进 [yuè jìn] make progress by leaps and bounds;make a leap; leap forward

跃跃欲试 [yuè yuè yù shì] anxious to try;itch to have a go

岳 [yuè] 1 (n) 高大的山 a lofty mountain 2 (n) 称妻的父母 parents of one's wife

岳母 [yuè mǔ] mother-in-law

粤 [yuè] (n) 广东省的简称 the Kwangtung Province

yūn

晕(暈) [yūn] 1 (v)头脑发昏 be giddy;feel dizzy＊机器转动得很快，看久了会头晕。 The machine turns very fast；one feels giddy when looking at it for a long time. 2 (v) 昏迷 faint ＊他晕倒了。 He had fainted.

另见 [yùn]

yún

云 [yún] (v) 说 say ＊ 人云亦云 to say what others have said; does not have one's opinion.

云(雲) [yún] (n) 水蒸气上升遇冷凝聚成微小的水滴或冰晶，成团地在空中飘浮，叫"云" clouds

云彩 [yún cǎi] clouds

云层 [yún céng] cloud layer

云集 [yún jí] gather together

云消雾散 [yún xiāo wù sàn] the sky has cleared up;clear up;disappear

耘 [yún] (v)除草 weed;remove grass and other plants from the field ＊ 春耕夏耘 to plough in spring and weed in summer.

芸 [yún] (n)草本植物，有强烈香味，可供药用 a fragrant plant

匀 [yún] 1 (adj) 平均；齐 equal; even;average;same ＊ 颜色涂得不均匀。The colour is not evenly painted.2 (v)使平均 divide equally; balance 3 (v)分出一部分来给别人 share with others＊把稻种匀一些给兄弟队。 Share the padi seeds with our brother-teams.

匀称 [yún · chèn] well balanced; well-proportioned

匀净 [yún·jing] well balanced; well-proportioned

匀速转动 [yún sù zhuǎn dòng] uniform rotation

yǔn

陨(隕) [yǔn] (v) 从空中落下 fall or drop from the sky

陨星 [yǔn xīng] a meteor

殒(殞) [yǔn] (v)死亡 die

允 [yǔn] 1 (v)答应 promise;consent; approve;allow;permit ＊ 她母亲不允许她参加太多活动。Her mother does not allow her to take part in too many activities. 2 (adj) 公平；得当fair;appropriate ＊他办事公允。He is fair in his dealing.

允诺 [yǔn nuò] give consent;promise

yùn

愠 [yùn] (adj)恼怒；怨恨 angry;bear resentment ＊ 他父亲面有愠色。 His father looks angry.

蕴(藴) [yùn] (v) 含；藏 contain;hide ＊中东各地蕴藏的石油很丰富。The petroleum hidden in various parts of the Middle East is abundant.

晕(暈) [yùn] (n)太阳、月亮周围的光圈 the halo of the moon or sun

另见 [yūn]

晕车 [yùn chē] train sick;car sick

酝(醖) [yùn] (v) 酿酒 brew

运(運) [yùn] 1 (v) 移动；旋转 move;revolve＊月球绕着

地球运转。The moon revolves round the earth. 2 (v) 搬动；输送 carry;transport;deliver 3 (n) 也用来指客观规律发展的趋势 fate; luck; ✱ 他没有运气。He has no luck. 4 (v) 应用 apply; utilize; put to use

运筹学 [yùn chóu xué] operations research

运动 [yùn dòng] move;be in motion;sports;athletics;campaign

运动会 [yùn dòng huì] athletics meet ;sports meet ;games

运动员 [yùn dòng yuán] athlete

运河 [yùn hé] canal

运输 [yùn shū] transport

运送 [yùn sòng] deliver;transit; transport

运行 [yùn xíng] circulate;move

运载 [yùn zài] carry;deliver

韵 [yùn] 1 (n)和谐的声音 tone;rhyme ✱ 琴韵悠扬 The tone from the musical instrument is beautiful. 2 (n) 元音; 母音 vowels 3 (n) 风致；情趣 charm;interest;taste ✱ 他的唱腔很有韵味。His singing tone is charming.

韵脚 [yùn jiǎo] the last word in a verse which rhymes with another

韵律 [yùn lǜ] rhythm

孕 [yùn] 1 (adj) 怀胎 pregnant ✱ 孕妇应避免做粗重的工作。A pregnant woman should avoid doing heavy jobs. 2 (v) 从已有的事物中培养出新生事物 be filled with ;breed ;·generate ✱ 他的文学作品孕育着新思想。His literary work is filled with new ideas.

孕期 [yùn qī] gestation

熨 [yùn] 1 (v) 把衣物烫平 to iron clothes ✱ 妈妈在熨衣服。Mother is ironing the clothes. 2 (n)熨斗；烫衣服用的金属器具 iron

Z

zā

扎 [zā] (v)捆；束 to tie;to bind;to fasten ＊护士包扎他的伤口。The nurse binds up his wound.
另见 [zhā]

zá

咱 [zá] (pron) 我 I;one
另见 [zán]

杂(雜) [zá] 1 (adj) 不纯粹的，多种多样的 mixed;miscellaneous; assorted ＊我的杂用费包括买邮票和理发的钱。My miscellaneous expenses include stamps and haircuts. 2 (v)混合；渗入 to mix;to blend

杂费 [zá fèi] miscellaneous fees; miscellaneous charges

杂感 [zá gǎn] fleeting impression; random thoughts

杂货 [zá huò] sundry goods;groceries

杂货店 [zá huò diàn] grocery;grocer's

杂记 [zá jì] random note; miscellanies

杂技 [zá jì] acrobatics

杂交 [zá jiāo] cross-breed;hybridize

杂粮 [zá liáng] coarse cereals;miscellaneous grain crops(e.g. maize, millet etc.)

杂乱 [zá luàn] disorderly;disarranged;confused

杂乱无章 [zá luàn wú zhāng] out of order;untidy;in a mess

杂文 [zá wén] short essays;essay; satirical essay

杂务 [zá wù] odd job;miscellaneous business

杂音 [zá yīn] interference(e.g.radio);confused noise

杂志 [zá zhì] magazine;periodical

杂质 [zá zhì] impurity;pollution

砸 [zá] (v) 敲打 to bash;to smash ＊我把炭块砸碎。I smash the charcoal block into pieces.

zāi

栽 [zāi] 1 (v) 种植 to plant;to grow;to cultivate ＊我在屋子前面栽了一些果树。I have planted some fruit trees in front of the house. 2 (v)跌倒 to fall down;to tumble ＊杰克栽破了头。Jack fell down and broke his crown. 3 (n)供移植的秧苗或切枝 saplings; young tree slips or cuttings for planting ＊桃栽 peach slips for planting;peach saplings ＊花栽。flower cuttings

栽培 [zāi péi] to plant and cultivate; to educate;to train;to foster;to cultivate

栽赃 [zāi zāng] to place stolen goods with a person to implicate him;to shift the blame on to;to plant.....on somebody

灾 [zāi] (n) 祸害disaster;calamity *战争是可怕的灾难。War is a frightful calamity

灾害 [zāi hài] disaster;calamity

灾荒 [zāi huāng] famine

灾祸 [zāi huò] disaster;calamity;sufferings;catastrophic consequences

灾黎 [zāi lí] the calamity-stricken people

灾难 [zāi nàn] misfortune;calamity;catastrophe

灾情 [zāi qíng] extent of a famine or natural disaster

灾殃 [zāi yāng] natural disaster;misfortune;catastrophe

灾异 [zāi yì] portents

zǎi

宰 [zǎi] (v)屠杀牲畜to slaughter;to kill;to butcher*节日里，村民杀猪宰羊。During the festivals, the villagers slaughter pigs and goats.

宰割 [zǎi gè] to cut up;to trample underfoot;to oppress and exploit

仔 [zǎi] 1 (n)幼小的动物young animal*猪仔 piglet 2 (n) 对男孩子的昵称 sonny;a nickname for boys *明仔。Sonny Ming

另见 [zī]

载(載) [zǎi] 1 (n)年 year *这是千载难逢的好机会。This is a good opportunity you will hardly find in a thousand years. 2 (v)记录；刊登 to record;to register;to publish *报上刊载了一篇有关空气污染的文章。The newspaper has published an article on air pollution.

另见 [zài]

zài

载(載) [zài] 1 (v) 装运to load;to carry;to convey;to transport *巴士通常在侧门载客。The bus usually loads at side door. 2 (v) 充满to fill with *苛政之下，怨声载道。Under the oppressive rule,murmurs fill the streets 3(conj) 又；且 and *少女们载歌载舞。The young girls sang and danced.

另见 [zǎi]

再 [zài] 1 (adv) 又一次或第二次 again;once more;once again *他出狱后不久再度被捕。He was arrested again soon after he had been released from jail. 2 (adv) 更加 further;more *如果你肯帮忙那是再好也没有了。There will be nothing better if you are willing to help. 3 (adv) 然后；才 then ;till;till then *我们工作完了再说。We shall discuss it till we have finished our work.

再版 [zài bǎn] to reprint; to republish;second edition

再度 [zài dù] once more;again;once again

再见 [zài jiàn] see you again;goodbye

再接再厉 [zài jiē zài lì] to make unremitting efforts;to make sustained and redoubled efforts

再三 [zài sān] repeatedly;again and again;time and again

再生产 [zài shēng chǎn] to reproduce

再说 [zài shuō] to see to something later;to attend to something later;furthermore

再现 [zài xiàn] to reappear

在 [zài] 1 (v) 存；生存；活着 to exist;to be present;to be alive;live *他父母健在。His parents are soundly alive. 2 (v) 处于（某动作或过程）to be (in the act or process of)..... *他在睡觉，别打扰他。He is sleeping ; do not disturb him. 3 (prep) 处于某时间、地点或范围 at; in; on; over;

among;amidst ＊他们在礼堂里开会。They are having their meeting in the hall. 4(v)依赖;全靠 lie in;to rest with;to depend on ＊挽救之道在于教育。The cure lies in education.

在案 [zài àn] on record

在场 [zài chǎng] in the presence; on the spot;be present

在后 [zài hòu] behind

在乎 [zài·hu] be particular about; mindful of;to care about;to lie on; to rest in;to depend on

在即 [zài jí] at once;immediately; near at hand

在假 [zài jià] on leave

在···看來 [zài ... kàn laí] from the point of view of;as ... sees it

在···里 [zài ..... lǐ] inside;in

在···內 [zài ..... nèi] included;in; among

在前 [zài qián] beforehand; that time;then

在···上 [zài .... shàng] above;over; up

在世 [zài shì] alive;live

在所不免 [zài suǒ bù miǎn] it cannot but be;unavoidable

在外 [zài wài] extra;outside;over and above

在望 [zai wàng] within reach;within sight

在···下 [zài ..... xià] below;under; underneath;beneath

在野 [zài yě] out of office;in obscurity

在意 [zài yì] to be particular about; mindful of;to care about;to mind

在于 [zài yú] to lie in;to rest with;to depend on

在在 [zài zài] in every case; everywhere

在职 [zài zhí] in office;at one's post;at work

在···中 [zài ..... zhōng] in;among; in the midst of

在座 [zài zuò] to be present at;in the presence of

zān

簪 [zān] (n) 插在发上的一种饰物 a hairpin

zán

咱 [zán] (pron) 我 I;me
另见 [zá]

咱们 [zán men] we;us

zǎn

攒(攢) [zǎn] (v) 积蓄；积聚 to save; to accumulate;to bring together

zàn

赞(贊) [zàn] 1 (v) 资助；支持 to patronize; to support ＊李氏基金赞助这项社会调查计划。The Lee Foundation patronizes this social survey project. 2 (v) 夸奖；称许 to praise;to commend;to admire＊好人好事应该受到赞扬。Good personalities and good deeds should be praised. 3 (v) 同意 to approve;to second＊我赞成林先生的意见。I second Mr. Lin's idea.

赞不绝口 [zàn bù jué kǒu] to praise (somebody or something) unceasingly

赞成 [zàn chéng] to approve;to assent;to favour;to agree;to second

赞歌 [zàn gē] song of praise;ode

赞美 [zàn měi] to admire;to praise

赞赏 [zàn shǎng] to appreciate; to praise

赞叹 [zàn tàn] to praise highly;to admire

赞同 [zàn tóng] to assent;to agree; to second;to favour

赞许 [zàn xǔ] to approve commendation

赞扬 [zàn yáng] to extol;to speak favourably of

赞助 [zàn zhù] to support;to aid; assistance

暂(暫) [zàn] (adv) 临时；短时间 temporarily; for a short time *机器出毛病使工作暂停。A breakdown of machinery temporarily stopped the work.

暂且 [zàn qiě] for the time being; for the moment;for the present

暂时 [zàn shí] temporary;provisional;not permanent.

錾(鏨) [zàn] (n) 凿石头的小凿子 a chisel

zāng

脏(髒) [zāng] (adj) 肮脏；不干净 dirty;filthy *不要用脏手帕擦眼。Do not rub the eye with a dirty handkerchief.

zàng

赃(贓) [zàng] (n) 贪污受贿或偷盗所得的财物 bribes; stolen goods; booty; pilfered property *典当的物品中有些是贼赃。Some of the pawned articles are stolen goods.

赃官 [zāng guān] a corrupt official

赃物 [zāng wù] stolen articles (goods); pilfered property

藏 [zàng] 1 (n) 储放东西的地方 a storehouse;a reserve;a hoard 宝藏。treasure-trove;buried treasure 矿藏mineral reserves. 2 (n) 佛道教经典总称the Buddhist or Taoist classics 3 (n) 西藏简称abbreviated term for Xizang (Tibet)

另见[cáng]

脏(臟) [zàng] (n) 内脏，身体内部各种器官的总称 viscera;the entrails

葬 [zàng] (v)掩埋死人 to bury*他们把飞机失事蒙难者的尸体埋葬在同一处。They buried the bodies of the air crash victims at the same place.

葬礼 [zàng lǐ] funeral ceremony; obsequies

葬送 [zàng sòng] to bring ..... to ruin;to ruin

zāo

糟 [zāo] 1 (n) 渣滓 sediment;dregs; grains from a distillery 2 (adj) 腐烂to decay ; to rot *木头 糟了 The wood has rotted. 3 (adj) 坏；不好bad;in a mess;in chaos and ruin *他把事情弄糟了。He has made a mess of the matter.

糟糕 [zāo gāo] a cake made of dregs; too bad luck;what a mess!

糟糠 [zāo kāng] poor men's food; distiller's grains

糟粕 [zāo pò] slag; scum; dregs; waste matter;dross.

糟蹋 [zāo tá] to spoil;to waste;to misuse;to disgrace;to trample;to ravage

遭 [zāo] 1 (v) 遇到；碰上 to meet with (calamity, death, etc.);to suffer (e.g. setbacks);to sustain *当雨季来临时，住在低地的村民就要遭殃。When the rainy season sets in, villagers living in the low-lying area will meet with disaster. 2 (n) 次a measure word (for time, occasion turn, etc.) *参加国际球赛，他还是第一遭。This is the first time he takes part in an international tournament.

遭到 [zāo dào] to meet with;to come under;to sustain

遭受 [zāo shòu] to suffer;to endure;to undergo

遭殃 [zāo yāng] to suffer a catastrophe;to meet with disaster;to run into calamity;to suffer

遭遇 [zāo yù] to meet with (disaster, difficulties, etc.);to come under;to encounter suffering;sad lot

záo

凿(鑿) [záo] 1 (n) 挖槽或打孔用的工具 a chisel; a punch 2 (v)打孔；挖掘 to chisel;to punch;to dig *他在铁板上凿一个孔。He punched a hole on the iron plate.

zǎo

澡 [zǎo] (v) 洗浴 to bathe

藻 [zǎo] 1 (n) 水草的总称 aquatic grasses;water weed;algae 2 (adj)华丽;文采;高雅 elegant * 词藻 。ornate phraseology (in pedantic writing)

早 [zǎo] 1 (n) 清晨，太阳出来的时候morning *劳动人民从早忙到晚。The working people work from morning till night. 2(adj)先前；在一定时间以前 early *忙什么，离开演出时间还早呢。 Why hurry? it's still early for the show. *人类早已懂得武器的用处。Man early learned the usefulness of weapons.

早操 [zǎo cāo] morning exercise
早晨 [zǎo·chen] morning
早点 [zǎo diǎn] a light breakfast
早期 [zǎo qī] earlier period;early stage
早日 [zǎo rì] soon;earlier
早上 [zǎo·shang] morning
早熟 [zǎo shú] early ripening;precocity;premature
早晚 [zǎo wǎn] morning and evening; sooner or later
早先 [zǎo xiān] in former times;formerly
早已 [zǎo yǐ] already
早知如此 [zǎo zhī rú cǐ] if I had only known it .....

枣(棗) [zǎo] (n)落叶亚乔木。果椭圆形，成熟后红色，可食。 木质坚硬，可制车 船和用具 the date tree;the dates

枣红 [zǎo hóng] reddish-brown; date-red

蚤 [zǎo] (n) 也叫“跳蚤”，昆虫。体侧扁，褐色，无翅， 善跳跃。寄在人畜身上，吸血，能传 播鼠疫等病症the flea

zào

噪 [zào] (v) 喧哗to make noises *群鸦乱噪。The crows are making a lot of noises.

噪音 [zào yīn] unharmonious noises

燥 [zào] (adj) 没有水分或水分很少 dry;arid *沙漠是干燥炎热的地方。The desert is a dry and hot place.

躁 [zào] (adj) 性急不冷静 quick-tempered;impatient;rash *他性情急躁，不适于做领导工作。 He is too quick-tempered to be suitable for leadership work.

造 [zào] 1 (v)制造 to make;to do;to create;to manufacture *社会财富是劳动人民创造的。The wealth of society is created by the working people. 2 (v) 建筑 to build *这船是包工建造的。 The ship was built by contract. 3 (v)教养；培养 to cultivate;to train;to bring up *这学府造就了不少人才。This institute has brought up many men of talent. 4 (v) 往；到 to reach;to go to *我将登门造访。I shall go to your house to pay my respects. (I shall pay you a visit) 5 (n) 方；方面 ；一方面的人 party;side *两造。the two parties—the plaintiff and the defendant. 6 (n) 农作物的收成。 harvests;crops ＊一年三造皆丰收。All the three crops in the year have proved to be good.

造成 [zào chéng] to form;to make; to manufacture;to cause

造次 [zào cì] to venture

造反 [zào fǎn] to rebel against;to revolt;rebellion

造福 [zào fú] to bring benefit to;to benefit

造化 [zào·hua] luck

造就 [zào jiù] to train;to bring up;to cultivate

造句 [zào jú] to make a sentence

造林 [zào lín] afforest;afforestation

造型 [zào xíng] model

造谣 [zào yáo] to start a rumour; rumour mongering

造诣 [zào yì] literary or artistic attainments

造作 [zào·zuo] pretentious;affected;artificial;laboured

皂 [zào] 1 (adj) 黑 black;dark＊他做事糊涂，皂白不分。He worked in a muddle-headed manner and could not distinguish black from white. 2 (n) 肥皂：洗濯用的碱性物质soap

灶（竈） [zào] (n) 用砖土或其他材料做成的烧水、饭、菜等的设备 a kitchen-range;an oven

zé

责（責） [zé] 1 (n) 责任；应做的事responsibility;duty＊他没有负起做父亲的责任。He did not fulfill his responsibility as a father. 2 (v)吩咐；委托to enjoin; to entrust ＊校长责成教师改进教学工作。The school principal enjoins the teachers to improve their teaching.3 (v) 非难 to censure ;to reprimand;to reproach;to rebuke ;to reprove ＊我责备他粗心大意。I reproved him for his carelessness.

责备 [zé bèi] to reproach;to blame; to censure

责成 [zé chéng] to enjoin;to entrust

责罚 [zé fá] to punish

责怪 [zé guài] to reprimand;to blame

责骂 [zé mà] to abuse;to rail;to reproach

责难 [zé nàn] to censure;to rebuke

责任 [zé rèn] responsibility;duty; obligation

责任心 [zé rèn xīn] sense of responsibility

责问 [zé wèn] to question;to take somebody to task

责无旁贷 [zé wú páng dài] bounden duty;an inescapable duty

啧（嘖） [zé] 1 (n) 争辩的声音voices of dispute ＊啧有烦言。There are voices of dissatisfaction. 2 (n) 赞美的声音 voices of praise

啧啧 [zé zé] voices of dissatisfaction;voices of praise

泽（澤） [zé] 1 (n) 聚水的地方 a marsh;a bog;a swamp 2 (n) 光滑 glossiness; lustre ＊这块玉的色泽不错。The colour and lustre of this piece of jade is good.

泽国 [zé gúo] a heavily flooded place;a country submerged in water

择（擇） [zé] (v) 选择；挑选 to select; to choose;to pick out ＊饥不择食。A starveling will not choose his food.

择善而从 [zé shàn ér cóng] to choose and follow what is good

则（則） [zé] 1 (n) 榜样；模范 example;model ＊班长必须以身作则。The monitor must set himself as an example. 2 (n) 规章、条文 rules; article ＊我们一定要遵守交通规则。We must obey the traffic rules.3 (n) 量词 a measure word;item ＊寓言两则。two (items of) fables. 4 (adv) 那么；所以 so;therefore＊有错则改之。You have commited mistakes, so you must correct them. 5 (adv) 于是 then;and then ＊ 陈旧的事物即将腐朽，新生事物则如旭日东升。The old things would decay and the new ones then emerged like the morning sun rising from the east.

zéi

贼 (賊) [zéi] (n) 偷盗东西的人 a thief;a burglar＊昨晚窃贼闯进他的家里。A thief broke into his house last night. 2 (n) 叛逆；敌人；坏人 a rebel;an enemy; an undesirable person ＊卖国贼。a traitor＊叛贼, a rebel

贼兵 [zéi bīng] rebel troops

贼巢 [zéi cháo] robbers' den;bandits' lair

贼党 [zéi dǎng] rebels;robbers;brigands

贼喊捉贼 [zéi hǎn zhuō zèi] a theif cries "stop, thief"to cover himself up by shouting with the crowd

贼眉鼠眼 [zéi méi shǔ yǎn] having an appearance of guilt

贼头贼脑 [zéi tóu zéi nǎo] villainous-looking

贼赃 [zéi zāng] stolen goods; spoils;pillage

zěn

怎 [zěn] (pron) 如何 how? why?

怎么 [zěn·me] what? how? why?

怎么样 [zěn · me yàng] what about? how?

怎样 [zěn yàng] how? why?

zēng

曾 [zēng] (adj) 隔两代的亲属 great grand(e.g. child)

曾孙 [zēng sūn] great grand son

曾祖父 [zēng zǔ fǔ] great grand father

另见 [céng]

增 [zēng] (v) 加多；添 to add; to multiply;to increase;to grow ＊在经济不景气时， 失业人数激增。Unemployment increases in time of economic depression .

增产 [zēng chǎn] to increase production

增光 [zēng guāng] to add to the glory

增加 [zēng jiā] to increase;to add; to enhance;to enlarge;to grow

增进 [zēng jìn] to increase;to promote;to develop;to heighten;to enhance

增刊 [zeng kān] supplement — as to a newspaper

增率 [zēng lù] rate of increase

增强 [zēng qiáng] to strengthen;to multiply;to intensify

增删 [zēng shān] emendation ;to emend;to revise

增援 [zēng yuán] to reinforce

增长 [zēng zhǎng] to enhance;to grow;to increase

憎 [zēng] (v)厌恶；恨 to detest;to hate＊我们做人要爱憎分明。To be a man, we should draw a clear line between whom or what to love and whom or what to hate.

憎恨 [zēng hèn] to hate;to detest

憎恶 [zēng wù] to detest;to hate;to disgust

zèng

赠 (贈) [zèng](v) 送给 to present; to offer (e.g. gift) ＊出版社赠送了一套书给学校。The publishing house has presented a set of books to the school.

赠品 [zèng pǐn] a present;a memento;a gift

赠送[zèng sòng] to present; to grant;to give;to bestow;to confer

赠阅 [zèng yuè] to give somebody ....to read

zhā

喳 [zhā] 〔喳喳〕 [zhā zhā] (n)鸟叫的声音 chirping of birds *喜鹊喳喳地叫。The magpie chirps noisily.

渣 [zhā] (n) 物质经过提炼或使用后剩下的东西 residue;scum ;dregs; dross *豆渣。soya bean residue.

渣滓 [zhā zǐ] dregs;scum;refuse; dross;waste

zhá

扎 [zhá] 1 (v)刺 to prick;to puncture; to stab;to pierce*歹徒扎死一名无辜的人 The gangster stabbed an innocent person to death. 2 (v) 安居;安置to settle;to station *军官在山顶驻扎部队。 The officer stationed his troop on the hill-top. 另见[zā]

扎根 [zhá gēn] to take root;to settle down

扎实 [zhá shí] solid;in a down-to-earth way;sturdy

扎营 [zhá yíng] to camp;to encamp;to make a stockade

札 [zhá] (n) 信件 letters * 信札。letters *手札。 a hand-written letter

轧(軋) [zhá] (v)滚压 to roll

轧钢 [zhá gāng] steel-rolling 另见[ya]

闸(閘) [zhá] (n)调节水库、河道水流的建筑物 a sluice gate;a lockgate;a lock

闸门 [zhá mén] lockgate;lock;sluice gate

炸 [zhá] (v) 把食物放在多量的沸油里弄熟 to fry 另见[zhà]

铡(鍘) [zhá] 1 (n) 一种切草或其他东西的器具 a lever knife;a guillotine 2 (v) 用铡刀切东西 to cut with a guillotine;to guillotine

zhǎ

眨 [zhǎ] (v) 眼睛闭上立刻又睁开 to wink;to blink *他向我眨眼示意。He winks at me.

zhà

乍 [zhà] 1 (adv) 忽然;突然 suddenly *天气乍冷乍热。 It is a changing weather, now cold, now hot. 2 (adv) 起初;刚刚开始 at first;just;newly

乍冷乍热 [zhà lěng zhà rè] now cold;now hot — of the weather;by fits and starts

诈(詐) [zhà] 1 (v) 欺骗 to deceive;to cheat;to defraud; to swindle;to blackmail *他时常诈骗朋友的钱。He often cheated his friends out of their money. 2 (v) 假装 to pretend;to feint *敌人诈降,想引诱我军中伏。The enemy pretended to surrender ; they were trying to ambush us.

诈骗 [zhà piàn] to deceive;to swindle;to defraud

咋 [zhà] 咬 to bite

咋舌 [zhà shé] shocked;so shocked that one bites his tongue and cannot utter a word

炸 [zhà] (v) 爆破 to explode;to blow up;to bomb;to blast *我军炸毁了敌人的碉堡。 Our army blew up the enemy's pill-box. 另见[zhá]

炸弹 [zhà dàn] bomb

炸药 [zhà yào] explosives;dynamite

蚱 [zhà] (n) 蚱蜢 [zhà měng] 昆虫,像蝗虫,吃农作物的叶,是害虫 grasshoppers

榨 [zhà] (v) 把物体里的液汁压出来 to squeeze;to extract;to press out ＊ 小贩在榨甘蔗汁。The hawker is extracting juice from sugar-canes.

榨取 [zhà qǔ] to obtain by pressing;to drain;to extract;to exploit;to exact

榨油机 [zhà yóu jī] oil extracting machine

榨油厂 [zhà yóu chǎng] oil press

栅 [zhà] (n) 用竹、木或铁条做成的栏 fence;palisade;barrier gate;balustrade

栅栏 [zhà·lan] balustrade;fence

栅极 [zhà jí] grid

zhāi

斋(齋) [zhāi] 1 (v) 禁食 to fast ＊ 回教徒每年守斋一个月。The Muslims keep a fast for one month in every year. 2 (n) 屋子；房间 house ; room 3 (n) 素食 vegetarian food

摘 [zhāi] 1 (v)采；取下 to pick;to pluck ＊ 姑娘们在摘苹果。The girls are plucking apples. 2 (v) 选取 to select;to excerpt ＊ 这篇文章很好，我特地摘录了几段给你们看看。This essay is excellent. I have specially selected a few paragraphs for you to read.

摘抄 [zhāi chāo] to copy something selectively

摘记 [zhāi jì] summarize; sum up

摘录 [zhāi lù] to record;excerpts

摘要 [zhāi yào] digest;to make an extract;summary;to abstract

摘引 [zhāi yǐn] to quote

zhái

宅 [zhái] (n)住所 a house;a residence ＊ 这是有钱人家的住宅区。This is a residential area of the rich.

zhǎi

窄 [zhǎi] 1(adj)狭小，跟“宽”相对 narrow ＊ 这条路很窄。This road is very narrow. 2 (adj)气量小；不开朗 narrow-minded ＊ 他心眼窄，想不开。He is narrow-minded and takes things too hard.

zhài

债(債) [zhài] (n) 欠别人的钱财 a debt ＊ 他没钱还债。He has no money to pay the debt.

债户 [zhài hù] debtor

债台高筑 [zhài tái gāo zhù] to run heavily into debt;deep in debt

债券 [zhài quàn] debentures;bonds

债务 [zhài wù] debt,obligation

债主 [zhài zhǔ] creditor

寨 [zhài] 1(n)防卫用的木栅栏、围墙等建筑物 a stockade;a stronghold;a camp 2 (n) 有围墙或围栅的村子 a walled or fenced village

zhān

占 [zhān] (v)预测吉凶 to divine;to foretell

另见 [zhàn]

占卜 [zhān bǔ] to divine; to cast lots

沾 [zhān] 1 (v) 浸湿 to moisten;to wet ＊ 孩子的尿把床沾湿了。The child wets the bed with urine. 2 (v)因接触而附着 to tinge;to stain; to be touched with ＊ 他的手沾了一些血。His hand is stained with some blood. 3 (v)得到好处 to benefit by ＊ 朋友们因他的成就而沾光不少。Friends benefit by his achievement.

沾光 [zhān guāng] to get an advantage;to benefit by

沾染 [zhān rǎn] to be affected with;to be contaminated with (e.g. bad habits);to be stained with(e.g.

the blood of)

沾沾自喜 [zhān zhān zì xǐ] complacent;self-satisfied

沾污 [zhān wū] to pollute;to defile

粘 [zhān] (v) 糊贴 to paste up ; to stick on;to affix to ＊ 他们粘贴标语。They paste up the posters. 另见 [nián]

毡(氈) [zhān] (n) 用以垫衬防寒的毛织品 felt; fabrics; used for rugs,carpets,wrappers,etc

毡帽 [zhān mào] felt caps

毡袜 [zhān wà] felt socks

瞻 zhān] 1(v)看；望 to look;to look ahead 2 (v) 尊敬；尊崇 to look up to; to reverence

瞻前顾后 [zhān qián gù hòu] to look fore and aft — to be filled with misgivings

瞻望 [zhān wàng] to look forward; to look ahead

瞻仰 [zhān yǎng] to look up with respect;to admire

zhǎn

展 [zhǎn] 1(v) 张开 to open;to launch;to unfold ＊ 鸟儿展翅高飞。The bird unfolds its wings and flies high. 2 (v) 延迟 to delay;to postpone;to extend ＊ 机场展期开幕。The opening ceremony of the airport is postponed. 3 (v) 陈列 to exhibit;to be on display;to put on display ＊ 学生的美术作品将在最近期间展出。The art work of the students will be put on display very soon.

展开 [zhǎn kaī] to open up;to expand;to launch;to unfold;to develop;to spread out

展览 [zhǎn lǎn] to exhibit;to be on display;exhibition

展览会 [zhǎn lǎn huì] exhibition

展期 [zhǎn qī] to postpone;to extend a time limit

展示 [zhǎn shi] to show;to display

展望 [zhǎn wàng] to forecast;to look forward;to prospect

展现 [zhǎn xiǎn] to fold;to open and spread out;to lay open and view

展性 [zhǎn xíng] malleability

辗(輾) [zhǎn] (v) 滚转 to roll; turn over

辗转 [zhǎn zhuǎn] to mill around; to turn over and over again;to toss and turn

辗转反侧 [zhǎn zhuǎn fǎn cè] to toss to and fro — as when sleepless

辗床 [zhǎn chuáng] a rolling mill

斩(斬) [zhǎn] (v) 砍断 to chop off;to cut in two ＊ 捕奴人斩断黑奴的十个脚趾。The slave hunter chopped off ten toes from the feet of the black slave.

斩草除根 [zhǎn cǎo chú gēn] to uproot;to pull up weeds by the root;to eliminate the cause of

斩钉截铁 [zhǎn dīng jié tě] resolute;determined;adamant;in a clear-cut-way

斩首 [zhǎn shǒu] to behead;to execute;to decapitate

崭(嶄) [zhǎn] (adj) 高峻；突出 high;lofty;prominent

崭新 [zhǎn xīn] brand-new

盏(盞) [zhǎn] 1(n) 浅杯；小杯 a shallow cup;a small cup ＊ 酒盏。wine cup 灯盏 the oil cup for the lamp 2 (n) 量词 a measure word (e.g. a lamp, a cup)

zhàn

占 [zhàn] 1(v) 据有 to occupy;to possess ＊ 敌人占据了我们的堡垒。The enemy occupied our fort. 2(v) 构成；形成；包含 to constitute; to make up;to embrace ＊ 赞成两种语文政策的占大多数。Those who are in favour of bi-lingualism constitute the moiority.

另见 [zhān]
占据 [zhàn jù] to occupy;to take over;to hold
占领 [zhàn lǐng] to occupy;to seize
占便宜 [zhàn pián·yi] to take advantage of;to gain advantage over
占上风 [zhàn shǎng fèng] to prevail;to gain the upper hand
占有 [zhàn yǒu] to posses;to own; to hold
占优势 [zhàn yōu shì] to get the better hand of

站 [zhàn] 1(v) 直立 to stand * 不要站在巴士门口的梯级上。Do not stand on the doorsteps of the bus. 2 (n) 停留转运或服务的地方 station; stop (e.g. bus);service centre * 火车站 railway station * 汽车服务站 automobile service station * 电力站。electric power station
站不住脚 [zhàn bù zhú jiǎo] untenable;cannot be justified;unable to stand on one's ground
站得住脚 [zhàn dé zhù jiǎo] tenable;convincing;to hold water
站队 [zhàn duì] to fall in;to line up;to take up one's position;to take sides
站岗 [zhàn gǎng] to keep guard;to stand sentry
站台 [zhàn tái] platform (at railway station)
站住 [zhàn zhù] to stop;to stand still;to stay

战 (戰) [zhàn] 1 (v) 相打；打战 war; battle; struggle ; to fight; to combat * 战争不是解决国家间争端的最好办法。War is not the best way to decide quarrels between different countries. * 英国同法国对德国作战。England fought with France against Germany. * 我们为自由而战 We battle for freedom. 2 (v) 发抖；哆嗦 to tremble;to quiver * 一听到地雷爆炸声，官兵们个个心惊胆战。The government troops trembled at the sound of exploding landmines.
战败 [zhàn bài] to be defeated;to lose the battle; beat;to overcome (the enemy);to over-power
战报 [zhàn bào] war communique
战备 [zhàn beì] preparation against war
战场 [zhàn chǎng] battle field;field of operations (war)
战斗 [zhàn dòu] battle;fight combat;struggle
战斗力 [zhàn dòu lì]fighting strength;fighting capacity
战斗性 [zhàn dòu xíng] fighting spirit;militancy;combativeness
战犯 [zhàn fàn] war criminal
战俘 [zhàn fú] prisoner-of-war;captive
战歌 [zhàn gē] war song; battle march
战鼓 [zhàn gǔ] war drum
战果 [zhàn guǒ] outcome of battle; results
战壕 [zhàn háo] dugout; trenches
战火 [zhàn huǒ] flames of war
战绩 [zhàn jī] military success
战机 [zhàn jī] combat opportunity; the right time to strike
战局 [zhàn jú] war situation
战栗 [zhàn lì] to shudder;to shiver
战利品 [zhàn lì pǐn] spoils; war booty;prize of war
战略 [zhàn luè] strategy
战旗 [zhàn qí] the colours;flag of an army
战胜 [zhàn shèng] to defeat (the enemy);to triumph over;to be victorious
战士 [zhàn shì] a soldier;a fighter
战术 [zhàn shù] tactics
战天斗地 [zhàn tian dǒu dì] to fight against heaven and earth;to combat all forces of nature
战无不胜 [zhàn wú bù shèng] in-

vincible;ever-victorious
战线 [zhàn xiàn] front
战役 [zhàn yì] campaign;battle
战友 [zhàn yǒu] comrade-in-arms
战战兢兢 [zhàn zhàn jīng jīng] quaking with terror;to tremble with fright;very cautious
战争 [zhàn zhēng] war;warfare
战争贩子 [zhàn zhēng fàn·zi] a warmonger

栈(棧) [zhàn] 1 (n) 旅馆或存放货物的地方 a hotel; a warehouse; a godown * 客栈。 a hotel 2 (n) 养牲畜的竹木棚或棚栏 a stable;an enclosure for livestock * 马栈。a stable * 羊栈。a sheep pen 3 (n) 山崖间的道路 a way made along a cliff
栈道 [zhàn dào]planks laid across a dangerous precipitous point;a covered way along a precipice
栈房 [zhàn fáng] a warehouse;a storehouse;a godown

绽(綻) [zhàn] (v)(n) 破裂；裂缝 to split;a rent

颤(顫) [zhàn] (v) 发抖；哆嗦 to shiver;to shudder * 他见了血便全身打颤 He shuddered at the sight of blood.
另见 [chàn]

湛 [zhàn] (adj) 深厚；清澈 deep; clear

蘸 [zhàn] (v)以物件沾液体、粉末或糊 to dip (in liquid,powder or paste)*酸芒果蘸糖和黑酱油非常好吃。Sour mango dipped in sugared black soy tastes very delicious.

zhāng

章 [zhāng] 1(n) 诗歌、文字的段落 chapter * 全书共分十章。There are ten chapters in the book. 2 (n)规则；条例 rules;regulations * 我们要求取消不合理的规章制度。We demand the abolition of the unreasonable rules and regulations. 3 (n) 印 a seal *校长在我们的毕业证书上盖章。The principal affixes his seal on our graduation certificates. 4 (n) 标志 a symbol;a badge
章程 [zhāng·cheng] rules and regulations;charter
章法 [zhāng fǎ] style;phraseology
章节 [zhāng jié] chapter;section
章魚 [zhāng yú] an octopus

樟 [zhāng] (n) 常绿乔木。根、茎、枝、叶都有樟脑香味，可提取樟脑和樟油，供工业和医药用。木材可做箱柜，能防蛀 the camphor tree
樟脑 [zhāng nǎo] camphor

蟑 [zhāng] (n) 蟑螂 [zhāng láng]昆虫。黑褐色，体扁平，两对翅有光泽，是厨房里的害虫 the cockroach

彰 [zhāng] (adj)明显；显著 obvious; apparent;showy

张(張) [zhāng] 1(v) 分开；展开 to open up;to stretch * 伤者慢慢地张开眼睛。The wounded person slowly opens his eyes. 2(v)扩大；夸大 to expand;to exaggerate * 不用怕，我们的对手只是虚张声势。Do not be afraid; our opponents are merely making an empty show of power. 3 (v) 看，望 to look * 他在月台上

东张西望地找他的女朋友。 He looked around at the platform hunting for his girl friend. 4 (n)量词 a measure word, (leaf. sheet,piece,etc) *一张纸。 a sheet of paper. *一张桌子。a (piece of) table

张冠李戴 [zhāng guān lǐ dài] Li is putting on zhang's hat — the cap is on the wrong head;to mistake one thing for another

张皇失措 [zhāng huáng shì cuò] to be scared out of one's wits;to be frightened and at a loss of what to do

张口结舌 [zhāng kǒu jié shé] to stare open-mouthed;to gape with astonishment

张力 [zhāng lì] tension

张罗 [zhāng luó] to make arrangements;to try to find something for certain needs

张望 [zhāng wàng] to look about;to look around

张三李四 [zhāng sān lǐ sì] anybody;this one or that

张牙舞爪 [zhāng yá wǔ zhǎo] to show one's claws;to bare one's teeth;rampant and overbearing

张扬 [zhāng yáng] to publish abroad;to proclaim

zhǎng

掌 [zhǎng] 1(n) 手心 palm (of hand) *这件事对我来说易如反掌。To me, this matter is as easy as turning one's palm. 2 (n) 禽兽的足心paw;claw *熊掌 。bear's paw *鹅掌 goose's claws 3 (v)把握；主管to control;to handle;in charge of *他掌管一切有关生产的事务。He is in charge of everything concerning production.

掌舵 [zhǎng duò] to take the helm of;to be at the helm

掌权 [zhǎng quán] to be in power; to take power

掌管 [zhǎng guǎn] in charge of;to handle;to control

掌声 [zhǎng shēng] applause;clapping;the sound of clapping

掌握 [zhǎng wò] to grasp;to gain control of;to possess;to master

长(長) [zhǎng] 1(v)发育；生长 to grow *木瓜树长得快。The papaya tree grows fast. 2 (v) 增进；增加；提高 to increase; to rise;to raise *多看书可以增长见识。One can increase one's knowledge by reading more books. 3 (adj) 辈分、年龄或排行较高的 older ;elder *兄长。elder brothers *官长。superior;senior 4 (n) 负责人 person -in-charge;head;chief *代表团团长。the head of a delegation. *部长。head of department;minister
另见 [cháng]

长辈 [zhǎng bèi] seniors;elders

长成 [zhǎng chéng] grown up

长进 [zhǎng jìn] to progress

长势 [zhǎng shì] growing

长兄 [zhǎng xīng] the eldest brother

长子 [zhǎng zǐ] the eldest son

涨(漲) [zhǎng] (v) 升高 to rise; to go upward; to soar; to grow *涨潮了。The tide is rising. *物价飞涨。The prices of commodities are soaring high.
另见 [zhàng]

涨潮 [zhǎng cháo] flood-tide;rising tide

漲风 [zhǎng fēng] upward trend (of prices)

漲价 [zhǎng jià] price hike

zhàng

帐(帳) [zhàng] (n) 帷幕 camp; tent *童子军搭起一个营帐。 The boy scouts pitched a camp. *蚊帐 a mosquito net

* 祭帐。a scroll sent to mourners

帐房 [zhàng fáng] an accountant

帐目 [zhàng mù] accounts

帐篷 [zhàng·peng] a tent

账（賬） [zhàng] (n) 金钱财物进出的记录 an account * 这账房窜改他的账目。The accountant cooked his accounts. * 他是来收账的 He has come for his account * 清账 to settle an account * 查账 to audit * 开账 to open an account * 结账。to close an account. * 算账 to cast up an account;to settle up * 倒账。to become bankrupt * 赖账。to deny debts * 放账。to give credit

账簿 [zhàng bù] account book

账单 [zhàng dān] bill;invoice

账房 [zhàng fáng] account

账目 [zhàng mù] accounts

账台 [zhàng taí] a counter in a shop

账尾 [zhàng weǐ] the balance of an account

胀（脹） [zhàng] 1(v) 体积变大 to expand;to swell up * 气体遇热膨胀。Gas expands by heat * 通货膨胀。inflation (of currency) 2 (adj) 身体因肠胃气体滞留而不舒适 flatulent;dropsical;pot-bellied * 水胀。dropsy (of the abdomen) 蛊胀。ascites

涨（漲） [zhàng] 1(v) 增大；扩大 to swell; to expand; to inflate * 黄豆泡涨了。The soya bean has been soaked in water to become swollen. 2 (v) 充满；布满 to fill up;to overspread * 他气得涨红了脸。He was so angry that a blush overspread his face. 另见 [zhǎng]

障 [zhàng] (v) (n) 阻碍 to obstruct;to stand in the way;to hinder;barrier; obstruction;obstacle * 小心，前面有障碍物。Beware, obstacle in front.

瘴 [zhàng] (n) 瘴气，热带或亚热带山林里的一种能使人生病的空气 pestilential vapour; miasma; unwholesome atmosphere

丈 [zhàng] 1(n) 长度单位，十尺为一丈 a unit of length equivalent to ten Chinese feet (or 3 metres approximately) 2 (v) 测量 to measure;to survey 3 (n) 对年老的人的尊称 an address to the elders * 姑丈。father's sister's husband;uncle * 岳丈 father-in-law * 老丈。an old gentleman

丈夫 [zhàng fū] husband;a man of spirit;a hero

丈量 [zhàng liáng] to measure;to survey

丈母娘 [zhàng mǔ niáng] mother-in-law

丈人 [zhàng·ren] father-in-law

仗 [zhàng] 1 (n) 兵器 arms;weapons of war * 兵仗。weapon of war 2 (n) 战争 war;battle * 打仗。to fight a battle * 胜仗。a winning battle;a victory * 败仗。a losing battle;a defeat 3 (v) 依靠；凭借 to rely on;to depend on 4 (n) 护卫 guard * 仪仗队。guard of honour

仗恃 [zhàng shì] to rely upon

仗势 [zhàng shì] to trust to power in influence

仗义疏财 [zhàng yì shū cái] to help others economically on the grounds of justice

仗义执言 [zhàng yì zhí yán] to speak for righteousness sake

杖 [zhàng] (n) 扶着走路的棍棒 a walking stick;a crutch * 拐杖。a crutch

zhāo

招 [zhāo] 1 (v) 用手势叫人或致意 to beckon, to call * 他招手要我进去。

He beckoned me in .2 (v) 征求，邀请, to recruit;to enrol;to enlist;to invite ＊ 大学将在六月招生。The university will enrol its freshmen in June. 3 (v) 引；惹 to attract;to incur;to incite;to provoke ＊ 爱斯基摩人猎熊时招致很大的危险。The Eskimos incur great danger in hunting bears. 4 (v) 供认；承认罪行 to admit;to confess ＊ 嫌犯最后终于招供了。The suspect confessed at last. 5 (n) 计策；手段 tactic; mean;tricks ＊ 狡猾的老板很会耍花招。The cunning boss is good at playing various tricks.

招标 [zhāo biāo] to invite to bid (for a tender)

招兵买马 [zhāo bīn mǎi mǎ] to hire men and buy horses;to enlist followers

招待 [zhāo dài] to receive;to entertain;to give a reception to

招待会 [zhāo dài huì] a reception

招待所 [zhāo dài suǒ] a reception centre;a guest house

招呼 [zhāo · hu] to call;to hail;to greet;to wave to somebody;to tell; to inform;to attend to;to look after

招架 [zhāo jià] to defend;to ward off;to resist

招领 [zhāo lǐng] notice for owner to claim last things

招募 [zhāo mù] to enlist;to recruit

招牌 [zhāo · pai] a sign-board;a shop sign

招惹 [zhāo·re] to provoke;to incur; to arouse

招认 [zhāo rèn] to confess

招生 [zhāo shēng] to enrol students

招收 [zhāo shōu] to enrol

招手 [zhāo shǒu] to beckon;to wave to

招贴 [zhāo tiē] a placard;a poster;a bill

招降纳叛 [zhāo xiáng nà pàn] to recruit turncoats and accept renegades

招摇撞骗 [zhāo yáo zhuàng piàn] to use the name or authority of others to swindle;to bluff and deceive

招展 [zhāo zhǎn] to wave;to flutter

招致 [zhāo zhì] to enrol;to accept; to take in;to cause;to give rise to;to result in

昭

[zhāo] (adj) 显著；明显 apparent; evident;clear ＊ 他是一个臭名昭著的政客。He is a notorious politician.

昭然 [zhāo rán] apparent

昭然若揭 [zhāo rán ruò jiē] clear as daylight;everything above board

昭示 [zhāo shì] clear explanation

昭雪 [zhāo xuě] to settle a grievance satisfactorily; innocence clearly manifested

昭著 [zhāo zhù] bright;clear;evident

朝

[zhāo] (n) 早晨；早 morning; early 2 (n) 日，天 day ＊ 任何语文並非一朝一夕所能学成的。One can never master a language within one day.

另见 [cháo]

朝不保夕 [zhāo bù bǎo xí] the morning cannot guarantee the evening — in imminent danger

朝不虑夕 [zhāo bù lǜ xī] in the morning one doesn't worry what will happen in the evening;shortsighted

朝令夕改 [zhāo lìng xī gǎi] to fickle (in policy,feelings etc.);changeable

朝气 [zhāo qì] vigour;ardour;vitality;animation

朝气蓬勃 [zhāo qì péng bó] full of vigour and vitality

朝三暮四 [zhāo sān mù sì] changeable;shift and veer;play fast and loose;blow hot and cold

朝夕 [zhāo xī] everyday; morning and evening;a short time

朝霞 [zhāo xiá] rays and clouds in the morning sun

朝阳 [zhāo yáng] morning sun;rising sun

zháo

着 [zháo] 1(v)接触；挨上 to touch;to hit ＊直升机要着地了。The helicopter is going to touch down.2 (v) 感受；受到 to feel;to catch(e.g.cold) ＊孩子着凉了。The child has caught a cold. ＊着火了。The house caught fire. 3 (v)助动词;表示动作已完成 a helping word for the formation of the past participle ＊ 他睡着了。He was fast asleep.

另见 [zhuó] [·zhe]

着火 [zháo huǒ] to catch fire

着慌 [zháo huōng] to arouse fear; panic

着急 [zháo jí] anxious;worried

着凉 [zháo liáng] to catch cold

zhǎo

爪 [zhǎo] (n)鸟兽的脚指claws ＊虎爪。the claws of a tiger ＊鹰爪 the claws of an eagle

爪牙 [zhǎo yá] cat's paw;accomplice;lackey;henchman

找 [zhǎo] 1(v)寻 to look for;to find; to seek;to search ＊我找你很久了。I have been looking for you for a long time 2(v)付还余额 to pay a balance;to pay the change ＊ 我还没有找钱给你。I have not given you the change yet.

找换 [zhǎo huàn] to exchange money

找麻烦 [zhǎo má·fan] to look for trouble

找门路 [zhǎo mén lù] to seek employment;to seek an opening

找钱 [zhǎo qián] to give (one his) change;small change

找寻 [zhǎo xún] to look for;to seek for;to search for;to hunt for

沼 [zhǎo] (n) 水池 a pond;a pool

沼泽 [zhǎo gé] marsh;swamp;bog; quagmire

沼气 [zhǎo qì] methane gas;marshgas

zhào

兆 [zhào] 1(n) 事情发生前的迹象 an omen;a sign ＊凶兆。 an evil omen;a portent ＊吉兆。 a lucky omen ＊预兆。 signs of the time 2 (n) 数词：百万 million

兆头 [zhào·tóu] an omen

兆周 [zhào zhōu] megacycle

召 [zhào] (v)叫人来to call;to beckon ＊ 队长召开全体队员会议。The team leader called a meeting of all members. ＊会长号召会员为社会福利而努力工作。 The President of the Association called upon his members to work hard for social welfare.

召唤 [zhào huàn] to call

召回 [zhào huí] to recall;to call back

召集 [zhào jí] to call up;to convene ; to assemble;to summon;to gather

召见 [zhào jiàn] to summon;to send for

召开 [zhào kāi] to call (e.g. a meeting);to hold;to summon

诏（詔）[zhào] (n) 封建帝王所发的命令 an imperial mandate;a decree

照 [zhào] 1 (v) 光线射在物体上 to shine;to illuminate ＊他用手电筒照射房间。He shines the room with a torchlight.2(v) 面对镜子或其他反光面 to face a mirror or other reflective surface ＊ 他在照镜子。He is facing (looking at his reflection in) a mirror. 3 (v) 摄影 to take (a photograph);to photograph ＊ 我

们把它照下来。Let's photograph it. 4 (v) 根据;遵循 in accordance with;according to;in the light of * 我们照章办事。We work according to rules. 5 (v)知道,明白 to know;to understand * 对这件事,他们两人心照不宣。They knew this matter thoroughly but neither wanted to say anything about it. 6 (n) 凭证 a certificate;an evidence;a licence *护照。a passport

照办 [zhào bàn] to do as one is told

照常 [zhào cháng] as usual;to function as usual

照管 [zhào guǎn] to take charge of;to look after;to take care of

照顾 [zhòu·gù] to consider;to give due consideration to;to take care of;to look after

照会 [zhào huì] to send a note to.....;note (diplomatic)

照旧 [zhào jìu] as usual

照例 [zhào jì] according to the rules;as usual

照料 [zhào liào] to take care of

照明 [zhào míng] to illuminate;to light (up)

照片 [zhào piàn] photograph; photo;picture

照相 [zhào xiàng] to take photograph;photographing

照相馆 [zhào xiàng guǎn] a photo studio;a graphic studio

照相机 [zhào xiàng jī] a camera

照样 [zhào yàng] in the same way; likewise ; as usual

照耀 [zhào yào] to shine;to illuminate

照应 [zhào·yìng] to look after;to take care of;to give consideration

罩 [zhào] 1(n) 泛指一切覆盖在外的器物 a cover;a shade ; a lampshade *灯罩。a veil 2 (v) 覆盖 to cover; to shade * 黑夜笼罩着大地。Night envelopes the whole earth.

赵(趙) [zhào] (n) 姓 a surname

肇 [zhào] (v)发生 to occur,to happen;to cause * 肇祸的摩多单车已经逃跑了。The motor-bike which caused the accident has escaped.

肇事 [zhào shì] to stir up trouble; to create a disturbance

zhē

蜇 [zhē] (v)昆虫叮刺 to sting * 我的手给黄蜂蜇了一下。My hand was stung by a wasp.
另见 [zhé]

遮 [zhē] (v) 挡;掩盖 to block off; to conceal;to cover * 太阳给乌云遮住了。The sun is covered by the dark cloud.

遮蔽 [zhē bì] to shade;to cover;to block off

遮盖 [zhē gài] to cover up;to overcast;to conceal

遮羞布 [zhē xīu bù] figleaf

遮掩 [zhē yǎn] to cover;to overcast;to conceal;to hide

折 [zhē] (v) 翻转 to tumble *叔父天天折跟斗使身体健康。My uncle tumbles every day to keep himself fit.

折腾 [zhē·teng] to tumble;to repeat (doing something);to torture

zhé

折(摺) [zhé] 1 (v)断;弄断 to break *一名建筑工友从二楼摔下来,折断了腿骨。A construction worker fell from the first floor and broke his leg. 2 (v) 转弯 to turn back; to turn over * 他刚走出大门又折了回来。He turned back just after he had walked out of the main gate. 3 (v) 扣减 to give a discount;to discount * 这本书打八折。This book is given a twenty per cent discount. 4 (v) 拗曲 to bend;to fall * 表演者把钢杆折成圆环。The performer bent a steel bar into a loop. 5 (v)兑换；换算to convert into;to exchange;depreciation *一百元星币折合 人民币七十八元左右。One hundred Singapore dollars will exchange Renminbi seventy-eight dollars.

折迭 [zhé dié] to fold
折服 [zhé fú] be convinced
折合 [zhé hé] to convert into; to be worth;to amount to
折旧 [zhé jiù] depreciation
折扣 [zhé·kou] to discount
折磨 [zhé · mo] to torture;to grind down;to undergo an ordeal
折射 [zhé shè] to refract;refraction
折衷 [zhé zhōng] compromise; eclecticism

蜇 [zhé] (n) 海蜇，腔肠动物，伞形软体，生活在海中，皮制干可食 a jellyfish

哲 [zhé]哲学[zhé xué](n)研究宇宙万有原理原则的学问philosophy

蛰（蟄）[zhé] (v) 动物冬眠 to hibernate; hibernation
蛰伏 [zhé fú] to hibernate;to lie concealed

辙（轍）[zhé] (n)车轮轧出来的浅沟或印子 the track of a wheel

摺 [zhé] (v)迭合 to fold;to double together;to bend *手摺。a small folding paper;a pass book
摺尺 [zhé chǐ] a folding rule
摺刀 [zhé dāo] a folding knife;a pocket knife
摺迭 [zhé dié] to fold up
摺扇 [zhé shàn] a folding fan

zhě

者 [zhě] (n) 代词；代替人或事物 a pronoun for person or thing;that who;those who;that which;those which * 读者。readers (those who read) 善者 those who are meek 学者。a scholar;that who learns 两者 both (items, conditions, persons, etc)

褶 [zhě] (n) 衣服、布料的皺纹 pleat * 百褶裙。a pleated skirt

zhè

鹧（鷓）[zhè] (n) 鸟，背部和腹部黑白两色相杂，头顶棕色，脚黄色。吃昆虫、蚯蚓等 the common partridge

蔗 [zhè] (n) 甘蔗，草本植物。茎含糖质，可以吃，也可以制糖 sugar cane

这（這）[zhè] (adj);(adv) 指较近的时间、地点、事物，跟"那"相对 this;here *这个人是谁？ Who is this man?
这个 [zhè gè] this
这会儿 [zhè hǔ ír] at this moment
这里 [zhè lǐ] here
这么 [zhè me] such;so
这儿 [zhèr] here
这些 [zhè xiē] these
这样 [zhè yàng] such;in this way; thus

·zhe

着 [zhe] 1(part)助词，表示动作的持续 a help word for the formation of present participle *汽车在门口等着。The car is waiting at the door. *他们正谈着话呢。They are talking with each other 2 (part) 助词，表示 状态的持续 helping word to show the continuation of state of things * 茶几上放着一瓶花。A vase of flowers is placed on the tea table. *大门敞开着。The gate is open.
另见 [zhúo] [zhaó]

zhēn

贞（貞）[zhēn] (adj)纯洁的；有节操的 pure;chaste

贞操 [zhēn cāo] pure;moral rectitude
贞洁 [zhēn jiě] chaste and undefiled ;virgin purity
贞节 [zhēn jié] pure;undefiled

侦(偵) [zhēn] (v)探听，暗中查访察看 to spy;to detect ＊ 我们派人去侦察敌军的行动。We send people to spy into the actions of the enemy troops.
侦察 [zhēn chá] to scout;to reconnoitre;reconnaissance
侦查 [zhēn chá] to inquire secretly
侦察兵 [zhēn chá bīng] a scout
侦察机 [zhēn chà jī] a reconnaissance plane
侦察轰炸机 [zhēn chá hōng zhà jī] a reconnaissance bomber
侦缉 [zhēn qī] to examine and arrest
侦探 [zhēn tàn] a detective;a secret service agent;a spy;to detect

斟 [zhēn] (v)把液体倒出 to pour out ＊ 主人替我斟酒。The host pours me a glass of wine.
斟酌 [zhēn zhuó] to consult;to weigh and consider
斟酌办理 [zhēn zhuó bàn lǐ] at one's discretion
斟酌情况 [zhēn zhuó qíng kuàng] in the light of specific circumstances;according to circumstances

砧 [zhēn] (n)捶、砸或切东西时垫在底下的墩子 block;an anvil
砧板 [zhēnbǎn] chopping board

珍 [zhēn] 1 (n)宝贝贵重的东西 the precious things;curiosities;rarities;treasure ＊ 奇珍异宝。Presious and rare objects 2 (adj) 贵重的；宝贵的 precious;valuable;scarce;excellent;beautiful;delicate ＊ 鱼翅是筵席上的珍品。Shark's fin makes a delicate dish in the feast. 3 (v)重视 to value highly;to value and treasure ＊我们必须珍惜时间。We must value and treasure our time.
珍藏 [zhēn cáng] to treasure
珍贵 [zhēn guì] valuable;precious
珍品 [zhēn pǐn] precious thing
珍视 [zhēn shì] to cherish;to treasure;to prize
珍饰 [zhēn shì] jewelry
珍惜 [zhēn xī] to love dearly;to treasure and value;to value highly
珍重 [zhēn zhòng] to take good care;to hold dear
珍珠 [zhēn zhū] pearl

针(針) [zhēn] (n) 尖细的利器 a needle ＊ 缝纫机针。sewing machine needlec ＊缝纫手针 hand sewing needles ＊大头针 pins ＊别针。a clip ＊时针。an hour hand (of a clock or watch)＊分针。a minute hand ＊ 秒针 a second hand ＊ 指南针 a compass
针刺麻醉 [zhēn cì má zhì] acupuncture anaesthesia
针对 [zhēn duì] to direct towards; to point at;in point of;in light of
针对性 [zhēn duì xìng] to the point;with a clear aim in mind
针锋相对 [zhēn fēng xiāng duì] tit for tat
针灸 [zhēn jiǔ] acupuncture and moxibustion
针线 [zhēn· xian] needle and thread;needlework
针织品 [zhēn zuī pǐn] knitted goods;knitwear;hosiery

真 [zhēn] (adj) 符合客观事实，跟"假"相对 real;genuine; true; actual ＊ 我还没弄清事情的真相。I am still not clear in the real facts of the matter.＊这位巴士售票员为人真好。This bus conductor is a really nice person.＊货真价实。(We provide) genuine goods and honest prices
真诚 [zhēn chéng] honest;earnest; sincere;truly

真空 [zhēn kōng] vacuum
真金不怕火 [zhēn jīn bù pà huǒ] pure gold is not afraid of being burnt — men of abilities fear nothing
真理 [zhēn lǐ] truth
真面目 [zhēn miàn mù] true feature;true colours
真凭实据 [zhēn píng shí jù] factual evidence;indisputable evidence
真切 [zhēn qiè] realistic;distinct
真情 [zhēn qíng] reality; actual state;real situation;real emotion or feeling
真实 [zhēn shì] real;true;actual
真相 [zhēn xíang] truth;true state; real facts
真象 [zhēn xiang] the real image
真相大白 [zhēn xiāng dà bái] the actual state of affairs has been made clear
真正 [zhēn zhèng] real;genuine
真挚 [zhēn zhì] sincere; cordial; genuine

甄 [zhēn] (v)审查;鉴定(优劣、真伪)to examine;to distinguish ✽ 他们在甄选球员。They are examining and selecting the players.
甄别 [zhēn bié] to screen;to determine the true nature of a case

zhěn

诊(診) [zhěn] (v) 检查病情to examine;to consult;to diagnose ✽ 医生诊断他的病为肺炎。The doctor diagnosed his illness as pneumonia.
诊断 [zhěn duàn] diagnosis;to diagnose
诊疗 [zhěn liáo] to consult and give medical treatment
诊疗所 [zhěn liáo suǒ] a clinic;a dispensary;a doctor's consulting room
诊脉 [zhěn mài] to feel the pulse of a patient
诊治 [zhěn zhì] to treat;to cure;to heal

疹 [zhěn] (n) 一般指皮肤上起红色小点，小颗粒或小块的病症 rash; pock ✽ 麻疹 measles

缜(縝) [zhěn] (adj)细密;小心 meticulous;careful
缜密 [zhěn mì] meticulous;careful

枕 [zhěn] 1(n)睡觉时垫在头下的东西 pillow 2 (v)睡觉时头放在垫头的东西上to rest head on (e.g pillow)
枕袋 [zhěn dài] a pillow-case
枕戈待旦 [zhěn gē dài dàn] to make a pillow of one's spear waiting for day break
枕巾 [zhěn jīn] a pillow cover
枕木 [zhěn mù] wooden sleepers of a rail road
枕头 [zhěn tóu] a pillow

zhèn

振 [zhèn] 1 (v)摇动，挥动to shake;to oscillate;to move;to wave ✽ 他振笔疾书。He moves his pen and writes rapidly. 2(v)奋发 to stimulate; to pluck up; to inspire; to arouse ✽ 这是一个振奋人心的好消息。This is a good news that inspires all of us.
振拨 [zhèn bà] raise; pull up
振动 [zhèn dòng] to oscillate;to vibrate
振奋 [zhèn fèn] to inspire;to stimulate;to enliven;to animate
振奋人心 [zhèn fèn rén xīn] encouraging;exciting;inspiring
振幅 [zhèn fù] amplitude
振兴 [zhén xīng] to revive;to develop;to promote;to enliven
振振有辞 [zhèn zhèn yǒu cí] to say plausibly;high-sounding
振作 [zhèn zǔo] to pull oneself together;to inspire;to hearten;to encourage

赈(賑) [zhèn] (v) 用财物救济 to relieve;to assist;to give alms ＊学生响应赈济水灾灾民的工作。The students responded to the call for the relief of flood victims

赈济 [zhèn jì] to subscribe towards relief funds

赈款 [zhèn kuǎn] relief funds

赈灾 [zhèn zāi] to relieve famine or other distress

震 [zhèn] 1 (v)剧烈或迅速地颤动 to shake;to quake;to shock ＊地震。earthquake 2 (v) 惊惧或情绪激动to be alarmed;to be shocked＊听到他死去的消息，我们感到震惊。We are shocked to learn that he was dead.

震荡 [zhen dìng] to shake;to tremor;to oscillate

震悼 [zhèn dào] to be shocked with grief

震动 [zhèn dòng] to tremor;to vibrate;to shock;to alarm

震耳欲聋 [zhèněryùlóng] deafening

震撼 [zhèn hàn] to shake;to shock

震惊 [zhèn jīng] to shock; to startle;to alarm

震惧 [zhèn jù] to tremble with fear;to shake with fear

震怒 [zhèn nù] to thunder;to tremble with rage

镇(鎮) [zhèn] 1 (v)安定 calm; composed＊他面对凶残的敌人仍镇静自若。He remains composed in face of the ferocious enemy. 2(v)压服 to suppress;to quell ＊当局派兵镇压破坏行为。The authority sent troops to suppress the sabotage. 3 (n) 市集 a town

镇定 [zhèn dìng] (to remain) calm; to calm down;(to keep) cool; steady

镇静 [zhèn jìng] sedative;mollified calm;steady

镇守 [zhèn shǒu] to guard at strategic military point

镇压 [zhèn yà] to repress;to suppress;to put down;to quell

阵(陣) [zhèn] 1 (n)军事布置的局势 a line-up of troops;an array of military force or weapons＊军队严阵以待，迎击来犯者The army was in battle array to wait for the invaders. 2 (n) 量词指事情或动作的段落 a measure word: a time or an occasion of wind,rain,applause,etc ＊一阵又一阵、now and again;at intervals ＊一阵烟，a puff of smoke ＊一阵雨。a shower of rain＊一阵掌声。a burst of applause

阵地 [zhòn dì] position;battlefield; front

阵地战 [zhèn dì shàn] a positional warfare

阵脚 [zhèn jiáo] fore-front (mostly figurative)

阵容 [zhèn rǒng] line-up;battle array

阵势 [zhèn shì] battle array;disposition of forces situation

阵痛 [zhèn tòng] twinge;twitch; spasm;sudden sharp pain

阵亡 [zhèn wáng] to die in battle; to bite the dust

阵线 [zhèn xiàn] battle front;front

阵营 [zhèn yíng] camp

阵雨 [zhèn yǔ] shower

zhēng

争 [zhēng] 1 (v)抢先；竞取；竞赛；竞胜 to compete;to contest;to win over;to fight for;to contend for ＊每个人都争着发言。Everybody competes to give a speech.＊寸土必争。to contest every inch of ground＊健儿们决心为国家争光。The sportsmen are determined to win honour for the country. 2

(v) 奋勉；奋斗 to endeavour; to strive;to struggle ＊史前人类必需向大自然展开斗争以图生存。The pre-historic man had to struggle against the nature for existence. 3 (v)吵闹；对抗；辩论 to quarrel;to dispute;to argue ＊ 两派之间争论不休。There are endless arguments between the two factions.

争霸 [zhēng bà] to seek hegemony; to strive for hegemony

争辩 [zhēng biàn] to argue;to debate;to refute

争吵 [zhēng chǎo] to quarrel;to squabble

争端 [zhēng duān] point of contention;cause of dispute

争夺 [zhēng duó] to strive for;to seize;to fight for;to scramble for; to contend for

争分夺秒 [zhēng fēn duó miǎo] to seize every minute and every second — to race against time

争风 [zhēng fēng] a quarrel from jealousy

争光 [zhēng guāng] to win honour

争论 [zhēng lún] to argue;to debate;controversy

争气 [zhēngqì] to try to be a credit to;to strive to live up to;to work hard to win honour for

争取 [zhēngqǔ] to win over;to obtain ; to strive for

争权夺利 [zhēng quán duó lì] to struggle for power and wealth

争先 [zhēng xiān] to contend for first place;compete to be the first

争先恐后 [zhēng xiān kǒng hòu] to struggle to be at fore-front and not willing to lag behind

争雄 [zhēng xíong] to strive for supremacy

争议 [zhēng yì] to argue;to dispute;to debate;controversy

争执 [zhēng zhí] to dispute with; to contend;to be at odds with

挣 [zhēng] (v) 用力支撑；摆脱 to struggle;to get free from

挣脱 [zhēngtuō] to struggle to free oneself;to shake off;to get rid of

挣扎 [zhēng zhá] to struggle desperately;to flounder desperately

狰 [zhēng]狰狞 [zhēng níng] (adj) 样子凶恶 hideous;ferocious;vile;vicious ＊这事件暴露了伪善者的狰狞面目。 The incident exposed the hideous feature of the hypocrite.

峥 [zhēng]〔峥嵘〕[zhēng róng] 1 (adj) 山势高而险 steep;sheer 2 (adj) 突出；不平常 outstanding;prominent;eminent

铮（錚）[zhēng] 〔铮铮〕 [zhēng zhēng] (n) 金属相击声 the clang of metals

睁 [zhēng] (v) 张开（眼睛） to open (e.g. eyes)＊他睁开眼睛瞪着我。 He opened his eyes to stare at me.

筝 [zhēng] (n) 一种弦乐器，用手指弹拨发声 a stringed instrument ＊古筝。A stringed instrument

正 [zhēng]〔正月〕[zhēng yuè] (n) 一年的第一个月 January; the first month of the year
另见 [zhèng]

怔 [zhēng] (v) 呆；楞 to be stunned; to become stupefied ＊他儿子被捕的消息使他怔住了。He was stunned by the news of his son's arrest.

怔忡 [zhēng chōng] heart beating very fast

怔忪 [zhēng zhōng] astound

征 [zhēng] 1 (v)远行 to travel;to take a long journey ＊ 军队已踏上征途了。The army has begun their long journey. 2 (v)讨伐 to attack; to conquer ＊ 波斯无法征服希腊。Persia failed to conquer Greece.

征服 [zhēng fú] to conquer;to overcome

征途 [zhēng tú] underway (of a long journey)

征(徵) [zhēng] 1 (v) 寻求；求取 to seek;to ask for;to request * 报社向读者们征稿。The newspaper office requests articles from its readers. 2 (v) 抽收(税捐) to levy (e.g. taxes);to impose * 政府今年将征收更高的所得税率。The government will impose a higher rate on the income tax this year. 3 (n) 现象；迹象 phenomenon; symbol; symptom; sign * 病人已有好转的征象。The patient has shown signs of improvement. 4 (v) 召集；传召 to draft;to recruit * 他被征召当兵。He was drafted as a soldier.

征兵 [zhēng bīng] conscription;recruit;draft

征购 [zhēng gòu] requisition; purchase by the state

征候 [zhēng hòu] omen;symtoms of a disease;sign

征集 [zhēng jí] to collect;to gather

征求 [zhēng qíu] to consult;to ask for (opinion);to solicit

征收 [zhēng shōu] to levy and collect;to impose (a duty)

征象 [zhēng xiàng] symbol;symptom

征用 [zhēng yòng] requisition;expropriation

症(癥) [zhēng] (n) 肚子里的积块 a tumour in the stomach—key-point * 我们必须先找到问题的症结。We must first find out the key-point to the problem.
另见 [zhèng]

症结 [zhēng jié] key-point;knotty problem

蒸 [zhēng] 1 (v) 液体受热化成气体上升 to evaporate * 热蒸发水 Heat evaporates water. 2 (v)隔水煮食物 to steam (food) * 我在蒸蕃薯 I am steaming the sweet potatoes

蒸馏水 [zhēng líu shuǐ] distilled water

蒸汽机 [zhēng qì jī] a steam engine

蒸蒸日上 [zhēng zhēng rì shàng] ever more flourishing;become more prosperous; more thriving with each passing day

zhěng

拯 [zhěng] (v) 救；援助 to save;to rescue;to help * 救生员拯救了那沉溺的小孩。The life-guard saved the child from drowning.

整 [zhěng] 1 (adj) 有秩序，不乱 in order;neat;orderly * 游行队伍非常整齐。The parading procession is in good order. 2 (adj)全部在内，不缺 whole; total; entire; complete; overall * 他工作了一整天。He has been working for the whole day. 3 (v) 修理 to repair;to mend 他花了很多钱整修机器。He spent a lot of money to repair his machine. 4 (v) 使有组织；使有条理 to reorganise; to rectify; to put in order;to arrange * 军队整装待发。The army troop arranged the equipment in good order and got ready to march off.

整编 [zhěng biān] to reorganize;to reshuffle

整风 [zhěng fēng] rectification of style of work;to rectify incorrect styles of work

整个 [zhěng gè] whole;total;entire

整洁 [zhěng jié] neat and tidy

整理 [zhěng lǐ] to regulate; to put things in order;to rehabilitate;to adjust

整流器 [zhěng líu qì] rectifier;commutator

整齐 [zhěng qí] uniform;in good order;tidy

整数 [zhěng shú] whole number;integer

整肃 [zhěng sù] to purge

整体 [zhěng tǐ] the whole;as a whole; integration;entity

整体化 [zhěng tǐ huà] to integrate; integration

整训 [zhěng xiàn] to train and consolidate

整形外科 [zhěng xíng wài kē] plastic surgery

整修 [zhěng xiū] to repair;to put in order

整整 [zhěng zhěng] exactly;whole

正 [zhěng] (adj) 完整的whole;entire;with-out fraction;only (added to numeral expressions)＊二百万元正 dollars two hundred only ＊下午七时正 7.00p.m.
另见 [zhēng] [zhèng]

zhèng

正 [zhèng] 1 (adj) 直的；平的；当中的 upright;straight;central ＊ 请摆正这幅画。Please put the picture straight. 2 (adj) 公认的；传统的；例常的；对的 orthodox; authorised;regular;correct ＊ 这酒店供应正宗北京菜。 Traditional Peking cuisines are provided in this restaurant. 3 (adj) 商合的；恰当的；合规矩的 exact; proper; formal ＊ 对这问题，总经理不予正式答复。The general manager declined to give a formal reply to the question. 4 (adv) 恰好；刚好 just;at the time of;during ＊ 他正在读报。He is just reading newspaper. ＊ 那正是我所需要的。That is just what I want. 5 (v) 调整；整理；修改to adjust;to regulate;to correct ＊如发现有拼错的字，请改正之Please correct any wrong spelling that you find. 6 (adj) 主要的，主体的，跟〃副〃相对 chief;main;principal (contracted with;vice-, deputy) ＊ 正会长不在时，副会长代行其职务 The vice-President shall deputise for the Chief President in the latter's absence. 7 (adj)真的；纯粹的real;genuine;pure＊本药房只卖正牌药Only real medicines are sold in this drugstore. 8 (adj;n) 肯定的；跟"反"、"负"相对 positive;affirmative ＊ 负负得正。Two negatives make an affirmative.
另见 [zhēng] [zhěng]

正比 [zhèng bǐ] direct ratio

正本 [zhèng běn] authentic writing; original copy

正常 [zhèng cháng] normal

正常化 [zhèng cháng huà] to normalize;to render normal;to bring back to normal

正当 [zhèng dāng] at a time when; just when;when;while

正当 [zhèng dàng] proper;legitimate;rightful;due

正电 [zhèng diàn] positive electricity

正方体 [zhèng fāng tǐ] a cube

正方形 [zhèng fāng xíng] a square

正告 [zhèng gào] to inform in all seriousness;to solemnly inform;to serve notice on

正规 [zhèng guī] regular

正规军 [zhèng guī jūn] regular army;regular forces

正轨 [zhèng guǐ] the right track

正好 [zhèng gǎo] fit;suitable;just; just all right;a good chance

正号 [zhèng hào] positive sign

正经 [zhèng· jing] decent; honest; real;proper

正面 [zhèng miàn] front;frontal; frontage ; positive side;in positive way

正面冲突 [zhèng miàn chōng tū] a head-on collision

正面人物 [zhèng miàn rén wù] a

positive character
正派 [zhèng pài] upright;honest; decent
正气 [zhèng qì] uprightness;integrity;probity;open and above-board
正巧 [zhèng qiǎo] by (a happy) chance;by coincidence
正确 [zhèng què] correct;right
正式 [zhèng shì] official;recorded; formal;full
正视 [zhèng shì] to envisage;to face squarely
正数 [zhèng shù] positive number
正统 [zhèng tǒng] orthodox;legitimate;lineal
正文 [zhèng wén] the main text;the original text
正午 [zhèng wǔ] noon
正义 [zhèng yì] just;right;righteous ;justice
正音 [zhèng yìn] correct pronunciation
正义战争 [zhèng yì zhàn zhēng] a just war
正在 [zhèng zaì] in the process of;in the act of
正值 [zhèng zhí] just at the time of
正直 [zhèng zhí] just;upright;far-minded;honest
正中 [zhèng zhōng] exactly in the middle
正中下怀 [zhèng zhòng xià huái] exactly to one's wish
正宗 [zhàng zōng] orthodox;traditional

证(証) [zhèng] 1 (v) 用人或事物来表明或断定 to prove;to testify ＊事实证明这个判断是正确的。Facts have proved that the judgement is correct. 2 (n)凭据，帮助断定事理的人或事物 an evidence;a proof;a certificate ＊他将出庭作证。He is going to give evidence in the court.
证件 [zhèng jiàn] papers;certificates
证据 [zhèng jù] evidence;proof
证明 [zhèng míng] to prove;to confirm;to testify;certificate
证券 [zhèng quàn] bills;bonds;securities
证券交易所 [zhèng quàn jiāo yì suǒ] the stock exchange
证人 [zhèng·ren] a witness
证实 [zhèng shí] to confirm;to corroborate;to verify;to testify
证书 [zhèng shū] a certificate;a testimonial

政 [zhèng] 1 (n)统卸全国的事情 government;administration ＊新加坡施行共和政体。Republican government is practised in Singapore. 2 (n)办事的规则，方法 regulations;managements ＊家政 domestic regulations;household art ＊财政。finance (financial management)
政变 [zhèng biàn] coup;coup d'etat
政策 [zhèng cè] policy
政党 [zhèng dǎng] political party
政府 [zhèng fǔ] government
政纲 [zhèng gāng] political platform
政界 [zhèng jiè] political circles
政局 [zhèng jú] political situation; political scene
政客 [zhèng kè] politician;political hack
政论 [zhèng lùn] political comment
政权 [zhèng quán] political power
政体 [zhèng tǐ] political constitution;system of government;form of government
政委 [zhèng wěi] political commissar
政治 [zhèng zhì] politics
政治避难 [zhèng zhì bì nàn] political asylum;political refuge
政治犯 [zhèng zhì fàn] political detainee
政治家 [zhèng zhì jiā] statesman
政治经济学 [zhèng zhì jīng jì xuē]

political economy
政治觉悟 [zhèng zhì jué wù] political understanding;political awakening;political consciousness
政治路线 [zhèng zhì lù xiàn] political course

症 [zhèng] (n) 病;疾病的情况disease ;illness;symptom *他得了不治之症。He is suffering from an incurable disease.
另见 [zhēng]
症状 [zhèng zhuàng] symptom

郑(鄭) [zhèng] 1 (n) 姓 a surname 2. (adj)郑重 [zhèng zhòng] 认真;严肃 serious;solemn

zhī

支 [zhī] 1 (n) 分出来的 branch; branching *委员会决定在市区多设一个支部。The committee decides to establish one more branch office in town area. 2 (v) 架起;搭起to erect;to raise;to lift *他用竹竿支起帐篷。He erected the tent with bamboo poles. 3 (v)撑持 to support;to sustain*木桥没有足够支持一列火车的力量。A wooden bridge is not strong enough to support a railway train. 4 (v)调度;指使 to send;to dominate;to control * 他不愿意受人支配。He does not want to be controlled by others. 5 (v) 付款 to pay *我必须在月底前支付公用事业局的水电费。I must pay the PUB's bill before the end of the month. 6 (n) 量词 piece: a measure word for candle, pen, rifle, etc.
支部 [zhī bù] a branch of an organization
支撑 [zhī cheng] to prop up;to support;to sustain
支出 [zhī chū] to pay out;to disburse expenditure
支解 [zhī jiě] to dismember
支离破碎 [zhī lí pò suì] shattered; splintered;split
支流 [zhī liú] tributary ;subsidiary trend;secondary stream
支配 [zhī pèi] to control;to dominate;to manipulate
支票 [zhī piào] a cheque
支吾 [zhī·wu] quibble;stall
支线 [zhī xiàn] branch line;extension
支援 [zhī yuán] to support;to aid;to hold up;to help;to back
支柱 [zhī zhù] mainstay;brace;pillar

枝 [zhī] (n) 植物主干旁出的茎条 branches of a plant
枝节 [zhī jié] side issue; minor issue;minor problem

肢 [zhī] (n) 人的手和脚;兽的脚;鸟的翼和脚 the limbs of the man; the limbs of animals;the wings and legs of birds * 他冷得四肢麻木。His limbs are numb with cold.

知 [zhī] (v) 认识;了解;晓得 to know;to perceive;to be aware of *知无不言,言无不尽。 to tell the truth and the whole truth * 知己知彼,百战不殆。Know your enemy and know yourself and you can fight a hundred battles without disaster.
知道 [zhī dào] to know;to be aware of
知己 [zhī jǐ] intimate;an intimate friend;one who knows me
知交 [zhī jiāo] intimacy
知觉 [zhī jué] consciousness
知名人士 [zhī míng rén shì] well-known people;famous people;outstanding personalities
知趣 [zhī qù] to know how to act on different occasions;tactful
知识 [zhī·shi] knowledge
知识分子 [zhī·shi fèn zǐ] intellectuals;intelligentsia
知识界 [zhī·shi jiè] intellectual circle

蜘 [zhī] 蜘蛛 [zhī zhū] (n) 节肢动物，有足四对。腹部突起，能分泌粘液，结网捕捉小虫 the spider

之 [zhī] 1 (part) 助词。相当于"的" of (possessive particle) ✻失败乃成功之母。 Failure is the mother of success. 2 (pron) 第三人称代词，相当于"它"，"他"，"她"，"他们" it;him;her;them (objective case) ✻凡事不可操之过急。 Generally, when we do anything, we should not do it too hurriedly.

之后 [zhī hòu] after..., behind...; later

之间 [zhī jiàn] in the midst of...; between...

……之类 [zhī lèi] such...;...alike

……之流 [zhī liú] such as...,...and his like

之前 [zhī qián] before...

之外 [zhī wài] besides...; in addition to...

之一 [zhī yī] one of...

……之中 [zhī zhōng] in the midst of...;among...

之字路 [zhī zì lù] a zigzag course

芝 [zhī] (n) 灵芝，寄生于枯树的一种菌，可供药用 a medical fungus

芝麻 [zhī·ma] sesame

只(隻) [zhī] (n) 量词 a measure word (referring to one of a pair of things such as shoe, sock, ear, hand, etc);measure word for animal ✻一只手。one hand; 一只鸭。a duck

织(織) [zhī] (v) 用棉、毛、丝、麻线等制布或衣物 to knit;to weave ✻她用羊毛线编织一件毛背心。 She knitted a cardigan with wool.

织补 [zhī bǔ] to knit up;to darn

织工 [zhī gōng] a weaver

汁 [zhī] (n) 含有某种物质的液体 juice ✻橙汁。orange juice

脂 [zhī] 1 (n) 动物体内的油质 the fat of animal lard;grease 2 (n) 凝固的膏 ointment 3 (n) 红色的化妆品 rouge;cosmetics

脂肪 [zhī fáng] fat;grease

脂粉 [zhī fěn] rouge and powder; cosmetics;feminine beauty

脂膏 [zhī gāo] fat; wealth from the people

zhí

直 [zhí] 1 (adj) 不弯的 straight ✻山中有直树，世上无直人。 There are straight trees in the mountains, but there is no straight man in the world. 2 (adj) 竖，纵，跟"横"相对 vertical;erect ✻杂技演员直立在钢索上。The acrobat stands erect on the steel rope. 3 (adj) 公正；无私 righteous;honest; just ✻有时法律会被利用来迫害正直的人。Sometimes the law could be used to persecute a righteous person. 4 (adj) 爽快；坦率 outspoken;frank;straightforward ✻他的评语是率直的。He is straightforward in his remarks. 5 (v) 伸长使不曲 to straighten; to stretch ✻他直起腰来。 He straightens himself. 6 (adj) 不转折的 directly ✻所得税是一种直接税 A tax on income is a direct tax.

直达 [zhí dá] through (train); through—traffic

直到 [zhí dào] until; till;up to

直观 [zhí guān] intuition;visual (e.g. aids)

直角 [zhí jiǎo] right angle

直接 [zhí jiē] direct;immediate

直截了当 [zhí jié liǎo dàng] outspoken;straight;bluntly

直径 [zhí jìng] diameter

直流电 [zhí liú diàn] direct current (d.c.)

直升机 [zhí shēng jī] a helicopter

直属 [zhí shǔ] directly under...

直率 [zhí shuài] frank;straightforward;plain spoken;outright
直系亲属 [zhí xì qīn shǔ] lineal relative
直辖 [zhí xiá] directly under the central authorities
直线 [zhí xiàn] straight line
直言不讳 [zhí yán bù huì] to speak without reservation;to mince no words
直译 [zhí yì] literal translation;word for word translation

值 [zhí] 1 (n) 价钱 price;value *我国的币值是稳定的。The value of our currency is stable. 2 (v) 相抵;相当 to cost;to be worth *这个相机现在值五百元。The camera now costs five hundred dollars. 3 (v) 遇到;碰着 to meet; to encounter *他上回旅行东海岸时,正值雨季。In his last trip to the East Coast, he was just in time to meet with the rainy season. 4 (v) 担任职务 to be on duty *今天该谁值日?Who should be on duty today?
值班 [zhí bān] to be on duty
值得 [zhí dé] to be worth; to merit; to deserve
值钱 [zhí qián] valuable
值勤 [zhí qín] to be on duty
值日 [zhí rì] to be on duty for the day

植 [zhí] (v) 栽种 to plant;to grow;to cultivate*学生们在路旁植树。The students plant trees at the roadside.
植林 [zhí lín] afforestation
植树节 [zhí shù jú] Arbour Day
植物 [zhí wù] plants
植物学 [zhí wù xué] botany
植物园 [zhí wù yuán] botanical garden

殖 [zhí] (v) 生育 to reproduce: to breed *蚊子繁殖得非常快。The mosquitoes breed very fast.
殖民地 [zhí mín dì] colony
殖民主义 [zhí mín zhǔ yì] colonialism

职(職) [zhí] 1 (n 责任;分内应做的事 duty *他从来没有失职。He never fails in his duty. 2 (n) 工作的地位 position; post *他在国防部担任要职。He is holding an important post in the Ministry of Defence.
职别 [zhí bié] classification of profession
职工 [zhí gōng] staff and workers; employees
职能 [zhí néng] function
职权 [zhí quán] positions and powers
职位 [zhí wèi] position;post
职务 [zhí wù] official duties
职业 [zhí yè] occupation;profession;vocation
职业病 [zhí yè bìng] occupational disease
职员 [zhí yuán] staff;office worker
职责 [zhí zé] responsibility;duty

执(執) [zhí] 1 (v) 拿;持 to hold;to grasp *她执着他的手。She held him by the hand. 2 (v) 掌管 to preside;to manage *真的有命运之神执掌人们的命运吗?Is it true that the Fates preside over man's destiny? 3(v) 坚持 to presist in;to stick to;to adhere to *在会议上,他固执己见,不肯让步。He adhered to his own opinion and refused to give way at the meeting. 4 (v) 实行 to carry out;to perform;to execute *委员会的职务,是执行会员大会的议决案。The duty of the Committee is to execute the resolution of the General Meeting of Members.
执拗 [zhíaò] obstinate; pig headed
执笔 [zhí bǐ] to hold a pen — to

write down
执迷不悟 [zhí mí bù wù] to persist in error;to refuse to come to one's senses;to refuse to mend one's way
执行 [zhí xíng] to carry out;to perform;to put into effect;to execute
执行委员会 [zhí xíng wěi yuán huì] the executive committee
执照 [zhí zhào] a certificate;a licence
执政 [zhí zhèng] to govern;to be in power;to rule

侄 [zhí] 1 (n)弟兄的儿子 nephew
侄女 [zhí nǚ] niece (brother's daughter)
侄子 [zhí zǐ] nephew

zhǐ

止 [zhǐ] 1 (v)停住 to stop;to cease ✱ 比赛因雨停止 The game was stopped by rain. 2 (v)阻挡；使停住 to check;to hold back;to allay ✱ 没有人能够阻止历史车轮的前进。No one can hold back the wheel of history.
止步 [zhǐ bù] to stop;to halt
止境 [zhǐ jìng] limit;boundary
止痛 [zhǐ tòng] analgesic;allay pains;pain killing
止血 [zhǐ xuè] to stanch;to stop bleeding

址 [zhǐ] 1 (n) 地点 a place ✱ 住址 。a dwelling;a house; an address 2 (n)基地 a foundation ✱ 遗址。remains of an old building;old ruins

趾 [zhǐ] (n) 脚指头 the toe
趾高气扬 [zhǐ gāo qì yáng] give oneself airs and swagger about; breed pride and arrogance;cocky

纸（紙） [zhǐ] (n) 供人写字作画包物的制品，用植物纤维制成 paper
纸币 [zhǐ bì] bank note;paper currency
纸浆 [zhǐ jiāng] paper pulp
纸老虎 [zhǐ lǎo hǔ] paper tiger
纸牌 [zhǐ pái] playing cards
纸上谈兵 [zhǐ shàng tán bīng] empty talk;armchair strategy;fight only on paper

只（衹） [zhǐ] (adj) 仅；单 merely;only ✱ 只许州官放火，不许百姓点灯。Only the magistrates were allowed to burn down houses, while the common people were forbidden even to light lamps — only the powerful can do what they want, the weak are not allowed to do anything. 另见 [zhī]
只不过 [zhǐ bù guò] simply...
只得 [zhǐ dé] have to;cannot but;-have no choice but to...
只顾 [zhǐ gù] merely;just;be preoccupied only with
只管 [zhǐ guǎn] go ahead;by all means ; just;merely;be concerned only with...
只好 [zhǐ hǎo] could not but;cannot help but
只要 [zhǐ yào] so long as;if only; provided that;on condition that
只有 [zhǐ yǒu] only (by) ;can only be...; only in this way;only thus; not otherwise
只争朝夕 [zhǐ zhēng zhāo xī] to seize the hour;to seize the time

旨 [zhǐ] (n)意思；目的 meaning;aim; intention;object ✱ 文艺创作比赛的宗旨是发扬健康文化。The main aim of this literary competition is to promote healthy culture.

指 [zhǐ] 1 (n) 人手末端分歧的部份 fingers ✱ 房间里黑暗得伸手不见五指。It is so dark in the room that one cannot see the five fingers before the face. 拇指 the thumb 食

指the index finger 中指the middle finger 无名指the ring finger 小指the little finger 2 (v) 针对；导向；表明to point;to direct;to indicate * 他指着地图解释战后世界政治形势。He pointed at the map to explain the post-war world political situation.

指标 [zhǐ biāo] quota;aim;target

指斥 [zhǐ chì] to reprove

指出 [zhǐ chù] to point out;to indicate

指导 [zhǐ dǎo] to instruct;to guide; to direct;to lead

指点 [zhǐ diǎn] to instruct;to point; to show;to indicate

指定 [zhǐ dìng] to appoint; to assign;to name;to charge with

指挥 [zhǐ huī] to command;to conduct;to direct

指挥部 [zhǐ huī bù] headquarters; command post

指挥棒 [zhǐ huī bàng] a baton;a club

指挥员 [zhǐ huī yuán] commander; commanding officer

指教 [zhǐ jiào] to instruct;to teach; to comment;to advise

指控 [zhǐ kòng] to lay a charge;to accuse

指名 [zhǐ míng] to point out somebody's name;to mention... by name

指明 [zhǐmíng] clearly demonstrate; clearly point out

指南 [zhǐ nán] to guide

指南针 [zhǐ nán zhēn] a compass

指认 [zhǐrén] to identify

指日可待 [zhǐ rì kě dài] the day is not far off;just round the corner

指桑骂槐 [zhǐ sāng mà huái] to revile the locust while pointing to the mulberry — to curse one thing while pointing at another;to make oblique accusations

指使 [zhǐ shǐ] to instigate;to incite

指示 [zhǐ shì] to indicate;to instruct directive

指手画脚 [zhǐ shǒu huà jiǎo] to talk (others) about with wild gestures;to carp and cavil

指数 [zhǐ shù] index

指望 [zhǐ• wang] to look forward to;to expect;to pin one's hopes on;to count on

指纹 [zhǐ wén] finger-print

指引 [zhǐ yǐn] to guide;to conduct; to lead

指责 [zhǐ zé] to censure; to blame; to denounce; to charge; to accuse

指针 [zhǐ zhēn] guidance; direction

指正 [zhǐ zhèng] to correct

zhì

至 [zhì] 1 (adj) (v) 到 until;till;to;up to;to approach;to reach * 直至现在，他仍然沉迷于赌，不思悔改。Up to now he still deeply indulges himself in gambling and does not think of mending his ways. 2 (adj) 极；最 extremely; mostly;super- * 在封建时代，帝王对臣民有至高无上的权力。In the Feudal Age, an emperor had the supreme power over his subjects

至多 [zhì duō] at most

至高无上 [zhì gāo wú shàng] most lofty;supreme;paramount

至今 [zhì jīn] up to now;until now; hitherto

至理名言 [zhì lǐ míng yán] a golden saying;an axiom

至上 [zhì shàng] highest; supreme

至少 [zhì shǎo] at least;minimum

至于 [zhì yú] as for;as to;concerning;with regard to

桎 [zhì] (n)脚镣 fetters

桎梏 [zhì gù] fetters and handcuffs; shackles; yokes

蛭 [zhì] (n) 环节动物。体形扁平，前后各有一个吸盘，能吸人畜的血 leeches

致(緻) [zhì] 1 (v)给与，送给，向对方表示 to pay (e.g. respects);to send (e.g. letter, congratulation, etc.);to salute;to extend (e.g. greetings) *我们每天向国旗致敬。We salute the national flag everyday. 2 (v) 引来；造成 to cause * 火灾招致重大的损害。The fire caused much damage. 3 (v)集中于；专心从事于 to concentrate on;to devote oneself to *他致力于科学研究工作。He devotes himself to scientific research.

致哀 [zhì āi] to convey lamentation

致词 [zhì cí] to make a speech;to address

致贺 [zhì hè] to convey congratulations

致敬 [zhì jìng] to salute

致力 [zhì lì] to devote oneself to;to make efforts in;to concentrate effort on

致命 [zhì mìng] fatal;vital;lethal; mortal

致使 [zhì shǐ] to cause;to bring about

致谢 [zhì xiè] to extend thanks to

致意 [zhì yì] to send one's regards; to give one's compliments to;to extend greetings

窒 [zhì] (adj) 阻塞不通blocked;choked;stifled;suffocated *火患发生时，他被困在舱底下窒息而死。During the fire, he was trapped under the cabin and was suffocated to death

痔 [zhì] (n) 痔疮，肛门附近直肠静脉扩张郁血而引起的一种病 piles ;bleeding piles *内痔。internal piles *外痔。external piles

质(質) [zhì] 1 (n) 特性；本性 disposition;character;nature;quality *我们重质不重量。We aim at quality rather than quantity. 2 (n)实物；物体 matter ;substance;element *冰和水是不同形式的同一物。Ice and water are the same substance in different forms. 3 (adj) 朴素；单纯 plain; simple *他为人质朴忠厚。He is simple and honest. 4 (v) 对证；当面；面对；碰面 to call as witness; to confront;to present oneself before *被告和原告对质。The defendant was confronted with his accusers. 5 (v) (n) 抵押；抵押品 a pledge;a hostage; mortgage *劫机者扣押三名搭客作人质。The hijackers kept three passengers as hostages

质变 [zhì biàn] qualitative change

质地 [zhì dì] natural constitution and quality (of materials)

质量 [zhì liàng] quality

质问 [zhì wèn] to query;to interrogate;to take somebody to task

质子 [zhì zǐ] proton

帜(幟) [zhì] (n) 旗 a flag;a banner

秩 [zhì] (n) 秩序[zhì xù]次序；条理 order *球赛观众都能遵守会场秩序。All the football match spectators were able to observe orders in the stadium.

挚(摯) [zhì] (adj) 诚恳；亲密 true;close *他渴望得到真挚的友情。He longs for true friendship.

挚友 [zhì yǒu] close friend;intimate friend

制 [zhì] 1 (v)订立；规定to stipulate; to enact;to lay down;to draw up;to work out *新政府将制定新的宪法。The new government will enact a new constitution. 2 (v) 限定；约

束；管束 to restrain;to restrict；to control ＊政府将限制某些货物入口。The government will restrict the import of certain goods. 3 (n) 法则；体统 system ＊新加坡现行民主政制。Democratic system of government is being practised in Singapore.

制(製) [zhì] (v) 造；做 to make;to create ;to produce;to manufacture ＊这家工厂制造鞋子。This factory manufactures shoes.

制裁 [zhì cái] to impose sanction on;to be dealt with according to law

制定 [zhì dìng] to enact;to lay down;to regulate;to work out;to adopt;to devise

制动 [zhì dòng] to brake

制度 [zhì du] system; rule principle; institution; policy; regulations

制服 [zhì fú] uniform

制服 [zhì fú] to subdue;to conquer

制空权 [zhì kōng quán] air control; air supremacy

制胜 [zhì shèng] to come out victorious;to gain mastery over

制图 [zhì tú] to make charts or blueprints

制约 [zhì yuē] to restrain

制造 [zhì zào] to produce;to make; to manufacture;to fabricate (e.g. tension);to foment (dissension, split, etc.)

制止 [zhì zhǐ] to stop;to check;to restrain;to prevent

制作 [zhì zuò] to create;to manufacture;to form

志 [zhì] (n) 意向 will;ambition;aspiration;aim ＊青年人应该有雄心壮志。Young people should have lofty aspirations and high aims.

志气 [zhì qì] will;ambition;noble aspirations;lofty ideals

志趣 [zhì qù] will and interest;aspirations

志士 [zhì shì] people with lofty ideals;honest patriot

志同道合 [zhì tóng dào hé] to cherish the same ideals and follow the same path;two minds with but a single thought

志向 [zhì·xiang] aspiration

志愿 [zhì yuàn] will;desire;wish of one's own free will;voluntary

志愿兵 [zhì yuàn bìng] a volunteer soldier

志(誌) [zhì] 1 (v) 记住 remember ＊您的恩情我永志不忘。I shall remember your kindness forever. 2 (n) 记载的文字 annals;record ＊三国志。The Annal of The Three Kingdoms.

痣 [zhì] (n) 皮肤上的斑点 spots on the body;moles

置 [zhì] 1 (v) 放；搁；摆 to place; to put ＊这么重要的事你不可置之不理。You cannot put such an important matter aside. 2 (v) 摆设；装设；设立 arrange ;install; establish ＊他在房里装置了冷气设备。He has installed an air-conditioner in the room. 3 (v) 购买 to purchase;to buy ＊他最近添置了一些家具。He has bought some furniture recently.

置办 [zhì bàn] to buy

置换 [zhì huàn] to displace;to replace;to substitute

置若罔闻 [zhì ruò wǎng wén] to ignore completely;to take no notice of;turn a deaf ear

置身 [zhì shēn] to place oneself in;to put oneself in

置于 [zhì yú] to place in;to put in

置之不理 [zhì zhī bù lǐ] to ignore;to pay no attention to;to leave alone

置之度外 [zhì zhī dù wài] to ignore; not to take into account;to disregard

智 [zhì] 1 (n) 才识 wisdom;intelligence;wit * 群众的智慧是无穷的。The wisdom of the masses is inexhaustible. 2 (adj) 明白事理的 wise * 他不去是明智之举。It is wise of him not to go.

智慧 [zhì huì] wisdom

智力 [zhì lì] intelligence

智谋 [zhì móu] wisdom;strategy;wit

智取 [zhì qǔ] to outwith ; to take by strategy

智育 [zhì yù] education to develop intellectually

稚 [zhì] (adj) 幼小 tender;young;immature;infantile

滞(滯) [zhì] (adj) 凝聚;不流通 stagnant ;not moving * 当经济危机出现时生产停滞。When economic crisis occurs, production becomes stagnant.

滞货 [zhì huò] goods which do not sell well

滞销 [zhì xiāo] not selling well (of commodities)

治 [zhì] 1 (v) 管理;整理 to govern;to administer;to manage;to run;to treat * 皇帝研究治国安民的办法。The emperor studied ways to govern a state and to look after the welfare of his subjects. 2 (v) 惩办 to punish * 这些坏人应如何治罪?How should we punish these bad hats?

治安 [zhì ān] public security;public order

治本 [zhì běn] to give fundamental treatment

治标 [zhì biāo] to alleviate symptoms (of disease or social illness)

治病救人 [zhì bìng jiù rén] to cure the sickness and save the patient.

治理 [zhì lǐ] to govern;to run;to manage;to harness;to tame;to bring under control

治疗 [zhì liáo] to remedy;to cure;to treat;to heal

治丧 [zhìsāng] funeral service; mourning service

治水 [zhìshuǐ] to reduce the waters to order

治外法权 [zhì wài fǎ quán] extraterritoriality

掷(擲) [zhì] (v) 抛;扔 to throw; to cast * 他练习投掷标枪。He practised throwing the javelin.

炙 [zhì] 1 (v) 烤 to roast 2 (n) 烤熟的肉 roasted meat

炙手可热 [zhì shǒu kě rè] to put your hand near him and you can feel the heat — great influence and power

栉(櫛) [zhì] 1 (n) 梳子、篦子等梳头发的用具 combs * 山坡上的木屋鳞次栉比。The squatter houses on the hill slope line up closely like fish scales and teeth of a comb. 2 (v) 梳(头发) to comb (the hair)

栉风沐雨 [zhì fēng mù yǔ] combed by wind and bathed by rain — the hazards of travelling in the open

zhōng

中 [zhōng] 1 (adj) (n) 跟四周的距离相对 middle;centre * 草场中心有一根旗杆。There is a flagstaff in the centre of the field. 2 (prep) 在一定范围内,里面 in, among;inside * 他消失在人群中。He disappeared among the crowd. 3 (prep) 位置在两端之间 in between;halfway * 汽车在中途被拦截。The car was stopped halfway on the journey. 4 (adj) 等级在两端之间 middle (of grade);medium;average * 他来自中等家庭。He came from a middle class family 5(prep) 表示动作正在进行 in...;under... (to show an action in progress) * 这宗案件正在调查中。This case is now under investigation. 6 (adj) 适合 suitable * 这种器皿中看不中用。This ware is

suitable for decorative purpose but unsuitable for utility.
另见 [zhòng]
中波 [zhōng bō] medium wave
中餐 [zhōng cān] Chinese meal; lunch
中草药 [zhōng cǎo yào] traditional Chinese medicinal herbs
中等 [zhōng děng] average;moderate;medium
中点 [zhōng diǎn] middle point
中断 [zhōng duàn] to break off;to interrupt;to come to a stop;to disrupt
中国 [zhōng gúo] China
中和 [zhōng hé] to neutralize
中华民族 [zhōng huá mín zú] the Chinese nation
中华人民共和国 [zhōng huá rén mín gòng hé gúo] the People's Republic of China
中级 [zhōng jí] intermediate;middle rank;secondary
中坚 [zhōng jiān] centre;pillar;backbone;mainstay;nucleus of
中间 [zhōng jiān] the inside;the middle;among ;in the middle;halfway;in the process
中间派 [zhōng jiān paì] middle-of-the-roaders;middle section
中立 [zhōng lì] neutrality;neutral; standing in the middle;neither on one side or the other
中立国 [zhōng lì guó] a neutral country
中立化 [zhōng lì huò] to neutralize
中流砥柱 [zhōng liú dì zhù] pillar; rock;mainstay
中年 [zhōng nían] middle age
中篇小说 [zhōng piān xiǎo shuō] novella;novelette
中秋节 [zhōng qiū jíe] Middle Autumn Festival; The Moon Festival
中山装 [zhōng shān zhuāngl] man's jacket with closed collar
中世纪 [zhōng shì jì] the Middle Ages;medieval
中枢 [zhōng shū] axis
中途 [zhōng tú] midway
中文 [zhōng wén] Chinese language
中午 [zhōng wǔ] midday;noon
中心 [zhōng xīn] centre;core;heart; key;central
中性 [zhōng xìng] neutral character; neutrality
中学 [zhōng xué] middle school; secondary school
中旬 [zhōng xún] the second ten days of a month;mid-month
中央 [zhōng yāng] centre;central leading organ (e.g. central committee)
中央集权 [zhōng yāng jì quán] centralization;centralization of authority
中央委员 [zhōng yāng wěi yuán] member of the central committee
中药 [zhōng yào] traditional Chinese medicine
中叶 [zhōng yè] middle period (e.g. dynasty;century)
中医 [zhōng yī] doctor of the traditional Chinese school of medicine; traditional Chinese medical science
中游 [zhōng yóu] middle reaches (of a river)
中原 [zhōng yuán] the Central Plain of China
中子 [zhōng zǐ] neutron

钟(鐘) [zhōng] 1 (n) 金属制成的响器 bell * 钟声。ringing of the bell. 2 (n) 计时的器具 clock * 电钟。electric clock
钟表 [zhōng bǐǎo] clocks and watches
钟点 [zhōng diǎn] time hour
钟头 [zhōng toú] hour

钟(鍾) [zhōng] 1 (n) 姓 a Chinese surname 2 (n) 杯子a cup;a goblet 3 (v) 聚集 to bring together
钟爱 [zhōng aì] to love faithfully

and ardently

钟情 [zhōng qín] to fall in love with

钟乳 [zhōng rǔ] stalactite

忠 [zhōng] (adj) 赤诚；全心全意 loyal;faithful;devoted *公务员应忠于职守。A civil servant should be faithful to his duty.

忠诚 [zhōng chéng] loyal;faithful; truthful;be staunch;be loyal;be devoted

忠告 [zhōng gào] to counsel;to admonish;to advise ; earnest advice

忠实 [zhōng shí] loyal; faithful;devoted;staunch

忠心 [zhōng xīn] loyalty;faithfulness;devotion

忠心耿耿 [zhōng xīn gěng gěng] infinitely loyal; loyal and devoted; most faithful and loyal

忠言逆耳 [zhōng yán nì ěr] honest advice is hard to take;sincere advice jars on the ear

忠于 [zhōng yú] be true to;be loyal to;be faithful to

盅 [zhōng] (n) 杯子 a cup

衷 [zhōng] (adv) 内心 heart; mind; sincerity *他言不由衷。His words do not come from his heart.

衷情 [zhōng qíng] the feelings

衷心 [zhōng xīn] heart-felt;whole-hearted; sincere

终（終） [zhōng) 1 (n) 最后；末了 the end;close;conclusion *他年终有一个长假。He has a long holiday at the end of the year. 2 (n) 死亡 death *他临终还念念不忘他的工作。At the door of his death, he still worried about his work. 3 (adj) 表示整个一段时间 whole;all;entire *这座山终年积雪。This tall mountain is covered with snow the whole year round.

终点 [zhōng diǎn] terminal (point)

终归 [zhōng guī] after all;in the end; be bound to

终结 [zhōng jié] to wind up;to end up

终究 [zhōng jiū] after all;in the end;finally

终了 [zhōng liǎo] to be over;to be finished;to end up

终日 [zhōng rì] all day long

终身 [zhōng shēn] whole life long; life-time

终于 [zhōng yú] in the end; finally; after all

终止 [zhōng zhǐ] stop;cease;put an end to;conclude;close

zhǒng

肿（腫） [zhǒng] (v) 皮肉或内脏浮肿、发炎 be swollen *他的脸被打得浮肿。His faoo becomes swollen after being beaten.

肿瘤 [zhǒng liú] a tumour

种（種） [zhǒng] 1 (n) 植物的子 the seed *农人在播种。The farmer is sowing the seeds. 2 (n) 类别；样式 kind;sort;variety; species; type *你要那一种书？What sort of book do you want? 人种 race;human race 物种species of things

种类 [zhǒng lèi] class;kind;variety; species

种子 [zhǒng zǐ] seed

种族 [zhǒng zú] race;racial

种族歧视 [zhǒng zú qí shì] racial discrimination

种族主义 [zhǒng zú zhǔ yì] racialism;racism

踵 [zhǒng] (n)脚后跟 the heel *人们接踵而来。The people come one after another .

冢（塚） [zhǒng] (n)坟墓 tomb; grave

zhòng

中 [zhòng] 1 (v) 正对上，恰好合上 to hit (e.g. target) *他被击中要害

。He was hit right at the vital part of his body. 2 (v) 受到；遭到 to suffer;to sustain;to be liable to ＊在炎阳底下工作很容易中暑。One who works under the hot sun is liable to sunstroke.

另见 [zhōng]

中毒 [zhòng dú] be poisoned

中肯 [zhòng kěn] sincere and to the point (e.g. advice)

中伤 [zhòng shāng] cast slanderous remarks; hurt with damaging remarks

中暑 [zhòng shǔ] sunstroke;heat stroke

仲 [zhòng] 1 (adj) 在当中的，居间的意思 middle;in between ＊仲夏。mid-summer 2 (n) 兄弟排行，常用孟、仲、季作次序，仲是第二 the second (brother)

仲裁 [zhòng cái] to arbitrate;to interpose;to intermediate

仲裁庭 [zhòng cái tíng] an arbitration court

种(種) [zhòng] (v) 使植物生长 to plant;to grow;to cultivate;to sow ＊种瓜得瓜，种豆得豆。Plant melons and get melons; sow beans and get beans — to reap what one has sown

另见 [zhǒng]

种地 [zhòng dì] to do farm work

种痘 [zhòng dòu] to vaccinate;vaccination

种植 [zhòng zhí] to plant

众(衆) [zhòng] 1 (adj) 很多 many;numerous ＊他子女众多。He has many children. 2 (n) 很多的人 the people;the masses ＊人民群众有无限的创造力。The masses have boundless creative power ＊电视是很有效的大众传播工具 Television is a very effective mass media.

众多 [zhòng duō] numerous

众叛亲离 [zhòng pàn qīn lí] opposed by the masses and deserted by one's followers

众矢之的 [zhòng shǐ zhī dì] under attack on all sides

众说纷纭 [zhòng shuō fēn yún] many different opinions

众所周知 [zhòng suǒ zhōu zhī] as all know;it is known to all

众志成城 [zhòng zhì chéng chéng] a united people is like a strong city fortification;unity is strength

重 [zhòng] 1 (adj) 分量大 heavy; weighty ＊铁比木头重。Iron is heavier than wood. 2 (n) 分量 weight ＊这块钢板的重量是一吨。The weight of this steel plate is one ton. 3 (adj) 程度深 serious; deep ;thick ＊他得了重病。He was seriously ill. 4 (adj) 主要；要紧 main;important; strategic ＊他被委以重任。He was given an important task.

另见 [chóng]

重兵 [zhòng bīng] strong forces

重大 [zhòng dà] important;great; major

重担 [zhòng dàn] heavy burden; heavy loads;heavy responsibility

重地 [zhòng dì] vital centres

重点 [zhòng diǎn] focal point; emphasis;main point;key point

重读 [zhòng dú] to stress (pron)

重工业 [zhòng gōng yè] heavy industry

重活 [zhòng huó] heavy work

重力 [zhòng lì] gravitation;gravity

重量 [zhòng liàng] weight

重任 [zhòng rèn] a task of importance; prime task; a task of great significance

重伤 [zhòng shāng] heavy wound; heavily wounded

重视 [zhòng shì] to pay great attention to;to take...seriously;to attach importance to

重心 [zhòng xīn] centre of gravity

重型 [zhòng xíng] heavy type;heavy (e.g. machine, building, equipment, etc.)
重压 [zhòng yā] heavy pressure (eg. of work)
重要 [zhòng yào] important;significant;essential;major
重音 [zhòng yīn] a stress;an accent
重用 [zhòng yòng] to put somebody in important position
重于泰山 [zhòng yú tài shān] to be weightier than Mount Tai;to be of great significance

zhōu

周 [zhōu] 1 (n) 圈子 circle; circuit; round;circumference ＊运动员绕场一周。The sportmen ran a round in the stadium. 2 (adj) 普遍；完全 general;whole;entire ＊众所周知，华侨是刻苦耐劳的。It is generally known that the overseas Chinese are a hardworking lot. 3 (adj) 完备 complete;thorough＊为了保证成功，我们必须要有一个周密的计划。In order to ensure success we must have a complete and thorough plan. 4 (n) 星期 a week
周报 [zhōu bào] a weekly publication;a weekly
周长 [zhōu cháng] perimeter;circumference
周到 [zhōu dào] thoughtful;considerate
周而复始 [zhōu ér fù shǐ] to go round
周济 [zhōu jì] to relieve;to give charity;to assist
周刊 [zhōu kān] a weekly magazine;a weekly
周密 [zhōu mì] careful;thorough; well-considered
周年 [zhōu nián] anniversary
周期 [zhōu qī] a period
周期表 [zhōu qī biǎo] a periodic table
周期性 [zhōu qī xìng] periodicity; cyclical character
周岁 [zhōu suì] a full year of life from one birthday to another
周围 [zhōu wéi] surrounding
周详 [zhōu xiáng] detailed and complete
周旋 [zhōu xuán] to treat;to deal with;to tackle
周游 [zhōu yóu] to tour
周折 [zhōu zhé] twists and turns; tortuous course
周知 [zhōu zhī] to make known to all
周转 [zhōu zhuǎn] to revolve;to turn over;to circulate;to turn round

舟 [zhōu] (n) 船 a boat

州 [zhōu] (n) 一种行政区划 state; county;prefecture
州务大臣 [zhōu wù dà chén] the chief minister of state
州长 [zhōu zhuán] state governor

洲 [zhōu] 1 (n) 沙滩；浅滩 a shoal; a sandbank 2 (n) 小岛 an islet;an island ＊星洲。the Island of Singapore 3 (n) 大陆 the continent ＊亚洲。Asia ＊非洲。Africa ＊北美洲。North America ＊南美洲。South America＊欧洲 Europe ＊大洋洲。Oceania ＊南极洲。Antarctic ＊澳洲。Australia
洲际导弹 [zhōu jì dǎo dàn] intercontinental missile

诌（謅）[zhōu] (v) 编造故事 to make up story ＊不要听他胡诌。Do not listen to his non sense.

粥 [zhōu] (n) 稀饭 porridge;congee; rice gruel

zhóu

妯 [zhóu] 妯娌 [zhóu lǐ] (n) 嫂子和弟媳合称 sisters-in-law

轴（軸）[zhóu] 1 (n)旋转物的中心 an axis;an axle ＊轮轴 wheel axle 2 (n)量词 a measure word : reel ＊ 两轴线 two reels of thread.

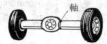

轴承 [zhóu chéng] bearing;axle bearing;shaft bearing
轴心 [zhóu xīn] centre of axis;axial centre

zhǒu

帚 [zhǒu] (n)扫除尘土、垃圾等的用具 a broom ＊扫帚 a broom ＊鸡毛帚 a feather broom

扫帚

肘 [zhǒu] (n) 上臂和下臂相接关节的外部 the elbow ＊ 掣肘 to impede the elbow — hindrances
肘关节[zhǒu guān jíe] the elbow joint
肘腋 [zhǒu yè] elbow and armpit—near relatives, friendship

zhòu

宙 [zhòu] (n)指古往今来所有的时间 all ages;all times＊宇宙 the universe;all spaces and times
绉（縐）[zhòu] (n) 绉纱；有一种丝纺织品 crape
皱（皺）[zhòu](n) 摺纹 wrinkle; crease;fold ＊ 他因年老而皮肤皱缩。He is wrinkled with age.
皱眉 [zhòu méi] to frown
咒 [zhòu] 1 (n)宗教、迷信或巫术中的密语 a charm;a spell ＊ 符咒 written and spoken charms or spells 2 (v)骂 to curse;to damn;to swear at ＊ 那个妇人在咒她的媳妇。The woman is abusing her daughter-in-law
咒骂 [zhòu mà] to curse ; to damn; to swear at
咒语 [zhòu yǔ] curse;imprecation
昼（晝）[zhòu] (n)白天 daytime ＊机器昼夜不停地转动。The machine whirs incessantly day and night.
骤（驟）[zhòu] (adj)突然；急；快 sudden;unexpected ＊ 狂风骤起。A strong wind blows suddenly
骤然 [zhòu rán] suddenly; unexpectedly
胄 [zhòu] 1 (n) 皇族的后代 descendants of the imperial family. 2 (n) 战帽；盔 a helmet ＊ 甲胄 armour and helmet

zhū

朱（硃）[zhū] (n) 大红色 red; scarlet
朱红 [zhū hóng] vermilion ;scarlet
朱砂 [zhū shā] cinnabar;vermilion
侏 [zhū] (n) 矮小的人；如：侏儒 pigmy; a dwarf
诛（誅）[zhū] 1 (v)处死 to put to death;to execute ＊毒贩业已伏诛。The drug trafficker has been executed. 2 (v) 责罚；斥责 to punish;to denounce ＊ 人人口诛笔伐他的卖国行为。All denounced him orally and in writings for his traitorship.
诛除 [zhū chú] to eradicate;to exterminate
诛求 [zhū qiú] to demand booty;to exact;to blackmail
珠 [zhū] 1 (n) 蚌壳内所生的珍品，称珍珠或真珠 a pearl 2 (n)圆粒形状的东西 beads; balls; drops. ＊ 水珠 water drops＊串珠 a string of beads ＊念珠 a rosary ＊ 圆珠笔 a ball-pen ＊ 滚珠轴承

ball bearing

珠宝 [zhū bǎo] pearls, gems and jewels; jewellery; jewelry

珠母 [zhū mǔ] the pearl oyster;the mother-of-pearl

珠算 [zhū suàn] abacus calculational method

珠子 [zhū·zi] pearls;beads

株 [zhū] 1 (n) 露出地面的树根泛指全树 the exposed roots of a tree — a tree * 守株待兔。to wait for a passing rabbit at the tree — wishful thinking of obtaining something without effort;strictly abiding by limited experience and refusing to seek new ways and methods. 2 (n) 量词；指植物 a measure word for plants * 一株桃树。a peach tree.

蛛 [zhū] 蜘蛛 [zhí zhú] (n) the spider

蛛丝马迹 [zhū sī mǎ jī] spider's web and horse's footprint — traces;clues;hints

诸（諸）[zhū] 1 (adj) 全体的；各；许多的 all ;every ;many ;various * 诸子百家。all schools of thought 2 (prep) 于；之于 to ;at;in;with;from * 这些条例不久将付诸实施。These rules will be brought to implementation soon.

诸侯 [zhū hóu] the various feudal princes

诸如 [zhū rú] like;such as

诸如此类 [zhū rú cǐ lèi] so on and so forth; things like this ; all such things

诸位 [zhū wèi] sirs! gentlemen! ladies and gentlemen! everybody

诸子百家 [zhū zǐ bǎi jiā] all schools of thought;all classes of philosophers

猪（豬）[zhū] (n)家畜;头大;口吻长;四肢短小;体肥；肉可供食用;皮和鬃是工业原料 a pig;a hog;a swine *小猪。a piglet *野猪 a wild pig;a boar * 公猪 a boar * 母猪 a sow

猪圈 [zhū juān] a pigsty;a pigpen

猪肉 [zhū ròu] pork

猪瘟 [zhū wēn] hog cholera

猪油 [zhū yóu] lard

猪鬃 [zhū zōng] hog's bristles

zhú

烛（燭）[zhú] (n) 用线绳或苇子做中心，周围包上蜡油，点着取亮的东西 candle * 蜡烛 wax candles

烛光 [zhú guāng] candlelight; candle-power

烛台 [zhú tái] a candlestick

烛心 [zhú xīn] candlewick

竹 [zhú] (n) 多年生常绿植物。茎干有节中空可制器具 ，也是建筑、造纸的材料 bamboo

竹竿 [zhú gān] bamboo pole; bamboo stick

竹笋 [zhú sǔn] bamboo shoot

逐 [zhú] 1 (v) 追赶；强迫离开 to chase;to drive out;to expel * 一名间谍被驱逐出境。A spy was expelled from the country 2 (adj)按照次序，一一挨着 one after another;one by one * 他逐字逐句地替我解释这项条例。He explains this regulation to me word for word

逐步 [zhú bù] little by little; gradually;bit by bit;step by step

逐个 [zhǘ gè] one by one
逐渐 [zhú jiàn] gradually;step by step
逐年 [zhú nián] year by year;with each passing year
逐一 [zhú yī] one by one
逐字逐句 [zhúzìzhújù] word for word; literal; literally

zhǔ

主 [zhǔ] 1 (n) 权力或财物的所有者 a master;an owner;a possessor * 车主。a car owner *地主。a land owner;a landlord 2 (n) "客"的反义词 the host *宾主欢聚一堂。The host and guests are in a happy gathering 3 (n) 事件中的当事人 the person concerned * 事主向警方报案。The person concerned reported the case to the police 4 (v) 预示 to foretell *早霞主雨；晚霞主晴。Rosy cloud in the morning foretells a rainy day while that in the evening, a fine day.

主笔 [zhǔ bǐ] editor (as of a newspaper)
主编 [zhǔ biān] editor;head of compiling staff ; to edit
主持 [zhǔ chí] to manage;to sponsor;to uphold;to stand for
主次 [zhǔ cì] primary and secondary (e.g. importance)
主导 [zhǔ dǎo] leading (factor, role, etc.);dominant (e.g. ideas, thought, etc.)
主动 [zhǔ dòng] initiative
主妇 [zhǔ fù] mistress of a house
主观 [zhǔ guān] subjective;subjectivity
主管 [zhǔ guān] to be responsible for;to be in charge of
主观性 [zhǔ guān xìng] subjectivity
主观主义 [zhǔ guān zhǔ yì] subjectivism
主将 [zhǔ jiàng] the commanding general
主教 [zhǔ jiào] the bishop
主句 [zhǔ jù] principal clause (grammar)
主角 [zhǔ juě] leading actor or act tress;mian role;title-role
主力 [zhǔ lì] main forces
主力军 [zhǔl lì jūn] the main force; principal force
主流 [zhǔ liú] main stream;main current;main trend
主谋 [zhǔ móu] chief instigator
主权 [zhǔ quán] sovereignty
主人 [zhǔ rén] host;master;owner; proprietor;possessor
主任 [zhǔ rèn] chairman;director; the supervisor
主人翁 [zhǔ rén wēng] a master (of one's own house, country, etc.) a hero (in story, novel, etc.)
主食 [zhǔ shí] staple food
主使 [zhǔ shǐ] to instigate
主题 [zhǔ tí] main theme;the chief subject
主体 [zhǔ tǐ] mainstay;main body; essential part
主席 [zhǔ xí] chairman
主席团 [zhǔ xí tuán] presidium
主演 [zhǔ yǎn] to be the main performer
主要 [zhǔ yào] main;principal; essential;leading;important;major; key
主意 [zhǔ yì] opinion;decision;idea
主义 [zhǔ yì] ism;theory;doctrine; policy
主语 [zhǔ yǔ] subject (grammar)
主宰 [zhǔ zǎi] to dominate;to master;to control;to dictate
主张 [zhǔ zhāng] proposal;opinion; assertion;to maintain;to advocate; to hold
主子 [zhǔ zǐ] boss;master;wire-puller

嘱(囑) [zhǔ] (v) 吩咐；托付to enjoin;to charge;to order *他叮嘱孩子努力学习。He enjoined his child to study hard.

嘱咐 [zhǔ·fu] to bid; to enjoin;to direct;to instruct

嘱托 [zhǔ tuō] to entrust ;to require somebody to do something

瞩(矚) [zhǔ] (v)注视 to watch attentively;to gaze at＊妇女爬山队攀登喜马拉雅山高峰的壮举,举世瞩目。The whole world watch attentively the great undertaking of a team of women climbers scaling the high peaks of Himalayas

煮 [zhǔ] (v) 放食物在锅里加热 to cook;to boil ＊ 她每天煮饭洗衣。She cooks and washes everyday

zhù

住 [zhù] 1 (v)居；宿 to live;to reside;to stay;to lodge ＊ 他住在乡村。He lives in a village. 2 (v)停止 to stop; to cease ＊ 住手！Stop! Hands off!

住房 [zhù fáng] housing;living quarters

住户 [zhù hù] an inhabitant

住口 [zhù kǒu] to shut up

住宿 [zhù sù] to stay for the night

住宅 [zhù zhái] a residence;a house;a dwelling

住址 [zhù zhǐ] an address

注 [zhù] 1 (v)灌入；倒 to pour;to instil;to inject ＊医生把葡萄糖注射入病人的静脉。The doctor injects glucose into the patient's vein. 2 (v)思想集中于 to concentrate;to pay attention to;to take notice of ＊驾车者要多注意行人的安全。The drivers of motor vehicles should pay greater attention to the safety of the pedestrains. 3 (v) 用文字给书中的字句作解释 to comment on: notes ＊ 编者在注解译文。The editor is giving explanatory notes to the translation. 4 (v)登记；记录 register;record;to make an entry＊请认明注册商标，方不致误。Please identify the registered trade mark so that you may make no mistakes 5 (n) 赌博所下的钱和财物 a bet;a stake ＊ 他孤注一掷。He staked all on a single throw.

注册 [zhù cì] to enroll;to register

注定 [zhù dìng] to be doomed to (failure);to be bound to

注解 [zhù jiě] to explain;explanation;notes

注目 [zhù mù] to focus attention;to bring to one's notice

注入 [zhù rù] to instil,to imbue; inject

注射 [zhù shì] to inject;injection

注释 [zhù shì] to explain;explanation;notes

注视 [zhù shì] to watch attentively; to watch with concern

注销 [zhù xiāo] to write off;to cancel

注意 [zhù yì] to pay attention to;to be attentive;to take notice of

注意力 [zhù yì lì] attention

注音 [zhù yīn] phonetic annotation

注重 [zhù zhòng] to attach attention to;to pay great attention to;to claim one's attention;to lay stress on

驻(駐) [zhù] (v)停留；屯扎 to encamp;to be stationed ＊部队驻扎在一座山上。The troops were stationed on a hill.

驻地 [zhù dì] station;garrison

驻防 [zhù fáng] garrison

驻军 [zhù jūn] station troops

驻守 [zhù shǒu] to defend with stationed troops;to garrison

驻扎 [zhù zhā] to encamp;to garrison

柱 [zhù] 1 (n) 直立的长条建筑材料 a pillar; a post ＊ 店屋前面有两根柱子。There are two pillars at the front of the shop house. 2 (n) 象柱子形的东西 column ＊水银柱。Mercury column

柱石 [zhù shì] the stone base of a pillar;a plinth;mainstay (figuratively)

蛀 [zhù] (v)虫食木、纸、衣、米等物 (insects) eat or bore (wood, paper, clothes, rice, etc.)＊这块木板给虫蛀了一个洞。 Insects bored a hole on the piece of wood.

蛀虫 [zhù chóng] moth;(insect) borers

蛀牙 [zhù yá] decayed tooth

贮（貯） [zhù] (v)积存；储藏to store up;to keep;to reserve 农民们贮粮备荒。The peasants store up the grain against famine.

贮藏 [zhù cáng] to hoard;to save

贮存 [zhù cún] to stock;to store up

苎（苧） [zhù] 苎麻[zhù má] (n) 草本植物。茎部韧皮纤维坚韧有光泽，可供纺织、造纸和制鱼网等用。根可供药用 ramee,a kind of hemp

著 [zhù] 1 (adj)显明；显出conspicuous; prominent; famous; well-known ＊ 他是著名的物理学家。He is a famous physicist. 2 (v) 写文章；写书to write;to compose ＊ 他撰著了一本现代史。 He has written a book on modern history. 3 (n)写出来的作品 writings ＊他的著作被译成几种文字。His writings had been translated into various languages.

著称 [zhù chēng] to be noted for;to be known for

著名 [zhù míng] famous;well-known;celebrated

著者 [zhù zhě] author

著作 [zhù zuò] works;writings

箸 [zhù] (n)筷子 chopsticks

祝 [zhù] (v) 表示美好愿望 to wish; to greet;to congratulate;to offer (one's) compliments to ＊祝你成功。I wish you success.

祝词 [zhù cí] text of a felicitation; congratulations

祝福 [zhù fú] to bless;to wish; blessing

祝贺 [zhù hè] to congratulate;to greet congratulation

祝酒 [zhù jiǔ] to toast;to drink a toast

祝寿 [zhù shòu] to congratulate;to greet congratulation

祝愿 [zhù yuàn] to wish;good wishes

助 [zhù] (v) 帮 to help;to aid;to assist ＊助人为快乐之本。 To help others is a source of happiness

助词 [zhù cí] particle (grammar)

助动词 [zhù dòng cí] auxiliary verb (grammar)

助理 [zhù lǐ] assistant;helper

助理秘书 [zhù lǐ mì shū] assistant secretary

助燃 [zhù rán]helping to combust; combustion supporting

助人为乐 [zhù rén wéi lè] to take pleasure in helping others;ready to help others

助手 [zhù shǒu] assistant;helper; helping hands

助威 [zhù wēi] to give oral or moral support;to cheer somebody up

助兴 [zhù xìng] to join in merry-making

助学金 [zhù xué jīn] student subsidies;student grant

助长 [zhù zhǎng] to indulge;to give a loose rein to (something bad)

筑（築） [zhù] (v)建造；修造to build; to construct ＊ 筑路工程正在进行中。The road construction work is in progress.

铸（鑄） [zhù] (v) 把金属熔化后倒在模子里制成器物 to cast (e.g.metals) ＊ 工友在铸造一座

不锈钢的胸象。The workers are casting a stainless steel bust.
铸成大错 [zhù chéng dài cùo] to make a great mistake
铸工 [zhù gōng] a foundry worker
铸件 [zhù jiàn] a casting;a cast
铸模机 [zhù mó jī] a moulding machine
铸铁 [zhù tiě] cast iron
铸造 [zhù zào] to cast;foundry
铸造厂 [zhù zào chǎng] a foundry

zhuā

抓 [zhuā] 1 (v)搔 to scratch ＊他抓抓头，想出一条妙计来。As he scratched his head, he made a decision on a trick. 2 (v) 用手提取物件 to grasp;to seize; to grab ＊那个特务一把抓住他的头发用力摇。The spy grabbed his hair and shook furiously. 3 (v) 捕捉to arrest;to catch ＊我们抓到了一个奸细。We have caught a secret agent.
抓紧 [zhuā jǐn] to grasp firmly
抓重点 [zhuā zhòng diàn]to grasp the essential point
抓住 [zhuā zhù] to seize;to catch; to get hold of

zhuān

专(專) [zhuān] 1 (adj) 单一，集中在一件事上 single-minded; attentive ＊学生上课时要专心。A student should be attentive during class lessons . 2 (adj) 特别 specialized;special ＊他是搞化学工艺的专门人才。He is a specialized personnel in chemical technology.
专长 [zhuān cháng] professional ability; technical skill; speciality
专车 [zhuān chē] special train; special vehicle
专程 [zhuān chéng] to be on a special trip to
专诚 [zhuān chéng] in full sincerity
专横跋扈 [zhuān héng bá hù] arbitrary;tyrannical;despotic;to ride roughshod over
专机 [zhuān jī] special plane
专家 [zhuān jiā] a specialist;an expert
专刊 [zhuān kān] a special issue
专科 [zhuān kē] a special course of study;a specialty, as in medicine
专科学校 [zhuān kē xúe xiào] a technical college;a vocational school
专栏 [zhuān lán] (newspaper) column;special column
专利 [zhuān lì] to monopolize; monopoly
专门 [zhuān mén] specialized; special
专权 [zhuān quán] having the whole power
专题 [zhuān tí] a special theme
专心 [zhuān xīn] wholehearted; attentive
专心致志 [zhuān xīn zhì zhì] to devote oneself to;to set one's heart on;whole-hearted and exclusive
专业 [zhuān yè] special line;profession;speciality
专用 [zhuān yòng] (reserved) for special use
专一 [zhuān yī] concentration;to be devoted to one thing
专政 [zhuān zhèng] dictatorship;to exercise dictatorship over;to dictate
专职 [zhuān zhí] post taken by appointed people
专制 [zhuān zhì] to tyrannise;autocratic;despotic

砖(磚) [zhuān] (n) 用土坯烧成的建筑材料 brick;tile ＊耐火砖。refractory bricks.
砖土 [zhuān tǔ] brick-clay
砖窑 [zhuān yáo] a brick kiln

zhuǎn

转(轉) [zhuǎn] 1 (v) 绕着中心运动 to revolve;to rotate; to turn ＊地球绕太阳公转，同时又绕自己的轴自转 ＊ The earth revolves round the sun and at the same time rotates on its axis. 2 (v) 改变方向、地位或形势等 to turn;to change ＊汽车转右了。The car turned right. 3 (v) 间接送交 to transfer;to pass ＊ 她托我转交这封信给你。 She asked me to hand over this letter to you.
另见 [zhuàn]

转变 [zhuǎn biàn] to change into; to be transformed;to remould ; change;transformation;alteration

转播 [zhuǎn bō] to relay

转车 [zhuǎn chē] to change train or bus halfway

转达 [zhuǎn dá] to convey

转动 [zhuǎn dòng] to revolve;to rotate;to turn about

转化 [zhuǎn huà] to transform into; to change into;to invert;to turn into;to transmute

转机 [zhuǎn jī] a change for the better;favourable turn

转嫁 [zhuǎn jià] to shift ... to;to divert from;to transfer

转交 [zhuǎn jiāo] to hand over;to forward through ; care of (c/o)

转念 [zhuǎn niàn] to be on second thought

转让 [zhuǎn ràng] to make over;to convey;to transfer;to alienate

转身 [zhuǎn shēn] to turn around

转述 [zhuǎn shù] to convey (e.g. opinion);to transmit

转瞬之间 [zhuǎn shuǎn zhī jiān] in a twinkling;in no time;on the instant

转弯 [zhuǎn wān] to turn a corner

转弯抹角 [zhuǎn wān mò jiǎn] to beat about the bush;in a round about way;oblique

转危为安 [zhuǎn wēi wéi ān] to carry over the danger;to be past danger

转校 [zhuǎn xiáo] to transfer to another school

转眼 [zhuǎn yǎn] in the twinkling of the eye

转业 [zhuǎn yè] to change one's occupation or profession;to switch to another type of enterprise;to shift one's occupation

转移 [zhuǎn yí] to shift;to divert from;to switch;to move from;to transfer

转运 [zhuǎn yùn] to transport;to forward

转载 [zhuǎn zaì] to reprint;to reproduce

转战 [zhuǎn zhàn] to fight from place to place

转折 [zhuǎn zhé] to change course; to turn (e.g. direction);to take a turn

转折点 [zhuǎn zhé diǎn] turning point

转租 [zhuǎn zū] to sublet

zhuàn

传(傳) [zhuàn] 1 (n)解释经书的著作或文字 a commentary ＊《左传》。 Tzuo's Commentary (on Spring and Autumn Annal) 2 (n) 记叙某人生平事迹的文字 a biography ＊自传。autobiography ＊ 阿Q正传 The True Biography of Ah Q
另见 [chuán]

传记 [zhuàn jì] biography

转(轉) [zhuàn] (v) 以力旋动物体 to turn (something) ; to twist;to wrench＊技工转松螺丝钉，把电动机卸下。The technician turned the screws loose and dismount the electrical motor.

转炉 [zhuàn lú] converter
另见[zhuǎn]

篆 [zhuàn] (n) 篆字，汉字的一种字体 the seal character of Chinese calligraphy

撰 [zhuàn] (v) 著述 to write;to compose ＊他替报馆撰稿。He wrote articles for a newspaper office.

赚 (賺) [zhuàn] (v) 获得利润 to gain;to make (money); to earn;to reap ＊他靠劳力赚钱。He earned his money with toil.

zhuāng

装 (裝) [zhuāng] 1 (v) 穿衣打扮 to dress up;to make up ＊男孩子不喜装扮。 Boys hate to be dressed up. 2 (v) 假扮 to pretend;to disguise 3 (v) 载 to load;to stuff; to pack ＊货物还没装箱。The goods have not been packed into cases 4 (v) 配置 to install;to fix up ＊机器已经装好了。 The machine has been fixed up.

装扮 [zhuāng bàn] to dress oneself up as;to deck out as;to guise;to make up

装备 [zhuāng bèi] to equip;to furnish with;to install;to fit out equipment;installation

装订 [zhuāng dìng] to bind (e.g. a book)

装潢 [zhuāng huáng] to furnish and decorate;furnishing and decorations

装甲兵 [zhuāng jiǎ bīng] armoured corps

装模作样 [zhuāng mó zùo yàng] to pose;to strike air

装配 [zhuāng pèi] to assemble;to install

装腔作势 [zhuāng qiāng zuò shì] to strike a pose;to give oneself airs; to have a pretentious manner

装饰 [zhuāng shì] to decorate;to embellish;to bedeck;to adorn

装饰品 [zhuāng shì pǐn] decorations;ornaments

装束 [zhuāng shù] attire;dress up

装卸 [zhuāng xiè] loading and unloading

装载 [zhuāng zài] to transport;to carry (from one place to another)

装置 [zhuāng zhì] to install;to furnish with;to equip with;installation;device

庄 (莊) [zhuāng] 1 (n) 农民集居的地方 a village ＊这村庄是美丽的场所。 This village is a beautiful spot. 2 (adj) 严肃 solemn; dignified ＊国务院发表了一项庄重的声明。The State Council issued a solemn declaration. 3 (n) 店铺 a shop;a store ＊布庄 a textile shop 4 (n) 大路 a thoroughfare;a highroad ＊康庄大道 a level highway

庄稼 [zhuāng·jia] crops

庄严 [zhuāng yán] solemn;magnificent;grand;dignified

庄园 [zhuāng yuán] a manor;an estate

庄重 [zhuāng zhòng] solemn; serious

桩 (樁) [zhuāng] (n) 插进地里的柱 a pile driven into the ground ＊工人在打桩。 The workers are driving the pile into the ground.

妆 (妝) [zhuāng] (v) 修饰容貌 to adorn oneself ＊梳妆台。a dressing table

妆奁 [zhuāng lián] bride's trousseau; marriage portion

zhuàng

撞 [zhuàng] 1 (v)碰；击 to collide; to knock;to clash;to strike with force ＊两辆汽车相撞。The two cars collided. 2 (v) 偶遇 to meet unexpectedly ＊我想避开她，偏偏在这里撞见她。I try to avoid her, yet unexpectedly I meet her here.

撞见 [zhuàng jiàn] to meet by chance

撞骗 [zhuàng piàn] to swindle;to embezzle

壮(壯) [zhuàng] (adj) 强健;有力量 strong;robust; stout;dauntless * 他年轻力壮。 He is young and strong.

壮大 [zhuàng dà] to become big and lusty;strengthen;to grow in strength;to expand

壮胆 [zhuàng dǎn] to strengthen one's courage

壮观 [zhuàng guān] grandeur;grand and impressive sight

壮举 [zhuàng jǔ] a great undertaking; heroic undertaking

壮阔 [zhuàng kuò] grand and expensive

壮丽 [zhuàng lì] grand-looking; magnificent

壮烈 [zhuàng liè] courageous; heroic

壮年 [zhuàng nián] in one's prime; middle age

壮志 [zhuàng zhì] lofty ambition; great aspiration

壮志凌云 [zhuàng zhì líng yún] soaring determination

状(狀) [zhuàng] 1 (n) 样子 appearance; shape; form * 山洞里有各种形状的岩石。There are rocks of various shapes in the cave. 2 (n) 情形 condition; state of affairs * 这个国家的经济状况越来越糟。The economic condition of this country is going from bad to worse. 3 (n)诉讼词 an accusation;a plaint *告状。 to file a plaint. 4(n)凭证 a certificate * 奖状。 a certificate of merit.

状词 [zhuàng cí] a written accusation

状况 [zhuàng kuàng] conditions; general aspects

状态 [zhuàng tài] manner;appearance;state of things

状语 [zhuàng yǔ] adverbial adjunct (grammar)

zhuī

椎 [zhuī] (n) 构成高等动物脊柱的短骨 vertebra

锥(錐) [zhuī] 1 (n) 钻孔的工具 an awl;a gimlet;a drill

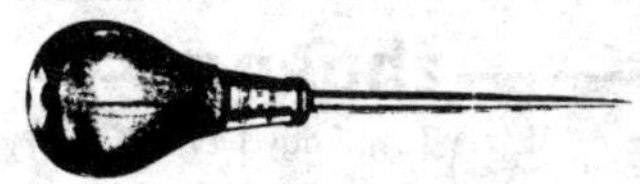

追 [zhuī] 1 (v)赶;紧跟着to chase after;to pursue;to catch up *警方正在追查一个逃犯的下落。 The police is pursuing the whereabout of an escaped convict. 2. (v) 回溯过去 trace back,to recall;to retrospect * 要了解这两国之间的冲突,我们得追溯它们早期的纠纷。 In order to understand the conflict between the two countries, we may trace back to their disputes in an earlier period.

追查 [zhuī chá] to investigate;to inquire;to search into;to find out

追悼 [zhuī dào] to grieve for person's death;memorial

追肥 [zhuī féi] additional fertilizer; additional manure

追赶 [zhuī gǎn] to chase;to run after;to race with

追击 [zhuī jī] to pursue;pursuit

追究 [zhuī jiū] to search into;to find out;to carry on an inquiry

追求 [zhuī qiú] to seek after; pursuit of

追认 [zhuī rèn] subsequent confirmation;to confer posthumously; to ratify

追溯 [zhuī sù] to trace back

追算 [zhuī suàn] to calculate subsequently;to back-date

追随 [zhuī suí] to follow;to go after;to tail behind

追问 [zhuī wèn] to cross-examine; to get to the roots of things

追逐 [zhuī zhú] to chase after;to pursue

追踪 [zhuī zōng] to pursue

zhuì

缀(綴) [zhuì] (v) 缝联 to baste together * 她在缀补一条破袖。She basted her torn sleeve together.

坠(墜) [zhuì] 1 (v) 落；掉下 to fall down;to sink * 那少女从窗口坠下。The young girl fell out of the window. 2 (v) 下垂 to hang;to sag * 探险者坠下石块，探测洞的深浅。The explorers hanged a stone down the hole to test its depth.

坠毁 [zhuì huǐ] to crash (e.g. aeroplane)

坠落 [zhuì luò] to crash;to fall

坠马 [zhuì mǎ] to fall off a horse

坠子 [zhuì zi] pendant eardrops

惴 [zhuì] (adj) 恐惧；担心 afraid; worried * 他听了这个消息后，心里惴惴不安。He got worried after he had heard the news.

赘(贅) [zhuì] (adj) 多余的，不必要的 redundant;superfluous

zhūn

谆(諄) [zhūn] [谆谆] (adj) 恳切地，不厌倦地；细心地(教诲) (to teach) earnestly;untiringly;carefully * 师长谆谆地教诲学生。The teachers teach the students with care.

zhǔn

准(準) [zhǔn] 1 (v) 允许；许可 to allow;to permit;to consent * 当局不准小贩在街边摆卖。The authority does not allow hawkers to sell at the roadside. 2 (adj) 正确 correct; exact; accurate; precise * 这个真理放之四海皆准。This truth is correct anywhere in the world. 3 (adv) 一定 certainly; surely * 任务准能完成。The task would certainly be accomplished.

准备 [zhǔn bèi] to prepare;to pave the way for;to be ready;preparation;preparedness;readiness

准将 [zhǔn jiàng] a brigadier-general

准确 [zhǔn què] accurate;exact; precise

准绳 [zhǔn shéng] criteria for; accepted standards

准时 [zhǔn shí] punctual;on time

准许 [zhǔn xǔ) to permit;to allow; to consent;to approve of

准予 [zhǔn yǔ] to give permission to

准则 [zhǔn zé] guiding principle; code;accepted standards

zhuō

卓 [zhuō] (adj)高；不平凡 high;distinguished; prominent; outstanding * 这些知识分子对国家作出了卓越的贡献。These intellectuals have made outstanding contributions to the country.

卓绝 [zhuō jué] extremely;unsurpassed;exceedingly;outstanding

卓见 [zhuōjiàn] highly commendable idea; distinguished opinion

卓越 [zhuō yuè] outstanding; brilliant;distinguished

卓有成效 [zhuō yoǔ chéng xiào] very effective

桌 [zhuō] (n) 几案 a table * 饭桌 a dining table * 书桌 a desk

捉 [zhuō] (v) 捕；拿 to catch; to capture;to seize;to arrest ＊那扒手当场被捉。The pickpocket was caught on the spot.

捉襟见肘 [zhuō jīn jiàn zhǒu] to expose one's elbow when drawing tight the lapel of one's jacket — to be in financial difficulties

捉迷藏 [zhuō mí cáng] hide-and seek

捉摸 [zhuō mō] to conjecture;to guess

捉拿 [zhuō ná] to arrest;to catch

捉弄 [zhuō nòng] to play trick upon somebody

拙 [zhuō] (adj) 笨 stupid;unskilled; clumsy ＊ 勤能补拙。Being diligent, one is able to mend one's stupidity

拙笨 [zhuō bèn] clumsy;awkward

拙劣 [zhuō liè] poor;clumsy;unskilful

zhuó

浊(濁) [zhuó] (adj)水不清；不干净 muddy; turbid; dirty ＊ 污浊。dirty

浊流 [zhuó liú] turbid stream

浊音 [zhuó yīn] voiced consonant

啄 [zhuó] (v) 鸟类用嘴尖叩击并夹住东西 to peck; ＊ 小鸡啄米。The chickens peck the rice grains.

啄木鸟 [zhuó mù niǎo] wood pecker

琢 [zhuó] (v) 雕刻玉石to work on gem;to cut;to polish;to chisel ＊玉不琢，不成器。A raw gem will not be a treasure unless it is worked.

琢磨 [zhuó mó] chisel (e.g. jade) polish by slow painstaking work; think hard;chew over

灼 [zhuó] 1 (v)烧；火烫to burn;to scald ＊他皮肤被灼伤的面积很大。A large area of his skin is burnt. 2 (adj)明白；透彻clear; penetrating ＊这个老人所说的都是真知灼见。What the old man said is true and penetrating.

灼热 [zhuó rè] scalding hot

镯(鐲) [zhuó] (n) 套在手腕的环形装饰品 bracelet ＊ 玉镯。jade bracelet

擢 [zhuó] (v)提升；选拔to promote; to raise;to select ＊他被擢升为总经理。He was promoted to the position of a general manager.

茁 [zhuó] (n) 植物生长出来的样子 the budding of plants;the sprouting of seeds

茁壮 [zhuó zhuang] sturdy;healthy and strong

酌 [zhuó] 1 (v) 斟酒pour out wine; drink ＊他自斟自酌。He is drinking wine alone. 2 (v) 斟酌；考虑 weigh and consider;consider＊我们将酌情处理。We shall handle the matter according to circumstances.

酌量 [zhuó liáng] to deal with on the merits of each case;appropriately

酌情 [zhuó qíng] according to circumstances;on the merits of each case;at discretion

着 [zhuó] 1 (v)穿衣 to put on;to dress ＊他着上工作服。He puts on a working dress. 2 (v) 接触；挨上 to touch ＊飞机安全着陆了。The aeroplane has touched down safely. 3 (v) 动手to begin;to set on;to set to ＊我们已着手订制本年度的活动计划了。We have begun to draw up a plan for our activities this year. 4 (v) 加上；附上to add;to apply ＊我还没有给这幅画着色。I have not applied colours on this drawing. 5(v) 使；派遣 to send (somebody to do something) ＊我会着人来取这包东西。I shall send somebody to fetch this parcel.

另见[zhāo] [·zhe]
着陆[zhuó lù] to land;landing
着落[zhuó luò] whereabout; a satisfactory result or settlement
着手[zhuó shǒu] to begin;to set to;to get down to;to carry out
着想[zhuó xiǎng] to bear........in mind;to consider the interest of;to think of
着眼[zhuó yǎn] to fix one's attention on;to have.....in mind
着重[zhuó zhòng] to make a special effort to;to stress;to centre on;to concentrate

zī

咨(諮)[zī](v)跟别人商量;询问 consult;inquire
咨文[zī wén] a message (a formal official communication)
咨询[zī xún] to seek advice;to consult
咨询委员会[zī xún wěi yuán huì] advisory committee

姿[zī] 1 (n)容貌appearance;look *她姿容秀美。She has a pretty look. 2 (n)形态;样子posture;gesture *演员的舞姿非常优美。The dancing posture of the actor is beautiful.
姿势[zī shì] gesture;gesticulation;posture
姿态[zī tài] gesture;one's bearing or carriage;form;attitude

资(資)[zī] 1 (n)财物;钱财 wealth ;property ;capital;money *许多外国人来这里投资。Many foreigners come here to invest their money. 2 (v)给;助 to give;to provide;to aid;to assist *我现在开列几本书,以资各位参考。Now I list several books for (as an aid in) your reference. 3 (n)本性;质素 disposition ;natural gift *这孩子天资聪敏,将来必成大器。This boy is naturally gifted and will certainly be a great man in future. 4 (n) 出身;经历 qualifications ; experiences *你有足够的资格应征这肥缺。You have the fullest qualifications to apply for this fat vacant post.
资本[zī běn] capital
资本家[zī běn jiā] capitalist
资本主义[zī běn zhǔ yì] capitalism
资产[zī chǎn] assets
资产阶级[zī chǎn jiē jí] bourgeoisie
资格[zī gé] qualifications
资格证书[zī gé zhèng shū] credentials
资金[zī jīn] funds;capital
资历[zī lì] work record;qualifications and previous
资料[zī liào] materials for some specific use ; data experience
资望[zī wàng] reputation
资源[zī yuán] resources
资源勘探[zī yuán kān tàn] prospecting of resources
资质[zī zhì] natural disposition
资助[zī zhù] to susidize;to assist financially;to give financial backing to

髭[zī](n)嘴上边的胡子 moustaches

孜[zī](adj)勤 diligent;unwearied
孜孜不倦[zī zī bú juàn] persevering;indefatigable;industrious;tireless; diligently

兹[zī] (adv)现在;这里;这 now;here;this *兹订于明日下午三时召开会员大会。Now it has been decided that a general meeting will be held at 3 p.m. tomorrow.

滋[zī] (v)生长;繁殖to grow;to sprout;to spring up;to multiply;to flourish *我们要及时清除污水,以防蚊虫滋生。We should clear the filthy water in time to prevent the mosquitoes from multiplying.

滋润 [zī rùn] moist;to moisten

滋生 [zī shēng] to multiply;to sprout;to spring up

滋事 [zī shì] to make troubles

滋味 [zī wei] taste;flavour

滋养 [zī yǎng] to nourish

滋长 [zī zhǎng] to grow;to spring up

辎(輜) [zī] (n) 有幕的车；行李车 a curtained wagon ;a baggage wagon

辎重 [zī zhòng] baggage;impediments;supplies for troops

吱 [zī] (n) 表示声音 used in transliterating

zǐ

子 [zǐ] 1 (n) 儿；儿女 a son;a child ＊父子。father and son ＊妻子。wife and children 2 (n) 人 a person ＊戏子。an actor (actress) ＊男子。a man ＊女子。a girl ＊舟子。a boatman ＊天子。the emperor 3 (n) 古代对有道德学问的人的尊称；先生 a respectful term for a moral and learned man in ancient China;Sir; Master ＊孔子。Master Kung (latinized into Confucius) ＊孟子 Master Meng (latinized into Mencius) 4 (n) 植物的种；动物的卵 seeds;eggs ＊鱼子。fish-roe 5 (n) 地支的第一位，用作次序的第一 the first of the Earthly Branches ; first

另见 [·zi]

子弹 [zǐ dàn] bullet;shell

子弟 [zǐ dì] son;younger brother

子母钱 [zǐ mǔ qiàn] interest and principal

子女 [zǐ nǚ] sons and daughters

子时 [zǐ shí] 11 p.m. to 1 a.m.

子孙 [zǐ sūn] children and grandchildren;sons and grandsons;descendants;future generation

子午 [zǐ wǔ] midnight and noon

子午线 [zǐ wǔ xiàn] the meridian

子音 [zǐ yīn] consonants

仔 [zǐ] 仔细 [zǐ xì] (adj) 周密；小心 careful; prudent; cautious ＊他做事很仔细。He is very careful in his work.

另见 [zāi]

紫 [zǐ] (adj) 蓝、红合成的颜色 purple;violet

紫外线 [zǐ wài xiàn] ultra-violet rays

紫罗兰 [zǐ lo lán] the violet

紫菜 [zǐ cài] laver;an edible marine algae

姊 [zǐ] (n) 姐姐 an elder sister

滓 [zǐ] (n) 渣子；沉淀物 residues; dregs

zì

字 [zì] (n) 用来记录语言的符号 a word;a written character;a letter ＊常用字。common words ＊汉字 Chinese characters

字典 [zì diǎn] a dictionary

字迹 [zì jì] one's hand-writing

字据 [zì jù] a written receipt

字里行间 [zì lǐ háng jiān] between the lines

字面 [zì miàn] literal sense (of the word)

字母 [zì mǔ] letters of the alphabet

字幕 [zì mù] captions;subtitle

字体 [zì tǐ] the form of a written character

字帖 [zì tiè] copy book;reproductions of the works of master calligraphers

字眼 [zì yǎn] a phrase;an expression

自 [zì] 1 (pron) 本身 self;oneself ＊我们主张自力更生。We stand for self-reliance 2 (adv) 当然 of course;certainly;naturally ＊两人久别重逢，自有许多话说。Having reunited after a long departure, the two certainly have a lot to talk about. 3 (adv) 从；由 from;since ＊欢迎来自半岛的朋友们。Welcome to our friends from the Peninsular.

自白 [zì bái] confession;to make a clean breast of

自暴自弃 [zì bào zì qì] self forsaking;to abandon oneself to despair;to give oneself up to vice

自卑 [zì bēi] inferiority;self-abased

自吹自擂 [zì chuī zì léi] to brag and boast;to blow one's own trumpet;self-praise

自从 [zì cóng] from;since

自大 [zì dà] self-important;arrogant ; conceited

自动 [zì dòng] automatic

自动化 [zì dòng huà] to automate; automation;to automatize

自发 [zì fā] spontaneous (e.g. trend, force, struggle, etc.)

自费 [zì fèi] at one's own expense

自封 [zì fēng] self-appointed;to proclaim oneself;self-styled

自负 [zì fù] conceited;proud;sole responsibility for (e.g. one's own profits or losses)

自告奋勇 [zì gào fèn yǒng] to volunteer one's service for;willingly to take the responsibility upon oneself

自供状 [zì gòng zhùang] self-confession

自高自大 [zì gāo zì dà] full of vain glory ;conceited ;be disgustingly self-satisfied;arrogance

自顾不暇 [zì gù bù xiá] unable even to fend for oneself

自豪 [zì háo] pride;proud of

自己 [zì jǐ] oneself;one's own

自给 [zì jǐ] be self-supporting;self-sufficiency

自己人 [zì jǐ rén] one of us

自给自足 [zì jǐ zì zú] self-reliant; self-sufficiency;able to support oneself

自居 [zì jū] to style oneself;to claim to be;to consider oneself to be

自觉 [zì jué] self-conscious; awakened;aware

自绝 [zì jué] to alienate oneself from .

自觉性 [zì jué xìng] self-awakening;conciousness;awareness

自觉自愿 [zì jué zì yuàn] voluntary and concious;of one's own accord; willing;be ready to

自夸 [zì kuā] to boast;to talk big;to plume oneself

自来水 [zì lái shuǐ] tap water;pipe water

自立 [zì lì] to support oneself;to rely on oneself

自力更生 [zì lì gēng shēng] to rely on one's own efforts;self-reliance; self-reliant

自留地 [zì líu dì] private plots; plots for private use

自满 [zì mǎn] complacent;self-satisfied;conceited

自命不凡 [zì mìng bù fán] to think of oneself as superior being; to pride oneself for being out of the ordinary

自欺欺人 [zì qī qī rén] to try to deceive others only to end in deceiving oneself;to deceive oneself and others;sheer hypocrisy

自谦 [zì qiān] humble;modest

自燃 [zì rán] spontaneous combustion;self-ignite

自然 [zì rán] nature;natural;naturally;spontaneously

自然规律 [zì rán guī lì] natural laws;law of nature

自然科学 [zì rán kē xué] natural sciences

自然主义 [zì rán zhǔ yì] naturalism
自如 [zì rú] skilfully (e.g. apply); freely
自杀 [zì shā] to commit suicide
自身 [zì shēn] oneself
自食其力 [zì shí qí lì] to earn one's own living;to live on one's own toil;self-supporting
自食其果 [zì shí qí guǒ] to reap what one has sown;to be made to pay for one's evil doing;to court self-destruction
自首 [zì shǒu] to give oneself up (to law);to make confession
自私 [zì sī] selfish;selfishness
自私自利 [zì sī zì lì] selfish;selfishness
自投罗网 [zì tóu luó wǎng] to fall into a trap through one's own fault
自卫 [zì wèi] to defend oneself; self-defence
自卫战争 [zì wèi zhàn zhēng] war of self-defence
自我 [zì wǒ] oneself ; ego
自我改造 [zì wǒ gǎi zào] self-remoulding
自我批评 [zì wǒ pī píng] self-criticism
自习 [zì xí] to review one's lessons
自相矛盾 [zì xiāng máo dǔn] self-contradictory
自新 [zì xīn] to improve oneself
自信 [zì xìn] to believe in oneself; self-confidence
自行 [zì xíng] by oneself;of one's own accord;spontaneously
自修 [zì xiū] to study on one's own
自诩 [zì xǔ] to brag and boast;self-important
自学 [zì xué] to study by oneself
自以为是 [zì yǐ wéi shì] to consider oneself always in the right;to be cock-sure
自由 [zì yóu] freedom;liberty
自由竞争 [zì yóu jìng zhēng] free competition
自由落体 [zì yóu luò tǐ] free falling body
自由贸易 [zì yóu mào yì] free trade
自由职业者 [zì yóu zhí yè zhě] professionals; professional men
自由主义 [zì yóu zhǔ yì] liberalism
自愿 [zì yuàn] to be of one's own free will;on one's own initiative; voluntarily;willingly
自圆其说 [zì yuán qí shuō] to make out a good case;to justify oneself; to justify one's argument
自在 [zì zai] carefree;without the least worry;comfortable;pleasant
自治权 [zì zhì quán] autonomy
自知之明 [zì zhī zhī míng] to know oneself
自治 [zì zhì] to exercise autonomy; autonomous rule;self-government
自治区 [zì zhì qū] autonomous region
自主 [zì zhǔ] to be independent;to be one's own master
自转 [zì zhuǎn] to rotate
自传 [zì zhuàn] autobiography
自尊心 [zì zūn xīn] self-respect
自作聪明 [zì zuò cōng míng] to fancy oneself clever;to consider oneself to be clever

恣 [zì] (adj) 放荡的；无拘束的 licentious;loose;profligate;without restraint *在老师面前，不得放恣。Don't throw off restraint before your teacher.
恣意 [zì yì] to do at will;to follow one's fancies

渍（漬） [zì] 1 (v) 浸泡 to soak; to steep;to pickle * 厨子把切好的卷心菜浸渍在盐水里。The cook soaks the sliced cabbage in salt water. 2 (v) 污染 to stain * 他每天擦机器，不让渍一点油泥。He wipes the machine everyday to keep it free from stain of grease and dirt.

·zi

子 [·zi] (part)轻音后缀字 a suffix;an enclitic ＊胖子 a fat person ＊瞎子 a blind person ＊椅子 a chair ＊果子 fruit ＊桶子 a pail ＊刀子 a knife ＊鼻子 a nose ＊房子 a house
另见 [zǐ]

zōng

宗 [zōng] 1 (n) 祖先；种族；同祖的同族的 ancestors;clans ancestral; kindred ＊祖宗an ancestor ＊同宗 clansmen 2 (n)派别 a faction;a sect;a school (as of art, teaching, etc.) ＊中国武术，大别为南北二宗。The Chinese martial arts may mainly be divided into Northern and Southern schools. 3 (adj) 主要的；根本的；根源 main;original; origin＊万变不离其宗。Things will stick to their origin however they change. 4 (n)量词 a measure word (for money, goods, etc.) ＊公司最近订购了大宗货物。The company has recently ordered for a large amount of goods.

宗教 [zōng jiào] religion
宗派 [zōng pài] faction;sectarian; group;sect
宗派主义 [zōng pài zhǔ yì] factionalism;sectarianism
宗族 [zōng zú] clan;tribe
宗旨 [zōng zhǐ] purpose;aim;intention;object
宗主国 [zōng zǔ guó] suzerain; metropolitan country
宗主权 [zōng zǔ quán] suzerainty

综(綜) [zōng] (v) 聚集；集合 to sum up ;to integrate; to synthe size ＊戏剧是一门综合的艺术。Drama is an integrated form of art.

综合 [zōng hé] to sum up;to integrate; to synthesize;synthetic
综合报导 [zōng hé báo dǎo] summing up report;pooled dispatch
综合利用 [zōng hé lì yòng] multipurpose use
综合治疗 [zōng hé zhì liáo] composite treatment
综合中学 [zōnghézhōngxué] comprehensive secondary school
综括 [zōng kuò] to sum up ;to summarize

棕 zōng] (n) 常绿乔木 叶鞘纤维(棕衣)很坚韧，可做绳索、毛刷、地毡或制床绷子等 a palm tree

棕色 [zōng sè] brown
棕榈 [zōng lǘ] the coir palm
棕绳 [zōng shéng] the coir rope
棕树 [zōng shù] a palm tree
棕油 [zōng yóu] palm oil

踪 [zōng] (n)人或动物走过留下的脚印。trace; footprint ＊我们在追踪逃跑的敌人。We are tracing the fleeing enemies.

踪迹 [zōng jī] trace;footprint;track; vestige
踪影 [zōng yǐng] trace;sight

鬃 [zōng] (n)马等颈上的长毛。也指猪的硬毛horse's mane;pig's bristles

zǒng

总(總) [zǒng] 1 (adj)概括全部的，主要的，为首的 general; main;chief ＊他被调到总邮政局工作。He was transferred to the General Post Office. 2 (adv) 一直；经常 always;constantly＊事物总是不断发展的。Matters are always in continuous development. 3 (adv) 毕竟；无论如何；anyway; anyhow; at any rate; in a word ＊个人的力量总是有限的。The strength of an individual is limited anyway.

总代理 [zǒng dài lǐ] general agent; sole agent
总得 [zǒng děi] have to;must

总动员 [zǒng dòng yuán] general mobilization
总额 [zǒng é] grand total;total sum;total
总而言之 [zǒng ér yán zhī] in a word;in short;put it briefly
总纲 [zǒng gāng] general programme
总共 [zǒng gòng] altogether;in all; in sum;gross amount
总归 [zǒng guī] in the end;anyway;anyhow
总和 [zǒng hé] the sum and substance of
总汇 [zǒng huì] a pool;a centre
总会 [zǒng huì] a general office
总计 [zǒng jì] amount to;add up; total
总结 [zǒng jié] to sum up;summary
总机关 [zǒng jī guān] head-quarters
总括 [zǒng kuò] to sum up;to put in a nutshell
总理 [zǒng lǐ] premier;prime minister
总量 [zǒng liàng] the grand total
总数 [zǒng shù] total amount;sum total
总算 [zǒng suàn] finally; at least
总体 [zǒng tǐ] sum total;totality
总统 [zǒng tǒng] president
总务 [zǒng wù] general affairs
总则 [zǒng zé] general rules;general provisions
总之 [zǒng zhī] in short;in a word; at any rate
总路线 [zǒng lù xiàn] a general line
总是 [zǒng shì] always;generally
总司令 [zǒng sī lìng] Commander-in-Chief

zòng

纵（縱） [zòng] 1 (v)放 to set loose;to let go ＊纵虎归山（比喻把坏人放走）。To set loose the tiger back to the mountain (to allow the enemy or bad element to escape). 2 (v) 放任；不加约束 to let things take their course;to connive at ＊母亲纵容孩子反而害了他。 Mother who connives at her child will do him harm instead. 3 (v) 跳跃 to leap ＊他纵身一跃，就跨上了马。 He gives a leap and lands himself on the saddle of the horse. 4 (conj) 即使 even if ＊ 纵有千山万水也挡不住英勇的勘探队员。Even thousands of mountains and rivers will not hold back the courageous surveyors 5 (adj) 竖直，跟"横"相对 vertical;perpendicular;longitudinal
纵切面 [zòng qīe miàn] vertical section
纵队 [zòng duì] column;brigade (military)
纵横 [zòng héng] vertically and horizontally;perpendicular and horizontal;length and breadth
纵横交错 [zòng héng jīao cuò] criss-cross;crosswise
纵火 [zòng huǒ] to set fire to
纵情 [zòng qíng] to indulge one's passions;to indulge oneself
纵然 [zòng rán] even if
纵容 [zòng róng] to connive at;to be indulgent;to tolerate;to pamper
纵使 [zòng shǐ] even if
纵身 [zòng shēn] to leap
纵欲 [zòng yù] to give rein to the passions

粽 [zòng] (n) 用竹叶或苇叶裹糯米制成的食品 glutinous rice dumplings wrapped in leaves ＊端午节我们吃粽子。We eat glutinous rice dumplings during the Dragon Boat Festival

zǒu

走 [zǒu] 1 (v)步行；行；移动 to walk;to go;to move ＊ 钟不走了。

The clock has stopped moving. 2 (v) 离开 to leave;to depart ✱ 他刚走。He has just left.

走调 [zǒu diào] to change in tone

走动 [zǒu dòng] to walk around;to move about

走狗 [zǒu gǒu] lackey;running dog; stooge

走火 [zǒu huǒ] to fire accidentally; short-circuited

走后门 [zǒu hòu mén] a backdoor deal

走廊 [zǒu láng] corridor;balustrade

走漏 [zǒu lòu] to leak out;to let out (a secret)

走路 [zǒu lù] to walk

走马看花 [zǒu mǎ kan huā] to take a hurried glance;to glance over something

走入歧途 [zǒu rù qí tú] to go astray;to deviate from the right path

走私 [zǒu sī] to smuggle

走投无路 [zǒu tóu wú lù] to find oneself cornered;to go down a blind alley;to come to an impasse

走向 [zǒu xiàng] to head towards; to walk towards; alignment

走样 [zǒu yàng] change in shape

走卒 [zǒu zú] cat's paw;stooge; lackey

zòu

奏 [zòu] 1 (v) 吹弹乐器 to play music ✱ 我们将以华乐演奏这首马来歌曲。We shall play this Malay song with Chinese musical instruments. 2 (v) 取得；发生 to obtain;to prove ✱这药一服就能奏效。Once you take it, this medicine will prove efficacious.

奏捷 [zòu jié] to obtain victory

奏鸣曲 [zòu míng qǔ] sonata

奏乐 [zòu yuè] to play music;to strike up

奏效 [zòu xiàn] to show results;to prove effective

揍 [zòu] (v) 打 to hit;to beat;to strike ✱他挨揍了。He was beaten up (by somebody).

zū

租 [zū] 1 (v)有代价地借用房地·器物等 to rent;to lease ✱ 他租了一间房。He has rented a room. 2 (n) 借用房、地、器物等的代价 rent; rental ✱ 房租又起了。The house rental has increased again.

租户 [zū hù] a tenant

租界 [zū jiè] concession;foreign settlement;leased territory

租借 [zū jiè] to lease

租金 [zū jīn] rent

租税 [zū shuì] tax

租约 [zu yuē] a deed of lease;title deed

zú

卒 [zú] 1 (n)士兵 a soldier ✱士卒 a soldier 2 (n) 差役 a servant ✱ 他心甘情愿当外国大老板的走卒。He willingly acts as a running servant for his foreign boss. 3 (v)完毕；结束 to end;to conclude;to complete;to finish ✱他在今年底卒业。He will finish his course of study at the end of this year. 4 (v) 死 die ✱屈原的生卒年月不详。The date of birth and death of Qu Yuan is unknown.

族 [zú] 1 (n) 聚居而有血统关系的人群 a group of the same blood living in a community ✱家族。a family ✱宗族。a clan ✱民族 a nation ✱ 种族 a race 2 (n)同类 a class; ✱ 水族 aquatic animals

足 [zú] 1 (n) 脚 the foot;the leg ✱兄弟如手足。Brothers are like hands and feet. 2 (adj)满；充分 full;sufficient;ample ✱ 他们资金不足。They have not enough capital. 3 (v)值得 to be worth ✱ 不必言谢

，我对你的帮助是微不足道的。You need not thank me ; my help to you is not worth mentioning.
足够 [zú gòu] sufficient;adequate; ample
足迹 [zú jī] trace;footprints
足见 [zú jiàn] can well see that.....
足球 [zú qiú] football
足以 [zú yǐ] enough to .....
足智多谋 [zú zhì duō móu] wise and full of strategems

zǔ

诅(詛) [zǔ] (v)咒骂 to curse;to abuse
诅咒 [zǔ zhòu] to curse;to rail at;to revile
阻 [zǔ] (v)挡；拦to hinder;to prevent;to obstruct;to stop ＊他阻止我继续说下去。He prevents me from continuing my speech.
阻碍 [zǔ ài] to stand in the way;to obstruct;to hinder
阻挡 [zǔ dǎng] to block;to hold back;to stop
阻击 [zǔ jī] to intercept;to hold off and attack (e.g. the enemy)
阻拦 [zǔ lán] to hinder;to obstruct; to stop
阻力 [zǔ lì] resistance
阻挠 [zǔ náo] to hamper;to hinder; to check
阻塞 [zǔ sè] to block;to obstruct
阻止 [zǔ zhǐ] to prevent; to obstruct;to hold up;to check;to hinder
组(組) [zǔ] 1 (v)结合；构成to constitute;to form;to organise ＊十个人可以组成一个分队。Ten persons can form a contingent. 2 (n) 机关团体中的一个部门，结合成的集体 a unit;a section;a group ＊出版组。publication unit.
组成 [zǔ chéng] to constitute; to be composed of;to make up;to consist of
组阁 [zǔ gé] to form a cabinet
组合 [zǔ hè] to be composed of;to make up combinations (maths)
组长 [zǔ zhǎng] group leader
组织 [zǔ zhī] to organise ; organisation
组织层次 [zǔ zhī céng cì] organisation structure
组织处分 [zǔ zhī chǔ fèn] organisation discipline
组织力量 [zǔ zhī lì liàng] organisation strength
组织学 [zǔ zhī xué] histology
祖 [zǔ] 1 (n)父母亲的上一辈 the generation before one's parents 2 (n) 先代人的通称 forefathers; ancestors ＊我们的祖先很早就来南洋了。Our forefathers came to South East Asia long, long ago.
祖传 [zǔ chuán] handed down from one's ancestors
祖父 [zǔ fù] grandfather
祖国 [zǔ guó] motherland
祖母 [zǔ mǔ] grandmother
祖先 [zǔ xiān] forefathers;ancestors
祖宗 [zǔ zōng] ancestry;ancestor

zuān

钻(鑽) [zuān] 1 (v)穿孔；打眼 to bore to drill ＊他在墙上钻了一个孔。He bored a hole into the wall. 2 (v)进入 to go into ＊老鼠钻进洞里了。The rat has gone into the hole. 3(v)深入 to penetrate ＊他刻苦钻研社会科学著作。He takes the pain to penetrate into books on social sciences.
另见[zuàn]
钻空子 [zuān kòng·zi] to avail oneself of loopholes
钻牛角尖 [zuān niú jiǎo jiān] to penetrate into the point of a buffalo's horn — to penetrate into the study of impracticable

subjects
钻探 [zuān tàn] drill;bore
钻研 [zuān yán] to make a penetrating study of

zuǎn

纂 [zuǎn] (v) 编纂，收集材料编书 to edit books

zuàn

钻(鑽) [zuàn] 1 (n)打眼用的工具 an auger;a drill *电钻。electric drill. 2 (n) 金刚石 diamond *钻石戒指。a diamond ring
另见 [zuān]
钻床 [zuàn chuáng] a driller;a drilling machine
钻机 [zuàn jī] a drilling machine ; a boring machine
钻头 [zuàn tóu] a drill;a boring head

zuǐ

嘴 [zuǐ] (n) 口 mouth
嘴巴 [zuǐ•ba] mouth
嘴唇 [zuǐ chún] lip
嘴脸 [zuǐ liǎn] face(derogatory); physiognomy(derogatory)

zuì

醉 [zuì] (adj) 喝酒过多，神志不清 to be drunk * 他喝醉了。He is drunk.
醉汉 [zuì hàn] a drunkard;a sot;a heavy toper
醉生梦死 [zuì shēng mèng sǐ] to lead a befuddled life, as if drunk or in a dream
醉心 [zuì xīn] to be preoccupied with;to be fascinated with;to be infatuated with;to be obsessed with;to be drunk with
醉醺醺 [zuì xūn xūn] tipsy;fuddled (drunk)

最 [zuì] (adv) 极；顶 most; best; to the highest degree * 他是我最要好的朋友。He is my best friend.
最初 [zuì chū] at first;at the very beginning;original;initial
最大 [zuì dà] the greatest;maximum
最多 [zuì dūo] the most
最好 [zuì hǎo] best of all;had better
最后 [zuì hòu] final;the last;eventual;ultimate
最后通牒 [zuì hòu tōng dié] ultimatum
最惠国 [zuì huì gūo] the most-favoured nation
最近 [zuì jìn] recently;of late;lately
最少 [zuì shǎo] the least
最小 [zuì xiǎo] the least;minimum

罪 [zuì] 1 (n) 犯法的行为a crime; offence;guilt *这个战犯罪大恶极。The war criminal had committed towering crimes. 2 (n) 苦难；报应 suffering;retribution *母亲无论如何也不能让孩子受罪。 Under any circumstances the mother will not let her child suffer.
罪大恶极 [zuì dà è jí] most heinous crimes;to be guilty of terrible crimes
罪恶 [zuì è] evil;sin;wickedness; crime
罪恶滔天 [zuì è tāo tiān] monstrous crimes
罪犯 [zuì fàn] criminal;convict
罪过 [zuì•guo] crime;sin;wrong
罪魁祸首 [zuì kuí huò shǒu] chief criminal;arch-criminal
罪名 [zuì míng] criminal charge
罪孽 [zuì niè] sin;crime;evil;iniquity
罪行 [zuì xíng] criminal act;vicious act
罪证 [zuì zhèng] evidence of crimes
罪状 [zuì zhuàng] crime;guilt; charge

zūn

尊 [zūn] 1 (n) 地位或辈分高 honourable;senior ＊职业无尊卑之分。Occupations should not be classified into honourable and mean types. 2 (v) 敬重 to respect;to honour ＊他很受人尊敬。He is highly respected by others. 3 (n) 量词 a measure word for cannon

尊称 [zūn chēng] term of respect; respectful appellation

尊重 [zūn chòng] to hold in high esteem;to honour;to respect

尊贵 [zūn guì] respectful;honourable

尊敬 [zūn jìng] to respect;esteem; to revere

尊严 [zūn yán] dignity

尊长 [zūn zhǎng] an elder

尊崇 [zūn zhóng] to hold in high esteem; to honour; to respect

樽 [zūn] (n)酒杯 a wine cup

遵 [zūn] (v)依照；按照 to abide by; to follow;to observe ＊团员们应遵守纪律。Members of the delegation should observe the rules.

遵从 [zūn cóng] obey;follow

遵命 [zūn mìng] in compliance with

遵守 [zūn shǒu] to observe;to adhere to;to abide by

遵循 [zūn xún] to follow;to abide by;to comply with;to act in accordance with

遵照 [zūn zhào] to adhere to;to conform to;according to;to comply with

zuó

昨 [zuó] (adv) 今天的上一天 yesterday ＊昨天我去看戏。Yesterday I went for a show .

昨晚 [zuó wǎn] last evening

昨夜 [zuó yè] last night

zuǒ

左 [zuǒ] 1 (n) 方位名，面向南时靠东的一边 left;the left hand side ＊他站在我的左边。He stands on my left. 2 (adj) 偏差；不对头 deviation;different ＊两个人的意见相左。Two persons have different opinions. 3 (adj) 偏；邪 abnormal; evil;vicious ＊不要给旁门左道的学说所误导。Do not be misled by the queer and vicious theory.

左边 [zuǒ biān] left side

左顾右盼 [zuǒ gù yòu pàn] to peep right and left

左面 [zuǒ miàn] left side

左派 [zuǒ pài] leftist

左倾 [zuǒ qīng] Left deviation

左思右想 [zuǒ sī yòu xiǎng] to think of this and that;to turn over in the mind;to rack one's brains;to keep thinking

左袒 [zuǒ tǎn]] to take sides

左翼 [zuǒ yì] left wing;left flank

左右 [zuǒ yòu] both sides;the left and the right;about;approximately; to dominate;to hold(somebody) under one's thumb;to control

左右逢源 [zuǒ yòu féng yuán] to win advantage from both sides

左右手 [zuǒ yòu shǒu] right-hand man;a valuable assistant

佐 [zuǒ] (v) 帮助 to assist;to help;to aid

撮 [zuǒ] (n) 量词 a measure word (handful) ＊一撮儿毛 a handful of hair.
另见 [cuō]

zuò

作 [zuò] 1 (v)做；制作 to make ＊她懂得制作糕饼。She knows how to make cakes and biscuits. 2 (v)写文章 write;compose;work at ＊他练习写作。He practises writing articles. 3 (v) 起；兴起 to start;to rise ＊枪声大作。Gun shots start noisily. 4 (v) 视为 to take something as ＊火车票过期作废。The overdue train tickets are to be taken as invalid.

作罢 [zuò bà] to give up;to dismiss

作弊 [zuò bì] to practise fraud;to indulge in corrupt practises

作对 [zuò duì] to set against;to be opposed to

作法 [zuò fǎ] method;step;way of doing things

作废 [zuò fèi] to declare invalid;to make null and void

作风 [zuò fēng] style of work;working style

作梗 [zuò gěng] to obstruct;to impede;to hamper;to hinder

作怪 [zuò guài] to make trouble;to play tricks;to be a nuisance;to do mischief

作家 [zuò jiā] writer;author

作践 [zuò jiàn] to disgrace;to trample;to ravage

作茧自缚 [zuò jiǎn zì fù] to be caught in one's own trap

作客 [zuò kè] to be a guest

作料 [zuò liào] condiment;ingredient

作孽 [zuò niè] evil-doing

作陪 [zuò péi] to keep company

作品 [zuò pǐn] a literary or artistic work;composition

作曲 [zuò qǔ] to compose musical composition

作曲家 [zuò qǔ jiā] composer

作祟 [zuò suì] to cause trouble;to make mischief;to play tricks

作为 [zuò wéi] behaviour;accomplishments;achievements;to regard as;to serve as

作威作福 [zuò wēi zuò fú] to abuse one's power tyrannically;to ride roughshod over;to play the tyrant

作文 [zuò wén] composition;essay; article

作息 [zuò xī] to work and rest

作业 [zuò yè] work;homework

作用 [zuò yòng] function;result; consequence;work;produce effect; act

作战 [zuò zhàn] to fight;to make war;operations;fighting

作者 [zuò zhě] author

坐

[zuò] 1 (v) 把臂部平放在椅上 to sit 2 (v) 乘；搭 to go by;to ride in (car, boat, airplane, etc.);to take ＊我坐火车去怡保。I went to Ipoh by train.

坐标 [zuò biāo] coordinates

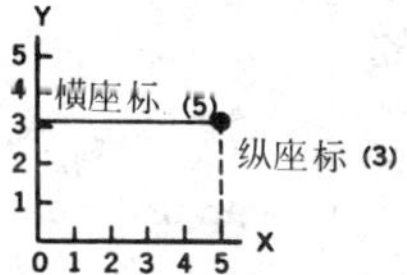

坐标轴 [zuò biāo zhóu] coordinate axis

坐井观天 [zuò jǐng guān tiān] to see the sky from the bottom of a well — to take a narrow view of things

坐牢 [zuò láo] to be put in prison; to be imprisoned;to be sent to jail

坐立不安 [zuò lì bù ān] restless;on pins and needles

坐落 [zuò luò] to situate ;to locate

坐山观虎斗 [zuò shān guān hǔ dòu] to sit on top of the mountain to watch the tigers fight — see both sides jump on each other and not get involved in it

坐视 [zuò shì] to look on with indifference;to sit by and watch

坐失时机 [zoù shì shí jī] to allow an opportunity slip past

坐卧不宁 [zuò wò bū níng] unable to sit down or sleep at ease;to be uneasy in one's sitting and sleeping

坐享其成 [zuò xiǎng qí chéng] to

sit around waiting to share the victory or success of others with folded arms

座 [zuò] 1 (n)坐位 seat ＊ 满座。full house. 2 (n)量词 a measure word (for mountain, bridge, tall building, reservoir, etc.)

座次 [zuò cì] order of seats

座谈 [zuò tán] to have a discussion meeting

座谈会 [zuò tán huì] forum;symposium;discussion;meeting

座位 [zuò wèi] seat

座无虚席 [zuò wū xū xì] no empty seat; full house

座右铭 [zuò yòu míng] motto; maxim

做 [zuò] 1 (v) 进行工作或活动 to do;to work;to undertake ＊ 他在船厂做工。He works in the shipyard. 2 (v)当；为 to become;to be ＊ 他要做一个好教员。He wants to be a good teacher.

做伴 [zuò bàn] keep somebody company

做法 [zuò fǎ] way of making things;ways and means;tactics

做工 [zou kòng] to do (manual) work

做客 [zuò kè] to be a guest

做梦 [zuò mèng] to dream

做贼心虚 [zuò zéi xīn xū] to have a guilty conscience like a thief

做主 [zuò zhǔ] to decide (things) for oneself;to take (matter) into one's own hand

做作 [zuò·zuo] unnatural;pretentious;affected

本词典查阅方法简介

METHOD OF LOOKING FOR WORDS

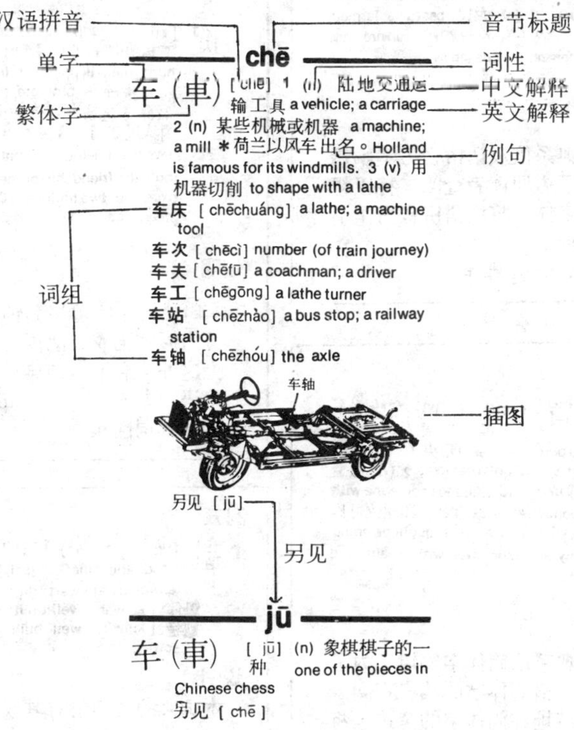

汉语拼音
音节标题
单字
chē
词性
车(車)
[chē] 1 (n) 陆地交通运输工具 a vehicle; a carriage
中文解释
英文解释
繁体字
2 (n) 某些机械或机器 a machine; a mill ＊荷兰以风车出名。Holland is famous for its windmills. 3 (v) 用机器切削 to shape with a lathe
例句
车床 [chēchuáng] a lathe; a machine tool
车次 [chēcì] number (of train journey)
车夫 [chēfū] a coachman; a driver
词组
车工 [chēgōng] a lathe turner
车站 [chēzhàn] a bus stop; a railway station
车轴 [chēzhóu] the axle
车轴
插图
另见 [jū]
另见
jū
车(車) [jū] (n) 象棋棋子的一种 one of the pieces in Chinese chess
另见 [chē]

例一

nìu

拗 [niù] (adj) 固执，任性 stubborn; having one's own way ＊他脾气很拗。He has a stubborn character.

拗不过 [niu bú guò] unable to change one's idea

另见 [ǎo]

nóng

农（農）[nóng] 1 (n) 耕种事业 agriculture ＊青年们下乡务农。The youths go to the countryside to cultivate the soil (to deal with agriculture). 2 (n) 农民 peasants; farmers ＊工农一家亲。The workers and peasants are one family.

说明

本词典系依汉语拼音方案编辑。为了方便读者查阅，特以粗大的字体，将汉语拼音当作小标题标出。

例nìu, nóng即是

例二

买（買）[mǎi] 1 (v) 拿钱换东西，跟"卖"相对 to buy; to purchase ＊ 我买了一个照相机。I bought a camera. 2 (v) 用金钱拉拢 to influence someone with money ＊他以为金钱和地位可以收买一个人。He thought he could buy a person over with wealth and status.

说明

本词典系依简体字编辑。为了方便不谙简体字的读者查阅，我们特地在简体字的旁边，将其繁体字写在括号（　）内。例买（買）即是。

例三

聘 [pìn] 1 (v) 请人担任职务 to employ ＊他被解聘了。He is suspended frm employment 2 (v) 订婚 to betroth; to espouse

聘金 [pìn jīn] money paid at a betrothal

说明

本词典的每个字都有中英文注释，所属的词组则只有英文注释。

促 [cù] 1 (adj) 赶快 to hurry ＊不必匆促，还有很多时间。Don't hurry, there is plenty of time. 2 (v) 催，推动 to promote ; to spur ＊我深信这场足球赛能促进我们两国人民之间的友谊。I deeply believe that the football match will promote the friendship of the people between our two nations. 3 (adj) 靠近 near; close

说明

有时，一个字可当名词同时也可当形容词或其他词类用。遇上这种情形，本词典都分别以略语的方式——(n),(adj)等——标明其词性。

例五

魁 [kuí] 1 (n) 为首的，头子 the head; the chief 2 (adj) 高大 great; eminent; stalwart; gigantic

魁伟 [kuíwěi] well built; stately

魁梧 [kuíwú] well built (of a person)

说明

本词典的文字附有其汉语拼音、全部文字皆按其汉语拼音的字母次序排列。

例六

募 [mù] (v) 广泛征求 to solicit; to raise; to canvass ＊学生们到处筹募建校基金。The students went everywhere to solicit for building funds.

说明

为了协助读者能进一步认识某一个字的意义与用法，本词典在常用字的解释后，附有例句或用法示例。以＊号代表例子的开端。

例七

劳(勞) [láo] 1 (v)(n)出大力工作 labour; work; labour; manual labour ＊经过一天的劳作，他觉得很疲倦。After a day of labour, he feels very tired. 2 (adj)(n)辛苦，疲乏 care-worn; fatigued; fatigue ＊他为大家的事忙了几个星期，十分劳累。Having been busy in public matters for weeks, he becomes worn out. 3 (part)烦劳，请人做事的客气话 an excuse for putting others to the trouble of doing a favour＊劳驾你代我向大家问好。Would you mind sending my regards to all the people? 4 (n)功劳 merits

说明

一个字有时会有多个不同的意义。在遇上这一类的文字时，本词典以阿拉伯数1,2,3…等分别说明它数个不同的意义。

例八

玳 [dài]〔玳瑁〕[dàimaò] (n) 一种海龟，甲可做装饰品 a trutle

说明

有时候，图解比起文字的说明更能使读者一目了然。本词典为了使读者能更深刻地了解一些字与词的意义，特选辑了两百余张插图。

例九

bǎ

把 [bǎ] 1 (v) 抓住，掌握住 to grasp; to hold; to seize ＊把住栏杆慢慢下来。Grasp the railings and go down slowly. 2 (v) 将用来移置句中宾词于动词之前的字。to have (somebody or something done) ＊把这封信寄了去Have this letter sent out.
另见 [bà]

bà

把 [bà](n) 器物上便于手拿的部份，柄 a handle
另见 把 [bǎ]

说明

一个字有时会有两个或两个以上的读音。遇上这种情形，我们在字意的解释之后，加上另见〔××〕，即可在〔××〕音节之处查阅这个字的另一种解释。
例把〔bǎ〕，把〔bà〕即是。

汉语拼音方案

SCHEME FOR THE CHINESE PHONETIC ALPHABET TRANSCRIPTION

一 字母表
1. Alphabetical Table

Aa	Bb	Cc	Dd	Ee	Ff	Gg
ㄚ	ㄅㄝ	ㄘㄝ	ㄉㄝ	ㄜ	ㄝㄈ	ㄍㄝ
Hh	Ii	Jj	Kk	Ll	Mm	Nn
ㄏㄚ	ㄧ	ㄐㄧㄝ	ㄎㄝ	ㄝㄌ	ㄝㄇ	ㄋㄝ
Oo	Pp	Qq	Rr	Ss	Tt	
ㄛ	ㄆㄝ	ㄑㄧㄡ	ㄚㄦ	ㄝㄙ	ㄊㄝ	
Uu	Vv	Ww	Xx	Yy	Zz	
ㄨ	ㄪㄝ	ㄨㄚ	ㄒㄧ	ㄧㄚ	ㄗㄝ	

v 只用来拼写外来语、少数民族语言和方言。字母的手写体依照拉丁字母的一般书写习惯。

"v" is only used to spell or transcribe borrowed words (which are foreign words adopted and adapted into the Chinese language), the languages of the national minority races and local dialects. The alphabets are written according to the normal form of the Latin alphabets.

二 声母表
2. Table of consonants

b	p	m	f	d	t	n	l
ㄅ玻	ㄆ坡	ㄇ摸	ㄈ佛	ㄉ得	ㄊ特	ㄋ讷	ㄌ勒
g	k	h		j	q	x	
ㄍ哥	ㄎ科	ㄏ喝		ㄐ基	ㄑ欺	ㄒ希	
zh	ch	sh	r	z	c	s	
ㄓ知	ㄔ蚩	ㄕ诗	ㄖ日	ㄗ资	ㄘ雌	ㄙ思	

在给汉字注音的时候，为了使拼式简短，zh ch sh 可以省作 ẑ ĉ ŝ。

When Chinese characters are given phonetic annotation, in order to simplify the transcription, zh ch sh could be written as Ẑ Ĉ Ŝ

三 韵母表

3. Table of Final Parts of Syllables

	i ㄧ 衣	u ㄨ 烏	ü ㄩ 迂
a ㄚ 啊	ia ㄧㄚ 呀	ua ㄨㄚ 蛙	
o ㄛ 喔		uo ㄨㄛ 窩	
e ㄜ 鹅	ie ㄧㄝ 耶		üe ㄩㄝ 约
ai ㄞ 哀		uai ㄨㄞ 歪	
ei ㄟ 欸		uei ㄨㄟ 威	
ao ㄠ 熬	iao ㄧㄠ 腰		
ou ㄡ 欧	iou ㄧㄡ 忧		
an ㄢ 安	ian ㄧㄢ 烟	uan ㄨㄢ 弯	üan ㄩㄢ 冤
en ㄣ 恩	in ㄧㄣ 因	uen ㄨㄣ 温	ün ㄩㄣ 晕
ang ㄤ 昂	iang ㄧㄤ 央	uang ㄨㄤ 汪	
eng ㄥ 亨的韵母 (the final part of [heng])	ing ㄧㄥ 英	ueng ㄨㄥ 翁	
ong （ㄨㄥ）轰的韵母 (the final part of [hong])	iong ㄩㄥ 雍		

(1)“知、蚩、诗、日、资、雌、”等七个音节的韵母用 **i**，即：知、蚩、诗、日、资、雌、思等字拼作 **zhi, chi, shi, ri, zi, ci, si**。

(1) The final part of the seven syllables（知、蚩、诗、日、资、雌、思）is "i", so 知、蚩、诗、日、资、雌、思 are transcribed as [zhi], [chi], [shi], [ri], [zi], [ci], [si]

(2) 韵母儿写成 **er**，用做韵尾的时候写成 **r**。例如："儿童"拼作 **ertong**，"花儿"拼作 **huar**。

(2) 儿 which is a final part of a syllable, is written as "er". But when it is used at the very end part of a syllable, it is written as "r" For example, "儿童" is transcribed as [ertong] while "花儿" is transcribed as [huar]

(3) 韵母ㄝ单用的时候写成 **ê**。

(3) ㄝ which is a final part of a syllable, is written as "ê" when it is used singly.

(4) **i** 行的韵母，前面没有声母的时候，写成：**yi**（衣），**ya**（呀），**ye**（耶），**yao**（腰），**you**（忧），**yan**（烟），**yin**（因），**yang**（央），**ying**（英），**yong**（雍）。

(4) In the case of the final parts of syllables which are grouped under "i", when there are no initial sounds, they are written as [yi]（衣），[ya]（呀），[ye]（耶），[yao]（腰），[you]（忧），[yan]（烟），[yin]（因），[yang]（央），[ying]（英），[yong]（雍）

u 行的韵母，前面没有声母的时候，写成：**wu**（乌），**wa**（蛙），**wo**（窝），**wai**（歪），**wei**（威），**wan**（弯），**wen**（温），**wang**（汪），**weng**（翁）。

In the case of the final parts of syllables which are grouped under "U", when there are no initial sounds, they are written as [wu]（乌），[wa]（蛙），[wo]（窝），[wai]（歪），[wei]（威），[wan]（弯），[wen]（温），[wang]（汪），[weng]（翁）

ü 行的韵母，前面没有声母的时候，写成：**yu**（迂），**yue**（约），**yuan**（冤），**yun**（晕）；**ü** 上两点省略。

In the case of the final parts of syllables which are grouped under "ü", when there are no initial sounds, they are written as [yu]（迂），[yue]（约），[yuan]（冤）[yun]（晕）. The two dots placed on top of "ü" are omitted.

ü 行的韵母跟声母 **j, q, x** 拼的时候写成 **ju**（居），**qu**（区），**xu**（虚）**ü** 上两点也省略；但是跟声母 **n, l** 拼的时候，仍然写成：**nü**（女），**lü**（吕）。

The final parts of syllables which are grouped under "ü", when they are transcribed with the initial sounds "j", "q", "x", They are written as [ju]（居），[qu]（区），[xu]（虚）. The two dots placed on top of "u" are also omitted. But when they are transcribed with the initial sounds "n", "l", they are written as [nü]（女），[lü]（吕） (The two dots are not omitted).

(5) **iou, uei, uen** 前面加声母的時候，写成：**iu, ui, un**。例如 **niu**（牛），

gui(归), **lun**(论)。

(5) In the case of "iou", "uei", "uen", when initial sounds are added, they are written as "iu" "ui" and "un", for example, [niu] 牛 , [gui] 归 , [lun] 论

(6) 在给汉字注音的时候，为了使拼式简短，ng 可以省作 ŋ。

(6) When Chinese characters are given phonetic annotation, in order to simplify the transcription, [ng] could be written as [ŋ]

四 声调符号
4. Tone Marks

阴平 ˉ	阳平 ˊ	上声 ˇ	去声 ˋ
1st tone	2nd tone	3rd tone	4th tone

声调符号标在音节的主要母音上。例如：

Tone marks are put above the main vowel of syllables. Thus:

妈 mā （阴平）	麻 má （阳平）	马 mǎ （上声）	骂 mà （去声）	吗·ma （輕声）
1st tone	2nd tone	3rd tone	4th tone	neutral tone

五 隔音符号
5. The Dividing Sign

a, o, e 开头的音节连接在其他音节后面的时候， 如果音节的界限发生混淆，用隔音符号（ ' ）隔开，例如：（皮袄）。**pi'ao**

When a syllable which is preceded by "a", "o", "e", follows another syllable, a situation arises in which the two syllables are likely to get into each other's boundary, causing confusion. In such a situation, the dividing sign (,) is used, as in [pi'ao]

化学元素表
TABLE OF CHEMICAL ELEMENTS

序数 No.	元素名称 Name of Elements	符号 sym-bols	英文名称 English Names	序数 No.	元素名称 Name of Elements	符号 sym-bols	英文名称 English Names
1	氢 qīng	H	hydrogen	29	铜 tóng	Cu	copper
2	氦 hài	He	helium	30	锌 xīn	Zn	zinc
3	锂 lí	Li	lithium	31	镓 jiā	Ga	gallium
4	铍 pí	Be	beryllium	32	锗 zhě	Ge	germanium
5	硼 péng	B	boron	33	砷 shēn	As	arsenic
6	碳 tàn	C	carbon	34	硒 xī	Se	selenium
7	氮 dàn	N	nitrogen	35	溴 xiù	Br	bromine
8	氧 yǎng	O	oxygen	36	氪 kè	Kr	krypton
9	氟 fú	F	fluorine	37	铷 rú	Rb	rubidium
10	氖 nǎi	Ne	neon	38	锶 sī	Sr	strontium
11	钠 nà	Na	sodium	39	钇 yǐ	Y	yttrium
12	镁 měi	Mg	magnesium	40	锆 gào	Zr	zirconium
13	铝 lǚ	Al	aluminium	41	铌 ní	Nb	niobium
14	硅 guī	Si	silicon	42	钼 mù	Mo	molybdenum
15	磷 lín	P	phosphorus	43	锝 dé	Tc	technetium
16	硫 liú	S	sulphur	44	钌 liǎo	Ru	ruthenium
17	氯 lǜ	Cl	chiorine	45	铑 lǎo	Rh	rhodium
18	氩 yà	Ar	argon	46	钯 bǎ	Pd	palladium
19	钾 jiǎ	K	potassium	47	银 yín	Ag	silver
20	钙 gài	Ca	calcium	48	镉 gé	Cd	cadmium
21	钪 kàng	Sc	scandium	49	铟 yīn	In	indium
22	钛 tài	Ti	titanium	50	锡 xí	Sn	tin
23	钒 fán	V	vanadium	51	锑 tī	Sb	antimony
24	铬 gè	Cr	chromium	52	碲 dì	Te	tellurium
25	锰 měng	Mn	manganese	53	碘 diǎn	I	iodine
26	铁 tiě	Fe	iron	54	氙 xiān	Xe	xenon
27	钴 gǔ	Co	cobalt	55	铯 sè	Cs	cesium
28	镍 niè	Ni	nickel	56	钡 bèi	Ba	barium

序数 No.	元素名称 Name of Elements	符号 Sym-bols	英文名称 English Names	序数 No.	元素名称 Name of Elements	符号 Sym-bols	英文名称 English Names
57	镧 lán	La	lanthanum	81	铊 tā	Tl	thallium
58	铈 shì	Ce	cerium	82	铅 qiān	Pb	lead
59	镨 pǔ	Pr	praseodymium	83	铋 bì	Bi	bismuth
60	钕 nǚ	Nd	neodymium	84	钋 pō	Po	polonium
61	钷 pǒ	Pm	promethium	85	砹 ài	At	astatine
62	钐 shān	Sm	samarium	86	氡 dōng	Rn	radon
63	铕 yǒu	Eu	europium	87	钫 fāng	Fr	francium
64	钆 gá	Gd	gadolinium	88	镭 léi	Ra	radium
65	铽 tè	Tb	terbium	89	锕 ā	Ac	actinium
66	镝 dī	Dy	dysprosium	90	钍 tǔ	Th	thorium
67	钬 huǒ	Ho	holmium	91	镤 pú	Pa	protactinium
68	铒 ěr	Er	erbium	92	铀 yóu	U	uranium
69	铥 diū	Tm	thulium	93	镎 ná	Np	neptunium
70	镱 yì	Yb	ytterbium	94	钚 bù	Pu	plutonium
71	镥 lǔ	Lu	lutetium	95	镅 méi	Am	americium
72	铪 hā	Hf	hafnium	96	锔 jú	Cm	curium
73	钽 tǎn	Ta	tantalum	97	锫 péi	Bk	berkelium
74	钨 wū	W	tungsten	98	锎 kāi	Cf	californium
75	铼 lái	Re	rhenium	99	锿 āi	Es	einsteinium
76	锇 é	Os	osmium	100	镄 fèi	Fm	fermium
77	铱 yī	Ir	iridium	101	钔 mén	Md	mendelevium
78	铂 bó	Pt	platinum	102	锘 nuò	No	nobelium
79	金 jīn	Au	gold	103	铹 láo	Lr	lawrencium
80	汞 gǒng	Hg	mercury				

计量单位简表
TABLES ON WEIGHTS AND MEASURES

1. 公制 The Metric System

类别 Classification	英语名称 English Name	缩写或符号 Abbreviation or Symbol	汉语名称 Chinese Name	对主单位的比 Ratio to the Primary Unit	折合英制 Convert to British System
长度 Length	millimicron	mu	毫微米	1/1,000,000,000	
	micron	u	微米	1/1,000,000	
	centimillimetre	cmm.	忽米	1/100,000	
	decimillimetre	dmm.	絲米	1/10,000	
	millimetre	mm.	毫米	1/1,000	
	centimetre	cm.	厘米	1/100	
	decimetre	dm.	分米	1/10	
	metre	m.	米	Primary Unit主单位	= 3.28呎
	decametre	dam.	十米	10	
	hectometre	hm.	百米	100	
	kilometre	km.	公里	1,000	= 0.6214 哩

类别 Classification	英语名称 English Name	缩写或符号 Abbreviation or Symbol	汉语名称 Chinese Name	对主单位的比 Ratio to the Primary Unit	折合英制 Convert to British System
Area 面积及地积	square metre	sq. m	平方米	Primary Unit 主單位	
	are	a.	公亩	100	
	hectare	ha.	公顷	10,000	＝2.471 亩
	square kilometre	sq. km.	平方公里	1,000,000	＝0.3861 平方哩
Weight and Mass 重量和质量	milligram (me)	mg.	毫克	1/1,000,000	
	centigram (me)	cg.	厘克	1/100,000	
	decigram (me)	dg.	分克	1/10,000	
	gram (me)	g.	克	1/1,000	
	decagram (me)	dag.	十克	1/100	
	hectogram (me)	hg.	百克	1/10	
	kilogram (me)	kg.	公斤	Primary Unit 主单位	＝2.205 磅
	quintal	q.	公担	100	
	metric ton	MT (或 t.)	公吨	1,000	＝0.9843 噸
Capacity 容量	microlitre	ul.	微升	1/1,000,000	
	millilitre	ml.	毫升	1/1,000	
	centilitre	cl.	厘升	1/100	
	decilitre	dl.	分升	1/10	
	litre	l.	升	Primary Unit 王单位	＝0.2200 加侖
	decalitre	dal.	十升	10	
	hectolitre	hl.	百升	100	
	kilolitre	kl.	千升	1,000	

2. 英美制 The British and U.S. System

类别 Classification		名称 Name	缩写 Abbreviation	汉译 Chinese Translation	等值 Equivalent	折合公制 Metric Value
Length 长度		mile	mi.	哩	880 fm.	=1.609 公里
		fathom	fm.	㖊	2 yd.	=1.829 米
		yard	yd.	码	3 ft.	=0.914 米
		foot	ft.	呎	12 in.	=30.48 厘米
		inch	in.	吋		=2.54 厘米
Weight 重量	*Avoirdupois* 常衡	ton	tn. (或 t.)	吨	20 cwt.	
		英 long ton		长吨	2,240 lb.	=1.016 公吨
		美 short ton		短吨	2,000 lb.	=0.907 公吨
		hundredweight	cwt.	英担	英 112 lb. 美 100 lb.	=50.802 公斤 =45.359 公斤
		pound	lb.	磅	16 oz.	=0.454 公斤
		ounce	oz.	盎司，唡	16 dr.	=28.35 克
		dram	dr.	打兰，英錢		=1.771 克
	Troy 金衡	pound	lb. t.	磅	12 oz. t.	=0.373 公斤
		ounce	oz. t.	盎司，唡	20 dwt.	=31.103 克
		pennyweight	dwt.	英錢	24 gr.	=1.555 克
		grain	gr.	谷，喱		=64.8 毫克
	Apothecaries' 葯衡	pound	lb. ap.	磅	12 oz. ap.	=0.373 公斤
		ounce	oz. ap.	盎司，唡	8 dr. ap.	=31.103 克
		dram	dr. ap.	打兰，英錢	3 scr. ap.	=3.887 克
		scruple	scr. ap.	吩	20 gr.	=1.295 克
		grain	gr.	谷，喱		=64.8 毫克

2. 英美制 The British and U.S. System

类别 Classification		名称 Name	缩写 Abbreviation	汉译 Chinese Translation	等值 Ecuivalent	折合公制 Metric Value
Area 面积及地积		square mile	sq. mi.	平方哩	640 a.	=2.59 平方公里
		acre	a.	英亩	4,840 sq. yd.	=4,047 平方米
		square yard	sq. yd.	平方碼	9 sq. ft.	=0.836 平方米
		square foot	sq. ft.	平方呎	144 sq. in.	=929 平方厘米
		square inch	sq. in.	平方吋		=6.451 平方厘米
Capacity 容量	*Dry Measure* 干量	bushel	bu.	蒲式耳	4 pks.	英=36.368 升 美=35.238 升
		peck	pk.	配克	8 qts.	英=9.092 升 美=8.809 升
		gallon (英)*	gal.	加仑	4 qts.	=4.546 升
		quart	qt.	夸脱	2 pts.	英=1.136 升 美=1.101 升
		pint	pt.	品脱		英=0.568 升 美=0.55 升
	Liquid Measure 液量	gallon	gal.	加仑	4 qts.	英=4.546 升 美=3.785 升
		quart	qt.	夸脱	2 pts.	英=1.136 升 美=0.946 升
		pint	pt.	品脱	4 gi.	英=0.568 升 美=0.473 升
		gill	gi.	及耳		英=0.142 升 美=0.118 升

* Gallon 作干量单位仅用于英制。

常用符号简介

COMMON MARKS AND SYMBOLS

1. 标点符号 Punctuation Marks

符号 Mark	英语名称 English Name	汉语名称 Chinese Name
.	period (或 full stop, full point)	句号
,	comma	逗号
;	semicolon	分号
:	colon	冒号
?	question mark (或 interrogation point)	问号
!	exclamation mark (或 exclamation point)	感叹号（或感情号，惊叹号）
“ ” (或 " ")	(double) quotation marks	引号
‘ ’ (或 ' ')	single quotation marks	单引号
——	dash	破折号
-	hyphen	连字号

1. 标点符号 Punctuation Marks

符号 Mark	英语名称 English Name	汉语名称 Chinese Name
’（或'）	apostrophe	撇号，省字号
…	ellipsis (或 suspension points)	省略号
( )	parentheses (或 curves)	(圓) 括号
[ ]	square brackets	方括号
〚 〛	double brackets	双方括号
〈 〉	angle brackets	角括号
{ }	braces	大括号
~	swung dash (或 tilde)	代字号
∧	caret	脫字号
/	virgule (或 slant)	斜綫号
*	asterisk	星号
†	dagger	劍号
‡	double dagger	双劍号
¶（或¶，⁋）	paragraph	段落号
§	section (或 numbered clause)	分节号
‖	parallels	平行号
☞	index (或 fist)	參見号
⟶	arrow	箭号

2. 商业符号 Commercial Symbols

符号 Symbol	英语读法或名称 English Reading or Name	汉语读法或名称 Chinese Reading or Name
@	at; each	单价
%	percent	百分之…
‰	per thousand	千分之…
#	1 number (before a figure): as, track #3	①…号(在数字前表示数目，如 track #3 即 3 号轨道)
	2 pounds (s) (after a figure): as, 5#	②…磅(在数字后表示磅，如 5# 即 5 磅)
¥	1 Renminbi yuan	①人民币元
	2 yen	②日元
£	pound (s) sterling	(英) 镑
$ (或 $)	dollar (s)	(美) 元
/	shilling (s)	先令
¢	cent (s)	分
℔	pound (s) (in weight)	磅
®	registered trademark	注册商标
©	copyrighted	版权所有

繁简体字对照表

LIST OF SIMPLIFIED CHARACTERS AND THEIR ORIGINAL COMPLEX FORMS

7 笔

〔車〕车
〔夾〕夹
〔貝〕贝
〔見〕见
〔壯〕壮
〔妝〕妆

8 笔

〔長〕长
〔亞〕亚
〔軋〕轧
〔東〕东
〔兩〕两
〔協〕协
〔來〕来
〔戔〕戋
〔門〕门
〔岡〕冈
〔侖〕仑
〔兒〕儿
〔狀〕状
〔糾〕纠

9 笔

〔剋〕克
〔軌〕轨
〔庫〕库
〔頁〕页
〔郟〕郏
〔剄〕刭
〔勁〕劲
〔貞〕贞
〔則〕则
〔閂〕闩
〔迴〕回
〔俠〕侠
〔係〕系
〔鳧〕凫
〔帥〕帅
〔後〕后
〔釓〕钆
〔釔〕钇
〔負〕负
〔風〕风
〔訂〕订
〔計〕计
〔訃〕讣
〔軍〕军
〔衹〕只
〔陣〕阵
〔韋〕韦
〔陝〕陕
〔陘〕陉
〔飛〕飞
〔紆〕纡
〔紅〕红
〔紂〕纣
〔紈〕纨
〔級〕级
〔約〕约
〔紇〕纥
〔紀〕纪
〔紉〕纫

10 笔

〔馬〕马
〔挾〕挟
〔貢〕贡
〔華〕华
〔莢〕荚
〔莖〕茎
〔莧〕苋
〔莊〕庄
〔軒〕轩
〔連〕连
〔軔〕轫
〔剗〕刬
〔鬥〕斗
〔時〕时
〔畢〕毕
〔財〕财
〔閃〕闪
〔唄〕呗
〔員〕员
〔豈〕岂
〔峽〕峡
〔峴〕岘
〔剛〕刚
〔剮〕剐
〔氣〕气
〔郵〕邮
〔倀〕伥
〔倆〕俩
〔條〕条
〔們〕们
〔個〕个
〔倫〕伦
〔隻〕只
〔島〕岛
〔烏〕乌
〔師〕师
〔徑〕径
〔釘〕钉
〔針〕针
〔釗〕钊
〔釙〕钋
〔釕〕钌
〔殺〕杀
〔倉〕仓
〔脅〕胁
〔狹〕狭
〔狽〕狈
〔芻〕刍
〔訐〕讦
〔訌〕讧
〔討〕讨
〔訕〕讪

〔訖〕讫
〔訓〕训
〔這〕这
〔訊〕讯
〔記〕记
〔凍〕冻
〔畝〕亩
〔庫〕库
〔浹〕浃
〔涇〕泾
〔書〕书
〔陸〕陆
〔陳〕陈
〔孫〕孙
〔陰〕阴
〔務〕务
〔紜〕纭
〔純〕纯
〔紕〕纰
〔紗〕纱
〔納〕纳
〔紝〕纴
〔紛〕纷
〔紙〕纸
〔紋〕纹
〔紡〕纺
〔紖〕纼
〔紐〕纽
〔紓〕纾

11笔

〔責〕责
〔現〕现
〔匭〕匦
〔規〕规
〔殼〕壳
〔埡〕垭
〔掗〕挜
〔捨〕舍
〔捫〕扪
〔掆〕掆
〔堝〕埚
〔頂〕顶
〔掄〕抡
〔執〕执
〔捲〕卷
〔掃〕扫
〔堊〕垩
〔萊〕莱
〔萵〕莴
〔乾〕干
〔梘〕枧
〔軛〕轭
〔斬〕斩
〔軟〕软
〔專〕专
〔區〕区
〔堅〕坚
〔帶〕带
〔厠〕厕
〔硃〕朱
〔麥〕麦

〔頃〕顷
〔鹵〕卤
〔處〕处
〔敗〕败
〔販〕贩
〔貶〕贬
〔啞〕哑
〔閉〕闭
〔問〕问
〔婁〕娄
〔啢〕唡
〔國〕国
〔喎〕㖞
〔帳〕帐
〔崍〕崃
〔崗〕岗
〔圇〕囵
〔過〕过
〔氫〕氢
〔動〕动
〔偵〕侦
〔側〕侧
〔貨〕货
〔進〕进
〔梟〕枭
〔鳥〕鸟
〔偉〕伟
〔徠〕徕
〔術〕术
〔從〕从
〔釷〕钍

〔釺〕钎
〔釧〕钏
〔釤〕钐
〔釣〕钓
〔釩〕钒
〔鈙〕钕
〔釵〕钗
〔貪〕贪
〔覓〕觅
〔飥〕饦
〔貧〕贫
〔脛〕胫
〔魚〕鱼
〔訝〕讶
〔訥〕讷
〔許〕许
〔訛〕讹
〔訢〕䜣
〔訩〕讻
〔訟〕讼
〔設〕设
〔訪〕访
〔訣〕诀
〔產〕产
〔牽〕牵
〔烴〕烃
〔淶〕涞
〔淺〕浅
〔渦〕涡
〔淪〕沦
〔悵〕怅

〔鄆〕郓
〔啓〕启
〔視〕视
〔將〕将
〔晝〕昼
〔張〕张
〔階〕阶
〔陽〕阳
〔隊〕队
〔婭〕娅
〔媧〕娲
〔婦〕妇
〔習〕习
〔參〕参
〔紺〕绀
〔紲〕绁
〔紱〕绂
〔組〕组
〔紳〕绅
〔紬〕䌷
〔細〕细
〔終〕终
〔絆〕绊
〔紼〕绋
〔絀〕绌
〔紹〕绍
〔紿〕绐
〔貫〕贯
〔鄉〕乡

12笔

〔貳〕贰
〔預〕预
〔堯〕尧
〔揀〕拣
〔馭〕驭
〔項〕项
〔賁〕贲
〔場〕场
〔塊〕块
〔達〕达
〔報〕报
〔揮〕挥
〔壺〕壶
〔惡〕恶
〔葉〕叶
〔貰〕贳
〔萬〕万
〔葷〕荤
〔喪〕丧
〔葦〕苇
〔棖〕枨
〔棟〕栋
〔棧〕栈
〔棡〕㭎
〔極〕极
〔軲〕轱
〔軻〕轲
〔軸〕轴
〔軼〕轶
〔軤〕轷
〔軫〕轸
〔軺〕轺
〔畫〕画
〔腎〕肾
〔棗〕枣
〔硨〕砗
〔硤〕硖
〔硯〕砚
〔殘〕残
〔雲〕云
〔覘〕觇
〔睏〕困
〔貼〕贴
〔貺〕贶
〔貯〕贮
〔貽〕贻
〔閏〕闰
〔開〕开
〔閑〕闲
〔間〕间
〔閔〕闵
〔悶〕闷
〔貴〕贵
〔鄖〕郧
〔勛〕勋
〔單〕单
〔喲〕哟
〔買〕买
〔剴〕剀
〔凱〕凯
〔幀〕帧
〔嵐〕岚
〔幃〕帏
〔圍〕围
〔無〕无
〔氫〕氢
〔喬〕乔
〔筆〕笔
〔備〕备
〔貸〕贷
〔順〕顺
〔傖〕伧
〔㑳〕㑇
〔傢〕家
〔鄔〕邬
〔衆〕众
〔復〕复
〔須〕须
〔鈣〕钙
〔鈈〕钚
〔鈦〕钛
〔鈃〕钘
〔鈍〕钝
〔鈔〕钞
〔鈉〕钠
〔鈐〕钤
〔欽〕钦
〔鈞〕钧
〔鈎〕钩
〔鈧〕钪
〔鈁〕钫
〔鈥〕钬
〔鈄〕钭
〔鈕〕钮
〔鈀〕钯
〔傘〕伞
〔爺〕爷
〔創〕创
〔飩〕饨
〔飪〕饪
〔飫〕饫
〔飯〕饭
〔爲〕为
〔脹〕胀
〔腖〕胨
〔腡〕脶
〔勝〕胜
〔猶〕犹
〔貿〕贸
〔鄒〕邹
〔詁〕诂
〔訶〕诃
〔評〕评
〔詛〕诅
〔詗〕诇
〔詐〕诈
〔訴〕诉
〔診〕诊
〔詆〕诋
〔詞〕词
〔詘〕诎
〔詔〕诏
〔詒〕诒
〔馮〕冯
〔痙〕痉
〔勞〕劳
〔湞〕浈
〔測〕测
〔湯〕汤
〔淵〕渊
〔渢〕沨
〔渾〕浑
〔愜〕惬
〔惻〕恻
〔惲〕恽
〔惱〕恼
〔運〕运
〔補〕补
〔禍〕祸
〔尋〕寻
〔費〕费
〔違〕违
〔韌〕韧
〔隕〕陨
〔賀〕贺
〔發〕发
〔綁〕绑
〔絨〕绒
〔結〕结
〔絝〕绔
〔經〕经
〔給〕给
〔絢〕绚
〔絳〕绛
〔絡〕络

〔絞〕绞
〔統〕统
〔絕〕绝
〔絲〕丝
〔幾〕几

13笔

〔項〕项
〔琿〕珲
〔瑋〕玮
〔頑〕顽
〔載〕载
〔馱〕驮
〔馴〕驯
〔馳〕驰
〔塒〕埘
〔塤〕埙
〔損〕损
〔遠〕远
〔塏〕垲
〔勢〕势
〔搶〕抢
〔搗〕捣
〔塢〕坞
〔聖〕圣
〔蓋〕盖
〔蓮〕莲
〔蒔〕莳
〔蓽〕荜
〔夢〕梦
〔蒼〕苍
〔幹〕干
〔蓀〕荪
〔蔭〕荫
〔蒓〕莼
〔楨〕桢
〔楊〕杨
〔嗇〕啬
〔楓〕枫
〔軾〕轼
〔輊〕轾
〔輅〕辂
〔較〕较
〔竪〕竖
〔賈〕贾
〔滙〕汇
〔電〕电
〔頓〕顿
〔盞〕盏
〔歲〕岁
〔虜〕虏
〔業〕业
〔當〕当
〔睞〕睐
〔賊〕贼
〔賄〕贿
〔賂〕赂
〔賅〕赅
〔嗎〕吗
〔嘩〕哗
〔嗊〕唝
〔暘〕旸
〔閘〕闸
〔黽〕黾
〔暈〕晕
〔號〕号
〔園〕园
〔蛺〕蛱
〔蜆〕蚬
〔農〕农
〔嗩〕唢
〔嗶〕哔
〔鳴〕鸣
〔嗆〕呛
〔圓〕圆
〔骯〕肮
〔筧〕笕
〔節〕节
〔與〕与
〔債〕债
〔僅〕仅
〔傳〕传
〔傴〕伛
〔傾〕倾
〔僂〕偻
〔賃〕赁
〔傷〕伤
〔傭〕佣
〔梟〕枭
〔頎〕颀
〔鈺〕钰
〔鉦〕钲
〔鉗〕钳
〔鈷〕钴
〔鉢〕钵
〔鉕〕钶
〔鈸〕钹
〔鉞〕钺
〔鉬〕钼
〔鉏〕钽
〔鉀〕钾
〔鈾〕铀
〔鈿〕钿
〔鉑〕铂
〔鈴〕铃
〔鉛〕铅
〔鉚〕铆
〔鈰〕铈
〔鉉〕铉
〔鉈〕铊
〔鉍〕铋
〔鈮〕铌
〔鈹〕铍
〔僉〕佥
〔會〕会
〔亂〕乱
〔愛〕爱
〔飾〕饰
〔飽〕饱
〔飼〕饲
〔飴〕饴
〔頒〕颁
〔頌〕颂
〔腸〕肠
〔腫〕肿
〔腦〕脑
〔像〕象
〔獁〕犸
〔鳩〕鸠
〔獅〕狮
〔猻〕狲
〔誆〕诓
〔誄〕诔
〔試〕试
〔詿〕诖
〔詩〕诗
〔詰〕诘
〔誇〕夸
〔詼〕诙
〔誠〕诚
〔誅〕诛
〔話〕话
〔誕〕诞
〔詬〕诟
〔詮〕诠
〔詭〕诡
〔詢〕询
〔詣〕诣
〔諍〕诤
〔該〕该
〔詳〕详
〔詫〕诧
〔詡〕诩
〔裏〕里
〔準〕准

〔頎〕颀
〔資〕资
〔羥〕羟
〔義〕义
〔煉〕炼
〔煩〕烦
〔煬〕炀
〔塋〕茔
〔煢〕茕
〔煒〕炜
〔遞〕递
〔溝〕沟
〔漣〕涟
〔滅〕灭
〔溳〕涢
〔滌〕涤
〔溮〕浉
〔塗〕涂
〔滄〕沧
〔愷〕恺
〔愾〕忾
〔愴〕怆
〔㥮〕㤘
〔窩〕窝
〔禎〕祯
〔禕〕祎
〔肅〕肃
〔裝〕装
〔遜〕逊
〔際〕际
〔媽〕妈
〔預〕预
〔綆〕绠
〔經〕经
〔綃〕绡
〔絹〕绢
〔綉〕绣
〔綏〕绥
〔綈〕绨

14笔

〔瑪〕玛
〔璉〕琏
〔瑣〕琐
〔瑲〕玱
〔駁〕驳
〔摶〕抟
〔摳〕抠
〔趙〕赵
〔趕〕赶
〔摟〕搂
〔摑〕掴
〔臺〕台
〔撾〕挝
〔摯〕垫
〔壽〕寿
〔摺〕折
〔摻〕掺
〔摜〕掼
〔勩〕勚
〔婁〕蒌
〔蔦〕茑
〔蓯〕苁
〔蔔〕卜
〔蔣〕蒋
〔薌〕芗
〔構〕构
〔樺〕桦
〔榿〕桤
〔覡〕觋
〔槍〕枪
〔輒〕辄
〔輔〕辅
〔輕〕轻
〔塹〕堑
〔匱〕匮
〔監〕监
〔緊〕紧
〔厲〕厉
〔厭〕厌
〔碩〕硕
〔碭〕砀
〔碸〕砜
〔奩〕奁
〔爾〕尔
〔奪〕夺
〔殞〕殒
〔鳶〕鸢
〔蔬〕蔬
〔對〕对
〔幣〕币
〔彆〕别
〔嘗〕尝
〔嘖〕啧
〔嘩〕哗
〔夥〕伙
〔賑〕赈
〔賒〕赊
〔嘆〕叹
〔暢〕畅
〔嘜〕唛
〔閨〕闺
〔聞〕闻
〔閩〕闽
〔閭〕闾
〔閥〕阀
〔閤〕合
〔閣〕阁
〔閡〕阂
〔嘔〕呕
〔蝸〕蜗
〔團〕团
〔嘍〕喽
〔鄲〕郸
〔鳴〕鸣
〔幘〕帻
〔嶄〕崭
〔嶇〕岖
〔罰〕罚
〔嶁〕嵝
〔幗〕帼
〔圖〕图
〔製〕制
〔種〕种
〔稱〕称
〔箋〕笺
〔僥〕侥
〔僨〕偾
〔僕〕仆
〔僑〕侨
〔僞〕伪
〔銜〕衔
〔鉶〕铏
〔銬〕铐
〔銠〕铑
〔鉺〕铒
〔鋩〕铓
〔鋪〕铺
〔鋁〕铝
〔銅〕铜
〔銦〕铟
〔銖〕铢
〔銑〕铣
〔銩〕铥
〔鋌〕铤
〔銓〕铨
〔鉿〕铪
〔銚〕铫
〔銘〕铭
〔鉻〕铬
〔錚〕铮
〔銫〕铯
〔鉸〕铰
〔銥〕铱
〔銃〕铳

〔銨〕铵
〔銀〕银
〔鉫〕铆
〔戧〕戗
〔餌〕饵
〔蝕〕蚀
〔餉〕饷
〔餄〕饸
〔餎〕饹
〔餃〕饺
〔餏〕饻
〔餅〕饼
〔領〕领
〔鳳〕凤
〔颱〕台
〔獄〕狱
〔誡〕诫
〔誣〕诬
〔語〕语
〔誚〕诮
〔誤〕误
〔誥〕诰
〔誘〕诱
〔誨〕诲
〔誑〕诳
〔說〕说
〔認〕认
〔誦〕诵
〔誒〕诶
〔廣〕广
〔麼〕么

〔瘧〕疟
〔瘍〕疡
〔瘋〕疯
〔塵〕尘
〔颯〕飒
〔適〕适
〔齊〕齐
〔養〕养
〔鄰〕邻
〔鄭〕郑
〔燁〕烨
〔熗〕炝
〔榮〕荣
〔滎〕荥
〔犖〕荦
〔熒〕荧
〔漬〕渍
〔漢〕汉
〔滿〕满
〔漸〕渐
〔漚〕沤
〔滯〕滞
〔滷〕卤
〔漊〕溇
〔漁〕渔
〔滸〕浒
〔滻〕浐
〔滬〕沪
〔漲〕涨
〔滲〕渗
〔慚〕惭

〔慪〕怄
〔慳〕悭
〔慟〕恸
〔慘〕惨
〔慣〕惯
〔寬〕宽
〔賓〕宾
〔窪〕洼
〔寧〕宁
〔寢〕寝
〔實〕实
〔皸〕皲
〔複〕复
〔劃〕划
〔盡〕尽
〔屢〕屡
〔獎〕奖
〔墮〕堕
〔隨〕随
〔韍〕韨
〔墜〕坠
〔嫗〕妪
〔頗〕颇
〔態〕态
〔鄧〕邓
〔緒〕绪
〔綾〕绫
〔綺〕绮
〔綫〕线
〔緋〕绯
〔綽〕绰

〔緄〕绲
〔網〕网
〔網〕网
〔維〕维
〔綿〕绵
〔綸〕纶
〔綬〕绶
〔綳〕绷
〔綢〕绸
〔綹〕绺
〔綣〕绻
〔綜〕综
〔綻〕绽
〔綰〕绾
〔綠〕绿
〔綴〕缀
〔緇〕缁

15笔

〔鬧〕闹
〔靚〕靓
〔輦〕辇
〔髮〕发
〔撓〕挠
〔墳〕坟
〔撻〕挞
〔駔〕驵
〔駛〕驶
〔駟〕驷
〔駙〕驸
〔駒〕驹

〔駐〕驻
〔駝〕驼
〔駘〕骀
〔撲〕扑
〔頡〕颉
〔撣〕掸
〔賣〕卖
〔撫〕抚
〔撟〕挢
〔撳〕揿
〔熱〕热
〔鞏〕巩
〔摯〕挚
〔撈〕捞
〔穀〕谷
〔慤〕悫
〔撥〕拨
〔蕘〕荛
〔蕆〕蒇
〔邁〕迈
〔蕢〕蒉
〔蕪〕芜
〔蕎〕荞
〔蕕〕莸
〔蕩〕荡
〔蕁〕荨
〔樁〕桩
〔樞〕枢
〔標〕标
〔樓〕楼

〔樅〕枞
〔麩〕麸
〔賚〕赉
〔樣〕样
〔橢〕椭
〔輛〕辆
〔輥〕辊
〔輞〕辋
〔槧〕椠
〔暫〕暂
〔輪〕轮
〔輟〕辍
〔輜〕辎
〔甌〕瓯
〔歐〕欧
〔毆〕殴
〔賢〕贤
〔遷〕迁
〔憂〕忧
〔碼〕码
〔磑〕硙
〔確〕确
〔賫〕赍
〔遼〕辽
〔殤〕殇
〔鴉〕鸦
〔輩〕辈
〔劌〕刿
〔齒〕齿
〔劇〕剧
〔膚〕肤

〔慮〕虑
〔鄴〕邺
〔輝〕辉
〔賞〕赏
〔賦〕赋
〔䞍〕䝼
〔賬〕账
〔賭〕赌
〔賤〕贱
〔賜〕赐
〔賙〕赒
〔賠〕赔
〔賧〕赕
〔嘵〕哓
〔噴〕喷
〔噠〕哒
〔噁〕恶
〔閫〕阃
〔閱〕阅
〔閬〕阆
〔數〕数
〔踐〕践
〔遺〕遗
〔蝦〕虾
〔嘸〕呒
〔嘮〕唠
〔嘰〕叽
〔嶢〕峣
〔罷〕罢
〔嶠〕峤
〔嶔〕嵚

〔幟〕帜
〔嶗〕崂
〔篋〕箧
〔範〕范
〔價〕价
〔儂〕侬
〔儉〕俭
〔儈〕侩
〔億〕亿
〔儀〕仪
〔皚〕皑
〔樂〕乐
〔質〕质
〔徵〕征
〔衝〕冲
〔慫〕怂
〔徹〕彻
〔衛〕卫
〔盤〕盘
〔鋪〕铺
〔鋏〕铗
〔鋱〕铽
〔銷〕销
〔鋰〕锂
〔鋇〕钡
〔鋤〕锄
〔鋯〕锆
〔鋨〕锇
〔銹〕锈
〔銼〕锉
〔鋒〕锋

〔鋅〕锌
〔銳〕锐
〔銻〕锑
〔鋃〕锒
〔鋟〕锓
〔錒〕锕
〔鍋〕锅
〔領〕领
〔劍〕剑
〔劊〕刽
〔鄶〕郐
〔餑〕饽
〔餓〕饿
〔餘〕余
〔餒〕馁
〔膞〕䏝
〔膕〕腘
〔膠〕胶
〔鴇〕鸨
〔魷〕鱿
〔魯〕鲁
〔魴〕鲂
〔穎〕颖
〔颳〕刮
〔劉〕刘
〔皺〕皱
〔請〕请
〔諸〕诸
〔諏〕诹
〔諾〕诺
〔諑〕诼

〔誹〕诽
〔課〕课
〔諉〕诿
〔諛〕谀
〔誰〕谁
〔論〕论
〔諗〕谂
〔調〕调
〔諂〕谄
〔諒〕谅
〔諄〕谆
〔誶〕谇
〔談〕谈
〔誼〕谊
〔廟〕庙
〔廠〕厂
〔廡〕庑
〔瘞〕瘗
〔瘡〕疮
〔賡〕赓
〔慶〕庆
〔廢〕废
〔敵〕敌
〔頦〕颏
〔導〕导
〔塋〕茔
〔潔〕洁
〔澆〕浇
〔澾〕㳠
〔潤〕润
〔澗〕涧

〔潰〕溃
〔潙〕沩
〔澇〕涝
〔潯〕浔
〔潑〕泼
〔憤〕愤
〔憫〕悯
〔憒〕愦
〔憚〕惮
〔憮〕怃
〔憐〕怜
〔寫〕写
〔審〕审
〔窮〕穷
〔褳〕裢
〔褲〕裤
〔鴆〕鸩
〔遲〕迟
〔層〕层
〔彈〕弹
〔選〕选
〔槳〕桨
〔漿〕浆
〔險〕险
〔嬈〕娆
〔嫻〕娴
〔駕〕驾
〔嬋〕婵
〔嫵〕妩
〔嬌〕娇
〔嬀〕妫
〔駑〕驽
〔翬〕翚
〔毿〕毵
〔緗〕缃
〔練〕练
〔緘〕缄
〔緬〕缅
〔緹〕缇
〔緲〕缈
〔緝〕缉
〔縕〕缊
〔緦〕缌
〔緞〕缎
〔緱〕缑
〔縋〕缒
〔緩〕缓
〔締〕缔
〔編〕编
〔緡〕缗
〔緯〕纬
〔緣〕缘

16笔

〔璣〕玑
〔墻〕墙
〔駱〕骆
〔駭〕骇
〔駢〕骈
〔擄〕掳
〔擋〕挡
〔擇〕择
〔撿〕捡
〔擔〕担
〔壇〕坛
〔擁〕拥
〔據〕据
〔薔〕蔷
〔薑〕姜
〔薈〕荟
〔薊〕蓟
〔薦〕荐
〔蕭〕萧
〔頤〕颐
〔鴣〕鸪
〔薩〕萨
〔蕢〕蒉
〔橈〕桡
〔樹〕树
〔樸〕朴
〔橋〕桥
〔機〕机
〔輳〕辏
〔輻〕辐
〔輯〕辑
〔輸〕输
〔賴〕赖
〔頭〕头
〔醞〕酝
〔醜〕丑
〔勵〕励
〔磧〕碛
〔磚〕砖
〔磣〕碜
〔歷〕历
〔曆〕历
〔奮〕奋
〔頰〕颊
〔殨〕殨
〔殫〕殚
〔頸〕颈
〔頻〕频
〔盧〕卢
〔曉〕晓
〔瞞〕瞒
〔縣〕县
〔瞘〕眍
〔瞜〕䁖
〔賵〕赗
〔鴨〕鸭
〔閾〕阈
〔閹〕阉
〔閶〕阊
〔閿〕阌
〔閽〕阍
〔閻〕阎
〔閼〕阏
〔曇〕昙
〔噸〕吨
〔鴞〕鸮
〔噦〕哕
〔踴〕踊
〔螞〕蚂
〔螄〕蛳
〔噹〕当
〔罵〕骂
〔噥〕哝
〔戰〕战
〔噲〕哙
〔鴦〕鸯
〔嗳〕嗳
〔嘯〕啸
〔還〕还
〔嶧〕峄
〔嶼〕屿
〔積〕积
〔頹〕颓
〔穇〕䅟
〔篤〕笃
〔築〕筑
〔篳〕筚
〔篩〕筛
〔舉〕举
〔興〕兴
〔學〕学
〔儔〕俦
〔憊〕惫
〔儕〕侪
〔儐〕傧
〔儘〕尽
〔艙〕舱
〔錶〕表
〔鍺〕锗
〔錯〕错
〔鍩〕锘

〔錨〕锚
〔錸〕铼
〔錢〕钱
〔鍀〕锝
〔錁〕锞
〔錕〕锟
〔鍆〕钔
〔錫〕锡
〔錮〕锢
〔鋼〕钢
〔鍋〕锅
〔錘〕锤
〔錐〕锥
〔錦〕锦
〔鍁〕锨
〔錇〕锫
〔錠〕锭
〔鍵〕键
〔錄〕录
〔鋸〕锯
〔錳〕锰
〔錙〕锱
〔覦〕觎
〔墾〕垦
〔餞〕饯
〔餜〕馃
〔餛〕馄
〔餡〕馅
〔館〕馆
〔頷〕颔
〔鴿〕鸽

〔膩〕腻
〔鴟〕鸱
〔鮁〕鲅
〔鮃〕鲆
〔鮎〕鲇
〔鮓〕鲊
〔穌〕稣
〔鮒〕鲋
〔鮑〕鲍
〔鮍〕鲏
〔鮐〕鲐
〔鴝〕鸲
〔獲〕获
〔穎〕颖
〔獨〕独
〔獫〕猃
〔獪〕狯
〔鴛〕鸳
〔謀〕谋
〔諜〕谍
〔謊〕谎
〔諫〕谏
〔諧〕谐
〔謔〕谑
〔謁〕谒
〔謂〕谓
〔諤〕谔
〔諭〕谕
〔諼〕谖
〔諷〕讽
〔諮〕谘

〔諳〕谙
〔諺〕谚
〔諦〕谛
〔謎〕谜
〔諢〕诨
〔諞〕谝
〔諱〕讳
〔諝〕谞
〔憑〕凭
〔鄺〕邝
〔瘻〕瘘
〔親〕亲
〔辦〕办
〔龍〕龙
〔劑〕剂
〔燒〕烧
〔燜〕焖
〔熾〕炽
〔螢〕萤
〔營〕营
〔縈〕萦
〔燈〕灯
〔濛〕蒙
〔燙〕烫
〔澠〕渑
〔濃〕浓
〔澤〕泽
〔濁〕浊
〔澮〕浍
〔澱〕淀
〔懞〕蒙

〔懌〕怿
〔憶〕忆
〔憲〕宪
〔窺〕窥
〔窶〕窭
〔窵〕窎
〔褸〕褛
〔禪〕禅
〔隱〕隐
〔嬙〕嫱
〔嬡〕嫒
〔縝〕缜
〔縛〕缚
〔縟〕缛
〔緻〕致
〔縧〕绦
〔縫〕缝
〔縐〕绉
〔縗〕缞
〔縞〕缟
〔縭〕缡
〔縑〕缣
〔縊〕缢

17笔

〔耬〕耧
〔環〕环
〔贅〕赘
〔璦〕瑷
〔覯〕觏

〔黿〕鼋
〔幫〕帮
〔騁〕骋
〔駸〕骎
〔駿〕骏
〔趨〕趋
〔擱〕搁
〔擬〕拟
〔擴〕扩
〔壙〕圹
〔擠〕挤
〔蟄〕蛰
〔縶〕絷
〔擲〕掷
〔擯〕摈
〔擰〕拧
〔轂〕毂
〔聲〕声
〔藉〕借
〔聰〕聪
〔聯〕联
〔艱〕艰
〔藍〕蓝
〔舊〕旧
〔薺〕荠
〔藎〕荩
〔韓〕韩
〔隸〕隶
〔檉〕柽
〔檣〕樯
〔檔〕档

〔櫛〕栉
〔檢〕检
〔檜〕桧
〔麯〕曲
〔轅〕辕
〔轄〕辖
〔輾〕辗
〔擊〕击
〔臨〕临
〔磽〕硗
〔壓〕压
〔礄〕硚
〔磯〕矶
〔邇〕迩
〔尷〕尴
〔殮〕殓
〔齔〕龀
〔戲〕戏
〔虧〕亏
〔斃〕毙
〔瞭〕了
〔顆〕颗
〔購〕购
〔賻〕赙
〔嬰〕婴
〔賺〕赚
〔嚇〕吓
〔闌〕阑
〔闃〕阒
〔闆〕板
〔闊〕阔

〔闈〕闱
〔闋〕阕
〔曖〕暧
〔蹕〕跸
〔蹌〕跄
〔蟎〕螨
〔螻〕蝼
〔蟈〕蝈
〔雖〕虽
〔嚀〕咛
〔覬〕觊
〔嶺〕岭
〔嶸〕嵘
〔點〕点
〔矯〕矫
〔鴰〕鸹
〔簀〕箦
〔簍〕篓
〔輿〕與
〔歟〕欤
〔龜〕龟
〔優〕优
〔償〕偿
〔儲〕储
〔魎〕魉
〔禦〕御
〔聳〕耸
〔鵃〕鸼
〔鍥〕锲
〔鍇〕锴
〔鍘〕铡

〔鍚〕钖
〔鍶〕锶
〔鍔〕锷
〔鍤〕锸
〔鍾〕钟
〔鍛〕锻
〔鎪〕锼
〔鍬〕锹
〔鍰〕锾
〔鍍〕镀
〔鎂〕镁
〔懇〕恳
〔餳〕饧
〔餿〕馊
〔斂〕敛
〔鴿〕鸽
〔膿〕脓
〔臉〕脸
〔膾〕脍
〔膽〕胆
〔謄〕誊
〔鮭〕鲑
〔鮪〕鲔
〔鮫〕鲛
〔鮮〕鲜
〔颶〕飓
〔獷〕犷
〔獰〕狞
〔講〕讲
〔謨〕谟
〔謖〕谡

〔謝〕谢
〔謠〕谣
〔謅〕诌
〔謗〕谤
〔謚〕谥
〔謙〕谦
〔謐〕谧
〔褻〕亵
〔氈〕毡
〔應〕应
〔癘〕疠
〔療〕疗
〔癇〕痫
〔癉〕瘅
〔癆〕痨
〔齋〕斋
〔羴〕羶
〔鮝〕鲞
〔糞〕粪
〔糝〕糁
〔燦〕灿
〔燭〕烛
〔鴻〕鸿
〔濤〕涛
〔濫〕滥
〔濕〕湿
〔濟〕济
〔濱〕滨
〔濘〕泞
〔澀〕涩
〔濰〕潍

〔懨〕恹
〔賽〕赛
〔襇〕裥
〔襖〕袄
〔禮〕礼
〔屨〕屦
〔彌〕弥
〔嬪〕嫔
〔績〕绩
〔縹〕缥
〔縷〕缕
〔縵〕缦
〔縲〕缧
〔總〕总
〔縱〕纵
〔縮〕缩
〔繆〕缪
〔繅〕缫
〔嚮〕向

18笔

〔擷〕撷
〔擾〕扰
〔騏〕骐
〔騎〕骑
〔騅〕骓
〔攄〕摅
〔擻〕擞
〔鼕〕冬
〔擺〕摆
〔贄〕贽

〔燾〕焘
〔聶〕聂
〔聵〕聩
〔職〕职
〔藝〕艺
〔覲〕觐
〔鞦〕秋
〔藪〕薮
〔繭〕茧
〔藥〕药
〔藭〕䓖
〔藴〕蕴
〔檯〕台
〔櫃〕柜
〔檻〕槛
〔櫚〕榈
〔檳〕槟
〔檸〕柠
〔轉〕转
〔轆〕辘
〔覆〕复
〔醫〕医
〔礎〕础
〔殯〕殡
〔霧〕雾
〔豐〕丰
〔覷〕觑
〔懟〕怼
〔叢〕丛
〔矇〕蒙
〔題〕题

〔韙〕韪
〔瞼〕睑
〔闖〕闯
〔闔〕阖
〔闐〕阗
〔闓〕闿
〔闕〕阙
〔顒〕颙
〔曠〕旷
〔蹣〕蹒
〔嚙〕啮
〔壘〕垒
〔蟯〕蛲
〔蟲〕虫
〔蟬〕蝉
〔鵑〕鹃
〔嚕〕噜
〔顓〕颛
〔鵠〕鹄
〔鵝〕鹅
〔穫〕获
〔穡〕穑
〔穢〕秽
〔簡〕简
〔簣〕篑
〔簞〕箪
〔雙〕双
〔軀〕躯
〔邊〕边
〔歸〕归
〔鏵〕铧

〔鎮〕镇
〔鏈〕链
〔鎘〕镉
〔鎖〕锁
〔鎧〕铠
〔鎳〕镍
〔鎢〕钨
〔鎦〕镏
〔鎬〕镐
〔鎊〕镑
〔鎰〕镒
〔鎵〕镓
〔鵒〕鹆
〔餼〕饩
〔餾〕馏
〔饈〕馐
〔鯁〕鲠
〔鯉〕鲤
〔鯀〕鲧
〔鯇〕鲩
〔鯽〕鲫
〔颸〕飔
〔颼〕飕
〔觴〕觞
〔獵〕猎
〔雛〕雏
〔臏〕膑
〔謹〕谨
〔謳〕讴
〔謾〕谩
〔謫〕谪

〔謭〕谫
〔謬〕谬
〔癤〕疖
〔雜〕杂
〔離〕离
〔顏〕颜
〔糧〕粮
〔燼〕烬
〔鵜〕鹈
〔瀆〕渎
〔瀠〕潆
〔濾〕滤
〔鯊〕鲨
〔濺〕溅
〔瀏〕浏
〔濼〕泺
〔瀉〕泻
〔瀋〕沈
〔竄〕窜
〔竅〕窍
〔額〕额
〔襠〕裆
〔闃〕阒
〔瓊〕琼
〔攆〕撵
〔鬆〕松
〔翹〕翘
〔襝〕裣
〔禱〕祷
〔醬〕酱
〔隴〕陇

〔嬸〕婶
〔繞〕绕
〔繚〕缭
〔織〕织
〔繕〕缮
〔繒〕缯
〔斷〕断

19笔

〔鵡〕鹉
〔鬍〕胡
〔騙〕骗
〔騷〕骚
〔壚〕垆
〔壞〕坏
〔攏〕拢
〔蘀〕萚
〔難〕难
〔鵲〕鹊
〔藶〕苈
〔蘋〕苹
〔蘆〕芦
〔藺〕蔺
〔躉〕趸
〔蘄〕蕲
〔勸〕劝
〔蘇〕苏
〔藹〕蔼
〔蘢〕茏
〔顛〕颠
〔櫝〕椟

〔櫟〕栎
〔櫓〕橹
〔櫧〕槠
〔轎〕轿
〔鏨〕錾
〔轍〕辙
〔轔〕辚
〔繫〕系
〔麗〕丽
〔礪〕砺
〔礙〕碍
〔礦〕矿
〔贋〕赝
〔願〕愿
〔鶴〕鹌
〔璽〕玺
〔贈〕赠
〔闞〕阚
〔關〕关
〔嚦〕呖
〔疇〕畴
〔蹺〕跷
〔蟶〕蛏
〔蠅〕蝇
〔蟻〕蚁
〔嚴〕严
〔獸〕兽
〔嚨〕咙
〔羆〕罴
〔羅〕罗
〔犢〕犊

〔贊〕赞
〔穩〕稳
〔簽〕签
〔簾〕帘
〔簫〕箫
〔牘〕牍
〔懲〕惩
〔鏗〕铿
〔鏢〕镖
〔鏜〕镗
〔鏤〕镂
〔鏝〕镘
〔鏞〕镛
〔鏡〕镜
〔鏟〕铲
〔饉〕馑
〔饅〕馒
〔鵬〕鹏
〔臘〕腊
〔鯖〕鲭
〔鯡〕鲱
〔鯤〕鲲
〔鯢〕鲵
〔鯰〕鲶
〔鯛〕鲷
〔鯨〕鲸
〔獺〕獭
〔譚〕谭
〔譖〕谮
〔譙〕谯
〔識〕识

〔譜〕谱
〔證〕证
〔譎〕谲
〔譏〕讥
〔鶉〕鹑
〔廬〕庐
〔癢〕痒
〔龐〕庞
〔壟〕垄
〔類〕类
〔爍〕烁
〔瀟〕潇
〔瀨〕濑
〔瀝〕沥
〔瀕〕濒
〔瀘〕泸
〔瀧〕泷
〔懶〕懒
〔懷〕怀
〔寵〕宠
〔襪〕袜
〔襤〕褴
〔韜〕韬
〔騭〕骘
〔騖〕骛
〔顙〕颡
〔繮〕缰
〔繩〕绳
〔繾〕缱
〔繹〕绎
〔繯〕缳

〔繳〕缴
〔繪〕绘

20笔

〔瓏〕珑
〔驁〕骜
〔驊〕骅
〔騮〕骝
〔騶〕驺
〔騙〕骗
〔攖〕撄
〔攔〕拦
〔攙〕搀
〔顢〕颟
〔驀〕蓦
〔蘭〕兰
〔蘞〕蔹
〔蘚〕藓
〔鶘〕鹕
〔飄〕飘
〔櫪〕枥
〔櫸〕榉
〔礬〕矾
〔麵〕面
〔櫬〕榇
〔櫳〕栊
〔礫〕砾
〔鹹〕咸
〔鹺〕鹾
〔齟〕龃
〔齡〕龄

〔齣〕出
〔齠〕龆
〔獻〕献
〔黨〕党
〔懸〕悬
〔鼉〕鼍
〔贍〕赡
〔闥〕闼
〔闡〕阐
〔曨〕昽
〔蠣〕蛎
〔蠐〕蛴
〔嚶〕嘤
〔鶚〕鹗
〔髏〕髅
〔鶻〕鹘
〔鶩〕鹜
〔籌〕筹
〔籃〕篮
〔譽〕誉
〔覺〕觉
〔嚳〕喾
〔衊〕蔑
〔艦〕舰
〔鐃〕铙
〔鐐〕镣
〔鐓〕镦
〔鐘〕钟
〔鐒〕铹
〔鐙〕镫

〔釋〕释
〔饒〕饶
〔饊〕馓
〔饋〕馈
〔饌〕馔
〔饑〕饥
〔臚〕胪
〔朧〕胧
〔騰〕腾
〔鰈〕鲽
〔鰂〕鲗
〔鰓〕鳃
〔鰐〕鳄
〔鰍〕鳅
〔鰒〕鳆
〔鰉〕鳇
〔鰌〕鳍
〔鯿〕鳊
〔獼〕猕
〔觸〕触
〔護〕护
〔譴〕谴
〔譯〕译
〔譫〕谵
〔議〕议
〔癥〕症
〔辮〕辫
〔競〕竞
〔贏〕赢
〔糲〕粝
〔爐〕炉
〔瀾〕澜
〔瀲〕潋
〔瀰〕弥
〔懺〕忏
〔寶〕宝
〔騫〕骞
〔竇〕窦
〔襬〕摆
〔騖〕骛
〔纊〕纩
〔繽〕缤
〔繼〕继
〔饗〕飨
〔響〕响

21笔

〔鰲〕鳌
〔攝〕摄
〔騾〕骡
〔驅〕驱
〔驃〕骠
〔驄〕骢
〔驂〕骖
〔擷〕撷
〔韃〕鞑
〔歡〕欢
〔權〕权
〔櫻〕樱
〔欄〕栏
〔轟〕轰
〔覽〕览
〔酈〕郦
〔飆〕飙
〔殲〕歼
〔齦〕龈
〔贐〕赆
〔囁〕嗫
〔囈〕呓
〔闢〕辟
〔囀〕啭
〔顥〕颢
〔躊〕踌
〔躋〕跻
〔躑〕踯
〔躍〕跃
〔纍〕累
〔蠟〕蜡
〔囂〕嚣
〔巋〕岿
〔髒〕脏
〔儺〕傩
〔儷〕俪
〔儼〕俨
〔鐵〕铁
〔鑊〕镬
〔鐳〕镭
〔鐺〕铛
〔鐸〕铎
〔鐶〕镮
〔鐲〕镯
〔鐮〕镰
〔鐿〕镱
〔鶬〕鸧
〔鷂〕鹞
〔鷄〕鸡
〔臟〕脏
〔鰭〕鳍
〔鰱〕鲢
〔鰣〕鲥
〔鰥〕鳏
〔鰷〕鲦
〔鰜〕鳒
〔癩〕癞
〔癧〕疬
〔癮〕瘾
〔斕〕斓
〔辯〕辩
〔礱〕砻
〔鶿〕鹚
〔爛〕烂
〔鶯〕莺
〔灃〕沣
〔灕〕漓
〔懾〕慑
〔懼〕惧
〔竈〕灶
〔顧〕顾
〔鶴〕鹤
〔屬〕属
〔襯〕衬
〔續〕续
〔纏〕缠

22笔

〔鬚〕须
〔驍〕骁
〔驕〕骄
〔攤〕摊
〔覿〕觌
〔攢〕攒
〔鷙〕鸷
〔聽〕听
〔蘿〕萝
〔驚〕惊
〔轢〕轹
〔鷗〕鸥
〔鑒〕鉴
〔邐〕逦
〔霽〕霁
〔齬〕龉
〔齪〕龊
〔鱉〕鳖
〔贖〕赎
〔躚〕跹
〔躓〕踬
〔囌〕苏
〔囉〕罗
〔巔〕巅
〔邏〕逻
〔體〕体
〔罎〕坛
〔籜〕箨
〔籟〕籁

〔籙〕箓
〔籠〕笼
〔鰲〕鳌
〔儻〕傥
〔艫〕舻
〔鑄〕铸
〔鑌〕镔
〔龕〕龛
〔糴〕籴
〔鰾〕鳔
〔鱈〕鳕
〔鰻〕鳗
〔鱅〕鳙
〔讀〕读
〔巒〕峦
〔彎〕弯
〔孿〕孪
〔孌〕娈
〔顫〕颤
〔鷓〕鹧
〔癭〕瘿
〔癬〕癣
〔聾〕聋
〔龔〕龚
〔襲〕袭
〔灘〕滩
〔灑〕洒
〔竊〕窃
〔鷚〕鹨
〔轡〕辔

23笔

〔瓚〕瓒
〔驛〕驿
〔驗〕验
〔攪〕搅
〔欏〕椤
〔轤〕轳
〔靨〕靥
〔魘〕魇
〔饜〕餍
〔鷯〕鹩
〔靆〕叇
〔顬〕颥
〔曬〕晒
〔顯〕显
〔蠱〕蛊
〔髕〕髌
〔籤〕签
〔讎〕雠
〔鷦〕鹪
〔黴〕霉
〔鑠〕铄
〔鑕〕锧
〔鑣〕镳
〔鑞〕镴
〔鱖〕鳜
〔鱔〕鳝
〔讌〕谶
〔欒〕栾
〔攣〕挛

〔變〕变
〔戀〕恋
〔鷲〕鹫
〔癰〕痈
〔齏〕齑
〔讋〕詟
〔鷸〕鹬
〔纓〕缨
〔纖〕纤
〔纔〕才
〔鷥〕鸶
〔鱗〕鳞

24笔

〔鬢〕鬓
〔攬〕揽
〔驟〕骤
〔壩〕坝
〔韆〕千
〔觀〕观
〔鹽〕盐
〔釀〕酿
〔靂〕雳
〔靈〕灵
〔靄〕霭
〔蠶〕蚕
〔艷〕艳
〔顰〕颦
〔齲〕龋
〔齷〕龌
〔鹼〕硷

〔贓〕赃
〔鷺〕鹭
〔囑〕嘱
〔羈〕羁
〔籩〕笾
〔籬〕篱
〔黌〕黉
〔鱠〕鲙
〔鱣〕鳣
〔讕〕谰
〔讖〕谶
〔讒〕谗
〔讓〕让
〔鸇〕鹯
〔鷹〕鹰
〔癱〕瘫
〔癲〕癫
〔贛〕赣
〔灝〕灏

25笔

〔欖〕榄
〔靉〕叆
〔躡〕蹑
〔躥〕蹿
〔鼉〕鼍
〔籮〕箩
〔鑭〕镧
〔鑰〕钥
〔鑲〕镶
〔饞〕馋

〔鱠〕鲙
〔鱭〕鲚
〔蠻〕蛮
〔臠〕脔
〔廳〕厅
〔灣〕湾
〔糶〕粜
〔纘〕缵

26笔

〔驥〕骥
〔驢〕驴
〔趲〕趱
〔顴〕颧
〔黶〕黡
〔釃〕酾
〔釅〕酽
〔矚〕瞩
〔躪〕躏
〔釁〕衅
〔鑷〕镊
〔灤〕滦

27笔

〔顳〕颞
〔鸕〕鸬
〔黷〕黩
〔鑼〕锣
〔鑽〕钻
〔鱸〕鲈
〔讞〕谳

28笔

〔欞〕棂
〔鑿〕凿
〔鸚〕鹦
〔钁〕镢
〔戇〕戆

29笔

〔驪〕骊
〔鬱〕郁

30笔

〔鸝〕鹂
〔鱺〕鲡
〔鸞〕鸾

32笔

〔籲〕吁

笔画查字表

CHARACTER STROKE INDEX

再 552
耳 107
吏 265
亘 141
共 144
列 271
夸 247
夺 103
压 503
厌 509
有 536
灰 182
在 552
存 77
达 79
迈 290
戍 407
成 56
百 11
而 107
页 516
死 413
夹 198
199
扛 135
扣 246
托 446
执 578
扩 252
扪 296
扫 375
375
扬 511
邪 486

划 177
178
轨 156
毕 25
尧 513
过 157
159
臣 55
匡 249
匠 209
至 580
夷 520
此 73
乩 191
贞 568
师 391
尘 55
尖 203
劣 272
当 84
85
光 154
吁 494
544
吐 443
443
吓 475
169
吃 59
吸 470
吗 289
吆 513
屿 541
屹 525
帆 111
则 556

刚 135
岁 420
岂 344
吊 93
早 555
网 453
同 438
因 526
团 444
444
回 183
曲 358
358
曳 516
虫 61
肉 370
竹 589
牝 335
丢 96
舌 384
先 475
迁 346
迄 344
廷 436
乔 350
年 316
朱 588
缶 123
伍 466
伎 196
伏 125
优 534
伛 541
伐 110
仲 586
件 207

任 367
伤 380
价 201
伦 284
份 120
伧 43
仰 512
仿 115
伉 240
伙 187
伪 458
伊 517
似 414
传 68
休 493
伟 457
华 176
延 506
自 600
血 500
臼 227
向 482
乒 336
乓 326
行 490
164
后 173
舟 587
创 70
69
全 359
会 184
248
合 167
139

企 344
伞 374
众 586
杀 377
爷 515
犷 155
兆 566
舛 69
肌 190
肋 260
刎 462
杂 551
朵 103
旨 579
名 304
各 139
多 103
负 129
争 571
危 455
色 376
凫 126
旬 500
旭 496
刘 277
齐 343
充 61
妄 454
亦 524
交 209
衣 517
产 49
亥 162
庄 595
庆 356
忖 77

忏 49
忙 292
闭 26
问 462
闯 70
灯 88
州 587
冲 61
62
次 73
决 233
冰 32
汗 163
污 464
江 208
汛 501
汐 470
汲 192
池 59
汝 371
汤 427
壮 596
妆 595
宇 541
守 401
宅 559
安 3
字 600
并 33
关 152
羊 510
兴 490
492
米 299
讲 208
讳 185
讴 322
讵 230

讶 505
许 495
讹 105
论 285
284
讼 416
讽 122
设 384
访 115
诀 233
军 235
农 319
弛 59
那 311
异 525
导 86
寻 500
尽 218
219
阱 223
阵 571
阳 511
阪 13
阶 213
阴 527
防 114
收 400
迅 501
奸 202
如 370
妇 129
妃 117
她 423
妈 288
好 165
166
戏 473
观 152
153

8

10

11

15

16

19

25

26 以上 above